UNDERSTANDING BUSINESS

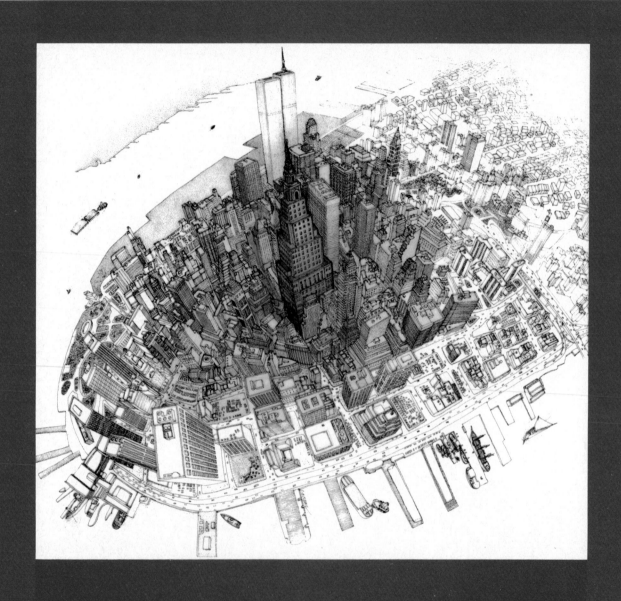

UNDERSTANDING
BUSINESS

WILLIAM G. NICKELS

University of Maryland

with 434 illustrations

TIMES MIRROR/MOSBY COLLEGE PUBLISHING

ST. LOUIS · TORONTO · SANTA CLARA

1987

Acquisition Editor **Elizabeth J. Schilling**
Developmental Editor **Catherine C. Bailey**
Developmental Editor for Supplements **Julie Powers**
Project Editor **Suzanne Seeley**
Production Editor **Tim O'Brien**
Art Director **Kay M. Kramer**
Designer **Diane M. Beasley**
Production **Jeanne B. Genz, Jan Shelly, Sheila Jones,**
   Kathy Burmann, Gail Morey Hudson,
   Teresa Breckwoldt
Photo Research **Lars Etzkorn**
Cover Illustration **"Lower Manhattan with the**
   Bank of New York" by Albert Lorenz

Copyright © 1987 by
Times Mirror/Mosby College Publishing
A division of The C. V. Mosby Company
11830 Westline Industrial Drive, St. Louis, Missouri 63146

Every effort has been made to locate the copyright holders
for all borrowed material, but in a few instances this has
proved to be impossible.

Library of Congress Cataloging in Publication Data

Nickels, William G.
   Understanding business.

   Bibliography: p.
   Includes Index.
   1. Business. 2. Business—Vocational guidance.
I. Title.
HF5351.N53 1987   650   86-23080
ISBN 0-8016-3627-2

GW/VH/VH 9 8 7 6 5 4 3 2 1   02/A/241

DEDICATION

This book is dedicated to my wife, Marsha, and my son, Joel, who spent many a day and night in silent vigil while I worked on the manuscript. It is also dedicated to students and instructors everywhere who provided the incentive to write a text that would be both interesting and challenging.

ABOUT THE AUTHOR

Dr. William G. Nickels is an associate professor of business at the University of Maryland, College Park, Md. He has more than 15 years of teaching experience and has taught the introduction to business course for several years. During his teaching career, he has received many awards, including the Outstanding Teacher on Campus Award at the University of Maryland in 1985; the Teaching Excellence Award, Division of Behavioral Science, University of Maryland, 1983-1984; and the George Washington Honor Medal for Excellence in Economic Education.

Dr. Nickels received his Ph.D. from The Ohio State University.

PREFACE

If the son or daughter of a friend came into your office to ask you about business, what is it that they would be most interested in discussing? What would you be most interested in telling them? This is the exact situation I have faced for the last several years as a teacher of an introduction to business course at the University of Maryland. I found that the students were most confused about and interested in possible careers. They were also interested in what people actually did in the various business functions.

I was never comfortable telling students to read one of the present introduction to business books because they were written more like an encyclopedia than a user-friendly guide to business and its functions. It was disappointing that the texts were similar in coverage and style. Where was the coverage of economics that students needed in order to read and understand the business journals? Why was management placed so early in the text when students were so far from management positions? Why wasn't there more on the service industry, since that's where over 70% of the jobs will be? And why so many examples from major industries when small business was providing most of the jobs? And why was there so little emphasis on careers when that was the major concern of students?

CONTENT DIFFERENCES

Times Mirror/Mosby, it turns out, was asking the same questions. They asked me if I would be interested in writing a new, different introduction to business book that more closely met student and instructor needs. This text is a result of that conversation.

Careers Emphasis

Although this book may cover most of the same material as competing texts, it does so in a more logical manner, and the style of presentation is quite different. First of all, there is a much greater emphasis on careers. The unique Prologue is devoted to careers in business. It illustrates how the text and the course will help students start thinking about their own futures and what resources are available to assist them. There is also a career orientation throughout the book and every career section is highlighted in the same background color, so that students can find the material quickly.

Coverage of Economics

To prepare students for reading and understanding the business literature, there are two chapters on economics. Such topics as fiscal and monetary policy, trade deficits, and free markets are covered so that students can read business periodicals with greater comprehension.

After extensive new market research, one focus group, and reviews by over 40 instructors, we found that most introduction to business teachers prefer this strong economics foundation. Because some groups of students may already have a strong economics background, you may elect to assign these chapters as supplemental readings without losing continuity.

Entrepreneurship and Franchising

A separate chapter on entrepreneurship and franchising is included because these two aspects of business are rapidly growing and will offer students numerous job opportunities.

Small Business Coverage

One entire chapter devoted to managing a small business allows the students to fully understand and appreciate the numerous opportunities available in small firms. Excellent examples of small business managers are highlighted.

Marketing/Management Organization

You will notice that marketing is presented *before* management. The book *In Search of Excellence* was popular in the 1980s because of its marketing orientation. Students are more likely to seek jobs in marketing and to use marketing skills before they get involved in management. Reviewers agreed that it is more logical to discuss marketing before management.

Service and Nonprofit Marketing

There is a separate chapter on the marketing of services and nonprofit organizations because such organizations will provide about 72% of the future jobs.

Personal Financial Planning

There is also a separate chapter on personal financial planning because many students today seem to have forgotten the benefits of saving for the future and how to use credit prudently. This optional chapter explores such concepts as saving, investing, and achieving financial independence.

International Business

I recognize the importance of international business in today's markets and introduce the topic in Chapter 1. However, a detailed discussion of international topics is held to the very end because students cannot fully discuss international marketing or international finance until they know what these two functions are. This organization allows you to end the class on an important and interesting topic—international business.

Style Differences

The major difference in this book is the style of presentation. Unlike its competitors, it is written in a style designed to get the students *involved* and *active* as they read it. The style is very personal, engaging, and easy to read. Reviewers were enthusiastic throughout in their praise of its style. There are many pedagogical devices to help students learn the material. Please read "To the Student" for details. In order to get the flavor of the text, I encourage you to read the Prologue. It introduces the themes of the text—careers and understanding business—and sets the tone. Glance through the text and you will see that it is carefully designed both to be interesting and to facilitate comprehension and retention.

EXTENSIVE DEVELOPMENT

How do we know that this text meets the needs of today's instructors? Throughout the evolution of this project, constant market research was conducted to ensure that the book would meet your needs in terms of coverage, organization, and pedagogical approach. Instructors at over 400 schools were asked how their present text met their needs and what they would want in a new introduction to business text.

After the first draft was completed, it was reviewed by 20 different instructors and revised accordingly. The second draft was reviewed by 25 instructors who provided additional commentary and recommendations. Seven key reviewers were then brought to St. Louis for a 2-day focus group to discuss their reactions to the second draft, the needs of this course, the approach of the text, its pedagogical format, and the importance and composition of the supplements package.

After this process was completed and revisions made, certain chapters were sent to experts in the various areas for their review. Experts reviewed the chapters on economics, computers, accounting, money and banking, finance, insurance, and law. They verified the accuracy, currentness, and clarity of presentation. I still assume complete responsibility for the book's content, however, in that I am the one who wrote the final draft.

The text then went through a third draft review by 15 instructors. All of this effort was made to provide you with the highest-quality, most market-driven introduction to business text ever prepared.

Classroom Testing

The ultimate test of a text is its utility for students, I have used the text in three different classes over a 2-year period. Students were very enthusiastic about its content and style, and made many recommendations that were incorporated into the various drafts.

PEDAGOGY

There are many pedagogical devices in *Understanding Business,* some unique, to help your students learn and retain the material in the text. We believe that the text has the most comprehensive pedagogy available in this market.

Learning Goals

Each chapter has several learning goals that students can use as guidelines for what they are expected to know when they complete the material. The Study Guide is closely linked to the Learning Goals so that students have clear objectives when they study.

Opening Profiles

Each chapter begins with a profile of a person who illustrates an important point that will be covered in the chapter. Not all the personalities are famous because they represent the full gamut from small business owners to the president of Pepsico and the chairman of the Federal Reserve. These profiles provide a transition between chapters and a good introduction to the text material.

Progress Checks

After each major topic within a chapter, there is a unique learning tool called "Progress Check." It stops the student in the middle of the chapter and asks a few questions to test recall. If the student is not retaining the material, the Progress Check will reveal that fact and help the student get back on track.

Thinking It Through

These inserts, found throughout each chapter, ask students to pause and think about how the material they are reading applies in their own lives. This device is an excellent tool for linking the text material to the student's past experience to enhance memory.

Interactive Summaries

The summaries are written in a question and answer format rather than as a short restatement of the text. This enables students to see sample questions and answers, thus preparing them better for quizzes and exams.

Key Terms

Key terms appear in boldface in the text the first time they are introduced to the student. They are defined in the margin, listed at the end of each chapter, and defined in a glossary at the end of the text.

Getting Involved

The goal of the Progress Checks and the Thinking It Through boxes is to increase student involvement in the learning process. The same is true of the section called "Getting Involved." It assigns students miniprojects that they can do to learn more about the subject. Some of it is library work, but most of it involves talking with people to obtain their reactions and advice on certain subjects. The Instructor's Manual places the Getting Involved questions in the chapter *before* the actual ones in the text so that they can be assigned before the class. If your students divide the work among themselves, they can learn much from outside sources without any one student having to do too much work.

Practice Cases

Each chapter concludes with two cases to practice management decision making. These are relatively short cases that are great for discussion starters. The answers to the cases are in the Instructor's Manual.

Photos and Illustrations

While the revision process was underway, a professional photo researcher worked with me in selecting illustrations that would complement and reinforce key concepts. Each photograph and illustration that appears in the text is *directly* related to the example and application. More than 30 of the photographs were specifically commissioned for use in this text. Look through the book and you will see for yourself that the illustrations beautifully and effectively enhance the written material.

SUPPLEMENTS

The supplements package went through extensive review. The Test Bank, the Study Guide, the Instructor's Manual, and the other supplements were reviewed and revised so that the total package is qualitatively the most usable on the market. All of the supplements are available free to adopters through their local Times Mirror/Mosby representative or through Times Mirror/Mosby's central office, 800-325-4177.

The Test Bank

If you were to sit down with instructors who teach introduction to business, as we have, you would see that the one teaching aid of crucial importance to them is the Test Bank. Unlike the majority of competition, this Test Bank was thoroughly reviewed and developed. It not only contains more than 2,000 questions, but also includes a rationale and page number for each correct answer and why the answer is correct. The level of difficulty of each question is indicated. All adopters of *Understanding Business* may obtain MICROTEST II, a computerized version of the test bank. James McHugh, himself a teacher of introduction to business at St. Louis Community College–Forest Park, prepared the test bank.

The Instructor's Manual

The second most important ingredient in the teaching package, according to our research, is the Instructor's Manual. I prepared the Instructor's Manual myself and included lectures that are up-to-date and material not covered in the text.

To facilitate the transition from your current book to *Understanding Business,* I have included conversion notes in the Instructors' Manual. These notes delineate exactly how this book differs from the leading competitors in both coverage and terminology on a chapter-by-chapter basis.

Color Acetates

Frank Falcetta of Middlesex Community College and Alan Kardoff of Northern Illinois University prepared 100 original color acetates on material that will augment that covered in the text. These acetates enable you to design your own lectures and illustrate them with colorful visual aids.

Transparency Masters

In addition to the acetates, every chart, graph, and table in the text is reproduced as a transparency master for your easy use in the classroom.

Study Guide

A very important component of our teacher's package is the Study Guide. Ours is uniquely designed to help students become involved in the learning process. The study guide to *Understanding Business,* written by Barbara Barrett of St. Louis Community College–Meramec, is not merely a synopsis of the text. Rather, it is a learning device that forces students to write answers and to apply what they have learned. If your students use this guide, they will be fully prepared for class discussion and exams.

Business Forms

The instructor's package includes a comprehensive group of 59 business forms with which students should become familiar. They include sample bonds, agreements, job applications, and wills. These were prepared by Frank Falcetta of Middlesex Community College and are drawn from a variety of real business firms.

Computer Simulation Exercises

Our research also uncovered many instructors who wanted a computer simulation exercise to enable their students to become more familiar with computer usage. The computer-assisted instruction to supplement *Understanding Business* is based on a small business. The interactive disks and the accompanying Instructor's Manual contain exercises that require students to apply concepts they have learned for each part of the text. Also included are a business career guidance module and management simulation. This complete computer-aided instruction system provides instructors who wish to use microcomputers with a user-friendly learning tool. It was prepared by John Lloyd and Myron Mandiak of Monroe Community College.

Stock Market Game

Free to adopters, this package of forms and instructions encourages students to choose actual stocks, simulate investment decisions, and chart their success or failure. This is an excellent tool to get students involved in reading the business section of their local newspaper or *The Wall Street Journal*. This game was prepared by Robert Ulbrich of Parkland College.

Videotape

A videotape is also free to adopters and provides an introduction to the course and case materials to supplement lectures. The videotape to accompany *Understanding Business* consists of five 8- to 12-minute segments on various subjects covered in the text. The segments are interesting minicases that can be used individually or shown consecutively during one class period.

Supplemental Lecture Topics

These comprehensive lecture topics present alternative lecture ideas for each chapter of the text. Written by Alan Kardoff of Northern Illinois University, these ideas complement 50 of the 100 color acetates.

Instructor's Resource File Box

One complaint that instructors had about the supplements of competing texts was that they were difficult to use. Some competitors have even found it necessary to provide a guide on how to use the supplements. The Nickels supplements are as user-friendly as the text. Organized by chapter, each element included in the package is integrated with an unbound copy of the text, allowing you to insert it into the three-ring binder that is provided. The unbound study guide is also provided. You can thus remove all of the material dealing with one chapter and go to class without searching through a whole series of supplementary materials.

■ ■ ■

As you can see, the text and the supplementary package are among the most comprehensive and thoroughly tested on the market. All of these steps were taken so that you could make the introduction to business course one of the best at your school. In spite of all the reviews and rewritings, there may be some parts of the text you would like to have changed or removed. I am quite open to suggestions and am eager to hear from you by mail or at professional meetings where our paths may cross. I do not view this text as my book, but as a book that belongs to you and your students and anyone else who is trying to understand business. We can work on our book until it meets all of our wants and needs, if you provide the input I need to make those changes.

ACKNOWLEDGMENTS

The market for introduction to business books is a crowded one, led by a few books that are very similar to each other. It takes a publisher who is confident and forward-looking to enter that market with a conceptually different book that was designed for students and instructors, not as a "me-too" entry. Glenn Turner at Times Mirror/Mosby is a man of vision and daring. His expertise in business publishing is exceptional. It was he who approved this project and guided it through to completion.

His staff at Times Mirror/Mosby are also dedicated and talented. They all deserve praise for their efforts on this book. Special credit goes to Cathy Bailey, who was the developmental editor for the text. She coordinated the effort, found reviewers, arranged focus groups, helped select illustrations, and developed the text. In many ways, having her work on the text was like having a co-author who was knowledgeable and efficient.

Julie Powers handled the development of the supplements package. She was able to juggle many balls at the same time so that everything was concluded on schedule. Designer Diane Beasley is responsible for the exciting look of the book and enhancing the utility of the text with highlighted pedagogical elements. Lars Etzkorn found the cover illustration and all those beautiful photos you see throughout the text. Jeanne Genz carefully wove all elements into cohesive, clear page form. Elizabeth Schilling came in late to rally the troops when they needed it most. Suzanne Seeley did a skillful job of getting the book through the production process under difficult time constraints. She was a joy to work with because she kept her head and calm in the storm.

To create a text that meets the needs of faculty and students in a wide variety of schools, one needs the input from dozens of reviewers. Many faculty members reviewed several drafts of each chapter, spent hours making suggestions and changes, and enthusiastically supported the results. A dedicated group spent an entire weekend in a focus group going over each chapter in detail and discussing the supplements one by one. They won my respect and my sincere thanks. They were Barbara Barrett of St. Louis Community College–Meramec, Paul Jenner of Southwest Missouri State University, Robert Kersten of St. Louis Community College–Florissant Valley, James McHugh and Bernard Weinrich of St. Louis Community College–Forest Park, Robert Ulbrich of Parkland College, and John Rich of Illinois State University.

Some 20 faculty were involved in reviewing the first draft. Twenty-five reviewed the second draft, some of them repeats from the first panel. Another 15 reviewers went over a third draft. All of them were careful and thorough in their reviews and suggestions. Ultimately, we had to stop the process, but these dedicated people stuck with it to the end. The faculty members who participated in the review process or who acted as experts on selected chapters include the following:

Ed Aronson
Golden West College

Barbara Barrett
St. Louis Community College–Meramec

John Beem
College of DuPage

John Blackburn
The Ohio State University

John Bowdidge
Southwest Missouri State University

Stephen Branz
Triton College

Harvey Bronstein
Oakland Community College

B.J. Campsey
San Jose State University

Monico Cisneros
Austin Community College

R.K. Davis
University of Akron

Alton Evans
Tarrant County Community College

C.S. Everett
Des Moines Area Community College

Frank Falcetta
Middlesex Community College

Robert Fishco
Middlesex County Community College

Charles FitzPatrick
Central Michigan University

Donald Gordon
Illinois Central College

Roberta Greene
Central Piedmont Community College

Paul Jenner
Southwest Missouri State University

Alan Kardoff
Northern Illinois University

Warren Keller
Grossmont College

Robert Kersten
St. Louis Community College–Florissant
Valley

Roger Lattanza
University of New Mexico

George Leonard
St. Petersburg Junior College

John Lloyd
Monroe Community College

Paul Londrigan
C.S. Mott Community College

Jerry Lynch
Purdue University

James McHugh
St. Louis Community College–Forest Park

Eugene O'Connor
California Polytechnical University–San Luis
Obispo

Dennis Pappas
Columbus Technical Institute

Joseph Platts
Miami-Dade Community College

Roderick Powers
Iowa State University

Robert Redick
Lincoln Land Community College

John Rich
Illinois State University

Guy Sessions
Spokane Falls Community College

Richard Shapiro
Cuyahoga Community College

Jerry Sitek
Southern Illinois University

Michelle Slagle
The George Washington University

Paul Solomon
San Jose State University

David Stringer
DeAnza College

Ray Tewell
American River College

J. Robert Ulbrich
Parkland College

Pablo Ulloa
El Paso Community College

Heidi Vernon-Wortzel
Northeastern University

Bernard Weinrich
St. Louis Community College–Forest Park

In addition to the faculty reviews, this text was reviewed by three separate classes at the University of Maryland. They read photocopied chapters and wrote reviews. This was a major commitment on their part and provided helpful student input. The students especially liked the career orientation of the text and the readability. Special thanks goes to Lucette Comer and Aruna Rao for their inputs.

Some people contributed written material for the manuscript. Robert Ulbrich of Parkland College contributed information about the farm crisis for Chapter 1, James McHugh of St. Louis Community College (Forest Park) wrote most of the union material for Chapter 18, and Michael Chattalas wrote part of the material on banking for Chapter 20. They did an excellent job and their contribution shows.

My wife, Marsha, was my permissions manager, typist (in emergencies) and overall supporter. In spite of all these supporters and reviewers, the book may still have errors because of my stubbornness or oversight. I assume responsibility for any such errors. They were probably pointed out to me more than once, but I may still have missed them. If we are lucky, there will be a second edition and you can participate in the process of improving the text. I would appreciate the input.

Bill Nickels

To the Student

Before you begin reading *Understanding Business,* you may want to know something about the book and the overall purpose of the course. First, let's explore the objectives of the text. The primary objective is to help you learn the basic fundamentals of business. That is, you will learn the basics of what people do in marketing, management, finance, personnel, accounting, production management, and other business areas. You will also learn the basic terms and concepts of economics so you can better understand the business literature. When you are finished with the course, therefore, you should be able to read with comprehension all the business publications to continue your goal of truly understanding business.

In the text, you will be encouraged to read business newspapers and magazines such as *The Wall Street Journal* and *Business Week.* The idea is to expose you to as many information sources as possible so you can learn about business from many perspectives. You will get much more out of this class if you really immerse yourself in business by talking with business people, reading the literature, and completing the "Getting Involved" exercises and cases at the end of each chapter.

Why should you bother spending so much time on this class? Because a second objective of the text is to help you decide what kind of career would be rewarding and interesting for you *and* to show you how to get the job you want through effective resumé writing and interviewing. There are dozens of other introduction to business texts on the market, but your instructor chose the one that was designed to guide you in your own personal search to understand what business is all about so that you can become more focused on a career. Because of that orientation, this should be one of the most valuable courses you take in school.

You'll notice that I use a conversational tone in the text. My goal in doing so is to help you understand business by keeping the text highly readable and interesting. You should be able to retain more if you enjoy reading the text. Another feature of this text that should increase its effectiveness for you is the number of examples taken from businesses with which you are probably familiar.

There are many resources available to you when taking a college-level course. They include your instructor, the text, your classmates, the library, and outside experts who are working in the business world. The Prologue to the text discusses these resources and outlines a strategy for getting the most out of this course. Your college and business days will be much more productive if you start a file system and follow the other advice in the Prologue.

Making Learning a Game

Business is an important and serious subject. However, experience shows that you learn more when you enjoy what you are doing. So let's make the 26 chapters in this text into 26 parts of an *Understanding Business* game. You will see how well you are playing the game when you get your grades back from the various quizzes and exams you take. But the real test of your game skills will occur when you go out into the marketplace, use the skills from this text to get a good job, and then begin practicing what you have learned. Several features have been included in the text to help you win the game.

Learning Goals

The *Understanding Business* game looks like this. You start the game by reading through a series of goals. The objective of the game is to accomplish those goals so that you can reach the final objective: a challenging and rewarding career. To play the game right, you should read the learning goals first, before you attempt to read any of the 26 parts of the game book.

Progress Checks

Several times as you are going through the various parts of the game, I will stop you from reading and ask you some questions. If you know all the answers, you are winning the game. If you don't know the answers, it is easy to go back and find the answers before you go on. These short pauses in the game are called "Progress Checks" because that's what they are—checks to measure your progress in understanding the material.

Thinking it Through

It is much easier to remember text material if you pause periodically and think of how the material specifically applies to you. The boxes called "Thinking It Through" challenge you to think about how the material you are reading applies in your own life. That way the game has more meaning to you. Together, the Progress Checks and the Thinking it Through sections will give you plenty of opportunity to test both your knowledge and your ability to apply that knowledge.

Summaries

The summaries at the end of each chapter are written in a question and answer format. That gives you one more chance to score yourself as you play the game. Read each question and try to answer it yourself before reading the answers in the summaries. If you have used the Progress Checks, then every summary should show you that you are winning the game and that you do understand more and more about business.

Key Terms

All games have new terms you have to learn, such as "icing the puck" in hockey, "double dribble" in basketball, and "clipping" in football. Once you know all the terms, the game is much easier to follow and understand. The same is true of the *Understanding Business* game. Therefore, key terms will be printed in bold and defined in the margin. If you learn the terms as you go through each of the 26 parts, it will be easy to remember them when the game gets even more serious— out in the business world.

Career Information

There are sections and boxes throughout the text describing careers, future job opportunities in those careers, and salaries. Each of those parts is highlighted by having the same color background so you can search for career information at a glance. If you play the game right, one of those careers may be waiting for you when you complete your education.

Learning by Doing

Each chapter ends with some exercises that encourage you to go out and do some research or somehow get involved in the learning process. This is designed to be an action course or game. You may find that it is easier to win the game when each person does his or her own research and then shares the results with the instructor and the class. Your instructor may divide the assignments so that no one has so much to do. There are many ways to play the game.

Practicing Management Decisions

There are two cases at the end of each chapter that enable you to think through what you have learned in a real-world situation. You may enjoy working through these cases as game practice whether or not they are assigned in class.

Game Experience

In the work world, you will be expected to come on time, to complete your work when it is due and turn it in, and to be a responsible contributor to the organization. That means you will be expected to communicate effectively in both oral and written form. There is no better place to practice those skills than in class. Now is the time to commit yourself to being prepared when you come to class, to contribute if you are asked, and to do the assigned work on time. If you do this in all your classes, you will have work habits that will serve you well all your life.

The main reason most people play games is because they are fun. I have done everything I can to make this text a rewarding experience. That is true of Times Mirror/Mosby as well. As you can see, we have chosen an attractive cover, colorful illustrations, clear and readable charts, and a very readable format. All of this was done to make the game enjoyable and a great learning experience. Good luck. I hope you win the game.

Bill Nickels

CONTENTS

PART I   BUSINESS TRENDS AND THE ECONOMIC ENVIRONMENT

Prologue: Career and Course Resources, 3

Business careers, 4
  Assessing your skills and personality, 4
  Establishing a resource file, 5
  Career opportunities today, 7
  Career preparation, 7
Resources for the course, 8
  The professor as a resource, 10
  The text as a resource, 10
  Outside readings as a resource, 11
  Your classmates as a resource, 12
  Outside contacts as a resource, 13
  The library as a resource, 14

1 Trends Affecting Business, 19

The service revolution, 20
  Where the jobs will be, 22
  The business of nonprofit organizations, 23
Megatrends, 24
  Trend toward small business, 24
  Service and repair job opportunities, 27
  The computer revolution, 27
  The social revolution, 29
International markets, 38
  Opportunities in international business, 38
Summary, 40

Appendix: Arts Administration Internships, 42

2 Capitalism and Business, 47

The importance of economics to business, 48
What is economics? 48
The study of economics, 49
  Macroeconomics, 49
  Microeconomics, 50
Early economic thought: Malthus (1766-1834), 50
Capitalist economics: Adam Smith (1723-1790), 52
  Capitalism: freedom and incentives, 53
  The basic rights of capitalism vs. communism, 53
How free markets work, 54
  How prices are determined, 55
  Equilibrium point, 56
  World markets: supply and demand, 57
Limitations of the free market system, 58
The socialist experiment, 60
The communist experiment, 61
  Capitalist inroads, 61
Experimenting with a mixed economy, 62
Summary, 63

3 Economic Issues Affecting Business, 69

Gross national product, 71
   Dividing GNP, 71
   Productivity, 72
The issue of unemployment, 74
   Unemployment compensation, 76
The issue of inflation, 77
   Measures of inflation, 77
The issue of recession versus inflation, 80
   Stagflation and supply-side economics, 80

The issue of monetary policy, 82
   Tight versus loose monetary policy, 82
   The federal deficit, 82
The issue of fiscal policy, 83
   Taxes and spending, 83
The issue of the national debt, 85
The issue of trade deficits, 88
Summary, 89

PART II   BUSINESS FORMATION

4 Forms of Business Organization, 97

Getting started in business, 98
What is a business? 98
Forms of business ownership, 98
   Advantages of sole proprietorship, 99
   Disadvantages of sole proprietorships, 100
Partnership, 102
   Advantages of partnerships, 102
   Disadvantages of partnerships, 103
Corporations, 104
   Advantages of corporations, 104
   Disadvantages of corporations, 106
   How to incorporate, 108
Subchapter S corporations, 110
Cooperatives, 110
Joint ventures, 111
Which form for you? 113
Summary, 114

5 Managing a Small Business, 119

Small versus big business, 120
   Importance of small businesses, 120
   Small business categories, 122
Starting a small business, 125
   Small business success and failure, 125
   The entrepreneurial spirit, 127
How to start a successful small business, 128
   Learn from others, 128
   Get some experience, 128
   Take over a successful firm, 129
Managing a small business, 129
   Begin with planning, 131
   Accounting, 132
   Finance, 132
   Human resource management, 134
   Computers in small business, 135
   The small business administration, 137
International small business prospects, 138
Summary, 139

6 Entrepreneurship and Franchising, 145

The entrepreneurial spirit, 146
   The entrepreneurial explosion, 147
   What does it take to be an entrepreneur? 149
   Individual entrepreneurs, 149
   Entrepreneurial teams, 149
   Women entrepreneurs, 150
   Minority entrepreneurs, 151
   Skunkworks, 151
   Intrapreneuring, 152
Franchises, 153
   Advantages of franchising, 153
   Disadvantages of franchises, 155
   Buying a franchise, 157
   Franchising in international markets, 158
Summary, 159

PART III   FUNDAMENTALS OF MARKETING

Adia temporaries have appeal.

7   Marketing Principles, 165

The importance of marketing, 166
What marketing is, 166
   Marketing management: the four *P*'s, 167
Product differentiation—from chickens to sneakers, 169
What do marketers do? 169
   The marketing communication function, 171
   The market segmentation function, 172
   Marketing research, 176
Business orientation: from production to marketing, 178
The marketing concept, 179
   Consumer orientation, 179
   Coordination and integration of the firm, 180
   Profit orientation, 181
Applying the marketing concept in the 1980s, 181
   Applying a more societal marketing concept, 182
   Broadening the concept of marketing, 182
Industrial marketing, 183
Summary, 186

8   Marketing Communication, 193

The importance of communication, 194
   Communication versus promotion, 195
   Marketing publics, 196
Marketing communication in action, 196
   Internal marketing comes first, 198
   Good communication begins with listening, 198
Marketing communication systems, 199
   Listening to publics: marketing intelligence, 199
   Marketing intelligence versus marketing research, 200
   Responding to publics, 200

Promotion, 201
   Advertising, 202
   Sales promotion, 205
   Word of mouth, 207
   Public relations, 208
   Personal selling, 210
Summary, 215

9   Product Development and Pricing, 221

Product importance, 222
   What is a product? 223
   Different product views, 223
   The product mix, 225
   Marketing different classes of consumer goods, 226
   Marketing industrial products, 227
Packaging changes the product, 227
   The growing importance of packaging, 228
   Different packaging functions, 228
Branding, 229
   Brand categories, 229
   Labeling legislation, 230
   Brand images, 230
Product management, 230
   New product success, 231
   The new product-development process, 231
Product strategy and the product life cycle, 234
   The product life cycle, 235
Pricing, 236
   Importance of pricing, 236
Pricing objectives, 237
   How are prices determined? 238
   Pricing strategies, 239
   Retail pricing (markups), 241
   Nonprice competition, 242
Summary, 242

10   Distribution: Wholesaling and Retailing, 249

Place–the fourth *P* of the marketing mix, 250
Why we need middlemen, 251
   How middlemen add value, 252
   Middlemen and exchange efficiency, 254
Retail middlemen, 255
   Retail store categories, 257
   Out-of-store shopping, 258
   Scrambled merchandising, 259
   Retail distribution strategy, 259

Wholesale middlemen, 260
  Functional discounts, 261
  Merchant wholesalers, 262
  Manufacturer-owned wholesale outlets, 264
Physical distribution, 264
  Importance of distribution, 265
  The physical distribution manager, 266
  Transportation modes, 266
  Criteria for selecting distribution systems, 268
  The storage function, 269
  Materials handling, 269
Channel systems, 269
  Cooperative channel systems, 270
  Corporate systems, 270
  Contractual systems, 270
  Administered systems, 270
  The channel captain, 271
  Channel systems of the future, 271
  Summary, 273

11 Service and Nonprofit Marketing, 279

The service sector, 280
  The difference between goods and services, 281
Your involvement with services, 283
  Half of consumer expenditures go for services, 283
Strategies for marketing services, 285
  Strategies for marketing convenience services, 285
  Strategies for marketing shopping services, 286
  Strategies for marketing specialty services, 287
  Strategies for marketing industrial and professional
    services, 288
Nonprofit organization marketing and management, 289
  Special types of nonprofit marketing, 290
  Political marketing, 291
  Marketing for charities, 292
Community Service, 292
  Social catalyst, 292
  Targeting volunteers, 292
  Giving direction, 293
  Structuring the organization, 293
  Visible success, 293
  Maintaining enthusiasm, 294
Universally applicable business concepts, 294
Summary, 294

PART IV   MANAGEMENT

The Trouble With Surrounding Yourself With
Yes-Men Is That The Results Are Usually Negative.

12 Management and Leadership, 301

The changing role of management, 302
  Managers are needed everywhere, 303
What do managers do? 304
Planning, 305
  Planning in action, 306
Organization, 307
Leadership, 308
  Leadership styles, 309
Control, 313
  Setting standards, 314
Tasks at different levels of management, 315
  Delegating, 317
  Decision making, 318
Learning managerial skills, 318
  Verbal skills, 319
  Writing skills, 319
  Computer skills, 319
  Human relations skills, 320
  Other technical skills, 321
  Summary, 321

13 **Organizing a Business,** 327

Organizational trends, 328
  What is organization structure? 330
  Formal versus informal organization, 331
The importance of organizational design, 332
  Departmentalization, 333
Organization theory: Fayol, 335
  Max Weber and organizational theory, 336
Designing organizations, 338
  Tall versus flat organization structures, 338
  Span of control, 339
  Centralization versus decentralization of authority, 340
  Organization at Campbell Soup Company, 341
Organization types, 343
  A line and staff system, 343
  The matrix organization, 344
Organizational culture, 347
  Informal organization, 349
Summary, 350

14 **Production and Operations Management,** 357

America's manufacturing base, 358
  The reindustrialization controversy, 359
  Globalization and deindustrialization, 359
Fundamentals of production, 360
  Keeping costs low: site selection, 362
  Locating close to markets, 364
Production utility, 364
The production process, 365
  Materials requirement planning (MRP), 366
  Just-in-time inventory control, 366
Making changes in the production process, 368
  The use of CAD and CAM, 369
The computerized factory, 371
  Computer-integrated manufacturing (CIM), 373
  Local area networks (LANs), 374
  Control procedures: PERT, critical path, and
    Gantt charts, 374
People versus machines, 377
Quality control, 378
  Quality circles, 378
Automating the service sector, 379
  Automating the salesperson, 380
Preparing for the future, 381
Summary, 383

15 **Computers, Robots, and Other Business
Tools,** 389

The information age is here, 390
Careers in computers, 391
  Systems analysts, 393
  Computer service, 393
  Other computer careers, 393
Five generations of computers, 395
  Parallel processing, 395
Computer hardware, 396
  Technological changes in computers, 398
  More power on a chip, 398
Computer software, 399
Planning and designing computer systems, 400
  Identify information needs, 400
  Involve all departments, 401
  Seek input from the data processing department, 401
  Seek other expert advice, 402
  Choose software first, 402
  Decide whether to buy or use a computer service, 402
  Evaluate equipment and vendors, 403
  Train employees, 403
  Update system, including training, 404
  Integrate computer and personal communication, 404
The future of computers, 404
  Modems, 405
Computers and high-tech growth, 405
  Robotics, 405
  Telephone technology, 407
  Microwave and satellite transmission, 409
  Telemarketing, 410
  Videotex: linking you with the computer age, 412
Summary, 412

Appendix: Helpful Computer Terms, 417

PART V   MANAGEMENT OF HUMAN RESOURCES

16 Motivation of Workers, 421

Motivation and leadership, 422
Early management studies (Taylor), 422
  The Hawthorne studies (Mayo), 423
Motivation and Maslow's need hierarchy, 424
  Applying Maslow's theory, 426
McGregor's theory X and theory Y, 427
  Theory X, 428
  Theory Y, 428
Theory Z (Ouchi), 430
Motivation factors: Herzberg, 430
Job enrichment, 432
Management by objectives, 433
  Motivation through communication, 435
Implementing the new concepts, 437
  A model for the future, 437
Management by walking around, 439
Summary, 440

17 Human Resource Management, 447

The personnel function, 448
  The importance of personnel, 448
  The human resource problem, 450
Human resource planning, 451
  Recruiting, 452
  Selection, 453
  Employee orientation, 454

Employee training and development, 456
  Apprentice programs, 456
  Off-the-job training, 457
  Vestibule training, 457
  Job simulation, 457
Performance appraisals, 458
Compensation and benefits, 459
  Pay systems, 460
  Scanlon plans, 461
  Fringe benefits, 461
Management development, 462
  The importance of networking, 463
Adjusting to worker needs, 464
  Job sharing plans, 465
  Flextime plans, 465
  Compressed work weeks, 466
Human resource management, 466
Laws affecting human resource management, 467
  Laws protecting the handicapped, 468
  Minimum wage legislation, 468
  Other legislation, 468
Summary, 470

Appendix, 474

A five-step job search strategy, 474
  The job search, 474
Preparing a resumé and cover letters, 476
  Writing a resumé, 477
  Writing a cover letter, 480
Preparing for job interviews, 482
Be prepared to change jobs, 483

18 Employee-Management Issues: Unions, Executive Pay, and Comparable Worth, 487

Management-employee issues, 488
The development of labor unions, 489
  The early history of organized labor, 490
Labor legislation and collective bargaining, 492
  Objectives of organized labor, 492
  Labor-management conflicts, 495
The future of labor-management relations, 497
The issue of executive compensation, 500
The issue of comparable worth, 502
  Recent public-sector comparable worth action, 503
  Comparable worth in industry, 503
The issue of employee ownership (ESOPs), 504
  Benefits of ESOPs, 504
  Problems with ESOPs, 506
The issue of employee satisfaction, 506
Summary, 508

PART VI   ACCOUNTING AND FINANCE

19 Accounting Principles, 515

The importance of accounting, 516
What is accounting? 517
    Accounting is user-oriented, 517
    Managerial accounting, 518
    Financial accounting, 519
Accounting versus bookkeeping, 519
    Accounting documents, 521
The "accounts" of accounting, 522
    The asset account, 522
    The liabilities account, 524
    The owners' equity account, 524
    The revenue account, 524
    The expense account, 524
Accounting journals, 525
Accounting ledgers, 525
Financial statements, 525
    The income statement, 526
The balance sheet, 528
    The fundamental accounting equation, 529
Accounting creativity, 531
Cash flow problems, 533
    Cash flow and the bank, 534
Careers in accounting, 534
    Bookkeepers, 535
    Accountants, 535
    Becoming a Certified Public Accountant (CPA) or
        Certified Management Accountant (CMA), 535
Summary, 538

Appendix: Financial Ratios, 542

Average collection period of receivables, 542
Credit terms, 543
    Return on sales, 543
Return on investment (ROI), 543
Inventory turnover, 544
Debt-to-equity ratio, 544
Other ratios, 545

20 Financial Institutions, Money, and Banking, 547

The banking industry, 548
The American banking system, 548
    Commercial banks, 549
    Savings and loan associations, 553
    Credit unions, 554
    Mutual savings banks, 554
    The Federal Deposit Insurance Corporation, 555
    The Federal Savings and Loan Insurance Corporation, 555
Other financial institutions, 555
    Electronic funds transfer systems (EFTS), 556
    Financial supermarkets, 558
The Federal Reserve System, 559
    Organization of the Federal Reserve System, 559
    Operations of the Federal Reserve System, 560
    Regulating the money supply, 560
    Other functions of the Fed, 562
Early banking history, 565
    The Great Depression, 566
Bank failures—1930s and 1980s, 567
Summary, 569

21 Financial Management, 575

The role of finance, 576
    What is finance? 576
    Internal auditing, 578
    Financial problems, 578
Long-term financing, 578
    Venture capital, 579
    Equity financing, 580
    Debt financing, 583
Short-term financing, 587
    Trade credit, 587
    Family and friends, 588
    Commercial banks, 588
    Different forms of bank loans, 589
    Factoring, 590
    Commercial paper, 591
    Internal sources of funds, 591

The romance of finance, 591
Financial planning, 592
　Short-term forecasting, 592
　Long-term forecasting, 592
Budgeting, 593
Financial controls, 594
　Spreadsheet analysis, 594
Tax preparation, 595
Summary, 596

22 Stocks and Bonds, 601

Securities markets, 602
Stock exchanges, 602
　U.S. exchanges, 603
　The over-the-counter (OTC) market, 603
How to buy stock, 604
　Market orders and limit orders, 604
　Buying on margin, 605
　Odd lot trading, 605
　Stock splits, 605
　Bulls and bears, 605
Choosing the right investment, 606
　Investment criteria, 606
　Diversification, 607
　Mutual funds, 607
　The bond market, 609
Commodity exchanges, 610
　Hedging, 611

Understanding financial data in the media, 611
　Stock quotations, 612
　Mutual fund quotations, 614
　Bond quotations, 615
Securities regulations, 615
　Federal regulation, 616
　Additional regulation, 616
Summary, 618

23 Personal Financial Planning, 623

Financial management, 624
　Saving for the future, 624
Building your capital account, 624
　Applying the strategy, 626
Real estate—the number-one investment, 626
　Tax deduction and home ownership, 627
Money management, 628
　Credit cards, 628
Insurance coverage, 630
　Health insurance, 631
Education—the best investment, 632
Planning your retirement, 632
　Social Security, 633
　Individual retirement accounts (IRAs), 633
　Keogh plans, 635
　Financial planners, 635
Summary, 636

PART VII   RISK MANAGEMENT, ETHICS, AND INTERNATIONAL BUSINESS

24 Risk Management and Insurance, 641

Managing risk, 642
Identifying risk, 642
　Reducing risk, 643
　Self-insurance, 643
　Avoiding risk, 644
　The insurance crisis, 646
Insurance companies, 647
The law of large numbers, 648
　Rule of indemnity, 648
　Coinsurance clause, 648
　Deductible clauses, 649
Business risk insurance, 649
Property insurance, 650
　Automobile insurance, 650
　Marine and aviation insurance, 651
Liability insurance, 651
　Workers' compensation insurance, 651
　The issue of product liability insurance, 652
　Commercial multiline policies, 654

Criminal loss and nonperformance protection, 654
Business interruption insurance, 654
Health insurance, 655
Life insurance for businesses, 655
  Group life insurance, 655
  Owner or key executive insurance, 655
  Retirement and pension plans, 656
Farm insurance, 656
Homeowner's insurance (apartment insurance), 656
The risk of damaging the environment, 657
Careers in risk management, 658
  Insurance sales, 659
  Insurance adjusters and actuaries, 659
Summary, 661

25 Business Law and Ethics, 667

Business law, 668
Contract law, 669
  Breach of contract, 669
The uniform commercial code, 670
  Warranties, 670
  Negotiable instruments, 670
Patent law, 670
Bankruptcy laws, 671
Statutory and common law, 671
Laws to promote fair and competitive practices, 672
  The Sherman Act of 1890, 672
  The Clayton Act of 1914, 673
  The Federal Trade Commission Act of 1914, 674
  The Robinson-Patman Act of 1936, 674
  The Pure Food and Drug Act of 1906, 675
  The Fair Packaging and Labeling Act of 1966, 675
  The tort system, 676
  Recent legislation, 677
Consumerism, 679
  Environmental issues, 681
Corporate social responsibility, 682
  Social auditing, 683
Business integrity begins at the top, 685
  Ethical standards, 686
Summary, 687

26 International Business, 693

The international market, 694
Terms of international trade, 695
  Other terms regarding world trade, 696
The trade deficit, 697
Why trade with other nations? 699
  Getting involved, 700
Restrictions on foreign trade, 702
  Trade protectionism, 703
  Other trade constraints, 704
Trading in world markets, 705
  Exporting, 706
  Licensing, 706
  Creating subsidiaries, 706
  Franchising, 707
Global marketing, 707
  Export trading firms, 708
  Joint ventures, 708
  Countertrading, 710
Multinational corporations, 711
  Global corporations, 711
  International trade organizations, 713
The future of world trade, 715
Summary, 717

Glossary, G1

Chapter Notes, C1

Author Index, AI1

Company and Product Index, CPI1

General Index, GI1

BUSINESS TRENDS AND THE ECONOMIC ENVIRONMENT

PART I

PROLOGUE
CAREER AND COURSE RESOURCES

CHAPTER 1
TRENDS AFFECTING BUSINESS

CHAPTER 2
CAPITALISM AND BUSINESS

CHAPTER 3
ECONOMIC ISSUES AFFECTING BUSINESS

CAREER AND COURSE RESOURCES

Alan Kutz's story is a good example of why *every* college student should take a course in business. Alan began his college career as a political science major. While in college, he became fascinated by history and decided to become a history teacher. Alan got a B.A. in history from The George Washington University and an M.A. in history from Howard University. Alan took *no* courses in business.

The job market was such that a career in government looked more attractive to Alan than teaching. Thus he began his career as a research associate at the Library of Congress.

Alan wanted to move into management, but found he lacked the managerial background and business education needed for such a position. He decided to drop out of government for a while and go back to school to get an M.A. in public administration. Alan learned a little late that a knowledge of business is necessary in *any* organization.

Armed with some managerial training, Alan became a management intern for the U.S. Department of Labor. With this experience and his managerial education, Alan was able to obtain a position as coordinator of the Comprehensive Employment Training Act (CETA) program for Montgomery County, Maryland. Using the knowledge of business, economics, and management that he gained in the CETA program, Alan left to become the Executive Director of the Corporation for Technological Training. None of Alan's jobs was in a *business* yet (these were all nonprofit, government organizations), but he was certainly using his business knowledge and skills.

Alan found that working for others, especially the government, could be very frustrating. He simply did not have the freedom to do what he wanted to do. Today, Alan is part-owner of his own firm, called Career Lab. Alan's firm tests people for specific aptitudes and skills and places them in today's challenging new jobs. His advice to today's college student is to learn business skills such as computer use and effective writing and oral communication. ▪

Alan Kutz.

3

BUSINESS CAREERS

Almost all of us want to find a rewarding career and to be successful and happy. We just find it hard to decide what that career should be. Even those who have relatively successful careers tend to look for something more fulfilling, more challenging, and more interesting.

One purpose of this text is to introduce you to the wide variety of careers available in business and management. You will learn about marketing, finance, accounting, economics, personnel, management, and more. When you are finished, you should have a much better idea about what kind of business career would be best for you. Not only that, you will also be prepared to use basic business terms and concepts to be a success in *any* organization, including government agencies, charities, and social causes—or in your own small business.

This book is written in a different style from most textbooks. It is written to you and for you, the student. It is not just a text full of facts and figures; it is a guidebook for understanding business. Special attention is given to career opportunities, techniques for starting your own business or for managing a small business, and strategies for finding and getting the rewarding career that you want. A great place to start in your career search is with a course like this one. It should be one of the most valuable courses you take, regardless of your major. Each chapter in this book will begin with a Profile of someone in the business world. Many of the people you'll meet in the Profiles learned the hard way that it is easy to fail in business if you don't know what you are doing. These stories are a good way to learn from the experiences of others. The Profile of Alan Kutz (p. 3) is an example of this.

Assessing Your Skills and Personality

There are hundreds of men and women like Alan out in the world, people who are fantastic resources for career information because they have *been there*. Alan kept changing jobs, searching for the right one until he was in his 40s. Now he counsels people who are successful in making money but unhappy with their jobs. To help them find the right career, Alan gives them a general aptitude and interest test and then advises them about the careers that are best suited for their skills and personality.

After working with thousands of clients, Alan has learned that many people choose an occupation that doesn't fit their personality. The result is that these people are unhappy at work. They then come to the Career Lab at age 35 or 40 to learn what they should have done and try to start over. Clearly, this is not the best way to find the right career.

The earlier you can do a personal assessment of your interests, skills, and values, the better it will be for finding some career direction. In recognition of this need, many colleges have assessment programs you can take. About 300 schools use a software exercise called SIGI (System for Interactive Guidance and Information). A different version, called DISCOVER is used at 400 other schools. Both feature self-assessment exercises, create personalized lists of occupations based on *your* interests and skills, and provide information about careers and the preparation required. The Strong-Campbell Interest Inventory can be used to supplement DISCOVER and reinforce the results.

SIGI-Plus is a self-assessment exercise.

It would be helpful to take such programs early in this course so you can discover, while you are learning about the different business fields, which ones most closely fit *your* interests and skills.

These self-assessment programs will help you assess the kind of work *environment* you would prefer (for example, technical, social service, or business), what *values* you seek to fulfill in a career (for example, security, variety, independence), what *abilities* you have (for example, creative/artistic, numerical, sales), and what important *job characteristics* you prefer (for example, income, travel, amount of pressure on the job). Armed with such information, you are more likely to make a career choice that will be personally fulfilling. Such assessment tests are available in college placement centers, career labs, and libraries.

Establishing a Resource File

While it is essential to read information about careers, various businesses, and useful facts and figures, one tends to forget such data. It is extremely important to keep the names of contact people at various organizations. It is also important to have access to facts and figures of all kinds about the economy and business-related subjects.

An effective way to become an expert on almost any business subject is to set up your own information system. Eventually you may want to store data on computer disks for retrieval on your personal computer. Meanwhile, it is effective to establish a comprehensive paper filing system.

Each time you read a story about a firm that interests you, either cut it out of the magazine or photocopy it and place it in an appropriate file. You might begin with files labeled "Careers," "Small business," "Economics," "Management," and "Resource people." Soon you will have a tremendous resource file. Later, you

WHICH JOBS PAY THE MOST IN DIFFERENT BUSINESS CAREERS?

MAJOR	1985 SALARY
Finance, economics	$20,916
Accounting, auditing	20,460
Business administration	19,620
Communications	19,620
Nontechnical sales	19,116
Retail sales	18,012

Salary differences are not so significant that you should choose a major you don't like just for the money it pays. Do what you enjoy, and the pay will follow.
Source: College Placement Council, 1985.

GROWTH IN SELECTED BUSINESS JOBS FOR THE FUTURE (1995)

	NUMBER OF JOBS
Technical sales representatives	387,000
Accountants, auditors	344,000
Retail store managers	291,000
Systems analysts	217,000
Nontechnical sales representatives	100,000
Restaurant and bar managers	137,000
Insurance salespeople	91,000
Retail store buyers	75,000
Wholesale employees	55,000
Purchasing agents	51,000
Personnel and labor relations	47,000
Employment interviewers	29,000
Public relations	25,000
Tax preparers	14,000
Special agents for insurance	13,000
Real estate brokers	12,000
Financial services sales	11,000
Credit analysts	9,000
Stockbrokers	2,000

Note that the greatest number of future jobs are in sales and marketing in general; next is accounting, then systems analysis and personnel-related jobs.

Source: Bureau of Labor Statistics, 1985.

might add to these initial files so that at a minimum they would include the following topics:

- Accounting
- Career information
- Computers (applications, new capabilities, and so on)
- Economics
- Government (statistics, regulations, and so on)
- International business
- Investments
- Marketing
- Resource people
- Small business management
- Social issues

If you start now, you will have at your fingertips information that will prove invaluable for use in term papers and throughout your career. Few college students do this filing and as a consequence lose most of the information they read in college or even after college. It is one of *the* most effective ways of educating yourself and having the information available when you need it. The only space you will need to start is a 12-inch by 12-inch corner of your room to hold a portable file box.

In these files you might put your course notes, the names of your professors, the books you used, and so on. You may need this information later for references. Also, be sure to keep all the notes you make when talking with people about careers, including salary information, courses needed, and contacts.

Television shows such as *Wall Street Week* are another good way to learn about business and investments. Have you watched *Adam Smith's Money World,*

Shows such as *Wall Street Week* can increase your learning experience.

Nightly Business Report, or other business shows? Try watching some of them and see which ones you like best.

Apple is an example of a new firm with challenging careers.

Career Opportunities Today

This is an exciting time for college students. Not since the dawn of the industrial age have there been more new career opportunities. About 700,000 new businesses were formed in the United States in 1986 and hundreds of thousands of new businesses are being started every year. Some of these businesses are in traditional areas such as restaurants and retail stores, but many new firms are in challenging areas that are opening whole new careers for tomorrow's graduates (see the box below).

The names of some of the modern firms may be familiar to you; for example Apple Computer and Domino's Pizza. Most firms, though, are small and are in new fields such as cable television (e.g., Heritage Communications), robotics (e.g., GMF Robotics, Prab Robots, Intelledex), biotechnology (e.g., Cetus, Genentech), and electronics (e.g., Energy Conversion Devices, Healthdyne). You may never have heard of most of these firms, yet they represent the kinds of firms in which many of tomorrow's jobs will be.

THE AGE OF OPPORTUNITY

Charles H. Kaman, founder and chairman of Kaman Corp., a bearings, music, and aerospace concern, in the commencement program, University of Hartford, May 19, 1985:

"I started Kaman, which is now a half-billion dollar company, when I was 26 years old—not much older than most of you. I remember those days. They were tough. And even then, there were people talking about the 'good old days' of a generation before. The 'good old days' exist only in dreamers' minds as an excuse for inaction.

"I have seen many administrations in Washington, all economic conditions from boom to bust, and have lived with 40 years of changing tax codes and policy, some favorable and some unfavorable to business. With no reservations, I can say this is a very good time to start a career. This is, once again, the age of the entrepreneur. It is also the age of the scientist, the researcher, the teacher. It is the age of the talented manager, the professional and the artist. Today, an individual of character, intelligence and drive can, in fact, do almost anything. This country is absolutely bursting with opportunity."

Career Preparation

How does one prepare for careers in these new areas? How can students learn more about these new firms and what they do? What courses should students take to prepare themselves for the interesting new careers of tomorrow? These are the kinds of questions that this course and all the resources discussed in this prologue will help you answer.

If you are a typical college student, you may not have any idea what you would like to do for a career. That is not necessarily a big disadvantage in today's rapidly changing job market. There is no certain way to prepare for the most interesting and challenging jobs of tomorrow; many of them have not even been created yet. Rather, you should continue your college education; learn skills such as verbal communication, writing, and math; and remain flexible while you explore the job market. The box titled "How Important Is the Choice of College Major?" is the edited text of a speech given by William Raspberry to graduates at the University of Maryland. He focuses on the issue of not having a clear career objective.

HOW IMPORTANT IS THE CHOICE OF COLLEGE MAJOR?

William Raspberry, a columnist for *The Washington Post,* gave the following talk to graduates of the University of Maryland. It has been shortened for use in this text.

"Apart from the minority of you who will leave college for such trade schools as medicine or law or engineering, it is likely that by the time you are my age you will be doing something totally unrelated to your undergraduate major.

"That does not mean that your undergraduate years will have been a waste; it only means that *their value will consist primarily of the generalized information we call liberal arts.* What your college education will have given you is someplace to stand while you figure out where to go.

"It's all right. Take the word of someone whose major was, at various times, English, history, mathematics and pre-seminary, it's all right. You don't really need to know what you'll be doing 10, 15 or 20 years hence. And even if you wanted to know, you couldn't. Things are changing too fast.

"The new possibilities are unknown and unknowable. You cannot get ready for them in any specific way. I only hope that you have, during your college years, learned the art of flexibility; that you have learned how to learn. Because that will be your most valuable asset in the years ahead: your willingness to stay loose and to recognize opportunity when it comes along, even if it bears no direct relationship to your college major. . . .

"Your best shot at *happiness, self-worth* and *personal satisfaction*—the things that constitute real success—is not in earning as much as you can but in performing as well as you can something that you consider worthwhile. Whether that is healing the sick, giving hope to the hopeless, adding to the beauty of the world, or saving the world from nuclear holocaust, I cannot tell you.

"Your own talents, inclinations and ideals are your best guide. Just make sure that it is something that enriches your mind and your soul, not just your bank account."

Source: William Raspberry, "Good Major," *The Washington Post,* June 4, 1984. (Italics added for emphasis.)

RESOURCES FOR THE COURSE

College courses are best at teaching you terms and concepts and ways of thinking about business. To learn about real-world applications, you have to go out and learn for yourself. Textbooks are like comprehensive tour guides in that they tell you what to look for and where to look, but they can never replace experience.

This text, then, is not meant to be the only resource for this class. In fact, it is not the primary resource. Your professor is much better at responding to your questions and needs. This book is just one resource he or she can use with you to satisfy your desire to fully grasp what the business world is all about. Actually, there are six basic resources for the class:

1 *The professor.* Your instructor is more than a teacher of facts and figures. He or she is a resource person who is there to answer questions and guide you to the answers. One of the most valuable facets of college is the chance to study with experienced professors.

2 *The text, Understanding Business,* and the *Study Guide* that comes with it. The *Study Guide* will help you review the material and give you practice answering questions; that way you can practice taking tests before you have to take actual tests for a grade (see Figure P-1).

3 *Outside readings.* If you are not in the habit of reading business periodicals, now is the time to start. It is impossible to ask intelligent questions and carry on a meaningful dialogue about business topics without having some knowledge about current topics and terms from the literature. You may be pleasantly surprised to find you enjoy reading *The Wall Street Journal* and watching *Wall Street Week* and other business shows on television. You should at least give it a try.

4 *Your own experience and that of your classmates.* Many college students have had some experience working in a retail store, a restaurant, or some other business or nonprofit organization. Sharing those experiences exposes you to many real-life examples that are invaluable for understanding business.

5 *Outside contacts.* A good way to learn about business is to go out and visit businesses personally. Who can tell you more about what it's like to start a career in accounting than someone who is doing it now? The same is true of other jobs. The world will be your classroom if you let it be.

FIGURE P-1

The text is not the only resource for this course; it is not even the primary resource. You can gain knowledge and experience from everything you read and from all the people you meet.

6 *The library.* There are newspapers and magazines in the library on all phases of business. Take a day to review what is available. You might look for *The Wall Street Journal* newspaper and *Inc., Business Week, Forbes, Money,* and *Financial World* magazines. Also, check out the career section of the library for what is available. The library and the librarian are excellent resources.

The Professor as a Resource

It is important for you to develop a friendly relationship with your professors. One reason for this is that professors often get job leads that they can pass on to you. They are also excellent references for future jobs. But most of all, your professor is one more experienced person who can help you find materials and answer questions about business.

The Text as a Resource

There are many learning aids included throughout the text to assist you in understanding the material. A brief review of these follows.

The first learning aid is a list of Learning Goals at the beginning of each chapter. If you read through these objectives, it will help set the framework for the chapter material. Sometimes it is hard to get into studying; the Learning Goals provide an introduction to get your mind in a learning mode.

Periodically in the chapters, you will encounter a set-off section called a Progress Check. The purpose of these aids is to give you a chance to pause and think about what you have just read. We all have experienced having our minds wander while we read. These Progress Checks can help you realize whether you are really absorbing the material or not. They are also an excellent review device.

You may have noticed that all the key definitions in the book are highlighted in boldface type. This will help you improve your business vocabulary. The Key Terms are also defined in the margins, and page references to important terms are given at the end of each chapter. A full glossary is located in the back of the book. Terminology is a major part of an introductory course, and you should rely heavily on these learning aids to help you commit the terms to memory.

The sections titled Thinking It Through are designed to help you relate the material to your own experiences. They get you thinking about the meaning of what you have read *beyond* the course. It is much easier to retain material that you can relate to your own life.

The cartoons, photographs, boxes, figures, and other highlighted material are designed to reinforce and highlight key concepts, and to make the book a more effective learning tool as well as a pleasure to read. Great care has been used in selecting them to make sure these objectives are achieved.

The summaries are not mere reviews of what has been said. Rather, they are written in question-and-answer form, much like a classroom dialogue. This format makes the material more lively and should help you remember it better.

No matter how hard we try to make learning easier, the truth is that we forget most of what we read and hear. To really remember something, it is best to *do* it. That is why there is a section called Getting Involved in each chapter. These are not the typical textbook end-of-chapter questions. These are mini-projects that you can do now or later to reinforce what you have read by getting more involved.

You may find it easiest to divide these projects among the class and come back and share what you have learned.

The Practicing Management Decisions cases are another chance to think about the material and apply it in real-life situations. Don't skip the cases even if they are not reviewed in class. They are an integral part of the learning process because they enable you to apply what you have learned.

If you use all of these learning aids plus the *Study Guide,* you will not simply "take a course in business." Instead, you will have actively participated in a learning exercise that will help you greatly in your chosen career.

Outside Readings as a Resource

We have noted that business periodicals are one of the six major resources of the course. It is recommended that you review the following magazines and newspapers, as well as other resources, during the course and throughout your career:
- *The Wall Street Journal*
- *Forbes*
- *Inc.*
- *Business Week*
- *Fortune*
- The business section of your local paper

If you are not familiar with these sources, it is time to get to know them. You don't necessarily have to become a regular subscriber, but you should learn what

Business literature is a major resource for understanding business.

information is available in these sources over time, especially information that will help you get a job. All of these sources are available free of charge in your school or local library.

The Wall Street Journal is an excellent way to stay current with national and international news on business and economics. By reading just the front page of *The Wall Street Journal* daily, you can keep up with national and international news as well as business and economic conditions. The editorial pages discuss current issues in depth and explain them from a businessperson's perspective.

Forbes, Fortune, Business Week, and *Inc.* magazines are excellent sources also. They have stories about various large and small firms and their strategies for competing in today's markets. For your purposes, these magazines will introduce you to the firms that will be providing the job opportunities of the future. *Inc.* magazine, for example, picks the top 500 small businesses each year and discusses them in depth. It also introduces you to other new, growing companies and who their key people are. Using that information, you can contact those firms and explore career possibilities.

Your Classmates as a Resource

It is often quite productive to interact with your classmates out of class as well as in. They know people and have had experiences that would be very beneficial for you. Don't rely totally on the professor for "answers" to the cases and other exercises in this book. Often there is no "right" answer, and your classmates may open up whole new ways of looking at things for you.

Part of being a successful businessperson is knowing how to work with others, and college classrooms are excellent places to practice this skill. Some professors will encourage their students to work together in small groups by providing them opportunities to do so. Such exercises build teamwork as well as presentation and

THE RETURNING STUDENT

According to the U.S. Census Bureau, many college students now are 22 years old or older. Furthermore, a much larger percentage of the older students are women; the number of women students over 22 years of age more than doubled in the last decade. In urban institutions, the average age of students is 28 years. More students in such schools go to school *after* 4:00 PM than before. Returning students include:

- Veterans who are upgrading their job skills for more promising careers.
- Women who have returned to school because their children are grown or because they need to work due to divorce or other family circumstances.
- High school graduates who have been working for several years, but need skills in computers, writing, and other areas to find better jobs.

- Full-time employees seeking to further their career or to take courses "just for fun."
- People who have lost their jobs because of technological change (e.g., auto workers, miners, and farmers).

Returning students usually are more serious about college because they have experienced the need for certain skills in the real world. They often work harder and longer than traditional 18- to 22-year-old students.

Returning students often are as uncertain as traditional students about career choices and strategies for finding the right job in the right firm. There is little reason to take business courses if the ultimate result isn't a better job or a more rewarding career.

analytical skills. Some of the students in your class may be quite experienced in their use of these skills (see the box on p. 12).

Outside Contacts as a Resource

After you have done a personal assessment, it is a good idea to begin exploring potential career possibilities in the areas that seem to fit you best. The time to begin studying career opportunities is now, not when you are closer to graduation. As you read about the various business functions (marketing, finance, etc.), try to imagine what it would be like doing such a job. Does it sound interesting? Do you have the needed skills? This book will give you some guidance, but the best way to learn about careers is to visit various organizations and talk with people in the different occupations.

When you go shopping, for example, think about whether or not you would enjoy working in a store. Talk with the clerks and the manager and see how they feel about the job. Think about the possibilities of working for a restaurant, a body

Which job fits you best?

shop, an art supply store, or any other establishment you visit. If something looks interesting, talk to the employees and learn more about the job. Soon you may discover fascinating careers in places such as the zoo, theaters, amusement parks, and health clubs. Do these careers look interesting? How much do they pay? Is there a chance to advance? The only way to find out is to ask.

What is it like to be a salesperson for a sporting goods company? Call one and ask. What is it like to be an accountant in a major firm? What do stockbrokers do? Is it fun? How do people feel about selling real estate, life insurance, or computers?

What courses should a college student take to prepare for such jobs? You'll never know unless you ask people doing them. It is not enough to read about careers; articles can make jobs look more exciting and glamorous than they really are. Visit an accounting office and see about accounting for yourself. Go to an advertising agency if that's what you're interested in.

Don't make up your mind until you have investigated. In short, be constantly on the alert to find career possibilities, and do not hesitate to talk with people about their careers. They will be pleased to give you their time because they are talking about their favorite subject—themselves.

It is as important to learn which jobs you do not enjoy as it is to find those you do. Elimination of some jobs from your alternatives takes you that much closer to the best job for you.

Later in the text, after you have learned more about different career opportunities, we shall discuss a step-by-step procedure for getting a job, including writing a resumé, writing a cover letter, managing job interviews, and more. That information is in the Appendix of Chapter 17. Before you get involved in such details, you need to become familiar with some other resources. One of those resources is the use of business periodicals.

The Library as a Resource

Few exercises you do in this class will be more important to you than this one. Your assignment is to do some library research to find the resources you might use to begin a successful career search. While you are in college, you may want to work as an intern in various firms to get a better feel for what people do. Here are some sources you could use for finding such jobs:

- *Summer Jobs* (Princeton, N.J.: Peterson's Guides, 1985).
- 1986 Internships (Cincinnati, Ohio: Writer's Digest Books, 1986).
- *The Experienced Hand: A Student Manual for Making the Most of an Internship* (Carroll Press, 1982).

What other sources are available in your library for finding internships? Write this information down and put it in your career file.

If you would like a head start in finding businesses that are looking for students, there are many sources. See if you can find the following:

- *The Corporate Job Hunting Guide for the College Student* (Englewood Cliffs, N.J.: Prentice Hall, Inc., 1985).
- *101 Challenging Government Jobs for College Graduates* (N.Y.: Prentice-Hall Press, 1986).
- *Peterson's Business and Management Jobs 1985* (Princeton, New Jersey: Peterson's Guides, Inc., 1984). Lists jobs in various locations, company profiles, job hints, and opportunities.

- *Jobs! What They Are . . .Where They Are . . .What They Pay . . .* (Simon & Schuster, 1985). This book by Robert O. and Anne M. Snelling discusses entry-level jobs in seven fields: (1) computers, (2) engineering, (3) finance, (4) health resources, (5) marketing, (6) media and communications, and (7) sales.

When you find the section where such books are kept, look at the other titles and list them along with the call letters. See if you can find books on specific careers such as the following:

- *Careers in Marketing* (Prentice-Hall, Inc., 1984).
- *Business and Management Jobs* (Princeton, N.J.: Peterson's Guides, 1986).
- *Opportunities in Accounting* (National Textbook Co., 1983).

What books are available on the careers you prefer now? Add them to your resource file.

Finally, look for books that will help you set up a successful strategy for winning the job you want. Some good ones include the following:

- *What Color Is Your Parachute?* (Ten Speed Press, changes annually). (A classic; 1986 or latest edition.)
- *Merchandising Your Job Talents* (U.S. Government Printing Office, 1980).

Look for books on how to write cover letters and resumés, dressing for success, and special strategies for women and minorities. Examples include the following:

- *To Work: A Guide for Women College Graduates* (Prentice-Hall, Inc., 1982).
- *Designing Creative Resumes* (Los Altos, Calif.: William Kaufman, Inc., 1985).
- *Re-Entering: Successful Back-to-Work Strategies for Women Seeking a Fresh Start* (Crown Publishers, 1980).
- *Hispanic Employment: A Recruitment Source Booklet* (U.S. Government Printing Office, 1980).
- *Resources for Affirmative Action* (Garrett Park Press, 1982).
- *Revising Your Resume* (New York: John Wiley & Sons, Inc., 1986).

To make this assignment and all the other assignments in the book work the best for you, you should (1) do careful research, (2) keep careful notes, (3) share your notes with the class, and (4) discuss your findings. This means working with your professor and the other students in the class.

LOOKING AHEAD

At the end of each chapter, you will find a section titled Looking Ahead. The idea is to set the stage for the next chapter by relating it to what you have just read. This prologue may be a good place to look ahead to the whole book, how it is set up, and why.

The first chapter in the text is a follow-up to this prologue. The world is changing so rapidly that it is hard to plan a lifetime career. One year there are too many teachers and the next there is a teacher shortage. One day petroleum engineers are in great demand, and 3 months later, the demand collapses. To stay up with such changes, it is important to follow trends and patterns. Chapter 1 reviews some trends that will have a major effect on careers and your life. The business environment is important for everyone to understand.

The rest of Part I reviews the fundamentals of economics. Whether or not you have ever studied economics, it is a good idea to explore economics from a business perspective. The market for goods and services is now a world market, and the world market is seriously affected by world economic conditions. There is no way to understand business today without understanding economic principles.

entrepreneur
An innovator who organizes, manages, and assumes the risks of starting a business.

After we have reviewed economics, we shall begin discussing various forms of business, with special attention given to small businesses and **entrepreneurs** (innovators who organize, manage, and assume the risks of starting a business). This subject is fascinating because of the many new businesses that are being started today and the job opportunities they offer.

Then we will explore the functions of business: marketing, management, personnel, accounting, finance, and the major business tools (for example, computers).

We end the course discussing important issues such as risk management (insurance), ethics, and international business.

The logic is that we should study the *environment* of business first (trends, economic issues), then the *forms* of business, and finally the *functions*. There are, however, good reasons to discuss ethics and international business earlier, so your instructor may assign them sooner. That should not hurt the continuity of the book, because each chapter is a separate learning experience that links with the other chapters in various ways. Good luck in the course; I hope you enjoy it.

TRENDS AFFECTING BUSINESS

PROFILE   CHARLOTTA STEPHENS, ENTREPRENEUR

Many college students are thinking of owning their own businesses some day. Naturally, they will have to get some experience first and save some money to invest. There are thousands of career opportunities for such entrepreneurs. Many foreign minorities and American blacks are finding small business ownership *the* path to personal wealth and satisfaction. Chapter 1 is about trends, and the trend toward small business is one of the most important. Charlotta Stephens is a good example of the opportunities and challenges available in small business.

Charlotta was a senior attorney at the Department of Commerce earning $50,000 a year, but was bored and restless. She pictured herself as an entrepreneur, and she planned and saved for 9 years to start her own business. Now she has two McDonald's restaurants in Baltimore. A *Washington Post* article about her discusses the obstacles she had to overcome:

> Although any business person needs financing, management and technical skills, blacks begin with some unique cultural, racial, and social pressures. Many blacks are brought up with an almost antibusiness bias, for example, conditioned to believe they should play it safe with a secure 9-to-5 job rather than take risks.

Charlotta Stephens.

Trends will tell you the direction the country is moving in. The decisions are up to you. But trends, like horses, are easier to ride in the direction they are already going.

JOHN NAISBITT

Charlotta Stephens was willing to take those risks and put in the time needed to become a success. She worked from 6 AM until 10 PM for months and months in her first store and then brought in her brother as manager. Then she bought a second store.

The decision to start a small business is an especially challenging one for black entrepreneurs like Charlotta, but one that more and more are accepting and winning. Much of the future employment for blacks depends on the growth of such small businesses. Today's black college students should learn more about small business management while in school. All students will find more opportunities in small businesses than in big corporations. ▨

Source: Dorothy Gilliam, "On Her Own," *The Washington Post,* May 7, 1984, p. 131.

THE SERVICE REVOLUTION

industrial sector
Industries such as mining, manufacturing, and construction.

Part of what makes this era such an exciting time for college students is the fact that the United States has entered a new stage of development—the service age or the information age. Figure 1-1 tells the story in a dramatic picture. It shows that the **industrial sector** of the economy is still the heart of the business system,

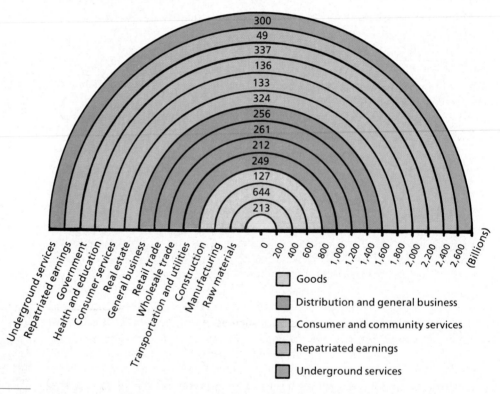

FIGURE 1-1

The U.S. economic system. The industrial sector of the economy is the core. Surrounding that core are distribution and general business services. Consumer and community services add to the system. Added to that are earnings from abroad (repatriated earnings) and underground services (those not officially reported to the Internal Revenue Service). About two thirds of the economic output in the early 1980s was generated from the service sector.
Source: Redrawn from *Forbes,* April 11, 1983, pp. 142-143.

WHAT IS THE SERVICE SECTOR?

There is much talk about the service sector, but few discussions actually list what it includes. Below is a representative list of services as classified by the government:

Lodging Services

Hotels, rooming houses, and other lodging places
Sporting and recreation camps
Trailering parks and camp sites for transients

Personal Services

Laundries	Child care
Linen supply	Shoe repair
Diaper service	Funeral homes
Carpet cleaning	Tax preparation
Photographic studios	Beauty shops
Health clubs	

Business Services

Accounting	Exterminating
Ad agencies	Employment agencies
Collection agencies	Computer programming
Commercial photography	Research and development labs
Commercial art	
Stenographic services	Management services
Window cleaning	Public relations
Consulting	Detective agencies
Equipment rental	Interior designing

Automotive Repair Services and Garages

Auto rental	Tire retreading
Truck rental	Exhaust system shops
Parking lots	Car washes
Paint shops	Transmission repair

Miscellaneous Repair Services

Radio and television	Welding
Watch	Sharpening
Reupholstery	Septic tank cleaning

Motion Picture Industry

Production	Theaters
Distribution	Drive-ins

Amusement and Recreation Services

Dance halls	Racetracks
Symphony orchestras	Golf courses
Pool halls	Amusement parks
Bowling alleys	Carnivals
Fairs	Ice skating rinks
Botanical gardens	Circuses

Health Services

Physicians	Nursery care
Dentists	Medical labs
Chiropractors	Dental labs

Legal Services

Educational Services

Libraries	Correspondence schools
Schools	Data processing schools

Social Services

Child care	Family services
Job training	

Noncommercial Museums, Art Galleries, and Botanical and Zoological Gardens

Selected Membership Organizations

Business associations
Civic associations

Miscellaneous Services

Architectural	Surveying
Engineering	Utilities

producing about *$1 trillion* ($1,000 billion) worth of goods. As the chart shows, the industrial sector consists of industries such as mining (raw materials), manufacturing, and construction. Surrounding that core are a variety of service industries ranging from transportation and utilities through wholesale and retail trade to government. Over *$2 trillion* were generated by the **service sector** of the economy, which consists of industries such as wholesale trade, retail trade, real estate, health and education, and the government.

Anyone who reads the papers knows that behind these figures is a "good news/ bad news" story. The good news is that there are millions of new jobs being created in the service sector. These jobs can be more interesting, more challenging, and more rewarding financially. Job titles range from retail clerk and auto repair person through more advanced titles such as computer-repair technicians, architects, phy-

service sector
Industries such as transportation and utilities, wholesale trade, retail trade, real estate, consumer services, health and education, and the government.

FIGURE 1-2

Industries providing services will continue to employ an increasing proportion of the work force. This figure shows that service jobs have been growing faster than manufacturing jobs since 1960 and will continue that trend well into the 1990s.

Number of workers represents wage and salary workers, except for agriculture, which includes self-employed and unpaid family workers.
NOTE: Dashed lines represent low, moderate, and high projections.
Source: Bureau of Labor Statistics.

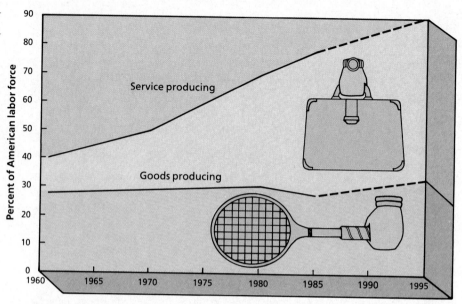

sicians, salespeople, fashion merchandisers, computer programmers, systems analysts, accountants, and brokers. To be totally honest, the sector also has job titles like clerk, barber, and garbage collector. For most college graduates, the jobs are relatively exciting and interesting.

The bad news is that the traditional manufacturing sector is growing more slowly and has been laying off workers at a fast pace. Many workers are being replaced by robots, computers, and other machines. Serious unemployment has resulted in cities like Detroit that relied heavily on automobile production for jobs. More statistics that will clarify the present situation are[1]:

- 74.7% of all American workers are now employed in service-producing sectors.
- Of 25 million net jobs created since 1970, 22 million, or 89%, were in the service sector.
- The service sector generates nearly 70% of the total output of goods and services.
- The growth in the service sector will continue throughout the 1980s and beyond (Figure 1-2).
- The vast majority of new jobs for women are being created in the service sector.

NONFARM BUSINESSES

	GOODS-PRODUCING INDUSTRIES	SERVICE-PRODUCING BUSINESSES
1956	40.3%	59.7%
1966	36.2%	63.8%
1976	29.4%	70.6%
1986	25.3%	74.7%

Where the Jobs Will Be

What do Figure 1-2 and these statistics mean to today's college graduates planning their career? It means that the chances are very high that you will be employed by a firm in the service sector. Literally millions of new jobs will open up for secretaries, retail store managers, salespeople, computer designers and software writers, and technicians in areas such as energy conservation and hazardous waste disposal. As you plan your college career, keep these trends in mind. You may want to take more computer courses, marketing courses, or technical training courses than you thought. Because there will be such a surge of older people, there is a tremendous need for geriatric social workers (that is, those who work with older people).

Nine of every 10 new jobs created in the next decade will be in service industries, with health and computer-related professions growing the fastest, while manufacturing jobs continue a sluggish growth.
Source: Bureau of Labor Statistics.

The Business of Nonprofit Organizations

A **business** is any organization that seeks profit by providing needed goods and services. Some students today are not interested in a career in business per se. They are more interested in working for the government, a social cause (for example, environmentalism), a church, a charity, a school (for example, teachers), a hospital, or some other **nonprofit organization.** These students should understand that in the future the successful career person in such organizations is more likely than not to have a degree in business. Along with the changeover from an industrial to a service economy, the United States has placed more and more resources into nonprofit organizations, including the government. Within that trend, the most significant change is the adoption of more and more business concepts in the management of such organizations (for example, computer operations, marketing, and accounting). Some current figures tell the story best:

- The **nonprofit sector,** which consists of all organizations whose goals do not include making a profit, accounts for 5% of the total output of goods and services and 6% of employment. This percentage is greater than that of the automobile industry.[2]
- Charities alone must compete for about $90 billion in available donations; therefore they must be effective marketers
- There are more than 16,000 trade associations and professional societies today (representing 173 million people and organizations). Such organiza-

business
Any organization that seeks profit by providing needed goods and services.

nonprofit sector
All organizations whose goals do not include making a profit.

Advertising for nonprofit organizations.

Make my day.
Visit the San Diego Zoo.

tions employ graduates from public relations, accounting, computer technology, marketing, and other business subjects.

- Of all those employed in the service sector, 26% are employed by the government—federal, state, and local.

What all these figures mean for today's students is that there are many jobs available in the nonprofit sector for business majors. The preparation for a career in a nonprofit organization is much the same as for a career in business; that is, one must become an expert in some business discipline such as accounting, marketing, information systems, personnel, management, or economics.

THINKING IT THROUGH

What difference does it make that the United States has changed from an industrial to a service economy? What kinds of jobs will be eliminated? What kind of jobs will experience tremendous growth? What is the difference between working in a nonprofit service organization such as a public school or hospital and a profit-making service organization such as a hotel?

PROGRESS CHECK

- What is a business, and how does it differ from a nonprofit organization? What percent of total economic output is generated by the service sector? (See Figure 1-1.)

- What percent of today's jobs are in the service sector?

MEGATRENDS

One person who has documented the shift from an industrial economy to a service economy is John Naisbitt, who wrote the popular book *Megatrends*.[3] His conclusions are based on over 2 million articles from local newspapers. From monitoring thousands of newspapers, Naisbitt follows the trends. The box on "Naisbitt's 10 'Megatrends'" summarizes findings from the book. Notice the trends from institutional help to self-help, from representative democracy to participatory democracy, and from either/or to multiple options. What this means for you is new opportunities in the business world and in government.

As far as careers are concerned, Naisbitt emphasizes the fact that most of the new service jobs involve creating, processing, and distributing *information*. Subtract those people dealing with information, and the service sector has remained relatively stable since 1950. Now 60% of us are information people, following careers in areas such as teaching, research, programming, accounting, and managing media.

Trend Toward Small Business

Naisbitt says, "The transition times between economies are the times entrepreneurship blooms. We are now in such a period."[4] New businesses were being created at a pace of about 93,000 per year in 1950, and today over 700,000 are

NAISBITT'S 10 "MEGATRENDS"*

1. From an industrial society to an information society. In the 19th century, the U.S. made the transition from an agricultural economy to an industrial economy. Over the past 30 years, the nation has made another transition—from the factory to the office. In the 1950s, Americans were predominantly blue-collar workers. Today, more than 60% are white-collar or "information" workers: computer programmers, teachers, clerks, secretaries, accountants, stockbrokers, managers, insurance agents, bureaucrats, lawyers, bankers, and technicians.

2. From forced technology to high-tech/high-touch. In other words, technological advances can no longer be forced on an unwilling population. For every high-tech action there is a high-touch reaction. For example, computers make it possible for people to work at home, but most of us will want to go to the office anyway because we need human interaction, or high-touch.

3. From a national economy to a world economy. The U.S. is no longer the world's industrial leader; it must move on to other (information) tasks. The U.S. cannot isolate itself economically from the rest of the world because it is no longer (if it ever was) self-sufficient. Third-World countries will manufacture our cars and TV sets while we specialize in communications and financial services.

4. From short-term to long-term. America's world market position was hurt by a short-sighted, self-defeating philosophy: make the highest profits in the shortest period of time. American companies and their MBA managers have tended to focus on the next quarter instead of the next decade. The result: they lost out to their far-sighted competitors in Japan, West Germany, and other developed nations. This is changing.

5. From centralization to decentralization. This trend applies to both government and business, where the ideas now come from the bottom up. Our complex society can no longer be administered by a large federal bureaucracy; states and local governments are better suited to the task. The political power is shifting to them. Small firms, rather than unwieldy conglomerates, are making the technological advances and creating the new jobs. National TV is being hurt by local cable firms.

6. From institutional help to self-help. People no longer want to depend on the government, the school system, the corporation, the union, or the medical establishment. Americans are increasingly shunning government "programs." They're demanding better schools (one million parents educate their children at home); exercising, dieting, and taking care of themselves to avoid doctors and hospitals; and starting their own companies.

7. From representative democracy to participatory democracy. People are demanding to be a part of the decisions that concern them—in the government, in the workplace, and in the marketplace. No more totalitarian fiefdoms.

8. From hierarchies to networking. The pyramid power structures in government, corporations, and world relations have been torn apart by the computer. Information is power, and the computer allows everyone access to information. Thus, people and countries treat each other as peers, exchanging information horizontally instead of from the top down. This process is called networking.

9. From North to South. Population, jobs, government power, etc. are moving from the northern states to the southern and western states, and the trend is irreversible. The shift has already created three "megastates"—California, Texas, and Florida. The top 10 American cities of the future will be Albuquerque, N.M.; Austin and San Antonio, Texas; Denver; Phoenix and Tucson, Ariz.; Salt Lake City; San Diego and San Jose, Calif.; and Tampa, Fla.

10. From either/or to multiple options. This is no longer a chocolate-or-vanilla world. People have alternatives, and they're exercising them. The individual, not the family, is now society's building block. We have moved from the myth of the melting pot to the celebration of cultural diversity. There are singles and child-free couples instead of married parents. There is part-time, flex-time, and job-sharing instead of the 9-to-5 grind.

Source: "John Naisbitt's Clip Joint," *Marketing News*, March 16, 1984, pp. 1, 18 (section 2).

small business
Business that is independently owned and operated, is not dominant in its field of operation, and meets certain standards of size in terms of employees (less than 100) or annual receipts.

started each year. During a 7-year period ending in 1984, 9 million jobs were added to the work force: 6 million were in *small* businesses, 3 million were in state and local (not federal) government, and *none* were added in the top 1,000 corporations. Figure 1-3 shows that this trend is continuing. A **small business** is defined as one that is independently operated, is not dominant in its field of operation, and meets certain standards of size in terms of employees (less than 100) or annual receipts.

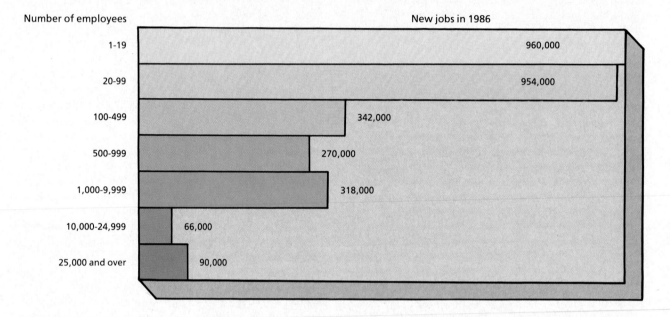

Number of employees

New jobs in 1986

Number of employees	New jobs in 1986
1-19	960,000
20-99	954,000
100-499	342,000
500-999	270,000
1,000-9,999	318,000
10,000-24,999	66,000
25,000 and over	90,000

FIGURE 1-3   New jobs by size of firm. A survey found that 64% of the new jobs in 1986 would be created in businesses with fewer than 100 workers.
Source: Dun and Bradstreet Corporation survey of 5,000 firms.

This means that it is extremely likely that tomorrow's graduates will find the most challenging jobs with growth potential in small- to medium-sized businesses. To learn about such businesses, interested students should read *Inc.* magazine, because other business publications tend to favor *big* business and government.

The future of small businesses is indicated by what is popular now, because the United States has already entered the transition period between old, large "smokestack" industries (that is, steel, auto, tires, chemicals, and utilities) and smaller, more efficient service and high-tech industries, including fast-food restaurants; auto rental firms; and firms producing computer chips, solar panels, and computers.

Small businesses will continue to be the source of new employment opportunities in the United States and will provide the base for future economic growth. The traditional established large firms will continue to provide basic materials (for example, steel, lumber, oil, automobiles, and aluminum), but most of the truly innovative economic miracles will continue to flow from the small- to medium-sized firms in new growth industries such as fiber optics, genetic engineering, robotics, satellite communications, electronics, and computers.[5]

Some 700,000 small businesses open every year.

Service and Repair Job Opportunities

No one influence has had a greater impact on business in the last decade than the growth in technology. **High-tech industries** are those that use or produce the latest in machinery (for example, computers, robots, solar cells, and lasers).

The problem today is that technological growth has exceeded our capacity to train or retrain people for the new jobs being created. Some of the fastest-growing high-tech jobs are for data processors, computer operators, computer analysts, office machine servicers, and computer programmers. But that is only the beginning. Traditional mechanics are no longer able to work on the sophisticated computer and electronic systems in cars. Trained people are also needed to service and repair videotape recorders, computers, robots, and all the new high-tech equipment.

Because the need for such people is very high, the pay tends to be relatively good. Have you noticed all those new retailers selling personal computers and software? What is missing are stores to service and repair those machines. The opportunities in 1990 and beyond for skilled technicians, service, and repair people will be phenomenal.

high-tech industries
Industries that make and use the most advanced equipment in industries such as computers, robotics, computer chips, solar panels, and electronics.

The Computer Revolution

Nobody needs to tell you that a major revolution in business has occurred because of the computer. What may not be as clear is that thousands of jobs are now becoming available in the computer field. You may know about programming and, perhaps, systems analysis. But other occupations in computers are not as well known. They include:

- Applications developer (usually a mechanical engineer)
- Computer-aided design (CAD) technicians
- Computer-aided manufacturing (CAM) designers
- Data base designers
- Digital systems engineer
- Electronic die maker
- Graphics specialist
- Information system manager
- Materials flow specialist
- Microprocessor technologist
- Project engineer
- Software systems analyst
- Tape librarian
- Teleprocessing engineer

This list is merely a hint of the many new jobs emerging. You may have no interest in math or working with computers and still find a rewarding career in computers as a tape librarian, a repair specialist, or in some other related occupation. An art major may enjoy being a graphics specialist. The way it looks today, it would probably be a mistake not to take a course or two to familiarize yourself with computers. Someday you will be writing memos, composing letters, and writing papers on a word processor. The time to learn to use such equipment is now. Have you looked at your handwriting lately? If you are a typical student, you'd better learn to type or use a word processor if you want to communicate with businesspeople. Computers are the future; prepare yourself.

There is a wide variety of computer-related careers.

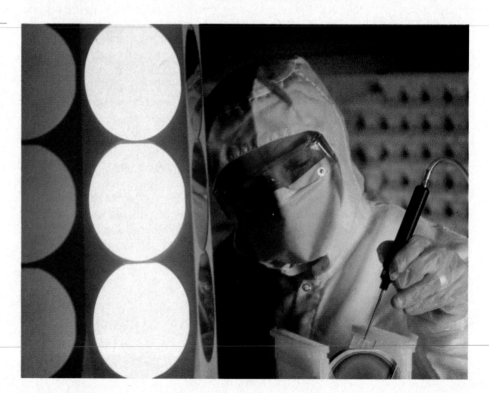

▨ Can you name more than four of Naisbitt's megatrends? Read through them again, and try to rank them in importance; that will help you picture the impact on society of such trends.

▨ Sometimes numbers lose their meaning when they get too big. Calculate how many new small businesses are started in the United States everyday, 365 days a year. How many would you guess without referring back to the text material?

The Social Revolution

Not all future changes will be technological. Many *social* changes will have a dramatic effect on your future. The next section discusses some of these changes.

The service revolution in business is being matched by a similar revolution in the social sector (Figure 1-4). Some of the more dramatic changes include:

- Americans are healthier, wealthier, and better educated.
- Big shifts in various age groups so that there are many more older people in society, fewer teenagers, and more middle-class, two-income families.
- A great surge of women into the labor force and into professional jobs has resulted in many changes in family, life-styles, and roles.
- Hispanics, blacks, and Asians have increased in percentage of the population and have made much progress in business, especially small business.
- A vast, new international market is opening to those who learn how to market overseas.

These trends and more are discussed below. Let's begin with population shifts because they help predict future areas of growth.

Population Shifts

Population trends have a tremendous influence on the future of business and economics in the United States. Almost everyone is aware of the "graying of America," the fact that a rapidly growing segment of the population is over 65. What is less well known is the fact that men and women over 85 constitute the *fastest-growing age group in the United States*. These people create a tremendous burden on the health care system and the social security system and create a growing market for retirement communities, senior citizen recreation programs, continuing education programs for the retired, and other services related to older citizens. Senior citizens want a higher quality of life, too. The government will have to do something about social security and Medicare for older people. For you, the aging of America provides dramatic new career opportunities in counseling, recreation, health care, and research on the aged.

The real crunch in old-age problems will come about the year 2010 when the baby boom children reach retirement age. Then there will be 16 million citizens over age 85, which is approximately 5.2% of the population. Long before then, the baby boom children will have caused major changes in society. First, they are now having children of their own and creating a mini–population boom. The graph in the upper right margin tells the story. Notice that about 1990 the second baby boom will peak. If past history is any guide, this will lead to a scramble to

POPULATION TRENDS: CHILDREN

Preschool children (1950-2000) (in millions)

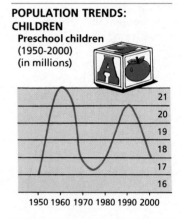

| 21 |
| 20 |
| 19 |
| 18 |
| 17 |
| 16 |

1950 1960 1970 1980 1990 2000

POPULATION TRENDS: OLDER PEOPLE

Year	Millions of Americans Over 65*
1980	26.3
2000	36.1
2040	68.4

Year	Millions of Americans Over 85*
1980	2.3
2000	5.1
2040	13.3

Note what happens in the years between 1980 and 2040. The number of Americans over 65 more than *doubles*, whereas the number over 85 increases almost *sixfold* in the same time period.

Source: Social Security Administration, 1986.

FIGURE 1-4

A, U.S. population gains, 1940-1984. **B,** Social and economic change in the U.S. since the 1940s. Social changes since the 1940s have been dramatic. Life expectancy has increased by over 10 years; spendable income more than doubled; almost three times as many people completed high school; the number of women in the work force almost doubled; the share of employment in manufacturing declined by 7%, but employment in trade went up by 6% and in services by 21%; and the number of farmers as percent of population declined from 23.2% to only 2.4%.

Source: U.S. Departments of Commerce, Agriculture, Labor, and Health and Human Services.

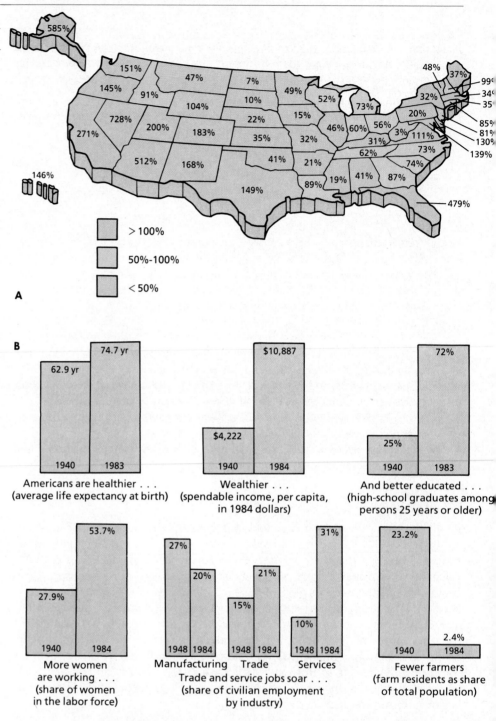

open new elementary schools. Naturally, there will be a surge in demand for baby food, diapers, children's furniture, toys, and other child-related products. In 1960, there were 20 million children under age 5 in the United States. In 1990, there will be about 19 million—close to the original boom years. Any student planning a future career must keep such trends in mind, because it will mean an increased

FOLLOWING THE INCREASE IN OLDER AMERICA

The old business adage of "Find a need and fill it" is as applicable today as it ever was. This chapter gives you some insight into the trends. Manor Care nursing home chain will show you what can happen if you anticipate such trends and do indeed "Find a need and fill it."

Manor Care now earns about $30.2 million a year compared with just $6.9 million in 1981. Furthermore, Manor Care feels it can keep expanding at a similar rate. It notes that the population of people over 85 should grow from 2.7 million to 5 million over the next 15 years. That represents a large potential for nursing home services.

Manor Care has 149 facilities in 24 states with a total population of 15,995 residents. The company plans to expand by 2,500 beds a year. The annual cost of Manor Care varies, but ranges from $10,000 to $30,000 in different states.

Clearly there will be many career opportunities for all kinds of people in the nursing home field. What other things will an aging population need besides housing? What does that mean for students planning careers today?

Source: Sarah Oates, "Manor Care Tries to Lure Affluent Elderly," *Washington Business,* August 26, 1985, pp. 1-17.

demand for elementary school teachers, camp counselors, and other such occupations related to children.

Population figures can give you all kinds of insights into the future (Figure 1-5). For example, it may be rather safely predicted from past experience that the U.S. population will grow more conservative as the average age of voters increases.

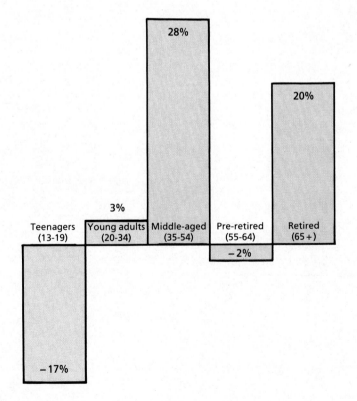

FIGURE 1-5

Projected population shifts, 1980-1990. The fastest growing segment of the population will be people over 85. That group will grow by more than 50% by the year 2000. Fewer teenagers mean less crime and less teen unemployment. More middle-aged people means more skilled workers with high incomes. More retired people means a bigger burden on social security. What else can you derive from this chart?

What are the consequences of the following statistics? The answers will determine the future of business and economics and *your* future as well.[6]

- Today about 25% of federal expenditures go to the aged. This is expected to rise to 32% by 2000 and 63% by 2025.
- The West is expected to have population growth of 22% in the 1980s and 18% in the 1990s, containing one fourth of the population by the year 2000. The South will grow by 16% in the 1980s and 13% in the 1990s (Figure 1-6).
- There will be a tremendous growth of workers between the ages of 25 and 54, the prime earning years. Add to that the trend toward two-income families, and spending will increase dramatically.
- Total U.S. population is expected to grow from 240 to 260 million in 1995. The median age will increase from 31 to almost 35 in 1995. World population will reach 6 billion by the year 2000 and 8 billion by 2025.
- A decline in the teenage population should make it harder to recruit for the military, lower teen crime rates, lower teenage unemployment, and result in a decline in sales of teen-related products and services (for example, records and movies).

Some of the effects population trends will have on today's students are as follows:

- They will be paying higher social security taxes to support retired workers and face the prospect of getting less from social security than they contribute.
- They will find tremendous opportunities opening up in fields related to the elderly (for example, health care) and babies (for example, teaching).

FIGURE 1-6

Changes in population will vary among the states. Projected percent changes in state populations, 1980-2000.

Source: *Occupational Outlook Handbook,* U.S. Department of Labor, Bureau of Labor Statistics, 1986-1987 edition, p. 14.

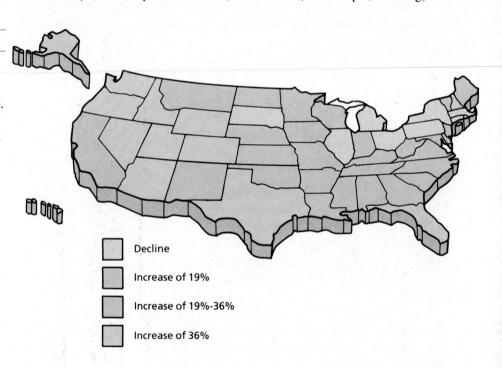

Decline

Increase of 19%

Increase of 19%-36%

Increase of 36%

- Their upward movement into management may be slowed by the huge block of management-age people before them; this may mean that they will need more education to enter managerial ranks.
- They will find tremendous opportunities in international business.

THINKING IT THROUGH

What career opportunities will arise as a result of the huge increase in people who are over 85 years old? What will happen to crime statistics and unemployment statistics when there is a fall-off in the number of teenagers in the population? What does an increase in two-income families mean for economic growth?

Women in the Work Force

Perhaps the most visible trend in the business world (after the changeover to a service economy) is the surge of women joining the work force. In 1960, it was rare for a married woman with a child to work outside her home; only 1 woman out of 5 did. Today more than half the mothers with children are in the labor force. An estimated 6 million preschool children spend all or part of their day in a nursery school or day-care center.[7] One of the rapidly growing services in the United States, therefore, is day care. There are now more than 25,000 day-care centers in this country.[8]

Mothers are entering the labor force in record numbers.

The trend toward more women working often means an increase in two-income families. In addition to a demand for day care, such trends indicate an increasing demand for recreation, restaurants, dry cleaning, household care, and personal care services. Of the new American Express cardholders, 30% are women. More than half are under age 35 and earn over $25,000 annually. The majority hold managerial or professional jobs.[9]

Businesses are providing new career opportunities for women in areas once dominated almost exclusively by men. At IBM, for example, the number of women managers increased 106% over 5 years. A Cleveland executive search firm had a 200% increase in high-tech jobs filled by women over a 3-year period. At Ask Computers, 21 of 53 managers are women.[10] Women college graduates should recognize these new opportunities and apply for jobs in nontraditional industries where salaries and opportunities are greatest.

Women in Small Businesses There has been a rapid growth of women starting small businesses in the last decade or so. According to the Bureau of Labor Statistics, the number of self-employed women grew by almost 70% between 1972 and 1982. Recent statistics show that there are over 3 million businesses owned by women, selling over $40 billion worth of goods and services.

Charlotte Taylor, a consultant to female entrepreneurs, says, "Women go into business for the same reasons men do—to make money and to be their own boss."[11] John Naisbitt *(Megatrends)* said, "It becomes increasingly clear that women will not only join their male counterparts as equals in business, they may pass them. At the very least, they bring perspectives, values, talents and skills, well-suited to the new economy we are building."[12] There is a National Association of Women Business Owners, and the Small Business Administration has an Office of Women's Business Ownership. Women must often be prepared to make sacrifices of time, money, and family togetherness to succeed in small business. The box has a questionnaire for men and women to determine whether or not they are ready for entrepreneurship.

WHAT IT TAKES TO START A SMALL BUSINESS

"**B**usiness success depends on more than a good idea, ambition and imagination," stresses consultant Charlotte Taylor. "It takes stamina, skills and perseverance." If you are considering going into business, she suggests testing your responses to these statements:

- I don't tend to get overly anxious in ambiguous or uncertain situations.
- I prefer games where I can use my skills to win, rather than games of chance.
- I believe my own actions are what are important in how my life turns out, not luck or fate.

- Money, for me, is more important as a measure of my success than for the things that it can buy.
- I am willing to put my work before my family and friends and make it my number-one priority.
- I am willing to change my standard of living to accommodate the new venture.
- I see building a business as a way of life and one I will be totally interested in.

Your answers, says Taylor, should be yes. And finally; "If I had a choice of earning twice as much working for someone else, I would still rather be my own boss." If you can say yes to that, she says you have what it takes.

Source: Sarah Ban Breathnach, "Trends: Women Entrepreneurs, *The Washington Post,* May 3, 1984, p. D5. © *The Washington Post,* 1984.

Marketing to Hispanics

The 1980 census showed that the Hispanic population of the United States had grown 61% in 10 years. The significance of this figure is more evident when one looks at the number of Hispanics in certain cities. In San Antonio, for example, 52% of the population is Hispanic; and the city's Hispanic mayor, Henry Cisneros, is a nationally known politician. There are over 3 million Hispanics in Los Angeles, 2.5 million in New York, 856,000 in Miami, 738,000 in San Antonio, and 737,000 in Chicago. In total there are about 20 million Hispanics in the United States with a family income totaling $70 billion.

The Hispanic market is huge and soon will be larger than the market for black citizens. There are several Hispanic magazines with names like *Temas* and *De Armos Hispanic Magazine Network* (national magazines), and *Miami Mensual* (Miami) and

The Hispanic market is large and growing.

Caminos (Southwest). There are also Hispanic newspapers, for example, *El Diario* (New York), *El Manana* (Chicago), and *La Opinion* (Los Angeles). In addition, several radio and TV stations are aimed at this market. In short, many opportunities exist to create businesses that have a special appeal to the Hispanic market.

The market is not necessarily unified; there are differences between Hispanics from Puerto Rico, Mexico, Cuba, and other countries. Hispanics are now graduating from colleges and universities throughout the country and are entering business and government. Opportunities have never been better for educated Hispanics in all areas of business. There is a real growth opportunity in small businesses that market directly to the Hispanic people.

Marketing to Blacks

The 1980 census showed that the black population had grown over 17% since 1970 and had reached over 26 million people. Total black income is $140 billion a year.[13] Like the Hispanic population, blacks are geographically concentrated. New York has about 1.8 million blacks (25% of the population), Chicago has about 1.2 million (39%), Detroit, 758,000 (63%), Washington, D.C., 448,000 (70%), New Orleans, 308,000 (55%).[14] As you can see, blacks are the dominant group in several major cities. The opportunity for black graduates in government and small businesses is thus wide open and growing all the time.

This is not to say black America has no problems. Black unemployment in 1984 was 17.6% (more than twice the level for whites). Unemployment among black *teenagers* reached about 50% in the 1980s. Many other statistics could be cited to show that blacks have a more difficult time sharing the American dream than other groups.

But the statistics hide tremendous progress among certain black groups. Naturally, the group doing best is black college graduates. Most figures show blacks earning much less than whites at comparable jobs. But black males in professional and technical occupations make 86% of the salary of white counterparts. Black females in these occupations make 98% as much as their counterparts.[15]

Black students who go on to get higher degrees have an almost unlimited opportunity for rewarding careers. There is a tremendous demand for black professors, for example. The reason that it is so hard to recruit black professors is that blacks with advanced degrees can earn far more in industry.[16] In short, black opportunity today is highest for college graduates, especially graduates with advanced degrees.

Blacks and other minorities are doing well in small businesses. We shall explore this trend in the sections that follow.

Marketing to Asians

There are now about 5 million Asians living in the United States, but their market impact is much greater than their numbers. Asian-Americans have median family incomes of about $23,000 versus $20,000 for the entire U.S. population. About one third of Asian adults are college graduates in contrast with only 17% of white adults. A report from the Population Reference Bureau in Washington predicts that the Asian community will have doubled in size by the year 2000.[17] The insert about "Asian Small Business Owners" will give you some insight into the success of Asians in small business. Such material emphasizes the trend toward small business and the opportunities available.

ASIAN SMALL BUSINESS OWNERS

A trip through the small businesses of most large cities will reveal something very interesting. Many, if not most, are owned and operated by people from various minority groups—Chinese, Korean, Vietnamese, and so on. Many are Asian, but all countries and races are represented. In some areas, Hispanics and blacks dominate.

The Asian phenomenon is particularly instructive, because Asians represent the most recent wave of new entrepreneurs to come to America. Many fled Vietnam and Cambodia to seek a new life. Most could not speak English and many had no previous business experience. Nonetheless, they prosper. Walter Park, a Korean who owns a business brokerage, says, "They are willing to sacrifice themselves for the next generation." His sales force sells about 100 small businesses a year for about $170,000 each, mostly to Koreans.

Hamburger stands and liquor stores are considered starter enterprises. The goal is to earn money and buy even larger businesses. Mr. Ahn was a musician in Korea. He came to the United States in 1976 and worked as a janitor to save money for a business. His wife worked in a garment factory. They bought a run-down hamburger stand for $30,000.

Asians often buy in neighborhoods that are unattractive to others. The businesses are cheaper and they seem to find acceptance among minority groups. The Ahns sold their hamburger place for $60,000 and now own Tommy's Charbroiled Hamburger, for which they paid $180,000.

Other stories could be told about successful minority small businesses, but you probably know some examples yourself. Minority businesspeople are a true American success story. But their success doesn't come easy.

A Korean brewery executive bought a liquor store for $120,000 down. (Sellers generally give buyers 5 years to pay off the balance at 12%. Banks seldom finance such ventures.) To make the business a success, this man and his wife work morning to night seven days a week. Minority business owners seem willing to put in long hours to make the money that small businesses offer. It is the free enterprise system at its best, and it is working.

Source: Sanford J. Jacobs, "Asian Immigrants Build Future in U.S. by Buying Cash Firms," *The Wall Street Journal*, October 1, 1984, p. 45. Reprinted by permission of *The Wall Street Journal;* © Dow Jones & Company, Inc., 1984. All rights reserved.

Opportunities For All Minorities

The primary financier of minority-owned businesses is the federal government. Contributions are also available from private investors who pool their funds and form Minority Enterprise Small Business Investment Companies, or MESBICS. These companies invest the combined federal and private funds in minority-owned businesses. There have been some problems with minority-owned small businesses simply because there are problems with small businesses overall. The failure rate is very high for all small businesses.

Recently, there has been a renewed interest in backing minority firms. A Boston venture capital firm is backing 12 companies: six started by blacks, three by Asians, and one each by a Hispanic, an American Indian, and an East Indian. The name of this venture capital firm is Urban National Corporation. It has $25 million to invest, raised mostly from large corporations.[18]

Minority firms are entering many of today's high-tech industries. For example, Micro Peripheral, Incorporated is a maker of disk drives for computers. Infolink Corporation makes data gathering systems. Santic Corporation makes computer printers. The Urban National Corporation recently invested in Air Atlanta, a re-

Air Atlanta is a minority-owned airline.

gional airline owned by blacks. There is a great potential for growth of minority-owned firms in the future. Minorities are pouring into U.S. cities, establishing themselves in communities, and starting successful small business ventures ranging from restaurants that cater to other minority groups to high-tech firms selling to industry. The new venture capital firms should help minority-owned businesses get started and prosper in tomorrow's dynamic markets, including international markets. Many new immigrants are able to start **import-export** businesses, trading with firms in their native countries. Let's look at international markets to see what the potential is.

imports
Goods and services bought from other countries.

exports
Goods and services sold to other countries

INTERNATIONAL MARKETS

In the last few years, the attention of many U.S. businesspeople has shifted away from domestic (U.S.) markets to international markets. There are several reasons why this happened:

- The population of the United States is about 240 million people, whereas the world population is about 5 billion; clearly, the growth potential is overseas.
- Foreign businesses have been capturing more and more of U.S. sales. By 1984, the United States was importing 20% of its steel; 30% of its cars; 40% of its calculators; 50% of its computerized machine tools; 60% of its TV sets, radios, tape recorders, and phonographs; and 95% of its motorcycles.[19] To offset these imports, the United States had to begin selling more of its goods overseas.
- The U.S. Government became concerned about the loss of jobs in the United States because people were buying goods made in other countries. There was much discussion of limiting imports of many goods. Every billion dollars in imports costs Americans 25,000 jobs.[20]

There are several reasons why the United States was buying more goods than it was selling in the mid-1980s. Foreign workers tended to make less money, so foreign goods were often cheaper. Foreign producers such as Japan paid more attention to quality control and often had more reliable or better quality goods. The U.S. dollar had risen in value relative to the money in other countries. This made foreign goods cheaper. It also made U.S. goods more expensive to foreign buyers.

Opportunities in International Business

The net effect of all these trends was that U.S. business began to focus more attention on international sales. This means that today's college graduates have a tremendous opportunity to become involved in international business. Naturally, that would probably mean learning a foreign language and traveling to foreign countries. The potential for exciting and rewarding careers in this area has never been greater.

Pacific Rim countries
Countries on the edge of the Pacific furthest from California: South Korea, Japan, China, Taiwan, Hong Kong, and Singapore.

At one time, the countries we traded with the most were the European countries and Canada. Today our attention has shifted to what is called the **Pacific Rim:** South Korea, Japan, China, Taiwan, Hong Kong, and Singapore. The figure on p. 39 is an indication of this. We still trade many goods with Europe, but we trade even more with those countries in the Pacific. This creates new challenges

Levi's are popular in Pacific Rim countries.

and opportunities for students willing to learn the appropriate languages and travel to these exotic countries.

Perhaps the most exciting element of international trade is the potential it has for improving the standard of living and quality of life in less developed countries.

Overall, the United States sold $59 billion worth of goods to the developing nations in 1983, fully 40% of American exports. The growth potential in these countries is substantial. Since 1960 the number of cities in the Third World with populations greater than 1 million has risen from 53 to 125. By 2000, it will be 295, of which 70 may have populations over 4 million each![21]

To further development in less developed countries and to compete with other developed countries, U.S. producers will have to adopt whole new strategies. Sophisticated machinery often hinders growth by taking jobs away from laborers. Developing nations often need more basic machinery that is cheaper and better adapted to the environment of those countries. Sometimes used equipment is very attractive, and this opens huge markets in parts and service.

The shift from an industrial economy to a service economy is happening in a few other developed countries such as Japan and West Germany.[22] It has been projected that 90% of Japanese workers will be in the service sector by 1990. The decline in industries such as automobiles and steel has affected most developed countries. The future growth in overseas sales, therefore, is in the service sector in professions such as banking, insurance, management, communications, transportation, retailing, and consulting.

In short, the revolution taking place in the United States (shifting from an industrial economy to a service economy) is having effects worldwide. As a result, less developed countries with cheaper labor and newer plants are capturing world markets for manufactured goods such as autos, steel, clothing, shoes, and electronic equipment. This is healthy from a world perspective because it enables poor countries to build an industrial base, be more productive, and become net contributors to the world economy. It is disruptive to the United States because it results in a loss of sales and temporary unemployment. To prosper in this new, competitive environment, all nations, including the United States, will have to think globally (world markets) and work cooperatively with other nations to assure continued economic growth for all of humankind.

PROGRESS CHECK

■ Which age group is growing fastest in the United States? What implications does this have for business?

■ About what percentage of married women with children now work outside of the home in the United States?

SUMMARY

1 "Trends, like horses, are easier to ride in the direction they are already going," is how John Naisbitt summarized the subject of this chapter. If you know the business trends, it is much easier to plan your career in an area that promises growth and opportunity.

■ Where is the growth going to be in the future?

No question about it, the growth sector of the economy is in the service sector. Of the 19 million net jobs created in the 1970s, 89% were in the service sector. This trend is continuing in the 1980s and will carry over into the 1990s.

■ I find I'm more attracted to the nonprofit sector; that is, either the government or maybe a trade association. Will there be jobs there?

Yes, but preparing for a career in the nonprofit sector is about the same as preparing for one in the business sector. Keep your options open, and take business courses.

2 There are certain "megatrends" that were said to dominate our culture in the 1980s. The book by that name is a bestseller.

■ What were those trends?

One is the trend toward small business. Some 700,000 new businesses are being formed each year. Of new jobs over a 7-year period, 6 of 9 million were in small businesses. The rest were in nonprofit organizations.

Another growth area is high-tech. This industry grew too rapidly at first and slowed in the mid-1980s, but there will be renewed strength in areas such as fiber optics, robotics, and biotechnology.

3 Accompanying the technological revolution is a social revolution. This includes major population changes, family composition changes, and more.

■ Which of the many statistics do you feel I should memorize from this section?

Most facts and figures are included for your information. It is the *trends* that count most. For example, the trend is for Americans to live longer, to be wealthier, and to be better educated. There are more women in the work force, and many more old people. Note the increase in the Hispanic and black populations and where the jobs are for these people (in business, with a college degree). Note, especially, the opportunities in small businesses.

4 Changes in the United States market will have profound effects on businesses and careers. But the greatest potential for business is overseas.

■ Why overseas?

The U.S. has only 234 million people or so, whereas the world market is made up of over 4.7 *billion* people. Clearly, there are many career opportunities in international trade and business.

business p. 23
exports p. 38
high-tech industries p. 27
imports p. 38
industrial sector p. 20

nonprofit organization p. 23
Pacific Rim countries p. 38
service sector p. 21
small business p. 26

APPENDIX: ARTS ADMINISTRATION INTERNSHIPS*

The following arts organizations have formal and informal internship programs. Some of the programs involve a stipend. Others involve work-study or college credit arrangements. If you are interested in pursuing one of these programs, write directly to the organization, requesting more information and guidelines concerning the internship. Upon receipt of the organization's information, you will be ready to send them your resume with a cover letter.

The Artists Foundation, Inc., 110 Broad St., Boston, Mass. 02110. Contact: Michele Schofield, acting director, Artists Services.

Aspen Music Festival, 1860 Broadway, Suite 401, New York, N.Y. 10023. Contact: director of public relations

Boston Visual Artists Union, Inc., 77 N. Washington St., Boston, Mass. 02114. Contact: Internship Programs.

British American Arts Assn., 1789 Columbia Rd., NW, Washington, D.C. 20009. Contact: Nan S. Levinson, executive director.

City Arts Workshop, Inc., 417 Lafayette St., New York, N.Y. 10003. Contact: Valerie Falk, public arts project coordinator.

Corcoran Gallery of Art, 17th St. and New York Ave., NW, Washington, D.C. 20006. Contact: curator of education.

Dallas Museum of Fine Arts, P.O. Box 26250, Dallas, Tex. 75226. Contact: Dr. Anne R. Bromberg, curator of education.

Denver Art Museum, 100 W. 14th Ave. Parkway, Denver, Colo. 80204. Contact: Daryl Fisher, coordinator of school programs.

Foundation for the Community of Artists, Suite 412, 280 Broadway, New York, N.Y. 10007. Contact: Jimmie Durham, executive director.

Institute for Movement Exploration, Inc., 15 Lewis St., Hartford, Conn. 06074. Contact: Alice Martin DeMund, executive director.

International Sculpture Center, 1050 Potomac St., NW, Washington, D.C. 20007. Contact: Andria Nicholson.

John F. Kennedy Center for the Performing Arts Education Program, Washington, D.C. 20566. Contact: Evelyn Dewey, intern coordinator.

John Michael Kohler Arts Center, 608 New York Ave., P.O. Box 489, Sheboygan, Wis. 53081. Contact: Nancy N. Dummer, administrative assistant.

Los Angeles Contemporary Exhibitions, Inc., 240 S. Broadway, Third Floor, Los Angeles, Calif. 90012. Contact: intern coordinator.

Los Angeles Institute of Contemporary Art, 2020 S. Robertson Blvd., Los Angeles, Calif. 90034. Contact: Tobi Smith, director of finance.

Minneapolis Institute of Arts, 2400 3rd Ave. S., Minneapolis, Minn. 55404. Contact: Theodore A. Park, intern coordinator.

Museum of Art, Washington State University, Pullman, Wash. 99164-7460. Contact: Sanford Sivitz Shaman, director.

Museum of Northern Arizona, Rt. 4, Box 720, Flagstaff, Ariz. 86001. Contact: Elizabeth W. Dobrinski, administrative assistant.

The National Committee, Arts for the Handicapped, 1825 Connecticut Ave., NW, Washington, D.C. 20009. Contact: Ralph Nappi, assoc. director.

National Dance Assn., 1900 Association Drive, Reston, Va. 22901. Contact: program assistant or executive director.

National Opera Institute, John F. Kennedy Center, Washington, D.C. 20566.

Ohio Foundation on the Arts, Inc./Statewide Arts Services Program, 440 Dublin Ave., Columbus, Ohio 43215. Contact: Barbara Andrews, registrar.

Real Art Ways, Inc., 40 State St., Box 3313, Hartford, Conn. 06103. Contact: Adrienne Pollard, administrative assistant.

Smithsonian Institution, Academic Internship Program, Smithsonian Institution, L'Enfant Plaza 3300, Washington, D.C. 20560. Contact: academic programs specialist, Office of Fellowships and Grants.

South Street Dance Co., 759 S. 6th St., Philadelphia, Pa. 19147. Contact: Ellen Forman, director.

Washington Project for the Arts, 400 7th St., NW, Washington, D.C. 20004. Contact: Olivia Georgia, assistant director.

Wisconsin Conservatory of Music, 1584 N. Prospect Ave., Milwaukee, Wis. 53202. Contact: Dr. Patricia Jones, academic dean.

Women's InterArt Center, Inc., 549 W. 52nd St., New York, N.Y. 10019. Contact: Sam Sweet, managing director.

*Reprinted from December 1984/January 1985 issue of *Business Week's Guide to Careers* by special permission, © 1985 by Mc Graw-Hill, Inc. All Rights Reserved.

1 Read current business publications to find which countries are growing the fastest economically. Read about those countries to see if you would like to work there, at least some of the time. What languages could you take in school to prepare you for working with people in these countries?

2 Do a thorough investigation of computer courses at your school and in your area. Talk with people about the best courses to take. Visit a local computer store and consider investing in a home computer to practice your skills. Consider this an investment in education and your career.

3 Review the statistics in the section titled "Population Shifts." Write a two-page report for your files discussing the possible effects of such trends on business and your career. Check the population shifts in your area of the country.

4 Review the latest issue of the *Inc.* 100. What kind of firm dominates the list? What are the trends? What do these trends mean for your career?

5 Observe the life-style and personal satisfaction of workers over 40 years old. Is their emphasis on work or family? What are the consequences? Are there any signs that people in your area are shifting attention to quality of life issues such as health, education, the environment, personal development, and family togetherness? How do your observations help in seeking balance in your life?

6 How has your career decision been affected by the data in this chapter?

CASE ONE   MINORITY-OWNED SMALL BUSINESSES

In the Prologue, we learned that businesspeople are a major resource for this course. In this case, we shall study new immigrants who have started small businesses to see what we can learn from them. They must be doing something right, because they are so successful. For example, although there are only about 100,000 Koreans in New York City, they now operate more than half of the fruit and vegetable stores. A *Wall Street Journal* article begins with this line, "It's rare to see a coffee shop in New York that is not owned by Greeks, a produce store that is not owned by Koreans, or a newsstand not owned by Indians."

Nicholaos Merges was a stowaway on a ship from Greece to the United States. He started his career as a dishwasher and advanced to short-order cook, baker, and waiter. Mr. Merges saved his money and invested $20,000 in a coffee shop called Tiffany Restaurant. He works 10 to 12 hours a day. Gracie's Corner, another coffee shop, is owned by Victor Sgantzos. He works 10 to 15 hours a day, and two of his three children work at the shop.

Bipin Patel, an East Indian, earns over $25,000 a year from his newsstand. Kirtisingh Chudasama is one of the biggest newsstand owners. He bought a franchise for $1,800. With his profits he bought a newsstand in a building lobby for his daughter to run. Now he has 21 stands and estimates that about 60% of the 1,500 newsstands in New York are owned by people from India, Pakistan, and Bangladesh. Mr. Chudasama's 14-year-old daughter does his payroll.

DECISION QUESTIONS

1 What are the secrets to success for these entrepreneurs? What do their experiences say about opportunities in small business?

2 What social trends in America made it possible for poor immigrants, often with very little command of English, to take over small businesses in New York, California, and other areas of the country?

3 Is there any significance to the fact that these immigrants chose the service sector rather than the traditional industrial sector to get their start?

4 Read Naisbitt's megatrend number 6 and relate it to this case.

Source: Trish Hall, "The Old Country Network", *The Wall Street Journal*, May 20, 1985, p. 51c of a special section on Small Business Marketing. All the examples in this case are from her article. Reprinted by permission of *The Wall Street Journal;* © Dow Jones & Co., Inc. All rights reserved.

**PRACTICING
MANAGEMENT DECISIONS**

CASE TWO   DEALING WITH CHANGING FAMILY STRUCTURES

Economic and social changes have had a dramatic impact on the nature of the family. It used to be that a "typical" family was one with a mother, father and two kids. Only 11% of all families now fit that description! In 1970, 40% of the families consisted of a husband, a wife, and children. Today, about 28% match that description. To show you how significant that change is, let's look at another figure. Since 1970, there has been an *increase* in "families" of 22 million, but a *decrease* of over 1 million in married-couple families with children. The number of single-person households has increased by about 9 million since 1970 and now accounts for 23% of all households.

Today, couples with *no children* are the largest group of American households (30%). These are mostly older couples (two of three are over 50). About 4% of American households consist of unmarried couples living together. If we were to add up all those people who live alone with those married couples without children (including those who live together without being married), we find that 57% of all households fall into a category that might be called new-style family.

Think what that means when communities are trying to get more money for schools. Some 57% of the voters have no children in school and could resist the increase. Think also of how many schools are closing because of declining enrollments. Family changes are affecting all kinds of institutions in society.

Think also of the economic potential of two-income families with no children. These people have been called "yuppies," or young urban professionals, and are stereotyped as driving fancy sports cars, living in elaborately decorated apartments, and enjoying the good life. There is some truth in that image. On the other hand, such couples tend to work long hours and seem to have no time for starting a family.

The tensions of having two-income families plus the social changes that have happened over the last 25 years or so have led to divorce and the phenomenon called the single-parent family. The number of households headed by a woman with one or more children has doubled since 1970. There are about 6 million such families, and most of them live in poverty. Another 800,000 single-parent households are headed by a man. These are the statistics. What do they mean for business?

DECISION QUESTIONS

1 What effects have the changes in family structure had on businesses thus far? Think of the products that have been designed for couples with no children and for individuals living alone. Think also of the working woman phenomenon. What does that mean in the long run for businesses?

2 Couples are having fewer and fewer children, and are beginning to have children later. What effect will these changes have on schools and businesses?

3 What is the significance of the fact that two of three of the married couples with no children at home are over 50? What market opportunities does that create?

4 What is the relationship between the breakup of the family and poverty in the United States?

LOOKING AHEAD

To understand the language of business, you will have to understand basic economics. The language of business is largely the language of economics. Furthermore, it is important to understand the roots of the American business system. America is being challenged for the political and economic allegiance of other countries. There is a clash of values among capitalist, socialist, and communist systems. The survival of free markets depends on knowledgeable businesspeople who understand the system and can market its benefits to the rest of the world. Chapter 3 discusses the various world economic systems and the advantages and disadvantages of each.

CAPITALISM AND BUSINESS

LEARNING GOALS

After you have read and studied this chapter, you should be able to:

■ Define economics and its components: macroeconomics and microeconomics.

■ Identify the three economic systems and compare the level of government involvement in each.

■ Compare and contrast the economic views of Thomas Malthus and Adam Smith.

■ Discuss the role of freedom and incentives in capitalism.

■ Outline the four basic rights of capitalism, and compare capitalism to communism.

■ Explain how the free market system works in terms of supply and demand.

■ Illustrate the relationships among supply, demand, and price level, using a graph.

■ Describe the limitations of the free market system.

■ Discuss the limitations of socialism and communism.

PROFILE   JOSEPH A. SCHUMPETER, ECONOMIST

Joseph A. Schumpeter (pronounced *Shoom-pater*) was one of the first economists to give a clear explanation of business profits. His doctoral dissertation, *The Theory of Economic Development*, became popular and was published when Schumpeter was only 28. That was back in 1911. The year is significant, because way back then Schumpeter anticipated the rapid structural changes the economy is now experiencing; that is, the rise of innovative small businesses and service organizations.

Schumpeter felt that an expanding economy needed more and more capital investment. The source of that investment was *profit*. Schumpeter considered profit a necessary cost of doing business. He felt profits were the only way to maintain jobs and create new ones. For the first time in economic history, profit became a moral obligation and goal.

Later, Schumpeter wrote *The Tax State* to describe the government's power to redistribute income from the productive to the unproductive. He felt such power would lead to political irresponsibility and inflation. He wrote this in 1918, long before his prediction came true in country after country.

The best-known work of Schumpeter is *Capitalism, Socialism, and Democracy*, published in 1942. In this book, he argues that capitalism would be destroyed by its own success. He felt that, to be popular, a freely elected government would cause the nation to become more and more like the "welfare state." Eventually the

Joseph A. Schumpeter.

The ideas of economists and political philosophers, both when they are right and when they are wrong, are more powerful than is commonly understood. Indeed the world is ruled by little else.

JOHN MAYNARD KEYNES

government burden and the inflation it caused would destroy both democracy and capitalism.

Someday you may want to read Schumpeter in the original. Meanwhile, to get some feel for the ideas of John Maynard Keynes and Schumpeter, two of the great economists of the modern era, you may want to read the *Forbes* article cited below. It is one of the most interesting, but brief, reviews I have ever read. ∎

Source: Peter F. Drucker, "Schumpeter and Keynes," *Forbes,* May 23, 1983, pp. 124-132. Reprinted by permission of *Forbes* magazine; © Forbes Inc., 1983.

THE IMPORTANCE OF ECONOMICS TO BUSINESS

The success of the American system is based on an economic and political climate that allows business to prosper. Any change in the economic or political system has a major influence on the success of the business system. The *world* economic situation and world politics also have a major influence on businesses in the United States. Therefore, to understand business, one must also understand basic economics and politics. Most universities require students to take economics courses *before* they take business courses, because economic concepts are the basis for most business decision-making.

For this reason, the next two chapters will be devoted to teaching you the *fundamentals* of economics. The basic objective of this section is to teach you some basic terms and concepts from economics so that when you read business periodicals you will understand what they mean when they discuss economic terms and organizations. Another objective is to learn how the United States system can be strengthened to help everyone prosper.

WHAT IS ECONOMICS?

economics
The study of the allocation of scarce resources among competing individuals.

factors of production
Land, materials, human labor, and capital.

communist systems
Systems in which resource allocation is largely government controlled.

capitalist systems
Systems in which resources are allocated by consumers bargaining in the marketplace and trading goods and services.

socialist systems
Systems in which allocation of resources is done partially by the market (the free trade of goods and services), and partially by the government.

Economics is the study of the allocation of scarce resources among competing individuals. You understand what it means to "economize" in your own life. It means we have to learn to "make do" because we do not have all that we want. The world is in a similar situation. There are **factors of production** (resources) available: land and natural resources, human labor, and capital (machines, tools, and buildings). Those resources are used to produce goods and services to satisfy our need for food, shelter, and clothing, and our other needs. The economic questions are: "*Who* decides how to allocate those resources?" and "*How* should they be allocated?"

Today, resource allocation in some countries is largely government controlled. That is the nature of **communist systems** (for example, the Soviet Union). Resource allocation may also be left to individual consumers, bargaining in the marketplace and trading goods and services. That is the nature of **capitalist systems** (for example, the United States and Canada). In between are systems that are based on private exchange *and* some government ownership. That is the nature of **socialist systems** (for example, Sweden and Denmark). Even socialist countries such as Norway rely mostly on *private* business for wealth. There are no pure capitalist or communist systems; all systems have some mixture of consumer choice plus government-controlled allocation. Regardless of the system used, the ultimate goal of economics is to make optimum use of resources so that people can attain a good

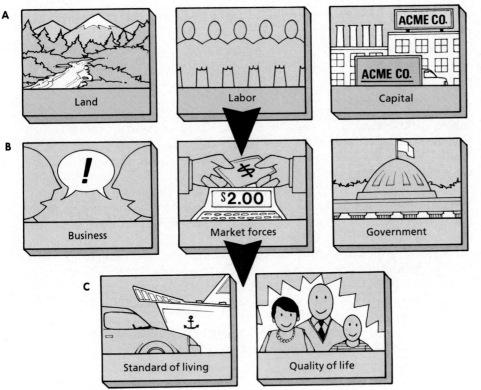

FIGURE 2-1

Economics in action. Economics studies how various resources, **A,** are best allocated, **B,** to produce the highest standard of living and quality of life, **C.** The inputs are known as the "factors of production."

---

standard of living (that is, have homes, cars, clothes, and other tangibles) and enjoy a good *quality of life* (that is, education, health, a clean environment, and happiness).[1] Figure 2-1 shows the economic system and its ultimate goals.

THE STUDY OF ECONOMICS

If you were to go through the course list in economics at most colleges, you would find courses in both macroeconomics and microeconomics. You would likely find other courses on the history of economic thought. The following sections define some basic terms in economics and give you some feel for what is covered in various economics courses.

Macroeconomics

What causes one country to prosper and grow while other countries, with similar resources, remain poor? What causes unemployment? How much of a country's wealth should be spent on government programs such as defense, welfare, and education?

These and other similar questions are the subject of macroeconomics. **Macroeconomics** is the study of the nation's economy as a whole. Macroeconomics can be a fascinating subject to study, because it looks at such important issues as whether or not taxes should be raised, the problems of inflation and depression,

macroeconomics
The study of the nation's economy as a whole.

and much more. Nearly every major social, political, or economic issue can be discussed more intelligently and objectively once one understands basic macroeconomics.

Microeconomics

microeconomics
The study of the behavior of people and organizations in particular markets.

What happens to the price of corn when there is a drought in the Midwest? What happens to the supply of farm products when the government subsidizes farmers or keeps farm prices artificially low? What is the impact of income taxes versus value-added taxes on consumers? How does one determine the value of leisure time? These and other similar questions are the subject of microeconomics. **Microeconomics** is the study of the behavior of people and organizations in particular markets. It looks at how prices are determined and how people and businesses respond to changes in the market (for example, changes in the demand for and supply of products).

Microeconomics can also be challenging to study because it teaches principles that can be used in everyday buying and selling transactions with others.

PROGRESS CHECK

■ What is the difference between microeconomics and macroeconomics? Which would be concerned with international trade fluctuations?

■ What is the difference between a high standard of living and a high quality of life? What are some of the components of each?

EARLY ECONOMIC THOUGHT: MALTHUS (1766–1834)

Thomas R. Malthus.

Most early economists had no idea of how to make a country grow to be prosperous or to help people become healthy and happy. In fact, economics was once known as the "dismal science," because economists were so pessimistic. In England, for example, an economist named Thomas R. Malthus saw that most of his countrymen were starving. Poverty, hunger, and disease were the norm. Malthus felt conditions could only get worse, because population was increasing geometrically (for example, 200, 400, 800) while food supplies were only slowly increasing. (He published this idea in 1798.) He anticipated *more* hunger and disease as a result. Today there are some people who feel Malthus was right, and it is just a matter of time before there are too many people in the world and too few resources. (See the box on p. 51 for a discussion of the issue.)

Recently, economists have predicted that the world would run out of resources such as oil, water, and coal and that pollution would get worse and worse.[2] They cite nations such as Mexico as their model of the future. Other writers are more optimistic and predict world prosperity. They feel that population growth can be an asset. Their model of the future is the United States.[3] Which predictions are correct? Nobody knows for sure, but we do know some strategies for creating prosperity. The basis for optimism began in 1776. What was needed was a social and political base for growth. That base was established in America.

GOVERNMENTS, NOT PEOPLE, ARE THE PROBLEM

To hear most experts tell it, rapid population growth is the curse of underdeveloped countries. More mouths to feed and care for make it difficult for poor nations to pull themselves out of poverty. Resources are limited. More births mean less for everyone else.

That notion is flawed. Whether people are an asset or a liability depends on what kind of society they live in.

South Korea, Taiwan, Singapore and Hong Kong are the great economic success stories among developing nations. Yet all have population densities in excess of China. Not coincidentally, all have far more of what we call free enterprise than most other states.

Even socialist India is making enormous progress in feeding itself, thanks to more market-oriented agricultural policies. At the time of Independence in 1947, India's 350 million people lived in constant fear of cataclysmic famines that took the lives of millions. Today, India's 700 million people are almost self-sufficient in food production.

Population problems are usually most acute in countries that have state-dominated economies.

Numerous countries, for instance, have crippled their farmers by making it illegal for them to get a fair price for their output. They must sell their produce to government boards, often far below market prices. Nigeria, once a food exporter, has done this—and then wonders why people abandon the countryside and flood the cities and why it has become a major food importer.

The American position is fundamental and correct: If people are permitted to be productive, they usually will be, and the population problem will be far less acute than modern Malthusians would lead us to believe.

Source: M.S. Forbes, Jr., *Forbes*, October 1, 1984, p. 17. Reprinted by permission of *Forbes* magazine; © Forbes, Inc., 1984.

Even cities like Honolulu have rapidly expanded, leading Malthusians to believe that it is only a matter of time before population exceeds available resources.

Adam Smith.

invisible hand
The idea that countries prosper when individuals within the country prosper because the way to make money is to provide needed goods and services to others through trade; the invisible hand turns self-directed gain into social benefit.

CAPITALIST ECONOMICS: ADAM SMITH (1723–1790)

The year was 1776. The Declaration of Independence stated that everyone had the right to life, liberty, and the pursuit of happiness. Certainly those early Americans felt they knew how to make a country prosper. They felt that the key was *freedom,* and they fought to get it.

There was an economist who understood the American dream and helped shape it, even though he was not an American. His name was Adam Smith. He published his book, *An Inquiry into the Nature and Causes of the Wealth of Nations,* in 1776, the same year that the Declaration of Independence was signed. Adam Smith, too, felt he knew what would cause a nation to prosper. Like the founding fathers of America, he believed in the power of freedom.

Adam Smith believed that people would work hard if they knew they could make a lot of money by doing so. He made the desire for money the foundation of his theory. He pictured farmers working long hours growing food to sell locally and to other countries. He pictured businesspeople working long hours to make shoes, tools, and other products to sell locally and internationally. As long as they were free to make as much money as they could, Adam Smith felt that farmers and businesspeople would work long hours. Case One in Chapter 1 illustrates how new immigrants are proving Adam Smith correct. The result, Smith believed, would be plenty of food to eat and products of all kinds available to buy. He said that people *trying to improve their own situation in life* would benefit society as a whole (like an invisible hand) by producing needed goods, services, and ideas. Adam Smith's **invisible hand** concept referred to the idea that countries would prosper as individuals within the country prospered, because the way to make money was to provide needed goods and services to others through trade. The invisible hand turns self-directed gain into social benefit.

Capitalism has greatly increased farm output in China.

Capitalism: Freedom and Incentives

According to Adam Smith, two keys to economic success were freedom and incentives.

Freedom of religion, the press, opportunity, and speech, and freedom from government oppression, were the foundations of the U.S. Constitution and Adam Smith's economic theory. Incentives to produce were built into the system; farmers and businesspeople were allowed to keep what they made or sell it as they pleased. The more they worked, the more they earned. Such freedom and incentives made the United States one of the most prosperous nations in the world. The name that was used to describe the powerful economic system that created prosperity for all who were willing to work hard was capitalism. **Capitalism** is an economic system is which all or most of the means of production and distribution (for example, land, factories, railroads, and stores) are privately owned and operated for profit.

capitalism
An economic system in which all or most of the means of production and distribution are privately owned and operated for profit.

The Basic Rights of Capitalism Versus Communism

The most fundamental of all rights under capitalism is the right to private property. This means that people can buy, sell, and use land, buildings, machinery, inventions, and other forms of property, and pass the property on to their children. On the other hand, Karl Marx said in *The Communist Manifesto* that "The theory of the communists may be summed up in the single sentence: abolition of private property."[4] Another major element in communism was the abolition of all right to inheritance.[5] Clearly, capitalism and communism have different beliefs entirely.

A second basic right under capitalism is the right to keep all profits, after taxes, of a business. Under communism, organizations are owned by the state and any profit goes to the state.

A third basic right under capitalism is freedom of competition. Within certain guidelines established by the government, a company is free to compete with new products, promotions, and other strategies.

The fourth basic right under capitalism is freedom of choice. People are free to choose where they want to work, whether or not they will join a union, and what career they want to follow. Other freedoms of choice include where to live and what to buy or sell. One simply cannot appreciate such freedoms until they are taken away. In the Soviet Union, for example, citizens are not free to choose careers, to select among many competitive products in the market, or to move from city to city. The benefits of capitalism are best seen in the results. We shall explore the results of communism in Case One at the end of the chapter and on pp. 61-62.

The results of capitalism are best shown with some examples. In the 1780s, four fifths of French families devoted 90% of their incomes simply to buying bread—only bread—to stay alive. Life expectancy in France in 1795 was 23.4 years for men and 27.3 years for women. This was the era, remember, when Adam Smith wrote his *Wealth of Nations*. Soon after, the market economy took over. A **market economy** is one in which free trade is encouraged and people have the freedom and incentives to profit from that free trade. This is how Michael Novak describes what happened next[6]:

> The invention of the market economy in Great Britain and the United States more profoundly revolutionized the world between 1800 and the present than any other single force. . . . Human beings finally figured out how wealth may be produced in a

There are no limits to what free men and free women and free enterprise and free markets and a free society can accomplish when people are free to follow their dreams.

Jack Kemp

market economy
Economy in which free trade is encouraged and people have the freedom and incentives to profit from that free trade.

real wages
Money wages divided by the price level.

sustained, systematic way. In Great Britain, **real wages** doubled between 1800 and 1850, and doubled again between 1850 and 1900.

Similar gains occurred in France and most of the free world. We shall now explore how free markets work; they are the source of such growth.

HOW FREE MARKETS WORK

free market system
System in which decisions about what to produce and in what quantities are decided by the market; that is, by buyers and sellers negotiating prices for goods and services.

A **free market system** is one in which decisions about what to produce and in what quantities are decided by the market, that is, by buyers and sellers negotiating prices for goods and services.

You and I and other consumers in the United States send signals to tell producers what to make, how many, in what color, and so on. The way we do that is by going to the store and buying products and services. For example, if all of us decided we wanted more fish (rather than red meat), we would signal fishermen to catch more fish. The message is sent by the *price*. As the demand for fish goes up, the price goes up as well, because people are willing to pay more. Fishermen notice this price increase and know they can make more money by catching more fish. Thus they have the *incentive* to get up earlier and fish later. Furthermore, more people go fishing. These are people who previously could not make a profit fishing but now can because of the higher price. The kind of fish they go for depends on the kind of fish we prefer (requests in the store).

Supply and demand ultimately sets the fish market price.

The same process occurs with all products. The *price* tells producers how much to produce. As a consequence, there is rarely a long-term shortage of goods in the United States. If anything were wanted but not available, the price would tend to go up until someone would begin making that product or sell the ones they already had, given free markets.

How Prices Are Determined

The previous discussion about supply, demand, and pricing is an important part of microeconomics. It illustrates the fact that prices are not determined by sellers. Rather, they are determined by buyers and sellers negotiating in the marketplace. A seller may want to receive $10 a pound for fish, but the quantity demanded at that price may be quite low. The lower the price the fisherman can charge, the higher the quantity demanded is likely to be. Many more people can and will buy fish at $1 a pound than at $10 a pound. How is a price determined that is acceptable to both buyers and sellers? The answer is provided by understanding the economic concepts of supply and demand.

Supply

Supply refers to the quantity of products that manufacturers or owners are willing to sell at different prices at a specific time. Generally speaking, the amount supplied will increase as the price increases. Economists usually show this relationship between quantity supplied and price on a graph. Figure 2-2 shows a simple supply curve. The price of an item in dollars is shown vertically on the left of the graph. Quantity is given horizontally at the bottom of the graph. The various points on the graph indicate how many fish a fisherman would provide at different prices. For example, at a price of $2, a fisherman would provide only two fish, but at $8, he would supply eight fish. The line connecting the dots is a supply line

supply
The quantity of products that manufacturers or owners are willing to sell at different prices at a specific time.

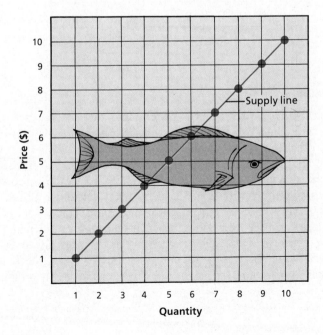

FIGURE 2-2

A simple supply line showing the quantity of fish supplied at different prices. The supply line rises from left to right. Think it through. The higher the price of fish goes (the left margin), the greater the quantity that fishermen will be willing to supply.

supply curve
Shows the relationship between price and the quantity supplied.

demand
The quantity of products that people are willing to buy at different prices at a specific time.

demand curve
Shows the relationship between quantity demanded and price.

or **supply curve.*** It indicates the relationship between the price and the quantity supplied. All things being equal, the higher the price, the more fishermen will be willing to supply.

Demand

Demand refers to the quantity of products that people are willing to buy at different prices at a specific time. Generally speaking, the quantity demanded will decrease as the price increases. Again, the relationship between price and quantity demanded can be shown in a graph. Figure 2-3 shows a simple demand line. The various points on the graph indicate the quantity demanded at various prices. For example, at a price of $8, the quantity demanded is just two fish. But if the price were $2, the quantity demanded would increase to eight. The line connecting the dots is a **demand curve.** It shows the relationship between quantity demanded and price.

FIGURE 2-3

A simple demand line showing the quantity of fish demanded at different prices. The demand line falls from left to right. It is easy to understand why the higher the price of fish, the lower the quantity demanded. As the price falls, the quantity demanded goes up.

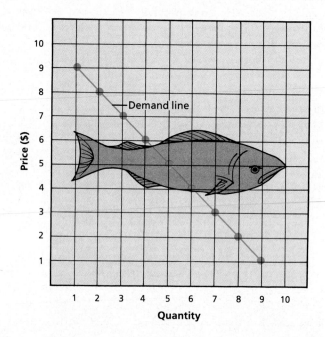

Equilibrium Point

equilibrium point
Point at which supply and demand are equal.

market price
Price determined by supply and demand.

It should be clear to you after reviewing the graphs that the key factor in determining supply and demand is price. Sellers prefer a high price and buyers prefer a low price, all other things being equal. If you were to lay the two graphs on top of one another, the supply line and the demand line would cross. At that crossing point, the quantity demanded and the quantity supplied would be equal. Figure 2-4 illustrates that point. At a price of $5, the quantity demanded and the quantity supplied are equal. It is known as the **equilibrium point.** That would become the market price. **Market price,** then, is determined by supply and demand.

What would happen if the seller moved his or her price up to $6? At that price, the buyer would be willing to buy only four fish, but the seller would be willing to sell six fish. Similarly, if the price were cut to $4, then buyers would

---

*Such lines are usually curved, but are shown straight to keep the example easier to understand.

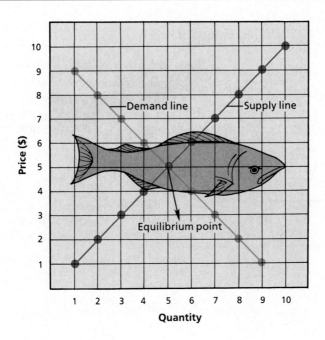

FIGURE 2-4

The interaction of quantity demanded and supplied at the equilibrium point. When we put supply and demand lines on one graph, we find that they interact at a price where the quantity supplied and the quantity demanded are equal. This is therefore called the equilibrium point. In the long run, the market price will tend toward the equilibrium point.

be willing to buy six fish, but sellers would be willing to sell only four. In a free market, prices will always tend toward the equilibrium price.

It is the interaction between supply and demand, then, that determines the market price in the long run. There is no need for government involvement or government planning. If surpluses develop, a signal is sent to sellers to lower the price. If shortages develop, a signal is sent to sellers to increase the price. Eventually supply will again equal demand if nothing interferes with market forces.

World Markets: Supply and Demand

Every day billions of consumers throughout the world are sending signals to millions of producers throughout the world telling them what they want. The signal is sent by the price of various goods and services. The signals are sent very quickly, so that there should be little delay in ending surpluses and shortages. In the real world, there are many interferences to the free exchange of goods and services among countries. Consequently, some countries have surpluses (for example, the United States has a surplus of many crops) and others suffer from scarcity (many countries do not have sufficient food). A free market system would seem to be the best system for improving the world's economic condition. Given the advantages of such a system, there must be offsetting disadvantages or else the world would be joined in one, united free market.

> No better weapon against poverty, disease, illiteracy, and tyranny has yet been found than capitalism.
>
> Michael Novak

PROGRESS CHECK

▪ What are the two keys to economic success, according to Adam Smith?

▪ Who says *what* should get produced in the United States and in what quantity?

▪ What is the significance of the equilibrium point?

LIMITATIONS OF THE FREE MARKET SYSTEM

The free market system, with its freedom and incentives, was a major factor in creating the wealth that advanced countries now enjoy. It was truly an economic miracle. On the other hand, certain inequities seem to be inherent in the system. Rich people can buy almost everything that they need, and poor people often cannot. We shall explore how this happens and then we'll discuss what can be done about it.

FIGURE 2-5

The number of buyers and sellers at different prices.

						Equilibrium point				
Price	$11	$10	$9	$8	$7	$6	$5	$4	$3	$2	$1
Number willing to buy a steak at this price	0	1	2	3	4	5	6	7	8	9	10
Number willing to sell a steak at this price	10	9	8	7	6	5	4	3	2	1	0

Picture a market with ten buyers all willing to *buy* one unit of a commodity (for example, a large steak), but with each person willing to pay a different *price*. Picture also ten sellers who are calling to *sell*, but at different prices. Figure 2-5 shows how this market may look.

As you can see, the price where supply equals demand (the equilibrium point) is at $6. If the steak were priced at $6, there would be no excess supply nor any excess demand. But notice this also. At the price of $6, there are some buyers who want steak, but are shut out by the market. All the buyers willing to pay from $1 to $5 (the majority) don't get what they want. Similarly, all the sellers who were willing to sell at prices from $7 to $11 are effectively shut out from the market. The market thus *excludes* buyers with too little money and sellers that cannot survive at low prices.

Thus we have the situation in the United States where some poor people cannot afford enough food or adequate housing. The same thing is true with health care, clothing, and other goods and services. The wealthy seem to get all they need, and the poor get less than they need.

When people criticize these *results,* they are saying, in effect, that they do not approve of the price mechanism (free markets) as the means for allocating scarce resources. Remember, economics is the study of how to allocate scarce resources. The free market brought us prosperity, but it brought inequality as well. It is that inequality that has caused much national and world tension.

In the search to create more equality in the United States, the government has intervened in the free market system to create more social fairness and a more even distribution of wealth. See the box on p. 59 for a discussion of government involvement in the agriculture market. We shall discuss such government involvement in greater depth in Chapter 3. Before we do, let's review what other countries have done to allocate scarce resources. One alternative system is socialism. Socialism is an interesting contrast, because it is a combination of free market allocation and government allocation.

THE FARM CRISIS

For many years, the U.S. government has been directly involved in the farm market. It has artificially set some prices and encouraged or discouraged the production of selected animals and crops. Thus the farm economy is not completely ruled by the laws of supply and demand. Price is often set by the government, or is at least manipulated by the government.

The farm crisis in the mid-1980s was partially a result of government interference. Uncontrolled by the laws of supply and demand, many marginal farms that would have failed gradually over the years have instead survived. Furthermore, attracted by artificial prices and the rising price of land, farmers went into debt to buy more land and produce more.

The crisis occurred when farm values fell along with the prices of most commodities, including farm products. Farmers could not earn enough from selling their output to pay off loans at the bank. Some banks were in danger of failing and began closing down farms to sell the land and equipment to recover part of the loans. Thousands of small farms and many large farms were forced out of business.

What should we do now? Many farmers want the government out. They would prefer operating under a system of free markets, but the market is so involved with federal and international governments that a sudden shift to free markets may cause many more failures. There is no "answer" to this crisis; only questions. But the farm market is a good example of the problem of trying to control markets centrally (that is, by the government rather than by the price mechanism).

THINKING IT THROUGH

How much government involvement should there be in an economy? How important is freedom versus equality? How much control should the government have over ownership of production and distribution facilities? How much of the wealth of a nation should go to support those in need? These are the issues that businesses and government face throughout the world.

PROGRESS CHECK

- Could you draw a chart to illustrate the idea that free markets may shut out the majority of buyers and sellers and lead to a situation of haves and have nots?

- Could you explain the problems of government-controlled economies using the farm crisis as an example?

THE SOCIALIST EXPERIMENT

The United States could be *the* economic model for the rest of the world. Adam Smith's free market economic principles are clearly a means to prosperity. How is it, then, that most Third World countries (mostly poor countries) have adopted socialism as their economic model?[7] Why has the Soviet Union adopted a communist model for its economy? These are important questions, because the answers spell out the future of American businesses. If free market capitalism is to expand worldwide and create prosperity for all the world's citizens, capitalism will have to prove itself a better system *overall*.

What is capitalism's weak point? One answer is *equality*. Capitalism needs to meet the needs of *all* people, especially the poor, the sick, the old, and the unemployed. Socialist countries have tried to address these problems, but may go too far in letting government allocate resources. For example:

- In Denmark, two thirds of the population is sustained by the state. A breadwinner with a meager salary pays at least 55% in taxes and *marginal rates* (rates for earning above a certain amount) of at least 60%. A plumber who charges $20 for a job pays $4 in sales taxes, $5 in income tax, and $8 for expenses, leaving him or her $3.[8]
- In Holland, there are almost as many inactive people (including retired) as there are private-sector workers. There is not much incentive to go back to work if you lose your job. An unemployed worker gets 80% of his or her previous salary for 6 months and 75% for the next 2 years.[9]

In Sweden, the government benefits seem good. To minimize unemployment, the government pays $5.25 per hour toward the wages of workers who would otherwise be laid off. Hospital care is just $4 a day. Dental care for children is free. But, as they say, "There is no such thing as a free lunch." A manager earning around $42,000 pays all but $14,750 in national and local taxes. If that person were to get a raise, 85% of it would go to taxes![10] "In Sweden, the government keeps the salary and leaves you the tip—15%," says the president of a Swedish firm.[11]

One country that may have found the right balance between free markets and a fair distribution of income is Finland. Finland is about the size of California and has only 4.9 million people, yet it is eighth in the world for per capita output ($10,440 per person). Finland did it mostly by relying on *private* companies. Whereas government spending accounts for 62% of Sweden's economy and 58% of Denmark's, it is 36% of Finland's, which is less than the United States' 37%. Economic growth in Finland over the last 5 years is double that of the rest of Europe.[12]

| **THINKING IT THROUGH** | Socialism depends upon capitalism for wealth creation and then depends on the government to distribute the wealth more evenly. Can you explain why that eventually may cut off the source of wealth? How hard would you study in school if you knew everyone would get a C regardless of how they did on the tests? Would you give your car as much care and attention if it were owned by the state? Do such questions help you to see what may happen to job incentives (for example, maintenance of apartment buildings) in a communist economy? |

THE COMMUNIST EXPERIMENT

According to *U.S. News and World Report,* "The Soviet Union today is a nation in distress, its people trying to cope with a faltering economy." The article summarizes interviews with several communist citizens. They report that it is "all but impossible for a family to live on a single salary." The Soviet system provides citizens with many benefits—low-rent apartments, free medical service, access to free education—but still there are problems.[13]

Many of the Soviet Union's problems are economic. There are perennial food shortages. There are shortages in many other products as well, and the quality is often poor. *Newsweek,* in an article called "A System That Doesn't Work," reported that 50% or 60% of all Soviet industrial capacity may be devoted to arms production. Furthermore, Soviet bureaucrats generally prefer to keep prices artificially low to show there is no inflation under communism. "In fact, however, the low prices only result in the misallocation of resources, and inflation is measured in shortages and lines outside the shops. Another basic problem is that without the ability to bring output and prices in line with demand, no manager has any incentive to be flexible."[14] The *Newsweek* article cites inefficiency in agriculture (25% of Soviet workers work on farms versus 4% in the United States) and slow decision making among government planners. Free market forces do not operate in the Soviet Union, and the result is often great imbalances. You should be able to explain why now that you understand how supply and demand works to control markets quickly and efficiently.

The meltdown of a Soviet nuclear power plant in the Spring of 1986 drew attention to poor construction practices, maintenance problems, and faulty safety precautions in the Soviet Union.[15] Such a disaster has had a serious economic impact on the Soviet Union at a time when the country is economically weak.

Capitalist Inroads

Some communist countries are experimenting with capitalism, especially the incentives of profit. In China, for example, agriculture and industry has been infused

A rice seedling nursery in Shandong Province, China.

with many capitalist experiments with highly rewarding results (see Case Two at the end of this chapter). Several Third World countries have had great success with capitalism as well. (See the box below.)

THIRD WORLD CAPITALISM

South Korea is a good example of capitalist-led growth. In the early 1960s, gross national product (GNP) in South Korea was $3 billion. Twenty years later, it was $65 billion.

North Korea, by contrast, is communist controlled. Its growth has been stagnant compared with South Korea's, even though North Korea was the more developed half of the nation with 55% of the arable land, 90% of electrical power, and 70% of mineral production.

Malaysia is also a capitalist bright spot among Third World countries. Its record? Gross national product in 1970 was $3.9 billion; by 1980 it was $12.6 billion. There is plenty of food, even some for export, and only half of the arable land is under cultivation. Could capitalism create the same advances in the rest of the less developed countries?

Figures are from Edwin Hartrich, *The American Opportunity,* New York: Macmillan Publishing, Inc., 1983, pp. 182, 189.

EXPERIMENTING WITH A MIXED ECONOMY

mixed economy
An economy that combines free markets with some government allocation of resources.

The United States is not a purely capitalist nation. Rather, it has a **mixed economy;** that is, a combination of free markets plus government allocation of resources. As a mixed economy, the United States falls somewhere between a pure capitalist state and a socialist state. The degree of government involvement in the economy is a matter of some debate in the United States today. In 1986, the Congress proposed the largest change in the tax system since it was started. Top tax rates would be lowered, and rates for low income families cut to nothing. These changes were proposed to simplify the tax codes and to stimulate the economy. The new tax code would discourage investments that were made to avoid taxes and encourage investments that promoted business growth.

The government has a great effect on the success of business in the United States and throughout the world. In Chapter 3 we shall explore many issues having to do with the government and the economy. Keep in mind as you read Chapter 3 that the foundation of the U.S. economy is capitalism. The government serves as a means to supplement that basic system and thus promote growth and greater equality. Changes in the tax codes will have a significant effect on the economy over the next few years. You will be better able to understand what is happening in the economy and how it affects business after you read the next chapter. But first, let's pause and review what we have learned so far about economics.

PROGRESS CHECK

- How much are the economies of socialist countries like Sweden and Denmark controlled by the government?
- What are some of the benefits and drawbacks of communism as practiced in the Soviet Union?

1 Economics is the study of the allocation of scarce resources among competing individuals.

- What is macroeconomics?

  It is the study of the nation's economy as a whole.

- What is microeconomics?

  It is the study of economic decisions by specific organizations and individuals. It looks at how prices are determined and how businesses and people respond to changes in supply and demand.

2 Malthus believed that economic conditions would worsen over time because resources (food) were scarce and the population was multiplying geometrically. Adam Smith felt that the world economy could become prosperous if people were given *freedom* to work and freedom to keep the profits. This would give them *incentive* to work hard and produce needed goods and services for others. Prosperity for individuals would lead (like an invisible hand) to prosperity for all.

- How does the free market system work?

  Consumers vote in the marketplace with their purchases. Consumer demand either raises or lowers prices, and those price changes signal sellers about *what* to produce and *how much*. The market controls production.

- What are the mechanisms that control the free market?

  Supply, demand, and prices. As prices rise, quantity demanded falls and quantity supplied increases, and vice versa.

- What are supply and demand curves?

  A *supply curve* indicates the relationship between price and the quantity supplied. A *demand curve* shows the relationship between quantity demanded and price. Where they intersect is called the equilibrium point; it is the point where the quantity supplied and the quantity demanded are equal. The *market price* is determined by supply and demand forces.

- Does the free market satisfy everyone's needs?

  No, the rich tend to get all they need and the poor often do not. That is why there are no totally free market systems. Some government programs seem necessary.

- Which is more important: freedom or equality?

  Both are clearly important goals. The world economies are split over the relative importance of each, with communism favoring equality and capitalism favoring freedom.

3 The farm crisis resulted partially from government interference in the pricing mechanism of the farm market.

- The government has been involved in the farm market for years; what caused the sudden crisis?

  The value of farm land had increased steadily for years and rose even faster in the inflationary 1970s. Farmers bought more land to share in the rising values. In the early 1980s, farm values fell, crop prices dropped, and farmers could not repay their loans. This caused not only the farms, but also some banks that lent them money, to fail.

4 Some people (socialists) feel that capitalism has run its course and the next step in economics should be socialism. The socialist idea is to take the wealth created by capitalism and distribute it more equally.

- What has happened to the socialist experiment?

Socialism around the world often undermines the freedom and *incentives* of capitalism by taking too much from the productive members of society and giving it to the unproductive members. Marginal tax rates can reach 85%.

- How is the communist system working?

  The Soviet Union's economy is very weak, but some other communist countries are improving their economies (namely China). What is making some communist countries stronger economically is increased capitalism.

KEY TERMS

capitalism p. 53	macroeconomics p. 49
capitalist system p. 48	market economy p. 53
communist system p. 48	market price p. 56
demand p. 56	microeconomics p. 50
demand curve p. 56	mixed economy p. 62
economics p. 48	real wages p. 54
equilibrium point p. 56	socialist system p. 48
factors of production p. 48	supply p. 55
free market system p. 54	supply curve p. 56
invisible hand p. 52	trickle-down theory p. 65

GETTING INVOLVED

1 Go to your local or school library and find a couple of Introduction to Economics texts. Look through the Tables of Contents and briefly leaf through the books. What are the major topics? How hard are the books to read? Share your findings with others in the class.

2 What are some of the *disadvantages* of living in a free society? How could such disadvantages be minimized? What are the advantages? Write a short essay describing why a poor person in India might reject capitalism and prefer a socialist/communist state. How could the United States overcome this situation to broaden the base of the free market system? Perhaps two students could debate capitalist versus communist societies to further reveal the issues.

3 Democratic capitalism is said to be based on a Judeo-Christian base of ethics. Write a short essay showing that the moral and ethical foundation of our country is weakening. What would you recommend? Discuss with your class.

4 The leaders of both communist and capitalist societies feel so strongly about the benefits of their systems that they are sometimes willing to go to war to defend them. Show that such tensions are created largely by *economic* pressures, and discuss how such tensions can be minimized or eliminated. Would you support free trade with communist countries? Give arguments for both sides.

PRACTICING MANAGEMENT DECISIONS

CASE ONE   ECONOMIC CONSEQUENCES OF COMMUNIST SYSTEMS

Although the capitalism system led to prosperity in much of the world, there were some people, especially Karl Marx, who felt that capitalism would eventually be replaced by socialism. He felt that the wealth of capitalism should be distributed more evenly and that the people should own businesses and farms collectively. Socialism got a real boost in the 1930s when the United States went through the Great Depression. Government involvement in the economy increased greatly in the United States and even more so in socialist countries.

In the Soviet Union, China, and a few other countries, socialism took the form of communism. That is, the government became the principal mechanism for allocating resources, and the government (not the people) owned businesses and farms.

To create a more equal distribution of wealth, communist governments felt they had to suppress many of the freedoms enjoyed in capitalist nations. That included freedom of religion, press, travel, expression, and business ownership. The government became very powerful. The problem is that government allocation of resources is not as fast, efficient, or effective as free market choices. As a consequence, shortages and surpluses occur in many goods and services.

A major problem of communism is that the suppression of freedom also takes away the incentive to produce quality goods and to maintain them. Therefore, many goods produced in communist countries are of inferior quality and suffer from lack of service. Government directives simply cannot motivate people to work as hard and as carefully as the profit motive.

DECISION QUESTIONS

1 Given the apparent economic success of capitalist countries and the relative economic failure of communist countries, why would a Third World nation adopt the communist system?

2 What would happen if communist countries introduced capitalist concepts? (See Case 2.)

3 Could more open exchange of goods and services between the United States and the Soviet Union lessen international tensions? Are there two sides to this question?

CASE TWO   THE CAPITALIST EXPERIMENT IN CHINA

China is a land of over 1 billion people, most of whom live in poverty. Per capita income is only $350, about the same as Haiti. There are 400,000 state-owned enterprises in China. It was and is a communist/socialist country. However, China is trying to introduce some capitalism into the system to see what happens. It watched Taiwan raise its per capita income to over $2,500 with capitalist incentives and decided to try it at home.

The announcement was made October 20, 1984. The plan was adopted by the Communist Party's Central Committee after a week-long meeting in Beijing. The plan calls for dismantling of the state planning system, greater freedom for business enterprises, heavier reliance on market forces to determine output, free-floating prices on certain goods, higher wages for skilled workers, and more private entrepreneurs. (This was quite a drastic change from the previous state control of wages, prices, production and trade.)

In the past, prices were kept artificially low, subsidized by the state. Ignoring market signals, the system often had shortages of some goods and huge stockpiles of unwanted merchandise. The government was careful to retain control over some major products (steel, coal, machinery, and synthetic fibers). The plan says things like:

"Only when some individuals are allowed and encouraged to get better off first through diligent work will more and more people be prompted to take the road of prosperity." Adam Smith would be proud. In this country, we call it the **trickle-down theory**.

The report also said that, as the economy diversifies, the role of private entrepreneurs should expand and take over enterprises now run by the state. The driving force

PRACTICING MANAGEMENT DECISIONS

trickle-down theory
Assumes that when wealthy people get wealthier, they will buy goods and services that will boost the economy so that their wealth will trickle down to less wealthy people.

behind these changes is Deng Xiaoping. He began this move by taking the commune out of communism and restoring family farms and free market incentives. Production jumped by 89%. The experiment worked. The plan was to try a similar experiment in industry. It could be called "market socialism." State enterprises will now function as independent companies responsible for making profits. Here are some of the results, as reported in the U.S. press:

- At the Beijing Television Factory, monthly output went up 30% since the managers began offering piece-rate bonuses for each set produced above target. Profits rose by $81,000.
- Bicycles, radios, and watches that once were scarce are now plentiful.
- Farmers are setting up small agribusinesses such as papaya growing and are trucking fresh vegetables to market.
- Chinese factories are starting to sell large quantities of higher quality but inexpensive goods to the United States and other international markets. Exports went from $12.7 billion in 1983 to $15 billion in 1984.
- Jialing Machinery made only military equipment in the past. Market opportunity led it to make motorcycles because the demand was high. Now the factory turns out 200,000 units a year of quality high enough to wear the Honda label. Profits tripled in 1984.
- There is spirited competition between the Coca Cola bottler and Asia Cola. Asia Cola spends $1,200 a month to advertise on a large neon sign. China now has 168 ad agencies to "encourage competition."
- China's first fast-food restaurant has Donald Duck on the roof. It sells hamburgers, french fries, hot dogs, fried rice, sweet and sour pork, and other "Chinese" meals.
- Bu Xinsheng is a national hero for raising productivity at his factory and improving quality. How did he do it? He switched from wages to piece work. Maximum wages went from $18 to $41 a month, but workers had to work harder to earn them. They did.
- In the cities, literally millions of people have set up shops or stalls where they sell just about everything. There are now a few millionaires in China.

Along with the prosperity has come some of the Western culture China's leaders had worried about. Young Chinese are listening to rock and roll music, watching TV, and wearing makeup. Western clothes are the rage. Some entrepreneurs are making huge profits by selling hard-to-get consumer goods. The old values of sharing and caring seem to be losing out to profiting and affluence.

DECISION QUESTIONS

1 What are the capitalist principles that enabled China to raise productivity so quickly?
2 What effect has the new capitalism had on workers? Consumers? Small business-people? Farmers? Who is hurt by the new reforms?
3 What are the negatives associated with the new capitalism? Can they be minimized?
4 What does the new system mean for future relationships between the United States and China?

Sources: "The Greatest Leap Yet Toward a Free Market," *Business Week,* November 5, 1984, p. 45; Amanda Bennett, "Bu Xinsheng: China's Model Manager," *The Wall Street Journal,* May 30, 1984, p. 36; "Capitalism in China," *Business Week,* January 14, 1985, pp. 53-59; Michael Weisskopf, "China Recasts Its Economy," *The Washington Post,* October 21, 1984, p. 1; and other current articles.

The United States Government recognizes the inequality of a free market system. As a consequence, more and more funds are being diverted to the government for care of the aged (social security), the poor (welfare), and the sick (Medicare). In spite of increased spending, the problems persist.

Funds are also spent on defense, crime prevention, and regulation of business. Too much government spending slows business growth. Too little may result in social decay.

Chapter 3 looks at economic issues affecting business. They include productivity, unemployment, taxes, money creation by the government, inflation, the national debt, and trade deficits. The health of the economy is directly related to the health of business. Chapter 3 will teach you terms and concepts you can use to read and understand the business literature.

ECONOMIC ISSUES AFFECTING BUSINESS

LEARNING GOALS

After you have read and studied this chapter, you should be able to:

- Outline six key economic issues of the coming decades.
- Discuss the concepts of gross national product and productivity.
- Explain four types of unemployment.
- Describe two major causes of inflation and major inflation measuring indices.
- Define *recession, depression, stagflation,* and *supply-side economics.*
- Explain monetary policy and its impact on business.
- Explain fiscal policy and its impact on business.
- Discuss the issues surrounding the national debt.
- Explain the issues of trade deficits.

PROFILE   JOHN MAYNARD KEYNES, INTERVENTIONIST

John Maynard Keynes (pronounced *Canes*) was one of the economists who had a great influence on U.S. economic policy. It was he who advocated stabilizing the economy by the use of fiscal policy. That is, he thought that inflation could best be slowed by increasing taxes and/or lowering government spending. If unemployment got too high, he proposed cutting taxes and/or increasing government expenditures. Such a strategy is known as Keynesian economics and was a guiding philosophy in the U.S. for decades (and still is for many people).

Keynes' father was a lecturer in economics at Cambridge University. John Maynard began his studies at Cambridge (math and philosophy) and was encouraged to go into economics. Eventually he too became a lecturer at Cambridge.

He published his most famous book, *General Theory of Employment, Interest and Money,* in 1936. Until that time, American economic thinking was dominated by Adam Smith's *classical economics.* Smith felt that the economy would *automatically* function at full employment if there was minimal government intervention. The depression of the 1930s changed that view, and Keynesian economics took over. ■

John Maynard Keynes.

The free market system in America has been replaced by a *mixed economy.* A mixed economy is one in which resources are allocated both by free trade and by government agencies. The government has become an integral part of economic plan-

The character inherent in the American people has done all that has been accomplished; and it would have done somewhat more, if the government had not sometimes got in its way.
HENRY DAVID THOREAU

How much for defense is a major economic issue.

prime rate
The most favorable interest rate that businesses can get from banks.

ning and strategy. There are hundreds of trade associations in Washington, D.C., the function of which is to provide a dialogue between business and government. Naturally, one objective is to convince legislators to support business and minimize regulation, corporate taxes, and other restrictions.

The key political and social issues of the 1980s are basically economic issues. The economic changes discussed in Chapter 1 (for example, the service revolution, the growth of small businesses, and women in the work force) have focused attention on the government and its role in managing the disruptions caused by those changes. Some of the key issues of the late 1980s and 1990s will be:

- *Unemployment,* especially unemployment among those laid off by the "smokestack" industries (for example, autos and steel) who need retraining or relocation or both.
- *Interest rates* and their effect on economic growth (that is, inflation, recession, and stability).
- *Foreign trade* and its effect on jobs and the economy.
- The size of the *national debt* and the policies necessary to pay off the debt.
- *Social programs* such as social security and Medicare and their funding.
- The size of the *defense budget.*

All of these issues have a major impact on business. Government policy toward unemployment affects hiring and training practices. Interest rates have a major effect on the ability of firms to grow through borrowing (see box below). Foreign markets are so big that government restrictions on foreign trade have a tremendous impact on businesses. Many businesses are involved in building defense systems, including aircraft, missiles, weapons, and tanks. Any change in government policy affects all of those firms.

What is the state of the economy today? What are the factors that must be considered in addressing these issues? What is the business position on these subjects?

For college students, the issues are particularly important. How big a ta. burden will students have because of social security debts? What will the state of the economy be when today's students graduate? These are the kinds of issues that this chapter addresses.

HOW INTEREST RATES AFFECT SMALL BUSINESS

Articles from business journals tend to say things like, "High interest rates are slowing the search by Acme-Cleveland Corporation, a machine-tool producer, for a major acquisition to help diversify the company." Another article may say, "With fixed mortgage rates dropping toward 10%, home builders are expected to increase production."

Such quotes are meant to show the impact of interest rates on the economy. They affect every kind of industry from banking to farming and manufacturing. When rates are rising, business confidence and consumer confidence tend to fall, because things are going to be more expensive to buy. When they fall, people get more optimistic.

The **prime rate** is the most favorable interest rate that businesses can get from banks. Small businesses and consumers like you and me must pay higher rates than the prime.

What are interest rates today? Check your local paper's business section to find out. Is business confidence high or low? Businesspeople watch interest rates very closely. You should learn to do so also if you want to understand the business environment.

We begin with some definitions. Two terms that appear in almost all economic discussions, *gross national product* (GNP) and *productivity,* are discussed below.

GROSS NATIONAL PRODUCT

Almost every discussion about a nation's economy is based on a concept called gross national product. The reason is obvious once you learn what GNP is.

Gross national product (GNP) is the total value of a country's output of goods and services in a given year. It is a measure of economic growth or decline. When people discuss what share of the "economic pie" should go to government, they mean what percent of GNP should be spent on defense, welfare, education, and other government programs. Also, GNP gives business owners some measure of how the economy is functioning. If GNP is rising rapidly, the economy is said to be relatively strong. If GNP is stable or falling, the economy is said to be relatively weak (see Figure 3-1).

gross national product (GNP)
The total value of a country's output of goods and services.

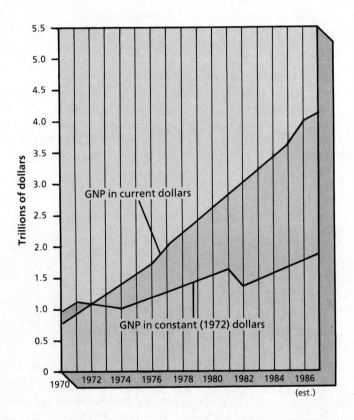

GNP in current dollars

GNP in constant (1972) dollars

1970   1972   1974   1976   1978   1980   1982   1984   1986
(est.)

FIGURE 3-1

Gross national product (GNP), 1970-1986. Although GNP is rising rapidly in dollar amounts, real growth in constant dollars (less inflation) is slight. If an economy doesn't grow, money is not available for the increasing costs of defense, welfare, and social security. GNP is now around $4 trillion. Since there are more people in the U.S. every year, if GNP does not grow, each of us will have less to spend.

Dividing GNP

An ongoing major controversy is the share of gross national product that goes to the government in taxes. In the U.S., the percentage of GNP taken by the government at all levels (federal, state, and local) was about 20% in the early 1950s. By the early 1980s, that figure had risen to 34%.

**net national product
(NNP)**
The output of goods and services beyond that which is
needed to replace worn-out
machinery, equipment, and
capital goods.

This figure is misleading in some ways, because the economic pie that is divided between the government and business is not gross national product, but net national product (NNP). **Net national product** measures the output of goods and services beyond what is needed to replace worn-out machinery, equipment, and capital goods. Of total GNP, about 12% is for replacement capital. Thus the total percent of the net economic pie being taken by government is not 34% but is closer to 40%.[1] To maintain our standard of living, we need to have a steady increase in GNP, and that means we must have more productivity.

From 1979 to 1985, GNP, adjusted for inflation, grew only 2.1% annually. That compares with 3.1% during the 1970s and 4.2% during the 1960s. Clearly, growth is slowing. The annual rate of gain in productivity has been about 1.3% since 1979. It was 1.5% in the 1970s and 2.9% in the 1960s. Thus both GNP and productivity have been falling slowly for 25 years.

Productivity

productivity
The total output of goods and
services in a given period of
time divided by work hours
(output per work hour).

Another term that is widely used in economic discussions is *productivity*. **Productivity** is *the total output of goods and services in a given period of time divided by workhours (output per workhour)*. An *increase in productivity* means that the same amount of labor input is now able to produce more goods and services. The higher productivity is, the lower costs are in producing goods and services, and the lower prices can be. Therefore businesspeople are eager to increase productivity.

Productivity is one of the major ingredients of capitalist growth. The word *capitalism* is based on the word *capital*. Capital refers to machinery and materials that are used on farms and in businesses to help workers produce more. At the beginning of the twentieth century in the United States, 1 out of 3 workers was needed to produce enough food to feed everyone and create some surplus for world use. Today less than 1 out of 20 workers can produce far greater quantities of

Machinery makes workers
more productive.

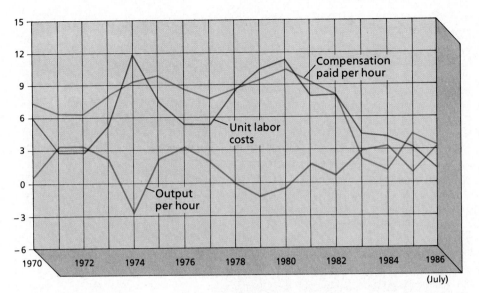

FIGURE 3-2

Productivity (output), hourly compensation, and unit labor costs: 1970 to 1984. Note that output has shown little gain over the 16-year period.

Source: Statistical Abstract of the United States, Department of Commerce, Bureau of the Census, 1986, p. 386.

food that contribute a much larger share of world production. What made the difference? The answer is that the use of tractors, chemical fertilizer, combines, silos, and other machines and materials (capital) raised farmers' *productivity*.

The increase in farm productivity was the basis for economic growth in the United States for years. The next revolution in productivity occurred in the manufacturing industry. The use of machines made mass production possible (that is, production of thousands of items such as shoes and cars by just a few workers). Again, it was capital that made such gains possible.

Now that we are in a third type of economy, a service economy, productivity is again an issue because service firms are so labor intensive. Machinery, not labor, increases productivity. Productivity in farming and manufacturing have slowed so that annual increases in productivity are low in the United States (Figure 3-2). However, productivity is still increasing in those countries that are just now introducing machinery into their farms and factories.

Productivity in the Service Sector

In the service sector, computers, word processors, and other machines are making service workers more productive. The Unites States is ahead of much of the world in service productivity, but there is much competition from Japan, South Korea, and other countries.

A major issue in the coming years will be business productivity. More money will be invested in machines such as robots, lasers, and computers to keep production high for each worker. The problem is that many workers are being replaced by machines in the quest for higher and higher productivity. This has resulted in another major economic issue: unemployment. We shall discuss this issue next.

ANNUAL PRODUCTIVITY GAINS, 1973-1984

United States	2.1%
Belgium	6.2%
Japan	5.9%
France	4.6%
Netherlands	4.6%
Italy	3.8%
West Germany	3.4%
Great Britain	2.3%

Source: U.S. Department of Labor.

PROGRESS CHECK

■ Can you define gross national product, net national product, and productivity?

■ Why are productivity increases slower in service industries?

Robots replace workers on the assembly line.

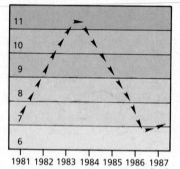

U.S. unemployment rate over time.

frictional unemployment
Occurs because of people who have quit work and have not yet found a new job and also because of new entrants in the labor force.

THE ISSUE OF UNEMPLOYMENT

Any student preparing to enter the job market has to be concerned about unemployment. So much is said and written about the jobless in various cities that one could get depressed thinking about the future prospects for jobs. The fact is that, in the 1980s, the unemployment rate has varied from just below 7% to 10%. That means some 7 million or more people were unemployed. Such figures seem overwhelming and must be put in some perspective.

First of all, there are more people working in America than ever before in history. So, along with high unemployment there is high employment. How can that be? The answer is that more people are seeking work. For example, you have already learned that the number of women seeking work has risen dramatically over the last decade or so.

There are four types of unemployment: frictional, structural, cyclical, and seasonal. Each type has a different effect on the economy. New people wanting to enter the labor force are part of the frictionally unemployed. **Frictional unemployment** refers to those people who have quit work because they did not like the job, the boss, or working conditions and who have not yet found a new job. It also refers to those people who are entering the labor force for the first time (for example, new graduates) or are returning to the labor force. There will always be some frictional unemployment, because it takes some time to find a new job or a first job. Frictional unemployment has little effect on the economy.

THEY WANT TO WORK.

YOU TRAIN THEM. WE'LL HELP PAY FOR IT.
Now there's a program that shares training costs when a business hires and trains the jobless. It is called The Job Training Partnership Act.
    This program establishes a

partnership between business and government. It provides up to 50% of on-the-job training costs. And you may qualify for tax credits of up to 50% of the first year's salary.
    The program is administered by local Private Industry Councils—organizations

made up in the majority by local business leaders who tailor it to meet specific local needs.
    Put the Job Training Partnership Act to work now. Write:

National Alliance of Business
P.O. Box 7207, Washington, D.C. 20044

Ad Council
A Public Service of This Publication

NATIONAL ALLIANCE OF BUSINESS CAMPAIGN
BUSINESS PRESS AD NO. NAB-1893-85—7" x 10" [110 Screen]
Volunteer Agency: Campbell-Mithun, Inc. Volunteer Coordinator: James Flieder, Allstate Insurance Companies

BP-6-85

Structural unemployment calls for retraining programs.

There is a second important group called the structurally unemployed. **Structural unemployment** refers to that unemployment caused by a mismatch between the skills (or location) of job seekers and the requirements (or location) of available jobs. For example, one finds coal miners in an area where the mines have been closed. You have learned that a major cause of this type of unemployment is the decline of the manufacturing sector. Another cause is the replacement of workers by robots and other technology. Structural unemployment calls for industry retraining programs to move workers into growth industries.

A third kind of unemployment is **cyclical unemployment.** It occurs because of a recession or a similar downturn in the business cycle. This type of unemployment lasts until the economy recovers and businesses begin rehiring.

The fourth type of unemployment is **seasonal unemployment.** It occurs where the demand for labor varies over the year, as with the harvesting of crops.

Figure 3-3, p. 76, shows the number of people unemployed for various reasons. What is the trend?

structural unemployment
That unemployment caused by people losing jobs because their occupation is no longer part of the main structure of the economy.

cyclical unemployment
Occurs because of a recession or a similar downturn in the business cycle.

seasonal unemployment
Occurs where the demand for labor varies over the year.

FIGURE 3-3

Note that in 1983, 6,258 of 10,717 unemployed people were job losers, largely because of structural changes. Note too the steady trend in job losers and new entrants since 1970.

Source: U.S. Bureau of Labor Statistics, *Employment and Earnings, Monthly*, and *Bulletin 2096*.

UNEMPLOYED PERSONS, BY SEX AND REASON: 1970 TO 1983
(IN THOUSANDS OF CIVILIAN PERSONS 16 YEARS OLD AND OVER. ANNUAL AVERAGES OF MONTHLY FIGURES)

Sex and reason unemployed	1970	1973	1977	1980	1983
Total	**4,093**	**4,365**	**6,991**	**7,637**	**10,717**
Job losers	1,811	1,694	3,166	3,947	6,258
Job leavers	550	683	909	891	830
Reentrants	1,228	1,340	1,963	1,927	2,412
New entrants	504	649	953	872	1,216
Male	**2,238**	**2,275**	**3,667**	**4,267**	**6,260**
Job losers	1,199	1,099	2,021	2,649	4,331
Job leavers	282	338	413	438	386
Reentrants	533	536	794	776	953
New entrants	224	301	441	405	589
Female	**1,855**	**2,089**	**3,324**	**3,370**	**4,457**
Job losers	614	593	1,145	1,297	1,926
Job leavers	267	345	496	454	444
Reentrants	696	803	1,170	1,151	1,459
New entrants	279	346	513	468	627

In summary, some of the people who are unemployed are out of work because they just entered the labor force or are just returning. They present no long-term problem because there must be *some* time when a person seeks a job. Many people are unemployed because their industry is declining. In the long run, that can be a healthy sign, because new industries will replace older, obsolete industries. Meanwhile, these people need to be retrained, and that is a major concern today.

THINKING IT THROUGH

Would the United States be better off today if we had not introduced modern farm machinery? There *would* be more people employed on the farm if we had not. Would the world be better off in the future if we did not introduce new computers, robots, and machinery? They *do* take away jobs in the short run. What happened to the farmers who were displaced by machines? What will happen to today's workers who are being replaced by machines?

Unemployment Compensation

The government has tried to cushion the effects of unemployment by paying people *unemployment benefits* for a limited period while they seek new jobs. Such payments may affect the unemployment roles in that they lessen the incentive to hurry and find new jobs. In Florida, for example, a laid-off worker who had made $16,000 annually and has a wife and two children may find that unemployment and public-assistance benefits available to the family are equal to his former take-home pay. His disposable income (that is, income after taxes) may actually increase. This is how *The Wall Street Journal* reported the situation[2]:

Even with Florida's relatively low benefit levels, government programs can provide considerable inducement for staying off the job. Unemployment compensation provides as much as $537.50 a month for each unemployed worker. And a family of four may be eligible for as much as $253 a month in food stamps, as much as $443 for rent and utilities assistance, about $50 in Low Income Energy Assistance, $150 in Emergency Energy Assistance, and school breakfast and lunch valued at $70.90. Two dozen other sources of "in-kind" income could also be available to them. . .

The Census Bureau announcement noted that these benefits increased from $2 billion in 1965 to $72 billion in 1980 and that had the value of these benefits been counted, the poverty rate would have been reduced by as much as 42%.

The United States, in other words, is trying to protect those people who are unemployed because of factors such as recessions and industry shifts. One problem is that such payments may get high enough to further, rather than relieve, unemployment problems because they may destroy the incentive to find new work until the payments end.

PROGRESS CHECK

- Can you explain the differences among frictional, structural, and cyclical unemployment? Which is causing the largest unemployment today? (See Figure 3-3.)

- What is the effect of unemployment compensation on unemployment figures?

THE ISSUE OF INFLATION

Another major concern of business and government in the early 1980s was inflation. **Inflation** basically refers to a general rise in the price level of goods and services over time. Inflation had gone over 10% early in the 1980s, and people were afraid it would go even higher. There are many causes of inflation, according to economists. Two of the most important are:

- Cost-push inflation. **Cost-push inflation** refers to the fact that businesspeople raise prices when the costs of various factors of production go up. For example, increases in the cost of labor, machinery, raw materials, fuels, and credit necessitate higher prices.
- Demand-pull inflation. **Demand-pull inflation** refers to a condition in which buyers want to buy more goods and services than are available at the time. The demand for goods and services is related to the amount of money in the economy. If the supply of money increases faster than production increases, the result is inflation. This is called "too much money chasing too few goods."

Measures of Inflation

Two of the more popular measures of price changes over time (inflation indicators) are the consumer price index (CPI) and the producer price index (PPI), also known as the wholesale price index. The **consumer price index** (see Figure 3-4) measures

inflation
A general rise in the prices of goods and services over time.

cost-push inflation
Refers to inflation caused by rising business costs.

demand-pull inflation
Refers to inflation caused by excessive demand for goods and services.

consumer price index (CPI)
Measures changes in the prices of about 400 goods and services that consumers buy.

FIGURE 3-4

Consumer price indexes: 1970 to 1986. Note that the cost of food tripled, and the cost of medical care has quadrupled in 16 years.

Source: Statistical Abstract of the United States, Department of Commerce, Bureau of the Census, 1986, p. 466; data updated per Bureau September 1986.

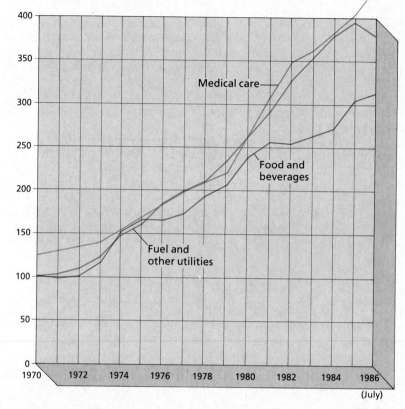

FIGURE 3-5

Producer price indexes by stage of processing: 1970 to 1986. Note that the cost of crude materials rose faster than the cost of finished goods. Note how oil price increases raised costs in 1974 and 1980 and lowered them in 1986.

Source: Statistical Abstract of the United States, Department of Commerce, Bureau of the Census, 1986, p. 466; data updated per Bureau September 1986.

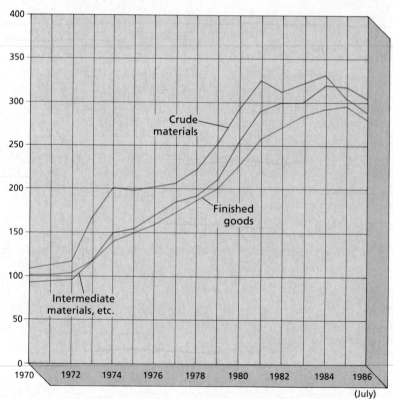

changes in the prices of about 400 goods and services that consumers buy. It measures the price of an average market basket of goods for an average family over time. Such an index gives a vivid picture of the effects of inflation on consumer prices. For example, goods and services costing $264.50 in 1980 cost only $116.30 in 1970 and a little less than $80 in 1952. (See Figure 3-4 for the annual rate of increase between 1970 and 1986.)

The **producer price index** measures changes in the prices businesses pay for goods and services over time. Both the consumer price index and the producer price index are calculated monthly and published in business periodicals. The consumer price index is the most closely followed, because many companies and government programs base their salary and payment increases on it. Many people also follow the producer price index closely, because it usually indicates future consumer prices and is therefore a barometer of future inflation (see Figure 3-5).

producer price index
Measures changes in the prices businesses pay for goods and services over time.

INFLATION AND THE RULE OF 72

No formula is more useful for understanding inflation than the rule of 72. Basically, the idea is to compute quickly how long it takes the cost of goods and services to double at various compounded rates of growth. For example, if houses were increasing in cost at 9% a year, how long would it take for the price of a home to double? The answer is easy to calculate. Simply divide the annual increase (9%) into 72* and you get the number of years it takes to double the price (8). If houses go up in price by 12%, it only takes 6 years to double in price ($72/12 = 6$), and so on. Of course, the same calculation can be used to predict how high food prices will be or the price of a car 10 years from now.

Let's go over an example of how you can use this formula. Let's say you wanted to buy a house for $100,000 but found interest rates were so high that you would end up paying almost $500,000 for the house after 30 years (assuming no money down). It sounds as if you would be paying way too much for the house, given the information so far. But if you calculate how much the house may be worth after 30 years, you may change your mind. If housing prices increase 10% per year, prices will double every 7 years or so ($72/10 = 7.2$). In 30 years, then, the price will double about four times ($30/7 = 4.5$). Your $100,000 house would then sell for about $1.6 million in 30 years. Since you would have paid less than $500,000, the home would be a good deal (assuming a 10% increase). What if the price only went up 6% a year? Then the price would be what after 30 years? It would double in 12 years, so it would double about 2.5 times in 30 years. In other words, it would be worth about $600,000, still more than you paid for it.

It works in reverse, too. Let's say, for example, that someone tells you to buy real estate in Florida. He says, "I bought land for $5,000 10 years ago and it's worth $10,000 today. It doubled already, isn't that great?"

Well, how did he do? If something doubles in 10 years, that means they made about 7.2% per year compounded ($72/10 = 7.2$). That is less than a tax-free government bond earns. In short, that is *not* a good return, especially since the real estate salesperson takes part of the sale price.

*Don't ask where the number 72 came from. It simply works out that 72 is the number that gives the desired results.

THINKING IT THROUGH

If one year in college costs $9,000 today, how much will it cost when a 4-year-old goes to school 14 years from now, if college costs go up 10% a year? The answer is that college costs will quadruple. So the cost will be $36,000 a year! Are you ready for that?

THE ISSUE OF RECESSION VERSUS INFLATION

recession
Two consecutive quarters of negative growth in real GNP (GNP adjusted for inflation).

A **recession** is defined as two consecutive quarters of negative growth in real GNP (GNP adjusted for inflation). When recession occurs, prices fall and businesses begin to fail. A recession has severe consequences for an economy: large unemployment, business failures, and an overall drop in living standards. For years (since 1930 when the Great Depression occurred), the government has put much of its effort into preventing another recession or **depression**. A depression is a severe recession. Whenever business slowed or unemployment increased, the government pumped money into the economy to revive it.

depression
A severe form of recession (see *recession*).

The United States government now becomes concerned when inflation is in the range of 5% to 10%. However, these figures must be put in some perspective. In 1984, inflation in Mexico was up to 70%; in Brazil it was 220%, in Israel 400%, and in Argentina 500%. Inflation rates like these can destroy an economy and business. Such rates also set the stage for major revolutions.

In Germany, inflation rates in 1923 were unbelievable. The price of coffee or bread often doubled in an *hour!* At the height of the problem, a loaf of bread cost 200 *billion* marks. People had to carry baskets filled with money to buy groceries. Is it any wonder that Germany today is *very* concerned about inflation?

Stagflation and Supply-Side Economics

A new economic phenomenon occurred in the late 1970s and early 1980s. Inflation kept rising even though the economy was slipping into recession. This was an unexpected economic event that called for a new term. The word used was **stagflation**, or high unemployment and slow growth combined with inflation. Thus two bad situations were occurring at once. To slow inflation, the government took money out of the economy. This slowed growth, plunging the economy into a deeper recession. Inflation finally came down, but there were still two bad situations: economic stagnation combined with high unemployment (above 10%).

stagflation
Stagnant economic conditions (no growth) combined with inflation.

Unemployment lines are long when there is stagflation.

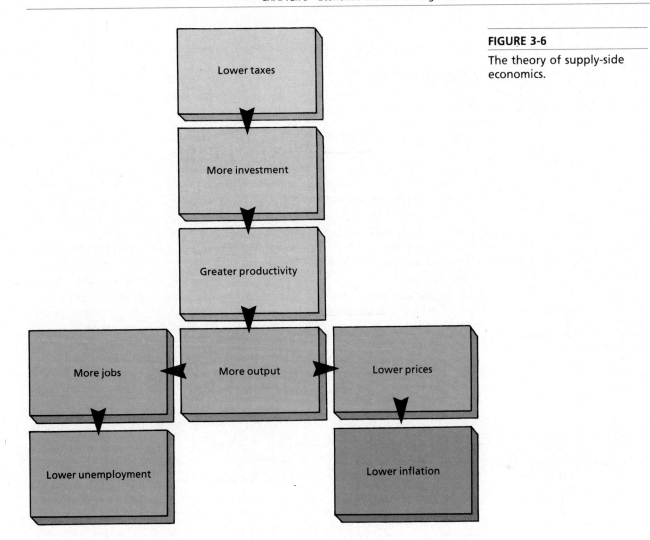

FIGURE 3-6
The theory of supply-side economics.

Later in the 1980s, economic attention turned toward lowering the unemployment rate and getting the economy moving again. The money supply was increased and taxes were cut. By 1986, unemployment had fallen to below 7% while the economy picked up. The term used to describe the policy of lowering taxes so that more money would be invested in production, leading to an increase in production activity, causing a drop in unemployment was **supply-side econom-ics**. In diagram form, supply-side economics looks like Figure 3-6. There remains much debate about the future of the United States economy as the government tries to keep employment high, inflation low, and business growing. Government stimulation of the economy in the mid-1980s could lead to inflation again in the late 1980s.

To fight inflation and recession, the government and the Federal Reserve Bank try to manage the economy. To understand the economic situation in the United States and the world today with regard to inflation, recession, unemployment, and other economic matters, you must understand the government's and the Federal Reserve Bank's roles. Two terms that are crucial to your understanding are: monetary policy and fiscal policy.

supply-side economics
The policy of lowering taxes so that more money is invested in production, leading to an increase in production activity, causing a drop in unemployment.

PROGRESS CHECK

- Can you explain cost-push versus demand-pull inflation?
- What is the difference between a recession and a depression?

THE ISSUE OF MONETARY POLICY

In learning about monetary policy, the first thing one must understand is the role of the Federal Reserve Bank (the Fed). The Fed is one of the sources of money; it can add or subtract money from the economy as it sees fit. For example, the Fed can simply produce more dollars or cut the amount it lends to banks, if it thinks one of those actions is warranted.

Managing the money supply is the responsibility of the Federal Reserve System. It operates independently of the President or Congress and has the goal of keeping the economy growing without causing inflation. It does that by trying to manage the money supply and interest rates. This process is called monetary policy.

A nation's **monetary policy** is the management of the money placed into the economy and the management of interest rates. Inflation is sometimes caused by having too much money in the economy. When that happens, the Fed cuts the money supply and increases interest rates. That makes less money available for spending and discourages businesses and consumers from borrowing money (because of high interest rates). When businesses find it hard to borrow money, they often cut back on production and lay off workers. This slows the economy and lowers inflation.

monetary policy
The management of the amount of money placed into the economy by the government and the management of interest rates.

Tight Versus Loose Monetary Policy

When unemployment gets too high, the Federal Reserve Bank may put more money into the economy and lower credit rates. This stimulates spending and encourages business growth, which leads to the hiring of more people.

When you read that the Fed is "loosening up on the money supply" or "lowering interest rates," it means that the Fed is trying to stimulate the economy (that is, increase consumer spending and increase business investment). A *tight monetary policy* is one in which the Fed is restricting the supply of money and increasing credit costs to lower inflation. (We shall discuss the Federal Reserve System in more detail when we explore money and banking.)

As you can imagine, such intervention into free markets has serious consequences for businesses. They watch the Fed very closely to see what the monetary policy is now and will be in the future.

The Federal Deficit

Sometimes the Fed is forced to put more money into the economy than it planned. This happens, for example, when government spending exceeds the revenue from taxes. The **federal deficit** (the difference between government revenue from taxes and government spending) is often corrected by increasing the supply of money, and that is inflationary. There is much concern about deficit spending throughout the 1980s, because government spending is exceeding revenue by as much as $200 billion a year. To understand this issue, we must turn to *fiscal* policy.

federal deficit
The difference between government revenue from taxes and government spending.

THE ISSUE OF FISCAL POLICY

The term **fiscal policy** refers to government efforts to keep the economy stable by increasing or decreasing taxes and/or government spending. For many years, the government has tended to raise taxes to fund more and more social and defense programs. The government tried to cut spending to balance the budget (that is, make income equal spending). But such attempts were rather unsuccessful in that they merely cut the *growth* in spending rather than spending itself. Most people have no idea where their tax dollars go. Figure 3-7 will give you some feel for who benefits from government programs.

fiscal policy
Government efforts to keep the economy stable by increasing or decreasing taxes or government spending.

Despite attempts to trim the federal government, millions upon millions still benefit directly from U.S. spending. Here are some who gain from the budget:

People collecting Social Security	36,896,000
People under Medicare	30,213,000
Children in school-lunch programs	24,600,000
Medicaid beneficiaries	22,900,000
People receiving food stamps	20,030,000
Members of families receiving Aid to Families With Dependent Children	10,354,000
Veterans or survivors collecting pensions or compensation	4,148,000
Households in subsidized housing	4,018,000
Needy, aged, blind and disabled	3,716,000
Government workers	2,800,000
Workers on unemployment compensation (weekly average)	2,800,000
Military personnel	2,200,000
Civil-service retirees	2,032,000
Military retirees	1,462,000
Railroad-retirement beneficiaries	951,000
Disabled coal miners	398,000

On top of that: Millions are helped by farm price supports, college-student loans, small-business loans and veterans' medical care, among other programs.

NOTE: Figures cannot add to a total because many people receive government help under more than one program.

FIGURE 3-7

Something for nearly everyone.

Source: "What Reagan's Budget Will Mean for You," *U.S. News & World Report,* February 13, 1984, p. 24.

Taxes and Spending

A major issue in the 1984 political campaign concerned fiscal policy, especially taxes. Some candidates favored increasing income taxes to pay for government programs. Others resisted increased taxes and called for less spending instead. Still others proposed a whole new tax system, a flat tax, that would greatly lower tax rates but increase government revenue by eliminating tax loopholes (strategies for avoiding taxes).

Some people felt that taxes should be raised just for the rich. They felt that rich people were not paying their fair share. The box below discusses that issue. The point is that people are divided in the United States over economic issues such as taxation and fiscal policy in general. Such issues will dominate government/business/economic thinking in the future. Business periodicals and current newspapers, TV, and radio news shows will keep you abreast of the debate.

The problem is that government spending has exceeded government income for so long that the **national debt** (the sum of government money borrowed and not paid back) is $2 trillion. That is about $8,500 for every man, woman, and child in the United States! To borrow money to pay the debt, the government goes to the same sources (banks) as businesspeople do. Government bonds may be more attractive to these sources, and this can drive businesspeople out of the credit market. Such a situation can hurt business and be inflationary. Most people feel that something must be done about the national debt before it becomes unmanageable. Let's see what the problem is.

national debt
The sum of money the government has borrowed and not paid back.

ECONOMIC MYTH: RICH PEOPLE DON'T PAY TAXES

The fairness issue in the U.S. tax structure has always been a major debate among politicians. The problem is that many people think that rich people do not pay any taxes; they use tax shelters to avoid them. Roger A. Freeman of the American Enterprise Institute tried to end such myths by publishing a pamphlet called "Tax Loopholes: The Legend and the Reality." In the year of his study, there *were* 112 people with incomes over $200,000 who did not pay any taxes! "Ah ha," the critics say. But that is not the end of the story. Those 112 represented only .07% of Americans reporting incomes over $200,000, and they had good reasons for not paying. Some paid taxes in other countries and others had huge donations to charity or severe business losses.

The key point was that 99.3% of taxpayers reporting incomes of more than $200,000 (15,323 people) *did* pay federal taxes. They paid an average of $177,161, equal to 44% of adjusted gross income and 60% of taxable income. There were 621 people who made over $1 million that year. They paid an average of $989,862 in taxes, equal to 46% of their adjusted gross and 65%

of their taxable income. In short, rich people have paid a considerable share of taxes. Since then, the tax rate has been cut to a maximum of 50% of taxable income. When that happened, rich people actually paid a *larger* share of the tax burden. The tax cut was made in 1981. This is how *Forbes* reported the results of that cut:

> In 1982 the top 5% of taxpayers—those earning more than $49,633—paid an average federal bite of $21,354, just $4 less than the year before. Their share of the load, however, went from 35% in 1981 to 36% in 1982, according to the foundation (Tax Foundation, Inc.) . . . Despite the economy (there was a recession that year), the foundation found almost 50% more millionaires; 5,512 reported income of a million or more in 1981, 8,203 in 1982. The millionnaires' average tax payment: $844,339.

In short, "rich" people pay a good share of the total tax burden. Today, if *all* earnings and income in excess of $50,000 were completely confiscated by the government, it would be enough to run the federal government for 1 week!

Source: "The Rich Man's Burden," *Forbes,* July 16, 1984, p. 8. Reprinted by permission of *Forbes* magazine, © *Forbes* Inc., 1984.

PROGRESS CHECK

■ How does the government manage the economy using monetary policy?

■ How does the government manage the economy using fiscal policy?

THE ISSUE OF THE NATIONAL DEBT

The national debt reached the $2 trillion level in 1986. The questions are: What is the national debt? How did it get so high? What can be done about it?

First, let's look at how the national debt got so high. Figure 3-8 gives some details about the sources of government funds and the way that money is spent. As you can see, income for 1986 was expected to be $793.7 billion, and expenditures were expected to be $973.7 billion, leaving a $180 billion deficit. When you look at Figure 3-8, you will see that such deficits have occurred for several years. Notice too where the increased spending is going: defense and health and human services are the biggest expenditures. The government is growing faster than the economy's ability to support its programs. Most government programs have automatic increases built into them, so government spending goes up automatically every year.

One question that economists, government officials, and, ultimately, you and other taxpayers must answer is, "What are our national priorities?" Do we want a strong military capability, including nuclear weapons, and how much are we willing to pay for such capability?

Another huge chunk of the budget goes for Social Security payments. Social Security was not meant to be a retirement program, but a *supplement* to savings. Many people ignored that fact and rely on Social Security for survival. Can the government cut their benefits now? Could people retire later? Figure 3-7 shows that nearly 37 million people are receiving Social Security now, and the number will rise dramatically when the baby boom adults retire. Can the nation afford to support so many people for so long?

Millions of people also receive Medicare treatment, school lunches, Medicaid, food stamps, housing subsidies, and other government-paid (taxpayer-paid) assis-

If you had a stack of $1,000 bills in your hand only four inches high, you'd be a millionaire. A trillion dollars would be a stack of $1,000 bills 67 miles high.

President Ronald Reagan

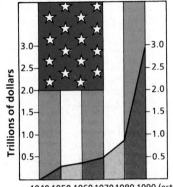

1940 1950 1960 1970 1980 1990 (est.)

By spending more than it takes in, the government has gone deeply into debt. The dollar amount is huge—approaching $3 trillion. What to do about it is *the* question for the near future

---

HIGH DOLLAR, LOW INFLATION—AND VICE VERSA?

The inflation rate is staying low. The exchange rate of the dollar is staying high. There is a connection between those two circumstances.

A high dollar makes American imports cheap. It also holds down, very effectively, the prices of American products that have to compete with imports. Because oil is priced in American dollars worldwide, a high dollar makes it very expensive in other countries and contributes to the current slackness in the oil markets.

When the government published the consumer price index for July this week, it showed that inflation has been very well behaved over the past year. Consumer prices had risen, on the average, only 4.1 percent. But within that broad average of prices, there were some instructive variations. The lowest inflation rates were among the things that are traded internationally, and

under pressure from the dollar. Food prices, for example, rose less over the past year than the CPI did. Clothing prices rose much less. Prices of fuel oil and gasoline actually fell.

In 1984 the American dollar became substantially overvalued in terms of its actual purchasing power. It was being held up by the financial pressures generated by foreign capital coming into this country to take advantage of the high American interest rates.

In 1986 the value of the dollar began to fall. This made prices for American goods lower and prices for foreign goods higher. This should improve the balance of trade—but could lead to the return of inflation. Both the value of the dollar and inflation will be economic issues for the next several years.

Source: Editorial modified from *The Washington Post*, August 24, 1984. © *The Washington Post, 1984.*

FIGURE 3-8

Government receipts and expenditures. Note that deficits are expected
to continue for the next several years

SOURCE	1984 ACTUAL	ESTIMATES					
		1985	1986	1987	1988	1989	1990
Receipts (in billions of dollars)							
Individual income taxes	296.2	329.7	358.9	392.5	433.6	475.5	512.6
Corporation income taxes	56.9	66.4	74.1	87.5	99.0	106.7	112.5
Social insurance taxes and contributions	241.7	268.4	289.4	309.5	346.5	376.5	409.1
Excise taxes	37.4	37.0	35.0	35.0	33.6	33.1	33.5
Estate and gift taxes	6.0	5.6	5.3	5.0	4.7	4.7	5.1
Custom duties	11.4	11.8	12.3	12.8	13.4	14.0	14.7
Miscellaneous receipts	17.0	18.0	18.6	19.5	19.6	19.5	20.1
TOTAL	666.5	736.9	793.7	861.7	950.4	1,029.9	1,107.7
Expenditures (by agency; in billions of dollars)							
Legislative branch	1.6	1.8	1.8	1.7	1.7	1.7	1.8
The Judiciary	.9	1.0	1.1	1.2	1.2	1.3	1.3
Executive Office of the President	.1	.1	.1	.1	.1	.1	.1
Funds appropriated to the President	8.5	11.1	12.1	12.4	12.0	11.6	10.8
Agriculture	37.5	45.1	38.5	37.0	36.3	32.8	32.8
Commerce	1.9	2.1	2.0	1.9	1.9	1.9	2.4
Defense—Military	220.8	246.3	277.5	312.3	348.6	382.3	418.3
Defense—Civil	19.5	19.0	20.3	21.1	22.5	23.7	24.9
Education	15.5	17.4	16.9	16.0	15.7	15.8	16.1
Energy	10.6	11.0	9.3	10.2	11.0	11.5	12.0
Health and Human Services	292.3	318.5	330.3	350.2	374.6	398.6	423.7
Housing and Urban Development	16.5	28.9	15.4	14.3	13.8	13.6	14.1
Interior	4.9	5.0	4.4	4.2	4.2	4.2	4.2
Justice	3.2	3.9	4.0	4.0	3.9	4.0	4.0
Labor	24.5	23.5	22.8	22.6	22.8	23.1	23.4
State	2.4	2.7	3.3	3.3	3.4	3.3	3.4
Transportation	23.9	26.2	25.1	23.9	23.4	23.6	23.6
Treasury	148.3	176.7	181.0	190.6	200.5	193.6	187.8
Environmental Protection Agency	4.1	4.4	4.6	4.6	4.6	4.4	4.0
General Services Administration	.2	.4	.1	.2	.2	.2	.3
National Aeronautics and Space Administration	7.0	7.3	7.8	7.8	7.9	8.6	9.3
Office of Personnel Management	22.6	23.6	24.8	26.0	27.3	28.5	29.8
Small Business Administration	.3	.7	.1	—	—	—	—
Veterans Administration	25.6	26.8	26.7	26.8	27.4	27.7	28.1
Other agencies	11.3	12.3	10.8	8.0	6.3	5.0	4.0
Allowances	—	1.1	.4	.7	1.8	2.9	4.0
Undistributed offsetting receipts	−52.3	−57.9	−67.6	−74.5	−78.3	−86.5	−94.0
TOTAL BUDGET OUTLAYS	851.8	959.1	973.7	1,026.6	1,094.8	1,137.4	1,190.0
BUDGET SURPLUS OR DEFICIT (−)	−185.3	−222.2	−180.0	−164.9	−144.4	−107.5	−82.4

Source: Budget of the United States Government, Fiscal Year 1986, pp. 9-12.

A

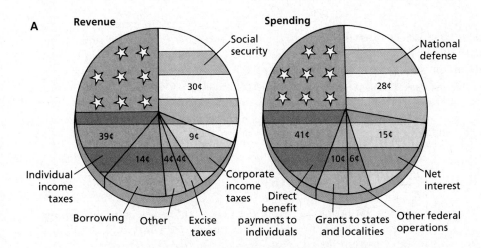

Revenue

Spending

Social security
30¢

National defense
28¢

39¢

9¢

41¢

15¢

14¢ 4¢ 4¢

10¢ 6¢

Individual income taxes

Corporate income taxes

Net interest

Borrowing   Other   Excise taxes

Direct benefit payments to individuals

Grants to states and localities

Other federal operations

FIGURE 3-9

Some congresspeople have been calling for a balanced budget amendment to the Constitution so that annual expenditures could not exceed revenues. Look at the charts on the left, and you will see why there is interest in such a bill. **A,** Government revenue and spending. **B,** The federal deficit. **C,** How the deficit is growing.

B

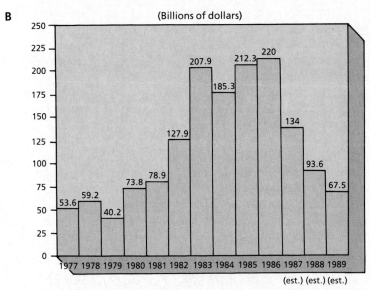

(Billions of dollars)

1977: 53.6 1978: 59.2 1979: 40.2 1980: 73.8 1981: 78.9 1982: 127.9 1983: 207.9 1984: 185.3 1985: 212.3 1986: 220 1987: 134 1988: 93.6 1989: 67.5

1987 (est.) 1988 (est.) 1989 (est.)

C

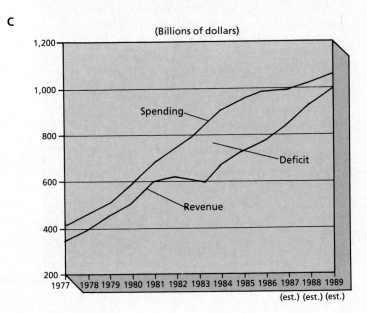

(Billions of dollars)

Spending

Deficit

Revenue

1977 1978 1979 1980 1981 1982 1983 1984 1985 1986 1987 1988 1989

(est.) (est.) (est.)

tance. What is the national priority regarding such payments? Should the government continue such payments and expand the programs when hard times come, or should such payments be limited somehow? Are such payments more or less important than defense or social security? What should the policy be if such payments threaten the economy by siphoning too much money from business? These are the issues you should be following in the various media. They have a direct effect on you (in taxes) and on business. Figure 3-9 shows that budget deficits are increasing every year.

THE ISSUE OF TRADE DEFICITS

Historically, the United States has sold more goods and services to other nations than it has bought. Recently, however, that situation reversed, and the United States began buying more goods than it sold. The term used to describe the situation where imports (purchases from abroad) exceed exports (sales abroad) is **trade deficit**. The trade deficit in 1985 was $148.5 billion.

trade deficit
The situation where imports (purchases from abroad) exceed exports (sales abroad).

One reason that deficits were so high was that the U.S. dollar increased in value relative to foreign money. This made foreign goods cheaper and U.S. goods more expensive in world trade.

There were other reasons for the deficit as well. Foreign products such as Japanese cars were perceived to be of better quality. Furthermore, American labor costs were much higher than those of other countries such as South Korea, Mexico, and Brazil. See the box on p. 85 for further discussion of the trade deficit. It discusses many of the issues mentioned in this chapter. Note the warning about the return of inflation. In the future, you should be able to read and understand such articles and recommend policies to improve world conditions.

The United States government worked with other nations to lower the value of the dollar relative to other currencies and improve the trade balance. The trade deficit may improve as a result. The health of the United States economy affects

Foreign imports such as these TV sets can lead to trade deficits.

the success of economies throughout the world. I hope you now see the relationship between the success of businesses worldwide and economics. If you study economics, you will learn more about how the system functions. The concepts and terms in Chapters 2 and 3 should give you a good foundation for reading more about economics in business journals.

PROGRESS CHECK

■ What percent of the national budget goes for defense? (See Figure 3-9).

■ How did the national debt get so high? (Study Figure 3-8 carefully.)

CAREER INFORMATION—ECONOMIST

NATURE OF THE WORK

The business economist's primary function is to apply economics to business problems. They are employed by manufacturing firms, utilities, banks, transportation companies, insurance firms, retailing companies, and more. Many economists work for various government agencies.

An *industrial economist* does sales forecasts and projects how events occuring outside of the organization will affect the organization. A *bank economist* does short- and long-term forecasts of the markets for money and credit. A *government economist* does forecasting, but also does research on public policy issues. The general function of an economist is to analyze and interpret government policies and their effect on the economy and business firms.

JOB OUTLOOK

Economics will be one of the faster-growing careers in the next decade. The Bureau of Labor Statistics ranked it 18th of the 20 jobs to grow the fastest. Business and industry, research organizations, and consulting firms will provide the most opportunities for economists. Employment in government agencies is expected to grow in response to the heavy responsibilities of government officials in areas such as housing, transportation, environmental planning, health, and so on.

EARNINGS

The median salary for economists was about $38,000 in 1980. Naturally it has gone up since then, but this gives you a ballpark figure. The highest-paid economists work in consulting firms and in securities firms (i.e., those that sell stocks and bonds). Trade associations are the next highest paying organizations followed by manufacturing, and retail trade.

SOURCE OF ADDITIONAL INFORMATION

National Association of Business Economists, Washington, D.C.

Source: *Occupational Outlook Handbook*, 1986-1987 (U.S. Department of Labor).

SUMMARY

1 Almost every discussion about a nation's economy is based on a concept called gross national product (GNP). If GNP is rising, the economy is said to be strong. If GNP is stable or falling, the economy is said to be weak.
  ■ What is GNP?
    GNP is the total value of a country's output of goods and services produced over a given period of time. It can be used to measure economic growth or decline.
  ■ What percentage of GNP goes to the government?
    In the mid-1980s, the government took 34% of GNP or 40% of net national product (NNP).

2 To increase GNP, a country needs to be more productive. An increase in productivity means that the same amount of labor is able to produce more goods and services.

■ Why is productivity slowing in the United States?

At the beginning of this century, 1 out of 3 workers were farmers. Today, less than 1 out of 20 workers are farmers, yet we produce much more food. The reason is that farm productivity increased because of *capital* inputs (for example, tractors, plows, and fertilizer). When farm productivity leveled off, the industrial revolution began, and capital (machinery) made industrial laborers more productive. Industrial productivity is now leveling off as we enter a third revolution, the service revolution. Thus productivity is slowing.

■ What will increase productivity in the future?

The service sector is now introducing more capital goods (for example, robots and computers) to make white collar (service) workers more productive.

3 When an economic system introduces new technology, temporary unemployment often occurs. Farm employment, for example, fell dramatically over the last 50 years and continues to fall.

■ What are the types of unemployment?

Frictional unemployment refers to those people just entering the labor force or who are between jobs. *Structural unemployment* refers to those who are laid off because their type of work is no longer needed in such quantity (farmers over the last 50 years are one example. Today it is steel workers). *Cyclical unemployment* is caused by ups and downs in the economy. *Seasonal unemployment* occurs where the demand for labor varies over the year.

■ How does the United States protect the unemployed?

Unemployed people get *unemployment benefits* from the government for a limited period until they can find new jobs.

4 A general rise in the price of goods and services over time is called *inflation*.

■ What are the major causes of inflation?

Cost-push inflation means that products cost more as the cost of producing them goes up. *Demand-pull inflation* is caused when the demand for goods exceeds the supply.

■ How is inflation measured?

The government measures the increase in the cost of consumer items with the consumer price index (CPI) and the cost of wholesale items with the producer price index (PPI).

■ How can I measure the effects of inflation over time?

Using the rule of 72, you can easily determine how long it takes the cost of an item to double. Just take the yearly rate of increase and divide it into 72. Thus, if prices go up 9% a year, things will double in 8 years.

5 When real GNP declines for two quarters, an economy is said to be in a *recession*. A deep recession is known as a depression.

■ What happens in a recession or depression?

There is likely to be an increase in unemployment, prices fall, and businesses fail.

■ What is the opposite of a depression?

The opposite of depression is inflation. During inflation, prices rise, some businesses prosper (others may fail), and employment picks up.

6 In its attempt to keep the economy from going into a depression or from too rapid inflation, the government has two weapons: monetary policy and fiscal policy.

■ What is monetary policy?

Monetary policy refers to the manipulation of the amount of money placed into the economy and the management of interest rates.

■ How does monetary policy work?

When money is "tight" and interest rates are high, the economy slows, and there is less investment in capital equipment. When money is poured into the economy and interest rates fall, the economy picks up, capital spending increases, and employment rises. One danger of too much money being placed into the economy is inflation.

■ What is fiscal policy?

Fiscal policy refers to government efforts to manage the economy through taxes and government spending.

■ What are the issues today about monetary and fiscal policy?

Some people feel the government is spending too much money (fiscal policy). They want to cut back on government programs. Others feel that taxes are too low. They want to keep or increase government programs (fiscal policy). To increase government revenues, some people propose putting more money into the economy and lowering interest rates. That is supposed to increase production and thereby increase government income (supply-side economics). But that could cause inflation. Meanwhile, the national debt is going up because the government is spending more than it is receiving in taxes.

7 Recently, the United States has had *trade deficits;* that is, it buys more from other countries than it sells to them.

■ How can the United States create a better balance of trade?

The United States should sell more overseas when our products are cheaper (a result of higher productivity or lower labor costs), when the quality of our products increases, and when the value of the dollar declines.

KEY TERMS

consumer price index (CPI)   p. 77
cost-push inflation   p. 77
cyclical unemployment   p. 75
demand-pull inflation   p. 77
depression   p. 80
federal deficit   p. 82
fiscal policy   p. 83
frictional unemployment   p. 74
gross national product (GNP)
   p. 71
inflation   p. 77
monetary policy   p. 82
national debt   p. 84
net national product (NNP)
   p. 72
prime rate   p. 70
productivity   p. 72
producer price index (PPI)   p. 79
recession   p. 80
seasonal unemployment   p. 75
stagflation   p. 80
structural unemployment   p. 75
supply-side economics   p. 81
trade deficit   p. 88

GETTING INVOLVED

1 Is the economy now experiencing inflation, recession, economic growth with little inflation, or stagflation (inflation with no economic growth)? What government policies have led to that situation? What should the policy now be? Read current business literature to get their views and discuss the alternatives. What economic priorities should be considered?

2 How large is the national debt today? Is it rising or falling and at what rate? What is being done to reduce the debt? Discuss.

3 What is the situation today regarding the trade balance with other nations? Is the United States importing more than it sells or vice versa? What is being done in this area? Is free trade being promoted or restricted? Discuss.

4 Have some fun using the rule of 72 to anticipate future prices. For example, calculate how much a new car will cost a child now 5 years old when he or she reaches age 17 if the car prices go up by 6% a year. Assume the cost of a new car is now $15,000. How much will a textbook cost if prices go up by 12% a year, and the book now costs $30? These exercises will teach you about the problems of inflation!

5 Everyone is for peace, but nobody seems to know how to create it. Discuss the proposition that some percent of the world's military expenditures should go to help develop poor countries. Would that be a step toward peace? How would you promote such a step? Discuss both sides of the issue, including a defense for high military spending in the United States, to understand both sides of the issue.

6 Discuss other current economic issues with your classmates and instructor. Pick two issues of general concern and discuss various viewpoints. Be ready to defend your position by finding facts and figures to support it. Have you set up a file system yet to keep such figures?

PRACTICING MANAGEMENT DECISIONS

CASE ONE   DIVIDING THE ECONOMIC PIE

Any economic system should benefit *all* of the people if it is to be a model for the world. The term distribution of income refers to the way in which income is divided among the members of society. One of the major concerns about the U.S. economy is the uneven distribution of income. For example, the top 20% of the population may receive over 40% of the total whereas the lowest 20% may get 5% or less. These figures tend to be misleading, however, in that the top 20% are usually older, more experienced men and women with college degrees. The lower 20% is made up partially of young people just getting started and new immigrants.

The bottom 20% may be tomorrow's top 20%, given the freedom and opportunity of the U.S. economy. In other words, there is always a group of people in the lowest 20% bracket, but they are not all the same people over time. To enter the upper 20%, people may have to get more education, work several years, and choose the right career path.

Some nations point to the poverty figures in the United States to prove that free markets and capitalism do not work. To counter such charges, you should know some facts about poverty.

In 1984, official government statistics showed that 33.7 million Americans (14.4% of the population) lived in poverty. Poverty was defined as having an income of $10,609 for a family of four. Of course, the term *poverty* is a relative one. In most countries, $10,609 for a family of four would be considered affluence.

The poverty figure tends to be overstated because it does not measure income received in the form of noncash payments from the government, including food stamps, Medicaid, and the value of subsidized housing. Such programs were designed to help poor people and have done so, but the effort is not reflected in the poverty statistics. Including such income would lower the percentage of people reportedly living temporarily in poverty.

Another group of people included in the poverty statistics have unreported income that would take them off the list. Many men and women work as maids, window cleaners, car repairers, and other jobs, but some do not report the income and thus are considered poorer than they are.

There are obviously some families in the United States who fit the description of people living in poverty. Many of those families are headed by unmarried women in their teens. Others are headed by unemployed men with handicaps or such low skills as to be virtually unemployable. These are the families that most need public assistance. They number far fewer than 34 million, however.

It is instructive to note that only 2% of American families remain on welfare for more than 7 years. Research has shown that if income distribution is divided into fifths, 25% of those in the lowest fifth move into the top third by the end of a decade. These figures show that poverty is usually only temporary and that upward mobility is quite high in the United States.

DECISION QUESTIONS

1 Do you know someone who started in the lower range of the economy and who, over time, rose to the higher ranks? What does that tell you about the system?

2 Is any level of poverty acceptable in affluent America? Allocating more money to poor people has done little to relieve poverty. Why?

3 Is it healthy or not to have a wide separation in income between new wage earners and those who have worked for years? If you wanted to even the distribution more, how would you do it? What would be the advantages and disadvantages?

4 What can be done to aid the 2% of the population who are semi-permanently in poverty?

Source: "Many Americans Experience a Taste of Poverty," *Business Week,* August 20, 1984, p. 18.

CASE TWO   PIECEWORK AT LINCOLN ELECTRIC

One manufacturing facility that has had little problem with productivity for over 50 years is the Lincoln Electric Company of Cleveland. The secret behind Lincoln's success is that it pays its employees well for a job well done, but it expects much in return. How much does it pay? The *average* worker at Lincoln Electric makes about $45,000 a year. What do employees have to do to earn that money? Oh, there's the trick.

Lincoln's employees are paid by the piecework system. That is, workers earn so much per piece. The more they produce, the more they make. The incentive to work hard is more money.

Is the company easy on its workers? Not at all. The company has employees punch a time clock every day, and often expects overtime work. There are no unions at Lincoln Electric. The workers feel they are well paid and do not have any need for unions.

In addition to the piecework system, Lincoln also has a profit-sharing plan. Each job is evaluated as to its importance to the company, and a rate is established for it. Workers are then graded on the quantity and quality of their work as well as on their attitudes. These ratings determine the bonuses they receive. The company president reports that productivity has increased 15% per year compared with an industry average of about 3%. Employee turnover is only 6% compared with the 36% of other manufacturers. Because of its high productivity, Lincoln can pay its employees more. Lincoln spends only 25% of its revenues on wages versus about 37% for competitors.

DECISION QUESTIONS

1 You are starting a business that sells sandwiches in vending machines and from vendors who go to various locations in the city selling sandwiches and related food from trucks. You are setting up a production system for making sandwiches. Would you pay your workers on a piecework basis? What would be the benefits and possible problems? What evidence from the Lincoln Electric example could you use to support such a decision?

2 The American free enterprise system is based on freedom and incentives. Compare the incentives of a piecework system with jobs you have had or have observed where people were paid by the hour. What does that tell you about increasing worker productivity in America?

3 Would you share profits with employees on the basis of quantity and quality of work *plus attitudes* as Lincoln Electric does? How would that benefit both the firm and the workers? How would you measure attitudes?

LOOKING AHEAD

Now that you are familiar with some economic terms and can read the business literature, we can focus our attention on business itself. We shall start by looking at different ways of starting a business. You can start a business by yourself. You can take on one or more partners. Or, you can form a corporation or a multinational firm. Each of these forms of business has its advantages and disadvantages that we shall discuss in Chapter 4.

Today, much of the excitement in the business world involves two areas: entrepreneurship and franchising. These two subjects are so interesting that they deserve a chapter of their own—Chapter 5.

BUSINESS FORMATION

PART

II

CHAPTER 4
**FORMS OF BUSINESS
ORGANIZATION**

CHAPTER 5
**MANAGING A
SMALL BUSINESS**

CHAPTER 6
**ENTREPRENEURSHIP
AND FRANCHISING**

FORMS OF BUSINESS ORGANIZATION

LEARNING GOALS

After you have read and studied this chapter, you should be able to:

- Identify and explain the three basic forms of business ownership.
- Describe the advantages and disadvantages of sole proprietorship.
- Outline the advantages and disadvantages of partnerships.
- Explain the differences between limited and general partnerships.
- Compare the advantages and disadvantages of corporations.
- Explain the process of incorporation.
- Differentiate among corporate types.
- Discuss cooperatives and joint ventures.

PROFILE DAVID MINTZ, INVENTOR OF TOFUTTI DESSERT

David Mintz found that success does not come easily to an entrepreneur. He owned a kosher restaurant and catering service that followed the Jewish dietary laws. One of those laws prohibits the eating of dairy products at the same meal with meat. That eliminated ice cream and yogurt as desserts. Mr. Mintz knew that an alternative dessert would bring more business and more profit. He began experimenting in his laboratory/kitchen. After years of throwing away thousands of new dessert efforts and losing thousands of dollars in the process, David came up with a promising new dessert.

One ingredient was tofu (soybean curd), hardly the stuff dreams are made of. Yet the stuff tasted remarkably good—much like ice cream. He called his frozen dessert "Toffuti." The no-cholesterol, no-butterfat product made a big hit with his customers and with health-conscious people all over the country.

In August of 1981, David Mintz formed his own company—Tofu Time Inc. You could buy shares of the company on the over-the-counter market. The trading symbol was TOFU. Mr. Mintz owned 61% of the shares, which were worth over $10 million.

Mr. Mintz's story is just one of many success stories in the United States. The company took years to build, but Mr. Mintz stuck with it. He found that the best way to benefit from his work was to incorporate and sell part ownership of the company to others. ■

Source: Mark Estren, "Small Businesses: Beating the Odds," *Dial*, August, 1984, p. 8.

David Mintz.

GETTING STARTED IN BUSINESS

Have you ever thought about starting your own business? Do you think it would be too hard or too risky? Are you the type who would prefer sailing on a big and placid lake, like the people mentioned in the margin? Are you the "go-for-it" white-water type? Or aren't you sure?

One way to find out is to start your own business while you're in school. Brett Kingstone's *The Student Entrepreneur Guide*[1] may help. Brett lists about 50 different businesses you could start. One student buys large cookies for 25¢ and sells them for 35¢. Selling 600 cookies a night, the Cookie Craze owner makes $60 a night for just a few hours work. Kevin Wilson set up a snack bar (natural foods and juices) in the student library. Eric Rahn gathers up dry cleaning and contracts the work out to a local cleaner. Two women at Wellesley contact parents and sell them on the idea of sending cakes to their children for birthdays and other events. There are lots of businesses you could start.

But how do you *start* a business? How much paperwork is involved? Is it better to own a business by yourself or take on partners? What are the advantages and disadvantages of different forms of business? That is what this chapter is about. There is no better way to learn about business than to start one—and now is as good a time as any. Even if you have no intentions of starting a business, it is interesting to see what is involved.

WHAT IS A BUSINESS?

nonprofit organization
Provides goods and services to the economic system, but does not have profit as an objective.

A *business* is any organization that seeks profit by providing goods and services to the economic system. A **nonprofit organization** also provides goods and services to the economic system, but does not have profit as an objective. The United Way, the Catholic church, and the U.S. Army are examples of nonprofit organizations. Business takes different forms, which we shall explore next.

FORMS OF BUSINESS OWNERSHIP

sole proprietorship
The ownership of an organization by one person.

partnership (general)
A legal form of business with two or more owners.

corporation
A state-chartered legal entity with authority to act and have liability separate from its owners.

People can form a business in several ways. They can begin a typing service out of their home, open a car-repair center, start a new restaurant, or go about meeting other wants and needs of the community on their own. An organization that is owned, and usually managed, by one person is called a **sole proprietorship.** That is the most common form of business ownership (over 12 million firms).

Many people do not have the money, time, or desire to run a business on their own. They prefer to have someone else or some group of people get together to form the business. When two or more people become co-owners of a business, the organization is called a **partnership** (about 1.4 million firms).

Mr. Mintz of Tofu Time Inc. learned that there are advantages to creating a business that is separate and distinct from the owners. A legal entity that has an existence separate from the people who own it is called a **corporation**. There are only 2.8 million corporations in the United States (17% of all businesses), but they do 87% of the business (see Figure 4-1).

There are many advantages to going into business by yourself. The fact that most people choose this form of organization indicates that the perceived advantages outweigh the disadvantages.

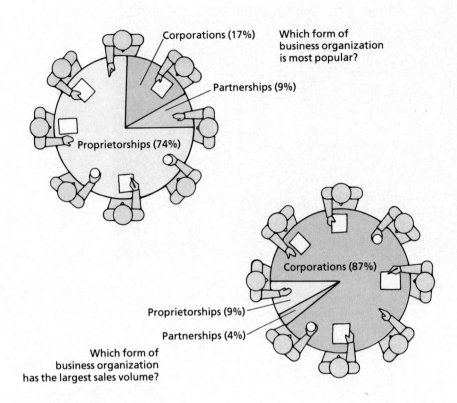

Which form of
business organization
is most popular?

Which form of
business organization
has the largest sales volume?

FIGURE 4-1

Although corporations make up only 17% of the total *number* of businesses, they make 87% of the sales volume. Sole proprietorships are the most common form of ownership (74%), but they make only 9% of sales volume.

Source: Based on 1985 Department of Commerce data.

SOLE PROPRIETORSHIPS

Advantages of Sole Proprietorships

There must be some major advantages to being a sole proprietor. After all, over 12 million people in the United States have formed this kind of business. These are also the easiest kind of businesses for you to explore in your quest for an interesting career. Every town has some sole proprietorships that you can visit. There's the local produce stand, the beauty shop, the auto repair garage, and the liquor store. If you look closely, you'll find sole proprietors who do income taxes, repair appliances and television sets, and provide all kinds of local services. Talk with them about the joys and frustrations of being on their own. Most people will mention the benefits of being their own boss and setting their own hours. Other advantages are likely to emerge, including:

1 *Ease of starting and ending the business.* All you have to do to start a sole proprietorship is buy the needed equipment (for example, a saw, a word processor, a tractor, a lawn mower, or a welder) and put up some announcements saying you are in business. It is just as easy to get out of business; you simply stop. There is no one to consult or to disagree with about such decisions. You may have to get a permit or license from the government, but that is usually no problem.

2 *Being your own boss.* "Working for others simply does not have the same excitement as working for yourself." That's the way sole proprietors feel. You may make mistakes, but they are *your* mistakes—and so are the many small victories each day.

A sole proprietorship.

3 *Pride of ownership.* People who own and manage their own businesses are rightfully proud of their work. They deserve all the credit for taking the risks and providing needed goods or services.

4 *Retention of profit.* Other than the joy of being your own boss, there is nothing like the pleasure of knowing that you can make as much as you can and do not have to share that money with anyone else (except the government, in taxes). Store owners and service people are often willing to start working early in the day and stay late because the money they earn is theirs to keep.

5 *No special taxes.* All the profits of a sole proprietorship are taxed as the personal income of the owner, and he or she pays the normal income tax on that money. Owners *do* have to file an estimated tax return and make quarterly payments. It is wise for small business owners to pick up a packet of information for small business owners from the local Internal Revenue Service office so that no hassles do develop.

It is for these reasons and others that there are more sole proprietorships than any other kind of business in the United States. Hundreds of thousands of new businesses are formed every year. However, thousands more fail. Many people dream of owning their own business, but there are also disadvantages to sole proprietorships.

Disadvantages of Sole Proprietorships

Not everyone is cut out to own and manage a business. Often it is difficult to save enough money to start a business *and* keep it going. Often the cost of inventory, supplies, insurance, advertising, rent, utilities, and other expenses are simply too much to cover alone. There are other disadvantages of owning your own business, including:

To open a shop is easy; the difficult thing is to keep it open.

Chinese proverb

1 *The risk of losses.* When you work for others, it is their problem if the business is not profitable. When you own your own business, you have the risk of losing almost everything—your time, your money, and your business. What you keep, if you fail, is the pride of having tried, and the experience.

2 Unlimited liability. When you own your own business, you and the business are considered one. That is, any debts or damages incurred by the business are *your* debts and *you* must pay them, even if it means selling your home, your car, and so forth. This is a serious risk and one that requires careful thought and discussion with a lawyer, insurance agent, and others. For example, someone may be injured and sue the business (you). As the owner, you are liable for everything!

3 *Difficulty in management.* Most businesses need some management; that is, someone must keep inventory records, accounting records, tax records, and so on. Many people who are skilled at selling things or providing a service are not so skilled in keeping records. Sole proprietors may have no one to help them. It is often difficult to find good, qualified people to help run the business. Some employees can be careless, tardy, dishonest, unreliable, and incompetent. It is hard to own a business, manage it, train people, and have time for anything else in life.

4 *Overwhelming time commitment.* Perhaps *the* most common complaint among sole proprietors is the fact that good employees are hard to find. Therefore, the owner must spend long hours working. The owner of a store, for example, may put in 12 hours a day, at least 6 days a week. That is almost twice the hours worked by a salaried laborer, who may make more money.

5 *Few fringe benefits.* If you are your own boss, you lose many of the fringe benefits that come from working for others. For example, you have no health insurance, no disability insurance, no sick leave, no vacation pay, and so on. These benefits may add up to 30% or more of a worker's income.

6 *Limited growth.* If the owner becomes incapacitated, the business often comes to a standstill. Furthermore, a sole proprietorship relies on its owner for most of its funding. Therefore expansion often is slow and there are serious limits to how much one person can do. That is one reason why many individuals seek partners to assist in a business.

7 *You are on your own.* The greatest advantage of a sole proprietorship can also be a major disadvantage. You have nobody to help or to blame if something goes wrong. You are it!

8 *Limited life span.* If the sole proprietor dies, the business no longer exists. Talk with a few entrepreneurs about the problems they have faced in being on their own. They are likely to have many interesting stories to tell, such as problems getting loans from the bank, problems with theft, and problems simply keeping up with the business. These problems are the reason that many sole proprietors discourage their children from following in their footsteps, although many would have it no other way. To learn more, talk with local businesspeople. They know more about the situation in your area than anyone else does.

unlimited liability
Means that the owner's personal assets (for example, home and car) are vulnerable to claims against the business; sole proprietors and general partners have unlimited liability.

THINKING IT THROUGH

Have you ever dreamed of opening your own business? If you did, what would it be? What talents or skills do you have that you could use? Could you start a business in your own home? About how much would it cost to start? Could you begin part time while you worked elsewhere? What could you get from owning your own business in the way of satisfaction and profit? What would you lose?

PARTNERSHIPS

Often, it is much easier to own and manage a business with one or more partners. (A partnership is a legal form of business with two or more owners.) Your partner can cover for you when you are sick or go on vacation. Your partner may be skilled at inventory keeping and accounting while you do the selling or servicing. A partner can also provide additional money, support, and expertise.

A partnership.

Advantages of Partnerships   – Single taxation.

There are many advantages of having one or more partners in a business. Some of the people who are enjoying the advantages of partnerships today more than ever before are doctors, lawyers, dentists, and other professionals. They have learned that it is easier to take vacations, stay home when they are sick, or relax a little when there are others available to help take care of clients.

It is not difficult to form a partnership, but it is wise to get the counsel of a lawyer experienced with such agreements. Lawyers' services are expensive, so would-be partners should read all about partnerships and reach some basic agreements before calling in a lawyer. It is often easier to *form* a partnership agreement than to operate one or end one, and many friendships have ended after friends became partners. With some care, however, partnerships have these advantages:

1 *More financial resources.* Naturally, when two or more people pool their money and credit, it is easier to pay the rent, utilities, and other bills incurred by a business. There is a concept called limited partnership that is specially designed to help raise capital (money). A **limited partner** invests money in the business, but does not have any management responsibility or any liability for business losses. The agreement form necessary for a limited part-

limited partner
Invests money in the business, but does not have any management responsibility or liability for losses (see *limited liability*).

nership is more complex than that needed for a simple partnership (called a **general partnership**). For example, the agreement must mention the amount of money involved, the share of profits each person receives, and so on. You will need a lawyer's help with such agreements. The point here is that partnerships feed more money into the business for growth.

2 *Ease of management*. It is simply much easier to manage the day-to-day activities of a business with carefully chosen partners. Partners give each other free time from the business, and provide different skills and perspectives. Many people find that the best partner is a spouse. That is why you see so many husband/wife teams managing restaurants, service shops, and other businesses.

general partner
An owner (partner) who has unlimited liability and is active in managing the firm.

Disadvantages of Partnerships

Any time two people must agree on anything, however, there is the possibility of conflict and tension. This is true of partnerships as well. Partnerships have caused splits among families, friends, and marriages. Let's explore the disadvantages of partnerships further:

1 *Unlimited liability*. Each general partner is liable for the debts of the firm, no matter who was responsible for causing those debts. Like a sole proprietor, partners can lose their homes, cars, and everything else they own if the business fails or is sued by someone. Such a risk is very serious and should be discussed with a lawyer and an insurance expert. A general partner, then, is an owner (partner) who has unlimited liability and is active in managing the firm. (As mentioned earlier, a limited partner risks an investment in the firm, but is not liable for the business's losses.)

2 *Division of profits*. Let's say two people form a partnership. One puts in more money and the other puts in more hours. Each may feel justified in asking for a bigger share of the profits. Sharing the risk means sharing the profit, and that can cause conflicts.

3 *Disagreements among partners*. Disagreements over money are just one example of potential conflict in a partnership. Who has final authority over employees? Who hires and fires employees? Who works what hours? What if one partner wants to buy expensive equipment for the firm and the other partner disagrees? Potential conflicts are many. Because of such problems, all terms of partnership should be spelled out in writing to protect all parties and to minimize misunderstanding in the future.

4 *Difficult to terminate*. Once you have committed yourself to a partnership, it is not easy to get out of it. Questions about who gets what and what happens next are often very difficult to solve when the business is closed.

Again, the best way to learn about the advantages and disadvantages of partnerships is to interview several people who have experience with such agreements. They will give you additional insights and hints on how to avoid problems.

Abraham Lincoln and a partner bought a small country store in New Salem, Ill. in 1832. Lincoln wasn't very good at business, or his partner at staying away from whiskey. Within a year, his partner died, and Lincoln was left owing $1,100 to his creditors, a huge sum he referred to as "the National Debt."
Source: *Inc.*, May, 1985, p. 18.

PROGRESS CHECK

■ Unlimited liability is one of the biggest drawbacks to sole proprietorships and general partnerships. Can you explain what that means?

■ What is the difference between a *limited* partner and a *general* partner?

CORPORATIONS

TOP 25 U.S. CORPORATIONS, 1985 (BY SALES)

1 General Motors
2 Exxon
3 AT&T
4 Mobil
5 Ford Motor
6 IBM
7 Texaco
8 Chevron
9 Sears, Roebuck
10 Du Pont
11 General Electric
12 Phibro Salomon
13 Amoco
14 K Mart
15 Citicorp
16 Atlantic Richfield
17 Chrysler
18 Safeway Stores
19 Aetna Life & Casualty
20 USX
21 Kroger
22 Cigna
23 GTE
24 Phillips Petroleum
25 Tenneco

Source: *Business Week*, April 18, 1986, p. 123.

Although the word *corporation* makes people think of big businesses like General Motors, IBM, Ford, Exxon, GE, Westinghouse, and USX (formerly U.S. Steel), it is not necessary to be big in order to *incorporate* (start a corporation). Obviously, many corporations *are* big. However, incorporating may be beneficial for small businesses, also.

The purpose of forming a corporation is to get away from the disadvantages of sole proprietorships and partnerships. One of the more worrisome aspects of owning your own business or having a partner is the fear of losing everything you own if someone sues the business or the business loses a lot of money.

A corporation is a state-chartered legal entity with authority to act and have liability separate from its owners. What this means for the corporation's owners (stockholders) is that they are not liable for the debts or any other problems of the corporation beyond the money they invest. Owners no longer must worry about losing their house, car, and other property because of some business problem—a very significant benefit. A corporation not only limits the liability of owners, it enables many people to share in the ownership (and profits) of a business without working there or having other commitments to it.

Advantages of Corporations

The concept of incorporation is not too difficult, even though the procedures for incorporating are often rather complex. Most people are not willing to risk everything to go into business. Yet, for businesses to grow and prosper and create abundance, many people would have to be willing to invest their money in business. The way to solve this problem was to create an artificial being, an entity that existed only in the eyes of the law. That artificial being is called a *corporation*. It is nothing more than a technique for involving people in business at a minimal risk. Let's explore the advantages of such an entity:

1 *More money for investment.* To raise money, a corporation sells ownership (stock) to anyone who is interested. This means that millions of people can own part of major companies like IBM, Xerox, and General Motors. If a company sold 10,000,000 shares for $50 each, it would have $500 million available to build plants, buy materials, hire people, build products, and so on. Such a large amount of money would be difficult to raise any other way. So a major advantage of corporations is their ability to raise large amounts of money.

2 *Limited liability.* It bears repeating that a major advantage of corporations is the limited liability of owners. Corporations in England and Canada have the letters "Ltd." after their name, as in British Motors, Ltd. The Ltd. stands for **limited liability** and is probably the most significant advantage of corporations. Limited liability means that the owners of a business are responsible for losses only up to the amount they invest.

3 *Size.* That one word summarizes many of the advantages of corporations. Because they have large amounts of money to work with, corporations can build large, modern factories with the latest equipment. They can also hire experts or specialists in all areas of operation. Furthermore, they can buy

limited liability
Means that the owners of a business are responsible for losses only up to the amount they invest.

other corporations in other fields to *diversify their risk.* (What this means is that a corporation can be involved in many businesses at once so that if one fails the effect on the total corporation is lessened.) In short, a major advantage of corporations is that they have the size and resources to take advantage of opportunities anywhere in the world. Corporations do not have to be large to enjoy the benefits of limited liability and more money for investment. Many doctors, lawyers, and individuals and partners in a variety of businesses have incorporated. Therefore, there are many small corporations in the United States.

Major corporation headquarters.

4 *Tax advantages.* Once a person, partnership, or group of individuals have incorporated, they often receive significant tax advantages. They can deduct expenses for automobiles, meals, trips, and much more from their taxes. They can reinvest profits into the corporation to postpone paying taxes, and more. One of the most important tax advantages is tax-free fringe benefits, such as retirement funds.

5 *Perpetual life.* Because corporations are separate from those who own them, the death of one or more owners does not terminate the corporation.

6 *Ease of ownership change.* It is easy to change the owners of a corporation. All that is necessary is to sell stock to someone else. This means that new owners can be brought in easily as well.

7 *Separation of ownership from management.* Corporations are able to raise money from many different investors without getting them involved in management. The corporate hierarchy looks like this:

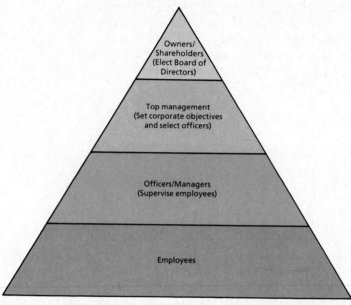

This pyramid shows that the owners/shareholders are separate from the managers and employers. The owners elect a board of directors. The directors select the officers. They, in turn, hire managers and employees. The owners thus have some say in who runs the corporation, but no control.

NONPROFIT CORPORATIONS

A nonprofit corporation is a special type of corporation formed for charitable and other purposes. It does not seek *profit*. Such a corporation has many of the features of business corporations with the major exception of its tax status. Owners of a nonprofit corporation can contact the Internal Revenue Service for forms to qualify for tax-exempt status (IRS booklet number 557).

The number of nonprofit corporations is remarkable, running into the hundreds of thousands. In states such as Ohio and New York, over one third of all corporations with state charters are nonprofit. In some towns and cities, over 50% of the property is tax exempt because it belongs to nonprofit organizations such as churches and hospitals.

Disadvantages of Corporations

There are so many sole proprietorships and partnerships in the United States that it is clear that there are real disadvantages to incorporating. Otherwise, more people would incorporate their businesses. Here are a few of the disadvantages:

1 *Initial cost.* Incorporation may cost thousands of dollars and involve expensive lawyers and accountants. There are less expensive ways of incorporating in certain states (see p. 109), but most people do not have the time or confidence to go through this procedure without the help of a lawyer.

2 *Paperwork.* The papers to be filed to start a corporation are just the beginning. Tax laws demand that a corporation prove all its expenses and deductions are legitimate. A corporation, therefore, must process many forms. A sole proprietor or partnership may keep rather casual accounting records; a corporation, on the other hand, must keep detailed records, the minutes of meetings, and more.

3 *Two tax returns.* If an individual incorporates, he or she must file both a corporate tax return and an individual tax return. The corporate return can be quite complex.

4 *Size.* Large corporations sometimes become too inflexible and too tied down in red tape to respond quickly to market changes.

5 *Social security.* A corporation has a high social security and unemployment compensation burden; that is, it must contribute to these funds.

6 *Termination difficult.* Once a corporation is started, it's relatively hard to end.

7 *Double taxation.* Corporate income is taxed twice. First the corporation pays tax on income before it can distribute any to stockholders. Then the stockholders pay tax on the income (dividends) they receive from the corporation. States often tax corporations more harshly than other enterprises. Sometimes they levy special taxes that apply to corporations, but not to other forms of business.

Many people are discouraged by the costs, paperwork, and special taxes corporations must pay. Partners may feel that the hassles of incorporation outweigh the advantages.

Figure 4-2 (p. 108) summarizes the advantages and disadvantages of the various forms of business organization.

BANKRUPTCY

Starting any kind of business involves risks. Sometimes things do not work out and the business simply cannot pay its bills. Let's say, for example, that a business bought new inventory for the next season. Suddenly, the owners find that the bank refuses to lend them more money or some similar financial catastrophe occurs. What can the owners do?

Bankruptcy is the legal procedure whereby a person or a business unable to meet financial obligations is relieved of debt by having the court divide its assets among its creditors.

The Bankruptcy Reform Act of 1978 provides for less drastic measures: Chapter 11 requires that if 51% of the creditors, by dollar and number, agree to settle for a portion of what the company owes them, then the other companies must accept the deal made by the majority.

Chapter 11 enables a company to stay in business, make a new financial plan, sell its inventory, and survive. Eventually it may pay back its creditors, rehire employees, and make a profit. The alternative is to declare bankruptcy. In that case, the company, its creditors, employees, and stockholders (if any) all lose out. Thousands of Chapter 11 petitions are filed each year, offering struggling firms one more chance to succeed.

FIGURE 4-2

Summary of the advantages and disadvantages of various business forms.

BUSINESS TYPE	ADVANTAGES	DISADVANTAGES
Sole proprietorship	■ Easy to start ■ Pride of ownership ■ You keep all the profits ■ No special taxes ■ Easy to terminate ■ You are your own boss	■ Risk of loss ■ Unlimited liability ■ Tremendous time commitment ■ Few fringe benefits ■ Difficulty in management ■ No backups ■ Limited growth ■ Higher taxes than corporations
General partnership	■ More money to start and operate ■ Shared responsibility and easier to manage with diverse skills ■ Most of the benefits of sole proprietorships, except profits are shared	■ Unlimited liability ■ Shared profits ■ Disagreements among partners ■ Difficult termination
Corporation	■ More money to start and operate than any other form ■ Limited liability ■ Size results in diversified risk and economies of scale ■ Tax advantages ■ Perpetual life ■ Ease of ownership change ■ Separate ownership from management	■ Initial cost ■ Paperwork ■ Two tax returns ■ Social Security ■ Difficult termination ■ Double taxation ■ Size can be a disadvantage if it results in poor adaptability

How to Incorporate

The process of forming a corporation varies somewhat from state to state. The *articles of incorporation* are usually filed with the secretary of state of the state in which the company incorporates. The articles contain the following information[2]:

■ The corporation's name
■ The names of the people who incorporated it
■ Its purposes
■ Its duration (usually perpetual)
■ The number of shares that can be issued, their voting rights, and any other rights the shareholders have
■ The corporation's minimum capital
■ The address of the corporation's office

- The name and address of the person responsible for the corporation's legal services
- The names and addresses of the first directors
- Any other public information the incorporators wish to include

In addition to the articles of incorporation listed, a corporation also has *by-laws*. These describe how the firm is to be operated from both a legal and managerial point of view. The by-laws include items such as:

- How, when, and where shareholders' and directors' meetings are held, and how long directors are to serve
- Directors' authority
- Duties and responsibilities of officers, and the length of their service
- How stock is issued
- Other matters, including employment contracts[3]

Individuals Can Incorporate

It is important to remember that a corporation does not need to have hundreds of employees or thousands of stockholders. Individuals (that is, doctors, lawyers, movie stars, rock stars, and so forth) can also incorporate. By doing so, they may save on taxes and receive other benefits of incorporation. It is not always as difficult as it sounds to form a corporation, especially if you choose to do it in a state with less complex rules. Many firms incorporate in Delaware because it is relatively easy to do so there. A book called *How to Form Your Own Corporation Without a Lawyer for Under $500* by Ted S. Nicholas (Enterprise Publications, 1986) tells you the steps to take. The title gives you a good idea of the difficulty involved.

CORPORATE TYPES

You may find some confusing terms when reading about corporations. Here are a few of the more widely-used terms:

An *alien corporation* does business in the United States, but is chartered (incorporated) in another country.

A *domestic corporation* does business in the state in which it was chartered (incorporated).

A *foreign corporation* does business in one state, but is chartered in another; about one third of all corporations are chartered in Delaware because of its relatively attractive rules for incorporation. A foreign corporation must register in states where it operates.

An *open corporation* sells stock to the general public.

A *closed corporation* is one whose stock is held by a few people and is not available to the general public.

THINKING IT THROUGH

What would the United States be like without major corporations? What products would be hard to get? What would be the benefits? Now that you've read about sole proprietorships, partnerships, and corporations, which sounds like the best place for you to work? Why? Which calls for taking the most risks? Which would be most fun? Most profitable? What part of your personality most determines where you fit in best?

PROGRESS CHECK

◼ What is the role of owners (stockholders) in the corporate hierarchy?

◼ If you buy stock in a corporation and someone gets injured by one of the corporation products, can you be sued? Why or why not? Could you be sued if you were a general partner in a partnership?

SUBCHAPTER S CORPORATIONS

Subchapter S corporation
A hybrid, half-corporate, half-partnership entity that looks like a corporation, but is taxed like a partnership.

A **Subchapter S corporation,** called an S corporation, is a unique government creation that is a hybrid, half-corporate, half-partnership entity. It looks like a corporation, but is taxed like a partnership. Originally S corporations seemed much like regular corporations. They had shareholders, directors, and employees. They also had the benefit of limited liability and some real tax advantages over partnerships, including deductible fringe benefits for owners.

However, the Subchapter S Revision Act of 1982 changed the rules. Now a Subchapter S corporation looks more like a partnership. It still has stockholders, directors, and officers, but fringe benefits of owners are no longer deductible.

The paperwork and details of Subchapter S corporations are similar to those of regular corporations. The best way to learn all the benefits is to go over the tax advantages and liability differences with a lawyer or accountant or both. The new tax laws being written make S corporations more attractive. The profits of such businesses are taxed as regular income, and that is now lower than corporate taxes.

COOPERATIVES

Some people dislike the notion of having owners, managers, workers, and buyers as separate individuals with separate goals. They envision a world where people cooperate with one another more fully and share the wealth more evenly. These people have formed a different kind of organization that reflects their social orientation. Such an organization is called a cooperative.

cooperative
An organization owned by members/customers who pay an annual membership fee and share in any profits, if it is a profit-making organization.

A **cooperative** is an organization that is owned by members/customers who pay an annual membership fee and share in any profits (if it is a profit-making organization). Often the members/customers work in the organization so many hours a month as part of their duties. Owners, managers, workers, and customers are all the same people. You may have a food cooperative near you. If so, stop by and chat with the people and learn more about this growing aspect of American trade.

There is another kind of cooperative in the United States, set up for different reasons. These cooperatives are formed to give members more economic power as a group than they would have as individuals. The best example is farm cooperatives. The idea at first was for farmers to join together to get better prices for their food products. Eventually, however, the organization expanded so that farm cooperatives now buy and sell fertilizer, farm equipment, seed, and other products needed on the farm. This has become a multibillion dollar industry. The cooperatives now

Cooperatives are important in agriculture.

own many manufacturing facilities. Farm cooperatives do not pay the same kind of taxes that corporations do, and thus have an advantage in the marketplace.

To give you some idea of the size of farm cooperatives, let's look at Farmland Industries, Inc. Recently this cooperative merged (joined) with FAR-MAR-CO to become a $5 billion organization. Farmland Industries owns manufacturing facilities, oil wells and refineries, fertilizer plants, feed mills, and plants that produce everything from grease and paint to steel buildings. It also owns a network of warehouses plus insurance, financial, and technical services for its 750,000 members. There are over 7,500 more smaller cooperatives in the country, some of which do a billion dollars of business a year. As you can see, cooperatives are a major force in agriculture today.

JOINT VENTURES

One of the latest trends in business is for two or more corporations (often from two different countries) to join together to accomplish some objective, such as creating an international car. A **joint venture,** then, is an effort by two or more business firms to capture new markets through cooperation and shared investment

joint venture
An agreement whereby two or more corporations join together to accomplish some objective.

Toyota's first American-built car, a joint venture with GM.

Tokyo Disneyland, a joint venture with Walt Disney Productions.

risk. This enables world markets to benefit from the expertise of all nation's business-people working together. For example, General Motors joined with Toyota to assemble Chevrolet Novas in the United States. These agreements are known as joint ventures, and are taking place all over the world. Britain's state-owned car company, BL, formed a joint venture with Japan's Honda to build cars in England. American Motors entered a joint venture with France's Renault. Ford plans to design cars in Japan, build them in Mexico, and sell them in the United States.

In other areas, Wheeling-Pittsburgh Steel Corp. formed a joint venture with Japan's Nisshin Steel Co. to make steel in the United States. IBM is trying to arrange a joint venture with Italy's Stet to enter Europe's telecommunications market. McDonald's has a joint venture in Thailand to franchise fast-food places.

One of the many interesting examples is the joint venture of Walt Disney Productions and Oriental Land in Japan. Their project was to create Tokyo Disneyland, a theme park much like the Disney parks in America. The results were fantastic. Over 10 million visitors came to the park in the first year.

WHICH FORM FOR YOU?

As you can see, you may participate in the business world in a variety of ways. You can start your own *sole proprietorship, partnership, corporation,* or *cooperative.* There are advantages and disadvantages to each. However, the risks are high no matter which form you choose. The miracle of free enterprise is that the freedom and incentives of capitalism make such risks acceptable to many people, who go on to create the great corporations of America. You know many of their names: J.C. Penney, Malcolm Forbes, Sears and Roebuck, Levi Strauss, Ford, Edison, and so on. They started small, accumulated capital, grew, and became industrial leaders. Could you do the same?

Most students prefer to take the more cautious route of working for a corporation. The advantages are many: a fixed salary, paid vacations, health coverage, limited risk, job security, promotional possibilities, and more. You know the advantages.

The disadvantages of working for others are also significant: limited income potential, fixed hours, repetitive work, close supervision, and limited freedom. Sometimes it is fun to work for others while starting your own business on the side. Apple Computer was started in a garage. Many firms were started in people's basements, garages, and attics.

The point is that business offers many different opportunities for tomorrow's graduates. Because the greatest opportunities are in small businesses, we shall devote the entire next chapter to that subject. First, however, let's review the material in this chapter and do some exercises.

PROGRESS CHECK

■ What is included in the articles of incorporation? Can you name three items?

■ What is the purpose of corporate by-laws?

■ What is the difference between a foreign and alien corporation? Be careful on this one.

SUMMARY

1 A *business* is any organization that seeks profit by providing goods and services to the economic system.
- What are the various ways businesses are formed?
  The three major forms of business are: sole proprietorships, partnerships, and corporations (including Subchapter S corporations).
- What are the advantages and disadvantages of each? Is there some way to quickly review them?
  See Figure 4-2 on p. 108.
- Which form of business is the most popular?
  About 74% of all businesses are sole proprietorships. They are the most popular form of ownership. Some 17% of businesses are corporations, and only 9% are partnerships.
- Which form sells the most?
  Corporations do 87% of the business in the United States. Proprietorships do 9% of the business and partnerships only 4%.

2 A major factor in choosing a form of business is liability for damages.
- What does *unlimited liability* mean?
  It means that the owners of a sole proprietorship or partnership (except limited partners) must pay all debts and damages caused by their business, to the point where they may have to sell their houses, cars, or other personal possessions.
- What does *limited liability* mean?
  Corporate owners (stockholders) are responsible for losses only up to the amount they invest. Their other personal property is not at risk.
- Why do people incorporate?
  Two important reasons are limited liability and special tax advantages, such as the deductibility of fringe benefits (for example, retirement funds).
- What does Chapter 11 of the bankruptcy act do?
  It enables firms to stay in business by paying creditors less and staying open until profits return.

3 The corporate hierarchy consists of stockholders (owners), who elect a board of directors, who hire managers to supervise employees.
- How do you form a corporation?
  Two major steps are needed: (1) file articles of incorporation in your state (the articles include the name, purpose, and duration of the corporation), and (2) write up by-laws telling how the firm will operate (authority of directors, dates and officers, and so forth).

4 A Subchapter S corporation is a hybrid form of corporation that has some of the advantages of a corporation (limited liability) and some of the advantages of a partnership (simpler taxes).

5 Cooperatives are organizations that are owned by members/customers.
- Aren't cooperatives little groups in neighborhoods?
  They can be, but they can grow to be multibillion dollar organizations like FAR-MAR-CO in agriculture.

6 It is time for the United States to look beyond its borders for corporate involvement. Joint ventures enable U.S. firms to join with foreign firms in new ventures.
- Are these ventures successful so far?
  Very. In industries as diverse as automotive and family entertainment (Disney), joint ventures have proved successful.

cooperative p. 110	nonprofit organization p. 98	**KEY TERMS**
corporation p. 98	partnership (general) p. 98	
general partner p. 103	sole proprietorship p. 98	
joint venture p. 111	Subchapter S corporation	
limited liability p. 104	p. 110	
limited partner p. 102	unlimited liability p. 101	

GETTING INVOLVED

1 You cannot learn about the spirit of entrepreneurship by reading books. Therefore you should go out and talk to at least four different sole proprietors and ask them about the joys and sorrows of being in business for yourself: How much does it cost to start? How many hours do they work? What are the specific benefits? Share the results with your class.

2 If you look around, you will be able to find people who are involved in partnerships, cooperatives, franchises, and corporations in your area. Since your career depends on such information, spend some time interviewing people from each form of ownership and get their impressions, hints, and warnings. Again, share your findings with the class to multiply the research benefits.

3 Visit a nonprofit organization and talk with people who work there in marketing, accounting, and so on. Is the work really different from a business? Are they paid well? What do they like and dislike? Do they feel part of a movement, a cause, a mission? Share your findings.

4 Debate the following statement with fellow students: "It is better for a college graduate to go to work for a large corporation than to start his or her own business because the risks are less, the salary is secure, the fringe benefits are ample, and the chances for promotion are good."

5 Explain to others the advantages and disadvantages of a corporation to test your knowledge. If you have trouble, reread those parts in the chapter and look up the subject in an encyclopedia or other source to learn more. Share what you found.

PRACTICING MANAGEMENT DECISIONS

CASE ONE   SEARS, ROEBUCK AND COMPANY—DIFFERENT BUSINESS FORMS

Perhaps no name is more closely associated with business in the United States than Sears. Today Sears sells more merchandise and has more employees than any other retailer. We can learn something about different forms of business by studying the evolution of Sears.

It all begin in the late 1800s with Richard Sears. He was working in a railroad station and sold watches on the side. Eventually he opened his own watch store in Minneapolis (R.W. Sears Watch Company). He was one of the first to use effective newspaper and magazine ads to promote such a store. The store was so successful that Sears sold it and opened another store in Chicago.

Sears needed a repairman to work in the store. A man named Alvah T. Roebuck answered Sears' ad. Eventually Richard and Alvah got together and formed a partnership in 1893. They called it Sears, Roebuck and Company. The partnership grew and began selling hundreds of items from a catalog. By 1895, Roebuck got nervous about Sears' aggressive marketing strategies and sold his shares back to Sears for $25,000—Not the best of deals as things turned out.

Sears found a couple of other investors and each of the three men owned 500 shares of stock in the Sears corporation. One partner sold his share in 1901 for $1.25 million. Still no bargain, as things began to grow.

Early in the 1900s, Sears decided to consolidate its plants and expand. It needed more money to do so. Therefore, it sold $9 million worth of preferred stock. Richard Sears made his partner president in 1908. Several stores were opened in 1925 under yet another president. The rest of the story is familiar to you. Now Sears has more stores and more employees than any other retailer, and the stores are located in many countries. The mail order catalog is still a leader. You, too, can own part of Sears. Its shares are listed on the New York Stock Exchange. Sears is expanding now, so you may become rich by being an investor.

Sears now handles auto servicing and rental, insurance, gardening, and home decorating. It is becoming a financial center (having acquired Dean Witter Reynolds) and a real estate broker (with Coldwell Banker & Company). Sears is also following the high-tech era by selling computers, word processors, and the newest phone systems.

DECISION QUESTIONS

1 How does the Sears story reflect the advantages and disadvantages of being a sole proprietor, a partner, and a corporation?

2 Sears had a partner who sold out. What does this tell you about partnerships in general, if anything?

3 What is the major factor that caused Sears to become a corporation?

PRACTICING MANAGEMENT DECISIONS

CASE TWO BUYING VERSUS STARTING YOUR OWN BUSINESS

Albert Lowry, an expert on investing in small business, recommends that you *buy* a business rather than start one on your own. The advantages are:

1. You might get a bargain price. Circumstances sometimes force an owner to sell for less than a business is worth (for example, health reasons or divorce).

2. You bypass start-up problems, which can be unforeseen and costly. You save the time and trouble of buying equipment and supplies. Operating methods are proven. There are customers!

3. Guesswork is minimized. If you start a new business, you can't be sure about the right location, the right size building, advertising, price, and so on. An established owner already knows many of these things.

4. The owner can give you information about competitors, seasonal fluctuations, and more.

5. You get time-tested suppliers and service people.

6. You may inherit employees who are experienced and can help you with the business.

Lowry's book is called *How to Become Financially Successful by Owning Your Own Business*. It gives you hints on where to look for business opportunities, how to evaluate the worth of a business, how to analyze the business's financial statements, how to finance such a business and more. Such books are an invaluable aid to someone thinking of becoming a business owner. This is true whether or not you intend to take on a partner in your business.

DECISION QUESTIONS

1 What are the disadvantages of buying a business rather than starting one fresh?

2 There is an old saying, "He doesn't have twelve years of experience; he has had one year's experience twelve times." What does this saying tell you about the managerial expertise of people selling their businesses?

3 Could you look at a business's financial statements and tell whether or not it was profitable and determine how much it was worth? Could most people? What does this tell you about the value of an accountant to someone anticipating buying a business?

Source: Albert J. Lowry, *How to Become Financially Successful By Owning Your Own Business* (New York: Simon & Schuster, Inc., 1981), p. 28

Because 74% of all businesses in the United States are sole proprietorships and another 9% are partnerships, you can see that small businesses are the heart of free enterprise. Most of the *new* jobs are in this area, as are many of the exciting new industries.

LOOKING AHEAD

Because small business is so important to America and to your future, we devote Chapter 5 to managing such organizations. We shall explore all phases of small business management, from starting a business to motivating employees.

Behind the growth of small business is a *spirit of entrepreneurship* that has swept the country. Even large businesses are restructuring to create smaller, more entrepreneurial units. Along with that trend is the movement toward franchising. Both of these subjects are covered in Chapter 6.

MANAGING A SMALL BUSINESS

LEARNING GOALS

After you have read and studied this chapter, you should be able to:

- Explain the risks and benefits of owning a small business.
- Define small business and discuss its importance to the American economy.
- List five categories of small business.
- List three ways to become involved in a small business.
- List and describe five areas of concern in managing a small business.
- Explain what a business plan is, and outline six general areas of information that should be included.
- Identify five types of outside assistance a small business owner needs, and why.
- Describe four advantages small business have in international markets.

PROFILE MARK GOLDMAN, BACKPACK MAN

Everywhere you go on most college campuses you will see students wearing backpacks. Wouldn't that be a great product to produce? That's exactly what Mark Goldman thought. His father owned a small manufacturing business called Eastern Canvas Products, Inc. Most of its business was with the Pentagon—duffel bags, canteen covers, ammo pouches, and the like. The company produced a few knapsacks for commercial customers, but that accounted for only 3% of sales. Mark saw an opportunity to go after the college market. His father was skeptical, but reluctantly agreed to produce a new line of backpacks with the trade name East-Pak.

Mark's dad resisted spending money for packaging design ($12,000) and fancy labels ($4,000 more), but Mark won. Eventually, the product line was expanded to 35 styles. The backpacks were promoted at college-store trade shows and in *College Store Journal.* In 1978, sales hit $1 million. In 1980, $2 million. In 1981, Mark became president of the company.

In 1983, sales went up to $7 million. Although most of the sales are in the East because of supply problems, students can thank Mark Goldman for making backpacks standard gear on campus.

By the way, the company makes even more money ($14 million) selling them to the military. Monte Goldman, Mark's dad, knew what he was doing, too! ■

Source: Johnnie L. Roberts, "Pentagon Supplier Finds Niche Selling Knapsacks to Students," *The Wall Street Journal,* September 17, 1984, p. 31. Reprinted by permission of *The Wall Street Journal,* © Dow Jones & Company, Inc., 1984. All rights reserved.

Mark Goldman.

small business
One that is independently owned and operated, not dominant in its field, and meets certain standards of size in terms of employees (fewer than 100) or annual receipts.

SMALL VERSUS BIG BUSINESS

There is so much talk today about "big business" that one would think that small business was not important to the United States economy. What is a "small" business, anyway? And how does it differ from a "big" business? The Small Business Administration (SBA) defines a **small business** as one that is independently owned and operated, not dominant in its field of operation, and meets certain standards of size in terms of employees (fewer than 100) or annual receipts (for example, less than $2 million a year for service businesses). See Figure 5-1 for some guidelines on the sizes of various kinds of small businesses.

A wholesaler may sell up to $22 million and still be considered a small business by the SBA. In manufacturing, a plant can have 1,500 employees and still be considered small. For example, American Motors is considered small because it is tiny compared to Ford, General Motors, and Chrysler. In short, a small business is considered "small" only in relation to other businesses in its industry. Let's look at some interesting statistics about small businesses:

- There are about 16 million businesses in the United States; about 14 million of them are small.
- Small businesses account for over 40% of the gross national product (GNP).
- Half the small businesses have sales of less than $500,000 and fewer than 10 employees.
- Of all nonfarm businesses in the United States, almost 97% are considered small by SBA standards. The percentage of small businesses in various categories is shown in Figure 5-2.

As you can see, small business is really a big part of the United States economy. How big a part? We'll explore that question next.

Importance of Small Businesses

Most people do not have any idea of the importance of small businesses in our economy. So much news is devoted to employment and problems in big businesses such as automobiles, steel, and textiles that we tend to feel that the economy is

FIGURE 5-1

There is no one definition of "small business," but the U.S. Small Business Administration uses these guidelines for classification.

Source: Office of Economic Research, U.S. Small Business Administration.

SMALL BUSINESS	EMPLOYMENT SIZE	ASSET SIZE	SALES SIZE
Independent contractor	0	0	Under 100,000
Family size	1-4	Under $100,000	$100,000-500,000
Small	5-19	$100-5,000	$500,000-$1 million
Medium	20-99	$500,000-5 million	$1-10 million
Large	100-499	$5-25 million	$10 million-50 million
Total small business	0-500	$0-25 million	$0-50 million
Medium business	500-999	$25-100 million	$50-250 million
Large business	1,000+	$100 million+	$250 million+
Government size business	10,000+	$2 billion	$2 billion+

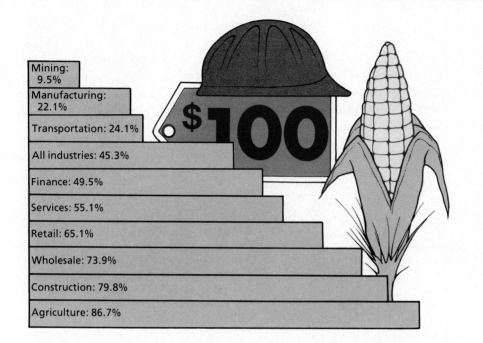

Mining: 9.5%

Manufacturing: 22.1%

Transportation: 24.1%

All industries: 45.3%

Finance: 49.5%

Services: 55.1%

Retail: 65.1%

Wholesale: 73.9%

Construction: 79.8%

Agriculture: 86.7%

FIGURE 5-2

Percentage of small businesses in different categories. Note the large percentage of small firms in agriculture, wholesaling, and retailing.
Source: Office of the President, *State of Small Business*, 1983.

dominated totally by large businesses. Yet according to the White House Commission on Small Business 87% of the nation's new jobs in the private sector are in small businesses and they should provide 50% of gross national product by 1990. That means there is a very good chance that you will be either employed by a small business someday or will start one.

The growth rate of small and medium-sized businesses has been obscured by the decline in employment in traditional "smokestack" industries. For example, between 1965 and 1984, America's population aged 16 to 65 grew 38%, to 178 million people. Jobs during that same period increased by 45%, to 103 million. It is important to note that in the last 5 years alone, employment in the *Fortune* 500 companies, the *largest* firms in the United States, *declined* by about 3 million jobs.[1]

No doubt media coverage leads you to believe that most of the new jobs are in "high-tech" industries—computers, robots, and the like. The truth is that only 10% of the jobs created in the last 10 years were in high technology. Most of the new jobs are in low-tech industries such as women's wear manufacturers and restaurants.

Another surprising statistic is that the growth in mid-size firms (sales of $25 million to $1 billion) was among *manufacturing* firms, not *service* firms, as many believe. Here is what Peter Drucker has to say about this new phenomenon[2]:

> There are many people around now who are risk-takers and who want material success badly enough to impose on themselves the grueling discipline and endless hours of the entrepreneur.
>
> But where does the money come from? A decade ago, we worried that there would be no capital available for new ventures—now it seems there is more venture capital than there are ventures. The biggest factor in the entrepreneurial explosion . . . is the development . . . of a body of organized knowledge of entrepreneurship and innovation.

Think of a job that nobody could pay you enough to do, and plunge right in. At first the hours will be inhuman and the work will probably be unromantic, but you'll be your own boss. Welcome to the wonderful world of small business.

Richard Grierre in *Forbes*, October 21, 1985.

The problem in the past with small businesses was that they failed because of managerial incompetence. That trend is changing now as more and more emphasis is being placed on small business management training. The result, as we have noted, is that most new jobs today are in small to medium-sized firms in traditional low-technology manufacturing and retailing industries.

A body of knowledge is available that will enable such entrepreneurs to survive and prosper for many years to come. Before we explore small business management, however, let's review the kinds of businesses we are talking about.

THINKING IT THROUGH

Imagine yourself working in a small business. What kind of business would it be? How much local competition is there? What could you do to make your business more attractive than competitors'? Would you be willing to work 60 to 70 hours per week in such a business?

Small Business Categories

The government tends to classify things, including small businesses. They talk about five different classes of small business: (1) service businesses, (2) retail businesses, (3) construction firms, (4) wholesalers, and (5) manufacturers. What kind of business would be the most attractive career choice for you? Let's review the industries:

1 *Service businesses*. You are already familiar with the services provided by dry cleaners, travel agencies, lawn-care firms, beauty parlors, and other services that cater to you and your family. In your career search, be sure to explore services such as hotels/motels, health clubs, amusement parks, income tax preparation organizations, employment agencies, accounting firms, rental firms of all kinds, management consulting, repair services (for example, computers, robots, VCRs), insurance agencies, real estate firms, stock brokers, and so on. There are many exciting careers available in such firms.

2 *Retail businesses*. You have only to go to a major shopping mall to see the possibilities in retailing. There are stores selling shoes, clothes, hats, skis, gloves, sporting goods, ice cream, groceries, and more. Much more. Watch the trends, and you will see new ideas like fancy popcorn stores, T-shirt shops, videotape rental stores, yogurt shops, and more. Do any of these retail stores look like interesting places to work?

3 *Construction firms*. Drive through any big city and you will see huge cranes towering over an empty lot where major construction is taking place. Would you enjoy supervising such work? Visit some areas where construction firms are building bridges, roads, homes, schools, buildings, and dams. There is a feeling of power and creativity in such work that excites many observers. How about you? Talk to some of the workers and supervisors and learn about the risks and rewards of small construction firms.

4 *Wholesalers*. Have you ever visited a wholesale food warehouse, a wholesale jewelry center, or similar wholesale firms? If not, you are missing an important link in the small business system, one with much potential. Whole-

Construction jobs can be challenging and rewarding.

sale representatives often make more money, have more free time, travel more, have more fringe benefits, and enjoy their jobs more than similar people in retailing. Check it out.

5 *Manufacturing.* Of course, manufacturing is still an attractive career for tomorrow's graduates. There are careers for designers, machinists, mechanics, engineers, supervisors, safety inspectors, and a host of other occupations.

Visit some small manufacturers in your area and inquire about such jobs. Naturally, there are thousands of small farmers who enjoy the rural life and the pace of farming. Small farms are usually not very profitable, but some that specialize in exotic crops do quite well. (See Case 2 at the end of the chapter.) Similarly, many small mining operations attract college students with a sense of adventure and daring. People who are not sure of what career they would like to follow have a busy time ahead. They need to visit service firms, construction firms, farms, mines, retailers, wholesalers, and all other kinds of small and large businesses to see the diversity and excitement available in American business (see Figure 5-3).

FIGURE 5-3

What's growing, what's not in small business. Note the growth of management/public relations firms, engineering/architectural services, and beauty shops.

Source: Dun & Bradstreet Corporation, *Dun's Census of American Business,* 1985.

Rank	Business	1984 Number	1979–84 % growth
1	Eating establishments	174,876	16.5
2	Gasoline service stations	100,213	−0.3
3	Drinking establishments	95,246	34.9
4	Grocery stores	95,127	9.3
5	Plumbing/heating/air-conditioning	84,721	57.5
6	General auto repair shops	62,949	59.4
7	Gift/novelty shops	59,762	12.8
8	Electrical work	55,948	66.2
9	Sporting goods/bicycle stores	47,952	9.2
10	Automotive home supply stores	47,645	7.6
11	Local trucking without storage	46,129	76.8
12	Management/public relations	44,697	181.9
13	Furniture stores	44,336	−3.0
14	Women's ready-to-wear	44,274	−1.5
15	Liquor stores	41,639	22.0
16	Hotels/motels/tourist cottages	37,948	65.7
17	Beauty shops	37,310	153.2
18	Hardware stores	34,017	−3.4
19	Engineering/architectural services	33,859	110.8
20	Auto equipment (wholesale)	33,177	−2.2

WOMEN IN SMALL BUSINESS

There has been a rapid growth in the number of women starting small businesses in the last decade or so. According to the Bureau of Labor Statistics, the number of self-employed women grew by almost 70% between 1972 and 1982. Recent statistics show that women own over 3 million businesses, selling over $40 billion worth of goods and services annually.

Judith A. Hayner, executive director of Every Woman's Place, Incorporated, describes the effect that some women are having on small business this way:

> According to a 1984 Small Business Administration report, women in the United States are starting small businesses at a rate five times faster than that of men. For every five women entering the work force, three are starting businesses. In the state of Michigan, women currently own 36% of the small businesses. In 1980, there were 2.8 million female-operated sole proprietorships in this country, which generated more than $40 billion in receipts. Of even greater significance to our economic recovery is the fact that the average number of full- and part-time jobs created by female-owned companies is 5.57, while the median for the population is 4.0. If it is true (and research substantiates this claim) that the small-business sector is responsible for at least 70% of all new job creation, then it is not difficult to deduce that the majority of new jobs in this decade of the entrepreneur are being created by women.

PROGRESS CHECK

■ What are the five different classes of small businesses?

■ What factors are used to classify a firm as a "small" business?

STARTING A SMALL BUSINESS

The free enterprise system is best represented not by firms such as General Motors or Exxon, but by small organizations such as Parsley Patch, Inc. This company was started on a shoestring budget by two women. It began when Elizabeth Bertani prepared salt-free seasonings for her husband who was on a salt-free diet. Her friend, Pat Sherwood, felt that the seasonings were good enough to sell. Mrs. Bertani agreed, and Parsley Patch, Inc. was born.

The business began with a modest investment of $5,000 that was supposed to go for their graduate school tuitions. Eventually the two women invested more than $100,000 and forgot about graduate school; running a small business was too enjoyable to give up.

But it was not easy. At first, the women decided to go after the gourmet market where people were willing to pay high prices for good quality seasonings. They selected expensive glass jars with cork stoppers for containers and spent almost $5,000 for a logo and a label design. The product line of six spice blends was introduced at a gourmet food show, and orders poured in. The families and five employees were soon working 6-day, 60-hour weeks to fill orders.

Everything was going well. Hundreds of gourmet shops adopted the line, but sales were still below expectations. It became clear that the health food market offered more potential because the salt-free seasonings were a natural for people with restricted diets. The problem was that the health food market is entirely different from the gourmet market—no fancy glass bottles with cork stoppers in health food stores. The containers were simply too expensive (final wholesale price—$2.75; retail—$4.15 or more). Therefore, the women selected a less expensive jar (17 cents) and lowered the retail price to a more competitive and attractive $2.25.

Sales took off and were approaching $30,000 a month. The problem was *no profits*. The women had been poorly advised not to worry about costs, and they hadn't. Furthermore, they had no idea how to go about cost control and other "sophisticated" managerial functions. A CPA (certified public accountant) and an experienced manager were hired to help. The women learned how to compute the costs of each blend, how to separate production and overhead costs, and how to control expenses. More effective purchasing lowered the cost per jar by 5 cents and cut ingredient costs by half. Sales now run $700,000 or so annually. The women maintain a 60% gross margin (sales minus cost of goods sold).

"Luckily enough we were able to turn it around," Mrs. Sherwood said. "You can't continue to be naive about business practices, or you go broke."[3]

Small Business Success and Failure

"You can't continue to be naive about business practices, or you go broke." Those words bear repeating, and the figures support that statement. If one hundred small businesses are started at any given point in time, the odds are that twenty of them will be gone by the end of the first year; seventeen more will go out of business in the second year; and by the end of the fifth year, a total of about sixty-seven will have failed![4] Only 33% are likely to survive! Truly, you can't continue to be naive about business practices or you *do* go broke (see Figure 5-4).

The purpose of this chapter is to explore small businesses, their role in the economy, and small business management. It is easier to identify with a small

Parsley Patch's line of seasonings.

FIGURE 5-4

Small business firms with the
lowest failure rates.

Source: Small Business Administration, 1984.

BUSINESS	FAILURES PER 100,000 (1983)
Funeral service and crematoriums	10.9
Wholesale tobacco and tobacco products	22.6
Fuel and ice dealers	36.2
Laundry, cleaning, and garment repair	38.0
Drugstores	39.7
Hotels	40.4
Wood products	44.7
Personal services (e.g., secretarial, consulting)	45.2
Beer and wine wholesalers	45.7
Service stations	46.2

neighborhood business than a giant multinational firm, yet the principles of management are very similar. So, if we can learn about small business management, we can make a giant step toward understanding management in general. The management of charities, social causes, government agencies, churches, schools, unions, and associations is much the same as the management of small and large businesses. All organizations demand capital, good ideas, planning, information management, budgets (and financial management in general), accounting, marketing, good employee relations, and good overall managerial know-how. We shall explore these areas as they relate to small businesses and then, later in the book, apply the concepts to large firms, even multinational organizations.

Small businesses are good places to learn managerial principles.

The Entrepreneurial Spirit

Given the fact that 67% of small businesses are doomed to fail within 5 years, why do so many people continue to try? First of all, you should understand that thousands of new businesses are started every year. In 1983, 600,000 new businesses were formed, 40,000 more than the year before.[5] But in that same year, 31,334 businesses failed.

Clearly, something in the American spirit motivates people to try, try again to start and run their own small business. As we learned earlier, the key words are *incentive* and *freedom*. Talk to any small business owners and they are likely to mention the concept of freedom very early in the conversation. They say things like, "I wanted to be my own boss," or "I wanted the freedom to succeed or fail on my own."

Besides the freedom, small businesses offer an unusually high incentive to work hard because all of the profit (or loss) goes to the owner/manager. Yet profit is not the greatest incentive for most entrepreneurs. Conversations with them almost invariably result in statements such as, "I had a dream; I wanted a small repair garage of my own," or "I had this great idea, a product that no one else had, and I wanted to make it myself."

Thus, in spite of overwhelming odds against them, entrepreneurs set out to conquer the business world, confidently and enthusiastically. How hard do they work? A survey of *Forbes'* "Up and Comers" found that 48% of the chief executives of up and coming firms work more than 70 hours a week. However, all this enthusiasm means nothing without a unique or superior product. Seventy percent of small business executives agreed that the product is the key to success.[6]

Figure 5-5 lists the fastest-growing small-business-dominated industries as well

SMALL-BUSINESS-DOMINATED INDUSTRIES	PERCENT EMPLOYMENT CHANGE
Fastest	
Savings & loan associations	42.6
Operative builders	39.0
Computer & data processing services	32.9
Carpentry & flooring	31.4
Radio, TV, & miscellaneous stores	30.8
Masonry, stonework, & plastering	30.4
Painting, paper hanging, & decorating	24.9
Roofing & sheet metal work	23.5
Mailing, reproduction, & stenographic	22.7
Residential building contractors	22.4
Slowest	
Combined real estate, insurance offices	−7.6
Taxicabs	−6.9
Petroleum & petroleum products	−6.0
Pipeline, except natural gas	−5.0
Household appliance stores	−4.6
Chemicals & allied products	−3.7
Liquor stores	−3.7
Real estate operators & lessors	2.9
Amusement & recreation services	1.6
Sporting goods, toys, & hobby goods	1.2

FIGURE 5-5

Fastest and slowest growing small-business-dominated industries as measured by employment change, October 1982–October 1984.

Source: *The State of Small Business* (Washington, D.C.: The United States Small Business Administration, 1985), p. 20.

as some slow-growth industries to help you in your career choices. Which of the fast-growing industries sound most interesting to you?

HOW TO START A SUCCESSFUL SMALL BUSINESS

Hundreds of would-be entrepreneurs of all ages have asked the same question: "How can I learn to run my own business?" Many of these people had no idea what kind of business they wanted to start; they simply wanted to be in business for themselves. That seems to be a major trend among students today. Here are some hints for starting a small business.

Learn from Others

Working for others in the same business is a good first step toward ownership.

There are a few courses available that teach small business management well. You might begin by investigating your local schools for such classes. The best thing about these courses is that they bring together entrepreneurs. *That* is how to learn to run a small business—talk to others who have done it.

The starting place for budding entrepreneurs is talking with small business owners and managers. Learn from their experience, especially their mistakes. They will tell you that location is critical. They will caution you not to be under-capitalized. They will warn you about the problems of finding and retaining good workers. And, most of all, they will tell you to keep good records and hire a good accountant and lawyer before you start. Small business owners can give you hundreds of good ideas, ranging from how to get bank loans to how to design creative advertising. This free advice is invaluable.

Get Some Experience

There is no better way for learning small business management than by becoming an apprentice or working for a successful entrepreneur. For example, Nancy Mount, a florist in Cheney, Kansas, worked part time for 8 months for the owner of The Cheney Florist. She did everything from cutting flowers to making flower arrangements for elaborate weddings. After that experience, she and her husband Tom took over the business.[7] The rule of thumb is: 3 years experience in a comparable business (Nancy was an exception).

SITUATIONS FOR SMALL BUSINESS SUCCESS

- When the customer requires a lot of personal attention as in a beauty parlor.
- When the product is not easily made by mass-production techniques (for example, custom-tailored clothes or custom auto body work).
- When sales are not large enough to appeal to a large firm (for example, small women's dress shop).

- When the neighborhood is not attractive because of crime or poverty. This provides a unique opportunity for small grocery stores, liquor stores, and laundries. The risk is higher, but often so are profits.
- When a large business sells a franchise operation to local buyers. Don't forget franchising as an excellent way to enter the world of small business.

Take Over a Successful Firm

One thing you will learn about small business management is that it takes long hours, dedication, and determination. Few succeed, but those who do are special and worth finding. Talk with them and you'll learn that often they work 12 hours a day, 6 days a week and rarely take vacations. Clearly, they are married to their business. After many years, however, they may feel stuck in their business. They often think that they can't get out because they have too much time and effort invested. Usually their children refuse to take over because the work is too hard and the hours too long. In short, there are millions of small businesses out there with owner/managers eager to get away, at least for a long vacation.

This is where you come in. Find a mature businessperson (that is, one who is 50 to 60 or more years old) who owns a small business. Tell him or her that you are eager to learn the business and would like to serve an apprenticeship, a training period. At the end of that period (1 year or so), you would like to help the owner/manager by becoming assistant manager. As assistant manager, you would free the owner to take off weekends and holidays, and to take a long vacation—a good deal for him or her. For another year or so, work very hard to learn all about the business—suppliers, inventory, bookkeeping, customers, promotion, and so on. At the end of 2 years, make the owner this offer. He or she can retire or work only part time, and you will take over the business. You can establish a profit-sharing plan for yourself plus a salary. Be generous with yourself; you will earn it if you manage the business. You can even ask for 40% or more of the profits.

The owner benefits by keeping ownership in the business and making 60% of what he or she earned before—without having to work. You benefit by making 40% of the profits of a successful firm. For example, if the firm were earning $120,000 after expenses, the owner would get $72,000 a year and you would get $48,000. Believe me, this is an excellent deal for an owner about to retire who is able to keep his or her firm and a healthy profit flow. It is also the most clever and successful way to share in the profits of a successful small business without any personal money investment.

Several students have been successful in managing shoe stores, liquor stores, and other such stores in this manner. They make several times the income of students who merely work for retailers. One student used this strategy to take over the territory of an older manufacturer's agent. Look around; the possibilities are many. If the deal falls through, you can quit and start your own business fully trained.

PROGRESS CHECK

▪ What is the "rule of thumb" for how many years experience you should have before starting a small business?

▪ What percent of businesses usually fail in the first year? How many after 5 years?

MANAGING A SMALL BUSINESS

The Small Business Administration has reported that 90% of all failures are a result of "poor management." The problem is that "poor management" covers a number of faults. It could mean poor planning, poor record keeping, poor inventory control, poor promotion, or poor employee relations. Most likely it would include poor capitalization (that is, insufficient money to operate the firm). This chapter will give us a chance to explore the functions of business in a small business setting. Often, it is easier to picture such functions in a small firm. Later, after we have discussed these functions in this setting, we shall explore each function more completely. The functions we shall explore are:

- Planning
- Accounting
- Finance
- Human resource management
- Computer assistance

OUTLINE OF A COMPREHENSIVE BUSINESS PLAN

Section 1—Introduction Begin with a two-page or three-page management overview of the proposed venture. Include a succinct description of the business and discuss major goals and objectives.

Section 2—Company background Describe company operations to date (if any), potential legal considerations, and areas of risk and opportunity. Summarize the firm's financial condition and include past and current balance sheets, income and cash-flow statements, and other relevant financial records.

Section 3—Management team Include an organization chart, job descriptions of listed positions, and detailed resumes of the current and proposed executives. Managers should have expertise in all disciplines necessary to start and run a business. If not, mention outside consultants who will serve in these roles and describe their qualifications.

Section 4—Financial plan Provide 5-year projections for income, expenses, and funding sources. Explain the rationale and assumptions used to determine the estimates. Assumptions should be reasonable and based on industry/historical trends. Make sure all totals add up and are consistent throughout the plan. If necessary, hire a professional accountant or financial analyst to prepare these statements.

Stay clear of excessively ambitious sales projections; rather, offer "best-case," expected, and "worst-case" scenarios. These not only reveal how sensitive the bottom line is to sales fluctuations but serve as good management guides.

Section 5—Capital required Indicate the amount of capital needed to commence or continue operations and describe how these funds are to be used. Make sure the totals are the same as the ones on the cash-flow statement. This area will receive a great deal of review from potential investors so it must be clear and concise.

Section 6—Marketing plan Review industry size, trends, and the target market segment. Discuss strengths and weaknesses of the product or service and pricing compared to competition. Forecast sales in dollars and units. Outline sales, advertising, promotion, and PR programs. Make sure the costs agree with those projected in the financial statements.

Section 7—Location analysis In retailing and certain other industries, the location of the business is one of the most important factors. Provide a comprehensive demographic analysis of consumers in the area of the proposed store as well as a traffic-pattern analysis and vehicular and pedestrian counts.

Section 8—Manufacturing plan Describe minimum plant size, machinery required, production capacity, inventory and inventory-control methods, quality control, plant personnel requirements, etc. Estimates of product costs should be based on primary research.

Section 9—Appendix Include all marketing research on the product or service (off-the-shelf reports, article reprints, etc.) and other information about the product concept or market size. Provide a bibliography of all the reference materials you consulted. This section should demonstrate that the proposed company won't be entering a declining industry or market segment.

Source: R. Richard Bruno, "How to Write a Business Plan for a New Venture," *Marketing News,* March 15, 1985, p. 10.

Begin with Planning

It is amazing how many people are eager to start a small business, but have only a vague notion of what they want to do. Eventually, they come up with an idea for a business and begin discussing the idea with professors, friends, and other businesspeople. It is at this stage that the entrepreneur needs a **business plan**. A business plan is a detailed written statement that describes the nature of the business, the target market, the advantage the business will have in relation to competition, and the resources and qualifications of the owner(s). See the box, "Outline of a Comprehensive Business Plan," p. 130, for details.

A business plan forces potential owners of small businesses to be quite specific about the products or services they intend to offer and to analyze the competition, the amount of money needed to start, and other details of operation. A business plan is also mandatory for talking with bankers or other investors. (See the box below, "Tips From a Banker.") To prepare a thorough plan, a person would most likely need the assistance of a good accountant. In general, a business plan should include the following:

1 A brief description of the industry and a detailed explanation of the products or services to be offered.
2 A thorough market analysis that discusses the size of the market, the need for the new product (service), and the nature of the competition.
3 A marketing plan that includes location, signs, advertising, and display.
4 An operating plan that includes a sales forecast, financial projections, accounting procedures, and personnel requirements.
5 A comprehensive capitalization plan describing how much money the owner(s) is committing. Few banks or venture capital companies will support a new firm unless the owner(s) has a substantial financial commitment.
6 A description of the experience and expertise of the owner(s). This may include a resume, letters of recommendation, and financial statements.

> **business plan**
> A detailed written statement that describes the nature of the business, the target market, the advantages the business will have over competitors, and the resources and qualifications of the owners.

> The business plan is the grammar of an entrepreneurial venture; without it you cannot construct coherent thoughts.
> Ned Heizer

TIPS FROM A BANKER

Michael Celello is president of the People's Commercial Bank. He says that fewer than 10% of prospective borrowers come to a bank adequately prepared. He offers several tips to small business owners:

1 Pick a bank that serves businesses the size of yours and choose the bank carefully. If you are rejected by one bank, other banks can learn of your inquiry through credit bureaus and turn you down also.
2 Have a good accountant prepare a complete set of financial statements as well as a business plan and personal balance sheet. If you come to the bank with an accountant and all the necessary financial information, you increase your odds of getting a loan by 75%.
3 Make an appointment before going to the bank.
4 Demonstrate to the banker that you're a person of good character: civic-minded and respected in business and community circles.
5 Read *The Wall Street Journal* and other business publications so you can demonstrate industry knowledge and economic knowledge.
6 Ask for all the money you need and be specific. The banker may want to make separate loans for different needs with varying life expectancies.
7 Be prepared to personally guarantee the loan.

Modified from Michael Celello, "Tips From a Banker," *Inc.*, November, 1981, p. 44.

Many sources of money are available to new business ventures, but all of them call for a comprehensive business plan. The time and effort invested *before* a business is started pays off many times later. With small businesses, the big payoff is survival. To do a good job initially, small businesspeople need help. We'll discuss that next.

How many small businesses do you think have a comprehensive business plan before they start? Which part of the plan is most important? How long do you think it would take to prepare such a plan? Is the investment in time worthwhile? Why?

Accounting

If you talk with small business owners, they are likely to say that the most important assistance they need in managing the business involves accounting. They may call it record keeping, for that is the foundation of accounting. A businessperson who sets up an accounting system early will save much grief later. Computers make record keeping 100% easier and enable a small business owner to follow the progress of the business (sales, expenses, profits) on a daily basis, if necessary. An inexpensive computer system can also help with inventory control, customer records, and payroll.

A good accountant is invaluable in setting up such systems and showing you how to keep the system operating smoothly. Many business failures are caused by poor accounting practices.

Finance

The problem with most new, small businesses is that the entrepreneurs have more enthusiasm than managerial skills and capital. The economic system in America is called capitalism for a reason. It is capital (money) that enables entrepreneurs to get started; buy needed goods, services, labor, and buildings; and keep the business

PROFILE OF SUCCESS

What kind of person succeeds in small business management? A look at the chief executives from *Inc.* magazine's 100 top firms finds that the founders were about 36 years old when they started. Most are men, but 3 of the 100 were women. Being a leader seems to run in the family in that 43% had parents who were entrepreneurs and 41% work with family members. This is a well-educated group; 81% have undergraduate degrees and 46% have graduate degrees (31% in engineering, 27% in business, and 12% in law).

One must be prepared to work hard. The *average* workweek is 60 hours (6 10-hour days). Many do not take even a 1-week vacation.

It is interesting to note that in 1983, 71% of the chief officers were *not* hands-on computer users. It will be interesting to follow this statistic as more and more decision making becomes computerized through new software systems.

going. Some of the *financial* reasons cited by the Small Business Administration for failure are:

- Starting with too little capital
- Starting with too much capital and being careless in its use
- Borrowing money without planning how and when to pay it back
- Trying to do too much business with not enough capital
- Not allowing for setbacks and unexpected expenses
- Extending credit too freely

Entrepreneurs, like most people, are not highly skilled at obtaining, managing, and using money. Inadequate capitalization or poor financial management can destroy a business even when the basic idea behind the business is good and the products are accepted in the marketplace.

Sources of Funds

One of the major problems of new entrepreneurs is misinformation and lack of information about capitalization and financial management. According to most sources, a new entrepreneur has several sources of capital: banks; finance companies; venture capital organizations; government agencies such as the Small Business Administration, the Farmers Home Administration, the Economic Development Authority; and more. But the truth is that obtaining money from these sources is very difficult for most small businesses. The costs of drawing up documents, hiring accountants and lawyers, added to the psychological costs of being turned down by organization after organization, is too high for most entrepreneurs to bear.

Most small business owners, like the women who started Parsley Patch, get their seed money from personal savings. Sometimes they turn to relatives and friends for backing, often including them in the business. Banks are another source, but they often charge a very high rate of interest, one most entrepreneurs feel they cannot afford.

Small Business Investment Companies

The Small Business Investment Act recently celebrated its twenty-fifth anniversary. Since its passage, more than $4.5 billion has been invested in approximately 60,000 small businesses through **small business investment companies** (SBICs). Today, about 500 SBICs are providing seed money for new ventures. Cuts in federal capital gains taxes brought more money into such organizations in the early 1980s, as did the relaxation of pension fund regulations allowing them to invest in such ventures. Now there are billions of dollars in venture capital available for new firms. Such figures can be misleading, however, in that venture capital is pouring into some firms (for example, high-tech industries), but not others (for example, restaurants). Access to such money takes a good business plan. You can follow the ups and downs of venture capital availability in *Inc.* and *Venture* magazines.

SOURCES OF FUNDS FOR SMALL BUSINESSES (in order)

1 Personal savings and savings from family and relatives
2 Loans from banks and other financial institutions
3 Assistance from friends
4 Small Business Administration and venture capitalists

MINORITY FINANCING

Minority Enterprise Small Business Investment Companies (MESBICS), the 150 small business investment companies that bankroll minority entrepreneurs, put $88.5 million into about 1,100 businesses in 1984. Radio stations got the biggest share (35%), followed by retail stores (27%), and manufacturing (12%). In spite of such statistics, the majority of small businesses are funded by savings or from friends and partners.

Source: *The Wall Street Journal*, August 12, 1985, p. 21. Reprinted by permission of *The Wall Street Journal*, © Dow Jones & Company, Inc., 1985. All rights reserved.

Small Business Investment Company (SBIC)
Provides seed money for new ventures.

PROGRESS CHECK

- There were nine sections in the business plan. This is probably *the* most important document a small businessperson will ever make. Can you describe at least five of those sections now?

- The U.S. Small Business Administration gives six reasons why small businesses fail financially. Can you name three?

Human Resource Management

human resource management
Involves hiring, training, motivating, and compensating employees and establishing fringe benefits.

Human resource management is the job of hiring, training, motivating, compensating, and establishing fringe benefits for employees. It is not easy to find good, qualified help, even when unemployment is high. It takes time and patience to train new employees, and turnover (employees quitting for various reasons) is usually very high. That means more hiring and more training. Also, absenteeism is often high. Employees sometimes come late and leave early. People get sick. Some must be fired. In each case, the owner/manager is forced to take time away from operating the business to handle personnel problems. Few consultants are available to handle such problems, either. That is why employee relations is such an important part of small business management. A dedicated, hard-working, honest, reliable work force is an invaluable resource and one that demands great attention. One way to get such a commitment from employees is to let them share in the profits. This is a common practice, as we shall see next.

EMPLOYEE RELATIONS PLUS

Victoria Dapena de Kuscher is from Puerto Rico. She owns a Dunkin' Donuts franchise in Rockville, Maryland. It is one of the highest volume shops in the Dunkin' Donuts system.

A visit to the shop is like a tour of the United Nations. Vicki employs an Egyptian, a Thai, a Vietnamese, several Hispanics, and a black American. The Kuschers bought a house across the street from the shop, which they use as a rooming house for employees. "This way if they come off the streets they have a clean place to

sleep and wash up, and that means they work better," she says.

Vicki has a family of her own (three children), but still has time to be active in the community. Most of all, she's known for saying, "I tell job-hunters my door is always open, but it opens both ways. I don't fire anyone—they fire themselves if they don't do the job."

Vicki is a model for today's modern Hispanic women in business. She works hard, she's fair, she treats her employees well, and she's successful.

Motivating Employees

It is no surprise to find that 96% of the top growth companies listed by *Inc.* magazine share ownership and profits with their employees.[8] We have noted that the two driving forces behind capitalism are freedom and incentives. Often, it is the incentive of ownership that encourages workers in organizations to work 60 or more hours a week. If you own your own car, you are more likely to wash it, polish it, and take good care of it, the researchers say. The same is true of companies. Those who have an ownership interest tend to be more careful, more involved, more committed.

A good example of employee involvement is that of Action Instruments, Inc., an electronics firm with sales of $15 million.[9] Jim Pinto, president of the firm, says, "The future of this company is to eliminate the differences between workers, managers, and owners by making them all capitalists. If you own a piece, if you feel a part of this, you do everything to increase productivity." Almost half of the company's 285 employees are shareholders. But Action goes beyond mere ownership. Action Instruments sends employees the equivalent of executive reports weekly, telling them about profits, shipments, and key bottlenecks. Furthermore, dress is casual, everyone goes by first name, and titles are not used.

What do the employees think? Ruth Valenti, an assembly line supervisor, says, "People feel at ease and do a better job. It's like I'm self-employed—everybody is. . . . It's like everybody has their own little business—yet we all work together." Turnover rate is less than half the norm for the industry. The idea is that the key to success in any corporation is people, and people need to be motivated. The best way to motivate people is to give them as much freedom as possible, and some incentive to work effectively and efficiently, such as partial ownership in the firm.

Computers in Small Business

Someone who has never managed a small business before is amazed at the paperwork involved. Just the tax information required would challenge most people's patience. On top of that there is the need for inventory control, order processing, billing, and more. The new, small computers are a real blessing for small businesses overwhelmed by paperwork. Computers can help with inventory control, order processing, accounts receivable, purchasing, payroll, general ledger accounting, production planning, sales forecasting, budgeting, and more. Computer technology changes almost daily, so selecting the best system is complicated at best. It is a good idea to have some outside assistance to help select an appropriate system. A system that is too small or too large or that cannot handle the system problems of the business is a waste of time, money, and effort.

Computers help manage the paperwork in small businesses.

For some firms, the best idea might be to use a service bureau; that is, an organization that performs computer services for small businesses. The best way to know whether or not to buy a computer or use an outside service and what kind of computer to buy or service to hire is to do a thorough survey of computer needs.

The time spent analyzing the business and implementing a computer system will pay off in huge dividends later. Everything from inventory control to customer record keeping is much, much easier when the data is available on the computer. Most small businesspeople do not have a computer system yet, and many are highly resistant to the idea. These traditional businesspeople may find it hard to compete against more efficient new firms that use the latest technology to assist them in management.

Outside Assistance

Small business owners have learned, sometimes the hard way, that they need outside consulting advice early in the process. This is especially true of legal, tax, and accounting advice, but may also be true of marketing, finance, and other areas. Most small and medium-sized firms cannot afford to hire such experts as employees, so they must turn to outside assistance.

A good **certified public accountant** (CPA) is invaluable to a small business. He or she can help make decisions such as whether to buy or lease equipment and whether to own or rent the building. Help may also be provided for tax planning, financial forecasting, choosing sources of financing, and writing up requests for funds.

certified public accountant (CPA)
An individual who is certified by one of the states after passing a rigorous examination and meeting certain educational, moral, and job experience requirements.

Small business owners often need outside assistance.

Other small businesses may give you an idea where to find a CPA experienced in small business. It pays to shop around for advice. CPAs provide a service and should be willing to answer questions, submit references, and otherwise show that they can help a business at a reasonable fee.

Another necessary and invaluable aid is a competent, experienced lawyer—one who knows and understands small businesses. Partners have a way of forgetting agreements unless the contract is written up by a lawyer and signed. Lawyers can help in a variety of matters including leases, contracts, protection against liabilities, and more. Again, it is wise to ask for references and interview people until a personality as well as professional fit is made. Pay your CPA and lawyer a fee rather than offering them a share of profits.

Marketing decisions should be made long before a product is produced or a store opened. An inexpensive marketing research study may help determine where to locate, whom to select as your target market, and what would be an effective strategy for reaching those people. Thus a marketing consultant with small business experience is also valuable.

Two other invaluable experts are a commercial loan officer and an insurance agent. The commercial loan officer can help you design an acceptable business plan and give you valuable financial advice as well as loan you money when you need it. An insurance agent will explain all the risks associated with a small business and how to cover them most efficiently with insurance and other means (for example, safety devices and sprinkler systems).

Small businesspeople tend to laugh when they hear how many consultants or "experts" they will need. They laugh because they don't have the money to hire such experts, and they wouldn't know what to ask if they could afford them. In fact, much of this expertise could come from *one* small-business consultant who knows marketing, accounting, and some law. (It is wise to seek a lawyer, however, in any case.)

Often a local university has business professors who will advise small businesspeople for a small fee. It also is wise to seek the counsel of other small businesspeople. SCORE, the Service Corps of Retired Executives, is another good source of expertise. It is part of the Small Business Administration. In short, small businesses need expert outside assistance in areas such as accounting, finance, and legal matters, and such assistance should be obtained as soon as possible, before any major decisions are made, including whether the business should be started or not.

The Small Business Administration

The Small Business Administration (SBA) has produced many publications to assist small businesspeople in all areas of management. Funding for the SBA is slated to be cut by 50% between 1986 and 1989. Nonetheless, you can get many of its booklets at your local library.

Many of the functions of the SBA are scheduled to go to the Department of Commerce. Included is the **Service Corps of Retired Executives** (SCORE). See the box on "Causes of Small Business Failure" put out by SCORE. This office provides consulting services for small businesses free (except for expenses). The SBA also sponsors volunteers from industry, trade associations, and education who counseled small businesses. They are called the Active Corps of Executives (ACE).

The **Small Business Institute** (SBI) arm of the SBA had an interesting program for college students. Colleges would join the program by contacting the local SBA office. Then students would counsel businesses, write up a report, and, if the report met SBA standards, the school received $400.

The SBA also made direct loans to *selected* small businesses (for example, handicapped owners, Vietnam veterans, and other special cases), and guaranteed loans for small businesses with special problems with the bank.

Service Corps of Retired Executives (SCORE)
Provides consulting services to small businesses for free (except expenses).

Small Business Institute
Sponsors college students who consult with small businesses, write a report, and are paid a fee by the Small Business Administration.

When this text was written, the SBA was still operating independently. Some of its operations may have been shifted to other government agencies by now, especially the Department of Commerce. You may want to write or call Washington, D.C. for the latest information about programs and report to the class. You might also go to the library and find out what SBA booklets are available.

CAUSES OF SMALL BUSINESS FAILURE

- Plunging in without first testing the waters on a small scale.
- Underpricing goods or services.
- Underestimating how much time it will take to build a market.
- Starting with too little capital.
- Starting with too much capital and being careless in its use.
- Going into business with little or no experience and without first learning something about it.
- Borrowing money without planning just how and when to pay it back.

- Attempting to do too much business with too little capital.
- Not allowing for setbacks and unexpected expenses.
- Buying too much on capital.
- Extending credit too freely.
- Expanding credit too rapidly.
- Failing to keep complete, accurate records, so that the proprietor drifts into trouble without realizing.
- Carrying habits of personal extravagance into the business.
- Mistaking the freedom of being in business for oneself, for liberty to work or not according to whim.

Source: SCORE, the Service Corps of Retired Executives.

Small Marketers Aids (SMAs)
Booklets published by the Small Business Administration that cover topics such as keeping records, cash management, public relations, and advertising.

The **Small Marketers Aids** (SMAs) are aimed at retail and service firms, but are helpful for all kinds of businesses. They are:
- No. 71, *Checklist for Going Into Business*
- No. 147, *Sound Cash Management and Borrowing*
- No. 155, *Keeping Records in Small Business*
- No. 163, 164, *Public Relations and Advertising*
- No. 165, *Checklist for Profit Watching*

The Management Aids (MA) brochures cover everything from pricing to budgeting, organizing, and staffing. No. 218, *Business Plan for Small Manufacturers*, is good. So is No. 224, *Association Services for Small Businesses*. Small businesses are going international, as we shall see next.

INTERNATIONAL SMALL BUSINESS PROSPECTS

There are only about 240 million people in the United States, but there are about 5 billion people in the world. Obviously, the world market is potentially a much larger, much more lucrative market for small businesses than the United States alone. In spite of that potential, most small businesses still do not think international, but the trend is shifting.

In 1981, it was reported that of all the companies in the United States, only 28,000 sold overseas. U.S. exports were only 6.7% of the gross national product.[10]

One person involved in generating more international involvement of small businesses is Maureen Reagan, daughter of U.S. President Ronald Reagan. She got involved, at first, with a magazine designed to promote products from California overseas. That project grew into Sell Overseas America, the Association of American Export. The idea is to sign small companies as members and overseas buyers as associates, and help guide the small companies with foreign commerce. This is what Maureen Reagan says of the potential[11]:

> There's a major role for small companies willing to take it [overseas sales] on. Last year we guided 740 of them into export trade, from the market research stage to completion of sale and final payment on their first transaction.

Small businesses have several advantages over large businesses in international trade:

- Overseas buyers enjoy dealing with individuals rather than large corporate bureaucracies.
- Small companies can usually begin shipping much faster.
- Small companies provide a wide variety of suppliers.
- Small companies can give more personal service and more undivided attention, because each overseas account is a major source of business to them.

The growth potential of small businesses overseas is truly phenomenal. The pioneers in overseas expansion were franchised organizations such as McDonald's, Avis, Hertz, and Kentucky Fried Chicken. They were soon followed by entrepreneurs who faced too much competition in the United States and saw the opportunity to start small businesses in a foreign country. For example, there is much less competition for pizza parlors, ice cream stands, rental firms, and other small businesses in other countries.

PROGRESS CHECK

- SCORE is one program of the Small Business Administration. What else does the SBA do for small business?

- What are some of the advantages small businesses have over large businesses in selling overseas?

SUMMARY

1 Of all the nonfarm businesses in the United States, 97% are considered small by the Small Business Administration. Small business accounts for over 40% of GNP. Perhaps more important to tomorrow's graduates, 87% of the nation's new jobs in the private sector are in small businesses.
- What are the various classes of small businesses?
  There are five classes: (1) service businesses, (2) retail businesses, (3) construction firms, (4) wholesalers, and (5) manufacturers.
- What does the "small" in small business mean?
  The Small Business Administration defines a small business as one that is independently owned and operated, not dominant in its field of operation, and meets certain standards of size in terms of employees (less than 100) or sales (depending on the size of others in the industry; for example, American Motors is considered small in the auto industry).

ONCE AN ACORN

Sometimes to make it big, you first have to make it small. Conrad Hilton started out sweeping floors in a dusty New Mexico hotel. He cleaned up as owner of a famous hotel chain. John Paul Getty started with a $500 oil lease in Oklahoma and become one of America's richest men. David Packard baked the paint onto his first product in a kitchen oven. Forty-five years later, he was running a $4.7 billion company. There are anonymous men and women starting small today whose names will be household words in 20 years. Will one of those names be yours? Get started!

> Harry J. Gray
> Chairman and chief
> executive officer
> United Technologies

2 Most people have no idea how to go about starting a small business. They have some ideas and the motivation; they simply don't have the know-how.
- What hints would you give someone starting a small business?

First, learn from others. Take courses and talk with some small business owners. Second, get some experience working for others. Third, take over a successful firm. Since 67% of small businesses fail within 5 years, if the business has succeeded that long it is doing *something* right. Finally, study the latest in small business management techniques, including the use of computer for things like payroll, inventory control, and mailing lists.

3 Begin with a plan. The more effort you put into a business plan, the less grief you'll have later.
- What goes into a business plan?

See the box on p. 130.
- Should you do it all yourself?

Most small business people advise new entrepreneurs to get outside assistance in at least two areas: you need a good lawyer and a good accountant. Also, seek help from Small Business Administration publications and any other sources you can find. The more knowledge you can gain early the better.

4 It is best to have some assistance in selecting and installing a computer system as soon as money permits; in fact, it should be included in the business plan.
- How do I select a computer?

It is best to begin by studying the ways you could use the computer for inventory, payroll, and so on. Then consider the need for word processing and other software. The software (programs you will use) will determine the hardware (computer equipment) you should buy.

5 The future growth of American business in general, and small businesses as well, is in foreign markets. The pioneers of overseas small business growth were franchises of firms such as McDonald's and Hertz.

KEY TERMS

business plan   p. 131
certified public accountant (CPA) p. 136
human resource management p. 134
Service Corps of Retired Executives (SCORE)   p. 137

small business   p. 120
Small Business Institute   p. 137
Small Business Investment Company (SBIC)   p. 133
Small Marketer's Aids (SMAs)   p. 138

GETTING INVOLVED

1 Find out about the Small Business Administration's programs, such as SCORE and ACE. Write for more information and share what you learn. Go to the library to see what publications are available from the SBA. Bring some of the publications to class to review.

2 Select a small business that looks attractive as a career possibility for you. Talk to at least three people who manage such businesses. Ask about financing, personnel problems (hiring, firing, training, scheduling), accounting problems, and other managerial matters. Pick their brains. Let them be your instructors. Share your findings with the class, including whether or not the job was rewarding, interesting, and challenging and why.

3 Go to the library and get *Inc.* magazine for the last 3 years. Look through the table of contents and briefly review several articles in each issue. What kind of information is available? Make copies of interesting articles for your career file. Share what you found with the class.

4 Do a survey of local schools and the local Chamber of Commerce. What classes are available in small business management? What other resources are available, if any? Discuss.

5 Go to a local banker and discuss the financing of small businesses. What do they suggest? What is their experience with such loans? Share what you learn.

CASE ONE   BMOC: STARTING A SMALL BUSINESS AT SCHOOL

PRACTICING
MANAGEMENT DECISIONS

Many students do not wait until they complete school before they try to get their feet wet in small business management. They look around them, see thousands of students, and try to develop small businesses that would appeal to students. For example, some students assemble and sell "Home Emergency Kits" for students returning in the fall. The kits contain items like pens, chocolate chip cookies, aspirin, and other college "necessities." The kits are sold to the parents and distributed to students the first week of class as a start-the-year-right gift from home.

Many students produce and sell calendars with pictures of beautiful women on campus or male "hunks." Others sell desk mats with advertising messages on the sides. More conservative students become salespeople for beer companies, cosmetic companies, and other traditional firms. They too feel as if they are in their own business on campus, because they have exclusive sales rights but don't have to assume as many risks.

One student makes more than his professors by selling ice cream from a truck. Others try to learn the retail business by delivering pizza or other fast foods.

Dick Gilbertson considered such options when he was a student at Indiana University. He felt students might enjoy having food other than pizza and subs delivered to the dorms. His research showed that students preferred McDonald's hamburgers and Taco Bell burritos. Students said they were willing to pay $1.00 more for a Big Mac, fries, and a Coke rather than ride the mile or so to the fast-food stores. Mr. Gilbertson's company, Fast Breaks, now serves the 13,000 students at his school. Guess who his partner is? A professor of entrepreneurship at Indiana University.

Jimmy Enriquez was busy getting a degree in accounting at the University of Texas when he started two companies. One is a construction-site cleaning business that is run by his sister. It has 15 employees, grosses about $4,000 a week, and has expanded to Dallas and Houston. The other business is a vending company that leases "foosball" games. Foosball was dead when Jimmy and his brother Rocky started. But they started foosball leagues, let beginners play for free, and built a prosperous business. Jimmy's advice to potential entrepreneurs:

> If you wait until you're out of school and working for somebody else, you're going to get used to that big car—and you're not going to want to gamble with that stuff. It's better to start a company when you're a student, while you're still used to driving a junker and living like a dog.

There are now more than 100 entrepreneurship clubs on college campuses. Jimmy started an entrepreneur club at the University of Texas that has 260 members. Some 250 schools now have entrepreneurship classes.

DECISION QUESTIONS

1 What are the advantages and potential problems of starting a business while in school?

2 What kinds of entrepreneurs are operating around your school? Talk to them and learn from their experiences.

3 What opportunities exist for satisfying student needs at your school? Pick one idea, write a business plan, and discuss it in class (unless it is so good you don't want to share it; in that case, good luck).

Source based on material from articles by Ellen Wojahn, "Reading Writing, and Revenues," *Forbes,* October, 1984; Robert Johnson, "Students Make Mark Ferrying Fast Foods," *The Wall Street Journal,* December 7, 1984; and miscellaneous other sources.

PRACTICING MANAGEMENT DECISIONS

CASE TWO   BOOKER WHATLEY: CAN SMALL FARMS BE PROFITABLE?

The newspapers are full of stories about the decline of the small farm. The government spends billions of dollars each year trying to save the farmer. Clearly, farming is not a business to be entering today, especially a small farm. That is what most people think. But not Booker T. Whatley.

Booker thinks he has a formula for successful small farming. His slogan: "Stay small, but get smart." Here is the formula:

Find a small farm on a paved road within 50 miles of a city of at least 50,000 people. Grow about 10 different crops such as sweet potatoes, berries, and sweet corn. If one crop fails, you see, you will have nine others to sell. Completely irrigate the farm with a drip irrigation system to ensure against drought. The farm doesn't have to be much bigger than 25 acres. The idea is to gross about $100,000 a year. You'll need a medium-sized tractor, but not much else in the form of equipment.

The secret to success is not the production, but the marketing function. The idea is to make this a "pick-your-own" farm products place. People in town would pay you a nominal membership fee for the right to pick fresh vegetables at a cost of about 40% below supermarket prices. The theme is, "Eliminate the middleman for cheap, farm-fresh produce." That is why the farm is located relatively close to town. You save the time and money of harvesting; your customers do it for you.

For year-round income, you might add a place to raise rabbits, quail, or bees. Building and stocking a pond with fish provides a source of entertainment for customers and another cash crop. You may also want to lease out a nut tree or grapevine. You see the possibilities. The details depend on the location, local tastes, and competition.

Mr. Whatley's model was designed using a $250,000 grant from the Rockefeller Foundation (at Tuskegee Institute). One farmer in Alabama followed these ideas and has a 45-acre farm with 1,000 bee hives that produce 17,000 pounds of honey. There are also pick-your-own blueberry patches and a plot of grapevines. Some land is leased for sheep grazing. The owner is now planning a fish pond.

DECISION QUESTIONS

1 Is a business plan as necessary for starting a small farm as for starting a small retail store? What are the differences, if any?

2 Could a farmer use the concepts of learning from others and taking over from others, as described in this chapter?

3 Can you anticipate any special problems a farmer might have in starting a business versus other small businesspeople?

4 Evaluate the Whatley formula.

This case is based on Ed Bean, "Booker T. Whatley Contends His Program Will Help Small Farmers Make Big Money," *The Wall Street Journal,* October 4, 1984, p. 35.

If you are a little excited about the idea of starting your own business someday, join the crowd. Entrepreneurship is the "in thing" for the near future. Entrepreneurs are starting the new high-tech firms that will be the IBMs and Xeroxes of tomorrow. Chapter 6 will discuss such entrepreneurs. Also, you will learn about the response of large corporations to competition from small firms—Intrapreneuring, or creating small entrepreneurial areas within the firm.

One area of strong interest today is franchising. Franchising is a way of getting into business with less risk and more certain managerial assistance. Chapter 6 also describes opportunities and pitfalls to watch out for in starting a franchise.

After that, the text will go into much greater detail about business functions—marketing, accounting, personnel, finance, and so forth. This chapter merely introduced the use of such functions in small business.

ENTREPRENEURSHIP AND FRANCHISING

LEARNING GOALS

After you have read and studied this chapter, you should be able to:

- Outline four reasons for the recent growth in entrepreneurship in the United States.
- Describe five attributes needed to be a successful entrepreneur.
- Compare the benefits of entrepreneurial teams with individual entrepreneurships.
- Discuss the reasons for the growing number of women and minorities in entrepreneurship.
- Describe skunkworks and intrepreneuring and their benefits for big businesses.
- List and describe four areas of concern in evaluating a franchise.

PROFILE   DOUGLAS SCHUMANN, ENTREPRENEUR

Douglas Schumann's story is one of hundreds of thousands of similar stories that develop every year. Every year, 365 days a year, almost 2,000 new small businesses are started. Someone is willing to take a risk, invest money, and go for the reward of entrepreneurship.

Mr. Schumann was a textile marketing consultant in his fifties when he got his idea for a new business. He was visiting New Orleans and overheard someone saying it was too bad that New York chefs didn't have Louisiana crayfish. Crayfish were popular in New Orleans; why not New York?

So, acting on his idea, Mr. Schumann found a crayfish supplier in New Orleans and began calling on New York chefs. Soon he was selling $3,000 worth of crayfish a week. That's when he decided to get serious about the business. The business began very simply: no inventory, no warehouse. Shipments were picked up at the airport, split up into deliveries in the airport parking lot, and delivered.

In 1983, Mr. Schumann bought a warehouse. As he went from restaurant to restaurant, he heard that chefs were interested in Dover sole from Europe. Naturally, Mr. Schumann found a European supplier and went into the fish business. This became the largest revenue producer for the firm.

Now in his sixties, Mr. Schumann is still looking for ways to expand his product line and markets. The company now has 4 trucks, 14 employees, 3 full-time salespeople, and 5 buyers in Europe.

If Mr. Schumann's experience were unusual, that would be the end of the story, but the fact that such stories are commonplace means that we are in the age of the entrepreneur. Those who want to take the risk, but want more assured

Douglas Schumann.

If there is one coefficient of entrepreneurial success, it is energy. You may have all the ambition in the world, gobs of capital, a gambling man's soul, and business degrees covering an entire wall, but if you are not a human dynamo, forget it.

JOSEPH R. MANCUSO in
Have You Got What It Takes?

entrepreneurial venture
A business enterprise founded by an entrepreneur or entrepreneurial team that provides not only employment for the founders, but also for a significant group of other people.

Some Procter & Gamble products.

returns, are turning to franchising as an alternative to creating their own firms. We shall discuss both kinds of risk-takers in this chapter. Maybe you will be inspired to become an entrepreneur yourself. ■

THE ENTREPRENEURIAL SPIRIT

Two words that fit together perfectly are *entrepreneur* and *spirit*. It is the *entrepreneurial spirit* that creates nearly 700,000 new businesses every year. Much of the material available on forms of business and small business management fails to communicate the *spirit* of free enterprise in America. All small business owners are entrepreneurs, but not all entrepreneurs are small business owners. An entrepreneur is an innovator who organizes, manages, and assumes the risks of starting a business to develop and market a new product. Joseph Mancuso defines an **entrepreneurial venture** as a "business enterprise founded by an entrepreneur or an entrepreneurial team dedicated to providing not only employment for the founder, but also for a significant group of other people. Moreover, it accomplishes this goal by delivering new and better products or services to the marketplace."[1] The history of the United States is the history of its entrepreneurs:

- Du Pont was started in 1802 by Eleuthere Irenee du Pont. Some 18 shareholders provided $36,000 in start-up money.
- Campbell Soup began in 1869 as a partnership of Joseph Campbell and Abraham Anderson. (It could have been Anderson Soup.)
- Avon started in 1886 on $500 David McConnell borrowed from a friend.
- Kodak was launched by George Eastman in 1880 with a $3,000 investment.
- Procter & Gamble was formed in 1837 by William Procter and James Gamble with $7,000 in capital.
- Ford Motor began with an investment of $28,000 by Henry Ford and eleven associates.

Some entrepreneurs started franchise organizations in which others could share in the wealth and the adventure:

- McDonald's was founded in 1954 by Ray Kroc, who bought the franchise rights from the McDonald brothers.
- D'Lites restaurants were formed in 1981 by Doug Sheley, who had owned franchises for 18 Wendy's restaurants.

These examples tell us some things about modern entrepreneurs as compared to ordinary owners of small businesses:

1 They may start off as small businesses, but that is not their goal.
2 An entrepreneur may form a sole proprietor or partnership at first; eventually, however, most form corporations to get more capital and to expand.
3 It doesn't take much to start: a good idea, a few dollars, and lots of determination.
4 Entrepreneurs are special people, the driving force behind innovation and growth.
5 Entrepreneurs are not the same as inventors. An entrepreneur may invent a product, but he or she also has the ability to develop that invention into a successfully marketed product.

This chapter will examine the implications of entrepreneurship for you and your career. It will also explore the many possibilities of franchising, and the potential here is impressive. In 1984, there were 462,000 franchised outlets in the United States selling $457 billion worth of goods and resources.[2]

The Entrepreneurial Explosion

The Internal Revenue Service reported in 1985 that 11 million Americans worked for themselves, nearly twice as many as compared with only 5.7 million in 1970. There are many reasons why people are willing to take the risks of ownership. These reasons include:

- *Profit.* Steve Wozniak and Steve Jobs started Apple Computer in a garage. Recently, Jobs left the company, sold 1.35 million shares of his company stock for $21.4 million, kept 5.5 million shares, and found a team of workers to start a new business. Nolan Bushnell founded Atari and sold it 5 years later for $28 million. Such incentives have led many engineers and risk takers of all kinds to seek their fortune in home laboratories and small businesses.
- *Independence.* The Center for Entrepreneurial Management reports that many entrepreneurs are not in it for the money. Rather, they simply do not enjoy

All societies have hero myths. The one who slays the dragon, searches for the Holy Grail or the Golden Fleece, removes the sword, unties the knot is the entrepreneur.

Bob Schwartz,
The School for Entrepreneurs

Restaurants provide an excellent start for entrepreneurial immigrants.

working for someone else. Ten years ago, money was the lure; today, half of the new owners are more interested in the freedom of ownership.

- *Opportunity*. Many immigrants do not have the necessary skills for working in today's complex organizations. They *do* have the initiative and drive to work the long hours demanded by entrepreneurship. To them, the opportunity to share in the American dream is a tremendous lure. They are willing to sacrifice to see that their children have a chance for a good life.
- *Challenge*. *Venture* magazine concluded that entrepreneurs were excitement junkies who flourished on taking risks, but others disagree. Nancy Flexman and Thomas Scanlan wrote a book called *Running Your Own Business*. They contend that entrepreneurs take moderate, calculated risks; they are not just gambling. In general, though, entrepreneurs seek *achievement* more than *power*.[3]

COLLEGIATE ENTREPRENEURS

The Association of College Entrepreneurs started with 7 member colleges in 1983 and grew to 170 member colleges by 1985. Edward Birch, vice-chancellor of the University of California, Santa Barbara says, "I think they see this as an exercise that's going to prepare them for the big game."

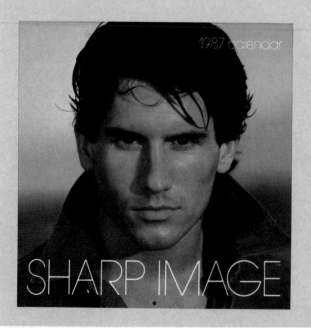

For many students, however, being an entrepreneur while in college is more than an exercise—it is an excellent way to pay for college and begin a career. For example, Jed Roth started a car-cleaning business that earned him $15,000 in his senior year. After graduation, he stayed in the business and soon had revenues of $100,000. Like all entrepreneurs, however, Jed is finding that it takes long hours and often 7-day weeks to succeed in such a business.

Naturally, many student-run businesses fail, but failure in a business is a learning tool too. Dan Bienenfeld began selling calendars featuring photos of good-looking men about campus at UC, Santa Barbara. He grossed $10,000, a modest start. He then took on a partner and a vice-president for production and someone to invest $80,000.

Using his experience, Dan began selling more effectively to card shops, boutiques, book stores, and other retailers. He also added new products to the line—posters and gift wrap. Now the business is expected to reach $3 million in sales. The line now includes 21 different items, including the popular 1986 Madonna and 1987 Sharp Image calendars.

Is there an entrepreneurs club on your campus? Would you like to start one? Write the Center for Entrepreneurship, Wichita State University, Wichita, Kansas, 67208. It is an excellent way for students to learn the secrets of success and failure from other student entrepreneurs.

Source: Karen Blumenthal, "On Campuses, Making Dean's List Comes Second to Making a Profit," *The Wall Street Journal*, April 4, 1985. Reprinted by permission of *The Wall Street Journal*; © Dow Jones & Company, Inc., 1985. All rights reserved.

What Does It Take to Be an Entrepreneur?

Would you succeed as an entrepreneur? A list of attributes you would look for in yourself includes[4]:

1 *Self-directed.* You should be thoroughly comfortable and thoroughly self-disciplined even though you are your own boss.
2 *Self-nurturing.* You must believe in your idea when no one else does, and be able to replenish your own enthusiasm.
3 *Action-oriented.* Great business ideas are not enough. The most important thing is a burning desire to realize, actualize, and build your dream into reality.
4 *High energy level.* You must be emotionally, mentally, and physically able to work long and hard.
5 *Tolerant of uncertainty.* Successful entrepreneurs take only *calculated* risks (if they can help it). Still, they must be able to take some risks.

Some advice for entrepreneurs is as follows[5]:

- Research your market, but do not take too long to act.
- Start your business when you have a customer.
- Try your venture as a sideline at first.
- Plan your objectives within specific time frames.
- Surround yourself with people who are smarter than yourself—including an outside board of directors.
- Do not be afraid to fail.
- Have a great accountant.

Percent of executives who operated a business while in high school or college

Small business executive 16%

Fortune's 500 top executives 19%

Inc.'s 500 fastest-growing entrepreneurs 32%

Individual Entrepreneurs

Maybe you cannot meet all of these requirements now, but now you know what to shoot for. Entrepreneurship in the 1970s and early 1980s was led by a few dynamic *individuals:* Adam Osborne of Osborne Computer, Sirjang Lai "Juge" Tandon of Tandon Corporation, Steve Jobs of Apple Computer, and Lore Hays of Vector Graphic, Incorporated. All these companies were highfliers at first, but got into trouble, and most are being run by someone else now. The trend in the late 1980s is to develop entrepreneurial *teams.* What makes teams more effective than individuals?

THINKING IT THROUGH

Do you know anyone who seems to have the entrepreneurial spirit? What about him or her makes you say that? Are there any similarities between the characteristics demanded of an entrepreneur and those of a professional athlete? Would an athlete be a good prospect for entrepreneurship? Why or why not?

Entrepreneurial Teams

An **entrepreneurial team** is a group of experienced people from different areas of business who join together to form a managerial team with the skills needed to develop, make, and market a new product. A team may be better than an individual entrepreneur because it combines creative skills with production and marketing skills right from the start. The team assures more cooperation and coordination among functions.

entrepreneurial team
A group of experienced people from different areas of business who join together to form a managerial team with the skills needed to develop, make, and market new products.

One of the exciting new companies of the 1980s is Compaq Computer.[6] It was started by three senior managers at Texas Instruments: Bill Murto, Jim Harris, and Rod Canion. All three were bitten by the entrepreneurial bug, and decided to go out on their own. They debated starting a Mexican restaurant, a company to produce hard disks for computers, or a business built around a beeping device for finding car keys. However, they finally decided to build a portable personal computer compatible with the IBM PC.

The key to Compaq's success was that it was built around this "smart team" of experienced managers. The chief executive officers in such firms are not order givers, but coordinators whose main task is to tap the potential of their "teams." A study of 90 West Coast companies found that a strong management team was the top priority for success.

At Compaq, the team wanted to combine the discipline of a big company with an environment where people could feel they were participating in a successful venture. The trio of entrepreneurs recruited seasoned managers with similar desires. A 14-year veteran of Texas Instruments set up a state-of-the-art accounting system. A senior vice president from Datapoint became operations manager, and an IBM veteran became sales and resource manager.

All of the managers work as a team. That is, the treasurer and top engineer contribute to production and marketing decisions. Everyone works together to conceive, develop, and market products. In its first year, Compaq generated $11 million in sales, the hottest performance in the history of American business.

In 1984, Compaq was faced with a challenge from IBM's new "super" PC. To combat the competition, Compaq set up an in-house entrepreneurial team. As engineers were designing the product, manufacturing managers were setting up a factory to produce it. Within *6 months,* Compaq began shipping its Deskpro 286s to retailers. They shipped 10,000 computers in the first 90 *days!* It is one of the company's most successful products.

Quick adaptation to the market is what enables entrepreneurial teams to start new businesses and to stay in business. Large corporations simply cannot move as quickly, or at least haven't until recently.

No group has taken more advantage of the entrepreneurial age than women. Women are not just *joining* the labor force; they are starting new firms to enlarge the need for labor.

Women Entrepreneurs

The entrepreneur is a poet and packager—an actualizer and a visualizer.

Bob Schwartz,
The School for Entrepreneurs

Women entrepreneurs are the fastest-growing segment of the nation's small business population. In 1984, there were 3.1 million women business owners. The number of female sole proprietors increased 46% in the 5-year period ending in 1982.

The U.S. Small Business Administration cites several reasons for this dramatic growth. Because of wider opportunities for female employees over the past several years, women have gained valuable work experience that is directly transferable to entrepreneurial skills. While employed in traditional occupations, women acquired the necessary experience for running all types of ventures, from retail stores to real estate companies. Always a path to upgrading personal potential, educational advancement has served as a direct avenue for women who desire to start their own businesses. More women are focusing on higher education in nontraditional fields such as aerospace, engineering and electronics. The narrowing income gap between men and women should continue to narrow as more women start businesses in those nontraditional professions and occupations.[7]

Minority Entrepreneurs

Throughout this book we have discussed minority businesspeople. The last survey of minority-owned enterprises found 393,000 *self-employed* nonwhite persons. They represented 70% of all minority-owned firms.[8]

Black managers who feel they are being passed over for high-level executive positions are turning to entrepreneurship instead. Lawrence Robertson, for example, was a financial manager at Ford. When the promotions stopped coming, he and six other minority finance managers and accountants formed Asset Management International.

Caroline Jones began as a secretary at the J. Walter Thompson ad agency. She became a copywriter and moved up through the ranks of several advertising agencies until she reached the vice-president level at Batten, Barton, Durstine, and Osborne (BBD&O). She then started Ming-Jones Advertising, Incorporated with two other black vice-presidents from big agencies.[9]

The new journal *Black Enterprise* is an interesting one for students to read. It has dozens of success stories about successful entrepreneurs and how they did it. The box below is from an article in *Black Enterprise*.

The major agency that implements federal policies to benefit minority entrepreneurs is the **Minority Business Development Agency** (MBDA) in the Department of Commerce. It funds minority development centers that provide management, marketing, and technical assistance at the local level. The Agency also awards grants to other organizations that assist minority firms. MBDA has six regional and six district offices. By contacting one of these offices, a minority businessperson can receive much guidance and assistance.[10]

Minority Business Development Agency
Awards grants to other organizations to assist minority enterprises, maintains an information clearing house for minority business development, conducts research, and otherwise helps minority enterprises.

TOP 15 BLACK-OWNED BUSINESSES

1 Johnson Publishing Co., Inc. (Publishing, cosmetics, and TV production)
2 Motown Industries (Entertainment)
3 H.J. Russell Construction, Inc. (Construction/development/communications)
4 Philadelphia Coca-Cola Bottling Company, Inc. (Soft drink bottling)
5 Soft Sheen Products, Inc. (Hair care products manufacturer)
6 G & M Oil Co., Inc. (Petroleum Products)
7 Interstate Landscaping Co. (General contracting)
8 TLC Group, Inc. (Paper patterns for home sewing)

9 Systems and Applied Sciences Corp. (Computer and electronic data systems)
10 Wardoco, Inc. (Commercial fuel oils)
11 Porterfield Wilson Pontiac-GMC Truck-Mazda, Inc. (Automobile sales and service)
12 Bing Steel, Inc. (Steel processing and distribution)
13 M&M Products Co., Inc. (Hair care products manufacturer and distributor)
14 Baranco Pontiac, Inc. (Automobile sales and service)
15 Dick Griffey Productions (Entertainment)

Source: "The Top 100 Black Businesses," *Black Enterprise*, June 1986, p. 105.

Skunkworks

Entrepreneurship has been so successful in small firms that larger corporations are trying to imitate the results. But how do you create an atmosphere of innovation and daring in a stodgy old firm? The answer is to break away from the traditional

skunkworks
A highly innovative, fast-moving entrepreneurial unit operating at the fringes of a corporation.

An intrapreneur developed the Pontiac Fiero.

An intrapreneur at 3M developed Post-it note pads.

tight organization structures and create small, creative entrepreneurial centers where innovative ideas are developed.

The name given to highly innovative, fast-moving entrepreneurial units operating at the fringes of the corporation is **skunkworks.** The term comes from the *L'il Abner* comic strip and was first used at the Lockheed California Company. A man named Clarence L. "Kelly" Johnson organized a division of the company in 1943 to design, build, and test the first tactical jet fighter in the United States—the XP 80.[11] The plane was designed, built, and flown 143 days after the project was started. Johnson's philosophy was, "Do the best possible job in the simplest way, at the cheapest cost, in the quickest time." He hand-picked a few good men, shared his vision, asked for their best, and provided the leadership needed to make the project work. Today, "skunkworks" describes any highly-motivated entrepreneurial team in a large corporation that emphasizes innovation.

Intrapreneuring

Intrapreneurs are people with entrepreneurial skills employed in corporations. The idea is to use a company's existing resources—human, financial, and physical—to launch new products and generate new profits. At 3M Company, for example, managers are expected to come up with at least 25% new products every 5 years.

Have you seen those yellow Post-it note pads people use to stick messages up on a wall? That product was developed by Art Fry, a 3M employee. He needed a piece of sticky paper for marking the pages of a hymnal without falling out. The 3M labs soon produced a sample, but distributors thought the product was silly, and market surveys were negative. Nonetheless, 3M kept sending samples to secretaries of top executives. Eventually, after 12 years, the orders began pouring in, and Post-its became a $12 million winner.

Hewlett-Packard call their entrepreneurial approach The Triad Development Process. The idea is to link the design engineer, the manufacturer, and the marketer (the Triad) in a team from the design phase on. Everything, even the assembly line, shuts down if the Triad team wants to test an innovation.

Some business schools are now teaching courses on how big corporations can develop new products and adapt to changing markets by using intrapreneuring. The first school for intrapreneurs was started in Sweden in 1980 by the Foresight Group. They now have a similar school in the United States.

If you are interested in this subject, a good book to read is Gifford Pinchot's *Intrapreneuring* (Harper & Row, 1985). He defines an intrapreneur as:

> Any of the "dreamers who do." Those who take hands-on responsibility for creating innovation of any kind within the organization. The intrapreneur may be the creator or inventor but is always the dreamer who figures out how to turn an idea with a profitable reality.

Some intrapreneurs cited by Pinchot include:
- Hulki Aldikacti, who developed the Pontiac Fiero
- Lee Iacocca and the Ford Mustang
- Michael Phillips and Master Charge
- John Webb and the Xerox 2600
- Stuart Sands and Intel's bubble memory[12]

The advantages of being an entrepreneur within a firm include:
- *Employee morale*. It is fun and exciting to be able to work on your own products with much freedom.

intrapreneur
A person with entrepreneurial skills who is employed in a corporation to launch new products; such people take hands-on responsibility for creating innovation of any kind in an organization.

- *Marketing clout.* P.D. Estridge developed a good personal computer, but it was infinitely more attractive with the IBM name on it.
- *Technology base.* The research laboratories at major corporations have everything one needs to launch a product.
- *Financial backing.* An obvious point, but entrepreneurs can find much venture capital too, *outside of major firms.*
- *People to help.* Some of the best minds are already in corporations where they can be of great help.
- *Information resources.* It is expensive to set up the complex computer systems that are already available in major firms.

> We have lived through the age of big industry and the age of the giant corporation. But I believe this is the age of the entrepreneur.
>
> President Ronald Reagan

PROGRESS CHECK

- What are "skunkworks" and how did they get started?

- What are some attributes you would need to be a successful entrepreneur?

- What are some advantages of being an entrepreneur within a large firm (intrapreneuring)?

FRANCHISES

Not everyone is cut out to be an entrepreneur, or an intrapreneur either. The personality called for is that of a risk-taker and innovator. Some people are more cautious or simply want more assurance of success. For them, there is a vastly different strategy for owning a business; that is, buying a franchise. Some entrepreneur has developed a winning product concept, and you can share in the dream by paying him or her for the right to use that concept by buying franchise rights. **Franchisees** are hard-working, dedicated businesspeople. They have the energy and the drive of an entrepreneur, but they may not have the innovativeness. Entrepreneurships and franchising are thus complementary processes. The entrepreneur develops the *idea* and the franchisee implements it at the local level.

Basically, a **franchise** is an arrangement whereby someone with a good idea for a business sells the rights to use the business name and to sell the products or services in a given territory. The **franchisor** (the company that developed the idea) may help you (the *franchisee*) find a place to locate the business; sell you (at low cost) signs, materials, and everything else you need to get started; teach you how to manage the business; and give you all kinds of help with promotion and other business-related problems. About one out of every three retailers is a franchise, so you shouldn't have much difficulty finding places to visit where you can get more information from franchise owner/managers.

franchisee
A person who buys a franchise (see *franchise*).

franchise
An arrangement whereby someone with a good idea for a business sells the rights to use the business name and sell its products or services in a given territory.

franchisor
A company that develops a product concept and sells others the rights to make and sell the products.

Advantages of Franchising

Perhaps McDonald's is the name most people associate with franchises. But names such as Pizza Hut, Burger King, Kentucky Fried Chicken, AAMCO, H&R Block, and others are also familiar to people, not only in the United States, but around the world. Franchised *service* companies provide services from lawn care and day care to real estate and legal counseling. (See Figure 6-1, p. 154, for a more comprehensive list.) Franchising has been a rapidly growing part of the economy throughout the world, so it must have advantages. Some of them are:

1 *Management assistance.* A franchisee (the person who buys a franchise) has

FIGURE 6-1

Franchising in the United States.

PRODUCTS/SERVICES	NO. OF ESTABLISHMENTS			SALES ($ IN MILLIONS)		
	TOTAL	COMPANY-OWNED	FRANCHISEE-OWNED	TOTAL	COMPANY-OWNED	FRANCHISEE-OWNED
Automotive products/services	38,660	4,358	34,302	9,782	3,052	6,730
Auto/truck rental	13,219	2,236	10,983	4,676	2,667	2,009
Business aids and services						
Accounting/credit/general	2,843	46	2,797	173	16	157
Employment services	4,666	1,484	3,182	2,094	939	1,155
Printing/copying	4,919	142	4,777	769	32	737
Tax preparation	9,742	4,285	5,457	399	204	195
Real estate	16,398	552	15,846	3,592	350	3,242
Miscellaneous	15,063	441	14,622	2,768	399	2,369
Construction/home improvement/maintenance/cleaning	18,881	660	18,221	2,975	1,007	1,968
Convenience stores	15,867	8,821	7,046	11,279	6,760	4,519
Educational products/services	7,504	861	6,643	733	140	593
Fast-food restaurants	74,842	23,087	51,755	44,148	15,361	28,787
Hotels/motels/campgrounds	6,830	1,058	5,772	13,352	3,553	9,799
Laundry/dry cleaning	3,746	122	3,624	328	31	297
Recreation/entertainment/travel	6,829	128	6,701	1,263	152	1,111
Rental (equipment) services	2,452	272	2,180	699	195	504
Retailing: Nonfood	43,266	13,192	30,074	15,579	5,297	10,282
Retailing: Food (Nonconvenience)	16,115	1,980	14,135	9,345	2,519	6,826
Miscellaneous	4,387	472	3,915	850	109	741
Total	306,229	64,197	242,032	124,804	42,783	82,021

Source: *Franchising in the Economy, 1982–1984,* U.S. Department of Commerce, Bureau of Industrial Economics, January, 1984. (1984 data are estimated by respondents to various government surveys.)

a much greater chance of succeeding in business because he or she has an established product (for example, McDonald's hamburgers), help with choosing a location and promotion, and assistance in all phases of operation. It is like having your own store with full-time consultants available when you need them.

2 *Personal ownership.* A franchise operation is still *your* store and you enjoy much of the freedom, incentives, and profit of any sole proprietor. You are still your own boss, although you must follow more rules, regulations, and procedures than you would with your own privately owned store.

3 *Nationally recognized name.* It is one thing to open a new hamburger outlet or ice cream store. It is quite another to open a new Burger King or a Baskin-Robbins ice cream shop. With an established franchise, you get instant recognition and established customers from around the world.

4 *Financial advice and assistance.* A major problem with small businesses is arranging financing and learning to keep good records. Franchisees get valuable assistance in these areas and periodic advice from people with expertise in these areas.

Disadvantages of Franchises

Of course, there are costs associated with joining a franchise that must be considered. You must be sure to check out any such arrangement with present franchisees and to discuss the idea with a lawyer. Some disadvantages of franchises include:

1 *Shared profit.* The franchisor often demands a large share of the profits, or a percentage commission based on *sales,* not profit. Often the share taken by the franchisor is so high that the owner does not make a profit that matches the time and effort involved in owning and managing a business.

2 *Management regulation.* Management assistance has a way of becoming managerial orders, directives, and limitations. Franchisees may feel burdened by the company's rules and regulations and lose the spirit and incentive of being their own boss with their own business. See Figure 6-2 below for more details.

BENEFITS	DRAWBACKS
■ Nationally recognized name and established reputation	■ High initial franchise fee
■ Help with finding a good location	■ Additional fees may be charged for marketing
■ A proven management system	■ A monthly percentage of gross sales may go to the franchisor
■ Tested methods for inventory and operations management	■ Possible competition from other nearby franchisees
■ Financial advice and assistance	■ No freedom to select decor or other design features
■ Training in all phases of operation	■ Little freedom to determine management procedures
■ Promotional assistance	■ Many rules and regulations to follow
■ Periodic management counseling	
■ Proven record of success	
■ It's your business!	

FIGURE 6-2

The benefits and drawbacks of an established franchise

On the whole, the benefits outweigh the drawbacks for many people. That is why franchising is so popular today.

FRANCHISING'S BILLIONAIRE

Forbes magazine has said that "Few American fortunes have grown so large as William Millard's." How did he do that? He was the franchisor for ComputerLand during the rapid rise of personal computers in the 1980s. By 1984, there were 783 ComputerLand stores doing $1.4 billion worth of business. Millard owned 96% of ComputerLand and received 9% of the revenue as the franchisor.

Much of the success of ComputerLand is credited to its president from 1976 to 1983, Ed Faber. Mr. Millard made Mr. Faber vice-chairman and made his daughter president in 1983.

ComputerLand franchisees became concerned in the mid-1980s with the slowdown in computer sales. There was even a chance of ComputerLand filing bankruptcy proceedings as a result of an investor disagreement.

ComputerLand provides a great example of opportunities in franchising in the 1980s. One can become a billionaire as a franchisor and a millionaire as a franchisee. But when competition stiffens and demand falls, franchises can fail as quickly as they rise.

Source: Kathleen K. Weigner, "The Beleaguered Billionaire," *Forbes,* August 26, 1985, pp. 33-35. Reprinted by permission of *Forbes* magazine; © Forbes Inc., 1985.

EXAMPLES OF FRANCHISE OPPORTUNITIES

MCDONALD'S CORPORATION

One McDonald's Plaza
Oak Brook, IL 60521

Douglas Moreland
License Dir.
(312) 887-6196

A McDonald's franchise grants the rights and authorizations necessary to operate a specific McDonald's restaurant facility for a period of time, usually 20 years.

HISTORY:		Full
Est-1955; 1st Fran-1955		
Units	09/83	12/84
Co-Owned	2302	2433
Franchised	5288	5682
Total	7590	8115
US:6131; CAN:437; FOR:999		
US:50 States:		
Full-Time Staff:		3K

FINANCIAL:	
Cash Investment:	$120-141K
Total Investment:	$299-353K
Fees: Franchise	$13K
Royalty 11%, Advert	4%
Contract Period:	26Yr/ 0Yr
Master Fran. Available:	No
Passive Owner:	Not Allowed
Parent:	
EXPANSION: US-	All US
Canada-Yes, Overseas-Yes	

SERVICES/MISCELLANEOUS:

Financial Assistance:	No
Site Selection:	NA
Lease Negotiation:	NA
Co-op Advertising:	Yes

Training: 12-18 mos. In-store Training, 2 Wks, Headquarters

On-Going: B,C,D,E,F,G,H,I

Avg. Employees: 3 full-time, 61 part-time

Exclusive Territory:	No
Expand in Territory:	No
Experience:	Unnecessary

REDD PEST CONTROL COMPANY, INC.

4114 Northview Drive
Jackson, Mississippi 39206
Marvin Jordon

Description of Operation: Pest and termite control
Number of Franchises: 5 in Tennessee, Louisiana, Mississippi and Florida
In Business Since: 1946
Equity Capital Needed: $15,000 minimum
Financial Assistance Available: Franchisee will be able to factor his accounts receivable and furnish financing for equipment and vehicles.
Training Provided: 3 to 6 months depending on background
Managerial Assistance Available: Extensive assistance for the first year; additional assistance thereafter, as required.
Information Submitted: March 1984

DAY'S EASE, INC.

12045 Francesca Dr.
Grand Blanc, MI 48439

Sally Tartoni
1976/Approx. $3,000
3 in MI and OH

Franchisor of house cleaning services. Four Daisy Girls, insured and bonded, work as a team to clean a house in less than 2 hours, allowing the lady or man of the house to have a day of ease.

These entries are from Robert Bond's *The Source Book of Franchise Opportunities* (McDonald's and Day's Ease) and the Department of Commerce's *Franchise Opportunity Handbook*. Note the cost of a franchise varies from $299,000 to $353,000 for McDonald's to as little as $3,000 for Day's Ease.

Buying a Franchise

Obviously, there are many advantages *and* disadvantages that need to be explored before buying a franchise (see Figure 6-2). Nonetheless, it *is* an excellent way to become an owner/manager and make a nice salary plus profit.

There are many things to do before jumping into a franchise. The Checklist for Evaluating a Franchise presented here points out that you should have a lawyer evaluate the franchise. Furthermore, you have to analyze yourself, the franchise, and the market. Take some time to go over the checklist; it will help you understand many of the questions that franchisees should ask if they want a successful venture.

CHECKLIST FOR EVALUATING A FRANCHISE

THE FRANCHISE

- Did your lawyer approve the franchise contract you are considering after he studied it paragraph by paragraph?
- Does the franchise give you an exclusive territory for the length of the franchise?
- Under what circumstances can you terminate the franchise contract and at what cost to you?
- If you sell your franchise, will you be compensated for your good will?

THE FRANCHISOR

- How many years has the firm offering you a franchise been in operation?
- Has it a reputation for honesty and fair dealing among the local firms holding its franchise?
- Has the franchisor shown you any certified figures indicating exact net profits of one or more going firms which you personally checked yourself with the franchisee?
- Will the firm assist you with:
  A management training program?
  An employee training program?
  A public relations program?
  Capital?
  Credit?
  Merchandising ideas?
- Will the firm help you find a good location for your new business?

- Has the franchisor investigated you carefully enough to assure itself that you can successfully operate one of their franchises at a profit both to them and to you?

YOU—THE FRANCHISEE

- How much equity capital will you have to have to purchase the franchise and operate it until your income equals your expenses?
- Are you prepared to give up some independence of action to secure the advantages offered by the franchise?
- Are you ready to spend much or all of the remainder of your business life with this franchisor, offering its product or service to your public?

YOUR MARKET

- Have you made any study to determine whether the product or service which you propose to sell under franchise has a market in your territory at the prices you will have to charge?
- Will the population in the territory given you increase, remain static, or decrease over the next 5 years?
- Will the product or service you are considering be in greater demand, about the same, or less demand 5 years from now than today?
- What competition exists in your territory already for the product or service you contemplate selling?

Source: *Franchise Opportunities Handbook,* U.S. Department of Commerce, 1984.

COMPETITION AMONG FRANCHISED BUSINESSES

For a potential entrepreneur, a franchise is often the path to quick riches. The parent organization provides guidance, sets standards, and supplies national advertising. The Commerce Department reported that only 4% of all franchises failed in 1 year.

Franchising is not a guarantee of success for a small business, however. Competition can be intense. Over 40% of all eating places are franchises, including 20,000 hamburger outlets, 12,000 pizza parlors, and 10,000 chicken outlets.

A franchise can cost as little as $1,000 for an Angie's Inc. industrial catering truck to $1.5 million for a Good Taco, Inc. store. To check out the possibilities, it is best to talk with several owners of the franchise that interests you. Learn about expenses and how much the franchisor takes "off the top" from sales. Often there is little profit left for the hard-working owner/manager. But sometimes the profits are great. Check carefully first, and the risks can be minimized.

Source: Teri Agins, "Owning Franchises Has Pluses, but Wealth Isn't Guaranteed," *The Wall Street Journal,* October 22, 1981, p. 33.

FAST-FOOD FRANCHISES IN INTERNATIONAL MARKETS (1985)

COMPANY	OVERSEAS UNITS
McDonald's	1,831
Kentucky Fried Chicken	1,773
Pizza Hut	481
Burger King	364
Wendy's	201

Source: Haya El Nasser, "U.S.A. Fast-Food Speeds Abroad," USA Today, January 27, 1986.

Franchising in International Markets

Anyone who has traveled overseas knows that large franchisors such as McDonald's, 7-Eleven stores and Hertz have many franchises overseas. If you go back to those countries now, you will find that newer, smaller franchises are going international as well.

Video Update, Inc., a franchisor of video rental stores, recently licensed a joint venture in Malaysia to open 100 Video Update stores. A similar venture is being negotiated for Singapore. What makes franchising successful in international mar-

A McDonald's franchise overseas.

kets is what makes them successful in the United States: convenience and a predictable level of service and quality.

Now you can go to Osaka, Japan and visit Studebaker's, a restaurant and bar franchise that features American songs from the 1950s and 1960s. A Wurlitzer jukebox plays the hully gully and the bunny hop while waitresses in 1950s dress serve the food and beverages. There are 542 McDonald's stores in Japan as well.

Many franchises are being solicited by potential overseas franchisees. That is what lured Gymboree, a franchisor of children's gym centers, to Spain, France, Japan, and South Korea.

Franchisors must be careful to adapt to the region, however. In France, the people thought a furniture stripping place called Dip 'N' Strip was a bar that featured strippers. In general, however, U.S. franchises are doing well all over the world and are adapting to the local customs and desires of consumers.[13]

PROGRESS CHECK

■ Which kinds of products/services have the most franchised outlets?

■ This chapter lists ten benefits of a franchise and seven drawbacks. How many do you recall?

SUMMARY

1 An *entrepreneur* is an innovator who organizes, manages, and assumes the risks of starting a business to develop and market a new product idea. E.I. du Pont, Henry Ford, William Procter, and Joseph Campbell were all entrepreneurs who started companies that have grown into corporate giants.

■ What is the difference between an entrepreneur and a typical small business owner?

An entrepreneur is more of an innovator, a dreamer, and an organizer who can take a product idea from conception stage through production and marketing.

■ Why the sudden interest in entrepreneurship?

People like Steve Jobs at Apple Computer and Nolan Bushnell at Atari are today's new business superstars with assets in the millions. The opportunity and challenge are clear.

■ What does it take to be an entrepreneur?

A person must be self-directed, self-nurtured, action-oriented, tolerant of uncertainty, and have a high energy level.

2 Individual entrepreneurs have often failed to maintain leadership of their firms.

■ What have modern entrepreneurs done to assure longer terms of management?

They have formed *entrepreneurial teams* that have expertise in more than innovation.

3 Women and minorities are especially attracted to entrepreneurship.

■ Why women and minorities?

Entrepreneurship enables a person to grow to his or her potential. Sexism and racism cannot hold an entrepreneur down.

4 *Intrapreneuring* is big business's answer to the entrepreneur.
  ■ What is intrapreneuring?
    It is the establishment of entrepreneurial centers within a larger firm where people can innovate and develop new product ideas internally.
  ■ Are there successful intrapreneurs?
    P.O. Estridge developed the IBM Personal Computer, and Lee Iacocca was the intrapreneur behind the Ford Mustang.
5 A franchisee can participate in the entrepreneurial age by buying the rights to market a new product innovation in his or her area.
  ■ Are franchisees entrepreneurs?
    All business owners have been called entrepreneurs because they have taken the risk of owning a business. The entrepreneurs we have discussed in this chapter, however, are a different breed. Clearly there is more than one definition of an entrepreneur.
6 A *franchisee* is a person who buys a franchise.
  ■ What are the benefits and drawbacks of being a franchisee?
    The benefits include a nationally recognized name and reputation, a proven management system, promotional assistance, and the pride of ownership. Drawbacks include high franchise fees, managerial regulation, and shared profits.

KEY TERMS

entrepreneurial venture p. 146	**franchisor** p. 153
entrepreneurial team p. 149	**intrapreneur** p. 152
franchise p. 153	**Minority Business Development**
franchisee p. 153	**Agency** p. 151
	skunkworks p. 152

GETTING INVOLVED

1 Go to the library and find past issues of *Venture* and *Inc.* magazines. Read about the entrepreneurs who are heading today's dynamic new businesses. Have several students in the class write profiles about various entrepreneurs and report to the class. A wonderful source is David Silver's *Entrepreneurial Megabucks*. It has profiles of 100 entrepreneurs from the last 25 years.

2 While at the library, go to the reference section and find the *Franchise Opportunities Handbook* or a similar listing of franchise opportunities. Glance through the listings looking for the cost of a franchise, the variety of franchises available, and other interesting information. If several people each write down two entries, the class will have enough information to give them a good feel for franchising opportunities.

3 Visit a franchise other than a fast food restaurant and see what the owner has to say about the benefits and drawbacks of franchising. Would they buy the franchise again if they could start all over? What mistakes did they make, if any? What advice would they give a student interested in franchising?

4 Research as many franchise possibilities as you can find and write a brief report (2 pages) on the one you find most attractive. Include the cost of obtaining the franchise, the training provided, the nature of the business, and other details. Put all the reports in a binder and make it available to the class.

CASE ONE   3M COMPANY, INTRAPRENEURIAL LEADER

This year the 3M Company will sell about 90,000 different products from 45 separate divisions employing more than 5,000 engineers and scientists making $7.7 billion in sales. A $7.7 billion company hardly sounds like an entrepreneurial hideout, but it is.

Employees are allowed to spend some 15% of their work time on new ideas without having to account for that time in any short-term way. In the long term, of course, the company expects results, and results they get. That's where the 90,000 products come from. Not all the discoveries are planned, however.

Patsy Sherman, for example, accidentally spilled a test chemical on her tennis shoe (people dress informally at 3M). She discovered that chemicals and dirt could not remove or stain the spot. This discovery led to the profitable Scotchgard fabric protector.

Remember those yellow Post-it notes that Art Fry developed for marking his Sunday hymnal? Well, Art started at the University of Minnesota and worked as an intern at 3M. The company was impressed with Fry's block-printing product for art schools. It was 20 years later that Fry developed Post-it notes.

Fry now works with 50 or so new products a year, 99% of which are not saleable. If a product *is* successful, Fry gets to follow it through production and marketing. Then it's back to the lab for more research.

To give you some idea of how wide the product line is at 3M, let's look at some products they are working on. One hot item is a programmable optical disk; others include bioelectronic ears and space shuttle insulation. There is an Electronic and Information Technologies Sector, a Graphics Sector, an Industrial and Consumer Sector, and a Life Sciences Sector. The company started out as Minnesota Mining and Manufacturing (3M) company. It has come a long way from the mining days. Most of its success is due to intrapreneuring.

DECISION QUESTIONS

1 Why is it important for laboratory people to follow their new product ideas through production and marketing?
2 How can a multibillion dollar corporation keep its entrepreneurial spirit alive?
3 Is it healthy for a corporation to be involved in such widely diverse industries as Scotch tape and bioelectronic ears? Doesn't that prevent the corporation from having expertise in all those areas?
4 Could 3M survive without intrapreneuring?

Source: Peter Hall, "What It's Like to Work for 3M," *Business Week's Guide to Careers*.

CASE TWO   OPPORTUNITIES IN FRANCHISING

In 1985, there were 500,000 franchised businesses in the United States. About one third of all retail sales are through franchises, which employ approximately 5.3 million people. The Department of Commerce reports that each year since 1971 less than 5% of franchise-owned outlets have discontinued organization (but many have been sold at big losses). Compare that with the failure rate of sole proprietorship (25% to 33 ⅓% in the first year), and franchises start to look rather attractive.

Hot franchises in 1985 included videogame, software, and home computer stores. The older fields, such as restaurants and auto repair shops, are growing more slowly. Some 20 or 30 years ago, you could get a McDonald's or AAMCO transmission franchise for about $10,000. Today, a McDonald's franchise will cost $250,000 to

$400,000 depending on the location. Nonetheless, McDonald's is still a good investment. An average McDonald's tops $1 million in revenue, and an operator may net $100,000 or more. Newer franchises cost less, but involve more risk. You can, for example, get a Uniforce Temporary Personnel franchise for $90,000.

The success stores are many. MAACO Enterprises was founded in 1972. It specializes in auto body repair and painting. By 1985, it had 384 units in 42 states and Canada selling $170 million worth of services. There are 1,920 units of Postal Instant Press (PIP) in the United States, Canada, the United Kingdom, and Japan. Many women own PIP franchises. Printing and high-tech reproduction franchises cost about $80,000. Alpha Graphics, for example, has 134 outlets. The initial cost is $36,000. Equipment, real estate, advertising, supplies and so on bring the total cost for this franchise to $218,000.

Maybe you would enjoy running one of the 23 Big Daddy's Lounge and Package Liquor Stores. If you are not sure about franchising, maybe you should contact the International Franchise Association for more information. The address is 1350 New York Avenue, N.W. (Suit 900), Washington, D.C., 2005. The phone number is (202) 628-8000. You can get the names, addresses, phone numbers, cash investment and qualifications needed, and other data on members. The association offers several interesting publications, including *Is Franchising For You?* and *How to Be a Franchisor.*

DISCUSSION QUESTIONS

1 What kinds of questions might you ask before buying a franchise?
2 Are the lower risks of franchise organizations worth giving up the freedom of ownership and control? How would you find information to answer such questions?
3 Look around your town and see which franchises seem successful. Is it true that the three most important promotional elements for a franchise are location, location, and location? Is there evidence of this around you?

LOOKING AHEAD

It is no accident that books like *In Search of Excellence* and *A Passion for Excellence* have been best-sellers in recent years. What these books emphasized was the need for businesses to work more closely with their customers, to listen, to be more responsive, and more innovative. One reason for the growth of entrepreneurship is the fact that smaller firms are more responsive to the market.

The key words are "responsive to the market." Business depends on customer relationships, and as with all relationships, customer relationships rely on open two-way communication. The function responsible for market responsiveness and communication is marketing.

The next five chapters will explore all phases of marketing: product design, packaging, branding, pricing, distribution, promotion, retailing, and more. Marketing finds out what people want, and then communicates those wants to production so that the firm produces what people want. Marketing (listening) comes first. That is why it is the first function we discuss in this text.

FUNDAMENTALS OF MARKETING

PART III

CHAPTER 7
MARKETING PRINCIPLES

CHAPTER 8
MARKETING COMMUNICATION

CHAPTER 9
PRODUCT DEVELOPMENT AND PRICING

CHAPTER 10
DISTRIBUTION: WHOLESALERS AND RETAILERS

CHAPTER 11
MARKETING OF SERVICE AND NONPROFIT ORGANIZATIONS

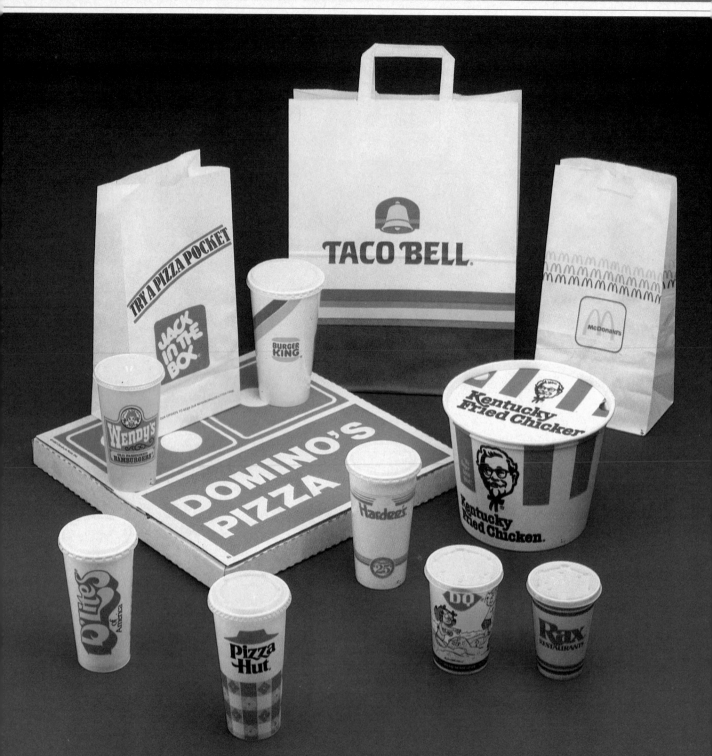

MARKETING PRINCIPLES

LEARNING GOALS

After you have read and studied this chapter, you should be able to:

- Define what marketing is and describe the 4 *P*'s of the marketing mix.
- Identify the eight traditional functions of marketing.
- Discuss market segmentation and list and explain the segmentation variables.
- Outline the consumer decision making process and describe outside influences on the process.
- Explain the marketing concept and its evolution.
- List and describe several ways industrial marketing is different from consumer marketing.

PROFILE GILBERTO GONZALEZ

Nothing shows the value of the free market system better than the success of immigrants from South America, Vietnam, and other less developed areas of the world. Gilberto Gonzalez is one of those new Americans who are adding their enthusiasm and willingness to work to the system.

In 1963, Gilberto had to choose: stay and work for communist Cuba or flee to the United States. He left. What he left behind was a career as manager of a sugar cane farm. When he arrived in the United States, he found work as a sugar cane cutter within two days. He was willing to accept such a job to live in the land of the free.

Soon Mr. Gonzalez and a partner saved enough money to open a small grocery store in Baltimore, Maryland. Using the profits from that store, Gonzalez moved to the nation's capital, Washington, D.C., and opened a grocery store in a Hispanic neighborhood.

Today, Mr. Gonzalez owns five stores and a distribution warehouse and grosses $11 million annually. To what does he attribute his success? "I worked hard," he said, "but it was this country that made my success. You can work hard in many places. Sometimes good things will happen, often not. . . . The United States is a wonderful country and I have never once changed my mind about being here." It

Gilberto Gonzalez.

Marketing is the whole business seen from the viewpoint of its final result, that is, from the customer's point of view.
PETER DRUCKER

is the free market system that makes it possible for people like Gilberto Gonzalez to prosper.

Mr. Gonzalez is a marketer. Distribution, warehousing, and retailing are all marketing activities. There are careers available in marketing in many different areas. Before we discuss careers, however, we shall learn all about marketing and how Mr. Gonzalez and other marketers keep the economy going. ■

Source: Luis Aguilar, Jr. and Alexander Kippen, "Cuban Immigrant Honored as American Success Story," *The Washington Post*, June 21, 1984, p. MD 5. © *The Washington Post*, 1984.

THE IMPORTANCE OF MARKETING

Two books that have shaped the discussion of business in the 1980s are *In Search of Excellence*[1] and *A Passion for Excellence*.[2] They should be on your reading list. Entrepreneurship is successful only when the product becomes a success in the market. That means that everything a business does begins and ends with customers. Here is how authors Thomas J. Peters and Robert H. Waterman put it[3]:

> The good news from the excellent companies is the extent to which, and the intensity with which, the customers intrude into every nook and cranny of the business—sales, manufacturing, research, accounting. . . . All business success rests on something labeled a sale, which at least momentarily weds company and customer. A simple summary of what our research uncovered . . . is this: the excellent companies *really are* close to their customers. . . . The excellent companies are better listeners.

The book, *A Passion for Excellence,* grew out of discussions created by *In Search of Excellence*. The emphasis was on getting out of the plant and *listening* to customers. The whole of the book is summed up in this passage[4]:

> In the private or public sector, in big business or small, we observe that there are only two ways to create and sustain superior performance over the long haul. First, take exceptional care of your customers . . . via superior service and superior quality. Second, constantly innovate. That's it.

Constant innovation is done by intrapreneuring and entrepreneuring. So we have discussed half of the way to create superior performance (Chapter 6). The other half is *marketing*—"taking exceptional care of customers via superior service and quality."

Marketing, then, has become a major focus of business in the 1980s, and will continue to be in the 1990s. The success of American business and thus the success of the economy depends on business's ability to market.

It is no wonder, then, that marketing is the first business function to be discussed in depth in this text. In fact, we shall devote five chapters to marketing, one more than business textbooks usually do. Why? Because what is true for business is true for nonprofit organizations as well. Their survival and growth depend on their marketing ability. Chapter 11 focuses on the marketing of services (where the future of business is) and nonprofit organizations.

WHAT MARKETING IS

A popular slogan that describes modern-day marketing is, "Find a need and fill it." The ad on p. 167 is a good example. What does "Find a need and

fill it" mean? It means that businesses must do some market research to find out what goods and services people and organizations want and need. Listening should come first. Then marketers must do whatever it takes to satisfy those wants and needs. The ultimate goal is to make money (profit) by producing and selling goods and services. Marketing, then, can be defined as follows:

Marketing is the process of studying wants and needs and satisfying those wants and needs by exchanging goods and services; this results in satisfied buyers and creates profits for sellers.

Marketing Management: The Four *P*'s

To maintain some control over the marketing functions in a firm, many businesses have created a position called marketing manager. A **marketing manager** plans and executes the conception, pricing, promotion, and distribution of ideas, goods, and services to create exchanges that satisfy individual and organizational goals.

When developing programs to satisfy market wants and needs, marketing managers work with several variables known as the marketing mix. A **marketing mix** is the strategic combination of product decisions with decisions on packaging, pricing, distribution, credit, branding, service, complaint handling, and other marketing activities. Some texts on business combine all the elements of the marketing

marketing
The process of planning and executing the conception, pricing, promotion, and distribution of ideas, goods, and services to create exchanges that satisfy individual and organizational objectives.

marketing manager
Plans and executes the conception, pricing, promotion, and distribution of ideas, goods, and services to create exchanges that satisfy individual and organizational goals.

marketing mix
The strategic combination of product decisions with decisions regarding packaging, pricing, distribution, credit, branding, service, complaint handling, and other marketing activities.

FIGURE 7-1

The four *P*'s and the marketing manager's role.

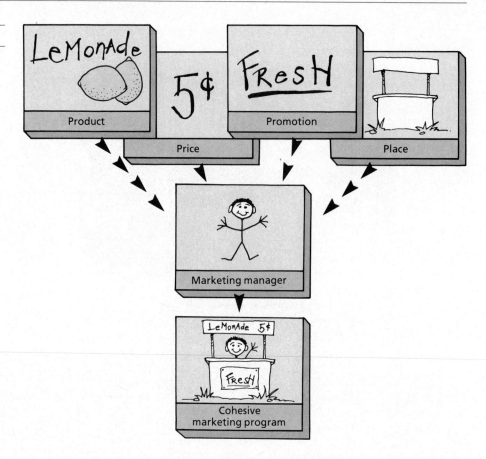

four *P*'s of marketing
Product, place, promotion, and price.

product differentiation
The creation of benefits and an image for a product that captures the imagination of the public and sets it apart from other, similar products.

mix under four easily remembered categories, called the **four *P*'s**: *p*roduct, *p*lace (distribution), *p*romotion, and *p*rice. These variables are partly controllable by the marketing manager (see Figure 7-1).

Competition is so severe today that the design of a *product* with some special appeal for consumers is critical. The creation of benefits and an image for a product that captures the imagination of the public is called **product differentiation.** The box on p. 169 will give you some insight into this important task. The development of products, including packaging and branding, is so important that Chapter 9 is devoted to that subject.

In today's competitive marketplace, *price* is a critical component of the marketing mix. No doubt you have noticed how the price of home computers has fallen as the market became more competitive. Because price is so important to product acceptance, we shall discuss price in that context in Chapter 9 also.

The *promotion* function in marketing includes listening as well as talking. In any relationship, including marketing relationships, communication seems to be the vital link. Promotion (including advertising) will be discussed as part of an overall communication process in Chapter 8.

The last element in the four *P*'s is *place* (distribution). The idea is to make goods and services available where and when they are needed. That means transporting them and storing them. The major institutions involved in distribution are wholesalers and retailers. They are the subject of Chapter 10.

PRODUCT DIFFERENTIATION—FROM CHICKENS TO SNEAKERS

Millions of chickens are raised on Maryland's Eastern Shore. One of the most famous producers there is Frank Perdue. Perdue chickens are sold at a premium to restaurants and in supermarkets in New York City and all through the eastern United States. These chickens can be distinguished from competing chickens because they are fed "secret ingredients" that make them yellow. Furthermore, Frank Perdue promises "your money back if you don't like the chickens." Frank Perdue is proof that a homogeneous product such as chickens can be "differentiated" from competition and sold at a premium. Most producers found it difficult to create product differentiation for chickens, but Frank Perdue did not.

A similar story can be told about tennis shoes. For years, no product lacked a special identity more than did tennis shoes (sneakers). But through careful promotion and product differentiation, tennis shoes with names such as Adidas, Nike, and Reebok have captured a large share of the market—again at premium prices. Whereas plain sneakers might cost $15, these new tennis shoes may cost $50 and more. Nike products are so popular that the name *Nike* on a T-shirt is a status symbol in some areas. Product differentiation and promotion made Nike stand out from "ordinary" tennis shoes. Then Reebok captured the aerobics market.

Similar stories could be told about sunglasses (Foster Grant), bananas (Chiquita), and oranges (Sunkist).

Product differentiation and promotion generated special interest in these products that is hard to beat. Could similar preferences be generated for other homogeneous products such as milk, eggs, butter, and gasoline? What about colleges, hospitals, movie theaters, and auto rental firms? Have you heard about the new brand-name tomatoes? McDonald's uses them on their new McD LTs.

THINKING IT THROUGH

Which of the four *P*'s of marketing do you think is most important? What are the interrelationships among the four *P*'s? Many people believe that marketing is synonymous with promotion. Would the four *P*'s help you to show them that their concept of marketing is incorrect?

Over time, the focus of marketing has changed in the United States. At first, the greatest need was for the distribution of goods. Later, attention shifted to consumer demand for services. We shall discuss that evolution next.

WHAT DO MARKETERS DO?

What marketers do depends on what needs to be done to satisfy consumer wants. In 1900, consumers needed the basic necessities of life—food, clothing, and shelter.

FIGURE 7-2

Eight basic marketing functions by category. Buying and selling (trading) are the heart of marketing. But buying and selling do not take place unless goods are transported to where they are wanted and stored there until buyers are ready to buy (distribution). Who can afford to buy a house or car without financing? Because credit was so critical to selling, it was a major *marketing* function at first. Now it is more a finance function. Storing goods meant taking the risk of theft, damage, or obsolescence. Thus marketers assumed the function of taking those risks (and buying insurance). Marketing of farm products and commodities (for example, steel) demanded standardization and grading of goods. Finally, the whole process begins and ends with researching the market to *find* wants and needs and then testing to see if needs are being satisfied.

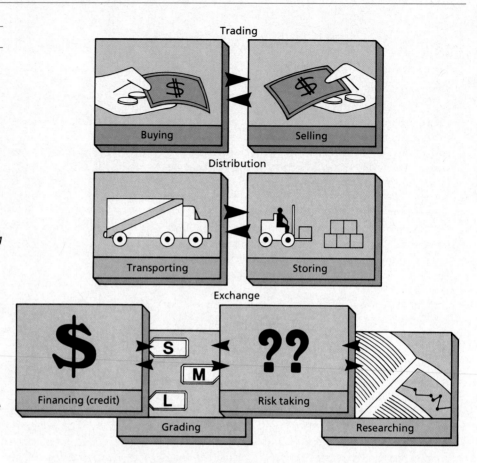

The problem was getting goods from the producer to the consumer. The most basic need was for food, so marketers concentrated on the transportation and storage of food products. Manufacturers needed raw materials to produce various products, so the distribution of industrial goods (coal, steel, wood) was also important. By the 1920s, marketers were described as performing eight basic functions[5] (see Figure 7-2):

1 Buying
2 Selling
3 Transporting
4 Storing
5 Financing
6 Standardizing (grading)
7 Risk taking
8 Research

By the 1980s, new consumer demands had changed what marketers had to do. Rather than focus on functions such as distribution and storage, marketers shifted their attention to more careful listening to consumers (communication), and more attention was given to identifying specific markets (segmentation). Some marketers still perform the basic eight functions, but now more attention is being placed on two others: marketing communication and market segmentation. Furthermore, marketers are also much more concerned with studying and understanding human behavior.

The Marketing Communication Function

Marketing communication involves talking with consumers to be sure the product, price, and all other aspects of the trade relationship are what is wanted. It is an ongoing process. A classic explanation of the process was given by John Marder of Grey Advertising. This is what he said[6]:

> In the beginning, there is the seller and there is the buyer. And if they are to interact . . . they must communicate with one another. And in fact they do . . . in a variety of ways. Typically, the buyer communicates with the seller through the answers he gives to the seller's market research. And the seller, in turn, communicates with the buyer through his advertising.
>
>   In greater detail . . . their communications go like this:
> - The buyer expresses his wants and needs, his desires and satisfactions.
> - The seller, sensing the opportunity for profit, makes the product or service that is called for.
> - Then, through his advertising, the seller tells the buyer that he has just the thing the buyer was asking for.
> - And if the seller has correctly understood what the buyer was saying . . . and if he has actually made what was asked of him . . . the buyer will probably buy.
>
> Of course, the transaction is not quite that brief, or that simple. In the course of the dialogue the seller has had to ask a lot of questions . . . and he has had to ask them quite skillfully . . . to benefit from what the buyer was saying.

marketing communication
Talking with target markets to be sure that the product, price, and all other aspects of the exchange situation are what is wanted.

Last year one million people bought quarter-inch drills—not because they wanted quarter-inch drills, but because they wanted one million quarter-inch holes!
   Sell the people what they want.

G. Worthington Hipple

Transportation is a basic marketing function.

TAKE THE CONRAIL CHALLENGE

YOU HAVE NOTHING TO LOSE BUT THE OLD WAY TO SHIP

We'll analyze your freight transportation needs—inbound, outbound, just in time—to prove how competitive our price and service package can be. And it won't cost you a cent. Take the Conrail challenge today. Write: Charles N. Marshall, Senior Vice President

Marketing & Sales, Conrail, Six Penn Center Plaza, Room 1040 D, Philadelphia, Pennsylvania 19103. Or call 1-800-8-ACTION. In Canada, call collect, 0-215-977-5825. You have nothing to lose but the old way to ship.

CONRAIL

Buying and selling (trading) are the heart of marketing. But buying and selling don't take place unless goods are transported to where they are wanted and stored there until buyers are ready to buy (distribution). Who can afford to buy a house or car without financing? Because credit was so critical to selling, it was a major *marketing* function at first. Now it is more a finance function. Storing goods meant taking the risk of theft, damage, or obsolescence. Thus marketers assumed the function of taking those risks (and buying insurance). Marketing of farm products and commodities (for example, steel) demanded standardization and grading of goods. Finally, the whole process begins and ends with researching the market to *find* wants and needs and then testing to see if needs are being satisfied.

PROGRESS CHECK

- What are the four *P*'s of marketing? Can you name two activities under each? (See Figure 7-1 on p. 168.)

- What are the traditional eight functions of marketing?

The Market Segmentation Function

Because no one seller can satisfy all buyers, and no one buyer can satisfy all sellers, a marketing activity is needed to narrow the market. As a consumer, you select a few stores where you shop and choose a few doctors and other service organizations and people to meet your needs. The seller goes through a similar process.

For the seller, market segmentation helps target marketing efforts toward those people who are in the right place at the right time and who most want the product in question. In a market, the seller has three targeting options: (1) Introduce only one product, hoping to get as many people to buy as possible. This is called undifferentiated marketing. (2) Go after one particular group and develop the ideal product for them. This is called concentrated marketing. (3) Introduce several product versions, each appealing to a different group. This is called differentiated marketing.[7] Note that the determination of market segments and the selection of market targets are separate problems. **Market segmentation** is the process of dividing the total market into several submarkets (segments) that have similar characteristics. **Market targeting** is the process by which an organization decides which market segments to serve.

Segmentation Variables

There are several ways in which a firm can divide the market for marketing purposes. Remember, the idea is to break the market down into smaller groups (segments) with similar characteristics (for example, all men, teenagers), and then aim the

market segmentation
Process of dividing the total market into several submarkets (segments) that have similar characteristics.

market targeting
The process by which an organization decides which markets to serve.

FIGURE 7-3

Geographic segmentation variables.

VARIABLE	TYPICAL SEGMENTS
Region	New England, Mideast, Great Lakes, Plains, Southeast, Southwest, Rocky Mountain, Far West
City or county size	Under 5,000; 5,000-19,999; 20,000-49,999; 50,000-99,999; and so on
Population density	Urban, suburban, rural

product at one or more of these groups. Let's say, for example, we were trying to sell a new, high-fiber, nutritious, low-sugar cereal. We could begin our marketing campaign by focusing on a certain region, such as the Far West, where fitness is a major issue. Dividing the market by geographic area is called **geographic segmentation** (see Figure 7-3).

We could aim our promotions toward people aged 25 to 45 who had some college training, and had high incomes—young urban professionals, or yuppies. Segmentation by age, income, and occupation is part of **demographic segmentation** (see Figure 7-4).

geographic segmentation
Divides the market into separate geographic areas.

demographic segmentation
Divides the market into groups by age, sex, income, and similar categories.

VARIABLE	TYPICAL SEGMENTS
Age	Under 5; 5–10; 11–18; 19–34; 35–49; 50–64; 65 and over
Education	Grade school or less; some high school; high school graduate; some college; college graduate; advanced college degree
Family size	1; 2–3; 4–5; over 6
Family life cycle	Young, single; young, married, no children; young, married, oldest child less than 6 years old; young, married, youngest child 6 or over; older, married, with children; older, married, no children; older, single; other
Income	Under $5,000; $5,000–$9,999; $10,000–$14,999; $15,000–$19,000; over $20,000
Nationality	American, Asian, British, Eastern European, French, German, Italian, Japanese, Latin American, Middle Eastern, Scandinavian, and so forth
Occupation	Professional, managerial; technical, officials, and proprietors; clerical, sales; supervisors; operatives; farmers; students; home managers; retired; unemployed
Race	White, black, Indian, Oriental, and so forth
Religion	Catholic, Protestant, Jewish, and so forth
Sex	Male, female
Social class	Lower lower, upper lower, lower middle, upper middle, lower upper, upper upper

FIGURE 7-4

Demographic segmentation variables

FIGURE 7-5

Psychographic segmentation
variables

VARIABLE	TYPICAL SEGMENTS
Attitudes Behavior patterns Interests Life-styles Opinions Personality Self-image Values	There are no typical breakdowns in psychographic analysis because the technique is new and still being developed.

FIGURE 7-6

Benefit segmentation
variables

VARIABLE	TYPICAL SEGMENTS
Comfort Convenience Durability Economy Health Luxury Safety Status	Benefit segmentation divides an already established market into smaller, more homogeneous segments. Those people who desire economy in a car would be an example. The benefit desired varies by product.

**psychographic
segmentation**
Divides the market by values,
attitudes, and interests.

benefit segmentation
Divides the market by benefits
desired.

situation segmentation
Separates out those situations
in which the product may be
used.

volume segmentation
Divides the market into user
categories: heavy, medium,
light, and nonusers.

We may want our ads to portray the life-style of this group. To do that, we could study the group's values, attitudes, and interests. This segmentation strategy is called **psychographic segmentation** (see Figure 7-5).

What benefits should we talk about? Should we emphasize high fiber, low sugar, price, health in general, or what? Determining which benefits are preferred is called **benefit segmentation** (see Figure 7-6).

Do we want people to eat the cereal for breakfast, for snacks, or at bedtime? Getting people to think of different times and places to use a product is called **situation segmentation.** Remember the orange juice ads that said, "Orange juice; it's not just for breakfast anymore"? They were trying to broaden the situations in which people drink orange juice.

Who are the big eaters of cereal? Children eat cereal, but so do adults. Separating the market by usage (volume of use) is called **volume segmentation.** Most of the cereal companies seem to aim at children. Why not go for the adults, a less competitive market? (See Figure 7-7.) The best segmentation strategy is to use all the variables to come up with a consumer profile (a target market) that is clear, reachable, and sizeable. A *target market,* therefore, is a group or groups of consumers that are selected for special marketing attention.

FIGURE 7-7

Volume market
segmentation

VARIABLE	TYPICAL SEGMENTS
Heavy users Light users Nonusers	Segmentation by usage is self-explanatory
Loyalty status	None; medium; strong; absolute (repeat purchases)

✳The segmentation variables we have discussed thus far are:
- Geographic
- Demographic
- Psychographic
- Benefit
- Situation
- Volume

For an interesting challenge, look through Case Number 2 on Kellogg at the end of this chapter. Write a report to Kellogg using these segmentation strategies to make a case for producing a high fiber, nutritious, low sugar cereal for adults.

Product differentiation and market segmentation are separate marketing functions. How are they related? How do they differ?

Consumer Behavior

In the late 1960s, marketing scholars took a more active interest in learning how consumers think and act. That led them to the literature of psychology, sociology, anthropology, and social psychology. Eventually, they developed textbooks in the area, and **consumer behavior** has become one of the major courses in marketing.

Figure 7-8 illustrates the kind of subjects that are studied in such a course. The core involves studying the consumer purchase decision process. "Problem

consumer behavior
The study of buyers' actions in the marketplace.

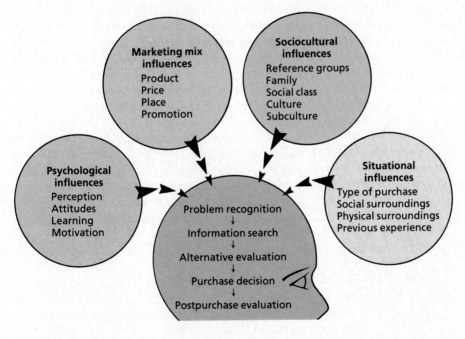

FIGURE 7-8

The consumer decision-making process and outside influences.

culture
The set of values, attitudes and ways of doing things that are transmitted from one generation to another in a given society.

learning
Involves changes in an individual's behavior resulting from previous experiences and information.

reference group
The group that an individual uses as a reference point in the formation of his or her beliefs, attitudes, values or behavior.

subculture
The set of values, attitudes, and ways of doing things that result from belonging to a certain nationality group, religious group, racial group, or other group to which one closely identifies.

recognition" may be the fact that your washing machine broke down. This leads to an information search. That is, you look for ads about washing machines and begin reading brochures about them. You may even consult *Consumer Reports* and other information sources. Then you evaluate alternatives and make a purchase decision. After the purchase, you may ask others how much they paid for their machines and do other comparisons, including the performance of your new machine. Marketing researchers investigate consumer thought processes and behavior at each stage to determine the best way to facilitate marketing exchanges.

Consumer behavior researchers also study the various influences on consumer behavior. Figure 7-8 shows that such influences include the marketing mix variables, psychological influences such as perception and attitudes, sociocultural influences such as reference groups and culture, and situational influences such as the type of purchase and the physical surroundings. Some terms that may be unfamiliar to you include:

- **Culture** is the set of values, attitudes and ways of doing things that are transmitted from one generation to another in a given society.
- **Learning** involves changes in an individual's behavior resulting from previous experiences and information.
- **Reference group** is the group that an individual uses as a reference point in the formation of his or her beliefs, attitudes, values, or behavior.
- **Subculture** is the set of values, attitudes, and ways of doing things that result from belonging to a certain nationality group, religious group, racial group, or other group with which one closely identifies, for example, teenagers.

✳ Marketing Research

If the goal of marketing is to "Find a need and fill it," then a major function must be to do research to find needs and to determine the most effective and efficient ways to satisfy those needs. **Marketing research** performs those tasks. Although marketing research can take many forms, it is helpful to review certain steps when conducting such studies. The steps are:

marketing research
A major function used to find needs and to determine the most effective and efficient ways to satisfy those needs.

- *Study the present situation.* How does the public perceive the company and its products? What products are profitable? These are the kinds of questions that determine the present situation.
- *Define the strengths and weaknesses of present programs.* It is as important to know what an organization does well as what it does not do well, and marketing research should report both sides.
- *Define the problem(s) to be resolved.* Marketing researchers should be given the freedom to help discover what the problems are, what the alternatives are, what information is needed, and how to go about gathering and analyzing it.
- *State research objectives in writing.*
- *Determine the scope and estimated costs.* Research can get quite expensive, so some trade-off must be made between information needs and cost.
- *Exhaust secondary data.* **Secondary data** means already published research results from journals, trade associations, the government, information services, libraries, and other sources. There is no sense in reinventing the wheel, so find out what other research has been done first. *The Statistical Abstract of the United States* is one secondary source often used in this book. The *Occupational Outlook Handbook, 1986-1987* is another secondary source cited.

secondary data
Already-published research results from journals, trade associations, the government, information services, libraries, and other sources.

- *Gather primary data.* **Primary data** refers to results from doing your own research. Many good books are available on research techniques. Interviews and questionnaires are two other ways to gather primary data.
- *Analyze and process the data.*
- *Prepare a report.*
- *Suggest alternative solutions.*
- *Recommend a course of action.*
- *Follow up on the implementation.*
- *Redefine the situation* (that is, evaluate the strengths and weaknesses of the new situation).

primary data
Refers to results of one's own research.

Focus Group Studies

A very popular research technique in the 1980s has been **focus group studies.** The idea is to bring together a group of about 6 to 15 people who represent the market you wish to reach. You let them discuss the research question in an unstructured manner (an open conversation) to see what they say without much prompting. This often gives researchers better insights into the beliefs and feelings of people than formal questionnaires. The results of the focus group studies can then be used to construct more formal research studies. Focus groups are a fast and efficient way to get input from selected markets.

focus group studies
Unstructured interviews with 6 to 15 people who represent a target market to obtain their beliefs and feelings about a company and its products and other, similar subjects.

Consumer advisory boards are similar to focus groups in that they are made up of consumers whose ideas are sought by managerial decision makers. The difference is that consumer advisory boards meet on a regular basis over time, and a focus group will generally meet only once.

consumer advisory boards
Panels of consumers who meet on a regular basis over time to advise managerial decision makers on ideas and products.

Survey Research

Survey research includes a variety of techniques designed to get the personal views of some sample of the target market. The basic forms of survey research are questionnaires and personal interviews. One of the most popular interviewing strategies today is to call people on WATS lines, that is, a separate phone line for long distance calls. Almost as popular is stopping people in shopping malls and inter-

survey research
Includes a variety of techniques designed to get the personal views of some sample of the target market.

Survey research includes personal interviews.

viewing them while they are in a shopping mood. Questionnaires can be targeted toward select groups to get their opinions and suggestions, and their reactions to products.

Observation Techniques

One of the most fundamental research techniques is simply to observe what is happening in the marketplace. For example, the newest cash registers record what items are being purchased (including colors, prices, and so on) and at which stores. At the end of the day, a researcher can observe the effects of a new display, a change in price, or other such changes. Some researchers follow customers as they shop and note where they stop, whether or not they read labels, and so on.

One classic case of the observation technique involved Charles Parlin, often acknowledged as the founder of marketing research. He wanted to prove to Campbell Soup that the wives of blue collar workers bought soup in a can rather than making their own. He did this by collecting garbage! He collected a scientific sample of garbage from various parts of the city, dumped the contents on an armory floor, and counted the number of soup cans. He was able to convince Campbell Soup that it should advertise in the *Saturday Evening Post* because it reached the working class people, who were prime customers for canned soup. The garbage count was the convincing argument.

Another popular technique used today is license plate surveys. This consists of going through the parking lot and looking at the license plates to see where the consumers are coming from.

Experimental Research

The most rigorous and controlled research process in marketing is experimental research. Experimental research studies groups and individuals in a setting where they can be exposed to products, advertisements, and other marketing efforts to test their reactions. It is called experimental research because it is run like a laboratory experiment, with many controls.

The whole purpose of such experiments is to create products and promotions that will result in satisfied customers and profit for the seller. Marketing has not always been so focused on consumer wants and needs. In fact, the marketing philosophy has changed dramatically over the last century. We shall end this chapter, therefore, with a brief history of where marketing has been. This will show you where marketing is going.

PROGRESS CHECK

- Can you give an example of how to use the six segmentation variables?

- Can you briefly describe what a focus group is? Survey research? Observation techniques?

BUSINESS ORIENTATION: FROM PRODUCTION TO MARKETING

From the time the first settlers began their struggle to survive in America until after the Civil War, the general philosophy of business was, "Produce as much as you can because there is a limitless market." Given the limited production capability and the vast demand for products in those days, such a philosophy was both logical and profitable. Business owners were mostly farmers, carpenters, and trade workers who were catering to the public's basic needs for housing, food, and clothing. There was a need for greater and greater productive capacity, and businesses naturally had a **production orientation**—that is, the goals of business centered on production rather than marketing. This was satisfactory at that time, because most goods were bought as soon as they became available. As we noted earlier, the marketing need was for distribution and storage.

During the period from 1890 to 1920, businesses developed mass-production techniques. Automobile assembly lines are a prime example of this development. Production capacity often exceeded the immediate market demand. The business philosophy turned in the 1920s from a production orientation to a **sales orientation.** Businesses turned their attention to promoting their products and mobilized much of the firm's resources in the sales effort. That was the era in which salespeople were trained to "get your foot in the door, overcome objections, and close the sale." Much time and money was spent on such selling strategies.

After World War II (1945), there was a tremendous demand for goods and services among the returning soldiers who were starting a new life with new families. These postwar years launched the baby boom (the sudden large increase in the birthrate after the war) and a boom in consumer spending. Competition for the consumer's dollar was fierce. Business owners recognized the need to be more responsive to consumers, and a new orientation emerged called the **marketing concept.**

> **production orientation**
> Means businesses focused on producing goods rather than marketing them.

> **sales orientation**
> Means a firm focuses all of its attention on the salesperson, teaching him or her techniques for winning customers.

> ✳ **marketing concept**
> Refers to a three-part business philosophy: (1) a consumer orientation, (2) the coordination and integration of the firm, and (3) a profit orientation.

THE MARKETING CONCEPT

The marketing concept that emerged in the 1950s and dominated marketing thought for 30 years had three parts:

1 A *consumer orientation;* that is, find out what consumers want and give it to them.

2 The *coordination and integration of the firm* so that everyone in the organization has the same objective—consumer satisfaction.

3 A *profit orientation;* that is, market those goods and services that will earn the firm a profit and enable it to survive and expand to serve more consumer wants and needs.

Consumer Orientation

Henry Ford is reported to have said, "You can have any color car as long as it's black." He seemed more interested in production than in adapting to consumer wants and needs. He felt that the best car was a good, reliable, inexpensive one. In fact, up until 1926 Ford sold half the new cars made in this country. But the people at General Motors talked with consumers and found a basic desire for individuality and status. They began making cars in all colors and shapes and eventually took away much of Ford's market. This is an example of a **consumer orientation** at work. Today, all the car companies are working harder than ever to be more responsive to consumer wants and needs. Foreign competition has become fierce, and only those firms that give consumers what they want will survive. But

> **consumer orientation**
> Means finding out and giving consumers what they want.

Chevrolet has long focused on quality at low cost.

is it enough to give individuals what they want? Don't firms have some obligation to society as well?

There is some evidence today that organizations are adopting a broader **societal orientation** that includes a consumer orientation. For example, many large business firms and nonprofit organizations have become involved in programs designed to train the disadvantaged, improve the community, reduce the use of energy, cut back pollution, provide consumer information and consumer education, involve employees in community projects, and generally respond to the broader needs of society. A consumer orientation thus has become only one of the many social goals of today's progressive organizations and marketing managers.

societal orientation
Includes a consumer orientation, but adds programs designed to improve the community, reduce pollution, and satisfy other social goals.

Coordination and Integration of the Firm

To provide optimum consumer satisfaction, all elements of marketing (product, place, promotion, and price) must be coordinated and integrated with other departments in that cause. For example, salespeople often promise delivery on a certain date, and then the delivery people fail to show up. Such lack of coordination annoys the consumer and prevents consumer satisfaction. Similarly, a salesperson may write up a sale and promise credit terms, only to find that the credit department turns down the customer's application. Again, this may cause resentment. Similar examples all show that marketing functions should be coordinated and integrated with other business functions.

A solution to achieving the goal of coordination and integration is to have one person responsible for all marketing activities—a marketing manager or vice president of marketing. Since the early 1950s there has been a consistent trend toward having such a position in larger firms.

Profit Orientation

The purpose of adopting a new business philosophy was to improve consumer relations because better relationships would also benefit the firm and increase profits. One goal of all business firms is to optimize profits. This is called a **profit orientation.** Profit enables a firm to grow and hire more people, to provide even more satisfaction to consumers, and to strengthen the economy as a whole.

Some people believe that profits are the only or the major goal toward which businesses should work.[8] But most firms have many goals, including providing a pleasant atmosphere for employees and managers. This is called a **human orientation.** All these goals of an organization, however, depend on the firm's survival and long-term growth, and these are not possible without profits.

profit orientation
Marketing those goods and services which will earn the firm a profit.

human orientation
The broadening of the profit orientation to include other corporate objectives, especially the satisfaction of the wants and needs of managers and employees.

THINKING IT THROUGH

In much of Africa, there are few roads or inland waterways and no trains. Many of the people are starving, have few clothes, and little shelter. If you were to begin a marketing program to help these people, can you see the advantage of starting where we started in the United States—building roads, bridges, railroads, and a few storage facilities? Should businesses be production oriented rather than marketing oriented in developing Africa?

APPLYING THE MARKETING CONCEPT IN THE 1980s

Everyone knows the troubles the automobile market had in the late 1970s and early 1980s. What did they turn to for solutions to their problems? Marketing. Lee Iacocca at Chrysler emphasized product quality. *Advertising Age* said of his success, "While he denies any claim to being a marketing genius, he nevertheless epitomizes that most important marketing fundamental, the very backbone of sound business practice: create a quality product; deliver it to the marketplace; and make sure you let everyone know about it."[9]

Polaroid is a leading name in photography, yet from 1978 to 1982 sales and earnings collapsed. It was time for a reassessment. What did they decide? "I think it is fair to say that as the company broadens, it is becoming more consumer-driven," said M. Carl Johnson III, a Polaroid vice president. An industry analyst observes, "Now Polaroid is marketing versus product-directed. It is trying to find out what the consumer wants, to do market research as it never did before."[10]

Applying a More Societal Marketing Concept

A number of firms have adopted a new societal marketing orientation and are providing leadership for other socially minded capitalists. For example, Andora Freeman and Joy Ernst started a toy recycling center to teach children the importance of conservation and to make a profit for themselves. Used toys are sold at bargain prices, and the original owners keep 50% of the take. The store, Toy Go Round, could earn higher profits if it carried toy guns and G.I. Joe dolls, but the owners refuse because they do not like the social effects on children of playing with war toys.[11]

Socially minded people are encouraging other companies besides their own to adopt a societal marketing concept. Two new investment funds—Calvert, and Working Assets—have been established to allow small investors to invest in firms with a societal orientation. Assets of the two funds total $45 million. Total investment in such funds is estimated at $1 billion dollars.[12] Profit and social responsibility can be mutually supportive goals.

Now that the United States has become relatively affluent, people are demanding satisfaction of wants and needs that businesses often cannot and do not provide. For example, people are demanding a cleaner environment, a greater involvement with the arts, and better educational programs. This has led to a whole new dimension of marketing—nonprofit organization marketing.[13]

Coca-Cola helped promote the "Hands Across America" campaign.

Broadening the Concept of Marketing

In the 1970s marketers broadened the scope of their activities to include the marketing of nonbusiness organizations. No longer is the objective simply to "Find individual needs and fill them." Rather, the goal is to meet the broader needs of society as well. Standard marketing practices were applied to tasks such as promoting public hospitals and universities, museums, associations, government programs, and more. But more sophisticated tools were needed to create new social attitudes and behaviors for such programs as stopping smoking, driving 55 miles

per hour, wearing seat belts, picking up litter, and so on. Much future growth in marketing will be in this area.

Furthermore, more attention in the future will be given to industrial marketing; that is, marketing from business to business. Marketing to consumers has reached a high level of effectiveness and efficiency. Marketing to business needs more development.

INDUSTRIAL MARKETING

As consumers, we have a tendency to think of marketing as a system designed to satisfy our needs. After all, there are about 240 million consumers in the United States, and we make up a huge market. On the other hand, there is another side of marketing that we know must exist, but do not encounter as often. That market consists of all the exchanges that go on among major organizations in society. For example, somebody has to sell coal to the electric utilities. Someone else sells electricity to the major manufacturers of cars, trucks, machinery, and computers. Then someone sells these manufactured goods to farmers, government agencies, and other large organizations. Using all the resources provided by these exchanges, producers, farmers, and government agencies begin the process of satisfying the needs of consumers. But there are still many middlemen who must be contacted before goods and services reach the final consumer. There are wholesalers who provide transportation and storage services; communications firms who keep the information flowing among the organizations (for example, ad agencies); and retailers who store the merchandise until we are ready to buy.

The marketing of goods and services to manufacturers, institutions (for example, hospitals or schools), commercial operations (retail stores), and the government is called **industrial marketing.** The basic principle of this kind of marketing is still "Find a need and fill it," but the strategies are different because the buyers are different. Some of the things that make industrial marketing different are as follows:

industrial marketing
The marketing of goods and services to manufacturers, institutions, commercial operations, and the government.

1 The market for industrial goods is a *derived* demand; that is, the demand for consumer products such as automobiles creates the demand for industrial goods and services including tires, batteries, glass, metal, plastics, and engines.

2 The demand for industrial goods is relatively inelastic; that is, the demand does not always change significantly with minor changes in price. The reason for this is that industrial products are made up of so many parts that a price increase for one part is not usually a significant problem.

3 The number of customers in the industrial market is relatively few; that is, there are just a few construction firms or mining operations compared to the consumer market of 70 million or so households.

4 The size of industrial customers is relatively large; that is, a few large organizations account for most of the employment and production of various goods and services.

5 Industrial markets tend to be concentrated; for example, oil fields tend to be concentrated in areas such as the Southwest and Alaska. Consequently marketing efforts often may be concentrated on a particular geographic area, and distribution problems are often minimized by locating warehouses near industrial "centers."

6 Industrial buyers generally are more rational in their selection of goods and services; they use specifications and carefully weigh the "total product offer" including quality, price, and service.

7 Industrial sales tend to be direct. Manufacturers will sell products such as tires directly to automobile manufacturers, but would tend to use wholesalers and retailers to sell to consumers.

Industrial markets are often more complex than consumer markets because the products are sold many times before they reach the ultimate consumer. Be sure to consider industrial marketing when you evaluate marketing careers; the opportunities are many and the pay is relatively good. Much of the future growth of marketing will be in this sector. The box on p. 185 lists the many careers available in marketing.

PROGRESS CHECK

▪ What were the orientations businesses had before the marketing concept? Why?

▪ What are the three parts of the marketing concept?

▪ What is a human orientation?

▪ What does "broadening the concept of marketing" mean?

SELECTED CAREERS IN MARKETING

PRODUCT MANAGEMENT

1 A product manager for consumer goods develops new products that can cost millions of dollars, with advice and consent of management—a job with great responsibility.

2 An administrative manager oversees the organization within a company that transports products to consumers and handles customer service.

3 An operations manager supervises warehousing and other physical distribution functions and often is directly involved in moving goods on the warehouse floor.

4 A traffic and transportation manager evaluates the costs and benefits of different types of transportation.

5 An inventory control manager forecasts demand for stockpiled goods, coordinates production with plant managers, and keeps track of current levels of shipments to keep customers supplied.

6 An administrative analyst planner performs cost analyses of physical distribution systems.

7 A customer service manager maintains good relations with customers by coordinating sales staffs, marketing management, and physical distribution management.

8 A physical distribution consultant is an expert in the transportation and distribution of goods.

ADVERTISING

9 An account executive maintains contact with clients while coordinating the creative work among artists and copywriters. In full-service ad agencies, account executives are considered partners with the client in promoting the product and helping to develop marketing strategy.

10 A media buyer analyst deals with media sales representatives in selecting advertising media and analyzes the value of media being purchased.

11 A copywriter works with art directors in conceptualizing advertisements and writes the text of print or radio ads or the storyboards of television ads.

12 An art director handles the visual component of advertisements.

13 A sales promotion manager designs promotions for consumer products and works at an ad agency or a sales promotion agency.

14 A public relations manager develops written or filmed messages for the public and handles contacts with the press.

15 A specialty advertising manager develops advertising for the sales staff and customers or distributors.

RETAILING

16 A buyer selects products a store sells, surveys consumer trends, and evaluates the past performance of products and suppliers.

17 A store manager oversees the staff and services at a store.

SALES

18 In direct (door-to-door or other) personal selling, compensation is based mostly on a commission.

19 In sales to channel members, the salesperson sells to those in another step of the distribution channel (between the manufacturer and the store or customer). Compensation includes salary plus bonus.

20 An industrial or semitechnical salesperson sells supplies and services to businesses. Compensation is salary plus bonus.

21 A complex or professional salesperson sells complicated or custom-designed products to business. This requires understanding of the technology of a product. Compensation is salary plus bonus.

MARKETING RESEARCH

22 A project manager for the supplier coordinates and oversees the market studies for a client.

23 An account executive for the supplier serves as a liaison between client and market research firm, like an advertising agency account executive.

24 An in-house project director acts as project manager (see No. 22) for the market studies conducted by the firm for which he works.

25 A marketing research specialist for an advertising agency performs or contracts for market studies for agency clients.

NONPROFIT MARKETING

26 The marketing manager for nonprofit organizations develops and directs mail campaigns, fund raising, and public relations.

Source: David W. Rosenthal and Michael A. Powell, *Careers in Marketing,* © 1984, pp. 352-354. Adapted by permission of Prentice-Hall, Englewood Cliffs, N.J.

SUMMARY

1 *Marketing* is the process of studying wants and needs and satisfying those wants and needs by exchanging goods and services. A *marketing manager* plans and executes the conception, pricing, promotion, and distribution of ideas, goods, and services to create exchanges that satisfy individual and organizational goals.

- Why is marketing more important now?

   Overseas competition and domestic competition have made marketing the major difference among firms.

- What do marketers do?

   The eight traditional marketing functions are: buying, selling, transportation, storage, finance (credit), risk bearing, standardization, and research.

- What are the newest functions?

   Two new functions are marketing communication and market segmentation.

2 The *marketing mix* consists of the four *P*'s: product, place, promotion, and price. The marketing manager uses these variables to try to capture the target market.

- What is a target market?

   It is that group or groups selected for special marketing effort.

- How are those groups chosen?

   Market segmentation breaks the total population down into segments with similar characteristics. The breakdown could be:

   Geographic: various areas of the country are targeted.

   Demographic: age, sex, income, religion, race, and other variables are used.

   Psychographic: values, attitudes, and interests are some of the variables.

   Benefit: comfort, convenience, and other benefit categories are chosen.

   Situation: when and where product is used.

   Volume: heavy, light, medium, and nonusers.

3 *Marketing research* is the "find a need" and "the most effective way to fill it" function.

- What are the various steps in the process?

   See pp. 176-177.

- Do marketing researchers use any special techniques?

   Focus groups are a fast and efficient way to get information. Surveying people in malls, at home, and on the phone are other popular techniques. Of course, nothing beats observing actual behavior in the market. The most rigorous and controlled research is *experimental*.

4 The *marketing philosophy* has changed over time. At first, emphasis was on production; then on sales. In the 1950s, the philosophy that emerged was called *the marketing concept*.

- What is the marketing concept?

   It is (1) a consumer orientation, (2) the coordination and integration of the firm to provide consumer satisfaction, and (3) a profit orientation.

- What is the future direction of marketing?

   The aim is to satisfy all needs, including needs not met by businesses. Businesses are adopting a *societal orientation* that broadens the consumer orientation and a *human orientation* that attempts to satisfy the needs of managers and employees while making a profit.

■ What about industrial marketing?

Much future growth will be in this area. Businesses selling computers, raw materials, and other goods and services to other businesses represent a true growth area.

KEY TERMS

benefit segmentation p. 174

consumer advisory boards p. 177

consumer behavior p. 175

consumer orientation p. 179

culture p. 176

demographic segmentation p. 173

focus group studies p. 177

four *P*'s of marketing p. 168

geographic segmentation p. 173

human orientation p. 181

industrial marketing p. 184

learning p. 176

market segmentation p. 172

marketing p. 167

marketing communication p. 171

marketing concept p. 179

marketing manager p. 167

marketing mix p. 167

marketing research p. 176

market targeting p. 172

primary data p. 177

product differentiation p. 168

production orientation p. 179

profit orientation p. 181

psychographic segmentation p. 174

reference group p. 176

situation segmentation p. 174

sales orientation p. 179

secondary data p. 176

societal orientation p. 180

subculture p. 176

survey research p. 177

volume segmentation p. 174

GETTING INVOLVED

1 Imagine you are the president of a small liberal arts college. Enrollment has declined dramatically. The college is in danger of closing. Show how you might revive the college by applying the marketing concept. How would you implement the three phases: (1) a consumer orientation; (2) coordination and integration among departments; and (3) a profit orientation? Would you recommend a more societal orientation as well? How would you do it?

2 It is easy to document the social ills for which marketing is partially responsible. Discuss the social benefits and social costs imposed by marketing. Take the position you have not held previously and defend it (that is, defend marketers if you have opposed them and vice versa). Discuss whether less developed countries would or would not benefit from more marketing.

3 Businesses began with a *production orientation,* producing what they wanted and selling it later. Discuss how some artists and colleges continue that orientation. What would happen if artists and colleges switched to the marketing concept? How would their interaction with consumers differ?

4 Talk to several people who work in marketing (for example, retailers, salespeople, marketing researchers, advertising people) and see how they enjoy their jobs. Which careers look best? Discuss your findings with the class.

5 Watch your local papers for evidence that firms are adopting a human orientation (that is, paying more attention to manager and employee satisfaction). For example, watch for references to company health programs, recreation programs, more flexible schedules (flextime), day-care programs, and so on. Debate both sides of this

statement: "Businesspeople are in business to make a profit; that is, and should be, their only objective."

6 Take a product and show how you would segment the market for it using the six variables listed in this chapter.

PRACTICING MANAGEMENT DECISIONS

CASE ONE   TRIVIAL PURSUIT: APPLYING MARKETING CONCEPTS

Here's a Trivial Pursuit question for you. What product is made by Horn Abbot Ltd.? The answer: Trivial Pursuit. Here's another one. What game generates over $50 million *per year* for the inventors and their friends? The answer: Trivial Pursuit. OK, one more. What game uses 70 million pounds of a special paper, requires the production of 20 billion cards, and involves almost 3,000 workers in its production? The answer: Trivial Pursuit.

Back in 1981, Chris Hanley (a high school dropout) and Scott Abott (a sports editor) invented the game. These two men plus two partners put up $250,000 to produce the game. They went to toy fairs in Canada and the United States in 1982 and received fewer than 500 orders. Then the game caught on. By 1984, the U.S. producer of Trivial Pursuit was producing 63,000 games a week and had back orders for 11 million games. The sales projection for 1985 was 20 million games.

By July of 1984, Chris, Scott, and Chris's brother John were holed up at the Ascot Inn in Toronto working on the sixth set of 6,000 questions (their second edition of general topics). The team has come up with an All-Star Sports Edition, a Baby Boomer edition, a Genus Edition, a Master Game edition, and so forth. The idea is to keep the game interesting by coming out with more new questions in interesting new categories.

Now the company is being swamped with requests to use the Trivial Pursuit name on everything from highball glasses to umbrellas. There are Trivial Pursuit T-shirts, four types of Trivial Pursuit calendars, a memo pad, and an appointment book. People have also asked to use the name on such products as athletic wear, linens, tablecloths, tables, and more.

A continuing major problem has been keeping retailers supplied with games. Retailers such as Sears place orders for 100,000 sets, and that takes up all the production capacity. Meanwhile, thousands of smaller retail stores cannot get the game at all.

New offshoots from the Trivial Pursuit concept include a music trivia game, Rock and Roll Replay (tape cassettes with 5-second bits of old rock and roll songs), Sexual Trivia, and Trivial Fever, a software package for playing the game on a computer.

DECISION QUESTIONS

1 What human need did Trivial Pursuit meet? Is this a good example of "find a need and fill it?"
2 Trivial Pursuit games have been designed for sports fans, baby boomers, rock and roll fans, and computer users. What other market segments could be targeted?
3 Of the four *P*'s of marketing, the company had the most trouble with *place*, making and distributing the product to meet an unexpected demand. How effective was the company with price and promotion? What could you do to keep retailers from getting upset?
4 What about designing a marketing edition of Trivial Pursuit? Example questions could include, what company used the slogan "Good to the last drop?" What did the names IBM, 3M, and NCR stand for originally?

Source: Gerald Lanson, "Big Game," *Inc.,* November, 1984, pp. 101-111.

CASE TWO   KELLOGG: MARKETING BREAKFAST CEREAL

It all started back in the 1800s with Dr. John H. Kellogg. He was a strict vegetarian and a leader in the Seventh Day Adventist community. Dr. Kellogg noticed that the typical American breakfast consisted of salt pork, biscuits, and ham gravy or pancakes and molasses. As director of a health spa, Dr. Kellogg fed his patients corn, wheat, and oatmeal—ground and baked. No salt and no sugar.

C.W. Post was one of his patients. He decided to go into business to market what was to become Post Grape Nuts. Post added sugar to make his cereal tastier. Dr. Kellogg and his brother, Will K. Kellogg, countered by offering a sweetened cereal of their own. The breakfast battle was on.

The big Kellogg cereal in the 1800s was Corn Flakes. Guess what their number-one best-seller is today? You guessed it: Corn Flakes. Number two is sugar-covered corn flakes (Frosted Flakes). All in all, Kellogg's has about 40% of the consumer market.

Let's see how Kellogg has attacked certain market segments. For adults, it has developed high fiber cereals like Nutri-Grain, Bran Products, and Cracklin' Oat Bran plus the vitamin-pill-in-a-cereal Special K. For children, it's Froot Loops, Sugar Pops, Sugar Smacks, and Apple Jacks. For traditionalists, there are Corn Flakes, Rice Krispies, and Raisin Bran.

Post Raisin Bran is now part of General Foods. It too has targeted certain markets. There is Grape-Nuts for the old-timers. Kids can feast on sugary cereals such as Smurf-Berry Crunch, Super Sugar Crisp, and Honey-Nut Crunch Raisin Bran. Joggers might go for C.W. Post Hearty Granola or just plain Bran Flakes. All together, General Foods has about 16% of the market.

The old Cheerios is still number one for General Mills. Honey Nut Cheerios is second. Anyone over 40 may remember eating graham crackers with milk. Now, General Mills makes it easy for you with Golden Grahams. Kids can sugar up on Donutz, Trix, and Lucky Charms. The General Mills market share is 23% or so.

A popular cereal in the Quaker Oats line is 100% Natural. They also make Life and Cap'n Crunch and Halfsies. Market share—about 9%.

We can't forget Ralston Purina with its 6% plus market share. They have given us Donkey Kong, Cookie Crisp, Waffelos, and Dinky Donuts. But their number-one cereal is still Chex.

Nabisco's number-one seller is Shredded Wheat. It has only about a 4% market share.

Going through the top sellers in each company is like going back to the 1940s or before. The top sellers—Corn Flakes, Cheerios, Post Raisin Bran, and Chex—are long-time favorites. Most of the best-sellers are relatively nutritious.

How far have we come from the original intent of Dr. Kellogg to give us a healthy, nutritious, sugar-free, salt-free breakfast food? Cookie Crisp is 47% sugar. A 1-ounce serving of Mr. T's Cereal has 230 milligrams of sodium. That's 30 more milligrams than Lay's packs into an equal amount of potato chips. Sugar Golden Crisp is 51% sugar, and Honey Smacks has 57% refined sweetener (including honey). In fact, there is little fiber in most kiddie-oriented cereals.

The cereal industry is now doing about $4 billion a year in sales. Some $100 million is spent on advertising.

DECISION QUESTIONS

1 Cereal makers have followed the marketing slogan of "Find a need and fill it" by giving us any kind of cereal we want, including cereals that are mostly sugar or very high in salt content. This is definitely an example of a consumer orientation. Would

the same mix of cereals be available if cereal companies adopted a more societal orientation?

2 Dropping those cereals with high sugar content would cut profits dramatically at cereal companies. Under what circumstances would a company make such cuts?

3 Cereal companies have provided us with high-fiber, high-vitamin cereals. Adults eat them, but children often choose the cereals that are half sugar. What reaction do you have to this trend?

4 Debate the following statement: "Cereal companies have made a major contribution to the American diet by giving us everything we have asked for in cereals."

Sources: John C. Maxwell, Jr., "Cereal Milks '83 Gains," *Advertising Age,* May 28, 1984, p. 32 and Robert Ferrigno, "Still a Breakfast of Champions?," *The Washington Times Magazine,* August 21, 1985, pp. 4M-6M.

LOOKING AHEAD

This chapter introduced the concept of the marketing communication function. An obvious recommendation: listen to consumers and respond. What makes the concept come alive is to picture it in practice. Chapter 8 will describe in detail the use of a marketing communication system in a small restaurant. You will be able to identify with the situation easily. We shall then discuss promotion as a follow-up to listening and producing what people want. The model we are following is very basic:

1 Find out what people want (marketing research).

2 Produce it (production; not a marketing function).

3 Tell them about it (promotion).

4 Make sure they can get one (distribution).

5 Apply the concepts in *all* organizations, including the government and other nonprofit organizations.

MARKETING COMMUNICATION

LEARNING GOALS

After you have read and studied this chapter, you should be able to:

- Define *marketing communication* and distinguish it from promotion.
- Outline and describe the steps to implement a marketing communication system.
- Explain the difference between marketing intelligence and marketing research.
- List and describe the elements in the promotion mix.
- Identify four classes of advertising.
- Explain how sales promotion supplements a promotional plan and list several sales promotion techniques.
- List the advantages and disadvantages of publicity.
- List the seven steps in the personal selling process.

PROFILE ERNEST P. (FOR POWER TOOLS) WORREL, STAR OF TV COMMERCIALS

Two lines from commercials in the 1980s will stand out for a long time. One is "Where's the beef?" for Wendy's. The other is "KnowhutImean, Vern?" a tag line for many commercials performed by Jim Varney, better known as Ernest P. Worrel (see p. 192). Mr. Varney performed his first professional role at age 16 as Puck in Shakespeare's *A Midsummer Night's Dream*. He also worked as a stand-up comic. But the role he is best known for is that of a goofy, bumbling rube in commercials. The character of Ernest P. Worrel features Varney's nose and mouth, which are rather large; you know what I mean?

The Ernest P. Worrel Fan Club has over 7,000 members. Varney has appeared in commercials for over 80 companies selling products ranging from milk and Toyotas to natural gas and pizza. Varney has made as many as 26 commercials in one day, and they are funny, funny, funny.

The Ernest P. Worrel character is an attention-getting device for product commercials. The ads also create publicity because so many people talk about them. ▪

Source: Timothy K. Smith, "Abominable Ernest of Commercials Noses Out Everyone," *The Wall Street Journal*, p. 1. © Dow Jones & Company, Inc. All rights reserved.

Doing business without advertising is like winking at a girl in the dark; you know what you are doing, but nobody else does.
STEWART H. BRITT

public
Any group that has a potential or actual relationship with an organization.

Everything begins with communication.

THE IMPORTANCE OF COMMUNICATION

Of all the marketing activities listed in Chapter 7, one stands out as vital. That is communication. We are entering the information age. Everyone seems to agree about that, but why is information so important? The answer is that the market system, the business system, and the world trade system all need an efficient two-way flow of information among producers, middlemen (for example, wholesalers and retailers), and consumers. That need has led to an explosive growth of computers to handle the information flow. The key to successful marketing is to establish such two-way flows with *all* of an organization's "publics," including stockholders, employees, suppliers, distributors, media personnel, customers, and potential customers. (A **public** is any group that has a potential or actual relationship with an organization.)

To communicate is the beginning of understanding.
Southwestern Bell

One of the leading firms in the United States, when it comes to marketing communication and promotion, is Procter & Gamble. Every year P&G spends more than a billion dollars on advertising, making it the number one advertiser in the United States (see Figure 8-1). Therefore, most people think of P&G as a firm that promotes heavily, and believe that is how P&G became so successful. But the truth is that P&G is equally or more proficient at listening to and working with customers as it is at promoting to them.

In one year, P&G will visit some 1.5 million people as part of about 1,000 research projects designed to discover what people like and dislike about P&G's products compared to competitive products.[1] Researchers at Procter & Gamble

RANK	COMPANY	ADVERTISING
1	Procter & Gamble	$1,600,000,000
2	Phillip Morris Cos.	1,400,000,000
3	RJR/Nabisco	1,093,000,000
4	Sears, Roebuck & Co.	800,000,000
5	General Motors Corp.	779,000,000
6	Beatrice Cos.	684,000,000
7	Ford Motor Co.	614,600,000
8	K mart Corp.	567,000,000
9	McDonald's Corp.	550,000,000
10	Anheuser-Busch Cos.	522,900,000
11	American Telephone & Telegraph	521,318,000
12	Ralston Purina Co.	508,365,000
13	Dart & Kraft	489,349,000
14	General Mills	484,146,000
15	J.C. Penney	478,892,000
16	PepsiCo Inc.	478,372,000
17	Pillsbury Co.	473,220,000
18	Warner Lambert Co.	469,339,000
19	Unilever U.S.	413,623,000
20	Johnson & Johnson	401,217,000
21	American Home Products Corp.	399,516,000
22	Chrysler Corp.	393,400,000
23	Coca-Cola Co.	390,000,000
24	GE/RCA	373,336,000
25	Kellogg Co.	364,299,000

FIGURE 8-1

Top 25 U.S. advertisers, 1986.
Source: *Advertising Age,* September 4, 1986.

study how people go about basic household chores such as washing clothes, doing dishes, and so on. Any problems present an opportunity for P&G to invent new products or create new solutions to people's needs. P&G truly operates on the principle of "Find a need and fill it and your needs will be met as well."

Communication Versus Promotion

Before we go any further in discussing how organizations communicate with their various publics, let's pause and discuss the difference between marketing communication and promotion.

- **Marketing communication** is a two-way exchange of information between buyers and sellers. Organizations communicate with various publics. *Listening* is the key to marketing communication.
- **Promotion** is a one-way attempt by marketers (buyers or sellers) to persuade others to participate in an exchange relationship with them. Promoters *talk to* others.

Marketing communication is a dialogue, and involves talking *with*. Promotion is talking *to*. Both are necessary in a successful marketing relationship, but the more *talking with* that occurs, the less *talking to* is necessary. Read that last sentence again. It is the key to marketing.

marketing communication
A two-way exchange of information between buyers and sellers.

promotion
A one-way attempt by marketers to persuade others to participate in an exchange relationship with them.

Selling can be an exciting and rewarding career.

Outdoor signs are part of promotion.

Marketing Publics

Successful marketers have learned that organizations have many "publics" that must be considered in a marketing program. The first "public" is the firm's employees. The marketing concept calls for coordination and cooperation from all members of the firm to provide consumer satisfaction. An **internal marketing program** is one designed to commit employees to the objectives of the firm. Like all marketing efforts, internal marketing begins with listening and being responsive to employees. In other words, marketing communication is the heart of all marketing programs. Note that marketing to employees is different from efforts by personnel to communicate with employees. This marketing effort is part of a total campaign aimed at all publics, including employees.

Other "publics" that marketers must communicate with include stockholders, suppliers, dealers, media representatives, government regulators—and customers and potential customers. In each case, marketing begins with listening to these people, adapting to what they say, and responding in a warm and friendly manner.

Marketing communication is actually quite easy once you see what its objectives are. Marketing communication is designed to establish friendly relationships. To do that, a person must be friendly, a good listener, helpful, responsive, honest, and open. The idea of marketing communication can be conveyed clearly in the following story—a composite of true experiences that illustrates the connections of marketing, communication, and the successful management of business.

internal marketing program
One designed to commit employees to the objectives of the firm.

MARKETING COMMUNICATION IN ACTION

The best way to envision good marketing communication is to see it in action. To do that, you will have to envision a small Italian restaurant named Barucci's. The restaurant has been owned and operated by the Barucci family for years (Mr. Barucci [Papa], Mrs. Barucci [Maria], and their sons, who are now aged 17 and 20). The restaurant was only marginally profitable, even though Papa worked 6 days a week, 12 to 14 hours a day. Maria helped whenever she could, as did the

Preparing an Italian dish with care.

boys. Everything was managed by Papa; he was the driving force behind the business.

One day Papa died. After a couple of months, the restaurant started faltering. No one was in charge. No one knew all the suppliers, the inventory system, or how to manage the restaurant. Papa had taken care of everything, so nobody else bothered learning.

Maria was desperate. She called the local college for some marketing advice. Several marketing students and a faculty advisor agreed to help. The first thing they recommended was to implement a *marketing communication system* (MCS) to learn about the business, its customers, the competition, suppliers, employee insights, internal records, and so forth. Maria learned that the first step in any marketing program is to listen. She wondered exactly what that meant, and the marketing team developed a list of people to whom Maria should listen. The list looked like this:

External information sources

    Customers

    Previous customers

    Suppliers

    Competitors

    Salespeople from potential suppliers

    Potential customers

    Members of the local community

    Government inspectors

    Other restaurant owners

Maria was eager to get started because she felt she had little time before the business failed. She wondered where to start. The faculty advisor suggested that she start internally to learn as much as possible about the business before going outside. He cited some key sources of information:

Internal information sources

    Employees

    Company records

    Other internal files

external information sources
Include discussions with competitors, suppliers, dealers, customers, consultants, trade associations, previous customers, potential customers, and others who have some interest in the firm.

internal information sources
Include employee discussions, accounting records, and other internal reports and data.

Internal Marketing Comes First

Maria quickly learned the secret to the success of marketing consultants: "If you want to know what is going right and wrong in a business, don't ask the managers, ask the employees. Make a list of their recommendations and insights, rewrite them, and turn them in as your consulting report." Maria did that. For the first time ever, the employees felt that they were part of a team. Their input was considered important. The psychological effect was amazing. Not only did the employees teach Maria all about how the business was run; they also gave her many helpful ideas for improvements. Naturally, because employees recommended them, the improvements were easily and swiftly implemented.

THINKING IT THROUGH

Why should a firm's marketing department be concerned about marketing to its own employees? Aren't they committed to the company's products already? Aren't stockholders fully supportive of everything the firm does already? How does one promote to government regulators? Is that what lobbyists do?

Good Communication Begins with Listening

Maria then decided it was time to further implement the marketing communication system. She began talking with competitors, other restaurant owners, suppliers, and salespeople from various computer firms.

The salespeople from potential suppliers were helpful in teaching Maria about the latest in restaurant management techniques and technology. Two of them designed some advanced management systems for Maria and taught her and her employees how to implement the changes.

The atmosphere at the restaurant became one of openness, helpfulness, loyalty, and genuine affection among all the people: suppliers, employees, and the Barucci family. Naturally, that feeling carried over to customers who felt that Barucci employees were friendly, helpful, and knowledgeable about food, wine, and food preparation. That atmosphere is one secret to successful marketing. The waiters and the chef were schooled together so that the waiters could talk intelligently about how the food was prepared, what to order with what, and which wines went with what. Because of this, the restaurant became a big success. Marketing insights from this case are:

- Data gathering is futile unless the data is turned into information and that information is shared among the employees.
- Information gathering and processing (marketing research or listening) is not an end in itself; it is a means to inform, train, motivate, and unite employees in a common effort to market the business.
- The goal of a comprehensive marketing program is to increase the satisfaction of *all* people associated with an organization—suppliers, owners, managers, employees, customers, neighbors, and so on.
- An effective total marketing communication program reduces the need for promotion; in this system, promotion is the organization's way of telling various publics that the firm is *responding* to their wants and needs. Promotion thus becomes a feedback device rather than merely a persuasive tool.

Now that we have seen a marketing communication system in action, we can discuss the concepts and principles with more understanding. First, let's define more carefully what we are talking about.

- What is the difference between marketing communication and promotion?
- Can you name five different publics of a restaurant?
- What are five sources of external information for a firm? What are two internal sources?

MARKETING COMMUNICATION SYSTEMS

Once a firm recognizes the fact that marketing communication is basically a process of making friends with those with whom one does business, it can formalize that goal by installing a **marketing communication system.** As we have learned, a marketing communication system (MCS) consists of three steps:

1 *Listening* to the various publics of an organization. This is called "marketing intelligence" and "marketing research."
2 *Responding* to that information by designing products and services that those publics want. This is called "corporate responsiveness."
3 *Promoting* the organization and its products to those publics to let them know that the firm is listening, is responding, and does have the desired products or services.

marketing communication system
Listening to various publics, responding to that information, and promoting the organization and its product.

Listening to Publics: Marketing Intelligence

Maria Barucci learned that there is simply no substitute for gathering marketing information other than physically going out and talking with people. That is what Procter & Gamble does. That is what IBM does. That is what all the excellent firms do.

Marketing research (listening to customers) is critical to an MCS.

Marketing Intelligence Versus Marketing Research

marketing intelligence
A constant stream of data from many sources, many of them unplanned.

The difference between marketing research and marketing intelligence is quite important for planners of a marketing communication system. **Marketing intelligence** is a constant stream of information from many sources, many of them unplanned. It consists of compliments and complaints from customers, letters, comments by employees, conversations overheard in airports, and millions of other bits and pieces of information picked up by corporate executives, employees, and friends. Marketing intelligence is simply there—to be used or ignored as the company wishes. If it is used, it is a powerful source of information.

marketing research
The formal gathering of data and information to learn about specific problems or issues; it is periodic and structured.

Marketing research, on the other hand, is the formal gathering of data and information to learn about specific problems or issues. Marketing research data become part of marketing intelligence. The problem with marketing research as the source for marketing decision making is that research is done infrequently. However, as a supplement to other marketing intelligence, marketing research (a formalized search for information) is invaluable.

MARKETING RESEARCH IN SMALL BUSINESS

For more than 30 years New York Twist Drill made a better industrial bit and the world beat a path to its doorstep. Sales doubled every five years until 1980, when the recession dried up business. During the next two years orders fell by 40 percent, and management searched frantically for a cure. After weeks of early-morning "skull" sessions, they finally found the answer—marketing. With the sales manager doubling as the marketing director and the salesmen providing the market research, the company quickly recruited customers for a new line of products. Since spring of 1983 the massive machine-tool lathes and grinders that once produced reamers and bits used to make airplanes and tractors have been sculpting delicate stainless-steel surgical drills and grinding out 13-piece drill sets for consumers. "We used to say, 'Who needs a marketing program?'" confesses vice president of sales C.J. Sirignano, who is happy to report that sales have jumped 30 percent since June. "Now, we're true believers."

"To Market, To Market," *Newsweek* (January 9, 1984), p. 70.

Service marketers must be responsive to customer wants.

Responding to Publics

The second part of an effective marketing communication system calls for responding to the wants and needs of various publics. This means that the organization must listen to those publics in the first place. And it means that somehow that information must get to decision makers who can respond. Most of the time, that does not happen. Salespeople often fail to report suggestions (or complaints) by customers. When employees do report information to managers, the information is often ignored or dismissed as being foolish or irrelevant. When managers refuse to listen, employees soon learn not to pass on information. That is the norm in many organizations. Nobody knows what's going on because everybody is afraid to speak up. I'm sure you have noticed that happening in many organizations, perhaps including your college.

A responsive firm adapts to changing wants and needs quickly and captures the market from other less responsive firms. That is why information is so vital to organizations today and why so much money is spent on computers to analyze data. The problem is that the computers are not getting the data they need. In fact, computers and data and information are no substitute for the close, personal contact that occurs when an executive talks face-to-face with customers.[2] That is one reason why small firms are capturing markets from large firms. Small firms tend to be better listeners, to have fewer layers of management in which information gets lost, and to be more responsive to changes in the market.

PROGRESS CHECK

- What are the three steps in a marketing communications system (MCS)?
- What is the difference between marketing intelligence and marketing research?

PROMOTION

After an organization has listened to its publics, studied its internal records, and adapted its policies and procedures to meet the desires of others, it is ready to promote. The promotional program should be relatively easy because listening tells the organization what information is wanted and needed. Pretesting of promotional messages helps assure the organization that the message will be effective (that is, do research to evaluate the commercials before they are shown to the general public). The elements a promotion manager uses to reach the public is called the promotion mix.

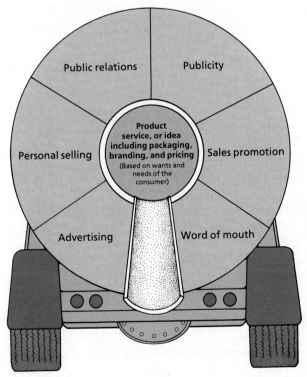

FIGURE 8-2

The promotion mix. This figure shows that the product offer is the central focus of the promotion mix. The offer is based on consumer wants and needs. All of the communication elements are designed to promote the exchange of the product offer for something of value.

promotion mix
Some combination of promotional tools (for example, advertising, personal selling, public relations, publicity, sales promotion, and word-of-mouth) that can be used to communicate to various publics.

A **promotion mix** is some combination of promotional tools (for example, advertising, personal selling, public relations, publicity, sales promotion, a good product or service, and word-of-mouth) that can be used to communicate to various publics (see Figure 8-2). Each public calls for a separate mix. For example, consumers are usually most efficiently reached through advertising. Large organizations are best reached through personal selling. To motivate people to buy now rather than later, sales promotion efforts such as coupons, discounts, special displays, premiums, and so on may be used. Publicity adds support to the other efforts and can create a good impression among all publics. Word-of-mouth is often the most powerful promotional tool and is generated effectively by listening, being responsive, and creating an impression worth passing on to others. Let's explore each element of the promotion mix to learn the fundamentals.

Advertising

advertising
Paid, nonpersonal communication through various media by organizations and individuals who are in some way identified in the advertising message.

Most people do not clearly understand the differences among promotional tools such as advertising, personal selling, publicity, and word of mouth. **Advertising** is limited to paid, nonpersonal communication through various media by organizations and individuals who are in some way identified in the advertising message. The advertisement for advertising below discusses some myths about ads. Word of mouth is not a form of advertising because it does not go through a medium, it is not paid for, and it is personal. Similarly, publicity is different from advertising in that it too is not paid for. Personal selling is face-to-face communication and does not go through a medium; thus it is not advertising. Note also that advertising may be used by anyone, including nonprofit organizations. Furthermore, advertising is different from propaganda in that the promoter is identified.

Advertisers also advertise advertising.

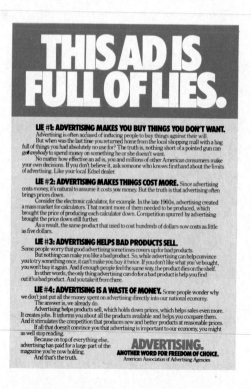

Advertising Statistics

The importance of advertising in the United States is easy to document; one need only look at the figures. The total ad volume exceeds $94 billion yearly. The number one medium in terms of total dollars spent is *newspapers* (see Figure 8-3) with almost 27% of the total. Many people erroneously think that the number one medium is TV, so take some time to learn the real figures.

MEDIUM	1984		1985		
	MILLIONS OF DOLLARS	PERCENT OF TOTAL	MILLIONS OF DOLLARS	PERCENT OF TOTAL	PERCENT CHANGE
Newspapers					
National	3,081	3.5	3,352	3.5	+8.8
Local	20,441	23.3	21,818	23.0	+6.7
Total	23,522	26.8	25,170	26.5	+7.0
Magazines					
Weeklies	2,224	2.5	2,297	2.4	+3.3
Women's	1,209	1.4	1,294	1.4	+7.0
Monthlies	1,499	1.7	1,564	1.6	+4.3
Total	4,932	5.6	5,155	5.4	+4.5
Farm publications	181	0.2	186	0.2	+3.0
Television					
Network	8,526	9.7	8,285	8.8	−2.8
Spot	5,488	6.2	6,004	6.3	+9.4
Cable (national)	492	0.6	637	0.7	+29.5
Local	5,084	5.8	5,714	6.0	+12.4
Cable (local)	80	0.1	130	0.1	+62.5
Total	19,670	22.4	20,770	21.9	+5.6
Radio					
Network	320	0.4	365	0.4	+14.0
Spot	1,197	1.3	1,335	1.4	+11.4
Local	4,300	4.9	4,790	5.1	+11.4
Total	5,817	6.6	6,490	6.9	+11.6
Direct mail	13,800	15.7	15,500	16.4	+12.3
Business papers	2,270	2.6	2,375	2.5	+4.6
Outdoor					
National	562	0.6	610	0.6	+8.3
Local	310	0.4	335	0.4	+8.3
Total	872	1.0	945	1.0	+8.3
Miscellaneous					
National	8,841	10.1	9,551	10.1	+8.0
Local	7,915	9.0	8,608	9.1	+8.8
Total	16,756	19.1	18,159	19.2	+8.4
Total					
National	49,690	56.6	53,355	56.3	+7.4
Local	38,130	43.4	41,395	43.7	+8.6
GRAND TOTAL	87,820	100.0	94,750	100.0	+7.9

FIGURE 8-3

U.S. advertising volume. The McCann-Erickson U.S. advertising volume reports represent all expenditures by U.S. advertisers—national, local, private individuals, and so on. The expenditures, by medium, include all commissions as well as the art, mechanical, and production expenses, which are part of advertisers' budgets for each medium.

Source: Prepared for *Advertising Age* by Robert J. Coen, McCann-Erickson Inc. Reprinted by permission from Robert J. Coen. From *Advertising Age,* May 12, 1986, p. 76.

When people refer to advertising, they are usually talking about TV advertising. For example, the debate about the effect of advertising on children is really a debate about TV advertising and children. Similarly, when people talk about advertising being offensive, intrusive, manipulative, and so on, they are thinking primarily of TV advertising. But only about 22% of advertising is TV advertising. Clearly, then, there is much more to advertising than people imagine.

People have the false impression that advertising is not very informative. But the number one medium, newspapers, is full of information about products, prices, features, and more. Does it surprise you to find that businesses spend more on direct mail than on radio and magazines? Direct mail (the use of mailing lists to reach an organization's most likely customers) is also very informative and a tremendous shopping aid for consumers. Each day consumers receive minicatalogs in their newspapers or in the mail that tell them what is on sale, where, at what price, for how long, and more. Thus advertising is informative.

The public benefits greatly from advertising expenditures. First, we learn about new products, new features, sale items, and more. But we also benefit from free radio and TV and subsidized newspapers and magazines. In short, advertising not only informs us about products but pays for us to watch TV and get the news from magazines and newspapers.

Figure 8-4 discusses the advantages and disadvantages of various advertising media to the advertiser. Newspapers and radio are especially attractive to local advertisers. Television has many advantages to national advertisers, but it is expensive. Figure 8-5 shows how the cost of 1 minute of advertising during the telecast of the Super Bowl has increased to exceed $1 million.

> In the factory we make cosmetics; in the store we sell hope.
>
> Charles Revson of Revlon

FIGURE 8-4

Advantages and disadvantages of different advertising media.

MEDIUM	ADVANTAGES	DISADVANTAGES
Newspapers *More info. content.*	Good coverage of local markets; ads can be placed quickly; high consumer acceptance; ads can be clipped and saved	Ads compete with other features in paper; poor color; ads get thrown away with paper (short life span)
Television *national local all senses*	Uses sight, sound, and motion; reaches all audiences; high attention with no competition from other material	High cost; short exposure time; takes time to prepare ads *low info. content.*
Radio	Low cost; can target specific audiences; very flexible; good for local marketing	People may not listen to ad; depends on one sense (listening); short exposure time; can't keep ad
Magazines	Can target specific audiences; good use of color; long life of ad; ads can be clipped and saved	Inflexible; ads often must be placed weeks before publication; cost is relatively high
Outdoor	High visibility and repeat exposures; low cost; local market focus	Limited message; low selectivity of audience
Direct mail	Best for targeting specific markets; very flexible; ad can be saved	High cost; consumer rejection as "junk mail"

SUPER BOWL	YEAR	COST OF "60 SPOT"
I	1967	$80,000
II	1968	$70,000
III	1969	$85,000
IV	1970	$200,000
V	1971	$200,000
VI	1972	$200,000
VII	1973	$207,000
VIII	1974	$214,000
IX	1975	$220,000
X	1976	$250,000
XI	1977	$324,000
XII	1978	$290,000
XIII	1979	$444,000
XIV	1980	$450,000
XV	1981	$550,000
XVI	1982	$670,000
XVII	1983	$800,000
XVIII	1984	$890,000
XIX	1985	$1,000,000
XX	1986	$1,100,000

FIGURE 8-5

Super Bowl marketing. The growth of America's premier sporting event is reflected in the rising cost of a 60-second TV commercial over the years. One minute of advertising during the Super Bowl costs over $1 million.

Source: Modified from *Advertising Age,* January 20, 1986.

Classes of Advertising

Different kinds of advertising are used by various organizations to reach different "publics." Some major classes include:

- *Retail advertising*—advertising to consumers by various retail stores such as supermarkets and shoe stores.
- *Trade advertising*—advertising to wholesalers and retailers by manufacturers to encourage them to carry their products.
- *Industrial advertising*—advertising from manufacturers to other manufacturers. A firm selling motors to automobile companies would use industrial advertising.
- *Institutional advertising*—designed to create an attractive image for an organization. "We Care About You" at Giant Food is an example. "Virginia Is For Lovers" and "I ♥ New York" are two institutional campaigns by government agencies.

sales promotion
Consists of those marketing activities that stimulate consumer purchasing and dealer interest by means of such things as displays, shows, exhibitions, and contests.

Sales Promotion

Sales promotion consists of those marketing activities that stimulate consumer purchasing and dealer interest by means of such things as displays, shows and exhibitions, and contests (see Figure 8-6).

Those free samples of products that people get in the mail; the cents-off coupons that they clip out of the newspapers; the contests that various retail stores sponsor; and those rebates that have been so popular in recent years all are examples of sales promotion activities. Sales promotion programs supplement personal selling, advertising, and public relations efforts by creating enthusiasm for the overall promotional program. Sales promotion activities also are directed at company

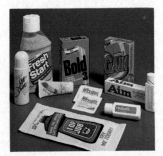

Product samples.

FIGURE 8-6

Sales promotion techniques.

Displays (store displays)
Contests ("You may have won $1 million!")
Samples (toothpaste, soap)
Coupons (10¢ off)
Premiums (free glass when you buy a meal)
Shows (fashion shows)
Deals (price reductions)
Trade shows
Bonuses (buy one, get one free)
Incentives (the gift in a Cracker Jack box)
Rebates (refunds from producers)

Lotteries
Audiovisual aids
Catalogues
Demonstrations
Special events
Exhibits
Portfolios for salespersons
Trading stamps
Conventions
Sweepstakes

VIDEO PROMOTIONS

Products of many types are now being sold directly through the medium of television. Perhaps the most successful of these shows is the Home Shopping Network (HSN).

Founded in 1982, this Clearwater, Florida–based company operates by establishing agreements with local cable companies who receive 5% of the total sales from within their area. The programs are broadcast live 24 hours a day. Hosts display housewares, appliances, jewelry, and other items one at a time, and shoppers dial a toll-free number to place their orders. They can pay by credit card or by personal check. Products carry a thirty-day, money-back guarantee, and are delivered via UPS within 7 to 10 days of the order. The company now routinely ships 18,000 to 20,000 packages per day.

Over a recent 11-month period, the average HSN customer purchased 17 items at an average price of $32 each. But others have become home shopping "junkies," charging over $1,000 per month on the show.

HSN's remarkable success has generated an equally impressive performance by its stock on Wall Street. With that kind of success, several new home shopping services are being started.

Videos are now being used to promote items via direct mail as well. PromoView Inc., of Newport Beach, California, has developed a video alternative to direct mail called V.I.P. (Visual Information Package). The idea is that videocassette promotions will be more cost effective, because they have higher response rates.

The way it works is that clients supply PromoView with the videos. The company then duplicates them, packages them in a gift box with the client's graphics, and ships them to prospects. A toll-free "800" number may be included for purchase of the items. PromoView also provides mailing list research. Response rate is expected to be 50 per 1,000 versus 5 per 1,000 for direct mail. Would you watch a promotional videotape on your VCR?

Sources: James Cox, "Airing Deals for Armchair Shoppers," *USA Today*, August 7, 1986, p. 1-2B; Lynn G. Reiling, "Cable, VCR Marketing Programs Being Beamed at Armchair Shoppers," *Marketing News*, January 21, 1985, p. 2.

employees (especially salespersons), wholesalers, retailers, and institutions such as schools and hospitals.

Sales promotion can be both internal and external. That is, it is just as important to get employees enthusiastic about a sale as it is potential customers. The most important internal sales promotion efforts are directed at salespeople and other customer-contact persons such as complaint handlers and clerks. Sales promotion tries to keep the salespeople enthusiastic about the company through sales training; the development of sales aids such as flip charts, portable audiovisual displays, and movies; and participation in trade shows where salespeople can get leads. Other employees who deal with the public may also be given special training to make them more aware of company programs and a more integral part of the total promotional effort.

After enthusiasm is generated internally, it is important to get distributors and dealers involved so that they too are enthusiastic and will cooperate by putting up signs and helping to promote the product.

After the company's employees and salespeople have been motivated with sales promotion efforts and middlemen are involved, the next step is to promote to final consumers using samples, coupons, cents-off deals, displays, store demonstrators, premiums, and other incentives such as contests, trading stamps, and rebates. Sales promotion is an ongoing effort to maintain enthusiasm, so different strategies are used over time to keep the ideas fresh. The box below discusses promotional strategy.

pull strategy
One in which heavy advertising and sales promotion is directed toward consumers.

push strategy
Means that the producer uses advertising, personal selling, sales promotion, and all other promotional tools to convince wholesalers and retailers to stock and sell merchandise.

PUSH STRATEGIES VERSUS PULL STRATEGIES

There are two ways to promote the movement of products from producers to consumers. The first is called a **push strategy.** In push strategy, the producer uses advertising, personal selling, sales promotion, and all other promotional tools to convince wholesalers and retailers to stock and sell merchandise. If it works, consumers will then walk into the store, see the product, and buy it. The idea is to push the product down the distribution system to the stores. One example of a push strategy is to offer dealers one free case of beer or soda for every dozen cases they purchase.

A second strategy is called a **pull strategy.** In a pull strategy heavy advertising and sales promotion is directed toward consumers. If it works, consumers will go to the store and order the products. The store owner will then order them from the wholesaler, who will order them from the producer. Products are thus pulled down through the distribution system. Dr. Pepper has used television advertising in a pull strategy to increase distribution. Of course, a company could use both a push and pull strategy at the same time in a major promotional effort.

PROGRESS CHECK

- What is the difference between trade advertising and industrial advertising?

- Can you name a dozen different sales promotion techniques?

Word of Mouth

Word-of-mouth promotion encourages people to tell other people about products they have enjoyed. Word of mouth is one of the most effective promotional tools, but one most marketers do not use to full effectiveness.[3]

word-of-mouth promotion
Encourages people to tell other people about products they have enjoyed.

Anything that encourages people to talk favorably about an organization is effective word of mouth. Notice, for example, how stores use clowns, banners, music, fairs, and other attention-getting devices to create word of mouth. Clever commercials can generate much word of mouth (for example, the Ernest P. Worrel ads mentioned in the Profile). You can ask people to tell others about your product or even pay them to do so. Samples are another way to generate word of mouth. But the best way to generate word of mouth is to have a good product, provide good services, and keep customers happy. We consumers are happy to tell others where to get good services and reliable products. However, we are also quick to tell others when we are unhappy with products and services. Negative word of mouth hurts a firm badly. Taking care of consumer complaints quickly and effectively is the best way to lessen negative word of mouth.

public relations
The management function that evaluates public attitudes, identifies the policies and procedures of an individual or an organization with the public interest, and executes a program of action to earn public understanding and acceptance.

Public Relations

Public relations (PR) is defined by the *Public Relations News* as the management function that evaluates public attitudes, identifies the policies and procedures of an individual or an organization with the public interest, and executes a program of action to earn public understanding and acceptance. Notice that public relations starts with good marketing research ("evaluates public attitudes").

ACTIVITIES OF THE PR DEPARTMENT

You may get a better idea of what public relations involves if we list some of the activities of PR departments:

- Establishing contact with civic groups, consumer organizations, and other concerned citizens to learn their views of the organization, to answer their questions, and to provide information (or education).
- Opening lines of communication with customers, suppliers, distributors, retailers, stockholders, government agencies, educators, and community leaders.
- Conducting studies to find the economic, environmental, and social consequences of organizational practices and to learn how to make a more positive contribution to customers, stockholders, and society.
- Providing any assistance needed to adjust the goals, policies, practices, personnel policies, products, and programs of the organization to meet the needs of changing markets.
- Assisting all members of the firm in developing effective programs of consumer information and education.

- Sending speakers to schools, clubs, and other such groups to maintain an open dialogue with students and other socially active members of society.
- Creating incentives for employees to participate in public-affairs activities such as raising funds for charitable groups, advising young people in Boy Scouts, Girl Scouts, or Junior Achievement groups, and being active in community associations.
- Answering consumer and other complaints promptly and correcting whatever it was that caused the complaint.
- Training employees or volunteers to provide prompt, friendly, courteous, and helpful service to anyone who contacts the organization in person, by phone, or by written correspondence.
- Demonstrating to society that the organization is listening, reacting, adjusting, and progressing in its attempt to satisfy its diverse publics.
- Opening two-way communications with employees to generate favorable employee opinion and to motivate employees to speak well of the organization to others.

This list is not a complete description of all the activities and responsibilities of the PR staff, but it should give you some feeling for what they do. The talking arm of the public relations function is called publicity.

Public relations is one department in an organization that has explicit responsibility for listening to the public. The second step in a good PR program, after listening, is the development of policies and procedures that are in the public interest. Public relations should not be just a promotional tool or a communications device; it should be an action-oriented department with responsibility to adapt the organization to the public's wants and needs. The final step in a PR program is to take action to earn public understanding and acceptance. One does not earn understanding by bombarding the public with propaganda; one *earns* understanding by having programs and practices in the public interest and letting people know that you have them. It is not enough to act in the public interest; you must also inform people of that fact.

Publicity

Publicity is one function of the public relations department. Here is how it works. Imagine that you have just invented a new product that enables people to dry-clean their clothes at home in their own washing machines. The problem is that

NEGATIVE VERSUS POSITIVE PUBLICITY

Publicity can have a powerful effect on consumers both positively and negatively. Positive publicity about William ("The Refrigerator") Perry made him a star in commercials in 1985.

In 1986, there was much negative publicity about terrorism in Europe and the Middle East. As a consequence, many people cancelled their vacations to those areas. When the nuclear power plant exploded in the Soviet Union in that same year, other people cancelled their vacation trips to Poland and other countries in the area.

When negative publicity occurs, the best response usually is to acknowledge the problem, describe in detail the steps being taken to resolve the problem, and counter the negative publicity with positive publicity about the organization's responsiveness. An excellent example was the case when Tylenol capsules were found to be tainted. The company, Johnson & Johnson, responded immediately by pulling the product from the shelves. Positive publicity for such fast reaction created a good impression for Johnson & Johnson.

An example of poor handling of negative publicity occurred as a result of the Chernobyl nuclear disaster. Soviet leaders failed to acknowledge the extent of the accident for days, and then provided only a few details. Negative publicity about the negative response compounded the problem.

TYLENOL Caplets are **SHAPED** so they're easier to swallow.

TYLENOL Caplets are **COATED** so they're easier to swallow.

TYLENOL Caplets are **EFFECTIVE** for extra-strength pain relief.

THAT'S WHY CAPLETS ARE THE FORM OF TYLENOL CONSUMERS PREFER MOST.

See Bill Powell and Martin Kasindorf, "The Tylenol Rescue," *Newsweek*, March 3, 1986, pp. 52-53; and "The Chernobyl Syndrome," a special report in *Newsweek*, May 12, 1986, pp. 20-49.

publicity
Any information about an individual, a product, or an organization that is distributed to the public through the media and that is not paid for or controlled by the sponsor.

you have very little money to promote the product, and you want to get some initial sales to generate funds. One effective way to reach the public is through publicity. **Publicity** is any information about an individual, a product, or an organization that is distributed to the public through the media, and that is not paid for, or controlled by, the sponsor. You might prepare a publicity release describing the new product and how it works and send it to the various media. (We shall not go into vast detail on how this is done, but there is much skill involved in writing the story so that the media will want to publish it.) Release of the news about the new product will reach many potential buyers (and investors, distributors, and dealers), and you will be on your way to becoming a wealthy marketer.

Publicity is an effective complement to other tools of marketing promotion such as advertising, personal selling, and sales promotion. The best thing about it is that the various media will publish publicity stories free if the material seems interesting or newsworthy. The idea, then, is to write publicity that meets these criteria.

Publicity often has several advantages over other marketing promotions, such as advertising. For example, publicity may reach people who would not read an advertising message. Publicity may be placed on the front page of a newspaper or in some other very prominent position. Perhaps the greatest advantage of publicity is its believability. When a newspaper or magazine publishes a story as news, the reader treats that story as news, and news is more believable than advertising. Of course, publicity is also much cheaper than advertising, because it is published free.

There are several disadvantages of publicity as well. The media do not have to publish a publicity release, and most are thrown away. Furthermore, the story may be altered so that it is not so positive. There is *good* publicity (IBM comes out with a new supercomputer) and *bad* publicity (poison found in Tylenol capsules). Once a story has run, it is not likely to be repeated. Advertising, on the other hand, can be repeated as often as needed. One way to see that publicity is handled well by the media is to establish a friendly relationship with media representatives, cooperating with them when they seek information. Then, when you want their support, they will cooperate as well.

personal selling
The face-to-face presentation and promotion of products and services plus the searching out of prospects and follow-up service.

Personal Selling

Personal selling is the face-to-face presentation and promotion of products and services plus the searching out of prospects and follow-up service. Effective selling is not simply a matter of persuading others to buy (see Figure 8-7). In fact, it is more accurately described as helping others to satisfy their wants and needs. Selling can be an exciting, rewarding, challenging, professional, and enjoyable career.

To suggest the importance of personal selling in our economy and the career opportunities it provides, let us look at a few figures. First, United States census data show that nearly 10% of the total labor force is employed in personal selling. When we add those who sell for nonprofit organizations, we find that over 7 million people are employed in sales.

The cost of a single sales call to a potential industrial buyer is over $200. Surely no firm would pay that much to send out anyone but a highly skilled, professional marketer and consultant. But how does one get to be that kind of sales representative? What are the steps along the way? Can women as well as men enter industrial sales? Such questions are answered in the story of Marge Burns.

[Salespeople] are lucky people. At a time when many discussions of work focus on such dismal topics as alienation, dehumanization, and boredom, [salespeople] do work that brings them into contact with other people, lets them establish productive human relationships, and is seldom repetitious or dull. At a time when many people feel estranged from, or indifferent about, their jobs, [salespeople] do work that can be engaging and engrossing. And, at a time when many people feel that their jobs lack challenge and exhilaration, [salespeople] do work that can be deeply satisfying and fulfilling.

V.R. Buzzotta, et al., in *Effective Selling Through Psychology*

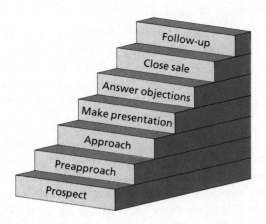

FIGURE 8-7

Steps in the selling process.

What the steps mean	
Prospect	This first step involves researching potential buyers and choosing those most likely to buy. These people are called *prospects*. You may learn the names of prospects from present customers, from surveys, from public records, and so forth.
Preapproach	Before making a sales call, the sales representative must do further research. As much as possible should be learned about the customer and his or her wants and needs. What products are they using now? Are they satisfied? Why or why not? Before a call, a salesperson should know the customer well and have a specific objective for the call. This is probably *the* most important step in selling.
Approach	"You don't have a second chance to make a good first impression." That is why the approach is so important. It involves learning all about the prospect and his or her needs (including hobbies and so forth). Good selling begins with good research.
Make presentation	This is the actual demonstration or presentation of the product and its benefits to the prospect. This may involve audiovisual aids. Showing advantages versus competition is often included.
Answer objections	Sometimes a prospect may question facts or figures and ask for more information. Often a sales representative must come back several times. The goal is to make sure that the customer is informed and committed to the purchase.
Close sale	You have to "ask for the sale" to finalize the sales process. "Would you like the red one or the green one?" "And when would you want delivery?" are examples of questions used to close the sale.
Follow-up	The selling process isn't over until the product is delivered, installed, and working satisfactorily. The selling relationship often continues for years as the salesperson responds to customer requests and introduces new products over time. Selling is a matter of establishing relationships; not just selling goods and services.

Climbing the Sales Ladder

Marge Burns was a hard-working person from the time she was very young. When Marge was 13, she was exposed to her first outside job in personal selling. She got a daily paper route and built her territory from 55 to 85 customers.

At 16 Marge went to work at a local drive-in restaurant as a waitress. She was paid $1.10 an hour, but with tips her weekly earnings often exceeded $120. Marge became more adept at working for and with people on this job, and she found that most people responded favorably (in this case with a tip) to a conscientious, friendly, dedicated salesperson (waitress).

After high school, Marge got a job at one of the leading department stores. She worked in various departments, but her tasks always included selling. Marge was surprised by her continual success in her various jobs, because she felt she was basically a rather shy person. She always believed that successful salespeople had to be outgoing, fast-talking individuals with lots of personality. Marge hardly fit that description. She was relatively quiet; she talked easily to people, but was not particularly quick with words, and she had a rather reserved personality. Nevertheless, Marge felt she had been successful at selling and was eager to try other selling jobs.

A year and a half after graduation from high school, Marge enrolled in State College. She was especially interested in potential marketing careers for women. But Marge was still very hesitant about selling, because she did not feel she had the right kind of personality. She eventually majored in marketing. One of her teachers encouraged her to pursue a sales career, because selling was an entry into all aspects of marketing management.

With great hesitancy and doubt, Marge began applying for sales jobs with Procter & Gamble, General Foods, and other consumer goods firms. Because of her past experience, she was much more comfortable in discussing careers in retailing with Sears and the other major stores. But when Procter & Gamble offered her a starting annual salary that was $2,000 over what most retailers offered, plus a company car and good benefits, Marge said "yes."

Procter & Gamble trained Marge in selling techniques, including the use of prepared sales talks that were used for practice and for gaining confidence. Marge enjoyed her contacts with retailers and the challenge of winning shelf space, setting up attractive displays, and introducing new products. Marge was surprised, though, at how little "selling" she had to do. She used her friendliness, sincerity, and professionalism to work with her customers to generate more satisfaction for them and more sales for her company. Marge did quite well in this job, and her salary was satisfactory.

THINKING IT THROUGH	**C**ould you be a sales representative? Could you be an effective one with some training? What sales experience have you had? Don't say "none" if you have persuaded your parents to buy you things, or persuaded others to go to the movies, and so forth. What is most scary about selling? How could those fears be overcome while in college? What courses could you take? How could extracurricular activities help?

One day Marge met a man who was in sales at IBM. He had heard about her through a friend and was impressed with her ability. He told her about sales opportunities at IBM and about some special opportunities for women. He talked Marge into meeting his boss at IBM and discussing career opportunities. Marge was hesitant, because technical skills were not one of her strengths.

After much discussion and interviewing, Marge decided to switch to IBM. She went through a comprehensive training program and eventually became a highly successful member of the sales force. Marge felt like a professional marketer at IBM because she was given so much responsibility. She was trained to be a consultant to her clients and to work with them in solving many different problems, not merely marketing problems.

Let us review some things you can learn from Marge and other sales representatives: Personal selling is a tool that may be applied in all aspects of a person's life. People can apply the same techniques to sell their ideas and their political philosophy as they use to sell soap and computers. Marge showed us that a person can begin very early to practice selling strategies. One misconception people have is that salespeople have a recognizable personality and sales approach. But Marge reveals that successful sales representatives do not differ from the general population on most measures. There is no correlation between sales success and intelligence, personality, age, level of education, or most other such measures.

In other words, one cannot group salespeople into a common bundle and analyze them. All of them are different, all use slightly different approaches, and all have different personalities, skills, and educational backgrounds. We have seen, though, that Marge was able to succeed at many different kinds of sales jobs, and so there must be some similarities among salespeople. Marge's story reveals several interesting facts:

- There is no such person as a "born" sales representative or sales manager. People become good in these fields by effectively applying certain well-established principles of the behavioral sciences (and, of course, by mastering the many technical aspects of their jobs).
- Selling strategies may be learned by anyone. But above all a sales representative must be flexible enough to adjust to the wants, needs, and demands of individual customers. Being a good listener and developing a warm, responsive manner is often more important than being a good talker or clever manipulator.

Part of sales training is personal development. It is important for all sales representatives to study their personal strengths and weaknesses. Self-knowledge enables a person to develop the interpersonal skills needed for successful selling.

America's highest paid salesman in 1984 was a computer firm's vice-president—marketing, who received $1.2 million, according to *Sales and Marketing Management* magazine's annual compensation survey. . . .The average compensation for the top 115 sales and marketing executives with 104 publicly-owned companies was $189,000.

Marketing News,
Sept. 27, 1985, p. 17

PROGRESS CHECK

- What are the seven steps in the selling process?
- Eleven public relations activities were listed in the text; can you recall six of them?

CAREER INFORMATION: MANUFACTURERS' SALES REPRESENTATIVES

NATURE OF THE WORK

Most manufacturers employ sales workers to market their products. Manufacturers' sales workers sell mainly to other businesses—factories, banks, wholesalers, and retailers. They also sell to institutions—hospitals, schools, libraries, and others.

Manufacturers' sales workers visit prospective buyers to inform them about the products they sell, analyze the buyers' needs, suggest how their products can meet these needs, and take orders. Sales workers visit firms in their territory, using an approach adapted to their line of merchandise. Those who handle bakery items, for example, may emphasize wholesomeness, packaging, and variety. Sometimes sales workers promote their firm's products at trade shows and conferences.

Sales workers who deal in technical products, such as electronic equipment, often are called industrial sales workers. Some engineers, often called sales engineers, also sell technical products. In addition to providing information on their firm's products, they help prospective buyers with technical problems. For example, they may recommend improved materials and machinery for a firm's manufacturing process, draw up plans of proposed machinery layout, and estimate cost savings from buying their equipment. They present this information to company officials and negotiate a sale, a process which may take many months. They may work with engineers in their own companies, adapting products to a customer's special needs. Technical sales workers sometimes train customers' employees to operate and maintain new equipment, and make frequent visits to make certain that it is functioning properly.

Manufacturers' sales workers spend most of their time visiting prospective customers. They also prepare reports on sales prospects or customers' credit ratings, plan their work schedules, draw up lists of prospects, make appointments, handle correspondence, and study literature about their products.

JOB OUTLOOK

Employment in this field is expected to grow more slowly than the average for all occupations through the mid-1990's. Industrial firms, chain stores, and institutions that purchase large quantities of goods at one time frequently buy directly from the manufacturer. The need for sales workers should continue as manufacturers emphasize sales activities to compete for the growing number of these valuable accounts. However, offsetting the demand somewhat will be the increased use by manufacturers of wholesalers and independent sales representatives to sell their products, particularly during economic downturns.

EARNINGS

Manufacturers' sales workers may be paid under different types of compensation plans. Some manufacturers pay experienced sales workers a straight commission, based on the dollar amount of their sales (as in the case of independent representatives); others pay a fixed salary. Most use a combination of salary and commission; salary and bonus; or salary, commission, and bonus. Bonus payments may depend on individual performance, on the performance of all sales workers in the group or district, or on the company's performance.

Median annual earnings of full-time manufacturers' sales workers were about $23,400 in 1984. The middle 50 percent earned between $16,600 and $33,800 a year. The bottom 10 percent earned less than $12,500; the top 10 percent earned more than $44,200 a year.

RELATED OCCUPATIONS

Manufacturers' sales workers must have sales ability and a specific knowledge of the products they sell. Some related occupations that require these skills are wholesale and retail buyers, field-contact technicians, wholesale trade sales workers, real estate sales workers, insurance sales workers, and securities sales workers.

SOURCES OF ADDITIONAL INFORMATION

For details about job opportunities for manufacturers' sales workers, contact manufacturers in your area.

Source: *Occupational Outlook Handbook,* 1986-1987 (U.S. Department of Labor).

1 Communication is one of the most vital of all the marketing activities. The idea is to establish an open dialogue with all of the organization's publics.

■ What is the difference between marketing communication and promotion?

Communication is a dialogue (talking *with*). Promotion is a one-way influence attempt (talking *to*).

■ Who are the publics of an organization?

Publics include any persons or groups that have an actual or potential relationship with the organization; that includes employees, stockholders, suppliers, dealers, customers, potential customers, media representatives, and government regulators.

2 To establish an open dialogue with its various publics, an organization needs a marketing communication system.

■ What does a marketing communication system look like?

There are three parts of an MCS: (1) *listening* to the various publics through marketing intelligence and marketing research, (2) *responding* to that information, and (3) *promoting* to those publics the fact that the organization is listening and now has or is doing what they want.

■ What is the first step in implementing a MCS?

Listening. Usually, listening to employees is the best start. Internal marketing gets all the employees committed to the company and its programs.

■ What is the difference between marketing intelligence and marketing research?

Marketing intelligence is a constant stream of data from many sources, many of them unplanned. Marketing research is a formal system for gathering information to learn about specific problems or issues. Marketing intelligence is constant; research occurs only periodically.

■ What does an organization do with all that information?

Information should be distributed to managers who should respond accordingly. It is responsiveness to market changes that makes a MCS effective.

3 Once an organization has listened to the various publics and has responded to that information, the next step in a MCS is to promote back to those publics. The various tools firms use to promote (advertising, selling, public relations, publicity, sales promotion, word-of-mouth) are collectively called the *promotion mix*. The product itself is part of the mix, along with packaging, branding, and pricing.

■ What do I need to know about advertising?

It is limited to paid, nonpersonal communication through various media where the sponsor is identified. By definition, then, word of mouth is not advertising. The number one medium in total dollars spent by advertisers is newspapers. TV is second and direct mail third. You should know the various classes of advertising and how objectives differ during the product life cycle.

■ What makes promotion effective?

The key to successful promotion is listening to customer wants and needs and responding to those wants and needs. Face-to-face communication through personal selling is often the most effective way to do this.

■ Why is publicity more effective than advertising?

Publicity is more believable. It can be placed on the front page or editorial page where it is more likely to be seen.

- What are problems with publicity?

  Publicity releases may be thrown away and never used, or altered so that they are less effective. Furthermore, publicity is rarely repeated. Worst of all, publicity can be negative.

- What is the secret of word-of-mouth promotion?

  Providing products and services that are so good that people cannot help but tell their friends about them.

4 Sales promotion consists of those marketing activities that stimulate consumer purchasing and dealer interest by means of such things as displays, shows, exhibitions, and contests.

- What are other sales promotion tools?

  Many are listed in Figure 8-6. They include samples, coupons, bonuses, catalogues, exhibits, and rebates.

- Is sales promotion the same as promotion?

  No; promotion includes personal selling, advertising, and all other elements of the promotion mix. Sales promotion is just one part of the promotion mix. It is really a catch-all term used to describe all the sales promotion tools.

5 Personal selling is the face-to-face presentation and promotion of products and services plus the searching out of prospects and follow-up service.

- What are the seven steps in the selling process?

  1. Prospect
  2. Preapproach
  3. Approach
  4. Make presentation
  5. Answer objections
  6. Close sale
  7. Follow-up

- What is the meaning of the Marge Burns story?

  That most people do some selling all of their lives. That selling is largely a matter of being friendly and helpful and responsive. And that there are many sales careers available to people who don't think they are the type for sales careers.

KEY TERMS

advertising p. 202
external information
   sources p. 197
internal information
   sources p. 197
internal marketing program
   p. 196
marketing communication
   p. 195
marketing communication
   system p. 199
marketing intelligence p. 200

marketing research p. 200
personal selling p. 210
promotion p. 195
promotion mix p. 202
public p. 194
publicity p. 210
public relations p. 208
pull strategy p. 207
push strategy p. 207
sales promotion p. 205
word-of-mouth promotion
   p. 207

1 If your school were to adopt a marketing communication system, where would it begin? To whom should it listen? How would it measure responsiveness? How would the students benefit? Discuss how schools that are failing because of decreasing enrollments could benefit from an MCS.

2 Give examples from your experience with businesses to prove that "the more communication with customers that occurs, the less promotion to customers is necessary." Are there successful firms in your area that do little promotion?

3 Explain the importance of internal marketing to a total marketing program. Give examples (from your experience or knowledge) of good and bad internal marketing. How does this differ from personnel's motivation efforts?

4 Bring in samples of advertising to show how informative consumer advertising can be. Bring in other ads that are not so informative. Discuss both sets of ads with the class to see which are more effective in attracting consumer interest.

5 Go through your paper and cut out examples of publicity (stories about products published in the paper) and sales promotion (coupons, contests, sweepstakes). Discuss the effectiveness of such promotional efforts with the class.

6 How would you go about generating word of mouth promotion for the following?
   a. An upcoming dance at school.
   b. A new restaurant in the area.
   c. A great vacation spot.
   d. A microwave oven.

CASE ONE   MARKETING COMMUNICATIONS IN HOSPITALS

In this chapter, you learned the benefits of a marketing communication system for Barucci's Restaurant. The procedures and principles are the same in all organizations, but some seem far behind in their application of the ideas. Take hospitals, for example. If you or anyone you know has been in a hospital lately, you know the problem. There are complaints about everything from parking and registering to food, service, medical treatment, and price. In fact, the nation's 5,800 general hospitals are a troubled industry.

Several factors have made hospital marketing more important. Most large companies have changed their health-care benefits to encourage employees to find the most cost-effective care. The government has changed its Medicare program from reimbursement for actual costs to set fees per diagnosis. Furthermore, people are going to the hospital less and staying for shorter periods. Admissions are down about 5% and the length of stay has dropped from 7.6 days to 6.7 days. Overall, occupancy rates are less than 70%. Health officials estimate that 1,000 hospitals may close by the end of the decade.

To counter such trends, hospitals are turning to marketing. One step has been to add new services, and hospitals have been nothing if not creative in adding new benefits:
   ■ Some hospitals are converting empty beds to motel rooms for friends and relatives of patients.
   ■ A hospital in Virginia started a catering service out of its kitchen.
   ■ Clinton Memorial in Michigan began a dry cleaning and laundry business, and rents carpet cleaning equipment.

The trend today is for hospitals to give up their independence and become part of larger health-care systems. In 1985, better than 35% of hospitals were part of such systems. Some 15% were owned by for-profit corporations. By joining systems, hospitals increase their buying power and get more clout from their advertising.

The move toward for-profit hospitals is accelerating. The largest chain, HCA, owns

200 hospitals. American Medical International has 117, and Humana has 90 facilities. Hospitals, in other words, are getting to be like hotel chains; they are profit-oriented, competitive, and customer-oriented.

There are many things a hospital could do to make its services more attractive to consumers. Hospitals are way behind hotels in that respect. Some areas that need attention include:

- Check-in, including the attitude and appearance of workers, attractiveness of lounges, and speed of service.
- Room service, including friendliness of nurses and other aides, noise control, and decor.
- Food service, including snacks for patients and guests and healthy, good-tasting meals.
- Physician's care, including time with patient, good two-way communication, consumer information and education.
- Follow-up care, including check-ups, out-patient care, and service evaluation.

Think of the different impressions you get from your visit to a hotel versus a hospital. Compare the attentiveness of workers, the decor, the attention to small details, the speed of service, and so on. Ask others about their impressions of various hospitals versus various hotels.

DECISION QUESTIONS

1 The first step in an effective marketing communications system is listening. Who are the publics to whom hospitals should listen?

2 Internal marketing comes first; that is, listening to and meeting the needs of employees. How does this concept apply to hospitals?

3 Once the staff is coordinated and motivated, the next phase of a marketing communication system is to listen to and satisfy consumers. How could that step be implemented in a hospital? How do hospitals compare to hotels at this step?

4 The last step in a marketing communication system is promotion. How important is promotion to a successful MCS for a hospital versus the other two steps: (1) listening and (2) responding to the needs and wants of various publics?

5 Would your answer differ for nonprofit hospitals versus for-profit hospitals?

PRACTICING MANAGEMENT DECISIONS

CASE TWO   REVIEWING THE COFFEE INDUSTRY

About 25 years ago, the number one drink in America was coffee. The trend was not good, however. From 1962 to 1976, the sales of coffee declined and the sales of soft drinks went up. By the end of 1976, soft drinks became the number one drink. The history of coffee sales is revealing.

The original colonists were mostly tea drinkers, bringing the habit with them from England. There were some coffee drinkers in the Dutch colony called New Amsterdam. In 1773, the colonists dumped hundreds of chests of tea into Boston harbor because of taxes, and America became a coffee-drinking nation.

By 1962, coffee sales were up to $1 billion a year and three fourths of the population drank an average of over 3 cups a day. The market looked so good at that time that Procter & Gamble bought Folger in 1963. From 1963 on, however, coffee sales have declined.

What happened in the 1960s to change the market? A major factor was the battle between Pepsi and Coke for the teenage drinker. Pepsi developed the theme of the "Pepsi Generation." Coke responded with themes directed toward young people as well. Coffee ads, meanwhile, were directed toward the over-35 crowd. The spokespeople for coffee were middle-aged women such as Mrs. Olsen, who promoted Folgers Coffee.

Fierce competition developed between Folgers and Maxwell House, both using a mature woman for a spokesperson. Both brands gained in market share at the expense of other brands. Competitors retaliated with a blitz of couponing, discounts, and heavy advertising. Customers became more price conscious. Sales continued to fall.

Meanwhile, the Pepsi generation grew up and took their preference for soft drinks with them. Coffee had the image of an older person's drink. Some figures reveal the trend:

| | PERCENT DRINKING COFFEE | |
AGE	1962	1982
10-19	25.1	8.5
20-29	81.0	43.0
30-59	90.8	73.3
60 +	88.4	83.1

Another factor that had an impact on coffee sales was the introduction of instant coffee and decaffeinated coffee. At one time, getting up and putting on the coffee was a daily chore. Instant coffee changed all that, and coffee was no longer a breakfast staple. The ambiance was gone and the taste changed.

There were big frosts in 1975 and 1985 that sent coffee prices soaring. Many people used high prices as a reason to quit. Consumption rose when prices fell again, but never to previous levels.

Decaffeinated coffee hurt sales by reminding people that regular coffee contained lots of caffeine. *Caffeine* became a "dirty" word in the 1980s. Decaffeinated coffee had neither the taste nor the wake-up power of "real" coffee. It was like new Coke taking over from old Coke; things were simply not the same. The most popular spokesman for decaffeinated coffee, Robert Young (Dr. Marcus Welby of TV fame) was an older man.

More recently, coffee producers have changed their ads. The appeal is to a younger but not young crowd. Some themes:

"Times Like These Were Made for Taster's Choice."

"The Thunder Was Loud—The Music Was Soft. The Coffee Was Brim."

Coffee ads are clearly being directed to a younger group (25 to 35). The market potential is huge. It is now over $4 billion.

DECISION QUESTIONS

1 What would you do if you were the marketing director of a firm that had major brands of regular coffee and decaffeinated coffee? How would you position your coffees?
2 Would you develop different strategies for regular versus decaffeinated coffee? Why or why not?
3 Discuss how you would recapture the market from soft drinks.
4 Could the coffee industry have prevented its decline by having a marketing communication system? Discuss.

LOOKING AHEAD

One of the most important functions of a marketing communication system is to work with potential customers to design products that most completely meet their wants and needs. Promotion of a bad product is money wasted in the long run. The product itself is such an important part of marketing that we shall devote an entire chapter to product concepts and management next.

PRODUCT DEVELOPMENT AND PRICING

LEARNING GOALS

After you have read and studied this chapter, you should be able to:

- Discuss how consumers develop their perception of a product.
- Describe classes of consumer products and industrial products.
- List and describe four functions of packaging.
- Outline the five steps of the new product development process.
- Identify and describe the stages of the product life cycle and describe marketing strategies at each stage.
- Outline different categories of pricing objectives.
- Discuss the use of break-even analysis in pricing.
- Differentiate between skimming and penetration pricing strategies.
- Discuss the strategies of psychological pricing and price lining.
- Describe retail pricing.

PROFILE   THOMAS S. MONAGHAN OF DOMINO'S PIZZA

In 1960, Tom Monaghan started in the food business by buying a small Italian restaurant (mostly pizza) near Eastern Michigan University. Things didn't go well at the restaurant and Tom decided to change his product offer. He felt that he could stand out from other pizza places by concentrating on delivery. Thus was born Domino's Pizza, Inc.

Sales doubled when Tom switched to delivery, and he opened four new outlets near college campuses and military bases (a total of seven outlets). All the stores were in Michigan. In 1968, Tom began opening outlets out of state. He extended himself too fast and Domino's got into financial difficulty.

Sticking to his belief that the concept was right, Tom continued working in the restaurants and regained financial stability by 1971. Over the next 4 years, he expanded to 100 franchises. "I began rebuilding by staking out a business niche— free delivery—and doing it better and faster than anyone else," Monaghan says.

Quality and service are the keys to Domino's success. Twenty four commissaries supply all the pizza ingredients, including fresh dough. Laboratory tests and taste tests help control quality and improve the product. But the unique selling prop-

Tom Monaghan.

If a man can . . . make a better mousetrap than his neighbor, though he builds his house in the woods the world will make a beaten path to his door.
RALPH WALDO EMERSON

osition (the thing that makes the product better) is delivery in 30 minutes—guaranteed! The pizza is free if the delivery person is late.

Using the concept of 30-minute delivery, Tom Monaghan expanded to over 1,000 outlets and set a goal of 5,000 outlets. What is Domino's product? It isn't just pizza; that product is available everywhere. It is good quality pizza delivered to your door.

How is Tom doing with this unique product offer? Well enough to buy the Detroit Tigers American League baseball team for $43 million. The company sponsors an Indy 500 racing team and the Michigan 500, Domino's Pizza 500, and several collegiate track and field events. ■

Source: Bernie Whalen, "'People-Oriented' Marketing Delivers a Lot of Dough for Domino's," *Marketing News,* March 16, 1984, pp. 4-5.

PRODUCT IMPORTANCE

The marketing mix consists of the four *P*'s of product, place, promotion, and price. Now that we have discussed marketing's role in society and marketing communication (the *p*romotion element of the four *P*'s), we are ready to discuss two more of the marketing mix variables: *p*roduct and *p*rice. Chapter 10 will focus on the final *P*: *p*lace, or distribution.

The reason marketers do so much listening, as discussed in Chapter 8, is to learn what consumers want and need in the products that companies make, including consumer preferences about price.

The problem of adapting products to markets is a continuous one. An organization cannot do a one-time survey of consumer wants and needs, design a line of products to meet those needs, put them in the stores, and relax. There must be a *constant* monitoring of consumer wants and needs because consumers change over time and seek variety in their choices.

Nowhere is the problem of consumer choice more keenly felt than in the fast-food business. Firms such as McDonald's and Burger King are constantly monitoring consumers to detect trends, preferences, and life-style changes that call for new offerings. The more sophisticated firms become in marketing, the more important it becomes for others to follow. This is what Ronald Fay, president of Wendy's International Inc., says about marketing research: "Four years ago we didn't even have a research and development staff. Today we have 42 people in that area."[1]

The number of products in the development stage range from 20 or so at McDonald's to more than 50 at Wendy's. Burger King uses a computer to predict how much labor a new product will require, what effect it might have on sales of other menu items, and how much total profit it will generate.[2]

Fast-food organizations must constantly monitor all sources of information for new product ideas. McDonald's got the idea for the Big Mac, the Filet-O-Fish sandwich and the Egg McMuffin from franchisees. Chicken McNuggets were developed when the head chef was experimenting with Onion McNuggets. McDonald's chairman suggested that the chef try chicken and after much market testing, a new product was born. Researchers also monitor grocery store shelves and cookbooks for new ideas. Product development, then, is a key activity in any modern business.

PRODUCT IMPORTANCE AT CHRYSLER

One of the people who recognize the importance of a good product in marketing is Lee Iacocca, the Chrysler chairman, who appeared on Chrysler's television ads saying, "If you can find a better car, buy it!" This is what *Advertising Age* said about his philosophy:

> "Product is king" for the veteran auto executive, who obviously is still very much guided by his engineering background. And his tenacity in making his credo a reality at Chrysler is at the core of his success.

> He would deny that what has been accomplished at Chrysler smacks of marketing acumen. . . . As he explains it:

You say it was a marketing task, but I don't look at it that way. I looked at [the job of turning around the company] as a very difficult *product* task and a quality and productivity task.

Marketing really means nothing if we didn't have the product that appeals to people. Not just convertibles, but across the board. Without that, our [market] penetration wouldn't have gone up.

And once you have solid product? Mr. Iacocca makes it sound almost routine. "Then you back the product and give some assurance you stand behind it, and that's the key to any marketing program."

Source: Ralph Gray, "Lee Iacocca of Chrysler: Crisis Plans Paying Off," *Advertising Age* (January 2, 1984), pp. 1 and 30.

What Is a Product?

From a marketing viewpoint a product is not just the physical good or service. A **product** consists of all the tangibles and intangibles that consumers evaluate when deciding whether or not to buy something. Thus a product is a washing machine, car, or bottle of beer, but the product also consists of:

- The price
- The package
- The store surroundings
- The image created by advertising
- The guarantee
- The reputation of the producer
- The brand name
- The service
- The buyers' past experience

product
Consists of all the tangibles and intangibles that consumers evaluate when deciding whether or not to buy something.

When people buy a product, they evaluate all these things and compare products in all these dimensions. Therefore a successful marketer must begin to think like a consumer and evaluate the product as a total collection of impressions created by all the factors listed. The box on p. 225 discusses the importance of understanding the consumer and of expert product design.

Different Product Views

Most people tend to think of products as tangible goods that can be seen and felt. They also tend to view products as what producers make in a factory. The following examples will help illustrate why traditional thinking about products needs to be changed.

What is the product of a library? For years librarians seemed to concentrate on books and reading groups as their main product. But these products failed to

The marketing view demands the active recognition of a new kind of competition. This is . . . not competition between what companies produce in their factories, but between what they add to their factory output in the form of packaging, services, advertising, customer advice, financing, delivery arrangements, warehousing, and other things people value.

Theodore Levitt

Libraries have broadened
their product offering.

You could plan a trip,   borrow a classic film,   get help finding a job,

learn to belly dance,   attend a concert,   get fast answers,

trace your family tree,   stay in shape,   or get your books by mail.

AT THE LIBRARY? At the library.
Come see what's new besides books.

attract enough people. So some librarians decided to look at the product from the perspective of the public, and as a result they made a drastic change in the product.

> In the Salinas, Calif., library, teen-agers have brightly painted a young-adult room where they hold guitar "jams." In the current events room of Pittsburgh's Carnegie Library, a United Press International newsprinter clatters away 12 hours a day. In Erie, Pa., a child can borrow a guinea pig from the library for a week; its juvenile department also boards mice, rats, gerbils and a 42-inch boa constrictor for children to play with. . . . The Whitmore Library in Salt Lake County, Utah, has opened piano and organ rooms. . . . [and] In Chicago, as part of an experiment for children aged two to five years, three branch libraries are lending out tools and playthings like toy workbenches, hand puppets, an abacus, a magnet, drums and tambourines.[3]

Clearly the product of a library today may be anything that will satisfy the needs of selected market segments, including videotaped movies, rental paintings, workshops, and concerts. (See the ad above, put out by the American Library Association). Libraries are much more successful today because they have designed their product to fit the needs of people. Previously they had designed a product (a wide selection of books) and then tried to find people to use it. Recognizing that people evaluate many aspects of a total product offer, libraries have made their product more convenient by means of mobile lending units, more fun by adding record collections and listening rooms, and more helpful by increasing over-the-phone services. In short, libraries have been designing consumer-oriented products.

What is the product of an automobile manufacturer? It could be good mileage (compact cars), luxury (full-size Cadillacs), sportiness (convertibles), speed, or safety or some combination of these features. Still, the product isn't what the manufacturer puts into the car; the product is the perception of these features by consumers. In conclusion, we can say the following about products:

- There often is a difference between the product as viewed from the perspective of the seller and as viewed by the buyer.
- Successful sellers design their products based on the needs of the buyer—those needs are determined through marketing research.
- A buyer evaluates a product by comparing many dimensions, including price, quality, convenience, safety, and satisfaction in use.
- A product is what a person perceives it to be.

AN EXPERT SKIER DESIGNS EXPERT SKIS

It helps to understand your customer's wants and needs to design good products. Who, for example, would know more about a skier's needs than a professional skier? C.B. Vaughan made the U.S. National Ski team twice and was clocked at a downhill speed record of 106 miles per hour.

Using his knowledge of skiing and a small investment of several thousand dollars, in 1970 Vaughan began a business out of the trunk of his car making and selling ski equipment. Gross sales the first year were $67,000. Now, C.B. Sports does over $35 million a year in sales, has six plants, and employs 560 people.

The surprising thing about this story is that Vaughan knew nothing about design when he started. He learned most of it from a book, and the rest by trial and error. His advantage over other producers is his meticulous workmanship and attractive details. The first success was "super pants," which featured an ankle to waist snag-free zipper. But parkas are his biggest success. They sell for about $200 and are a status symbol. It helps that Vaughan is from Vermont and has attracted a big following in that area. Vaughan says, though, that "the product has to speak for itself... we've managed to create a charisma in the marketplace."

Source: "From Moguls to Millions," *Marketing Communications*, November, 1984, pp. 10, 11.

What is the product of a college or university? Can you see that the product would differ for different students? Some would value the social life, others the educational standards, and still others the location and price. Faculty might see an entirely different product. The product, then, is what people think it is. The job of marketing, therefore, is to show people the benefits of the product so that they perceive value.

What is the product of a restaurant? Is it the food? Think about it.

THINKING IT THROUGH

The Product Mix

A **product mix** is the combination of products offered by a manufacturer. In the case of automobile manufacturers, the product mix consists of everything from automobiles to minivans, small trucks, large tractor trailers, and tanks.

product mix
The combination of products offered by a manufacturer.

product line
A group of products that are physically similar or are intended for a similar market.

convenience goods and services
Products that the consumer wants to purchase frequently and with a minimum of effort.

shopping goods and services
Products that the consumer buys only after comparing quality and price from a variety of sellers.

specialty goods and services
Products that have a special attraction to consumers, who are willing to go out of their way to obtain them.

A **product line** is a group of products that are physically similar or are intended for a similar market. In automobiles, one company's product line for passenger cars may include large luxury cars, midsize cars, compact cars, minivans, and station wagons. They are all part of the product line.

Manufacturers must decide what product mix is best. The mix may include both goods and services to spread the risk among several industries. Product line decisions are also important. Carrying too many different products can be inefficient. U.S. auto manufacturers, for example, are cutting back on options in colors, designs, and so on to make the production process more efficient. Carrying too few products in the line may also be a poor strategy because you may attract more customers with a full line of products than a reduced line. For example, a store that sells a full line of appliances is more attractive to shoppers than a store that carries just a couple of models.

Marketing Different Classes of Consumer Goods

Several attempts have been made to classify consumer goods and services. One of the more traditional classifications has three general categories: convenience goods and services, shopping goods and services, and specialty goods and services. These classifications are based on consumer shopping habits and preferences:

- **Convenience goods and services** are products that the consumer wants to purchase frequently and with a minimum of effort (for example, candy, snacks, banking). Location is very important for marketers of convenience goods and services. Brand awareness and image also are important.
- **Shopping goods and services** are those products that the consumer buys only after comparing value, quality, and price from a variety of sellers. Shopping goods and services are sold largely through shopping centers where consumers can "shop around." Because consumers carefully compare such products, marketers can emphasize price differences, quality differences, or some combination of the two. Examples include clothes, shoes, appliances, and auto repair shops.
- **Specialty goods and services** are products that have a special attraction to consumers, who are willing to go out of their way to obtain them. Examples include goods such as expensive fur coats, jewelry, and cars and services provided by medical specialists or business consultants. These products are often marketed through the classified section of the telephone book or by word of mouth.

ROLEX

Consumers are willing to expend different amounts of effort to acquire convenience goods, shopping goods, and specialty goods.

The marketing task varies depending on the kind of product; that is, convenience goods are marketed differently from specialty goods, and so forth. The best way to promote convenience goods is to make them readily available. Price or quality are the best appeals for shopping goods, and specialty goods rely heavily on word of mouth.

Whether or not a good or service falls into a particular class depends on the individual consumer. What is a shopping good for one consumer (for example, coffee) could be a specialty good for another consumer (for example, imported coffee). Some people shop around comparing different dry cleaners, so dry cleaning is a shopping service for them. Others go to the closest store, making it a convenience service.

Marketing Industrial Products

The industrial market is larger than you may think, because **industrial goods** may be sold several times before reaching the consumer market. For example, sand may be sold to a glass maker to make auto glass. The glass is then sold to an auto manufacturer who puts the glass in the car.

There are two major classes of industrial goods. **Capital goods** are products that cost a lot of money and last a long time, such as factories and machinery. **Expense items** are less costly and are used up more quickly, such as cleaning fluids and light bulbs. From the auto glass example, you may have noticed other classifications that could be used for industrial goods—products used in factories, utilities, mines, institutions (for example, hospitals, schools), government agencies, and wholesale and retail outlets:

- *Raw materials* are goods such as sand and coal.
- *Component parts* are goods such as engines, tires, and windshields.
- *Accessory equipment* includes typewriters and copy machines.
- *Installations* are factories and similar large facilities.
- *Supplies* include cleaning fluid and pencils.
- *Services* include consulting, accounting, and cleaning.

There are many careers in industrial marketing for college students because such goods and services are sold by sales representatives more than advertising (as most consumer goods are sold). This means a big demand for salespeople to sell everything from huge installations to supplies. Because industrial buyers buy in huge volume, comparatively speaking, the chance to make large commissions is very good.

industrial goods
Products used in factories, utilities, mines, institutions, government agencies, and wholesale and retail outlets.

capital goods
Products that cost a lot of money and last a long time, such as factories and machinery.

expense items
Less costly goods that are used up relatively quickly, such as cleaning fluids and light bulbs.

PROGRESS CHECK

- What is the product of a professional baseball team?

- Name the three classes of consumer goods and give examples of each. Can you do the same for industrial goods?

PACKAGING CHANGES THE PRODUCT

Many years ago people had problems with table salt, because it would stick together and form lumps whenever the weather was humid or damp. The Morton Salt Company solved that problem by designing a package that kept the salt dry in all kinds of weather. Thus the slogan, "When it rains, it pours." Packaging made Morton's salt more desirable than competing products, and it is still the best-known salt in the United States.

The Morton Salt Company knew how to use packaging to change and improve its basic product—salt. Other companies have used similar techniques. Thus we have had stackable potato chips in a can, cigarettes in a crush-proof box, beer in flip-top aluminum cans, dinners that can be boiled in a pouch and served immediately, whipped cream in dispenser cans, and so forth. In each case, the package changed the product in the minds of consumers and opened large markets. Packaging changes the product by changing its visibility, usefulness, or attractiveness.

The Growing Importance of Packaging

Packaging has always been an important aspect of the product offer, but today it is carrying more of the promotional burden. Many goods that were once sold by salespersons are now being sold in self-service outlets, and the package has been given more sales responsibility. As such the package must do the following: (1) it must attract the buyer's attention; (2) it must explain the benefits of the good inside; (3) it must provide information on warranties, warnings, and other consumer matters; and (4) it must give some indication of price, value, and uses.

Different Packaging Functions

One major function of packaging is to attract the attention of the buyer. To do this a package needs *visibility*. Visibility is achieved through the creative use of color, shape, texture, design, and size. Using these cues, one can easily identify most of the popular consumer products. For example, most people can recognize a Coke bottle, a box of Tide, a pack of Marlboro cigarettes, or a package of Crest toothpaste from several yards away.

Another function of packaging is to give consumers added convenience for their money. You are already familiar with the convenience that packaging has given products through the use of handy spray pumps, easy-open cans, squeezable ketchup bottles, clear plastic wraps, and so forth. In the future, we may expect to see more packaging innovations that will enable us to keep meat and milk without refrigeration, to serve instant gourmet meals from speedy microwave ovens, and to keep fresh vegetables and other perishables for months. Recently, Campbell introduced a salad with a shelf life of 28 days.

New, convenient forms of packaging.

Another function of packaging is to protect the goods from environmental factors such as rain and sun. Packaging must also protect against breakage, damage, and harm from animals.

Packaging helps the middleman by grouping goods into easily managed sizes. It may be designed, for instance, so that the shipping carton becomes a display rack. Packaging also helps retailers to price items, store them on their shelves, and process the item through their checkout counters. The new universal product codes (UPCs) that were developed for supermarket items and other retail goods may enable the retailer to reduce checkout time, reduce errors, and increase inventory control and the information flow from retailer to producer.

To summarize the functions of packaging we have discussed so far, remember that packaging (1) adds visibility, (2) adds convenience, (3) protects the goods from damage, and (4) keeps the goods in manageable, controllable sizes. We also mentioned that packaging benefits middlemen as well as consumers. Branding, like packaging, changes the product by changing consumer perceptions. The name *Del Monte* on a label makes the product different than one with the label *peaches*. We shall discuss such issues below.

BRANDING

A **brand** is a name, symbol, or design (or a combination of them) that identifies the goods or services of one seller or group of sellers and distinguishes them from those of competitors. The term *brand* is sufficiently comprehensive to include practically all means of identification of a product except perhaps the package and its shape. A **brand name** is that part of the brand consisting of a word, letter, or group of words or letters comprising a name that differentiates the goods or services of a seller from those of competitors. Brand names you may be familiar with include Chevrolet, Sony, Del Monte, Campbell, Winston, Jordache, Exxon, Borden, Michelob, and Colgate. Such brand names give products a distinction that tends to make them attractive to consumers.

A **trademark** is a brand that has been given legal protection. It includes the brand name and the pictorial design. The trademarks shown in the margin are widely recognized. So are trademarks such as McDonald's golden arches.

To measure the importance of brand names in our society, you might try the following experiment. Find a group of beer drinkers who say they greatly prefer one brand of beer and dislike another brand. Pour the brand they do not like into an empty bottle of the favored brand and serve it to them. Ask them how they like it. Most will say it tastes great, because the name on the bottle has a direct effect on the perceived taste. If they believe they are drinking their favorite beer, other brands will probably taste good to them. People's perceptions of a product's taste, value, and attractiveness are determined by preconceived notions that are partially maintained by branding. That is, if people expect something to be good, it usually is perceived as good. And if they expect something to be bad, it usually is perceived as bad.

People are often impressed by certain brand names, even though they say they know there is no difference between brands in a given product category. For example, when someone who says that all aspirin is alike asks for an aspirin, put two bottles in front of him or her—one with the Excedrin label and one labeled with an unknown brand. See which one he or she chooses. Most people choose the brand name even when they say there is no difference. What does this indicate?

Brand Categories

Several categories of brands are familiar to you. **National brand names** are the brand names of national manufacturers. They include well-known names such as Xerox, Polaroid, Kodak, Sony, and Chevrolet.

brand
A name, symbol, or design (or combination of these) that identifies the goods or services of one seller or group of sellers and distinguishes them from those of competitors.

brand name
That part of the brand consisting of a word, letter, or group of words or letters comprising a name that differentiates the goods or services of a seller from those of competitors.

trademark
A brand that has been given legal protection.

Trademarks for NBC, BMW, Shell, and 7-Up.

national brand
The brand name of a national manufacturer (for example, Xerox).

private brands
The name given products by distributors or retailers (also known as "house" or "distributor" brands).

generic name
The name of a product category.

Goods with generic names on display.

Private brands are names given to products by distributors or retailers. Well-known names include Kenmore and Diehard (Sears). These brands are also known as "house" brands or "distributor" brands.

What many manufacturers fear is having their brand names become generic names. A **generic name** is the name for a product *category*. Did you know that *aspirin* and *linoleum* were once brand names? So were *nylon, escalator, kerosene,* and *zipper.* All of those names became so popular, so identified with the product, that they lost their brand status and became **generic** (the name of the product class). The producers then had to come up with new names. The original *Aspirin,* for example, became *Bayer* aspirin. Some companies that are working hard to protect their brand names today include Xerox (one ad reads, "Don't say 'Xerox it;' say 'Copy it'") and Styrofoam.

Some products are popular today because they have no brand names. They are called *generic products* because they are called by the name of the product class. There are generic tissues, generic cigarettes, generic peaches, and so forth. All it says on the label of the can is "Peaches," no brand name. These products sell for less because they do not have to support heavy advertising and promotion budgets. Do you buy generic toothpaste? Generic mouthwash? Why or why not?

Labeling Legislation

Labeling and branding decisions are often made together. The Fair Packaging and Labeling Act of 1966 sets certain requirements for information on labels. The idea is to help consumers do comparison shopping. The Food and Drug Administration has rules covering the nutritional content of some foods. We shall discuss the psychological effects of creative branding and labeling in the next section.

Brand Images

You might try an experiment for yourself. Buy an attractive but inexpensive tie and put it in a very attractive box from an exclusive store. Then buy a similar tie from the exclusive store and put it in a box from an inexpensive discount store. Tell your friends that you can't decide which tie is better and ask them to choose. If past experience is any guide, most will choose the inexpensive tie in the more expensive box. Again, laboratory experiments support these suggestions. The concept that explains such behavior is that people often cannot determine the value of products by physical inspection; they therefore turn to other indicators of quality such as labels, packaging, brand names, and price. A higher-priced, expensively packaged item is usually perceived as better regardless of its actual physical qualities.

PRODUCT MANAGEMENT

product manager
Coordinates all the marketing efforts for a particular product (or product line) or brand.

A **product manager** coordinates all marketing efforts for a particular product (product line) or brand. The concept of product management originated over 50 years ago with Procter & Gamble, and over the last 25 years product managers have come to occupy important positions in many firms. An Association of National Advertisers survey of members found that 85% of the companies producing packaged goods, 34% of the companies producing other consumer goods, and 55% of manufacturers of industrial goods had a product-management system. Product management may offer a truly challenging career, if you are interested.

Product managers have direct responsibility for one brand or one product line, including all the elements of the marketing mix: product, place, promotion, and price. It's like being the president of a one-product business. One reason companies have created this position is to have greater control over new product development and product promotion. The following material explores the success rate for new product introductions. It then outlines steps to follow in product development, including strategies for marketing products over time.

New Product Success

For many years it was commonly believed that about 90% of new products failed. Consequently, many firms hesitated to bring out new products. Instead, they tended to copy proven products from other companies. More recently, The Conference Board conducted a study of medium- and large-sized firms that showed that failure rates were closer to 33%. One reason for the improved success rate is that firms are doing more careful consumer research and are not launching products until research shows a probable demand. (A "successful" product was one that was "sent to the market and met management's original expectations in all important respects."[4]) Some key findings from the study were:

- Firms selling mainly to industrial markets launched an average of eight major new products during the preceding 5 years, compared with six for consumer-oriented firms.
- Insufficient and poor market research is the leading cause of new-product failure. Cited next most often as reasons for failure are technical problems in design or production and errors in timing the product's introduction.

The emphasis today seems to be on new-product failures. A progressive firm should look to market successes. Smaller firms may experience a lower success rate, but not if they do proper product planning. We shall discuss such planning below.

The New-Product Development Process

Product development consists of several stages:
1 Generating new product ideas
2 Screening
3 Development
4 Testing
5 Commercialization (bringing the product to the market)

New products continue to pour into the market every year, and the profit potential looks tremendous. Think, for example, of the potential of two-way cable TV, large-screen TV sets, home computers, video disks, word processors, and other innovations. Where do these ideas come from? How are they tested? What is the life span for an innovation? That is what the following material is all about.

Generating New Product Ideas

Figure 9-1 gives you a good idea of where new product ideas come from. Note that 38% of the new product ideas for consumer goods come from analyzing competitors. This was true of 27% of new industrial products. Such copying of competitors in favor of discovering new products slows the introduction of new ideas.

A strong point can be made for listening to employee suggestions for new product ideas. The number-one source of ideas for new industrial products was

FIGURE 9-1

Where new product ideas come from.

Adapted from Leigh Lawton and A. Parasuraman, "So You Want Your New Product Planning to Be Productive," Table 1, *Business Horizons,* December 1980.

Consumer products (based on a survey of 79 new products)	(%)*
Analysis of the competition	38
Company sources other than research and development	31.6
Consumer research	17.7
Research and development	13.9
Consumer suggestions	12.7
Published information	11.4
Supplier suggestions	3.8

Industrial products (based on a survey of 152 new products)	(%)*
Company sources other than research and development	36.2
Analysis of the competition	27.0
Research and development	24.3
Product users	15.8
Supplier suggestions	12.5
Product user research	10.5
Published information	7.9

*Percentages add up to more than 100% because more than one source was named for some products.

company sources other than research and development. It was also a major source for new consumer goods. Part of that is because of successful marketing communication systems that monitor suggestions from all sources.

Look through Figure 9-1 carefully and think about the implications. Notice that more than a third of all new product ideas for industrial products came from

FIGURE 9-2

Marketing considerations for new brands.

Reprinted by permission of the A.C. Nielsen Company.

Areas of company strengths and weaknesses
Tie-ins with, or potential impact on, other company brands
Production capabilities
Consumer attitudes toward category, brands, product benefits
  Awareness
  Satisfaction with existing brands
Regional consumer differences
  Package sizes
  Flavors
  Product types
  Forms
Advertising and merchandising norms, timing and directions
Consumer promotional considerations
Nature of competition
  One brand dominance
  Fractionated market
  Local brand oriented
  Controlled label penetration

Market segments
Distribution channels
  Sales force coverage capabilities
  Brokers
  Trade class differences
Trade perceptions of category; new brand entries
Outlet importance by area
Pipeline requirements
Turnover rates/optimum inventory allocations
Shelf facing possibilities and reasonable expectations
Potential distribution of sizes by outlet type
Seasonal characteristics
Price points/differentials/margins

users, user research, or supplier suggestions. This reinforces the notion that a firm should listen to its suppliers and customers and give them what they want.

Product Screening and Analysis

Product screening is designed to reduce the number of ideas being worked on at any one time. Criteria needed for screening include whether the product fits in well with present products, profit potential, marketability, and personnel requirements (see Figure 9-2). Each of these factors may be assigned a weight and total scores computed.

Product analysis is done after product screening. It is largely a matter of making cost estimates and sales forecasts to get a feeling for profitability. Products that do not meet the established criteria are weeded from further consideration.

Product Development and Testing

If a product passes the screening and analysis phase, the firm begins to develop it further. A product idea can be developed into many different product concepts (alternative product offerings based on the same product idea that have different meanings and values to consumers). For example, a firm might want to test the concept of a chicken dog—a hot dog made of chicken that tastes like an all-beef hot dog.

Concept testing involves taking a product sample or product idea to consumers to test their reactions (see Figure 9-3). Do they see the benefits of this new product? How frequently would they buy it? At what price? What features do they like and dislike? What changes would they make? Different samples are tested using different packaging, branding, ingredients, and so forth, until a product emerges that is desirable from both a production and a marketing perspective.

PRODUCT DEVELOPMENT IN HISTORY

It was, perhaps, one of the longest development efforts on record for a consumer product. Whitcomb Judson received his first patents in the early 1890s. It took more than 15 years to perfect the product, but even then consumers weren't interested. The company suffered numerous financial setbacks, name changes, and relocations before settling in Meadville, Pa. Finally, the U.S. Navy started using Judson's zippers during World War I. Today, Talon Inc. is the leading U.S. maker of zippers, producing some 500 million of them a year.

Product development

Identify unfilled need
Preliminary profit/payout plan for each concept
Concept test
Determine whether the product can be made
Test the concept and product (and revise as indicated)
Develop the product
Run extended product use tests

Communication development

Select a name
Design a package and test
Create a copy theme and test
Develop complete ads and test

Strategy development

Set marketing goals
Establish marketing strategy
Develop marketing mix (after communication developed)
Estimate cost of marketing plan and payout (after product development)

FIGURE 9-3

Three basic elements before test marketing.
Reprinted by permission of the A.C. Nielsen Company.

PRODUCT STRATEGY AND THE PRODUCT LIFE CYCLE

Once a product has been developed, tested, and placed on the market it goes through a life cycle consisting of five stages: introduction, growth, maturity, saturation, and decline. This is called the product life cycle (see Figure 9-4). The **product life cycle** is a theoretical model of what happens to a product *class* (for example, all freeze-dried coffees) over time. Not all products follow the life cycle, and particular brands may act differently. For example, while frozen foods as a generic class may go through the entire cycle, one brand may never get beyond the introduction stage. Nonetheless, the product life cycle provides a basis for anticipating future market developments and for planning marketing strategies accordingly. Some products, such as microwave ovens, stay in the introductory stage for years. Other products, such as fad clothing, may go through the entire cycle in a couple of months.

product life cycle
The five-stage theoretical depiction of the process from birth to death of a product class: introduction, rapid growth, maturity, saturation, and decline.

FIGURE 9-4

The product life cycle and advertising objectives.

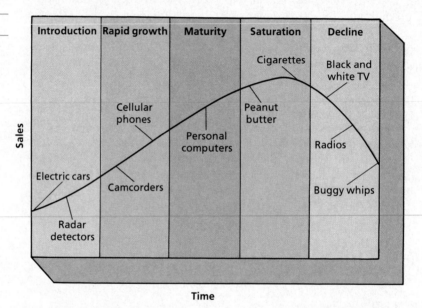

Figure 9-5 shows what happens to sales volume and profit/loss over time. Such figures are revealing. For instance, they show that a product at the mature stage may be realizing continued growth in sales volume while profit is decreasing. At that stage, a marketing manager may decide to create a new image for the product to start a new growth cycle. Note, for example, how Arm and Hammer

FIGURE 9-5

Sales and profit at various stages in the product life cycle.

LIFE CYCLE STAGE	SALES VOLUME	RATE OF CHANGE OF SALES VOLUME	PROFIT/LOSS
Introduction	Slow growth	Increasing	Loss
Growth	Rapid growth	Increasing/Decreasing	Very high profit
Maturity	Growth	Decreasing	Decreasing profit
Saturation	Stagnation	Negative	Decreasing profit
Decline	Decrease	Negative	Loss

baking soda gets a new image every few years to generate new sales. One year it is positioned as a deodorant for refrigerators and the next as a substitute for harsh chemicals in swimming pools. Knowing what stage in the cycle a product is in helps marketing managers to decide when such strategic changes are needed.

Figure 9-6 outlines the marketing mix decisions that might be made. As you go through the table, you will see that each stage calls for multiple marketing mix changes. Next, we shall walk through the product life cycle together and discuss what happens at each stage.

FIGURE 9-6

Strategies through the product life cycle.

LIFE CYCLE STAGE	PRODUCT POLICY	MARKETING MIX ELEMENTS		
		PRICING	DISTRIBUTION	ADVERTISING
Introduction	Offer market-tested product; keep product mix small	Go after innovators with high introductory price (skimming strategy)	Use wholesalers	Heavy investment in primary demand advertising
Growth	Improve product; keep product mix limited	Adjust price to meet competition	Increase distribution	Heavy competitive advertising
Maturity	Differentiate your product to satisfy different market segments	Further reduce price	Take over wholesaling function	Emphasize brand name
Saturation	Add to product mix; diversify markets	Stabilize pricing	Intensify distribution	Maintain advertising support
Decline	Cut product mix	Consider price increase	Consolidate distribution	Reduce advertising

THINKING IT THROUGH

In what stage of the product life cycle are personal computers? What does Figure 9-6 indicate firms should do at that stage? What will the next stage be? What might you do at that stage to optimize profits?

Most soft drinks are in the mature or decline stage of the product life cycle. Does that explain why Coke introduced new Coke? What other new soft drinks have been introduced in the last few years? Have any reached rapid growth?

The Product Life Cycle

We can see how the product life cycle works by looking at the introduction of instant coffee. When it was introduced, most people did not like it as well as "regular" coffee, and it took several years to gain general acceptance (introduction stage). At one point, though, instant coffee grew rapidly in popularity, and many brands were introduced (stage of rapid growth). After awhile, people became

Consumer electronics can be found in all stages of the product life cycle.

attached to one brand and sales leveled off (stage of maturity and saturation). Sales went into a slight decline when freeze-dried coffees were introduced (stage of decline). At present, freeze-dried coffee is at the maturity stage. Perhaps you can think through the product life cycle of products such as hot cereals, frozen orange juice, mechanical watches, and mechanical calculators.

The importance of the product life cycle to marketers is this: different stages in the product life cycle call for different strategies. Figure 9-6 summarizes the entire concept. It shows how a product manager changes his or her objectives and strategies over the life of a product. It is important to recognize what stage a product is in, because such an analysis leads to more intelligent marketing decisions.

Different stages in the product life cycle call for different pricing strategies. We shall discuss pricing—a key management decision in product design—next.

PROGRESS CHECK

■ What are the five steps in the new product development process?

■ Can you draw a product life cycle and label its parts? Can you give one marketing strategy in product, price, place, or advertising for each stage? (See Figure 9-6.)

PRICING

Pricing is so important to marketing that it has been singled out as one of the four *P*'s, along with product, place, and promotion. Price is also a critical ingredient in consumer evaluations of the product. In this section, therefore, we shall explore price as both an ingredient of the product and as a strategic marketing tool. Let's begin, as most marketers do, with the consumer.

Importance of Pricing

"How much is it?" This question is repeated many times a day in stores around the world. It shows that consumers and organizations will buy many things if the price is right. One can design the finest products in the world, but if the price is perceived as too high or too low, the effort may be for nothing. Pricing decisions, therefore, should be completely integrated with product decisions, because price is part of the product offer, just as the package and the brand are. Price is one way in which a seller can differentiate his or her offer from those of competitors.

PRICING OBJECTIVES

One of the factors that has raised pricing to the top of the strategic planning process is the tendency of marketing managers to concentrate on short-run pricing strategies. Figure 9-7 lists some of the pricing objectives a firm might take. Note that some of them, such as "build traffic" and "help in the sale of weak items in the line," are short-run objectives. Often the competitive and internal corporate environments are such that short-run considerations dominate decision making. The economic environment today is so unstable that long-run considerations such as "growth" and "maximum long-run profits" are becoming more important. In fact, survival in the market has become a major goal for many firms.

- Survival
- Maximum long-run profits
- Maximum short-run profits
- Growth
- Build traffic (attract people to the store)
- Maintain price-leadership
- Discourage entrants
- Speed exit of marginal firms
- Avoid government investigation and control
- Maintain loyalty of middlemen and get their sales support
- Enhance image of firm
- Be regarded as "fair" by customers (ultimate)
- Create interest and excitement about the item
- Make a product "visible"
- High return on investment
- Share of the market
- Meet competition
- Help in the sale of weak items in the line

FIGURE 9-7

Potential pricing objectives.

Firms must establish realistic and measurable pricing goals if marketing strategy is to be effective. Some firms aim for a target return on investment. Firms such as General Motors, du Pont, Alcoa, and General Electric have set such goals. A specific target return objective enables these firms to determine a required level of profit. This, in turn, helps in the setting of prices and other marketing mix variables.

Some firms use *market share* as a pricing goal. In the past, firms such as Sears, Exxon, and American Can have had such a strategy. There is sometimes a measurable link between share of market and return investment, but that link is much less reliable in the economic environment of the 1980s. In the search for increased share of the market, firms might cut prices and hurt their profit margins.

Another pricing objective used extensively in the past is to meet competition. Companies such as Goodyear and National Steel have used such strategies. The steel industry, the tire industry, and many other fundamental industries in the United States are suffering greatly from such past practices. Many firms are going bankrupt, and the survivors are being forced to radically change their marketing strategies, including pricing.

Some firms set a *profit-maximization objective,* where the goal is to earn "as much as possible." Such a policy cannot usually be implemented over the long run because of competitive and government forces, but in the short run it can be quite effective. Suppose, for example, a firm has spent millions of dollars developing a new product that can be copied relatively easily, but for which the set-up time is 2 years or more. The firm could price its product as high as "traffic will bear," hoping to get back all its research and development money and a reasonable profit return before competitors entered the market. As competition entered, the firm would probably shift to a more competitive pricing strategy, such as meeting competition.

Pricing objectives are based on a firm's overall objectives, the market segments being served, competition, market conditions, and many other variables. The basic overall objective is to establish mutually beneficial exchange relationships with selected target markets.

Pricing objectives should be influenced by other marketing decisions regarding product design, packaging, branding, and promotion. All these marketing decisions are interrelated.

✳ How Are Prices Determined?

We are so accustomed to thinking of pricing as something done by the seller that it is difficult to think of pricing decisions coming from anyone other than the seller. But a moment's reflection will show you that it is often the buyer who sets the price. For example, how many times have you told a seller that you would give him or her a certain amount of money for something? In this section we shall show how prices are determined by the *interactions* between buyers and sellers.

People also feel rather intuitively that the price charged for a product must bear some relation to the cost of producing the product. In fact, we would generally agree that prices are usually set somewhere above cost. But as we shall see, prices and cost are not always related.

Cost-Based Pricing

Karl Marx.

Karl Marx was perhaps the most widely known economist who tried to explain the relation between the cost of production and price. He felt that the price of a good was, and should be, based on the amount of labor needed to produce it. But it does not take much research to show this just is not so. In fact, there is often very little correlation between the price of something and its cost of production. Does a quarterback earn more than a physician because it costs more to produce a quarterback? Does a rare stamp cost a thousand times more than a regular stamp because one cost more to produce? Obviously not.

Nevertheless, producers often use cost as a primary basis for setting price. They develop elaborate cost accounting systems to measure production costs (including materials, labor, and overhead), add in some margin of profit, and come up with a satisfactory price. The question is whether the price will be satisfactory to the market as well. In the long run, the market determines what the price will be, not the producer.

Break-Even Analysis

One strategic decision marketing managers must make is whether or not to produce a product at all. Break-even analysis is one tool that helps in such decisions. It is used in both product and price decisions. **Break-even analysis** tells them whether the firm would be able to make money (or break even) at a particular price, given a certain sales volume.

Break-even analysis usually involves break-even charts that show total costs and total revenues. The total revenue curve shows the revenue expected *at a given price*. A different chart is constructed for each price and a break-even point (BEP) is determined. At the break-even point, total cost equals total revenue. Beyond that point the firm will make money on each unit; below that point the firm will lose money on each unit sold (see Figure 9-8).

Figure 9-8 shows that sales above 50 units would result in a profit given a particular price. Sales below 50 units would result in a loss. Marketers can develop a series of break-even charts to eliminate obviously unrealistic prices. Break-even analysis should be used only to give some general feeling for an appropriate price.

break-even analysis
Tells managers whether the firm will make money (or break even) at a particular price, given a certain sales volume.

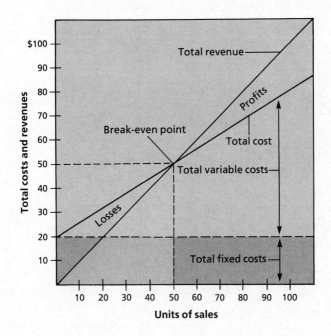

FIGURE 9-8

Break-even analysis for a particular price.

Pricing Strategies

Let's say a firm has just developed a new product, such as video recorders. The firm has to decide how to price these recorders. One strategy would be to price the recorders high to recover the costs of developing the recorder and to take advantage of the fact that there are few competitors. A **skimming price strategy** is one in which the product is priced high to make optimum profit while there is

skimming price strategy
One in which the product is priced high to make optimum profit while there is little competition.

little competition. Of course, those large profits will attract others to produce recorders. That is what is happening with the high-priced camcorders that were introduced recently.

A second strategy, therefore, is to price the recorders low. This would attract more buyers and discourage others from making recorders because the profit is so low. This strategy enables the firm to penetrate or capture a large share of the market quickly. A **penetration strategy**, therefore, is one in which a product is priced low to attract more customers and discourage competitors. The Japanese successfully used a penetration strategy with videotape recorders. No U.S. firm could compete with the low prices the Japanese offered.

Odd Pricing and Price Lining

Another pricing strategy is called psychological pricing. No doubt you have noticed that retailers often price goods at $9.98 or $19.98 instead of $10.00 or $20.00. That practice is known as **odd pricing**. Retailers believe that odd prices (for example, $99.95) are psychologically more attractive than even prices (for example, $100).

penetration strategy
One in which a product is priced low to attract more customers and discourage competitors.

odd pricing
Pricing items a few cents under a round price ($9.98 instead of $10) to make the product appear less expensive.

Advertisers often use "odd pricing" for psychological reasons.

Some retailers offer merchandise at a limited number of prices rather than have individual prices for each item. For example, a shoe store may offer several lines of shoes priced at $30, $40, and $50. This practice of having a few, set prices is known as **price lining**. The advantages of price lining are that (1) it makes pricing of goods easier, (2) it makes the checking out of goods easier, and (3) it appeals to a specific market segment that is looking for a given price level.

The disadvantages of price lining include (1) prices are more difficult to change, (2) cost increases from producers are difficult to pass on to consumers without

price lining
Pricing products at a certain set price rather than having separate prices for individual items.

changing the whole store image, and (3) the set prices may not appeal to a wide enough market segment.

Retail Pricing (Markups)

Retailers tend to base their price on some desired profit goal. The easiest way to calculate how much a retailer makes on each sale is to subtract cost from the sale price to find how much was made. **Markup** is the term retailers use to describe selling price minus cost. Thus the **markup percentage** (how much they make percentage-wise) is calculated as follows:

markup
Selling price minus cost.

markup percentage
Markup in dollars over selling price.

Selling price $3
Cost $2
Markup (in dollars) $1

$$\text{Markup percentage} = \frac{\text{Markup in dollars}}{\text{Selling price}} = \frac{\$1}{\$3} = \frac{1}{3} = 33\frac{1}{3}\%$$

SOME PRICING TERMS

It is impossible to cover all pricing concepts in detail in this book. However, you should at least be familiar with the following terms:

1 *Adaptive pricing* allows an organization to vary its prices based on factors such as competition, market conditions, and resource costs. Rather than relying on one set price, the firm adjusts the price to fit different situations.

2 *Competition-oriented pricing* is a strategy based on what competitors are doing. It may be the opposite of pricing leadership.

3 *Cost-oriented pricing* is the strategy of setting prices primarily on the basis of cost. For example, retailers often use cost plus a certain markup, and producers use a system of cost-plus pricing.

4 *Customary pricing* means that most sellers will adapt the product to some established, universally accepted price such as the price for gum or candy bars. Notice that when the customary price goes up, almost all producers adjust their price upward.

5 *Demand-oriented pricing* is the strategy of setting prices on the basis of consumer demand rather than cost. Sometimes different prices are charged different consumers (discriminatory pricing), as is the case with movie theaters (less for children), and drugstores (senior citizens get a discount).

6 *Market price* is that price that is determined by supply and demand and is not controllable by the seller. For example, farmers have little control over the price they receive for grain or cattle. Market prices exist for many goods and services besides farm products.

7 *Pricing leadership* is the procedure by which all the competitors in an industry follow the pricing practices of one or more dominant firms. When one firm lowers or raises its prices, the others follow almost immediately. You may have noticed this tendency among oil companies and cigarette companies.

8 *Product-line pricing* is the procedure used to set prices for a group of products that are similar but are aimed at different market segments. For example, a beer producer might have a low-priced beer, a popular-priced beer, and a premium-priced beer.

9 *Target pricing* means that an organization will set some goal such as a certain share of the market or a certain return on investment as a basis for setting a price. Usually market conditions prevent a firm from establishing prices this way, but such goals do give some direction to pricing policies.

10 *Uniform pricing*, also known as a "single-price policy," means that all customers buying the product (given similar circumstances) will pay the same price. Although the most common policy in the United States, uniform pricing is unusual in many foreign markets, especially among private sellers.

To calculate what the percentage markup on cost is, given the percentage markup on sales, you use this equation:

$$\text{Percentage markup on cost} = \frac{\text{Percentage markup on selling price}}{100\% - \text{Percentage markup on selling price}} = \frac{33\frac{1}{3}\%}{100\% - 33\frac{1}{3}\%} = \frac{33\frac{1}{3}\%}{66\frac{2}{3}\%} = \frac{1}{2} = 50\%$$

Although this equation may seem complicated, the calculations are done quickly and easily, once a person begins working with such figures. Furthermore, there are conversion charts that can be used to look up figures. It is important for a business major to be able to work with simple mathematics such as the equation above, because markup is such a fundamental concept.

Nonprice Competition

In spite of the emphasis placed on price in microeconomic theory, marketers often compete on product attributes other than price. You may have noted that price differences between products such as gasoline, cigarettes, candy bars, and even major products such as compact cars are often small, if there is any price difference at all. Very rarely will you see price used as a major promotional appeal on television. Instead marketers tend to stress product images and consumer benefits such as comfort, style, convenience, and durability.

Many organizations promote the services that accompany basic products rather than price. The idea is to make a relatively homogeneous product "better." For example, airlines stress friendliness, promptness, more flights, better meals, and other such services. Motels stress "no surprises" or cable TV, swimming pools, and other extras.

Quite often the reason marketers emphasize nonprice differences is because prices are so easy to match. Few competitors can match the image of a friendly, responsive, consumer-oriented company.

PROGRESS CHECK

■ Can you list most of the 18 pricing objectives shown in Figure 9-7?

■ Why is cost not an effective basis for pricing?

■ What is the markup on an item that sells for $6 if its cost were $4?

SUMMARY

1 If the goal of marketing is to find a need and fill it, the heart of marketing is finding what products people want and seeing that they get them. Product is one of the four Ps of the marketing mix.

■ What is a product?

The question is more complex than it seems. A product is much more than a physical object. A product also involves the price, the brand name, the quality, the satisfaction in use, and more. A product is what a buyer or potential buyer perceives it to be.

■ Are there different classes of consumer products?

Yes, there are convenience goods (minimum shopping effort), shopping goods (where people compare price and quality), and specialty goods (where consumers will go out of their way to get them).

■ Are there categories of industrial products?

Yes, industrial products can be placed in six categories: raw materials, components, accessory equipment, installations, supplies, and service.

■ Are consumer goods and services marketed differently than industrial goods and services?

Yes; convenience goods are best promoted by location; shopping goods by some price/quality appeal; and specialty goods by word of mouth. Industrial goods are usually sold by salespeople in the field.

2 Packaging changes the product and is becoming more important, taking over much of the sales function for consumer goods.

■ What are the functions of packaging?

Packaging adds visibility and convenience, minimizes damage, and keeps the goods in manageable sizes.

3 Branding also changes the product.

■ What are the categories of brand names?

There are *private* brands, *national* brands, and *generic* names. Can you define each?

4 Product managers coordinate product, place, promotion, and price decisions. They are like presidents of one-product firms.

■ How do product managers find new products?

There are many sources of new product ideas (see Figure 9-1).

■ What is the product development process?

It consists of generating new product ideas, screening, development, testing, and commercialization.

5 Once a product is placed on the market, marketing strategy varies as the product goes through various stages of acceptance—called the product life cycle.

■ What are the stages of the product life cycle?

They are introduction, growth, maturity, saturation, and decline.

■ How do strategies change at the various stages?

See Figure 9-6 on page 235.

6 Pricing is one of the four *P*'s of marketing. It can also be viewed as part of the product concept.

■ What are pricing objectives?

Some objectives include long-run or short-run profits, growth, maintenance of price leadership, fairness, generating product excitement, meeting competition, and capturing a larger share of the market.

■ How are prices determined?

Some firms use cost as a basis, but ultimately prices are set by the market; that is, supply and demand and competition.

7 Break-even analysis tells a firm whether or not it would be profitable to produce a product at all. At the break-even point, total cost equals total revenue. Sales beyond that point are profitable.

■ Is break-even point analysis the only technique for price setting?

No, it is just one way to get a feel for an appropriate price.

■ How do retailers set prices?

Retailers use a concept called *markup*. It is calculated on the selling price. A product purchased for $2.00 and sold for $3.00 would have a markup of $1.00 or 33⅓%.

KEY TERMS

brand p. 229
brand name p. 229
break-even analysis p. 239
capital goods p. 227
convenience goods and services p. 226
expense items p. 227
generic name p. 230
industrial goods p. 227
markup p. 241
markup percentage p. 241
national brand p. 229
odd pricing p. 240
penetration strategy p. 240
price lining p. 240

private brands p. 230
product p. 223
product life cycle p. 234
product line p. 226
product manager p. 230
product mix p. 225
shopping goods and
   services p. 226
skimming price strategy
   p. 239
specialty goods and services
   p. 226
trademark p. 229

GETTING INVOLVED

1 Look around at the different shoes that students are wearing. What product qualities were they looking for when they chose those shoes? What was the importance of price, style, brand name, manufacturer reputation, and color? Do different students buy shoes for different reasons?

2 Discuss how packaging has changed the attractiveness of the following products:
   a. Beer
   b. Mustard
   c. Salt
   d. Soda (pop)

3 For each of the following products, discuss whether a marketer should emphasize price, location, or word of mouth in his or her promotional campaign and explain why:
   a. Baby sitting
   b. A resort motel
   c. Bottled water
   d. A dentist
   e. A bank
   f. A candy bar

4 List at least seven sources of new product ideas and put them in the order you think is most important. Explain why you chose that order.

5 Discuss how the faculty at your college could increase student satisfaction by working more closely with students in developing new products (courses) and changing existing products (courses). Would it be a good idea for all marketers to work with their customers that way? Discuss.

PRACTICING MANAGEMENT DECISIONS

CASE ONE   SELLING PERSONAL COMPUTERS: PRODUCT ADD-ONS

The basic machine you get when you buy a personal computer is little different from others produced by competitors. That means that any little advantage can go a long way toward making one product seem better than others. For several years, the features that received special attention as a unique benefit were alternative ways to get information into and out of computers.

In October of 1983, Hewlett-Packard introduced the HP 150, the first personal computer you could command by touching the screen. It looked like a good idea on paper. But users discovered some problems. First, you get fingerprints all over the screen. Second, your fingers are fat and the picture elements on the screen are small. It's hard to see where to put your finger with your hand and arm in the way and it's inconvenient to take your hand off the keyboard.

Apple used a "mouse" for its Macintosh and other personal computers. Various versions of the mouse are available: one-, two-, and three-button varieties. The mouse is an alternative to moving data using keys on the keyboard. In fact, a mouse is often faster because you can move the pointer directly to where you want to go, whereas with keys you can only move horizontally or vertically. If you have even played video games, you are familiar with joysticks and how they are used.

The idea is to make computer use easier. Many consumers, though, seem to feel that computers have limited use. Those who had obvious use for computers have bought one (most of them). Others have bought them to "keep up with the Joneses." Many of the potential buyers, though, see little use for a computer. They cannot picture putting recipes on a computer or doing their taxes on a video screen.

Computer manufacturers have been talking more about capacity and ease of use than reasons for buying computers. Additional features like a mouse or a joystick often confuse the issue.

DECISION QUESTIONS

1 What is the product of a personal computer? How would you find out? Name at least three personal computer products and the segment they would appeal to.
2 What steps would you recommend for manufacturers to make the product better?
3 Have features like touch control and the mouse added to the perceived value of computers? How could such features be more readily introduced into the market?

CASE TWO   NEW COKE VERSUS COCA-COLA CLASSIC

PRACTICING MANAGEMENT DECISIONS

Nothing touched off more discussion and debate in marketing in the 1980s than the introduction of new Coca-Cola (Coke). The new Coke was made sweeter to taste more like Pepsi, and a marketing campaign was launched to sell this new taste. At first, sales were up as consumers rushed to try the new Coke. Soon the reaction became negative and people began hoarding the old Coke. Minor campaigns were started by old-Coke fans to bring back the old Coke.

A daily newspaper in Paris reported, "Coca-Cola, like the Chevrolet and Levi Strauss . . .were and are, for America, landmarks that one dare not touch. Ninety-nine years of existence, it is the equivalent of the Parthenon or the Sphinx. . . ." Articles questioned the marketing research done by Coke. They had asked people which taste they preferred, but they had failed to take into account tradition, brand loyalty, and habit.

Faced with hostile consumers from coast to coast, Coke relented and brought back old Coke under the name Coca-Cola Classic. It also kept the new Coke for those who preferred the taste. Coca-Cola Classic is doing better than new Coke thus far.

Through all of this, Coke was in the news day after day as people aired both sides of the issue. In the long run, Coke may win the marketing war because of the publicity and its willingness to listen to consumer protest.

Coke had a large share of the overseas market, even larger than the share it had of the U.S. market. Europeans and other foreign consumers preferred Coke—the old Coke that is. Nevertheless, Coke decided to introduce new Coke overseas as well. Again, there was much criticism in the trade press. Again, Coke got much free publicity—this time worldwide.

DECISION QUESTIONS

1 What lessons might brand-name marketers learn from the Coke case? Campbell soup is thinking of changing its soup cans. Is that a good idea? What are the possible benefits and problems?

2 Do you think that Coke's market research department goofed? Why or why not?

3 If you were Coke's president, would you continue to make new Coke? How would you decide? Would you take new Coke overseas? Why or why not?

4 Is Classic Coca-Cola a new product?

LOOKING AHEAD

A product cannot fully meet the wants and needs of consumers unless it is at the right place at the right time. Several marketing organizations have emerged to perform the functions needed to move goods from producers to consumers. Your neighborhood stores are one example. Chapter 10 looks at the distribution of products and the organizations that move and store goods on their way to your home.

DISTRIBUTION: WHOLESALING AND RETAILING

LEARNING GOALS

After you have read and studied this chapter, you should be able to:

- Explain why we need marketing middlemen and what functions they perform.
- Describe how middlemen add utility (value) to products.
- List various kinds of retailers and what makes them unique.
- Define terms such as *scrambled merchandising, wheel of retailing, merchant wholesalers, channel of distribution, wholesaling,* and *retailing.*
- Explain how and why manufacturers use functional discounts.
- Understand the importance of physical distribution and storage.
- Compare and contrast different distribution modes.
- Describe how members of a channel of distribution can cooperate to make the channel more efficient.

PROFILE   JOHN BLACKWELDER, FURNITURE RETAILER

Blackwelder Furniture Company grosses about $15 million and is growing at a pace of 20% a year. How does this retailer do so well? It sells top-line, brand-name furniture for markups averaging 35% rather than the usual 100% or more. This makes John Blackwelder "the most hated man in the Carolinas and Virginia" by other furniture retailers and the "greatest secret in the world" to furniture bargain hunters.

Mr. Blackwelder credits his low prices to location, volume, and cost controls. He's located in a furniture manufacturing center, he has a high volume because of low profit margins, and his display area is relatively inexpensive.

What customers do is shop the exclusive department stores in major cities across the United States, find the furniture they want, copy the code numbers, and call Blackwelder to buy it. Naturally, the department stores are crying "unfair." Customers feel happy that they are getting good quality furniture at discount prices.

Such is the nature of retailing today—competitive, price conscious, and eager to capture new markets with innovative pricing, store designs, and more. John Blackwelder found a market niche (discount top-grade furniture) and went after

John Blackwelder.

To the extent that any middleman can do so, he should think of himself primarily as a purchasing agent for his customers, and only secondarily as a selling agent for his suppliers.
PHILIP McVEY

the market aggressively. Levitz Furniture found another niche (discount house brand furniture or moderately priced furniture). The people who benefit from such competition are you and me. Retailers are our suppliers of goods and services, and competition has lowered prices for careful shoppers like those who call Black-welder. ■

PLACE—THE FOURTH *P* OF THE MARKETING MIX

We have discussed product, promotion, and price as elements of the marketing mix. This chapter focuses on *place,* getting goods to the right *place* at the right *time* in the right *quantity.* We use the word *place* because it is a fourth *P,* but the traditional marketing term for place is *distribution.* The **distribution mix** is all those functions marketers perform to move goods from producer to consumer (see Figure 10-1).

distribution mix
All those functions marketers perform to move goods from producers to consumers.

FIGURE 10-1

The distribution mix. These eight functions are the same as the original eight functions of marketing because at one time marketing was synonymous with distribution.

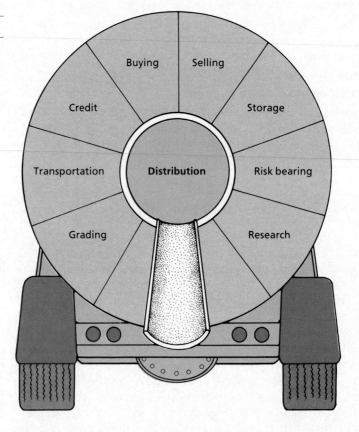

Buying Selling
Credit Storage
Transportation **Distribution** Risk bearing
Grading Research

marketing middlemen
Institutions such as wholesalers and retailers that are in the middle of the distribution network from producers to consumers.

Two institutions have emerged to perform the distribution function: wholesalers and retailers. They are known as **marketing middlemen** because they are in the middle of a distribution network that connects producers with consumers.

WHY WE NEED MIDDLEMEN

Marketing middlemen have always been viewed by the public with some suspicion. Surveys have shown that about half the cost of the things we buy are marketing costs that are largely to pay for the work of middlemen! People reason that if we could only get rid of middlemen, we could greatly reduce the cost of everything we buy. Sounds good, but is the solution really that simple?

Let's take as an example a can of tomato soup. How could we, as consumers, get it for less? Well, we could all drive to Ohio where some of the soup is produced and save some shipping costs. But would that be practical? Can you imagine millions of people getting in their cars and driving to Ohio just to get some soup? No, it doesn't make sense. It is much cheaper to have some middlemen bring the soup to the major cities. That might involve transportation and warehousing by wholesalers. But these steps add cost, don't they? Yes, but they add value as well, the value of not having to drive to Ohio.

The soup is now somewhere on the outskirts of the city. We could all drive down to the wholesaler's outlet store and pick up the soup; in fact, some people do just that. But that is not really the most economical way to buy soup. If we figure in the cost of gas and time, the soup would be rather expensive. Instead, we prefer to have someone move the soup from the warehouse to another truck, drive it to the corner supermarket, unload it, unpack it, stamp it with a price, put it on the shelf, and wait for us to come in to buy it. To make it even more convenient, the supermarket may stay open for 24 hours a day, 7 days a week. Think of the *costs*. Think also of the *value!* For less than 40 cents, we can get tomato soup when we want, where we want, and with little effort on our part.

Middlemen add value to a can of soup.

If we were to get rid of the retailer, we could buy a can of tomato soup for a little less, but we would have to drive miles more and spend time in the warehouse looking for soup. If we got rid of the wholesaler, we could save a little more, but then we would have to drive to Ohio. But a few cents here and a few cents there add up—to the point where marketing may add up to 50 cents for every 50 cents in manufacturing costs. Figure 10-2 shows how middlemen share your food dollar for beef, eggs, and milk. Note that the retail margin varies widely. Also note that the total marketing cost ranges from 30% to 50%. We do not like to pay such

FIGURE 10-2

How middlemen share your food dollar.

Source: U.S. Department of Agriculture.

ITEM	FARMER	PROCESSOR	WHOLESALER	RETAILER
1 pound choice beef	66.3%	5.4%	7.4%	20.9%
1 dozen grade A large eggs	69.7%	11.5%	5.1%	13.7%
1 half-gallon milk	50.8%	21.6%	19.8%	7.8%

This table shows that the farmer gets only 50.8¢ of the dollar you spend for milk. Some 21.6¢ goes to processors, 19.8¢ to wholesalers, and 7.8¢ to retailers. The question is, is the value added by middlemen worth the cost? Marketers say yes, as the soup story in the text illustrates.

high costs for marketing, but there is no other way to get what we want when we want it at a reasonable cost. The cost of marketing is well worth it when you see what you get for your money.

It should be clear that businesses are not the only organizations in which a high proportion of costs are due to marketing middlemen. It also costs much to have several churches in one city when people "need" only one. It also is expensive to have post offices, libraries, health clinics, and other such nonbusiness middleman organizations. But again, the convenience and efficiency of having such facilities usually far outweigh the cost. Three basic points about middlemen are:

- Marketing middlemen can be eliminated, but their activities cannot be eliminated; that is, you can get rid of retailers, but then consumers or someone else would have to perform the retailer's tasks, including transportation, storage, finding suppliers, and establishing communication with suppliers.
- Middleman organizations survive because they perform marketing functions more effectively and efficiently than they could be performed by others.
- Middlemen add costs to products, but these costs are usually more than offset by the values they create.

How Middlemen Add Value

utility
Value added to raw materials.

Of the five utilities (**utility** is value added to raw materials) mentioned in the literature of economics—form, time, place, possession, and information—four are created primarily by marketing middlemen. The first mentioned, form utility, is often performed by middlemen. For example, supermarkets add form utility to meats by cutting, wrapping, pricing, and displaying them. Of course restaurants and other retailers also create form utility. But marketing middlemen are noted more for the creation of time, place, possession, and information utility. Following are some examples.

Time Utility

7-Eleven stores give you time utility.

Rudy Lynch was watching TV with his brother when he suddenly got the urge to have a hot dog and a Coke. The problem was that there were no hot dogs or Cokes in the house. Rudy ran down to the corner delicatessen and bought some hot dogs, buns, Cokes, and potato chips. Rudy was able to get these groceries at 10 PM because the store was open from 8 AM to 11 PM.

- Middlemen, such as retailers, add *time utility* to products by making them available *when* they are needed.

Place Utility

Mary Margaret Melchak was traveling through the badlands of South Dakota and was getting hungry and thirsty. She saw a sign saying that Wall Drugs with fountain service was up ahead. She stopped at the store for some refreshments. She also bought sunglasses and souvenir items while she was there.

- Middlemen add *place utility* to products by having them *where* people want them.

Possession Utility

William Nathan wanted to buy a nice home in the suburbs. He found just what he wanted, but he did not have the money he needed. So he went with the real estate man to a local savings and loan and borrowed the money to buy the home. Both the real estate broker and the savings and loan were marketing middlemen.

- Middlemen add *possession utility* by doing whatever is necessary to transfer ownership from one party to another, including providing *credit*.

Information Utility

Fernando Gomez could not decide what kind of TV set to buy. He looked at various ads in the newspaper, talked to the salespersons at several stores, and read material at the library. He also got some material from the government about radiation hazards and consumer buying tips. The newspaper, salesperson, library, and government publications were all information sources made available by middlemen.

- Middlemen add information utility by opening two-way flows of *information* between marketing participants.

HIGH-TECH HITS SUPERMARKETS

You may think that computers and robots are a fad and that you have seen about as far as they'll go in retailing and consumer marketing. But, as they say, "You ain't seen nothing yet."

In supermarkets, it all began with electronic scanners that "read" the codes on products. Next, the machine started talking: "Green beans, 79 cents, ice cream, $3.29."

In Nokendai, Japan, there is a store called Seiyu's that makes U.S. supermarkets look ancient. In Seiyu's, shopping carts are equipped with built-in calculators to keep a running total of purchases. A motorized cart runs up and down the aisles advertising specials, holding samples, playing jingles, and giving sales pitches. At the meat counter, customers punch their order into a computer that automatically cuts the meat, weighs it, and wraps it. Stocking is done by a robotlike forklift truck that fills shelves as it moves along on a track in the aisles.

Ultimately, though, you will be able to pick up your phone, connect with a supermarket computer, punch in your order, and have your order delivered. This will be the ultimate in convenience; your order will be picked up by robots and packaged by them. Computers will also determine the most efficient delivery routes. Humans will drive the trucks, at least in the foreseeable future. After that, who knows?

How will computer ordering and delivery affect supermarket selling? What will be the impact on packaging and branding? How will you be assured of quality meats and produce?

If you think of how convenient it is to buy gas, food, clothing, housing, and almost anything else you want or need, you will realize the value of having marketing middlemen. Think of the bother it could be to try to buy stocks and bonds if there were no stockbrokers. Or how hard it would be to buy or sell a home without a real estate broker. Note that these middlemen serve both the buyer and the seller. The box on p. 253 discusses the role of technology in stores.

Middlemen and Exchange Efficiency

The benefits of marketing middlemen can be illustrated rather easily. Suppose that five manufacturers of various food products tried to sell directly to five retailers. The number of exchange relationships that would have to be established is five times five, or 25. But picture what happens when a wholesaler enters the system. The five manufacturers would contact one wholesaler to establish five exchange relationships. The wholesaler would have to establish contact with the five retailers. That would mean another five exchange relationships. Note that the number of exchanges is reduced from 25 to only 10 by the addition of a wholesaler. This process can be visualized as shown in Figure 10-3 where the number of exchanges is reduced from 25 to 10.

FIGURE 10-3

How middlemen create exchange efficiency.

Source: U.S. Department of Agriculture.

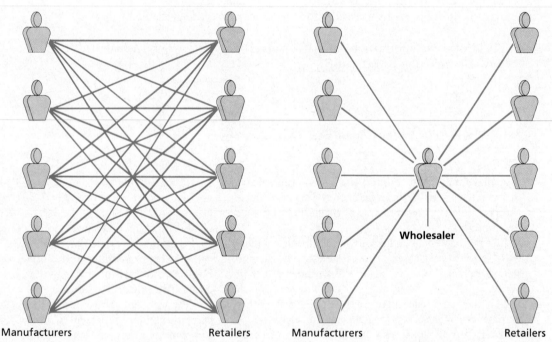

Manufacturers   Retailers   Manufacturers   Retailers

Wholesaler

Figure 10-3 shows how middlemen create exchange efficiency by lessening the number of contacts needed to establish marketing exchanges. Not only are middlemen an efficient way to conduct exchanges, but they are often more effective as well. This means that middlemen are often better at performing their functions than a manufacturer or consumer would be. Figure 10-4 shows how middlemen join to form *channels of distribution* for consumer and industrial goods.

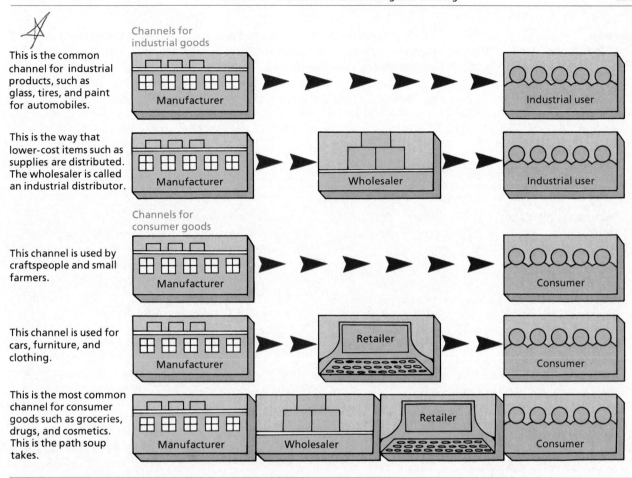

This is the common channel for industrial products, such as glass, tires, and paint for automobiles.

This is the way that lower-cost items such as supplies are distributed. The wholesaler is called an industrial distributor.

This channel is used by craftspeople and small farmers.

This channel is used for cars, furniture, and clothing.

This is the most common channel for consumer goods such as groceries, drugs, and cosmetics. This is the path soup takes.

Channels of distribution for industrial and consumer goods.   **FIGURE 10-4**

PROGRESS CHECK

■ What are the eight functions in the distribution mix?

■ Can you explain how middlemen add form, time, place, possession, and information utility?

RETAIL MIDDLEMEN

Next time you go to the supermarket to buy groceries, stop for a minute and look at the tremendous variety of products in the store. Think of how many marketing exchanges were involved to bring you the 12,000 or so items that you see. Some products (spices, for example) may have been imported from halfway around the world. Other products have been processed and frozen so that you can eat them out of season (for example, strawberries).

retailer
A marketing middleman that sells to consumers.

A supermarket is a retailer. A **retailer** is a marketing middleman who sells to consumers. In the United States there are approximately 2.3 million retail stores, selling everything from soup to automobiles. Retail organizations employ more than 11 million people. They are one of the major employers of marketing graduates. There are many careers available in retailing in all kinds of firms.

CAREER INFORMATION: RETAIL SALES

NATURE OF THE WORK

The success of any retail establishment depends largely on its sales workers. Courteous and efficient service from behind the counter or on the sales floor does much to satisfy customers and build a store's reputation.

Whether selling furniture, electrical appliances, or clothing, a sales worker's primary job is to interest customers in the merchandise. This is done by describing the product's construction, demonstrating its use, and showing various models and colors. For some jobs, particularly those selling expensive, "big ticket" items, special knowledge or skills are needed. Personal computer sales workers, for example, must have sufficient knowledge of electronics to explain to customers the features of various brands and models and the meaning of manufacturers' specifications.

In addition to selling, most retail sales workers make out sales checks, receive cash payments, and give change and receipts. More and more stores are installing point-of-sale terminals that register sales, adjust inventory figures, and perform simple calculations. This equipment increases workers' productivity—enabling them to provide better customer service. They also handle returns and exchanges of merchandise and keep their work areas neat. In addition, they may help stock shelves or racks, mark price tags, take inventory, and prepare displays.

JOB OUTLOOK

Employment of retail sales workers is expected to grow about as fast as the average for all workers through the mid-1990's. While the volume of goods sold is expected to grow rapidly, the continuation of self-service and the increase in computerized checkout systems will reduce somewhat the need for additional sales workers. However, employment in stores selling "big ticket" items will be much less affected since these items are not likely to be sold self-service.

Retail trade sales work will continue to provide more job openings than almost any other occupation through the mid-1990s. Prospects for sales jobs are good because retail selling is a large occupation and turnover is high. There will continue to be many opportunities for part-time workers, as well as for temporary workers during peak selling periods such as the Christmas season.

EARNINGS

In 1984, the starting wage for most retail sales positions (including part time and temporary) not covered by union contracts was the federal minimum wage, $3.35 an hour. Some stores doing less than $362,500 in business per year paid less, since they are not required to pay the minimum wage. Median weekly earnings of full-time retail sales workers were about $290 in 1984. The middle 50 percent earned between $170 and $360 a week; 10 percent earned less than $130 a week; and 10 percent earned more than $510. Earnings vary widely by type of goods sold.

Some sales workers receive salary plus commissions—that is, a percentage of the sales they make. Others are paid only on a commission or salary basis. Those paid by commission may find their earnings greatly affected by ups and downs in the economy.

Sales workers in many retail stores may buy merchandise at a discount, often from 10 to 25 percent below regular prices. This privilege sometimes is extended to the employee's family. Some stores, especially the large ones, pay part or all of the cost of life insurance, health insurance, and a pension.

SOURCES OF ADDITIONAL INFORMATION

Information on careers in retail sales may be obtained from the personnel offices of local stores; from state merchants' associations; or from local unions of the United Food and Commercial Workers International Union.

Source: *Occupational Outlook Handbook*, 1986-1987, U.S. Department of Labor.

Retail Store Categories

There are so many new retail establishments opening today that it is difficult to keep up. Nevertheless, some of the more important categories include the following.

Department Stores

A department store has 25 or more employees, sells home furnishings, appliances, family apparel, and household linens in different departments of the store. Most large suburban malls have one or two department stores as *anchors*. An anchor store is one that is large enough and popular enough to attract business to a shopping center or mall.

Discount Stores

Discount stores are self-service outlets that sell general merchandise below department store prices. The leading discount chains (in sales volume) are K-mart, Wal-mart, Target, Gemco, and T.G.&Y. See the box on "The Wheel of Retailing" (p. 259) for what sometimes happens to discount stores.

Specialty Stores

A specialty store sells a single category of merchandise such as shoes, cameras, flowers, or books. Some better-known names include Toys 'Я' Us, Hickory Farms, and Radio Shack.

Supermarkets

A supermarket is a large, self-service store that offers a wide variety of food items (meat, produce, canned goods, etc.) and some nonfood items. The largest chains include Safeway, Kroger, Lucky Stores, Winn-Dixie, and A&P. A small version of a supermarket is called a grocery store.

Hypermarkets

A hypermarket is a giant food and general merchandise store. Such stores are popular in France and are becoming more widespread in the United States. The Fred Meyer stores in the Northwest are an example.

Convenience Stores

A convenience store is a small food store with a limited selection that emphasizes convenient locations and hours. Some popular chains are 7-Eleven, White Hen, and Open Pantry.

Catalog Stores

A catalog store sends catalogs to consumers and displays merchandise in showrooms where customers can shop and order merchandise from an attached warehouse. Examples are Best Products, Zale, Service Merchandise, Giant Stores, and Vornado.

General Stores

A general store is an early style of retail store offering a wide variety of merchandise. Many smaller towns have a general store to serve their needs.

R.H. Macy went broke with his first three dry-goods stores.

Toys 'Я' Us is a specialty store.

TOP 10 SUPERMARKET CHAINS

1 Safeway
2 Kroger
3 American Stores
4 Lucky
5 Winn-Dixie
6 A&P
7 Albertson's
8 Supermarkets General
9 Stop & Shop
10 Grand Union

THE 10 LARGEST RETAILERS

1 Sears Roebuck
2 K-mart
3 Safeway Stores
4 Kroger
5 J.C. Penney
6 American Stores
7 Southland
8 Federated Department Stores
9 Lucky Stores
10 Household International

Source: *Fortune* (June 10, 1985), pp. 190-91.

Vending machines usually sell convenience goods.

Chain Stores

Chain stores are two or more retailers with the same name offering the same product line. Shoe stores, specialty stores, department stores, and other categories of stores can also be called chain stores if there are two or more stores. Some popular chain stores are Florsheim Shoes, Western Auto, and Sears.

Out-of-Store Shopping

For every dollar consumers spend in stores like those listed above, they spend 37.5¢ at home ordering goods and services by mail and by phone.[1] The store figures do not include supermarkets, service stations, restaurants, and car dealerships. Still, the out-of-store shopping trend is growing. Some of the categories include the following.

Telemarketing

telemarketing
The sale of goods and services by telephone.

Telemarketing is the sale of goods and services by telephone. Some 80,000 companies use telemarketing today to supplement or replace in-store selling.[2] Many send a catalog to consumers and let them order by calling an "800" toll-free number. Some $100 billion worth of business was done in 1984 using telemarketing.[3]

Vending Machines

vending machine
Dispenses convenience goods when consumers deposit sufficient money in the machine.

A **vending machine** dispenses convenience goods when consumers deposit sufficient money in the machine. The benefit of vending machines is their convenient location in airports, office buildings, schools, service stations, and other areas where people want convenience items.

Door-to-Door Sales

door-to-door sales
Selling to consumers in their homes.

Door-to-door sales involves selling to consumers in their homes. Major users of this category include encyclopedia publishers (Britannica), cosmetics producers (Avon), and vacuum cleaner manufacturers (Electrolux). The newest trend is to sell lingerie, art work, plants, and other goods at house "parties" sponsored by sellers. No doubt you have heard of Tupperware parties.

Mail Order Retailers

mail order retailer
Sends catalogs to consumers who then order goods by mail (or phone).

A **mail order retailer** sends catalogs to consumers who then order goods by mail. Two popular mail order catalogs are those for L.L. Bean and Sharper Image. Some of this business is now being shifted to telemarketing.

L.L. Bean is a popular mail order retailer.

Even though we have covered most of the major categories of retailers, there are more that could be mentioned. Think of all the gasoline stations, restaurants, video stores, bakeries, butcher shops, rental stores, dry cleaning establishments, and more that you see in your travels. Certainly, retailing offers a variety of careers in many different settings. There are malls that feature only outlet stores and others that sell only home-made crafts. Retailing can be an exciting career.

THE WHEEL OF RETAILING

The *wheel of retailing* describes a situation that has occurred in retailing over the years. What happens is that new retailers tend to enter a market by emphasizing low price, limited service, and out-of-the way locations. As business improves, they add services and get better locations. Soon prices must be raised to cover the added services and the store must now compete with traditional department stores and specialty stores. Once a store has added services, it is difficult to go back. Often the stores fail (for example, Korvette's and Robert Hall). However, new stores can enter the market at low prices and repeat the cycle. The wheel of retailing, therefore, looks like the illustration at right:

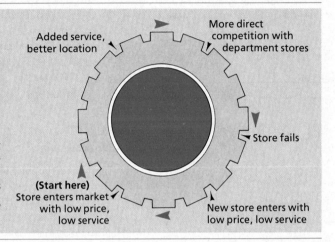

Added service, better location

More direct competition with department stores

Store fails

(Start here) Store enters market with low price, low service

New store enters with low price, low service

THINKING IT THROUGH

How important are middlemen such as wholesalers, retailers, trucking firms, and warehouse operators to the progress of less developed countries? What products should be distributed first? Is there a lack of middlemen in poor countries? How much are such middlemen worth to a poor country?

Scrambled Merchandising

One long-running trend that makes categorizing retailers difficult is the trend toward scrambled merchandising. **Scrambled merchandising** is the adding of product lines (to a retail store) that are not normally carried (such as auto supplies in a supermarket). A moment's reflection will remind you of how often you have seen this occur. You can buy lawn furniture and fertilizer in a drug store, drug sundries in a supermarket, and TV sets virtually anywhere. Discount stores are selling food, and food stores are selling merchandise normally found in discount stores. No wonder it is called *scrambled* merchandising.

scrambled merchandising The adding of product lines that are not normally carried by a retail store.

Retail Distribution Strategy

A major decision marketers must make is selecting retailers to sell their products. Different products call for different retail distribution strategies. There are three categories of retail distribution: intensive distribution, selective distribution, and exclusive distribution.

✳ intensive distribution
Puts products into as many retail outlets as possible.

✳ selective distribution
The use of only a preferred group of the available retailers in an area.

✳ exclusive distribution
The use of only one retail outlet in a given geographic area.

Intensive distribution puts products into as many retail outlets as possible, including vending machines. Products that need intensive distribution include candy, cigarettes, gum, and popular magazines (convenience goods).

Selective distribution is the use of only a preferred group of the available retailers in an area. Such selection helps assure the producers of quality sales and service. Manufacturers of appliances, TV sets, furniture, and clothing (shopping goods) usually use selective distribution.

Exclusive distribution is the use of only one retail outlet in a given geographic area. Because the retailer has exclusive rights to sell the product, he or she is more likely to carry more inventory, give better service, and pay more attention to this brand than others. Automobile manufacturers usually use exclusive distribution, as do producers of specialty goods.

Regardless of the strategy used, manufacturers often ship their goods through wholesalers. The reason is that wholesalers are more efficient at performing the distribution functions.

PROGRESS CHECK

▪ Can you name six categories of retailers and describe the stores?

▪ Can you explain the wheel of retailing and scrambled merchandising?

WHOLESALE MIDDLEMEN

wholesaler
A marketing middleman that sells to organizations and individuals, but not final consumers.

A **wholesaler** is a marketing middleman who sells to organizations and individuals, but not final consumers. For years no clear distinction was made in marketing between wholesaling and retailing. An early attempt to differentiate these two marketing middlemen occurred in 1932, when the government made a census of wholesale distributors. Today there is still much confusion as to the difference between wholesalers and retailers. For example, many retail outlets have signs that say "wholesale distributors" or something similar.

Wholesalers handle volume shipments for sale to organizations.

What difference does it make whether an organization is called a wholesaler or a retailer? One difference is that many states impose a sales tax on retail sales. To collect such a tax, the state must know which sales are retail sales and which are not. Retailers are sometimes subject to other rules and regulations that do not apply to wholesalers. On the other hand, the minimum wage laws have tended to exempt small, local retail stores, but not wholesalers.

For practical marketing purposes, it is helpful to distinguish wholesaling from retailing and to clearly define the functions performed so that more effective systems of distribution can be designed. Some producers will not sell directly to retailers but will deal only with wholesalers. Some producers will give wholesalers a bigger discount than retailers. What confuses the issue is that some organizations sell much of their merchandise to other middlemen (a wholesale sale) but also sell to ultimate consumers (a retail sale).

The issue is really rather simple: A retailer sells products to consumers for their own use; a wholesaler does not. Wholesalers sell products to businesses and institutions (e.g., hospitals) for use in the business or to wholesalers, retailers, and individuals *for resale*. It bears repeating that wholesalers *do not* sell to consumers for their own use.

Functional Discounts

Because wholesalers perform *functions* for manufacturers that retailers do not, manufacturers may give wholesalers a different discount on products than they would retailers.[2] Similarly, retailers get a discount that is not available to consumers. This is called a **functional discount.** An example may help clarify how this works.

Imagine a manufacturer of bicycles that makes a bike that *lists* (retail price to you, the consumer) for $100. The retailer may get a functional discount of 30%. The cost to the retailer would then be $70 ($100 − $30 = $70). The wholesaler that serviced the retailer, stored the bikes, and provided other assistance to the manufacturer might get an additional 10% off the price to the retailer ($70 × 10% = $7). The wholesaler would pay $63 for the bike ($70 − $7). Another wholesale middleman may help the manufacturer find regional wholesalers. That wholesaler would get a functional discount of say 5% off the wholesaler's price ($63 × 5% = $3.15). That wholesaler would pay $59.85 for the bike ($63 − $3.15). The price of the bike to the first wholesaler would be $59.85 and the price to you, the consumer, would be $100. Note that about 40% of the cost of the bike would go to middlemen for performing functions like transportation, storage, credit, delivery, market information, and sales assistance. Figure 10-5 illustrates the case.

functional discount
One given to wholesalers and retailers for the functions they perform.

Retail price	$100.00
Less discount to retailer (30%)	− 30.00
Retail cost	$ 70.00
Less second wholesaler's discount (10%)	− 7.00
Wholesaler's cost	$ 63.00
Less discount for first wholesaler (5%)	− 3.15
First wholesaler's cost (manufacturer's price to wholesaler)	$ 59.85

FIGURE 10-5

Functional discounts at different levels of the distribution network (two wholesalers and one retailer). Note that discounting begins with the retail price and works backward up the distribution network.

Let's look at different wholesalers to see what they do for manufacturers to earn their discount. We begin with merchant wholesalers because they do the most.

Merchant Wholesalers

merchant wholesalers
Independently owned firms that take title to goods that they handle.

Merchant wholesalers are independently owned firms that take title to goods that they handle. About 80% of wholesalers fall in this category.[4] General merchandise or full-line wholesalers carry a broad assortment of merchandise. They are found in industries such as drug, hardware, and clothing. They perform all eight distribution functions: transportation, storage, risk bearing, credit, market information, grading, buying, and selling.

rack jobber
Furnishes racks or shelves to retailers, displays products, and sells on consignment.

full-service wholesalers
Perform all eight distribution functions.

Limited-line wholesalers do the same functions with a narrower range of products such as health foods or automotive parts. Rack jobbers furnish racks or shelves full of merchandise to retailers, display products, and sell on consignment. This means that they keep title to the goods until they are sold, and then they share the profits with the retailer. Merchandise such as toys, hosiery, and health and beauty aids are sold by **rack jobbers.** These wholesalers are known as **full-service wholesalers** because they do many functions (see Figure 10-6). If a rack jobber does not supply credit to customers, he or she is classified as a limited-function wholesaler.

FIGURE 10-6

Functions performed by a full-function wholesaler.

Source: Thomas C. Kinnear and Kenneth L. Bernhardt, *Principles of Marketing*, Second Edition (Glenview, Ill.: Scott, Foresman & Co., 1986), p. 369.

1. *Provide a sales force* to sell the goods to retailers and other buyers.
2. *Communicate* manufacturers' advertising deals and plans.
3. *Maintain inventory*, thus reducing the level of the inventory suppliers have to carry.
4. Arrange or undertake *transportation*.
5. *Provide capital* by paying cash or quick payments for goods.
6. Provide suppliers with *market information* they cannot afford or are unable to obtain themselves.
7. Undertake *credit risk* by granting credit to customers and absorbing any bad debts, thus relieving the supplier of this burden.
8. *Assume the risk* for the product by taking title.

The wholesaler may perform the services listed below for *its customers:*

1. *Buy* goods the end market will desire and make them available to customers.
2. Maintain *inventory*, thus reducing customer's costs.
3. *Transport* goods to customers quickly.
4. Provide *market information* and business consulting services.
5. Provide *financing* through granting credit, critical to small retailers especially.
6. *Order* goods in the types and quantities customers desire.

limited-function wholesalers
Perform only selected distribution functions, such as transportation.

cash-and-carry wholesalers
Serve mostly smaller retailers with a limited assortment of products they sell for cash.

Limited-function wholesalers perform only selected functions, but do them especially well. **Cash-and-carry wholesalers** serve mostly smaller retailers with a limited assortment of products. Retailers go to them, pay cash, and carry the goods home; thus the term *cash-and-carry wholesaler*. Cash-and-carry wholesalers have begun selling to the general public in what are called *warehouse outlets*. One has to qualify as a nonconsumer by showing that one is a member of a government agency, small business, or other nonconsumer group.* It is surprisingly easy, however, to qualify and buy merchandise at "wholesale" for yourself.

*Wholesalers, remember, cannot sell to the general public.

CAREER INFORMATION: RETAIL AND WHOLESALE BUYING

Nature of the Work

Buyers purchase, for resale, the best available merchandise at the lowest possible prices and expedite the delivery of goods from the producer to the consumer. The responsibilities of buyers vary by industry and product and range from the mundane to the glamorous. For example, wholesale grocery buyers may spend many hours deciding which brand of cereal should be promoted in the grocery stores they supply. In sharp contrast, apparel buyers in department stores may attend a fashion show in Paris and buy thousands of dollars worth of evening dresses at one time.

Training, Other Qualifications, and Advancement

Familiarity with merchandise and with wholesaling and retailing practices is important for buyers, and many persons with such experience transfer into this occupation. Marketing and distributive education programs can launch careers in wholesaling and retailing that lead eventually to a buyer's position. Vocational schools, technical institutes, and community colleges offer postsecondary training that prepares students for careers in merchandising. Many colleges and universities offer associate degree or bachelor's degree programs in marketing and purchasing. An increasing number of employers prefer applicants who have a college degree.

Courses in merchandising or marketing may help in getting started in wholesaling and retailing. However, most employers accept college graduates from any field of study for buyer trainee programs, which combine classroom instruction in merchandising and purchasing with short rotations to various jobs in the store. This training introduces the new worker to store operations and policies and to the fundamentals of merchandising and management.

Job Outlook

Employment of buyers is expected to grow about as fast as the average for all occupations through the mid-1990s, as the wholesale and retail trade industries expand in response to a growing population and higher personal incomes.

Somewhat offsetting increased demand for buyers will be productivity gains resulting from the increased use of computers to control inventory, maintain records, and to reorder merchandise. The number of qualified jobseekers will continue to exceed the number of openings because merchandising attracts many college graduates. Prospects are likely to be best for qualified applicants who enjoy the competitive, fast-paced nature of merchandising.

Earnings

Median annual earnings of buyers were $19,500 in 1984. Most earned between $15,100 and $28,500 a year. The lowest 10 percent averaged less than $10,700, while the top 10 percent earned more than $38,000. A buyer's income depends upon the amount and type of product purchased, the employer's sales volume and, to some extent, the buyer's seniority. Buyers for large wholesale distributors and for mass merchandisers such as discount or large chain department stores are among the most highly paid.

Related Occupations

Workers in other occupations who need a knowledge of marketing and the ability to assess consumer demand are sales managers, comparison shoppers, manufacturers' sales representatives, insurance sales agents, wholesale trade sales representatives, and travel agents.

Sources of Additional Information

General information about a career in retailing is available from: National Mass Retailing Institute, 570 Seventh Ave., New York, N.Y. 10018.

Source: *Occupational Outlook Handbook*, 1986-1987, U.S. Department of Labor.

drop shippers
Solicit orders from retailers and other wholesalers and have the merchandise shipped directly from a producer to a buyer.

truck jobbers
Deliver goods by truck to retailers.

Drop shippers solicit orders from retailers and other wholesalers and have the merchandise shipped directly from a producer to a buyer. They own the merchandise, but do not handle, stock, or deliver it. That is done by the producer. Drop shippers tend to handle bulky products such as coal, lumber, and chemicals.

Truck jobbers are small wholesalers who deliver goods by truck to retailers. They are like a cash and carry wholesaler on wheels. They provide no credit. They handle items like bakery goods, dairy products, and tobacco products.

Manufacturer-Owned Wholesale Outlets

Manufacturers may prefer to do some wholesaling functions themselves, especially for perishable or highly competitive products that require exceptional promotional effort. There are two kinds:

sales branch
A manufacturer-owned wholesale facility that stocks the goods it sells and processes orders from its own inventory.

sales office
A manufacturer-owned wholesale facility in which sales are made, but no inventory is carried.

A sales branch stocks the goods they sell and process orders from their own inventory. They are popular in industries such as chemicals and machinery.

A **sales office** is a facility where sales are made, but no inventory is carried. Distribution is from warehouses located elsewhere.

Regardless of who does the wholesaling function, the greatest costs are involved in transportation and storage. Next we shall look at these functions and strategies for making the relationships in the distribution network more friendly and efficient.

PROGRESS CHECK

- What is a rack jobber?

- How much would a $100 item cost the wholesaler if the retailer got a 25% functional discount and the wholesaler got a 10% discount?

PHYSICAL DISTRIBUTION

If you want to be successful as a marketing agent, you must first determine when, where, who, and at what price consumers want your product, and then you must arrange to tell people about your product, motivate them to buy it, get it to the right parties where and when they want it and in the way they want it.

William McInnes

physical distribution
The movement of goods from producer to consumer.

Historically, the reason for middlemen was to help perform the physical distribution function. In fact the first courses in marketing had titles such as "The Distribution of Products." Physical distribution is still the most costly marketing function. Every year organizations in the United States spend about 20% of GNP on physical distribution, far more than for any other marketing function. This figure changes as GNP changes. Today, it would be almost $800 billion. **Physical distribution** is the movement of goods from producer to consumer and involves functions such as transportation and storage.

This section will introduce you to the principles of physical distribution and give you some insights into physical distribution management. If you are attracted to careers in this area, you can find courses available covering transportation, distribution management, and related topics such as carrier management. Sometimes these courses have the word "logistics" in the title. Although logistics is sometimes viewed as a slightly different concept, the course content is largely physical distribution and transportation.

Importance of Distribution

One cannot overemphasize the importance of physical distribution, even in an era when the service sector is dominant. Physical distribution begins with raw materials (at the mine) that have to be shipped to manufacturers who change them into useful products. Physical distribution also includes those functions involved in purchasing goods, receiving them, moving them through the plant, inventorying them, storing them, and shipping finished goods all the way to final users (including all the warehousing, reshipping, and physical movements of all kinds involved).

Physical distribution often means sending goods overseas.

A smart physical distribution manager can do wonders for a firm's profitability. For example, one firm was shipping finished cabinets in carload lots to four warehouses. The traffic manager found that the company could save 40% by shipping the shelving separately from the bolts and nuts. This was possible because the shipping rates for components were much less than for finished parts. The increase in cost for handling and packaging the component parts was $40,000, but the savings in shipping costs was $320,000, or a net saving of $280,000. Such are the savings possible when physical distribution is carefully managed.

HOW COMPLEX IS THE DISTRIBUTION SYSTEM?

Researchers once studied the distribution system of building materials to construct a two-story, masonry dwelling with six rooms and one bath. They studied 43 different materials amounting to 186 tons of products. In traveling from place to place, these products (and their antecedents) were loaded onto carriers, moved, and unloaded 424 separate times. Some 366 business entities were involved, including 148 transportation agencies. The 217 business entities that participated in the ownership flow of materials participated in 374 transactions, including 330 purchase/sale transactions.

The Physical Distribution Manager

physical distribution manager
Responsible for coordinating and integrating all movement of materials, including transportation, internal movement, and warehousing.

Physical distribution costs have been a concern of marketers for many years, but there has been more talk and theory development than action. Recently, however, the development of computers, marketing information systems, and integrated channel networks have led to a new position called **physical distribution manager.** This person is responsible for coordinating and integrating all movement of materials including transportation, internal movement (materials handling), and warehousing. Few organizations actually have such a position, but many have accepted the concept, and the process of implementing a "total systems approach" is slowly being carried out. Only very recently have firms begun to recognize the need for physical distribution management *throughout the channel system,* rather than just within the firm itself. That is, a department in one firm could coordinate and integrate as much of the movement of goods through the entire channel as possible. The idea is to keep distribution costs low for the whole system as well as for each individual organization in the channel.

When different modes of transportation are compared, ships transport most cheaply and trucks offer the most flexibility. Pipelines offer continuous delivery; airlines transport with greatest speed.

Transportion Modes

A primary concern of distribution managers is the selection of a transportation mode that will minimize costs and assure a certain level of service. (Physical distribution management is sometimes called logistics management, or rhocrematics, but the meaning is the same.)

The largest percentage of goods are shipped by rail. Railroad shipment is best for bulky items such as coal, wheat, and heavy equipment. For the last 20 years or so, railroads have handled about 40% of the total volume of goods in the United States, and this represents a decline in railroad shipping. As recently as 1950 railroads were handling up to 60% of volume. As you are no doubt aware, railroad lines are in a state of transition. As a result of practices such as piggyback shipments, railroads should continue to hold a 40% share of the market. (Piggyback means that a truck trailer is loaded onto a flatcar and taken to a destination where it will be driven to separate plants by a truck driver.) Railroad shipment is a relatively energy-efficient way to move goods and could therefore experience significant gains if energy prices climb.

The second largest surface transportation mode is motor vehicles (trucks, vans, and so forth). Such vehicles handle a little over 20% of the volume. Trucks are more flexible than railroads in that they can deliver almost any commodity door-to-door.

Trucks are a very flexible transportation mode.

Water transportation moves a greater volume of goods than you might expect. Over the last 20 years, water transportation has carried 16% to 17% of the total. If you live near the Mississippi River, you have likely seen towboats hauling as many as 30 barges at a time with a cargo of up to 35,000 tons. On smaller rivers, about eight barges can be hauled carrying up to 20,000 tons—that is the equivalent of four 100-car railroad trains. Thus you can see the importance of river traffic. Add to that Great Lakes shipping, shipping from coast to coast and along the coasts, and international shipments, and water transportation takes on a new dimension as a key transportation mode.

Another transportation mode that is not visible to the average consumer is movement by pipeline. Yet almost 25% of the total volume moves this way. Pipelines are used primarily for the transportation of petroleum and petroleum products. But the Cleveland Electric Illuminating Company has experimented with a coal pipeline, and several more are either planned or in operation now. In this method the coal is broken down into small pieces, mixed with water to form what is called a slurry, and piped to its destination, where it often must be dried before using. There have been experiments with sending other solids in pipelines, and this could be a major mode of distribution in the future.

Today only a small fraction of shipping is done by air. Nonetheless, air transportation is a critical factor in many industries. Airlines carry everything from small packages to luxury cars and elephants and could expand to be a very competitive mode for other goods.

The primary benefit of air transportation is speed. No firm knows this better than Federal Express. Its theme is, "When it absolutely, positively has to be there overnight." Federal Express is just one of several competitors vying for the fast-delivery market.

Federal Express moves goods rapidly and efficiently.

- Transportation modes vary from relatively slow carriers, such as barges, to high-speed jet airplanes. Generally speaking, the faster the mode, the higher the cost.
- Marketers must select those transportation modes that deliver goods at a reasonable price and maintain an acceptable level of customer service.

Some marketers have found huge savings by switching transportation modes. For example, one firm found tremendous savings by eliminating most of its warehouses and flying goods to customers when speed was demanded. Otherwise, deliveries were made by truck.

There are many trade-offs in physical distribution, such as the trade-off of increased transportation costs for lower warehouse costs. We now explore the criteria to be used in making such decisions.

Criteria for Selecting Distribution Systems

From a marketing perspective, two criteria dominate all thinking in physical distribution planning. One criterion is *customer service*. Customer wants and needs come first. A goal would be to serve all a firm's customers' needs with 100% reliability. Such a goal would be prohibitively expensive. But distribution managers do strive for an 85% to 95% level of customer satisfaction.

The other criterion, obviously, is *profit*. Marketing systems are designed to accomplish mutually satisfying exchanges, which means that the buyer *and* the seller must be satisfied. That means profit for the seller.

The Storage Function

About 25% to 30% of the total cost of physical distribution is for storage. This includes the cost of the warehouse and its operation plus movement of goods within the warehouse. There are two kinds of warehouses: storage and distribution. A storage warehouse stores products for a relatively long time. Seasonal goods such as lawn mowers would be stored in such a warehouse.

Distribution warehouses are facilities used to gather and redistribute products. You can picture a distribution warehouse for Federal Express or United Parcel Service handling thousands of packages for a very short time. Many college students work part-time in such facilities while in school and go on to be traffic managers who control the shipment of goods.

Materials Handling

Materials handling is the movement of goods within a warehouse, factory, or store. It is instructive to go to a warehouse and watch the operations for a while. You may see forklift trucks picking up stacks of merchandise and moving them around. In more modern warehouses, computerized vehicles will move the materials. Warehouse management is a possible career for business students.

materials handling
The movement of goods within a warehouse, factory, or store.

DELIVERY BY AIR

Customer service was the primary goal of Bob Alexander, manager of international sales for Goodman Equipment. He had to deliver a 67,000-pound excavating machine to Switzerland in the fall. The customer wanted the machine as quickly as possible, because he was afraid snows would come and prevent delivery of the machine until spring. Following the buyer's specifications, Bob *flew* the machine to Switzerland, and the buyer paid the extra shipping costs. Speed, not cost, was the major consideration, because the machine was needed to help dig a railway tunnel. This is just one example of a buyer working with a small business to develop a delivery system that is satisfactory to both.

CHANNEL SYSTEMS

Often marketers become so concerned about managing materials flows to, through, and from their own firm that they neglect the interfirm relationships and agreements that keep goods moving freely from manufacturer to wholesaler to retailer to consumer. All the firms involved in moving goods from producer to consumer are known collectively as a **channel of distribution.** Marketing managers tend to concentrate on product decisions, price decisions, and promotion decisions, while channels of distribution tend to grow in an uncontrolled, uncoordinated manner. In this section we shall look at the channel, not as an economic system, but as a behavioral system. We have already discussed how channels create exchange efficiency and add value to goods and services. We shall now look at the human problems in channels and techniques for minimizing such problems.

channel of distribution
All the firms involved in moving goods from producer to consumer.

Cooperative Channel Systems

At one time, channel relationships were rather informal in that manufacturers, wholesalers, retailers, and other channel members were tied together only loosely by short-term agreements. Each organization remained rather independent of the other organizations in the channel, and conflict was as typical as cooperation. Many retailers were especially proud of their independence and often cooperated with manufacturers or wholesalers only when they felt that it was to their advantage. Similarly, manufacturers and wholesalers often had different philosophies of business.

Some answer had to be found to the question, how can manufacturers get wholesalers and retailers to cooperate to form an efficient distribution system? One answer was to link the firms together somehow in a formal relationship. Two systems emerged to tie firms together: corporate systems and contractual systems.

corporate system
One in which all the organizations in this channel are owned by one firm.

contractual system
One whose members are bound to cooperate through contractual agreements.

administered system
The management by producers of all the marketing functions at the retail level.

Corporate Systems

A **corporate system** is one in which all the organizations in the channel are owned by one firm. If the manufacturer *owns* the retail firm, clearly it can influence much greater control over its operations. Sherwin Williams, for example, owns its own retail stores and thus coordinates everything: display, pricing, promotion, inventory control, and so on. Hart, Schaffner, & Marx owns its own clothing stores for the same reason. Other companies that have tried corporate systems include GE, Firestone, and Xerox.

Contractual Systems

If a manufacturer cannot buy retail stores, it can try to get the retailers to sign a *contract* to cooperate. A **contractual system** is one in which members are bound to cooperate through contractual agreements. There are three forms of contractual systems: First, there are franchise systems such as McDonald's, Kentucky Fried Chicken, Baskin-Robbins, and AAMCO. The franchisee agrees to all of the rules, regulations, and procedures established by the franchisor. This results in the consistent quality and level of service you find in most franchised organizations.

Second, there are wholesaler-sponsored chains such as IGA food stores. Each store signs an agreement to use the same name, participate in chain promotions, and cooperate as a unified system of stores, even though each store is independently owned and managed.

A third system is a retail cooperative. This arrangement is much like a wholesaler-sponsored chain except it is initiated by the retailers. The same cooperation is agreed to, however, and the stores remain independent.

IGA stores are independently-owned members of a contractual system.

Administered Systems

What does a producer do if it cannot buy retailers or get them to sign an agreement to cooperate? The best thing to do is to manage all the marketing functions yourself, including display, inventory, control, pricing, and promotion. The management by producers of all the marketing functions at the retail level is called an **administered system**. Kraft does that for its cheeses and Scott does it for its seed and other lawn-care products. Retailers cooperate with producers in such systems be-

Eagle snacks are marketed using an administered system.

cause they get so much help for free. All the retailer has to do is ring up the sale and make money.

The Channel Captain

The greatest problems in traditional *independent* systems are human problems. People just do not want to give up some of their freedom to benefit the system. Thus retailers do not like to do what wholesalers want, wholesalers do not want to do what manufacturers want, and manufacturers do not respond to their suppliers, distributors, and dealers. The channel becomes a source of conflict, antagonism, and inefficiency.

But in the wings there stands a champion of cooperation and coordination—the so-called channel captains. The channel captain's role is to somehow gain control over the channel members and get them to work together. The captain may be the manufacturer, the wholesaler, or the retailer. For example, in the automobile distribution system the manufacturer has much control over what the dealers do and when and how they do it. Retailers such as Sears have the power to control manufacturers that supply them. In other cases, it is the wholesaler who takes charge.

In each case, however, a channel captain usually has the power to get the other channel members to cooperate. A **channel captain** therefore is one organization in the channel that gets the other members to work together in a cooperative effort. The captain may have more financial resources, better marketing intelligence, or more managerial know-how. Regardless of the source of power, this organization maintains control.

channel captain
One organization in the channel that gets the other members to work together in a cooperative effort.

Sears is a good example of a channel captain. Because of its size, financial strength, and managerial know-how, Sears is able to get wholesalers and manufacturers to cooperate fully in whatever Sears wants. Manufacturers even make products to Sears' specifications. This is good for Sears—it gets control over the channel system. Management of the entire channel system, from producer to consumer, is the best way to stay competitive in today's markets.

Channel Systems of the Future

It is the year 2000, and Diane Winton wants to go grocery shopping. What kind of store do you think she will go to? Or will she go to a store? There is some evidence that much of our grocery shopping in the future will be done from home. There will be a handy catalog of everyday grocery items in the kitchen. When we want something, we will just pick up the phone, call the local food distribution center, order what we want, and have it delivered in an hour or two. The principle is, move goods, not people. Those items which we like to shop for, such as meats, bakery goods, and produce, we could buy at a local farmer's market, where such goods are on display in a wide variety of shops.

If in the future people do go shopping for food as they do today, it is quite likely that they will shop at hypermarkets, where many nonfood items will also be sold. The idea is to minimize the number of places a person must visit to shop and to increase the margin on items sold at supermarkets. (The markup on nonfood items tends to be much higher than that on foods.)

More significant than the changes in the retail system, which will go through a slow, evolutionary change, will be the increased movement toward vertically integrated channel systems. The most significant development in channel systems could be the growth of interfirm marketing communication systems that will involve computerized inventory systems, systemwide promotional programs, and a generally more efficient physical distribution flow. This may mean lower prices for consumers, but it would lead to more centralization of market power among a few giant corporations. Such corporations would be diversified into many areas, such as food, clothing, appliances, books, and furniture.

CAREER INFORMATION: ENTRY-LEVEL TRAFFIC AND SHIPPING JOBS

NATURE OF THE WORK

Traffic, shipping, and receiving clerks keep track of goods transferred between businesses and their customers and suppliers. In small companies, they may be assigned tasks requiring a good deal of independent judgment, such as handling problems with damaged merchandise, or supervising other workers in shipping or receiving rooms.

A job as a traffic, shipping, or receiving clerk offers a good opportunity for new workers in a firm to learn about their company's products and business practices. Some clerks may be promoted to head traffic, shipping, or receiving clerk; warehouse manager; or purchasing agent. Very experienced workers with a broad understanding of shipping and receiving may enter related fields such as industrial traffic management.

JOB OUTLOOK

Employment of traffic, shipping, and receiving clerks is expected to increase more slowly than the average for all occupations through the mid-1990's, in part because so many clerks work in manufacturing and wholesale trade, industry sectors that are expected to grow more slowly than the overall economy.

Employment growth will continue to be affected by automation, as all but the smallest firms move to hold down labor costs by using computers to store and retrieve shipping and receiving records. Methods of materials handling have changed significantly in recent years. Large warehouses are increasingly automated, using equipment such as computerized conveyor systems, robots, computer-directed trucks, and automatic storage and retrieval systems. This automation, coupled with the growing use of hand-held scanners and personal computers in receiving departments, is expected to hold down employment growth.

EARNINGS

Median weekly earnings of full-time traffic, shipping, and receiving clerks were about $280 in 1984; the middle 50 percent earned between $220 and $380 a week. Ten percent earned less than $170 and 10 percent more than $500.

Shipping and receiving clerks in urban areas earned average weekly salaries of $321 in 1984. This was about as much as the average for all nonsupervisory workers in private industry, except farming. Salaries varied substantially, however, by type of employer. Shipping and receiving clerks employed in the services industry averaged $292, those working for wholesale houses averaged $324, and those employed by public utilities averaged $354.

Shipping and receiving clerks employed in the private sector averaged $280 a week in 1985.

RELATED OCCUPATIONS

Traffic, shipping, and receiving clerks record, check, and often store the materials that a company receives. They also process and pack goods for shipment. Other workers who perform similar duties are stock clerks, material clerks, distributing clerks, routing clerks, and order fillers.

Source: *Occupational Outlook Handbook*, 1986-1987, U.S. Department of Labor.

THINKING IT THROUGH

Picture yourself picking up a phone attached to a computer and ordering all kinds of goods and services—from food and clothing to TV sets, automobiles, and stocks and bonds. How will such computer shopping affect the marketing functions of packaging, branding, and distribution? What will happen to retail supermarkets and department stores?

What distribution mode do you feel will grow the fastest in the future? What kinds of goods could be sent through a pipeline other than oil? Will airplanes take over the role of railroads? Consider the transport of coal, steel, and other commodities. What could be the ultimate transportation mode of the future?

PROGRESS CHECK

▪ Which transportation mode is the best at serving multiple locations?

▪ How does an administered system work?

SUMMARY

1 Distribution (place) is the fourth *P* of the marketing mix.
  ▪ What is the distribution mix?
      The functions are buying, selling, transportation, storage, credit, risk taking, grading, and research.
  ▪ Wouldn't it be cheaper to get rid of middlemen?
      You can get rid of middlemen, but not their function, which they can do less expensively.
  ▪ What utilities do middlemen add?
      All five: form, time, place, possession, and information.
2 A retailer is a marketing middleman who sells to consumers.
  ▪ Are there different categories of retailers?
      There are many, including department stores, supermarkets, discount stores, and catalog stores.
  ▪ What are the out-of-store categories?
      They include telemarketing, vending, and door-to-door sales.
  ▪ What is the "wheel of retailing?"
      It is the tendency for stores to start with low prices, few services, and poor locations and then add services and better locations until they are priced competitively with department stores; then they often fail.
  ▪ What is scrambled merchandising?
      Selling product lines not normally found in a particular type of store.
  ▪ What are the three retail distribution strategies?
      Intensive, selective, and exclusive distribution.
3 A wholesaler is a marketing middleman that sells to organizations and individuals, but not final consumers.
  ▪ What is a functional discount?
      One given to wholesalers or retailers for the functions they perform.

■ What are the different types of wholesalers?

Basically, there are two types: full-function wholesalers that do all eight functions and limited-function wholesalers that do a few functions well (e.g., drop shippers and truck jobbers).

4 Physical distribution is the movement of goods from producer to consumer.

■ What is a physical distribution manager?

A person responsible for coordinating and integrating all movement of materials, including transportation, materials handling, and warehousing. The concept may extend to the whole channel system.

■ What are the major transportation modes?

Airplanes, trucks, trains, water transport, and pipelines.

■ What is the storage function?

It involves warehouse management and materials handling.

5 A channel of distribution is all the firms involved in moving goods from producers to consumer.

■ How can the channel be made more efficient?

By having the manufacturer buy all the firms (corporate system), by having members contract to cooperate (contractual system), or by having the producer control all the marketing activities at the retail level (administered system).

KEY TERMS

administered system p. 270
cash-and-carry wholesalers p. 262
channel captain p. 271
channel of distribution p. 269
contractual system p. 270
corporate system p. 270
distribution mix p. 250
door-to-door sales p. 258
drop shippers p. 264
exclusive distribution p. 260
full-service wholesalers p. 262
functional discount p. 261
intensive distribution p. 260
limited-function wholesalers p. 262
mail order retailer p. 258
marketing middlemen p. 250

materials handling p. 269
merchant wholesalers p. 262
physical distribution p. 264
physical distribution manager p. 266
rack jobber p. 262
retailer p. 256
sales branch p. 264
sales office p. 264
scrambled merchandising p. 259
selective distribution p. 260
telemarketing p. 258
truck jobber p. 264
utility p. 252
wholesaler p. 260
vending machine p. 258

GETTING INVOLVED

1 Visit different retailers in your area and walk around the store for awhile. Which places would be the most fun to work for? Check on salaries, chances for promotion, and hours. Does retailing look like a good career? Discuss your findings with the class.

2 When you are visiting retailers, ask who their suppliers are. Call up a few wholesale organizations and visit their facilities. Do they look like nice places to work? What are the opportunities, salaries, and chances for advancement? What kinds of jobs are available?

3 Check the prices in your local convenience store, if you have one. They have names like 7-Eleven and High's. How do their prices compare to supermarket prices? Why can convenience stores charge more? What values (utilities) do they provide better than supermarkets?

4 Talk to a truck driver and other people involved in distribution (e.g., warehouse operators, Federal Express workers, and so on). Do any of these careers look interesting?

5 Go to the library and get a book on logistics or physical distribution. Look through the table of contents and briefly glance through the book. Does this subject interest you? What material does the book cover? Discuss your findings with the class.

CASE ONE   SHOPPING AT RETAIL MALLS

**PRACTICING
MANAGEMENT DECISIONS**

No phenomenon better describes the marketing habits of Americans than shopping at malls. Recently, *Shopping Center Age* found that 93% of the population had been to a mall at least once in the last 6 months. Some 78% of us go to the mall at least once a month.

What is the attraction of the mall? Some sociologists feel that the mall has replaced the downtown plaza as a place to gather and visit. Certainly, malls have become a gathering spot for teenagers and younger "mall rats." Best of all, though, a mall is good for window-shopping.

It is no mistake that malls are called "shopping centers" by many people. The key to malls was developed by a man named Victor Gruen about 30 years ago. His goal was to change "destination shoppers" into "impulse shoppers." Here's how it works. You run to the mall to buy a pair of shoes. You go into a shoe store to get what you want, but cannot find it. You then proceed to walk through the mall to another shoe store. During that walk, you may stop for an ice cream cone, drop in to a bookstore for a paperback novel, and window-shop at several clothing stores. You went to the mall for shoes (a destination shopper) and ended up buying ice cream, books, and maybe a sweater (an impulse shopper).

Malls are ingeniously designed to foster impulse shopping. Shoe stores are usually widely separated so you have to travel the length of the mall to "shop for shoes." Most malls are "anchored" by a couple of major department stores (e.g., Sears) that are at opposite ends, like anchors holding the mall together. Notice how the malls have spread the distance between clothing stores and other places to shop.

At Southwest Plaza in Colorado, there are 18 shoe stores. There are over two dozen women's clothing outlets and 31 eateries. In addition, there are five major department stores, five movie theaters, and 190 other retail outlets. The latest trend in malls is to have professionals such as doctors, dentists, and lawyers. Southwest Plaza has a tower with dozens of such professionals. You can go to a doctor's office in some malls and shop while you wait. You are called by a "beeper" when they are ready for you.

Countering the trend for huge malls like Southwest Plaza are smaller, more product-specific malls. Across the street from Southwest, for example, is a strip mall (stores all in a row) with seven furniture stores. This lets consumers shop for furniture conveniently, but does not lead to much impulse buying. Other shopping centers may feature several automobile dealers. Lately, a major attraction is "outlet" malls or "off-price" malls that contain many discount stores. On the other extreme are malls catering to the rich, anchored by stores such as Neiman-Marcus and filled with exclusive jewelry shops and high-fashion clothing stores.

DECISION QUESTIONS

1 Most of the new malls have no supermarkets. Why do you suppose this is?

2 Do malls sell convenience goods, shopping goods, or specialty goods (or some combination)?

3 What are the benefits and drawbacks of shopping malls in a community?

4 How can independent retailers compete with malls?

PRACTICING MANAGEMENT DECISIONS

CASE TWO   SUPERMARKET COMPETITION

What is it like to run a grocery store for fun and profit? Could you compete with the giants like Safeway, A&P, Kroger, and Winn-Dixie? What could you do to compete? Let's look at Gromer's supermarket in Elgin, Illinois to see how they do it.

First of all, let's check to see how the supermarket is doing. It makes a little over 2% on each dollar of sales. That's better than Safeway's .99%, Kroger's .98%, or Winn-Dixie's 1.59%, but not as good as A&P's 3.67%. Most stores have about 7,500 customers a week. Gromer's has over 34,200. He grosses about $900,000 a week in sales. In other words, Gromer's is doing quite well.

How do they do it? For one thing, Gromer's tries to meet as many needs as possible. It has a magazine rack, a deli, a carryout service, a bakery on the premises, film processing, videocassette rentals, catering, and more. Gromer's listens to customers and gives them what they want. Most stores carry almost 10,500 different brands and sizes; Gromer's carries almost twice that. A typical supermarket carries 1,200 varieties of frozen food. Gromer's has 1,500. It sells 18 varieties of croutons. There are 152 barrels of bulk foods. You get the idea.

What about pricing? Well, a cup of coffee is free. Ice cream at the cone bar is 25¢. The meat department loses money. The bakery earns just a little. The stamp-selling and utility-bill collection services lose money. Not only that, but the store stays open 24 hours a day, so the lighting bill and other such costs are high. Mind you, this is in a town of about 65,000 people where very few go shopping at night.

So where does profit come in? The salad bar is one profit center. Everything but the soup costs $2.19 a pound. Gross profit runs as high as 65% in season. This compares to a gross profit of 8% on items such as soup, sugar, and flour. Shish kebab is $4.98 a pound, and much of the weight is stick and vegetables. Fresh-squeezed orange juice goes for $2.49. All these items are highly profitable, and there are thousands more like this throughout the store, along with the great bargains.

Mr. Gromer carries a notebook and jots down consumer requests. He uses up a lot of notebooks in a year. The employees are trained to be attentive equally to customer wants and to profit. Each manager is given much responsibility for his or her area. In-store competition for profits and customers is intense. For example, the bakery competes for sales against baked goods from outside suppliers (which are sold in another department).

Of course, it is difficult to talk of small business success without mentioning computers. Gromer's was one of the early users of checkout scanners. The scanners and an estimated quarter of a million dollars worth of computer hardware and software are the heart of Gromer's marketing intelligence system. For example, computer print-outs tell Mr. Gromer which sizes of Rice Krispies sell fast and which do not. That way, unpopular sizes can be eliminated. Computer data can also tell Gromer's how to cut up a piece of meat to optimize profit. Gromer's knows how many groceries go through the lines for every 15-minute period every hour of every day. This helps immeasurably in scheduling check-out people, baggers, and so forth. The computer is an invaluable asset in inventory control and in virtually every phase of operation.

To contrast all this with the big operators, it is instructive to know that A&P once had almost 16,000 stores in 34 states, but now has some 1,088 stores in only 25 states. Small retailers can compete against the giants, if they do it right.

DECISION QUESTIONS

1 In which kind of store would you prefer to shop—Gromer's or a typical supermarket? Why? What makes Gromer's special?

2 Does it make sense to have a huge mark-up on some goods and lose money on others? Why not have a small mark-up on everything?

3 Gromer employees will jump-start your car, collect your bill payments, sell you stamps, roast your turkey, handle your banking, handle your auto license plates, and peel and core your pineapple. Do such services belong in a supermarket? Why? What can you learn about the marketing concept of "find a need and fill it" from Gromer's?

LOOKING AHEAD

Most of the strategies used to market goods are now being used also to market services and nonprofit organizations. You have already learned that most of the careers of the future will be in the service sector. The marketing problems of service and nonprofit organizations are often more difficult than those of businesses that deal in goods. For one reason, the study of nonprofit marketing is relatively new. However, the career opportunities are fantastic. In Chapter 11, we shall explore the challenges and opportunities of service and nonbusiness marketing.

SERVICE AND NONPROFIT MARKETING

LEARNING GOALS

After you have read and studied this chapter, you should be able to:

▪ Differentiate between goods and services.

▪ Distinguish between consumer and industrial services.

▪ Explain marketing strategies for consumer services.

▪ Describe the role of marketing in nonprofit organizations.

▪ List and describe the elements of a marketing plan for community service organizations.

PROFILE   DICK DOTT OF PEDUS INTERNATIONAL

The number one firm on the *Inc.* 500 list* in 1984 was a firm called Pedus International. A look at Pedus and its CEO, Dick Dott, gives an indication of what it is like to be an executive in one of the fastest growing U.S. *service* firms.

Pedus is named for Munich entrepreneur Peter Dussman, who parlayed $500 and a job cleaning bachelor apartments into a major European janitorial company. Dussman provided Dick Dott with the initial capital to start Pedus.

Dick Dott was a good choice for top manager. Dott had some experience with service firms before starting Pedus. He worked 5 years for Pacific Telephone & Telegraph and 10 years at Bekins Moving & Storage. Pedus started as a relatively small (68-employee) security firm. It has grown into a service giant with 7,000 employees and $70 million in sales. It is now a service conglomerate providing guard services, janitorial staffing, food workers, and more throughout the West and Southwest.

Pedus grew by finding eager entrepreneurs to manage service businesses that had growth potential but were only marginally profitable. Pedus would buy the service firm and put managers in charge. They were given freedom and incentives as if they were the sole owners. For example, Tim Gilmore of Pedus Security Services, Inc. says, "My autonomy is nearly total. . . .But that freedom is what makes me tick." In fact, Gilmore built the business from $12 million to $30 million.

Another acquisition Dott made was Metroplex Maintenance Services, Inc. It

Inc. magazine's annual list of the top 500 U.S. small businesses.

Dick Dott.

The evolution of the United States into a service economy has significant implications for U.S. economic growth and for economic policy formation. Services are less cyclical than goods—growing less in booms, and falling less in recessions. Services tend to be more labor intensive and to use less capital equipment than manufacturing. Productivity increases have been slower in services, and price increases have been more rapid.

U.S. DEPARTMENT OF COMMERCE

was undercapitalized and only marginally profitable when Pedus bought it. Along with Metroplex came its top manager, Eddie Neel. Neel pushed sales from $1 million in 1979 to $10 million in 1984. "The difference is management," Neel says. "They told me, 'This area is yours; you're responsible for the growth; you're responsible for the P&L (profit and loss).' Then they left everything else up to me. It's almost like having my own company."

Dott says of Pedus, "There's no philosophy other than having fun doing what you do . . . the company doesn't grow because I pull people up. It grows because they push me up."

Pedus is a model of the growth firms of the 1990s—service organizations run by modern managers who stress freedom and incentives. Harold Shapiro is a typical manager at Pedus. He says he has one mandate—to take care of his customers. His compensation, like that of all other managers, is tied to a personal incentive plan based on his division's growth. ▪

Source: Curtis Hartman, "The Cleanup Crew," *Inc.,* December, 1984, pp. 61-62.

Stevie Wonder.

Growth of jobs in the service sector.

THE SERVICE SECTOR

We have learned that over 70% of the jobs in the United States today are in the service sector (including the government and other nonprofit organizations). Furthermore, almost all the growth in employment is in this sector. Therefore it is wise for us to pay special attention to marketing and management in service and nonprofit organizations. The Profile of Dick Dott and Pedus International is just one illustration of the growth firms of tomorrow.

The Stevie Wonder poster at left was the winning kick-off poster for the *Reader's Digest* "$500,000 Don't Drive and Drink College Scholarship Challenge"—a good example of social advertising to solve a social problem.

As you will see in this chapter, marketing and management are often more difficult in service and nonprofit organizations than in companies producing goods, because the product is intangible. This provides a real opportunity for students who are willing to study and learn how to manage such organizations. The path to the top is less cluttered. Managerial expertise is less widespread. The chances for advancement are great. Besides, it is often interesting to work for service organizations in fields such as recreation, fitness, communications, education, transportation, and travel assistance. Talk to people who work for various airlines, health clubs, travel bureaus, ski resorts, consulting firms, and resort hotels and you may find that employment in the service sector can be quite rewarding for you.

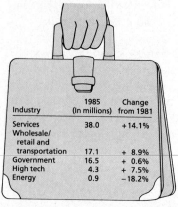

Industry	1985 (In millions)	Change from 1981
Services	38.0	+14.1%
Wholesale/ retail and transportation	17.1	+ 8.9%
Government	16.5	+ 0.6%
High tech	4.3	+ 7.5%
Energy	0.9	−18.2%

The Difference Between Goods and Services

There is much confusion in business literature about the definition and scope of the service sector. For example, some people say that if you can't hold the product you buy in your hand, you have bought a service. They mean that there is no way you can hold a haircut, a vacation, a car wash, an education, or a plane trip in your hand, and these are all services. But you *can* hold plane *tickets,* consulting *reports,* and *water* (in a glass) in your hand—and these are services, too. Utilities (gas, water, electricity, phone) are all service organizations, and included in government statistics on service organizations. So are retail stores and wholesale facilities (see Figure 11-1).

SERVICE CATEGORY	PERCENTAGE OF TOTAL SERVICE EMPLOYMENT
Retail and wholesale trade	32%
Business and personal service	30
Government	23
Finance, insurance, and real estate	8
Transportation, communications, and utilities	7
TOTAL	100%

FIGURE 11-1

Employment in the service sector. Note that the largest percentage of jobs is in retailing and wholesaling.

Source: "Employees on Nonagricultural Payrolls by Industry, Annual Averages, 1985," U.S. Department of Labor, Bureau of Labor Statistics, 1986.

There are about as many definitions of services as there are writers in the area. Perhaps the best strategy, therefore, would be to find the points that most writers generally agree on and then reach some conclusions that can help us understand the differences between goods and services.

First, it is clear that goods are basically tangible (physical) and can be examined, purchased, stored, resold, and carried from place to place. Services, on the other hand, are basically intangible and cannot be easily examined, nor can they be stored, resold, or carried from place to place. Thus **goods** include clothes, food, books, household furniture, and the like. **Services** include consulting, repairs, cleaning, renting, banking, and communications (such as radio, TV, telephone).

Second, goods are produced at one time and sold at a later time. Because services cannot be stored, they must be produced and sold simultaneously. Furthermore, the quality of a good is determined almost exclusively by the manufacturers of that good. They have rather complete control over raw materials, production processes, and quality control. Services, on the other hand, depend greatly on the input of buyers for their quality. For example, the quality (benefits) of a college education depends upon the faculty (the producer) and the student (the buyer). If buyers do not do their part, service satisfaction or quality will be lowered; for example, students must study to learn the material. The satisfaction you get from school is as much a matter of how much *you* put into it as it is how good the instructor is. (Can you see how this principle would apply at a vacation resort?) Service marketing and management call for much closer communication and cooperation between buyers and sellers. Thus we can reach the following conclusions about the differences between goods and services:

- *Goods* are tangible products that can be examined, purchased, stored, resold, and transported (for example, TV sets and furniture).

goods
Tangible products that can be examined, purchased, stored, resold and transported—for example, TV sets and furniture.

services
Intangible products that often cannot be examined before purchase and cannot be stored, resold, or transported.

The meal you buy at a restaurant has both goods and
services components.

- *Services* are intangible products that often cannot be examined before purchase and cannot be stored, resold or transported (for example, a haircut, an airplane trip, or legal advice).
- Goods are produced and sold separately.
- Services are produced and sold simultaneously.
- The quality of a service is the result of an interaction between buyer and seller, whereas quality control with goods is managed by the producer.

Thus far we have made rather clear distinctions between goods and services, but the two tend to mingle in the real world. For example, when you buy a meal at a fine restaurant, you get food (a tangible) and you get a bundle of services that include cooking, serving, recommendations of which foods to get, and clean-up. When you buy a washing machine, you get a tangible good (the washer) plus a bundle of services that may include credit, delivery, installation, demonstration, and follow-up repairs. Thus goods and services are often sold together, and the customer buys some combination of tangible and intangible benefits (see Figure 11-2). The separation between goods and services is neither clear nor obvious. Given that problem, we can still discuss service marketing and management.

FIGURE 11-2

A comparison of various
goods and services packages.

Source: W. Earl Sasser, R. Paul Olsen,
and D. Daryl Wykoff, *Management of
Service Operations: Text, Cases, and
Readings* (Boston: Allyn & Bacon, Inc.
1978), p. 11.

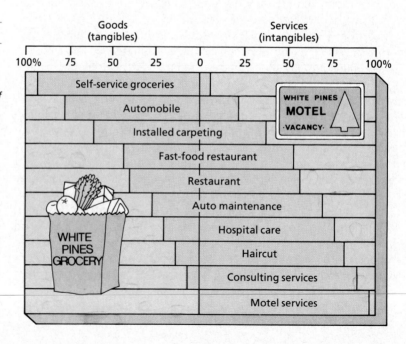

Figure 11-2 shows that services vary from those closely associated with goods (for example, a retail store selling groceries) to those with almost no goods involved (for example, motel services).

YOUR INVOLVEMENT WITH SERVICES

Because the United States has been dominated by the industrial sector for so long, it may be difficult for you to imagine the service sector being so important. "After all," you say, "I don't buy or use many services, but I do buy lots of goods such as food, clothing, cars, TVs, and radios." Let's pause, therefore, and explore how you can become more familiar with the service sector.

Half of Consumer Expenditures Go for Services

Jennifer Carroll was a sophomore at a midwest community college. During an introductory course in business she heard that almost half of what consumers spend is for services. Jennifer found this hard to believe, because she did not spend much of her money on services, or so she thought. After all, how much does one spend on haircuts, laundry, and the like?

Jennifer's professor suggested she make note of her expenditures for services throughout the semester to see for herself where the money went. Jennifer agreed, and this is what she found.

She discovered that one of the major service expenditures she made was for rent. In fact, housing is one of the largest service expenditures for all consumers (about 35%). Another major outlay was for tuition at the university (educational expenses are about 3% of all service expenditures). In the middle of the semester, Jennifer went on an outing with the ski club on a chartered bus. After some investigation, Jennifer learned that transportation services were an important factor in total service costs (about 7%) and recreation was another (over 4%). One of Jennifer's friends sprained her ankle while skiing and had to go to the hospital. Jennifer was surprised at the cost of medical care and how much it took of the consumer's service dollar (about 16%) (see Figure 11-3).

SERVICE CATEGORY	PERCENTAGE OF TOTAL SPENDING
Housing	35%
Medical care	16
Household operation	14
Personal business	13
Transportation	7
Recreation	4
Private education	3
Personal care	4
Religion and charities	3
Foreign travel	1
	100%

FIGURE 11-3

Consumer spending for services. Figures rounded to nearest percent. These figures were the basis for much of Jennifer's class report and represent after-tax expenditures.

Source: Adapted from figures published by the U.S. Department of Commerce, "Survey of Current Business: National Income Issue."

During the semester Jennifer had her hair cut and styled, took her clothes to the dry cleaner, went to a music festival, attended services at her church, sent letters to her friends, telephoned her parents, saw a couple of movies, joined some friends at football games, and helped her sorority gather funds for a charity. Each of these activities involved a service organization, and Jennifer saw more clearly where consumers spend their money on services. Of course, a good share of a person's income goes in taxes for government services; some may be given away for religious activities, charities, and social causes (about 3%); and the rest goes for service expenditures such as insurance, health care, entertainment, utilities (water, electricity, telephone, gas), repairs, transportation, credit charges, education, communications (radio, TV, telegraph), and legal aid. Figure 11-4 lists the major consumer services.

FIGURE 11-4

Selected consumer services.

Amusement (movie theaters, bowling alleys, and so forth)
Automobile (insurance, parking, repair, rental, and storage)
Barber shop, beauty parlor, and shoeshine services
Brokerage services for stocks and bonds
Child-care, babysitting, and animal-sitting services
Cleaning, painting, repair, and maintenance (of homes, for example)
Clothes cleaning, alterations, and repair
Delivery services
Financial services (banking and credit)
Funeral services
Home utility services (gas and electricity)
Income tax preparation services
Legal services
Life insurance services
Lodging (hotels, motels, and camper parks)
Medical care and sickness prevention
Photography sales and processing
Private education
Radio and television broadcasting and repair
Real estate services
Rental services (boats, cars, homes, and so forth)

Jennifer reported her findings to the class. The professor reminded her that she had not mentioned services to businesses; to institutions such as hotels, motels, schools, and hospitals; and to the government. The class then discussed the phenomenal growth of computer services, leasing services (for example, of cars, trucks, copiers, buildings, and so forth), and consulting services (see Figure 11-5).

Because the service sector is so important, we need to discuss strategies for marketing various services, consumer and professional. There are few experts in such areas, thus the potential for you to progress rapidly is greatest in these fields.

PROGRESS CHECK

▪ Which service categories employ the most people?

▪ On which services do consumers spend the most money?

STRATEGIES FOR MARKETING SERVICES

Services may be divided into two broad classifications. The first is **industrial services**. These services are provided for a broad range of organizations, including manufacturing, mining, agriculture, nonprofit, and the government. A selected list of such services may be found in Figure 11-5.

industrial services
Services that are provided to organizations engaged in such fields as mining, agriculture, and government.

Accounting, auditing, and bookkeeping
Architectural services
Building maintenance
Cleaning (building, linen, uniforms)
Communication
Computer services
Consulting
Credit
Detective agencies and other protective services
Educational services
Employment
Engineering services
Financial services
Insurance
Leasing services (auto, building, computers, and so forth)
Legal services
Marketing intelligence and research services
Medical
Promotional services including all the media
Repair
Stenographic services
Testing laboratories
Transportation
Utilities (gas, water, electricity)
Window cleaning

FIGURE 11-5

Selected industrial services.

The second broad class is consumer services. **Consumer services** are products such as rental housing and medical care that service organizations provide to consumers. Like goods, consumer services can be divided into three types—convenience, shopping, and specialty. This section will explore how the emphasis in marketing changes for these three types of consumer services. Figure 11-4 lists a few selected consumer services.

consumer services
Products such as rental housing and medical care that service organizations provide consumers.

It is the consumer who determines to which category a service belongs. For example, one person might consider dry cleaning a convenience service and go to the closest store. Someone else might be very fussy about dry cleaning and might drive way across town to have his or her clothes cleaned. To this person, dry cleaning is a specialty service. A service is classified as a convenience, shopping, or specialty on the basis of the shopping behavior of individual consumers.

Strategies for Marketing Convenience Services

Convenience services are those consumer services that the public purchases rather frequently and with a minimum of effort. Examples include repair services (auto,

convenience services
Consumer services that the public purchases rather frequently and with a minimum of effort.

shoe, watch) and dry-cleaning services. The definition is based on the method of purchase employed by the typical consumer. The convenience involved may be in terms of nearness to the buyer's home, easy accessibility to some means of transportation, or nearness to places where the buyer shops or works.

It has been said that the three most effective appeals for convenience services are location, location, and location. Most consumers want to obtain convenience services with a minimum of time and effort. Often they are willing to pay extra for that convenience. For example, the neighborhood dry cleaner may be more expensive than another dry cleaner farther away, but most people would prefer to pay extra rather than drive across town. In fact, dry cleaners that pick up and deliver clothes are usually both the most expensive and the most convenient.

THINKING IT THROUGH   **W**here do you spend most of your service-related dollars? How much goes for rent, travel, recreation, and health care? What service costs are rising most rapidly? How much have movies increased in price since you started going?

What service organizations might be fun to investigate for career possibilities? How well do they pay?

Image is important for convenience services.

Although location is usually the most important marketing variable for convenience services, other factors may be critical. One such factor is *image*. If a service outlet can establish a reputation (an image) for fast, friendly, and reliable service, its marketing task is much easier. Word of mouth is very important in establishing an image, and so is advertising. For example, consider the convenience service offered by a motel. Consumers want to stop when they get tired and where they do not have to go out of their way. But they will go slightly out of their way for a particular motel if the image is one they prefer. Names such as Best Western motels, Holiday Inn, and Howard Johnson's mean a certain standard of quality at a certain price. It is important for all convenience services to have a clear, attractive image and to be located close to where people will be when the service is needed. Some services, including motels, have established such a positive image in the minds of consumers that they have become classified as shopping goods rather than convenience goods.

Strategies for Marketing Shopping Services

Shopping services are those consumer services that the public selects after comparing quality, price, and reputation. Examples include auto repair shops, insurance companies (auto and life), and various rental services (such as auto and home). Consumers need information to compare shopping services, and so marketing communication rather than location may be the key marketing variable.

shopping services
Services that the consumer buys only after comparing quality and price from a variety of sellers.

Look at the life insurance industry, for example. Most consumers do not fully understand basic concepts such as whole-life policies, term policies, and mutual life insurance companies. To get a person's business, a life insurance company must communicate effectively with the buyer. This means hiring and training good salespeople who can relate to the people they serve. For shopping services, such as life insurance, information provided by sales representatives often is the key difference between sellers.

How do you select which bank or savings and loan to use? Do you go to the least expensive barber or beauty parlor—and how did you decide? Was word of mouth important? Often consumers do not feel comfortable choosing among shopping services because they do not feel that they have sufficient information. The company that provides that information can often win their business.

Medical specialists offer specialty services.

Strategies for Marketing Specialty Services

Specialty services are those consumer services for which buyers are willing to make a special purchasing effort by traveling out of their way or by paying a premium. Examples include services of medical specialists, lawyers, and financial advisors. Marketing emphasis for these people and organizations should be placed on providing consumer satisfaction. Word of mouth and publicity are good promotional tools.

Consumer satisfaction for such services means giving the client the time and attention he or she wants and deserves. It also means providing the consumer with pleasant surroundings and keeping waiting time to a minimum. But most of all, it means performing the service better than competitors. A financial analyst who can help people make money and minimize taxes will soon be in demand. A criminal lawyer who wins important cases will always be in demand. Again, emphasis is on success and performance.

Price and location are relatively minor factors in specialty-service marketing. By definition, people will go out of their way to get such a service and will pay a premium price. But they demand satisfaction and set high standards of perfor-

specialty services
Consumer services for which buyers are willing to make a special purchasing effort by traveling out of their way or paying a premium.

mance. Word of mouth spreads the word among potential consumers if the service is exceptional.

Strategies for Marketing Industrial and Professional Services

In recent years there has been a tremendous increase in the use of industrial and professional services by individuals, businesses, and government executives. Such services cover a wide range of areas and activities including legal problems, marketing strategies, financial plans, computer system design, advertising campaigns, personnel practices, sales training, executive development, and more. Although the firms that provide such services are experts in their areas, they often lack the marketing expertise to communicate their value to others. Even marketing consultants sometimes have difficulty marketing their own services. The reason is that professional-service marketing is a relatively new and unrefined process. Nonetheless, some concepts are effective if properly implemented:

- Professional services must first establish clear corporate objectives and designate one or more people to be responsible for marketing; those people should receive special marketing training.
- Target markets should be established, beginning with present accounts and expanding along lines of specialization (for example, providing similar professional services for all associations or all private schools).
- Professional services need to develop referral sources.

One of the better ways to reach new clients is to ask present customers whether they know people who have similar problems. Successful solutions to corporate problems should be spread by word of mouth to other firms. How? By getting permission from clients to use their names when soliciting new accounts and by bringing new and old accounts together where word of mouth can take place. The concept is:

- Professional services should conduct periodic free seminars where clients and potential clients can discuss similar problems and learn about the problem-solving potential of the professional service.
- Someone in a professional service organization should be responsible for writing articles for trade journals that discuss the successful implementation of new management concepts such as management information systems; such articles gain exposure for the firm.

Professional services are usually specialty services. Therefore the concepts discussed above about specialty services apply. The major difference with consulting services is that most potential customers do not know where to go to find help, what kinds of questions to ask, and how much to budget for such help. That is why professional services need to conduct regular free seminars—to educate users as to the best way to deal with service firms.

Joel Hyatt uses television to promote his professional legal services.

professional services
Services provided by experts to other businesses, the government, and consumers.

PROGRESS CHECK

- Can you distinguish between convenience, shopping, and specialty services and give an example of each?

- Can you briefly describe a marketing strategy for convenience, shopping, and specialty services?

- What can professionals do to market their services?

NONPROFIT ORGANIZATION MARKETING AND MANAGEMENT

Today more than ever nonprofit organizations are seeking students trained in marketing, finance, accounting, personnel, and other business functions. Training in business does not mean you have to work in business. The following examples will give you some feel for opportunities in the nonprofit sector:

- The Baltimore Aquarium was being built on the waterfront. It promised to be a major tourist attraction for the city. During the construction phase, the Director of Marketing conducted a series of focus group interviews among several potential target audiences. The information that was gathered was very helpful in designing pricing strategies, promotional programs, parking places, transportation systems, and more.

Creativity in nonprofit organization advertising.

- Fred Mindlin, executive director of Opportunities Resources for the Arts, received a letter from 30 second-year Harvard MBA students interested in arts administration. These students had learned that various symphony groups, ballet companies, and similar arts organizations were eager to find administrators who could conduct marketing research studies; develop a salable product offer; set a pricing policy; promote the arts to the public; raise funds from patrons, foundations, and various government agencies; and generally manage the communications function.
- The United States government spends millions of dollars every year for advertising. This money goes to 21 different government accounts, most of which are military recruitment programs. Other government programs that spend millions in advertising are the Postal Service, the Department of Energy (DOE), the Department of Agriculture, AMTRAK (the passenger railroad service), the U.S. Travel Service, the National Institute on Drug Abuse, the IRS, and the Office of Education.
- Over 500 credit union executives attended a marketing conference in Montreal. These managers of nonprofit savings institutions were discussing how to compete with banks, savings and loan organizations, and other profit-making institutions. Topics included: When should a smaller credit union hire a full-time marketing officer, how elaborate should an annual report be, and how do you conduct employee incentive programs?

An example of military recruitment advertising.

NONPROFIT ADVERTISING

Bill Kardash runs a rather different direct-mail advertising firm. He was responsible for the first Earth Day and has conducted campaigns to save the whales, save the dolphins, and boycott tuna. Mr. Kardash knows the donor market well (for example, cat and dog lovers come from lower economic and educational strata and tend to be older, but giraffes and endangered African wildlife appeal primarily to the rich and well educated). He also knows not to use a "live stamp," but instead to use a postage-guaranteed return envelope because environmentalists are fussy about saving money. Such marketing tricks come with practice.

We could go on listing programs of churches, boys' and girls' clubs, unions, charities, social causes, hospitals, foundations, and other nonprofit organizations. But the point is clear. Nonprofit organizations, which have tended to actively scorn marketing and other business functions, are now turning to business school graduates for help in soliciting more funds and better serving all their publics.

nonprofit marketing
The use of marketing concepts and tools to establish exchange relationships among individuals or groups and organizations, other than businesses, that can partially satisfy their wants and needs.

Special Types of Nonprofit Marketing

This text cannot possibly discuss in detail the special marketing problems of nonbusinesses such as churches, schools, charities, foundations, social causes, unions, fraternities, politicians, youth groups, libraries, and nonprofit health care agencies.[1] However, a brief look at some of these organizations will give you some feeling for the problems involved.

Nonprofit organizations need advertising too.

It's like being grounded for eighteen years.

Having a baby when you're a teenager can do more than just take away your freedom, it can take away your dreams.
The Children's Defense Fund.

Marketing of Social Causes

Often the goals of marketing are to mobilize the public behind some cause that seems beneficial to everyone. Many of these causes develop a slogan or some basic statement that everyone can recognize and support. You are probably familiar with campaigns such as the following:

Give blood.
Love your neighbor.
Drive defensively.
Fasten your seat belt.
See America first.
Stop smoking.
Buy bonds.
America, love it or leave it.
Help fight pollution.
Give to the college of your choice.
Help prevent forest fires.
Stay in school.
Support your local police.
Help prevent crime.
Hire the handicapped.

The promotion of such causes is part of the area called *social marketing*. **Social marketing** is the marketing of social ideas, causes, or practices. Social causes that people are concerned with today include pollution control, world freedom, women's and men's liberation, racial integration, and world hunger. All these social causes must generate support among the public if they are to be successful. This calls for effective and efficient marketing programs.

social marketing
The marketing of programs that seek to foster the acceptance of a social idea, cause, or practice.

Political Marketing

Politics is a very important part of American life, and marketing is becoming an increasingly important part of the political scene. **Political marketing,** then, is the application of marketing strategies in the political arena. Market research, market segmentation, marketing communication, and the other marketing functions are as important to politicians as they are to any other marketer. Some concepts of note are:

political marketing
The application of marketing strategies in the political arena.

- Mass advertising for a political candidate has the same function as national advertising for products—to establish the name and a favorable image.
- Political candidates must rely heavily on organization—getting their supporters to recruit other supporters and to keep the momentum going throughout the campaign, including getting voters to the polls.
- Political candidates need very careful market-segmentation strategies to ensure that pertinent issues will be discussed with different market segments as needed.

Politicians need marketing middlemen for the same reasons that manufacturers do. It is impossible for a candidate to contact every one of his or her constituents, and so middlemen must be organized to contact various market segments. If a candidate has a hundred close political supporters and each of those supporters contacts five people each and asks those five to contact five more through five layers, then potentially 312,500 people will be personally contacted and encouraged to vote for the candidate. In the case of presidential elections, such pyramiding often takes place within each state and within each city.

Marketing for Charities

There are more than half a million charitable organizations in the United States today. Each of them is competing for the public's support. The National Center for Voluntary Action estimates that 50 to 60 million people belong to volunteer groups of some sort. John Dixon from the Center for a Voluntary Society estimates volunteerism's "gross national product" at about $50 billion a year.

In spite of the willingness of Americans to volunteer their time and money for charitable causes, there is much discontent and hesitancy about charitable giving. One of the most damaging criticisms of charities has been their inefficiencies in one area—you guessed it, marketing. Some charities spend as much as 70% to 90% of their income on fund raising. There is little doubt that charitable organizations are desperately in need of marketing assistance.

COMMUNITY SERVICE

Most businesspeople today are involved in community organizations as part of their social responsibility. One reason such people are asked to assist in these organizations is their business expertise. Without the incentive of profit and paid workers, however, it is difficult to manage a successful program. Nonetheless, business concepts can be applied effectively to such organizations. There are six elements to a strategic marketing plan for community organizations:

1 A social catalyst or person who provides leadership
2 Targeting volunteers
3 Giving direction
4 Structuring the organization
5 Visible success and feedback
6 Maintaining enthusiasm

Social Catalyst

social catalyst
A person or organization that recognizes a social need and mobilizes others to support the cause.

A **social catalyst** is a person who sees a social need and mobilizes others to support an organization to satisfy that need. Businesspeople have always provided leadership in such causes. There is a need today to find and train students for tomorrow's leadership positions. A dozen chief executive officers from America's leading firms are on the board of the National Business Consortium for Gifted and Talented. They are getting business involved in educational programs for young people. Business leaders are involved in many such organizations from Junior Achievement and United Appeal to the local boys' and girls' clubs and scouts.

Targeting Volunteers

The segmentation variable that works best for nonprofit organizations is the degree of interest in the cause. Business organizations for such organizations must find people who are already highly committed to participating.

The targeting strategy goes like this: Get highly committed people to contact a few other highly committed people. Usually they either know these people already or can find them easily. Each contacted person is asked to contact several more in a pyramiding scheme that generates dozens of concerned and partially committed volunteers. They then may be called together at one or several meeting places.

Who put over 500,000 people to work last year providing $800 million worth of service to their communities?

America's 387 Volunteer Centers, that's who.

As the leaders for local problem-solving, Volunteer Centers placed volunteers in programs confronting such problems as hunger, illiteracy and unemployment. They helped over 100,000 agencies serving youth, the elderly, and the physically and mentally handicapped.

And they helped a half million Americans give their time, talent and creative energy to help themselves through their service to others.

Get Involved! Call your local Volunteer Center!

Volunteer Centers
VOLUNTEER — The National Center
Working together to help America get involved!

> Marketing for volunteers is important to nonbusiness organizations.

Politicians have used this strategy for years. Business owners can use similar strategies for solving problems such as neighborhood crime, hunger, pollution (for example, clean-up campaigns), and gaining support for organizations such as local schools, churches, charities, causes, and clubs.

Giving Direction

Volunteers must be told what to do, when, where, and how often. Volunteering is not a priority for most people, and they need someone to guide them in what they do. Businesspeople are experienced in planning, organizing, directing, and controlling people. Volunteers need even more management control because they are not being paid and often feel less commitment.

Structuring the Organization

It is important for nonprofit organizations to have some structure; that is, a place to meet, a name, a slogan, and some clear objectives. Think of the change that has occurred because of organizations with names like Neighborhood Watch, MADD (Mothers Against Drunk Driving), and Red Cross. Businesspeople are often highly skilled at creating such organizations.

Visible Success

Few things motivate people more than seeing that their work makes a difference. To motivate volunteers, an organization must provide them with feedback about the success of each effort. Volunteers need recognition for what they do. They also must feel that the effort is accomplishing something or they will lose motivation.

Maintaining Enthusiasm

Because of the new two-career family life-styles, volunteers are harder to find today. More flexibility is needed in scheduling times and days for people to work. To maintain enthusiasm, a volunteer job must be personally rewarding. Time must be taken to acknowledge volunteers and give them incentives, much like any worker: prizes, certificates, recognition dinners, newspaper articles, and so forth. The easier an organization can make volunteering the better.

THINKING IT THROUGH

What cause most interests you? Would you like to fix up your neighborhood park, cut down on neighborhood crime, or start a neighborhood co-op? Just follow the six steps. Can you see how the organizers of Live Aid used these six steps to fight world hunger? You see, business concepts can be used for all kinds of causes.

UNIVERSALLY APPLICABLE BUSINESS CONCEPTS

The growth and prosperity of business is directly tied to the growth and prosperity of the national and local economy. Businesspeople recognize this interdependency, and are active in all phases of national and local political and social organizations. Business tools (for example, computers) and business concepts (for example, planning, organizing, staffing, and controlling) are equally applicable in nonprofit organizations as in business organizations.

The next several chapters will focus on management principles. Keep in mind as you read them that the same concepts can be applied in any organization. Business courses are not just for businesspeople. They are the foundation for managing all successful organizations. Note also that you can learn much about business techniques and strategies (for example, motivation, human relations skills, and marketing) by volunteering to participate in a nonprofit organization.

PROGRESS CHECK

■ Can you define social marketing and give several examples?

■ What are the six steps in a strategic marketing plan for a community organization?

SUMMARY

1 Many exciting careers await tomorrow's graduates in service and nonprofit organizations. The marketing and management tasks are often more difficult to perform, but are usually more rewarding as well.
   ■ Why is service marketing more difficult?
      Services are more difficult to market because they are intangible, quality varies, and there are no middlemen to help.
   ■ Where will the jobs be in the service sector?
      The greatest number of jobs in the service sector are in retail and wholesale trade and personal and business services.

2 Different kinds of service organizations need different marketing programs. No one formula applies to all.

- How does service marketing differ among organizations?

    Consumer services are marketed differently based on their classification. Convenience services are best marketed by choosing a good location and working on the firm's image. Shopping services demand open, two-way communication with consumers to establish a clear price/quality image. Specialty services are promoted through word of mouth. That means providing attractive facilities and giving consumers what they want. Professional services rely heavily on referrals and can reach bigger markets by providing free seminars. Markets can also be reached by writing articles in professional journals.

- What is the future of the service sector?

    It will continue to provide the bulk of new jobs. Tremendous growth will occur in the communications area, in education, in transportation, and in health care. Review Chapter One for some trends.

3 Today, more than ever, nonprofit organizations are seeking students trained in marketing, finance, personnel, and other business functions. Just because you go to a business school doesn't mean you have to follow a career in business.

- What other kinds of organizations are looking for people trained in business?

    All organizations need people with such training. Great opportunities can be found in the government, associations, charities, causes, unions, clubs, arboretums, museums, theaters, universities, and more.

4 Most businesspeople today are actively involved in the marketing and management of community organizations.

- What steps could a person take to generate volunteer support for a community organization?

    There are six steps: (1) a social catalyst is needed to mobilize others, (2) highly committed people must be targeted and asked to recruit others, (3) volunteers must be told what to do, when, where, and how often, (4) the organization needs structure (a name, slogan, objectives), (5) communicate successes to volunteers and give volunteers recognition, (6) maintain enthusiasm with rewards, certificates, recognition dinners, and so forth.

- Why should businesspeople get involved in nonprofit groups?

    Because the growth and prosperity of business is directly related to the success of schools, hospitals, political groups, and other elements of society.

- Why should I get involved?

    Because volunteering is not only a community service, but an excellent way to learn business skills.

KEY TERMS

convenience services p. 285
consumer satisfaction
  p. 287
consumer services p. 285
goods p. 281
industrial services p. 285
nonprofit marketing p. 290

political marketing p. 291
professional services p. 288
services p. 281
shopping services p. 286
social marketing p. 291
specialty services p. 287
social catalyst p. 292

GETTING INVOLVED

1 Make a list of service organizations in your area. Mentally go through the list and notice how effective they are at marketing. What problems do they have? What are the opportunities for you and other students to do a better job? Discuss.

2 One of the trends in the future will be for consumers to rent rather than own goods. Make a list of items that consumers might want to rent rather than own if consumer prices rise dramatically. Imagine a centrally-located rental firm providing these goods. What would be the problems? The opportunities? Discuss with the class.

3 Give an example of two organizations involved in the marketing of convenience services, shopping services, and specialty services. Discuss how marketing differs within and among categories. How could marketing be improved in each category? Give specific examples.

4 Choose some cause about which you feel strongly. Write a paper describing how you would use the six-step marketing strategy to further that cause. What seem to be the major stumbling blocks? Discuss your cause with the class, get their input, and do the same for them.

PRACTICING MANAGEMENT DECISIONS

CASE ONE   MALLS: NEW LOCATION FOR SERVICES?

Everyone knows what you go to a shopping mall for. You buy shopping goods like shoes, clothes, appliances, TV sets, and furniture. More recently, however, shopping centers have been invaded by a whole host of service organizations, including doctors, dentists, lawyers, and income tax services.

At the Sears store in Costa Mesa, California, you can visit a dentist's office. At various Sears stores around the country, you can buy stock, buy a house, and get all kinds of financial advice and assistance. What is this? Services are taking over the economy. Will they take over the malls as well?

In Cleveland, there are two dental clinics in Clarkin department stores. They employ 25 dentists and are open 7 days a week for a total of 72 hours. Prices are 40% to 50% lower than prevailing rates.

At the Montgomery Ward stores in San Diego, shoppers can go to the Law Store, pay a receptionist $10, and go into a booth to discuss one legal problem with a lawyer by phone.

In various malls around the country, you can find all kinds of services: beauty parlors, law clinics, social workers, doctors, dentists, health spas, travel agencies, recreation centers, and more.

DECISION QUESTIONS

1 What are the advantages and disadvantages of locating a service in a shopping center?

2 What kind of services that are not yet in shopping centers could possibly thrive there?

3 What kind of services might fit best in a mall: convenience, shopping, or specialty? Why?

4 What kind of nonprofit organizations might consider locating in shopping centers?

CASE TWO MARKETING ARMY CAREERS

One of the major nonprofit employers in the United States is the military. Recruiting men and women into the various military services is a major marketing problem, and the Army uses all the marketing tools to accomplish that objective.

The Army's marketing research department is responsible for monitoring sales, analyzing the effectiveness of promotional programs, and recommending marketing changes. Surveys, studies, and extensive data on each recruit create a glut of statistics to be analyzed. The Recruiting Command stores such data in a Sperry Univac mainframe. When a recruit signs a contract, a record involving more than 330 variables is entered. An analysis of 5 years involves 4 million records. Each Army specialty has a certain number of openings and requires certain qualifications. Computer models are used to match recruits with specifications.

The total recruitment budget is nearly $200 million, including $62 million in advertising. The Army has to make 780,000 sales a year. Most of those are soldiers who reenlist. Army salespeople must generate about 140,000 contracts with new recruits each year.

The Army uses special incentives to recruit and retain soldiers. For example, there is a $15,200 continuing education benefit for 2-year enlistees. There is a $5,000 bonus for 4-year enlistees. The "Be All You Can Be" campaign was developed by the N.W. Ayer ad agency to show the growth possibilities in the Army.

The Army has a special need for college graduates and people who want to be doctors, dentists, and other professionals. Like all big businesses, the Army also needs people skilled in computer science.

The military services provide many career opportunities for college graduates with business skills in accounting, marketing, management, logistics, and more. There is an unusually good recruitment program and some attractive fringe benefits, including overseas assignments and special skills training.

DECISION QUESTIONS

1 What are some of the advantages and disadvantages of a career in the military service versus a private business?
2 What could the Army do to make a military career more attractive to college graduates?
3 How would you evaluate the television advertising campaigns of the various military services?

Source: "Today's Army Relying on Marketing Research to Attain Recruitment Goals," *Marketing News,* July 6, 1984, pp. 1-16.

This chapter made it clear that sound business practices based on solid principles are just as important in nonbusiness organizations—which have as their main goal something other than making a profit—as they are in profit-oriented businesses. Businesses and nonbusinesses alike need effective management and structure. They also need to make the best possible use of the business tools available, including computers. Part IV covers all of these important topics. Management is the basis for success in any organizational endeavor.

LOOKING AHEAD

MANAGEMENT

PART IV

CHAPTER 12
MANAGEMENT AND LEADERSHIP

CHAPTER 13
ORGANIZING A BUSINESS

CHAPTER 14
PRODUCTION AND OPERATIONS MANAGEMENT

CHAPTER 15
COMPUTERS, ROBOTS, AND OTHER BUSINESS TOOLS

MANAGEMENT AND LEADERSHIP

LEARNING GOALS

After you have read and studied this chapter, you should be able to:

- Describe the four functions of management.
- Distinguish between strategic planning, tactical planning, and contingency planning.
- Explain four basic concepts of organizing.
- Describe the various leadership styles and when they are used.
- List the four steps in the organizational control process.
- Identify the three levels of management, and explain the skills needed at each level.
- Outline 5 skills needed for managerial success.

PROFILE ROGER ENRICO OF PEPSICO

The next few chapters are about management and management functions. No manager's story is better to introduce this subject than that of the president of Pepsi-Cola USA, Mr. Roger Enrico (pictured with Michael Jackson on p. 300).

Mr. Enrico worked his way up through the ranks. A 1965 graduate of Babson College, he worked in marketing for General Mills until 1971. In 1971, he joined Pepsico, Incorporated as an associate product manager for Frito-Lay. In 1972, he became a product manager and in 1974, a marketing director at Frito-Lay.

His next move was to president of Pepsico Foods/Japan in 1975. In 1977, he became area vice president for South Latin America for Pepsi International. He became Frito-Lay's vice president of marketing in 1978 and senior vice president of sales and marketing of the Pepsi-Cola bottling group in 1980. By 1982, he was executive vice president of Pepsi-Cola USA and became president in 1983. As you can see, Mr. Enrico was willing to change jobs and locations on his move up the corporate ladder. Along the way, he learned managerial skills that he now applies effectively to keep Pepsi competitive. It was he, for example, who supervised the

Roger Enrico.

There is no management philosophy that you can apply to everybody. Management is personalized motivation.
CHRISTIE HEFNER

hiring of Michael Jackson, Lionel Ritchie, and Geraldine Ferraro for Pepsi's advertising.

Mr. Enrico works 12-hour days and travels 40% of the time. He is boss to 1,200 employees, but avoids structured staff meetings. He writes few memos, preferring to call or visit in person. He likes to delegate responsibility, a skill he had to learn. He says, "If you allow people to take more risks, they work harder and come up with more ideas."

Mr. Enrico can't answer all his calls, but he answers important ones quickly. That lets people know he's listening and that their requests are important.

Mr. Enrico, in short, is a modern manager: hard working, responsive, talented, and creative. In Chapter 12, we shall explore managerial tasks and skills. Mr. Enrico is a good model to keep in mind as you read.   ■

Source: Based on Haren Heller, "Pepsi Chief Unbottles a Winning Formula at Work," *USA Today,* October 11, 1985, p. 50.

THE CHANGING ROLE OF MANAGEMENT

One reason people go to college is because college prepares them to become managers. Students have told me, "I don't know *what* I want to do, really. I guess I would like to be in management." Management is attractive to students because it represents authority, more money, prestige, and so on. But few students are able to describe just what it is that managers do. That is what this chapter is for: it describes what managers are, what they do, and how they do it.

management
The art of getting things done through people and other resources.

Management is the art of getting things done through people and other resources. At one time, that meant that managers were called *bosses,* and their job was to tell people what to do and watch over them to be sure they did it. Bosses tended to reprimand those who didn't do things correctly, and generally acted stern and "bossy." Many managers still behave that way. Perhaps you have witnessed such managers yelling at employees at fast-food restaurants or on shop floors.

Today, management is changing from that image. Managers are being trained to *guide* and *coach* employees rather than to boss them around. Modern managers emphasize teamwork and cooperation rather than discipline and order giving. Managers in some high-tech and progressive firms dress more casually, are more friendly, and generally treat employees as partners rather than unruly workers.

In general, therefore, management is experiencing a revolution. Books like *The One Minute Manager* encourage supervisors to actively praise employees. A new concept called **management by walking around** (MBWA) encourages managers to get out of their offices and mingle with workers and customers.[1] This does not mean that managers are becoming mere cheerleaders. It does mean, though, that managers are working more closely with employees in a joint effort to accomplish common goals.

management by walking around
Getting out of the office to personally interact with employees and customers.

What this means for tomorrow's graduates is that managerial careers demand a new kind of person. That person is a skilled communicator as well as a planner, coordinator, organizer, and supervisor. Managers today believe that they are part of a team and enjoy the new responsibility and flexibility that comes with more open and casual management systems. These trends will be discussed in the next few chapters to help you decide whether or not management is the kind of thing you would like to do.

AMERICA'S MOST WANTED MANAGERS

Roger Enrico of Pepsi-Cola USA is one of ten people cited by Fortune magazine as "America's Most Wanted Managers." Other selections included Nolan Archibald of Black & Decker, Donald Beall of Rockwell International, and Jane Evans of Monet, Crystal Brands, Incorporated.

What these managers have in common is that they are action-oriented. A manager today has to be able to effectively manage change. A second characteristic such managers have is the ability to build a sense of shared values—an ability to motivate and generate loyalty.

Nine attributes were listed by one executive recruiter: an advanced degree; profit and loss experience; steady progress through the ranks, with an occasional detour to a staff position; some background in international business; excellent communications skills; a vision that can be imparted to others; self-confidence; the ability to take risks without undue worry; and high integrity.

These are the traits that make top executives attractive to other firms. The favorites typically have a healthy ego, a fondness for competitive sports, and a lot of experience moving from city to city.

Source: Roy Rowan, "America's Most Wanted Managers," *Fortune,* February 3, 1986, pp. 18-19.

Managers Are Needed Everywhere

One of the exciting things about studying management is that it prepares you for a career in any organization. Managers are needed in schools, churches, charities, government organizations, unions, associations, clubs, and all other organizations. Naturally, an important need for managers is in business.

When selecting a career in management, a student has several decisions to make:

- What kind of organization is most attractive? That is, would you like to work for government, business, or some nonprofit organization?
- What type of managerial position seems most interesting? A person may become a production manager, a sales manager, a personnel manager, an accounting manager, a traffic (distribution) manager, a credit manager, and so on. There are dozens of managerial positions from which to choose.
- What type of industry appeals to you—computer, auto, steel, railroad, or what? Would you prefer to work for a relatively new firm or an established one?
- What courses and training are needed to prepare for various managerial careers? Only careful research will answer this question.

Regardless of the managerial position you choose, there are certain fundamental concepts and principles you must learn. The next few chapters will broaden the discussion so that you will be better prepared, if you choose, to pursue a rewarding career in management.

THINKING IT THROUGH

What kind of management are you best suited for: personnel, marketing, finance, accounting, production, credit, or what? Why do you feel this area is most appropriate?

Would you like to work for a large or small firm? Private or government? In an office or out in the field? Would you like being a manager? If you are not sure, read on and see what is involved.

WHAT DO MANAGERS DO?

Management texts tend to group management activities under a few easily-remembered categories, much as the marketing texts do with the four *P*'s. The four primary managerial functions are planning, organization, leadership, and control[2] (see Figure 12-1). Other functions include staffing (personnel), directing, reporting, and budgeting.[3] You have some familiarity with management tasks already: You have planned to go to college to learn something about business. You have organized your time and materials to do that. Periodically, you will have to evaluate and control your progress to decide whether or not you are meeting your objectives.

FIGURE 12-1

The primary functions of management.

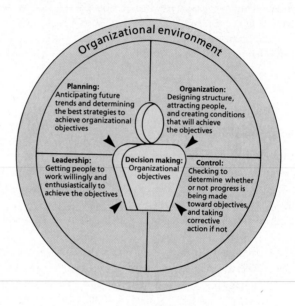

planning
Anticipating future trends and determining the best strategies and tactics to achieve organizational objectives.

organization
Includes designing the organizational structure, attracting people to the organization (staffing), and creating conditions and systems that ensure that everyone and everything work together to achieve the objectives of the organization.

leadership
Getting others to work willingly and enthusiastically to achieve the objectives of the organization.

control
Checking to determine whether or not an organization is progressing toward its objectives, and taking corrective action if it is not.

But management is much more complex than doing a few tasks. A good manager must know about the industry the firm is in and all the technological, political, competitive, and social factors affecting that industry. He or she must also understand the kind of people who work in the industry and what motivates them. Finally, a manager must be skilled in performing various managerial tasks, especially technical tasks, human relations tasks, and communications tasks. You may have the goal of becoming a manager some day. Here are the functions you will be expected to perform:

- **Planning** includes anticipating future trends and determining the best strategies and tactics to achieve organizational objectives.
- **Organization** includes designing the organizational structure, attracting people to the organization (staffing), and creating conditions and systems that ensure that everyone and everything works together to achieve the objectives of the organization.
- **Leadership** is getting others to work willingly and enthusiastically to achieve the objectives of the organization.
- **Control** is checking to determine whether or not an organization is progressing toward its objectives, and taking corrective action if it is not.

These four functions are the heart of management, so let's explore them in more detail. The process begins with planning.

Managers plan, organize, lead, and control.

PLANNING

Most planning follows similar patterns. The procedure you would follow in planning your life and career is basically the same as those used by businesses for their plans. Planning answers three fundamental questions for businesses:

1 What is the situation now? What is the state of the economy? What opportunities exist for meeting people's needs? How much competition is there? (See Figure 12-2.)

FIGURE 12-2

Questions to resolve during the strategic planning process.

■ Situation analysis
  Where are we now?
  What products are most profitable? Customers?
  Why do people buy our products?
  Who are our major competitors?
  How did we get to this point?
■ Forecasting
  What is the future of the economy?
  What is the future of the industry?
  What is the size of the future market for our products?
  What market share might we get?
■ Setting objectives
  How much growth do we want?
  What is our profit goal?
  What are our social objectives?
  What are our personal development objectives for employees?
■ Action programs
  What are short-term (tactical) objectives?
  What are our long-range (strategic) objectives?
  What are our alternatives if the situation changes (contingency planning)?
  How can we accomplish these objectives?
■ Budgeting
  How much will our plans cost?
  How shall we allocate those funds to functions?
  How shall we obtain these funds?

objective
Something that you want to accomplish in the future.

strategic (long-range) planning
Determines major objectives of the organization and the policies and strategies for obtaining and using resources to achieve those objectives.

tactical planning
The process of developing detailed short-term decisions about what is to be done, who is to do it, and how it is to be done.

contingency planning
The preparation of alternative courses of action that may be used if the primary plans are not achieving the objectives.

2 Where do we want to go? (An **objective** is something that you want to accomplish in the future. Planning involves the process of setting objectives.)

3 How can we get there from here? This is the most important part of planning. It takes three forms:

a **Strategic (long-range) planning** determines the major objectives of the organization and the policies and strategies for obtaining and using resources to achieve those objectives. In this definition, *policies* are broad guides to action, and *strategies* determine the best way to use resources. At the strategic planning stage, the company decides which customers to serve, what products or services to sell, and the geographic areas in which the firm will compete.

b **Tactical planning** is the process of developing detailed, short-term decisions about what is to be done, who is to do it, and how it is to be done. Whereas strategic planning is done by the top managers of the firm (for example, the president), tactical planning is more often done by managers at lower levels of the organization. Tactical planning may involve setting annual budgets and deciding on the details of how to meet the strategic objectives.

c **Contingency planning** is the preparation of alternative courses of action that may be used if the primary plans do not achieve the objectives of the organization. The economic and competitive environments change so rapidly that it is wise to have alternative plans of action ready in anticipation of such changes.

Planning in Action

Daniel Merkel, president of American Orthodontics, says that planning is very important to his firm. He says that both long-term (strategic) and short-term (tactical) planning play extremely important roles in the company. He believes that planning is a continuous process:

> To take the same plan that worked yesterday and use it with any degree of success in today's market is impossible. Every two months, I meet with our entire management team specifically to address short-term planning. Some of the issues we discuss include the alignment of sales territories, production needs, pricing, and other marketing strategies, and personnel requirements.
>
> In our long-range planning, we address wider issues, such as present and future competition, and tapping opportunities available to our company through penetration of new markets.[4]

Each year, the company makes detailed long-range plans that cover the next 3 years and less detailed plans that look 6 years into the future.

As president, Mr. Merkel focuses on strategic issues and encourages managers to come up with action plans. After planning meetings, formal plans are written down and distributed to managers. The plan acts as a reference tool (control measure) to ensure that daily activities are compatible with the general plan. This example is typical of how planning fits with a firm. The second key function is organization.

ORGANIZATION

How often have you heard the comment, "One of these days we'll have to get organized"? Clearly, organization is an important managerial task. Basically, organizing means allocating resources, assigning tasks, and establishing procedures for accomplishing the organizational objectives. When organizing, a manager develops a structure or framework that relates all workers, tasks, and resources to each other. That framework is called the organization structure. Most organizations draw a chart showing these relationships. This is called an organization chart. A very simple chart would look like this:

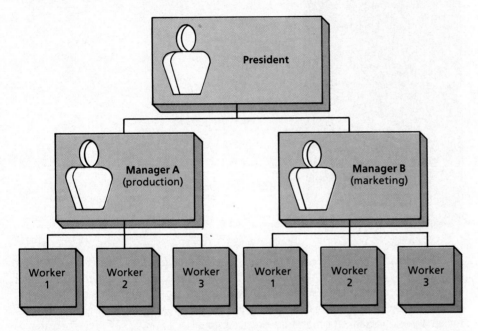

The organization chart pictures who reports to whom and who is responsible for each task. The problem of developing organization structure will be discussed in more detail later.

The basic concepts are rather easy because you already have some experience organizing. For example, to play baseball, you have to gather together some materials: gloves, ball, bat. Then you have to find people to play the various positions. (In business, this is called *staffing*.) Then each person is assigned some task: first base, pitcher, outfield, and so on. Someone must decide who bats first, who second, and so on.

All of this work of gathering materials and people together and assigning tasks is called organizing. If you were to draw a baseball field to show everyone where to stand, you would have an organization chart. A list of who bats in what order could be part of the chart. In short, organizing is a necessary part of all human effort, and is not too difficult if you know what you are doing.

An important part of organizing is staffing, getting the right people on the business team. You are probably most familiar with the term *personnel* to describe that function. Today it is called *human resource management* because it is as important to develop the potential of employees as it is to recruit good people in the first place.

The four most important things in running a business are management, management, management, and a superior product.

David Mintz,
inventor of Tofutti

The Disney corporate culture is apparent in its clean and attractive parks.

LEADERSHIP

The test of leadership is followership. Today's excellent corporations, more often than not, are reflections of their leaders.[5] They have had a vision of excellence and have led others to share that vision. Walt Disney's leadership can still be seen in Disney amusement parks and movies. J. Willard Marriott, Sr., and the other Marriotts have also created a corporate culture that spells excellence in their hotels and restaurants.

corporate culture
The use of stories, slogans, and legends to convey clearly felt values so that those values become part of what the corporation is.

Corporate culture refers to the use of stories, slogans, and legends to convey deeply-felt values so that those values (for example, integrity, dedication, and excellence) become part of what the corporation is. Leadership by example is what establishes corporate culture. Leadership, then, is what makes the difference between a good organization and an excellent one.

WHAT MANAGERS DO

PLANNING

- Setting organizational goals
- Developing strategies to reach those goals
- Determining resources needed
- Setting standards

ORGANIZING

- Allocating resources, assigning tasks, and establishing procedures for accomplishing goals
- Preparing a structure (organization chart) showing lines of authority and responsibility
- Recruiting, selecting, training, and developing employees
- Placing employees where they will be most effective

LEADING

- Providing leadership by example and communicating with employees
- Guiding, assisting, and motivating employees

CONTROLLING

- Measuring results against corporate objectives
- Monitoring performance relative to standards
- Taking corrective action

If you haven't read *In Search of Excellence* and *A Passion for Excellence,* you may want to do so soon. These two books are widely quoted in this text because they reflect the management values of the 1980s. For example, *A Passion for Excellence* talks about leadership in a whole new way. Read for yourself[6]:

> Fine performance comes from people at all levels who . . . communicate unshakable core values and patiently develop the skills that will enable them to make sustained contributions to their organizations. In a word, it recasts the detached, analytical manager as the dedicated, enthusiastic coach.
>
> Coaching is face-to-face leadership that pulls together people with diverse backgrounds, talents, experiences, and interests, encourages them to step up to responsibility and continual achievement, and treats them as full-scale partners and contributors. . . . It is about really paying attention to people—really believing them, really caring about them, really involving them. . . . the most vital aspects of coaching: visibility, listening, limit-setting, value-shaping, and skill stretching.

Leadership today, then, is not just good management. It is also a matter of establishing values, sharing visions, creating enthusiasm, and maintaining focus on a few, clear objectives.

Leadership Styles

Nothing has challenged researchers in the area of management more than the search for the "best" leadership traits, behaviors, or styles. Thousands of studies have been made just to find leadership *traits*; that is, characteristics that make leaders different from others.[7] Intuitively, you would conclude about the same thing that researchers found, that leaders tend to have more of the following traits than nonleaders:

Sociability	Popularity	Tact
Intelligence	Vision	Courage
Judgment	Good appearance	Cooperativeness
Ambition	Adaptability	Sense of humor
Energy	Decisiveness	

Other similar traits were discovered, but the general conclusion was that such findings were neither statistically valid nor reliable. You and I know that some leaders seem to have traits such as those listed above and others do not. In fact, observation will tell you that successful leadership depends largely on who is being led and in what situations.

For example, many businesspeople who are sports leaders seem to use rather successfully an autocratic leadership style that consists of issuing orders and telling players what to do. Motivation comes from threats, punishment, and intimidation of all kinds. This may be called the Vince Lombardi, George Allen, and Bobby Knight school of management. Such a style is effective in emergencies and when absolute followership is needed (for example, on army maneuvers).

Government organizations and government-like organizations (for example, universities) seem to prosper by using bureaucratic leadership. That is, they have rules to cover almost everything, and most employees live by the rules. There is little flexibility in such organizations and unique situations often cause indecision and paralysis among the leaders.

Many new, high-tech, and other progressive organizations are highly successful using a democratic style of leadership where traits such as flexibility, good listening skills, and empathy are dominant.

■ What are the four functions of management?

■ What is the difference between strategic planning and tactical planning?

In certain professional organizations, where managers deal with doctors, engineers, and other professionals, the most successful leadership style is often one of laissez-faire or free rein leadership. The traits needed by managers in such organizations include warmth, friendliness, and understanding.

Before we discuss such leadership styles in more detail, let's pause for some clarification of terms:

* ■ *Autocratic leadership* means making managerial decisions without consulting others, and implies power over others.
* ■ *Bureaucratic leadership* is based on inflexible routine supported by rules, regulations, and policies.
* ■ *Diplomatic leadership* is based on skill and tact in convincing employees to follow the leader's decisions.
* ■ *Democratic leadership* means that managers and employees work together to make decisions.
* ■ *Laissez-faire leadership* means that managers set objectives and employees are relatively free to do whatever it takes to accomplish those objectives. Many scientists and doctors work best under laissez-faire leadership.
* ■ *Employee-controlled leadership* consists of having employees set objectives, and management handle administrative matters. Many universities are run this way.
* ■ *Participative management* involves employees in setting objectives and making decisions; consultative, democratic, and laissez-faire leadership are all forms of participative management.

RESISTANCE TO PARTICIPATIVE MANAGEMENT

You might expect managers to be very responsive to a participative leadership style, but that is not always the case. This is especially true when companies try to get middle managers to switch from an autocratic style to a more participative style. At Florida Power & Light Company, for example, middle managers became confused about their new roles and needed special training sessions on how to conduct meetings, listen to suggestions, and follow up on those suggestions. Mr. Ricco of S.C. Johnson says getting middle managers to change is *the* problem among top managers. Mr. Eggers of Eggers Industries says that participative management calls for people skills, and those are difficult to teach.

Corning Glass had trouble implementing the new style, but is pleased with the results. In one plant, supervisors put five machinists in a room and gave them a die-manufacturing problem. In 5 hours, the group had a solution to the problem; this solution cost less than $200. Such results tend to make believers out of even the most resistant managers.

Other examples could be cited to show that implementing a system of participative management is not as easy as it sounds. The president of Mark Andy, Incorporated says "It's like pulling teeth." Nonetheless, changes are occurring, and the results are favorable.

Source: Leonard M. Apcar, "Middle Managers and Supervisors Resist Moves to More Participatory Management," *The Wall Street Journal*, September 16, 1985. © Dow Jones & Company, Inc., 1985. All rights reserved.

AUTOCRATIC LEADERSHIP IS FADING

James Dutt built Beatrice Company into a $12.6 billion giant. His managerial style, however, was not modern. Some 39 of the company's top 50 executives either quit or were fired under Dutt. One analyst described his approach as "The disposable-diaper theory of management."

Morale at Beatrice was low. Senior executives had to explain to Mr. Dutt's assistant why they wanted to see him. Mr. Dutt ended up in self-imposed isolation. When he finally resigned, Beatrice stock went up by $2 in one day.

Source: "James Dutt's Reign of Error," *Advertising Age,* August 19, 1985, p. 10.

Now that you are more familiar with the terminology, we can use these terms to explore different leadership styles. Some managers use a variety of leadership styles as the situation demands. What kind of leadership style do you think you would use in a business situation?

When to Use Various Leadership Styles

Research supports the idea that effective leadership depends on the people being led and the situation. It also supports the notion that different leadership styles ranging from autocratic to employee-controlled may be successful depending on the people and the situation. (See Figure 12-3 for a continuum of styles.)

FIGURE 12-3

A continuum of managerial styles.*

not successful.
Use to be like

AUTOCRATIC	BUREAUCRATIC	DIPLOMATIC	DEMOCRATIC	LAISSEZ-FAIRE	EMPLOYEE CONTROLLED
Issue orders Manager decides, employee follows orders	Manager decides and sets up rules to enforce decisions; employee follows rules	Manager decides and discusses decisions with employees (sells idea) who implement them	Employees participate in decision making. May decide by committee	Manager sets goals and employees function somewhat independently	Employees set goals and make decisions. Managers handle administrative matters

Dominant managerial traits

Decisiveness	Stability	Tact	Sociability	Empathy	Responsiveness
Dominance	Strength of conviction	Popularity	Flexibility	Understanding	High ethics
Aggressiveness	Deliberateness	Friendliness	Cooperativeness	Integrity	Tact
Self-assurance	Persistence	Initiative	Judgment	Judgment	Popularity
Intelligence			Insight	Sense of direction	Adaptability
Initiative			Communicativeness	Vision	Intelligence
			Openness	Trust	Flexibility
			Friendliness	Warmth	
			Empathy	Friendliness	

*This table is meant to illustrate different styles and traits and is not descriptive of any particular manager. It gives you a feel for the wide range of managerial styles that may be effective in various situations.

RULES OF LEADERSHIP

THE 12 GOLDEN RULES OF LEADERSHIP

1 *Set a good example.* Your subordinates will take their cue from you. If your work habits are good, theirs are likely to be too.

2 *Give your people a set of objectives and a sense of direction.* Good people seldom like to work aimlessly from day to day. They want to know not only what they're doing but why.

3 *Keep your people informed* of new developments at the company and how they'll affect them. Let people know where they stand with you. Let your close assistants in on your plans at an early stage. Let people know as early as possible of any changes that'll affect them. Let them know of changes that won't affect them but about which they may be worrying.

4 *Ask your people for advice.* Let them know that they have a say in your decisions whenever possible. Make them feel a problem is their problem, too. Encourage individual thinking.

5 *Let your people know that you support them.* There's no greater morale killer than a boss who resents a subordinate's ambition.

6 *Don't give orders.* Suggest, direct, and request.

7 *Emphasize skills, not rules.* Judge results, not methods. Give a person a job to do and let him or her do it. Let an employee improve his or her own job methods.

8 *Give credit where credit is due.* Appreciation for a job well done is the most appreciated of "fringe benefits."

9 *Praise in public.* This is where it'll do the most good.

10 *Criticize in private.*

11 *Criticize constructively.* Concentrate on correction, not blame. Allow a person to retain his or her dignity. Suggest specific steps to prevent recurrence of the mistake. Forgive and encourage desired results.

12 *Make it known that you welcome new ideas.* No idea is too small for a hearing or too wild for consideration. Make it easy for them to communicate their ideas to you. Follow through on their ideas.

THE 7 SINS OF LEADERSHIP

On the other hand, these items can cancel any constructive image you might try to establish.

1 *Trying to be liked rather than respected.* Don't accept favors from your subordinates. Don't do special favors trying to be liked. Don't try for popular decisions. Don't be soft about discipline. Have a sense of humor. Don't give up.

2 *Failing to ask subordinates for their advice and help.*

3 *Failing to develop a sense of responsibility in subordinates.* Allow freedom of expression. Give each person a chance to learn his superior's job. When you give responsibility, give authority too. Hold subordinates accountable for results.

4 *Emphasizing rules rather than skill.*

5 *Failing to keep criticism constructive.* When something goes wrong, do you tend to assume who's at fault? Do you do your best to get all the facts first? Do you control your temper? Do you praise before you criticize? Do you listen to the other side of the story?

6 *Not paying attention to employee gripes and complaints.* Make it easy for them to come to you. Get rid of red tape. Explain the grievance machinery. Help a person voice his or her complaint. Always grant a hearing. Practice patience. Ask a complainant what he or she wants you to do. Don't render a hasty or biased judgment. Get all the facts. Let the complainant know what your decision is. Double-check your results. Be concerned.

7 *Failing to keep people informed.*

Source: "To Become an 'Effective Executive,' Develop Leadership and Other Skills," *Marketing News,* April 1984, p. 1.

In fact, any one manager may use a variety of leadership styles depending on whom he is dealing with and the situation. A manager may be autocratic but friendly with a new trainee; democratic with an experienced employee who has many good ideas that can only be fostered by a manager who is a good listener and flexible; and laissez faire with a trusted, long-term supervisor who probably knows more about operations than the manager does. To summarize:

- In general, managers have certain traits such as judgment, liveliness, and sociability that differentiate them from nonmanagers, but those traits differ in different managerial situations.
- Different styles of leadership can be used effectively, ranging from autocratic to laissez faire; which style is most effective depends on the people and the situation.
- A truly successful manager has the ability to use a managerial style most appropriate to the situation and the employee involved.

A **manager** is a person who is able to get things done through others. How he or she accomplishes goals depends on the situation. There is no such thing as leadership traits that are effective in all situations, nor are there leadership styles that always work best. Leadership depends on followership, and followership depends on the traits and circumstances of the follower. In general, though, one could say that good leaders tend to be flexible, able to identify with the goals and values of followers, good communicators, sensitive to the needs of others, and decisive when the situation demands it. The box on p. 312 discusses the 12 golden rules and the 7 sins of leadership.

manager
Person who is able to get things done through others.

THINKING IT THROUGH

Do you see any problems with the new, more participative managerial style? Do you think it will be adopted by football teams? It is already practiced by some baseball teams. What is the difference between football and baseball players, what they do, and how they are managed? How does that relate to the business world?

 Can you see a manager getting frustrated when he or she cannot be bossy? Can someone who is trained to give orders (for example, a military sergeant) be retrained to be a participative manager? What problems may emerge? What kind of boss would you be? Do you have evidence to show that?

CONTROL

Often managers get so involved with the planning process and the day-to-day crisis management of the firm that they tend to short-change the control function. The **control function** involves measuring performance relative to objectives and standards and taking corrective action when necessary. The control function, therefore, is the heart of the management system because it provides the feedback that enables managers to adjust to any deviations from plans and to changes that have occurred in the environment that have affected performance (see Figure 12-4, p. 314). Controlling consists of the following steps:

1 Setting clear standards
2 Monitoring and recording performance (results)
3 Comparing results against plans and standards
4 Communicating results and deviations to the employees involved
5 Taking corrective action when needed

control function
Measuring performance relative to objectives and standards and taking corrective action when necessary.

FIGURE 12-4

The control process.

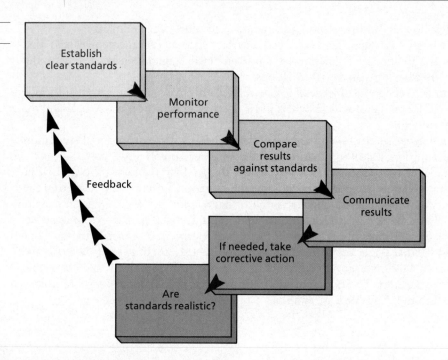

Setting Standards

Managers must set clear procedures for measuring progress.

The control system's weakest link tends to be the setting of standards. To measure results against standards, the standards must be specific, quantifiable, attainable, and subject to measurement. Vague goals and standards such as "better quality," "more efficiency," and "improved performance" are not sufficient. It is also important to have a time period established when goals are to be met. Examples of goals and standards that meet these criteria include:

- Cutting the number of finished product rejects from 10 per 1,000 to 5 per 1,000 by March 31.
- Increasing the times managers praise employees from three times per week to twelve per week.
- Increasing the sales of product X from 10,000 in the month of July to 12,000 in that same period.

One key to making control systems work is the establishment of clear procedures for monitoring performance. Naturally, management should not be burdened with such control procedures unless the goals are important enough to justify such reporting. Most managers have seen, for example, elaborate accident reports that took hours of management time, and that reported, "All is well." To minimize paperwork, such reports could be limited to exceptions. At the University of Maryland, to cite one example, all faculty are required to report daily on whether or not they performed their regular duties. This report is designed to measure sick leave. The paperwork could be cut by 98% or better if faculty merely reported sick days rather than every day. Many companies have similar examples where there is too much reporting of trivial details and too little reporting of significant performance results. To assure a free flow of communication on performance results versus standards, the number of elements measured should be kept to a minimum; those elements measured must be written; and management must provide feedback to those reporting that action is being taken on deviations.

■ Can you explain the differences between autocratic and democratic leadership styles?

■ What are the five steps in the control process?

TASKS AND SKILLS AT DIFFERENT LEVELS OF MANAGEMENT

Anyone who has ever played a sport such as basketball, football, or soccer knows there is a tremendous difference between being an excellent player and an excellent coach (manager). Often a good player will volunteer to coach the neighborhood team and is a disaster as a manager. The same thing happens in business. Few people are trained to be managers. Rather, the process of becoming a manager is similar to the sports example above. A person learns how to be a skilled accountant or salesperson or production line worker, and because of his or her skill, is selected to be a manager. The tendency is for such managers to become deeply involved in showing others how to do things, helping them, supervising them, and generally being very active in the operating task. The farther up the managerial ladder a person moves, the less such skills are required. Instead, the need is for people who are good planners, organizers, coordinators, communicators, morale builders, and motivators. Figure 12-5 shows that a manager must have three categories of skills:

1 Technical skills
2 Conceptual skills
3 Human relations skills

Pete Rose is one of the few people who can be worker and manager at the same time.

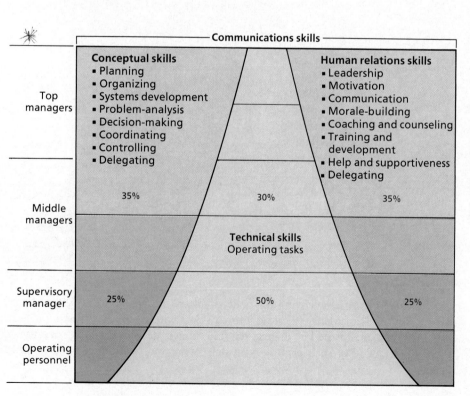

FIGURE 12-5

Management skills. Note that the higher up one goes in management, the more time is spent on conceptual and human relations functions and less on technical functions (operating tasks). Communication skills are needed at all levels of management.

Source: James Owens, *The Theory and Practice of Managing* (Tantallon, Md.: Management Education, Ltd.), 1982.

As you look at Figure 12-5, you will notice that first-level managers need to be skilled in all three areas. Half of their time is spent on operating tasks (assisting operating personnel, giving direction, and so forth). Top managers, on the other hand, need few technical skills. Instead, almost all their time is devoted to pure managerial skills: decision-making and human relations. One who is competent at one level of management may not be competent at higher levels. The skills needed are different. Let's pause here to clarify some more terms:

- *Technical skills* involve the ability to perform tasks of a specific department such as selling (marketing) or bookkeeping (accounting).
- *Conceptual skills* refer to a manager's ability to picture the organization as a whole and the relationship of various parts to perform tasks such as planning and controlling.
- *Human relations skills* include leadership, communication motivation, coaching, and training.

Top management is the highest level of management and consists of the president and other key company executives who develop strategic plans. *Middle management* includes plant managers and department heads who are responsible for tactical plans. *Supervisory management* includes people directly responsible for assigning specific jobs to workers and evaluating their daily performance; they are often known as first-line managers because they are the first level above workers (see Figure 12-6).

FIGURE 12-6

The managerial hierarchy.

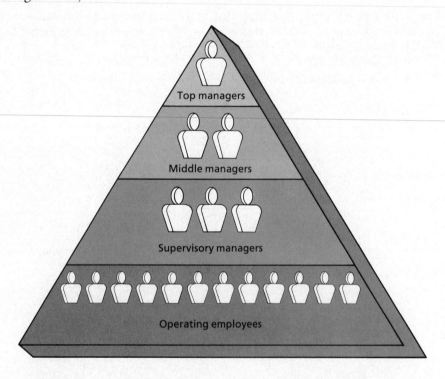

Top managers

Middle managers

Supervisory managers

Operating employees

Spend some time reviewing the conceptual and human relations skills needed by the top levels of management (Figure 12-5). Note that delegating is on both lists. Another one of the key managerial functions is decision making. Because of their importance, we shall explore both delegating and decision making in more detail.

PROFILE OF TOP MANAGERS

Becoming chief executive officer of a major corporation is the goal of many in today's long lines of pin-striped executives. What does it take to get there, and what is it like?

Heidrick & Struggles, the executive search firm, periodically puts together a composite of the typical CEO, based on questionnaires sent to 1,000 top corporations. Their findings:

He is 57, married to his first wife, Protestant, and has a bachelor's degree and perhaps an M.B.A. or legal degree. He is a workaholic, putting in 60 or more hours a week, and sits on three boards. He regrets not spending enough time with the family or at other nonbusiness pursuits, but

his $473,500 annual compensation package is some consolation. His career path involved only one or two previous job changes, as well as only one or two relocations, and he has been with the same company for 23 years. He looks forward to retiring there, at 65. He already has 7 years in as CEO and his last job was chief operating officer of the same company. He came out of marketing or finance.

His corporate heroes are Lee Iacocca of Chrysler, John Opel of IBM, and Walter Wriston of Citicorp. Although he enjoys his work very much, it gets tougher and tougher every year. As one chairman of a billion-dollar industrial company put it, "The corporate world is a jungle today. One must have physical stamina in addition to an alert mind."

Source: *Forbes,* May 7, 1984. Reprinted by permission of *Forbes* Inc., 1984.

Delegating

The most difficult task for most managers to learn is **delegating** (assigning authority and accountability to others and letting them do it while retaining responsibility for results). Remember, managers are usually selected from those who are most skilled at doing what the people they manage are doing. The inclination is for managers to pitch in and help or do it themselves. Of course, this keeps workers from learning and having the satisfaction of doing it themselves.

Managerial skills such as decision making, motivating, and morale building are usually much more important than technical skills, but managers are not often as well trained in these important areas.

delegating
Assigning authority and accountability to others while keeping responsibility for results.

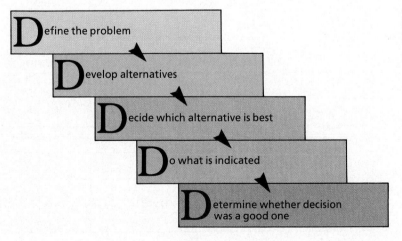

FIGURE 12-7

The five *D*'s of decision making.

Decision Making

Decision making is choosing among two or more alternatives. It sounds easier than it is in practice. In fact, decision making is the heart of all the management functions: planning, organization, leadership, and control. The **rational decision-making model** is a series of steps managers should follow to make logical, intelligent, and well-founded decisions. These five steps are:

1 Define the problem
2 Develop alternatives
3 Decide which alternative is best
4 Do what is indicated (implement solution)
5 Determine whether the decision was a good one and follow up (see Figure 12-7)

The best decisions are based on sound information. That is why this is known as the information age. Managers often have computer terminals at their desks so they can get internal records and external data of all kinds. But all the data in the world cannot replace a manager who is creative and makes brilliant decisions. Decision making is more an art than a science. It is the one skill most needed by managers in that all the other functions depend on it.

rational decision making model
Consists of five steps: (1) define the problem, (2) develop alternatives, (3) decide which alternative is best, (4) do what is indicated, and (5) determine whether the decision was a good one and follow up.

LEARNING MANAGERIAL SKILLS

Now that you have examined what managers do and some of the new managerial styles demanded by tomorrow's organizations, we can look at the skills you will need to be a good manager. In general, it's a good idea to take as many courses as you can in speech, writing, computers, and human relations. In all managerial jobs, these are the skills that are in greatest demand. Naturally, you will also have to develop technical skills in your chosen area. Figure 12-8 lists the five skills you will need to develop your managerial potential: verbal skills, writing skills, computer skills, human relations skills, and technical skills (in addition to computer skills).

FIGURE 12-8

Skill development (evaluating your managerial potential).

Evaluating your managerial potential

Skill needed	Personal evaluation			
	Excellent	Good	Fair	Need work
Verbal skills				
Writing skills				
Human relations skills				
Computer skills				
Other technical skills				

Verbal Skills

The bulk of your duties as a manager will involve communicating with others. You will have to give talks, conduct meetings, make presentations, and generally communicate your ideas to others. To prepare for such tasks, you should take speech courses and become active in various student groups. Become an officer so that you are responsible for conducting meetings and giving speeches. You may want to join a choir or other group to become comfortable performing in front of others.

Half or better of communication is skilled listening. A good manager mingles with other managers, workers, and clients. He or she listens to recommendations and complaints and acts on them. **Active listening** requires the asking of questions and feeding back what you have heard to let others know you are truly interested in what they say.

active listening
The asking of questions and feeding back what you have heard to let others know you are truly interested in what they say.

Writing Skills

Managers must also be able to write clearly and precisely. Much of what you want others to do must be communicated through memos, reports, policies, and letters you must write. Organizations everywhere are complaining about the inability of many college graduates to write clearly. If you develop good writing skills, you will be miles ahead of your competition. That means you should take courses in grammar and composition. Volunteer to write term papers, even if they are not assigned. To learn to write, you must practice writing! It helps to write anything: a diary, letters, notes, and so on. With practice, you will develop the ability to write easily—just as you speak. With this skill, you will be more ready for a career in management.

Computer Skills

The office of the future will be an office full of computers. Memos, charts, letters, and most of your other communication efforts will involve the computer. When you are practicing writing, practice on a typewriter or word processor. The truly efficient manager of the future will be able to compose on a word processor and send messages electronically throughout the world.

The office of the future will be computer-based.

To prepare for such an environment, you can begin by taking a course or two in typing. You will not need many advanced computer courses. The new software will make computer use relatively easy.

Human Relations Skills

A manager works with people, and that means that good managers know how to get along with people, motivate them, and inspire them. People skills are learned working with people. That means you should join student groups, volunteer to help at your church and local charities, and get involved in political organizations. Try to assume leadership positions where you have the responsibility for contacting others, assigning them work, and motivating them. Good leaders begin early by assuming leadership positions in sports, community groups, and so on.

CAREER INFORMATION: MANAGERS

JOB OUTLOOK

Employment of salaried managers and administrators is expected to increase faster than the average for all occupations through the mid-1990s as business operations become more complex.

Employment of managers generally changes along with employment in the industries in which they work. Much faster than average growth is expected in the employment of managers in many service industries—for example, business services, including computer and data processing as well as personnel supply services; miscellaneous services, including accounting, auditing, and bookkeeping services.

Industries in which faster than average growth in the employment of managers is expected include wholesale trade in nondurable goods, food stores, electrical and electronic machinery and equipment manufacturing, and apparel and accessories stores.

EARNINGS

Managers tend to earn more than workers in other occupations. In 1984, median annual earnings of all full-time managers and administrators, excluding self-employed, were over $27,400—compared to $17,000 for all occupations. The middle 50 percent earned between $18,000 and $40,000. More than 12 percent—over 4 times the proportion for all workers—earned $52,000 or more.

Earnings vary widely by occupation, employer, and level of responsibility. Median annual earnings of property and real estate managers were $16,900 in 1984, whereas marketing, advertising, and public relations managers earned $31,400. As in most fields, large employers tend to pay higher salaries than small employers, and earnings are higher in major metropolitan areas than in rural areas.

Management trainees may start at salaries not much higher than those of workers they supervise, whereas salaries of executives may be several times larger. Top-level managers in large corporations—among the highest paid workers in the country—can earn 10 times as much as their counterparts in small firms. A small number of corporate executives earn over $1 million a year.

Most managers in the private sector receive additional compensation in the form of bonuses, stock awards, and cash-equivalent fringe benefits such as company-paid insurance premiums and use of company cars.

SOURCES OF ADDITIONAL INFORMATION

General information about managerial functions, training programs, and career development is available from:

American Management Association, Management Information Service, 135 West 50th St., New York, N.Y. 10020.

National Management Association, 2210 Arbor Blvd., Dayton, Ohio 45439.

Source: *Occupational Outlook Handbook,* 1986-1987 (U.S. Department of Labor).

Be aware of how others react to you, and if you cause negative feelings or reactions, learn why. Don't be afraid to make mistakes and upset others. That is how you learn. But do learn how to work with others. Ask your friends what you could do to be a more effective and attractive leader.

Other Technical Skills

To rise up through the ranks of accounting, marketing, finance, production, or any other functional area, you will have to be proficient in that area. Therefore you should begin now to choose some area of specialization. You may start with a liberal arts education to practice your oral, written, and human relations skills. But to rise to top management, you might supplement that knowledge with an MBA (masters in business administration) or some similar degree in government, economics, or hospital administration. More and more students are going on to take advanced degrees. About 60% of top managers have taken courses beyond the bachelor's degree. The most common areas of technical expertise among top managers are marketing, finance, production, law, and engineering, in that order.

Management will be discussed in more detail in the next few chapters. Let's pause now, review, and do some exercises. Management is doing, not just reading.

PROGRESS CHECK

▪ What skills do supervisors need more of than do top managers and vice versa?

▪ What are the five *D*'s of decision-making?

SUMMARY

1 *Management* is the art of getting things done through other people.
  ▪ What are the four functions of management?
    Planning, organization, leadership, and control.
  ▪ What is the difference between strategic planning and tactical planning?
    Strategic planning is *long-range* and determines the major objectives of the firm, such as which customers to serve, products to sell, and areas to serve. *Tactical planning* involves developing detailed *short-term* decisions about what is to be done, who is to do it, and how it is to be done.
2 *Organization* includes designing the organization structure, attracting people to the organization, and creating conditions and systems that ensure that everyone and everything works together to achieve the objectives of the organization.
  ▪ Is staffing part of organizing?
    Yes; both people and materials are organized.
3 *Leadership* is getting others to work willingly and enthusiastically to achieve the objectives of the organization.
  ▪ What are the major leadership styles?
    Autocratic, bureaucratic, diplomatic, democratic, laissez faire, and employee-controlled.
  ▪ What is participative management?
    Involving employees in setting objectives and making decisions.
4 *Control* is checking to determine whether or not an organization is progressing toward its objectives, and taking corrective action if it is not.

■ What are the five steps in the control process?
(1) Set clear standards, (2) monitor and record performance, (3) compare results against plans and standards, (4) communicate results and deviations to the employees involved, (5) take corrective action.

5 Different skills are needed at different levels of management.
■ What are the various levels of management?
Top management (president, executive vice-president); middle management (plant managers, department heads); and supervisory management (foremen).
■ What skills vary at various managerial levels?
Supervisors spend half of their time on operating tasks; top managers almost none. Top managers spend most of their time using conceptual skills and human relations skills.
■ What is rational decision making?
It involves 5 *D*'s: (1) define the problem, (2) develop alternatives, (3) decide which alternative is best, (4) do what is indicated, (5) determine whether decision was a good one and follow up.

6 College students will have to learn certain skills if they want to be managers.
■ What skills?
Verbal skills, writing skills, computer skills, human relations skills, and other technical skills.

GETTING INVOLVED

1 Discuss the merits of working as a manager in government, business, and non-business organizations. To learn the advantages of each, talk to managers from each area and share what you learn with the class.
2 Talk with local managers and find out what they spend the most time doing. Is it planning, organizing, leading, or controlling? Or some entirely different, other task, like paperwork? Which tasks are most interesting to do; which are hardest? Which would you most enjoy? Discuss results with class.
3 Discuss the advantages of not becoming a manager. Do managers or workers seem to enjoy better life-styles? Discuss.
4 Go through *Forbes, Inc.,* and other business journals and read about managers. How much do they make? (See *Business Week's* annual survey.) How many hours do they work? Do they earn their pay? Discuss.
5 Review Figure 12-3 (p. 311) and discuss managers you have known or read about who have practiced each style. Which did you like best? Why? Which were most effective? Why? Which would *you* most like to be? Why?
6 Recall all of the situations where you have worked under a manager. How well did he or she delegate? Did the manager assign tasks and give you freedom to work or not? How did you feel about that? Discuss those feelings and the importance of learning to delegate.

KEY TERMS

active listening p. 319	corporate culture p. 308
contingency planning p. 306	delegating p. 317
control p. 304	leadership p. 304
control function p. 313	management p. 302

management by walking
   around   p. 302
manager   p. 313
objective   p. 306
organization   p. 304
planning   p. 304

rational decision making
   model   p. 318
strategic (long-range)
   planning   p. 306
tactical planning   p. 306

CASE ONE   IN SEARCH OF EXCELLENCE

PRACTICING MANAGEMENT DECISIONS

In the 1980s, the most popular book on management was called *In Search of Excellence*. It was on the best-seller list for over a year. Clearly, managers saw in it some advice worth taking. The authors visited many of the top firms in the United States to find out what made them different; better than the other firms. They were searching for excellence. Their findings support what you have read in this book thus far. Basically, excellent organizations insisted on top quality. They cared for their customers. They listened to their employees and treated them like adults. They emphasized human creativity over analysis and high-tech tools. The eight attributes of successful firms were:

a. *A bias for action.* "Do it, fix it, try it" was one slogan. The idea is to get on with it and not try to analyze decisions to death. If someone has a new idea, try it and see what happens. Remain flexible. "Ready. Fire. Aim. Learn from your tries. That's enough."

b. *Close to the customer.* Excellent companies listen to their customers intently and regularly. They then provide unparalleled quality, service, and reliability. "Probably the most important management function . . . is staying close to the customer to satisfy his needs and anticipate his wants." In this text, that was called "Find a need and fill it."

c. *Autonomy and entrepreneurship.* Excellent companies encourage risk taking and support good tries. "Make sure you generate a reasonable number of mistakes." The key to remaining competitive is innovation, and the way to assure innovation is to support the creative thinkers in the firm. "No support systems, no champions. No champions, no innovations."

d. *Productivity through people.* Basically, this was support for participative management. Treat employees like adults. Seek their input. Treat them as the primary source of productivity gains. "Many of the best companies really do view themselves as an extended family."

e. *Hands on, value driven.* A belief in doing the best, in the importance of details, in superior quality and service, in the importance of informality to enhance communication, and in economic growth and profits.

f. *Stick to your knitting.* Do what you are good at. That is, don't acquire businesses that you don't know how to run. Do one thing well rather than many things in a mediocre way.

g. *Simple form, lean staff.* Keep the organization form simple. Keep staff positions to a minimum. This is the KISS formula: Keep it simple, Sam!

h. *Simultaneous loose-tight properties.* Establish a strong corporate culture emphasizing quality, service and excellence and then delegate authority to let the people do it.

DECISION QUESTIONS

1 Most of the advice in *In Search of Excellence* is plain common sense. Why was the book so popular, then?
2 Although the eight steps listed are clearly a good way to manage, most firms do not practice all of the steps. Which ones seem to be neglected most?
3 What managerial style or styles are advocated in this book?

Source: Thomas J. Peters and Robert H. Waterman, Jr., *In Search of Excellence* (New York: Harper & Row, Publishers), 1982.

**PRACTICING
MANAGEMENT DECISIONS**

CASE TWO   ONE-MINUTE MANAGING

Many managers do not seem to have mastered the art of praising their employees so that workers feel their accomplishments are recognized. Because of this, a very popular book in the 1980s was one called *The One Minute Manager*. It was a how-to book on creating a feeling of achievement, responsibility, growth, and recognition among employees. The book was short and easy to read, but the message was strong and useful. Here is what the book said.

The way to praise employees such that they feel recognized is:

- Tell employees ahead of time that you are going to let them know how they are doing (good or bad).
- Praise employees immediately (look for a good thing to say); this only takes a minute.
- Tell them specifically what they did right.
- Tell them how good you feel about what they did and how it helps the organization.
- Encourage them to do more of the same.
- Shake hands or touch employees to show your support. (A touch on the shoulder is the idea.) The personal touch is important.

The way to instill feelings of achievement, responsibility and growth is to encourage employees to:

- Agree on some specific goals.
- Write out the goals in less than 250 words.
- Read the goals carefully.
- Take a minute periodically to review results as compared to goals.

Clear goals give employees a feeling of responsibility, and meeting those goals creates a feeling of achievement and growth. If employees get off track, a one-minute reprimand is in order. This is, reprimand immediately; be specific about what they did wrong; tell them how you feel; touch them for reassurance; remind them of their value; tell them you know they are good workers, but not in this instance; and drop the matter (no further consequences).

DECISION QUESTIONS

1 How would you feel if at least once a day you were given one minute of praise for something you were doing well? Does that help explain the popularity of the book? Would it motivate you?
2 All of this book is really common sense. Why would managers pay to read what they already know intuitively? Is it one thing to know, another to do?
3 What is your reaction to the one-minute reprimand?
4 What is your reaction to the idea of touching employees whenever you praise or reprimand them to show support?

"One of these days we're going to have to get organized," the saying goes. True enough. Businesses today are not just "getting organized," they are going through major re-organizations. Why? Companies got so big during the 1960s and 1970s that management became very difficult. The idea today is to make firms smaller by breaking them up into smaller divisions. All of this and more is discussed in Chapter 13.

ORGANIZING A BUSINESS

LEARNING GOALS

After you have read and studied this chapter, you should be able to:

■ Discuss current organizational trends in big business.

■ Differentiate between formal and informal organizations.

■ Identify the major forms of departmentalization.

■ Describe the organizational theories of Fayol and Weber.

■ Discuss tall versus flat organizations.

■ Describe span of control and list the determinants.

■ Differentiate between centralization and decentralization.

■ Compare and contrast line and staff organizations with matrix organizations.

■ Explain corporate culture and its impact on long term success.

■ Discuss the importance of the informal organization and its major aspects.

PROFILE   LEE IACOCCA OF CHRYSLER

When *Forbes* published the list of the 25 highest-paid executives of 1985, Lee Iacocca was number one. His total compensation was over $11 million. Few would deny that Lee Iacocca is the best-known, most controversial manager of the 1980s. His autobiography, *Iacocca,* was on the best-seller list for months. Its publisher says that it has become one of the best-selling nonfiction books in history. Many followers have encouraged him to run for President of the United States. What made Lee Iacocca so famous?

First of all, Iacocca is known as a great manager. Son of an Italian-born father, Lee went to Lehigh University, where he majored in engineering. Then he spent a year at Princeton working towards a master's degree. He began selling trucks for Ford. He was so good that he moved up through the sales ranks until he became marketing manager.

His biggest accomplishment at Ford was probably his promotion of the Ford Mustang. He made the covers of both *Time* and *Newsweek* because of his automotive marketing expertise.

Lee Iacocca.

A successful merchant does not build a business. He builds an organization and that organization builds the business. It is done successfully no other way.

A SCROLL HANGING IN THE OFFICE OF ROBERT ELLIOTT, CEO OF LEVITZ FURNITURE

He became Ford's president in 1970. Some eight years later, Iacocca again made the news when he was fired by Henry Ford II. There was much controversy over the firing.

On November 3, 1978, the Detroit Free Press had two headlines: "Chrysler Losses Are Worst Ever," and "Lee Iacocca Joins Chrysler." The company had lost $160 million in the third quarter alone that year. When Iacocca took over, Chrysler had 32 vice-presidents and communication among them was poor. Tremendous management changes were needed fast, and financial controls were also badly needed. In spite of brilliant leadership by Iacocca, Chrysler remained in deep trouble.

Another controversy erupted when he went to Washington for government backing of a $1.5 billion loan. Many considered it a big business bail-out, but Iacocca argued that the country would lose $2.75 billion in the first year if Chrysler collapsed. He got the backing.

Iacocca cut his salary to $1 per year. He cut executive salaries, and union workers accepted pay cuts also. Chrysler began building better cars and Iacocca appeared on Chrysler's television commercials and said, "If you can find a better car, buy it."

Stressing quality, Iacocca began selling more cars. He made headlines when he paid the government back. He made headlines again when Chrysler profits reached $2.4 billion and when his salary reached over $11 million.

Most recently, Iacocca served as Chairman of the Statue of Liberty–Ellis Island Centennial Commission. He raised millions of dollars to restore the Statue of Liberty. More controversy centered on his plans for developing the area around the Statue.

Many years from now, when people look back at the career of Lee Iacocca, what they are most likely to remember is his magnificent job of reorganizing Chrysler. It is difficult to manage a company effectively if it is not organized in a way that makes communication and cooperation possible. This chapter is about the function of organizing, which is a key management responsibility. ■

Source: Kurt Andersen, "A Spunky Tycoon Turned Superstar," *Time*, April 1, 1985.

If Lee Iacocca decides not to run for president, it may be because he won't take a demotion. When admissions officers at the University of Pennsylvania asked prospective students to fill in certain blanks to say whom they would most like to spend an evening with, the name of the Chrysler chairman, who has lately been An Item with Miss Liberty, was among those appearing most frequently. In fact, the three names that most often appeared on 8,000 applications were God, Jesus Christ—and Lee Iacocca.

Source: *The Washington Times,* July 11, 1986, p. 3A.

ORGANIZATIONAL TRENDS

One of the decisions high school students must make if they are going on to college is the choice between a large, state school or a smaller, more intimate school. Many students prefer the smaller school, where they can get to know the other students and where they are more than just another number. They feel they would get "lost" in a big, impersonal university. On the other hand, some students choose to go to a big school. When there, they find that there are many small social groups they can join to get that feeling of being part of a small, meaningful group. They do this by joining a fraternity, sorority, professional club, political group, religious group, or whatever. The point is that often people do not feel comfortable in large, impersonal groups. They want to feel that they *belong,* and that someone knows they are there and *cares*. They get that feeling by joining small, intimate groups.

The same feelings occur in the business world. Employees usually prefer to work in small, cohesive units where people work together, know each other, and cooperate in a common cause. The trend toward small business in many ways

Sororities give students at large institutions a feeling of belonging.

reflects the advantages of small units: camaraderie, involvement, flexibility, intimacy, and a feeling of oneness.

Like big universities, big businesses often suffer from too much bureaucracy, too many people to manage and keep track of, and too little clear responsibility for decision making. The idea that "big is better" has shifted to "small is beautiful" in the 1980s. The idea has been to reduce the size of units to make them more responsive to the market and more motivated because of group cooperation and commitment. In other words, many businesses have created the equivalent of fraternities and sororities (that is, small homogenous units) where employees work together on projects. This is how the trend toward smallness was discussed in the business best-seller *In Search of Excellence*[1]:

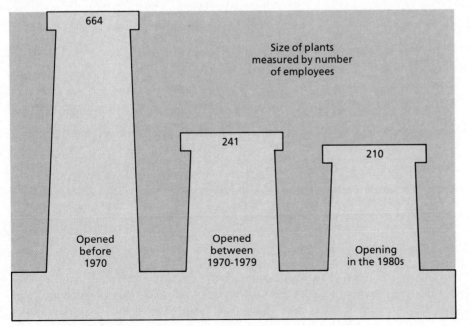

How plant size is shrinking.

664

Size of plants measured by number of employees

241

210

Opened before 1970

Opened between 1970-1979

Opening in the 1980s

The point of smallness is that it induces manageability and, above all, commitment. A manager really can understand something that is small. . . . More important, even in institutions that employ hundreds of thousands of people, if the divisions are small enough or if there are other ways of simulating autonomy, the individual still counts and can stand out. We asserted earlier that the need to stick out, to count as an individual is vital. We simply know no other way individuals can stick out unless the size of units—divisions, plants, and teams—is of human scale. Smallness works. Smallness *is* beautiful. The economic theorists may disagree, but the excellent companies' evidence is crystal clear.

The main purpose of this chapter is to discuss principles of organization such as the notion that companies function better when the operating units are small and manageable. There are other, similar organizational decisions that are just as important, such as: How many people should report to one manager? How much authority and responsibility should be delegated to lower-level managers and workers? As we have tried to indicate from the college example, organizational structure is critical to the creation of morale, commitment, and overall employee/manager satisfaction.

MERGER MANIA

It may seem contradictory to you to read in this book that the trend in organization design is toward smallness when you read in newspapers that big businesses are merging to become even bigger. In 1985, for example, over 3,000 mergers were announced. There were 36 transactions of over $1 bilion. Surely this is a sign of a trend toward bigness.

The reasons for buying businesses include the need for diversification, the relatively low cost of businesses in the 1980s, the increased use of bonds as a tool for raising funds to acquire firms, and more. None of these reasons is directly related to the best size of an organization for managerial purposes. Big firms often reorganize after an acquisition to make the separate organizations more manageable. In other words, a large firm can be reorganized into a series of smaller firms. That is exactly what is happening today. Bigness is good for financial and other reasons. Smallness is good for managerial reasons. There is no reason why a firm can't have both: a large organization and smaller, more manageable divisions.

Source: Laurie Meisler, "Mergers and Acquisitions 1986," *Forbes,* June 2, 1986, pp. 82 ff. Reprinted by permission of *Forbes* magazine; © Forbes Inc., 1986.

THINKING IT THROUGH   Business is finding that "Small Is Beautiful." How might this idea apply to the government? Could some national government programs be handled better on a state or local basis? Is there any evidence of that happening?

Have you joined any smaller groups in your college such as a fraternity, sorority, or professional society? What has that taught you about the benefits of having small groups within large firms?

What Is Organization Structure?

You have been following the principles of organization all of your life. Take, for example, a game of baseball. Someone has to pitch, someone else catches, others play the bases, outfield, and so on. Each person knows what their function is (after some coaching), and the team works together to accomplish some goal (winning the game). As the game gets more sophisticated, you may add a first base coach, a third base coach, and others who advise the players on what to do. Sometimes the organization becomes so formal, so structured, that the game is not as much fun. All the decisions are left to managers. The team may work efficiently, but it may lose the enthusiasm, the creativity, and the esprit de corps that makes winners out of even mediocre players. The questions then become, "How much structure should there be? How much decision making should be centralized with the managers? How much freedom should the players have to bat, to steal bases, and to try different positions?" The ideas are:

- An **organization** is a group of people working together to accomplish a goal.
- The structure and formality of an organization affects the morale and enthusiasm of the people in the organization.

organization
A group of people working together to accomplish a goal.

Formal Versus Informal Organization

All organizations have two organizational systems. One is the formal organization. It is the official system that details the responsibility, authority, and position of each person. Formal organization is used for baseball teams and for companies such as Campbell Soup. But there is also an informal organization. It consists of the various cliques, relationships, and lines of authority that develop outside the formal organization.

No organization can operate effectively without both types of organization. The formal system is often too slow and bureaucratic to enable the organization to adapt quickly. However, formal organization does provide helpful guidelines and lines of authority to follow in routine situations.

The informal organization is often too unstructured and emotional to allow careful, reasoned decision making on critical matters. It is extremely effective, however, in generating creative solutions to short-term problems and providing a feeling of camaraderie and teamwork among employees. The key terms and concepts are:

- A **formal organization** is the structure that details lines of responsibility, authority, and position. It is the structure that is shown on *organization charts*.
- The **informal organization** is the system of relationships and lines of authority that develops spontaneously as employees meet and form power centers. It is the human side of the organization that does not show on any organization chart.
- **Authority** is the right to make decisions and take action.
- **Responsibility** means that when a person is given a task to do, he or she has an obligation to do it.

In any organization, it is wise to learn quickly who the important people are in the *informal* organization. There are rules and procedures to follow for using certain equipment, but those procedures often take days. Who in the organization knows how to get you the equipment immediately without following the normal procedures? Which secretaries should you see if you want your work given first priority?

There is a story about the principal of an elementary school who finds that the informal leader is the teacher of the third grade—an older, motherly, dignified professional. The principal knows the situation and doesn't make a move unless

formal organization
The structure that details lines of responsibility, authority, and position. It is the structure that is shown on organizational charts.

informal organization
The system of relationships and lines of authority that develops spontaneously as employees meet and form power centers. It is the human side of the organization and does not show on any formal charts.

authority
The right to make decisions and take actions.

responsibility
Means that when a person is given a task to do, he or she has an obligation to do it.

he is sure of the support of that third-grade teacher. When the principal retires and is replaced by an energetic youngster from the big city, the new principal cannot figure out why his ideas are not being implemented. He will continue to have trouble until he has identified that informal leader and learned how to enlist her support for his initiatives. That is how the informal organization works.*

THE IMPORTANCE OF ORGANIZATIONAL DESIGN

One of the key questions of the 1980s and 1990s is whether or not business organizations in the United States will be able to adapt to new international competition and become more responsive to new consumer demands. The implication of the question is that America's huge corporations—IBM, USX, General Motors, AT&T, General Electric, Westinghouse, and so on—may simply be too big and cumbersome to adapt to changing markets. Certainly, the trouble AT&T has had in adjusting to new competition from MCI and other, smaller telephone companies indicates that there may be serious problems in the near future as large organizations are challenged by newer, smaller, more flexible firms. The answer will show whether or not the United States can maintain a leadership position in business or will continue to lose leadership to Japan, Korea, and other competing nations. In short, reorganization is one of the main managerial issues of this era. Generally, as we have noted, the move is toward smaller, more responsive units[2]:

- General Electric Company's Aircraft Engine Group changed from *two* mammoth complexes to *eight* smaller "satellite" plants. Similar reorganizing is occurring in the Major Appliance Group.

*Thanks to Professor John Bowdidge of Southwest Missouri State University for this story.

Hewlett-Packard operates smaller, people-oriented plants.

- AT&T shut down many of its large assembly lines at its Western Electric Subsidiary (now called AT&T Technologies, Inc.) and put in smaller, automated facilities to make more specialized products.
- S.C. Johnson & Son, Inc. (consumer goods) divided its 1,200-person work force into four smaller groups.
- Hewlett-Packard Company owes much of its success to the fact that it has always operated under the premise that small, people-oriented plants that are responsive to customer needs are best.

The problem with some organizations is that communication among units and among managers is simply too slow and complex. Kollmorgen Corporation, for example, produces printed circuit boards, industrial motors, and other industrial goods. Its main competitors were small mom-and-pop operations. This is how John Endee, Division President, described the situation[3]:

> The problem was that by the time our salesman in the field conferred with his regional sales manager, who would then confer with the division sales manager, who then went to manufacturing to schedule the order, "Pop" had the boards made and delivered to the customer.

To meet the efforts of smaller competitors, Kollmorgen created five separate product groups, each with a manager to oversee his or her own sales force and production capacity. Kollmorgen learned that it is difficult to get things done quickly in large organizations. This is especially true of very large organizations such as the government.

The importance of organizational design therefore is that the survival of many firms depends on the creation of more responsive organizations. Particular attention must be given communication, employee morale, and manageability. **Manageability** means that the organization is set up such that everyone knows who is responsible for everything that must be done, who reports to whom, what to do when problems arise, and so forth. This discussion helps us define what organization design is.

Organizational design is the establishment of manageable groups of people who have clear responsibilities and who know how to accomplish the objectives of the organization and the group.

Departmentalization

One way to form an organization into manageable units is to group them by their major activity. Separate departments of the firm are assigned different activities such as production, marketing, and accounting.

manageability
Organization such that everyone knows who is responsible for what, who reports to whom, what to do when problems arise, and so forth.

organizational design
The establishment of manageable groups of people who have clear responsibilities and who know how to accomplish the objectives of the organization and the group.

The top of a functionally oriented organizational chart.

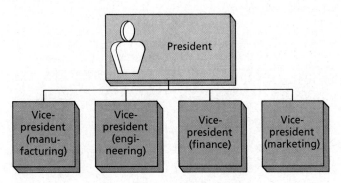

FIGURE 13-1

Line authority within a firm.

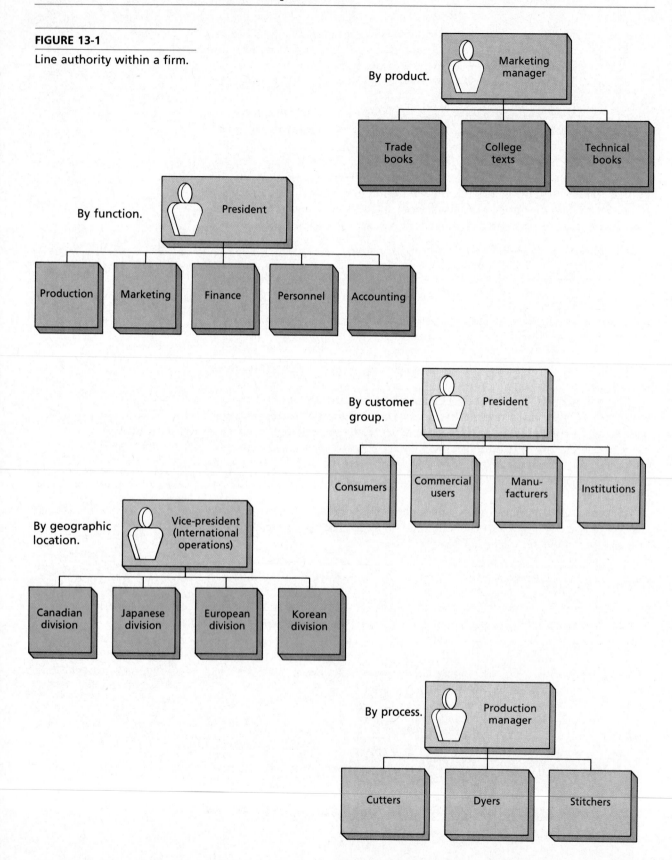

The dividing of organizational activities into separate units is called **depart-mentalization.** Many colleges of business are divided into separate departments: management, marketing, finance, and so forth. In businesses and in other organization, such units enable employees to specialize and work together more efficiently.

Figure 13-1 shows five ways a firm can departmentalize. One is by product. A book publisher might have a trade book department, a textbook department, and a technical books department. The development and marketing processes vary greatly among such books, so each department specializes in those functions.

A second way to departmentalize is by function. This text is divided by business function because such groupings are so popular. Production, marketing, finance, personnel, and accounting are all distinct functions calling for separate skills.

It makes more sense in some organizations to departmentalize by customer group. A pharmaceutical company, for example, might have one department that focuses on the consumer market, another that called on hospitals (institutional market) and another that targets doctors.

Some firms group their units geographically. The United States is usually considered one market area. Japan, Europe, and Korea may involve separate departments. The decision about which way to departmentalize depends greatly on the nature of the product and the customers served. A few firms departmentalize by process because it is more efficient to separate the activities that way. For example, a firm that makes leather coats may have one department cut the leather, another dye it, and a third sew the coat together.

Departmentalization is just one step in organizing a firm. Within departments, for example, it must be decided who reports to whom, who is responsible for what, and so on. These issues have concerned management specialists for many years. Many of the organizational principles we use today were developed in other countries more than 50 years ago.

departmentalization
Dividing tasks into homogeneous departments such as manufacturing and marketing.

ORGANIZATION THEORY: FAYOL

Until very recently in history, most organizations were rather small, the processes for producing goods were rather simple, and organization of workers was fairly easy to do. Not until the twentieth century and the introduction of mass production did business organizations grow complex and difficult to manage. The bigger the plant, the more efficient production became, or so it seemed. The concept was called *economy of scale,* which meant that large plants could produce many products with just a few pieces of equipment.

It was in this period that organization theorists emerged. In France, Henri Fayol published his book *Administration Industrielle et Générale* in 1919. It was popularized in the United States in 1949 under the title *General and Industrial Management.* Note that it was only about 40 years ago that organization theory became popular. Fayol introduced "principles" such as:

- *Unity of command.* That is, each worker was to report to one, and only one, boss. The benefits of this principle are obvious.
- *Hierarchy of authority.* Fayol suggested that each person should know to whom they should report and managers should have the right to give orders and expect others to follow.
- *Division of labor.* Functions were to be divided into areas of specialization such as production, marketing, finance, etc.

- *Subordination of individual interests to the general interest.* Again, an obvious concept.
- *Centralization of authority.* That is, authority should be clearly established and centralization and decentralization of authority needs to be balanced.
- Clear definition of communication channels.
- *Order.* Materials and people should be placed and maintained in the proper location.
- *Equity.* Fayol believed in good relations (and fair) between managers and workers.
- *Esprit de corps.* That is, the creation of a spirit of pride and loyalty among people in the firm.

Management courses in colleges throughout the world taught these principles, and they became synonymous with the concept of management. Organizations were designed so that no person had more than one boss, lines of authority were clear, and everyone knew to whom they were to report. Naturally, these principles tended to become rules and policies as organizations got larger. That led to more rigid organizations and a feeling among workers that they belonged to a *system* rather than a group of friendly, cooperative workers joined together in a common effort. People used the term *bureaucracy* to describe layer after layer of managers who seemed to do nothing but make and enforce rules and policies.

Max Weber and Organizational Theory

Max Weber (pronounced *Vayber*) was writing organization theories in Germany about the same time Fayol was writing his books in France. Weber used the term **bureaucrat** to describe middle managers whose function was to implement top management's orders. His book, *The Theory of Social and Economic Organizations* was introduced to the United States in the late 1940s. Weber's *bureaucratic organization* basically consisted of three layers of authority: (1) top managers who were the decision makers, (2) middle managers (the bureaucracy) who developed rules and procedures for implementing the decisions, and (3) workers and supervisors who did the work:

bureaucrat

A middle manager whose function is to implement top management's orders.

Max Weber.

FIGURE 13-2

This chart shows Weber's concept of a bureaucratic organization, one with clear lines of authority and several layers of management.

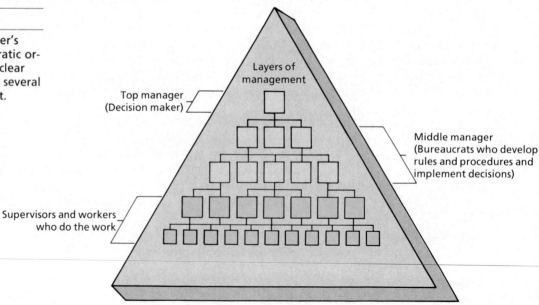

BUREAUCRACY AT UPS

United Parcel Service (UPS) is a firm that delivers small packages. It competes with firms such as Federal Express, Purolator, and the U.S. Postal Service. Competition is stiff, so UPS has to be very efficient. One way to achieve such efficiency is through bureaucracy.

The company is run strictly, with many rules and regulations. These are safety rules for all levels of employees, and strict dress codes are enforced. Other rules cover the cleanliness of trucks and buildings. Each manager has bound copies of policy books and is expected to follow them.

UPS also keeps careful records. Daily worksheets that specify performance goals and work output are kept on every employee and department. Daily employee quotas and achievements are accumulated weekly and monthly with the help of computers.

The other half of UPS's efficiency results from automation. It has 100 mechanized hubs that can sort 40,000 packages per hour. UPS handles 6 *million* packages a day. With such precision necessary, there's little room for deviation from set practices.

Source: R. Daft, *Organizations: Theory and Design* (St. Paul, Minn.: West Publishing Company, 1983), pp. 129-149.

It was Weber, then, who promoted the pyramid-shaped organization structure that became so popular in large firms. It is seen in Figure 13-2.

Weber's principles of organization were similar to Fayol's. In addition, however, Weber emphasized the following:

- Job descriptions. Every job was to be described in detail and written down.
- Written rules, decision guidelines, and detailed records.
- Consistent procedures, regulations, and policies.
- Staffing and promotions based on qualifications.

You can thank Weber when you go to a store or government agency and have trouble getting things done because the clerk says, "That's not company policy," or "I can't do that; it's against the rules." Weber felt large organizations demanded clearly established rules and guidelines that were to be followed precisely. Overzealous enforcement led to inflexibility and insensitivity to customer needs. Although the word *bureaucrat* did not have any negative connotations as used by Weber, the *practice* of establishing rules and procedures became so rigid that one of the worst things one can say about an organization now is that it is a *bureaucracy*.

Together, Fayol and Weber introduced organizational concepts such as (1) unity of command (one man, one boss); (2) division of labor (specialized jobs); (3) job descriptions; (4) rules, guidelines, procedures, and policies; (5) clear lines of authority and communication; (6) placement of materials and people in some established order; (7) the establishment of departments; (8) detailed record keeping; (9) the establishment of an esprit de corps or feeling of enthusiasm and devotion to the firm; and (10) the assignment of a limited number of people to each manager (limited span of control).

■ What is the difference between a *formal* and an *informal* organization?

■ Can you define authority and responsibility?

■ Can you name four of Fayol's principles and show how they link with Weber's principles?

An organization chart is really only a piece of paper . . . that identifies a chain of command of people and functions. True management begins only when you put all these people together, functioning together, in a vital, human interrelationship so that the company performs as a single team, driving onward toward the goals set by the chief executive.

Harold Geneen, Former President and CEO of ITT

TALL ORGANIZATIONAL STRUCTURE OF THE U.S. ARMY

President
Joint Chiefs of Staff
5 Star General
4 Star General
3 Star Lt. General
2 Star Major General
1 Star Brigadier General
Colonel
Lt. Colonel
Major
Captain
1st Lieutenant
2nd Lieutenant
Warrant Officer 4
Warrant Officer 3
Warrant Officer 2
Warrant Officer 1
Sergeant Major
Master Sergeant
Sergeant 1st Class
Staff Sergeant
Buck Sergeant
Corporal
Private 1st Class
Private
Note that the Army has many levels of management.

DESIGNING ORGANIZATIONS

Following the principles of Fayol and Weber, managers all around the world began designing organizations. First, division of labor led to *departmentalization* of firms. That is, the firms had separate departments for manufacturing, engineering, finance, and marketing. The top of the organization charts looked like this example:

The tendency was to construct organization charts that looked like pyramids. Many workers reported to a group of supervisors, who reported to plant managers, who reported to regional managers, who reported to national managers, who reported to vice presidents, who reported to the president, who reported to the chairman of the board. Such a complex organization called for many rules, guidelines, and procedures. In other words, it took many years to *implement* the organizational principles outlined in the late 1940s. During the 1950s and 1960s, there was much discussion about delegating authority, developing appropriate "managerial styles," and dealing with unions and other complications in the system. The goal seemed to be to get bigger by any means, including the purchase of other firms. Organization charts grew more complicated and complex. It wasn't until the late 1970s and early 1980s that management began the process of *reorganizing* firms, making them smaller, less complex, and more efficient. National and international competition forced these changes. We shall now discuss some of the organizational decisions that are being made, including:

1 The issue of tall versus flat organization structures.
2 The issue of span of control.
3 The issue of centralization versus decentralization.
4 The issue of organization design: line, line and staff, matrix, or what?

Tall Versus Flat Organization Structures

As organizations got bigger, some began adding layer after layer of management, sometimes resulting in a dozen or more managerial steps in firms such as General Motors. Such organizations had what are called **tall organization structures.** What this means, simply, is that the organization chart would be quite tall because of the various levels of management.

The organizations were divided into regions, divisions, centers, and plants. Each plant might have several layers of management. The net effect was a huge complex of managers, management assistants, secretaries, assistant secretaries, supervisors, trainers, and so on. Office workers were known as *white-collar workers* as opposed to the *blue-collar workers* who worked on the assembly line. As you can imagine, the cost of keeping all these managers and support people was quite high. The paperwork they generated was unbelievable, and the inefficiencies in communication and decision making became intolerable.

The development of small computers is helping to bring more efficiency to white-collar operations. But, more importantly, the trend is to eliminate white-collar positions, including several layers of management[4]:

- Dana Corporation cut its corporate staff from 500 in 1970 to about 100 in the 1980s.
- Acme Cleveland Corporation cut corporate staff from 120 to 50 in just a few months.
- Ford Motor Company cut more than 26% of its middle management staff and more cuts were planned—to a total of 50% or even 75%.

To give you a feel for the problem, there are *five* levels of management between the chairman and first-line supervisor at Toyota, a Japanese firm. Ford had over *fifteen* levels. You can see why American firms are now cutting down.

The trend is toward more **flat organization structures.** That is, organizations are cutting out layers of management and are expanding sideways instead. The idea is to have many, small semiautonomous units that report to vice presidents, who report to the president. Johnson & Johnson, for example, is a $5 billion company made up of 150 independent divisions that sell over $30 million each. The divisions are called "companies."

tall organization structures
One with many levels of management.

flat organization structures
One with relatively few layers of management.

Span of Control

Span of control refers to the optimum number of subordinates a manager supervises or should supervise. There are many factors to consider when determining span of control. At the lower levels, where the work is standardized, it is possible to implement a wide span of control (15 to 40 workers). However, the number should gradually narrow at higher levels of the organization, because work is less standardized and there is more need for face-to-face communication. Variables in span of control include:

span of control
The optimum number of subordinates a manager should supervise.

- *Functional complexity.* The more complex the functions are, the narrower the span of control (fewer workers report to one supervisor).
- *Need for direction.* The more subordinates need supervision, the narrower the span of control.
- *Need for coordination.* The greater the need for coordination is, the narrower the span of control.
- *Planning demands.* The more involved the plan, the narrower the span of control.
- *Managerial help.* The more help the superior receives, the broader the span of control (more workers can report to one supervisor).
- *Functional similarity.* The more similar the functions are, the broader the span of control.
- *Geographical closeness.* The more concentrated the work area is, the broader the span of control.[5]

Other factors to consider include the competence of superiors and subordinates, their degree of professionalism, and the number of new problems that occur in a day. In business, the span of control varies widely. The number of people reporting to the president may range from 1 to 80.[6] Andrew Grove, one of the founders of Intel Corporation, says the following about his experience with span of control[7]:

An important component of managerial leverage is the number of subordinates a manager has. If he does not have enough, his leverage is obviously reduced. If he has too many, he gets bogged down. . . . As a rule of thumb, a manager whose work is largely supervisory should have six to eight subordinates; three or four are too few and ten are too many . . . two days a week per subordinate would probably lead to meddling; an hour a week does not provide enough opportunity for monitoring.

Figure 13-3 ties together span of control and tall and flat organization structures. The tall organization with a narrow span of control might describe a lawn-care service with two supervisors who manage four employees each (two of whom are more experienced). The flat structure with a wide span of control may work in a plant where all ten workers are picking crabmeat.

FIGURE 13-3

Two ways to structure an organization with the same number of employees. Just looking at the pictures gives you some feel for where such structures are most appropriate.

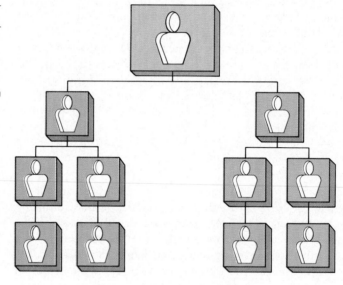

Tall structure with narrow span of control.

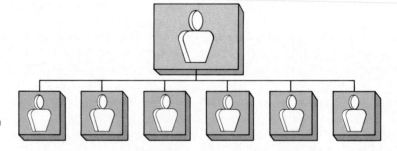

Flat structure with wide span of control.

Centralization Versus Decentralization of Authority

centralized authority
Maintaining decision-making authority with the top level of management at its headquarters.

decentralized authority
Delegating decision-making authority to lower-level managers who are more familiar with local conditions.

Imagine for a minute that you are a top manager at a store such as Montgomery Ward. Your temptation may be to maintain control over all your stores to maintain a uniformity of image and merchandise. You have noticed such control works well for McDonald's; why not Montgomery Ward? The degree to which an organization allows managers at the lower levels of the managerial hierarchy to make decisions determines the degree of *decentralization* that organization practices:

- **Centralized authority** means that decision-making authority is maintained at the top level of management at headquarters, or *central management*.
- **Decentralized authority** means that decision-making authority is delegated to lower-level managers who are more familiar with local conditions.

At Montgomery Ward, for example, the customers in California are likely to demand clothing styles different from those in Minnesota or Maine. It makes sense, therefore, to give store managers in various cities the authority to buy, price, and promote merchandise appropriate for each area. Such a **delegation of authority** is an example of decentralized management.

On the other hand, McDonald's feels that purchasing, promotion, and other such decisions are best handled centrally. There is little need for each McDonald's store to carry different food products. McDonald's, therefore, would lean toward centralized authority.

In reality, most organizations have some degree of centralized authority and some decentralized authority. Today's rapidly changing markets, added to geographic differences in consumer tastes, tend to favor more decentralization and thus more delegation of authority. The following discussion of the Campbell Soup Company will illustrate this point.

delegation of authority
Assigning part of a manager's duties to subordinates.

Organization at Campbell Soup Company

A real-life example is the best way to understand the importance of organization structure, the differences between centralized and decentralized structures, and the trend toward making firms more responsive to the market. For such an example, let's look at a company with which you are very familiar—the Campbell Soup Company. As you might imagine, Campbell was a relatively conservative company that had a few leading products. It introduced very few new products. There was almost no feeling of entrepreneurship or creativity among managers, and little freedom was allowed to explore new markets or try new ideas. Market share was declining, yet emphasis remained on production rather than marketing.[7]

Part of Campbell Soup's product mix.

In 1980, a new chief executive officer (CEO) took over. His name is Gordon McGovern. He came from Campbell's Pepperidge Farm division where he increased sales from $60 million to $300 million in 5 years. The previous president had an engineering background and was operations oriented. In contrast, McGovern is a progressive marketer.

One of the first things McGovern did was to change the organization structure! The old structure divided the company into *two* basic groups—canned and frozen foods—based on the way the products were manufactured. Marketing, new product development, and production were all done centrally (centralized management). McGovern felt that too much power was centralized among too few people and that prevented the free flow of ideas.

To foster entrepreneurship and to create more incentives for creative solutions to problems, McGovern created approximately 50 *decentralized* business units headed by general managers, most of whom had marketing backgrounds. These managers are responsible for profits (or losses) and new product development. They also have freedom to set up marketing in their units. Internal competition among unit managers is encouraged. Each unit has its own controller and financial planning analyst. Under this *decentralized* corporate structure, each general manager acts like the president of his or her own firm. Such responsibility is accompanied by the necessary authority, freedom, and incentives to create vibrant new enterprises within the larger organization.

The overall goal of this restructuring was to make Campbell more consumer oriented, more dynamic, and more innovative. McGovern feels that the United States is not a "melting pot," but a nation of specialized groups that need unique marketing efforts. The concept is called *target marketing* and is reflected in special promotions for Hispanics in New York and Chicago and special promotions aimed at the upscale consumer with products like Le Menu.

The Campbell Soup Company is really an organization of organizations. There is an organization that develops and markets soups. Another organization develops frozen foods, and still others are involved with beverages, pet foods, and so forth. Each unit is like a separate team competing in a different league with different rules.

Running the organization called "Soups" is a general manager. Under this manager are three marketing directors: one each for condensed soups, ready-to-serve soups, and soups and special projects. Under the three directors are marketing managers and assistant marketing managers. Assisting them are advertising, accounting, finance, and manufacturing specialists. As you can see, the organization is still quite complex with many layers of management. Although Campbell retains a relatively tall organization structure, the delegation of authority has resulted in a much flatter organization structure in reality.

Related to the questions of tall versus flat and centralized versus decentralized organizations is the question of designing the lines of authority. Several different organization designs are possible. We shall discuss them now.

PROGRESS CHECK

■ Are U.S. businesses moving toward having taller or flatter organization structures? Why?

■ What are some reasons for having a narrow span of control?

ORGANIZATION TYPES

A **line organization structure** is one in which there are direct two-way lines of responsibility, authority, and communication running from the top to the bottom of the organization, with all people reporting to only one supervisor. The most obvious example is the Army, which has a clear line of authority going from general to colonel to major to lieutenant to sergeant to corporal to private and back (See p. 338). A private reports to *a* corporal, the corporal to *a* sergeant, and so on back up to the generals. A line organization has the advantages of having clearly defined responsibility and authority, of being easy to understand, and of providing one supervisor for each person. The principles of good organization design are met.

However, a line organization has the disadvantages of being too inflexible, of having few specialists or experts to advise people along the line, of having lines of communication that are too long, and of being unable to handle the complex decisions involved in an organization with thousands of sometimes unrelated products and literally tons of paperwork.

line organization structure
One in which there are direct two-way lines of responsibility, authority, and communication running from the top to the bottom of the organization, with all employees reporting to only one supervisor.

A Line and Staff System

To minimize the disadvantages of simple line organizations, most organizations today have both *line* and *staff* personnel. A couple of definitions will help:

- **Line personnel** perform functions that contribute directly to the primary goals of the organization (e.g., making the product, distributing it, and selling it).
- **Staff personnel** perform functions that *assist* line personnel in performing their goals (e.g., marketing research, legal advising, and personnel). (See Figure 13-4, p. 344.)

Most organizations have benefited from the expert advice of staff assistants in areas such as safety, quality control, computer technology, personnel, investing, and so forth. Such positions strengthen the line positions and are by no means inferior or lower-paid positions. It is like having well-paid consultants on the organization's payroll.

Staff usually serve an advisory function; that is, they cannot tell line managers *or their workers* what to do. Naturally, this can cause conflicts, in that staff experts often know more about correct procedures to follow than line managers. This can be very frustrating for staff people. In fact, different organizations handle line-staff relationships in different ways. In some organizations, line managers must *consult* with staff managers on some issues; on others, they must get staff *approval* for certain actions; and in others, staff people may actually *give orders*.

The benefits of the line and staff organization structure are rather clear. The disadvantages are not so obvious at first. Today, however, many organizations are suffering from too many staff personnel (overstaffing). To justify their existence, staff people often conduct research and generate reports that no one asks for or needs (overanalyzing). The resulting paperwork can be astounding. Lines of authority and communication often get blurred when staff people get involved in decision making (overmanaging). For example, by the time a line manager clears a decision with the legal department, the safety department, and personnel, the initial problem could have become much more serious.

The trend today is to cut staff positions or assign staff to smaller, functional units where they truly assist, rather than work independently from line managers. Much of the attention of top managers today is focused on designing systems that

line personnel
Perform functions that contribute directly to the primary goals of the organization.

staff personnel
Perform functions that assist line personnel in performing their goals.

enable line and staff managers to cooperate more fully and to move more quickly to respond to market changes.

FIGURE 13-4

Line and staff organization. Fine lines indicate line authority; heavy lines indicate staff authority (advising, recommending). If you were to remove the staff personnel, this would be a line organization. Staff personnel act as advisors (in-house experts).

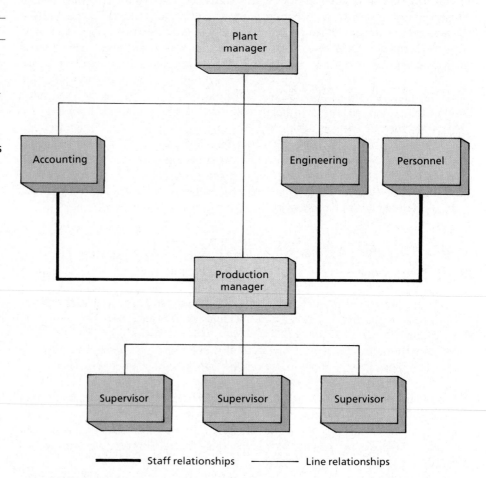

Staff relationships   Line relationships

The Matrix Organization

Both line and line and staff structures suffer from a certain inflexibility. Both have established lines of authority and communication and both work well in organizations with a relatively stable environment and evolutionary development (such as firms selling consumer products like toasters and refrigerators). In such firms, clear lines of authority and relatively fixed organization structures are assets that assure efficient operations.

Today's economic scene is dominated by new kinds of organizations in high-growth industries unlike anything seen in the past. They include industries such as robotics, biotechnology, and aerospace. In such industries, new projects are developed, competition with similar projects elsewhere is stiff, and the life cycle of new ideas is very short. The economic, technological, and competitive environments are rapidly changing. In such organizations, emphasis is on new product development, creativity, special projects, rapid communication, and interdepartmental teamwork. From that environment grew the popularity of the matrix organization. A **matrix organization** is one where specialists from different parts of

matrix organization
One where specialists from different parts of the organization are brought together to work on specific projects, but still remain part of a traditional line and staff structure.

the organization are brought together to work on specific projects, but still remain part of a line and staff structure (see Figure 13-5). In other words, a project manager can borrow people from different departments to help design and market new product ideas. This violates the rule of "one person, one manager," but allows for much creativity and teamwork—when it works.

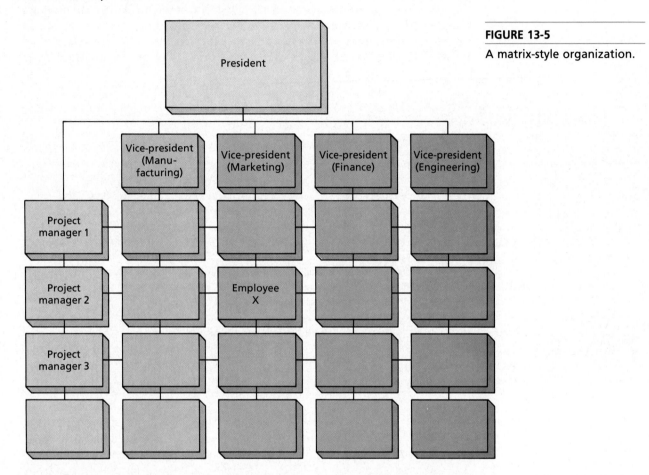

FIGURE 13-5

A matrix-style organization.

Matrix structures were developed in the aerospace industry at firms such as Boeing, Lockheed, and McDonnell Douglas. The structure is now used in banking, management consulting firms, accounting firms, ad agencies, and school systems. Although it works well in some organizations, it does not work in others. The box on Bausch & Lomb gives one example where such a structure failed (see p. 346). The advantages of a matrix structure are:

- It gives flexibility to managers in assigning people to projects.
- It encourages interorganizational cooperation and teamwork.
- It is flexible and can result in creative solutions to problems such as new product development.

The disadvantages are:

- It is costly to implement and complex.
- It can cause confusion among employees as to where their loyalty belongs— to the project manager or to their functional unit.
- It requires good interpersonal skills and cooperative employees and managers.

A rather basic form of matrix organization occurs in most business schools. The faculty members work in departments such as marketing, finance, management, and accounting. There may also be a director of undergraduate studies. If the director has a project, such as the development of an executive development program, he or she may ask several faculty members to serve on a task force to design the program. While on the task force, a faculty member reports both to the program director *and* the area chairperson. This is how the matrix form works, and it works well in situations like this. It is not a permanent structure in all cases. It is more a way of handling special projects with a wide variety of people from various areas.

A MATRIX-STYLE FAILURE

The Instruments Division at Bausch and Lomb needed organizing badly. Morale and motivation were low. There was a lack of coordination, and some questionable decision-making was occurring. There was not sufficient delegation of authority, and sales calls were not coordinated. Naturally, this meant that the division's objectives were not being met.

The Instruments Division had some 30 different products that competed against IBM, Hewlett-Packard, and others. Jim Edwards was given the responsibility to reorganize the division. He introduced the matrix management system he had used at IBM. Under the system, the head of a manufacturing division maintained responsibility for profits, but had little control over the sales force. Salespeople reported to marketing.

The reorganization didn't work. Income dropped 32%. Managers complained that they had lost authority over the sales force.

Dan Gill, Bausch & Lomb's President, decided to end the matrix-style organization and gave sales and marketing authority back to the manufacturing divisions. The organization that worked at IBM did not work as well at Bausch & Lomb. This example shows that organizations often must try different organization structures before they find the best one.

Source: Based on S. Stratford, "Troubles at Bausch & Lomb," *Fortune*, January 23, 1983, pp. 104-105.

If it seems to you that matrix organizations violate some traditional managerial principles, you are right. Normally a person cannot work effectively for two bosses. (Who has the *real* authority? Which directive has the first priority—the one from the project manager or from one's immediate supervisor?) Figure 13-6 shows how decisions regarding a matrix organization fit in with other organizational decisions.

In reality, the system functions more effectively than one may imagine. Here is how it works best:

- Underlying the matrix system is a traditional line and staff organization with clear and recognized lines of authority.
- To develop a new product idea, a project manager may be given *temporary* authority to "borrow" line personnel from engineering, production, marketing, and other line functions. Together, they work to complete the project and then return to their regular positions. In fact, then, they really do not report to more than one manager at a time.
- Such a system evolves in an organization where the informal communication system is more important than the formal organization, anyhow. That is, the corporate culture encourages interaction among departments and ad hoc committees to solve problems.

Departmentalization	How should departments be established—by product, by function, by customer, by geographic location, or some combination of these?
Span of control	How many employees should report to each manager? (A narrow span means few people reporting; a wide span means many people reporting to one manager).
Lines of authority	What will be the lines of authority and responsibility in the firm? What positions will be staff (support positions) and what positions will be line (directly in the chain of command)?
Delegation of authority	Should all key decisions be made by top management? What decisions should be delegated to managers and supervisors, if any?
Matrix organization formation	Who should be assigned to various committees? What authority should be given line managers to borrow employees from other areas for special committee assignments (See matrix organization discussion.)
Job design	Who is responsible for doing what? How much job rotation will we have? How much specialization?
Work procedures	What are the rules and procedures of operation? What are the lines of communication?
Follow-through	Delegation without follow-through is abdication. You can never wash your hands of a task. Even if you delegate it, you are still responsible for its accomplishment.

FIGURE 13-6

Some questions to ask at various stages of organization design.

- The unit of operation is small enough for such flexibility to be applied and yet everyone remain informed and clear as to relationships, goals, and procedures.

ORGANIZATIONAL CULTURE

One of the most important elements of success in any organization is the overall **organizational culture.** It may be defined as widely shared values within an organization that provide coherence and cooperation to achieve common goals. Usually the culture of an organization is reflected in stories, traditions, and myths. Anyone who has been to Disneyland or Disneyworld cannot fail to be impressed by the obvious values instilled by Walt Disney that permeate the organization. One may have heard about or read about the focus on cleanliness, helpfulness, and friendliness, but such stories cannot prepare you for the near-perfect implementation of those values at the parks. The workers seem to have absorbed the ideals into their very being so that they work joyfully with total attention given the customer.

organizational culture
Widely shared values within an organization that provide coherence and cooperation to achieve common goals.

The corporate culture at the license bureau often seems lacking a consumer orientation.

It is also obvious from visiting any McDonald's restaurant that every effort has been made to maintain a culture that emphasizes "quality, service, cleanliness, and value." Each restaurant has the same "feel," the same "look," and the same "atmosphere." In short, each has a similar organizational culture.

Disney and McDonald's are two examples of favorable corporate cultures that lead to successful operations. But an organizational culture can also be negative. Have you ever been in an organization where you feel that no one cares about service or quality? In our area, a visit to almost any motor vehicle licensing bureau is a quick lesson in negative shared values (organizational culture). The clerks seem uniformly glum, indifferent, and testy. The mood seems to pervade the atmosphere so that the patrons become moody and upset. There are exceptions, but you know the feeling. It gets so that one can hardly believe that an organization can be run so badly and survive, especially profit-making organizations. (Many people have written off government agencies as hopelessly lost in bureaucratic cultures that seem anticustomer and, consequently, depressing to workers as well as customers.)

The very best organizations have cultures that emphasize service to others, especially customers. The atmosphere is one of friendly, concerned, caring people who enjoy working together to provide a good product at a reasonable price. Those companies that have such cultures have less need for close supervision of employees, policy manuals, organization charts, and formal rules, procedures, and controls. The ideas are as follows:

- Organizational cultures are created by organizational leaders who create an atmosphere of shared values that have either a positive or negative effect on the relationships within the organization and with the various publics of the organization.
- Good organizational leaders create a culture that emphasizes cooperation and joy in serving customers, and that culture results in self-motivated employees who need minimal supervision.

Thus far we have been talking as if organizational matters were mostly controllable by management. The fact is that the *formal organization structure* is just one element of the total organizational system. To create organizational culture, the *informal organization* is of equal or greater importance. Let's explore this notion next.

THINKING IT THROUGH

What is the organizational culture at your college? Is it known for its excellence, quality, and student orientation? If not, what is it known for? How is that reflected in student attitudes, community support, and faculty attitudes? How could the culture be improved?

---

*Informal Organization

We noted earlier that the informal organization is the spontaneous system of open communications, relationships, loyalties, and power centers that naturally emerges in any group of people. The informal organization's nerve center is the "grapevine" or the system of unofficial information flows between and among managers and employees. It consists of rumors, facts, suspicions, accusations, and all kinds of accurate and inaccurate information. The key people in the information system usually have the most influence in the organization.

In the old "we versus they" system of organizations, where managers and employees were often at odds, the informal system often hindered effective management. In the new, more open organizations, where managers and employees work together to set objectives and design procedures, the informal organization can be an invaluable managerial asset that often promotes harmony among workers and establishes the corporate culture. Some of the more important aspects of the informal organization are:

1. **Group norms.** Group norms are the informal rules and procedures that guide the behavior of group members. They include often unspoken but very clear guidelines regarding things like proper dress, language, work habits (e.g., how fast one works, how many breaks one takes, who one turns to for assistance, and so on), and social behavior (where one goes for recreation, with whom, how often, and more). Deviants from the norm are often verbally abused, isolated, and harassed.

group norms
The informal rules and procedures that guide the behavior of group members.

2. **Group cohesiveness.** Often a work group will develop alliances and commitments over time that tie them together strongly. The term used to describe such feelings of group loyalty is *cohesiveness.* Historically, unions have been a strong cohesive force as workers united to fight management. The goal today is to generate such cohesiveness among all corporate employees to create excellence in all phases of operation. For such cohesiveness to develop, employees must feel that they are part of a total corporate team. Often, the informal network created by corporate athletic teams, unions, and other such affiliations can assist in the creation of teamwork and cooperation. In summary, the informal organization of a firm can strongly reinforce a feeling of teamwork and cooperation or can effectively prevent any such unity; managers who maintain open, honest communication with employees can create an informal atmosphere that promotes willing commitment and group cohesiveness.

group cohesiveness
A feeling of group loyalty.

PROGRESS CHECK

■ What are the advantages of a line and staff organization versus a pure line organization?

■ Why would a firm use a matrix organization?

■ What is organizational culture? Can you cite an example?

SUMMARY

1 One of the major movements in today's organizations, business and non-business, is toward increasing efficiency and productivity. At one time, the goal was to increase organization *size*. With size came *economies of scale* and greater productivity. Over time, however, organizations in the United States tended to become too big. Communication was slow to move up and down through level after level of management. Smaller, more flexible domestic and foreign firms began to steal markets. The result was the major restructuring of organizations now occurring.

■ What are some of the trends in restructuring?

The most obvious trend is toward smallness. Large firms are breaking up into smaller, more self-sufficient (autonomous) units. Layers of middle management positions are being eliminated. So are many staff positions (e.g., safety inspectors, advisors, analysts, etc.). This is making organization structures flatter and wider, that is, there are fewer layers of management, but more units.

2 An *organization* is a group of people working together to accomplish a goal. Decision making in an organization may be centralized or decentralized.

■ What do these terms mean?

Centralization is the extent to which decision-making power is concentrated in the hands of one or a few people. *Decentralization* means that decisions are made at lower levels of the organization.

3 There are two lines of authority in an organization: formal and informal.

■ What do these terms mean?

A *formal organization* is the structure that details lines of authority, responsibility, and position. It is what is drawn on the organization chart. The *informal organization* is the system of relationships and lines of authority that form spontaneously as employees meet and form power centers.

■ What do the terms authority and responsibility mean?

Authority is the right to make decisions and take actions. *Responsibility* means that when a person is given a task to do, he or she has an obligation to do it.

4 Organization theory is the foundation for organization design. Many organizational concepts go back 40 years or more to men such as Fayol and Weber.

■ What concepts did Fayol introduce?

They include unity of command, division of labor, centralization of authority, and clear lines of communication.

■ What was the contribution of Weber?

He emphasized job descriptions, written rules and procedures and regu-

lations, and consistent policies. He was the father of *bureaucratic* organizations.

5 Several issues dominate the discussion of organizational design: tall versus flat
structures, span of control, and centralization versus decentralization of authority.

  ■ What is the issue of tall versus flat organizations?
    U.S. firms got so big that there were a dozen or more layers of management
    between the president and workers. Information flows and flexibility were
    hurt. The trend is to break up firms into smaller, more autonomous *flatter*
    units.

  ■ What does *span of control* mean?
    It refers to the number of subordinates that report to a manager. The best
    number depends on the complexity of the task, the level in the organi-
    zation, and other factors. The ideal span for managers is said to be some-
    where between 6 and 10.

  ■ What is the decentralization issue?
    The "small is beautiful" movement not only breaks up larger corporations
    into smaller units, but gives those units more authority and responsibility
    for results.

6 There are several types of organization: line, line and staff, and matrix.

  ■ What's the difference among systems?
    Line organizations have clear lines of authority with each person having
    one boss; there are no internal staff advisors. A *line and staff organization*
    brings in staff personnel (advisors) in areas such as personnel, legal ad-
    vising, and quality control. A *matrix organization* is one where different
    specialists are brought together to work on a project while maintaining
    positions in the line or staff. A faculty member working with a program
    director is an example.

7 The key to organizational success is not just organizing, but the creation of a
corporate culture that emphasizes excellence in customer service and quality.

  ■ How does a leader create such a culture?
    By working with the informal organization to create teamwork and esprit
    de corps.

KEY TERMS

authority   p. 331
bureaucrat   p. 336
centralized authority   p. 340
decentralized authority   p. 340
delegation of authority   p. 341
departmentalization   p. 335
flat organization structures
   p. 339
formal organization   p. 331
group cohesiveness   p. 349
group norms   p. 349
informal organization   p. 331

line organization structure
   p. 343
line personnel   p. 343
manageability   p. 333
matrix organization   p. 345
organization   p. 331
organizational culture   p. 347
organizational design   p. 333
responsibility   p. 331
span of control   p. 339
staff personnel   p. 343
tall organization structures
   p. 339

GETTING INVOLVED

1 There is no way to better understand the effects of having 15 layers of management on communication accuracy than to play the children's game of "Message Relay." Take 15 members of the class and have them line up from one to fifteen. Have the first person read the following story and whisper it to number two, who whispers it to number three and so on through all fifteen. Have number fifteen tell the story out loud and compare it to the original. The distortions and mistakes are often quite humorous, but are not so funny in organizations such as Ford that *had* fifteen layers of management. Here's the story:

"Dealers in the Midwest region have received over 130 complaints about steering on the new Commander and Roadhandler models of our mini-vans. Apparently, the front suspension system is weak and the ball joints are wearing too fast. This causes slippage in the linkage and results in oversteering. Mr. Berenstein has been notified, but so far only 213 out of 4,300 dealers have received repair kits."

2 Write a short description of a situation where you were frustrated because a clerk in a bank, government agency, school, or hospital followed "the rules" or "policy" to the letter and caused you much grief and lost time. Share your story with others in the class. Compare stories and then discuss strategies for minimizing such bureaucratic hassles in organizations.

3 Discuss situations in your experience either at home, at work, or in sports when you had more than one person telling you what to do and the orders conflicted. Share several such situations and discuss the principle of one man, one boss. How many people can one person manage? Does it depend on the circumstances? Discuss.

4 Did you choose a large school or a small one for college? Why? Discuss the merits and drawbacks of being in a large organization. How does your experience apply to business?

5 No doubt you are familiar with the informal network of communication in schools, communities, and various organizations. Discuss the power of such informal groups. How can business use that power to become more productive *and* meet the needs of workers at the same time?

6 Imagine you are working for an appliance manufacturer that produces, among other things, dishwashers for the home. Imagine further that a competitor introduces a new dishwasher that uses sound waves to clean dishes. The result is a dishwasher that cleans even the worst burnt-on food and sterilizes the dishes and silverware as well. You need to develop a similar offering fast or lose the market. Discuss how a matrix form of management would help in the process.

7 If you were free to start all over, how would you organize your college or university? Would you have the same departments? What kind of staff people would you hire? How would your organization differ from the one you have? What keeps the school from adopting a more flexible, more responsive organization structure? Discuss.

CASE ONE   READING AN ORGANIZATION CHART

This is the organization chart for Donahue Manufacturing Company:

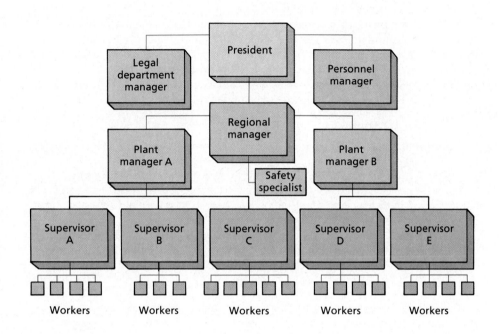

DECISION QUESTIONS

1 Which people are line managers and which are staff?
2 Which supervisor has the largest span of control? Which plant manager?
3 Would this be considered a tall or flat organization structure?
4 How many line managers are under the direct control of the personnel manager?

CASE TWO   RESTRUCTURING HITS MANAGEMENT POSITIONS

In the fall of 1985, AT&T announced that it was eliminating 24,000 jobs by the end of 1986. A big percentage of those jobs (30%) are in management. In similar fashion, United Technologies Corporation's semiconductor subsidiary laid off 2,600 of its 9,800 employees, over 20% of whom were managers. The list of companies with similar stories is quite long. In fact, since 1980, 89 of the 100 largest companies in the U.S. have reorganized to reduce the number of management levels.

W. James Fish, Ford Motor Company's personnel planning manager says, "We're looking at a total restructuring of American business." Ford wants to cut the white-collar work force in its Ford North American Automotive Operations by 20%, or about 9,600 jobs, over the next five years.

Such a restructuring is inevitable in a period when competition from foreign firms is intensifying. American firms had grown fat around the middle, and needed to because "lean and mean" to be more efficient and productive. Lots of lower-level employees were being eliminated; managers logically followed.

Tom Peters, coauthor of *In Search of Excellence,* believes the staffs of the Fortune 500 companies are still hopelessly bloated despite cuts of 40% to 50%. Peters feels that many of those managers have their MBA degree and got to top positions without ever getting real-world experience in designing, making, selling, and servicing products. They tend to rely on technology, rather than people for their answers—and ignore the retraining and redeployment of the workforce.

Peters recommends that managers get out of their offices and ask their workers how to make the firm more productive. Then they should visit customers to learn what they would like to see changed. Management is no longer viewed as an intellectual position involving planning, organizing, staffing, and controlling. Rather it is a hands-on job where managers and employees work as a team to make the firm productive. Those who used to sit and ponder are out of there. More cuts may be coming.

DECISION QUESTIONS

1 What does the reduction in middle management jobs mean for tomorrow's undergraduate and graduate business students?
2 How could you, as the president of a firm, decide which managers to let go?
3 What are the advantages and disadvantages of cutting staff personnel in areas like personnel, quality control, planning, and auditing? Could there be serious consequences of rapid cut-backs in management?

Sources: Statistics are from Cynthia Green, "Middle Managers are Sitting Ducks," *Business Week,* September 16, 1985, p. 34; and Tom Peter's comments are from Alvin P. Sanoff, "Something Is Out of Whack in U.S. Business Management," *U.S. News & World Report,* July 15, 1985, p. 54.

LOOKING AHEAD

So far, we have learned what customers want through *marketing.* We also know something about basic management, including how to structure organizations to accomplish our objectives. It is time, then, to begin producing products.

The problem is that America's industrial base is declining. Many factories are old and obsolete. Foreign competitors are producing goods for less and are making high-quality goods as well. How can we compete?

Chapter 14 discusses production and operations management. To regain a competitive position in manufacturing, American industry will have to improve everything from order processing to manufacturing, quality control, and shipping. We shall discuss how to do all that in Chapter 14. We shall discuss basic production issues first and then show how American business can recapture the industrial market.

PRODUCTION AND OPERATIONS MANAGEMENT

LEARNING GOALS

After you have read and studied this chapter, you should be able to:

- Discuss the conditions that have led to the decline of the industrial sector in the United States.
- List the factors managers consider in site selection.
- Describe the major production processes.
- Discuss the importance of materials requirement planning and just in time inventory control.
- Explain the uses of CAD/CAM and other elements of the computerized factory.
- Discuss the uses of PERT and CPM.
- Enumerate steps needed to combine people and machines in manufacturing.
- Describe quality circles.
- Discuss the impact of automation on the service sector.

PROFILE   DAVID HOUCK, STEEL PRODUCER

No place in the United States better illustrates the decline in the manufacturing sector than Youngstown, Ohio. The area has 40,000 or more unemployed steel workers. Since 1973, employment in the steel industry has fallen from 500,000 to 250,000. The Mahoning Valley has felt the sting of that decline more than most. Stretched out in that valley are 20 miles of steel mills, railroad tracks, and other steel-related facilities.

On September 19, 1977 (Black Monday), Youngstown Sheet & Tube closed, putting 5,500 people out of work. On November 19, 1979 (Black Monday Two), U.S. Steel closed its plant. It was a sad time in Youngstown. Steel had pretty much abandoned the valley, leaving behind thousands of unemployed steel workers and thousands more who would soon be unemployed, having lost the business created by the mills and their well-paid employees.

David Houck was a superintendent at U.S. Steel (now USX) when it closed, and he was convinced that the plant could be saved. He calculated that with cutbacks in labor, increases in productivity, and a focusing of product line, the

David Houck.

You're seeing a substantial deindustrialization of the U.S., and I can't imagine any country maintaining its position in the world without an industrial base.

ROBERT A. LUTZ, CHAIRMAN OF FORD OF EUROPE INC.

mill could be restored. Houck went to the men closing the plant and told them to be careful not to damage anything. He intended to reopen it—and he did. He found some venture capital, got some credit, and opened McDonald Steel Company.

Houck started with just one mill and 75 workers. He produced specialty steel products that few others could make. David Houck's favorite phrase is "skinny down." Huge plants and huge work forces have no place in scaled-back times; fewer bodies, more productivity, and a carefully culled product line are the orders of the day. "Skinny down" means keep the work force small and the operation small.

You learned in the last chapter that one password for today's corporations is "Small is Beautiful." David Houck once was superintendent of 32 managers who oversaw a work force of 800. Another 600 plus staffed the offices. You learned also about bureaucracy. U.S. Steel had a collection of work rules the size of the Sears catalog that had evolved over time. Layer after layer of management made decision making difficult. The system was inflexible, bureaucratic, and obsolete.

Now, David Houck works with a staff of eight, and the workforce is up to 126 in two mills. One cannot say with enthusiasm, "Youngstown is back," but David Houck is a model for industry in the future: small, productive, closely managed organizations with a cooperative workforce that shares in profits. This chapter is about production management. David Houck is a fine example of tomorrow's production manager.   ▪

Source: Based on Craig R. Waters, "Born-Again Steel," *Inc.,* November, 1984, pp. 52-64.

AMERICA'S MANUFACTURING BASE

The heart of the free enterprise system in the United States has always been its manufacturers. Names such as General Electric, USX, Westinghouse, American Can, and Navistar (formerly International Harvester) have represented the finest in production technology since the turn of the century. But, as we have learned, we are in a new era in social evolution. Today, manufacturing produces only one fourth of the U.S. gross national product. U.S. Steel, International Harvester, and other manufacturing giants and leaders from the past have been in a state of decline. Foreign manufacturers have been capturing huge chunks of the market for basic products such as steel, cement, machinery, and farm equipment.

What do those trends mean for tomorrow's college graduates? Is production and operations management a dying field? The answer is, absolutely not. Production management remains a challenging and vital element of American business. What has changed is the competitive, technological, social, and political environment. The very foundations of American business are being eroded because manufacturers have not kept up with some foreign producers in the latest technologies. This is an opportunity and a challenge, not the final word on the subject.

The rebuilding of America's manufacturing base is likely to continue to be one of the major business issues in the near future. There will be debates about the merits of moving production facilities overseas. Serious questions will be raised about the replacement of workers with robots and other machinery. Major political decisions will be made regarding protection of American manufacturers through quotas and other free trade restrictions. Regardless of how these issues are decided, however, tomorrow's college graduates will face tremendous challenges (and opportunities) in redesigning and rebuilding America's manufacturing base. Included in that challenge will be rebuilding America's **infrastructure**; that is, its bridges, roads, dams, water systems, and utilities.

The purpose of this chapter, therefore, is to introduce the concepts and issues in production management. You may want to visit a modern factory to experience for yourself what these new facilities look like. Would you enjoy the challenge of running such a facility? What are its advantages and disadvantages? The only way to be sure about such questions is to do your own personal research and talk to people in manufacturing. See if you can work on an assembly line for a day to get a feel for the production process.

The Reindustrialization Controversy

Throughout the 1980s there was much talk about the need to strengthen the U.S. manufacturing base. The debate started when *Business Week* devoted the bulk of its June 30, 1980 issue to "The Reindustrialization of America." Here is how the article began[1]:

> The U.S. economy must undergo a fundamental change if it is to retain a measure of economic viability, let alone leadership in the remaining 20 years of this century. The goal must be nothing less than the **reindustrialization** of America. A conscious effort to rebuild America's productive capacity is the only real alternative to the precipitous loss of competitiveness of the last 15 years, of which this year's wave of plant closings across the continent is only the most vivid manifestation.

The article cited effective business/government cooperation in West Germany and in Japan, and suggested that the United States adopt a comparable or better policy. The writers gave many statistics to prove that America's manufacturing power was declining:

- Economic growth had declined from 4.1% to 2.9% in the 1960s.
- In the 1970s, America lost 23% of its share of world markets.
- In 1960, 95% of radios, TV sets, and the like were supplied by United States producers. By 1980, imports had taken half the market. Today we import 90% of our electronics.
- Productivity had declined to almost zero.
- Plants were obsolete, managers were cautious, government policy was obscure, and unions were resistant to change.

You may want to make a copy of the *Business Week* article for your files. That article was the opening shot of a war against production decline that will be historically as important as any military battle the United States has fought.

Globalization and Deindustrialization

In 1986, *Business Week* again looked at industry to see what progress had been made. What it discovered was that industry continued to decline, with one added feature—globalization. **Globalization** involves searching the world for the plant site that offers the best financial breaks, building or using production facilities there, and shipping products back in finished form. For example, Apple picked a plant in Singapore to manufacture its personal computer, while Hewlett-Packard has a plant in Taiwan for manufacturing its printed circuit boards. Experts worry that this trend will leave the United States with an empty manufacturing shell.[2]

infrastructure
A country's network of facilities and plants, such as bridges, roads, dams, water systems, and utilities, that are essential for the operation of the economy. (A country's infrastructure can also be visualized as the skeleton on which the economy is built).

reindustrialization
The rebuilding of factories to make them more competitive in world markets.

globalization
Involves searching the world for the plant site that offers the best financial breaks, building or using production facilities there, and shipping products back in finished form.

networking
A business relationship where a small central organization relies on other companies and suppliers to perform manufacturing, marketing, or other crucial business functions on a contractual basis.

The trend is toward **networking**. Networking is a business relationship where a small central organization relies on other companies and suppliers to perform manufacturing, distribution, marketing, or other crucial business functions on a contractual basis. The problem is that the manufacturing is often being done overseas.

For example, Lewis Galoob Toys Inc. is known for its sword-wielding Golden Girls "action figures" and other trendy toys. This firm, with only 115 employees, sold $58 million worth of toys in 1985. Independent inventors dream up the products; and outside specialists do the design and engineering. A dozen or so manufacturers in Hong Kong produce the toys, passing on the most labor-intensive work to factories in China.[3]

Schwinn Bicycle Company has become a design, distribution, and promotion company with manufacturing done mostly in Asia. The popular Ocean Pacific (OP) Company is largely a marketing firm. Its clothes are designed and produced by others. Sales bloomed from $7 million to $270 million in 10 years. Other firms involved in networking include some familiar names: Nike, Esprit, and Liz Claiborne.[4]

The net effect of this trend is that the United States is becoming a nation of service firms (doing such things as design, marketing, banking, and insurance) while the Third World countries and other developed countries (for example, Japan) are taking over the production process. See Figure 14-1 for the historical development of production in the United States. You may also want to copy this *Business Week* Special Report for your files. It is a classic.

THINKING IT THROUGH

What are the advantages, if any, of having America's industrial base challenged by overseas competitors? Is competition normally a good thing or a bad thing for a business? Why?
What are some of the causes of America's industrial decline? What remedies would you propose?

PROGRESS CHECK

■ What do globalization and networking in business production mean?

■ What are some of the factors that have led to the need for a reindustrialization of the United States?

✳ FUNDAMENTALS OF PRODUCTION

To understand how America got into a position where it is fighting to regain leadership in production, we need to go back to fundamental concepts and build from there. You know what it takes to build a model of an airplane or make a dress. You need a place to work, you need money to buy the materials, and you need to be organized to get the task done. The same is true of the production process. It uses basic inputs (land, labor [and management], and capital [machinery]) to produce outputs (products, services, ideas) (see Figure 14-2). To

1850 Vertical   Companies grow larger and hire more managers, each to oversee a stage of the chain from raw materials to finished product.

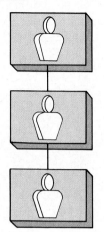

1800 Owner-managed Small companies, generally making one product for a regional market, are controlled by one person who performs many administrative tasks.

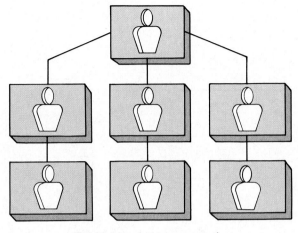

1900 Divisional   Large companies organize around a series of vertical chains of command to manage each product, or group of related products, that the company makes.

1950 Matrix   Large companies with vertical structures add a second, informal reporting chain that links managers with allied responsibilities or managers working together on temporary projects.

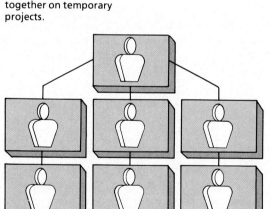

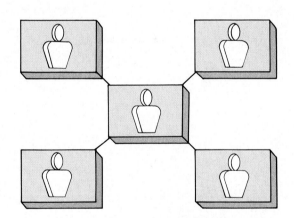

2000 Network   Small central organizations rely on other companies and suppliers to perform manufacturing, distri- bution, marketing, or other crucial business functions on a contract basis.

Organizational design for production, 1800-2000.

FIGURE 14-1

Source: John W. Wilson and Judith H. Dobrzynski, "And now the post-industrial corporation," *Business Week*, March 3, 1986, pp. 64-65.

be competitive, manufacturers must keep the costs of inputs down. That is, the costs of workers, machinery, and so on must be kept as low as possible. Similarly, the amount of output must be relatively high. Remember, the term for output per worker is *productivity*. How does a producer keep costs low and still produce more, that is, increase productivity? That is the question that will dominate thinking in the production sector for years to come.

FIGURE 14-2

The production process.

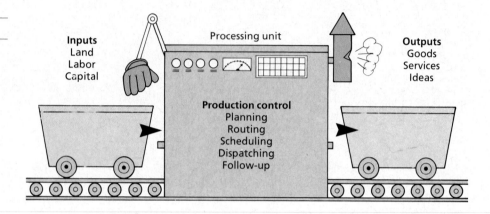

Keeping Costs Low: Site Selection

One of the major issues of the 1980s and 1990s is the shift of manufacturing facilities from one city or state to another in the United States. Such shifts have sometimes resulted in pockets of unemployment in some parts of the country and have also led to tremendous economic growth in others. Why would producers spend millions of dollars to move their manufacturing plants from one location to another? (See the box on p. 363.) One major reason is the availability of cheap labor and cheap resources. Many states in the southern United States have mostly nonunion labor. In general, such workers demand lower wages and fringe benefits. By moving South, U.S. business is able to compete more effectively with foreign producers who have much lower labor costs. That is a major reason why many businesses are shifting their production operations to Mexico, South Korea, and other overseas locations—to take advantage of cheaper labor costs. To keep their jobs, U.S. laborers must either become more productive or lower their demands for wages and fringe benefits. Naturally, such a suggestion causes much debate and controversy. Businesses are said to be greedy and uncaring when they move production facilities. But the fact is that the very survival of the U.S. manufacturing industry depends upon its ability to remain competitive, and that means either cheaper inputs or increased outputs from present inputs (this is called increased productivity).

Cheaper resources are a major reason for moving production facilities. Companies often need water, electricity, wood, coal, and other basic resources. By moving to areas where such resources are cheap and plentiful, costs can be lowered significantly—not only the cost of buying such resources, but the cost of shipping as well. Water shortages in the West, for example, often discourage the location of manufacturing plants there.

America simply works better in some places than it does in others.

Corporate America once fell in love with South Carolina without really knowing why.

Many companies, no doubt, were attracted by all the attributes indigenous to many of the Sunbelt states at the time.

But they did not invest nearly $15 billion in new plants solely on the basis of "cheap labor, cheap taxes, and cheap country club dues."

Ironically, the executives who moved here to manage those plants have become our biggest boosters.

Many, in fact, have changed jobs or changed careers, to avoid being transferred back home.

And what they tell us is that South Carolina simply works better than most other places in America.

There are quite a few reasons, of course. But chief among them is the fact that our people work better.

That's no surprise when you consider that our grandparents and great-grandparents, in most cases, grew up on a farm.

It's just a matter of fact that the work ethic is a way of life here, not a hollow phrase dreamed up by an advertising agency.

As a result, we consistently have the highest levels of worker productivity, and the lowest levels of work stoppages, in America.

To find out how our people can make your business work better, write J. Mac Holladay, Director, State Development Board, Suite 600, P.O. Box 927, Columbia, S.C. 29202, or call 803-758-3145.

You'll find there are a great many things that seem to work better in South Carolina, and many of them have nothing to do with business.

And that may help to explain why so many people come to live in South Carolina and never want to live anywhere else.

There's more to South Carolina than making a profit.

States compete for businesses with advertising.

The cost of land is also a critical factor in choosing a plant location. Many businesses are leaving cities, where land is expensive, and moving to rural areas where land is much, much cheaper. Some employers also enjoy living away from the noise, pollution, and traffic of big cities.

Another incentive to locate or relocate in a particular city is the tax situation and government support. Some states have higher taxes than others. Some states even give tax incentives and other support, such as zoning changes and financial aid, so that businesses will locate there.

HIGH-TECH PRODUCTION AND ECONOMIC GROWTH

A major issue of the 1980s and 1990s is finding locations in which to build the new high-tech manufacturing facilities. Ohio attracted a Honda plant. Tennessee was able to land General Motors' new Saturn plant and the auto manufacturing facilities of Nissan. The Nashville area is becoming another Detroit because of inexpensive labor and a central location.

A senior engineer for NCR was struck by the beauty and possibilities of Colorado Springs for a computer-chip plant. NCR did build its plant there in 1975, and since then 20 more high-tech companies and a hundred related research firms have located in Colorado Springs. It has become another Silicon Valley.

How did Colorado Springs do it? It was flexible on zoning changes, for one thing. But it also has low union activities, low utility rates, cheap housing, and great natural beauty. The economic development team targeted high-tech firms because of their clean image, and they won. Now Honeywell is there along with Ford Aerospace, Texas Instruments, TRW, United Technologies, and more. The town grew from 236,000 to 332,000 between 1970 and 1984. Some 6,000 jobs are added each year.

Source: Charles F. McCoy, "High-Tech Prosperity-Basic Industry Gloom Mingle in the Rockies," *The Wall Street Journal*, August 3, 1984, p. 1. © Dow Jones & Company, Inc., 1984.

Naturally, some places are more attractive than others because of climate, educational facilities, and other factors. The quality of life is better in some areas than others. If you have a chance to build a plant anywhere, why not choose sunny California, Florida, or Arizona? In summary, then, businesses try to cut production costs and improve lifestyles by locating their plants where:

- Resources are plentiful and inexpensive
- Skilled workers are available
- Labor is inexpensive
- Taxes are low and local government offers support
- Energy and water are available
- Land is available, inexpensive, and close to markets
- Transportation costs are low
- Quality of life is high
- Quality of education is high

Locating Close to Markets

One reason businesses choose to remain in areas such as Chicago, New York, New Jersey, and California is because that's where their customers are. In spite of all the talk about the booming Southwest, much of the buying power of the United States is still centered in the Midwest, Northeast and far West (California). By locating close to their customers, businesses lower the costs of transportation and can be more responsive to customer needs for service. It is especially important for service organizations to be located in urban areas where they can serve their customers best.

Once a location is selected, production can begin. After the Progress Check, let's begin at the beginning and go through the entire production process to see how it can be made more competitive.

A location close to markets is important.

PROGRESS CHECK

- What are the five steps in the production process?

- What are five of the nine criteria businesses use when selecting a production site?

- What is the production process called when you take a raw material and break it down into components, as firms do with crude oil?

form utility
The value added by the creation of finished goods and services using raw materials, components, and other inputs.

production process
Uses basic inputs (land, labor, and capital) to produce outputs (products, services, and ideas).

PRODUCTION UTILITY

Earlier you learned that five utilities were created by businesspeople: form, time, place, possession, and information. Four of these utilities are created mostly by marketing: time, place, possession, and information. Marketing also creates some form utility, but this is basically done by production people.

Form utility is the value added by the creation of finished goods and services using raw materials, components, and other inputs. It follows then that **the production process** is the creation of final goods and services using the factors of production: land, labor (machinery), and materials. Production is a broad term that includes all industries that produce goods and services, including mining, lumber, manufacturing, education, and health care.

Manufacturing is one part of production. It means making goods by hand or with machinery as opposed to extracting things from the earth (mining and fishing) or the production of services as opposed to goods. We shall discuss both manufacturing and the production of services in this chapter.

manufacturing
Making goods by hand or with machinery as opposed to extracting things from the earth (mining or fishing) or producing services.

THE PRODUCTION PROCESS

Andrew S. Grove, chief executive officer of Intel, uses a great analogy to explain the production process[5]:

> To understand the principles of production, imagine that you're a waiter . . . and that your task is to serve a breakfast consisting of a three-minute soft-boiled egg, buttered toast, and coffee. Your job is to prepare and deliver the three items simultaneously, each of them fresh and hot.
>
> The task here encompasses the three basic requirements of production. They are to build and deliver products in response to the demands of the customer at a *scheduled* delivery time, at an *acceptable quality* level, and at the lowest possible cost. . .
>
> Other production principles underlie the preparation of our breakfast. In the making of it, we find present the three fundamental types of production operations: **process manufacturing,** an activity that physically or chemically changes material just as boiling changes an egg; *assembly,* in which components are put together to constitute a new entity just as the egg, the toast, and the coffee together make a breakfast; and *test* which subjects the components or the total to an examination of its characteristics. There are, for example, visual tests. . . .

See the box below for more details on the production process.

process manufacturing
Physically or chemically changing materials.

assembly process
Puts together components.

synthetic systems
Either change raw materials into other products or combine raw materials or parts into a finished product.

OTHER PRODUCTION PROCESSES

From the text, it is easy to understand two manufacturing processes: process and assembly. In process manufacturing, you physically or chemically change materials. In **assembly process,** you put together components, such as tires, frames, and windows in a car. These two processes are called synthetic systems. **Synthetic systems** either change raw materials into other products (process manufacturing) or combine raw materials or parts into a finished product (assembly process).

The reverse of a synthetic system is one called an analytic system. In an **analytic system** a raw material is broken down into components to extract other products. For example, crude oil can be reduced to gasoline, wax, jet fuel, and so on.

A **continuous process** is one in which long production runs turn out finished goods over time. In our breakfast shop, for example, you could have eggs on a conveyor belt that lowered them into boiling water for 3 minutes and then lifted them out on a continuous basis. A 3-minute egg would be available whenever you wanted one. An automobile factory is run on a continuous process.

It usually makes more sense when responding to specific customer orders (job-order production) to use an **intermittent process.** This is an operation where the production run is short (one or two eggs) and the machines are shut down frequently or changed to produce different products (like the oven in a bakery or the toaster in the breakfast shop). Manufacturers of custom-designed furniture or metal railings would use an intermittent process.

analytic systems
Break down raw materials into components to extract other products.

continuous process
One in which long production runs turn out finished goods over time.

intermittent process
An operation where the production run is short and the machines are shut down frequently or changed to produce different products.

Mr. Grove goes on to mention five indicators of whether or not you can meet your production goals on any given day. They are:

1 *Sales forecast.* How many breakfasts should you plan to deliver?
2 *Raw material inventory.* Do you have enough eggs, bread, butter, and coffee on hand?
3 *Equipment.* Is everything ready to produce the breakfast?
4 *Manpower.* Are there enough people available to make the sales forecasted number of breakfasts?
5 *Quality.* Are customers satisfied?

The production of breakfasts begins with the purchase of the needed food and equipment. The food and supplies must be stored in refrigerators and other storage equipment. The first place we can look for production efficiency and savings, therefore, is in purchasing and storage.

Materials Requirement Planning (MRP)

One thing for certain about the technological changes taking place in manufacturing is that they have resulted in a whole new terminology for production and operations management. Today's students need to be familiar with this terminology before they can discuss such advances in any depth.

One of the more important terms is *materials requirement planning (MRP)*. Materials requirement planning is a computer-based operations management system that uses sales forecasts to make sure that needed parts and materials are available at the right place and the right time. In our breakfast shop, we would feed the sales forecast into the computer and it would specify how many of each ingredient to order, and print out the proper scheduling and routing sequence.

Holly Carburetor used MRP to solve an inventory problem. The company had too many dollars tied up in inventory and yet bad problems with parts shortages. The company decided it needed a custom-designed computer program for materials requirement planning.

Using the new program, the company cut inventory costs from $30 million to $20 million, making it well worthwhile to invest $250,000 for the computer program. The system enables anyone in the organization to ask the computer where the company is with respect to satisfying a customer order—where it is in the production process, the status of inventory, what is on order, and so forth. The company is planning to add "just-in-time" inventory control next.[6]

Just-In-Time Inventory Control

just-in-time (JIT) inventory control
Delivery of the smallest possible quantities at the latest possible time to keep inventory as low as possible.

One of the major costs of production is holding parts, motors, and other items in warehouses. To cut such costs, the Japanese perfected an idea called **just-in-time (JIT) inventory control.** The idea is to have suppliers deliver their products "just in time" to go on the assembly line. A minimum of inventory is kept anywhere on the premises. Some U.S. manufacturers have adopted the practice, and are quite happy with the results.[7]

Here is how it works. A manufacturer sets a production schedule and determines what parts and supplies will be needed. It then informs its suppliers of what will be needed. Naturally, this calls for more effort on the supplier's part (and more costs). Efficiency is maintained by having the supplier linked by computer to the producer so that the supplier becomes more like another department in the firm than a separate business. The supplier delivers its materials just in time to be used in the production process, with a bare minimum kept in storage.

Some U.S. manufacturers have adopted just-in-time programs to cut the costs of warehousing inventory.

You can imagine how the system would work at Andrew Grove's breakfast shop. Rather than ordering enough eggs, butter, bread, and coffee for the week and storing it, we would have our suppliers deliver every morning. A moment's reflection will tell you some of the problems with just-in-time systems. What happens if the supplier doesn't deliver on time because of weather conditions or an accident? Are suppliers willing to assume the added costs of more frequent, smaller deliveries? Such questions have to be answered through planning and negotiation. The results are usually worth the effort.

Just-in-time inventory means delivery of the smallest possible quantities at the latest possible time to keep inventory as low as possible. Between 1982 and 1984, GM is said to have cut its annual cost of holding inventory from $8 billion to just $2 billion by using JIT. Chrysler operates thirteen JIT manufacturing plants.[8] Chrysler determines when carriers must arrive and what the carrier will be hauling. The traffic department at Chrysler coordinates with the trucking firm and the supplier and negotiates precise service standards.[9]

Just-In-Time Supplier Relationships

Fortune magazine reviewed the just-in-time experience of U.S. producers in 1986. They found that nearly 100 companies had tried the system. For many of them, implementation of JIT methods had been rather difficult. The main problem was that producers were using JIT as a way of getting suppliers to hold inventories instead of them. This meant that the producers had no back-up inventory if the suppliers delivered the wrong parts or faulty parts.[10]

For the system to work well, producers have to work closely with suppliers and carefully work out details of the system, making sure that the suppliers are happy with the system too. Xerox failed to do that when it first established its JIT system, and it caused much supplier discontent. Xerox then developed an elaborate program to develop better supplier relationships and now teaches others how to do that.

Xerox learned how to implement a JIT system from Harley-Davidson. Harley is one of the best practitioners of just-in-time. The U.S. motorcycle company was about to fail because of Japanese competition. Operating costs in Japan were 30% lower, largely due to just-in-time manufacturing and quality control procedures such as those discussed later in the chapter. Using Japanese-style techniques, Harley cut its costs for warranty repairs, scrap, and reworking of parts by 60%.

MRP and JIT systems make sure the right materials are at the right place at the right time at the cheapest cost to meet customer needs and production needs. That is the first step in modern production innovation. The next step in innovation is to change the production process itself. We shall discuss this next.

MAKING CHANGES IN THE PRODUCTION PROCESS

Another major area for cost saving involves the design of the process used to make final products. You no doubt are familiar with the idea of a production line or assembly line. The workers are lined up on both sides of a long assembly line and perform one or more simple processes as the product goes by. For example, in making an automobile, one person puts in the seats, another installs the windows, and still others put on tires, bumpers, headlights, and so on. The process involves many, many workers doing a few not-too-complex tasks. (There are about 10,000 parts in a car.)

Recently, GM announced plans to completely redesign its production process, abandoning the assembly line. The name given the changeover was "Project Saturn." The fundamental purpose of the restructuring was to compensate for the Japanese $8- to $10-an-hour advantage in labor costs by dramatically cutting the number of man-hours needed to build a car. It was estimated that GM intended to cut the number of man-hours per car from 175 to only 30.[11]

The changes GM made were many, but the most dramatic was to switch to modular construction. This means that most parts will be preassembled into a few large components called *modules*. Workers are no longer strung out along miles of assembly line. Instead, they are grouped at various work stations where they put the modules together. Rather than do a few tasks, workers perform a whole cluster of tasks. Trolleys carry the partly completed car from station to station. Such a process takes up less space and calls for fewer workers—both money-saving steps. Suppliers were asked to provide a wider variety of parts and to subassemble certain parts before shipping them.

Robot spray painting a car.

robot
A computer-controlled machine capable of performing many tasks that require the use of materials and tools.

In addition to these changes, GM designed a casting process to build the engine block that uses 40% less machinery. This too saves money and time. And finally, GM greatly expanded its use of robots in the manufacturing process. A **robot** is a computer-controlled machine capable of performing many tasks requiring the use of materials and tools. Robots for example, spray paint cars and do welding. Robots are fast, efficient, and accurate.

GM is just one example of how innovations are now occurring in manufacturing. In general, firms are using more robots, more computers, and less labor. See Figure 14-3 for a look at the future of automation for the auto industry. Manufacturing plants tend to be smaller and more fuel efficient. Again, the goal is to cut costs and increase productivity to keep American business competitive. Next we shall explore the dramatic changes that are occurring that could restore American dominance in manufacturing in the next decade. The first change we shall explore is called *computer-aided design* and *computer-aided manufacturing (CAD/CAM)*.

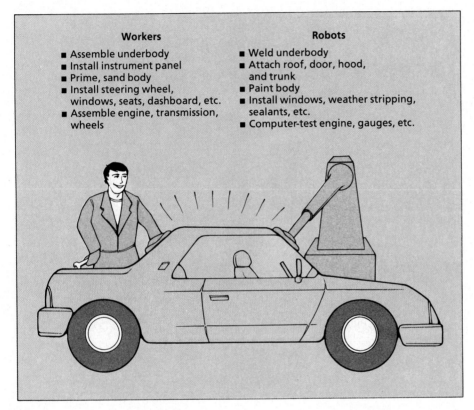

Workers	Robots
■ Assemble underbody ■ Install instrument panel ■ Prime, sand body ■ Install steering wheel, windows, seats, dashboard, etc. ■ Assemble engine, transmission, wheels	■ Weld underbody ■ Attach roof, door, hood, and trunk ■ Paint body ■ Install windows, weather stripping, sealants, etc. ■ Computer-test engine, gauges, etc.

FIGURE 14-3

Auto-mation—robot innovations for the auto industry.

The Use of CAD and CAM

If one development in the 1980s changed production techniques and strategies more than any other, it was the integration of computers into the design and manufacturing of products. The first thing computers did was help in the design of products. The idea is called **computer aided design,** or **CAD.** The next step was to involve computers directly in the production process. That was called **computer aided manufacturing (CAM).**

CAD/CAM has made it possible to design products to meet the tastes of small markets with very little increase in costs. A producer programs the computer to make a simple design change, and that change can be incorporated right into the production line. Custom products can thus be designed for narrow markets. For example, consumers in the Midwest like hamburger on their pizza rather than pepperoni or sausage. The Pillsbury Company added a hamburger pizza to their Midwest line by making a few simple changes in the computer program for pizzas.

CAD/CAM (computer aided design/computer aided manufacturing)
The integration of computers into the design and manufacturing of products.

Another example reveals how helpful the computer can be. In 1906, a Viennese architect named Josef Hoffman designed a beautiful silver-plated bowl as a gift for Albert Einstein. The original bowl has disappeared; only a photograph remains. To duplicate the bowl by hand through trial and error would have been costly and difficult. Instead, two men used the computer-aided design (CAD) process to program the dimensions of the bowl. They made 100,000 copies and sold them for $120 each. They could now make a slight change in the design on the computer and produce a new, unique design of their own.[12]

Designing tennis shoes with computer-aided design (CAD).

Computer-aided manufacturing (CAM) is used to make cookies in those new fresh-baked cookie shops. On-site, small-scale, semiautomated, sensor-controlled baking makes consistency easy.

Computer-aided design and manufacturing are also invading the clothing industry. A computer program establishes a pattern and cuts the cloth automatically. Soon, a person's dimensions will be programmed into the machines to create custom-cut clothing at very little additional cost.

The same flexibility is possible in large plants that produce automobiles, appliances, construction equipment, and other large, expensive items. In the past, any model change resulted in large increases in inventory and set-up costs. (All plant operations—machining, welding, assembling, and so forth—require *set-up time;* that is, time to prepare for the new process.) Today, many such changes are computerized, and the costs lowered dramatically. One manufacturer over a 5-year period roughly tripled its number of models while reducing inventory by half and doubling the output per worker.[13] How? Computer-aided manufacturing.

In summary, computer-aided design and computer-aided manufacturing (CAD/CAM) have revolutionized the production process. Now, everything from cookies to automobiles can be designed and manufactured much more cheaply.

Furthermore, customized changes can be made with very little increase in cost. Think what that will mean for the clothing industry, the shoe industry, and other fashion-conscious industries. The age of custom-designed consumer and industrial goods has arrived. Figure 14-4 illustrates how consumers will be able to order custom-built cars in the future.

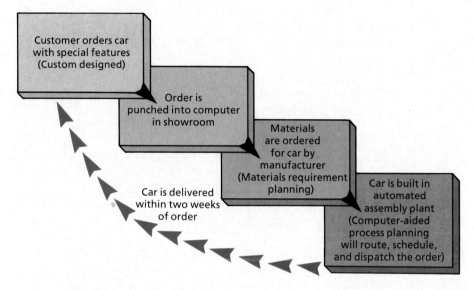

FIGURE 14-4

Buying a car in the future.

THE COMPUTERIZED FACTORY

Because of new ideas such as CAD/CAM, the United States is now on the brink of a whole new era in production management. No longer should the discussion be on the decline of American industry. Instead, the focus may be on the reemergence of American industry from its ashes. The force behind the change is new technology, especially computers and robots. Some terms you will be seeing over the next decade are:

- **Computer aided engineering (CAE).**[14] CAE includes the design and analysis of products, programming of robots and machine tools, designing of molds and tools, and planning of the production process and quality control. In the past, engineering involved a lot of paperwork—blueprints, drawings, and so forth. Many inefficiencies resulted from the shuffling of such papers from desk to desk to shop floor and so on. Today, the whole engineering process from conception to production can be and is being done by computer.
- **Computer aided design/computer aided manufacturing (CAD/CAM).** We have already discussed some applications of CAD/CAM. Properly applied, CAD/CAM can cut design cycle time by over 30% and increase productivity by 20% to 30%.[15]
- **Group technology (GT)** is the process of grouping or assembling parts based on the similarity of their geometry, size, and manufacturing processes. The idea is to design a parts supply system so that robots can select and assemble the parts.
- **Computer-aided process planning (CAPP)** is a system for converting engineering designs into manufacturing instructions. It takes into account in-

CAE (computer aided engineering)
The computer-generated design and analysis of products, programming of robots and machine tools, designing of molds and tools, and planning of the production process and quality control.

group technology (GT)
The process of grouping or assembling parts based on the similarity of their geometry, size, and manufacturing processes with the objective of designing a parts supply system so that robots can select and assemble the parts.

CAPP (computer aided process planning)
A system of converting engineering designs into manufacturing instructions.

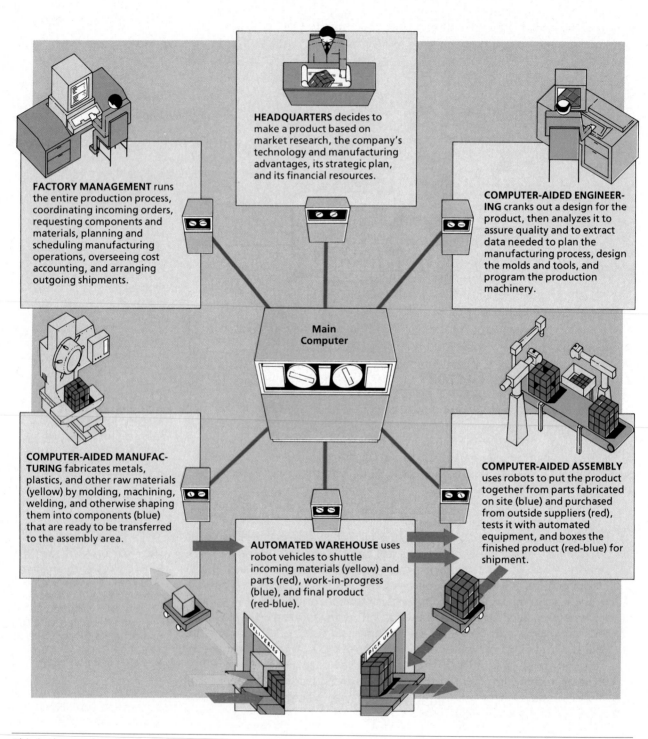

FACTORY MANAGEMENT runs the entire production process, coordinating incoming orders, requesting components and materials, planning and scheduling manufacturing operations, overseeing cost accounting, and arranging outgoing shipments.

HEADQUARTERS decides to make a product based on market research, the company's technology and manufacturing advantages, its strategic plan, and its financial resources.

COMPUTER-AIDED ENGINEER-ING cranks out a design for the product, then analyzes it to assure quality and to extract data needed to plan the manufacturing process, design the molds and tools, and program the production machinery.

COMPUTER-AIDED MANUFAC-TURING fabricates metals, plastics, and other raw materials (yellow) by molding, machining, welding, and otherwise shaping them into components (blue) that are ready to be transferred to the assembly area.

AUTOMATED WAREHOUSE uses robot vehicles to shuttle incoming materials (yellow) and parts (red), work-in-progress (blue), and final product (red-blue).

COMPUTER-AIDED ASSEMBLY uses robots to put the product together from parts fabricated on site (blue) and purchased from outside suppliers (red), tests it with automated equipment, and boxes the finished product (red-blue) for shipment.

Main Computer

This is the modern kind of factory that can compete in world markets.
Source: Roger Gorman, *Business Week,* March 3, 1986, p. 73.

formation about machine capacities, optional routing paths, and materials. It tells the operations people how to best use machines and tools to produce products in the most efficient way.

- **Materials requirement planning (MRP)** is a technique for managing inventories and issuing orders for parts and materials. MRP is linked with CAPP to determine what parts are needed in what quantities for production. It then checks inventory to see if the parts are available and, if not, generates orders for those parts.[16]

- **Flexible manufacturing systems (FMS)** are totally automated production centers that include robots, automatic materials handling equipment, and computer-controlled machine tools. A recent report mentioned a Japanese manufacturer who put in a flexible manufacturing system (FMS). This enabled the plant to cut back the number of machines from 68 to 18, the number of employees from 215 to 12, and space requirements from 103,000 sq. ft. to 30,000 sq. ft. Process time was cut from 35 days to a day-and-a-half.[17] GM's new plant uses flexible manufacturing with similar cost-saving results.

We could go on describing other systems, but the discussion would get too complex to absorb. What you should learn from all this is that factories are being fully automated. Everything from customer order processing, inventory control planning, and forecasting through production, quality control, and shipping is being made more productive through the use of computers and robots.

Today this process is rather uncoordinated. Factories have computer-controlled centers performing various functions, but these centers are not linked. The goal is to integrate the whole production process. As you can guess, this is easier said than done. A few firms, however, have integrated the entire process. They call the total system computer integrated manufacturing (CIM). Let's look at how this works.

Computer-Integrated Manufacturing (CIM)

Computer-integrated manufacturing combines computer-aided design (CAD) with computer-aided manufacturing (CAM). It then further integrates CAD/CAM with other corporate functions such as purchasing, inventory control, cost accounting, materials handling, and shipping.

The Ingersoll Milling Machine Company was an early user of CIM. This machine tool firm makes products in small lots—one or two at a time—and needed a huge amount of information processing to schedule products through design and production. Their computer-integrated manufacturing system includes scheduling, engineering design (CAE), inventory control, computer-aided design (CAD), computer-aided manufacturing (CAM), purchasing, accounts payable, cost accounting, and assembly. The system saves Ingersoll over $1 million a year, mostly in machinery design.[18]

New computer breakthroughs will make computer integrated manufacturing a reality in thousands of manufacturing firms in the next decade. Leading firms that are developing such systems for others include IBM, GE, Schlumberger, Control Data, Xerox, and Sperry Univac.

Just-in-time inventory supply systems will link suppliers with producers by computer to form networks of computer-linked firms. One problem with such integration is that different manufacturers producing computers, robots, computer

MRP (materials requirement planning)
A computer-based operations management system that uses sales forecasts to make sure that needed parts and materials are available at the right place and time.

FMS (flexible manufacturing systems)
Totally automated production centers that include robots, automatic materials-handling equipment, and computer-controlled machine tools.

CIM (computer-integrated manufacturing)
Computer aided design (CAD) combined with computer aided manufacturing (CAM). It then further integrates CAD/CAM with other corporate functions such as purchasing, inventory control, cost accounting, materials handling, and shipping.

software, and data transmission systems have not standardized their equipment. Thus it has been difficult in the past to integrate systems within the firm, much less among firms. This problem introduces the concept of local area networks (LANs). We'll discuss them next.

PROBLEMS WITH IMPLEMENTING AUTOMATION

Implementation of the new technologies into production facilities has not gone as smoothly as planned. General Motors, for example, built a $600 million assembly plant in Hamtramck, Michigan that has 260 robots for welding, 50 automated guided vehicles to carry parts to the assembly line, and a battery of cameras and computers that use laser beams to inspect and control the production process. Some problems include:

- The automated guided vehicles sat idle for a while because of software problems.
- Robots sometimes spray-paint each other instead of the cars.
- The plant was turning out only 30 to 35 cars per hour in 1986, far less than the 60 an hour for which it was planned.

Ford had similar start-up troubles making its minivan. The car arrived from the St. Louis plant 7 months later than planned. At first, there were problems getting the computer-controlled machinery from various manufacturers to communicate. Then the system was too complicated even for operators with months of training.

The computer/robot age came very quickly, and it is taking time to adjust to it. Some plants tried to fully automate before the operators were sufficiently trained and the equipment was fully tested in an assembly-line setting. The glitches are now being worked out, however, and computer automation is here to stay.

Source: Amal Nag, "Tricky Technology," *The Wall Street Journal*, May 13, 1986, pp. 1, 10.

Local Area Networks (LANs)

LAN (local area networks)
Unified systems that integrate the appropriate software and hardware and the computers, robots, and machines to use programs, as well as provide communication lines with the various functions of the organization.

For computer integrated manufacturing to reach its full potential, a company has to solve two problems: (1) it has to find the appropriate software (computer programs) and hardware and the computers, robots, and machines to use the programs; (2) the system must be connected somehow so that the various functions are linked in a unified communication system. The unified system is called a **local area network** or LAN.[19] See the Apollo ad on p. 375 for an example.

Control Procedures: PERT, Critical Path, and Gantt Charts

PERT (program evaluation and review technique)
A method for analyzing the activities involved in performing a given task, evaluating alternative means of meeting the goal, choosing the best method, and setting up controls that ensure the completion of the task on time.

Obviously, one of the important functions of a production manager is to be sure that products are manufactured and delivered *on time*. The question is, how can one be sure that all of the assembly processes will go smoothly and end up completed by the required time? One of the more popular strategies for maintaining some feel for the progress of the production process is called PERT (Program Evaluation and Review Technique). **PERT** is a method for analyzing the activities involved in performing a given task, evaluating alternative ways of meeting the goal, choosing the best method, and setting up controls to be sure the task is completed on time.

Note the various steps: (1) analyze activities that need to be done, (2) brainstorm different ways of doing those tasks, (3) choose the best way, and (4) set up control points to measure progress.

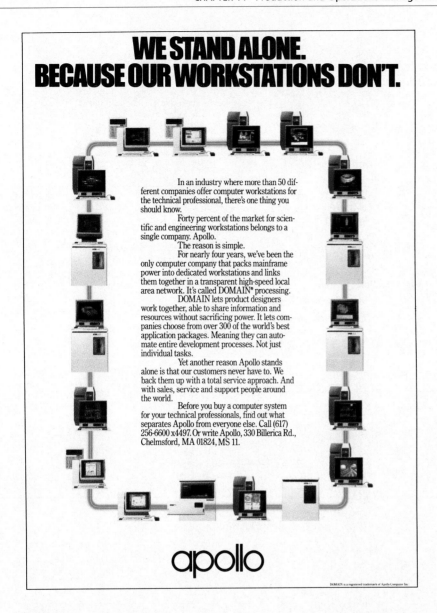

An ad for a local area network (LAN) system.

PERT is especially popular as a technique for evaluating alternative distribution systems or for scheduling production. The amount of time each step would take is calculated and the alternative paths are mapped. The maximum time needed for completion of a process is called the *critical path*. The various alternatives are evaluated and one is selected. Any deviations from the path are likely to delay completion of the project unless corrective action is taken.

When a manager follows the path a product takes from the beginning of the production process until the end and assigns specific times for each step, he is using the **critical path method (CPM)** of production scheduling (see Figure 14-5). It is easy, then, to follow whether or not the product is being completed on time. The manager merely checks each point along the way to see if everything is finished. If not, corrective action can be taken to speed things up and complete the total project on time.

CPM (critical path method) A production scheduling method through which a manager follows the path a product takes from the beginning of the production process until the end and assigns specific times for each step.

FIGURE 14-5

A, Understanding the critical path method.

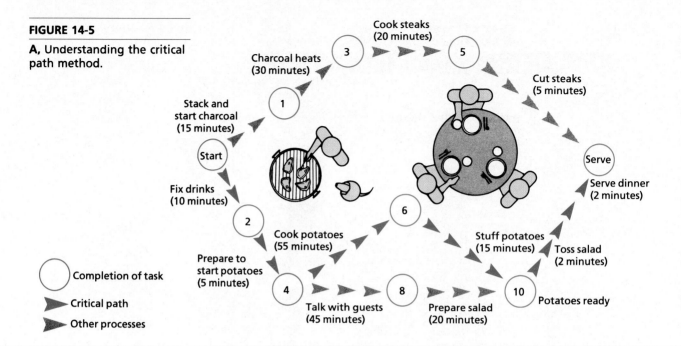

Cook steaks
(20 minutes)

Charcoal heats
(30 minutes)

Stack and
start charcoal
(15 minutes)

Cut steaks
(5 minutes)

Fix drinks
(10 minutes)

Serve dinner
(2 minutes)

Cook potatoes
(55 minutes)

Stuff potatoes
(15 minutes)

Prepare to
start potatoes
(5 minutes)

Toss salad
(2 minutes)

Talk with guests
(45 minutes)

Prepare salad
(20 minutes)

Potatoes ready

◯ Completion of task

▶ Critical path

▶ Other processes

B, A Gantt chart enables a production manager to see at a glance when projects are scheduled to be completed and what the status now is. For example, the dolls' heads and bodies should be completed before the clothing is sewn, but could be a little late, as long as everything is ready for assembly in week 6. This chart shows that at the end of week 3, the dolls' bodies are ready, but the heads are about half a week behind.

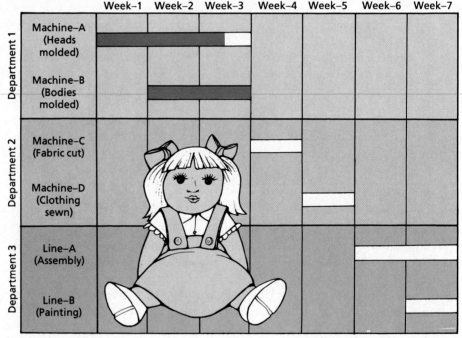

		Week–1	Week–2	Week–3	Week–4	Week–5	Week–6	Week–7
Department 1	Machine–A (Heads molded)							
	Machine–B (Bodies molded)							
Department 2	Machine–C (Fabric cut)							
	Machine–D (Clothing sewn)							
Department 3	Line–A (Assembly)							
	Line–B (Painting)							

Manufacturers have also used something called a *Gantt chart* for measuring production progress. This is nothing more than a chart listing what projects are being worked on and what stage they were in on a daily basis. All of this was once done by hand. Now the computer has taken over, and Gantt charts are becoming obsolete.

▓ What do you call the production process of taking a raw material and breaking it down into components, as firms do with crude oil?

▓ *Computer-integrated manufacturing* describes the linking together of computer-aided processes in production. Name four of those processes.

▓ Could you draw a PERT chart for making a breakfast of 3-minute eggs, buttered toast, and coffee? Which process would be the critical path, the longest process?

PEOPLE VERSUS MACHINES

PERT, CPM, and Gantt calculations were once done slowly and carefully by skilled production managers who had years of experience. Today, production alternatives can be simulated on the computer. Calculations that once took days can now be made in minutes. Thus it appears the future of production is secure. It seems that computers, robots, and automatic machinery will take over the whole process. The truth is that production is still dependent upon people, and it will be people who will determine the success or failure of future systems. Several steps must occur before people and machines will be combined to revolutionize manufacturing:

■ There is an obvious need to train future production workers in the use and repair of computers, robots, and automatic machinery.

■ Today's production workers must be retrained or relocated to adapt to the new high-tech systems.

■ Major adjustments must be made in the relationships between suppliers and producers to implement concepts such as just-in-time inventory programs and local area networking.

■ Production managers must be retrained to deal with more highly skilled workers who demand a much more participative managerial style. The box below shows how, with training, a businessperson can become quite successful in production.

DAVE BING: FROM BASKETBALL STAR TO STEEL PRODUCER

Dave Bing was a star guard for the Detroit Pistons basketball team in the 1970s. He was a National Basketball Association All-Star seven times. Now Dave Bing is a star in a different field.

In 1984, President Reagan named Dave Bing the National Minority Small Business Person of the Year. Mr. Bing started a steel fabricating plant soon after retiring from basketball in 1978. He is an example of today's modern production man.

Dave earned his B.A. in economics and marketing at Syracuse University. During the off-season over 8 years, he worked for the National Bank of Detroit and for two years as a Chrysler management trainee. When he left basketball, Mr. Bing spent 2 years training at Paragon Steel. Using that experience and his other managerial training, he started his own firm.

Using some of his basketball earnings to help finance the firm, Bing struggled at first. Now sales are in the $40 million range. His is the first black-owned steel company in the country. His customers include GM, Ford, and John Deere. Dave Bing's career shows that there are opportunities in production for talented people, even in declining industries such as steel.

Source: Katherine Blood, "Steel Star," *Forbes,* February 25, 1985, p. 162. Reprinted by permission of *Forbes* magazine; © *Forbes* Inc., 1985.

QUALITY CONTROL

quality control
The measurement of products and services against set standards.

Quality control is the measurement of products and services against set standards. In America, quality control was often done at the end of the production. It was done by a quality control department. Today, things have changed. As Ford says in its ads, "Quality Is Job One." **Total quality control** includes planning for quality, preventing quality defects, correcting any defects that occur, and a philosophy of continuous effort to build quality into products.

total quality control
Includes planning for quality, preventing quality defects, correcting any defects that occur, and a philosophy of continuous effort to build quality into products.

The president of Signetics (a producer of integrated circuits) reports that total quality control at his firm has resulted in $20 million in savings from 1980 to 1987. On-time deliveries have increased 50% and returns decreased by 90%.[20]

High-quality Japanese goods such as Toyota automobiles gave U.S. producers the incentive for quality control. Who taught Toyota about total quality control? An American consultant named Dr. W. Edward Deming. Total quality control means building in and ensuring quality from product planning to production, purchasing, sales, and service. Deming teaches firms to: (1) use statistical quality control during the process; (2) select supplies based on quality; (3) use statistical methods, not slogans to get quality; and (4) find sources of poor quality and eliminate them.[21] Now U.S. firms are listening to Deming and applying his strategies.

Quality Circles

quality circles
Groups of employees that are formed to develop ideas for solving quality problems and other problems in the workplace.

Management strategies for improving quality and productivity vary depending on the latest fad. One technique that was "hot" in the mid-1980s has tended to fade. Yet the idea is so good that it deserves more attention. The concept is called **quality circles**. The general idea is to form groups of employees with the hope of developing ideas for solving problems in the workplace such as how to improve quality, increase productivity, cut back on paperwork, reduce inventory costs, or introduce new processes such as computer integrated manufacturing.

Quality circles are made up of a dozen or so employees, generally from the same department, who meet frequently to solve problems that occur at work. Two benefits can emerge from such programs: (1) the company learns many cost-efficient ways to operate, thus increasing productivity; and (2) employees feel that their ideas are sought and are valuable, and that increases morale. To get participation, some companies ask for volunteers; others *require* employees to participate.

One technique used in such groups is called *brainstorming*. Basically, that means that group members generate as many ideas as possible about what the problems are, or solutions to a stated problem, and someone writes all the ideas down. The ideas are neither censored or evaluated. The purpose is to generate as many thoughts and perspectives as possible. Later, the ideas will be analyzed and discussed and the best ones implemented.

Pareto analysis
A strategy that ranks problems in the order of frequency or importance to focus corrective efforts.

One brainstorming strategy now gaining popularity is called Pareto analysis. In **Pareto analysis** problems are ranked in the order of frequency or importance. This procedure helps to focus on the major issues first to make the greatest possible gains.

Companies that have tried quality circles have found that employees often come up with answers to problems that managers knew nothing about:[22]

■ At a Teledyne Semiconductor plant, employees reported that silicon wafers worth $148 each were breaking because of ill-fitting lids on storage boxes. Correcting the problem was estimated to save the company $44,000 a year.

■ As a result of employee suggestions, a San Francisco public television station (KQED) reallocated space for employees, redesigned a membership form, and developed a procedures manual for accounting that significantly cut bookkeeping errors.

A quality circle in action.

Hundreds of such stories could be told. The International Association of Quality Circles went from 860 members to 5,000 members in 1 year in the early 1980s.

THINKING IT THROUGH

What are some of the ways technology could affect higher education? What will be the role of videotape recorders, computers, and interactive TV? How will this affect the cost of college tuition?

What other service organizations might be changed dramatically by the new technological revolution? Think of the effect on banks, government services, health-care institutions, and hospitals.

AUTOMATING THE SERVICE SECTOR

U.S. business cannot remain competitive in world markets, simply by automating production facilities in factories. The service sector will have to become more productive as well. We have already learned that 7 of 10 jobs in the United States are already in the service sector, with more to come. A truly strong America, therefore, has to be as progressive in introducing the latest technology to services as well as manufacturing.

One reason that service productivity lags behind manufacturing is because services are more labor intensive. That is, factories can more readily substitute machines for people and thus get more output from the remaining people. Traditional thinking has been that no machine can replace people in services such as banking, insurance, education, medicine, and consulting.

However, Theodore Levitt has presented a convincing argument that a production-line approach can be applied to services as well as goods.[23] He cites McDonald's as an example of this. McDonald's straddles the fine line between a retailer that offers mostly goods, such as an antique dealer, and one dealing almost exclusively in services, such as an income tax preparation service. The goods part of McDonald's was under the control of management. But the service personnel were less controllable. To gain some control, McDonald's has made almost every movement as standardized as possible:

> The tissue paper used to wrap each hamburger is color-coded to denote the mix of condiments. Heated reservoirs hold pre-prepared hamburgers for rush demand. . . . Nothing is left to chance or the employees' discretion.
>
> The entire system is engineered and executed according to a tight technological discipline that ensures fast, clean, reliable service in an atmosphere that gives the modestly-paid employees a sense of pride and dignity. . . .
>
> What is important to understand about this remarkably successful organization is not only that it has created a highly sophisticated piece of technology, but also that it has done this by applying a manufacturing style of thinking to a people-intensive service situation.[24]

Automatic teller machines make banking services more efficient.

Most of us have been exposed to similar productivity gains in banking. For example, people in many towns no longer have to wait in long lines for harassed tellers to help them deposit and withdraw money. Instead, they use automatic tellers that take a few seconds and are available 24 hours a day.

Another service that was once often very annoying because of slowness was the checkout counter at the grocery. The new system of marking goods with universal product codes enables computerized checkout, and allows cashiers to be much more productive when providing this service.

Airlines represent another service industry that is experiencing tremendous productivity increases through the use of computers for processing reservations, through the heavy use of prepackaged meals on board, and through more standardization of all movements of luggage, passengers, and so on.

Automating the Salesperson

It takes only a little imagination and more technologically-based thinking to make tremendous productivity advances in services that are now viewed as people intensive, one-on-one industries. Take life insurance sales, for example:

> A life insurance agent is said to be in a service industry. Yet what does he or she really do? They research the prospect's needs by talking with them, design several policy models for them, and then "consumer-use test" these models by seeking their reactions. Then the agent redesigns the final model and delivers it for sale to the customer. This is the ultimate example of manufacturing in the field. The factory is in the customer's living room, and the producer is the insurance agent, whom we incorrectly think of as being largely a salesperson. Once we think of him or her as a manufacturer . . . we begin to think of how best to design and manufacture the product rather than how to best sell it.
>
> The agent, for example, could be provided with a booklet of overlay sheets showing the insurance plans of people who are similar to the customer. This gives the customer a more credible and informed basis for making a choice. In time, the agent could be further supported by similar information stored in telephone-access computers.
>
> In short, we begin to think of building a system that will allow the agent to produce his product efficiently and effectively by serving the customer's needs instead of performing a manipulative selling job.[25]

The point is that the service sector will continue to gain very slowly in productivity as long as people believe that services have to be personalized and labor intensive. But as various service industries begin to substitute machines for people, productivity will increase more quickly. Note that many of the changes will be in consumer-related areas such as personal selling (insurance), delivery (order by phone supermarkets, drugstores, and variety stores), credit (advanced credit card systems), and consumer research plus problem solving (consulting, income tax preparation, real estate, stockbroking).

PREPARING FOR THE FUTURE

What does all this mean to you? It means that college graduates of the future will have marvelous new technological advances available to them. It means new opportunities and a higher standard of living and quality of life. But it also means preparing for such changes. Clearly, the workplace will be dominated by computers, word processors, and other advanced machinery. Even the service sector will require the use of hand-held computers.

If all of this sounds terribly cold and impersonal, then you recognize one of the needs of the future. People will need much more contact with people outside the work environment. There will be new demands for recreation, social clubs, travel, and other diversions. The America of the next century will be radically different from the America of the 1980s. It will take both technically trained people and people skilled in human relationships to guide us through the transition.

Laptop computers provide invaluable assistance to service providers.

Carnegie Mellon University now requires a course in manufacturing management for its MBA degree. Other courses are offered in robotics and manufacturing strategy. Some students act as consultants to manufacturers in the Pittsburgh area. Stanford University has an Institute for Manufacturing and Automation. Such programs will become commonplace as other schools follow the leadership of these schools in introducing such courses at both the undergraduate and graduate levels.

Other schools are training students to manage the new high-tech managers and workers. Emphasis is on participative management and the design of attractive work environments. All of this will come together in the 1990s to mean a new era in both the manufacturing and service sectors. You have every reason to be optimistic about the future for both U.S. and world economic growth because of these changes. You can also expect to find many exciting new careers in America's new industrial boom.

PROGRESS CHECK

■ What are some of the ways corporations can improve quality control?

■ Is a quality circle only a technique for improving quality?

CAREER INFORMATION: PRODUCTION SUPERVISORS

NATURE OF THE WORK

In any organization, someone has to be boss. For the millions of workers who assemble manufactured goods, service motor vehicles, lay bricks, unload ships, or perform any of thousands of other activities, a supervisor is the boss. These supervisors direct the activities of other employees and frequently ensure that millions of dollars worth of equipment and materials are used properly and efficiently. Supervisors are most commonly known as foremen or forewomen.

Although titles may differ, the jobs of all blue-collar worker supervisors are similar. They tell other employees what work has to be done and make sure the work is done correctly. For example, manufacturing supervisors may inspect products during and after the production process to make sure that they conform to customer specifications and company standards. Loading supervisors at truck terminals assign workers to load trucks, and then check that the material is loaded correctly and that each truck is fully used. They may mark freight bills and record the load and weight of each truck. Mine car dispatchers control the transport of coal through underground mines.

Supervisors make work schedules and keep production and employee records. They plan employees' activities and must allow for unforeseen problems such as absent workers and machine breakdowns. Supervisors teach employees safe work practices and enforce safety rules and regulations. They also may demonstrate time-saving or laborsaving techniques to workers and insure that new employees are properly trained.

Supervisors tell their subordinates about company plans and policies; recommend good performers for wage increases, awards, or promotions; and deal with poor performers by retraining them in proper methods, issuing warnings, or recommending that they be disciplined or fired. In companies where employees belong to labor unions, supervisors meet with union representatives to discuss work problems and grievances. They must know the provisions of labor-management contracts and run their operations according to these agreements.

Outstanding supervisors, particularly those with college education, may move up to higher management positions. In manufacturing, for example, they may advance to jobs such as department head and plant manager. Some supervisors, particularly in the construction industry, use the experience and skills they gain to go into business for themselves.

JOB OUTLOOK

Employment of blue-collar worker supervisors is expected to increase more slowly than the average for all occupations through the mid-1990s. Although rising incomes will stimulate demand for goods such as air-conditioners, home entertainment equipment, personal computers, and automobiles, employment in manufacturing industries will grow slowly due to increasing foreign competition. This will dampen demand for supervisors. Although most of these supervisors will continue to work in manufacturing, a large part of the increase in jobs will be in nonmanufacturing industries, especially in the trade and service sectors.

EARNINGS

Median weekly earnings for blue-collar worker supervisors were about $460 in 1984. The middle 50 percent earned between $350 and $630. The lowest 10 percent earned less than $265 and the highest 10 percent earned over $790. Supervisors receive a salary determined by the wage rates of the highest paid workers they supervise. For example, most companies keep wages of supervisors about 10 to 30 percent higher than those of their subordinates. Some supervisors receive overtime pay.

Source: *Occupational Outlook Handbook*, 1986-1987, U.S. Department of Labor.

1 In 1980, *Business Week* magazine called for "The Reindustrialization of America." Economic growth in manufacturing was declining, productivity was low, and many plants were obsolete.

▪ What has happened since?

Deindustrialization has continued with a new concept called *globalization*, leading American firms to seek production facilities overseas.

▪ Is that related to networking?

Yes; networking is where a firm in the United States relies on other companies to do its design and manufacturing. Often these other companies are overseas.

▪ What are the consequences of these trends?

America could lose its industrial base and become more of a service economy with less growth.

2 The answer to *Business Week's* call for reindustrialization is now occurring through automation.

▪ What is the basic production process?

It involves production planning, routing, scheduling, dispatching, and controlling.

▪ What is an initial step toward cost cutting?

Site selection using criteria such as qualified and inexpensive labor, resources (water, energy, land) are available, markets are close, taxes are low, and the quality of life is high.

3 Production adds *form utility*—the value added by the creation of finished goods and services from raw materials, components, and other inputs.

▪ What are the production process indicators?

They are the sales forecast, raw material inventory, equipment, manpower, and quality.

▪ What are the different processes?

They include process manufacturing, assembly process (synthetic systems) and analytic systems. The systems can be continuous process or intermittent process.

4 Materials Requirement Planning (MRP) uses sales forecasts to make sure that needed parts and materials are available at the right time and place.

▪ Is just-in-time inventory control part of MRP?

It can be. The idea is to have delivery of the smallest possible quantities at the latest possible time to keep inventory as low as possible.

5 Many new techniques are being used to make production more efficient (less expensive).

▪ What are some techniques?

Computer-aided design (CAD), computer-aided manufacturing (CAM), computer-aided engineering (CAE), computer-aided process planning (CAPP), and flexible manufacturing systems (FMS).

6 All the systems are being linked in a total system called *computer-integrated manufacturing* (CIM). What links the system is a network called *local area networks* (LAN).

▪ What control procedures are used?

The old PERT, CPM, and Gantt systems are now computerized so that progress can be checked moment by moment. The *critical path* is the longest series of steps in the process.

7 The new orientation in production is quality control. *Total quality control* includes planning for quality, preventing defects, correcting sources of defects, and a philosophy of continuous effort to build quality into products, purchasing, sales, and service.
- Is that what quality circles are for?
  Partly. They are also used for improving efficiency and generally to involve employees in decision making.

8 Because the United States is a service society now, automation of the service sector is extremely important.
- What does this mean for me?
  New careers in both the industrial and service sectors in areas not even developed yet.

KEY TERMS

analytic systems   p. 366
assembly process   p. 365
CAD/CAM (computer aided design/computer aided manufacturing)   p. 369
CAE (computer aided engineering)   p. 371
CAPP (computer aided process planning)   p. 371
CIM (computer-integrated manufacturing)   p. 373
continuous process   p. 366
CPM (critical path method)   p. 375
FMS (flexible manufacturing systems)   p. 373
form utility   p. 364
globalization   p. 359
group technology   p. 371
infrastructure   p. 359
intermittent process   p. 366

just-in-time (JIT) inventory control   p. 366
LAN (local area networks)   p. 374
manufacturing   p. 365
MRP (materials requirement planning)   p. 373
networking   p. 360
Pareto analysis   p. 378
PERT (program evaluation and review technique)   p. 374
process manufacturing   p. 365
production process   p. 364
quality circles   p. 378
quality control   p. 378
reindustrialization   p. 359
robot   p. 368
synthetic systems   p. 365
total quality control   p. 378

GETTING INVOLVED

1 Find the latest articles on computer integrated manufacturing (CIM) and local area networks (LAN). Which companies are making the greatest advances toward having integrated networks? What companies have installed the systems? Share your articles with the class. If everyone brings in one article, you should have quite a collection for your file on the industrial sector.

2 Review all the terms in this chapter: CAD, CAM, CIM, MRP, just-in-time inventory control, FMS, CAPP, CAE, and so on. These are the business terms of the 1990s. Try to use them in class so that they become familiar in different settings. Soon you will be thinking of new ways to advance business yourself, based on your understanding of these terms.

3 Have the class brainstorm all of the applications of high technology in the service sector that have already occurred. (Brainstorming is explained in the chapter.) Using this information, brainstorm further uses of technology in areas such as recreation, travel, retailing, wholesaling, insurance, banking, finance, and the government.

4 Debate the following proposition: "Resolved, that the federal government should become more involved in the future of U.S. industry through a national industrial policy." Take whichever side of the issue you did not previously agree with to broaden your thinking on this issue.

5 Debate the following proposition: "Resolved, that U.S. manufacturers should halt the spread of computers and robots used in manufacturing to save jobs for U.S. workers." Again, take the other side of this issue from your normal position.

CASE ONE   THE AUTOMATION OF GENERAL MOTORS

PRACTICING MANAGEMENT DECISIONS

No firm is more committed to computerizing production than General Motors. GM paid $2.5 billion to buy Electronic Data Systems (EDS) in 1984. EDS is a computer-services company that has been asked to bring its values of productivity to GM.

The model for future GM plants may be the Saturn plant in Tennessee. Saturn will cost about $5 billion to put into production, and will provide 6,000 jobs in the plant and 10,000 more in nearby facilities. Here are some of the impacts of Saturn.

Soon you will be able to go into a GM dealer and order a car, including colors, optional equipment, financing arrangements, and delivery date—all at a computer terminal. The computer will translate your order into parts orders. Radios, air conditioners, tires, and thousands of other parts will be ordered from suppliers all over the world. Computer designed inventory control will allow just-in-time delivery to the production floor. From order to delivery could take less than two weeks.

Meanwhile, at the factory the car is being designed and built using computer aided design and manufacturing. Robots will do much of the assembling and moving of parts. Workers will not be on assembly lines; rather, they will work in small groups (modules) to build subassemblies. Testing of parts will be done in the modules to raise quality control. The robots and computers will be able to talk to each other, and control systems will catch flaws almost immediately. Productivity in some areas will increase over present plants by 800%.

Workers will be paid a salary, not hourly wages. Workers as a whole will have no more than six job categories, and each worker will do a wider variety of work. Workers will have a much larger say in how jobs are performed and at what pace.

The whole plant will be virtually paperless. Everything from order forms to engineering drawings will be on computers. EDS computer specialists will link the system into computer integrated manufacturing. When a car is ordered, computers will begin designing an inventory of spark plugs, air filters, and other parts to be sent to automobile dealerships to service the cars for the foreseeable future.

DECISION QUESTIONS

1 What will be the impact of such plants on blue collar jobs and white collar jobs in manufacturing? GM feels the impact on white collar jobs will be greater. Why would that be?

2 How will such new manufacturing techniques affect the job market in the 1990s?

3 What will be the impact of such plants on suppliers, competitors, and dealers? What about unions?

PRACTICING MANAGEMENT DECISIONS

CASE TWO QUALITY—AMERICA IS BACK

Ask any production manager in Japan what person has had the greatest influence on their tremendous increase in quality products, and they are sure to answer "W. Edwards Deming." He taught them the concepts of statistical control of quality, and they applied the principles. Japanese businesses do not need as many quality control people at the *end* of assembly lines because they test for quality all along the production line. As a consequence, many Japanese products are not only priced well, they are higher in quality as well.

Another American named Philip Crosby wrote a book called *Quality Is Free* that has had a big impact on the thinking of managers at IBM and other leading firms. He followed that successful book with two others: *Quality Without Tears* and *The Art of Getting Your Own Sweet Way*. What do all these books boil down to? The answer? Why not do things right the first time? Or, "Set high standards and meet them every time."

It is no accident that Ford used the theme of "Quality is Job One" for its 1980s ad campaign. Quality is king in the 1980s, and America is starting to listen to its experts—as Japan did.

One example of the new quality approach is provided by Spectrum Control, Incorporated. The company had trouble soldering terminals to capacitors because the capacitors wouldn't accept solder. Rejects jumped from 3% to 32% and 50% to 75% of engineering time was taken up by this problem. Eventually the whole operation was shut down and Spectrum began a new quality program.

First, it had to reject the notion of acceptable quality levels (AQLs). Its customers (for example, IBM and Hewlett-Packard) were requiring something close to zero defects. Furthermore, a Japanese company (Murata Erie North American, Incorporated) was a competitor, and it was emphasizing Japanese-level quality.

Spectrum bought $15,000 worth of videotapes on quality by Deming (14 tapes, 16 hours). They also hired Philip Crosby (at $46,000 a week) to consult with them about quality.

The result? Spectrum estimates that its first year's savings on sales returns and allowances would be $767,000. Quality is now a fixture at Spectrum, and Crosby was right. Quality *is* free; in fact, it pays huge dividends.

DECISION QUESTIONS

1 How did it happen that American businesses let the quality of their products slip below that of foreign producers? Is it too late to meet the challenge?

2 How can computers and robots add to product quality? What effect does that have on labor?

3 Have you seen quality improvements in American cars in the last few years? What other products need more attention to quality?

Source: The Spectrum story is detailed in Craig R. Waters, *"Quality Begins at Home," Inc.*, August, 1985, pp. 68-71.

LOOKING AHEAD

Are you ready for the information age? Do you understand the language of computers? Do you understand how important robots and other high-tech machines will be in the future?

Chapter 15 will help you whether or not you are up to date in these areas. It is a good review of the terms and concepts from the computer area and other high-tech industries. Before we go on, however, be sure to take some time with the exercises and cases in this chapter. They set the stage for the next chapter.

COMPUTERS, ROBOTS, AND OTHER BUSINESS TOOLS

LEARNING GOALS

After you have read and studied this chapter, you should be able to:

- Discuss various careers in computers.
- Describe the five generations of computers.
- Distinguish between computer hardware and software, and identify several types of computers.
- Discuss high-tech computer applications.
- Explain the advances in telephone technology, microwave transmission, and videotex.

PROFILE   ELLEN WESSEL OF MOVING COMFORT, INCORPORATED

Perhaps no other movement better represents the 1980s than the increase in jogging, aerobics, and physical fitness in general. Naturally, such a trend called for new clothes and shoes for exercising. At first, exercise clothes for women were cut like men's clothes, and the shorts were too tight in the rear and too bunched up in the crotch.

Ellen Wessel felt that other women joggers would be willing to pay a little more for comfortable shorts. Ellen began a company called Moving Comfort, Inc. to produce such clothes. Sales went well, and gross income eventually reached the millions.

Actually, the process of achieving success was not that easy. At first, Ellen made the kind of mistakes you or I would make when learning a new business. She began buying material at retail prices, so profits were low. Her first partner dropped out after a few months because the profits were so small. For a year, Ellen lived off her savings. When she did finally order in quantity, she was overwhelmed when a huge truck dropped 1,000 yards of material off at her apartment.

Then Elizabeth Goecke bought a pair of Moving Comfort shorts and found them unflattering and uncomfortable. She offered to redesign them. Eventually, Elizabeth became a partner in the firm, and sales took off.

Ellen Wessel and Elizabeth Goecke.

Trouble returned. The rapid growth in sales caused problems throughout the firm. Two full-time and four temporary typists couldn't send out bills fast enough, and that delayed the receipt of income. The warehouse was in chaos. Things were hard to find, inventory turnover was slow, and the company was paying huge interest rates to finance the inventory.

Ellen was frustrated and felt like selling the business. We talked earlier about the need for consultants in small businesses, especially accounting help. Ellen called in such a consultant, and he recommended a computer system. The company put in a $26,000 computer system and spent $6,000 more for programming. The computer now saves the company $75,000 a year in interest alone. The company no longer needs temporary typists and still gets its bills out in 1 day after shipment.

The computer helps with all phases of the business, but is especially handy for inventory control and management. Inventory turnover doubled, and Moving Comfort became quite profitable. Ellen Wessel had a good idea and a good product, but that isn't always enough to succeed in business. Today's organizations, large and small, are much more likely to succeed with the use of a computer to assist in bookkeeping, payroll, inventory control, billing, and other everyday tasks. ■

Source: Mary Williams, "Fresh Idea, Optimism, Luck Helped Running-Wear Maker," *The Wall Street Journal,* June 27, 1983, p. 31. © Dow Jones & Company, Inc., 1983. All rights reserved.

THE INFORMATION AGE IS HERE

The introduction of new procedures and new technology is always disruptive. People tend to be afraid of the new systems. They believe that they won't be able to learn the new skills and will appear awkward or dumb. Certainly, the introduction of computers has followed that pattern. Slowly but surely, however, computers have crept into organizations, so that the pressure on those who still are unfamiliar with computers and their uses is even greater.

Are you comfortable using a computer? If not, it is time to learn. Computers are becoming more and more "user friendly." That is, they are becoming much easier to use and understand. To use a computer in the past, one had to learn computer languages such as FORTRAN (FORmula TRANslation) or COBOL (COmmon Business-Oriented Language). The learning process was slow, errors were plentiful, and the whole process was difficult for many students.

Today's computers are much easier to use (see Figure 15-1). Focus in many schools is shifting away from programming computers to using computers for managerial decision making, a more enjoyable high-level function. There will be many new jobs in computer programming, repair, and design. But more important to the majority of students, almost all jobs can be made more efficient through the use of computers. Someday soon we will all be able to buy items by using home computers. We will also be able to send letters by computer (electronic mail), find information by computer, and generally be more connected with information resources. In other words, you will not be able to function fully in tomorrow's business or consumer world unless you learn to use the computer. It will be almost as commonplace for businesspeople to use a computer as it is to drive a car.

The purpose of this chapter is to introduce you to some of the terms and uses of computers, robots, and other high-tech equipment in today's organizations. If you haven't done so already, stop in a computer store and have the salesperson show you how to do simple processes such as word processing (typing). Also, visit a computer center in a firm to see how computer data are processed and stored.

15 years ago, you had to be a programmer

```
Do 1050 I = 1, NVAR
Reads (5,1100) ISALE
1050 Write (6,1150) NP,
    ISALE
1100 Format (1X,15)
1150 (1X, 'Sales in period,'
    12, 15)
```

5 years ago, you had to learn a second language

```
Limit month to Oct 83
Limit product to my
    product
Display sales
```

Today, you just have to turn your PC on

```
Next request:
1. Browse:
    Look at some data
    tables
2. Report:
    Prepare a
    formal report
3. Graph:
    Graph the data
4. Analyze:
    Perform a special
    analysis
5. Info:
    Provide info
    about database
6. Manage:
    Make changes to
    database
7. Explains choice:
    Done choosing
    top menu utility

Choose one: > Browse
```

FIGURE 15-1

Computer use is getting easier. The list on the right is called a *menu*. You choose one of the seven and punch a key to see what you requested.

Source: John D.C. Little and James J. Findley. "Blueprint for a Revolution," *Marketing Communications*, March, 1984, p. C-21.

As you read newspapers and magazines, watch for articles on office automation, robots, cellular phones, interactive video systems, and other high-tech developments to see what is happening in the market now. The information age is here, and it's going to be interesting and challenging.

CAREERS IN COMPUTERS

A wide variety of careers is available to people in the computer field. Not all of them require a college education, and some are not technical. Let's review some of the major career possibilities first. Then we'll explore some related jobs.

Many careers are available in the computer field.

According to government statistics the greatest number of job openings in the future will be for computer and peripheral equipment operators. Some **40%** of the jobs will be in that category (see Figure 15-2). The growth in this area is being generated by the general increase in computer usage and the introduction of computers into smaller businesses. **Computer operators** are the people responsible for running and monitoring the overall computer operation. They collect the data input (tapes or disks) and read and follow the programmers' instructions. They also decide what equipment to use, which jobs should be done in what order, and whether the computer is functioning properly.

computer operators
Responsible for monitoring the overall computer operation for a system and troubleshooting problems that occur.

FIGURE 15-2

Projected computer employment (1990).

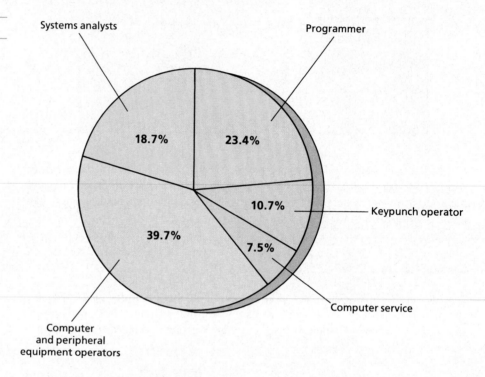

Systems analysts — 18.7%
Programmer — 23.4%
Keypunch operator — 10.7%
Computer service — 7.5%
Computer and peripheral equipment operators — 39.7%

peripheral equipment operators
Run the equipment (such as printers and disk drives) that is part of the computer system.

Peripheral equipment operators load and unload magnetic tapes and disk drives. They also run the printers and other equipment related to the computer. *Peripheral equipment* refers to all the tangible parts of a computer system other than the computer itself, input devices that feed information to the computer, and output devices that produce desired information.

programmers
People who write the instructions for the computer.

The second largest number of career openings will be in computer programming. **Programmers** are the people who write the instructions for the computer. The step-by-step instructions are called *programs* or *software*. They are fed into the computer on disks much as a record is played on a record player. This job may be as complex as designing an inventory system for a major automobile company or flight patterns for Chicago's airports.

To do this, programmers must talk with the departments involved and the computer analysts to find out what needs to be done. Then they prepare a *flow chart*, a diagram of the steps to follow in doing the job. Then the flow chart must be translated into a language the computer understands (see the box on p. 393). People who perform these functions are called *applications programmers*.

SELECTED COMPUTER LANGUAGES

Ada: A government (especially military) computer language

ALGOL (*Algo*rithmic *L*anguage): math-oriented language used most often for larger computers

APL (*A P*rogramming *L*anguage): IBM-devised language useful for math

BASIC (*B*eginners *A*ll-purpose *S*ymbolic *I*nstructional *C*ode): used mostly for math and statistics

COBOL (*Co*mmon *B*usiness-*O*riented *L*anguage): used for business applications such as billing, payroll, or inventory

FORTRAN (*For*mula *Tran*slation): used most often for scientific problems

LISP: Advanced artificial intelligence language for programs that deal with human languages

LOGO: Language useful for graphics; widely used in schools

PASCAL: Language that teaches a structured approach to programming; in the same class as Ada

PL1 (*P*rogramming *L*anguage *1*): similar to ALGOL, but handles business files better

PROLOG (*Pro*gramming in *Log*ic): basic artificial intelligence program

Systems Analysts

Some 19% of the careers in computers, according to the government, will involve systems analysts. **Systems analysts** have the challenging job of analyzing the many functions of the firm and designing a computer system to perform those functions more efficiently. First the systems analysts study how the job is now being performed. Then they design a system to do the job better. To do that, they must learn what information must be collected and processed, what output is needed, what computer capacity is needed, and the costs involved. Systems analysts must explain the system to the various computer users and tell the programmers what the system needs to do.

systems analysts
Study the many functions of the firm and design a computer system to perform those functions more efficiently.

Computer Service

The greatest increase in computer jobs (versus total number of computer jobs) in the future may be for computer service technicians. During the 1980s, companies were busy installing computers. During the 1990s, someone will have to maintain and fix those computers. This is a great opportunity for someone to start his or her own service business.

Other Computer Careers

Dozens of careers have evolved because of computers and the information revolution. Someone, for example, must teach people how to use computers (*computer trainers*). There are *computer consultants* who advise firms on which computer to buy. *Computer librarians* keep track of all the tapes, disks, and other data storage devices. A *data processing manager* supervises the data processing center. *Computer security specialists* try to prevent computer crime. *Technical writers* write the manuals that tell how to use the computer. Naturally, there are also *computer engineers* who design computers and manufacturers that produce computers.

LEADING MAGAZINES FOR MICROCOMPUTER USERS

Byte
Personal Computing
P.C. Magazine
Creative Computing
Computers & Electronics
InfoWorld
PC World
Compute!
Popular Computing

CAREER INFORMATION: COMPUTER SYSTEMS ANALYST

NATURE OF THE WORK

Systems analysts plan and develop methods for computerizing business and scientific tasks or improving computer systems already in use. They may work for the organization that wants to install a system or for a consulting firm that develops systems under contract.

Analysts begin an assignment by discussing the data processing problem with managers or specialists to determine the exact nature of the problem and to break it down into its component parts. If a retail chain wishes to computerize its inventory system, for example, systems analysts will determine what information must be collected, how it is to be processed, and the type and frequency of reports to be produced. After they have defined the goals of the system, they use techniques such as mathematical model building, sampling, and cost accounting to plan the system.

Once a design for the system has been developed, systems analysts prepare charts and diagrams that describe it in terms that managers and other users can understand. They also may prepare a cost-benefit and return-on-investment analysis to help management decide whether the proposed system is satisfactory.

If the system is accepted, systems analysts may determine what computer hardware and software will be needed to set up the system. They also prepare specifications for programmers to follow and work with them to "debug," or eliminate errors from the system.

JOB OUTLOOK

Employment of systems analysts is expected to grow much faster than the average for all occupations through the mid-1990s. The demand for systems analysts is expected to rise as advances in technology lead to new applications for computers. Factory and office automation, telecommunications, and scientific research are just a few areas where use of computer systems will expand.

College graduates who have had courses in computer programming, systems analysis, and other data processing areas as well as training or experience in an applied field should enjoy the best prospects for employment. Persons without a college degree and college graduates unfamiliar with data processing will face competition from the large number of experienced workers seeking jobs as systems analysts.

EARNINGS

Median weekly earnings of systems analysts who worked full time in 1984 were about $600. The middle 50 percent earned between $485 and $745 a week. The lowest 10 percent earned less than $345; the highest tenth, more than $870.

Earnings for beginning systems analysts in private industry average about $490 a week in 1984. Experienced workers earned about $585, and lead systems analysts earned about $690 weekly. In the Federal Government, the entrance salary for recent college graduates with a bachelor's degree was about $345 a week in early 1985.

SOURCES OF ADDITIONAL INFORMATION

Further information about the occupation of systems analyst is available from: Association for Systems Management, 24587 Bagley Rd., Cleveland, Ohio 44138 or Data Processing Management Association, 505 Busse Hwy., Park Ridge, Ill. 60068.

Source: *Occupational Outlook Handbook,* 1986-1987, U.S. Department of Labor, Bureau of Labor Statistics, pp. 74-75.

There are so many career possibilities involved that it is difficult to know which career might be most interesting for you. Again, the best way to find out is to visit several large computer operations and watch the people for a day or so. Interview a few systems analysts, programmers, and other specialists. Maybe you will find a rewarding career in this fast-growing field.

computer hardware
Includes all the tangible machines that process and store data.

To prepare for such research, you should know something about computer hardware and software and basic computer terms. We'll begin by looking at **computer hardware**; that is, all the tangible machines that process and store data.

Ellen Wessel (see the Profile) learned the hard way that a small business needs computer technology to be efficient. You have been exposed to computers for several years now. Notice that many people have computer anxiety. They are avoiding buying one or learning how to use one. This is the modern version of math anxiety. You may not be interested in a career in computer technology, but can you see the need for computer literacy no matter what you hope to do?

Can you visualize artists using computers? Could a ballet be designed on a computer? Are there limits to the use of computers in your chosen field?

FIVE GENERATIONS OF COMPUTERS

We are now in the fifth generation of computers. It is amazing to see the progress of computers over the last 25 years or so. The first generation of computers used vacuum tubes, were very bulky, and generated much heat—like thousands of light bulbs. Such computers filled whole rooms. The second generation used smaller, cooler transistors and diodes. The third generation was the introduction of integrated circuits. An integrated circuit is a network of transistors all contained on a silicon chip about the size of the top of a pencil. The fourth generation used very large scale integrated circuits (VLSI). These computers can fit on the top of a desk, but have much greater processing ability than the original room-sized computers. The fifth generation of computers is much faster. They are being programmed to be a source of **artificial intelligence**. That is, the computer is able to mimic human thought processes. Such systems are now being used in financial management, medical diagnosis, and petroleum refinery monitoring. Organizations such as NASA's Goddard Space Flight Center, GE's Space Division, and Motorola's Radar Operations Service use this new generation of computers.

artificial intelligence
The ability of computers to mimic human thought processes.

Once computers were just big calculators; then they became storehouses of information. Now they are giving advice; for example, financial expert systems are starting to do such tasks as guide an individual's investments, warn manufacturers about foreign competition, and reject bad insurance risks.[1]

Expert systems can store and manipulate knowledge and rules-of-thumb as well as data. They can "reason" by drawing inferences from stored knowledge.[2] This is the first stage of artificial intelligence. The computer can't think for you, but it can help you formulate questions and teach you how to reach logical conclusions.

expert systems
Store and manipulate knowledge and rules of thumb as well as data.

Parallel Processing

A big step toward providing computers with more intelligence is called **parallel processing**. The principle is that two heads are better than one. A company called Thinking Machines Corporation has developed parallel computers that link many fingernail-sized microprocessors (computers on a chip) so that they can work together. You can compare parallel processing to painting a fence. A dozen painters dividing up the work can outperform any single painter. Similarly, parallel processing strings together hundreds or thousands of processors to build faster computers.[3] In the next section we'll look at the lineup of today's computers.

parallel processing
Links hundreds or thousands of processors to build faster computers.

COMPUTER HARDWARE

There is an unbelievably wide range in computer size, price, and capability. New additions are constantly being introduced, from lap-top portables on the small end to supercomputers that can perform in the "1,000 megaflop range"; that means 1 billion operations per *second!*[4] Computers generally fall into the following catagories:

- *Microcomputers* are at the small end of the computer line. They include the home computers that you can buy for $1000 or so to more sophisticated portable and personal computers that businesses use. These computers can do up to 500,000 8-bit operations per second. Bit is short for binary digit and is expressed as either 0 or 1. Computer speed is measured in millions of instructions per second **(MIPS)**. Therefore a minicomputer's speed is .0005 MIPS. The parts of a microcomputer are illustrated below.

MIPS
Millions of instructions per second.

Key parts of a microcomputer system.

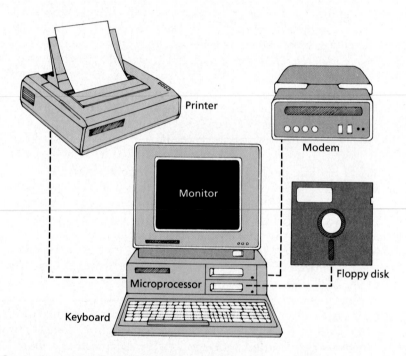

- *Supermicrocomputers* cost around $10,000 and can do .36 MIPS. Digital Equipment Corporation sells a Micro VAX1 that falls in this range.
- *Superminicomputers* cost from $100,000 to $500,000. They do over a million instructions per second.
- *Mainframe computers,* like the IBM Sierra (Series 3090), cost over $700,000 and do over 28 million instructions per second. These were once considered to be monster computers with fantastic capability. But now there's more.
- *Minisupercomputers,* like the Convex C-1, can do 60 million instructions per second. They cost about $500,000.
- *Supercomputers,* like the CRAY X-MP, can do a billion or more instructions per second and cost up to $16 million. Such computers are practical only for very large users such as the Defense Department or major research institutions. The goal now is for a trillion instructions per second.

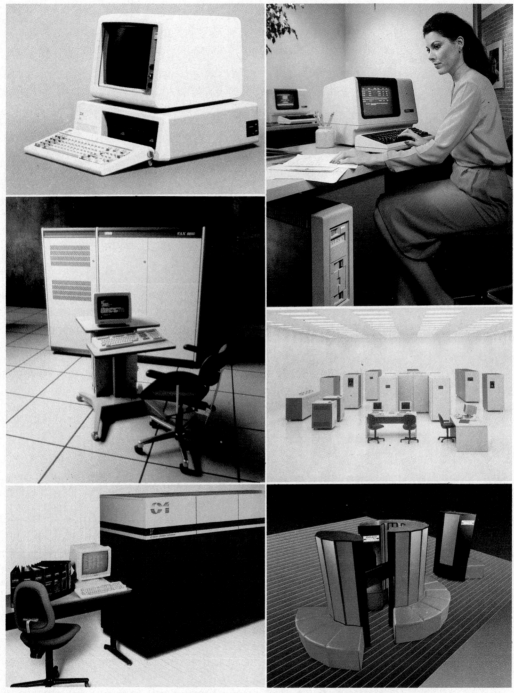

Left to right: The IBM PC is a microcomputer; Digital Equipment Corporation's Micro PDP-11 is a supermicrocomputer; the Digital Vax 8800 is a superminicomputer; the IBM 3090 is a mainframe computer; the Convex C-1 is a minisupercomputer; and the CRAY is a supercomputer.

■ Which computer careers will provide the most new jobs in the near future?

■ What are the five generations of computers?

Technological Changes in Computers

Computer manufacturers are working on new technologies that will greatly increase the speed and lower the cost of computers. You may enjoy following the new developments over time as computers become more sophisticated.

How much have prices fallen for the bigger computers? How fast will innovation occur? A look back will give you some perspective. John Blankenbaker built the first personal computer in 1971.[5] It was called the Kenbak 1, and it had no keyboard or screen. About that same time, Edward Roberts introduced a computer called the Altair. Its storage capacity was about one paragraph. But it and the Kenbak 1 began the microcomputer era—only a little more than a decade ago. The Altair was displayed at the Homebrew Computer Club in Palo Alto, California. Two club members, Stephen Wozniak and Stephen Jobs, liked the idea and proceeded to build their own similar computer in a garage. They named their product Apple 1.

In just a few years we have gone from these primitive models to today's sophisticated personal computers, and technology is changing even faster today. What will computers be like in the future? They will be as different in 10 years as they were 10 years ago. Many, like some IBM models today, will be able to understand voice commands. Others will come close to being "intelligent computers," that is, able to think through problems. It is safe to say that such developments will be as significant as the industrial revolution. It is also safe to say that computers will be as common as telephones, TV sets, and radios. And that means jobs for you. The very first computer was used by a business in 1954, when GE installed one at its Appliance Park in Kentucky. Think of all the computer jobs that have been created since then, and think of all the jobs that will come in the next 35 years!

More Power on a Chip

A hair from your head has a diameter of about 100 microns. Imagine, if you can, 4,500 transistors in that space. Before the end of the century (little more than 20 years from now), James Meindl, codirector of Stanford University's Center for Integrated Systems, predicts that there will be "gigascale integration," or a billion components to a chip.[6] Experts predict that within 5 years one chip will be able to do the work of today's mainframes. For example, there is currently an attempt to recreate the sounds of an entire orchestra, all on one chip.

Imagine further a pocket secretary that speaks and can be spoken to. It organizes messages, schedules meetings, and issues reminders. Such consumer aids will soon be available and will be inexpensive. The cost of storing data on computers is predicted to fall by 35% a year.

Imagine being able to carry a mainframe computer on your arm like a wristwatch. What are the possibilities for robotics, automotives, and electronics? To realize the full potential of computer hardware and the new integrated circuits (chips), new software must be developed.

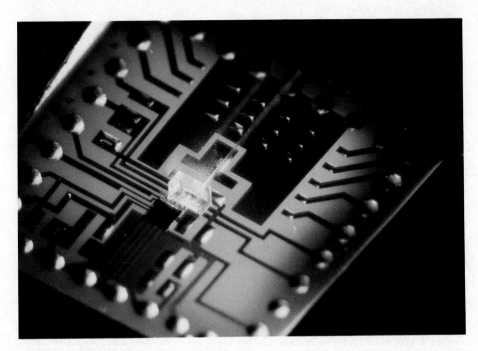

An enlarged view of a computer chip.

COMPUTER SOFTWARE

Computer software (programs) provide the instructions that enable you to tell the computer what to do. At one time, computer users developed much of their own software. To do that, they had to learn a computer language.

    Many businesspeople today are more concerned about finding the right software (instructions) than they are about the right hardware (the specific kind of computer they buy). The idea is to choose software that will do the jobs you want, and then find a computer that will accept that software.

    Software is like a record. If you want to hear a certain singer or orchestra, you buy that particular record. The record may be an old 78 or a new laser disk. The type of records you buy dictates the kind of record player (hardware) you need.

computer software
The instructions for telling the computer what to do.

Stores like Computerland help in the selection of computers.

Some software programs are easier to use than others. Some are more so-phisticated and can perform more functions. A businessperson must decide what functions he or she wants performed by a computer and then choose the appropriate software. That choice will help decide what make and size computer to buy.

It is important to recognize the fact that we are in the pioneering stage of computer software development. When selecting a computer, therefore, it is a good idea to anticipate what kind of software is likely to come out in the future. Software writers tend to develop programs that fit the most popular computers (for example, IBM, Apple). If you were to buy a record player that played the old 78s, you wouldn't be able to play the newest records when they came out. That is what happened to many people who bought certain inexpensive home computers when the company that made those computers went out of business. Nobody is writing new programs for those computers and they are rapidly becoming obsolete.

PLANNING AND DESIGNING COMPUTER SYSTEMS

Thus far the integration of computers into the workplace has been rather disor-ganized and uncoordinated. One manager may order a word processor for his or her staff, another may order personal computers for workers, and so on. What results is a mishmash of machines, most of which are not compatible and many of which go unused. Not until the last few years has it been possible to integrate data processing, word processing, interoffice communications, external commu-nications, printing, and other office-related functions. This was done using both new hardware and software. Now that such systems are available, the manager of any organization (small or large, profit or nonprofit) should follow these ten steps when planning office automation:

1 Identify the information needs of all the workers and managers and decide if additional computer resources are needed.
2 Involve all the departments in the planning process.
3 Seek input from the existing data processing department, if there is one.
4 Seek other expert advice.
5 Choose software first and integrate existing equipment with new equip-ment if possible.
6 Decide whether to buy equipment or use a computer service.
7 Evaluate equipment to be purchased and the vendor for price, quality, and service.
8 Train employees in computer use.
9 Update the system and training periodically.
10 Integrate computer communications with other communication efforts and other corporate operations.

Identify Information Needs

"What the growing business needs is a solution to the problem of getting the right data to the right person at the right time," says Burton Grad, computer industry specialist. "*Owning* a computer may or may not be the most cost-effective solution to such problems."[7] To determine what system is best, the starting point is to work with managers and workers to find what their needs are. A needs-assessment program looks at information needs, equipment needs, space needs, human involvement needs, and more. Needs assessment is also the first step in buying your own home computer.

Involve All Departments

Every business or organization has some primary function, such as accounting, production, marketing, or retailing. But each organization also has multiple tasks it must perform to assist in the primary function. Some obvious tasks involve payroll, inventory control, billing, employee records (for example, sick leave or vacations), and more. To design the most effective and efficient computer system, the needs of all departments must be considered. The real efficiencies in the future will come from integrated computer systems that allow managers of various departments to communicate with each other by computer and get needed data from a central information storage area. (See the illustration below.)

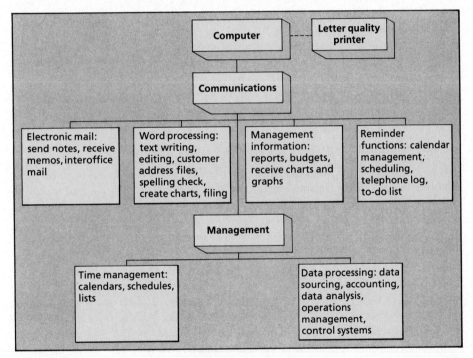

The computer as a management assistant.

Seek Input from the Data Processing Department

In the past, the information systems department tended to be located off by itself, and the managers and workers were treated as aliens who spoke a strange language called *computerese*. Periodically these "computer jocks" would send out reports on funny-looking computer paper that contained columns of numbers and graphs that were understood by few and used by fewer. The gulf between information systems specialists and line managers was often wide.

Today that lack of understanding and rapport can no longer be tolerated. Computers are supposed to make management and decision making easier and more accurate, not harder and more complex. The planning phase of computer development must involve all managers, including data processing experts, from the beginning. If the needs of one group of managers are given special attention, it should be the users, not the data processing people.

Seek Other Expert Advice

The cost of hiring an outside expert to evaluate the needs of the organization and recommend a solution is well worth it in the long run. An inside expert may be too committed to the present system or too biased by his or her own department's needs to provide the objective analysis needed. An experienced consultant may recommend an outside computer service or some kind of time-sharing system that would prove significantly cheaper and more flexible than other options.

Choose Software First

"Selection of the software precedes any deep or serious consideration of hardware," counsels Douglas Altenbern of Endata, Incorporated. He says, "Too many people select the hardware first, then try to find the right software package. It's a common mistake and a serious one that a seasoned computer consultant is not likely to make."[8] Note this step when selecting a personal computer for yourself.

At one time, people had to develop their own software to meet their specific needs. Today, however, the new software programs available for purchase are flexible enough to be used by most businesses.

Decide Whether to Buy or Use a Computer Service

Before running out to buy equipment that could soon become obsolete or need costly servicing, an organization may consider contracting with computer service companies to perform various functions. Just one such firm, Automatic Data Processing (ADP) of Roseland, New Jersey, handles computer problems, including payroll, of 100,000 customers averaging 70 employees each.

One type of service, called *remote processing,* works like this: An organization obtains special forms from a computer service company and fills in all the necessary information. The service company picks up the forms and processes them at its own "remote" facility (thus the term *remote processing*). The service company then provides the desired results—sales analyses, paychecks, bills, and so forth.

Another version of computer service is called *on-line remote processing.* A service company provides the organization with a computer terminal. The service company then trains someone at the organization to input the necessary data. The information then travels over phone lines to the service company and is sent back in processed form to the organization. Large national service firms as well as smaller regional firms provide such services.

A third option for a firm wishing to use outside services is called *time-sharing.* Time-sharing gives small and large firms the capability of using complex software programs and data files too expensive to be purchased by any one firm. Sometimes the data simply are not available any other way.

Individuals and smaller firms have found it valuable to use computer services that contain much information and sources. Two popular firms providing such data are The Source and Compuserve.

All of these options should be considered before equipment is purchased.

Nonetheless, the new computers are so small, inexpensive, and powerful that they are affordable by individuals and very small firms. The problem may then become one of deciding which functions to do internally and which to farm out to computer service firms.

Evaluate Equipment and Vendors

It is not always a good idea to buy a computer from the producer. The tendency is for the producer to sell you a computer, printer, software, and other accessories all made by that firm. As with stereo systems, however, it is sometimes best to buy different components from different manufacturers.

Like stereo stores, computer stores are often helpful in putting together a package system of various brand-name components to form a useful (and often cheaper) computer system. Such stores may also provide helpful training and service.

Train Employees

Many firms have seriously neglected the task of training their workers and managers to use the new word processing and data processing equipment. It is not enough to put people through a 1-week training course and assume that they are now proficient workers. Training must continue over time to help workers become familiar with all of the capabilities of the computers. Often the people least skilled in the use of computers are top managers. Certainly they should leave the more complex analyses to lower level workers, but top managers should be able to access even the most sophisticated information if needed. Productivity is the real goal of office automation, including top management productivity. And that takes training and retraining.

Training workers on computers.

Update System, Including Training

It bears repeating that computer technology, software, and procedures are changing week by week. To keep up, managers must be flexible and open to new ideas, and retraining must occur regularly.

Integrate Computer and Personal Communication

One danger of automating offices is that the firm becomes too impersonal, too mechanical. People are often hidden in cubicles behind a computer terminal, and human contact is minimized. Such isolation can be stressful and demoralizing. Managers of such workers need to practice more management by walking around, have more social functions, and provide more opportunities for interpersonal contact during breaks, at lunch, and after work.

Electronic communication can never replace human communication for creating enthusiasm and esprit de corps. Efficiency and productivity can become so important to a firm that people are treated like robots. In the long run, that results in less efficiency and productivity. Computers are a tool, not a total replacement for managers or workers. Nothing is as creative or as fast at computing and integrating complex variables as the human mind. Creativity is still a human trait. Computers should aid creativity by giving people more freedom and more time.

PROGRESS CHECK

- What is the difference between computer hardware and computer software?

- Which should you choose first when designing a computer system for home or office use: hardware or software?

THE FUTURE OF COMPUTERS

The development of integrated computers will have a significant effect on top management in the future. Many bureaucratic functions can be replaced by technology. We talked in Chapter 13 about tall versus flat organization structures. Computers will tend to eliminate middle management functions and thus flatten organization structures:

- A sophisticated combination of word processing, electronic and voice mail, videoconferencing, and high-speed communications enabled Hercules Corporation to cut the levels of management from twelve to six.[9]
- Citicorp's North American Banking Group developed an information system to improve customer service and make account and market information available to clients more quickly. As a result, the staff was reduced by 500 people.

Perhaps the most revolutionary effect of computers may be the ability to allow employees to stay home and do their work from there.[10]

- Mrs. Donna Puccini works for Continental Illinois Bank. She and three other women work at home using word processors to type letters, memos, and statistical tables. The word processing machine is in a bedroom and is linked to Continental's downtown office. Donna's work is transmitted to the office and back as easily as walking into the boss's office.
- Control Data has about 100 employees working at home or at satellite offices. Employees in the program are analysts, programmers, managers, writers, and clerks.

Naturally such work involves less travel time and costs and often increases productivity. It enables men and women to stay home with small children and is a tremendous boon for disabled workers.

Modems

The device that allows people to stay at home and work with a computer at work is called a **modem.** A modem converts data into a form that can be sent over phone lines so that one computer can "talk" to another.

A problem with computers today and in the future will be *hackers,* people who break into computer systems for illegal purposes such as transferring funds from someone's bank account to their own without authorization. There is also a problem with privacy as more and more personal information is stored in computers, and people are able to access that data illegally. The person who develops a foolproof lock for computer data will make a fortune.

modem
Converts data into a form that can be sent over phone lines so that one computer can "talk" to another.

COMPUTERS AND HIGH-TECH GROWTH

Thus far we have been talking about using computers to process numbers (data processing) and words (word processing). Another major revolution is occurring in the use of computers to run machines, including robots. We have already discussed the use of computers in production firms in Chapter 14. Below we shall briefly review the consequences of such uses and discuss the linkages of computers, robots, phones, and other high-tech equipment.

Robotics

The computer revolution is obvious to anyone who watches TV or reads any of the business publications. What is less obvious is the slow but sure trend toward replacing American production workers with robots. The driving force behind the automation of factories is overseas competition. In 1965, for example, almost all the clothes American men wore were made in the United States. By 1986, half of the clothes were estimated to be foreign made. Employment in the clothing industry fell at a similar rate. The answer was to introduce robots.[11] One machine can fold and sew pieces of fabric to make sleeves, the backs of suit coats and vests, with a speed and precision that few humans can manage. A camera "eye" can locate pieces of material and guide the sewing head to the proper position.

robotics
The use of computer-driven machines to do work formerly done by humans.

ROBOTS GO NONPROFIT

In Miami, Florida, the Dade County police use a robot to retrieve and disarm bombs and incendiary devices. In some cities, robots carry fire hoses into areas where no human could go.

In Japan, shoebox-size "intellibots" travel between racks of videotapes and audiotapes in the stacks of a university library. It takes only 40 seconds from the time a student requests a tape until the robot finds and loads the tape into a recorder.

Personal robots are available that can vacuum your carpet. Others will watch for burglars and get the newspaper. So far, none are available to clean windows.

Won't machines replace workers and cause more unemployment? The answer is both *yes* and *no*. Machines will replace workers, but those workers might have lost their jobs anyway to foreign workers. By automating, American producers can remain competitive and maintain some employment. The net effect is likely to be better for workers than no robots. In fact, the clothing workers see robots as a way to save the industry.[12] Robots are used in nonprofit organizations as well. (See the box on p. 405.)

A robotic work station.

A visit to General Electric's newly automated locomotive plant in Erie, Pennsylvania will give you a feel for how the production plants of the twenty-first century will look. Running up and down a track is a robot-like vehicle carrying 2500-pound castings to nine large "smart" machines that are computer controlled and perform dozens of operations in sequence. This job once took 70 workers 16 days to complete. Now one computer technician and two semiskilled workers complete the job, using robots, in 16 hours. This new productivity enables GE to successfully compete with foreign producers of locomotives.

Similar success stories could be told of robot efficiencies in the steel and auto industries. From 1978 to 1984, Detroit employed 23% fewer auto workers to make 2% more cars during the same period. GM's newest auto plants are fully automated; computer-run robots make the plants more efficient than ever.

Intelligent Robots

Robot technology has improved dramatically in the last few years (see the box on p. 407). Today, "intelligent" robots are being used in factories. Some robots can "see" and "read" using cameras. One GE robot, for example, detects irregularities in welded seams and corrects any mistakes. Another GE robot reads identifying numbers in nuclear fuel rods. The newest robots can "feel" the difference between an egg and a piece of steel and handle each of them accordingly. Some robots even respond to voice commands.

WHAT CAN ROBOTS DO?

- When the Nippon Hoso Kyoku Symphony Orchestra played a concert in 1985, a robot was guest organist. The robot can sight-read musical scores.
- A robot in Australia sheared a whole flock of sheep.
- A computer program named Hitech joined 765 humans as a chess master.
- A Ping-Pong match was held in San Francisco between an English robot and an American one.

- A robot in Palo Alto, California can listen to music and then print out the score.
- A patent has been issued for a robot tractor that can plant, tend, and harvest crops.
- Two robots replaced 20 humans packaging lipstick.
- The RM3 robot can wash the hulls of ships and repaint them at a rate of 1¼ acres a day.

Source: Noel Perrin, "We Aren't Ready for Robots," *The Wall Street Journal*, February 25, 1986, p. 30.

It has been estimated that 70% to 90% of America's industrial workers could be replaced by robots. This possibility exists, but it won't necessarily happen. The point is that computers linked with robots can perform dirty, difficult, repetitive tasks faster, cheaper, and better than people. To remain competitive, American industry will have to adopt the new technologies. By facing that reality now, industry can begin retraining workers, and schools can begin preparing future workers for the jobs of tomorrow.

However, some computer advances have largely positive effects for everyone. Especially interesting are the new technological breakthroughs in phone systems and videotex.

Telephone Technology

There have been great advances in phone technology over the last decade, and more innovations are coming. Part of the success of the computer revolution will be the interfirm transfer of information from computer to computer, and much of that linkage will be over phone lines. In addition to that growth in phone transmission will be the growth of telemarketing, cellular phones, teleconferencing, and picturephones (videophones).

Cellular Phones

For many years, people who wanted a mobile phone in their car, truck, or other vehicle were frustrated by the limitations of use. The problem was that under the old system (called IMTS, for Improved Mobile Telephone Service), it was difficult to get a dial tone. The reason was that each metropolitan area had only 12 channels broadcast from a single antenna; therefore, only a dozen customers could use the system at one time. Clearly this severely limited the growth and use of mobile phones.

Recently, however, there has been a breakthrough in mobile phone technology called *cellular telephone service*. **Cellular phone systems** get their name from the way that the phone signals are relayed from one geographical cell to another, making it easier to get an open line. The way it works is this. Each city or metropolitan area is divided into sectors or cells, each with its own antenna. All the cells use the same frequencies, which enables a conversation to be traded off from cell to cell as needed.

cellular phone systems
The latest mobile phone technology that transfers calls between "cells" as the user moves from one geographical area to another.

Cellular phones.

"How I work my CyberPhone to accelerate my drive for success."

Larry LeGrand, one of the youngest partners in the history of Peat, Marwick, Mitchell & Co. Today at 34, a leader in Peat, Marwick's Private Business Advisory Services group and one of the firm's numerous partners who use CyberTel Cellular.

A superior time-manager, LeGrand works his CyberTel Cellular telephone service to accelerate his daily effectiveness, accomplishing more in one day than some accomplish in a month. And driving him closer to his peak of personal success.

Today's log:

07.15: Heading downtown for breakfast meeting. Called Denny McDaniel, Capital Bank and Trust. Discussed Florida real estate deal and new business opportunities for bank.

09.10: Off to Clayton. Called CyberTel's Traffic Cybermation. "How's the traffic on westbound 40?"

09.15: Called Pierre LaBarge, LaBarge, Inc. Discussed sale of investment property and its effect on '86 taxes.

09.35: Called office. Will have Steve Laux re-run LaBarge's projections based on sale of above properties. Will review when I get to office.

10.45: Now east on 40. Discussed new international currency fund and tax consequences to investors with Richard Grote, Grote Financial Futures.

10.55: Called Sister Margaret Gregg at St. Joseph Institute for the Deaf. Reviewed agenda for next board meeting.

01.10: Head for office. Returned call to E. Schultz, Code Consultants. Reviewed potential investments and discussed children's trust fund.

03.10: Back to Clayton. Arranged for meeting with Jim Samson, Community Federal. Discussed tax advantages of investing in adjustable rate preferred stocks.

03.20: Returned call to Randy Whitelaw, The Whitelaw Group. Discussed year-end planning, including potential for deferred compensation program.

03.25: Called Tom Erickson at PMM. "Review Whitelaw's '86 projections and come up with planning ideas. Will discuss when I return."

03.27: Called CyberTel's Business Cybermation for today's business news update.

06.20: Returned call to Denny McDaniel. Florida real estate deal is a go.

06.35: Called Dot. I'm on the way home.

All over St. Louis, achievers like Larry LeGrand are discovering the increased speed and efficiency harnessed in every CyberTel Cellular CyberPhone.

Isn't it time you discovered it as well? Make the sound business move and call 444-4444. In Illinois, 1-800 MOBILE 4.

‖‖‖ CyberTel
CyberTel Cellular Telephone Company

Each of the cells has a minimum of 78 channels, and this results in far fewer busy signals. Each city will have a couple of cellular systems operating, making it possible to have 100,000 calls per hour.

Such systems will enable executives to dictate work to their office and conduct business by phone from anywhere. Big-city executives who spend a couple of hours commuting will be able to use that time productively. Phone calls are now possible from airplanes too, and some phones make it possible to access computer data from public areas such as airports and hotel lobbies.

CELLULAR PHONES IN REAL ESTATE

Salespeople will likely be the biggest users of cellular phones. Appointments can be made and verified over the phone (to prevent calling on someone who is not in, even though the salesperson had made an appointment). Salespeople will be able to phone in orders and do all kinds of work over the phone (in the car) that once required much more time. Salespeople will also be able to receive information and messages. This will make them much more aware and in touch.

Los Angeles real estate broker Walter Sanford uses his car as a mobile office with a cellular phone system. Sanford specializes in rental properties. Using his cel-lular phone, he can call his office, obtain new listings, and compute projected rental earnings without leaving his car. Using a Texas Instruments 707 portable computer terminal and his phone, he can hook into a Long Beach Board of Realtors data base and obtain current information on available property or tap into specially designed computer software to do computations on possible deals. In a sprawling and fast-moving real estate market such as Los Angeles, such mobility is very valu-able. In fact, Sanford increased sales by 20% to 30% with the new cellular system.

Source: Roger Beynon, Joseph Fulvio, and Reed Trask, "Emerging Computer/Telecommunication Solutions for Growing Corporation," *Inc.*, February, 1985, p. 106.

THINKING IT THROUGH

Are you familiar with all the terms discussed in this chapter? Can you see that they will soon be as commonplace as terms such as *steering wheel, fender, drive shaft,* and *spark plug* are now? Computers and other high-tech machinery will soon be as widespread as TV sets and automobiles. How can you take advantage of this in your career planning? How will it affect market-ing? Management? Retailing?

Microwave and Satellite Transmission

Businesses are not limited to communication through cable systems. Messages can also be sent through the air using microwave technology and satellites. These systems allow for the integration of voice, data, and images in a single data stream. This makes it possible to send phone conversations or electronic mail, to link computers, or to conduct teleconferences. A **teleconference** is a business meeting held by executives located in different buildings in different parts of the world who talk to each other while watching each other on TV screens. This is clearly much cheaper than having everyone fly to a central meeting place for a conference.

The least expensive way to transmit data is from one microwave dish to another dish. No doubt you have seen such dishes on the tops of buildings. If not, look around in major cities and you will see them. The problem is that such systems are limited to 20 miles or so. There must be a clear line of sight between dishes for the system to work well.

For long-distance communication, it is best to use satellite networks. Satellite communication is often less expensive than land-based communication. Even smaller companies can participate by sharing satellite use with other firms on a fee basis.

teleconference
Conducting business meetings over phone lines and TV screens so that executives lo-cated in different geographic areas can see and talk to each other.

A satellite dish.

A combination of microwave dishes and satellites has been developed. Signals are shot at satellites by microwave dishes and are rebounded to receiving dishes on the ground. Using such a system, Mary Kay Cosmetics held a conference at the Dallas Convention Center that was fed through a combination microwave/satellite system to 100,000 employees and agents.[13] The reason for discussing such uses is to introduce you to the possibilities for the future. We are in a primitive stage of communications technology. To become part of the growth of this new industry, you will have to read the business literature and take some courses to get hands-on experience. It is a good idea to visit firms with advanced communication systems to see and touch and experience for yourself the possibilities.

Telemarketing

telemarketing
Uses the telephone to allow consumers to order merchandise, ask questions, and keep in contact with businesses.

We must not forget that one goal of business is to communicate more effectively with consumers. Telemarketing is a big boost in that direction. **Telemarketing** is the use of the telephone to establish two-way communication links with consumers that enable them to order merchandise by phone, ask questions, and generally keep in close contact with businesses. Telemarketing is also a way for a business to screen potential customers, ask them questions, and aid them in buying goods and services.

There is a natural link between cable TV and telemarketing. Ads on special cable programs have promoted everything from *Sports Illustrated* on the sports network to *Prevention* magazine on the health network. All customers had to do was dial the 800 number on the screen to place an order.

Increased credit card use has also helped with such sales. A customer can call an 800 number to buy a product, give the credit card number over the phone, and have the order delivered immediately. People could also call 800 numbers to find the nearest dealer or service center.

Computers are often used to screen potential customers and to pinpoint markets where telemarketing promotions are aimed. Another growth area is 900 numbers. These numbers are used for people to "vote" for issues presented on TV shows. Think of the possibilities for doing market research over the phone; TV viewers can call to register their reaction to new products or product changes. The final link in the communications revolution is the one between producers and consumers, and the phone will be a critical part of that communications chain.

CAREER INFORMATION: COMPUTER AND PERIPHERAL EQUIPMENT OPERATORS

NATURE OF THE WORK

The duties of computers and peripheral equipment operators vary with the size of the installation, the type of equipment used, and the policies of the employer. In organizations with small computer systems, for example, computer operators may run both the computer and all the peripheral equipment such as printers, disk drives, and tape readers. In large computer installations, computer operators specialize in console operation while peripheral equipment operators run the related devices. Generally, the duties of computer operators and peripheral equipment operators involve the following tasks.

Working from operating instructions prepared by programmers or operations managers, computer operators set controls on the computer and on peripheral devices required to run a particular job. Computer operators or, in large installations, peripheral equipment operators, load the equipment with tapes, disks, and paper as needed. While the computer is running—which may be 24 hours a day for large computers—computer operators monitor the computer console and respond to operating and computer messages. If an error message occurs, for example, operators must locate the problem and solve it or terminate the program.

Peripheral equipment operators may have to prepare printouts and other output for distribution to computer users. Operators also maintain log books listing events such as machine malfunctions that occurred during their shift. Computer operators also may supervise and train peripheral equipment operators and computer operator trainees. They also may help programmers and systems analysts test and debug new programs.

JOB OUTLOOK

Employment of computer and peripheral equipment operators is expected to rise much faster than the average for all occupations through the mid 1990s.

Advances in technology have reduced both the size and the cost of computer equipment while at the same time increasing their capacity for data storage and processing. These improvements in technology have fueled an expansion in the use of computers in such areas as factory and office automation, telecommunications, medicine, and education. As computer usage grows, so will the need for computer operators and peripheral equipment operators. Because computer and peripheral equipment operators work mainly with large computer systems—the part of the overall computer market that has slowed down—employment of operators is not expected to rise as rapidly as in previous years.

EARNINGS

In 1984, median weekly earnings of full-time computer operators were $300. The middle 50 percent earned between $230 and $415. The lowest 10 percent of computer operators earned $190 or less a week, and the top 10 percent earned more than $540.

Weekly earnings of beginning computer operators averaged about $340 in 1984. Experienced workers averaged about $345, and lead operators about $415. Peripheral equipment operators earned about $325 a week. In the Federal Government, computer operators without work experience started at about $245 a week in 1985. Operators employed in manufacturing, transportation and public utilities, and wholesale trade had higher earnings than those employed in retail trade, banking, insurance, and services.

RELATED OCCUPATIONS

Other occupations involving work with computers include systems analysts, programmers, and computer service technicians. Other occupations in which workers operate electronic office equipment include data entry keyers, secretaries, typists, and printing typesetters and compositors.

SOURCES OF ADDITIONAL INFORMATION

People who want further information about work opportunities in computer operations should contact firms that use computers such as banks, manufacturing and insurance firms, colleges and universities, and data processing service organizations. The local office of the State employment service is another source of information about employment and training opportunities.

Source: *Occupational Outlook Handbook,* 1986-1987 (U.S. Department of Labor, Bureau of Labor Statistics).

Videotex: Linking You with the Computer Age

videotex
A system that allows the general public to access a central computer that provides various services such as news, games, banking, and electronic mail.

There was great excitement and anticipation in the early 1980s about the future of videotex. **Videotex,** basically, is a system that allows the general public to tap into a central computer that provides a variety of services such as news, shopping hints, games, banking, advertising messages, electronic mail (sending notes to other users), and educational programs. You can see why there is excitement in the industry. This seems like a great idea once the system is operating efficiently.

An early experiment with videotex was conducted in test markets by Times Mirror Videotex Services in 1982.[14] Some 350 volunteers used the service and gave their reactions. The service included 70,000 pages of information on subjects such as sports, recreation, health, travel, home decorating, and the Yellow Pages. It also included over 200,000 words of up-to-date news, shopping services (merchandise, tickets, flight schedules), home banking, games, and more.

Users particularly enjoyed the games, shopping information, bill paying, late-breaking news, educational programs, and electronic note sending. Other experiments have found that consumers like the idea of connecting their homes to fire and burglar alarm systems, automatic reading of gas and electric meters, making travel reservations, and storing information such as addresses, phone numbers, and recipes for later retrieval. Early attempts at marketing this technology have not been highly successful. It could be that these early tries just came too soon.

Someday some form of interactive video may become necessary to optimize information links among consumers and businesses. It may be called *videotex* or something else, but there likely will be such systems. This discussion has introduced some uses that are already available. Can you think of more? Think of electronic gambling and contests among users. What about exchanging recipes, handling license plate applications, and conducting job searches? The potential seems unlimited, and you have the opportunity to be in on the ground floor of this exciting new industry.

PROGRESS CHECK

■ Can you describe the advances in telephone technology?

■ What are some uses of videotex?

SUMMARY

1 Because we are now in the information age, it is wise to consider some of the possibilities for careers in computers. At least, you need to know computer terms and uses.

■ What careers are growing fastest in the computer field?
   Computer and peripheral equipment operators are first, next comes programmers, then systems analysts.

2 We are in the fifth generation of computers, the era of *artificial intelligence*.

■ What were the first four generations?
   1. Computers used vacuum tubes and were hot and bulky.
   2. Computers used smaller, cooler transistors and diodes.
   3. Computers used integrated circuits on silicon chips.
   4. Computers used very large-scale integrated circuits (VLSI).

- How do *expert* systems relate to artificial intelligence?

  Expert systems can store and manipulate knowledge and rules-of-thumb as well as data. They can "reason" by drawing inferences from this knowledge.

- How does parallel processing fit the new generation?

  Parallel processing strings together thousands of processors so that computers can work faster. Such speed and linkages are needed to simulate thinking.

3 *Computer hardware* includes all the tangible machines that process and store data.

- What are the categories of hardware?

  Microcomputers are the personal computers used at home or in the office (.0005 MIPs or *million instructions per second*).

  Supermicrocomputers are much faster and more expensive than microcomputers (.36 MIPS).

  Superminicomputers do 1 MIPS.

  Mainframe computers do 28 MIPS.

  Minisupercomputers do 60 MIPS.

  Supercomputers do 1,000 MIPS.

  Parallel systems do more MIPS than supercomputers.

4 *Computer software* is the instructions that tell a computer what to do. Most software today is on disks of some kind.

- What steps should be followed in choosing computer hardware and software?

  The ten steps recommended in this chapter are: (1) identify the information needs of all managers, (2) involve all departments in the planning process, (3) seek input from the data processing department, (4) get external advice, (5) choose software first and try to integrate old with new equipment, (6) decide whether to buy or rent equipment or use a service, (7) evaluate equipment, (8) train employees, (9) update the system periodically, and (10) integrate computer communications with other communication efforts.

5 In future, computers will automate the office and cut out staff personnel.

- Will work habits change as well?

  Absolutely. Many computer workers could work from home. Disabled workers would benefit greatly. A *modem* is the device that enables computers to "talk" with one another.

6 Robots will link with computers to do many dirty, repetitive, and skilled jobs.

- What can robots do?

  They can read, play, and write music; play Ping-Pong; paint, weld, play chess, shear sheep, run tractors; and more.

7 Other high-tech tools are available to business as well.

- What are some of these tools?

  They include cellular phones for cars, microwave and satellite communications, teleconferencing, telemarketing, and videotex.

GETTING INVOLVED

1 Talk to a computer programmer, a systems analyst, a data processing manager, and others in the computer field. Have others in the class do the same. Share your findings.

2 Go to the local magazine stand and buy a couple of the latest magazines for computer buffs. What is the latest in hardware and software? How do speed and costs compare to those mentioned in this chapter? How small are portables getting? Discuss your findings with the class.

3 Go to the computer lab at school and become as familiar as possible with the system. Then write a 3-page report on the hardware used, the software available, the procedures, hours, and so forth. Keep the report for any future computer use you may have and share it with the class.

4 There are emerging careers in several high-tech industries (for example, biotechnology). Read the latest computer magazines and find out what these careers are.

5 Find a secretary who has used both a typewriter and a word processor. Ask which is easier and why. Ask for a demonstration. You can do this at a computer store. Try to get some hands-on experience doing word processing. Try to have the copy printed on a letter-quality printer.

6 If you are completely computer literate, find someone in your class or in high school who is not and teach that person how to use the computer. Nothing increases learning as much as teaching others.

KEY TERMS

artificial intelligence p. 395	**peripheral equipment operators**
cellular phone systems p. 408	p. 392
computer hardware p. 394	**programmers** p. 392
computer operators p. 392	**robotics** p. 405
computer software p. 399	**systems analysts** p. 393
expert systems p. 395	**teleconference** p. 409
MIPS p. 396	**telemarketing** p. 410
modem p. 405	**videotex** p. 412
parallel processing p. 395	

PRACTICING MANAGEMENT DECISIONS

CASE ONE   IMPLEMENTING COMPUTER TECHNOLOGY AT GENERAL FOODS

Not too long ago the managers at General Foods got their data from a central data processing department. Reports were slow in coming, and their format was inflexible. If an answer led to further questions, it often took weeks to get the desired information. The marketing people simply were not able to respond quickly enough to market conditions.

Two events changed all of this. One was the development of personal computers and software that could perform multiple functions. The second was the realization by General Foods management that they needed better decision-making tools. Now, survey results that once took 5 months to process, and cost $5,000, can be done in 5 minutes on a spreadsheet.

At first, new computer technology was not introduced in any organized manner at GF. It started when the vice-president of information management bought a Radio Shack Computer. A man in the tax department bought an Apple computer. In both cases the computers added to productivity and lowered costs. As more and more people brought in their own PCs, it became apparent that such machines were the wave of the future.

The firm then created a management information system group to make data available to marketing personnel. The idea was not just to bring in PCs, but to optimize data availability. Decisions had to be made about where PCs should be placed and who would be responsible for them. To answer such questions, a marketing advisory council was formed. Input was sought from information systems people as well as marketing managers. Both long-range and short-range needs were analyzed to be sure the technology would not become obsolete too quickly.

Input was sought from all departments. It was decided to introduce the program from the top down. The theory was that top managers needed to understand the system to support it. Special training programs were introduced to show top managers the technology and functions. Managers were encouraged to take computers home. Eventually, courses were offered to spouses and children.

After this training, vice-presidents, directors, and functional heads were consulted, and they were trained. Finally, a training facility was set up for employees. An internal marketing campaign was launched to get employees interested and involved.

Because top management was involved from the beginning, they were more accepting of the program and flexible in allowing users to come up with new uses. Soon there were 300 personal computers in use at General Foods, and 4,000 people had been trained in their use.

Today General Foods has a mainframe computer; a minicomputer is set up in each division; and several microcomputer systems are in use: Apple, Radio Shack, IBM, and Compaq. Wang word processors were replaced with Wang PCs for secretaries.

The biggest limitation now at General Foods is not hardware, but software. People want to do more, and the programs are simply not available. Users are responsible for getting their own funding if they want more equipment. Management wants the system to serve users, so users design the program to fit their needs. The computer center is a service department that provides training, education, research, and testing of hardware and software. It also acts as an in-house consulting group to help end users.

General Foods is linked to several external data suppliers. The divisional minicomputers store internal sales data plus data from external suppliers. The mainframe has sales data and financial data that is accessible by both minis and micros. Overall, the system is well integrated, even though many different manufacturers are involved.

DECISION QUESTIONS

1 Evaluate the process General Foods followed in designing and implementing its computer system. Did it use the ten steps in the text?

2 What is your reaction to the fact that General Foods uses several different computer makers (Apple, Radio Shack, IBM, Compaq, and Wang)? Do you see advantages and disadvantages?

3 What is your reaction to the idea of introducing computers to top management first rather than give them to operating-level employees first?

This case is from Virginia Dudek, "The Plugged-in Marketers at General Foods," *Marketing Communications,* March, 1984, pp. C9-C13.

CASE TWO   ELECTRONIC SHOPPING—WHAT NEXT?

PRACTICING MANAGEMENT DECISIONS

Picture this. You walk into one of the new, large shopping malls. Maybe it is as big as the mile-long mall in Canada with 57 entrances. You dread the idea of going from store to store on a busy Saturday shopping for gifts for the holidays. Suddenly you notice something new in the center. It is a kiosk with a video screen inside. It looks like a giant video game. It is called an *Electronistore.*

Curious, you step inside and sit down. On the screen appears a hostess who welcomes you and asks whether or not you've used the service before. You say "No" by pressing a button, and step-by-step instructions appear.

You decide to explore the household appliances listing to see what's available. A subcategory of microwave ovens appears in the list. You ask for that list and see prices and product descriptions. If you want more details, you push the "details" button and get answers to questions such as whether or not the oven has a browning element.

Fascinated by the possibilities, you push buttons other categories, such as stereo equipment, shoes, and so on. If you see what you want for yourself and for gifts, you can insert your credit card and place an order. There is no salesperson and no standing in line.

The company that makes the Electronistore (Donnelley) expected sales of $256 million in 1985 and $17 billion by 1990. The Electronistore has several advantages:

- It allows for quick and easy comparison shopping.
- It provides in-depth product information.
- Merchandise can be demonstrated.
- Some 500 different items can be displayed.
- Shoppers enjoy using the service.

Electronistores are just the beginning of interactive electronic shopping, however. You still have to go to the kiosk and wait if others are using it. What if you could call up all the information desired on your own TV screen using interactive cable TV? Then you could do all of your shopping at home. Your computer would be the equivalent of a giant catalog capable of demonstrating products and taking your order. That is the reality of the late 1980s. What is next? Now that consumers can interact with producers electronically, what information needs to be exchanged with what result?

DECISION QUESTIONS

1 Which system seems to have the greater potential for success: electronic kiosks in stores or interactive TV in the home?
2 What kinds of *services* (not goods) could be sold over interactive TV systems?
3 Many people (especially those over 45) say that there is no need for a home computer. "What do you use them for, anyhow?" they say. Discuss the future of interactive TV and its uses for obtaining the latest news, banking, shopping, and more. Brainstorm all the possibilities to get a view of the future.

LOOKING AHEAD

Computers are fine for doing many tasks, and robots are fantastic as well. Still, no machine is as creative and flexible as a human being. But human beings need motivation. They need careful attention too. Chapter 16 explores the motivation of workers. We shall look at motivation theory and practice. This material is part of a broader topic called *human resource management*. We have learned how to select and program machines. In the following chapter, we'll learn how to select and motivate people.

Appendix:
Helpful Computer Terms

One of the more intimidating parts of getting involved with computers is the terminology. People can feel so overwhelmed by the words used to explain computers that they are overly nervous about actually working with computers. Playing computer games is a good way to learn that working with a computer is easier than it may appear at first. Let's review some of the more common terms, so you are comfortable discussing computers with others:

accessing Transferring data to or, more commonly, getting data from a storage device such as a floppy disk, to view, manipulate, and process it.

applications programs (software) Programs that do functions (for example, word processing, games, spreadsheet analysis, data base management, accounting) that are relatively complicated and specific to one area, such as accounting or inventory control.

artificial intelligence The attempt to get computers to think like humans. AI programs can learn from their mistakes and correct themselves. "The computer chess programs keep getting better by using artificial intelligence." A "smart" computer is not quite as brainy as an "intelligent" computer.

BASIC A programming language. "I programmed the computer using BASIC."

batch processing Data are collected for a predetermined time period before being processed and are run automatically by the computer in some priority order (that is, the user need not be there).

BDOS Pronounced *bee doss,* this means "basic disk operating system." It refers to that part of the program that customizes it to your particular system.

binary number The numbers that computers understand. Basically, computers use only two symbols (0 and 1) to express any number, no matter how large.

bit Short for *binary digit,* a bit is the smallest unit of information. A bit is expressed in binary numbers as either 0 or 1.

byte A byte is eight *bits.* This is the amount of information required to define one character (for example, one letter).

chip Chips are the basic building blocks of computers. They are also called *integrated circuits* or *ICs.* A computer chip is smaller than a baby's fingernail and yet contains thousands of switches (transistors). The brain of a computer is a chip called the *microprocessor* or *central processing unit* (CPU). It performs all the calculations and handles all information coming in to the computer and sends it back out.

COBOL A more advanced computer language for businesses.

command Anything you tell a computer to do.

cps "Characters per second;" refers to how fast printers make words. You multiply cps by 10 to get actual words per minute.

CRT Cathode ray tube; a screen like the one on your TV set. It is an input and output device that shows users desired information.

cursor A signal that tells you where you are on the CRT screen.

data base A large collection of data that a computer can look through to find needed information. An example would be all the names, addresses, and phone numbers of customers.

dedicated word processor A computer designed to do nothing but word processing.

disk drive A device that writes information onto and reads information from a disk (also spelled *disc*). Disks may be floppy or hard. Floppy disks come in different sizes. Hard disks hold more data and cost more money. Disks store both the data the computer generates and computer programs (software).

Dvorak keyboard A different arrangement of keys from the standard; this arrangement allows you to type faster.

EDP Electronic data processing.

electronic mail The sending and receiving of messages over a computer network.

electronic spreadsheet program A software program that makes financial projection, budgeting, and planning easier.

FORTRAN A high-level computer language mainly for scientific and mathematical use.

hardware The physical components of the computer system as opposed to software (the instructions).

integrated circuit An electronic circuit that has been put on a chip.

joystick The stick used to move objects in video games and also to move the cursor where desired.

K   See *byte*.

keyboard   That part of the computer that looks like a typewriter. It is handy if it is portable or attached with a flexible cable to allow you to set it in a comfortable position. A keyboard is usually attached to a CRT (video screen).

kilobyte   1024 bytes. This is about 170 actual words. A kilobyte takes up about two-thirds of a double-spaced page (1-inch margins, pica type). The amount of memory in a computer and floppy disk capacity are often measured in kilobytes (K). "My computer has 640K of memory."

letter-quality printer   A printer attached to a computer that prints out words in a form acceptable for business correspondence.

memory   Where information and programs are stored and manipulated in the computer. *RAM* means "random access memory." Larger computers have 512K bytes of memory or more. *ROM* stands for "read-only memory." It tells the computer what to do, but you can't change what it says, like RAM. ROM goes away when you turn off the machine.

menu   A list of commands that you can choose from that is displayed on the screen.

message   Anything the computer tells you.

MIPS   Million instructions per second.

modem   A device that converts data into a form that can be transmitted over phone lines so one computer can "talk" to another.

mouse   Like a joystick, it moves the cursor to where you want it.

nanosecond   A billionth of a second.

network   The linking of several computers or computer terminals.

printer   An attachment to a computer that forms words like a typewriter.

software   The instructions (programs) that tell a computer what to do.

terminal   A device that looks like a TV set attached to a typewriter that sends information to a computer and receives information from the computer.

tutorial   A training manual explaining how to use hardware and/or software.

user friendly   A computer or software that is easy to use. The ultimate would be one that could understand voice commands and respond accordingly.

window   The part of a file that is on the screen at one time. Sometimes you can have more than one window displayed at the same time (with split screen).

word processing   Writing (typing) and editing material on a computer. Very much like typing, but said to be easier.

MANAGEMENT OF HUMAN RESOURCES

PART

V

CHAPTER 16
MOTIVATION OF WORKERS

CHAPTER 17
HUMAN RESOURCE MANAGEMENT

CHAPTER 18
EMPLOYEE-MANAGEMENT ISSUES: UNIONS, EXECUTIVE PAY, AND COMPARABLE WORTH

MOTIVATION OF WORKERS

After you have read and studied this chapter, you should be able to:

- Explain Taylor's scientific management and contrast it with modern motivation theories.
- Discuss the Hawthorne studies and their significance.
- Identify the needs in Maslow's hierarchy and demonstrate their relationship to modern motivation theories.
- Differentiate between X and Y managers.
- Describe Theory Z and its application in the United States.
- Explain motivators and hygiene factors in a job.
- Identify the steps involved in implementing a management by objectives (MBO) program.
- Discuss management by walking around.

PROFILE CHARLES P. McCORMICK OF McCORMICK & COMPANY

Look in your spice rack and you are likely to find spices from McCormick & Company, Inc. The man who founded the company was Willoughby McCormick. He was a stern master who reprimanded his employees for everything they did wrong. When old Willoughby left his office, the employees signaled each other by beating on the pipes and ringing the phone to warn others that Willoughby was coming. Everyone worked hard when Willoughby was around. But when he left, they let down. When Willoughby died, the plant was in trouble, in large part because of working conditions.

Willoughby's nephew Charles took over operations and turned things around; he cut hours, increased pay, and listened to the workers. A year later, the firm was in the black to stay. "Charlie" ran the company for 37 years.

Several things contribute to employee satisfaction at McCormick today: (1) workers are rarely let go; (2) employees can compete for better jobs; and (3) workers feel free to discuss problems with managers. (Executives come to the plant for lunch about once a month.)

Workers respond by working hard. They are motivated by the chance to move up and by the feeling that McCormick really cares about them. Charles McCormick

Charles P. McCormick.

421

The test of leadership is not to put greatness into humanity, but to elicit it, for the greatness is already there.

JAMES BUCHANAN

is a model for tomorrow's managers. We will discuss the book *Re-inventing the Corporation* at the end of this chapter. It and this chapter are about motivation—the kind practiced at McCormick now. ■

Source: Henry Jaffe, "Sour McCormick, Now 'Sweet' Shop," *Washington Business,* April 30, 1984, p. 31.

MOTIVATION AND LEADERSHIP

No matter where you end up being a leader—in school, in business, in sports, in the military, wherever—the key to your success will be whether or not you can motivate others to do the best they can. That is no easy job today when so many people feel bored and disinterested in work. Yet the fact is that people are willing to work and work hard *if* they feel that their work is appreciated and makes a difference. People are motivated by a variety of things, such as recognition, accomplishment, and status.

The purpose of this chapter is to teach you the concepts, theories, and practice of motivation. The most important person to motivate, of course, is yourself. One way to do that is to find the right job in the right organization that enables you to reach your goals in life. The whole purpose of this book is to help you in that search and to teach you how to succeed once you get there. One secret of success is to recognize that everyone else is on a similar search. Naturally, some are more committed than others. The job of a manager is to find that commitment, encourage it, and focus it on some common goal.

This chapter will begin with a look at some of the traditional theories of motivation. We shall then discuss the Hawthorne studies because they created a whole new interest in worker satisfaction and motivation. Next, we'll look at some assumptions about employees: Are they basically lazy, or willing to work if given the proper incentives? We shall also explore the traditional theorists. You will see their names over and over in the business literature: Mayo, Herzberg, Maslow, and McGregor. Finally, we shall look at the modern applications of these theories and the managerial procedures for implementing them.

EARLY MANAGEMENT STUDIES (TAYLOR)

The Beginning of Scientific Management Studies: Frederick Taylor

Frederick Taylor is known as the father of scientific management. His book, *The Principles of Scientific Management,* was published in 1911. Taylor's goal was to increase worker productivity so that both the firm and the worker could benefit from higher earnings. The way to improve productivity, Taylor thought, was to scientifically study the most efficient way to do things and then teach people those methods. Three elements were basic to his approach: time, methods, and rules of work. His most important tools were observation and the stopwatch.

A classic Taylor story involves his study of men shoveling rice coal and iron ore with the same shovel. Taylor felt that different materials called for different shovels. He proceeded to invent a wide variety of sizes and shapes of shovels and, with stopwatch in hand, measured output over time in what were called **time-motion studies.** Sure enough, an average person could shovel more (from 25 tons

time-motion studies
Studying the most efficient way of doing a job using a stopwatch.

to 35 tons per day) with the proper shovel using the most efficient motions. This led to time-motion studies of virtually every factory job. The most efficient way of doing things was determined and became the standard for setting goals.

Taylor's scientific management became the dominant strategy for improving productivity in the early 1900s. There were hundreds of time-motion specialists in plants throughout the country. One follower of Taylor was H. L. Gantt. He developed charts by which managers plotted the work of employees a day in advance down to the smallest detail. Frank and Lillian Gilbreth used Taylor's ideas in a 3-year study of bricklaying. They developed the principle of *motion economy*, which showed that every job could be broken down into a series of elementary motions called "therbligs"—Gilbreth spelled backward. They then analyzed each motion to make it more efficient.

You can imagine how workers felt having time and motion people studying their every move. **Scientific management** viewed people largely as robots that needed to be properly programmed. There was little concern for the psychological or human aspects of work.

scientific management
The process of studying workers to find the most efficient way of doing things and then teaching people those techniques.

The Hawthorne Studies (Mayo)

One of the studies that grew out of Taylor's research was conducted at the Western Electric Company's Hawthorne plant outside of Chicago. The study began in 1924 and ended 8 years later as one of the major studies in management literature. Let's see why.

The Western Electric Hawthorne plant.

The studies were conducted by Elton Mayo and colleagues from Harvard University. The idea was to test the degree of lighting associated with optimum productivity. In this respect, it was a traditional scientific management study: keep records of productivity under different levels of illumination.

The problem with the initial experiments was that the productivity of the experimental group compared to other workers doing the same job went up regardless of whether the lighting was bright or dim. This was true even when the lighting was reduced to about the level of moonlight. These results confused and frustrated the researchers.

A second series of experiments was conducted. A separate test room was set up where temperature, humidity, and other environmental factors could be manipulated. A series of 13 experimental periods were recorded and productivity went up each time. Productivity went up by 50%. When the experimenters repeated the original condition (expecting productivity to fall to original levels), productivity kept increasing. The experiments were a total failure at this point. No matter what the experimenters did, productivity went up. What was causing the increase?

Mayo guessed that some human or psychological factor was involved. Thus, workers were interviewed about their feelings and attitudes toward the experiment. What the researchers found was to have a profound change in management thinking that continues today. Here is what they concluded:

- The women in the test room thought of themselves as a social group. The atmosphere was informal, they could talk freely, and interacted regularly with their supervisors and the experimenters. They felt special and worked hard to stay in the group. This motivated them.
- The women were involved in the planning of the experiments. For example, they rejected one kind of pay schedule and recommended another, which was used. The women felt that their ideas were respected and that they were involved in managerial decision making. This too motivated them.
- The women enjoyed the atmosphere of their special room and the additional pay they got from more productivity. Job satisfaction increased dramatically.

From the results, researchers began to study human motivation and the managerial styles that led to more productivity. The emphasis of research then shifted away from Taylor's scientific management to Mayo's newly discovered human-based management.

Mayo's findings led to completely new assumptions about employees. That change in assumptions led to many theories about the human side of motivation. None of these theories, however, has received more attention than that of Abraham Maslow.

MOTIVATION AND MASLOW'S NEED HIERARCHY

Abraham Maslow believed that to understand motivation at work, one must understand human motivation in general. It seemed to him that motivation arises from need; that is, one is motivated to satisfy *unmet needs;* needs that have been satisfied no longer provide motivation. He thought that needs could be placed on a hierarchy of importance. When one need is satisfied, another, higher-level need emerges and motivates the person to do something to satisfy it.[1] In fact, lower level needs (for example, hunger, thirst) may emerge at any time they are not met

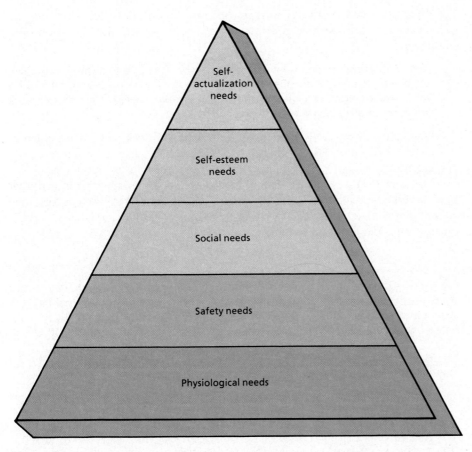

FIGURE 16-1

Maslow's need hierarchy. (Metaneeds are not in the hierarchy; they are above it.)

physiological needs
The needs for basic, life-giving elements such as food, water, and shelter.

safety needs
Include the needs for peace and security.

social needs
The need to feel loved, accepted, and part of the group.

self-esteem needs
Include the needs for self-confidence and status.

self-actualization needs
The needs for achievement and to be all you can be.

metaneeds
Needs that go beyond self, such as the needs for justice, truth, and honesty.

transcendence needs
See *metaneeds*.

and take our attention away from higher level needs such as the need for recognition or status.

Figure 16-1 shows Maslow's hierarchy of needs. The basic needs are **physiological needs** (including the need to drink, eat, and rest) and **safety needs** (including the need to feel secure at work and at home). Most of the world's workers struggle all day simply to meet these basic needs for food, shelter, and safety. In developed countries, such needs no longer dominate, and workers seek to satisfy growth needs such as **social needs** (including the need to feel loved, accepted, and part of the group), **self-esteem needs** (including the need for recognition, acknowledgement, and status), and **self-actualization needs** (including the need to accomplish established goals and be all you can be).

Beyond these fundamental needs, Maslow saw people striving to satisfy what he called *metaneeds*. These needs were not hierarchical; rather, they were equal in their power to motivate. **Metaneeds** lead people beyond considerations of self. When a person's fundamental personal needs are satisfied, Maslow believed that he or she instinctively turns to help others. Maslow's "ultimate satisfiers" (or those values that make one fully human), therefore, include the desire for unity, truth, goodness, beauty, justice, order, playfulness, aliveness, and simplicity (what he called **transcendence needs**).

What ultimately motivates workers, in other words, is to feel that they are participating in a cause that goes beyond self-actualization and self-realization. Maslow says[2]:

> They are devoted, working at something which is very precious to them—some calling or vocation in the old sense, the priestly sense. They are working at something which fate has called them to somehow and which fate they love, so that the joy-work dichotomy in them disappears.

Have you ever watched people caught up in the spirit of a cause, or experienced it yourself? The enthusiasm and energy level is unbelievable. It is fun, exciting, and all-encompassing. That is the spirit that successful firms try to create.

To compete successfully, U.S. firms must create a corporate environment that motivates the best and the brightest workers. That means establishing a corporate culture that includes goals such as social contribution, honesty, reliability, service, quality, dependability, and unity.

THINKING IT THROUGH

When in your life have you felt strongly motivated to do something? Try to think of several different incidents. Now look at Maslow's need hierarchy to see what need was motivating you. Have you ever experienced being motivated by metaneeds (for example, helping others, spiritual growth)? What kind of job would enable you to satisfy your metaneeds while meeting your other needs as well? Can you see how helpful Maslow's theory is in understanding motivation by applying it to your own life?

Applying Maslow's Theory

Andrew Grove of Intel observed Maslow's concepts in action in his firm. One woman, for example, took a low-paying job, which did little for her family's standard of living. Why? Because she needed the companionship her work offered (social/affiliation need). One of Grove's friends had a mid-life crisis when he was made a vice president. This position had been a lifelong goal, and when the man reached it he had to find another way to motivate himself. People at a research and development lab were knowledge centered. They were self-actualized by the desire to know more, but they had little desire to produce results, thus little was achieved.[3] Grove had to find new people who were results oriented.

MOTIVATION COMES FROM WITHIN

When a person is not doing his job, there can only be two reasons for it. The person either can't do it or won't do it; he is either not capable or not motivated. To determine which, we can employ a simple mental test: if the person's life depended on doing the work, could he do it? If the answer is yes, that person is not motivated; if the answer is no, he is not capable. . . .

The single most important task of a manager is to elicit peak performance from his subordinates. So if two things limit high output, a manager has two ways to tackle the issue: through training and motivation . . . motivation has to come from within somebody. Accordingly, all a manager can do is create an environment in which motivated people can flourish.

Andrew S. Grove, *High Output Management* (New York: Random House, 1983), pp. 157-158.

Once one understands the need level of employees, it is easier to design programs that will trigger self-motivation. Grove believes that all motivation comes from within. (See the box on p. 426.) He believes that self-actualized persons are achievement oriented. He thus designed a managerial program that emphasized output. Now managers are highly motivated to achieve their objectives because they are rewarded for doing so.

Grove's assumption was that people naturally work toward goals to which they are committed and that people are quite capable. Those assumptions are all part of another theory that we shall discuss next.

PROGRESS CHECK

- What are the similarities and differences between Taylor's scientific management and Mayo's Hawthorne studies? How did Mayo's findings influence scientific management?

- Can you draw Maslow's need hierarchy and label the parts? What are meta-needs?

McGREGOR'S THEORY X AND THEORY Y

The way managers go about motivating people at work depends greatly upon their attitudes toward workers.

Douglas McGregor observed that managers had two different attitudes that led to entirely different managerial styles. He called the two systems *Theory X* and *Theory Y*.

Theory X calls for keeping careful watch and records on employees.

Theory X

The assumptions of Theory X management are much like those of a parent with an unruly child. They are:

- The average person dislikes work and will avoid it if possible.
- Because of this dislike, the average person must be forced, controlled, directed, or threatened with punishment to motivate him or her to put forth the effort to achieve the organization's goals.
- The average worker prefers to be directed, wishes to avoid responsibility, has relatively little ambition, and wants security.

The natural consequence of such attitudes, beliefs, and assumptions is a manager who is very "busy" and who hangs over people telling them what to do and how to do it. Motivation is more likely to take the form of punishment for bad work rather than reward for good work. Workers are given little responsibility, authority, or flexibility. No doubt you have seen such managers in action. How did this make you feel? Is that how you prefer to be managed? Are these assumptions accurate regarding your work attitudes? For years, the typical manager operated from such assumptions. That is why management literature focused on time and motion studies that calculated the "one best" way to perform a task and the "optimum" time to be devoted to a task. It was assumed that workers needed to be trained and carefully watched to see that they conformed to the standards. Would you like to be told exactly how to do something in a given amount of time with no room for creativity, flexibility, or time to relax and take a breather?

Theory Y

In fact, some people do prefer much direction and close supervision (an autocratic management style) but most do not. Theory Y makes entirely different assumptions about people:

- The average person likes work; it is as natural as play or rest.
- The average person naturally works toward goals to which he or she is committed.
- The depth of a person's commitment to goals depends on the perceived rewards for achieving them.
- Under certain conditions, the average person not only accepts but seeks responsibility.
- People are capable of using a relatively high degree of imagination, creativity, and cleverness to solve problems.
- In industry, the average person's intellectual potential is only partially realized.

Rather than emphasize authority, direction, and close supervision, Theory Y emphasizes a relatively free managerial atmosphere in which workers are free to set objectives, be creative, be flexible, and go beyond the goals set by management.[4] Have you ever worked in such an atmosphere? How did that make you feel? Would you prefer to work under a Theory X or Theory Y manager? How willing would you be to be a Theory Y manager with your children or your workers? Traditional managerial styles were based on one of two major assumptions:

- Workers are basically lazy and must be given direction, threatened, and negatively motivated (Theory X); *or*
- Workers are basically goal-oriented and self-motivated, and the best managerial style is to offer them incentives and freedom (Theory Y).

Theory Y emphasizes a managerial atmosphere in which workers set objectives and are relatively free to be flexible and creative.

Your natural inclination would be to choose a Theory Y–type manager as your supervisor. On the other hand, most people feel that they need to be flexible in applying Theory X or Y to those they supervise. Some people do better with direction; others do better with more freedom.

In fact, the trend in most U.S. businesses is toward Theory Y management. One reason for a more flexible, permissive managerial style is to meet competition from foreign firms such as those in Japan. William Ouchi recently wrote a best-selling book on management called *Theory Z: How American Business Can Meet The Japanese Challenge*. Next we will explore this new theory.

APPLYING X AND Y

The trouble with these neat theories . . . is that no company that I know of is run in strict accordance with either Theory Y or Theory X. Not even the Army. . . . I have known managers who prefer to be told what to do, men who do not want responsibility for making crucial decisions . . . and once they are given precise instructions perform their assigned tasks with care and diligence. I have also known managers who are self-starters and perform best only when they have shared in the decision-making process; in fact, they resent being given orders. Both these types of managers were working for the same company. If you were the chief executive, how would you run that company—by Theory X or Theory Y? Or, would you use your common sense and act according to the circumstances at hand?

"Theory G: You cannot run a business, or anything else, on a theory."

Harold Geneen, *Managing* (New York: Avon Books, 1984), pp. 17-25.

THEORY Z (OUCHI)

Most organizations in Japan are run quite differently from those in the United States. Out of the Japanese system has come a concept called *Theory Z*.[5]

There are several major elements to this theory:

- Long-term employment, virtually guaranteed, for all employees
- Emphasis on collective decision making
- Relatively slow evaluation and promotion
- Creation of a sense of involvement, closeness, and cooperation in the organization (family atmosphere)
- Expectation of individual responsibility (like Theory Y)
- Trust among all managers and workers
- Few levels of management

Several U.S. firms are attempting to adopt this managerial style. Ouchi cites Hewlett-Packard as one such American firm. He quotes from a preamble to corporate objectives written by David Packard and William Hewlett.

The preamble begins by saying, "The achievements of an organization are the results of the combined efforts of each individual in the organization working toward common objectives." It goes on to list several requirements including (1) the most capable people should be selected for each assignment, (2) enthusiasm should exist at all levels, and (3) all levels should work in unison toward common objectives.

The corporate philosophy at Hewlett-Packard is to have overall objectives that are clearly stated and agreed to and to give people the freedom to work toward those goals in ways they determine best for their own areas of responsibility.

When Harold Geneen was chief executive officer of ITT, he reviewed Theory Z. He noted that U.S. corporate life is just the opposite from the basics of Theory Z: relatively short-term employment, rapid promotions and dismissals, individual decision making and responsibilities, and a sense of personal rather than corporate loyalty. He questioned whether Americans would want to trade our heritage of personal freedoms and individual opportunity for the ingrown paternalism, humility, and selflessness of the Japanese. He doubted whether we could instill such feelings, even if we wanted to.[6] A job for life in a firm may sound good until you think of the implications: no chance to change jobs and no opportunity to move up quickly through the ranks. There are fewer layers of management in Japan, thus fewer management positions. Geneen concluded that theory Z would not work as well in the U.S. as in Japan because of cultural differences. This emphasizes the fact that the appropriate managerial style is one that matches the culture, the situation, and the specific needs of individual employees. Next we shall look at motivating factors.

MOTIVATING FACTORS: HERZBERG

Theories X, Y, and Z are concerned with styles of management. Another direction in managerial theory is to explore what managers can do with the job itself to motivate employees (a modern-day look at Taylor's research). Of all the factors controllable by managers, which are most effective in generating an enthusiastic work effort? In other words, this section is more concerned with the *content of work* than style of management.

The most discussed study in this area was conducted by Frederick Herzberg.[7] He asked workers to rank the following job-related factors in the order of importance relative to motivation. That is, what creates enthusiasm for them and makes them work to full potential? The results, in order of importance, were:

1 Sense of achievement
2 Earned recognition
3 Interest in the work itself
4 Opportunity for growth
5 Opportunity for advancement
6 Importance of responsibility
7 Peer and group relationships
8 Pay
9 Supervisor's fairness
10 Company policies and rules
11 Status
12 Job security
13 Supervisor's friendliness
14 Working conditions

Herzberg noted that the factors receiving the most votes were all clustered around job content. Workers like to feel that they contribute (sense of achievement was #1). They want to earn recognition (#2) and feel their jobs are important (#6). They want responsibility (which is why learning is so important), but want recognition for that responsibility by having a chance for growth and advancement. Of course, workers also want the job to be interesting.

Herzberg noted further that factors having to do with the job environment were not considered motivators by workers. It was interesting to find that one of those factors was pay. Workers felt that the absence of good pay, job security, friendly supervisors, and the like could cause dissatisfaction, but the presence of those factors did not motivate them; they just provided satisfaction.

The conclusions of Herzberg's study were that certain factors of management did motivate employees (motivators) and gave them a great deal of satisfaction (see Figure 16-2). These factors mostly had to do with job content and were grouped as follows:

- Work itself
- Achievement
- Recognition
- Responsibility
- Growth and advancement

MOTIVATORS	HYGIENE FACTORS
(These factors can be used to motivate workers.)	(These factors can cause dissatisfaction, but changing them will have little motivational effect.)
Work itself	Company policy and administration
Achievement	Supervision
Recognition	Working conditions
Responsibility	Interpersonal relations (coworkers)
Growth and advancement	Salary, status, and job security

FIGURE 16-2

Herzberg's motivators and hygiene factors. There is some controversy over Herzberg's results. For example, sales managers often use money as a motivator.

Other factors of management were merely what Herzberg called hygiene factors. These had to do mostly with job environment and could cause dissatisfaction if missing but would not necessarily motivate if increased. They were:

- Company policy and administration
- Supervision
- Working conditions
- Interpersonal relations
- Salary

If we combined McGregor's Theory Y with Herzberg's motivating factors, we would come up with these conclusions:

- Employees work best when management assumes that employees are competent and self-motivated (Theory Y). Theory Y calls for a participative style of management.
- The best way to motivate employees is to make the job interesting, help them to achieve their objectives, and recognize that achievement through advancement and added responsibility.

JOB ENRICHMENT

⋇ **job enrichment**
Describes efforts to make jobs more interesting, challenging, and rewarding.

Both Maslow's and Herzberg's theories were extended by job enrichment theory. **Job enrichment** is a motivational strategy that emphasizes motivating the worker through the job itself. Work is assigned to individuals so that they have the opportunity to complete an identifiable task from beginning to end. They are held responsible for successful completion of the task. The motivational effect of job enrichment can come from the opportunity for personal achievement, challenge, and recognition.[8] Go back and review Maslow's and Herzberg's work to see how job enrichment grew out of those theories. Five characteristics of work are believed to be important in affecting individual motivation and performance:

1 *Skill variety.* The extent to which a job demands different skills of the person.
2 *Task identity.* The degree to which the job requires doing a job with a visible outcome from beginning to end.
3 *Task significance.* The degree to which the job has a substantial impact on the lives or work of others in the company.
4 *Autonomy.* The degree of freedom, independence, and discretion in scheduling work and determining procedures.
5 *Feedback.* The amount of direct and clear information that is received about job performance.

Variety, identity, and significance contribute to the meaningfulness of the job. Autonomy gives employees a feeling of responsibility, and feedback contributes to feeling achievement and recognition.

Sherwin Williams began a job enrichment program in its Richmond, Kentucky plant in 1980. Employees were grouped into teams and each member was trained to do all the jobs assigned the team. The teams have autonomy to decide where members work, what they do, and how they train others.[9] The group is responsible for results. Raises are based on performance as evaluated by team leaders and peers. Employees are encouraged to feel responsible for the entire production process.

The program was quite successful. Absenteeism is 63% lower than at other Sherwin Williams plants. Turnover is low and productivity is 30% higher than at other plants. Cost per gallon of paint is 45% lower.[10]

The job enrichment program at Sherwin Williams has led to lower absenteeism and turnover and higher productivity.

Job enrichment is clearly a way to design jobs so that people feel responsibility and a sense of accomplishment. The next step is to get everyone to agree on specific corporate objectives.

PROGRESS CHECK

- Briefly describe the managerial attitudes behind Theories X, Y, and Z.

- Relate job enrichment to Herzberg's motivating factors.

MANAGEMENT BY OBJECTIVES

Nothing makes more sense intuitively than the idea that all members of an organization should have some basic agreement about the overall goals of the organization and the specific objectives to be met by each department and individual in the organization. It follows, then, that someone would develop a system to involve everyone in the organization in goal setting and implementation. The system is called *management by objectives* (MBO). MBO was very popular in the 1960s. Big corporations such as Ford Motor Company used it. Ford executives taught the method to the U.S. Defense Department, and from there it spread to other government agencies.

Management by objectives is a system of goal setting and implementation that involves a cycle of discussion, review, and evaluation of objectives among top- and middle-level managers, supervisors, and employees. There are five steps in the MBO process (see Figure 16-3):

management by objectives (MBO)
A system of goal setting and implementation that involves a cycle of discussion, review, and evaluation of objectives among top-level managers, middle-level managers, supervisors, and employees.

1 Top management consults with managers throughout the organization to set long-range goals and the means to determine whether or not those goals are being met over time.

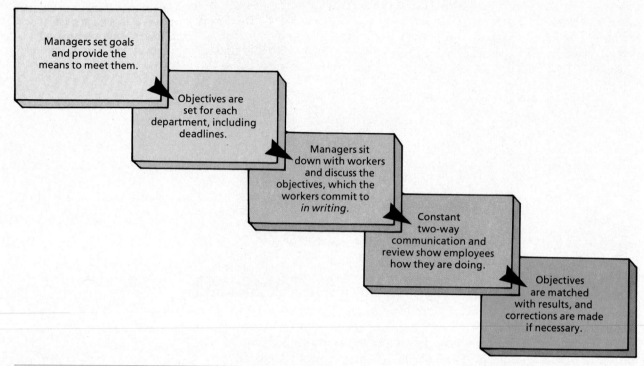

Managers set goals and provide the means to meet them.

Objectives are set for each department, including deadlines.

Managers sit down with workers and discuss the objectives, which the workers commit to *in writing*.

Constant two-way communication and review show employees how they are doing.

Objectives are matched with results, and corrections are made if necessary.

✳ FIGURE 16-3   Management by objectives.

2 Overall corporate goals are clearly formulated and subgoals are determined for each department. These subgoals are further divided into objectives for each unit and each individual within a unit. All of this is done with the full participation and cooperation of the people involved, including the means for reaching those goals and the deadlines.

3 The key to success of MBO systems is a third step where managers and workers sit down with their superiors, review the objectives and adjust them if necessary, and then commit themselves to those objectives in a written contract or agreement that states clearly the objectives, the means for reaching the objectives, and the time periods involved. The idea is that participation in goal setting involves everyone in the goals and motivates them by making them feel part of a team.

4 Implementation of the plan calls for periodic reviews of progress, constant two-way communication among all participants, and the application of good management so that the spirit of mutual cooperation and agreed-upon goals is maintained.

5 The last step is to monitor progress by matching objectives to accomplishments, noting deviations, making needed corrections, communicating the results to all participants, and adjusting to any unanticipated situations.

Management by objectives is most effective in relatively stable situations where long-range plans can be made and implemented with little need for major changes. Even in high-tech, rapidly-changing industries, such as computers and biotechnology, the concept of MBO may be effective. That is, managers should formulate plans in cooperation with everyone, commit people to those plans, and monitor results. To summarize, management by objectives is a strategy for involving all members of an organization in goal-setting and implementation, and, properly conducted, generates a feeling of involvement and cooperation (motivation). MBO is also an excellent way to determine who deserves a promotion and increased pay and who does not, based on results.

Problems arise when management uses MBO as a strategy for forcing managers and workers to commit to goals that are not really mutually agreed upon, but are set by top management. Care must also be taken to maintain open two-way communication and an organizational culture that values the stated objectives. For example, all universities talk about the importance of teaching, but few give full recognition to good teachers in promotion decisions. The objectives are clear, but the reward system contradicts the objectives. The same kind of conflict may occur in all organizations.

HELPING VERSUS COACHING

It is important for managers to understand the difference between helping and coaching subordinates. *Helping* means to work with the subordinate, doing part of the work if necessary. *Coaching* means acting as a resource—teaching, guiding, recommending—but not helping (that is, not participating actively in the task).

Helping subordinates tends to make them weak and dependent and irresponsible. Coaching subordinates tends to make them feel part of a team and capable of doing it on their own once they learn the system.

Motivation Through Communication

Management by objectives teaches us that one key to successful management, in any organization, is the establishment and maintenance of open two-way communication between and among managers and workers so that everyone understands the objectives and works together effectively and efficiently to achieve them. Communication must flow two ways among all members of an organization. The problem today is that most communication flows are one way; from top management down. This communication takes the form of directives, policies, announcements, memos, rules, procedures, and the like.

The flow upward, from workers to managers, is usually severely clogged. Rarely do organizations have any formal means of upward communication (from employees to management) equivalent to directives and announcements. Instead, the burden falls on workers to initiate contact with supervisors and present their ideas and suggestions. As you know, few people in any organization tell the boss when things are not going well. Children don't tell parents when they've broken something, students don't tell teachers when someone has goofed, and employees don't tell bosses. Such a system creates an "us against them" attitude, where workers feel united in their distrust and avoidance of managers. To create an atmosphere of "us working together," managers have to become active listeners and valued assistants to workers. Such a change demands radical retraining of managers and careful creation of new attitudes and beliefs among workers.

Teamwork between and among managers and employees does not just happen. The whole organization must be structured to facilitate dialogues. Some procedures for encouraging open communication include:

- Top management must first create an organizational culture that rewards listening by being listeners themselves; by creating facilities (for example, conference rooms) for having dialogues; and by showing others that talking with superiors counts—by providing feedback, adopting employee suggestions, and rewarding upward communication, even if it is negative. Employees must feel free to say anything.
- Supervisors and managers must be trained in listening skills. Most people receive no such training in school or anywhere else, so organizations must do the training themselves or hire someone to do it.
- Barriers to open communication must be removed and facilitating mechanisms installed. Barriers include separate offices, parking spaces, bathrooms, dining rooms, and other such facilities for various levels of management and workers. Such facilities foster an "us versus them" attitude. Other barriers include different dress codes, different ways of addressing one another (for example, calling workers by their first names and managers by their last),

APPLYING OPEN COMMUNICATIONS

Intel executives call their open communications policy *decision making by peers*. It has been described as "an open confrontation-oriented management style in which people go after blunt issues bluntly, straightforwardly. The main reason people need not hide is that they talk all the time. A meeting is not a rare, formal—and thus political—event."

Dana Corporation has a policy of caring, feeding, and unshackling the efforts of the average man or woman. They call it *productivity through people*.

Perhaps the best description of informal communications taking place within an organization and with customers describes the situation at the 3M Company:

> There were a score or more casual meetings in progress with salespeople, marketing people, manufacturing people, engineering people, R&D people . . . sitting around, chattering about new-product problems. We happened in on a session where a 3M customer had come to talk informally with about fifteen people from four divisions on how better to serve his company. . . . We didn't see a single structured presentation. It went on all day—people meeting in a seemingly random way to get things done.

Source: Thomas J. Peters and Robert H. Waterman, Jr., *In Search of Excellence* (N.Y.: Harper & Row, Publishers, 1982).

and so on. Removing such barriers takes imagination and a willingness to give up the special privileges of management. Facilitating efforts include large lunch tables where all organizational members eat, conference rooms, organizational picnics, organizational athletic teams, and other such outings where managers mix with and socialize with each other and with workers.

Team sports open communications between managers and workers.

IMPLEMENTING THE NEW CONCEPTS

We have come a long way from the time and motion studies of Fred Taylor. Maslow, Mayo, Herzberg, and others have taught us to treat employees as associates and to get them more involved in decision making. This increases motivation and leads to greater productivity.

The problem is that many managers were brought up under a different system. Some were in the military and are used to telling people what to do rather than consulting with them. Others come from the football-coach school of management. They too tend to yell and direct rather than consult and discuss.

Furthermore, employees are often not used to participative management. The transition from Theory X to Theory Y management, from Fred Taylor to Herzberg, is still going on. It is important, then, to have examples to follow when trying to implement the new approaches.

William Potter, the CEO of Preston Trucking Company, is one manager who has succeeded at the task of turning a disorganized, semihostile workforce into a cooperative, efficient team. Let's review his story to see what lessons he can teach us.

A Model for the Future

Employees at Preston Trucking Company wear a button on their shirts that says, "Preston People: We Make a Difference." The story of Preston Trucking is a parable that illustrates management principles of the future. High-tech may bring tremendous productivity increases through robotics, computers, word processors, and the like. But the truly successful firms will be those that get the most from their people. The machinery will be much the same in all firms; the creative use of that machinery will make the difference.

William Potter talking with an associate.

Preston was not always a model company. The Teamsters Union (truck drivers) filed 723 grievances against Preston in 1978. Surveys among workers elicited 40 negative comments for every compliment.[11] Labor-management relations were the equivalent of internal warfare. Cooperation was at a minimum.

There was talk of deregulation of the trucking industry, and Preston management knew that this would make improvements in productivity and labor relations critical to the firm's survival. A whole new attitude needed to be developed among top management. The philosophy to be adopted was that people (employees) were the firm's biggest asset, and that customer service was the primary goal. The question was whether or not management could motivate the truck drivers to join in the cause.

Implementing Change

The first step Preston took was to train managers to be facilitators and listeners rather than bosses and order givers. It was not easy to get management to give up their desire for control and authority over employees. Managers were all trained together, and encouraged one another to adopt the new philosophy.

Some of the changes involved terminology. Employees are now called *associates* and supervisors are called *coordinators*. The tradition in trucking firms was to record errors made by drivers and dockworkers, and management was accomplished by intimidation, threat, and negative reinforcement. Management at Preston changed that philosophy, and began keeping records of how often they complimented and encouraged employees.

When deregulation became a reality, the new system was in effect; that is, management had been trained to talk with employees, listening was emphasized over order-giving, employees were encouraged to become independent and responsible for their own operations, and a feeling of cooperation was established. Grievances decreased from 723 in 1978 to 472 in 1983.

The results show the benefit of a management philosophy that is people oriented. The number of trucking terminals in operation increased over 50% from 1978 to 1984. Because of better labor-management relations, it was possible to cut the number of coordinators by 4% (with more employees), to cut management personnel by 18%, and to eliminate a whole layer of management. The increase in employee morale raised productivity by 7.9% and resulted in a saving of $19,000,000.

Employees are now encouraged to buy company stock and share in the ownership and thus the profits of the firm. The attitude now is, "This is my company and I'm here to serve my customers to make a bigger profit for us." The button "Preston People: We Make a Difference" is more than a slogan. It is the reflection of a managerial philosophy.

The management team at Preston spends much of its time walking around visiting the various terminals and talking with the workers. They follow the concepts of the book *In Search of Excellence* in that they believe in "management by walking around" and "keeping close to the customer."

Lessons From the Preston Experience

Will Potter, the CEO at Preston Trucking Company, believes that college students preparing for business must get involved in campus activities and learn to (1) get along with people by learning listening skills; (2) be more concise and clear writers so that they can write memos and reports that are short and readable; and (3) be public speakers by becoming officers in campus clubs and giving talks. The best way to lead is by example, and the Preston management team is a model for employees and for managers in all types of firms as well. The lessons we can learn from the Preston example include:

- The future growth of industry and business in general depends on a motivated, productive work force.
- Motivation is largely internally generated by workers themselves; the process that releases that energy includes giving employees more freedom to be creative and rewarding achievement when it occurs.
- The first step in any motivational program is to establish open communication among workers and managers so that the feeling generated is one of cooperation and teamwork, a family-type atmosphere.

THINKING IT THROUGH

What do you think would have happened had top management at Preston decided to crack down on drivers and insist on better performance rather than seek their help? Would a participative managerial style work for a football team as well? What are the motivational differences, if any, between professional truck drivers and professional football players?

✴MANAGEMENT BY WALKING AROUND

One concept that the Preston Trucking Company adopted to improve employee relations and increase productivity is called management by walking around (MBWA). The idea is for managers to regularly wander among employees asking questions, being friendly, and being supportive[12]:

> In trying to explain the phenomenon [of walk-around management], a GM manager contrasted one key aspect of the striking difference between two giant plants: "I know this sounds like a caricature, but I guess that is how life is. At the poorly performing plant, the plant manager probably ventured out on the floor once a week, always in a suit. His comments were distant and perfunctory. At South Gate, the better plant, the plant manager was on the floor all the time. He wore a baseball cap and a UAW jacket. By the way, whose plant do you think was spotless? Whose looked like a junkyard?"

The best walk-around managers are on a first-name basis with employees and stop and chat informally about family and other personal subjects. Employees are made to feel part of a team, important, and part of the corporate family. To give an idea of how far this can go, at Activision (a videogame maker) the company telephone book is alphabetized by first names. The lessons are:

- There is a trend in organizations toward informality to create a feeling of teamwork and to make everyone feel part of a family of workers.
- One successful practice is called "management by walking around," in which managers periodically visit employees, call them by their first names, and act friendly and supportive.

Management by walking around often goes beyond the organization. Many managers apply the same concept with suppliers, dealers, customers, and other publics. That is, they get out and visit these people, ask if they need anything, and generally behave in a friendly, supportive, helpful manner.

Management by walking around is not effective if workers or other publics feel that the manager is there to snoop on them or to fake some camaraderie that isn't real. Managers who practice management by walking around effectively are sincere in their attempt to create a feeling of warmth and friendly cooperation—and it works.

PROGRESS CHECK

- What are the five steps in the MBO process?

- Where does management by walking around fit into Maslow's theory? Herzberg's theory?

SUMMARY

1 Willoughby McCormick of McCormick spices was a stern master. He would have loved having Frederick Taylor do time and motion studies to be sure his workers gave "an honest day's work for an honest day's pay." Charles McCormick, on the other hand, learned that workers are more productive when they feel management cares about them and makes it possible to move up in the organization.

- Who is Frederick Taylor?

  Frederick Taylor is the father of scientific management. He did time and motion studies to learn the most efficient way of doing a job and then trained workers in those procedures. He published his book on "scientific management" in 1911. The Gilbreths and H. L. Gantt were followers of Taylor.

2 Maslow studied basic human motivation and found that motivation was based on need—an unfilled need motivated people to satisfy it and a satisfied need no longer motivated.

- What were the various levels of need?

  From the bottom of the hierarchy up, the needs were physiological, safety, social, self-esteem, and self-actualization.

- What happens when self-actualization needs are met?

  A person moves up to metaneeds (for example, helping others, spiritual growth).

- Can managers use this theory?

  Yes; they can recognize what needs a person has and have work provide the satisfaction.

- What is the ultimate motivator?

  Maslow felt that working for others (service) was the ultimate motivator. Companies that stress social contribution, quality, and service can often inspire great things from their employees.

3 The newest managerial philosophies all stress human factors of motivation rather than Taylor's scientific management principles.

- What led to the more human managerial styles to increase motivation?

  The greatest impact on motivation management was generated by the Hawthorne studies in the late 1920s and early 1930s. Elton Mayo found that human factors such as feelings of involvement and participation led to greater productivity gains than did physical changes in the work place.

4 Managers can have two attitudes toward employees. They are called Theory X and Theory Y.

- What are these theories and who developed them?

  Theory X assumes that the average person dislikes work and will avoid it if possible. Therefore, people must be forced, controlled, and threatened with punishment to accomplish organizational goals. Theory Y assumes that people like working and will accept responsibility for achieving goals if rewarded for doing so. Douglas McGregor published these theories in 1970.

- What is Theory Z?

  Theory Z comes out of Japanese management and stresses long-term employment among other factors.

5 Herzberg found that some factors are motivators and others are hygiene factors; that is, they cause job dissatisfaction if missing, but are not motivators if present.

- What are the factors called motivators?

  The work itself, achievement, recognition, responsibility, growth, and advancement.

- What are the hygiene factors?

  Company policies, supervision, working conditions, interpersonal relations, and salary.

6 Job enrichment describes efforts to make jobs more interesting.

- What is the goal of job enrichment?

  The goal is to increase employee motivation and satisfaction.

7 One procedure for establishing objectives and gaining employee commitment to those objectives is called MBO (management by objectives).

- What are the steps in an MBO program?

  (1) Management sets goals, (2) objectives are established for each department, (3) workers discuss the objectives and commit themselves in writing to meeting them, (4) progress is reviewed, (5) feedback is provided and adjustments made.

- What is the key to successful management, including MBO systems?

  In a word, communication. That means training managers to listen and facilitating listening by removing barriers (for example, executive dining rooms) and providing necessary facilities (for example, conference rooms).

8 William Potter at Preston Trucking is a model for future managers.
- What did he do?

  He trained managers to be facilitators and listeners. He practiced "management by walking around." He made employees feel that Preston was their company and its customers their customers.

KEY TERMS

job enrichment   p. 432
management by objectives (MBO)   p. 433
metaneeds   p. 425
physiological needs   p. 425
safety needs   p. 425
scientific management   p. 423

self-actualization needs
  p. 425
self-esteem needs   p. 425
social needs   p. 425
time-motion studies   p. 422
transcendence needs   p. 425

GETTING INVOLVED

1 Think of all the bosses (managers/leaders) you have had over time in sports, clubs, and so forth. Did they assume a Theory X or Y style of leadership? How did you feel about that? Would you have worked harder or less hard if they had followed the other strategy? What does this tell you about motivation? Discuss with class.

2 Herzberg found that pay was not a motivator. If you were paid to get better grades, would you be able to get them? Have you worked harder as a result of a large raise? Discuss money as a motivator with your friends and class. Do you agree 100% with Herzberg?

3 Have you ever volunteered to work on a project where you felt your efforts really made a difference? How did you feel about that? If you haven't, how do you feel about that fact? Do you envy people with an obvious mission in life? How could you find a job that would satisfy your basic needs for food, shelter, safety, and esteem and feel as if you were making a difference in the world? Discuss options with classmates.

4 If you were made a manager, would you be willing to treat your employees as equals? Would you be willing to eat with them, socialize with them, and generally be their friend as well as their boss? Would it make a difference if they were from a different ethnic group, country, or social class? What kind of people do you feel need Theory X management? Discuss.

5 You have had the most experience in motivation working under various teachers in school. Which teachers got you to work hardest? How did they do it? What was their managerial style? What motivators did they use? Discuss your findings with the class.

PRACTICING MANAGEMENT DECISIONS

CASE ONE   THEORY X AND Y: THAT'S HOW THE COOKIE CRUMBLES

No two firms better illustrate Theory X and Theory Y than David's Cookies and Mrs. Fields Chocolate Chippery stores. You'll see what we mean.

First, let's look at David's Cookies. The owner is David Liederman. When his stores first opened, everyone criticized his cookies. However, when the *New York Times* had a cookie-tasting contest, David's won. Today David's Cookies has 80 stores in the New York area and stores in 24 states. David's is a big success!

What does he think about employees? Not much. David tries to minimize employee involvement in cookie making so they can't mess things up. He does that by making all the dough in a factory and shipping it to the stores. All the employee has to do is put the dough on a tray, put it in an automatic oven and take it out 7½ minutes later. David has hesitated to sell brownies because he feels workers might mess up the job of adding eggs. He says, "One of the reasons we do well . . . is that a chimpanzee could take cookies out of that bag and more often than not put them on the tray properly."

In contrast, let's go over to Mrs. Fields Chocolate Chippery. Debbi Fields has about 300 cookie stores selling about $45 million a year. Not bad either.

What does Mrs. Fields think about employees? She feels that people "will do their very best provided that they are getting proper support." Mrs. Fields says, "It's a people company. That's what it's all about. . . . What we really do is . . . we take care of people." This philosophy is reflected in how Mrs. Fields makes cookies. Store employees combine ingredients right in the store (some in proportioned containers). The ovens are not automatic. Employees put the raw dough in to bake and take out the finished cookies when it feels right. "We tell them that we want them to have fun," Mrs. Fields says. "People come to work because they need to be productive. They need to feel successful in whatever they do." Here is how Debbi sums up her job: "To make people feel important and to create an opportunity for them. That's really my role as cookie president, the cookie person."

DECISION QUESTIONS

1 What does the David's/Mrs. Fields story tell you about Theory X and Theory Y? Which works best?
2 Which store is more likely to build employee honesty and loyalty?
3 Which store is likely to be most profitable in the long run? Why?
4 In which company would you rather be a manager? Employee? Stockholder?

Sources: Tom Richman, "A Tale of Two Companies," *Inc.,* July, 1984, pp. 37-43; and "The Man Who Would Be Cookie King," *Marketing Communications,* December, 1984, p. 6.

CASE TWO   RE-INVENTING THE CORPORATION

PRACTICING MANAGEMENT DECISIONS

One way to determine managerial trends is to research all the articles written in hundreds of magazines and other publications and summarize the new directions indicated. That is what John Naisbitt did in his popular book, *Megatrends.* A new book he has coauthored with Patricia Aburdene is called *Re-Inventing the Corporation* (Warner Books, 1985). It reflects the attention generated by *In Search of Excellence.* The goal of management, according to Naisbitt and Aburdene, is to adopt "new humanistic values."

Steps for creating a new, better corporate atmosphere include: calling everyone by his or her first name, eliminating executive parking spots and bathrooms, having everyone answer his or her own phone, eliminating files, doing business only with pleasant people, and throwing out the organization chart.

The authors suggest that managers also "re-invent work." This means respecting workers, providing interesting work, rewarding good work, developing workers' skills, allowing some autonomy, and decentralizing authority.

Other points include: (1) the manager's role is that of teacher, mentor, and coach; (2) the best people want ownership in the firm; (3) the best managerial style is not top-down, but a networking, people style of management; (4) quality is the new key to success; (5) successful large corporations copy the entrepreneurial flavor of small businesses; and (6) the information age enables firms to locate where there is a high quality of life versus the more standard needs for raw materials and other industrial considerations.

DECISION QUESTIONS

1 The suggestions in this book follow the theories established by McGregor, Herzberg, and Maslow. These ideas go back 25 years or more. Why are they so popular today? What has changed in business, demographics, and the economy to make such ideas more popular?

2 What sort of motivation program is suggested by such books?

3 There is some mention of quality of life is Naisbitt's new book. Do you see any trends toward people searching for values beyond work such as Maslow's metaneeds: unity, goodness, aliveness, playfulness, and simplicity?

LOOKING AHEAD

Organizations succeed or fail on the ability of the people they employ. Therefore the hiring, training, motivating, and development of human resources is a vital element in business success. This task is becoming more difficult with new hiring rules, new employee demands, and new technologies. Certainly personnel will be an interesting and challenging position in the future. We discuss that function next in Chapter 17.

TWO
WORLD
TRADE
CENTER

HUMAN RESOURCE MANAGEMENT

LEARNING GOALS

After you have read and studied this chapter, you should be able to:

- Discuss several current issues in human resource management.
- Outline the steps involved in human resource planning.
- Describe recruitment and selection of employees.
- Identify and describe several types of training programs.
- Describe various compensation programs.
- Outline several types of management development programs.
- Describe several ways jobs are changing to meet the needs of a changing work force.
- Identify several pieces of legislation affecting personnel decisions, and explain the key provisions.

PROFILE   ALLAN R. THIEME OF AMIGO SALES, INCORPORATED

Often deciding who to hire can make all the difference in the world to the success of a firm. Allan Thieme's story is a good example. He designed a wheelchair for his wife, Marie, when she contracted multiple sclerosis. Mr. Thieme found that conventional wheelchairs were too wide to maneuver and too restricting of movement. His wheelchair is a motorized scooterlike device with a swivel seat that lets users exercise their legs.

Thieme had little capital and no reputation to begin a wheelchair business; he had been a plumbing contractor. After 5 years, Amigo Sales had sold only a few hundred chairs. Thieme was broke and about to drop the idea when he made a brilliant personnel decision. Why not hire disabled people to sell the wheelchairs? After all, who is a better salesperson than a user?

Today, 80% of Thieme's sales force is either disabled or has relatives who are. With the new sales force, sales rose. Soon they reached $9 million a year.

Amigo Sales learned the hard way that who you hire is one of the most critical decisions a firm can make. This chapter discusses human resource management in detail. It is another career alternative for you to consider. ■

Source: *Inc.,* December, 1982, p. 44.

Allan R. Thieme.

Obviously the most beautiful fate, the most wonderful good fortune that can happen to any human being, is to be paid for doing that which he passionately loves to do.
ABRAHAM MASLOW

human resource management
The process of evaluating human resource needs, finding people to fill those needs, and optimizing this important resource by providing the right incentives and job enrichment, all with the goal of meeting the objectives of the organization.

THE PERSONNEL FUNCTION

In your career search, you may be in and out of many personnel offices. While you are there, take a few minutes to observe. Talk to some of the employees and managers. Perhaps personnel is the field in which you would like to work.

There is an old story about the student who wanted to go into personnel, "because I want to work with people." It is true that personnel managers work with people, but they are also deeply involved in planning, record keeping, and other administrative duties. To begin a career in personnel, you need to develop a better reason than "I want to work with people." This chapter will discuss the personnel function, which involves recruiting, hiring, training, evaluating, and compensating people. Today, personnel management is often called human resource management. **Human resource management** is the process of evaluating human resource needs, finding people to fill those needs, and optimizing this important resource by providing the right incentives and job environment, all with the goal of meeting the objectives of the organization (see Figure 17-1). Let's find out why and explore some of the trends in the area of human resource management.

FIGURE 17-1

Human resource management.

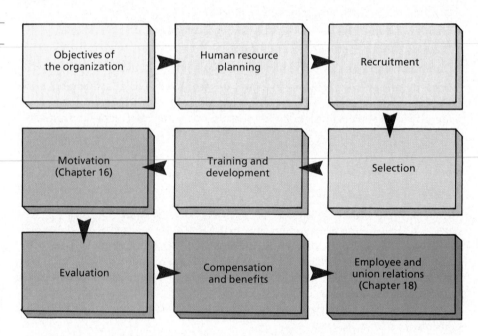

The Importance of Human Resource Management

One reason that human resource management (or personnel management) is receiving increased attention now is because of the major shift from traditional manufacturing industries to service industries and more technical jobs. A major problem today is retraining workers for new, more challenging jobs. For example, when Crown Zellerbach recently modernized a Louisiana pulp mill plant, it set up a training facility nearby and paid workers full wages to learn new skills. There are also other examples:

- Hewlett-Packard is spending $1 million to move 350 workers to new jobs, and Boeing enrolled laid-off electronics technicians in college to learn new microprocessor skills. The idea was to retrain their own people before going outside for skilled employees.

■ At GE's Louisville dishwasher plant, assembly line workers are learning how to read computer printouts. GE has a $6 million learning center in Pennsylvania and conducts training programs worldwide.[1]

GE has an active training program.

Julian Simon has called people "the ultimate resource," and when you think about it, nothing could be more true.[2] People develop the ideas that eventually become the products that satisfy our wants and needs. Take away their creative minds, and organizations such as IBM, GE, Hewlett-Packard, GM, and other leading firms would be nothing. The problem is that this resource has always been relatively plentiful, so there was little need to nurture and develop it. If you needed creative people, you simply went out and hired them. If they didn't work out, you fired them and found others.

Most firms assigned the job of recruiting, selecting, training, evaluating, compensating, motivating, and yes, firing people to the various functional departments. For years, personnel was viewed more or less as a clerical function responsible for screening applications, keeping records, processing payroll, and finding people when necessary.

Today personnel is called human resource management and has taken on an entirely new role in the firm. In the future, it may become the most critical function in that it is responsible for the most critical resource—people. In fact, the human resource function has become so important that it is no longer the function of just one department; it is a function of all managers. What are some of the problems in the human resource area?

The Human Resource Problem

No changes in the American business system have been more dramatic and had more impact on the future success of the free enterprise system than changes in the labor force. The ability of the U.S. business system to compete in international markets depends on an increase in new ideas, new products, and a higher level of productivity from its workers. All of these factors depend on the ultimate resource—people with good ideas. Problems in the human resource area include:

- Shortages in people trained to work in the growth areas of the future, such as computers, biotechnology, and the sciences.
- A huge population of skilled and unskilled workers from declining industries such as steel and automobiles who are unemployed or underemployed, and who need retraining.
- A complex set of laws and regulations involving hiring, safety, unionization, and equal pay that limits organizations' freedom to create an optimum labor force; for example, it is becoming very difficult to fire an inefficient or ineffective worker (see the box below).
- A tremendous influx of women into the labor force and the resulting demand for day care, job sharing, maternity leave programs, and special career advancement programs for women.
- A shift in the age composition of the work force, including many older workers.*
- A shift in employee attitudes toward work; leisure time has become a much higher priority, as have concepts such as flextime and a shorter work week.
- New technological changes demanding such skills as computer literacy and word processing abilities.
- New, more intense competition from overseas labor pools available for lower wages and subject to many fewer laws and regulations; this results in many jobs being shifted overseas.
- Growing concern over such issues as safety, health care, smoking on the job, and equal pay for jobs of comparable worth (discussed in Chapter 18).

*See Chapter 1 for a more complete coverage of demographic trends.

FIRING EMPLOYEES IS MORE DIFFICULT

At one time, it was relatively easy to fire an employee as long as you didn't violate any federal statutes such as the Civil Rights Act. That is no longer true. "Wrongful discharge is the tort of the 1980s," says H. Bradley Jones, a lawyer in Beverly Hills, California. "It's even more dangerous than medical malpractice," he says, "since few insurance companies sell insurance coverage to protect employers against wrongful discharge lawsuits." (A *tort* is a wrongful act resulting in an injury, loss, or damage for which the injured party can bring civil action.)

The number of cases and size of awards are increasing, and so is the accompanying publicity. Employers are getting much more cautious about who they fire and how. Some companies have gone as far as leasing rather than hiring employees to leave the problem to others.

The situation promises to get harder before it gets easier. Several states, for example, are considering passing "just cause" laws that would limit instances in which an employer could fire workers. Companies are responding to such actions by carefully reviewing employment contracts and watching what they say in interviews for employment. (See also Case One at the end of this chapter.)

Source: Jill Andresky, "Fear of Firing," *Forbes*, December 2, 1985, p. 90.

Given all these issues, you can see why human resource management has taken a more central position in management thinking. Let's see what is involved.

THINKING IT THROUGH

Does human resource management seem like a challenging career for the 1990s? Do you see any other issues likely to affect this function? What have been your experiences in dealing with people in personnel? Would you enjoy working in such an environment?

HUMAN RESOURCE PLANNING

All management, including human resource management, begins with planning. Six steps are involved in the human resource planning process. They include:

1 Preparing forecasts of future human resource needs.
2 Preparing a human resource inventory that includes ages, names, education, capabilities, training, specialized skills, and other information pertinent to the specific organization (for example, languages spoken). Such information reveals whether or not the labor force is technically up-to-date, thoroughly trained, and so forth.
3 Preparing a job analysis. A **job analysis** answers the question, "What do employees who fill various job titles do?" From job analyses come job descriptions and evaluations. **Job descriptions** specify the objectives of the job, the type of work to be done, the responsibilities, the necessary skills, the working conditions, and the relationship of the job to other functions. **Job specifications** are written descriptions of the qualifications required of a worker. Such information can be obtained through observation, interviews, and diaries, or some combination of techniques.

job analysis
A study of what is done by employees who fill various job titles.

job descriptions
Specify the objectives of a job, the type of work, the responsibilities of the job, the necessary skills, the working conditions, and the relationship of the job to other functions.

job specifications
Written descriptions of the qualifications required of workers.

FIGURE 17-2

Six steps in human resource planning.

Step 6
Prepare a comprehensive plan

Step 5
Assess future supply

Step 4
Assess future demand

Step 3
Prepare a job analysis

Step 2 Prepare a
human resource inventory

Step 1
Prepare a future needs forecast

4 Assessing future demand. Changing technology often means that training programs must be started long before the need is apparent. This enables resources to be available when needed.

5 Assessing future supply. The labor force is constantly shifting; getting older, becoming more technically oriented, attracting more women, and so forth. There are likely to be increased shortages of some skills in the future (for example, computer repair) and oversupply of others (for example, production line workers).

6 Establishing a plan for recruiting, hiring, educating, training, motivating, scheduling, and developing the labor force, given the previous analysis. See Figure 17-2 for an overview of the planning process.

recruitment
The set of activities used to legally obtain a sufficient number of the right people at the right time to select those who best meet the needs of the organization.

Recruiting

Recruitment is the set of activities used to legally obtain a sufficient number of the right people at the right time to select those that best meet the needs of the organization. One would think that, with about 7% unemployment and thousands

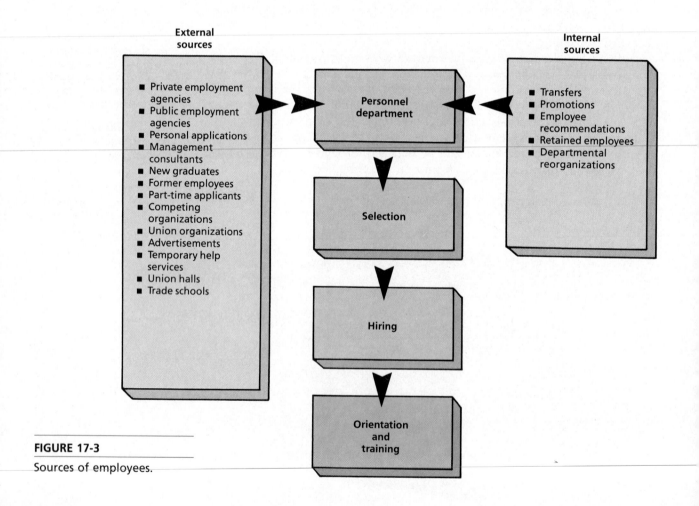

FIGURE 17-3

Sources of employees.

of new graduates with various levels of education, recruiting would be easy. But the truth is that recruiting has become very difficult for several reasons.

- Legal restrictions such as the Civil Rights Act make it necessary to recruit the proper mix of women, minorities, and other qualified individuals. Often people with the necessary skills are not available and must be hired and trained internally.
- The new emphasis on corporate cultures, teamwork, and participative management make it important to hire skilled people who also fit in socially.
- Firing unsatisfactory employees is often very difficult because of laws such as those involving discrimination by age, sex, and race. It is necessary to evaluate employees very carefully to be sure they will be effective long-term members of the organization.
- Some organizations have unattractive workplaces, have policies that demand promotions from within, operate under union regulations, or have low wages that make recruiting and keeping employees difficult or subject to outside influence and restrictions.

Because recruiting is a difficult chore that involves finding, hiring, and training people who are an appropriate technical and social fit, human resource managers turn to many sources for assistance (see Figure 17-3). These include internal promotions, advertisements, public and private employment agencies, college placement bureaus, management consultants, temporary help services (for example, Kelly and Manpower), professional organizations, referrals, and applicants who simply show up at the office.

Selection

Selection is the process of gathering information to decide who should be hired, under legal guidelines, for the best interests of the individual and the organization. Because of high turnover the cost of selecting and training employees has become prohibitively high in some firms. Think of the costs involved—interview time, medical exams, training costs, unproductive time spent learning the job, moving expenses, and so on—and you can see that such expenses can run over $50,000 for a manager. Even low-level workers cost thousands of dollars to recruit, process, and train. Thus the selection process is an important element in any human resource program. A typical selection process would involve six steps (see Figure 17-4):

selection
The process of gathering information to decide who should be hired, under legal guidelines, for the best interests of the individual and the organization.

1. Completion of an application form. Once this was a simple procedure with few complications. But new laws limit the kind of questions one can ask. Certainly such forms help discover educational background, past work experience, career objectives, and other information directly related to the requirements of the job (see the sample application form on p. 455).
2. Initial and follow-up interviews. Many managers and some human resource managers are not highly skilled in conducting job interviews. However, such interviews are helpful in testing an applicant's ability to communicate clearly, to adapt to a stressful situation, and to clarify his or her goals, career objective, and background.
3. Employment tests. Employment tests have been severely criticized because of charges of discrimination. Nonetheless, organizations continue to use them to measure basic competencies, to test specific job skills (for example, welding, typing), and to help evaluate applicants' personalities and interests.

FIGURE 17-4

Steps in passing the selection process.

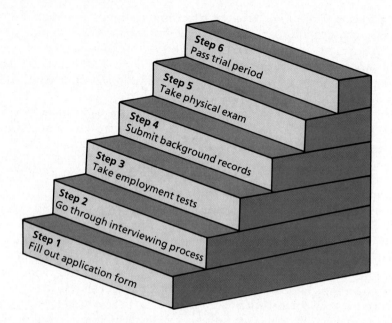

4   Background investigations. Most organizations are becoming more careful about investigating a candidate's work record, school record, and recommendations. It is simply too costly to hire, train, motivate, and lose people and then have to start the process over. Background checks help weed out candidates least likely to succeed and identify those most likely to succeed.

5   Physical exams. A complete medical background and checkup helps screen candidates. There are obvious benefits in hiring healthy people. Medical tests cannot be given just to screen out individuals. If such tests are given, they must be given everyone applying for the same position. A major controversy in the late 1980s was the proposal to use drug tests to screen employees in industry and the government. That debate is likely to continue for some time.

6   Trial periods. Often an organization will hire an employee conditionally. This enables the person to prove his or her worth on the job. After a period of 6 months or a year, the firm has the right to fire that employee based on evaluations from supervisors. Such systems make it easier to fire inefficient or problem employees, but do not eliminate the high cost of turnover.

The selection process is often long and difficult, but worth the effort because of the high costs of replacing workers. The process helps assure that the people an organization hires are competent in all relevant areas, including communication skills, education, technical skills, experience, social fit, and health.

Most firms recruit people who have the potential to be productive employees. Realizing that potential involves effective training programs and proper managerial incentives. The next step is employee orientation.

Employee Orientation

employee orientation
The activity that introduces new employees to the organization, to fellow employees, to their immediate supervisors, and to the policies, practices, and objectives of the firm.

Employee orientation is the activity that introduces new employees to the organization, to fellow employees, to their immediate supervisors, and to the policies, practices, and objectives of the firm. Orientation programs vary from quite infor-

Application form.

GENERAL DYNAMICS

GENERAL DYNAMICS IS AN EQUAL OPPORTUNITY EMPLOYER

APPLICATION FOR EMPLOYMENT

DATE		
Mo.	Day	Year

INSTRUCTIONS: FILL IN ALL INFORMATION. INCOMPLETE APPLICATIONS WILL NOT BE CONSIDERED FOR EMPLOYMENT. PRINT OR WRITE WITH BLACK INK OR TYPE IF PREFERRED. UPCOMING COLLEGE GRADUATES ATTACH A COURSE WORK TRANSCRIPT. OVERFLOW INFORMATION MAY BE PUT IN THE REMARKS SECTION.

PERSONAL

LAST NAME   FIRST NAME   MIDDLE NAME   SOCIAL SECURITY NUMBER

CURRENT ADDRESS   CITY   STATE   ZIP CODE   (A/C)   TELEPHONE

PERMANENT ADDRESS   CITY   STATE   ZIP CODE   (A/C)   TELEPHONE

IN CASE OF EMERGENCY NOTIFY: (A/C)   TELEPHONE

ADDRESS OF PERSON LISTED FOR EMERGENCY   CITY   STATE   ZIP CODE

IF EMPLOYED, CAN YOU PROVIDE PROOF OF UNITED STATES CITIZENSHIP? ☐ NO ☐ YES

IF NOT A U.S. CITIZEN, SPECIFY ALIEN REGISTRATION NUMBER:

HAVE YOU EVER BEEN KNOWN BY ANY OTHER NAMES (Include Nicknames); IF SO, WHAT?

DO YOU HAVE ANY PHYSICAL OR MENTAL LIMITATIONS WHICH COULD AFFECT YOUR ABILITY TO PERFORM THE JOB OR JOBS FOR WHICH YOU ARE APPLYING? IF YES, GIVE DETAILS. ☐ NO ☐ YES ACCOMMODATIONS REQUIRED:

ARE YOU AT LEAST 18 YEARS OF AGE? ☐ YES ☐ NO
HOW WERE YOU REFERRED?
☐ NEWSPAPER, WHICH ONE?
☐ AGENCY
☐ GOVERNMENTAL EMPLOYMENT SERVICE
☐ FRIEND/EMPLOYEE
☐ COLLEGE PLACEMENT OFFICE
☐ OTHER – PLEASE SPECIFY

GEOGRAPHICAL PREFERENCE _____ RELOCATION RESTRICTIONS _____ TRAVEL RESTRICTIONS _____

EDUCATION

CIRCLE HIGHEST EDUCATION COMPLETED

GRADE SCHOOL 1 2 3 4 5 6 7 8   HIGH SCHOOL 9 10 11 12   COLLEGE* 1 2 3 4 5   GRADUATE SCHOOL 1 2 3 4 5

	NAME & LOCATION	DATES ATTENDED MO./YR.	DATES ATTENDED MO./YR.	GRADUATED MO./YR.	DEGREE** CERTIFICATE DIPLOMA	MAJORED IN	MINORED IN	GPA/ POSSIBLE
HIGH SCHOOL								
COLLEGE(s)								
GRADUATE SCHOOL(s)								
MILITARY/ OTHER								

SCHOLASTIC HONORS, SCHOLARSHIPS, ETC. _____

LIST PUBLICATIONS, THESIS, ETC. _____

PROFESSIONAL LICENSES _____

*IF CO-OP GRADUATE, SPECIFY TOTAL WORK PERIODS .... SEMESTER _____ QUARTER _____

**SPECIFY NUMBER OF COLLEGE HOURS EARNED IF NO DEGREE OBTAINED .... SEMESTER _____ QUARTER _____

JOB INTEREST

TYPE OF WORK PREFERRED: ☐ FULL TIME ☐ PART TIME ☐ CO-OP ☐ SUMMER ☐ OTHER

HAVE YOU EVER WORKED FOR GENERAL DYNAMICS? ☐ NO ☐ YES DIVISION: DATES:

HAVE YOU EVER BEEN GRANTED A U.S. GOVERNMENT SECURITY CLEARANCE? ☐ NO ☐ YES TYPE/LEVEL: EMPLOYER: DATES:

HAVE YOU EVER HAD A SECURITY CLEARANCE SUSPENDED, DENIED OR REVOKED? ☐ NO ☐ YES EMPLOYER: DATE:

DO YOU HAVE RELATIVES EMPLOYED AT GD? ☐ NO ☐ YES NAME: RELATIONSHIP: GD DIVISION:

CAN YOU OPERATE WORD PROCESSING EQUIPMENT? ☐ NO ☐ YES MAKE/MODEL:

CAN YOU UTILIZE PERSONAL COMPUTERS? ☐ NO ☐ YES MAKE/MODEL:

WILL YOU WORK: YES NO
ANY SHIFT ☐ ☐
OVERTIME ☐ ☐
SATURDAYS ☐ ☐
SUNDAYS ☐ ☐

DATE AVAILABLE FOR EMPLOYMENT?

MAY WE CONTACT YOUR PRESENT EMPLOYER? ☐ NO ☐ YES

TYPING SPEED _____ WPM   SHORT-HAND SPEED _____ WPM

MILITARY STATUS

BRANCH OF U.S. ARMED FORCES	DATE ENTERED	DATE & TYPE OF DISCHARGE/RETIREMENT	RANK/RATE AT DISCHARGE
OTHER MILITARY SERVICE (Including Reserves)	DATE ENTERED	DATE & TYPE OF DISCHARGE/RETIREMENT	RANK/RATE AT DISCHARGE

mal, primarily verbal efforts to formal schedules that have employees visit various departments for a day or more and include lengthy handouts.[3] Formal programs may cover:

- History and general policies of the organization
- Descriptions of products or services provided by the organization to the public

- The formal organization chart
- Safety measures and regulations
- Human relations policies and practices
- Compensation, benefits, and employee services
- Daily routines and regulations
- Some introduction to the corporate culture—the values and orientation of the organization
- Organizational objectives and the role of the new recruit in accomplishing those objectives

PROGRESS CHECK

- What are the six steps in human resource planning?
- What are the six steps in the selection process?
- Can you define recruitment and selection?

EMPLOYEE TRAINING AND DEVELOPMENT

New technologies such as word processors and computers have made it necessary to do more training, and more sophisticated training as well. Furthermore, organizations are recognizing that people are their most vital resource and are getting much more involved in continued education and development programs for their employees. Career development is no longer just a haphazard system of promotions, moves, and occasional training programs. Rather, it is a long-term organizational strategy for assisting employees to optimize their skills and education.

training and development
All attempts to improve employee performance by increasing an employee's ability to perform through learning.

Training and development include all attempts to improve performance by increasing an employee's ability to perform through learning. The most fundamental training programs involve on-the-job training. **On-the-job training** means that the employee immediately begins his or her tasks and learns by doing, or watches others for a while and then imitates them, right at the workplace. Salespeople, for example, are often trained by watching experienced salespeople perform. Naturally, this can be either quite effective or disastrous, depending on the skills and habits of the person being watched. On-the-job training is obviously the easiest kind of training to implement and can be effective where the job is easily learned, such as clerking in a store, or performing repetitive physical tasks such as collecting refuse, cleaning carpets, and mowing lawns.

on-the-job training
The employee immediately begins his or her tasks and learns by doing, or watches others for a while and then imitates them, all right at the workplace.

Apprentice Programs

Many skilled crafts, such as bricklaying or plumbing, require a new worker to serve several years as an apprentice. An **apprenticeship** is a period of time when a learner works alongside a skilled worker to learn the skills and procedures of a craft. Unions often require such periods to assure excellence among their members as well as to limit entry to the union.

apprenticeship
A time when a new worker works alongside a master technician to learn the skills and procedures.

In the future, there are likely to be more but shorter apprenticeship programs to prepare people for skilled jobs in auto repair (the new computers and other electronics make the job much more complex), computers, and other skilled jobs.

Off-the-Job Training

Training is becoming more sophisticated as jobs become more sophisticated. Furthermore, training is expanding to include education (through the Ph.D.), personal development (for example, time management, stress management, health education, psychological training), and more (for example, physical education, health testing, and even classes in art and languages).

Some firms do such training internally and have elaborate training facilities. Other firms must assign such training to outside sources. **Off-the-job training** consists of internal and external programs to develop a variety of skills and to foster personal development that occur away from the workplace. This includes classroom lectures, conferences, films, as well as workshops, tapes, reading programs, and the like.

off-the-job training
Internal and external programs to develop a variety of skills and foster personal development away from the workplace.

Vestibule Training

Vestibule training is done in schools where employees are taught on equipment similar to that used on the job. Such schools enable employees to learn proper methods and safety procedures before joining the department.

vestibule training
Done in schools where employees are given instructions on equipment similar to that used on the job.

Job Simulation

One of the faster growing aspects of training is simulation exercises. **Job simulation** is the use of equipment that duplicates job conditions and tasks so that trainees can learn skills before attempting them on the job. This is the kind of training given astronauts, airline pilots, Army tank operators, ship captains, and others who must learn highly skilled jobs off the job. Astronauts, for example, must learn to work, eat, sleep, wash, and live in an environment of weightlessness. Simulation training sometimes takes place underwater (to simulate weightlessness) and in a variety of laboratories that can artificially create real-life experiences before attempting them.

job simulation
The use of equipment that duplicates job conditions and tasks so that trainees can learn skills before attempting them on the job.

A jet simulation.

Imagine the benefits of simulating the landing of an airplane in a major storm for the first time or docking a huge ocean liner in a small port facility. Such tasks are better learned in a simulator where many variables can be programmed to give people practical experience in a laboratory setting.

Computers can simulate the sounds, sights, smells, and emotions of the most trying circumstances (for example, fighting another jet plane in aerial combat). Given such capability it is easy to simulate other skills, such as managing the operating room of a nuclear power plant or operating new equipment of any kind.

PERFORMANCE APPRAISALS

All managers must supervise employees. (Remember, that is the definition of *management*—getting work done through others.) Therefore, they must be able to determine whether or not their workers are doing an effective and efficient job, with a minimum of errors and disruptions. Such a determination is called a performance appraisal and consists of these six steps:

1 *Establishing performance standards*. This is a crucial step. Standards must be understandable, subject to measurement, and reasonable.

2 *Communicating those standards*. Often managers assume that employees know what is expected of them, but such assumptions are dangerous at best. Employees must be told clearly and precisely what the standards and expectations are and how they are to be met.

3 *Evaluating performance*. If the first two steps are done correctly, performance evaluation is relatively easy. It is a matter of observing behavior to see if it matches standards.

4 *Discussing results with employees*. Most people will make mistakes and fail to meet expectations at first. It takes time to learn a new job and do it well. Discussing an employee's successes and areas that need improvement is an opportunity to be understanding and helpful and to guide the employee to better performance. Often managers feel that employees are to blame when standards are not met. But supervisors will learn that top management asks four questions when employees don't do well: (1) Who hired them? (2) Who trained them? (3) Who motivates them? and (4) Who should be fired if they fail? The answers make it pretty clear that supervisors are responsible for performance through others.

5 *Taking corrective action*. When needed.

6 *Using the results to make decisions*. Decisions about promotions, compensation, additional training, or firing are all based on performance evaluations.

If these steps sound like the management by objectives (MBO) you read about in Chapter 16, that is no accident. The measure of any employee's work is results. Were the objectives met or not? Management means getting results with top performance out of employees. That is what performance appraisals are for—at all levels of the organization. A **performance appraisal,** therefore, is an evaluation of the performance level of employees against established standards to make decisions about promotions, compensation, additional training, or firing.

performance appraisal
An evaluation of the performance level of employees against standards to make decisions about promotions, compensation, additional training, or firing.

PROGRESS CHECK

■ Can you name and describe four training techniques?

■ What are the six steps in a performance appraisal?

COMPENSATION AND BENEFITS

Employee compensation is one of the largest operating costs for many organizations. The long-term success of a firm—perhaps even its survival—may depend on how well it can control employee costs and optimize employee efficiency. Examples of organizations that have recently struggled with high employee costs include the auto industry, the steel industry, and the Kroger chain of supermarkets. Organizations such as these have asked employees to take reductions in wages to make the firm more competitive or risk going out of business and losing their jobs forever. Many employees have agreed, even union employees who had traditionally resisted such cuts. In other words, the competitive environment of the 1980s is such that compensation and benefit packages are being given special attention and are likely to remain of major concern in the near future.

The steel industry is working with employees on new compensation packages to be more competitive.

Several objectives can be accomplished by a compensation and benefit program. They include:

- Attracting the kind of people needed by the organization and in sufficient numbers
- Providing employees with the incentive to work efficiently and productively
- Keeping valued employees from leaving and going to competitors or starting competing firms
- Maintaining a competitive position in the marketplace by keeping costs low through high productivity
- Protecting employees from unexpected problems such as layoffs, sickness, and disability
- Assuring employees of funds to carry them through retirement

Pay Systems

The latest hero in China is a man named Bu Xinsheng.[4] He runs a highly successful shirt factory. From the mid-1970s to the mid-1980s, Mr. Bu raised the factory's assets and its number of workers from $10,000 and 73 respectively to $600,000 and 630. China is not known for its creative management techniques and highly productive work force. So, how did Mr. Bu do it? He switched his factory from straight wages to piecework. That increased the maximum possible wage from $18 a month to the equivalent of $41 a month, but workers had to work much harder to earn more. The government was thrilled with Mr. Bu's success and now supports Mr. Bu in implementing capitalist ideas such as market research, developing private brands, implementing graduated benefits for his workers, and buying equipment to expand production for export sales.

We see from this story that the type of pay system in an organization can have a dramatic effect on efficiency and productivity. Different systems include the following:

FIGURE 17-5

Alternate compensation techniques.

PAYMENT METHOD	DESCRIPTION
Straight salary	Weekly, monthly, or annual payment
Hourly wages	Number of hours worked times agreed-upon hourly wage
Commission system	Sales revenue times some fixed percentage
Salary plus commission	Base salary (weekly, monthly, or annual) plus sales revenue times some fixed percentage
Piecework	Number of items produced times some agreed-on rate per unit
ADDED COMPENSATION	
Overtime	Number of hours worked beyond standard (for example, 40 hours) times hourly wages for weekdays and double time for weekends and holidays
Bonuses	Varies by company; basically extra pay for meeting or exceeding objectives
Profit sharing	Additional payments based on company profits
Cost-of-living allowances (COLAs)	Annual increases in wages based on consumer price increases

- Salary systems, where compensation is computed on weekly, biweekly, or monthly pay periods. The typical college graduate is paid a salary.
- Hourly wage or daywork is the system used for most blue collar workers. Often employees must punch a time clock when they arrive at work and when they leave. Hourly wages vary greatly. Minimum wage is $3.35 and top wages go as high as $15 to $25 for skilled auto workers. This does not include benefits such as retirement systems that add 25% to 30% more to the total package.
- Piecework means that employees are paid according to the number of items they produce rather than by the hour or day. This system creates powerful incentives to work efficiently and productively. It was so effective for Mr. Bu that he has become a model manager in China.

- Commission plans are used to compensate salespeople. They resemble piecework; the commission is based on some percentage of sales.
- Bonus plans are used for executives, salespeople, and other employees. They earn bonuses for accomplishing or surpassing certain objectives.
- Profit-sharing plans give employees some share of profits over and above their normal pay.

Scanlon Plans

The pay systems discussed above can be combined in many creative ways. One effective strategy for involving employees in productivity programs is called the **Scanlon plan.** Under the Scanlon plan, committees are formed to make suggestions for productivity improvements. Members of the committee work closely with management to plan all areas of work, including equipment usage, quality standards, production standards, and so forth. Using such information, a norm is established for production levels. If the employees exceed the norm, a bonus fund is created and is shared 75/25, with 75% going to the employees and the rest kept in the firm. As you can imagine, this plan encourages participation among employees and many suggestions for improving productivity.

Scanlon plan
Uses committees to set performance standards, and if the employees exceed the standards, a bonus is created, with 75% going to the employee.

Fringe Benefits

Fringe benefits include sick-leave pay, vacation pay, pension plans, and health plans that provide additional compensation to employees. Fringe benefits in the 1980s grew faster than wages. According to a recent study by the United States Chamber of Commerce, U.S. companies now spend an average of $6,627 a year per employee for benefits. That is about 37% of the average worker's salary, compared with 30% a decade ago.[5] Many employees request more fringe benefits instead of more salary to avoid higher taxes. This has resulted in much debate and much government investigation.

fringe benefits
Benefits such as sick-leave pay, vacation pay, pension plans, and health plans that represent additional compensation to employees.

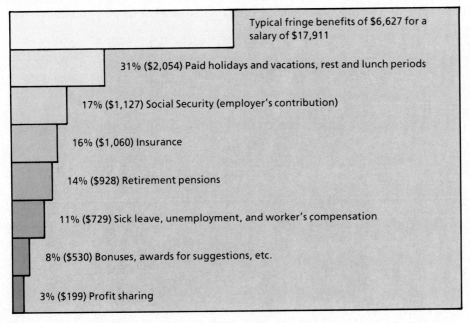

Typical fringe benefits of $6,627 for a salary of $17,911

31% ($2,054) Paid holidays and vacations, rest and lunch periods

17% ($1,127) Social Security (employer's contribution)

16% ($1,060) Insurance

14% ($928) Retirement pensions

11% ($729) Sick leave, unemployment, and worker's compensation

8% ($530) Bonuses, awards for suggestions, etc.

3% ($199) Profit sharing

The average employee receives over $6,600 in fringe benefits per year. This represents 37% of the total wage cost.

Source: U.S. Department of Commerce.

Fringe benefits include everything from paid vacations to health care programs, recreation facilities, company cars, and executive dining rooms. Managing the benefit package will be a major human resource issue in the 1990s. Employees want packages to include dental care, eye care, and shorter work weeks. Many firms are offering a cafeteria-style list of fringe benefits from which employees can choose up to a certain dollar amount. In other words, benefits are as important to wage negotiations now as salary. In the future, they may be more important.

Fringe benefits for employees include exercise rooms.

MANAGEMENT DEVELOPMENT

In the past employees were eager to become managers and were quite willing to make sacrifices for that honor. For example, people were willing to relocate often. (There was once a joke that *IBM* meant "I've been moved.") People were also willing to work longer hours, take on additional responsibilities, and "do what it takes" to move up the corporate ladder.

Things have changed today. Moving is not only costly, but affects the employee's children, friendships, community ties, and more. Management responsibilities are stressful, tiring, and affect family life. For these reasons and more it is becoming more difficult to find and keep good managers. Those who are willing must be trained to assume an entirely diffferent role: one of counselor, advisor, trainer, educator, coach, and assistant. As we have noted, managers are no longer mere bosses or rule makers and enforcers.

Managers need different training than most employees. They need to be good communicators and especially need to learn listening skills and empathy. They also need time management, planning, and human relations skills.

Management development, then, is the process of training and educating employees to become good managers and then developing managerial skills over time. Management development programs have sprung up everywhere, especially at colleges, universities, and private management development firms. Managers participate in various role-playing exercises, solve various management cases, and are exposed to films, lectures, and all kinds of management development processes.

management development
The process of training and educating employees to become good managers and then developing managerial skills over time.

A management development class.

Many managers are paid to take college-level courses through the doctorate level. Most management training programs also include several of the following:

- *On-the-job coaching*. This means that a senior manager will assist a lower-level manager by teaching him or her needed skills and generally providing direction, advice, and helpful criticism. Such programs are only effective when the senior managers are skilled themselves and have the ability to educate others. This is not always the case.
- *Understudy positions*. Job titles such as "Undersecretary of . . ." and "Assistant to . . ." reveal a relatively successful way of developing managers. They work as assistants to higher level managers and participate in planning and other managerial functions until they are ready to assume such positions themselves. Such assistants may take over when higher level managers are on vacation or on business trips.
- *Job rotation*. To expose managers to different functions of the organization, they are often given assignments in a variety of departments. Top managers, of course, must have a broad picture of the organization and such rotation gives them that exposure.
- *Off-the-job courses and training*. Managers periodically go to schools or seminars for a week or more to hone their technical and human relations skills. Such courses expose them to the latest concepts and create a sense of camaraderie as the managers live, eat, and work together in a college-type atmosphere. This is often where case studies and simulation exercises of all kinds are employed.

The Importance of Networking

Over time, men have developed what has been called an "old boy" network, through which certain senior managers become mentors to certain junior managers. They introduce them to the important managers, enroll them in the "right" clubs, and guide them into the "right" social groups. Young male managers are thus socialized regarding proper dress, behavior, and procedures to follow to rise up the corporate hierarchy.

Country clubs are part of the "old boy" network.

networking
The process of establishing and maintaining contacts with key managers in one's own organization and in other organizations and using those contacts to weave strong relationships that serve as informal development systems.

Women managers are just now learning the importance and the value of such networking and of having mentors. Women managers were often excluded (and many still are) from the country clubs and social clubs where men have carried on the tradition of corporate socialization and contact making. More and more, however, women are now entering this system or creating their own systems. **Networking,** then, is the process of establishing and maintaining contacts with key managers in one's own organization and in other organizations and using those contacts to weave strong relationships that serve as informal development systems.

NETWORKING AMONG BLACKS

Networking, exchanging everything from tips on job openings to advice on handling personnel problems, has expanded significantly among blacks in the last decade. Both professional women and blacks have learned from the "old boy" networks practiced by white male professionals for years.

Charles Grant, a former president of the National Black MBA Association, says that "Fifteen years ago, blacks didn't have the position, time, know-how or inclination to network. Now they're recognizing it as a tool." Blacks have always networked in churches, social clubs, and community groups. Now they are moving into business's professional ranks.

In 1981, a nine-member Federation of Corporate Professionals was started for networking of black organizations. In 1983, the Atlanta Exchange, a group of eleven black business and professional associations, was begun. These are just a couple of examples of blacks giving each other support, counsel, and information. Such networking should result in quicker advancements for black businesspeople.

Source: Carmen J. Lee, "Rise in Networking Among Blacks is Yielding Sizable Career Benefits," *The Wall Street Journal*, October 12, 1984, p. 33.

mentors
Corporate managers who supervise, coach, and guide lower level people by introducing them to the right people and groups and generally being their organizational sponsors.

Of equal or greater importance to women is the need for **mentors,** corporate managers who supervise, coach, and guide selected lower level people by introducing them to the right people and groups and generally being their organizational sponsors. Historically, there have been relatively few top-level women managers. Today this is changing, and women are developing networks and mentor relationships that are tremendous aids in the development process.

PROGRESS CHECK

■ Can you name and describe five alternative compensation techniques?

■ Can you define the terms *fringe benefits, networking,* and *mentors?*

ADJUSTING TO WORKER NEEDS

By now, you are quite familiar with the trends occurring in the workforce. You know, for example, that many more women are working now. You also know that managers and workers are demanding more from jobs in the way of flexibility and responsiveness. From these trends have emerged several new or renewed ideas such as job sharing, flextime, and networking. We shall discuss these ideas next.

Job Sharing Plans

Job sharing is an arrangement whereby two part-time employees share one full-time job. The concept has received great attention in recent years as more and more mothers with small children enter the labor force. Job sharing enables these mothers to work part time while the children are in school. Job sharing is also good for students, older people who want to work part time before fully retiring, and others who can only work part time. The benefits are:

- It offers employment opportunities to those who cannot or prefer not to work full time.
- An employee is more likely to maintain a high level of enthusiasm and productivity for 4 hours than 8 hours; therefore two part-time employees are often much more productive than one full-time employee.
- Part-time employees have time to shop, visit the doctor, and do other personal chores; therefore, absenteeism for such reasons is lowered.
- Employers are better able to schedule people into peak demand periods (for example, banks on payday) when part-time people are available.

Disadvantages include having to hire, train, motivate, and supervise twice as many people and prorating some fringe benefits. But most firms that were at first reluctant to try job sharing are finding the benefits outweigh the disadvantages.

job sharing
An arrangement whereby two part-time employees share one full-time job.

Flextime plans

Flextime plans give employees some freedom to adjust when they work as long as they work the required number of hours. The most popular plans allow employees to come to work at 7, 8, or 9 AM and leave between 4 and 7 PM. There usually is some **core time** (for example, 10 to 12 and 2 to 4) when everyone must be present. Flextime plans, like job-sharing plans, are designed to allow employees to adjust to the new demands of the times, especially the trend toward two-income families. The advantages of flextime include:

- Working mothers and fathers can schedule their days so that someone can be home to see the children off to school and the other partner can be home soon after school.
- Employees can schedule doctor's appointments and other personal tasks during working hours by coming in early and leaving at 3 or 4 PM.
- Traffic congestion is greatly reduced as employees arrive over several hours instead of all at once.

flextime plans
Give employees some freedom to adjust when they work as long as they work the required number of hours.

core time
The time when all employees are present in a flextime system.

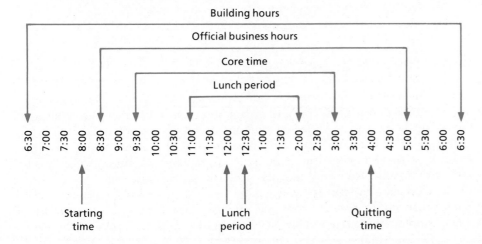

A flextime chart. Employees can start any time between 6:30 and 9:30. They then take half an hour for lunch and can quit from 3:00 to 6:30. Everyone works an 8-hour day. The red arrows show a typical flextime day.

- Employees can work when they are most productive; some people are most alert early in the morning, while others can't get going until 9 AM.
- A big psychological boost comes when an employee has some choice about sleeping late once in a while or taking off early on Friday afternoon in the spring.

There are some real disadvantages to flextime as well. Flextime does not work, for example, for assembly lines where everyone must be at work at the same time. It also is not effective for shift work.

Where flextime is employed, managers often have to work longer days to be there to assist and supervise employees. Some organizations operate from 6 AM to 6 PM under flextime, a potentially long day for supervisors. Flextime also makes communication more difficult; certain employees may not be there when others need to talk to them. Furthermore, some employees could abuse the system, if not carefully supervised, and that could cause resentment among others. You can imagine how you'd feel if half the work force left at 3 PM on Friday and you had to work until 7 PM. Longer working hours also means more energy use.

In spite of the difficulties, flextime has become quite popular. It has obvious advantages for creative people who are most productive at certain times of the day. But it also is helpful for anyone who likes the flexibility of sleeping late once in a while or working long hours when a proposal is due.

Compressed Work Weeks

compressed work week
Four 10-hour days.

A popular option in some organizations today is a **compressed work week.** That means that an employee would work four 10-hour days and have a long weekend instead of working five 8-hour days. There are the obvious advantages of working only 4 days and having 3 days off, but some employees get tired working such long hours, and productivity could decline. Most employees find such a system of great benefit, however, and are quite enthusiastic about it.

THINKING IT THROUGH

What effect have dual career families had on the personnel function? Have you noticed any changes in nepotism rules with so many marriages involving two professionals? (*Nepotism* means hiring relatives.) What problems can arise when family members work together in the same firm? What is your reaction to employees who date one another? Are such questions interesting enough to make you think about becoming a human resource manager?

HUMAN RESOURCE MANAGEMENT

As you can see from this discussion, human resource management has become a major element in the management of organizations. New laws have made hiring, promoting, firing, and employee relations in general very complex and subject to many legal complications. New competitive pressures have created the need for more careful compensation planning and administration. New concerns with health and safety have created completely new problems for management.

In short, human resource management has become a job for professionals. Those professionals are called personnel managers. The American Society of Personnel Administration (ASPA) has given recognition to the professional nature of this function and has developed categories for managers: (1) Accredited Executive in Personnel (AEP); (2) Accredited Personnel Manager (APM); (3) Accredited Personnel Diplomat (APD); and (4) Accredited Personnel Specialist (APS). In addition to the American Society of Personnel Administration, personnel specialists may join the American Society of Training Directors, the American Management Association, the International Personnel Management Association, and more.

Professional personnel managers are responsible for all levels of human resource management from resource planning to retirement plans. Specialists handle various aspects of resource management such as executive training, compensation, and so on. In short, there are a variety of exciting and challenging careers in human resource management that are becoming even more challenging in the new dynamic high-tech era where the recruiting, motivating, and retaining of highly skilled professionals will be the key to success or failure of many firms.

LAWS AFFECTING HUMAN RESOURCE MANAGEMENT

The government had little to do with personnel decisions until the 1930s. Since then, though, legislation and legal decisions have greatly impacted all areas of human resource management, from hiring to training and working conditions (see Figure 17-6).

■ National Labor Relations Act of 1935	Established collective bargaining in labor-management relations and limits management interference in the right of employees to have a collective bargaining agent.	**FIGURE 17-6** Some laws affecting personnel decisions.
■ Fair Labor Standards Act of 1938	Established a minimum wage and overtime pay for employees working more than 40 hours a week.	
■ Manpower Development and Training Act of 1962	Provided for the training and retraining of unemployed workers.	
■ Equal Pay Act of 1963	Specified that men and women who are doing equal jobs must be paid the same wage.	
■ The Civil Rights Act of 1964	Outlawed discrimination in employment based on sex, race, color, religion, or national origin.	
■ Age Discrimination in Employment Act of 1967	Outlawed personnel practices that discriminate against people aged 40 to 69. An amendment outlaws company policies that require employees to retire before age 70.	
■ Occupational Safety and Health Act of 1970 (OSHA)	Regulated the degree to which employees can be exposed to hazardous substances and specified the safety equipment to be provided by the employer.	
■ The Comprehensive Employment and Training Act of 1973	Provided funds for training unemployed workers (was known as the CETA program).	
■ Employee Retirement Income Security Act of 1974	Regulated company retirement programs and provided a federal insurance program for bankrupt retirement plans.	

One of the most important pieces of legislation was the Civil Rights Act of 1964. Title VII of that act prohibits discrimination in hiring, compensation, terms, conditions, or privileges of employment based on race, religion, creed, sex, or national origin. Interpretation of this law eventually led employers to actively recruit and give preference to minority groups. Supreme Court Justice William Brennan wrote in 1986, "A court may have to resort to race-conscious affirmative action when confronted with an employer or labor union that has engaged in persistent or egregious discrimination."

College women seeking jobs might take note of the fact that Title VII includes discrimination by sex. Equal pay for equal work is the law.

In 1972, the Equal Employment Opportunity Act (EEOA) was added as an amendment to Title VII. It established the Equal Employment Opportunity Commission (EEOC). The commission has the power to file suits against employers if it cannot secure an acceptable resolution of discrimination charges within 30 days.

Another significant piece of legislation was the Age Discrimination in Employment Act of 1967. This act protects 40 to 69-year-olds from discrimination. It will have special significance as baby boom adults reach this age.

In the area of training, the government passed the 1962 Manpower Development and Training Act. The goal was to train and retrain unemployed workers and those whose jobs were threatened by technological advances. The act was extended in 1965 so that on-the-job training could be done by corporations at government expense.

Laws Protecting the Disabled

The courts are looking carefully into hiring and selection procedures to prevent discrimination as much as possible. This is true for the disabled as well as minorities. The Vocational Rehabilitation Act (1973) extended the same protection given minorities and women to the disabled, including making reasonable accommodations to their physical and mental limitations.

Minimum Wage Legislation

Some controversy has been raised about legislation regarding wages. Of major concern is the minimum wage law. The minimum hourly wage went from $1.60 in 1968 to $2.65 in 1978. It is now $3.35 per hour. The controversy is over the effect of such minimum wages on teenage employment, especially among blacks. People have noted that the higher the minimum wage went, the higher teenage unemployment among blacks became; it has reached 50% or more. No cause-effect proof was offered, but it has been proposed that teenagers be exempt from minimum wage to enable employers to hire them for less. There is great resistance to this idea, however, because it is feared teenagers would then replace older, higher paid workers.

Other Legislation

Legislation also affects employee benefits, working conditions, and compensation, including time-and-a-half for overtime. Such legislation includes the Social Security Act (1935), the Occupational Safety and Health Act (OSHA) of 1970, and the Employment Retirement Income Security Act (ERISA) of 1974. New tax laws affecting Keogh and IRA accounts add to the effects of government on benefits

CAREER INFORMATION: PERSONNEL AND HUMAN RESOURCE DEVELOPMENT

NATURE OF THE WORK

Personnel, training, and labor relations specialists concentrate on different aspects of employer-employee relations. *Personnel specialists* interview, select, and recommend applicants for job openings; stay abreast of rules and regulations pertaining to affirmative action and equal employment opportunity; and help develop policies on hiring and advancement. They also handle wage and salary administration, pensions and benefits, and employee assistance programs. *Training specialists* develop courses, workshops, and other programs tailored to the training needs of an organization and its employees. Trainers consult with managers and supervisors about specific training needs, prepare manuals and other materials for use in training sessions, and keep employees informed about training opportunities. "Labor relations" means union-management relations, and *labor relations specialists* work in unionized establishments, for the most part. They help company officials prepare for collective bargaining sessions, participate in contract negotiations, and handle labor relations matters that come up every day.

In a small organization, one person can handle all aspects of personnel administration. By contrast, the personnel department in a large firm is likely to include recruiters, interviewers, job analysts, benefits specialists, training specialists, and labor relations specialists. Personnel clerks and assistants handle routine tasks such as issuing forms, maintaining files, compiling statistics, and answering inquiries.

JOB OUTLOOK

The number of personnel, training, and labor relations specialists is expected to grow about as fast as the average for all occupations through the mid-1990s. Most growth will occur in the private sector as employers try to provide effective employee relations programs for an expanding and aging work force. Relatively little growth is anticipated in public personnel administration.

Corporate recognition of the importance of human resource development is expected to result in greater investment in job-specific, employer-sponsored training and retraining as a response to productivity concerns, the aging of the workforce, and technological advances that can suddenly leave large numbers of employees with obsolete skills.

Although the number of jobs in this field is projected to increase through the mid-1990s, the job market is likely to remain competitive, given the abundant supply of recent college graduates and experienced workers with suitable qualifications.

EARNINGS

Typical entry level jobs in the personnel field include job analyst, EEO representative, benefits analyst, and training specialist. These positions generally require a bachelor's degree but no experience. Salaries vary widely, and depend on the size and location of the firm as well as the nature of its business.

In the federal government, new graduates with a bachelor's degree generally started at about $13,800 a year in 1985.

In 1984, the median salary for compensation analysts was $25,150; for benefits planning analysts, $23,989; for employee counselors, $26,712; for recruiters (professional/managerial), $26,460; and for personnel information specialists, $24,300. The median salary for EEO affirmative action managers was $35,000; for compensation and benefits managers, $33,417; for training and organizational development managers, $37,682; and for labor relations managers, $37,500.

According to a Bureau of Labor Statistics survey, average annual salaries of personnel directors in private industry ranged from $35,444 to $65,874 in 1984. Top personnel and labor relations executives in large corporations earned considerably more.

RELATED OCCUPATIONS

All personnel, training, and labor relations occupations are closely related. Other workers who help people find jobs or help to make the work environment safe and pleasant include health and regulatory inspectors, occupational safety and health workers, employment counselors, rehabilitation counselors, college career planning and placement counselors, industrial engineers, psychologists, and sociologists.

SOURCES OF ADDITIONAL INFORMATION

For general information on careers in personnel and industrial relations, write to:

American Society for Personnel Administration, 606 N. Washington St., Alexandria, Va. 22314.

Source: *Occupational Outlook Handbook,* 1986-1987 (U.S. Department of Labor).

planning, retirement, and other human resource areas. It is best to read *The Wall Street Journal, Business Week,* and other current magazines to keep current with all human resource legislation and rulings.

We have devoted this much space to the legislation affecting human resource management because such decisions have had an enormous impact on personnel programs, and will continue to do so. Recent suits charging male managers with sexual harassment of women are intensifying the sensitivity of all employers to the legal rights not only of women, but of minorities, the disabled, and older employees as well. In summary:

- Employers must be sensitive to the legal rights of women, minorities, disabled, and older employees or risk costly court cases.
- Legislation affects all areas of human resource management, from hiring and training to wages and benefits.
- Court cases have made it clear that it is sometimes legal to go beyond providing equal rights for minorities to provide special employment (affirmative action) and training to correct discrimination in the past.
- New court cases and legislation change human resource management almost daily; the only way to keep current is to read the business literature and become familiar with the issues.

PROGRESS CHECK

▪ Can you explain what was covered by the following laws?
1. The Equal Pay Act of 1963
2. The Civil Rights Act of 1964
3. The Occupational Safety and Health Act (OSHA) of 1970

SUMMARY

1 *Human resource management* is the process of evaluating human resource needs, finding people to fill those needs, and optimizing this important resource by providing the right incentives and job environment, all with the goal of meeting organizational objectives. *Personnel* is the traditional name for the human resource management office.

- What are the steps in human resource planning?
    The six steps are: (1) preparing forecasts of future human resource needs; (2) preparing human resource inventory; (3) preparing job analyses; (4) assessing future demands; (5) assessing future supply; (6) establishing a plan for recruiting, hiring, educating, and developing employees.

2 *Recruitment* is the set of activities used to legally obtain a sufficient number of the right people at the right time to select those that best meet the needs of the organization.

- What is selection?
    It is the process of gathering information to decide who should be hired.
- What are the six steps in the selection process?
    The steps are: (1) obtaining complete application forms; (2) giving initial interview and follow-up interview; (3) giving employment tests; (4) conducting background investigations; (5) giving physical exams; and (6) conducting a trial period of employment.
- What happens on the first day of employment?
    Employee orientation is the activity that introduces new employees to the

organization, to fellow employees, their immediate supervisors, and to the policies, practices, and objectives of the firm.

3 Employee *training and development* include all attempts to improve employee performance by increasing an employee's ability to perform through learning.

■ What are some of the procedures used for training?

They include on and off-the-job training, apprentice programs, vestibule training, and job simulation.

■ How is performance evaluated?

The steps are: (1) establish performance standards; (2) communicate those standards; (3) evaluate performance; (4) discuss results; (5) take corrective action when needed; (6) use the results for decisions about promotions, compensation, additional training, or firing.

4 Employee compensation is one of the largest operating costs for many organizations.

■ What kind of compensation systems are used?

They include salary systems, hourly wages, piecework, commission plans, bonus plans, and profit-sharing plans.

■ What are fringe benefits?

Benefits such as sick leave, vacation pay, pension plans, and health plans that provide additional compensation to employees.

5 *Management development* is the process of developing managerial skills over time.

■ How does networking fit in this process?

Networking is the process of establishing contacts with key managers within and outside the organization to get additional development assistance.

■ What are *mentors?*

Managers who coach and guide selected lower level people and act as their organizational sponsors.

■ Are there any new trends in human resource planning?

Yes, adjusting to the new demographics by trying job sharing plans, flextime plans, and other new employee-oriented plans.

6 There are many laws that affect human resource planning.

■ What are those laws?

See Figure 17-7 and review the section on laws. This is an important subject for future managers to study.

KEY TERMS

apprenticeship   p. 456
compressed work week
   p. 466
core time   p. 465
employee orientation   p. 454
flextime plans   p. 465
fringe benefits   p. 461
human resource management
   p. 448
job analysis   p. 451
job descriptions   p. 451
job sharing   p. 465
job simulation   p. 457
job specifications   p. 451

management development
   p. 462
mentors   p. 464
networking   p. 464
off-the-job training   p. 457
on-the-job training   p. 456
performance appraisal   p. 458
recruitment   p. 452
Scanlon plan   p. 461
selection   p. 453
training and development
   p. 456
vestibule training   p. 457

GETTING INVOLVED

1 Visit the personnel offices of your college and of several businesses. Talk with employees and several managers. What do they do all day? Do they enjoy the work? How did it appear to you? Share your impressions with others in the class.

2 Read the current business periodicals to find the latest court rulings on issues such as comparable worth, affirmative action, and other personnel-related issues. What seems to be the trend? What will this mean for tomorrow's college graduates?

3 Recall the various training programs you have experienced. Think of both on-the-job and off-the-job training sessions. What is your evaluation of such programs? How would you improve them? Share your ideas with the class.

4 Look up the unemployment figures for individual states. Notice there are pockets of very high unemployment. What causes such uneven unemployment? What can be done to retrain workers who are obsolete because of a restructured economy? Is that the role of government or of business? Discuss. Could government and business cooperate in this function?

5 Find several people who work under flextime or part-time systems. Ask them their reactions. Share your findings with the class.

PRACTICING MANAGEMENT DECISIONS

CASE ONE   THE DANGERS OF FIRING EMPLOYEES

The common law has previously maintained the right of an employer to fire an employee under something called the employment-at-will doctrine. But lately this doctrine has come under attack because of recent legal rulings. Employers can still fire people, but they may have some expensive consequences if employees sue. In California in 1983, 43 cases were decided in favor of employees, and the average settlement was over $500,000.

More than 50% of all discharge cases taken to arbitration are decided against the employer. Corporate personnel manuals are getting more detailed to protect against legal action. For example, the Del E. Webb Corporation struck the word *permanent* from employee descriptions.

NAS Insurance Services Inc. in California offers insurance for companies sued for wrongful discharge. It has been estimated that only two out of every 1,000 employees is fired unjustly, but that amounts to some 55,000 workers a year.

DECISION QUESTIONS

1 What are the implications for the personnel department of new legal rulings against firing for unjust cause?

2 If you were an employer, would you put more effort into screening and training employees, given these rulings? Who might be hurt by such changes? Who may benefit?

3 What is your reaction to the courts becoming involved in hiring, training, screening, and firing practices of business firms? Is it a positive step toward better employee treatment or not?

Source: Harikar Krishman, "Courts Restricting Power of Corporations to Fire Employees," *Washington Business*, September 9, 1985, p. 11 and "Firing Rights are Ended by Courts," *The Wall Street Journal*, October 1, 1985, p. 1.

CASE TWO   DUAL CAREER PLANNING

Carey Moler is a 32-year-old account executive for a communications company. She is married to Mitchell Moler, a lawyer. They have one child. Carey and Mitchell had not made any definite plans about how to juggle their careers and family life until Carey reached age 30. Then she decided to have a baby, and career planning took on whole new dimensions. A company named Catalyst talked to 815 dual-career couples and found most of them, like the Molers, had not made any long-range career decisions regarding family life-style.

From the business perspective, such dual career families create real concerns. There are problems with relocations, with child care, and so on that affect recruiting, productivity, morale, and promotion policies.

For a couple such as the Molers, having both career and family responsibilities is exhausting. But that is just one problem. If Carey is moving up in the firm, what happens if Mitchell gets a terrific job offer 1,500 miles away? What if Carey gets such an offer? Who is going to care for the baby? What happens if the baby gets ill? How do they plan their vacations when there are three schedules to balance? Who will do the housework?

Dual careers require careful planning and discussion, and those plans need to be reviewed over time. A couple who decide at age 22 to do certain things may change their minds at 30. Whether or not to have children. Where to locate. How to manage the household. All such issues and more can become major problems if not carefully planned.

The same is true for corporations. They too must plan for dual-career families. They must give more attention to job-sharing, flextime, paternity leave policies for men, transfer policies, nepotism rules, and more.

DECISION QUESTIONS

1   What are some of the issues you can see developing because of dual career families? How is this affecting children in such families?
2   What kind of corporate policies need changing to adapt to these new realities?
3   What can newlywed couples do to minimize the problems of dual careers? What are the advantages of dual careers? Disadvantages? How can a couple achieve the advantages with a minimum number of problems?

Human resource management is an area that has been receiving more attention lately because of issues such as comparable worth and executive pay. One major issue of the 1980s is the role of unions in corporations, both now and in the future.

Chapter 18 will discuss these issues, with special attention to the history and future of unions. Anyone who gets involved with business today should understand union issues and other employee-management concerns. Before we get into such issues, we will take some time to focus on a key objective of this course—helping you progress in your career. The following Appendix will teach you how to write a cover letter and resumé and how to prepare for job interviews.

APPENDIX

Now that we have explored human resource management from the business side, let's look at the process from your perspective. You now know that businesses are actively searching for good employees who can produce. Similarly, you are looking for an organization where your talents will be used to the fullest and where you would enjoy working. How can you find an organization that will provide the optimal satisfaction for both you and the organization? That is the goal of this appendix.

If you followed the advice in the Prologue, you have done a self-assessment to determine what kind of career would be best for you. You have also gone to the library and done some background research into organizations that need people with your skills and knowledge. It's time, therefore, to develop a strategy for finding and obtaining a personally satisfying first job.

A FIVE-STEP JOB SEARCH STRATEGY

There are several good books available that provide guidance for finding the right job. This appendix, will summarize the important steps. They are:

1 *Complete a self-analysis inventory.* A couple of such programs were discussed earlier. If you want to do an assessment on your own, see Richard Nelson Bolles, *What Color Is Your Parachute?* (Berkeley: Ten Speed Press, latest edition). See Figure A-1 for a sample assessment.

2 *Search for jobs you would enjoy.* Begin at your college placement office, if it has one. Keep interviewing people in various careers, even after you have found a job. Career progress demands continuous research.

3 *Begin the networking process as discussed in this chapter.* You can start with your family, relatives, neighbors, friends, professors, and local businesspeople. Be sure to keep a file with the names, addresses, and phone numbers of contacts, where they work, the person who recommended them to you, and the relationship between the source person and the contact.

4 *Prepare a good cover letter and resume.* Samples are provided in this appendix.

5 *Develop interviewing skills.*

The Job Search

The placement bureau at your school is a good place to begin reading about potential employers. On-campus interviewing is by far the number one source of jobs (see Figure A-2).

The second most important source of jobs involves writing to companies and sending a good cover letter and resume. The third best source is networking; that is, finding someone in a firm to recommend you. You find those people by asking friends, neighbors, family, and others if they know anyone who knows someone, and then you track those people down, interview them, and seek their recommendation. Other good sources include the placement center, want ads, summer and internship programs, and walking in to firms that appeal to you and asking for an interview.

FIGURE A-1

A personal assessment scale.

INTERESTS

1. How do I like to spend my time?
2. Do I enjoy being with people?
3. Do I like working with mechanical things?
4. Do I enjoy working with numbers?
5. Am I a member of many organizations?
6. Do I enjoy physical activities?
7. Do I like to read?

ABILITIES

1. Am I adept at working with numbers?
2. Am I adept at working with mechanical things?
3. Do I have good verbal and written communication skills?
4. What special talents do I have?
5. In which abilities do I wish I were more adept?

EDUCATION

1. Have I taken certain courses that have prepared me for a particular job?
2. In which subjects did I perform the best? The worst?
3. Which subjects did I enjoy the most? The least?
4. How have my extracurricular activities prepared me for a particular job?
5. Is my GPA an accurate picture of my academic ability? Why?
6. Do I aspire to a graduate degree? Do I want to earn it before beginning my job?
7. Why did I choose my major?

EXPERIENCE

1. What previous jobs have I held? What were my responsibilities in each?
2. Were any of my jobs applicable to positions I may be seeking? How?
3. What did I like the most about my previous jobs? Like the least?
4. Why did I work in the jobs I did?
5. If I had it to do over again, would I work in these jobs? Why?

PERSONALITY

1. What are my good and bad traits?
2. Am I competitive?
3. Do I work well with others?
4. Am I outspoken?
5. Am I a leader or a follower?
6. Do I work well under pressure?
7. Do I work quickly, or am I methodical?
8. Do I get along well with others?
9. Am I ambitious?
10. Do I work well independently of others?

DESIRED JOB ENVIRONMENT

1. Am I willing to relocate? Why?
2. Do I have a geographic preference? Why?
3. Would I mind traveling in my job?
4. Do I have to work for a large, nationally known firm to be satisfied?
5. Must I have a job that initially offers a high salary?
6. Must the job I assume offer rapid promotion opportunities?
7. In what kind of job environment would I feel most comfortable?
8. If I could design my own job, what characteristics would it have?

PERSONAL GOALS

1. What are my short- and long-term goals? Why?
2. Am I career oriented, or do I have broader interests?
3. What are my career goals?
4. What jobs are likely to help me achieve my goals?
5. What do I hope to be doing in 5 years? In 10 years?
6. What do I want out of life?

Source: Eric N. Berkowitz, Roger A. Kerin, and William Rudelius, *Marketing* (St. Louis: Times Mirror/Mosby College Publishing, 1986), pp. 636-637.

FIGURE A-2

Where college students find jobs.

Source: J. Singleton and P. Scheetz, *Recruiting Trends,* 1983–1984, Michigan State University.

SOURCE OF JOB	NEW EMPLOYEES
On-campus interviewing	49.3%
Write-ins	9.8%
Current employee referrals	7.2
Job listings with placement office	6.5
Responses from want ads	5.6
Walk-ins	5.5
Cooperative education programs	4.8
Summer employment	4.7
College faculty/staff referrals	4.5
Internship programs	4.5
High-demand major programs	4.4
Minority career programs	2.9
Part-time employment	2.4
Unsolicited referrals from placement	2.1
Women's career programs	2.1
Job listings with employment agencies	1.9
Referrals from campus organizations	1.8

THE IMPORTANCE OF SCHOOL ACTIVITIES

	F	E	SB
Lettered in high school sport	71%	50%	50%
Played on college varsity team	33%	18%	15%
Belonged to college fraternity or sorority	57%	39%	28%
Served as class officer in H.S. or college	77%	46%	50%
Were suspended or expelled	8%	16%	10%

This table summarizes the school activities of some people who have gone on to become successful businesspeople. *F* = *Fortune*'s 500 executives; *E* = *Inc.*'s 500 top entrepreneurs; *SB* = Leading small business owners.

Source: The Wall Street Journal, May 20, 1985, p. 6C.

Occupational Outlook Quarterly, produced by the Department of Labor, says this about job hunting:

> The skills that make a person employable are not so much the ones needed on the job as the ones needed to *get* the job, skills like the ability to find a job opening, complete an application, prepare the resume, and survive an interview.

Before you read on, check the Interview Rating Sheet in Figure A-3. Note what the recruiters want. Interviewers will be checking your appearance (clothes, haircut, fingernails, shoes), your attitude (friendliness is desired), your verbal ability (speak loud enough to be heard clearly), and your motivation (be enthusiastic). Note also that interviewers want you to have been active in clubs and activities and to have set goals. Have someone evaluate you on these scales now to see if you have any weak points. You can then work on those points before you have any actual job interviews.

PREPARING A RESUMÉ AND COVER LETTERS

It is never too early in your career to begin designing a resumé and thinking of cover letters. Preparing such documents reveals your strengths and weaknesses more clearly than most other techniques. Your resumé lists all your education, work experience, and activities. By preparing a resumé now, you may discover that you have not been active enough in outside activities to impress an employer. That information may prompt you to join some student groups, to become a volunteer, or to otherwise enhance your social skills. You may also discover that you are weak on experience, and seek an internship or part-time job to fill in that gap. In any event, it is not too soon to prepare a resumé. It will certainly be helpful in deciding what you would like to see in the area marked "education" and help you to choose

Candidate: "For each characteristic listed below there is a rating scale of 1 through 7, where "1" is generally the most unfavorable rating of the characteristic and "7" the most favorable. Rate each characteristic by *circling* just *one* number to represent the impression you gave in the interview that you have just completed."

NAME OF CANDIDATE _____

1. APPEARANCE
Sloppy   1 2 3 4 5 6 7   Neat

2. ATTITUDE
Unfriendly   1 2 3 4 5 6 7   Friendly

3. ASSERTIVENESS/VERBAL ABILITY
   a. Responded Completely to Questions Asked
      Poor   1 2 3 4 5 6 7   Excellent
   b. Clarified Personal Background and Related to Job Opening and Description
      Poor   1 2 3 4 5 6 7   Excellent
   c. Able to Explain and Sell Job Abilities
      Poor   1 2 3 4 5 6 7   Excellent
   d. Initiated Questions Regarding Position and Firm
      Poor   1 2 3 4 5 6 7   Excellent
   e. Expressed thorough Knowledge of Personal Goals and Abilities
      Poor   1 2 3 4 5 6 7   Excellent

4. MOTIVATION
Poor   1 2 3 4 5 6 7   High

5. SUBJECT/ACADEMIC KNOWLEDGE
Poor   1 2 3 4 5 6 7   Good

6. STABILITY
Poor   1 2 3 4 5 6 7   Good

7. COMPOSURE
Ill at Ease   1 2 3 4 5 6 7   Relaxed

8. PERSONAL INVOLVEMENT/ACTIVITIES, CLUBS, ETC.
Low   1 2 3 4 5 6 7   Very high

9. MENTAL IMPRESSION
Dull   1 2 3 4 5 6 7   Alert

10. ADAPTABILITY
Poor   1 2 3 4 5 6 7   Good

11. SPEECH PRONUNCIATION
Poor   1 2 3 4 5 6 7   Good

12. OVERALL IMPRESSION
Unsatisfactory   1 2 3 4 5 6 7   Highly satisfactory

13. Would you hire this individual if you were permitted to make that decision right now?
                 Yes   No

a major and other coursework. Given that background, let's discuss how to prepare these materials.

Writing A Resumé

A *resumé* is a document that lists all the information an employer would need to evaluate you and your background. It explains your immediate goals and career

Text continued on p. 480.

FIGURE A-4

Stamp out bad resumés. A good resumé should:

1. Invite you to read it, have a clear layout, top quality printing, and eliminate extraneous information.
2. Start sentences with action verbs such as organized, managed, and designed, rather than with lead-ins ("I was the person responsible for . . . ").
3. Highlight those accomplishments related to future work.
4. Be free of spelling, punctuation, and grammatical errors.
5. Speak the reader's language by using the vocabulary of the industry you are targeting.
6. Make a strong statement; this means using only the most relevant information—nothing less, nothing more.

Source: Special Advertising Section in *Business Week's Guide to Careers* ("The Chrysler-Plymouth Guide to Building a Resume").

Monica A. Thomas
18 Nautical Lane
Gloucester, Mass.

Age: 21
Height: 5'6''
Weight: 123 lbs
Hair: Red
Eyes: Hazel
Marital Status: Single
Health: Good

OBJECTIVE

To apply management experience and French language skills in a corporation overseas.

EDUCATION

B.A. Management, Georgia State University, Atlanta, Ga.

Also completed a semester of study abroad in London, England (Georgia State University)

Additional Areas of Academic Competence:

8 Credit Hours in computers using FORTRAN, Small Business Counseling.

College Courses included Marketing, French, English Literature, Computer Programming, Data Processing, Statistics, Sociology, Economics

High School Diploma: St. Agatha's High School Gloucester, MA: College Preparatory, National Honor Society, Graduated in top 25% of class.

WORK EXPERIENCE

6/81-Present   Flowers by Joann, Rockport, Mass. Responsibilities included: bookkeeping, inventory, floral design, selling merchandise, both person to person and by use of computer.

5/84-8/84   Waitress, Citronella's Taverna, London, England. Learned to work effectively with an international clientele.

5/83-9/83   Hostess, The Clam Shell, Salem, Mass.

Activities   American Marketing Association, Student Marketing Association, Fencing Club.

Monica A. Thomas
18 Nautical Lane
Gloucester, MA 01930
(617) 281-0568

EDUCATION

1984   B.A., Management GEORGIA STATE UNIVERSITY

1983   Semester, GSU-London, England

1982-83   8 Credit hours, FORTRAN, Small Business
              Training-Computer Science

OBJECTIVE

              To apply management experience and French
              language skills in a corporation overseas.

CAPABILITIES

■ Perceive motivations in others allowing them to produce
results based on their goals and commitments.

■ Listen to subtle communications and convert them into active
resolutions.

■ Provide spirit of trust and enthusiasm so that business
transactions can occur harmoniously.

■ Handle administrative details under pressure so as to allow
boss to pursue higher levels of thinking and decision making.

EXPERIENCE

■ Sold floral arrangements at $800-$1,200/month, in person and
by telephone and computer.

■ Managed all administrative details of medium-size floral shop
for five seasons (1981-85).

■ Recognized by British restaurant manager for outstanding
courtesy and efficiency.

■ Served as restaurant hostess/junior manager where patronage
increased over 33% in a three month period.

1981-   FLOWERS BY JOANN Rockport, MA
Present   Sales Assistant

1984   CITRONELLA'S TAVERNA London, England
(Summer)   Waitress

1983   THE CLAM SHELL Salem, MA
(Summer)   Hostess/Junior Manager

ACTIVITIES   Member: American Marketing Association
                      Student Marketing Association

objectives. This information is followed by an explanation of your educational background, experience, interests, and other relevant data.

If you have exceptional abilities and do not communicate them to the employer on the resumé, those abilities are not part of the person he or she will evaluate. You must be comprehensive and clear in your resumé if you are to communicate all your attributes.

Your resumé is an advertisement for yourself. If your ad is better than the other person's ad, you are more likely to get the job. In this case, "better" means that your ad highlights your attributes in an attractive way.

In discussing your education, for example, be sure to highlight your extra-curricular activities such as part-time jobs, sports, clubs, and other such activities. If you did well in school, put down your grades. The idea is to make yourself look as good on paper as you are in reality.

The same is true for your job experience. Be sure to describe what you did, any special projects in which you participated, and any responsibilities you had.

For the "other interests" section, if you include one, do not just list your interests, but describe how deeply you were involved. If you organized the club, volunteered your time, or participated more often than usual in an organization, make sure to say so in the resumé. Figure A-4 shows an unedited version of a resumé. It was a part of a "Guide to Building a Resume" prepared by the Chrysler-Plymouth Corporation. Look over the resumé and see what you think. Then turn to Figure A-5 for an improved version. Can you see how important planning and writing a resumé can be?

FIGURE A-6

Sample action words to use in your resumé.

Managed	Wrote	Budgeted	Improved
Planned	Produced	Designed	Increased
Organized	Scheduled	Directed	Investigated
Coordinated	Operated	Developed	Sold
Supervised	Conducted	Established	Served
Trained	Administered	Implemented	Handled

Writing a Cover Letter

A cover letter is used to announce your availability and to introduce the resumé. The cover letter is probably one of the most important advertisements anyone will write in a lifetime—so it should be done right.

First, the cover letter should indicate that you have researched the organization in question and are interested in a job there. Let the organization know what sources you used and what you know about it in the first paragraph to get the attention of the reader and show your interest.

You may have heard that "It is not what you know, but whom you know that counts." This is only partly true, but it is important nonetheless. If you do not now know someone, you can get to know someone. You do this by calling the organization (or better yet, visiting its offices) and talking to people who already have the kind of job you are hoping to get. Ask about training, salary, and other relevant issues. Then, in your cover letter, mention that you have talked with some of the firm's employees and that this discussion increased your interest. You thereby show the letter reader that you "know someone," if only casually, and that you are interested enough to actively pursue the organization. This is all part of networking.

Second, in the description of yourself, be sure to say how your attributes will benefit the organization. For example, do not just say, "I will be graduating with a degree in marketing." Say, "You will find that my college training in marketing and marketing research has prepared me to learn your marketing system quickly and begin making a contribution right away." The sample cover letter in Figure A-7 will give you a better feel for how this looks.

Third, be sure to "ask for the order." That is, say in your final paragraph that you are available for an interview at a time and place convenient for the interviewer. Again, see the sample cover letter in Figure A-7 for guidance. Notice in this letter how Tom subtly showed that he read business publications and drew attention to his resumé.

Dear Mr. Franklin:

A recent article in <u>Business Week</u> mentioned that Donahue Corporation is expanding its operations into the Southwest. I have always had an interest in your firm, and so I read more about you in <u>Forbes</u> and <u>Standard & Poor's</u>. It seems as though you will be needing good salespeople to handle your expanding business. Harold Jones, your Detroit sales representative, is a neighbor of mine. He told me about your training program, compensation system, and career opportunities. He convinced me that Donahue is the place for an ambitious college graduate.

I will be graduating from State College in June with a degree in marketing. My courses in marketing management, sales management, consumer behavior, and marketing research have given me some insight into marketing for a growing organization like yours. My 3 years' experience as a salesman for Korvalis Shoes has given me valuable skills that I could apply at Donahue. You will notice when you read the attached resumé that I have always been active in the organizations I have joined. Could I do as well at Donahue?

I will be in the New York area the week of November 17-25. Please let me know which time and date would be convenient for you to discuss a future at Donahue. I am looking forward to hearing from you.

Sincerely,

Thomas J. Smith

Thomas J. Smith

FIGURE A-7

A model cover letter. Things to notice:
1. The first paragraph of the letter mentions someone in the firm (a networking strategy).
2. The second paragraph mentions specific courses and experience applicable to the job.
3. The third paragraph asks for a specific time and date for the interview.

Some principles to follow in writing a cover letter and preparing your resumé are:
- Be self-confident. List all your good qualities and attributes.
- Do not be apologetic or negative. Write as one professional to another, not as a humble student begging for a job.

■ Research every prospective employer thoroughly before writing anything. Use a rifle approach rather than a shotgun approach. That is, write effective marketing-oriented letters to a few select companies rather than to a general list.

■ Have your materials typed on a good typewriter by an experienced typist or, better yet, have it printed.

■ Have someone edit your materials for spelling, grammar, and style.

■ Do not send the names of references until asked. Put "References furnished upon request" at the bottom of the last page of your resumé.

PREPARING FOR JOB INTERVIEWS

Companies usually do not conduct job interviews unless they are somewhat certain that the candidate has the requirements for the job. The interview, therefore, is pretty much a make-or-break situation. If it goes well, you have a much greater chance of being hired. Therefore, it is critical that you are prepared for your interviews. The five stages of interviews preparation are:

1. *Do research about the prospective employers.* Learn what industry the firm is in, its competitors, the products or services it produces and their acceptance in the market, and the title of your desired entry-level position. You can find such information in the firm's annual reports, in *Standard and Poor's*, *Moody's manuals*, and various business publications such as *Fortune, Business Week,* and *Forbes*. Ask your librarian for help. Together, you can look in the *Reader's Guide to Business Literature* and find the company name to look for articles on it. This is a very important first step. It shows you have initiative and interest in the firm.

2. *Practice the interview.* Figure A-8 lists some of the more frequently asked questions in an interview. Practice answering these questions and more at the placement office and with your roommate, parents, or friends. Do not memorize your answers, but be prepared—know what you are going to say. Also, develop a series of questions to ask the interviewer. Figure A-9 shows some sample questions you might ask. Be sure you know who to contact, and write down the names of everyone you meet. Review the action words in Figure A-6 and try to fit them into your answers.

FIGURE A-8

Be prepared for these frequently asked questions.

■ How would you describe yourself?

■ What are your greatest strengths and weaknesses?

■ How did you choose this company?

■ What do you know about the company?

■ What are your long-range career goals?

■ What courses did you like best? Least?

■ What are your hobbies?

■ Do you prefer a specific geographic location?

■ Are you willing to travel (or move)?

■ Which accomplishments have given you the most satisfaction?

■ What things are most important to you in a job?

■ Why should I hire you?

■ What experience have you had in this type of work?

■ How much do you expect to earn?

FIGURE A-9

Sample questions to ask the interviewer.

- How long does the training program last and what is included?
- How soon after school would I be expected to start?
- What are the advantages of working for this firm?
- How much travel is normally expected?
- What managerial style should I expect in my area?
- How would you describe the working environment in my area?
- How would I be evaluated?
- What is the company's promotion policy?
- What is the corporate culture?
- What is the next step in the selection procedures?
- How soon should I expect to hear from you?
- What other information would you like about my background, experience, or education?

3. *Be professional during the interview.* "You don't have a second chance to make a good first impression," the saying goes. That means that you should look and sound professional throughout the interview. Do your homework and find out how the managers dress at the firm. Then buy an appropriate outfit.

When you meet the interviewers, greet them by name, smile, and maintain good eye contact. Sit up straight in your chair and be alert and enthusiastic. If you have practiced, you should be able to relax and be confident. Other than that, be yourself, answer questions, and be friendly and responsive.

When you leave, thank the interviewers and, if you are still interested in the job, tell them so. If they don't tell you, ask them what the next step is. Maintain a positive attitude. Figure A-10 outlines what the interviewers will be evaluating.

4. *Follow up on the interview.* First, write down what you can remember from the interview: names of the interviewers and their titles, any salary figures mentioned, dates for training, and so on. Put the information in your career file. You can send a follow-up letter thanking each interviewer for his or her time. You can also send a letter of recommendation or some other piece of added information to keep their interest. "The squeaky wheel gets the grease" is the operating slogan. Your enthusiasm for working for the company could be a major factor in hiring you.

5. *Be prepared to act.* Know what you want to say if you do get a job offer. You may not want the job after hearing all the information. Do not expect to receive a job offer from everyone you meet, but do expect to learn something from every interview. With some practice and persistence, you should find a rewarding and challenging job.

Don't be concerned if upon graduation you have little understanding of your own talents or focus on your life's work. Only a minority are given such insights in their early years. Most have to find their way by diverse job experiences.

Frank Shakespeare,
President, RKO General

BE PREPARED TO CHANGE JOBS

If you are like most people, you will find that you will follow several different career paths over your lifetime. This is a good thing in that it enables you to try different jobs and stay fresh and enthusiastic. The key to moving forward in your career is a willingness to change jobs, always searching for the career that will bring the most personal satisfaction and growth. This means that you will have to write many cover letters and resumés and go through many interviews. Each time you change jobs, go through the steps in this Appendix to be sure you are fully prepared. Good luck.

FIGURE A-10

Sixteen traits recruiters seek in job prospects.

Source: "So You're Looking for a Job?" The College Placement Council.

1. *Ability to Communicate.* Do you have the ability to organize your thoughts and ideas effectively? Can you express them clearly when speaking or writing? Can you present your ideas to others in a persuasive way?
2. *Intelligence.* Do you have the ability to understand the job assignment? Learn the details of operation? Contribute original ideas to your work?
3. *Self-Confidence.* Do you demonstrate a sense of maturity that enables you to deal positively and effectively with situations and people?
4. *Willingness to Accept Responsibility.* Are you someone who recognizes what needs to be done and is willing to do it?
5. *Initiative.* Do you have the ability to identify the purpose for work and to take action?
6. *Leadership.* Can you guide and direct others to obtain the recognized objectives?
7. *Energy Level.* Do you demonstrate a forcefulness and capacity to make things move ahead? Can you maintain your work effort at an above-average rate?
8. *Imagination.* Can you confront and deal with problems that may not have standard solutions?
9. *Flexibility.* Are you capable of changing and being receptive to new situations and ideas?
10. *Interpersonal Skills.* Can you bring out the best efforts of individuals so they become effective, enthusiastic members of a team?
11. *Self-Knowledge.* Can you realistically assess your own capabilities? See yourself as others see you? Clearly recognize your strengths and weaknesses?
12. *Ability to Handle Conflict.* Can you successfully contend with stress situations and antagonism?
13. *Competitiveness.* Do you have the capacity to compete with others and the willingness to be measured by your performance in relation to that of others?
14. *Goal Achievement.* Do you have the ability to identify and work toward specific goals? Do such goals challenge your abilities?
15. *Vocational Skills.* Do you possess the positive combination of education and skills required for the position you are seeking?
16. *Direction.* Have you defined your basic personal needs? Have you determined what type of position will satisfy your knowledge, skills, and goals?

EMPLOYEE-MANAGEMENT ISSUES: UNIONS, EXECUTIVE PAY, AND COMPARABLE WORTH

LEARNING GOALS

After you have read and studied this chapter, you should be able to:

▥ Briefly trace the history of labor unions in the United States.

▥ Discuss the major legislation affecting labor unions.

▥ Outline the tactics used by labor and management during conflicts.

▥ Describe several ways today's labor unions have changed.

▥ Discuss the issue of executive compensation in the 1980s.

▥ Outline the issues surrounding the concept of comparable worth.

▥ Explain the benefits and problems of employee stock ownership programs (ESOPs).

PROFILES   RICHARD J. FERRIS OF UNITED AIRLINES TO BOONE PICKENS, Jr., OF MESA PETROLEUM

O ne of the main managerial issues of the 1980s is executive compensation. Both men discussed in this Profile made over $1 million in compensation in 1984. The debate focuses on whether or not these executives and others are worth what they make.

Business Week feels that the $1.38 million that Richard Ferris earned was "a bargain." The reason for this statement is that Ferris increased profits by 99% to $282 million and increased revenues by 16% to $7 billion. The company's return on equity was 16.8% compared to the industry average of 9.8%. Furthermore, Ferris had reduced debt to 34% of capitalization from 62% in 1982. A share of stock in UAL increased from 16⅝ in 1981 to 42 in 1985. All in all, Richard Ferris made the largest return on the money paid him of all the executives *Business Week* studied, whose *average* compensation exceeded $1 million per year!

Mr. Ferris is the kind of executive that one could admire for many reasons. He is making United Airlines a major force in international aviation by buying Pan American World Airways. He is also a family man and is on the national board

Richard Ferris.

By working faithfully eight hours a day, you may eventually get to be boss and work twelve hours a day.
ROBERT FROST

T. Boone Pickens, Jr.

of governors of United Way; he became its chairman in 1985. He also co-chaired a task force to study how to better market the city of Chicago. It's obvious that Richard Ferris is a model executive, but is he worth over $1 million a year? To compare, let's see what other executives make.

T. Boone Pickens, Jr., of Mesa Petroleum made $22.8 million in 1984, which made him the highest-paid executive that year. Mesa's dividend payment to *all* its stockholders was $14 million (less than Pickens' compensation). *Business Week* reports that a shareholder suit is possible over Pickens' pay.

Mesa's stock is down in value to about 17 from 34 in 1981. Though he made the *highest* income, Pickens produced the *lowest* profits and shareholder gains of all the executives studied.

There is much talk of employees being asked to take pay cuts to make American industry more competitive. Meanwhile, executive compensation is rising year after year. Here are some other examples: in 1984, Peter Magowan of Safeway Stores made about $1.7 million, An Wang of Wang Laboratories made $5.3 million, and Edward Telling of Sears made $7.3 million.

How does this pay compare with that of other important people? In 1984, Warren Burger, then Chief Justice of the Supreme Court, made $104,700; Tom Bradley, mayor of Los Angeles, made $76,865; and Tip O'Neill, Speaker of the House, made $94,600. What is "fair and equitable compensation" for executives? That is one issue explored in this chapter. The main topic of the chapter is employee-management relations, especially union relations. The issues of executive pay and comparable worth are relatively new issues that are directly related. ■

Sources: Reggi Ann Dubin and James E. Ellis, "UAL Chairman Ferris is a Bargain," *Business Week,* May 6, 1985, p. 80; and James R. Norman, "Does Boone Pickens Practice What He Preaches?" *Business Week,* May 6, 1985, p. 82.

MANAGEMENT-EMPLOYEE ISSUES

The relationship between owner/managers and employees has never been smooth throughout the history of business. To protect themselves from unfair managers, workers united to form unions. This gave workers more negotiating power with managers and more political power as well. The issue of worker pay and unions has been a major one in the 1980s and will continue to be controversial in the 1990s.

A new twist has been added to the issue of pay. Women receive less pay than men overall, and jobs traditionally held by women (for example, teacher, nurse, secretary) pay less than traditional "men's jobs" (for example, truck driver, garbage collector, miner). The issue of comparable worth adds to labor-management disputes.

The pay issue reached a new intensity in the 1980s for two reasons. First, foreign labor was so much cheaper than U.S. labor that jobs were being lost to foreign firms. This led workers at several firms (for example, Chrysler*) to take a pay cut to keep their company competitive with foreign firms. Second, executive pay was *increased* rather than decreased. This caused much debate over the issue of executive compensation.

---

*Chrysler employees went on strike in 1985 to get the money back, however.

To get a fairer share of profits, employees began asking for more equity in the firm. In fact, some companies that went bankrupt were purchased entirely by employees. Another issue, therefore, is the benefits versus drawbacks of ESOPs (employee stock ownership plans).

Employees are also interested in other benefits we have discussed, such as flextime, part-time work, day care, and more. Managers too are looking for more security, higher income, and better fringe benefits. The goal of this chapter is to present some of these issues. Like all other managerial problems, these issues must be worked out through open discussion, goodwill, and compromise. It is important to know both sides of the issues, however, to make reasoned decisions.

THE DEVELOPMENT OF LABOR UNIONS

Are labor unions essential in the American economy today? This question is certain to evoke emotional responses from various participants in the work place. The fisherman carrying a picket sign in Massachusetts will elaborate on the dangers to our free society if employers continue to try to bust authorized unions. The *autoworker* in Detroit, the *plumber* in St. Louis, the *farmworker* in Orange County, and millions of other union sympathizers will strongly affirm this conclusion. A different perspective is presented by the small manufacturer who is forced to operate under union wage and benefit obligations and work rules. Such a manager argues that competition is impossible under strict union conditions. The *automaker* in Detroit, the plumbing *contractor* in St. Louis, the large *grower* in Orange County, and millions of other small, medium, and large business enterprises will affirm this conclusion.

Labor unions have tried to improve working conditions in factories.

Fundamentally, most people would agree that the union movement of today is an outgrowth of the economic transition caused by the Industrial Revolution of the nineteenth and early twentieth centuries. The worker who once toiled in the fields, dependent on the mercies of nature for survival, suddenly became dependent on the continuous roll of the factory presses and assembly lines for survival. Additionally, periods of unemployment were severe on families, hours of work could extend to as long as 84 hours per week, pay was extremely low, safety standards were almost nonexistent, and the use and abuse of child laborers was rampant. Clearly the steps inherent in breaking away from an agrarian (farm) economy to an industrial economy were quite difficult. Nonetheless, over time workers learned that strength through unity could lead to improved job conditions, better wages, and job security.

Today, critics of organized labor maintain that none of the inhuman conditions that once dominated U.S. industry can be found in the work place. They charge that organized labor has in fact become a large industrial entity in itself, and the real issue of protecting workers has become secondary because the legal system and current management attitudes prohibit the reappearance of the sweatshops of the late nineteenth and early twentieth centuries.

The Early History of Organized Labor

The presence of formal labor organizations in the United States dates back to before the Revolutionary War. As early as 1792, cordwainers (shoemakers) in Philadelphia met to discuss the fundamental work issues of pay, hours, conditions, and job security. The cordwainers were a craft union, which is an organization of skilled specialists in a particular craft or trade. They were typical of the early labor organizations formed before the Civil War. The first truly national labor organization was the Noble Order of the Knights of Labor formed by Uriah Smith Stephens in 1869.

Knights of Labor
The first national labor union (1869).

By 1886 the **Knights of Labor** claimed a membership of 700,000 members. The Knights offered membership to all working people and promoted social causes as well as labor and economic issues. However, their stewardship was short lived because of the rather revolutionary attitudes of their leadership and the blame they received for a bomb that exploded at a labor rally at Haymarket Square in Chicago, which killed eight policemen.

American Federation of Labor (AFL)
A craft union formed in 1886.

A rival group to the Knights of Labor, the **American Federation of Labor (AFL),** was formed in 1886. By 1890, the AFL, under the dynamic leadership of Samuel Gompers, had moved to the forefront of the labor movement. The AFL was an organization of craft unions that championed nuts-and-bolts labor issues. In 1935 a powerful committee led by John L. Lewis, President of the United Mine Workers (UMW), emerged in the AFL. The UMW membership included unskilled workers who were members of new industrial unions, as opposed to the traditional craft-union focus of the AFL. Lewis defended their cause and split with the AFL, creating a new organization—the Congress of Industrial Organization (CIO)—in 1935. The CIO soon rivaled the AFL in membership because of the passage of the Wagner Act the same year (see Figure 18-1). In 1955, through the efforts and leadership of George Meany, the opposing factions merged to form the AFL-CIO.

Norris-La Guardia Act, 1932

Prohibited courts from issuing injunctions against nonviolent union activities; outlawed contracts forbidding union activities; outlawed the use of yellow-dog contracts by employers. (Yellow-dog contracts were contractual agreements forced on workers by employers whereby the employee agreed not to join a union as a condition of employment.)

National Labor Relations Act (Wagner Act), 1935

Gave employees the right to form or join labor organizations (or to refuse to form or join); the right to collectively bargain with employers through elected union representatives; and the right to engage in labor activities such as strikes, picketing, and boycotts. Prohibited certain unfair labor practices by the employer and the union, and established the National Labor Relations Board to oversee union election campaigns and investigate labor practices. This act gave great impetus to the union movement.

Labor-Management Relations Act (Taft-Hartley Act), 1947

Amended the Wagner Act; permitted states to pass laws prohibiting compulsory union membership (right-to-work laws); set up methods to deal with strikes that affect national health and safety; prohibited secondary boycotts, closed-shop agreements, and featherbedding (the requiring of wage payments for work not performed) by unions. This act gave more power to management.

Labor-Management Reporting and Disclosure Act (Landrum-Griffin Act), 1959

Amended the Taft-Hartley Act and the Wagner Act; guaranteed individual rights of union members in dealing with their union, such as the right to nominate candidates for union office, vote in union elections, attend and participate in union meetings, vote on union business and examine union records and accounts; required annual financial reports to be filed with the U.S. Department of Labor. One goal of this act was to clean up union corruption, but corruption continues today.

FIGURE 18-1

Major legislation affecting labor-management relations.

Norris-La Guardia Act
1932 law that prohibited courts from using injunctions against nonviolent union activities and outlawed the use of yellow-dog contracts.

National Labor Relations Act (Wagner Act)
1935 law that gave employees the right to join a union, to collectively bargain, and to engage in union activities such as strikes, picketing, and boycotts.

Labor-Management Relations Act (Taft-Hartley Act)
1947 law that permitted states to pass right-to-work laws; prohibited secondary boycotts, closed-shop agreements, and featherbedding; and set up methods to deal with strikes.

Labor Management Reporting and Disclosure Act (Landrum-Griffin Act)
1959 law that gave individual rights to union members to nominate candidates, vote in union elections, attend union meetings, examine union records, and required annual financial reports from unions to be filed with the Department of Labor.

LABOR LEGISLATION AND COLLECTIVE BARGAINING

The growth and strength of organized labor has always been dependent on two major factors; the law and public opinion. Figure 18-1 outlines four major pieces of federal legislation that have had impact on the rights and operations of labor unions. The Wagner Act provided labor with legal justification to pursue the issues supported by Samuel Gompers and the AFL. This act of Congress established an administrative agency, the National Labor Relations Board (NLRB), to oversee labor-management relations. It also provided guidelines and offered legal protection to workers seeking to vote on "organizing" a union to represent them in the work place. Figure 18-2 describes the steps involved in a union-organizing campaign.

FIGURE 18-2

Steps involved in a union organizing campaign.

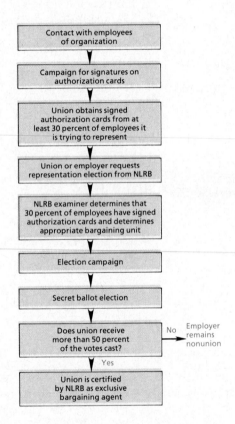

The equalization of unequals through collective bargaining was a vital issue, according to Gompers. The Wagner Act made collective bargaining legal and obligated employers to meet at reasonable times and bargain in good faith with respect to wages, hours, and other terms and conditions of employment.

Objectives of Organized Labor

As you might suspect, the objectives of organized labor frequently change according to shifts in social and economic trends. For example, in the 1970s the primary objective of most labor unions was additional pay and benefits for their membership. Throughout the 1980s, there was a significant shift toward issues related to job security and union recognition. The **negotiated labor-management agreement** sets the tone and clarifies the terms and conditions under which management and labor agree to function over a specific period of time. Figure 18-3 provides a list of topics commonly appearing in union-employer agreements.

negotiated labor-management agreement
Sets the tone and clarifies the terms under which management and labor agree to function over a period of time.

---

1. Union recognition and scope of bargaining unit
2. Management rights (management security)
3. Union security
4. Strikes and lockouts
5. Union activities and responsibilities
   a. Check-off of dues
   b. Union officers and stewards
   c. Union bulletin boards
   d. Wildcat strikes and slowdowns
6. Wages
   a. General wage adjustments
   b. Wage structure
   c. Job evaluation
   d. Wage incentives and time study
   e. Reporting and call-in pay
   f. Shift differentials
   g. Bonuses
7. Working time and time-off policies
   a. Regular hours of work
   b. Holidays
   c. Vacations
   d. Overtime regulations
   e. Leaves of absence
   f. Rest periods
   g. Meal periods
8. Job rights and seniority
   a. Seniority regulations
   b. Transfers
   c. Promotions
   d. Layoffs and recalls
   e. Job posting and bidding
9. Discipline, suspension, and discharge
10. Grievance handling and arbitration
11. Health and safety
12. Insurance and benefit programs
    a. Group life insurance
    b. Health insurance
    c. Pension programs
    d. Supplemental unemployment benefits

FIGURE 18-3

Topics commonly covered in union-employer agreements.

Source: Dale S. Beach, *Personnel: The Management of People at Work* (New York: Macmillan Publishing Co., 1985), p. 421.

Union security clauses stipulate that employees who reap benefits from a union must either join or pay dues to the union. After passage of the Wagner Act, labor sought security in the form of the closed shop. The **closed-shop agreement** specified that workers had to be members of a union before being hired. The Taft-Hartley Act outlawed this practice in 1947 (see Figure 18-4). Labor today favors the union shop as the primary means for ensuring security. Under the **union shop agreement,** workers do not have to be members of a union to be hired for a job, but must agree as a condition of employment to join the union within a prescribed period (usually 30, 60, or 90 days). The Taft-Hartley Act recognizes the legality of the union shop but grants individual states the power to outlaw the union shop through passage of **right-to-work laws.** To date, 20 states (plus one pending) have passed such legislation (see Figure 18-5). In a right-to-work state workers have the option under open shop to join a union, if one is present, or to not join.

closed-shop agreement
Specified that workers had to be members of a union before being hired (outlawed by the Taft-Hartley Act).

union shop agreement
One where workers do not have to be members of a union to be hired, but must agree to join the union within a prescribed period.

right-to-work laws
Give workers the right, under an open shop, to join a union—if it is present—or not.

FIGURE 18-4

Different forms of union contracts.

TYPE OF CONTRACT	DESCRIPTION
Union shop	The majority of union contracts are of this type. The employer can hire anyone, but employees must join the union to keep their jobs.
Simple-recognition shop	Roughly 15% of union contracts are in this category. The employer recognizes the union as the sole bargaining agent for all employees in the unit.
Agency shop	Employers may hire anyone. Employees need not join the union, but are required to pay a union fee. Less than 10% of union contracts are of this nature.
Maintenance-of-membership shop	Employees who join the union must remain in good standing. There is a period for considering union membership. Less than 5% of union contracts are in this form.
Closed shop (no longer used)	The Taft-Hartley Act made this form illegal. Only union members could be hired under this system.
Open shop	Union membership is voluntary for new and existing employees. Those who do not join the union do not have to pay union dues. Few union contracts are of this type.

simple recognition shop
One where the employer recognizes the union as the sole bargaining agent for all employees.

agency shop
One where employers may hire anyone and employees do not have to join the union, but must pay union fees.

maintenance-of-membership shop
One in which members of the union must remain in good standing.

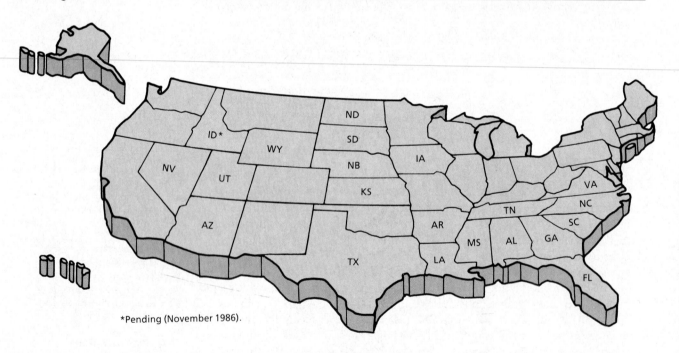

*Pending (November 1986).

FIGURE 18-5   States with right-to-work laws.

FIGURE 18-6
The growing costs of strikes.

Prestrike Costs

    Legal expenses
    Potential loss of orders from customers
    Expense of executive negotiations
    Potential slowdowns in productivity
    Downturn in worker morale
    Alterations in strategic planning scheme

Strike costs

    Legal expenditures
    Loss of profits from production stoppage or slowdown
    Cost of executive negotiations
    Added public relations costs
    Inventory-carrying costs
    Possible extra security costs
    Overtime in other plants
    Continuing salary expense for nonunion workers
    Cost of executive strike negotiations
    Continuing fringe benefits for strikers
    Management cost in performing operative tasks
    Potential loss of goodwill
    Cost of hiring strikebreakers

Poststrike costs

    Needed overtime to catch up on past orders
    Loss of customers who switched allegiance
    Productivity slump
    Possible training of replacement workers
    Chance of boycotts
    Loss of consumer goodwill and loyalties

Labor-Management Conflicts

When labor and management reach an impasse in their collective bargaining and negotiations break down, either side or both sides will use specific tactics to foster their objectives and perhaps sway public opinion. In the strategy of organized labor, the primary tactics are the strike and the boycott. Unions also use pickets and slowdowns as tactics to get desired changes.

The strike has historically been the most potent union tactic. It provides clear public focus on the situation and at times causes operations to totally shut down. Unfortunately, strikes have often generated violence and extended bitterness, because emotions on both sides frequently reach a boiling point. Today the strike is used less often as a labor tactic. Figure 18-6 identifies the major reasons why both labor and management seek to avoid strikes if at all possible. Nonetheless, as the USX and John Deere strikes in 1986 illustrated, the strike is not dead as a labor tactic. There were 54 major strikes in 1985, and 31 by July 1986.

Unions often revert to the boycott in an attempt to obtain their objectives. A **primary boycott** occurs when labor encourages their membership, as well as the general public, not to patronize the product(s) of a firm involved in a labor dispute. A **secondary boycott** is an attempt by labor to force an employer to stop doing

primary boycott
Union encouragement of members not to buy products of a firm involved in a labor dispute.

secondary boycott
An attempt by labor to force an employer to stop doing business with a firm that is the subject of a primary boycott.

Disneyland worker picketing.

lockouts
A tool for putting pressure on unions by closing the business.

yellow-dog contract
A contract agreement whereby employees agreed not to join a union as a condition of employment.

injunction
A court order directing some-one to do something or refrain from doing something.

business with a firm that is the subject of a primary boycott. The law permits labor to conduct authorized primary boycotts, but the Taft-Hartley Act prohibits the use of secondary boycotts by labor.

Management also uses specific tactics to attain its goals. Historically, management has made use of such tools as **lockouts** (putting pressure on unions by closing the business) and **yellow-dog contracts** (in which employees had agreed not to join a union) to thwart excessive labor demands. These methods are rarely used today. Today, management most often calls on the injunction and use of strike-breakers to stymie labor demands it sees as unreasonable.

An **injunction** is a court order directing someone to do something or refrain from doing something. Management has sought injunctions by courts to order striking workers back to work or limit the number of pickets that can be used during a strike. For a court to issue an injunction, management must show "just cause."

The use of strikebreakers has been a source of hostility and violence in labor relations. **Strikebreakers** (called *scabs* by unions) are workers who are hired to do the jobs of striking workers until the labor dispute is resolved. The Hormel meat packers strike and the TWA flight attendants' strike are two examples of management employing this tactic in the 1980s.

Which side has the advantage in the weapons available to them? Wide disparity would again be evident in our questioning of the fisherman from Massachusetts and the small unionized manufacturer.

THE FUTURE OF LABOR-MANAGEMENT RELATIONS

Organized labor is at a crossroads. The unionized share of the nonfarm workforce has declined from a peak of 35.5% in 1945 to 17% in 1986 (see Figure 18-7). The United Mine Workers alone has lost 84% of its membership since 1942. To save jobs, many unions are granting concessions to management (see Figure 18-8). Furthermore, public support for organized labor has drifted. Has the death knell sounded for organized labor?

Text continued on p. 499.

strikebreakers
Workers hired to do the jobs of striking workers until the labor dispute is resolved.

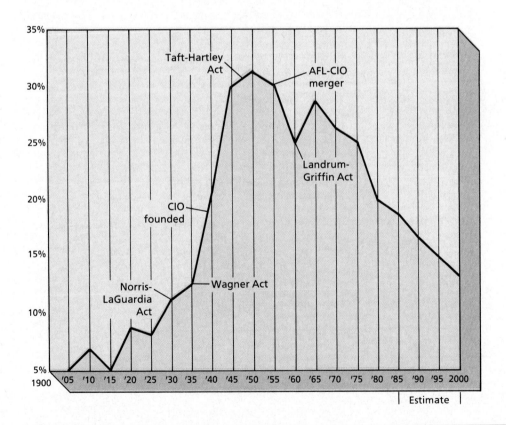

Percentage of union membership in the nonagricultural work force. Union membership as a percentage of the work force grew rather steadily until 1953 when it declined rather steadily. This trend has continued since then.
Source: Bureau of Labor Statistics.

FIGURE 18-7

FIGURE 18-8

Work rule changes granted by organized labor.

Copyright © 1983, *Business Week* Publishing.

UNIONS ARE GRANTING THESE MAJOR CHANGES IN WORK RULES . . .		. . . IN THESE INDUSTRIES
Job assignments	Cutting size of crews; enlarging jobs by adding duties; eliminating unneeded jobs	Steel, autos, railroads, meatpacking, airlines
Skilled maintenance and construction	Combining craft jobs such as millwright, welder, rigger, and boilermaker; allowing journeymen to perform helpers' duties; permitting equipment operators to run more than one machine	Autos, rubber, steel, petroleum, construction
Hours of work	Giving up relief and wash-up periods; allowing management more flexibility in scheduling daily and weekly hours; working more hours for the same pay	Autos, rubber, steel, meatpacking, trucking, airlines (pilots), textile
Seniority	Restricting use of seniority in filling job vacancies, 'bumping' during layoffs, and picking shifts	Autos, rubber, meatpacking, steel
Wages	Restricting pay to hours worked rather than miles traveled	Railroads, trucking
Incentive pay	Reducing incentives to reflect changing job conditions	Rubber, steel
Team work	Allowing team members to rotate jobs; permitting pay for knowledge instead of function; allowing management to change crew structure to cope with new technology	Autos, auto suppliers, steel, rubber

ORGANIZATION	MEMBERS (IN THOUSANDS)	ORGANIZATION	MEMBERS (IN THOUSANDS)
Unions		Government (NAGE)	200
Teamsters	1,891	Transportation Union	190
Automobile Workers (UAW)	1,357	Iron Workers	184
United Food and Commercial	1,300	Railway Clerks	180
Steelworkers	1,238	Fire Fighters	178
State, County (AFSCME)	1,098	Painters	164
Electrical (IBEW)	1,041	Oil, Chemicals	154
Carpenters	784	Electrical (UE) (Ind.)	162
Machinists	754	Bakery, Confectionery, Tobacco	161
Service Employees (SEIV)	650	Sheet Metal	161
Laborers	608	Transit Union	161
Communications Workers	551	Rubber	151
Teachers	551	Boilermakers	145
Clothing and Textile Workers	455	Transport Workers	130
Operating Engineers	423	Printing and Graphic	122
Hotel and Restaurant	400	Woodworkers	112
Plumbers	352	Office	107
Ladies' Garments (ILGWU)	323	Maintenance of Way	102
Musicians	299	**Associations**	
Paperworkers	275	National Education Association	1,684
Government (AFGE)	255	Nurses' Association	180
Postal Workers	251	Classified School Employees	150
Mine Workers	245	Police	140
Electrical (IUE)	233	California's Assembly of Governmental Employees (AGE)	105
Letter Carriers	230		
Retail, Wholesale	215		

FIGURE 18-9

National unions and employee associations reporting 100,000 members or more.

Source: U.S. Department of Labor, Bureau of Labor Statistics, *Directory of National Unions and Employee Associations, 1979, 1980*, updated with *Statistical Abstract of the U.S., 1982–83*, U.S. Department of Commerce, Bureau of the Census, p. 409, and unpublished union data.

Probably not. Nonetheless, to grow, unions will have to adapt to a workforce that is increasingly white collar, female, and professional. As Figure 18-9 highlights, the National Education Association is now the second-largest labor organization in the workplace. Additionally, unions must recognize the need for changes in work rules to permit U.S. companies to compete with growing international-based firms. Finally, labor and management must retreat from the "us versus them" attitude that has historically dominated labor relations and seek to build a "we" attitude between labor and management proponents. Pay concessions and givebacks by labor in the 1980s are a step in this direction. However, as the Profile at the beginning of the chapter highlights, executive compensation may be a sore spot for proponents of organized labor for years to come. The hourly wage of $13.75 and additional $9.25 in fringe benefits earned by some autoworkers may seem meager when compared with the $11 million earned by Lee Iacocca of Chrysler Corporation.

PROGRESS CHECK

■ What are the major laws affecting employee-management relations and unions?

■ Can you trace the history of unions from the Knights of Labor through today?

THE ISSUE OF EXECUTIVE COMPENSATION

How much should a top executive earn? In 1984, Michael Jackson sang his way to $35 million, Clint Eastwood squinted out $10 million, Martina Navratilova volleyed her way to $4 million, Marvelous Marvin Hagler boxed his way to $3.3 million, and Dan Rather reported the news for $2.2 million.

Is it not fair, therefore, that the President of Pepsico should make over $1 million or that Lee Iacocca of Chrysler should make $11 million? The U.S. free enterprise system is built on the incentives that allow executives to make that much. Stockholders seem to support such pay; nevertheless, some people feel that executive compensation is out of line (see Figure 18-10).

It is important to recognize that most of these executives are responsible for billion-dollar corporations and work 70-plus hours a week. Many can show their stockholders that their decisions turned failure to success (Lee Iacocca, for example). There is no "answer" to fair compensation for executives. This subject could be debated in class to get the views of a variety of people. After all, you may be one of those executives some day.

GOLDEN PARACHUTES—ANOTHER EXECUTIVE PAY ISSUE

A golden parachute is a fund set aside for corporate managers whose jobs may be threatened by a takeover by another firm. To attract an executive to a firm, the board may offer that executive a golden parachute to assure him or her that the job is a secure one—or else the golden parachute will protect against a crash. Why is this an issue? Because the golden parachutes are often huge.

The issue began when William Agee left Bendix with a $4 million golden parachute. In 1986, 30% of the top 250 companies had such plans, versus 15% 5 years ago, so the issue is growing in importance. So are the rewards. In 1986, Michael Bergerac got a $34 million golden parachute when he left Revlon after a takeover by Pantry Pride. William W. Granger, Jr., had been in charge of Beatrice Company less than 4 months when Kohlberg Kravis Roberts began negotiations to make the company private. Mr. Granger's golden parachute was $7 million. RCA created an estimated $33 million in bailout deals for some 60 executives when General Electric came bidding to buy them out.

Do executives deserve millions of dollars for losing their jobs? Are golden parachutes fair? These are serious questions being raised today.

Source: Eleanor Johnson Tracy, "Parachutes A-Popping," *Fortune*, March 31, 1986, p. 66; and "Executive Pay: How the Boss Did in '85," *Business Week*, May 5, 1986, pp. 48-58.

FIGURE 18-10

The 25 highest-paid executives.

	COMPANY	1985 SALARY AND BONUS	LONG-TERM COMPENSATION	TOTAL PAY
		THOUSANDS OF DOLLARS		
1. VICTOR POSNER, Chmn.	DWG	$12,739		$12,739
2. LEE A. IACOCCA, Chmn.	Chrysler	1,617	$9,809	11,426
3. T. BOONE PICKENS Jr., Chmn.	Mesa Petroleum	4,203	4,228	8,431
4. DREW LEWIS, Chmn.	Warner Amex	1,000	5,000	6,000
5. ROBERT L. MITCHELL, Vice-chmn.	Celanese	700	4,056	4,756
6. SIDNEY J. SHEINBERG, Pres.	MCA	509	3,975	4,484
7. ROBERT ANDERSON, Chmn.	Rockwell	1,326	2,310	3,636
8. CLIFTON C. GARVIN, Jr., Chmn.	Exxon	1,454	2,107	3,561
9. DAVID S. LEWIS, Chmn.	General Dynamics	1,062	2,289	3,351
10. JOHN H. GUTFREUND, Chmn.	Phibro-Salomon	3,066	140	3,206
11. GEORGE B. BEITZEL, Sr. v-p.	IBM	608	2,409	3,017
12. ROY A. ANDERSON, Chmn.	Lockheed	916	2,060	2,976
13. JOSEPH B. FLAVIN, Chmn.	Singer	660	2,312	2,972
14. PETER A. COHEN, Chmn.	Shearson Lehman Brothers	1,704	1,207	2,911
15. MICHAEL D. ROSE, Chmn.	Holiday	549	2,360	2,909
16. FRANK PRICE, V-p.	MCA	509	2,385	2,894
17. RICHARD J. SCHMEELK, Exec. v-p.	Phibro-Salomon	2,640	199	2,839
18. STEVEN J. ROSS, Chmn.	Warner Communications	2,800		2,800
19. GERALD GREENWALD, Vice-chmn.	Chrysler	1,167	1,613	2,780
20. DAVID R. BANKS, Pres.	Beverly Enterprises	423	2,355	2,778
21. RICHARD M. FURLAUD, Chmn.	Squibb	1,050	1,710	2,760
22. HENRY KAUFMAN, Vice-chmn.	Phibro-Salomon	2,640	120	2,760
23. HAROLD K. SPERLICH, Pres.	Chrysler	1,085	1,675	2,760
24. SPENCER SCOTT, Chmn.	Citadel Holding	356	2,291	2,647
25. PETER T. BUCHANAN, Pres.	First Boston	2,300	233	2,533

Source: *Business Week,* May 15, 1986, p. 49.

THE ISSUE OF COMPARABLE WORTH

An even more pressing issue than executive pay is that of pay equity for women. This question is taking on additional importance as more and more women enter the labor force. In 1890, only 15% of the labor force was women. By 1950, that figure had risen, but to only 25%. By 1980, women made up 40% of the labor force, and now the figure is over 50%. More women in the labor force mean more issues: day care centers, flextime, and so forth. But no issue has received more attention than pay equity or "comparable worth." **Comparable worth,** remember, is the demand for equal pay for jobs requiring similar levels of education, training, and skills.

For many years, women have earned about 64% of what men earn. One explanation for this is that women only work 50% to 60% of their available years once they leave school, whereas men, on the whole, work all of those years.[1] Another explanation is the idea that many women try to work as well as care for their families, and thus take more flexible jobs that pay less. But the main argument is that women make less because they are women and are discriminated against. The idea of pay equity is to correct past discrimination by raising the pay in "women's jobs" such as nursing, secretarial work, teaching, and so forth.

Part of the problem has been understanding just what "comparable worth" means. It does not mean that equal wages should be paid to men and women who do the *same* job. Federal law already requires "equal pay for equal work." It is against the law, for example, to pay a female nurse less than a male nurse. Rather, the issue of comparable worth centers on comparing the "value" of jobs such as nurse or librarian (women's jobs) with jobs such as truck driver or plumber (men's jobs). Such a comparison shows that "women's jobs" pay less—much less.

comparable worth
The demand for equal pay for jobs requiring similar levels of education, training, and skills.

Comparable worth proponents ask whether a truck driver should be paid more than a nurse.

One way women have fought such discrimination is to use the old tactic of forming unions. Technical and clerical workers at Yale University, for example, recently formed a union. A strike in 1984 won them a 24% pay hike over 3 years. The union members are computer technicians, librarians, secretaries, hospital aides, and research assistants. They earned, on the average, $13,500. The university paid its mostly male truck drivers about 36% more.[2] The union is pushing for even higher increases to correct what they perceive as unfair differences between male and female pay.

Recent Public-Sector Comparable Worth Action

The chances are good that women *will* receive adjustments in wages over time. The state of Minnesota, for example, has passed legislation requiring pay equity. To compare jobs, the state used an instrument called the **Hay Guide Chart Profile Method,** which awards points based on the employee's knowledge, problem-solving ability, accountability, and working conditions. For example, nurses and vocational-education field instructors both earned 275 points. Yet the nurses (94% of whom were female) made a maximum of $1,723 a month, and the instructors, who were all male, made up to $2,260 a month. The average female state worker with *20 years* of experience made *less* than the average newly-hired male worker.[3] Minnesota is correcting such inequities and has ordered its cities, counties, and school districts to adopt similar programs, affecting 163,000 workers.

Five other states—Iowa, Idaho, New Mexico, Washington, and South Dakota—are also adjusting pay scales. Two dozen other states are studying the idea. It certainly will be a major issue in the near future for all states.

Hay Guide Chart Profile Method
A technique for measuring pay equity based on an employee's knowledge, problem-solving ability, accountability, and working conditions.

Comparable Worth in Industry

Corporations see the writing on the wall, and are giving serious thought to pay equity issues. One tactic, of course, is to resist the movement. Some managers say that *the market* determines wages and that they have not discriminated. "If women want more pay," they say, "let them take jobs that pay more—truck driver, and other 'men's' jobs."

The problem becomes most acute when "the market" creates pay differences that aren't logically corrected by pay equity. For example, nurses in the state of Washington earned 573 points on their job-evaluation scale. Computer systems analysts received only 426 points. In the market, though, systems analysts make about 56% more than nurses. Clearly market factors are a consideration when the "value" of a job is weighed; a clerical supervisor received a higher rating than a chemist, but "the market" pays a chemist 40% more. Trying to compare all jobs on a pay equity scale would be virtually impossible and would play havoc with market forces. Today, for example, there is a glut of Ph.Ds of English. English professors thus earn low pay because of the market. Computer software writers are in short supply and receive high wages. Should public and private organizations be forced to pay Ph.Ds in English more because they score higher on some standardized pay-equity test? Clearly the problem is unmanageable at the national level. This does not mean, however, that some steps toward comparable worth should not be implemented in the private sector. It does mean that the process will be quite complex and will involve much debate—much like the union negotiations of the past.

Many firms have already started comparable-worth type analyses. AT&T, for example, evaluated 20 categories of employment using 14 measurements. The results of the study are now being implemented. Other firms have also implemented changes. The public sector is ahead of private firms on this issue, but comparable worth will be a major issue in businesses now that women make up such a large percentage of the labor force.

THINKING IT THROUGH

Professors in different departments of a university may make widely different wages, even though they all may have equal education and do equal work. For example, an engineering professor or business professor may make more than an English professor. Is that fair? Should English professors be paid the same using the comparable worth argument? How would that affect the supply and demand for English professors?

What role should the market play in determining wages? What about working conditions? Because a hod carrier does work that is harder than a bricklayer's, should he or she be paid more? Why isn't hard work rewarded more generously in the market?

THE ISSUE OF EMPLOYEE OWNERSHIP (ESOPs)

employee stock ownership plan (ESOP)
A plan whereby employees can buy part or total ownership of the firm where they work.

No matter how long and hard workers fight for better pay, they will never get as wealthy as people who actually own the companies. At least that is the theory behind **employee stock ownership plans (ESOPs)**. An *ESOP* is a plan whereby employees can buy part or total ownership of the firm where they work. The idea for ESOPs was started by Louis O. Kelso about 30 years ago. His idea was to turn workers into owners by selling them stock. Using this concept, he helped the employees of a newspaper buy their company. Since then, the idea of employees taking over all or some of the ownership of their companies has gained much favor. Since 1979, 16 laws have been passed giving tax breaks and other favorable treatment to such plans. Many people consider ESOPs examples of capitalism at its best. The facts are, however, that ESOPs have had mixed results.

Benefits of ESOPs

First, the good news. There are now some 7,000 businesses with ESOPs, affecting the wealth of some 8% of the work force. Corey Rosen of the National Center for Employee Ownership reports that 98% of the 7,000 firms are profitable. About 40% of the firms were sold to employees by owners who were ready to retire. ESOPs gave them a ready market (employees) and good tax breaks as well.[4]

A good example of an owner selling his firm to employees is that of 64-year-old Theodore Barry, who in 1985 sold his majority interest in the management consulting business he founded. Theodore Barry & Associates employed 100 professionals who generated $13 million in revenue. The management group, which owned 100% of TB&A (57% Theodore Barry; 43% balance of group), sold their interest. Through a complicated financial process, the ownership was redistributed; the new ownership became 50.1% all employees, 17% Theodore Barry, and 32.9% balance of the management group. No cash was required on the part of the all-employee group for their ownership.

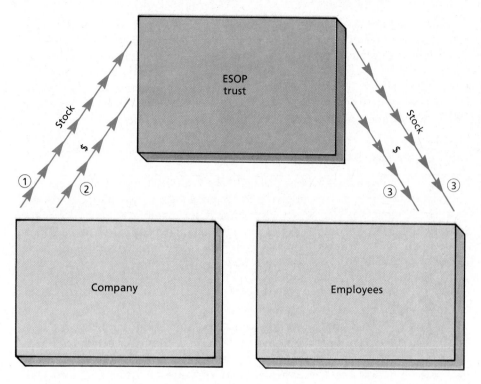

In a nonleveraged ESOP, annual contributions (to a maximum of 25% of payroll) are made as follows: *1,* Each year, company gives stock to ESOP, or *2,* gives cash to ESOP to buy stock. Employees pay nothing. ESOP holds stock for employees and periodically notifies them how much they own and how much it is worth. *3,* Employees collect stock or cash when they retire or otherwise leave company according to vesting schedule.

During the past few years, employee participation in ownership has emerged as an important issue in just about every industry and every type of company—in die-casting shops, steel foundries, airlines, bakeries, advertising agencies, industrial equipment suppliers, publishing companies, mutual fund organizations, radio stations, and on and on.

As might be expected, the trend is strongest in such places as California's Silicon Valley, where the passion for ownership has reached epidemic proportions. "Out here, everybody, including the janitors, expects to be an owner," says the president of a public relations firm in San Jose. But it can be seen in most other parts of the country as well—even in the Industrial Midwest, where basic manufacturing companies are finding it increasingly difficult to attract experienced managers without offering equity incentives.[8]

The basic purpose of employee ownership is to give employees a share in the profits of the firm and thus increase their involvement with the firm. Some of the advantages are:

- *Higher morale* as a result of being part-owner of the firm.
- *Incentives* to produce more efficiently—any increased profits are shared by the workers.
- *Tax benefits*. ESOPs are considered as a special type of pension plan by the government; thus there are tax breaks for employees.
- *More employee participation* in managerial decision making.
- *More commitment* by all workers to the firm and its success.
- *A lure* to attract highly skilled people at lower salaries with the promise that they will earn more in the long run as the *company* prospers.
- *Feelings of cooperation and participation* are generated that cannot be matched in any other way.

These are the actual results at firms such as American West Airlines. It *requires* employees to purchase stock equal to 20% of their first year's base pay. Mike Ehl, a 27-year-old customer service representative, says, "Every time I go to the airport, I feel excited by what I'm part of. Equity participation creates a bond that joins people and makes us think and work harder together."[6] Similar feelings are echoed at other companies with ESOPs. It would be misleading, however, to say that ESOPs are an unqualified success. Let's look at the other side.

Problems with ESOPs

Not all ESOP programs work as planned. They can be used to refinance a firm with employees' money without giving employees added participation or more job security. Employees at Dan River, Incorporated, for example, bought 70% of the company in a move to save jobs. Nevertheless, employment fell from 12,000 to 8,000 workers, and workers do not feel more involved in management. Employees cannot vote for directors nor on top policy matters. In short, management did very little to include employees in decision making. All employees got was ownership. Even at that, they got Class B common shares that did *not* share equally in profits with the Class A shares managers got.

Studies show that in 85% of the companies with ESOPs, employees do *not* have voting rights. ESOPs are also a more risky form of pension plan for employees.

At Pan American World Airways, workers took large pay cuts to get 11% of the company stock, but felt little was done to improve communications with management or to involve workers in solving problems. At Hyatt-Clark Industries, the leaders of the United Auto Workers Local 736 fought with management over daily operating decisions, staff appointments and salaries, and what to do with profits.

In summary, the goal of ESOPs is good—employee ownership, employee pride, and so on—but the *implementation* of such programs is often less than satisfactory. ESOPs are a relatively new managerial concept and thus have much improvement to make. Nonetheless, the good seems to outweigh the negative[7]:

- A survey of 360 high-tech firms found that those with ESOPs grew two to four times as fast as those where employees did not own stock.
- A study of 52 employee-owned companies in all industries found that the best performers were those that made the large stock payments to workers' ESOP accounts.

Those companies that have a strong "ownership culture" and give workers a powerful voice in decisions have "extremely motivated work forces" according to Corey Rosen, founder of the National Center for Employee Ownership.[8]

Therefore, when used correctly, ESOPs can be a powerful strategy for improving corporate profitability and increasing employee satisfaction, participation, and *income*.

THE ISSUE OF EMPLOYEE SATISFACTION

All this talk about pay would indicate that salary was the most important issue in employee satisfaction. The fact is that many other aspects of the job are important to employees' morale. Milt Moscowitz, Robert Levering, and Michael Katz wrote a book in 1984 called *The 100 Best Companies to Work For in America: An Insider's*

Guide to America's Favorite Employers (Addison-Wesley). The authors conclude that pay level doesn't appear to determine how happy employees are, although most of the top companies pay high salaries. Some of the qualities that make for a good employer include:

- Stressing quality, enabling employees to feel proud of the products and services they provide.
- Making people feel they are part of a team or even a family of workers.
- Reducing the distinctions of rank between top management and workers.
- Promoting from within by letting employees bid for jobs before hiring others.
- Allowing employees to share profits through profit-sharing plans or ESOPs.
- Devoting resources and attention to creating a pleasant work environment.
- Encouraging employees to be active in community service.
- Caring about the health of employees through fitness centers and medical programs.
- Expanding skills through training programs and payment for outside courses.
- Trying to avoid layoffs without first making an effort to place workers in other jobs in the firm or in other companies.

In case you're interested (for career purposes), some of the top names in the *Best Companies* book are IBM, Bell Labs, Delta, Goldman Sacks, Hallmark, Pitney Bowes, Trammell Crow, Hewlett-Packard, and Northwest Mutual Life. Big companies such as GE and Procter & Gamble made the list, but so did smaller firms such as Celestial Seasons, Gore, the Los Angeles Dodgers, Apple Computer, and People Express.

Procter & Gamble is one of *The 100 best companies to work for in America.*

At Reader's Digest, people work a 35-hour week, get 12 paid holidays a year, and have every Friday off during May. Why May? Because May is such a pretty month. A nice place to work, no?

There is some concern about the competitiveness of U.S. business in the future. Firms that provide employee satisfaction through the kinds of programs listed will do well, because their employees will work hard to keep the company productive. By the way, companies listed in the book are receiving an avalanche of resumés from people seeking work—a mixed blessing.

PROGRESS CHECK

■ What are the major reasons for and against using scales such as the Hay Guide Chart Profile for determining wages?

■ What are the advantages and disadvantages of ESOPs?

SUMMARY

1 The first national labor organization was the Knights of Labor, which was founded in 1869. Much legislation has been passed since then to balance the power of labor and management (see Figure 18-1).
   ■ What is a negotiated labor-management agreement?
      It clarifies the terms and conditions under which management and labor agree to function over a specific period.
   ■ What is a union shop?
      It is one in which employees may join a firm without being a member of the union, but must join the union to keep their job.
   ■ What other legal union contracts are there?
      Simple-recognition shop, agency shop, and maintenance-of-membership shop (see Figure 18-4).
   ■ What are the "weapons" used by unions and management in conflicts?
      Unions use strikes and boycotts. Management can use injunctions and lockouts.
2 Executive pay for many top managers is over $2 million per year.
   ■ What is a "fair" wage for managers?
      Manager's salaries are set by the market and organizations. What is "fair" is open to debate.
3 Women want "fair wages" too. In general they make about 64% of what men make. They are asking for pay equity, or comparable worth.
   ■ What is comparable worth?
      It is the demand for equal pay for jobs requiring similar levels of education, training, and skills.
   ■ Why is this an issue?
      Because "the market" has been the major factor in deciding who gets paid what, and overriding market forces is difficult.
   ■ Isn't pay inequity caused by sexism?
      There is evidence on both sides of that issue, but government or corporate actions would indicate that some remedial action will be taken regardless of causes.
4 Employees today are demanding "a piece of the action," ownership in the firm.
   ■ How are employee stock ownership plans (ESOPs) working?
      There are mixed results, but the overall trend is favorable. Some 7,000 businesses now have ESOPs. Properly implemented, such plans can increase morale, motivation, commitment, and job satisfaction. The problem is that many firms have used ESOPs as a capital-raising scheme and have not given employees more participation in management. The issue of the *administration* of ESOPs will be a major one in the next decade.
5 A major concern of yours is finding a good job in a company for which it is

nice to work. A book called *The 100 Best Companies to Work for in America* gives you some cues as to what to look for: a firm that stresses quality, makes employees feel part of a team, reduces distinctions between ranks, encourages communication, creates a happy environment, and so forth. Most of the "100 Best" are smaller firms, but others, such as IBM, GE, and Procter & Gamble, are quite large. Good luck in your search to find a company that provides a pleasant work environment.

KEY TERMS

agency shop   p. 494
**American Federation of
    Labor**   p. 490
closed-shop agreement   p. 493
comparable worth   p. 502
**employee stock ownership plan
    (ESOP)**   p. 504
**Hay Guide Chart Profile
    Method**   p. 503
injunction   p. 496
Knights of Labor   p. 490
**Labor-Management Relations
    Act (Taft-Hartley Act)**   p. 491
**Labor-Management Reporting
    and Disclosure Act (Landrum-
    Griffin Act)**   p. 491

lockouts   p. 496
**maintenance-of-membership
    shop**   p. 494
**National Labor Relations Act
    (Wagner Act)**   p. 491
**negotiated labor-management
    agreement**   p. 493
Norris-La Guardia Act   p. 491
primary boycott   p. 495
right-to-work laws   p. 493
secondary boycott   p. 495
simple recognition shop
    p. 494
strikebreaker   p. 497
union shop   p. 493
yellow-dog contract   p. 496

GETTING INVOLVED

1 Many college faculty members do not belong to a union. Faculty pay in many disciplines has fallen way behind pay in industry. Talk with several faculty members about their feelings toward unions. What are the chances that unions will be able to recruit more faculty members some day? Discuss your findings with the class.

2 Debate the following in class: "Business executives receive a total compensation package that is far beyond their value." Take the opposite side of the issue from your normal stance to get a better feel for the other point of view.

3 Read both sides of the debate on comparable worth in the current literature. Then debate the following: "Women's jobs must be paid more so that they are equal to the pay for men's jobs." Again, take the side you do not now support to learn more about the issue.

4 Buy or borrow the book *The 100 Best Companies to Work For in America*. What do the authors leave out that you would like to know? Are "women's" issues covered (for example, part-time work, job sharing, day care)? Report to the class.

5 Develop a list of three worker issues not covered in this chapter. Compare your list with others. Pick one or two popular ones and debate them in class.

CASE ONE   CLOSING UNION STORES AND FACTORIES

**PRACTICING
MANAGEMENT DECISIONS**

Mr. Arzberger worked for 37 years at a Kroger store in Pittsburgh. He lost his job recently when Kroger closed 43 Pittsburgh-area supermarkets because their 2,850 employees refused to accept pay cuts, benefit reductions, and other contract changes.

With wage rates as high as they were, Kroger was simply not competitive with the other food chains. A competing food chain paid $2 an hour less, and independent supermarkets were paying $3 to $4 less per hour. Kathy Koch was the head cashier at a Kroger store in Plymouth, Michigan. She too presided over the closing of her store as Kroger closed 70 of its 82 Michigan stores. Operating costs were simply too high, and unionized employees refused to accept contract concessions. The Michigan closings cost Kroger $10 million in severance pay and other benefits for more than 4,000 employees.

The Pittsburgh stores were purchased by Wetterau Inc., a food wholesaler that will sell the stores to independent operators, who will operate them with lower-paid help.

Other companies—Greyhound, USX, and Goodyear Tire and Rubber, to name just a few—are saying similar things to workers: your wages are too high. Either accept cutbacks or we may have to go out of business. The city of Dayton, Ohio is still recovering from the closing of NCR facilities there when union workers did not accept pay cuts years ago.

Greyhound worked through many of its labor concessions by means of an old strike-breaking effort. It hired replacements for 12,000 striking drivers and resumed limited operations. Trans World Airlines is farming out some of its maintenance work to nonunion concerns. Some 3,500 employees might have to work for the new firm for less pay or quit.

United Auto Workers, faced with the choice of closing plants or taking pay cuts, chose the pay cuts but put job security clauses into new contracts. Ford has threatened to move production facilities overseas unless labor concedes to cuts in pay.

DECISION QUESTIONS

1. What would you recommend to union workers whose plants are threatening to close unless they give wage concessions? What is your reaction to the huge salaries being paid corporate executives at Kroger, Greyhound, Ford, and other companies closing down facilities?
2. Is there some alternative to cutting wages or closing down? What is it?
3. Union workers often feel that the company is bluffing when it threatens to close. How can such doubts be settled so more open negotiations can take place?

PRACTICING MANAGEMENT DECISIONS

CASE TWO   TWO-TIER WAGE CONTRACTS

In 1983, the union at GM's Delco Products factory agreed to a two-tiered wage contract. What that means is that new workers are paid on a different (lower) scale than already-employed workers. Workers can thus be working side-by-side doing the same job, but making different wages. The conflicts are obvious.

What happened at GM is that the personnel director told the union that the plant would not hire any more people at the old wages (no new people had been hired for 3 years). If wages and benefits were lowered, the plant could hire new people. The new system was approved, and now assemblers make up to $9.68 per hour versus $13.00 under the old contract. The hourly work force increased to 3,550 workers from 2,200 over a two-year period. Naturally, the new workers have to have an extensive briefing session to explain to them why it was necessary to pay them less. (Otherwise, they would not have been hired.)

The Delco plant is an example of the two-tier wage system working relatively well. In other firms, the results are not as good. First of all, it should be noted that, in 1983 and 1984, some 450,000 workers were involved in two-tier contracts. That's about 8% of major union contracts and 17% of service industry contracts.

In 1981, Hughes aircraft gave raises to workers at its missile factory, but froze the starting wage at $3.63. The pay scales between old and new workers could never meet. The result? New workers didn't stay, morale fell, and workmanship declined.

American Airlines estimates that its two-tier system saved it $100 million in 1984. American had trouble recruiting pilots at the lower wages, however, and had to raise the rates. New flight attendants are not happy with the union. Many other companies are faced with the same situation as GM, American, and others. They cannot afford to hire people at old wage rates, but worry about morale problems under a two-tier system.

DECISION QUESTIONS

1 What economic conditions in the 1980s led to the issue of two-tier wage rates? Are these conditions improving or worsening, and what does that mean for future contracts?

2 Can anything be done to increase new-worker satisfaction with lower wages for the same job?

3 Will settling for two-tier contracts strengthen or weaken unions in the future?

Source: David Wessel, "Two-Tier Pay Spreads, But the Pioneer Firms Encounter Problems," *The Wall Street Journal*, October 14, 1985, pp. 1 and 11; and "The Two-tier System Is Working Well at GM's Delco Plant in Rochester, N.Y.," *The Wall Street Journal*, October 14, 1985, p. 11.

LOOKING AHEAD

We have now covered basic management and some of the issues involved. It is time to explore in more depth the inner workings of a firm. We shall begin with accounting. Then we shall explore finance and other important topics.

ACCOUNTING AND FINANCE

PART

VI

CHAPTER 19
ACCOUNTING PRINCIPLES

CHAPTER 20
**FINANCIAL INSTITUTIONS,
MONEY, AND BANKING**

CHAPTER 21
FINANCIAL MANAGEMENT

CHAPTER 22
STOCKS AND BONDS

CHAPTER 23
**PERSONAL FINANCIAL
MANAGEMENT**

ACCOUNTING PRINCIPLES

LEARNING GOALS

After you have read and studied this chapter, you should be able to:

- Explain the functions of accounting.
- Identify and describe the major accounts used to prepare financial statements.
- Distinguish between a journal and a ledger.
- Prepare a simple income statement, and explain its function.
- Prepare a simple balance sheet, and explain its function.
- Discuss how the method of determining depreciation and cost of goods sold affects net income.
- Explain the concept of cash flow.
- Calculate several financial ratios and discuss their significance.

PROFILE BRIAN STUTT, APPLIANCE DISCOUNTER

In 1977, Brian Stutt left the family appliance business in Brooklyn to see how well he could do on his own. He was 29 years old. Brian headed down to fast-growth Houston and worked for 8 months for an appliance wholesaler and for 2 months for a retailer. He noticed that the wholesalers were selling appliances to dealers for what retail customers (you and me) were paying in New York—or more. Brian saw an opportunity. He bought appliances in New York and sold them at deep discounts from his garage to customers willing to pay cash up front.

In 1980, Brian and his wife opened a store. It covered 2,000 square feet. They began to advertise aggressively. A year and a half later, the Stutts were doing $8.5 million in business. Things were going great.

About a year later, Brian realized that the business was consistently losing money. Later, he discovered why. As long as the business was growing, cash from this month's sales had always covered the previous month's bills. "What we never realized," his wife said, "was that we were spending $60 to make $50."

You see, Brian and Sharon knew how to sell appliances, but they knew almost nothing about accounting. Sharon had never even *seen* an income statement before. They did not pay any attention to costs because their cash flow always covered them. Furthermore, neither their banker nor the finance company that handled

Brian Stutt.

Accounting is the language of business.
ANONYMOUS

their inventory demanded financial reports on a routine basis. Their accountant never told them they had a problem. "We were paying our bills," Brian said. "Who worried?"

By December, 1983, the firm, Warehouse Appliance, had a deficit of almost $1 million. The Stutts had to sell their BMW and Mercedes. They also put their half-million-dollar house up for sale.

Sharon left the business for other pursuits. Brian cut back considerably. The sales force was cut from 28 to 5 people. Sales fell closer to $4.5 million. A consultant helped Brian with a 5-year plan and a budget. Now, Brian is determined to keep his house. He knows now that growth for its own sake is disastrous. He has learned the value of knowing accounting and finance, no matter what business you are in or what you are most skilled at doing. ▪

Source: "Through the Wringer," *Inc.,* December 1984, pp. 95-96.

THE IMPORTANCE OF ACCOUNTING

Brian Stutt's story is repeated hundreds of times everyday throughout the country. Small businesses (and often large businesses too) fail because they do not follow good accounting and financial procedures. Accounting is different from marketing, management, and personnel in that we know almost nothing about accounting from experience. We have all had some experience with marketing. We have observed and understand management concepts, and personnel procedures seem relatively easy to grasp. But accounting? What is it? What do accountants do? Is it interesting?*

The truth is that many people, including some business majors, are not interested in accounting at all. They would rather study marketing or management or finance—anything but accounting. The result is that there are literally thousands of businesspeople who are highly skilled in most areas of business, but relatively ignorant when it comes to accounting. The result? Like Brian Stutt, they plunge into the world of trade and seem to be doing well. Sales go up. Profits are high. But cash flow is poor; that is, the business simply does not have cash available to pay its bills. The net result is business failure—thousands every year.

The fact is that you will have to know something about accounting if you really want to understand business. Furthermore, accounting is not that hard. You will have to learn a few terms; that is mandatory. Then you have to understand bookkeeping and how accounts are kept. That is not too difficult either. From the figures accountants gather and record, they prepare reports, called financial statements. It is these reports that tell a businessperson how healthy the business is. It is almost impossible to run a business effectively without being able to read, understand, and analyze accounting reports and financial statements. Accounting reports and financial statements are as revealing of the health of a business as pulse rate and blood pressure reports are in revealing the health of a person.

The purpose of this chapter is to introduce you to basic accounting principles. By the end of it, you should have a good idea of what accounting is, how it works, and why it is important. Spend some time learning the terms and reviewing the

---

*The author wishes to acknowledge the assistance of Dr. Edward Lehman of American University for his guidance in preparing this chapter and the chapters on finance.

accounting statements. A few hours invested in learning this material will pay off repeatedly as you become more involved in business or investing, or simply understanding what's going on out there in the world of business and finance.

✳ WHAT IS ACCOUNTING?

Accounting is the recording, classifying, summarizing, and interpreting of financial events and transactions that affect an organization. *Transactions* include buying and selling goods and services, acquiring insurance, using supplies, and paying taxes. Transactions may be recorded by hand, or they may be recorded in a computer system. The trend is to use computers because the process is repetitive and complex, and computers greatly simplify the task.

After the transactions have been recorded, they are usually classified into groups that have common characteristics. For example, all purchases are grouped together, as are all sales transactions. The business is thus able to obtain needed information about purchases, sales, and other transactions that occur over a given period of time. The methods used to record and summarize accounting data into reports is called an *accounting system*.[1] Systems that use computers enable an organization to get financial reports daily if they so desire. One purpose of accounting is to help managers evaluate the financial condition and the operating performance of the firm so that they may make better decisions. Another is to report financial information to people outside the firm such as owners, creditors, suppliers, and the government (for tax purposes).

Accounting is User-Oriented

In more basic terms accounting is the measurement and reporting to various users (inside and outside the organization) financial information regarding the economic activities of the firm (see Figure 19-1). Accounting has been called "the language of business," but it is also the language used to report financial information about nonprofit organizations such as churches, schools, hospitals, fraternities, and governmental units. Accounting can be divided into two major categories: managerial accounting and financial accounting. An accountant working for a firm is likely to do both.

accounting
The recording, classifying, summarizing, and interpreting of financial events and transactions that affect the organization. It may also be viewed as the measurement and reporting (inside and outside the organization) of financial information about the economic activities of the firm to various users.

USERS	TYPE OF REPORT
Government taxing authorities (e.g., the Internal Revenue Service)	Tax returns
Government regulatory agencies	Required reports
People interested in the income and financial position of the organization: owners, creditors, financial analyst, suppliers, others	Financial statements found in annual reports (e.g., income statement, balance sheet)
Managers of the firm	Financial statements and various internally distributed financial reports

FIGURE 19-1

Users of accounting information and the required reports.

[handwritten notes:]
outside
- SEC
- IRS
- current stockholders
- potential stockholders
- creditors

Managerial Accounting

managerial accounting
Provides information and analyses to managers within the organization to assist them in decision making.

Managerial accounting is used to provide information and analyses to managers within the organization to assist them in decision making. Managerial accounting is concerned with measuring and reporting costs of production, marketing, and other functions (cost accounting); preparing budgets (planning); checking whether or not units are staying within their budgets (controlling); and designing strategies to minimize taxes (tax accounting).

Simple analysis of corporate figures can disclose very important information. For example, a slight month-to-month increase in payroll costs may not appear significant. But multiply that increase by 12 months and the increase in costs can be disastrous. Monitoring figures such as profit margins, unit sales, travel expenses, inventory turnover, and other such data is critical to the success of a firm. Top management decision making is based on such data.

Coca-Cola's annual report.

THE COCA-COLA COMPANY
ANNUAL REPORT 1985

Financial Accounting

Financial accounting differs from managerial accounting because the information and analyses are for people outside of the organization. This information goes to owners and prospective owners, creditors and lenders, employee unions, customers, governmental units, and the general public. These external users are interested in the organization's profits, its ability to pay its bills, and other financial information. Much of the information is contained in the annual report, a yearly statement of the financial condition and progress of the firm. Various quarterly reports keep the users more current.

financial accounting
The preparation of financial statements for people outside of the firm (for example, investors).

ACCOUNTING VERSUS BOOKKEEPING

Bookkeeping involves the recording of economic activities, and is a rather mechanical process. It does not demand much creativity. Bookkeeping is part of accounting, but accounting goes far beyond the mere recording of data. Accountants classify and summarize the data. They interpret the data and report it to management. They also suggest strategies for improving the financial condition and progress of the firm. Accountants are especially valuable for income tax preparation and analysis. Figure 19-2 shows the whole process:

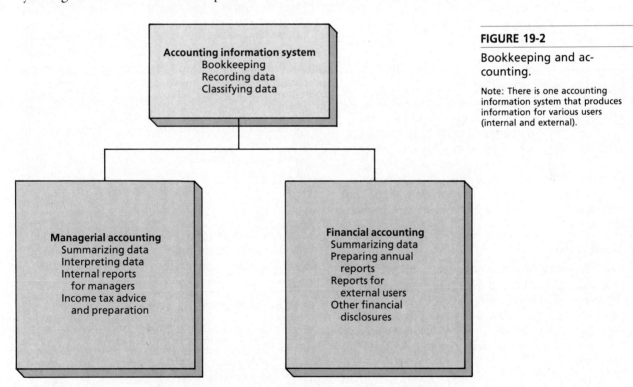

FIGURE 19-2

Bookkeeping and accounting.

Note: There is one accounting information system that produces information for various users (internal and external).

Now that you understand what accountants do and who they do it for, we can get down to the fundamental aspects of accounting. Accounting involves the gathering and recording of transactions (for example, the sale of merchandise, the payment of a bill, or the receipt of merchandise into storage), and the periodic preparation of financial statements that summarize those transactions.

CAREER INFORMATION: BOOKKEEPERS AND ACCOUNTING CLERKS

NATURE OF THE WORK

Every business needs systematic and up-to-date records of accounts and business transactions. Bookkeepers and accounting clerks maintain these records in journals and ledgers or in the memory of a computer. They also prepare periodic financial statements showing all money received and paid out. The duties of bookkeepers and the "tools of the trade" vary with the size of the business. However, virtually all of these workers use calculating machines and many work with computers.

In many small firms, a general bookkeeper handles all the bookkeeping. He or she analyzes and records all financial transactions, such as orders and cash sales. General bookkeepers also check money taken in against money paid out to be sure accounts balance, calculate the firm's payroll, and make up employee's paychecks. General bookkeepers also prepare and mail customers' bills and answer telephone requests for information about orders and bills.

In large businesses, several bookkeepers and accounting clerks work under the direction of of a head bookkeeper or accountant. In these organizations, bookkeeping workers often specialize in certain types of work. Some, for example, prepare statements of a company's income from sales or its daily operating expenses. Some enter information on accounts receivable and accounts payable into a computer and review computer printouts for accuracy and completeness. Others record business transactions, including payroll deductions and bills paid and due, and compute interest, rental, and freight charges. They also may type vouchers, invoices, and other financial records.

JOB OUTLOOK

Employment of bookkeepers and accounting clerks is expected to grow more slowly than the average for all occupations through the mid-1990s. Job prospects should be good, nonetheless, in view of the large number of openings that will occur because of the need to replace workers who transfer to other occupations or stop working.

The volume of business transactions is expected to grow rapidly, with a corresponding increase in the need for financial and accounting records. However, the need for bookkeepers, who maintain these records, will not increase nearly as fast because of the increasing use of computers to record, store, and manipulate data.

EARNINGS

Beginning accounting clerks in private firms averaged $11,704 a year in 1984. Salaries are higher for more complex jobs, up to an average of $20,244 a year for top level accounting clerks.

Median annual earnings of full-time bookkeepers and accounting clerks were about $13,500 in 1984; the middle 50 percent earned between $11,200 and $17,700 a year. Ten percent earned less than $9,000 and 10 percent more than $23,200.

In 1985, the federal government paid accounting clerks with 2 years of experience or postsecondary education a starting salary of $12,862 a year.

In 1984, the average beginning salary for accounting clerks in municipal, state, and federal government was $12,636 a year; the average salary for experienced workers was $16,248. Entry level accounting clerks averaged $13,832 a year in 1985, while accounting clerks with more responsibility averaged $16,484. Experienced bookkeepers in the private sector earned average annual salaries of $17,264 in 1985.

Accounting clerks' salaries vary by industry. They tend to be highest in public utilities and mining and lowest in finance, insurance, and real estate.

RELATED OCCUPATIONS

Workers in a number of other jobs also must be good at working with figures. Among such workers are bank tellers, collection workers, insurance clerks, and statistical clerks.

SOURCES OF ADDITIONAL INFORMATION

A brochure describing a career as a bookkeeper or accounting clerk is available upon request from:

Association of Independent Colleges and Schools, 1 Dupont Circle NW, Suite 350, Washington, D.C. 20036.

Source: *Occupational Outlook Handbook,* 1986-1987 (U.S. Department of Labor).

In the following sections, you will follow the steps accountants take in their day-to-day work. When we are finished, you should have a better idea of what accountants do and how they do it. You should also be able to read and understand financial statements and discuss accounting intelligently with an accountant and others in the world of business. The goal is not to learn how to be an accountant, just to learn the terms and concepts. So let's begin at the beginning.

Accounting Documents

If you were a bookkeeper the first task you would perform is to divide all of the firm's paperwork into meaningful categories. Those categories would probably include the following:

- Sales documents (sales slips, cash register receipts, and invoices)
- Purchasing documents
- Shipping documents
- Payroll records
- Bank documents (checks, deposit slips)
- Travel records
- Entertainment records

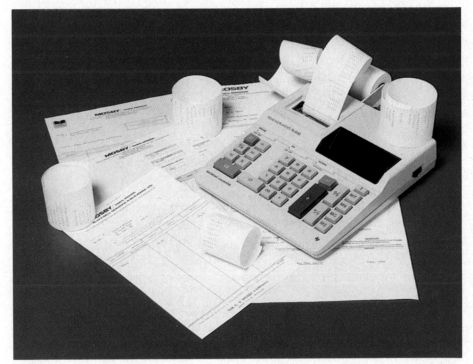

Transaction documents and an adding machine.

Now you would have several piles of papers, much like the piles that are generated in the preparation of income tax forms. You don't want the piles to get too high and unmanageable, so you must begin to record the data from the *original transaction documents* (the sales slips and so forth) into record books. (Thus the term *bookkeeping.*) These books are called **journals.** They are the books where accounting data are first entered.

journals
Recording devices used for the first recording of all transactions.

▪ Can you explain the difference between managerial and financial accounting?

▪ Could you define accounting to a friend so that he or she would clearly understand what is involved?

✳ THE "ACCOUNTS" OF ACCOUNTING

When recording the original transaction documents in a journal, the accountant or bookkeeper places them in certain accounts. Hence the term accounting. Accountants use five major accounts to prepare financial statements:

1 *Assets.* Economic resources owned by a firm (for example, land, buildings, machinery)

2 *Liabilities.* Amounts owed by the organization to others

3 *Owner's equity.* Assets minus liabilities

4 *Revenues.* The value of what is received for goods sold, services rendered, and from other sources

5 Expenses. Costs incurred in operating the business, such as rent, utilities, salaries, and insurance

expenses
Costs incurred in operating the business, such as rent, utilities, and salaries.

There is no way to understand accounting without learning a few accounting terms. The following material will give you further insight into the accounts used by accountants.

You know how much paperwork is involved in doing income taxes. There are often hundreds of sales slips and other documents to sort through, add up, and so forth. Imagine having many times that paperwork every day and you'll appreciate the valuable role a bookkeeper serves. Can you see why most businesses prefer to hire someone to do this work? Would it be worth the time for an owner to do all the paperwork? Can you understand why many businesses find it easier to do this work on a computer?

The Asset Account

assets
Economic resources owned by a firm, such as land, buildings, and machinery.

Assets are what a business owns, but they are also more than that. Assets include productive items (such as equipment, the building, land, furniture, fixtures, and motor vehicles) that contribute to income as well as intangibles such as patents or copyrights. Assets include the following:

▪ Cash (cash on hand, petty cash, and deposits in banks)
▪ Accounts receivable (money owed to a business from customers who bought goods on credit)
▪ Inventory
▪ Investments
▪ Land
▪ Equipment

Airplanes are assets.

- Buildings
- Motor vehicles
- Patents
- Copyrights

Assets, then, are things, such as property and machines, that have money value (see Figure 19-3). Assets are divided into three categories: (1) **current assets** (items that can be converted to cash within one year), (2) **fixed assets** (items such as land, buildings and fixtures that are relatively permanent) and (3) **other (intangible) assets** (this catch-all category includes items such as patents and copyrights). You can see why one of the key words in accounting is assets. Take a few minutes and go through the list, visualizing the assets.

current assets
Include cash or noncash items that can be converted to cash within 1 year.

fixed assets
Items of a permanent nature, such as land, buildings, furniture, and fixtures.

other (intangible) assets
Items that are not included in the current and fixed assets categories. This catch-all category includes items such as patents and copyrights.

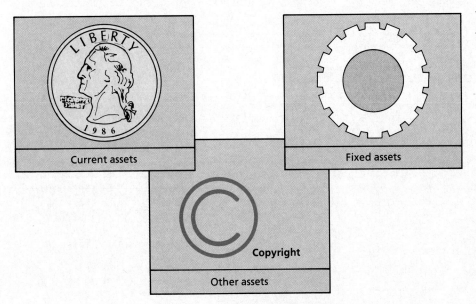

FIGURE 19-3

Assets.

The Liabilities Account

liabilities
Amounts owed by the organization to others. Current liabilities are due in 1 year or less.

A second important word in accounting is *liabilities*. **Liabilities** are what the business owes to others. As with assets, you will more easily understand what liabilities are when you see a list of some examples:

- Accounts payable (Money owed to others for merchandise and services purchased on credit, but not paid for yet.)
- Accrued expenses payable (Expenses the firm owes that haven't been paid.)
- Bonds payable (These represent money loaned to the firm that it must pay back.)

Liabilities are reported on financial statements. At this point, your objective is only to create a mental picture of what liabilities are by reviewing the list.

The Owners' Equity Account

owners' equity
Assets minus liabilities.

Owners' equity is assets minus liabilities. For sole proprietors, owner's equity means the value of everything owned by the business minus any liabilities of the owners (for example, outstanding loans). For corporations, the owners' equity account records the owners' claims to funds they have invested in the firm (capital stock) plus earnings kept in the business and not paid out in dividends (retained earnings). The formula *assets* minus *liabilities* equals *owners' equity* is the basis for a financial statement called the *balance sheet*.

The Revenue Account

income statement
Reports revenues and expenses for a specific period of time, showing the results of operations during that period. It summarizes all the resources that came into the firm (revenues), and all the resources that left the firm and the resulting net income.

The revenue account is where revenues from all sources are recorded. That includes sales revenues, rental revenues, commissions, royalties, and other revenue sources. Revenues are included in a financial statement called an **income statement.**

The Expense Account

The expense account is where the expenses of running the business are recorded, including such items as wages, rent, travel, insurance, supplies, advertising, and utilities. Expenses are recorded with revenues on the income statement. A review of all the accounts used in accounting is presented in Figure 19-4.

FIGURE 19-4

Sample of specific account titles in general account classifications.

FOR THE BALANCE SHEET			FOR THE INCOME STATEMENT		
ASSETS	LIABILITIES	OWNERS' EQUITY	REVENUES	EXPENSES	
Accounts receivable	Accounts payable	Capital stock	Sales revenue	Wages	Interest
Inventory	Notes payable	Retained earnings	Rental revenue	Rent	Donations
Investments	Bonds payable		Commissions revenue	Repairs	Licenses
Equipment	Taxes payable		Royalty revenue	Travel	Fees
Land				Insurance	Supplies
Buildings				Utilities	Advertising
Motor vehicles				Entertainment	Taxes
Goodwill				Storage	

ACCOUNTING JOURNALS

The day-to-day task of bookkeepers or accountants is to take information from original transaction documents (sales slips, payroll statements, travel records, and so on) and record them in a journal in the proper amount. The details of bookkeeping entries can be easily learned in a short class or on the job.

ACCOUNTING LEDGERS

Suppose that a businessperson wanted to determine how much was paid for office supplies in the first quarter of the year. That would be difficult even with accounting journals. The businessperson would have to go through every transaction seeking out those involving supplies and add them up. This is true of other categories, such as inventory and accounts receivable.

Clearly, what businesspeople need is another set of books that has pages labeled "Office Supplies," "Accounts Receivable," and so on. Then entries in the journal could be transferred *(posted)* to these pages, and information about various accounts can be found quickly and easily. A **ledger,** then, is a specialized accounting book in which information from accounting journals is categorized into homogeneous groups and posted so that managers can find all the information about one account in the same place. On a weekly, monthly, or quarterly basis, all the journals are totaled and posted (recorded) into ledgers. As you can see, bookkeepers and accountants are kept busy recording data in journals and posting them in ledgers.

ledger
Recording device in which information from accounting journals is categorized into homogeneous groups and posted so that managers can find all the information about one account in the same place.

PROGRESS CHECK

- Can you name the five "accounts" of accounting and give two examples of items that go into those accounts?

- Can you explain the difference between an accounting journal and a ledger?

FINANCIAL STATEMENTS

The accounting process consists of two major functions: (1) recording data from transactions; and (2) preparing **financial statements.** The two most important financial statements are:

1 The *income statement* (once called the *profit and loss statement* or *P&L statement*) reports revenue and expenses for a specific period of time, showing the results of operations during that period.

2 The *balance sheet* reports the financial position of a firm on a specific date. Financial statements provide the link between accounting and finance. An accountant's work is done when he or she prepares the financial statements, and that is where the finance person's work begins. The finance person's job is to analyze those statements and make recommendations to top management. A financial statement is merely the summary of all transactions that have occurred over a particular period. Financial statements tell the health of a firm. That is why they are of interest to stockholders (the owners of the firm), banks and bondholders

financial statements
Report the success and position (condition) of a firm; they include the income statement and balance sheet.

(people who have loaned money to the firm), investors (people who may want to own part of the firm), and, of course, the Internal Revenue Service, which wants its share of the profits.

ARE FINANCIAL STATEMENTS TOO CONFUSING?

There are many reasons for small business failure. One that is relatively easy to remedy is to learn how to read financial statements. According to Comprehensive Accounting Corporation, many companies fail because their owners don't understand their own financial statements. In fact the financial bookkeeping service company says that "95% of small business owners can't read their statements." The solution is now here, however. The new user-friendly computers can put statements into easily-read pie charts and graphs that show visually what's going on.

Source: *The Wall Street Journal*, March 18, 1985, p. 37. © Dow Jones & Company, Inc., 1985. All rights reserved.

Dr. Edward Lehman of American University, a management consultant, says, "In today's complex economic environment, no manager can do a good job without monthly financial statements."[2] Some managers try to make decisions based on annual statements, but that means working with data a year old. Brian Stutt, the discount store manager we discussed at the beginning of this chapter, didn't look at financial statements at all. As he learned, this is foolhardy. As we shall see, however, it is not enough just to read and understand financial statements. A businessperson also needs to understand cash flow. In the following sections, we shall explore financial statements and cash flow. If you pay attention and learn the concepts, you will know more about accounting than the majority of small business managers today.

The Income Statement

The most popular financial statement is the income statement, or profit and loss statement. The income statement summarizes all the resources that came into the firm from operating activities (called **revenue**), money resources that were used up (called **cost of goods sold** and *expenses*), and what resources were left after all costs and expenses were incurred (*net income* or *net loss*). It reports the results of operations over a particular period of time. The formulas for the income statement are as follows:

revenue
The value of what is received for goods sold, services rendered, and other sources.

cost of goods sold
A particular type of expense measured by the total cost of merchandise sold (including costs associated with the acquisition, storage, transportation in, and packaging of goods).

- Revenue *less* cost of goods sold *equals* gross profit or gross margin.
- Gross margin *less* operating expenses *equals* profit (income) before taxes.
- Income before taxes *less* taxes *equals* net profit (income) after taxes.

Let's review some of the terms used in the income statement and their significance. Naturally, stockholders and others want to know if the company is earning income or not. Also, it is instructive to note what income is made on sales and what profit is realized on the money invested by the owners (return on investment). Before we get to that, though, let's walk through the statement and learn what each step means.

Gross Sales, Net Sales, and Revenue

The figure that is most important at the top of the income statement is **net sales** (see Figure 19-5). To determine net sales, a firm must add up all of its sales revenues and subtract discounts, returns, and other adjustments made for customers.

Note the terms *revenues* and *sales*. Most revenue (money coming in to the firm) comes from sales, but there are other sources of revenue such as rents received, money paid to the firm for use of its patents, interest earned, and so forth. The top of the income statement looks only at sales revenues. Thus revenues and sales are synonymous at that point.

net sales

Sales revenue minus discounts, returns, and other adjustments made for customers.

Small Business, Inc.
INCOME STATEMENT
For the Year Ended December 31, 1986

Revenues			
Gross Sales		$720,000	
Less: Sales Returns and Allowances	$ 12,000		
Sales Discounts	8,000	20,000	
Net Sales			$700,000
Cost of Goods Sold			
Beginning Inventory, Jan. 1		$200,000	
Merchandise Purchases	400,000		
Freight	40,000	440,000	
Cost of Goods Available for Sale		$640,000	
Less Ending Inventory, Dec. 31		230,000	
Cost of Goods Sold			$410,000
Gross Profit (Gross Margin)			$290,000
Operating Expenses			
Selling Expenses			
Salaries for Salespeople	$ 90,000		
Advertising	15,000		
Supplies	2,000		
Other Sales Expenses	3,000		
Total Selling Expenses		$110,000	
General Expenses			
Office Salaries	67,000		
Depreciation	1,500		
Insurance	1,500		
Rent	28,000		
Light, Heat, Power	12,000		
Miscellaneous Expenses	2,000		
Total General Expenses		$112,000	
Total Operating Expenses			$222,000
Net Profit (Income) from Operations			68,000
Other Expenses	$ 10,000		
			10,000
Net Income Before Taxes			58,000
Less: Income Tax Expense			14,500
Net Income (Profit) After Taxes			$ 44,500

FIGURE 19-5

Example of an income statement.

Rev
- Exp
INCOME
(Loss)

net income
Revenue minus expenses.

Be careful not to confuse the terms *revenue* and *income*. Some people use them as if they were synonymous. But a glance at the income statement shows that revenues are at the top of the statement and income is at the bottom: **net income** *is revenue minus expenses.*

Cost of Goods Sold

To calculate how much money a business earned by selling merchandise over the year, you have to subtract how much it spent to buy the merchandise from the sales revenue. That cost includes the purchase price plus any freight charges paid to bring in the goods plus the costs associated with storing the goods. In other words, all the costs of buying and keeping merchandise for sale, including packaging, are included in the cost of goods sold.

gross margin
Net sales minus cost of goods sold.

The cost of shipping merchandise to customers is not a cost of goods sold. Only the cost of freight in is included in that category. When you subtract the cost of goods sold from net sales, you get what is called *gross margin* or *gross profit.* **Gross margin,** then, is how much the firm earned by buying and selling merchandise.

In a service firm, there may be no cost of goods sold; therefore, net sales equals gross margin. In either case (selling goods or services), the gross margin or gross profit figure doesn't tell you too much. What you are really interested in is net profit or net income. To get that, you must subtract expenses.

Operating Expenses

operating expenses
The various costs incurred in running a business, including rent, salaries, and utilities.

To sell goods or services, a business has certain **operating expenses.** Obvious ones include rent, salaries, supplies, utilities, insurance, and depreciation of equipment. Accountants can help you deduct other expenses, including travel expenses, entertainment, and so on.

After all expenses are deducted, you get what people call "the bottom line," which is net income. It answers the questions, "How much did the business earn?" and "How much of our income will be taxed?"

Net Income

retained earnings
The amount left after a company distributes some of its net income (profit) to stockholders in the form of dividends.

After taxes are paid, the company may want to distribute some of the income (profit) to stockholders in the form of dividends. The remainder is left in the firm to invest in a variety of other assets. This remainder is known as **retained earnings.** Keeping profits increases the value of the firm. Therefore, stockholders (owners) benefit from income whether they receive a share of it in the form of dividends or whether it is kept in the firm for reinvestment.

Pause here and review the income statement in Figure 19-5 until you feel you understand what is involved. Note that net income basically equals revenue minus expenses.

THE BALANCE SHEET

balance sheet
Reports the financial position of a firm at a specific date. Balance sheets are composed of assets, liabilities, and owners' equity.

A **balance sheet** is the financial statement that reports the financial position of a firm at a *specific time*. It is composed of assets, liabilities, and owners' equity. Note that the income statement reports on changes over a period of time and the balance sheet reports conditions at a specific point in time.

COMPUTERS IN ACCOUNTING

After reading the sections on bookkeeping and the number of accounts a firm must keep, you no doubt recognize how computers can help in the process. Even relatively small retailers and other small business owners are learning that data processing (like keeping and analyzing accounting records) is usually best done by a computer. Computers can record and analyze data and print out financial reports. But no computer is programmed to make good financial decisions, although they can be programmed to help in such decisions.

Soon it will be possible to have continuous auditing (that is, testing the accuracy and reliability of financial statements) because of computers. One auditing firm, Coopers & Lybrand, hopes to link its computers to clients' computers using Coopers' software to continuously analyze and to test the correct functioning of the clients' systems. Such continuous auditing would help prevent bank failures and other business bankruptcies by spotting trouble earlier.

Clever use of figures is not something that can be done with computers. Computers are a wonderful tool, however, in the hands of a creative accountant who can manipulate the data on a computer to see which strategy results in the best accounting procedures.

The words *balance sheet* imply that the report shows a balance, an equality between two figures. That is, the balance sheet shows a balance between assets and liabilities plus owner's equity. The following analogy will explain the idea of the balance sheet.

Let's say that you want to know what your financial condition is at a given point in time. Maybe you want to buy a new house or car and need to calculate the resources you have available to buy these things. First, you would add up everything you own—cash, property, money people owe you, and so forth. Subtract from that the money you owe others (for example, credit card debt, IOUs) and you have a figure that tells you that, as of today, you are worth so much. In the next section we shall discuss the same process as done by businesses.

CLARIFYING ACCOUNTING TERMS

- An *income statement* is sometimes called a *profit and loss statement*.
- *Income* and *profit* are synonyms. Be careful: *income* and *revenue* are *not* synonymous.
- *Gross profit* and *gross margin* are the same.
- *Net income, net profit,* and *net earnings* all refer to the same concept.

- *Revenues* and *sales* are nearly synonymous for many firms, although a firm can have revenues from services other than sales (such as rental fees).
- *Owners' equity, stockholders' equity,* and *investment* (as in "return on investment") are all the same. That is, you could say "return on equity," "return on investment," or "return on stockholders' equity" and mean the same thing.

The Fundamental Accounting Equation

Imagine that you don't owe anybody any money. That is, you don't have any liabilities. Then the assets you have (cash and so forth) are equal to what you own

fundamental accounting equation

Assets = liability + owners' equity; it is the basis for the balance sheet.

(equity). Translated into business terms, you have a **fundamental accounting equation** that is rather obvious. If a firm has no debts, then:

$$Assets = Owners' \ equity$$

This means that the owners of a firm own everything. If a firm has debts, the owners own everything except the money due others, or:

$$Assets - Liabilities = Owners' \ equity$$

FIGURE 19-6

Example of a balance sheet.

Small Business, Inc.
BALANCE SHEET
March 31, 1987

Assets		
Current Assets		
Cash	$ 15,000	
Accounts Receivable	200,000	
Notes Receivable	50,000	
Inventories At Cost	335,000	
Total Current Assets		$600,000
Fixed Assets		
Land	$ 40,000	
Buildings and Improvements	200,000	
Equipment and Vehicles	120,000	
Furniture and Fixtures	26,000	
Less: Accumulated Depreciation	(180,000)	
Total Fixed Assets		$206,000
Other Assets		
Goodwill	$ 20,000	
Research and Development	80,000	
Total Other Assets		$100,000
Total Assets		$906,000
Liabilities		
Current Liabilities		
Accounts Payable	$ 40,000	
Notes Payable	8,000	
Accrued Taxes	150,000	
Accrued Salaries	15,000	
Pension Fund	75,000	
Total Current Liabilities		$288,000
Long-Term Liabilities		
Notes Payable	$ 35,000	
Bonds	290,000	
Total Long-Term Liabilities		$325,000
Owner's Equity		
Common Stock	$100,000	
Retained Earnings	193,000	
Total Owner's Equity		$293,000
Total Liabilities and Owner's Equity		$906,000

If you add an equal amount to both sides of the equation (you remember this operation from algebra), you get a new formula:

$$\text{Assets} = \text{Liabilities} + \text{Owners' equity}$$

This formula is the basis for the balance sheet. On the balance sheet, you list assets in a separate column from liabilities and owners' equity. The assets are equal to or are balanced with the liabilities and owners' equity. It is that simple. The only complicated part is determining what is included in the term *assets* and what is included in the terms *liabilities* and *owners' equity*. Let's look at a balance sheet in Figure 19-6 (p. 530) and we'll get some clues.

First of all, the balance sheet shows that assets are divided into three categories: (1) current assets (those that can be used or consumed in one year or less); such as cash or accounts receivable; (2) fixed assets (land, building, furniture); and (3) other assets, such as patents and copyrights.

Liabilities are divided into two categories: (1) current liabilities or obligations that must be paid within one year, such as accounts payable; and (2) long-term liabilities or obligations that will not be paid within one year, such as bonds.

Owners' equity consists of common stock (certificates of ownership) and retained earnings (earnings not distributed to owners). There would be no common stock for a proprietorship or partnership.

Go back to the beginning of this chapter and reread the sections on The "Accounts" of Accounting, The Asset Account, The Liabilities Account, and so on, and you will see that the asset, liability, and owner equity accounts set up in the journals and ledgers are all part of the preparation for the balance sheet. Review the lists of items in these accounts and you will learn more about what is behind the figures on the balance sheet. Figure 19-7 summarizes the entire accounting system:

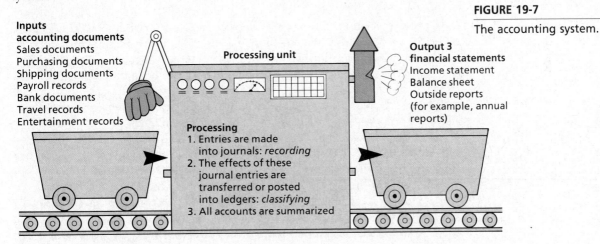

Inputs
accounting documents
Sales documents
Purchasing documents
Shipping documents
Payroll records
Bank documents
Travel records
Entertainment records

Processing unit

Processing
1. Entries are made into journals: *recording*
2. The effects of these journal entries are transferred or posted into ledgers: *classifying*
3. All accounts are summarized

Output 3
financial statements
Income statement
Balance sheet
Outside reports (for example, annual reports)

FIGURE 19-7

The accounting system.

ACCOUNTING CREATIVITY

If accounting were nothing more than the repetitive function of gathering and recording transactions and preparing financial statements, the major functions could be assigned to computers. In fact, most medium- to large-sized firms have done just that. The truth is that how you record and report data is critically important.

Inventory at the Converse plant.

Take depreciation, for example. Subject to certain technical rules, which are beyond the scope of this chapter, a firm may use one of several different techniques for calculating depreciation. However, once a method is chosen, it is difficult to change. Each technique results in a different bottom line; a different net income. Net incomes can change dramatically based on the specific accounting procedure that is used. Accountants can recommend ways of handling insurance, investments, and other accounts that will also affect the bottom line.

One of the more complex issues in accounting is how to handle inventory. This shows up in the "cost of goods sold" section of the income statement. When a firm takes merchandise from inventory and sells it, it has several different ways of calculating the cost of that item. One way is to take the oldest merchandise first, as is done in supermarkets. This is called the *FIFO* technique. *FIFO* stands for first in, first out. It is not whether or not the item was really first in or not; what counts is how much the accountants say that item cost. Let's say, for example, that a company has been buying bicycles for resale. They buy a bike in 1986 for $50. Because of inflation, they buy the same bike in 1987 for $60. Now thay have two bikes to sell. If the accountant used the FIFO technique, the cost of goods sold would be $50, because the bike that was bought first (in 1986) cost $50.

A second approach would be to use a technique called *LIFO*, or last in, first out. Using that strategy, a company's cost of goods sold for the bike would be $60. Can you see the difference in the two accounting approaches on the bottom line? FIFO would report $10 more of net income than LIFO (see Figure 19-8).

	FIFO	LIFO
REVENUE	$100	$100
Cost of goods sold	50	60
Income before taxes	$ 50	$ 40
Taxes of 50%	25	20
Net income	$ 25	$ 20

FIGURE 19-8

Accounting using LIFO versus FIFO inventory costing. By using a LIFO strategy, the accountant can lower taxes and appear to make less profit. By switching to FIFO, the firm would show an increase in profit, but taxes would be higher. Which strategy is best depends on the goals of the firm: to lower taxes, use LIFO; to attract stockholders with profit advances, use FIFO.

This is what is meant by accounting creativity. Accountants can use many such strategies and techniques to minimize taxes, maximize net income, or create the impression that the business is doing very well or very poorly—all by using legal, established accounting procedures. So you see there is more to accounting than meets the eye. It can be fascinating. What can be even more fascinating and challenging is to understand and use both accounting and finance. We shall explore that possibility in Chapter 21.

THINKING IT THROUGH

Can you see the challenge and reward of an accounting career? Do you enjoy working with figures and calculating ways to save on taxes? If so, maybe you would enjoy accounting. Have you visited an accounting firm and watched an accountant at work? What do you feel would be the advantages and disadvantages of such a career?

CASH FLOW PROBLEMS

If one term were selected to represent the greatest operating problem of the 1980s and 1990s, that term would likely be **cash flow.** The name of the game today is cash flow, not profit. *Profit* is an accounting term, a line on the income statement— but it is not cash. It is not always available for use. A firm can have increased sales and increased profit, and still suffer deeply from cash flow problems. That is what happened to Brian Stutt, the man in the Profile at the beginning of this chapter.

Cash flow is simply the difference between cash receipts and cash disbursements. You don't have to be an accountant to produce a cash flow analysis. It is just a matter of analyzing cash receipts versus cash disbursements.

Taking out a loan has no effect on profit. Similarly, repaying a loan has no effect on profit. But taking out and repaying loans has a lot to do with cash flow. This is essential to understand because the number one financial cause of small business failure today is not unprofitability; it is inadequate cash flow.

What a business has to do to prevent cash flow problems is to prepare a simple *cash flow forecast* (also known as a *cash flow budget*). That is, predict ahead of time cash receipts versus cash disbursements. For example, over the next 6 months, on a month-by-month basis, what will be the net cash balance at the end of each month? Let's say that January, February, and March show slight cash surpluses, but April shows a deficit. On January 2, you might go to the bank and show your banker your yearly forecast. Explain that you are expanding so fast that your cash

cash flow
The difference between cash receipts and cash disbursements.

resources are not growing as fast as your cash needs, and that will mean a deficit for April. You ask to borrow funds for April, showing the banker that the payments you receive for April sales (a big month for you) will be made in June, and that you will be able to repay the loan then.

UNDERSTANDING CASH FLOW

Cash flow management is one of the most critical issues in operating a business successfully. Although many businesses have difficulty with it, the issue is really rather simple.

Let's say you borrow money from a friend ($10) to buy a used bike and agree to pay him back at the end of the week. You sell the used bike to someone else for $15. He agrees to pay you in a week also.

It turns out that the person who bought the bike from you doesn't have the money in a week and tells you he will pay next month sometime. Meanwhile, your friend wants his $10. Eventually, you will make a $5 profit, but right now you have a cash flow problem. You owe $10 and have no cash. What would you do if your friend insisted on being paid? If you were a business, you might go bankrupt, even though you had the potential for profits.

Another alternative is to borrow money from the bank to pay your friend and pay the bank back when you receive the $15. That is what businesses try to do. But what if the bank refuses the loan?

Cash Flow and the Bank

A small firm should probably deal with a small bank and a large firm with a large bank. A large bank may not give a small firm the time and attention that a small bank might. That is why the least expensive (and often the best) consultant a small firm can find is often a local banker. If the banker is skilled in accounting and finance, he or she can provide all kinds of free financial advice. To assure that the advice comes regularly, a small businessperson might visit the banker periodically, as often as once a month. By keeping a skilled banker informed about sales, profits, and cash flow, a small businessperson makes sure of good financial advice and a more ready source of funds. Bankers, investment advisors, finance people, and a host of other businesspeople use the data from income statements and balance sheets to evaluate the health of firms and compare them to others. We shall discuss the techniques they use in the Appendix.

CAREERS IN ACCOUNTING

Would accounting be a good career for you? Certain aptitudes are important for those desiring to be an accountant. They include:

- An appreciation of accuracy
- A "feel" for figures
- An analytical mind
- An ability to handle masses of detail without losing perspective
- A sense of order

If you have not done well in math in school and don't particularly enjoy working with figures, you probably would not enjoy accounting. A good accountant must also be able to spot inaccuracies and work creatively with numbers, because he or she often works with figures prepared by others. If that sounds interesting and challenging to you, you might find accounting a rewarding career.

Bookkeepers

This chapter gave you some idea of what bookkeepers do. Almost all firms need one. Smaller firms often combine the job with secretarial duties. If you have an aptitude for working with figures, bookkeeping could be your entry into an accounting career.

Accountants

There are many different categories of accountants that fall into four major job sectors.

1 Public accounting
2 Management or internal accounting
3 Government accounting
4 Accounting education

Public accountants work for independent accounting firms. About one third of accountants become public accountants. Chances of making a high income are probably best in this area, but so is the chance for having a high-pressure, frustrating job. Public accounting firms vary from single proprietorship to the Big Eight accounting firms, which have thousands of employees (see Figure 19-9). Often accountants in public accounting firms work in such areas as tax accounting, auditing (checking the financial statements and analyzing accounting systems for accuracy), and management services (consulting work for other firms).

Management accountants work for corporations. Public accountants work with a wide variety of businesses; management accountants, in contrast, work for one firm. Every industry needs accountants, so the field provides many opportunities.

Government accounting involves working with federal, state, county, or local government agencies. The General Services Administration employs many accountants to audit other government agencies. The General Accounting Office monitors how government money is spent, and is an independent agency. The federal government employs about 25,000 accountants and auditors.

Accounting teachers are in great demand. To see what this career is like, observe your instructor and others in your school. There are many life-style advantages to teaching, as well as the satisfaction of working with students. There is a real shortage of accounting teachers in community colleges and universities because accountants with upper-level degrees can make more money elsewhere. However, the pay for accounting teachers in college tends to be higher, and more jobs are available than for college teachers in other fields.

Becoming a Certified Public Accountant (CPA) or Certified Management Accountant (CMA)

The most professional accountants are those who have been certified by passing professional exams much as physicians or lawyers do. Public accountants may take the Uniform Certified Public Accountant Examination. Those who pass are called

FIGURE 19-9

The top 48 accounting firms.

Note: Top 48 CPA firms, 1985, selected on basis of gross earnings; rankings within groups shift year-to-year. Source: Data courtesy American Institute of Certified Public Accountants, New York, N.Y.

The Big Eight

Arthur Anderson & Co., Chicago, Ill.
Arthur Young & Co., New York, N.Y.
Coopers & Lybrand, New York, N.Y.
Deloitte, Haskins, & Sells, New York, N.Y.
Ernst & Whinney, Cleveland, Ohio
Peat, Marwick, Mitchell & Co., New York, N.Y.
Price Waterhouse & Co., New York, N.Y.
Touche Ross & Co., New York, N.Y.

The Second Tier

Alexander Grant & Co., New York, N.Y.
Kenneth Leventhal & Co., Los Angeles, Calif.
Laventhol & Horwath, Philadelphia, Pa.
KMG Main Hurdman, New York, N.Y.
McGladrey Hendrickson & Pullen, Des Moines, Iowa.
Oppenheim, Appel Dixon & Co., New York, N.Y.
Pannell, Kerr, Forster & Co., New York, N.Y.
Seidman & Seidman, Grand Rapids, Mich.

The Third Tier

Altschuler, Melvoin and Glasser, Chicago, Ill.
Baird, Kurtz & Dobson, Kansas City, Mo.
Cherry, Bekaert & Holland, Charlotte, N.C.
Clifton, Gunderson & Co., Peoria, Ill.
Crowe, Chizek and Co., South Bend, Ind.

Moss Adams & Co., Seattle, Wash.
George S. Olive & Co., Indianapolis, Ind.
Plante & Moran, Southfield, Mich.

The Mid-Range 24

David Berdon & Co., New York, N.Y.
Brout & Co., New York, N.Y.
J.H. Cohn & Co., Newark, N.J.
Eide, Helmeke, Boelz & Pasch, Fargo, N.D.
Richard A. Eisner & Co., New York, N.Y.
John P. Forbes & Co., San Francisco, Calif.
Galusha Hihhins and Galusha, Helena, Mont.
Goldestein Golub Kessler & Co., New York, N.Y.
Goodman & Co., Norfolk, Va.
J.A. Grisette & Co., Lenoir, N.C.
Hausser & Taylor, Cleveland, Ohio
Kafoury Armstrong Turner & Co., PC, Reno, Nev.
Kemper CPA Group, Lawrenceville, Ill.
Kennedy & Coe, Salina, Kan.
Larson Allen Weishair & Co., Minneapolis, Minn.
Mann Judd Landau, New York, N.Y.
May Zima & Co., Atlanta, Ga.
Murphey Jenne & Jones, Decatur, Ill.
Murphy Hauser O'Connor & Quinn, New York, N.Y.
Neiml Holland & Scott, Kennewick, Wash.
A.M. Pullen & Co., Greensboro, N.C.
S.R. Snodgress & Co., Beaver Falls, Pa.
Wipfli Ullrich & Co., Wausau, Wis.
Lester Witte & Co., Chicago, Ill.

CPAs; they generally make good incomes and are true professionals. A firm's own internal auditors may take the Certified Internal Auditor's Examination for similar credentials. Management accountants may take the Certified Management Accountants' Examination and become CMAs. If accounting looks like the right field for you, find information describing what is required for certification and check out local schools for courses that will qualify you for the exam. One that can give you the needed information is Peter Muller's *The Fast Track to the Top Jobs in Accounting Careers* (New York: The Putnam Publishing Company, 1984). Your local bookstore should have this book or similar books.

CAREER INFORMATION: ACCOUNTING AND AUDITING

NATURE OF THE WORK

Accountants and auditors prepare, analyze, and verify financial reports that furnish information to managers in all business, industrial, and government organizations.

Four major fields are public, management, and government accounting, and internal auditing. Public accountants have their own businesses or work for accounting firms. Management accountants, also called industrial or private accountants, handle the financial records of their company. Government accountants and auditors maintain and examine the records of government agencies and audit private businesses and individuals whose dealings are subject to government regulations. Internal auditors verify the accuracy of their firm's financial records and check for waste or fraud.

JOB OUTLOOK

Employment of accountants and auditors is expected to grow much faster than the average for all occupations through the mid-1990s due to the key role these workers play in the management of all types of businesses. Small businesses are expected to rely more and more on the expertise of accountants in planning and managing their operations. In addition, increases in investment and lending associated with general economic growth also should spur demand for accountants and auditors. The increasing use of computers in accounting should stimulate the demand for accountants and auditors familiar with their operation.

EARNINGS

Bachelor's degree candidates in accounting received offers averaging around $19,500 a year; master's degree candidates, $23,200 in 1984.

Beginning public accountants averaged $19,100 a year. The middle 50 percent had starting salaries from $18,300 to $20,000. Salaries of junior public accountants averaged $22,600. Many owners and partners of firms earned considerably more.

The starting salary of management accountants in private industry averaged about $19,500 a year. The middle 50 percent had starting annual salaries from $17,700 to $21,800. Salaries of nonsupervisory management accountants averaged $32,200 in 1984. Chief management accountants who direct the accounting program of a company or one of its establishments averaged $47,400 a year.

Beginning trainee internal auditors averaged $19,700 a year in 1984. The middle 50 percent had annual starting salaries from $16,600 to $22,400. Internal auditors averaged $29,000.

In the federal government, the starting annual salary for junior accountants and auditors was about $14,400 in early 1985. Candidates who had a superior academic record could begin at $17,800. Accountants in the federal government averaged about $33,500 a year in 1984, auditors, about $34,200.

RELATED OCCUPATIONS

Accountants and auditors design internal control systems and analyze financial data. Others for whom training in accounting is invaluable include appraisers, budget officers, loan officials, financial analysts, bank officers, actuaries, underwriters, tax collectors and revenue agents, FBI special agents, securities sales workers, and purchasing agents.

SOURCES OF ADDITIONAL INFORMATION

Information about careers in public accounting and about competency tests administered in colleges and public accounting firms may be obtained from:

American Institute of Certified Public Accountants, 1211 Avenue of the Americas, New York, N.Y. 10036.

Information on specialized fields of accounting and auditing is available from:

National Association of Accountants, P.O. Box 433, 10 Paragon Dr., Montvale, N.J. 07645.

National Society of Public Accountants and Accreditation Council for Accountancy, 1010 North Fairfax St., Alexandria, Va. 22314.

The Institute of Internal Auditors, 249 Maitland Ave., P.O. Box 1119, Altamonte Springs, Fla. 32701.

The EDP Auditors Association, 373 South Schmale Rd., Carol Stream, Ill. 60188.

Source: *Occupational Outlook Handbook,* 1986-1987 (U.S. Department of Labor).

PROGRESS CHECK

■ Can you explain what income statements and balance sheets are and how they might be used?

■ Can you explain what LIFO and FIFO inventory techniques are and how each affects profits (net income)?

SUMMARY

1 *Accounting* is the recording, classifying, summarizing, and interpreting of financial events and transactions that affect an organization. The methods used to record and summarize accounting data into reports is called an *accounting system.*

■ How does managerial accounting differ from financial accounting?

Managerial accounting provides information and analyses to managers within the firm to assist them in decision making.

Financial accounting provides information and analyses to external users of data such as creditors and lenders.

2 There are five major accounts in accounting: assets, liabilities, owners' equity, revenues, and expenses.

■ What are *assets?*

Economic resources owned by the firm, such as buildings and machinery.

■ What are *liabilities?*

Money owned by the organization to others (for example, creditors, bond holders).

■ What is *owners' equity?*

Assets minus liabilities.

■ What are *revenues?*

The value of what is received from goods sold or services rendered.

■ What are *expenses?*

Costs incurred in operating the business, including salaries, rent, and utilities.

3 The original entry documents in accounting are called *journals.* Summaries of journal entries are recorded (posted) into *ledgers.* All of this is done to prepare financial statements.

■ What is an *income statement?*

It reports revenues and expenses for a specific period of time. The formula is *revenue less cost of goods sold equals gross margin less operating expenses equals income before taxes less taxes equals net income or net profit.* (Note that *income* and *profit* mean the same thing.)

■ What is a *balance sheet?*

It reports the financial position of a firm at a particular time. The formula is *assets = liabilities + owners' equity.*

4 Accounting creativity makes the reporting and analysis of data a challenging occupation.

■ What are LIFO and FIFO?

Two ways of pricing inventory. LIFO means *last in, first out.* FIFO means *first in, first out.* How you price inventory affects net income.

5 *Cash flow* is the difference between cash receipts and cash disbursements.

■ How does cash flow become a problem?

Businesses borrow money to buy products and to operate the business and do not collect revenues fast enough to have cash ready when bills come due.

6 There are many interesting careers in accounting.
  ■ Do all accountants work in business?
    No; many work for the government and other nonprofit organizations.

		KEY TERMS
accounting p. 517	**income statements** p. 524	
assets p. 522	**journals** p. 521	
balance sheets p. 528	**ledgers** p. 525	
cash flow p. 533	**liabilities** p. 524	
cost of goods sold p. 526	**managerial accounting** p. 518	
current assets p. 523	**net income** p. 528	
expenses p. 522	**net sales** p. 527	
financial accounting p. 519	**operating expenses** p. 528	
financial statements p. 525	**other assets** p. 523	
fixed assets p. 523	**owners' equity** p. 524	
fundamental accounting equation p. 530	**retained earnings** p. 528	
gross margin p. 528	**revenue** p. 526	

GETTING INVOLVED

1 Go to a local business and watch the people recording data in the journals and ledgers. Look over the ledger to see what it contains. Many firms now use computers for these tasks. Visit one that does and compare its ledgers to its journals. Spend some time observing accountants at work—the surroundings, the people, and so on. Report your reactions to the class.

2 Take a sheet of paper. On every fourth line, write one of the following headings: assets, liabilities, owners' equity, expenses and revenues. Then, list as many items as you can under each heading. When you are finished, look up the lists in the text and add to your own. Keep the lists for your notes. As you complete the lists, create a mental picture of each account so that you can understand the concepts behind accounts and accounting.

3 Prepare your own income statement. See how far you can get without looking back to Figure 19-5. Then look in the text to see what you have forgotten, if anything. Actually writing these things down does wonders for remembering the ideas later.

4 Prepare your own balance sheet. Remember the simple formula: *Assets = Liabilities + Owners' equity.* Go back and check your balance sheet against the one in Figure 19-6.

5 Write out your own explanation of how small businesses get into trouble with cash flow by expanding too rapidly. Think of several ways a business could avoid such problems. Discuss your thoughts with the class.

CASE ONE   CONSTRUCTING AN INCOME STATEMENT AND BALANCE SHEET

PRACTICING MANAGEMENT DECISIONS

Neighborhood Landscaping Service was started by Stuart Jenkins when he was in high school. As the business grew, Stu hired several of his friends and is now doing well. He is now in a position to begin keeping better records. Stu has written down some of his figures, but he doesn't know how to interpret them. He wants to take out a loan, and wants to prepare a balance sheet to calculate his financial position. These are his figures:

	Assets		Liabilities	
Cash	$ 5,350		Money owed bank	$7,500
Truck	13,500		Money owed supplier	545
Accounts receivable	2,400		Money owed for equipment	500
Equipment	4,520		Total liabilities	$8,545
Office furniture	945			
Supplies	550			
Trailer	500			
Total assets	$27,765			

Some other figures Stu had hastily put together in no consistent order are:

Income from work done	$74,000
Expenses incurred for trees, shrubs, etc.	22,000
Salaries of helpers (2)	16,000
Advertising	1,360
Insurance	2,000
Office costs (phone, heat, rent, etc.)	8,400
Depreciation on truck	$ 4,000

Stu paid $1,800 for other supplies, such as gravel, sand, and slate used for walkways.

DECISION QUESTIONS

1 What additional information, if any, would you need to construct a balance sheet? Is Stu in a strong or poor financial condition?
2 How much did Stu earn before taxes? Prepare an income statement to show Stu how such a financial statement looks.
3 Stu is unsure of the terminology of accounting. Study his list of figures and names and see if you can find any incorrect usage of terms.

PRACTICING MANAGEMENT DECISIONS

CASE TWO   WHERE DID KATHERINE GO WRONG?

Katherine Potter knew a good thing when she saw it. At least, it seemed so at first. She was traveling in Italy when she spotted pottery shops that made beautiful products ranging from ashtrays to lamps. Some of the pottery was stunning in design.

Katherine began importing the products to the United States, and sales took off. Customers immediately realized the quality of the items, and were willing to pay top price. Katherine decided to keep prices moderate to expand rapidly, and she did. Sales in the second 3 months were double those of the first few months. Sales in the second year were double those of the first year.

Every few months, Katherine had to run to the bank to borrow more money. She had no problems getting larger loans, because she always paid promptly. To save on the cost of buying goods, Katherine always took trade discounts. That is, she paid all bills within 10 days to save the 2% offered by her suppliers for paying so quickly.

Most customers bought Katherine's products on credit. They would buy a couple of lamps and a pot and Katherine would allow them to pay over time. Some were very slow in paying her, taking 6 months or more.

After 3 years, Katherine noticed a small drop in her business. The local economy was not doing well, because many people were being laid off from their jobs. Nonetheless, Katherine's business stayed level. One day the bank called Katherine and told her she was late in her payments. She had been so busy that she didn't notice the bills. The problem was that Katherine had no cash available to pay the bank. She frantically called several customers for payment, but they were not able to pay her either. Katherine was in a classic cash-flow bind.

Katherine immediately raised her prices and refused to make sales on credit. She started delaying payment on her bills and paid the extra costs. Then she went to the bank and went over her financial condition with the banker. The banker noted her accounts receivable and assets. He then prepared a cash budget and loaned Katherine more money. Her import business grew much more slowly thereafter, but her financial condition improved greatly. Katherine had gone nearly bankrupt, but she recovered at the last minute.

DECISION QUESTIONS

1 How is it possible to have high sales and high profits and run out of cash?
2 Why did Katherine do better when she raised her prices and refused to sell on credit?
3 What was the nature of Katherine's problem? Was she correct to go to the banker for help, even though she owed the bank money?

LOOKING AHEAD

The whole idea of accounting is to keep track of transactions to meet the requirements of the Internal Revenue Service and to keep management and outsiders informed as to the operations (income statement) and position (balance sheet) of the firm. Accounting's basic role ends when the financial statements are completed. At that point, finance's role begins. Finance and accounting personnel analyze the financial statements and make recommendations to management. The key to evaluating financial statements is a group of ratios that financial analysts use to compare firms. We shall look at those ratios in the Appendix. They are one link between accounting and finance.

Remember that accounting and finance are related so that a person cannot be fully expert in one field without understanding the other. In a firm, accounting and finance are often blended in the duties of a financial officer.

After we explore some financial ratios in the Appendix, we'll look at the money and banking system in the United States (Chapter 20). That will set the stage for an in-depth look at corporate finance (Chapter 21) and stocks and bonds (Chapter 22).

APPENDIX: FINANCIAL RATIOS

Every person interested in finance needs to understand basic accounting. What is especially helpful to financial analysis is the use of ratios to measure a company's health. You are familiar with ratios. They are used all the time to measure the success of sports teams. For example, in basketball, the ratio of shots made from the foul line versus attempts is measured. TV announcers say, "Jones is shooting 85% of his foul shots, so he is not the one to foul in the final minutes." We judge basketball players by such ratios: 80% is good for foul shots, 65% is not good. We calculate similar ratios for baseball ("He's batting .300," or 30%), football ("He's completed 50% of his passes"), and so on. So ratios are not hard to understand or compute, and they give a lot of information about the relative performance of sportspeople or of businesses. Now let's look at some key ratios that businesspeople use.

AVERAGE COLLECTION PERIOD OF RECEIVABLES

We have already noted that a major financial problem of small businesses is poor liquidity or cash flow. In most cases, poor cash flow is caused by not collecting accounts receivable fast enough. Many customers do not pay their bills until they are reminded or pressured to pay. Incentives such as discounts for paying early are often mandatory for minimizing collection time.

To determine whether or not a business is collecting its receivables in a reasonable period of time, an analyst calculates the average collection period. Unlike the other financial analysis calculations, this one takes two steps. The first step is to divide the annual credit sales by 365 to obtain the average daily credit sales. The second step is to divide accounts and notes receivable by the average daily credit sales (the first step) to get the average collection period in days. For example:

1. $\text{Average daily credit sales} = \dfrac{\text{Total annual credit sales}}{365 \text{ days}}$

2. $\text{Collection period in days} = \dfrac{\text{Notes and accounts receivable}}{\text{Average daily credit sales}}$

If total annual credit sales were $365,000, then the average daily credit sales would be $1,000:

$$\frac{\$365,000}{365} = \$1,000$$

If the notes and accounts receivable today were $60,000, then the collection period would be 60 days:

$$\frac{\$60,000}{\$1,000} = 60 = \text{Average collection period of receivables}$$

CREDIT TERMS

If you collect your accounts in 60 days but pay your accounts in 10 days, you will have a cash flow problem. To encourage people to pay more quickly, most companies give credit terms such as "2/10, net 30." This means that if customers pay within 10 days, they can deduct 2% from the price. Even if they don't take advantage of a discount, the total amount is due in 30 days.

Paying within 10 days is advantageous for buyers. Here's why. A 2% discount for paying within 10 days means that the company saves 2% by paying 20 days early—because the total amount is due within 30 days. Read the last sentence again slowly to be sure you understand. Each year there are 18 20-day periods. Therefore, by paying early (within 10 days) a firm can save 36% annually. That is why most small businesses pay their bills within 10 days. It is a bargain. Now that you've learned to save money on purchases, let's look at the ratio that measures sales effectiveness.

Return on Sales

Each industry has a different rate of return on sales. Such figures are well known in the industry. Therefore, a firm can determine whether or not it is doing as well as other businesses by calculating the return on sales ratio. This involves dividing net income by net sales. If net income were $10,000 and net sales were $200,000, the return on sales ratio would be 5%:

$$\text{Return on sales} = \frac{\text{Net income}}{\text{Net sales}}$$

$$\text{Return on sales} = 5\% = \frac{\$10,000}{\$200,000}$$

A good example of a company that showed a poor return on sales ratio was Compaq Computer. It had sales of $300 million in 1984 and earned only $9 million, a ratio of just over 3%. That was about half of IBM's return on sales ratio and 70% of Apple Computer's return on sales ratio. As a result, Compaq's stock fell from 11 to 3½ in that period. As you can see, investors pay attention to the return on sales ratio. One way to increase the ratio is to increase prices, but Compaq was facing a competitive market and wanted to keep its prices low. The results indicate that prices were too low. Stockholders compute ratios such as return on sales when evaluating a firm (or look up the ratios in business reports). Another ratio they look for is return on investment.

RETURN ON INVESTMENT (ROI)

Stockholders invest in a business expecting to make a greater return on their money than if they did something else with the money, such as depositing it in a bank or buying bonds. The way to calculate the return on equity (ownership) in a firm is to divide net income by the owners' equity. You are more likely to hear this formula referred to as *ROI* or *return on investment*. Investment, then, is synonymous with equity. If net income were $10,000 and stockholders' equity (investment) were $100,000, the ROI or return on investment would be 10%:

$$ROI = \frac{\text{Net income}}{\text{Owners' equity}}$$

$$ROI = 10\% = \frac{\$10,000}{\$100,000}$$

INVENTORY TURNOVER

A business supply store once asked a consultant why its inventory turnover ratio was so low. The consultant walked through the warehouse and found box after box filled with slide rules, stacked high. These obsolete items were being carried on the books as inventory and lowering the turnover ratio. What signaled the problem was that the owner compared his turnover ratio to the average industry ratio.

A lower than average ratio indicates obsolete merchandise or poor buying practices. A higher than average ratio may indicate an understocked condition where sales are lost because of inadequate stock. The ratio to determine inventory turnover is calculated by dividing the cost of goods sold by the average inventory for the period. For example, if the cost of goods sold were $160,000 and the average inventory were $20,000, the turnover ratio would be 8. This figure by itself is rather meaningless. It has to be compared to industry figures to tell a company how it is doing in relation to competitors. The calculation looks like this:

$$\text{Turnover} = \frac{\text{Cost of goods sold}}{\dfrac{\text{Jan. 1 inventory} + \text{Dec. 31 inventory}}{2}}$$

$$\text{Turnover} = \frac{\$160,000}{\dfrac{\$23,000 + \$17,000}{2}}$$

$$\text{Turnover} = \frac{\$160,000}{\$20,000} = 8$$

DEBT-TO-EQUITY RATIO

Every year *Forbes* magazine publishes an annual report on U.S. industry. This review looks at 1,000 different corporations and ranks them by return on equity, sales growth, and earnings per share. The two ratios *Forbes* uses for comparison are return on equity (which we've discussed) and debt/equity. Debt/equity is calculated by dividing total liabilities by owners' equity. Basically, this ratio tells you how much money, relatively, the company has borrowed compared to other firms in the industry. A high ratio triggers caution among investors. But again, high or low is relatively meaningless unless compared to the average of the same industry.

In the 1984 *Forbes* edition, for example, the highest figure in the health care industry was 1.6; that is, debt was 1.6 times equity. The median was 0.4. In heavy equipment, the median was 0.4 again, but International Harvester's figure was 5.3, Massey-Ferguson's was 6.1, and Pettibone's was 7.9. All of these firms with high figures were in deep trouble financially. The debt/equity ratio reflected that trouble.

It is calculated by dividing total liabilities by owners' equity. If total liabilities were $150,000 and owners' equity were $150,000, the debt/equity ratio would be 1:

$$\text{Debt/equity ratio} = \frac{\text{Total liabilities}}{\text{Owners' equity}}$$

$$\text{Debt/equity ratio} = 1 = \frac{\$150,000}{\$150,000}$$

Most consultants feel a ratio greater than one is not good, but again that varies by industry. Sometimes debt is a good sign if it means the company is trying to optimize the return to stockholders by assuming more risk.

OTHER RATIOS

Bankers are also interested in certain other ratios. We said earlier that a small businessperson should consult with his or her banker often. One calculation that a banker is sure to make is the current ratio. The ratio is:

$$\text{Current ratio} = \frac{\text{Current assets}}{\text{Current liabilities}}$$

This ratio measures a company's ability to pay its short-term debts. A ratio of 1.5 or higher is usually desired.

If we leave inventories out of the above equation, we get a more accurate feel for whether or not a business could quickly pay its current liabilities. Thus, another test is called the *quick ratio* or *acid-test ratio*. This is the supposed acid test of whether a firm is on solid financial ground, short term or not. The formula is:

$$\text{Quick ratio} = \frac{\text{Cash + Marketable securities +}\ \text{Accounts receivable + Notes receivable}}{\text{Liabilities}}$$

Finance people use several other ratios to learn more details about the condition of a business, but this will give you an idea of what ratios are and how they are used. The point is that financial analysis begins where accounting reports end. This appendix, then, represents the transition between accounting and finance.

Get the January issue of *Forbes* magazine that compares industries and look through the various industries. Note the variance in return on equity and debt/equity ratios. Think through the importance of inventory turnover and the ability to pay off debts with liquid assets such as cash and accounts receivable. Note how obvious it is to measure a firm's return (profit) on sales compared to that of other firms in the industry. Such reflections will show you the importance of ratios to investors, financial analysts, bankers, and business managers. Could you do business effectively without understanding such ratios? It is doubtful. If the thousands of *Forbes* readers are expected to understand such ratios, certainly a business executive should, and so should you if you want to understand the financial side of business.

FINANCIAL INSTITUTIONS, MONEY, AND BANKING

LEARNING GOALS

After you have read and studied this chapter, you should be able to:

- Identify types of banking institutions and describe the services available at each.
- Explain the involvement of nonbanks in the financial system.
- Discuss the functions of electronic funds transfer systems (EFTS).
- Explain the functions of the Federal Reserve system and describe the tools the "Fed" uses to control the money supply.
- Briefly trace the history of banking.
- Discuss the economic conditions that led to the Great Depression and steps the government has taken to prevent a recurrence.

PROFILE   PAUL VOLCKER OF THE FEDERAL RESERVE BOARD

No one man has had a greater impact on the U.S. economy over the last several years than Paul Volcker, Chairman of the Federal Reserve Board. Not only is he a powerful man, but he is an interesting man as well. He is an imposing figure in that he is 6 feet 7 inches tall, bald, and hefty. His trademark is a cigar in his hand. He is a giant both literally and figuratively.

Volcker went to Princeton University for a B. A. and then received an M. A. from Harvard University in political economy and government. He went on to attend the London School of Economics. His strong academic background landed him a job as an economist at the New York branch of the Federal Reserve Bank. (You may be interested in the fact that he had worked at the New York Fed for two summers previously. You too might consider an internship before you graduate.)

Volcker's next job was as a financial economist at Chase Manhattan Bank. This led to a position as Director of Financial Analysis at the United States Treasury and, eventually, the position of Undersecretary of the Treasury for Monetary Affairs.

In 1979, the economy was running at a 13% inflation rate and the dollar was weak. Volcker was appointed by President Carter as Chairman of the Federal Reserve (the Fed) to lower inflation and strengthen the dollar. He proceeded to

Paul Volcker.

do that effectively and efficiently. President Reagan was so impressed by Volcker's success that he kept him on as Chairman. Inflation dropped to below 5% and the dollar became so strong that other countries protested, and efforts had to be made to lower its value.

There is much fuss over who the next Chairman of the Fed will be. The Board influences monetary policy by participating in the 12-member open-market committee. The group decides whether or not to expand the money supply.

The Federal Reserve and the banking system in general have been the focus of much attention in the 1980s. The health of the economy is very much dependent on decisions by the Fed. Bank lending policies have much to do with the international debt crisis. Furthermore, the disinflationary trend of the mid-1980s has led to the failure of many banks and savings and loan organizations. Chapter 20 will explore such issues and more. ▪

TWENTY LARGEST BANKS

1	CITICORP	New York
2	BANK-AMERICA	San Francisco
3	CHASE MANHATTAN	New York
4	MANUFAC-TURERS HANOVER	New York
5	MORGAN (J.P.)	New York
6	CHEMICAL NEW YORK	New York
7	SECURITY PACIFIC	Los Angeles
8	BANKERS TRUST NEW YORK	New York
9	FIRST INTER-STATE BAN-CORP	Los Angeles
10	FIRST CHI-CAGO	Chicago
11	MELLON BANK	Pittsburgh
12	CONTINENTAL ILLINOIS	Chicago
13	WELLS FARGO	San Francisco
14	BANK OF BOSTON	Boston
15	FIRST BANK SYSTEM	Minneap-olis
16	MARINE MID-LAND BANKS	Buffalo
17	REPUBLIC-BANK	Dallas
18	MCORP	Dallas
19	INTERFIRST	Dallas
20	IRVING BANK	New York

Source: *Business Week,* April 7, 1986, p. 66.

THE BANKING INDUSTRY

Banks and savings and loan corporations have been in the news throughout the 1980s. Some banks were in the news because of the loans they made to foreign countries; loans that may not be paid back. Some savings and loan institutions were in the news because of failures in states like Ohio and Maryland, and in farm regions. (Some 120 banks went bankrupt in 1985.) Because of deflation, farm values declined, and farmers could not make their mortgage payments. This put great pressure on the savings and loan institutions and banks that had loaned money to farmers.

Finally, the Federal Reserve Bank was in the news because of its manipulation of the money supply. Paul Volcker, the head of the Federal Reserve, was a major player in the drama called "the economic policy for the 1980s."

Clearly, the banking industry has reached center stage in the 1980s, and the impact of what happens in it will have a direct bearing on you. If a local savings and loan fails, it may take a long time to retrieve the money you have worked so hard to get. Therefore, you and I have a real interest in what happens to the banking industry over the next few years.

Before we review the history of banking and discuss the current issues, let's pause and discuss the American banking system as it is today. We'll explore both the banking system and other financial institutions that are involved in banking-like activities.

THE AMERICAN BANKING SYSTEM

The American banking system consists of commercial banks, savings and loan associations, credit unions, and mutual savings banks. In addition, a variety of organizations perform several banking functions, although they are not true banks. These are *nondeposit* institutions, and are often referred to as *nonbanks*. These would include pension funds, insurance companies, commercial finance companies, consumer finance companies, and brokerage houses. We'll discuss the activities and services provided by each of these institutions, starting with the most important: commercial banks.

Commercial Banks

A **commercial bank** is a profit-making organization that receives deposits from individuals and corporations in the form of checking and savings accounts and uses some of these funds to make loans. It is important to note that commercial banks have two types of customers: (1) depositors; and (2) those who take out loans (borrowers). A commercial bank is equally responsible to both types of customers. Commercial banks try to make a profit by using the funds given them by depositors efficiently. In essence, a commercial bank uses customer deposits as inputs (on which they pay interest) to invest that money in interest-bearing loans to other customers. Commercial banks make a profit if the revenue generated by loans exceeds the interest paid to depositors plus all other operating expenses.

For legal operation, banks must be chartered by individual states or the federal government. Commercial banks chartered by states are called *state banks;* those chartered by the federal government are called *national banks*. Of approximately 14,800 commercial banks, two thirds are state banks. Nevertheless, national banks are larger since they hold about 65% of total commercial bank deposits.

✳ commercial bank
A profit-making organization that receives deposits from individuals and corporations in the form of checking and saving accounts and uses some of these funds to make loans.

Banks advertise to compete against other financial institutions.

© 1985, American Bankers Association

Services Provided by Commercial Banks

demand deposit
The technical name for a checking account because the money is available on demand from the depositor.

Individuals and corporations that deposit money in a checking account have the privilege of writing an unlimited number of personal checks that can be used to pay for almost any purchase or transaction. The technical name for a checking account is a **demand deposit,** because the money is available on demand from the depositor. Typically, banks charge individual consumers a service charge that ranges between $2 and $10 per month or demand a minimum deposit. In addition, banks might also charge a small handling fee for each check written. For corporate depositors, the amount of the service charge depends on the average daily balance in the checking account, the number of checks written, and the credit rating and credit history of the firm. The traditional checking account pays no interest to depositors, but new interest-bearing checking accounts have experienced phenomenol growth in recent years. Most commercial banks offer NOW and super NOW accounts to their depositors. A NOW (negotiable order of withdrawal) account typically pays an annual interest rate, but requires a certain minimum balance that must be maintained in the account at all times (for example, $500), and restricts the number of checks that can be written each month.

A Super NOW account pays higher interest in order to attract larger deposits. However, Super NOW account holders are required to maintain a minimum balance of $2,500. Super NOW accounts typically offer free and unlimited check-writing privileges. In addition to these types of checking accounts, commercial banks offer a variety of savings account options. A savings account is technically called a **time deposit** because the bank can require a prior notice before withdrawal.

time deposit
The technical name for a savings account, because the bank can require prior notice before withdrawal.

The most common form of savings account is called a passbook savings account. Under this savings option, depositors do not have checking privileges, but can withdraw money at any time. A **certificate of deposit (CD)** is a time-deposit (savings) account that earns an interest rate, to be delivered at the end of the certificate's maturity date. The depositor agrees not to withdraw any of the funds in the account until the end of the specified period. CDs are currently available for periods of from 3 months to 5 years, and the interest rates offered vary, depending on the period of the certificate. The interest rates offered depend on economic conditions and the prime rate at the time of the deposit. (A few years ago, CDs were yielding interest between 14% and 16%). In addition to the checking and savings accounts discussed above, commercial banks offer a variety of other services to their depositors. These include:

certificate of deposit (CD)
A savings account that earns a high rate of interest to be delivered at the end of the CD's period.

automated teller machines (ATMs)
Machines that allow bank customers to use access cards to make deposits and withdrawals at a variety of outlets, including supermarkets and department stores as well as outside the bank.

- **Automated teller machines (ATMs)** offer customers the convenience of 24-hour banking at a variety of outlets such as supermarkets, department stores, and drugstores in addition to the bank's regular branches. Depositors can now get cash, transfer funds, and make deposits at their own discretion with the use of a computer-coded personalized plastic access card.

FIGURE 20-1

Some services available at banks.

- Demand deposits (checking accounts)
- Time deposits (savings accounts)
- Loans
- Financial counseling
- Safe deposit boxes
- Certified checks
- Traveler's checks
- Credit cards
- Certificates of deposit (CDs)
- NOW accounts
- Super NOW accounts
- Telebanking

- Commercial banks also offer credit cards to their credit-worthy customers, inexpensive brokerage services, financial counseling, automatic payment of telephone bills, safe deposit boxes, tax-deferred individual retirement accounts (IRAs), traveler's checks, and overdraft checking account privileges (This means preferred customers can automatically get loans at reasonable rates when they have written checks exceeding their account balance). See Figure 20-1 for a list of key banking services.

Services to Borrowers

Commercial banks offer a variety of services to individuals and corporations in need of a loan. Generally, loans are given based on the creditworthiness of the recipient. Banks want to manage their funds effectively and thus carefully screen loan applicants to ensure that the loan plus interest will be paid back on time. To get a loan for a house or other large purchase in the future, it is very important for you to develop a good credit history as early as possible. Because this is easier said than done, you should carefully consider some of the tips provided in the box below on developing a credit history.

> A banker is a person who will loan you money only after he has determined you don't need it.
>
> Mark Twain

HOW TO DEVELOP A GOOD CREDIT HISTORY

Small businesses often have difficulty obtaining loans at reasonable interest rates from financial institutions. Commercial banks, for example, require small business loan applicants to provide adequate collateral—assets such as stock, for instance, that the bank could assume control over in the case of deliquency. Many small businesses, especially new ones that have low equity, might not be able to fulfill collateral requirements. In such cases it is the credit rating of the individual(s) owning the business that would decide whether or not the loan was granted.

How can an individual with little credit history develop a good credit rating? Here are some tips:

- Open up a checking and savings account at a financial institution. It is important that you manage these accounts in a way that would avoid bad checks, overdrawn balances, and so forth. It is also important to keep some money in savings at all times. This could be interpreted by prospective lenders as an indication of efficient money management.

- Establish credit with a department store or oil company. It is usually easier to get credit from such sources than from a financial institution in the form of a credit card. Pay your bills on time and avoid paying for finance charges. This should enhance your credibility when you apply for a credit card.
- Pay all your rent, utility, and telephone bills promptly. If you do so, you can obtain valuable references when you need them.
- Obtain a credit card from a financial institution. No matter how small the initial credit allowance might be, a credit card is one of the best ways to develop a good credit history quickly. Remember that the more responsible you are in managing your credit card account, the more credit you will be able to obtain in the future.

Business loans are normally characterized as short-term or long-term, depending on whether they are to be repaid within 1 year or over a longer period of time.

- **Short-term loans** are those that have to be paid within 1 year. Many businesses borrow on a short-term basis to obtain urgently-needed cash. Businesses find it useful to establish a line of credit before they actually need money. This would involve getting approval for a specified loan amount beforehand, so that the firm can immediately borrow the money whenever it is needed.

short-term loans
Loans that have to be paid in 1 year.

long-term loans
Loans that are payable in a period that exceeds 1 year.

■ **Long-term loans** are those payable in a period that exceeds 1 year. Typically, long-term loans must be repaid within 2 to 5 years but could also be extended for longer periods of time (up to 20 years). Banks give long-term loans to individuals, corporations, and domestic and foreign governments. The interest charged for most long-term loans for large corporations and governments is negotiated between the two parties. Often such loans require a long and exhausting round of bargaining before the terms of the loan (interest charged, repayment period, types and amount of collateral required, default options, and so forth), are mutually agreed upon. Most loans require collateral by law.

Airlines need long-term loans to finance their aircraft.

Savings and loan associations were set up to encourage home buying.

Savings and Loan Associations

A **savings and loan association** (S & L) is a financial institution that accepts both savings and checking deposits and provides home mortgage loans. (They are often known as **thrift institutions**). S & Ls were originally set up to encourage home ownership. As such, they were permitted to offer slightly higher interest rates on savings deposits in order to attract a larger pool of funds. These funds were then used to offer long-term fixed-rate mortgages at whatever rate prevailed at the time. With the abrupt rise in interest rates in the late 1970s, S & Ls found themselves in deep financial trouble. The problem occurred because they were forced to pay depositors higher interest rates than before, while their revenues from past mortgage loans held constant. Unable to pay a substantially higher interest rate than their competitors (that is, commercial banks), S & Ls began to lose a large proportion of their depositors, with catastrophic results for many of them. Between 1979 and 1983 about 20% of the nation's S & Ls failed because of unbearable financial pressure. Faced with this situation in 1981, the federal government permitted S & Ls to offer NOW and Super NOW accounts, to allocate up to 10% of their funds to commercial loans, and to offer mortgage loans with adjustable interest rates based on market conditions. In addition, S & Ls were permitted to offer a variety of other banking services, such as financial counseling to small businesses and credit cards. As a result, S & Ls became much more competitive with commercial banks.

savings and loan association
Financial institution that accepts both savings and checking deposits and provides home mortgate loans.

thrift institutions
Savings and loan associations.

PROGRESS CHECK

■ What are the services offered by a commercial bank?

■ What is the difference between a bank and a savings and loan association?

BANK OR SAVINGS AND LOAN?

The Sun Bank of Orlando, Florida is facing strong competition from the local savings and loan associations. The distinction between banks and savings and loan institutions has blurred in the 1980s. Some basic differences are that thrifts (savings and loan organizations) must have a majority of their assets in home mortgages, their mortgage rates tend to be more competitive, and they tend to offer higher returns on savings instruments and accounts. Commercial banks generally have more capital and more experience with a range of financial products.

In spite of these differences, thrifts are doing their best to look more like banks. Sun Bank emphasizes the word *bank* in its ads. Similarly, The First (the largest thrift institution in Florida) also looks a lot like a bank in its ads. It used to be called First Federal Savings and Loan of Orlando; it changed its name to improve its image.

The First is advertising its checking accounts, a service it could not offer before bank deregulation. The First also spent $1.5 million on image advertising in 1985 compared with $200 thousand to $300 thousand in the early 1980s.

Sun Bank is countering the competition of The First by training bank managers to make home mortgages and paying them $25 for each completed loan application. Sun Bank is also aggressively going after the personal loan business in the area. Sun already has more branches, automated teller machines, and drive-ins than The First.

This is just one example of the new competition between banks and thrift institutions. Throw in the competition from financial supermarkets, such as the services offered at Sears and some brokerage firms, and you see that competition in the financial industry has never been so strong.

Source: Leon Wynter, "Bank or Thrift?," *The Wall Street Journal,* June 10, 1986, p. 31. Reprinted by permission of *The Wall Street Journal;* © Dow Jones & Co., Inc. All rights reserved.

Credit Unions

credit unions
Nonprofit, member-owned financial cooperatives that offer basic banking services such as accepting deposits and making loans; they may also sell life insurance.

Credit unions are nonprofit, member-owned financial cooperatives that offer basic banking services such as accepting deposits and making loans to its members. Typically, credit unions offer interest-bearing checking accounts called share draft accounts at relatively high rates, short-term loans at relatively low rates, financial counseling, life insurance policies, and a limited number of home mortgage loans to their members. Credit unions may be thought of as financial cooperatives that are organized by government agencies, corporations, unions, or professional associations. The National Credit Union Administration insures savings at credit unions.

Mutual Savings Banks

mutual savings bank
Similar to a S & L, but owned by its depositors.

A **mutual savings bank** is similar to a savings and loan but is owned by its depositors. Most of the approximately 400 mutual savings banks operate in the northeastern sector of the United States, particularly in New England and New York. The range of services they provide are very similar to those offered by savings and loans. Don't be fooled by the word "bank" in the title—these are thrift institutions, not banks.

The Federal Deposit Insurance Corporation

The **Federal Deposit Insurance Corporation (FDIC)** is an independent agency of the United States government that insures bank deposits. If a bank were to fail, the FDIC would arrange to have the accounts at that bank transferred to another bank or pay off depositors up to a certain amount. (This amount has increased over the years, but is now at $100,000.)

Federal Deposit Insurance Corporation (FDIC)
Insures accounts in some banks against bank failures (up to a limit of $100,000 per account).

To be eligible for membership in the FDIC, a bank must meet certain standards. Furthermore, approved members undergo regular examinations by federal and state agencies. Members pay semiannual insurance fees to the FDIC based on the volume of their deposits. These fees are invested in government securities and are the FDIC's deposit insurance fund. This fund is small relative to the total reserves in many of the larger banks in the United States, as is expected of an insurance fund. This has never been a problem in the past, but recently some people have questioned the ability of the FDIC to cover the losses if a large bank or two were to fail.[1] The FDIC can borrow up to $3 billion from the U.S. Treasury in such cases, so the money you keep in an FDIC-insured bank is relatively safe.

The Federal Savings and Loan Insurance Corporation

The **Federal Savings and Loan Insurance Corporation (FSLIC)** is another independent agency of the United States government. It insures holders of accounts in savings and loan associations. Both the FDIC and the FSLIC were started in the 1930s, because bank and thrift institutions were failing and people had lost confidence in them. Some 1,700 institutions failed during that time. The FDIC was begun in 1933 and the FSLIC in 1934. Since then, both institutions have been successful in covering losses from bank and thrift institution failures.

Federal Savings and Loan Insurance Corporation (FSLIC)
Insures accounts in some savings and loan associations against failures (up to a limit of $100,000 per account).

The FSLIC receives its funds from fees paid by the member savings and loan associations. In addition to its own reserves, the FSLIC has the ability to borrow $750 million from the U.S. Department of the Treasury, to raise its fees, and to call upon insured associations to deposit up to 1% of total savings. In spite of all these resources, there was some question in the mid-1980s whether or not the reserves were sufficient.[2] At the end of this chapter, we shall explore the role of the Federal Reserve Bank and its role in keeping the economy stable so that financial institutions can remain strong.

OTHER FINANCIAL INSTITUTIONS

Nonbanks are financial organizations that accept no deposits, but offer many of the services provided by regular banks (see the ad for full-service banks). They include life insurance companies, pension funds, brokerage firms, and commercial finance companies. As competition between these organizations and banks increases, the dividing line between banks and nonbanks is becoming less and less apparent. The diversity of financial services and investment alternatives offered by nonbanks have caused banks to expand the services they offer. Today's consumer has the power to make decisions on his financial future much more easily than in the past. Consider that only a few years ago a typical customer might have been forced to open separate accounts at a commercial bank (checking account) and a savings and loan (interest-bearing savings account). Also, this consumer might

nonbanks
Financial organizations that accept no deposits, but offer many of the services provided by regular banks.

have obtained a car loan from a credit union while paying back a home mortgage loan at another S & L. In the meantime, he or she might have had a stock account with a brokerage house and an insurance policy with a separate insurance firm. Today, a consumer can shop for all these services and more at a single financial institution. The trend toward interstate banks should bring even more competition to the industry.

You know that life insurance companies provide financial protection for policy holders who periodically pay premiums. In addition, they invest the funds they receive from policyholders in corporate and government bonds. In recent years, more insurance companies have begun to provide long-term financing for real estate development projects.

Pension funds are amounts of money designated by corporations, nonprofit organizations, or unions to cover part of the financial needs of members when they retire. Contributions to pension funds are made either by employees alone or by both the employer and employees. A member may begin to collect a monthly draw on this fund upon reaching a certain retirement age. Pension funds typically invest in low return but safe corporate stocks or in other conservative investments such as government securities and corporate bonds to generate additional income.

Brokerage firms have traditionally offered services related to investments in the various stock exchanges in this country and abroad. However, brokerage houses have recently made serious inroads into the domain of regular banks by offering high-yield combination savings and checking accounts. In addition, brokerage firms now offer checking privileges on accounts (money market accounts). Also, investors can obtain loans from their broker, using their securities as collateral. Brokerage firms have experienced phenomenal growth during the past decade as more investors are becoming aware of the options they offer. It is likely that they will prove an increasingly strong challenge for regular banks in the future.

Commercial and consumer finance companies offer short-term loans to businesses or individuals who are either unable to meet the credit requirements of regular banks or have exceeded their credit limit and are in need of more funds. The interest rates charged by these finance companies are higher than those of regular banks. The primary customers of these companies are new businesses or individuals with no credit history. In fact, college students often turn to consumer finance companies for loans necessary to pay for their education.

pension funds
Amounts of money designated by corporations, nonprofit organizations, or unions to cover part of the financial needs of members when they retire.

brokerage firms
Organizations that buy and sell securities for their clients and provide other financial services.

consumer finance companies
Offer short-term loans to individuals at rates higher than those of commercial banks.

THINKING IT THROUGH

Do you understand the difference between the so-called banks and non-banks? Name a financial institution that could be called a nonbank. What are the primary functions of commercial banks? What are some of the new services offered by commercial banks? Describe the functions of credit unions.

Electronic Funds Transfer Systems (EFTS)

Today the whole banking system is on the brink of a major revolution in its day-to-day operations. The way things are done today—depositing money, writing checks, protecting against bad checks, and so on—is very expensive. You can imagine the cost of a bank approving a check, processing it through the banking system, and mailing it back to you. Something has to be done to make the system more efficient.

One step in the past was to issue credit cards. Credit cards cut down on the flow of checks, but they too have their costs. Paper still has to be processed, and there is a chance for credit card fraud.

What all of this is leading to is a society where exchanges of money are done electronically, with no paperwork involved. The system, as explained earlier, is called an **electronic funds transfer system (EFTS).** (See the box below for a summary of EFTS systems.) This means that you will be given a card much like a credit card. Retailers will put that card into a slot in their cash register (which will then be called a *point-of-sale terminal*). When the sale is recorded, an electronic signal will be sent to the bank transferring funds from your account to the store's account automatically. No paperwork will be involved. In fact, you will no longer receive a paycheck either. Rather, your employer will send the money electronically to the bank, and the bank will transfer funds from your employer's account to your account. You can see why it is called an electronic funds transfer system.

Naturally, such a system would be too complex if there were many banks dealing with many employers and individuals. To make the system work, it is better to have a few, large banks that operate most efficiently. These banks would not have to be located in expensive urban areas. Because most transactions will be done electronically, the banks can locate in inexpensive rural areas. All in all, the system will be much more efficient, and will have many benefits for both the banks and individuals. On the other hand, there is some consumer resistance to electronic banking because consumers are worried that electronic accounts are not very private. They also could miss having paper evidence of having paid bills. And banks and consumers both would lose the benefit of **float,** the time between when a check is given to a seller and the time it is cashed at the bank.

electronic funds transfer system (EFTS)
A system that allows for the payment of bills electronically; your paycheck may also be deposited electronically.

float
The delay between the time a check is given to a seller and the time it is cashed at the bank.

NEW DEVELOPMENTS IN BANKING SERVICES

The newest development in banking services is provided by electronic funds transfer systems (EFTS). This system facilitates the making of purchases and the payment of bills electronically. An EFTS is implemented through the use of a computer terminal or telephone connection that links the EFTS user with a central accounting system at the commercial bank. Here are some of the applications of an EFTS:

1 *Point-of-sale (POS) terminals.* A point-of-sale terminal is a computerized cash register that is used to electronically link a point of sale (a supermarket or a department store, for example) with a central accounting system at a nearby bank. Through the use of the POS, a consumer can make purchases that will be automatically deducted from his or her bank account. Consequently, purchases can be made without the use of cash, checks, or credit card. POS systems are currently being used successfully in certain test markets.

2 *Bill payment by telephone.* Depositors can ask their bank to transfer funds and make payments through the use of a touch-tone telephone in the convenience of their homes. The electronic transfer of funds is as simple as dialing to call a friend.

3 *Automated clearinghouse (ACHs).* Companies can use this service to transfer wages and salaries to their employee's bank accounts automatically at the scheduled pay date. Such systems make payroll accounting a much less complicated task.

4 *Electronic investment management.* As financial institutions expand the variety and scope of the services rendered, customers will be able to manage their investments in money deposits, bonds and securities, and money market funds from their living room. Brokerage firms already offer their most important customers the convenience of making investment decisions at home and electronically implementing them through a computer terminal link.

On the positive side, banks will be rid of the burden of processing checks and managing credit-card fraud and bad checks. Complete bank-at-home services will be available. That is, you will be able to transfer funds among accounts, make payments of various kinds (for example, utility bills and mortgage payments), and receive all kinds of information about your account. You could also buy and sell stock, get stock quotations, and more, once the system is finalized.

Financial Supermarkets

As the previous discussion indicates, the lines separating financial institutions such as banks, insurance companies, and stockbrokers are breaking down. Now you can go to Sears and buy stock, buy or sell a home, buy insurance, open a checking account, and get a credit card (Discover). In the future, the linkages among financial institutions will increase so that you will be able to complete almost all financial transactions from your home computer terminal. That will include electronic bank-

An ad for Sears' Discover card.

ing, electronic stock market transactions, electronic purchase and payment for insurance, electronic shopping from home, and more. It may even include the electronic payment of income taxes that will be computed from your other transactions.

Your immediate reaction may be to resist total reliance on such a system. It is obviously vulnerable to much government snooping and electronic fraud. All of these considerations must be worked out before the system is fully operational, but that may come sooner than you expect, especially if the costs of check processing continue to rise.

PROGRESS CHECK

▪ What do credit unions do?

▪ What are some examples of nonbanks?

▪ What are the advantages and disadvantages to consumers of electronic funds transfer systems?

THE FEDERAL RESERVE SYSTEM

Much of the future of banking will be decided by the Federal Reserve. Most people know very little about the operations of the Fed, so let's spend some time reviewing its function.

At the beginning of the twentieth century, banks operated in a largely unstable environment. This relative freedom in banking operations created many problems for banks, their customers, states, and the federal government. Because of poor management, illegal practices, low reserves, and very little communication among banks, the American banking system operated in an environment that threatened the financial security of everyone involved in it. Furthermore, it seriously undermined the federal government's ability to regulate the money supply.

The Federal Reserve Bank was established in 1913. It now serves as the *central bank* of the United States. Its primary responsibility is to promote economic stability and growth by regulating the flow of money and credit. Some of the functions of the Federal Reserve include:

- Managing the country's money and credit
- Providing short-term loans to banks that are temporarily short of reserves
- Issuing currency and coins
- Holding the reserves of commercial banks and other depository institutions
- Providing services to banks such as checking services and wire transfer services
- Being the government's banker by marketing its securities, paying its debts, and managing its international transactions
- Supervising banks and other financial institutions

Federal Reserve System
Consists of 12 Federal Reserve District banks that serve as a deposit for excess bank funds (for members) and loans member banks money.

Organization of the Federal Reserve System

The **Federal Reserve System** consists of twelve Federal Reserve District Banks (see Figure 20-2) located throughout the United States, and 25 branch territory banks. Each of the 12 district branches is collectively owned by member commercial banks. The Fed, however, is not controlled by the member banks. A seven-member board of governors that meets periodically in Washington, D. C., is responsible for managing the Fed. Each governor, who serves a 14-year term, is appointed by the President of the United States and is confirmed by the United States Senate. The Chairman and Vice-Chairman of the Board are also appointed by the President.

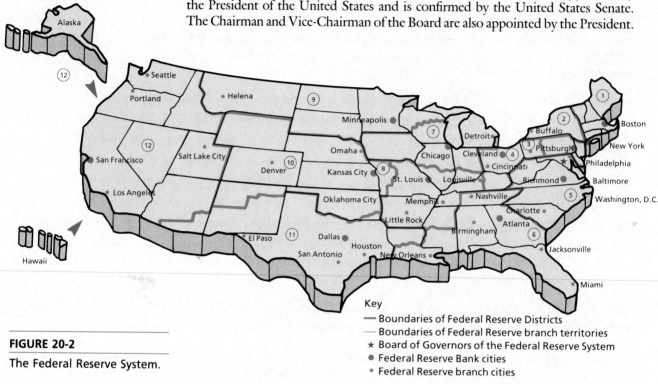

FIGURE 20-2

The Federal Reserve System.

Key
— Boundaries of Federal Reserve Districts
— Boundaries of Federal Reserve branch territories
★ Board of Governors of the Federal Reserve System
● Federal Reserve Bank cities
• Federal Reserve branch cities

Operations of the Federal Reserve System

reserve requirement
A percentage of member-bank funds that must be deposited in the Federal Reserve Bank.

All national banks are members of the Fed. State banks must also become members if they have checking accounts. The Fed's membership requirements are:

1 Member banks must purchase stock in their district reserve bank in proportion to their deposits relative to the other member banks in the district.

2 Member banks must keep funds at their district banks or in their own vaults to cover checks written by their depositors. These funds should be a certain percentage of the deposits they hold. This is called the **reserve requirement.**

On the other hand, member banks receive a number of important privileges:

1 Member banks can borrow funds from the district reserve banks.

2 Member banks use services, such as check clearing, provided by the Fed.

3 Member banks can obtain financial advice from the Fed.

4 Member banks are entitled to a dividend on the district reserve bank stock they own.

Regulating the Money Supply

The tools used by the Fed in its effort to regulate the money supply generally fall into three categories: reserve requirements, open-market operations, and the discount rate. Let's look at how the Fed uses these tools to perform its functions:

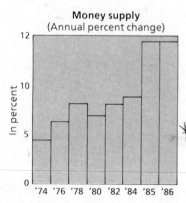

Money supply
(Annual percent change)

In percent

12

10

5

0

'74 '76 '78 '80 '82 '84 '85 '86

The Reserve Requirement

The reserve requirement is a percentage of commercial bank checking and savings accounts that must be physically retained in the bank (for example, as cash in the vault) or in a noninterest-paying deposit at the local Federal Reserve district bank. For instance, if Omaha Security Bank holds deposits of $100 million and the reserve requirement is, say, 10%, then the bank must retain $10 million to meet the reserve requirement. If the Fed were to increase the reserve requirement to 11%, then the bank would have to put an additional $1 million on reserve. This would reduce the funds available from the bank for loans. Consequently, the money supply would be reduced.

The reserve requirement is the Fed's most powerful tool. When it is increased, banks have less money for loans, fewer loans are made, money becomes more scarce, and in the long run that tends to reduce inflation. A decrease of the reserve requirement, on the other hand, increases the funds available to banks for loans, more loans are made, and money becomes more readily available. Such an increase in the money supply tends to stimulate the economy to achieve higher growth rates, but can also create inflationary pressures.

Open-Market Operations

Open-market operations is the tool most commonly used by the Fed. It involves the buying and selling of U. S. government securities by the Fed with the objective of regulating the money supply. U. S. government securities are issued by the federal government and sold to the public. These securities pay interest to owners and are guaranteed by the federal government. Consequently, they are considered to be a stable and relatively low-risk form of investment. How are U. S. government securities used by the Fed to control the money supply? When the Fed wants to decrease the money supply, it sells government securities. The money it obtains as payment is taken out of circulation, decreasing the money supply. If the Fed wants to increase the money supply, it buys government securities from individuals, corporations, or organizations that are willing to sell. The money paid by the Fed in return for these securities enters circulation, resulting in an increase in the money supply.

The Discount Rate

The Fed has often been called "the banker's bank." One of the reasons for this is that member banks can borrow funds from the Fed and then pass them on to their customers as loans. The **discount rate** is the interest rate that the Fed charges for loans to member banks. An increase in the discount rate by the Fed discourages banks from borrowing and consequently reduces the number of available loans, resulting in a decrease in the money supply (see Figure 20-3). On the other hand, a lowering of the discount rate encourages member bank borrowing and increases the amount of funds available for loans, resulting in an increase in the money supply.

Federal Funds

Federal funds are short-term loans of funds that can be transferred during one business day. Such immediately available funds include deposits at Federal Reserve Banks. Most federal funds are considered overnight money in that the money is loaned out in one day and paid back the next morning. What happens is that a lending institution with excess reserve funds in its reserve account can authorize

---

THE FEDERAL RESERVE SYSTEM'S TOOLS FOR CONTROLLING THE MONEY SUPPLY

TOOL	TO BOOST THE ECONOMY	TO COOL OFF THE ECONOMY
Reserve requirement	Decrease	Increase
Open-market operations	Buy	Sell
Discount rate	Lower	Raise

open-market operations Involve the buying and selling of U. S. government securities by the Federal Reserve to control the money supply.

discount rate The interest rate that the Federal Reserve Bank charges other banks for loans.

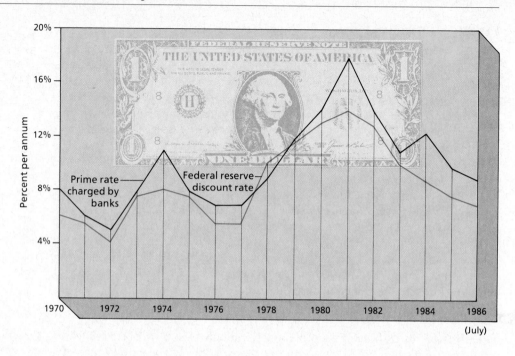

FIGURE 20-3

The discount rate and the prime rate. Note that the discount rate has a direct effect on the rate banks charge their best customer (the prime rate), thus controlling the flow of money going to business. The discount rate was lowered to 5.5% in 1986 and the prime rate fell to 7.5%.

Source: Statistical Abstract, 1985, and current data from the Department of Commerce.

a transfer from its reserve account to the reserve account of the borrower. The next morning, a transfer is arranged to put the money back plus an interest payment that is based on market conditions at the time. This interest rate is known as the *federal funds rate*.

Other Functions of the Fed

Checks have become the dominant medium through which payments are made in the economy. Some 95% of all business transactions today are paid in the form of checks. The process of handling and clearing the millions of checks written every hour would be extremely complicated and laborious if not for the Federal Reserve, which acts as a national clearing house for checks. The process by which a typical check is cleared through the Federal Reserve System is outlined step by step in Figure 20-4.

Setting Credit Controls

The Federal Reserve is responsible for controlling the credit practices of other financial institutions. These controls are of two major types:

    1 *Enforcing credit terms* for loans involving certain consumer durables (such as cars) and real estate loans. These terms may involve the amount of down payment required and the repayment period for such loans.

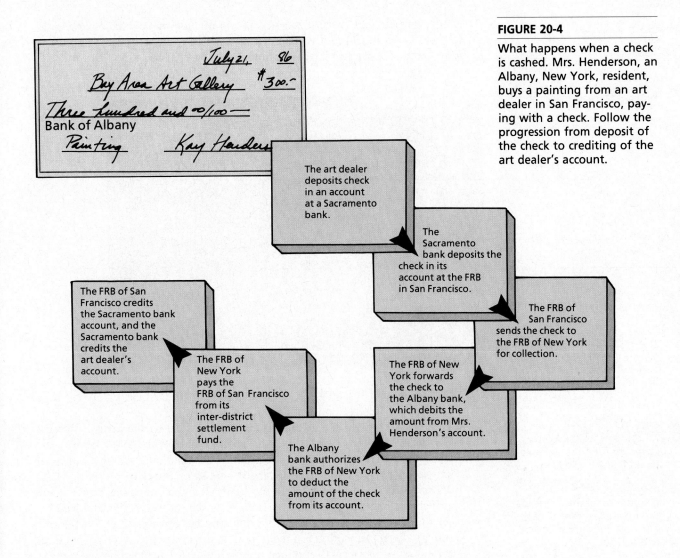

FIGURE 20-4

What happens when a check is cashed. Mrs. Henderson, an Albany, New York, resident, buys a painting from an art dealer in San Francisco, paying with a check. Follow the progression from deposit of the check to crediting of the art dealer's account.

2 *Setting the margin requirements* for certain transactions when buying stocks. Investors do not necessarily have to pay cash equivalent to a stock's selling price. Instead, they have the option of "buying on margin," which means that they would pay the minimum portion of the selling price that must be paid in cash at the time of the sale (this is called the *margin*) and use credit for the remainder. Since 1974, the margin requirement has been 50%. If an investor wants to buy $1,000 worth of XYZ Company's stock, he or she has to pay at least $500 in cash at the time of sale, while borrowing the remaining amount *"on margin."*

Issuance of Currency

The Fed is also responsible for issuing currency. All 12 Federal Reserve district banks are authorized to physically issue new money as it becomes needed. Also, the Fed is responsible for controlling the amount of money in circulation and for replacing worn-out bills with new ones. Given that the typical $1 bill has a life expectancy of about 18 months, you can imagine how many dollar bills have to be destroyed and replaced by newly printed ones every day.

Money being printed.

Some terms you will have to know in order to understand what you read about the Federal Reserve and banking in general include:

currency
All coin and paper money issued by the Federal Reserve Banks and all gold coins.

- **Currency** refers to all coin and paper money issued by the Federal Reserve Banks and all gold coins. It includes all coin and paper money held by the public in the United States. It also includes cash in the vaults of commercial and savings banks and currency carried abroad by travelers.

money supply
The sum of all the funds that the public has immediately available for buying goods and services.

- **Money supply** is the sum of all the funds that the public has immediately available for buying goods and services. Economists and the Federal Reserve use the money supply as a gauge for predicting and controlling U.S. economic activity. In implementing monetary policy, the Federal Reserve sets a target for money supply growth and then tries to influence bank lending and interest rates to achieve that target.

COMPUTERIZED BANKING AND COMPUTERIZED ERROR

A software error in the computer of the Bank of New York required the central bank to extend an unprecedented $22.6 billion loan overnight. The bank, which is a major clearing agent for government securities, had credited the accounts of securities *sellers,* but the computer glitch prevented it from debiting the accounts of the buyers.

As a result of the one computer error, the Bank of New York had to pay $5 *million* in interest for an 18-*hour* loan!

The U.S. money supply bulged with an extra $4.4 billion that week, leaving it far above its target range. The Chairman of the Federal Reserve is considering a special penalty for such errors to encourage better back-up systems.

Source: Mark Lewyn, *USA Today,* December, 1985.

Expanding the Role of the Federal Reserve

The regulatory functions of the Federal Reserve are vital to the survival and prosperity of not only the U. S. banking system but of the economy as a whole. Without the Fed, the money supply would be largely out of control. Recently, the Fed has been rather successful in managing the money supply, although the ups and downs have caused some disruptions in the market.

The Fed operates as the central bank of the United States and as such it has jurisdiction over all other banks. But what about nonbanks? The ongoing revolution of the banking industry is creating a highly competitive environment. Banks are being threatened by the new generation of financial institutions. As nonbank institutions begin to control an increasing share of the banking business, it is expected that the regulatory scope of the Fed will shift to the nonbanks as well. The Fed's current organization is very similar to the way it was when the Fed was started in the early part of this century. However, the structure of the banking industry has changed tremendously since then. Many experts believe that we can expect a big shift in the Fed's organization and scope of activities within the next decade. It is argued that the mission of the reorganized Fed would include supervising the nonbank as well as banking institutions.

Now that we have explored the various financial institutions and the role of the Federal Reserve, we can review the history of banking to see how the present structure evolved and examine some of the current issues in the financial world.

EARLY BANKING HISTORY

The history of banking goes back thousands of years. The Babylonians performed many of the banking functions of today, taking deposits, engaging in foreign exchange, and issuing paper with the same function as checks. Over time banks grew and prospered and became a vital part of the economy throughout the world.

In the United States, however, there were no banks at first, and strict laws limited the number of coins that could be brought to the colonies. Thus colonists were forced to barter; that is, to trade goods for goods (for example, cotton and tobacco for shoes and lumber).

The demand for money was so great that Massachusetts issued its own paper money in 1690. Other colonies soon followed suit. Land banks were established to lend money to farmers. Britain ended both practices by 1741. A new bank was formed in Pennsylvania during the Revolution to finance the war against England.

Alexander Hamilton persuaded Congress to form a central bank in 1781 over the objections of Thomas Jefferson and others. It closed in 1811 only to be replaced in 1816 because state-chartered banks couldn't support the War of 1812. Throughout this period, there was serious debate about the role and function of banking in this country. The battle between the Second (Central) Bank of the United States and state banks got really hot in the 1830s. Several banks in Andrew Jackson's home state were hurt by pressure from the Central Bank. The fight ended when the Central Bank was closed in 1836.

By the time of the Civil War, the banking system was a mess. Many different banks issued different kinds of currencies. During the war, coins were hoarded because they were worth more as gold and silver than as coins. The government began printing money ("greenbacks") that was money only because the government declared it so, not because the material it was made from had any value of its own.

Eventually, the government established federally chartered and state-chartered banks. The chaos continued and reached something of a climax in 1907, when many banks failed. People got nervous about their money and went to the bank to withdraw their funds. Shortly thereafter the cash ran out and some banks had to refuse money to depositors.

The cash shortage problems of 1907 led to the formation of a bank that could lend money to banks—the Federal Reserve System. It was a "lender of last resort" in such emergencies. We have noted that, under the Federal Reserve Act of 1913, all federally-chartered banks had to join the Fed. State banks could also join. The Federal Reserve became the banker's bank. If banks had excess funds, they could deposit them in the Fed and if extra money was needed, it could be borrowed. The Federal Reserve has been intimately related to banking ever since.

The Great Depression

The Federal Reserve Bank was designed to prevent a repeat of the panic that occurred in 1907. If banks were short of funds they were able to borrow funds from the Federal Reserve and cut off any doubt that the bank would survive. Nevertheless, the stock market crash of 1929 led to bank failures in the early 1930s. There are some interesting parallels between that period and now that should be explored.

For one thing, prices for farm products in the 1920s declined and farmers and retailers in rural areas could not pay off their loans. This led to many bank failures in rural parts of the country. Similar events happened in 1985 and 1986, with many rural banks failing.

There had been a rapid expansion of banks in the 1920s and many were undercapitalized. This too happened in the 1980s.

The stock market soared in the late 1920s much as it soared in 1986. Other events of the 1920s that are similar to today's situation are:

- There was a decline in demand for American products overseas in the 1920s. The high dollar caused a similar drop in 1985.
- The corporate structure of the United States was rather weak in the 1920s. Trusts and holding companies were using the dividends from one company to pay the interest and dividends of other companies. If one company failed, the whole trust was in trouble. The rapid growth of mergers today is being financed by bonds of questionable strength. The failure of one firm could have serious consequences again.

The economy today has its own unique problems. The national debt is about $2 trillion and rising. Total debt of households, corporations, and governments was $7.1 trillion in 1984. Credit market debt was 1.95 times GNP at that time.[3] In other words, the U.S. economy and U.S. banking system are in a relatively poor financial condition.

THINKING IT THROUGH

What happens to the prices of goods and services in a depression? Why is cash in hand the best thing to have in a depression? Why not keep your money in a bank? To prevent a recession, the Fed may loosen up greatly on the money supply. This leads to inflation. Why are gold and silver good investments in an inflationary economy? What happens to money in the bank?

BANK FAILURES—1930s AND 1980s

The failure of the banking system began on October 29, 1929. The stock market began tumbling and people had to rush to the bank to get money to cover their positions in the stock market. You should read about the Great Depression in some detail. The bottom line, however, was that businesses failed, jobs were lost, people went to the banks to withdraw their money, and the banks ran out of money. States were forced to close banks. President Franklin Roosevelt extended the period of the bank closings in 1933 to gain time to come up with some solution to the problem. (A similar scenario occurred in 1985 in Ohio and Maryland when savings and loan institutions began to fail.)

In 1933 and 1935, federal legislation was passed to strengthen the banking system. The most important move was to establish federal deposit insurance. However, during the 1960s and 1970s, many banks found that it was very costly giving up noninterest bearing reserves to the Federal Reserve Bank. They were attracted by the prospect of having interest-bearing reserves in state-chartered banks that were state insured. This withdrawal of reserves from the Fed left it with less money to use for fine-tuning the economy.

In 1980 the Monetary Control Act was passed. It required that almost all depository institutions have deposits in the Federal Reserve Bank. The act also gave thrift institutions the right to offer the NOW accounts, which were discussed earlier. These interest-bearing services, similar to checking accounts, were previously not allowed in most states. Banks and savings and loan institutions are now more competitive with one another. The interest-rate differential that once made thrifts more attractive is no longer there. All these steps were taken to strengthen the banking system in general.

In the 1980s, saving and loan institutions began failing in various states. Some were not insured by the Federal Savings and Loan Insurance Corporation, and the public was shocked to learn that state insurance was inadequate to cover the risk. State government officials closed the thrifts until federal insurance was obtained or other means were found to pay off depositors (for example, the thrifts were acquired by other, larger, more secure thrifts).

What will be the future of banks and savings and loans in the next decade? The answer lies in the decisions by the Federal Reserve and the overall strength of the U.S. and world economies. One thing that is certain is that the U.S. financial community is in a rather weak state. Many changes are needed to further strengthen the banking system. You would be wise to keep up with such events. Some things you should know about the banking system today are:

- Most banks are insured by the Federal Deposit Insurance Corporation, but there are not enough funds in the system to cover large bank failures.
- Most thrifts are insured by the Federal Savings and Loan Insurance Corporation, but again the funds are very small relative to the potential losses if thrifts continue failing. Some state insurance funds were depleted when just one major thrift failed.
- Deflation of crop prices puts great pressure on farmers and others who cannot pay their bills. This was a factor in the Great Depression of the 1930s and could lead to another, less severe recession today.
- To prevent recession, the Federal Reserve could continue to pump money into the economy. This could result in a return of inflation (too much money chasing too few goods).

What all of this says is that the financial condition of the United States is rather strained, and the consequences can be serious.[3] What can be done? For the answers, we must turn to the federal government and the Federal Reserve. Government monetary and fiscal policy will have a great influence on the economy as will decisions of the Federal Reserve Board (see Chapter 3).

CAREER INFORMATION: BANKING

NATURE OF THE WORK

Practically every banking institution—whether commercial bank, savings and loan association, or personal credit institution—has one or more vice presidents acting as general managers who coordinate the activities of the institution's departments or regional offices, and financial managers who oversee the activities of their branches. Most have a controller or cashier who is an executive officer generally responsible for all bank property. Large banks also may have treasurers and other officers to oversee several departments.

Each department is headed by a highly trained and experienced manager. Risk and insurance managers establish and oversee programs to control and minimize risks and losses. Credit card operations managers establish credit rating criteria, determine credit ceilings, and monitor their institution's extension of credit. Reserve officers review their institution's financial statements and direct the purchase and sale of bonds and other securities. User representatives in international accounting develop integrated international financial and accounting systems for the banking transactions of multinational organizations.

Bank officials must have a broad knowledge of business activities and also detailed knowledge of industries allied to banking, such as insurance, real estate, and securities. With growing competition, *promotion* of an expanding variety of financial services offered by banking institutions is an increasingly important function of bank managers. Besides supervising financial services, officers advise individuals and businesses and participate in community projects.

JOB OUTLOOK

Employment of bank officers is expected to increase faster than the average for all occupations through the mid-1990s. Expanded financial services offered by banks will spur demand for bank managers to provide sound management and effective quality control.

Because of the increasing number of qualified applicants, competition for bank managerial positions is expected to stiffen. Familiarity with other financial services—for example, insurance or securities—and with computers and data processing systems may enhance one's chances for employment.

EARNINGS

Officer trainees with a bachelor's degree generally earned between $13,200 and $22,800 a year in 1984. Those with master's degrees generally started at higher salaries. Graduates with a Master of Business Administration were offered starting salaries of $21,600 to $42,000 a year in 1984.

Salaries of bank officers averaged $28,600 in 1984 The salary level depends on the particular position and the size and location of the bank. For managers, as well as for other bank employees, earnings are likely to be lower in small towns than in big cities. The top 10 percent of all bank officers earned over $52,000 a year in 1984.

SOURCES OF ADDITIONAL INFORMATION

General information about banking occupations, training opportunities, and the banking industry itself is available from:

American Bankers Association, 1120 Connecticut Ave. NW., Washington, D.C. 20036.

Bank Administration Institute, 60 Gould Center, Rolling Meadows, Ill. 60008.

National Association of Bank Women, Inc., National Office, 500 N. Michigan Ave., Chicago, Ill. 60611.

The Institute of Financial Education, 111 E. Wacker Dr., Chicago, Ill. 60601.

Information on careers with the Federal Reserve System is available from:

Board of Governors, The Federal Reserve System, Personnel Division, Washington, D.C. 20551, or from the personnel department of the Federal Reserve bank serving each geographic area.

Source: *Occupational Outlook Handbook,* 1986-1987 (U.S. Department of Labor).

Given the information in this chapter, you are now prepared to read further about such decisions. Remember, the purpose of this text is to give you an introduction to business; the assumption is that you will keep up your studies. One of the ways to get more excited about financial matters is to learn more about stocks and bonds and personal finance. That is what we'll do in Chapters 21 and 22.

■ How does the Federal Reserve control the money supply? Why does it take the steps it does?

■ What are other functions of the Federal Reserve?

■ What did the government do after the Great Depression to prevent another such collapse of the banking system?

SUMMARY

1 The U.S. banking system consists of commercial banks, savings and loan associations (thrifts), credit unions, and mutual savings banks (depositor-owned thrifts).

■ What is unique about commercial banks?

They handle both deposits and checking accounts. The deregulation of the banking industry in 1980 closed the gaps between banks and S & Ls so that both now offer similar services.

■ What kind of services?

Everything from passbook savings accounts to NOW accounts, CDs, loans, Individual Retirement Accounts (IRAs), safe deposit boxes, traveler's checks, and more.

■ What is a thrift (savings and loan association)?

These organizations were designed to make mortgage loans and not to handle checking accounts. Originally, S & Ls paid more interest on deposits. Today, however, S & Ls offer interest-bearing checking accounts and their rates on deposits are closer to those offered by banks.

■ What is a mutual savings bank?

These are depositor-owned S & Ls. Note that they are thrift institutions, not banks.

■ What is a credit union?

A *credit union* is a member-owned cooperative that operates much like a bank in that it takes deposits, allows you to write checks, and makes loans. It also may sell life insurance and make home loans. Credit union interest rates are sometimes higher than those from banks and loan rates are often lower.

■ Who ensures that the money that I put into a bank, savings and loan corporation or credit union is safe?

Money deposited in banks is insured by an independent government agency called the Federal Deposit Insurance Corporation (FDIC). Money in S & Ls is insured by another independent government agency called the Federal Savings and Loan Insurance Corporation (FSLIC). Money in credit unions is insured by The National Credit Union Association.

2 Other financial institutions that make loans and do other bank-like things.
- What are these institutions?

    They include life insurance companies that loan out their funds, pension funds that invest in stocks and bonds and make loans, brokerage firms that offer interest-bearing checking accounts (money market funds), and commercial and consumer finance companies.

- What is the future of financial institutions?

    The trend is to merge functions, so that banks, S & Ls, and other financial institutions perform many of the same functions.

- What does this mean to me?

    In the future, you will be able to do much of your banking from home. Your paycheck will be deposited electronically at a local financial institution that will offer you electronic shopping, electronic bill paying, real estate services, and more.

3 The Federal Reserve was designed to control the banking system and the *money supply*.
- How does it control the money supply?

    It makes financial institutions (for example, banks) keep funds in the Federal Reserve (reserve requirements); buys and sells government securities (open-market operations); and loans money to banks (the discount rate). It also issues money on its own.

4 The history of banking and the Federal Reserve shows that periodically banks fail and depositors lose their money, even when the banks are insured. This has not happened under federal insurance, but it could.
- Are you trying to scare us with stories of bank failures?

    No, the truth is that these are stressful times for the U.S. economy and banks in particular. Not since the Great Depression of the 1930s have there been so many danger signals. The Great Depression began with lower farm profits, and more recent bank failures began in a similar way. The other parallels with the 1920s are spelled out in the chapter. Lessons from the past are valuable in preventing similar events in the present.

KEY TERMS

automated teller
  machines (ATMs) p. 550
brokerage firms p. 556
certificate of deposit p. 550
commercial bank p. 549
consumer finance
  companies p. 556
credit unions p. 554
currency p. 564
demand deposit p. 550
discount rate p. 561
electronic funds transfer
  system (EFTS) p. 557
Federal Deposit Insurance
  Corporation (FDIC) p. 555

Federal Savings and Loan
  Insurance Corporation
  (FSLIC) p. 555
Federal Reserve System p. 559
float p. 557
long-term loans p. 552
money supply p. 564
mutual savings bank p. 554
nonbanks p. 555
open-market operations p. 561
pension funds p. 556
reserve requirement p. 560
short-term loans p. 551
savings and loan associations
  p. 553
thrift institutions p. 553
time deposit p. 550

1 Paper money is issued by the 12 Federal Reserve district banks. Try to collect $1 bills issued by as many of these Fed banks as possible. Which district bank is responsible for issuing most of the bills you have looked at? Can you explain why?

2 Go to your commercial bank or the financial institution you do business with and talk with the accounts manager about the many services that are offered.

3 Open the business section of your daily newspaper and look at the exchange rates table that lists the equivalent price of foreign currency in U.S. dollars. Run through that list and try to learn some of the foreign currencies listed. Also, observe which foreign currencies are priced less than the dollar and which cost more. This will give you a feel for foreign currency exchange rates.

4 Go to your financial institution and ask for their high-yield interest rates (time deposits). Do you think they provide a satisfactory return-on-investment (ROI)? What would be the pros and cons of such an investment opportunity?

5 Read the business section of your local paper and the front page of *The Wall Street Journal* for a week. What is being said about banking and the Federal Reserve? How important does the financial community seem to think that Federal Reserve decisions are? What decisions have been announced lately?

CASE ONE   WHEN MONEY LOSES ITS MEANING

When money decreases in value because of inflation, people tend to place less trust in it as a method of storing value, and look for alternative means of storing their wealth that would be more efficient. Hyperinflation—extremely high inflation that can range from 100% to 10,000% annually—makes money particularly unstable. In fact, hyperinflation makes money meaningless. That is what happened in Germany during the 1920s. A pack of cigarettes, for example, had a price tag of 200 trillion marks. As a result, people ceased to use the official but worthless currency and resorted to using other objects as money (such as clothes, appliances, jewelry, antiques, diamonds, silver, and gold). These objects effectively became money. Subsequently, the German economy collapsed, setting the stage for the rise of Naziism.

Hyperinflation in post-World War I Germany is seen as the worst such case in this century. Nevertheless, there are numerous recent examples of hyperinflation. In the South American country of Bolivia, for example, prices during 1984 rose at an annual rate of 10,000%. A hamburger cost 1 million pesos, a loaf of bread sold for 300,000 pesos, and one night's lodging in a good hotel cost 35 million pesos. Hyperinflation in Bolivia has skyrocketed to the point where the peso is virtually worthless. The Bolivian example of hyperinflation is certainly an extreme one, but other countries have also experienced hyperinflation in recent times. Israel, for example, had an annual inflation rate of 400% in 1984; Argentina had annual inflation of about 200% for a number of years; and Iceland recently experienced an annual inflation rate of 150%.

DECISION QUESTIONS

1 Why did official money lose its meaning in Germany during the 1920s?

2 Do you believe that the United States could be facing a hyperinflation problem in the foreseeable future? Why or why not?

3 How can we deal with hyperinflation? What is the role of the Federal Reserve in controlling inflation? How does it perform this function?

**PRACTICING
MANAGEMENT DECISIONS**

CASE TWO   IS YOUR MONEY SAFE?

In 1983, Commonwealth Savings Company of Lincoln, Nebraska failed. The bank was insured by a private insurance fund that was wiped out by the failure. The depositors lost their money, and they still do not know if they will ever recover it.

In 1984, Western Community Money Center in Concord, California also failed. It was an industrial bank. The company that insured the bank, Thrift Guaranty Corporation, was hard-pressed to cover the losses to depositors.

In 1985, similar problems occurred in Ohio and Maryland. The Ohio Deposit Guarantee Fund, which insured 70 thrifts, collapsed because its largest member, Home State Savings Bank of Cincinnati, failed. (Home State was a savings and loan institution in spite of its name.) In Maryland, several S & Ls were closed and depositors could only withdraw limited funds until the organizations involved were purchased by larger, more financially secure S & Ls or federal insurance was obtained.

Several hundred savings and loan institutions are still insured by private insurers. They are located in Massachusetts, Pennsylvania, Maryland, and North Carolina. Recent events have shown that the funds available to fund failures in these organizations are insufficient. This is frightening when you realize that 300 banks and thrifts have failed in the last several years. In 1985, about 950 federally insured banks were on the Federal Deposit Insurance Corporation's problem list (potential failures), as were hundreds of S & Ls.

Even though banks and S & Ls protected by the federal government seem safe, the fact is that there is very little funding available if banks do begin to fail. Depositors would probably have to wait months or even years to get their funds back if their bank failed. Many depositors have spread their money among several banks to reduce the risk.

What about taking your money out of the bank and putting it into a credit union? Well, the safety is no better. Over 3,000 of the approximately 18,000 credit unions have private insurance (over 60 have *no* insurance).

People put their money into privately insured institutions and credit unions to make a percentage point or two more interest. Clearly, the risks associated with higher returns are great.

DECISION QUESTIONS

1   Do you know whether or not your money in the bank or credit union is insured by the federal government? If you don't know, you should find out.
2   What seems to be the cause of financial failures in the 1980s? Much of it has to do with deflation—falling housing and farm values. What else may be involved?
3   What would happen to the economy if banks and S & Ls began failing at a rapid rate? Has this happened before?

LOOKING AHEAD

We have discussed money and banking as an introduction to the important business function of finance. Finance is the function in a firm responsible for acquiring funds, managing funds within the firm, preparing budgets, and planning for the expenditure of funds. Financial officers must be familiar with money and banking and the Federal Reserve because much of what they do involves banks and economic conditions. Financial management will be discussed in Chapter 21.

Chapter 22 will cover the basics of stocks and bonds, and Chapter 23 will discuss personal financial management, ways for you to prosper by using financial strategies.

FINANCIAL MANAGEMENT

After you have read and studied this chapter, you should be able to:

▪ Explain finance and the functions of a financial manager.

▪ Compare and contrast the two major sources of long-term funds.

▪ Identify and describe several sources of short-term funds.

▪ Describe what is involved in financial planning.

▪ Discuss the role of spreadsheet analysis in financial control.

PROFILE   DANNY AND ANNETTE NOBLE, CLOTHING DESIGNERS

D anny and Annette Noble are two popular designers of colorful women's
clothing. They started their company, Danny Noble, Ltd., in 1983, and
soon after its clothes made the cover of Saks Fifth Avenue *Folio*. Sales in 1985
were over $5 million. Very successful in design, Danny Noble, Ltd. is also successful
in finance.

Their local accountant helped the Nobles write a business plan, and he acts as
a kind of finance and operations manager for the firm. The business plan attracted
a private investor to lend $150,000 to the firm for a one-third share in ownership.
The Nobles' had to put their house up for collateral against the loan.

The company grew so fast that it ran into a cash flow problem and couldn't
buy the $30,000 worth of materials to fill its fall orders. In hindsight, the Nobles
realized that their start-up capital was simply too small. Their finance advisor knew
someone at a local thrift institution, however, and the Nobles were able to swing
a $50,000 loan.

As the business prospered, it was able to get a line of credit for $250,000 and
a $75,000 term loan from a bank. Today Danny Noble, Ltd. is trying to grow at
a modest pace to maintain a strong financial position.

The Nobles' experience is a good example of what finance is all about. Finance
is the function that plans for the financial needs of the firm (part of the business
plan), obtains start-up and operating funds, controls those funds, and manages
other financial matters such as credit management and taxes.

Three financial problems that plague most businesses are poor cash flow,
insufficient start-up capital, and inadequate expense control. Danny Noble, Ltd.

Danny and Annette Noble.

suffered from the first two, but were very careful, with their accountant's advice, to watch expenses.

In this chapter, we shall examine financial management in more detail. It is a critical function in any firm, as the Nobles' experience indicates. ▪

This example is from Alix M. Freedman, "An Eye on the Bottom Line Aids Fashion Designer's Rise," *The Wall Street Journal*, January 28, 1985, p. 36.

THE ROLE OF FINANCE

An accountant may be compared to a skilled laboratory technician who takes blood samples and other measures of a person's health and writes the findings on a health report (financial statements). The physician is the one who interprets those reports and makes recommendations to the patient regarding changes that would improve health. The physician may be compared to the finance person in a business. Financial managers use the data prepared by the accountants and make recommendations to top management regarding strategies for improving the health (financial strength) of the firm.

A manager cannot be optimally effective at finance without understanding accounting. Similarly, a good accountant needs to understand finance. Accounting and finance, finance and accounting—the two go together like pizza and beer.

The purpose of this chapter is to introduce you to the role of finance in business. Like all the other areas we have discussed, the best way to get a true feel for finance as a career is to visit several finance departments, observe the surroundings, watch the people at work, ask questions, get involved, and see for yourself whether or not the work appears interesting.

One does not have to pursue finance as a career to be interested in finance, however. Financial understanding is important to anyone who wants to invest in stocks or bonds or plan a retirement fund. In short, finance is something everyone should study. In this chapter, the focus will be on finance from the businessperson's perspective. In Chapter 23 we'll discuss some *personal* finance topics so you'll be better prepared to manage your own funds.

What Is Finance?

Finance, basically, is the function in a business that is responsible for acquiring funds for the firm, managing funds within the firm (for example, preparing budgets, doing cash flow analysis, and planning for the expenditure of funds on such assets as plant, equipment, and machinery). The chief financial officer is often known as the **treasurer** or vice-president of finance. The most basic description of what a finance person does is to obtain money and then plan, use, and control money effectively (see Figure 21-1).

You are probably somewhat familiar with several finance functions, for example, the idea of buying merchandise on credit. The area of business usually responsible for *credit and collections* is finance. The finance manager must be sure that the company does not lose too much money to *bad debt losses* (people who don't pay). Naturally, this means that finance is responsible for *collecting overdue payments.* You no doubt have received reminder announcements from finance departments that gently remind you to pay your bill. Finance people are also responsible for **tax management,** that is, analyzing the tax implications of various

 finance
The function in a business responsible for acquiring funds for the firm, managing funds within the firm, and planning for the expenditure of funds on various assets.

treasurer
The chief financial officer of a company.

 tax management
The analysis of the tax implications of various managerial decisions and minimization of the taxes paid by the firm.

Assets ← Funds ← Liabilities
OWNERS EQUITY

Assets = Liabilities + E.O.

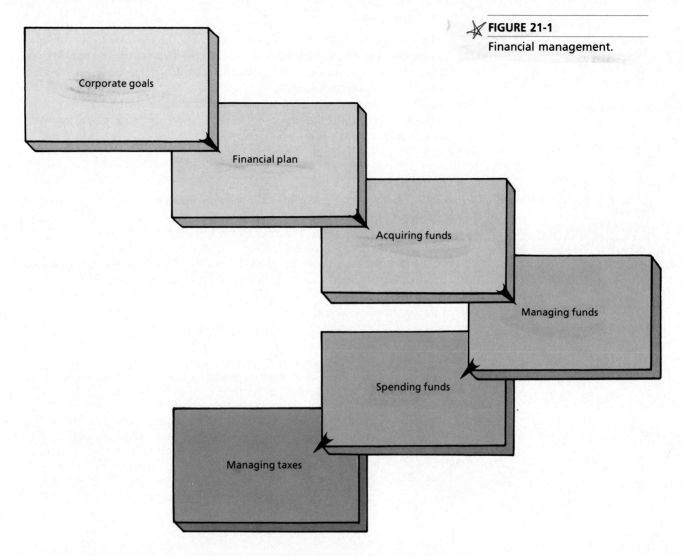

FIGURE 21-1

Financial management.

managerial decisions and minimizing the taxes paid by the business. Finance people also act as *internal auditors* to ensure that prescribed accounting procedures are being followed.

Somebody in a business must prepare budgets, just as a homeowner would. Finance people *plan* where money should be spent and then establish controls to be sure the funds are being spent wisely (see Figure 21-2).

- Planning
- Budgeting
- Obtaining funds
- Controlling funds (funds management)
- Collecting funds (credit management)
- Auditing
- Managing taxes
- Advising top management on financial matters

FIGURE 21-2

What financial managers do.

Internal Auditing

internal auditor
Financial person who makes sure that all transactions have been treated in accordance with established accounting rules and procedures.

Often someone in the finance department serves as an **internal auditor,** checking on the journals, ledgers, and financial statements prepared by the accounting department. The internal auditor makes sure that all transactions have been treated in accordance with established accounting rules and procedures. If there were no such audits, the accounting statements would be almost worthless. An internal audit, therefore, is simply one more check to see that the various financial accounts are being properly managed in a business.

✳Financial Problems

THREE CAUSES FOR FINANCIAL FAILURE
1 Poor cash flow
2 Undercapitalization (not enough funds to start with)
3 Inadequate expense control

Three of the most common ways for firms to fail *financially* are:
  1 Poor cash flow
  2 Undercapitalization (not enough funds to start with)
  3 Inadequate expense control

Let's focus our discussion of finance on the problem of obtaining funds. This is where finance begins and continues to be one of the key financial functions throughout the life of a business. It is also where the cash flow and undercapitalization problems are anticipated and resolved.

THINKING IT THROUGH

Can you see the link between accounting and finance? They are mutually supportive functions in a firm. A firm cannot get along without accounting but neither can it prosper without short- and long-term financing, managing its funds well, minimizing its taxes, and investing its funds properly. In fact, finance is so important to a firm that some finance executives go on to be presidents of firms. What would be the advantages and disadvantages of a president with a finance background versus a marketing background? Is there a danger of being too concerned with cost-cutting, budgeting, and controlling funds?

---

financial plan
Specifies the amount of money needed for various time periods and the most appropriate sources and uses of funds.

long-term financing
Money obtained from the owners of the firm and lenders who do not expect repayment within 2 or more years.

venture capital
Money that is invested in new companies with great profit potential.

retained earnings
Earnings that are retained rather than paid out in dividends

LONG-TERM FINANCING

You learned from the Nobles' example that one mistake businesses make from the very start is not having enough long-term funds (called capital) when they start. A **financial plan** for a business specifies the amount of money needed for various time periods and the most appropriate sources and uses of funds. **Long-term financing** is money obtained from the owners of the firm and lenders who do not expect repayment within 2 or more years. Long-term capital is used to buy long-term assets such as plant and equipment and to finance any expansions of the organization. Initial long-term capital usually comes from three sources:
  1 *Equity capital* comes from the owners of the firm. Part of equity capital is **venture capital.** It is money raised from organizations that fund (give capital to) new businesses (new ventures).
  2 A source of long-term capital *over time* is retained earnings. **Retained earnings** are the profits the firm keeps after distributing dividends (shares of the profit) to stockholders.

3 **Debt capital** comes from borrowing money through the sale of bonds or
   from banks and other lending institutions

Basically, long-term financing falls into two broad categories: equity capital and
debt capital (see Figure 21-3).

debt capital
Funds from borrowing money
through the sale of bonds or
from banks and other lending
institutions.

FIGURE 21-3
Sources of long-term funds.

Equity Capital
- Personal savings and second mortgages on homes
- Friends and family loans
- Partners
- Venture-capital firms
- Sale of stock (equity financing)
- Retained earnings

Debt Capital
- Sale of bonds (debt financing)
- Long-term loans from banks and other financial institutions

Venture Capital

The hardest time for a firm to raise money is when it is just starting. The company
typically has few assets; therefore the chance of borrowing significant amounts of
money from a bank are slim. The people starting the firm may be able to obtain
a second mortgage on their homes, but that is usually not enough to finance a
company through a year or more of operations. In Chapters 4 and 5, we talked
about the advantages and disadvantages of various forms of business and small
business management. We learned that the largest single source of start-up capital
is the savings of the initial owners plus those of partners, friends, and others willing
to risk some money on the chance that the firm will succeed. That is what happened
with the Nobles, as seen in the Profile at the beginning of this chapter. They found
an individual investor willing to lend them $100,000.

The modern source of start-up capital, however, is from venture capital firms.
Venture capital is money that is invested in new companies with great profit
potential. The search for such funds begins with a good business plan (see Chapter
5). This document must convince investors that the firm will be a success. Part of
the financial plan may be a financing proposal that spells out how much is needed,
how it is to be raised, and how it will be paid back.

The venture capital industry began about 50 years ago as an alternative investment vehicle for wealthy families such as the Rockefellers. They financed Sanford McDonnell, for example, when he was still operating out of a barn. That
small venture grew into McDonnell Douglas, the large aerospace and defense
contractor. The venture capital industry limped along for years until the early
1980s, when the new high-tech companies were being started. From 1979 to
1984, venture capital funding nearly tripled from $4 billion to $11.5 billion.[1]

A finance officer has to be careful in choosing a venture capital firm to help
finance a new business. For one thing, the venture capital firm will want at least
a one-third ownership of the business.[2] More importantly, the venture capital firm
should be able to come up with more financing if the firm needs it. The dangers
of having the wrong venture capital firm are illustrated in the experience of Jon
Birck.

Advertisements for venture
capital.

Jon Birck started Northwest Instrument Systems with money from a venture capital firm. He worked until 11:00 or 12:00 each night to build the company. One day he was asked to leave by the venture capital firm, which wanted a more experienced chief executive officer to protect their investment. Birck had dedicated 3 years to the company. He had left a secure job, put his marriage on the line, taken out a second mortgage on his house, and given himself a below-average salary; and then, just when the firm was ready for rapid growth, he was asked to resign.[3] Jon is starting a new firm with an entrepreneurial team and is approaching venture capital firms again.

Venture capital firms invest equity funds in small- to medium-sized (often high-tech) firms in hopes of receiving significant financial rewards. To learn more about venture capital and new firms in general, read *Venture* magazine.

Equity Financing

Regardless of whether or not a new firm can obtain venture capital funds, there usually comes a time when even more funds are required. One way to obtain needed funds is to sell ownership shares in the firm (called **stock**) to the public. If you look in the back of *The Wall Street Journal,* you will see thousands of small, medium, and large companies in every kind of industry listed, along with the current price of the firm's stock. This gives you some feel for the widespread use of **equity financing** as a way of obtaining capital. Now, we shall explore the advantages and disadvantages of equity financing.

stock
Shares of ownership in a company.

equity financing
A means a company uses to obtain capital that involves the public sale of stock.

Advantages of Selling Stock

Most large firms are listed on one of the several stock exchanges (for example, the New York or American Stock Exchange). This means that they feel equity financing (selling stock) is a good way to raise funds. The advantages are:

- Because stockholders are owners of the business, their investment never has to be repaid. That means the funds are available long-term for acquiring land, buildings, machinery, and other assets.
- There is no legal obligation to pay dividends (a share of the profits) to stockholders. Therefore, income can be plowed back into the firm for additional investment and growth.
- Selling stock improves the condition of the balance sheet. Because no debt is incurred, the corporation is stronger financially and able to borrow funds more easily.
- The public is often eager to buy ownership in new and growing firms to share in their potential profits. Selling stock is thus a relatively easy and quick source of funds for some firms.

Disadvantages of Selling Stock

"There is no such thing as a free lunch," the saying goes. There are disadvantages to selling ownership in a firm as well. They include:

- Because stockholders are owners of the firm, they can vote, through the board of directors, on who will manage the firm and what the policies will be. Having other owners takes away some freedom and control from those who started the firm and invested much time and effort in getting it started. Jon Birck learned that lesson the hard way when the owners asked him to leave as chief executive officer.

- Equity financing is a relatively expensive form of fund raising. Dividends are paid out of profit *after taxes*. It is thus more costly to pay dividends than interest. (Dividend income is taxed twice—it is taxed at the corporate level and taxed again as income to the stockholders. Interest, on the other hand, is a tax-deductible expense for the company.)
- Management decision making must be tempered by the need to keep stockholders happy. This often forces managers to use short-term tactics to keep earnings up rather than strategies to keep the firm profitable in the long run.

GREENMAIL—ISSUE OF THE 1980s

Greenmail is a transaction in which a company buys its own stock, usually at a premium price, from a shareholder who threatens to take over the firm by buying a controlling interest. In return, the shareholder (often referred to as a corporate raider) agrees to drop his takeover bid.

One of the most controversial greenmail deals involved the Walt Disney Company. It bought Saul Steinberg's stake in June, 1984 for $70.83 a share, giving him a $30 million pretax profit. Disney also picked up Mr. Steinberg's $28 million in expenses. In return, Mr. Steinberg stopped his $72.50-a-share takeover bid, an offer Disney management felt was not fair. History proved management correct in that Disney stock was selling at $146 a share 2 years later.

The Disney case supports the traditional promanagement argument for paying greenmail. Management says that paying greenmail stops a takeover threat from a raider who is trying to buy a company for less than fair value. Shareholders will supposedly benefit from a rise in stock much greater than the takeover bid, as happened in the Disney case.

The word *greenmail* comes from *greenback* (money) and *blackmail* (extortion). It sounds as if corporate officers bribe corporate raiders with dropping their high bids for company stock, hurting small stockholders who could sell their stock for a profit. The argument against greenmail, therefore, is that it hurts stockholders by preventing them from having a chance to receive a premium price for their stock. Small stockholders believe greenmail is a device by management to protect their own jobs. There are cases to illustrate both sides, but certainly greenmail is a major issue of the 1980s.

Source: © *The Washington Post*, 1986. David A. Vise, "Wall Street Piqued by Greenmail," *The Washington Post*, April 3, 1986, p. E1.

The Terminology of Stock

In Chapter 22 we shall talk about the stock market and how to buy stocks. In Chapter 23 we shall discuss *personal* finance and ways for you to profit by buying stocks and making other investments. Some of the terms you should know to understand stocks are discussed here.

Stocks are shares of ownership in a company. A **stock certificate** is evidence of ownership. It usually is a piece of paper that lists the name of the company, the number of shares it represents, and the type of stock it is (see Figure 21-4). Many stock certificates indicate some face value or **par value,** which is an arbitrary dollar amount that may be nowhere near the stock's market value—the amount for which the stock is selling. A **dividend** is a part of the firm's profits that is distributed to shareholders. The dividend may be in the form of cash or more stock.

A **prospectus** is printed material that enables prospective investors to evaluate stock. The requirements for the prospectus are set by the Securities and Exchange Commission (SEC) and include extensive financial and legal information. Technically, by voting for the board of directors of a corporation,

stock certificate
Evidence of stock ownership.

par value
An arbitrary dollar amount printed on the front of a stock certificate.

dividend
Part of the firm's profits that goes to stockholders.

prospectus
Printed material that enables prospective investors to evaluate stock.

FIGURE 21-4   A sample stock certificate for Apple Computer, Inc.

proxy
A temporary transfer of voting rights from stockholders to managers.

penny stock
A stock that sells for less than $1.00.

growth stocks
Stocks of corporations whose earnings have grown rapidly in the past in comparison with the economy and are expected to continue above-average growth in the future.

common stock
The most basic form of ownership of firms; it includes voting rights and dividends, if dividends are offered by the firm.

common stockholders can influence corporate policy, because the board selects the president. In reality, however, most stockholders give their voting rights to management, especially in large firms. A **proxy** is a temporary transfer of voting rights from stockholders to managers. Stockholders usually are willing to sign proxies, but sometimes proxies are solicited from other stockholders in an attempt to replace board members.

A **penny stock** is one that sells for less than $1. Such stocks often represent ownership in mining companies and are highly speculative. Some people are attracted to such stocks, feeling a stock will more easily double by going from 50 cents to $1 than from $150 to $300. **Growth stocks** are stocks of corporations whose earnings have grown rapidly in the past in comparison with the economy and are expected to continue their above-average growth in the future. Because such companies are growing rapidly, they often pay small dividends and use the retained earnings to finance further growth.

Common stock represents ownership privileges in a firm. These privileges include the right to vote and the right to receive some of the firm's profits (dividends) when distributed by management. Shares of common stock are relatively easy to sell. Common stockholders also have the first right to purchase any new shares of stock the company issues.

Preferred stock gives its owners preference in the payment of dividends and an earlier claim on assets if the company is sold, but does not include voting rights. Often the dividend rate paid to preferred stockholders is higher than that paid to common stockholders, and it is *fixed* whereas the common dividend varies. Furthermore, preferred stockholders get their dividend payments before common stockholders are paid, and are assured that payment will be made as long as the company makes sufficient profits. Preferred stockholders lose their voting privileges in return for this preferred treatment on dividends. In some respects, a preferred stockholder is similar to a bond holder. We shall explain *bonds* as a source of long-term funding next. See Figure 21-5 for a summary of other stock categories.

preferred stock
Stock that gives owners preference in the payment of dividends and an earlier claim on assets if the business is sold but does not include voting rights.

STOCK	DESCRIPTION
Classified common stock	This stock consists of two or more classes of common stock that have different voting rights or claims on dividends. For example, class A common stock may go to the general public and class B to the original owners. Class A stock may carry no voting rights, but its holders may receive larger dividends. The owners thus retain control of the firm.
Convertible preferred (no voting rights)	This stock can be exchanged for shares of common stock at a predetermined exchange rate.
Cumulative preferred (no voting rights)	This stock pays a dividend every year. If the dividend is not paid, the amount owed accumulates and must be paid before common stockholders receive any dividends.

FIGURE 21-5

Sample of different stock available in the market.

Retained Earnings

If you look up stock prices in *The Wall Street Journal, Barrons,* or some other source, you will see that many stocks pay a dividend. The dividend rate is there for you to see, and it ranges from a few cents to many dollars per share. However, some stocks pay no dividend.

A major source of long-term funds for a firm is income that it earns from its operations. *Dividends* are merely a share of that income given to stockholders. Remember, though, that dividends are taxed twice; both the corporation and the stockholder must pay taxes on those profits. Therefore, stockholders may prefer that the company keep (retain) those profits and reinvest them. This benefits the stockholders because the company can prosper and grow using those profits. It also benefits the firm in that it has more money to use. The profits that the company keeps are called *retained earnings,* therefore, because they are retained rather than paid out in dividends.

Debt Financing

A financing alternative to selling stock (called equity or ownership financing) is to sell bonds (debt financing). With debt financing, the company has a legal obligation

FIGURE 21-6   A sample bond certificate from IBM.

to pay principal and interest payments to bond holders. A *bond* is the certificate that shows that a person has loaned money to a firm (Figure 21-6).

Bonds are usually sold in $1,000 increments. The amount of interest a company is willing to pay to borrow funds is written on the bond. How high that interest rate must be depends on how risky the company is and what the *prevailing* interest rate is. Financial institutions will assist a company in selling either stocks or bonds.

Businesses compete with the government for the sale of bonds. Some local municipal bonds are tax-free bonds; that is, the interest earned is not taxed. Bonds sold by the federal government are relatively risk free, because they are backed by the power of the government to tax us. It is possible, therefore, for the government to make the sale of corporate bonds more difficult by selling its own, more attractive bonds. This is called "crowding out" of corporate bonds.

The Terminology of Bonds

A **bond** is a contract of indebtedness issued by a corporation or governmental unit that promises payment of a principal amount at a specified future time plus interest. **Interest** is the payment the issuer of the bond makes to bondholders for use of the borrowed money. The interest rate varies based on factors such as the state of

bond
A contract of indebtedness issued by a corporation or governmental unit that promises payment of a principal amount at a specified future time plus interest.

Borrowing money from the public.

BORROWING MONEY IN INTERNATIONAL MARKETS

When you read the financial section of the newspaper, you will discover that interest rates vary for money borrowed in different countries. Often interest rates in the United States are much higher than in Europe, Japan, or other areas of the world. Therefore more and more U.S. corporations are seeking funds overseas. For example ITT Financial Corporation recently formed a subsidiary in the Antilles to gain access to foreign investors.

A $100 million bond offering in the overseas market enabled the company to obtain funds for less than they would have cost in the United States. In fact, the bonds were originally designed to be sold in the United States but the overseas market proved better. The point is that financial officers must be able to think globally when planning to raise funds. The United States is a popular place for foreign firms to invest, and financial managers should take advantage of that desire.

the economy and the rate being paid for government bonds. **Principal** refers to the "face amount" of a bond, usually stated in multiples of $1,000. Bonds that sell below face value are called **discount bonds.** Those that sell above face value are called **premium bonds.**

Term to maturity refers to the period from the purchase date of the bond to the final principal-payment date. A **call** or **refunding provision** gives the issuer the right to pay off a bond prior to maturity. If, for example, the interest rate being paid were 12% and interest rates generally fall to 6%, the issuer may recall the bond with the 12% rate and issue new ones at the lower rates. A **sinking fund** requires the issuer to retire, on a periodic basis, some part of the bond issue before its final maturity.

Advantages of Selling Bonds

Most corporations that sell stock for long-term funds also sell bonds. There must be advantages and disadvantages of each. You can probably guess at the advantages of bonds after reading about stock. They include:

- Unlike stockholders, bondholders have no vote on corporate affairs, thus management retains control over the firm. Bondholders are creditors, not owners.
- Bonds are also more flexible than stock. Whereas stockholders have ownership forever, bondholders represent more temporary sources of funds that can be tapped when needed.

Disadvantages of Selling Bonds

Bonds also have their drawbacks. Among the most significant are:

- Bonds are an increase in debt (liabilities) and may make it more difficult to obtain other financing.
- Interest on bonds is a legal obligation. A corporation cannot delay or halt such payments as they may do with dividends.
- The face amount of bonds must be paid when due, unlike stock, which carries no such obligation.
- Interest payments on bonds affect a firm's cash flow negatively in that they come out of the cash account.

interest
The payment the issuer of a bond makes to bondholders for the use of borrowed money.

principal
The face amount of a bond.

discount bonds
Bonds that sell below face value.

premium bonds
Bonds that sell above face value

term to maturity
The period from the purchase date of a bond to the final principal-payment date.

call provision
Gives the issuer of a bond the right to retire a bond before its maturity.

sinking fund
Fund that requires the issuer to retire, on a periodic basis, some part of the bond issue prior to maturity.

Various Kinds of Bonds

debenture
A bond that is unsecured, i.e., not backed with any collateral such as equipment.

secured bonds
Bonds backed by some tangible asset that is pledged to the investor if the principal is not paid back.

A bond is basically an IOU that a firm gives people and organizations that lend the company money. There are two classes of bonds. The first is called *unsecured bonds (debentures)* that have only the credit rating of the firm as protection for the investor. Only companies with excellent credit ratings can sell debentures. The second class of bond is called **secured bonds.** These bonds are backed by some tangible asset that is pledged to the investor if the principal is not paid back. There are several kinds of secured bonds:

- *Mortgage bonds* are ensured by the company's real assets such as land and buildings. They are the most common of secured bonds.
- *Collateral trust bonds* are backed by stock that the company owns and that is held in trust by a commercial bank (thus the word "trust" in the title).
- *Equipment trust bonds* are backed by the equipment the company owns. This may include trucks, aircraft, and other equipment that is widely used in industry. A trustee holds title to the equipment until the bondholders are paid. Secured bonds, therefore, are a relatively safe investment. Figure 21-7 lists various kinds of bonds and their descriptions.

FIGURE 21-7

Sample of different bonds available in the market.

BOND	DESCRIPTION
Collateral trust	These bonds are secured by the general credit of the issuer as well as the specific property for which it is issued.
Convertible bond	These bonds can be exchanged for another security, usually common stock.
Coupon bond	These bonds have coupons attached; the bondholder submits the coupons to an agent for the payment of interest.
Debenture	These bonds are secured only by the general credit of the firm plus any unpledged assets.
Mortgage bond	These bonds are secured by real property (for example, buildings).
Municipal bond	A bond issued by the state or local government; interest rates are exempt from federal taxes.
Yankee bond	These bonds are issued by a foreign government and are payable in U. S. dollars.
Zero-coupon bond	These bonds pay no interest prior to maturity; the return comes from the difference between purchase price and the face (par) value.

As you can see, there are all kinds of bonds available with different risks, and bonds for every kind of investor.

Long-Term Loans

term loan agreement
A promissory note that requires the borrower to repay the loan in installments that are specified.

Once a business is established, it can get a long-term loan from a bank, insurance company, pension fund, or other financial institution relatively easily. Long-term loans are usually repaid within 3 to 7 years, but may extend to 15. For such loans, a business must sign a term-loan agreement. A **term-loan agreement** is a promissory note that requires the borrower to repay the loan in specified installments (for example, monthly, yearly).

Most long-term loans require some form of collateral, including real estate, machinery, equipment, and stock. The interest rate for such loans is based on factors such as whether or not there is collateral, the firm's credit rating, and the general level of market interest rates.

SUMMARY CHART COMPARING STOCKS AND BONDS

STOCKS	BONDS
1 Represent *ownership* of the business	**1** Represent *debt* of the business
2 Pay *dividends* to stockholders	**2** Pay *interest* to bondholders
3 Dividends are paid from after-tax profits	**3** Interest is tax deductible for firm
4 There is no legal obligation to pay dividends	**4** Interest is a legal obligation
5 Improve the condition of the balance sheet	**5** Interest hurts cash flow and weakens the conditions of the balance sheet
6 Stockholders can vote for the board of directors	**6** Bondholders have no vote
7 Stockholders are permanent owners	**7** Bondholders can be sought for funds when needed
8 Common stock never matures	**8** Face value of bonds must be paid when due

PROGRESS CHECK

▦ What are the six ways of raising equity capital and the two major ways of raising debt capital?

▦ What are the advantages and disadvantages of selling stock to raise long-term funds?

SHORT-TERM FINANCING

The bulk of a finance manager's job is *not* involved with stocks and bonds. Small businesses rarely use stocks and bonds as sources of capital. The nitty-gritty, day-to-day operations of the firm call for careful management of short-term financial needs. Cash may be needed for additional inventory, or bills may come due unexpectedly. Much like your personal financial needs, a business sometimes needs to obtain short-term funds when other funds run out. *Short-term funds* are those that are scheduled for repayment in less than a year.

Trade Credit

The most widely used source of short-term funding is called **trade credit.** This means that a business is able to buy goods today and pay for them sometime in the future. When a firm buys merchandise, it receives an invoice (bill) much like the one you receive when you buy something on credit.

As discussed in Chapter 19, a business invoice often contains terms such as "2/10, net 30." This means that the buyer can take a 2% discount for paying within 10 days. The total bill is due in 30 days if the discount is not taken. It is

trade credit
The practice of buying goods now and paying for them later or paying for them early and getting a discount.

important for the finance manager to pay attention to such discounts. In fact, they are so important, that the example is worth repeating here: If the discount is 2/10, net 30, the purchaser will pay 2 percent more for waiting an extra 20 days to pay the invoice. Some unsophisticated people feel that 2% is insignificant, and pay their bills after the discount period. Some quick calculations will show how costly such delay really is.

By not paying on time, the firm pays 2% for waiting just 20 days. If this continues over time, the firm would lose 2% for every 20-day period it doesn't pay its bills early. There are about eighteen 20-day periods in a year. Therefore the penalty for not taking discounts is approximately 36% a year ($18 \times 2\%$). Because about 10% of business transactions involve trade credit, this is an important element in the daily financial management of the firm.

Family and Friends

A second source of short-term funds for most smaller firms is money lent to them by family and friends. Because short-term funds are needed for periods of less than a year, often friends are willing to help. Such loans can be dangerous if the firm does not understand cash flow. As we discussed earlier, the firm may suddenly find several bills coming due at the same time and have no other sources of funds. It is better, therefore, not to borrow from friends, but instead go to a commercial bank that understands the risk and can help analyze future financial needs. If you do borrow from family or friends, it is best to be very professional about the deal and (1) agree on terms at the beginning, (2) write an agreement, and (3) pay them back the same way you would a bank loan.

Commercial Banks

As we discussed in Chapter 19, small to medium-sized businesses should have the person in charge of the finance function keep in very close touch with a local bank. It is wise to see a banker periodically (as often as once a month) and send the banker all financial statements.

A financial manager may obtain funds from a finance company, but the interest rates are usually higher than other sources. Commercial bank rates are usually lower.

Try to imagine different kinds of businesspeople going to the bank for a loan, and you'll get a better feel for the role of the finance manager. Picture, for example, a farmer going to the bank to borrow funds for seed, fertilizer, equipment, and other needs. Such supplies may be bought in the spring and paid for when the fall harvest comes in. Now picture a local toy store buying merchandise for Christmas sales. The money for such purchases might be borrowed in June and July and paid back after Christmas. A restaurant may borrow funds at the beginning of the month and pay by the end of the month. Can you see that *how much* a business borrows and for *how long* depends on the kind of business it is and how quickly the merchandise purchased with a bank loan can be resold or used to generate funds?

Have you ever found yourself going to the bank to take out funds for special emergencies such as a car accident? Sometimes such unexpected money needs arise monthly. One month it's a dentist bill, the next a need for snow tires, and so on. There are vacations to pay for, school supplies, Christmas presents, and more.

Similarly, a businessperson may have to go to the bank and borrow short-term funds often. A new shipment of goods may arrive unexpectedly, a machine may break down, an insurance bill may come due, and so forth.

Like you, a business sometimes finds itself in a position where many bills come due at once: utilities, insurance, payroll, new equipment, and more. Most times such sudden cash needs can be met; one can always ask the bank for more. But sometimes a business gets so far into debt, so far behind in its payments, that the bank refuses to lend it more. Suddenly the business is unable to pay its bills. More often than not, this results in bankruptcy or business failure, and you can chalk up another business failure to cash flow problems.

Can you see now how important it is for the finance or accounting person to do a cash flow forecast? By anticipating times when many bills will come due, a business can begin early to seek funds or sell other assets to prepare for the crunch. Can you see also why it is important for a businessperson to keep friendly and close relations with his or her banker? The banker may spot cash flow problems early and point out the danger. Or, the banker may be more willing to lend money in a crisis if the businessperson has established a strong, friendly relationship built on openness and trust.

Different Forms of Bank Loans

The most difficult kind of loan to get from a bank or other financial institution is an **unsecured loan.** It is a loan that is not backed by any collateral.

unsecured loan
A loan not backed by any collateral.

Loans are often secured by inventory or machinery.

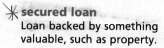**secured loan**
Loan backed by something
valuable, such as property.

A **secured loan** is one backed by something valuable, such as property. If the borrower fails to pay the loan, the lender may take possession of the collateral. That takes some of the risk out of lending money. *Pledging* is the term used for using accounts receivable as security. Some percentage of accounts receivable is accepted as collateral, and the cash received as payment for the merchandise is sent to the banker. **Inventory financing** means that inventory such as raw materials (for example, coal, steel) or other inventory is used as collateral for a loan. Other property can be used as collateral, including buildings, machinery, and other things of value (for example, company-owned stocks and bonds). If you develop a good relationship with a bank, it will open a line of credit for you.

inventory financing
Financing that uses inventory
such as raw materials as collateral for a loan.

Line of Credit

In the Profile about Danny Noble, Ltd., you read that at one point a bank gave the firm a **line of credit.** That means the bank will lend the business a given amount of unsecured short-term funds, provided the bank has the funds available. A line of credit is not a *guaranteed* loan, but it comes close. The purpose of a line of credit is to speed the borrowing process so that a firm does not have to go through the hassle of applying for a new loan every time it needs funds. The funds are available as long as the credit ceiling is not exceeded. Note that the amount of credit granted in the Danny Noble, Ltd. example was increased as the firm became more financially secure. A **revolving credit agreement** is a line of credit that is guaranteed. The bank usually charges a fee for guaranteeing the loan, a fee that applies to the unused balance of the account.

line of credit
The amount of unsecured
short-term credit a bank will
lend a borrower that is agreed
to ahead of time.

**revolving credit
agreement**
A line of credit that is guaranteed by the bank.

**SOURCES OF SHORT-TERM
FINANCING**
- Trade credit
- Family and friends
- Commercial banks
- Factoring
- Commercial paper
- Internal sources

Factoring

One relatively expensive source of funds for a firm is called *factoring*. The way it works is this: A firm sells many of its products on credit to consumers and other businesses. Some of these buyers are slow in paying their bills. The company may thus have a large amount of money due in accounts receivable. A *factor* buys the accounts receivable from the firm for cash (paying 50% to 70% of the value of the accounts receivable). The factor then collects the money due the firm. **Factoring,** then, is the process of selling accounts receivable for cash. How much this costs the firm depends on the rate the factor charges for this service. The discount rate for factoring depends on the *age* of the accounts receivable, the nature of the business, and the conditions of the economy.

factoring
Selling accounts receivable for
cash.

THE PRIME RATE

Periodically you will read that the *prime rate* has been raised or lowered. For most people, that report has little meaning. But for a financial manager, the level of the prime rate is very important. Here is why. The prime rate is the short-term interest rate that banks charge their preferred customers. Most firms pay slightly more than the prime rate for a loan, but some very good credit risks can negotiate loans below prime. In either case, the prime rate is the rate from which many loan rates are calculated.

Commercial Paper

Sometimes a large corporation needs funds for a few months and wants to get lower rates than those charged by banks. One strategy is to sell commercial paper. **Commercial paper** consists of promissory notes, in amounts ranging from $25,000 up, that mature in 270 days or less. Commercial paper is unsecured, so only the more financially stable firms can sell it. It is a way to get short-term funds for less than bank rates. Commercial paper is also a place where buyers of commercial paper can put cash for short periods to earn some interest.

commercial paper
A short-term corporate equivalent of an IOU that is sold in the marketplace by a firm. They mature in 270 days or less.

Internal Sources of Funds

Just like you and me, a business is wise to get its short-term funds from internal sources as much as possible. There are several ways a firm can generate more cash internally. One way is to collect accounts receivable more quickly. Often the company accountant works with the other finance people to find such sources of funds. Inventory may be reduced, costs may be reduced, or expenses may be cut. The healthier the balance sheet looks and the better the financial ratios are, the easier it is to borrow outside funds, if that is necessary. A wise accounting/finance team is able to save a business much money by finding internal sources of funds and freeing them, and by getting external funding at minimal rates (such as selling commercial paper).

PROGRESS CHECK

- What are the advantages and disadvantages of selling bonds to raise long-term capital?
- What is the difference between trade credit and a line of credit at a bank?

THE ROMANCE OF FINANCE

Cold, factual descriptions of what finance does cannot convey the drama and importance of finance in real life. Only a real-life example can do that. The box on p. 592 gives you a better feel for the excitement of finance. The problem in the example is how to raise and most efficiently spend the *billions* of dollars needed to make America's steel mills competitive again. Note the critical role finance plays in that problem.

THINKING IT THROUGH

After reading through the stories about finances at Danny Noble, Ltd. and Bethlehem Steel Corporation, does the job seem interesting to you? Do you understand the difference between stocks and bonds? Can you see the need for creatively obtaining short-term funds? Even if finance does not seem like an attractive career to you, you should spend some time reading about it. To understand business, you must understand the language of business—accounting—and the funding of business—finance.

STEEL COMPANIES TURN TO CREATIVE FINANCING

Creative financing is helping the steel industry to get back on its feet. For example, Bethlehem Steel's finance department recently halved its unfunded pension liability. The company sold $700 million of the stock in its $2.4 billion pension fund and switched into high-yield bonds. This saved the company $50 million in its annual pension-fund contributions. From late 1982 to fall of 1984, Bethlehem arranged $1.25 billion in special financing. The finance department accomplished as much in 2 years as it had in the previous 15—with a staff of 93, compared with 165 before 1982.

Financial executives at Bethlehem are often part of interdepartmental teams that are formed to accomplish specific tasks. A team may include departments such as law, accounting, and engineering. One such team recently completed a $540 million leasing arrangement. The deal took more than a year to complete. The fi-

nancial planning manager made eight trips to Austria to confer with a state-owned concern that won the contract to build needed machinery. Eight drafts of four separate documents were written, totaling more than 12,000 pages.

The finance department at Bethlehem is also arranging the sale of $500 million in assets and screening potential acquisitions for diversification. All in all, finance has become a critical function at Bethlehem Steel.

U. S. Steel made $200 million in improvements at its Gary, Indiana plant through a leasing arrangement with two Japanese lenders. U. S. Steel sold tax benefits to build a $750 million pipe-making plant that it now leases. Other stories could be told of creative financing to support the rebuilding of America's manufacturing base.

Source: Thomas F. O'Boyle, "Steel Companies Give Their Finance Staffs More Prominent Role in Solving Problems," *The Wall Street Journal*, August 8, 1984, p. 33.

FINANCIAL PLANNING

financial planning
Designed to provide a short-run and long-run picture of money flows to and from the firm with the objective of optimizing profits and making the best use of money.

It should be clear by now that the obtaining and managing of funds are as crucial to a business as manufacturing, marketing, or any other function. Good financial management begins with planning. **Financial planning** is designed to provide a short-run and long-run picture of money flows to and from the firm. The overall objective is to optimize profits and make the best use of money. We could all use more or better financial planning, so let's look at what is involved (see Figure 21-8).

Short-Term Forecasting tactical

short-term forecast
A prediction of revenues, costs, and expenses for a period of 1 year or less.

A **short-term forecast** is a prediction of revenues, costs, and expenses for a period of 1 year or less. This forecast is the foundation for most other financial plans, so its accuracy is critical. Part of short-term forecasting may be a cash-flow forecast. That is, the forecaster must ask at the end of each month, what will be the condition of the cash account? Naturally, the cash flow forecast is based on the forecast of sales revenues and on various costs and expenses and when they will come due.

long-term forecast
A prediction of revenues, costs, and expenses for a period longer than 1 year, sometimes extending 5 or 10 years into the future.

Long-Term Forecasting   strategic

A **long-term forecast** is a prediction of revenues, costs, and expenses for a period longer than 1 year, sometimes as far as 5 or 10 years into the future. This forecast plays a crucial part in the company's long-term strategic plan. The strategic plan

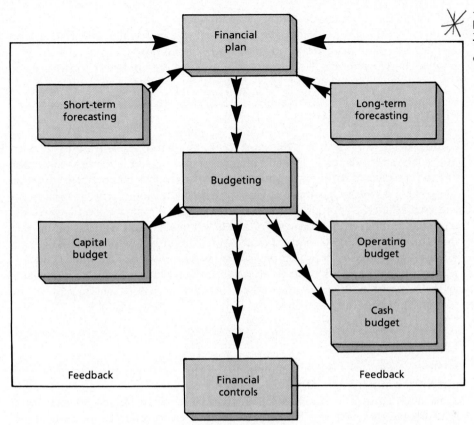

FIGURE 21-8

The financial planning and control process.

asks questions such as: What business are we in and should we be in the next 5 years? How much money should we invest in automation and new plant and equipment over the next decade? The long-term financial forecast gives top management some feel for the income or profit potential possible with different strategic plans.

BUDGETING

Long-term and short-term forecasts eventually are used to establish yearly budgets for a firm. There are usually several budgets:

- ■ An operating budget ·*DAY to DAY Daily*
- ■ A cash budget - *LONG TERM LAND*
- ■ A capital budget - *KNOWING BORROWING DAILY*

An operating budget is the projection of dollar allocations to various costs and expenses, given projected revenues.

The cash budget is the projected cash balance at the end of a given period (for example, monthly, quarterly).

The capital budget is the spending plan for assets whose returns are expected to occur over an extended period of time (more than 1 year). Some schools have whole courses on capital budgeting. At this point, what is important for you to know is that the financial officer plays a crucial role in deciding which long-term investments to purchase, based on an analysis of the returns (or profits) alternative investments would bring. We shall now discuss an important aspect of this analysis.

FINANCIAL CONTROLS

Inadequate expense control is the third most common financial reason why businesses fail (after poor cash flow and undercapitalization). It is the function of the finance department to monitor such expenses to see that controls are adequate.

financial control
A process that periodically compares the actual revenue, costs, and expenses with projections.

Once a company has projected its short-term and long-term financial needs and established the appropriate budgets to show how funds will be allocated, the final step in funds management is to establish **financial control.** This means that the actual revenues, costs, and expenses (including cash flow predictions) are periodically compared with projections. Deviations can thus be determined and corrective action taken. Such controls help reveal which accounts, which departments, and which people are varying from the plan. Such deviations may or may not be justified. In either case, some financial adjustment must be made.

Spreadsheet Analysis

spreadsheet analysis
A technique for determining the effect on one account of changes in other accounts.

A few years ago, when personal computers were just becoming popular, a company named VisiCorp introduced VisiCalc and opened up a whole new way of looking at business figures. The concept is called spreadsheet analysis. **Spreadsheet analysis** is a computerized technique for determining quickly the effect on one account of changes in other accounts. For example, a business can quickly calculate the effect on profit of a change in interest rates, a lowering of product prices, or an increase in shipping charges. Another popular program today is Lotus 1-2-3.

A Lotus 1-2-3 spreadsheet.

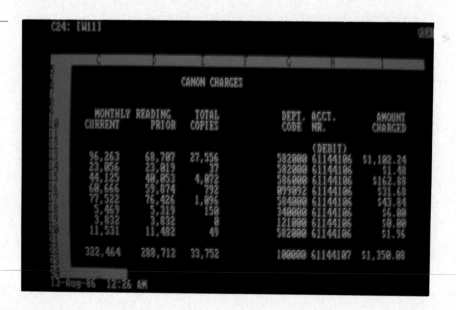

A spreadsheet is nothing more than an electronic grid. The user puts data into the rows and columns, and each intersecting block has a calculator that adds, subtracts, multiplies, or divides at great speed. The program begins with simple inserts, such as profit equals sales minus costs, or $C = A - B$. Any increase in A (sales) will result automatically in an increase in C (profit), given the simple formula.

After a financial model is built (and this is relatively easy to do), a user can begin playing with the numbers, asking "what if" questions. For example, if a computer retailer buys computers at $800 each and sells them for $1,000 each, he makes $200 per sale. On an average, he may sell 10 machines a week for a profit of $2,000. What if, anticipating he can sell 20 computers a week by discounting, he lowers his price by $50? What if, furthermore, his higher volume enables him to buy his machines at a bulk price $50 lower, but on the other hand requires him to hire an employee at $300 a week to handle the additional customers? By entering the altered values into the model he or she has constructed, the retailer immediately discovers the new profit level: $3,700.

Imagine a new restaurant owner trying to calculate start-up money requirements. He or she could enter various food costs and prices, cash flow, growth projections, and so on to determine capital needs. Similarly, a magazine publisher could forecast the circulation levels required for various projected selling prices and anticipated advertising revenues.[4] As you can see, spreadsheet analysis is one of the most helpful uses of a personal computer for small business entrepreneurs. It enables them to make all kinds of assumptions and test their impact immediately.

Because of the potential, spreadsheet programs have grown very rapidly. There are now hundreds of such programs available. Some have tutorial and on-line assistance features that make it easy to learn how to enter the data and do the analyses.

Spreadsheet analysis is a great aid to accountants and finance people as well. Spreadsheet analysis is helpful in evaluating alternative financing arrangements, changes in credit policies, and a host of other financial decisions.

TAX PREPARATION

Today's financial manager needs to be aware of all the strategies companies can use to avoid or defer taxes. None of this is illegal, mind you; it is simply minimizing the tax burden, as all citizens are trying to do.

The link between accounting and finance is clearest when the discussion swings to taxes, because creative accounting practices help minimize taxes. There are literally hundreds of ways corporations can take advantage of the tax codes to minimize their tax burden.

Most increases in corporate taxes are passed on to consumers in the form of higher prices for goods paid. It is one of the finance department's functions to see to it that corporate taxes are kept at a minimum so that everyone benefits—stockholders, employers, and the general public, who can buy the goods and services for less.

PROGRESS CHECK

- What is the difference between an operating budget, a cash budget, and a capital budget?

- What is involved in financial planning for a firm?

SUMMARY

1 *Finance* is that function in a business responsible for acquiring funds for the firm, managing funds within the firm (for example, preparing budgets, doing cash flow analysis), and planning for the expenditure of funds on various assets.

■ What do finance managers do?

   Plan, budget, control funds, obtain funds, collect funds, audit, manage taxes, and advise top management on financial matters.

2 One of the important functions of a finance manager is to obtain long-term capital. *Long-term financing* is money obtained from the owners of the firm and lenders who do not expect repayment within 1 year.

■ What are the two major sources of long-term capital?

   Equity capital: personal savings, friends, and family loans, partners, venture-capital firms, sale of stock, and retained earnings.

   Debt capital: sale of bonds and long-term loans from banks and other financial institutions.

■ What is *venture capital*?

   Money that is invested in new companies with great profit potential.

■ What are the advantages and disadvantages of selling stock for long-term financing?

   The advantages include the fact that owners need not be repaid, there is no legal obligation to pay dividends (so income can be reinvested), it improves the financial condition of the firm, and it is relatively easy to do. The disadvantages include the fact that owners can vote and affect management, it is a relatively expensive form of fund raising, and it forces management to be short-term, stockholder oriented.

■ What are other kinds of stock?

   Common stockholders can vote. If a firm wants to maintain its control over management, it may sell *preferred stock,* which carries no vote. The way to encourage stockholders to buy preferred stock is by paying a larger, fixed dividend and assuring its payment.

■ What are *retained earnings*?

   Profits retained by the firm rather than paid out in dividends.

3 There are two major forms of long-term debt financing: selling bonds and borrowing from banks and other financial institutions.

■ What is a bond?

   It is a contract of indebtedness that promises to pay the owner a principal amount (the face amount of the bond) plus interest. A bondholder is a *debtor* of the firm whereas a stockholder is an *owner*.

■ What are the advantages and disadvantages of raising long-term funds using bonds?

   The advantages are that bond interest is tax deductible, bondholders have no vote, and bonds are a more flexible financing vehicle. The disadvantages are that bonds are an increase in debt and may hurt chances for other financing, interest is a legal obligation, the face amount must be paid when due, and interest payments hurt cash flow.

■ Why are there different kinds of bonds?

   Different bonds appeal to different investors. Some investors want to pay no taxes on interest (municipal bonds); others want no interest, just appreciation in value (zero-coupon bonds); others want to be able to trade the bonds for stock (convertible bonds); and so on.

- What is the problem with getting long-term funds from financial institutions?
    You need good credit and most banks demand collateral.
4 As in long-term financing, there are many sources for short-term financing including trade credit, family and friends, commercial banks, factoring, commercial paper, and internal sources.
- Why should businesses use trade credit?
    Because even terms of 2/10, net 30 mean a savings of about 36% annually.
- What is a *line of credit*?
    It is an agreement by a bank to loan a specified amount of money to the business at any time, if the money is available. A *revolving credit agreement* is a line of credit that *guarantees* a loan will be available for a fee.
- What is the difference between a secured loan and an unsecured loan?
    An *unsecured loan* has no collateral backing it. A *secured* loan is backed by accounts receivable (called *pledging*), inventory, or other property of value.
- Is factoring a form of secured loan?
    No, *factoring* means *selling* accounts receivable at a discount.
- What is commercial paper?
    A promissory note maturing at 270 days or less.
5 Financial planning involves short- and long-term forecasting, budgeting, and financial controls.
- What are the three budgets of finance?
    The *cash budget* is the projected cash balance at the end of a given period. The *operating budget* is the projection of dollar allocations to various costs and expenses given various revenues. The *capital budget* is the spending plan for assets whose returns take over a year.
- What is *spreadsheet analysis*?
    A technique for determining quickly the effect on one account (for example, profit) by a change in another account (for example, sales).

KEY TERMS

bond   p. 584
call provision   p. 585
commercial paper   p. 591
common stock   p. 582
debenture   p. 586
debt capital   p. 579
discount bonds   p. 585
dividend   p. 581
equity financing   p. 580
factoring   p. 590
finance   p. 576
financial control   p. 594
financial plan   p. 578
financial planning   p. 592
growth stocks   p. 582
internal auditor   p. 578
interest   p. 585
inventory financing   p. 590
line of credit   p. 590
long-term financing   p. 578
long-term forecast   p. 592
par value   p. 581
penny stock   p. 582
principal   p. 585
preferred stock   p. 583
premium bonds   p. 585
prospectus   p. 581
proxy   p. 582
retained earnings   p. 578
revolving credit agreement   p. 590
secured bonds   p. 586
secured loan   p. 590
short-term forecast   p. 592
sinking fund   p. 585
spreadsheet analysis   p. 594

stock certificate   p. 581
stocks   p. 580
tax management   p. 576
term loan agreement   p. 586
term to maturity   p. 585

trade credit   p. 587
treasurer   p. 576
unsecured loan   p. 589
venture capital   p. 578

GETTING INVOLVED

1 Go to the library and find books on corporate finance. Briefly read through them and see what they cover, especially material that is not discussed in this chapter. Make notes and share what you found in class.

2 While you are in the library, look up *Venture* magazine and see what other financial magazines are carried. Look through several issues of *at least* two financial journals and report what is in them to class.

3 Continue your exploration of the library by looking up the *Standard & Poors* and *Value Line* reports. Ask the librarian what similar references are available. Report what you find to the class.

4 While in the library, find the last six issues of *Money* magazine. Look through them and see what kind of resource it could be in the future.

5 Spend another day at the library exploring other finance texts, journals, and newsletters. Report your most interesting discoveries to the class.

PRACTICING MANAGEMENT DECISIONS

CASE ONE   MERGERS AND TAKEOVERS

The 1980s witnessed a merger-mania as important as any in history. Some of the deals were huge. There was the purchase of Conoco by Du Pont in 1981 for $7.4 billion. In 1982, U.S. Steel bought Marathon Oil for $6.5 billion. In 1983, the merger of the Southern Pacific and Santa Fe Railroads took place, a $5.2 billion deal. In 1984 and 1985, Chevron purchased Gulf for $13.4 billion and RCA bought GE for $6.3 billion.

Not every firm wanted to merge or be taken over by another firm, however. Such mergers affect all aspects of the firm, including management control and stock values. When a firm tries to take control of another firm against the wishes of the takeover firm's management, it is called a "hostile takeover."

Some terms you have seen in the papers are confusing; terms that refer to takeover attempts and strategies for stopping them. One term is *white knight*. If a firm fears being taken over (purchased) by a firm that might fire top management or sell off valuable assets, it may seek another, more friendly firm to buy it instead. The friendly firm is called a "white knight" because it saves the firm from the hostile takeover "dragon."

If a firm tries to purchase the stock of another firm against its will, the takeover target may offer to buy the stock back at an inflated price. Buying back the stock is called *greenmail* because it's like blackmailing the purchaser by paying him off in greenbacks (money).

A popular tactic to avoid takeovers is to make the firm unattractive by piling up lots of debt in the form of *junk bonds* (bonds that are not highly rated, with little or no security behind them). No one wants to buy a firm with a poor debt position.

On the other hand, one way to acquire firms is by using junk bonds as funds to acquire the firm. Junk bonds are used in the 1980s to both acquire firms and to prevent being acquired. Remember, a junk bond is one that is more risky because it does not have any backing behind it and has a higher default rate than investment-grade bonds.

DECISION QUESTIONS

1 What does the rash of mergers and acquisitions say about the perceived value of firms by other firms?
2 If firms are going into debt to acquire other firms and takeover candidates are going into debt to prevent being acquired, what does that say about the financial strength of major firms today that are involved in such matters?
3 The federal government is deeply in debt. Consumers are also deeply in debt. Now, major corporations are going into debt financing. What does all this debt do to the strength of the economy?

CASE TWO   SEARS: THE FINANCIAL SUPERMARKET

PRACTICING MANAGEMENT DECISIONS

The new Chairman of Sears Roebuck and Company, Edward Brennan, believes that the company has all the parts it needs to offer a total financial package to consumers. This may be so, but the task of marketing this financial empire is yet to be completed. Sears has been called a *financial supermarket* because you can go there to buy life insurance, real estate, stocks, bonds, mutual funds, and consumer goods with Sears' own Discover credit card.

Sears is uniquely positioned to offer such services because it has such a huge customer base and is located in so many towns and cities. Furthermore, Sears has a reputation for dependability. Will Sears' reputation carry over into its financial operations? Can one company be so many things to so many people and still be effective?

DECISION QUESTIONS

1 What do you perceive as the advantages and disadvantages of having Sears as your broker and real estate agent?
2 Can you imagine other retail stores joining Sears in moving into financial services? Will such financial supermarkets provide a real challenge to traditional banks, brokers, and real estate firms?
3 Is it healthy for the economy to have a few, large firms dominant in both retailing and financial services? Why or why not?

LOOKING AHEAD

This chapter looked at finance from the viewpoint of the firm. The next chapter looks at stocks and bonds and other investment topics from the point of view of the investor. You will learn about the stock exchanges, how to buy and sell stock, how to choose the right investment, how to read the stock and bond quotations in *The Wall Street Journal* and other newspapers, and more. Finance takes on a whole new dimension when you see how you can participate in financial markets yourself.

STOCKS AND BONDS

LEARNING GOALS

After you have read and studied this chapter, you should be able to:

■ Identify the various stock exchanges.

■ Describe methods used to buy or sell stock listed on the stock exchanges.

■ Discuss five criteria used to select investment vehicles.

■ Describe mutual funds, the bond market, and commodities exchanges.

■ Understand securities quotations listed in the financial section of a newspaper.

■ Discuss regulation of securities trading.

PROFILE CHRISTOPHER FUNK, COMMODITY FUND MANAGER

Christopher Funk majored in neurophysiology at Purdue University. So how did he get involved in buying and selling commodities? Christopher's father operated a corn-seed business, and asked his son for help in devising corn futures strategies; that is, buying and selling corn for delivery sometime in the future. Christopher became fascinated by the process, and soon bought a seat (membership) on the Chicago Board of Trade. He spent several years learning the business and then left to form an investment management firm. He now co-manages Thompson Financial Partners I, a public commodity fund.

In 1985, Thompson Financial Partners I finished first among 72 funds with a 90% gain; the average gain for all funds was only 15.6%. This was the second year in a row that his fund was number one. Funk's own firm, Christopher M. Funk & Company, has averaged a 35% return over 11 years.

Clearly, Christopher Funk has been a man to follow. Most people know little about commodity markets, so investing with an expert like Christopher Funk can lead to a huge financial gain. ■

Source: John N. Frank, "Christopher Funk," *Business Week*, April 18, 1986, p. 218.

Christopher Funk.

If you're so smart, why aren't you rich?
ANONYMOUS

SECURITIES MARKETS

securities markets
Organizations that enable businesses and investors to buy and sell stocks, bonds, and mutual funds.

Corporations and individuals have several ways to make money. One way is to produce and sell goods and services. Another is to take the income from such ventures and invest it wisely. This chapter will explore the stock market and other ways to invest money, including commodities. Learning how to invest money is as important as learning how to earn it in the first place.

Securities markets are organizations that enable businesses and investors to buy and sell stocks, bonds, and mutual funds. Businesses benefit from securities markets by obtaining the capital they need to begin operations, expand, and buy goods and services. Securities markets also offer businesses a way to earn additional funds with their income. Investors also benefit from the securities markets, because it gives them a convenient place to buy and sell stocks, bonds, and mutual funds.

You will learn about securities markets in this chapter. If you make it a habit to read *The Wall Street Journal, Forbes,* and other business journals over time, you can learn more about securities and find out how to invest money wisely. Each year *The Wall Street Journal* publishes an Educational Edition that explains all the various sections in the paper. It would be wise to order a copy of that edition and spend some time learning the wealth of information available in *The Wall Street Journal.*

STOCK EXCHANGES

stock exchange
An organization whose members can buy and sell securities to the public.

As its name implies, a **stock exchange** is an organization whose members can buy and sell securities for the public. There are stock exchanges all over the world in cities such as Paris, London, Madrid, Sydney, Buenos Aires, and Tokyo. These exchanges enable businesses and individuals to buy securities from companies almost anywhere in the world. If you hear of a foreign company that has great

The Tokyo Stock Exchange.

potential for growth, you can usually obtain shares of stock with little difficulty from a U.S. broker who has access to the foreign stock exchanges.

U.S. Exchanges

The largest stock exchange in the United States is the New York Stock Exchange (NYSE). It does about 80% of all stock trading. The second-largest exchange in the United States is the American Stock Exchange (AMEX). It manages less than 10% of all exchanges. These two exchanges are called **national exchanges** because they handle stocks of companies from all over the United States.

In addition to the national exchanges, there are several *regional exchanges* in cities such as Chicago (Midwest), San Francisco (Pacific Coast), Philadelphia, Boston, Cincinnati, Spokane, and Salt Lake City. These regional exchanges deal mostly with firms in their own areas. Approximately 12% of all security trading done on America's organized stock exchanges occurs in these regional exchanges.

national exchanges
Exchanges that handle stocks of companies all over the United States (the New York Stock Exchange and the American Stock Exchange).

The Over-the-Counter (OTC) Market

The **over-the-counter (OTC) market** provides a means to trade stocks not listed on the national securities exchanges. The OTC market is made up of a network of several thousand brokers. These brokers maintain contact with each other and buy and sell securities for the public. A nationwide electronic system communicates trades to the brokers. The system is known as the National Association of Securities Dealers Automated Quotation system (**NASDAQ**—pronounced *"nazz-dak"*).

Originally the over-the-counter market dealt mostly with small firms that could not qualify for listing on the national exchanges or did not want to bother with the procedures. Today, however, well-known firms such as Apple, MCI, and Coors prefer to have their stock traded on the OTC market.

The over-the-counter market also handles most corporate and U.S. government bonds as well as many city and state government bonds. Common stock of most insurance companies and banks as well as the stock of many smaller firms is traded over-the-counter. If you look in *The Wall Street Journal* under "NASDAQ Bid and Ask Quotations," you will see that the price of over-the-counter stocks is determined by supply and demand as reflected in "bid" and "ask" prices.

over-the-counter (OTC) market
Exchange that provides a means to trade stocks not listed on the national exchanges.

NASDAQ
National Association of Securities Dealers Automated Quotation system.

COMPUTER SECURITIES TRADING

Computers are revolutionizing many industries, including stockbroking. It is now possible to obtain all kinds of stock information on your personal computer and to buy and sell stocks, all without human contact.

You can enter trades by writing an electronic order ticket. It is transmitted by phone to the brokerage's computers and then to its trading desk. A confirmation notice will appear on your computer screen.

Some restrictions apply to such computer trades. At Max Ule & Company, for example, computer orders can be made only after working hours. The fees vary for such services, and the services are getting more complex. Some brokerage houses now let clients check their portfolios, obtain research data, and make trades by computer. *Forbes* feels such advances are making customer-contact people an endangered species in this industry.

Source: Ruth Simon, *Forbes,* April 30, 1984, p. 130. © *Forbes* Inc., 1984.

HOW TO BUY STOCK

stockbroker
A middleman who buys and sells securities for clients.

The procedure for buying and selling stock is not at all difficult. First, you have to decide what stock or stocks you want to buy. That is the most difficult procedure. After deciding, you would call a stockbroker. A **stockbroker** is a middleman who buys and sells securities for clients. You would tell the broker what you want and the price you want to pay. The broker would call a member of the stock exchange who represents the firm for which the broker works. That member would go to the place where the stock you want is traded and negotiate a price. When the transaction is completed, the trade will be reported back to the broker, who will call you. The same procedure is followed to sell a stock. If you want, the broker will keep the stock certificates for you so that you can sell them easily and quickly, with just a telephone call.

Market Orders and Limit Orders

market order
Tells the broker to buy stock at the best price obtainable in the market now.

limit order
Tells the broker to purchase stock at a specific price.

When investors buy stock, they have an option on how to place the order. A **market order** tells the broker to buy stock at the best price obtainable in the market at the time. The order can be processed very quickly, and the trade price can be given to the investor in minutes. A **limit order** tells the broker to purchase stock at a *specific price*. Let's say, for example, that a stock is selling for $40 a share, and you feel it is likely to drop a little before it goes higher. You could, for example, place a limit order at $38, and the broker would purchase the stock at that amount (or lower if the stock were trading at a lower amount when the sale was completed). If the stock never fell to $38, no order would be processed.

A stockbroker at work.

Buying on Margin

Buying on margin involves the purchase of stocks by borrowing some of the purchase cost from the broker. Margin refers to the amount of equity an investor must have in the stock. Thus, if the margin is 40% the investor may borrow 60% of the stock's purchase price. Currently the Federal Reserve limits such borrowing to 50% of the market value. The investor's idea is to buy additional shares of a stock that he or she believes is going up in value. This increases the return to the investor, but also increases the risk. If the stock goes down, the investor loses money faster, in addition to paying interest on the borrowed funds. Buying on margin is more appropriate for speculators than investors.

buying on margin
The purchase of stocks by borrowing some of the purchase cost from the broker.

Odd Lot Trading

Stock purchases are conducted in **round lots,** that is, 100 shares at a time. Many investors cannot afford to buy 100 shares of a stock such as IBM, which may be selling for $150 or so per share, because the total cost would be $15,000. Such investors buy in **odd lots**—purchases of less than 100 shares. Such transactions are combined to make round lots, and then the shares are distributed accordingly.

round lots
100 shares of stock.

odd lots
A purchase of less than 100 shares of stock.

Stock Splits

To make it easier for investors to buy in round lots, companies often conduct **stock splits;** that is, they issue two or more shares for every share outstanding. For example, if IBM were selling for $150, it could declare a five-for-one split. Everyone who owned one share of IBM would then own five shares—but each share would be worth only $30. A round lot would then cost $3,000 instead of $15,000, which is a more manageable amount for investors. The advantage to the company is that it may be able to sell more shares at lower prices. The advantage to shareholders is that the demand for $30 shares may be greater than the demand for $150 shares, and the stock price may go up.

stock splits
Giving stockholders two or more shares of stock for each one they own.

Bulls and Bears

Two of the more frequently heard terms regarding investors are *bulls* and *bears*. **Bulls** are investors who believe that stock prices are going to rise. They buy stock in anticipation of the increase. When stock prices are rising, it is called a *bull market*.

Bears are investors who expect stock prices to decline. They would tend to sell their stocks before the prices fell. An investor can borrow stock from a stockbroker and sell it, hoping to buy the stock later at a lower price and return it to the broker. This is known as **selling short.** It is a way to make money when stock prices are going down. When the prices of stocks decline steadily, it is known as a *bear market*.

bulls
Investors who believe that stock prices are going to rise.

bears
Investors who expect stock prices to decline.

selling short
Borrowing stock from a broker and selling it, hoping to buy the stock later at a lower price and return it to the broker.

PROGRESS CHECK

■ Where are the bonds issued by city and state governments sold?

■ What does "buying on margin" mean?

■ What does "selling short" mean?

CHOOSING THE RIGHT INVESTMENT

investing
Committing capital with the expectation of making a profit.

Broadly speaking, **investing** means committing capital with the expectation of making a profit. *Active investing* means that the investor makes the decisions on how his or her money is invested, as in starting a business or buying real estate. *Passive investing* means that the investor commits funds, but someone else decides on the specific use of them. Investing in a mutual fund is a form of passive investing.

Investment Criteria

The first step in an investment program is to analyze the specific situation of the individual investor or organization. An analysis must be made of the situation in terms of income desired, cash requirements, and approximate level of risk.

FIGURE 22-1

Total returns on various investments, 1983 and 1984. Note that no one investment is good for all time. Stocks were up over 26% in 1983 (Dow Jones average), but only 1.35% in 1984. On the other hand, bank CDs went up from 6.18% in 1983 to 9.91% in 1984.

Source: *The Wall Street Journal*, January 2, 1985.

INVESTMENT	TOTAL RETURN*	
	1983	1984
Stocks		
Dow Jones Industrial Average (30 stocks)	26.06%	1.35%
Standard & Poor's 500 Stock Index	22.38	6.10
Wilshire 5000 Stock Index	23.45	3.05†
Bonds		
Shearson Lehman Long Term Treasury Index	1.99	14.68
Shearson Lehman Long Term AA-rated Bond Index	6.57	16.10†
Mutual Funds		
Lipper Growth Fund Index	22.13	−2.79
Lipper Growth and Income Fund Index	23.44	1.41
One-Year Certificate of Deposit		
Bank Rate Monitor National Index	6.18	9.91
Money Market Fund		
Donoghue's 12 month yield on all taxable money funds	8.58	10.04
Gold		
100 oz. bar of bullion	−14.5	−18.6
Silver		
1000 oz. bar of bullion	−17.5	−25.9
Residential Real Estate		
National Association of Homebuilder's yield on average priced new single family home	7	8.1
Art		
Sotheby's Old Master Paintings Index	16.6	16.3

*Includes reinvestment of dividends, if any.
†Estimate.

The second step is to select *general* investment vehicles that best fit the specific needs of the investor. For example, investors should decide how much, if any, of their assets should be committed to real estate, stocks, bonds, commodities (for example, silver or gold), bank accounts, and other investment choices. Figure 22-1 shows the returns for various general investments in 1983 and 1984.

The third step is to select specific investments within the general areas. For example, should the investor choose corporate bonds or tax-free municipal bonds? There are five criteria to use when selecting an investment vehicle: (1) investment risk, (2) yield, (3) duration, (4) liquidity, and (5) tax consequences.

Investment risk is the chance that an investment and all of its accumulated yields will be worth less at some future time than when the investment is made. There are specific risk measures for different investments. For example, common stocks have a measure called *beta*. **Beta** measures the riskiness of a specific stock relative to the stock market as a whole. The market as a whole has a beta of 1.0. A stock with a beta of 1.5 is considered 1½ times as risky as an average stock. All investments involve some risk. Generally speaking, the greater the risk an investor assumes, the greater the potential return may be on the investment.

Total yield is the increase in the value of an investment over time, usually a year. *After-tax yield* is the percentage of return after taxes are paid. Return from an investment comes from capital appreciation (for example, if the value of a home or stock goes up), profit distribution (dividends), interest, or some combination of these. **Real yield** is the yield after taxes and inflation are subtracted. For example, a person in the 30% tax bracket may buy a bond that yields 8% a year. After taxes, the yield would be 5.6%. If inflation were 4%, the real yield would be just 1.6%. *Tax consequences* refers to changes in the after-tax yield.

Duration is the length of time assets are committed. Investment decisions differ depending on whether one wants to make a large return in a few years or invest over the long term for retirement.

Liquidity is how quickly one can get back invested funds when desired. It takes time to sell assets such as a farm or business. On the other hand, stocks, bonds, and most commodities can be sold almost immediately and are thus considered more "liquid."

An investor must weigh risk, yield, duration, liquidity, and tax consequences when he or she chooses an investment vehicle. It is wise to choose several investments, as we shall see next.

Diversification

Diversification consists of buying several different general investment vehicles to spread the risk. For example, an investor may put 30% of his or her money into growth stocks with high risk. Another 30% may be invested in conservative government bonds, 15% in silver and other commodities, and the rest placed in the bank for emergencies and other investment opportunities. Most people put a significant percentage of their investment funds into real estate (namely, their own home).

Mutual Funds

A **mutual fund** is an organization that buys stocks and bonds and then sells shares in those securities to the public. Mutual funds have the expertise to pick what they

investment risk
The chance that an investment and all its accumulated yields will be worth less at some future time than when it is made.

beta
Measures the riskiness of a specific stock relative to the stock market as a whole.

total yield
The increase in the value of an investment over time, usually a year.

real yield
The yield after taxes and inflation are subtracted.

duration
The length of time assets are committed.

liquidity
How quickly one can get back invested funds when they are desired.

diversification
Buying several different general investment vehicles to spread the risk.

mutual fund
An organization that buys stocks and bonds and then sells shares in those securities to the public.

feel are the best stocks and bonds available. See the ad below for Twentieth Century Investors. The benefit to you is that you can buy shares of the mutual funds and thus share in the ownership of *many different companies*. This helps you to diversify. You pay a small management fee for the services of the fund's managers.

Most mutual fund companies, like the John Hancock Funds, have several different ways of investing your money. John Hancock has a bond fund, a growth stock fund, a U.S. government securities fund, and a tax-exempt fund. Some companies have even more variety.

An ad for a no load mutual fund; look at its record on the left.

The idea is this: you can buy shares in one or more of these funds, and leave the management of your money to them. This is probably the best way for smaller investors ($20,000 or less) to begin. The mutual fund will send you a list of the companies in which it owns shares and the bonds it owns. There are very conservative funds that invest only in government securities or bonds. Others specialize in high-tech firms, firms in other countries, and so on.

A stockbroker will be glad to help you buy shares in a mutual fund *for a fee*. With just a little research, you can avoid the broker's fee and buy some funds directly. The point is that the average small investor has a way to spread the risk of stock ownership by owning shares in many different companies through the purchase of shares in a mutual fund.

Most investment advisors put mutual funds high on the list of recommended investments for beginning investors.[1] It may be the best way to buy stocks or bonds. Some mutual funds make it possible to buy a mutual fund that invests in other mutual funds. That is a sure way to spread the risk even further and share in the success of U.S. business in general.

The Bond Market

We learned in the previous chapter that when a business wants to raise money but does not want to take on new owners, it may want to *borrow* money from the public. The way it does that is to sell bonds to the public. A bond is written or printed evidence of debt (a piece of paper) owed by a corporation or government.

A sample government treasury bond.

A bond is a promise made by the issuer (borrower) to return to the bondholder the *principal* (the amount borrowed) when the bond *matures* (becomes due at some future date). The bond states that a specific rate of interest (for example, 10%) will be paid at regular intervals until maturity.

Bonds make it possible for people to earn higher interest on their money than they would from putting it in a bank, *and* they provide financing for major corporations. Thus bonds create a mutually beneficial exchange relationship between businesses and the general public.

It does not take long to learn about bonds. It would be to your benefit to do so, because bonds usually do pay more interest than banks, are often quite safe (especially government bonds), and sometimes are tax free (for example, municipal bonds).

To minimize the hassle of buying bonds, some organizations have formed *bond mutual funds*. Investing in such a fund is as simple as making a phone call to a broker, filling out some forms, and sending in your money.

PROGRESS CHECK

▪ What is the difference between active and passive investing?

▪ What is the difference between total yield and real yield?

COMMODITY EXCHANGES

Christopher Funk, the man in the Profile who bought and sold commodities, works with people on the commodity exchanges. This can be a high-risk business for most people. It can also be a vehicle for protecting businesspeople, farmers, and others from wide fluctuations in commodity prices, and thus a very conservative investment strategy. Let's see how this works.

A **commodity exchange** specializes in the buying and selling of goods such as wheat, cattle, sugar, silver, gasoline, and foreign currencies. The Chicago Board of Trade is the largest exchange. It is involved with a wide range of commodities including corn, plywood, silver, gold, and U.S. Treasury bonds. The Chicago

commodity exchange
Specializes in the buying and selling of goods such as wheat, cattle, silver, sugar, gasoline, and foreign currencies.

The Chicago Board of Trade trades commodities.

Mercantile Exchange is the second largest, and deals in commodities such as cattle, hogs, pork bellies (bacon), potatoes, and various foreign currencies.

Commodity exchanges operate much like stock exchanges in that members of the exchange meet on the floor to exchange goods. The appearance of a commodities exchange is quite different, however, and interesting to observe. All transactions for a specific commodity take place in specific trading areas or "rings." Trades result from the meeting of a bid and offer in an open competition among exchange members. The bids and offers are made in a seemingly impossible-to-understand blending of voices, with all participants shouting at once.

Spot trading refers to the purchase and sale of commodities for immediate delivery. **Futures trading** is a more common practice, and involves the purchase and sale of goods for delivery sometime in the future. Commodities trading demands much expertise. Most people who speculate in commodities lose money. You can get expertise and share in commodity price increases by buying into a commodities mutual fund.

spot trading
The purchase and sale of commodities for immediate delivery.

futures trading
The purchase and sale of goods for delivery sometime in the future.

Hedging

Commodities trading is an important risk-management tool for those who produce, process, market, and use commodities. The technique they use is called hedging. **Hedging** in its pure form involves buying or selling commodities in the futures market equal and opposite to what you now have. This sounds more difficult than it is. Take, for example, a farmer who has wheat growing in the field. He or she is not sure what price the wheat will sell for at harvesttime. To be sure of a price, the farmer would *sell* the wheat on the futures market. The price would then be fixed, and the farmer could plan accordingly.

On the other hand, imagine a baker who is worried about the possibility of wheat prices rising. The baker could *buy* wheat on the futures market and plan accordingly. Hedging, therefore, gives businesses a form of price insurance that enables them to focus on their primary function without worrying about fluctuations in commodity prices. Those who own a commodity can offset the risk of a price decline by *selling* futures contracts. Those who will need a commodity in the future can offset a price rise by *purchasing* the commodity ahead of time. All of this is possible because of commodity exchanges.

hedging
In its pure form, buying or selling commodities in the futures market equal and opposite to what you now have.

UNDERSTANDING FINANCIAL DATA IN THE MEDIA

A wealth of investment information is made available to investors in daily newspapers and various magazines. Such information is meaningless, though, until you understand what the data are all about. Look through *The Wall Street Journal, Barron's,* and your local newspaper's business section. Pay attention to the data listed so you can picture what is available in your mind. Listen carefully to the business reports on radio and TV and watch a couple of business-oriented shows such as *Wall Street Week*. Listen for the terms and the different viewpoints. Investing is an inexact science, and few people are consistently right in predicting future stock and bond prices. Every time someone sells a stock believing it will go up no further, someone else is buying it, believing it will go up. The following material will give you a good start toward understanding some of the information that is available.

Stock Quotations

If you look in the back of *The Wall Street Journal*, you will see stock quotations from the New York Stock Exchange, the American Stock Exchange, and the NASDAQ over-the-counter markets. Look at the top of the columns and notice the headings. Figure 22-2 describes what the various figures say for the New York Stock Exchange and the American Stock Exchange. These figures tell you what the high price over the last 52 weeks has been; the low price; the dividend paid (if any); what the dividend yield is; the price/earnings ratio; and the high, low, close, and net change in price for the previous day. Look through the columns and find the stock that pays the highest yield. Spend a little time looking through the figures until they make some sense to you.

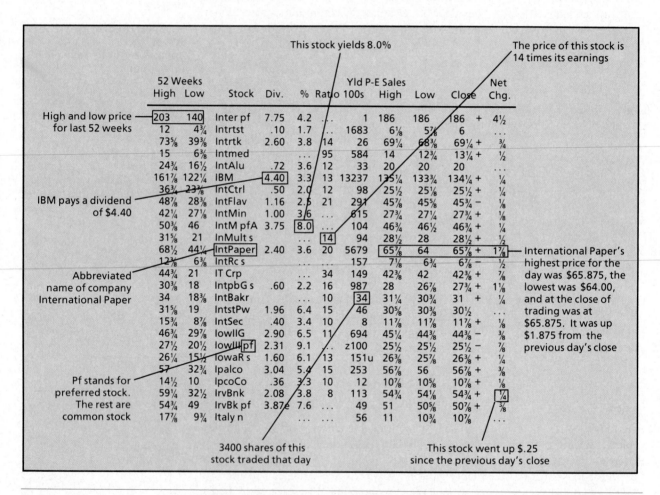

FIGURE 22-2 Understanding stock quotations in newspapers. Read across International Paper (Int. Paper), and you will see that the highest it sold for in the last 52 weeks was $68.50, and that the lowest was $44.25. The stock pays a dividend of $2.40 and yields 3.6%. The price divided by earnings is 20 (the PE ratio), and 567,900 shares were traded this day. The high for the day was $65.875, and the low was $64. The stock last sold for $65.875. The price went up $1.875 from the previous day's close.

WALL STREET NICKNAMES

The ticker symbols for stocks are often the source of some humorous nicknames for corporations. For example, the nickname for McDonnell Douglas (symbol *MD*) is "Mad Dog." Here are a few other names from The Street:

COMPANY	NICKNAME
Champion International (CHA)	Cha Cha
Beneficial Corporation (BNL)	Big Nose Louie
McDonalds	Hamburgers
AT&T	Big Phone
Helmerick & Payne (HP)	Hot Pants
Union Carbide (UK)	Ukelele
Dayton Hudson (DH)	Dead Head

Source: Beatrice E. Garcia, "If Big Nose Louie Turns You Off, Try Buying a Piece of Mad Dog," *The Wall Street Journal*, December 30, 1985, p. 15.

The Dow Jones Average

When you listen to stock reports on the radio, the announcer will say things like, "The Dow is up 2½ points today. Utilities are up 3, and transportations are down 1½." Charles Dow began the practice of measuring stock averages in 1884 when he added together the prices of 11 important stocks and divided the total by 11 to get an average.

Dow Jones Industrial Averages were broadened in 1982 to include 30 stocks, and new stocks are substituted when appropriate. There are 30 stocks in the Dow Jones Industrials; they include Du Pont, Eastman Kodak, GE, IBM, McDonald's, Sears, USX, and Woolworth.

Dow Jones Industrial Averages
The average cost of 30 industrial stocks.

The utility average is calculated by averaging the prices of 15 utilities, including Commonwealth Edison, Pacific Gas and Electric, and Southern California Edison. The transportation average is based on 20 stocks, including Burlington Northern Railroad, Eastern Air Lines, Federal Express, and TWA.

These Dow Jones averages give an indication of the direction of the market over time. An index compiled by NASDAQ covers all the over-the-counter stocks. Most comprehensive of all is the **Wilshire Index,** which covers all domestic common stocks on the New York and American Stock Exchanges plus 2,500 OTC stocks, for a total of about 5,000 issues.

Wilshire Index
A stock average based on all domestic common stock on the New York and American stock exchanges plus 2,500 OTC stocks.

INVESTMENT GAMES

Wizard of Wall Street is a computer game that lets you learn the ins and outs of investing without any risk. Players make decisions based on information from a tape that lists stock prices, news reports, and research reports.

Broderund Software sells the program for $44.95. It offered $1,000 to the school that used investments in any of 24 companies to record the highest gain. In 1986, the winner was Stanford University. Playing the game for 2 days, graduate students at Stanford parlayed a $1 million investment into $21.5 million. The Wharton School of Business made $9 million on a similar investment.

Computer games are an excellent way to learn about investments and try out your strategies with no real risk. The game becomes even more interesting when you begin playing with real money on Wall Street, especially if you have learned to do it well in school.

A comprehensive list of the Dow Jones Industrials, Transportations, and Utilities stocks, November 1986.

DOW JONES 30 STOCKS IN INDUSTRIAL AVERAGE	DOW JONES 20 STOCKS IN TRANSPORTATION AVERAGE	DOW JONES 15 STOCKS IN UTILITY AVERAGE
Allied-Signal	AMR Corp	Am Elec Power
Aluminum Co	Amer President	Centerior Energy
Amer Can	Burlington North	Colum Gas Sys
Amer Express	Canadian Pacific	Comwlth Edison
Am T&T	Carolina Freight	Consol Edison
Bethlehem Steel	Consolid Freight	Consol Nat Gas
Chevron	CSX Corp	Detroit Edison
DuPont	Delta Air Lines	Houston Indust
Eastman Kodak	Eastern Air Lines	Niag Mohawk P
Exxon	Federal Express	Pacific Gas & El
General Electric	Leaseway Transp	Panhandle Eastern
General Foods	Norfolk Southern	Peoples Energy
General Motors	NWA Inc	Phila Elec
Goodyear	Overnite Transp	Pub Serv Interp
Inco	Pan Am Corp	Sou Cal Edison
IBM	Santa Fe So Pacific	
Inter Paper	TWA	
McDonald's	UAL Inc	
Merck	Union Pac Corp	
Minnesota M&M	USAir Group	
Navistar Inter		
Owens-Illinois		
Philip Morris		
Procter & Gamb		
Sears Roebuck		
Texaco		
Union Carbide		
United Technologies		
USX		
Westinghouse El		
Woolworth		

Mutual Fund Quotations

We have noted that one way to get expert investment advice, to diversify your investments among various stocks and bonds, and to purchase such securities at a minimum cost is to buy into mutual funds. Look up the listing of mutual funds in *The Wall Street Journal*. Note that some funds have the letters NL after them (in the second to the last column). This means "no load," and refers to the fact that these funds can be bought without paying a commission to a salesperson. You do pay an annual fee for management advice, however. T. Rowe Price has a variety of funds available, including a growth fund, a high-yield fund, an international fund, and funds that yield tax-free returns. Various business periodicals evaluate the various funds for you. You can also buy mutual funds through your broker. This is a good way to start investing until you are experienced enough to select your own investments.

Bond Quotations

Bonds are issued by both corporations and government units. Government issues are covered in *The Wall Street Journal* in a table called "Treasury Issues." These issues are traded on the over-the-counter market. The price is quoted as a percentage of par (also called the face value). The interest rate is often followed by an "s" for easier pronunciation. For example, 9% bonds due in 1987 are called "nines of eighty-seven."

Figure 22-3 gives a sample of bond quotes for corporations. As you look through the sample quotes, note the variation in interest rates and the maturity dates. There are so many variables to consider in buying specific issues of stocks and bonds that most people rely on experts to help them choose the best investments. Nonetheless, the more one knows about these investments, the better one is prepared to talk intelligently with investment counselors and be sure their advice is consistent with one's best interests. It bears repeating that the easiest way to buy bonds and diversify at the same time is to buy into a bond mutual fund.

Bonds	Cur Yld	Vol	High	Low	Close	Net Chg.
LaQuin 10s02	cv	4	102	102	102	− 1¼
LearS 10s04	10.0	3	100	100	100	+ 1⅝
LearS 11½98	11.1	5	103½	103½	103½	− 1½
LearS 11¼98	10.8	2	104¼	104¼	104¼	− ¾
Leget 6½06	cv	36	103	102	102	...
LipGp 8⅝01	9.4	10	92⅛	92⅛	92⅛ −	1⅞
LincFI 8½96	8.7	5	97½	97½	97½ −	1⅜
LomN 7s11	cv	4	104	104	104	...
LonSI 11¾90	11.7	5	100⅜	100⅜	100⅜ −	2
Loral 7¼10	cv	2	121	121	121 −	½
Lorilld 6⅞93	7.6	62	90⅞	90⅜	90⅜	...
LouGs 9¼00	9.2	10	101⅛	101	101	...
Lowen 8½96	9.4	18	90	89	90 +	7
viLykes 7½94N f	...	35	19½	18	18 −	1
viLykes 7½94f	...	79	20½	19⅞	20½ +	⅞
viLykes 11s00f	...	25	21	20½	20½ −	½
MACOM 9¼06	cv	30	101	99¼	99¼ −	1¼

CV means convertible bond

500 bonds traded that day

This bond sold for a high of $900 and the low for the day was $890. It ended the day at $90, up $70 from the previous day

These Lowen bonds are due in 1996 and originally paid 8½%. The current yield is 9.4%

Understanding bond quotations in newspapers. Bonds are usually issued in $1,000 denominations, so a price of 90 is really $900. Note that some bonds yield as high as 11.7%. How does that compare to the yield from a bank account?

FIGURE 22-3

SECURITIES REGULATION

Most states have laws concerning securities trading. They are called *"blue-sky laws,"* because one legislator remarked that promoters would sell shares of the "blue sky" if not regulated. Most state laws include penalties for fraudulent statements or actions connected with the sale of stocks or bonds. Some require that dealers register or that all new issues be registered. The first state law of this nature was passed in 1911.

Federal Regulation

Securities and Exchange Commission (SEC)
Has responsibility at the federal level for regulating the various exchanges.

The **Securities and Exchange Commission (SEC)** has responsibility at the federal level for regulating the various exchanges. The Securities Act of 1934 created the SEC. An amendment to the act in 1964 extended the authority of the commission to the over-the-counter market. Those companies trading on the national exchanges or OTC market must register with the SEC and provide annual updates. Brokers are required to pass an examination, and all brokerage firms, brokers, and dealers selling over-the-counter are regulated by the SEC.

STUDENT INVESTORS

High school students from Delaware, Pennsylvania, Maryland, and Virginia compete in *The Stock Market Game* in which they invest an imaginary $100,000 to learn about finance. The contest is held each fall and spring, and is sponsored by the Securities Industry Foundation for Economic Education, which donates players' manuals.

The 1985 winner was Mike Shipe, 13, of Seaford High in Seaford, Delaware. He made $64,000 on the $100,000 investment in just 10 weeks. He bought just one stock, Rollins Environmental Services. It went from 11¼ on September 27th to 16⅞ on December 5th. *The Stock Market Game* created excitement in the classes. Some teams even tried short selling and selling on margin, two rather sophisticated stock market strategies.

Ari Kogut, a freshman at North Shore Country Day School in Illinois, took investing one step further. He took the $1,200 his classmates had earned selling candy and school jackets and, with school board approval, began investing in commodity futures. He began in the summer and by fall had increased the fund to $5,500. The money was used for the school prom. Ari's brother and father are both commodities traders, but Ari made the choices himself, based on his father's advice. You can imagine the interest in investing such a risk created in students at the school.

Securities Act of 1933
Protects investors by requiring full disclosure of financial information by firms selling new stocks and bonds.

The **Securities Act of 1933** protects investors by requiring full disclosure of financial information by firms selling new stocks or bonds. A registration statement with detailed information is filed with the SEC. A condensed version of that registration document—called a **prospectus**—must be sent to purchasers.

prospectus
A condensed version of financial information prepared for the Securities and Exchange Commission that is sent to purchasers.

Additional Regulation

An amendment to the Securities Exchange Act in 1938 created the National Association of Securities Dealers (NASD), which regulates over-the-counter businesses. Brokers and dealers must pass written examinations. Mutual funds were added under the Investment Company Act of 1940. Now mutual funds must also register with the SEC.

PROGRESS CHECK

▪ Why would a restaurant owner be interested in the futures market?

▪ How is spot trading different from futures trading in the commodities market?

▪ What does the Dow Jones Industrial Average measure and why is it so important?

NATURE OF THE WORK

Securities sales workers. Most investors—whether they are individuals with a few hundred dollars or a large institution with millions to invest—call on securities sales workers when buying or selling stocks, bonds, shares in mutual funds, or other financial products. Securities sales workers often are called *registered representatives, account executives,* or *brokers.*

When an investor wishes to buy or sell securities, sales workers may relay the order through their firms' offices to the floor of a securities exchange, such as the New York Stock Exchange. There, securities sales workers known as *brokers' floor representatives* buy and sell securities. If a security is not traded on an exchange, the sales worker sends the order to the firm's trading department, which trades it directly with a dealer in the over-the-counter market. After the transaction has been completed, the sales worker notifies the customer of the final price.

Securities sales workers also provide many related services for their customers. Depending on a customer's knowledge of the market, they may explain the meaning of stock market terms and trading practices; offer financial counseling; or devise an individual financial portfolio for the client including securities, life insurance, tax shelters, mutual funds, annuities, and other investments. Securities sales workers furnish information about the advantages and disadvantages of an investment based on each person's objectives. They also supply the latest price quotations on any security in which the investor is interested, as well as information on the activities and financial positions of the corporations issuing these securities.

Financial services sales workers. Financial services sales workers call on various businesses to solicit applications for loans and new deposit accounts for banks or savings and loan associations. They also locate and contact prospective customers to present the bank's financial services and to ascertain the customer's banking needs. At most smaller and medium-sized banks, branch managers and commercial loan officers are responsible for marketing the bank's financial services.

JOB OUTLOOK

The number of securities sales workers is expected to grow much faster than the average for all occupations through the mid-1990s. Most job openings, however, are expected to be created by workers who transfer to other jobs, retire, or stop working for other reasons.

Due to the highly competitive nature of securities sales work, many beginners leave the field because they are unable to establish sufficient clientele. Once established, however, securities sales workers have a relatively strong attachment to their occupation because of high earnings and the considerable investment in training.

Faster than average employment growth is expected among financial services sales workers as a result of the continued expansion in banking services and the need to finance an increasing level of commercial activity.

EARNINGS

According to the Securities Industry Association, earnings of full-time experienced securities sales workers who served individual investors averaged about $64,000 a year in 1984. The relatively small number of sales workers who handled institutional accounts averaged about $156,000.

Trainees usually are paid a salary until they meet licensing and registration requirements. After registration, a few firms continue to pay a salary until the new representative's commissions increase to a stated amount. The salaries paid during training range from $900 to $1,200 a month.

After candidates are licensed and registered, their earnings depend on commissions from the sale or purchase of stocks and bonds, life insurance, or other securities for customers. Commission earnings are likely to be high when there is much buying and selling and lower when there is a slump in market activity. Most firms provide sales workers with a steady income by paying a "draw against commission"—that is, a minimum salary based on the commissions which they can be expected to earn. Securities sales workers who can provide their clients with the most complete financial services should enjoy the greatest income stability.

Financial services sales workers are paid a salary; some receive bonuses if they meet certain established goals. Average earnings of financial services sales workers are considerably less than those of securities sales workers.

RELATED OCCUPATIONS

Similar sales jobs requiring special knowledge include insurance agents and real estate agents.

SOURCES OF ADDITIONAL INFORMATION

Further information concerning a career as a securities sales worker is available for $1 from:

Securities Industry Association, 120 Broadway, New York, N.Y. 10271.

Source: *Occupational Outlook Handbook,* 1986-1987 (U.S. Department of Labor).

SUMMARY

1 *Securities markets* are organizations that enable businesses and investors to buy and sell stock, bonds, and mutual funds.
- What is a stock exchange?
  An organization whose members can buy and sell securities.
- What are the different exchanges?
  There are stock exchanges all over the world. The largest U.S. exchange is the New York Stock Exchange (NYSE). It and the American Stock Exchange (ASE) together are known as national exchanges. In addition, there are several regional exchanges.
- What is the over-the-counter (OTC) market?
  It is a system for exchanging stocks not listed on the national exchanges. It also handles bonds issued by city and state governments.

2 To buy stock, you call a stockbroker who will arrange the deal.
- What is a market order?
  A *market order* tells the broker to buy the stock at the best price available now. A *limit order,* on the other hand, tells the broker to buy the stock at a specific price.
- What does buying on margin mean?
  It means that the investor borrows up to 50% of the cost of the stock from the broker so he or she can get more shares.
- What is odd lot trading?
  Buying less than 100 shares of a stock.
- What are bulls and bears?
  Bulls are investors who expect stock prices to rise; *bears* expect stock prices to fall.

3 *Investing* means committing capital with the expectation of making a profit.
- What is active investing?
  Active investing means the investor makes the decisions on how his or her money is invested. *Passive investing* means the investor lets someone else decide on the specific use of funds.
- What are the five investment criteria?
  They are (1) risk, (2) yield, (3) duration, (4) liquidity, and (5) tax consequences.
- What is diversification?
  It means buying several different general investment vehicles to spread the risk.

4 A *mutual fund* is an organization that buys stocks and bonds and then sells shares in those securities to the public.
- Is investing in a mutual fund easy?
  Yes. You can just call the company and order by phone.
- Is it wise to buy bonds?
  Yes. You can buy bonds directly or invest in a bond mutual fund. Figure 22-1 shows that there are times when bonds yield good returns and times when they do not.

5 *Commodity exchanges* specialize in the buying and selling of goods such as wheat, cattle, sugar, silver, gasoline, and foreign currencies.
- What is *spot trading*?
  Buying commodities for immediate delivery. *Futures trading* involves buying commodities for delivery some time in the future.

■ What is hedging?

Buying or selling commodities in the futures market equal and opposite to what you now have. For example, if you have wheat in the field, you sell in the futures market an amount equal to that crop.

6 Securities quotations are given in the daily papers.

■ What is the Dow Jones Industrial Average?

The average price of 30 stocks traded. There is also a utility average (15 stocks) and a transportation average (20 stocks).

7 Securities exchanges are regulated by the Securities and Exchange Commission (SEC).

■ Are there regulations regarding the training of brokers and false representation of securities?

Yes. They are discussed in this chapter.

KEY TERMS

bears p. 605
beta p. 607
bulls p. 605
buying on margin p. 605
commodity exchange p. 610
diversification p. 607
Dow Jones Industrial Average
  p. 613
duration p. 607
futures trading p. 611
hedging p. 611
investing p. 606
investment risk p. 607
limit order p. 604
liquidity p. 607
market order p. 604
mutual fund p. 607
NASDAQ p. 603

national exchanges p. 603
odd lots p. 605
over-the-counter (OTC) market
  p. 603
prospectus p. 616
real yield p. 607
round lots p. 605
Securities Act of 1933 p. 616
Securities and Exchange
  Commission (SEC) p. 616
securities markets p. 602
selling short p. 605
spot trading p. 611
stockbroker p. 604
stock exchange p. 602
stock splits p. 605
total yield p. 607
Wilshire Index p. 613

GETTING INVOLVED

1 Write the Education Department, *The Wall Street Journal,* 200 Burnett Rd., Chicopee, MA 01021, and have them send you the Student Edition. Look through it at your leisure. It explains all the columns and charts. Discuss this edition with your class.

2 Read *The Wall Street Journal* daily for several months. Notice the trends in stocks and bonds and read the articles. Each day choose a particularly interesting article and share it with the class.

3 See if your professor is interested in setting up an investment game in your class. Each student should choose one stock and one mutual fund. Each student's selections would be written in a book and the prices noted. In 6 weeks, you would look up the prices again. The students with the largest percentage gain would win.

4 Visit a brokerage firm and watch the ticker tape that reports stock transactions. Watch the brokers in action. Talk to a broker and discuss your investment situation. Learn as much as you can about the procedures for buying stocks, bonds, and mutual funds.

5 On April 17, 1986 the price of silver closed at 544.5, or less than $5.45 per troy ounce. Look up Futures Prices in *The Wall Street Journal* to see what the price for silver is now. How much gain or loss would I have made by buying 100 ounces in 1986? Also, check out the changes in gold, which closed at $339.40 on April 17; sugar, which closed at $7.98; and live cattle, which closed at $55.47.

PRACTICING MANAGEMENT DECISIONS

CASE ONE   WAS IT THE TIME TO INVEST IN BONDS?

In 1981, oil was $40 a barrel, and people were predicting prices of $80 or higher. A couple of years later, long-term bonds were yielding 15% on U.S. Treasury and 14% on tax-free municipal bonds. People were afraid of galloping inflation and hesitated to buy the bonds.

In mid-1986, oil was down to $10 a barrel and long-term Treasury bonds yielded only about 7½%. Many people were buying the bonds, convinced that inflation was conquered.

Inflation was bumping along at about 4% to 5%. If inflation increased to 5% or 7%, and long-term rates went up to 10%, the investor owning an 8% 25-year Treasury bond would have lost 20% of his or her capital. At 14%, the loss would have been 43%.

The stock market was reaching new highs all through the early part of 1986. Most signs pointed to a continuing rise in the market, but investors were unsure.

DECISION QUESTIONS

1 Given a 7½% yield on U.S. Treasury bonds in June, 1986, would an investor have made any real yield that year?
2 Discuss risk, yield, duration, and tax consequences of investing in bonds in 1986.
3 One investment decision may be to simply put your money in the bank at low interest rates when in doubt. What are the benefits and disadvantages of such a strategy?
4 Check your papers to see what today's inflation rate is and the yield in U.S. Treasury bonds. What would have happened had you bought a Treasury bond in mid-1986?

Source: Figures are from David Dreman, "The Short of the Decade," *Forbes,* April 28, 1986, pp. 334-335.

PRACTICING MANAGEMENT DECISIONS

CASE TWO   INVESTING AN INHERITANCE

Jason Heimberg's grandmother died and left him $30,000. Jason needed $5,000 of the inheritance to finish his last year at County Community College. He had $25,000 left to invest. Jason investigated several stocks that he felt were likely to grow rapidly. Most were high-tech stocks in industries such as gene splicing and robotics. Jason's stockbroker was encouraging him to diversify his investments by buying stock in two mutual funds. One was a fund that specializes in smaller growth companies. Another specialized in bonds.

A broker Jason met at a party suggested that he really need not use a broker at all. Her suggestion was to keep some funds in the bank for his use in an emergency. Other funds could be invested in several different mutual funds that were managed by one firm. She called them "no-load mutual funds," and explained that they could be bought for no brokerage fee. She said the funds have a notation that say NL in the various mutual fund quotations, as found in *The Wall Street Journal*.

A financial advisor has suggested that Jason buy insurance first, even though he is not married. The idea was to buy a policy that would invest money for Jason at what looked like a reasonable return. Any excess funds would be placed in a bank (for emergencies) and in mutual funds that the advisor would recommend.

DECISION QUESTIONS

1 What are the criteria Jason should use in evaluating investment alternatives?
2 Look up no-load mutual funds in a newspaper or magazine that lists them. Do you understand what is available? What are the advantages and disadvantages of buying a mutual fund through a broker?
3 What questions does this case raise that you need to have answered before you can invest your funds more intelligently? Where could you find answers to such questions?

LOOKING AHEAD

Finance really comes alive when you begin using the concepts to manage your own personal finances. Chapter 23 discusses ways for you to save capital to begin your own investment program. It then discusses investment alternatives, including real estate, insurance, and IRAs. We shall also learn how to read some financial data in *The Wall Street Journal* and how to buy stock.

PERSONAL FINANCIAL PLANNING

LEARNING GOALS

After you have read and studied this chapter, you should be able to:

▪ Describe a strategy to accumulate investment capital.

▪ Explain several benefits of owning real estate.

▪ Identify some fundamentals of personal money management.

▪ Differentiate between whole life and term life insurance, and their variations.

▪ Discuss the benefits of Individual Retirement Accounts (IRA) and Keogh plans.

▪ Describe the function of a financial planner.

PROFILE DAVE AND JAN PARKINSON OF TAMPA, FLORIDA

Planning for retirement should be part of any comprehensive financial plan, and it is never too early to begin. For example, David Parkinson would like to retire when he's 50. David is 32. His wife, Jan, is 31. When they retire, they would like to travel and live by the sea. The couple have already bought a retirement retreat on Anna Maria Island, and have saved $50,000 toward realizing their retirement dreams.

The Parkinsons accumulated this fund by holding down household expenses. While most couples spend 25% or more for housing, the Parkinsons spend much less because they bought a smaller home. They have no children and live frugally.

The couple has a combined income of $70,000. Rental of the beach house adds another $10,800. The Parkinsons own 100 shares of Hillenbrand Industries (NYSE), 104 shares of Jacklyn Inc. (ASE), and 600 shares of Claire's Stores (OTC). The couple has an IRA account in a mutual fund and other funds in a money market fund.

The Parkinsons are doing well; nonetheless, financial advisors have made suggestions that will help them protect their investments and save money on taxes.

College students are in an excellent position to plan their financial future like the Parkinsons did. Sometimes the best strategy is to live conservatively and save money for travel, retirement, and other long-range goals. To learn about strategies

Dave and Jan Parkinson.

Economy is half the battle of life; it is not so hard to earn money as to spend it well.

CHARLES SPURGEON

for becoming financially secure, one must study *personal* finance—the subject of this chapter.

One day you too may own a retirement retreat and have $50,000 in the bank. The time to start is now.

Robert McNatt, "An Early Retirement Is the Goal of Two Young Floridians," *Money*, April, 1985, pp. 39-40.

FINANCIAL MANAGEMENT

There are several reasons to study business subjects in college. One is to become a businessperson. Another is to understand subjects such as marketing and management so you can apply the concepts in churches, charities, social causes, unions, associations, and other nonbusiness pursuits. A third reason is to learn about subjects such as stocks, bonds, insurance, banking, credit, real estate and other topics that will help you become a better manager of your own funds (a financial manager). Did you know that the word *economist* means home manager? This chapter is designed to cover many of the topics that all people should know to be good economists—home managers.

This chapter will expose you to many subjects that will demand much further study before you feel competent dealing with them. Nonetheless, you will have a good start toward understanding personal finance—the management of your own funds.

Saving for the Future

Many people find successful careers in business and earn much money over the years, but have little to show for their efforts. Making money is one thing; saving it and spending it wisely is something else. Less than 10% of the population has saved enough money by retirement age to live comfortably off their savings.

This chapter begins with a strategy for accumulating money or capital. This money can then be invested in real estate and other investments. A careful investment plan will assure a fund for retirement purposes, so you can retire to an island like the Parkinsons, if you want. The following strategy may seem radical to you. Nonetheless, read it through to get the idea; then you can apply it to your own situation in whatever way seems most appropriate.

BUILDING YOUR CAPITAL ACCOUNT

The path to success in a capitalist system is to have capital (money) to invest, yet the trend today for young graduates is to not only be capital-poor, but to be in debt. Accumulating capital takes discipline and careful planning.

The principle is simple: to accumulate capital, you have to earn more than you spend. For a young couple, that process may be easier than one might expect, given the small number of young people with significant savings. Let's assume that a couple gets married soon after college. What to do next?

The first step is to find a job for both husband and wife. Both people will want to work for several years before the couple has any children.

Dorm room-style living after college builds capital.

During those years, the couple should try to live, as much as possible, on just *one* income. The other income can then be used to generate capital. It may be invested in a conservative mutual fund or some other relatively safe investment. Part of it could be invested in more risky investments for rapid capital accumulation.

Living on one income is extremely difficult for the average college graduate. Most graduates are eager to spend their money on a new car, a stereo, a videotape recorder, clothes, and the like. They tend to look for a fancy apartment with all the amenities. A capital-generating strategy calls for giving up most (not all) of these purchases to accumulate investment money. The living style required is close to the one adopted by most college students: a relatively inexpensive apartment furnished in early Sears Roebuck plus hand-me-downs from parents, friends, and Goodwill. For 5 or 6 years, the couple can manage with the old stereo, used cars, and a few nice clothes. The living style desired is one of sacrifice, not luxury. It is important not to feel burdened by this plan, but happy living together frugally for a better future.*

After 6 years of saving one income, the savings can grow to about $90,000 (after taxes) for a college graduate (saving $15,000 per year). What to do with the money? The first investment might be a moderately priced home. This investment should be made as early as possible. The purpose of the investment is to lock in payments for shelter at a given amount. This is possible with ownership, but not by renting. Through the years, home ownership has been a wise investment.

*An obvious alternative is to stay single and live frugally to generate capital.

Applying the Strategy

Some people have used the seed money from this strategy to buy duplex homes; that is, two attached homes. They lived in one of the homes and rented the other. The rent covered a good part of the payments for *both* homes, so they were able to live very cheaply while their investment in a home appreciated rapidly. They learned that it is quite possible to live comfortably, yet inexpensively, for several years. In this way they accumulated capital. When they grew older, they saw that such a strategy put them years ahead of their peers in terms of financial security. They eventually sold their duplex homes and bought single-family homes with the profits. The money saved has been invested in everything from stocks and bonds to silver, gold, insurance, additional real estate, and higher education (which is perhaps the best investment of all—an investment in yourself).

This strategy may seem too restrictive for you, but you still can apply the principles. The idea is to generate capital to invest. After all, this *is* a capitalist society, and in such a society you are lost without capital. A couple is wise to plan their financial future with the same excitement and dedication as they plan their lives together. Even a modest saving of $6,000 a year will allow a couple to buy a small home in 6 years and begin an investment program. Remember, money that earns 12% annually *doubles* in just 6 years! (See the rule of 72 on p. 79.) An investment of $6,000 for 6 years can grow to a total of over $50,000, a healthy start for any couple.

THINKING IT THROUGH

What would you have to sacrifice to live as you do now for another 6 years? Is it worth the sacrifice to become financially secure for the foreseeable future? Is there some halfway measure you feel would be better?

How much financial planning have you done for the future? Do you own life insurance? Do you have any savings? If you have accumulated debts while in school, how do you intend to pay them off?

REAL ESTATE—THE NUMBER-ONE INVESTMENT

As we have discussed, one of the better investments a person can make is in his or her own home. Homes grow in value each year (or have historically), and provide several other investment benefits. First of all, a home is the one investment that you can live in. Once you buy a home, the payments are relatively fixed (though taxes and utilities go up, as you'll see if you do buy). As your income rises, the house payments get easier and easier to make, but renters often find that rents tend to go up as fast or faster than income.

A home is a good way of forcing yourself to save. Every month you must make the payments. Those payments are an investment that will prove very rewarding over time for most people.

An investment in a duplex or small apartment building is also an excellent strategy. As capital accumulates and values rise, an investor can sell and buy an even larger apartment complex. Many fortunes have been made in real estate in just such a manner.

A home is one of the better investments people make.

Some figures will give you a better feel for the role of real estate in today's investment programs. For all people under age 45, one half of their assets are in real estate, and only $3,000 on average is invested in securities (stocks and bonds). For those over age 45, only 39% of assets are in real estate with $13,000 in securities.[1]

Tax Deduction and Home Ownership

Buying a home is likely to be the largest and most important investment you will make. It is nice to know that the federal government is willing to help you with that investment. Here's how. Interest on the payments you make for a home is tax deductible. So are the real estate taxes you pay. During the first few years, almost all the payments go for interest on the loan; therefore, almost all the early payments are tax deductible. That is a tremendous benefit for homeowners. If, for example, your payments are $800 a month and your joint income is in the 30% tax bracket, then Uncle Sam will, in effect, help pay about $240 of your mortgage payment, lowering your real cost to less than $600. This makes home ownership much more competitive with renting than may appear on the surface. Home ownership is one of the few tax shelters left in the new tax bill.

Real estate people will tell you that there are three keys to making the optimum return on a home; they are location, location, and location. A home in the "best part of town," near schools, shopping, and work, is the best financial investment. Most young couples tend to go further away from town where the homes are less expensive, but such homes are likely to appreciate in value much more slowly. It is better, from a financial viewpoint, to buy a smaller home in a great location.

To make payments on a home and pay the dozens of other bills a family encounters is no easy task. It takes planning and good money management. As for a businessperson, it is important for a homeowner to prepare a budget and stick to it. We'll explore this idea next.

MONEY MANAGEMENT

In hindsight, you realize that probably the silliest saying is, "Two can live as cheaply as one." Two people *eat* more than one, *wear* more than one, *drive* more than one, and *spend* more than one. In fact, the money just seems to disappear. "Where did it go?" couples ask each other. "Did *you* spend it?"

There is only one way for a couple to keep track of revenues and expenses, and it's the same way a business does: by writing it down. A couple should record *every single cent* they spend for over a year on various *accounts:* food, clothing, furniture, gas, rent, utilities, entertainment, vacations, gifts, and miscellaneous (a category that includes laundry, snacks, magazines, household items, and more). In this way they learn where the money is going, but may find it difficult to stem the flow. They learn that to become financially secure, a couple must learn to budget. Most of all, a couple must learn some discipline to live within that budget. Businesses are not alone in suffering from cash flow problems; most families have the same problem.

A budget is made by projecting revenues and expenses for the year and allocating the funds to various accounts. It is best to break down the figures to monthly revenues and expenses. At the end of the month, it is relatively easy to see if the family is living within the budget or not. The whole process is often painful, but usually is a necessary first step in getting some control over personal finances.

By keeping such a budget, you will learn the importance of setting aside money for the replacement of automobiles and appliances. If you don't add in such figures, you will find yourself suddenly in need of thousands of dollars for a replacement car—thousands of dollars you have not budgeted for.

Other items that are important in a household budget include life insurance, car insurance, and medical care costs. You will learn that running the finances of a household is very similar to running a small business. It takes the same careful record keeping (if only for taxes), the same budgeting process and forecasting, the same control procedures, and often (sadly) the same need to periodically borrow funds. Suddenly, concepts such as *credit* and *interest rates* become only too real. This is where some knowledge of finance, investments, and budgeting pays off.

Credit Cards

Known as "plastic" to young buyers, credit cards are no doubt familiar to you. Names like Visa, MasterCard, American Express, Diners Club, and Carte Blanche are as well known to most people as Sears. In a credit card purchase, finance charges after the first 25 or 30 days usually amount to 15% to 22% annually. This means that a person who finances a car, home appliances, and other purchases pays much more than if he or she paid with cash, even though such interest payments are tax deductible. A good personal financial manager, like a good businessperson, pays on time and takes advantage of savings made possible by paying early. Those couples who have established a capital fund can tap that fund to make large purchases and *pay the fund back* (with interest if so desired) rather than a bank.

Credit cards are an important element in a personal financial system, even if they are rarely used. First of all, many merchants demand credit cards as a form of identification. It is often difficult or impossible to buy certain goods or even rent a car without owning a credit card.

The use of money is all the advantage there is in having money.

Benjamin Franklin

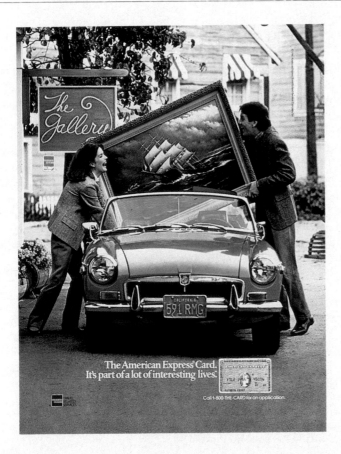

Credit cards must be used with care.

Secondly, credit cards are a way to keep track of purchases. A gasoline credit card, for example, enables you to have records of purchases over time for income tax and financial planning purposes. It is sometimes easier to write one check at the end of the month for several purchases than to carry cash around. Besides, cash may be stolen or lost.

Finally, a credit card is simply more convenient. If you come upon a special sale and need more money than you usually carry, a credit card is a quick and easy way to pay. You can carry less cash and don't have to worry about keeping your checkbook balanced as often.

The danger of a credit card is the flip side of its convenience. Too often consumers buy goods and services that they would not normally buy if they had to pay cash or write a check on funds in the bank. Consumers often pile up debts using credit cards to the point where they are unable to pay. If you are not the type who has a financial plan and a household budget, it may be better not to have a credit card at all. Credit cards are a helpful tool to the *financially careful* buyer. They are a financial disaster to somebody with little financial restraint and tastes beyond income.

PROGRESS CHECK

▓ What is the secret to accumulating capital?

▓ What are the three keys to making an optimum return on a home?

INSURANCE COVERAGE

One of the last things a young couple thinks about when they get married is the idea that one of them may get sick or have an accident and die. It is not a pleasant thought. Even more unpleasant, though, is the reality of thousands of young people dying every day in accidents and other unexpected ways. You have only to visit one of their families to see the emotional *and financial* havoc such a loss causes.

Today, with so many husbands and wives both working, the loss of a spouse means a sudden large drop in income. To protect each other from such devastation, a couple should invest in life insurance *for both husband and wife.* Both should be covered under the same policy, because it is cheaper that way.

Today, the preferred form of life insurance is called term insurance. **Term insurance** is pure insurance protection for a given number of years. Every few years, you must renew the policy, and the fee usually gets higher and higher. (See Figure 23-1.)

term insurance
Pure insurance protection for a given number of years that must be renewed periodically.

FIGURE 23-1

Why term insurance?

INSURANCE NEEDS IN EARLY YEARS ARE HIGH	INSURANCE NEEDS DECLINE AS YOU GROW OLDER
1 Children are young and need money for education. 2 Mortgage is high relative to income. 3 Often there are auto payments and other bills to pay. 4 Loss of income would be disastrous.	1 Children are grown. 2 Mortgage is low or completely paid off. 3 Debts are paid off. 4 Insurance needs are few. 5 Retirement income is needed.

whole life insurance
A combination insurance plan and savings plan that was popular in the past, but has declined in popularity in recent years.

variable life insurance
A whole life policy whose benefits vary based on the success of the insurance company in investing those funds.

universal life insurance
A combination of term insurance and an accumulation fund usually based mostly on short-term debt instruments (bonds).

A popular alternative in the past has been **whole life insurance.** This is a combination insurance plan and savings plan. The problem was that the savings portion simply was not competitive with the rates available in mutual funds and other investment alternatives.

Today, life insurance companies are becoming more aggressive in winning investment dollars. One new plan is called **variable life insurance.** This is a whole life policy whose benefits *vary* (thus the term *variable life*) based on the success of the insurance company in investing those funds. The money is placed in a portfolio that usually includes some stock, bonds, real estate, and other such investments. With such a policy, the benefits are guaranteed not to go below a certain amount. However, if the portfolio of stocks and bonds and other investments does well, the benefits will increase. Buying such a policy is a way to get insurance *and* have a diversified investment account for your family. It is also one other way that people like you and me have a vested interest in U.S. business. How much we get from insurance is tied to the success of the economy.

Another relatively new type of policy is called **universal life insurance.** It is a combination of term insurance and an accumulation fund, usually based mostly on debt instruments (bonds). Policy owners can switch funds to buy more insurance or more bonds. The interest rates earned are very close to those in the market after an initial fund of $1,000 is accumulated.

Even more creative policies are now coming on the market. They may give the policy holder the freedom to switch from whole life to term and back as life's circumstances change. This is called **adjustable life insurance.** Other policies combine the ideas from variable life, universal life, and adjustable life policies. Such policies may be considered as part of a total life savings and insurance plan. If people have the discipline to do it, though, the best option is straight term insurance with the idea that additional funds will be invested each year. That will result in the largest overall return *as long as the plan is followed*.

There are many career openings available in life insurance companies. The new policies are far superior to the old policies, and they should be relatively easy to sell. Now that so many women are working, there is a growing need to sell additional insurance to professional women. Talk to someone who sells these new policies. Are they enthusiastic? Would you enjoy such work? By now, you probably have gotten the idea that everyone you talk to is a potential source of information about careers. Right. Keep looking, and you will find hundreds of interesting and challenging careers.

adjustable life insurance
Gives the policyholder the freedom to switch from whole life to term and back as life's circumstances change.

Health Insurance

You are likely to have health insurance coverage through your employer. If not, you can buy insurance from a health insurance provider (for example, Blue Cross/Blue Shield) or a local health maintenance organization (HMO). Most people do not realize the benefit of having company-paid health insurance until they have to pay for the insurance on their own. The cost is quite high.

It is dangerous financially not to have health insurance.

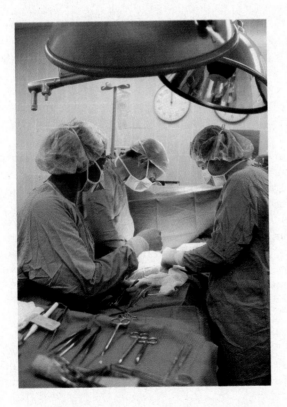

One decision you may have to make is to choose between Blue Cross/Blue Shield coverage or a HMO. For a young couple, a HMO is often an attractive alternative in that HMOs emphasize *preventive* health care. Emphasis is on checkups and the prevention of illness, although hospital care is also provided. Different plans have different policies regarding your freedom to select doctors and so on. Such a decision should not be taken lightly. Talk to people in town who have both options. Learn the advantages and disadvantages. Assess *your* family's needs, and then choose.

It is very dangerous financially not to have any health insurance. Hospital costs are simply too high to risk financial ruin by going uninsured. In fact, it is often a good idea to supplement health insurance policies with more **disability insurance** that pays part of the cost of a long-term sickness or an accident. The cost is relatively low to protect yourself from losing your livelihood for an extended period.

EDUCATION—THE BEST INVESTMENT

Throughout history, one investment strategy has paid off regardless of the state of the economy or political ups and downs. That investment is an investment in education. Everyone knows the benefits of getting graduate degrees in business and other areas. But those benefits are usually stated in terms of money or position (see Figure 23-2).

FIGURE 23-2

Median income comparisons of year-round workers by educational attainment, 1983.

YEARS OF SCHOOL COMPLETED	MEDIAN INCOME FOR MEN
Less than 8 years	$14,093
8 years	16,438
1 to 3 years high school	17,685
4 years high school	21,823
1 to 3 years college	24,613
4 years or more college	31,800

Source: 1986 Almanac.

Investing in education in curriculum areas such as art, literature, philosophy, psychology, music, and logic pays off in other ways. One can live a richer, fuller, and more enjoyable life when one fully appreciates music, drama, and knowledge for its own sake.

When planning for your financial future, it is wise to think of what you'll do when you become financially secure. Life is more than working and making money. An investment in education exposes you to other countries, other languages, new ideas, and different ways of life. If you invest in yourself, you will be making the best investment of all.

Make all you can, save all you can, give all you can.

Wesley

PLANNING YOUR RETIREMENT

It may seem too early to begin planning your retirement, but not to do so would be a big mistake. Successful financial planning means long-range planning, and retirement is a critical phase of life. What you do now could make a world of difference in the quality of life you will experience from age 65 to 85, and up.

Social Security

Social Security is the term used to describe the Old-Age, Survivors, and Disability Insurance Program established by the Social Security Act of 1935. There is no question that by the time you retire there will be huge changes in the Social Security system. The problem is that the system cannot afford to pay out more than it takes in. The number of people retiring and living longer is increasing dramatically, though the number of workers paying into social security per retiree is declining. The end result is likely to be (1) a bankrupt program; (2) serious cuts in benefits, likely including much later retirement and reduced cost of living adjustments (COLAs); or (3) much higher social security taxes. What happens to Social Security is important to you in that you probably should not count on it to provide you with ample funds for retirement. Rather, you should plan now to save funds for your nonworking years. The government has recognized the potential downfall of Social Security and has established incentives for you to save money now for retirement. Here are the specifics.

When you are young is the time to plan for retirement financing.

Individual Retirement Accounts (IRAs)

An **IRA** is a tax-deferred investment plan that enables you and your spouse to save part of your income for retirement. It is, in effect, a government-sponsored tax shelter. The money you put into the fund is not taxed, nor are the earnings taxed until you take them out when you retire. At that time, your tax rate should be lower.

individual retirement account (IRA)
A tax-deferred investment plan that enables one's self and one's spouse to save part of their income for retirement.

IRA accounts are probably the most important tax break ever made for workers. Everyone who works is eligible, even part-time workers. This includes people who are already covered by company retirement plans.

The amount you can put into an IRA has increased through the years. Now

IRA LIMITS

Under the new tax plan, people who have employee pension plans and who have an adjusted gross income that exceeds $35,000 ($50,000 per couple), cannot deduct the $2,000, but can still make contributions to an IRA, and the earnings are tax deferred. Single people earning less than $25,000 can still deduct the full amount ($2,000) and those earning $25,000 to $35,000 can deduct part of the contribution.

the dollar amount is $2,000 per year (check the latest figures). If you begin saving now, the money will compound over and over and become quite a nest egg by the time you retire. Opening an IRA account may be one of the wisest investments you can make.

A wide range of choices is available to you when you open an IRA. Your local bank, savings and loan, and credit union all have IRA savings plans available. Insurance companies offer such plans as well. You may prefer to be a little more aggressive with this money to earn a higher return. In that case, you can put your IRA funds into stocks, bonds, or mutual funds. Some mutual funds have multiple options (gold stocks, government securities, high-tech stocks, and more). You can switch from fund to fund or from investment to investment with your IRA funds. You can even open several different IRA accounts as long as the total amount invested doesn't exceed the government's limit. Talk to a broker, and learn your options.

Let's see why an IRA account is such a good deal for a young investor. The tremendous benefit is the fact that the invested money is not taxed, and neither are the earnings. That means fast returns and huge returns for you. For example, say you put $2,000 a year into an IRA. Normally, you would pay taxes on that $2,000. But because you put the money into an IRA, you won't have to pay those taxes. If you're in the 25% tax bracket, that means you save $500 in taxes! Put another way, the $2,000 you save only costs you $1,500—a huge bargain.

If you save $2,000 a year for 20 years and earn 12% a year, you will accumulate savings of over $160,000 in just 20 years and over $540,000 in 30 years. If you start when you are just out of school, you will be a millionaire by the time you retire. All you have to do is save $2,000 a year and earn 12%. Can you see why investment advisors often say that an IRA account is *the* best way to invest in your retirement?

You cannot take the money out until you are 59½ years old without paying a 10% penalty and paying taxes on the income. That is really a benefit for you, because it is less tempting to tap the fund when an emergency comes up or you see the car of your dreams. On the other hand, the money *is* there if a real emergency arises.

When you make financial plans, be sure to include an IRA. It's a sure path to being a millionaire some day and to having the funds available to enjoy your retirement years. You might consider contributing to an IRA through payroll deductions to assure the money is invested before you are tempted to spend it.

The new tax codes may limit the use of IRAs. This is a major issue in the passing of any tax reform in the future. The plan now is to continue the deduction for interest earned on IRAs, but not to make the initial contribution tax free if you already have a company retirement plan and make over $35,000.

THINKING IT THROUGH

From what you have heard about the Social Security system, does it seem like a good idea to open an IRA account? Do you understand the benefits? If not reread this section and seek outside counseling. An IRA is worth investigating.

You may want to find a broker too. Do you know anyone who has a broker he or she likes? Is he or she making money? Do you know how to contact a mutual fund broker? Now is the time to do the groundwork to assure yourself financial security later.

Keogh Plans

Millions of small businesspeople do not have the benefit of a corporate retirement system. Such people can contribute to an IRA account, but the amount they can invest is limited. The alternative for all those doctors, lawyers, real estate salespeople, artists, writers, small businesspeople, and other self-employed people is to establish their own Keogh Plan. It is like an IRA plan for entrepreneurs.

The advantage of Keogh Plans is that the maximum that can be invested is more than $30,000 per year. (The limit was $30,000 in 1984, and cost of living adjustments are added from 1986 on.) The original amount was much lower, but the government wanted to encourage self-employed people to build retirement funds. Both IRA and Keogh plans could be considered back-up plans to protect people against the likely declines in the value of the Social Security system. Even without any cuts, it looks like Social Security simply will not provide enough for a comfortable retirement.

Like IRA accounts, Keogh funds are not taxed nor are the returns the funds earn. Thus a person in the 25% tax bracket who invests $10,000 yearly in a Keogh saves $2,500 in taxes. That means, in essence, that the government is financing 25% of his or her retirement fund. As with an IRA, this is a good deal; no, an excellent deal.

If a person were to put the full $30,000 a year into a Keogh plan that earns a modest 10% a year, he or she would have over $5 million in the account after 30 years. Remember that this same person could put another $2,000 per year into an IRA account!

As with an IRA account, there is a 10% penalty for early withdrawal. Also like an IRA, funds may be withdrawn in a lump sum or spread out over the years. However, the key decision is the one you make now—to begin early to put funds into an IRA or Keogh plan (or both), so that the magic of compounding can turn that money into a sizeable retirement fund.

Financial Planners

If the idea of developing a comprehensive financial plan for your family seems overwhelming, relax; help is available. The people who assist families in developing a comprehensive program that covers investments, taxes, insurance, and other financial matters are called **financial planners.** Be careful, though; everybody and his brother are claiming to be financial planners today. Many are simply life insurance salespeople or mutual fund salespeople who call themselves "financial planners."

In the last few years, there has been an explosion in the number of companies offering financial services. Such companies are sometimes called "one-stop financial centers" or "financial supermarkets," because they provide a variety of financial services ranging from banking service to mutual funds, insurance, tax assistance, stocks, bonds, and real estate. It pays to shop around for financial advice. You can go to an independent financial planner or a financial service company. In either case, ask around among your friends and family. Find someone who understands your situation and is willing to spend some time with you.

Most financial planners begin with life insurance. They feel that most people should have basic term insurance coverage. They also explore your health insurance plans. They look for both medical expense and disability coverage. They may also recommend *major medical protection* to cover catastrophic illnesses.

financial planners
People who assist families in developing a comprehensive program that covers investments, taxes, insurance, and other financial matters.

Financial planning covers all aspects of investing, all the way to retirement and death. (Planning for estate taxes is important early in life.) Financial planners can steer you into the proper mix of IRA investments, stocks, bonds, precious metals (for example, gold), real estate, and so on.

If all of this sounds interesting to you, maybe you would enjoy a career as a financial planner. You could work independently and be a real asset to young people in need of counsel and advice. Find a financial planner in your area. Discuss what financial planners do and what recommendations they are now making for a person in your position. This is a fascinating field to study and could be a rewarding career.

PROGRESS CHECK

■ What is an IRA and why is it such a good investment?

■ What is a Keogh plan, and how does it differ from an IRA?

SUMMARY

1 The path to success in a capitalist system is to have money to invest. To do that, you must earn more than you spend.

■ Is there a proven strategy for a young couple to save and invest?

One effective strategy for a couple is to find two jobs and live off the salary of one. Save one income until you have the downpayment for a house. Buy the home and use other accumulated funds for furnishings, autos, and so on. Child rearing starts later.

■ What is the best investment?

Two investments that almost everyone should make are life insurance and real estate (your own home).

■ What is a major mistake most young people make with regard to finance?

They begin to use and then abuse credit cards. It is good discipline not to use credit cards at all.

2 Life insurance is recommended by most financial advisors for young couples. Certainly everyone should have some form of health insurance.

■ Are some life insurance policies better than others?

In general, it is better to buy term insurance and invest the additional money that whole life would cost in stocks, bonds, or other investments.

■ Should I have any additional health insurance other than that provided by my company?

Check and see if you have disability insurance. If not, the small additional cost is worth it.

3 It is important to begin planning for your retirement while you are still young.

■ Are there certain investments that are best for everyone?

Probably not. But everyone who invests would be wise to take advantage of IRA and Keogh plans, when applicable. This allows you to invest your money *before taxes*, and the income you make is tax free until you take it out. This increases your return dramatically. The best investment, however, you have already started to make; that is an investment in educating yourself.

KEY TERMS

adjustable life insurance
    p. 631
financial planners   p. 635
individual retirement
    account (IRA)   p. 633

term insurance   p. 630
universal life insurance   p. 630
variable life insurance   p. 630
whole life insurance   p. 630

GETTING INVOLVED

1 Few things are more surprising to a new college graduate than the cost of living, single or married, in an apartment. To prevent such surprises, calculate such costs now and share them with the class. Be sure to include rent, utilities, food, clothes, insurance (life, auto, disability), auto expenses, vacation, charity, recreation, doctors, furniture, and depreciation (auto). Then discuss the concept of living on *one* income, given these figures.

2 Go to the library and take out a couple of personal finance books and briefly read through them. Pay special attention to the material that is *not* covered in this chapter. Share highlights with the class.

3 Talk with your parents or others you know who have invested in a family home. What appreciation have they gained on the purchase price? What other benefits has the home brought? Discuss the benefits and drawbacks of owning a home and real estate in general as an investment now.

4 For just 1 month, write down *every cent* that you spend. Share what you learn with your class. If you find the exercise worthwhile, try it for a *year* and you'll really gain some insights.

5 Debate the following statement: "Resolved that the best investment one can make is in education, including education in the arts, literature, music, and dance." Take the side you do not now believe to see how others think.

CASE ONE   DECIDING WHEN TO START YOUR SAVINGS PLAN

**PRACTICING
MANAGEMENT DECISIONS**

The time to start a savings plan for your financial security in the future is now, not when you graduate and make more money. Why now? The miracle of compound interest needs time to do its magic. The more time, the better. For example, if you save just $10 a month, after 20 years (at 12%) you will have $9,198. After 40 years you will have over $97,000 dollars, and after 60 years you will have almost $1,000,000. The more you put in early, the better. For example, let's say you were given $120 in gifts for graduation. If you saved *that* money and added $10 per month, you would have almost $110,000 in 40 years (versus $97,000, without the extra $120). See what I mean? Invest now for big returns later. A lump sum of $1,000 invested now will return about $290,000 50 years from now at 12% ($391,583 if compounded monthly).

The idea is to consistently save a small percentage of your income. A goal might be 10% of your gross income per month or some dollar figure like $100 a month. Would you believe that saving $100 a month from the time you are 20 will add up to over $1,400,000 by the time you are 70 years old (at just a 10% return)? At 12%, you would have over $3,000,000! ($3,905,834 if compounded monthly.)

DECISION QUESTIONS

1 Are you ready to commit yourself to financial security in a few years? How much are you willing to save each month to get that security?

2 Could you save a dollar a day by making your own lunches or cutting back just a little on extras? Would it help to know that $1 a day would amount to almost $300,000 when you are 65 if you start at age 25 and earn 12%?

3 It's hard not to spend an extra $1,000 to get fancy equipment for your car or some other "luxury." Would it be easier to economize if you knew that $1,000 would grow to almost $30,000 in just 30 years at 12%? By the way, put that money into an IRA so Uncle Sam doesn't take a big bite out of it.

PRACTICING MANAGEMENT DECISIONS

CASE TWO   IS A WORD TO THE WISE REALLY SUFFICIENT?

There is a lot of talk about Social Security in the news these days, and no wonder. When the system was started, it was estimated that there would be 30 workers supporting each person who retired. By 1955, the ratio was down to six people supporting one retiree. Today the ratio is about three workers to one retiree. This means that you are going to be a terrible burden to tomorrow's workers *or* that tomorrow's workers may refuse to support the system, and you will be in big trouble. Best not to rely on Social Security for your retirement.

No one wants to frighten you, but the facts are rather grim. The 1980 U.S. Census found that 60% of America's retired people had income of less than $5,000 a year. Only 13% made over $10,000 a year. Because people are living longer all the time, you are likely to live for 20 or more years after retirement. Is it your goal to live on just $5,000 a year? If not, the time to plan for retirement is now.

If you save $10 a month now, you will have about $98,000 for your retirement (assuming you are age 25 or less). If you put in more, you will have more. Americans save less than people in all the other developed countries. We save less than 5% of our income compared to almost 15% by the West Germans and French and nearly 20% by the Japanese. Your retirement years can be spent in poverty—or on the beaches in the Bahamas. The managerial decision is yours to make now: save some reasonable part of every month's income or not.

DECISION QUESTIONS

1 Why do you suppose Americans do not save more money for their retirement years? Is the lure of pleasure now too great to resist saving just $10 a month? Do people put too much reliance on Social Security?

2 How many people under 30 years of age do you know who are saving for retirement? Do you think they would start saving earlier if they knew that at age 45 you have to save *ten times more* per month (that is, over $100 versus just over $10) to have $100,000 at age 65? Do such figures encourage you to save now?

LOOKING AHEAD

Like you, businesses must protect themselves against accidents, illness, and other catastrophes. They too must decide whether or not to buy insurance and what kind to buy if they do. Chapter 24 explores the function of risk management in firms and looks at a few major issues in this area, including the issue of the growth in lawsuits in the last decade or so.

RISK MANAGEMENT, ETHICS, AND INTERNATIONAL BUSINESS

PART VII

CHAPTER 24
RISK MANAGEMENT AND INSURANCE

CHAPTER 25
BUSINESS LAW AND ETHICS

CHAPTER 26
INTERNATIONAL BUSINESS

WHAT KIND OF COMPANY WOULD INSURE A 98-YEAR-OLD WOMAN IN POOR HEALTH?

A very proud one.

A very pleased one.

And a very thorough one.

You see, while we recognized the Statue of Liberty as a national monument to freedom and hope, we also saw the monumental amount of restoration it sorely needed.

So in 1984, when the CIGNA companies were first asked to provide insurance for the statue's renovation, we tried to provide more than insurance.

We brought in our own engineers to do an analysis of the project.

We assembled teams of specialists to look through designs and plans for the statue and the torch.

We looked for weaknesses.

We looked for risks.

In effect, we looked for trouble.

And when we found potential problems, we made suggestions to avoid them.

To help protect workers working on the statue.

And to help protect the statue itself.

We approached this task with the same high standards and dedication to thoroughness we apply to any major construction or reconstruction project we inspect. Although in this case, our efforts took on added significance.

After all, this time Liberty was at stake.

If you would like to know more about CIGNA Special Risk Facilities, write CIGNA Corporation, Department R10, One Logan Square, Philadelphia, Pennsylvania 19103.

Our continuing involvement in the restoration of the Statue of Liberty is just one more example of CIGNA's commitment to personalized service to each and every client.

RISK MANAGEMENT AND INSURANCE

LEARNING GOALS

After you have read and studied this chapter, you should be able to:

- Define risk, and distinguish between different kinds of risk faced by businesses and individuals.
- Discuss four ways to manage risk.
- Explain the causes of the insurance crisis of the 1980s.
- Describe the law of large numbers and several techniques used to reduce the cost of insurance.
- Discuss the issues involved in product liability.
- Describe careers in risk management.

PROFILE   HEINZ POPP, AUTOMOBILE DEALER

The costs of running a small business increase every year. Usually small business managers can adapt to such changes. In the 1980s, however, one cost of small business management has grown so fast that owners are finding it hard to adjust. Heinz Popp is one of those people. Like most of us, Mr. Popp had read about the large amounts that people were receiving from insurance companies as a result of accidents and other claims. Doctors seemed to be particularly hard hit because of the cost of malpractice insurance. But what did that have to do with Popp's auto dealership?

In 1985, Mr. Popp noticed that the insurance policy for his Porsche-Audi dealership in Brooklyn was about to expire. Mr. Popp got nervous when two insurance brokers told him they could not find a company that would issue a new policy. There was a possibility that the dealership would have to close.

Mr. Popp went to an auto dealers' group and found an insurance company willing to sell him a policy. That was the good news. The bad news was that Mr. Popp would have to pay whatever the insurance company decided to charge.

Mr. Popp learned that the new policy would cost $110,000, or nearly three times his old premium of $40,000. Mr. Popp needed the insurance, though, to cover his $2.3 million worth of new cars and auto parts against loss or damage.

Mr. Popp is not the only one who has had such problems recently. Across the nation, businesses of all sizes are facing premium increases ranging from 25% to 1,000% for property and liability insurance. The reason is that insurance companies are paying out more and more each year in claims. Statistics show that many insurance companies are paying out more than they are taking in. That is bad news

Heinz Popp.

CNA is vigorously championing a wide spectrum of actions to reform the civil justice system . . . unless this occurs, the affordability and availability of liability insurance is in grave jeopardy.

EDWARD J. NOHA, CEO, THE CNA INSURANCE COMPANIES

for the insurance companies. But, in the long run, the people who have to pay for such increases are business owners like Mr. Popp. Ultimately, you and I pay through higher prices for automobiles and other goods and services.

This chapter is about risk management. In the past, the best way to protect against risk was to buy insurance. Today the cost of insurance is so high that other options besides insurance coverage must be explored, along with insurance coverage. ■

Source: David B. Hilden, "Small Firms Face Sharp Cost Hikes for Insurance—If they Can Get It" *The Wall Street Journal,* August 5, 1985, p. 23. © Dow Jones & Co., Inc., 1985.

MANAGING RISK

The management of risk has become a major issue for businesses throughout the country. Every day you read or hear about a major earthquake, flood, fire, airplane crash, or truck accident that destroyed property or injured someone. Such reports are so much a part of the news that we tend to accept these calamitous events as part of everyday life.

Such events mean much more to businesspeople. They must pay to restore the property and compensate those who are injured. In addition to the newsmaking stories, there are thousands of other incidents that might involve businesspeople in lawsuits. They include everything from job-related accidents to people being injured from using a business's products.

What Mr. Popp learned, and what all businesspeople are learning, is that the courts are rewarding higher and higher dollar awards to people who are hurt[1]:

- Two Maryland men tried to dry their hot air balloon in a commercial laundry dryer. The dryer exploded, injuring them both. They received $885,000 in damages.
- A 41-year-old bodybuilder entered a race with a refrigerator strapped to his back to show his strength. During the race, one of the straps came loose and he was hurt. He sued and won $1 million.

These are not isolated cases of unusual awards. Rather, they represent the trend in litigation in the U.S. In 1984, the *average* product liability award was $1.07 million, up from about $350,000 ten years earlier. The average medical malpractice award was close to $1 million. In 1983, 360 personal-injury cases were settled for $1 million or more. This is 13 times the number that were settled for $1 million in 1973.[2]

Organizations must recognize this upward trend in insurance claims and develop strategies for dealing with it. One way to manage risk is to buy insurance, but insurance is getting very expensive, as you learned in the case of Heinz Popp. This chapter is concerned with risk management. Let's begin by defining some terms.

risk
The *chance* of loss, the degree of *probability* of loss, and the *amount* of possible loss.

speculative risk
A type of risk that involves a chance of either profit or loss.

IDENTIFYING RISK

The term **risk** refers to the *chance* of loss, the degree of *probability* of loss, and the *amount* of possible loss. In business there are different kinds of risk:

- **Speculative risk** is a type of risk that involves a chance of either profit or loss. It includes the chance a firm takes to make extra money by expanding its options, buying new machinery, acquiring more inventory, and making other decisions with which the probability of loss may be relatively low and the amount of loss is known. Speculative risk is the kind of risk you take when you bet on a horse race or play poker. One takes speculative risk on the chance of making a profit. In business, building a new plant is a speculative risk in that it may result in a loss.

pure risk
The threat of loss with no chance for profit.

- **Pure risk** is defined as the threat of loss with no chance for profit. Pure risk involves the threat of fire, accident, or loss. If such events occur, a company loses money; but if the events do not occur, the company gains nothing.

The risk that is of most concern to businesspeople is *pure risk*. Pure risk threatens the very existence of some firms. Once such risks are identified, firms have several options:

1 Reduce the risk
2 Self-insure against the risk
3 Avoid the risk
4 Buy insurance to cover the risk

INTERNATIONAL PERSPECTIVE ON INSURANCE

Insurance is designed to protect us from all kinds of risk. In Japan, there is a rather unique need for insurance: insurance to protect you in case you get a hole in one in golf.

Anyone who gets a hole in one is expected to have a party and send presents to friends, coworkers, and everyone who saw the event. The cost can be thousands of dollars.

The solution? Hole in one insurance. For a fee of $5 to $10 per year, a Japanese golfer is protected if such misfortune (or luck) occurs.

Source: E.S. Browning, "A Stroke of Luck Is Bad News in Japan If One Isn't Insured" *The Wall Street Journal*, August 12, 1985, p. 1.

Reducing Risk

A firm can reduce the chance of risk occurring by establishing loss-prevention programs such as fire drills, health education, safety inspections, equipment maintenance, accident prevention programs, and so on. Many retail stores, for example, have mirrors, video cameras, and other devices to spot and prevent shoplifting. Water sprinklers are used to minimize fire loss. Most machines have safety devices to protect workers' fingers, eyes, and so on.

Self-Insurance

Many companies and municipalities have turned to self-insurance because they either can't find or can't afford conventional property/casualty policies. Such firms set aside money to cover routine claims, and buy only "catastrophe" policies to cover big losses. The *amount* of loss is managed this way. At the Illinois insurance brokerage Arthur J. Gallagher & Company, the number of self-insured clients doubled from 1984 to 1985. Business is up 50% at a Dallas-based firm that administers claims and provides loss control services for self-insurers.[3]

Self-insurance is most appropriate when a firm has several widely distributed facilities. The risk from fire, theft, or other catastrophe is then more manageable.

mutual insurance company
Firm owned by its policyholders.

Firms with huge facilities, in which a major fire or earthquake could destroy the entire operation, usually turn to insurance companies to cover the risk.

One way to self-insure with others is to set up a **mutual insurance company** (that is, an insurance company owned by the policyholders). Such companies are being established by drug, chemical, railroad, utility, hazardous waste disposal, banking, and thrift industries. Already in operation is A.C.E. Insurance Company, which was started in 1985 by 34 major companies from a variety of industries, including auto, steel, oil, retailing, and entertainment.[4] The rash of new mutual companies is in response to escalating insurance rates from insurance companies. High rates are also forcing people to *avoid* risks, sometimes by going out of business.

INSURANCE TURNS DISASTER INTO OPPORTUNITY

The Allen-Edmonds Shoe Corporation of Belgium, Wisconsin had been in business for over 60 years when fire struck the company's main production facility. Only the chimney was left standing. Everything else was destroyed, including 50,000 pairs of shoes.

The company had insurance to cover such a loss. The old manufacturing plant was inefficient. The insurance money enabled the firm to build a modern manufacturing facility.

The fire occurred on a Friday night. By Monday, other small shoe manufacturers were helping, and offices were set up in an abandoned school. Within 2 weeks, the company was producing 1,000 pairs of shoes—on weekends in a factory owned by another company, 45 miles away. Production was then shifted to a site only a few miles from the original plant while a new facility was constructed.

Meanwhile, quality is up, efficiency is up, and worker morale is up. The workers seem to value their jobs more after facing the possibility of losing them.

Source: Sanford L. Jacobs, "Shoe Concern Turns Disaster Into Means of Raising Quality," *The Wall Street Journal*, April 16, 1984, p. 35. © Dow Jones & Co., Inc., 1984.

Avoiding Risk

Most risks cannot be avoided. There is always the chance of fire, theft, automobile accident, or injury. On the other hand, some companies are avoiding risk by not accepting hazardous jobs and by contracting out shipping and other functions to others. The threat of lawsuits has driven some drug companies from manufacturing vaccines; consulting engineers refuse to work hazardous sites. Some companies are losing outside directors for lack of liability coverage.[5]

In 1985, Cessna Aircraft Company stopped making five types of small planes because product liability premiums, which account for 30% of a plane's cost, had driven the price of new models beyond the reach of most customers. The city of Miami cancelled plans for an experimental railbus line because it couldn't find insurance coverage.[6] Several ice-skating rinks and ski resorts closed rather than pay sky-high insurance payments.

Other examples could be cited of doctors, municipalities, day care centers, and other businesses, professionals, and nonprofit organizations avoiding risk by going out of business or ceasing services. Many are calling the high cost of insurance a "liability crisis" (see Figure 24-1).

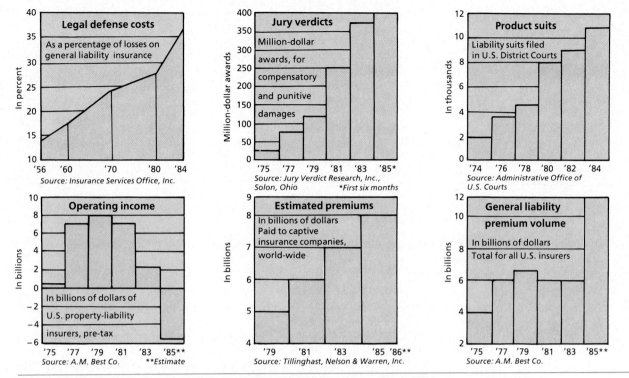

The rising cost of insurance and falling profits. This figure shows that million-dollar awards went up over 800% from 1976 to 1984-1985. Product suits almost tripled in that same period. Insurance premiums more than doubled, but insurance company profits were *negative* in 1984-1985.

Source: "Business Struggling to Adapt as Insurance Crisis Spreads," *The Wall Street Journal*, January 21, 1986, p. 31. © Dow Jones & Co., Inc., 1986.

FIGURE 24-1

CHANGING "DEEP POCKET" RULES

The tort (personal injury) system in the United States is going through a period of change. The U.S. Chamber of Commerce is especially concerned about the erosion of long-held doctrines requiring that fault be found before monetary damages can be recovered. As it is now, "compensation without fault" encourages legal actions against "deep pocket" defendants. That is, people are suing businesses, utilities, cities, and counties because they can afford to pay or have insurance, rather than because they are at fault. An example is the insurance company that was required to pay $260,000 plus $1,500 a month to a man who was injured when he fell through a skylight while burglarizing a school.

Another example is a woman who was injured when she fell asleep with a cigarette in her hand and set a hotel mattress on fire. She sued the cigarette company, the mattress maker, and the hotel. Even though she failed in her suit, her case illustrates the trend toward suing those with the most money regardless of fault (suing those with "deep pockets").

The federal government is in the process of establishing laws that would limit liability awards to strictly defined negligence or fault, preempting state laws. Senate Commerce Committee Chairman John C. Danforth is working on such legislation. It could go a long way toward lessening the liability burden of businesses and government organizations.

Source: "Capping the Courts," *The Wall Street Journal*, December 3, 1985, p. 30, "The Insurance Crisis: Now Everyone Is in a Risky Business," *Business Week*, March 10, 1986, pp. 88-92, and Theo Stamos, "Liability Insurance Crisis Is Looming," *The Washington Times*, December 4, 1985, p. 7c.

THINKING IT THROUGH

What kind of risks are you incurring every day? Which risks are you reducing through *loss prevention programs?* For example, do you lock your home and car doors? Do you eat healthy foods and exercise?

For what risks are you self-insured? (Do you have health insurance, car insurance, and life insurance?)

What other insurance should you have? Do you have major disability insurance for long-term illnesses? Do you have liability insurance? Are you insured against fire and theft? Can you see that you are a risk manager already?

The Insurance Crisis

The insurance crisis is illustrated best by this opening from a *Washington Post* article[7]:

> You cannot use a sled in Denver city parks. You cannot have a baby delivered in Monroe County, Alabama. You cannot buy any of the 58,000 published copies of Barbara Hutton's biography.
>
> If you have the stomach upset known as hyperemesis, you cannot get the pill that is certified as safe. . . . You can no longer buy the classic Jeep sedan. . . . You may not find a fireworks display next Fourth of July. You cannot set foot on dozens of the finest hiking trails in Yellowstone National Park. . . .
>
> Each of these diverse prohibitions, and many others as well, stems from the same central problem, a problem that will be one of the preeminent legal, economic and political issues of the late 1980s: the civil liability crisis.

The article goes on to say that the big insurance companies can't or won't provide all the coverage needed. Figure 24-1 tells why. Insurance losses have risen dramatically, and insurance companies are losing money. They can't raise premium prices high enough to cover the risks, so coverage for day care centers, bus lines, nurse-midwives, commercial fishing companies, and others are simply not being renewed. If insurance can be found, it is at unbelievably higher prices. For example, the Southern California Rapid Transit District had *no* accidents last year and its insurance went up from $67,000 to $3.2 million, a 4,700% jump in 1 year! The tripling of costs for Mr. Popp's Porsche-Audi dealer (See the Profile) seems cheap by comparison.

The insurance crisis has several causes. One is the huge increase in the number of lawsuits and the large damage awards. Another cause is the fact that people can sue organizations for injuries for which the organization was not at fault (see the box on p. 645). Yet another cause is the fact that insurance companies cut premiums a few years ago to compete for business when interest rates and investment earnings were high. Lower interest rates drastically cut the return on the investments, and losses occurred. Others feel that the number of lawyers in the United States (675,000 in 1985) contributes to the number of court cases. The number of product liability cases rose from 1,579 in 1975 to 10,745 in 1985.[8] See the insert titled "Too Many Lawyers?"

Regardless of the causes, the late 1980s will witness a focus on insurance unparalleled in the history of the United States. You can prepare for reading about these issues by learning the terms and concepts that follow.

TOO MANY LAWYERS?

Between 1967 and 1983, the number of lawyers in the United States more than doubled. If the number of lawyers continues to increase at that rate, by the year 2074 every man, woman, and child in the United States will be a lawyer. Since 1980, American law schools have graduated more than 35,000 new lawyers each year. In 1954, about 8,000 graduated. So the number of new lawyers coming out of school has more than quadrupled since the 1950s. What will all these lawyers do? If the early 1980s are any indication, they will see that more and more people spend time in court, at a cost that is becoming unbearable.

Source: A speech by John Silber, president of Boston University, reported by Jeff Jacoby in "Legal Locusts Are Swarming," *The Washington Times,* August 27, 1985, p. 14A.

© *The New Yorker,* 1986.

INSURANCE COMPANIES

There are two major types of insurance companies. A **stock insurance company** is owned by stockholders, just like any other investor-owned company. A *mutual insurance company* is owned by its policyholders. The largest life insurance company, Prudential, is a mutual insurance company (see the margin at right). Note that Northwestern Mutual has the word "mutual" in its company name. Aetna, on the other hand, is a stock insurance company.

A mutual insurance company issues *participating insurance.* That means that any excess profits (over losses, expenses, and growth costs) go to the policyholder/investor in the form of dividends. There are many small mutual insurance companies in the East and Midwest that provide limited coverage for fire, theft, vandalism, and natural disasters for farmers. As you have just learned, many new mutual insurance companies are being started by businesses because they cannot get insurance at reasonable rates from stock insurance companies.

stock insurance company
Owned by stockholders, just like any other investor-owned company.

THE 10 LARGEST LIFE INSURANCE COMPANIES, 1985

1 Prudential (M)
2 Metropolitan (M)
3 Equitable (M)
4 Aetna (S)
5 New York Life (M)
6 John Hancock (M)
7 Travelers (S)
8 Connecticut General (M)
9 Teachers Insurance & Annuity (TIAA) (M)
10 Northwestern Mutual (M)

Source: *Fortune,* June 10, 1985

M, Mutual company.
S, Stock company.

▪ What are the four ways to handle pure risks?

▪ What are some of the causes of the "insurance crisis" of the 1980s?

THE LAW OF LARGE NUMBERS

insurance policy
A written contract between the insured and an insurance company that promises to pay for all or part of a loss.

premium
The fee charged by an insurance company.

law of large numbers
States that if a large number of people or organizations are exposed to the same risk, a predictable number of losses will occur.

An **insurance policy** is a written contract between the insured (an individual or organization) and an insurance company that promises to pay for all or part of a loss. A **premium** is the cost of the policy to the insured or the fee charged by the insurance company.

As it is for all private businesses, the objective of an insurance company is to make a profit. To assure that it makes a profit, an insurance company gathers data to determine the extent of the risk. What makes the acceptance of risk possible for insurance companies is the law of large numbers.

The **law of large numbers** states that if a large number of people or organizations are exposed to the same risk, a predictable number of losses will occur during a given period of time. Once the insurance company calculates these figures, it can determine the appropriate premiums. The premium is supposed to be high enough to cover expected losses and yet earn a profit for the firm and stockholders. Today, insurance companies are charging high premiums, not for past risks, but for the anticipated costs associated with more court cases and higher damage awards.

Rule of Indemnity

rule of indemnity
States that an insured person or organization cannot collect more than the actual loss from an insurable risk.

The **rule of indemnity** says that an insured person or organization cannot collect more than the actual loss from an insurable risk. One cannot gain from risk management, only minimize losses. One cannot, for example, buy two insurance policies and collect from both for the same loss. If a company or person carried two policies, the two insurance companies would calculate any loss and split the reimbursement.

Coinsurance Clause

coinsurance clause
Requires businesses to carry insurance equal to a certain percentage of a building's actual value, usually 80%.

One way that individuals and corporations have tried to cut insurance costs is by underinsuring property. Most fires and other losses only damage part of the property, so rather than insure a building for its total worth, say $1,000,000, the policyholder may buy just $500,000 worth of insurance. This kind of thinking seems rational, but it throws off the calculations for the law of large numbers. Therefore, insurance companies have adopted a coinsurance clause.

A **coinsurance clause** requires businesses to carry insurance equal to a certain percentage of a building's actual value, usually 80%. If a firm were to buy only $500,000 worth of insurance on a $1,000,000 property and had a $300,000 loss, the insurance company would pay only a portion of the loss. The insurance company would calculate the payment as follows:

$$\frac{\text{Amount of actual insurance}}{\text{Amount demanded by coinsurance}} = \frac{\$500,000}{\$800,000} = \frac{5}{8}$$

$$\text{Loss} = \$300,000 \times \frac{5}{8} = \$187,000 = \text{insurance payment.}$$

Deductible Clauses

A **deductible clause** says that the insurance company will pay only that part of a loss in excess of some figure (the deductible amount) stated in the policy. This is another way that people and businesses use to cut insurance costs. The higher the deductible amount, the lower the premium. Thus a policy on an automobile may have a $300 deductible clause. That means the insured is responsible for the first $300 of a loss. A similar clause may be available in health insurance policies and other insurance coverages. Given these basic terms, we can discuss specific coverages for businesses.

deductible clause
States that the insurance company will pay only that part of a loss that exceeds some figure (the deductible amount) stated in the policy.

BUSINESS RISK INSURANCE

As we have discussed, risk management consists of reducing risk, self-insurance, avoiding risk, and buying insurance. In this section, we shall discuss some of the insurance policies that businesses can buy. Figure 24-2 briefly reviews such policies. We shall now discuss various areas in more detail.

Fire	A comprehensive policy of this type covers damage from fire, theft, windstorm, and earthquake.
Auto and truck	Such insurance usually covers property damage, bodily injury, collision (including damage to company cars), fire, theft, vandalism, and other related vehicle losses.
Marine and aviation	Covers boats and their cargo and airplanes and their cargo.
Liability	This very important insurance protects against legal claims from the firm's products or operations.
Workers compensation	Covers injuries sustained on the job.
Criminal loss	Special insurance may be needed to cover employee theft and losses from break-ins.
Credit	Protects against nonpayment by customers.
Business interruption	Covers losses from the firm being closed because of various events such as power outages.
Health	Usually the firm pays part of the cost of employee health insurance.
Life	Firms buy life insurance to protect against the loss of key executives and workers. Small businesses are especially vulnerable to losing their owner or manager.
Farm insurance	Covers property and liability risks on farms.

FIGURE 24-2

Examples of business risk insurance.

fire insurance
Covers losses to buildings and their contents from fire.

rider
Addition to a fire insurance policy that covers losses from wind, hail, explosion, riot, smoke, and falling aircraft.

PROPERTY INSURANCE

Fire insurance covers losses to buildings and their contents from fire. A **rider** (addition) to most policies also covers losses such as wind, hail, explosion, riot, smoke, and falling aircraft. Fire insurance is getting more expensive, along with other insurance coverage, because of the rise of arson. Each year arson destroys $3 billion worth of property and kills 1,000 people. It is the United States' most costly crime.[9]

THE 20 LARGEST U.S. PROPERTY/CASUALTY INSURANCE GROUPS

Ranked by net premium written as of December 31, 1984. Consolidated group data with interownership eliminated.

RANK (1984)	GROUP	ADMITTED ASSETS (THOUSANDS OF DOLLARS)
1	State Farm	19,961,140
2	Allstate	11,336,824
3	Aetna L&C	11,380,032
4	Travelers Insurance	9,702,031
5	CIGNA	10,140,345
6	Farmers Insurance	4,926,104
7	Liberty Mutual	8,210,288
8	Nationwide	5,003,762
9	Fireman's Fund	6,430,163
10	Continental Insurance	5,794,918
11	Hartford	6,720,277
12	USF&G	4,582,313
13	Crum & Forster	4,879,936
14	St. Paul	4,550,830
15	CNA	6,256,189
16	American International	4,811,695
17	Kemper	4,363,969
18	Chubb	3,224,924
19	Home Insurance	3,830,356
20	American Financial	2,552,559

Source: An ad for Insurance '86, *Fortune*, November 11, 1985, p. 71.

Automobile Insurance

Automobile insurance is the most widely purchased of all property/liability coverage. There are 10 types of coverage. Each policy pays up to the limit of the coverage.

bodily injury insurance
Covers bodily injury to others resulting from the ownership, maintenance, or use of a car.

- **Bodily injury insurance** covers bodily injury to others resulting from the ownership, maintenance, or use of a car.
- *Collision insurance* pays for damage to the insured's car as the result of collision with another car or object. The worth of the car sets a limit for the insurance.
- *Property damage insurance* covers accidental damage or destruction of property of another person.
- *Uninsured motorist insurance* pays the insured and any passengers for losses

resulting from injury, sickness, disease, or death caused by the owner or operator of an *uninsured* car or a hit-and-run driver.

■ *Underinsured motorist insurance* covers unpaid losses because the at-fault party's insurance was not sufficient.

■ *Medical payments insurance* pays the reasonable and necessary medical expenses incurred by the insured, resident family members, and guests in the insured's car. It also covers medical expenses for injuries caused by a vehicle while the insured is walking, riding in another car, or riding a bicycle.

■ *Personal injury protection* pays for medical expenses (in "no-fault" states), loss of income, death and/or disability, and loss of services. Coverage varies by state.

■ *Auto death indemnity* provides limited life-insurance protection from death in an auto accident that is not intentional.

■ *Auto disability income* provides weekly benefits in the event of total disability from an auto accident.

■ *Comprehensive coverage* covers losses from theft or damage from causes other than collision, including fire, glass breakage, vandalism, falling objects, hail, windstorm, flood, or collision with an animal.

It is usually best to have one policy that covers all these risks. For collision damage, insurance is cheaper if you have a *deductible clause*. That means you pay the first $100 to $1,000 (whatever level of deductible you choose), and the insurance company pays the rest. This means you avoid going to the insurance company and getting estimates every time you have a slight bump or scrape.

Marine and Aviation Insurance

Marine insurance is of two types: **ocean marine insurance,** which protects shippers from losses of property from damages to a ship or its cargo while at sea or in port, and **inland marine insurance,** which covers transportation-related or transportable property while goods are being transported by ship, rail, truck, or plane. *Ocean marine* insurance covers boats and cargo. *Inland marine* insurance covers virtually any transportable item from white mice used in the space program to corpses. **Aviation insurance** covers aircraft and any damage and liability from the use of aircraft.

ocean marine insurance
Protects shippers from losses of property from damage to a ship or its cargo while at sea or in port.

inland marine insurance
Covers transportation-related or transportable property while goods are being transported by ship, rail, truck, or plane.

aviation insurance
Covers aircraft and damage and liability from the use of aircraft.

LIABILITY INSURANCE

Public liability insurance provides protection for businesses and individuals against losses resulting from personal injuries or damage to the property of others for which the insured is responsible. A *public liability* policy was once adequate, but not today with lawsuits being brought from many unexpected sources. Now a firm needs *extended product liability* insurance to cover potentially *toxic substances* in products, *environmental liability,* and *directors and officer liability insurance*. All these new risks led to an *umbrella liability insurance* policy that covers all such risks and extends the amount of coverage to $1 million or more.

public liability insurance
Protects against losses resulting from personal injuries or damage to the property of others for which the insured is responsible.

Workers' Compensation Insurance

All states have laws that provide compensation for workers injured on the job. Some states sell **workers' compensation insurance** themselves. Other states allow

workers' compensation insurance
Provides compensation for workers injured on the job.

a firm to choose between private or state coverage, and still others leave coverage to private insurance companies. Regardless of the system, businesses must buy this insurance. The cost varies with the size of the firm's payroll and the risks involved. If a worker is injured on the job, medical and hospitalization costs are paid. The worker also receives some percentage of lost wages, usually after a short waiting period.

The Issue of Product Liability Insurance

Few issues in the insurance field received more attention in the 1980s than that of product liability. Once, the standard for measuring product defects was **strict liability.** In essence, this meant that there was no legal defense for placing a product on the market that was dangerous to the consumer *because of a known or knowable defect.* This standard seemed reasonable to businesses; no one should sell a defective product.

Recently, however, the courts have fashioned a new policy that extends liability in ways unexpected by producers. The new standard is called **absolute liability,** and it means a manufacturer can be held liable for failure to warn of a hazard even if the hazard was scientifically unknowable at the time of sale. Absolute liability may even be undesirable for consumers, because they ultimately must pay for the added cost of insurance through higher-priced products.

The most publicized case illustrating absolute liability involved the Manville Corporation in 1982. Manville filed for bankruptcy because it could not pay the claims made by tens of thousands of workers who had been exposed to asbestos on the job. The company denied knowing that asbestos was dangerous until recently. In the 1970s, $1 billion was spent in the U.S. on asbestos-exposure litigation.

The rule of absolute liability has had serious consequences for manufacturers of chemicals and drugs. A producer may place a drug or chemical on the market that everyone (including government inspectors and testers) agrees is safe. Years later, a side-effect or other health problem could emerge; the drug or chemical may have caused sickness, injury, or death. Under the doctrine of absolute liability, the manufacturer is held liable. This puts much more uncertainty and risk into the

strict liability
States that there is no legal defense for placing a product on the market that is dangerous to the consumer because of a known or knowable defect.

absolute liability
Means a manufacturer can be held liable for failure to warn of a hazard, even if the hazard was scientifically unknowable at the time of sale.

Careless use of equipment can lead to lawsuits.

business of making such products. Some notable cases will illustrate how strict the courts have become[10]:

- International Harvester Company was held liable for the operation of a skid loader it built. The farmer who bought the machinery had the maker remove the standard protective cage so the loader could pass through his barn door. The operator was subsequently crushed by a boom arm. This could not have happened had the protective cage been attached. The product was found defective by a jury.

- The Supreme Court of Appeals of West Virginia upheld a $500,000 award against a manufacturer of radial tires for damages suffered in an accident. The driver had purchased the car used, and the previous owner had put two radials and two nonradials on the car. The radial tire maker had advertised that this shouldn't be done. The court held that the tire maker should have stamped this warning on the side of the tires so used-car buyers would be aware of the problem.

Other cases that could be cited reveal unexpected conclusions by the courts. Producers feel totally exposed to lawsuits for almost any accident involving almost anything, and people *will* do stupid and dangerous things with products. Several people have lost fingers by picking up electric lawn mowers to clip their bushes; the producer was held liable.

Recently, new legislation was proposed to introduce a new **reasonable prudence** standard for product liability. Under this bill, a product would be held to be unreasonably dangerous if "the manufacturer knew, or through the exercise of reasonable prudence, should have known about the danger that allegedly caused the claimant's harm," and if "a reasonably prudent person in the same or similar circumstances would not have manufactured the product or used the design or formulation that the manufacturer used."

Naturally most manufacturers support such legislation, because it would protect them from paying for damages that no "prudent person" could have avoided. Such legislation could do much to lower the costs of insurance to producers and to you as a customer of those firms. On the other hand, consumers would have to assume more responsibility for using products with care (or at least "reasonable prudence").

reasonable prudence
States that a product is unreasonably dangerous if the manufacturer knew, or through the exercise of reasonable prudence should have known, about the danger that allegedly caused the claimant's harm and if a reasonably prudent person in the same or similar circumstances would not have manufactured the product.

THINKING IT THROUGH

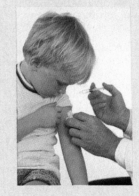

Pharmaceutical firms are being held liable for illnesses caused by shots given for childhood diseases. Diphtheria-tetanus-pertussis (DTP) vaccine saves thousands of lives each year, but a few children get sick and die from the shots. Consequently, to avoid lawsuits, many pharmaceutical companies are refusing to produce serum. This could mean the return of certain childhood diseases if something isn't done about the problem.

Does the court system seem unreasonable in its liability judgments? Who pays in the long run for huge rewards for injuries?

Physicians, especially obstetricians who deliver babies, must pay up to $56,000 a year for malpractice insurance. These doctors could be sued for a delivery they performed 20 years ago. Many doctors are shying away from the specialty of obstetrics for that reason. Is this a case of the courts being too strict, or is it merely a good example of the government (in the form of judges) protecting the consumer in a reasonable and prudent manner?

Commercial Multiline Policies

multiline policies
Insurance "packages" that include both property and liability coverage.

Multiline policies are insurance "packages" that include both property and liability coverage. They are specifically designed to meet the insurance needs of businesses and other organizations. Multiline policies are meant to cover virtually all of the insurance needs of the organization. The obvious advantage is having *one* policy with *one* company for everything.

PROGRESS CHECK

- What is the difference between a mutual insurance company and a stock insurance company?
- What is the law of large numbers?
- Can you define the following?
  1 Rule of indemnity
  2 Coinsurance clause
  3 Liability insurance
  4 Deductible clause
  5 Comprehensive coverage (auto insurance)

criminal loss protection
Insurance against theft, burglary, or robbery.

nonperformance loss protection
Insurance against failure of a contractor, supplier, or other person to fulfill an obligation.

fidelity bond
Protects an employer for financial loss resulting from employee dishonesty such as theft or forgery.

surety bond
Protects against the failure of a second party to fulfill an obligation.

credit life insurance
Guarantees the payment of the amount due on a loan if the debtor dies.

commercial credit insurance
Protects manufacturers and wholesalers from credit losses due to insolvency or default.

business interruption insurance
Provides protection for a business that shuts down because of fire, storm, or other insured causes; it covers lost income, continuing expenses, and utility expenses.

CRIMINAL LOSS AND NONPERFORMANCE PROTECTION

Criminal loss protection is insurance against theft (stealing of unprotected property), burglary (forcible entry), or robbery (taking of property by threat of violence or actual violence). **Nonperformance loss protection** is insurance against failure of a contractor, supplier, or other person to fulfill an obligation.

A **fidelity bond** protects an employer from financial loss resulting from employee dishonesty such as theft or forgery. It is common to buy fidelity bonds for retail clerks, bank tellers, salespeople who carry expensive samples, and other employees with ready access to cash or valuable property.

A **surety bond** protects against the failure of a second party to fulfill an obligation. In public construction projects, for example, the government requires surety bonds for every contract. Such bonds are also required for contracts on garbage collecting and snow removal. If you were to have a home built, and the bonded construction firm used improper materials or refused to finish the job, the bonding company would find another firm to correct or finish the work. Other forms of criminal and nonperformance insurance include:

- **Credit life insurance,** which guarantees the payment of the amount due on a loan if the debtor dies. It is a form of nonperformance insurance and is paid by the borrower.
- **Commercial credit insurance** protects manufacturers and wholesalers from credit losses due to insolvency or default.

BUSINESS INTERRUPTION INSURANCE

Business interruption insurance provides protection for a business that shuts down because of fire, storms, or other insured perils. It covers lost income, continuing expenses (for example, payroll and mortgage payments), and utility expenses.

HEALTH INSURANCE

Business and nonprofit organizations may offer their employees an array of health care benefits to choose from. Everything from hospitalization to physician fees, eye exams, dental exams, and prescriptions can be covered. Employees often may choose between options from health care providers (for example, Blue Cross/Blue Shield), health maintenance organizations (HMOs) that emphasize preventive medicine, or preferred provider organizations (PPOs) that are like HMOs, but allow employees to choose their own physicians.

In addition, major medical insurance is usually available to cover major long-term illnesses. Employees may also want accident insurance, cancer insurance, and other specialized health insurance policies.

Because of the many options available, some firms are offering flex or cafeteria plans. Employees can pick the benefits they want from a whole smorgasboard of possibilities. Options vary widely, including extra vacations rather than health insurance.

LIFE INSURANCE FOR BUSINESSES

We have already discussed life insurance in Chapter 23. There the focus was on life insurance for you and your family. Everything said there applies to life insurance for business executives as well. The best coverage for most individuals is term insurance, but dozens of new policies with interesting features have been emerging recently.

In business, risk managers are interested in life insurance for executives and employees. Some of the life insurance plans that risk managers deal with include (1) group life insurance, (2) owner or executive insurance, and (3) retirement and pension plans.

Group Life Insurance

A **group life policy** covers all the employees of a firm or member of a group. Rates for group insurance are lower than for individual policies. One reason is that insurance agents make up to 50% of the first year's payment, so buying in volume saves a lot of money. Usually group policies are based on the earnings of the employee. A policy may be for 1 or 2 years' salary. These are usually 1-year renewable term policies. The employer often pays most of the premium.

Often you can save money by joining some group to buy group term insurance. For example, teachers, union members, and members of various organizations can buy term insurance for much less by buying it as a member of the group. A good risk manager in a firm will tell you about such options and make policies beyond the corporate coverage available to employees.

group life policy
Covers all employees of a firm or member of a group.

Owner or Key Executive Insurance

If a sole proprietor or a partner in a business dies, the assets may have to be sold to pay off debts, financial expenses, and taxes. An owner or key executive insurance policy would enable the firm to pay off all bills and continue operating, saving jobs for the employees. In a partnership, the beneficiary of the policy is often the other partner, who uses the funds to buy the partner's shares. A risk manager would be sure that top executives were covered by life insurance so the money would be available to hire and train or relocate another manager with no loss to the firm.

Retirement and Pension Plans

With the Social Security system in financial difficulty, it is almost mandatory that firms provide their employees with supplemental retirement and pension plans. Many different arrangements can be made relative to how much the firm contributes and how much the employee contributes, but the important thing is to have some plan.

LIFE INSURANCE FOR SMALL BUSINESS

More than half of the privately-owned businesses in the United States would go out of business if their principal stockholder died. What's more, over half of these companies lack sufficient disability protection for their owners. One obvious answer is insurance, but there are other creative solutions. For example, the owner can leave his business to a charity and have his heirs use insurance on the owner's life to buy the company back. That way, the family gets the business, the charity gets the cash, and the estate pays no taxes.

Source: "After You've Gone," *Forbes,* October 21, 1985, p. 10.

FARM INSURANCE

A farm includes many pieces of property—barns, sheds, equipment, machinery, hay and grain—that are not covered by the standard homeowner's policy. Several different kinds of policies are available to farmers to cover the risks of ownership of such property:

- *Basic coverage* covers the house and all personal property against perils such as fire, theft, windstorm or hail, explosion, riot, smoke, and vandalism.
- *Scheduled farm personal property* covers property needed for operating the farm including hay, grain, fertilizers, machinery, farm vehicles and equipment, farm records, and livestock.
- *Blanket coverage* is like scheduled farm personal property and applies to goats, horses, mules, and donkeys. (Other animals and poultry are not covered.) Some crops, including tobacco, cotton, vegetables, and fruit are not included.
- *Liability insurance* covers claims by people injured on the farm.
- *Crop-failure insurance* covers losses from fires, lightning, hail, wind, insects, excessive moisture, and drought.

HOMEOWNER'S INSURANCE (APARTMENT INSURANCE)

homeowner's insurance
Protects farmers and other individuals from losses associated with residential living.

Homeowner's insurance protects farmers and others individuals from losses associated with residential living. With the exception of automobile insurance, there is probably no form of property-casualty insurance carried by more people. Homeowner's policies vary, but usually cover the home, other structures on the premises, home contents (furniture, stereo, TV, clothing, and so on), expenses if forced from home because of an insured peril, third party liability, and medical payments to others.

The range of coverage is broad, including fire, smoke, theft, wind damage, water damage, vandalism, and collapse. Not covered usually are flood, earthquake, neglect, power loss, or nuclear accident.

It is usually best to buy a package that covers all the above-named risks. Different policies have different names, but it's the coverage you are looking for, not the name. Homeowner's insurance may be called apartment insurance, but regardless of the name such insurance is important to a person who has a major investment in property and clothes.

THE RISK OF DAMAGING THE ENVIRONMENT

Several incidents over the last few years have focused attention on a major risk that businesses face—pollution liability. One of the most publicized cases recently was the Manville Corporation's problems with asbestos. When the health hazards of asbestos were discovered, Manville was hit with 16,500 lawsuits, and the prospects were for 32,000 more lawsuits. The total cost of the lawsuits was estimated to be $2 billion. To minimize the cost of such lawsuits, Manville asked for court protection under Chapter 11 of the Federal Bankruptcy Code.

COMMUNITY LIABILITY

It is natural to think of businesses taking risks and needing insurance to protect against fire, liability, and other catastrophes. It is not so usual to think of cities and towns having the same problems, but they do.

- Plainfield, Massachusetts had a nonalcoholic bicentennial because the town couldn't find an insurance company willing to issue liquor liability coverage.
- Columbus, Georgia is facing an annual increase in insurance premiums from $84,000 to $213,000.

A 1978 case that went to the New York Supreme Court gave citizens the right to sue government for the negligent acts of employees. The lawsuits came roaring in. A New York State Assembly committee counted 11,296 lawsuits seeking damages of $26 *billion* from local governments in the state.

Just as in cases against businesses, the courts have been rewarding huge claims to injured parties against communities:

- Newport Beach, Rhode Island was ordered to pay $6 million to a man who dove into water at a beach, hit a sandbar, and became paraplegic.
- Torrington, Connecticut was ordered to pay $2.6 million because police failed to protect a woman from her estranged husband.
- A California teenager was awarded $300,000 after he fell through a skylight while he was stealing high-intensity lights!

Cities, like businesses, feel that the courts have gone out of control. If a city loses a major suit because of a bridge collapse, faulty dam, or similar problem, insurance becomes unbelievably expensive or impossible to obtain. Many cities have become self-insured.

Can you see the potential for careers in risk management in the government? Do the courts seem out of control to you? Who ultimately pays for multi-million-dollar claims against cities? What can be done about this situation?

Source: Resa W. King, "The Coverage Crisis at Town Hall," *Business Week,* August 26, 1985, pp. 72-75.

Picking up dioxin-contaminated trash at Times Beach, Missouri.

A continuing controversy involves the environmental threat from hazardous waste disposal. This issue reached the headlines because of the events in Times Beach, Missouri. The Northeastern Pharmaceutical Chemical Company used to manufacture a product called hexachlorophene. When the market for the product collapsed, the company hired a disposal firm to get rid of the leftover waste. An employee of the firm sprayed the waste on the dirt roads of Times Beach, not knowing that the waste contained dioxin, a deadly chemical. In 1983, the federal government stepped in to buy the whole town and evacuate the people. A federal "superfund" was established to clean up toxic waste dumps all across the United States. Meanwhile, chemical and oil companies are faced with huge damage claims from the potential harm these dumps may cause.

The risk of environmental harm reaches international proportions in issues such as acid rain. But a recent international incident that had dramatic consequences for businesses was the disaster in Bhopal, India. A chemical leak from a Union Carbide plant killed over 2,000 people and seriously injured thousands more. Public concern was raised over a similar Union Carbide plant in Institute, West Virginia.

Because of incidents such as these, with potential damages in the billions of dollars, insurance companies have raised their rates dramatically and have often refused to sell insurance to such high-risk companies. Environmental impairment risk management will certainly be a major issue in corporations for many years to come.

CAREERS IN RISK MANAGEMENT

Risk management has become one of the more dynamic functions in business in the last few years. At one time, most risks (fire, theft, environmental damage, and so on) were covered by basic *insurance* policies from one or more firms. Today, corporations have **risk managers** who do sophisticated analyses of corporate risks and design elaborate solutions to those problems that provide optimum coverage at a minimum cost. The growth in numbers of such managers is evidenced by the fact that there were only 2,200 members of the Risk and Insurance Management Society in 1974 and 3,700 members in 1984—a 67% increase.

risk managers
People who do sophisticated analyses of corporate risks and design elaborate solutions to those problems.

Insurance Sales

Selling life insurance is one of the easier jobs to get after graduation from college. The median salary for an agent is over $22,000, and thousands of agents earn from $40,000 to $100,000, according to the Bureau of Labor Statistics. The problem is that the failure rate is unbelievable. Almost 90% of new agents are gone after 2 years. For those who persist, however, the career possibilities are good. Demographic studies show that there is a huge market for life insurance. Furthermore, because insurance companies are broadening into other financial areas, many insurance agents are calling themselves financial advisors and are selling mutual funds and other financial instruments along with insurance policies.

Insurance sales can be a rewarding career.

   Other careers in insurance sales are available, including health insurance, fire and theft insurance, automobile insurance, and more. Talk to several different insurance agents and get their views of the job. Some of these agents may be quite successful. Could you be?

Insurance Adjusters and Actuaries

Another career in risk management is for **insurance adjusters.** When you have a loss, the insurance company sends out an insurance adjuster to calculate the extent

insurance adjuster
Person who calculates the extent of a loss.

CAREER INFORMATION: ACTUARY

NATURE OF THE WORK

Why do young persons pay more for automobile insurance than older persons? How much should an insurance policy cost? How much should an organization contribute each year to its pension fund? Answers to these and similar questions are provided by actuaries who design insurance and pension plans and keep informed on their operation to make sure that they are maintained on a sound financial basis. Actuaries assemble and analyze statistics to calculate probabilities of death, sickness, injury, disability, unemployment, retirement, and property loss from accident, theft, fire, and other hazards. They use this information to determine the expected insured loss. For example, they may calculate how many persons who are 21 years old today can be expected to die before age 65—the probability that an insured person might die during this period is a risk to the company. They must make sure that the price charged for the insurance will enable the company to pay all claims and expenses as they occur. Finally, this price must be profitable and yet be competitive with other insurance companies. In a similar manner, the actuary calculates premium rates and determines policy contract provisions for each type of insurance offered. Most actuaries specialize in either life and health insurance or property and liability (casualty) insurance; a growing number specialize in pension plans.

JOB OUTLOOK

Employment of actuaries is expected to grow much faster than the average for all occupations through the mid-1990s. Job opportunities should be favorable for college graduates who have passed at least two actuarial examinations while still in school and have a strong mathematical and statistical background.

Employment in this occupation is influenced by the volume of insurance sales and pension plans, which is expected to grow over the next decade. Shifts in the age distribution of the population will result in a large increase in the number of people with established careers and family responsibilities. This is the group that traditionally has accounted for the bulk of private insurance sales.

As people live longer, they draw health and pension benefits for a longer period, and more actuaries are needed to recalculate the probabilities of such factors as death, sickness, and length of retirement. As insurance companies branch out into more than one kind of insurance coverage, more actuaries will be needed to establish rates. Growth in new forms of protection, such as dental, prepaid legal, and kidnap insurance also will stimulate demand.

The liability of companies for damage resulting from their products has received much attention in recent years. Actuaries will continue to be involved in the development of product liability insurance, as well as medical malpractice and workers' compensation coverage.

EARNINGS

In 1984, new college graduates entering the life insurance field without having passed any actuarial exams averaged about $18,000-$21,000, according to estimates by the Society of Actuaries. Beginners who had completed the first exam received between $20,000 and $23,000, and those who had passed the second exam averaged between $22,000 and $25,000. Top actuarial executives received salaries of $55,000 a year and higher.

SOURCES OF ADDITIONAL INFORMATION

For facts about actuarial qualifications and opportunities, contact:

American Society of Pension Actuaries, 1413 K St. NW., 5th Floor, Washington, D.C. 20005.

Casualty Actuarial Society, One Penn Plaza, 250 West 34th St., New York, N.Y. 10119.

Society of Actuaries, 500 Park Blvd., Suite 440, Itasca, Ill. 60143.

American Academy of Actuaries, 1835 K St. NW., Suite 515, Washington, D.C. 20006.

Source: *Occupational Outlook Handbook,* 1986-1987 (U.S. Department of Commerce, Bureau of Labor Statistics), pp. 72-74.

of the loss. When a tornado hits a town, for example, insurance adjusters will be out within hours or days to estimate the losses to reimburse the insured.

The people who predict future losses based on the analysis of historical data are called **actuaries**. If you are mathematically inclined, you may enjoy such a job. By now, you know how I recommend you learn about such jobs—go out and talk with people. I know I sound repetitive in making this suggestion, but so many students fail to do this invaluable kind of career research that it bears repeating. Are you the exception? If so, you have a real head start on other students.

actuaries
People who predict future losses based on the analysis of historical data.

PROGRESS CHECK

- What is the difference between a fidelity and a surety bond?
- What are three careers in risk management?

SUMMARY

1 The term *risk* refers to the chance of loss, the degree of probability of loss, and the amount of possible loss.
- What are the two kinds of risks?
  Speculative risk is the risk one takes with the hope of making a profit (for example, investing in stock, buying new equipment). *Pure risk* is the threat of loss with no chance for profit.
- How do organizations manage risks?
  They can either reduce risk, self-insure against the risk, avoid the risk, or buy insurance. Risk reduction calls for safety programs, fire drills, and the like. Self-insurance means setting aside funds for losses. Some businesses are starting *mutual insurance companies* to cooperatively self-insure. Risk avoidance may mean not producing certain products, avoiding hazardous sites, and leaving certain businesses entirely.

2 An insurance crisis occurred in the mid-1980s. It was caused by more lawsuits, higher court awards, and mistakes made by insurance companies.
- The term *mutual insurance* was mentioned; what does that mean?
  A *mutual insurance company* is owned by its policyholders. These companies are more popular today as more firms join together to start new mutual companies. They do so because *stock* companies (which are investor-owned) cannot or will not sell policies at "reasonable" prices.

3 The factor that makes insurance an effective way to cover risk is the *law of large numbers*. It states that if a large number of people or organizations are exposed to the same risk, a predictable number of losses will occur during a given period of time.
- What are some key terms used by insurance companies?
  An *insurance policy* is a written contract between the insured and an insurance company that promises to pay all or part of a loss. A *premium* is the fee charged by the insurance company. The *rule of indemnity* says an insured person cannot collect more than the actual loss. A *deductible clause* says that the insurance company will pay only the part of a loss that exceeds the deductible amount. A *coinsurance clause* requires businesses to carry insurance equal to 80% of a building's value.

4 Businesses carry a variety of insurance coverages including fire, auto and truck, liability, health, life, criminal loss, and workers' compensation.

- What is property insurance?

    It includes fire insurance and its *rider,* which covers wind, hail, smoke and other damage. It also includes auto insurance (including bodily injury, property damage, collision and comprehensive coverage), marine, and aviation insurance.

- What is *liability insurance?*

    It provides protection against losses resulting from personal injuries or damage to the property of others. A variety of liability policies are available, including an *umbrella liability* policy that covers virtually everything. *Workers' compensation* is a form of liability insurance for on-the-job injuries.

- Why is *product liability* insurance in the news?

    Because a new standard of *absolute liability* makes firms liable for hazards even if such hazards were unknowable at the time of sale.

- What is covered by criminal loss and nonperformance insurance policies?

    Criminal loss policies cover against theft, burglary, and robbery. Nonperformance insurance covers the failure of a second party to fulfill an obligation. A *fidelity bond* covers employee dishonesty, and a *surety bond* protects against second party nonperformance. Other coverage includes *credit life insurance* (losses if a debtor dies), *crime insurance* (non-employee theft, burglary, or robbery) and *commercial credit insurance* (losses from insolvency or default).

5 *Business interruption insurance* covers the operating losses from fire and other perils. *Health and life insurance* covers illnesses and the deaths of employees and key executives.

6 *Farm insurance* covers all farm property, including buildings, vehicles, machinery, livestock, and most crops.

7 A major risk of the 1980s is that of environmental damage from business operations.

- What is being done about such risks?

    The government is helping correct past damage, and firms are buying insurance to cover future losses.

8 There are many careers in risk management including risk management, insurance sales, insurance adjustment, and actuarial work.

KEY TERMS

absolute liability   p. 652
actuaries   p. 661
aviation insurance   p. 651
bodily injury insurance   p. 650
business interruption insurance
   p. 654
coinsurance clause   p. 648
commercial credit insurance
   p. 654
credit life insurance   p. 654
criminal loss protection   p. 654
deductible clause   p. 649

fidelity bond   p. 654
fire insurance   p. 650
group life insurance   p. 655
homeowner's insurance
   p. 656
inland marine insurance
   p. 651
insurance adjuster   p. 659
insurance policy   p. 648
law of large numbers   p. 648
liability insurance   p. 651
multiline policies   p. 654

mutual insurance company
   p. 644
nonperformance loss
   protection   p. 654
ocean marine insurance   p. 651
premium   p. 648
pure risk   p. 643
reasonable prudence   p. 653
rider   p. 650
risk   p. 642

risk managers   p. 659
rule of indemnity   p. 648
speculative risk   p. 642
stock insurance company
   p. 647
strict liability   p. 652
surety bond   p. 654
workers' compensation
   insurance   p. 651

GETTING INVOLVED

1 Visit a risk manager in a major corporation and talk about what he or she does and what the challenges are. Have two or three in your class do this and report back. What is new and exciting in the field?

2 Look at any insurance policies you have. Do you understand what is covered and what is not? Should policies be clearer? Why aren't they? Bring some policies to class and discuss them.

3 Look through recent newspapers and magazines for stories about lawsuits against firms. How much was the award? What was the issue? Are the damages awarded too little, too much, or about right?

4 Debate the following statement: "Businesses are responsible for the products they make and should be liable for any and all injuries sustained by customers using them."

5 Talk to insurance salespeople in several areas: life, accident, fire and theft, auto, and so forth. How much do they earn? Do they think their work is fun? Encourage several students do this and report back to the class. Check with your career development center and see if any insurance companies are hiring. If so, get their literature and bring it to class.

6 Find an actuary and a claims adjuster for an insurance company. Discuss their careers with them, and report your findings to class.

CASE ONE   SHARING THE RISK

PRACTICING MANAGEMENT DECISIONS

Businesses have an obligation to protect their employees against various risks. As you have read in this chapter, though, the costs of such coverage are rising dramatically. Take health coverage, for example. The costs of health care are going up so quickly that firms are asking employees to share the increased costs.

A survey of 250 corporations found that the number of companies picking up the entire cost of health insurance dropped from 75% in 1983 to 50% in 1984. Workers are being asked to pay a front-end deductible; this discourages them from going to the hospital for every minor ailment. The number of corporations asking workers to pay a deductible rose from 17% in 1982 to 52% in 1984. Furthermore, only 50% cover the entire hospital bill, and only 27% pay the entire surgical bill.

DECISION QUESTIONS

1 Is it fair to ask employees to pay a larger share of health care costs?

2 Have you seen evidence of hospitals becoming more efficient to halt the increasing costs? Have such efforts affected patient care?

3 Watch the newspapers for reports of large insurance claims against corporations. Who ultimately pays for those losses? What would you recommend that businesses do to lower those claims?

Source: Sanford L. Jacobs, "Regan Says He Is Listening, and Owners Provide an Earful," *The Wall Street Journal,* November 4, 1985, p. 27.

PRACTICING MANAGEMENT DECISIONS

CASE TWO   LIABILITY INSURANCE COSTS

Some 57 conferences were held in preparation for the White House Conference on Small Businesses. One of the major issues resulting from those conferences was the high cost of liability insurance. Liability insurance premiums soared in 1985, burdening some small businesses with up to four times the insurance expense they had been paying. Suggestions included limiting attorney fees, putting a ceiling on liability settlements, and replacing state regulation of insurance rates with federal regulation. Some worried that the whole liability insurance system would collapse because of enormous liability awards.

Small businesses are not the only organizations suffering from the skyrocketing cost of insurance. The problem is just as acute for big businesses and nonprofit organizations such as schools, churches, and local government agencies.

DECISION QUESTIONS

1 Which of the suggestions of small businesspeople make the most sense for the overall public good?
2 What could the courts do to protect citizens and still lower the costs of insurance for businesses and nonprofit organizations?

Source: "Splitting the Health Care Bill," *Forbes,* October 28, 1985, pp. 12-13. Reprinted by permission of *Forbes* Magazine; © Forbes Inc., 1985.

LOOKING AHEAD

In the next chapter, we shall further discuss business and the law. We shall look at laws affecting contracts, sales, negotiable instruments (checks), and more. We will learn about laws that promote competition and fair trade. In addition, we will explore the whole area of business ethics and morality, including consumerism and the social responsibility of business.

BUSINESS LAW AND ETHICS

LEARNING GOALS

After you have read and studied this chapter, you should be able to:

- List and describe the conditions necessary to make a legally enforceable contract.
- Discuss the UCC and patent law.
- Explain the different chapters of bankruptcy law.
- Enumerate several laws that regulate competition in the United States.
- Discuss various federal regulatory agencies.
- Describe consumerism and the key aspects of major consumer protection laws.
- Outline corporate social responsibility and social auditing.
- Describe different views toward corporate ethical standards.

PROFILE   WILLIAM C. NORRIS OF CONTROL DATA CORPORATION

William Norris started Control Data Corporation in 1957. Control Data was the first publicly financed start-up firm in the high-growth computer industry. It has survived the rise and fall of computer companies in the turbulent 1980s.

About 10 years after the firm began, Control Data acquired Commercial Credit Corporation, a huge financial company. It was said that the acquisition helped both firms, but it was particularly helpful to Control Data, because the firm needed $1 billion for the development, sale, and lease of its computers.

Over the years, Control Data had its financial ups and downs. William Norris was credited with having the vision to adapt the firm to market changes and keep it competitive. Control Data thus remained a strong competitor in the computer field, and Commercial Credit proved to be a profitable merger partner.

What made William Norris stand out, however, was not his success as an executive of a big computer firm, but his devotion to social involvement. Mr. Norris' philosophy was to do good things in order to do well. In other words, he considered his investments in the community as opportunities for profit in the long run. The criteria Control Data used in selecting social projects included (1) the importance of the problem to society, (2) Control Data's ability to address the problem, and (3) the likelihood that methods developed would result in a business opportunity. A good example of "doing good to do well" was the placement of

William C. Norris.

The performance of the corporation must be not only legal but ethical, fair, open, and considerate; it must accord with the total well-being requirements set by society.

COY G. ECKLAND, CEO OF EQUITABLE LIFE ASSURANCE

seven manufacturing plants in blighted communities, which provided 2,000 jobs and a payroll of $40 million.

Some of the social needs Norris saw as profitable business opportunities included (1) reduced unemployment; (2) better, more relevant and less costly education and training; (3) better health; (4) revitalization of urban and rural areas; (5) more environmental protection; and (6) lower cost and more efficient public services.

Commercial Credit has been similarly involved in social programs. It has been involved, for example, in the Adult Learning Center, which teaches basic reading and math skills to adults who perform below the eighth-grade level; a neighborhood business advisory center; a city school for pregnant students; and many volunteer efforts.

Control Data and Commercial Credit are dedicated to competitive business practices *and* social responsibility as well. They see no conflict between the two objectives. William Norris was criticized for devoting so much time and effort to social programs, but he remained committed. He became a model for future executives who feel that the future survival and growth of the United States and the world depend on concerned businesspeople who see the health of society as a necessary ingredient for corporate success in the long run.

Chapter 25 is about business law, but business law does not enforce social responsibility; that comes from the heart. This chapter will also look at corporate ethics and social responsibility. ▪

Source: This profile comes from a case prepared by Mark Heuer at the Center for Public and Business Policy, the University of Maryland.

BUSINESS LAW

business law
Rules, statutes, codes, and regulations established to provide a legal framework within which business may be conducted and that is enforceable in court.

Business law refers to rules, statutes, codes, and regulations established to provide a legal framework within which business may be conducted and which is enforceable by court action.[1] In the United States, there are more than 630,000 lawyers, that is, one for every 384 people. For every 1,000 people, the United States has three times as many lawyers as Germany, ten times as many as Sweden, and 20 times as many as Japan. Lawyers outnumber physicians almost two to one. There are also more lawyers than teachers.[2]

Corporations hire many lawyers. AT&T, for example, employs 905 attorneys; Exxon has 551, GE 415, and Ford 210. Clearly, corporate law is an important profession and a possible career for you.[3]

The purpose of this chapter is to review the legal environment of business, discuss the more important laws and regulations affecting business, and explore the social and ethical obligations of businesspeople.

Several topics we have covered in this text have indicated the importance of law to businesspeople. We learned, for example, that a major benefit of incorporating is that it gave investors limited liability from lawsuits. The discussion of risk management showed that lawsuits today resulting from product injuries or other liability suits may be so costly that insurance is difficult, if not impossible, to buy. In addition to the laws regarding liability, a businessperson should be familiar with the laws regarding contracts, negotiable instruments (for example, checks), and bankruptcy.

CONTRACT LAW

If I offer to sell you my bike for $35 and later change my mind, can you force me to sell the bike, saying we had a contract? If I lose $120 to you in a poker game, can you sue in court to get your money? If I agree to sing at your wedding for free and back out at the last minute, can you claim we had a contract? These are the kinds of questions that contract law answers.

A **contract** is a legally enforceable agreement between two or more parties. **Contract law** specifies what a legally enforceable agreement is. Basically, a contract is legally binding if the following conditions are met:

1 *An offer is made*. An offer to do something or sell something can be oral or written. If I agree to sell you my bike for $35, I have made an *offer*. That offer is not legally binding, however, until other conditions are met.

2 *There must be voluntary acceptance of the offer*. If I use "duress or undue influence" to get you to agree to buy my bike, the contract would not be legal. The *principle of mutual acceptance* means that both parties to a contract must agree on the terms. You couldn't use "duress" to get me to sell either. Even if we both agree, though, the contract is still not legally binding.

3 *Both parties must give consideration*. **Consideration** means something of value. If I agree to sell you my bike for $35 and you give me $5 to hold it until you earn the rest, the $5 is *consideration,* and we have a legally binding contract. If I agree to sing at your wedding and you do not give me anything in return, we have no contract.

4 *Both parties must be competent*. An insane person (one who has been legally declared incompetent) for example, cannot be held to a contract. In many cases, a minor may not be held either. For example, if a 15-year-old agrees to pay $10,000 for a car, the seller may not be able to enforce the contract.

5 *The contract must be legal*. Gambling losses are not legally collectible. If I lose money to you in poker, you cannot legally collect. The sale of illegal drugs is another example of an unenforceable contract.

6 *The contract must be in proper form*. An agreement for the sale of goods worth $500 or more must be in writing. Contracts that cannot be fulfilled within 1 year also must be put in writing. Real property contracts must be in writing.

contract
A legally enforceable agreement between two or more parties.

contract law
Specifies what constitutes a legally enforceable agreement (see *contract*).

consideration
Something of value; it is one of the requirements of a legal contract.

Breach of Contract

Breach of contract means that one party fails to follow the terms of the contract. Both parties may agree to end a contract, but if just one person violates the contract, the following may occur:

1 *Specific performance*. The person who violated the contract may be required to live up to the agreement if no money damages would be adequate. For example, if I offered to sell you a rare painting, I would have to sell you that painting.

2 *Payment of damages*. If I fail to live up to a contract, you can sue me for damages, usually the amount you would lose from my nonperformance. If we had a legally binding contract for me to sing at your wedding, for example, and I failed to come, you could sue me for the cost of a new singer.

breach of contract
Means that one party fails to follow the terms of a contract.

3 *Discharge of obligation.* If I fail to live up to my end of a contract, you could agree to drop the matter, and then you would not have to live up to your agreement either.

Lawyers would not make so much money if the law were as simple as implied in these rules of contract. In fact, it is always best to have a contract *in writing*. The offer and consideration should be clearly specified, and the contract should be signed and dated. A contract does not have to be long and complicated as long as it has these elements: (1) it is in writing, (2) the consideration is specified, and (3) there is a clear offer and agreement.

THE UNIFORM COMMERCIAL CODE

Uniform Commercial Code
Covers sales laws and other commercial law.

Laws involving businesses varied from state to state at one time. Today, the **Uniform Commercial Code** has been adopted by all the states. The Code covers sales laws and other commercial law. For example, the Code defines the rights of parties to a sale of goods contract relative to specific performance and damages.

Warranties

One of the items under article 2 of the Uniform Commercial Code is warranties. **Express warranties** are specific representations by the seller and relied upon by the buyer regarding the goods. The warranty you receive in the box with a clock or toaster is the express warranty. It spells out the seller's warranty agreement. **Implied warranties** are legally imposed on the seller. It is implied, for example, that the product will conform to the customary standards of the trade in which it passes. Many of the rights of buyers, including the acceptance and rejection of goods, are spelled out in Article 2 of the Uniform Commercial Code. Both buyers and sellers should become familiar with the Code. You can read more about it in business law books in the library.

express warranties
Specific representations by the seller regarding the goods.

implied warranties
Legally imposed on the seller and assume products are safe; if not, legal remedies may be enforced.

Negotiable Instruments

negotiable instruments
Forms of commercial paper that are transferrable among businesses and individuals, such as checks.

Negotiable instruments are forms of commercial paper that are transferable among businesses and individuals (such as checks). Article 3 of the Uniform Commercial Code states that a negotiable instrument (for example, a check) must be written and (1) signed by the maker, (2) made payable on demand at a certain time, (3) made payable to the bearer or to order, and (4) contain an unconditional promise to pay a specified amount of money.

PATENT LAW

patent
Exclusive rights for inventors to their inventions for 17 years.

Many students invent products that they feel are of commercial value, and then they wonder what to do next. One step may be to apply for a patent. A **patent** gives inventors exclusive rights to their inventions for 17 years. Patent owners may sell or license the use of the patent to others. Filing a patent with the U.S. Patent Office requires a search to make sure the patent is truly unique, followed by the filing of forms. The advice of a lawyer is usually recommended. Polaroid was able to force Kodak to recall all of its instant cameras because Polaroid had several patents that Kodak violated. Kodak lost millions of dollars, and Polaroid maintained market leadership in instant cameras.

A **copyright** protects an individual's rights to materials such as books, articles, photos, and cartoons. Copyrights are filed with the Library of Congress and involve a minimum of paperwork. You may charge a fee to allow someone to use copyrighted material.

copyright
Protects an individual's rights to materials such as books, articles, photos, and cartoons.

BANKRUPTCY LAWS

Bankruptcy is the legal process by which a person or business that is unable to meet financial obligations is relieved of those debts by the court. The court divides any assets among creditors, freeing the debtor to begin anew. The U.S. Constitution gives Congress the power to establish bankruptcy laws. There has been bankruptcy legislation since the 1890s, but the Bankruptcy Code was amended by the Bankruptcy Amendments and Federal Judgeships Act of 1984. This act allows a person who is bankrupt to keep part of the equity in a house, $1,200 in a car, and some other personal property. Exemptions vary by state. Most bankruptcies are filed under one of the following three sections of the act:

bankruptcy
The legal process by which a person or business, unable to meet financial obligations, is relieved of those debts by having the court divide any assets among creditors, freeing the debtor to begin anew.

- *Chapter 7* calls for "straight bankruptcy," which requires the sale of nonexempt assets of debtors. When the sale of assets is over, the assets are divided among creditors, including the government. Almost 70% of bankruptcies follow these procedures.
- *Chapter 11* allows a company to reorganize and continue operations while paying only a limited proportion of its debts. Chapter 11 applies only to businesses, not individuals. Less than 5% of all bankruptcies are handled this way. Under some conditions, the company can sell assets, borrow money, and change officers to strengthen its position. All such matters usually are supervised by a trustee appointed by the court to protect the interests of creditors. Chapter 11 is designed to help both debtors and creditors find the best solution.
- *Chapter 13* permits individuals, including small business owners, to pay back creditors over a 3-to-5-year period. It is less complicated and less expensive than Chapter 7 proceedings. About 25% of all bankruptcies take this form.

There were over 95,000 business bankruptcies in the United States in 1984.[4] Most of those were small businesses.

STATUTORY AND COMMON LAW

What makes law difficult is that the rules are not all written down clearly and precisely. There are two major kinds of law: statutory law and common law.

Statutory law includes legislative enactments, treaties, and ordinances (written laws). You can read these laws, but many are written in such a form that they call for interpretation. That is one reason why there are so many lawyers.

Common law is the body of law that comes from judges' decisions. Common law is often referred to as an "unwritten law," because it does not appear in any legislative enactments, treaties, or so forth. In law classes, therefore, students study case after case to learn about common law as well as statutory law.

statutory law
State and federal constitutions, legislative enactments, treaties, and ordinances (written laws).

common law
The body of law that comes from judges' decisions; also known as "unwritten law."

PROGRESS CHECK

▣ What are the six conditions for making a contract legally enforceable?

▣ Which chapter of the bankruptcy laws allows a company to reorganize and continue operations?

LAWS TO PROMOTE FAIR AND COMPETITIVE PRACTICES

One objective of legislators and judges is to pass laws that will maintain a competitive atmosphere among business and promote fair business practices. There was a time when businesses operated under relatively free market conditions. Business leaders became very powerful and were able to drive smaller competitors out of business. The following discussion shows what the government response was to this situation.

The Sherman Act of 1890

In the late nineteenth century big oil companies, big railroads, big steel companies, and other large firms dominated the U.S. economy. People were afraid that such large and powerful companies would crush any competitors and would therefore be able to charge high prices. It was in that atmosphere that Congress passed the Sherman Act in 1890.

Sherman Act
Forbids contracts, combinations, or conspiracies in restraint of trade and actual monopolies or attempts to monopolize any part of trade or commerce.

The **Sherman Act** was designed to prevent large organizations from stifling the competition of smaller or newer firms. The Sherman Act forbids the following: (1) contracts, combinations, or conspiracies in restraint of trade, and (2) actual monopolies or attempts to monopolize any part of trade or commerce.

The Sherman Act and the laws that followed it are most effective, not because the government has been so diligent in enforcing them, but because businesses are forced to make decisions knowing that the threat of legal action exists. Government thus becomes a pervasive force in business decision making.

Periodically the government gives businesspeople a stiff reminder that the law is not to be ignored. One such reminder was the "electrical equipment" cases of the 1960s. Several producers of electrical equipment were charged with violating one section of the Sherman Act by conspiring (1) to fix and maintain prices, terms, and conditions for the sale of specified products; (2) to allocate among themselves the business in heavy electrical equipment; (3) to submit noncompetitive bids for supplying specified equipment to various organizations; and (4) to refrain from selling certain types of equipment to other manufacturers of electrical equipment.

As a consequence of this case, some top managers of several electrical equipment companies were given prison sentences. Several served time in prison, and others were given suspended sentences. Furthermore, some companies were charged with triple damage claims for alleged overcharges on various pieces of equipment, with penalties reaching as much as $16 million. Such actions by the government force businesses to be very concerned about any actions that might be construed as violating the Sherman Act or any of the other laws affecting businesses.

MORE THAN A NEW LOOK, A NEW OUTLOOK.

AT&T

We're the new AT&T. A new company with a new symbol. But we're not exactly a newcomer. We have more than a hundred years' experience and a worldwide reputation. With the breakup of the Bell System, we know we must earn your confidence all over again—under new circumstances.

As we compete for your business, we'll stand out from the crowd by giving you better service than anyone. That's a commitment.

And we'll offer you the most advanced technology from our world-renowned Bell Laboratories. That's a guarantee.

We'll be the brand name that means dependable, state-of-the-art phones for your home, the best information systems for your business and the one and only long distance service that lets you reach out and touch anyone, any time –across the nation and around the world.

We'll use our research, development and marketing talents to keep American communications technology the best in the world.

We're the new AT&T. Our new outlook is also our competitive strategy and our goal: to give you every reason, every day, to choose us.

AT&T ran this advertisement in 1983 after an out-of-court antitrust settlement with the Justice Department broke up the Bell System, forcing the company to develop a corporate identity separate from its local phone companies.

The Clayton Act of 1914

There was some doubt about just what practices were prohibited under the Sherman Act of 1890. The **Clayton Act** of 1914 was an attempt to clarify some of the legal concepts in the Sherman Act. Various practices are prohibited "where the effect will be to substantially lessen competition or to create a monopoly." This language is also unclear and open to much interpretation.

The act prohibits organizations from selling or leasing goods with the condition or agreement that the "buyer" will not deal in goods supplied by a competitor (when the effect lessens competition). This is called *exclusive dealing*. The law also prohibits *interlocking directorates* (where a member of the board of directors is on

Clayton Act
Prohibits practices whose effect will be to substantially lessen competition or to create a monopoly.

a competitor's board) in competing corporations (except banks and common carriers) where one of the corporations has capital and surplus of more than $1 million and where the elimination of competition between them would constitute a violation of any of the provisions of the antitrust laws. The law also prohibits any corporation engaged in commerce from acquiring the shares of a competing corporation or from purchasing the stocks of two or more competitors. Notice that the Clayton Act is concerned with the *prevention* of practices that would lessen competition.

The government continued its actions to minimize restraint of trade with the Celler-Kefauver Act of 1950. It was an amendment to the Clayton Act and prohibited the acquisition of stocks or assets where in any line of commerce, in any section of the country, the effect of such an acquisition may be substantially to lessen competition, or to tend to create a monopoly. The government has kept a watchful eye on businesses throughout the last 100 years or so and has progressively cleared up the language of legislation regarding competitive practices. Only common law, that is, court cases, will really clarify the extent of such laws.

The Federal Trade Commission Act of 1914

Federal Trade Commission Act
Prohibits unfair methods of competition in commerce.

Like the Clayton Act, the Federal Trade Commission Act supplements the Sherman Act with additional prohibitions and makes the provisions clearer. The Federal Trade Commission (FTC) is an independent regulatory agency with enforcement responsibility. The **Federal Trade Commission Act** prohibits unfair methods of competition in commerce.* Note the words *in commerce;* it was not until 1938 that the *Wheeler-Lea Act* gave the FTC power to prevent practices that injure *the public.*

The FTC enforces the Federal Trade Commission Act, the Sherman Act, and the Clayton Act. It also enforces various labeling acts covering products such as wool, furs, and flammable fabrics.

Of most interest to the public in the last decade or so have been the FTC's actions against deceptive advertising. The FTC has a group of lawyers who screen national ads and process complaints from the public. The FTC may force an advertiser to cease and desist deceptive advertising and may even force an advertiser to place "corrective ads" that explain past deceptive actions. This has thus far occurred in only a few cases, but the threat is there. Most advertisers have learned to avoid creating advertisements that would come under FTC investigation. Obviously this has not made ads any more informative or interesting—it has only made them less blatantly deceptive.

The Robinson-Patman Act of 1936

Robinson-Patman Act
Makes it unlawful to discriminate in price, to grant false brokerage fees, or to make disproportional payments to buyers; protects merchants, the public, and manufacturers from unfair competition.

The **Robinson-Patman Act** expanded federal regulation of businesses even further than previous laws. This act had four basic purposes: (1) to make it unlawful for any person engaged in interstate commerce to discriminate in price between purchasers of commodities of like grade and quality; (2) to prohibit the granting of brokerage fees to large buyers who purchase directly from producers or through

---

Unfair competition includes individual practices against a competitor involving misrepresentation, deception, and fraud, and methods of competition having a tendency to unduly hinder competition or to create a monopoly.

"dummy" brokerage houses manned by regular employees of the purchasing organization; (3) to prohibit any payment to a customer unless such payment is made on proportionally equal terms to all other competing customers (for example, special advertising allowances); and (4) to protect independent merchants, the public, and manufacturers from unfair competition.

One interesting aspect of the Robinson-Patman Act is that it applies to both sellers *and buyers* who "knowingly" induce or receive an unlawful discrimination in price. It also stipulates that certain types of price cutting shall be criminal offenses punishable by fine and imprisonment. As you can see, the laws have grown more precise and the punishment more definite as the years have passed. Congress is continuing to monitor business practices and to pass laws to regulate those practices when necessary.

The Pure Food and Drug Act of 1906

Anyone who watches cowboy movies on television is familiar with the fast-talking salesman who sold snake oil and other all-purpose medicines off the back of a horse-drawn wagon. During the 1800s, sanitary conditions in food plants were deplorable. There was special concern about the sale of contaminated meat. There were many questionable business practices associated with the sale of food and drugs in that period. Nevertheless, it took 10 years of debate in Congress to get final passage of the Pure Food and Drug Act in 1906.

Now known as the Food, Drug, and Cosmetic Act, this 1938 law requires the truthful disclosure of ingredients on certain products. Before such laws were passed, some businesses were putting things like sawdust into ground meat products. Consumers were almost totally unaware of what they were eating, or putting on their skin with cosmetics. The law also prohibits false labeling and packaging of foods, drugs, cosmetics, and certain devices. Examples of mislabeling included using unnecessarily large containers and untruthful claims on labels.

The Fair Packaging and Labeling Act of 1966

When you go shopping now, you can read what the ingredients are on the foods you buy. Because the ingredients are listed in order, with the primary ingredient listed first and the others listed in descending order, you can get an idea of how much of each ingredient is in the product. Notice, for example, how much sugar goes into the cereals we eat. Note too all the artificial coloring and flavoring that is used. This labeling is especially important for people who must be careful how much salt they eat or who are allergic to foods, such as eggs or wheat. The **Fair Packaging and Labeling Act** of 1966 gave the Food and Drug Administration authority to *require* information on labels. That is one reason why you see so much information on labels today.

Fair Packaging and Labeling Act
Gave the Food and Drug Administration authority to require information on labels.

More recently, Congress passed the Drug Listing Act of 1972. This act gives the Food and Drug Administration (FDA) a comprehensive list by established name and by proprietary name of all drugs sold. The FDA is concerned about drug safety in light of the harmful effects certain drugs have caused. The Tylenol poisoning problem, in which people died when someone put poison into Tylenol capsules, led to new packaging rules that tried to prevent such tampering. Nonetheless, the problem recurred in 1986, and Tylenol scrapped the production of capsules.

Ingredients labels provide helpful information for consumers.

VITAMIN A	*	2
VITAMIN C	*	2
THIAMINE (VITAMIN B_1)	25	30
RIBOFLAVIN (VITAMIN B_2)	15	25
NIACIN	25	25
CALCIUM	*	15
IRON	25	25
VITAMIN B_6	25	25
FOLIC ACID	25	25
VITAMIN B_{12}	15	20
ZINC	15	15
PANTOTHENIC ACID	20	20

*CONTAINS LESS THAN 2 PERCENT OF THE U.S. RDA OF THESE NUTRIENTS.

INGREDIENTS

SUGAR, MARSHMALLOWS (SUGAR, MODIFIED FOOD STARCH, CORN SYRUP, DEXTROSE, GELATIN, ARTIFICIAL AND NATURAL FLAVORS, SODIUM HEXA-METAPHOSPHATE AND ARTIFICIAL COLORS), WHEAT FLOUR, CORN FLOUR, OAT FLOUR, RICE FLOUR, COCONUT OIL, SALT, ARTIFICIAL COLOR, REDUCED IRON, NIACINAMIDE, CALCIUM PANTOTHENATE, NATURAL FLAVORS, ZINC OXIDE, THIAMINE MONO-NITRATE (VITAMIN B_1), BHT (A PRESERVATIVE), PYRIDOXINE HYDROCHLORIDE (VITAMIN B_6), RIBO-FLAVIN (VITAMIN B_2), FOLIC ACID AND VITAMIN B_{12}.

MADE BY:
RALSTON PURINA COMPANY
CHECKERBOARD SQUARE
ST. LOUIS, MO 63164 U.S.A.
®

NIACIN	25	25
CALCIUM	**	15
IRON	6	6
VITAMIN D	10	25
VITAMIN E	25	25
VITAMIN B_6	25	25
FOLIC ACID	25	25
VITAMIN B_{12}	25	35
PHOSPHORUS	10	20
MAGNESIUM	8	10
ZINC	25	30
COPPER	6	8

*WHOLE MILK SUPPLIES AN ADDITIONAL 30 CALORIES, 4 g FAT, AND 15 mg CHOLESTEROL.
**CONTAINS LESS THAN 2% OF THE U.S. RDA OF THIS NUTRIENT.

INGREDIENTS: WHOLE WHEAT KERNELS, MALT FLAVORING, SALT.
VITAMINS AND ZINC: VITAMIN C (SODIUM ASCOR-BATE AND ASCORBIC ACID), VITAMIN E (ACETATE), VITAMIN B_3 (NIACINAMIDE), ZINC (ZINC OXIDE), VITAMIN A (PALMITATE), VITAMIN B_6 (PYRIDOXINE HY-DROCHLORIDE), VITAMIN B_2 (RIBOFLAVIN), VITAMIN B_1 (THIAMIN HYDROCHLORIDE), FOLIC ACID, VITAMIN B_{12}, AND VITAMIN D.

MADE BY KELLOGG CO.
BATTLE CREEK, MICH. 49016, U.S.A.
©1983 BY KELLOGG CO.
®KELLOGG COMPANY

CARBOHYDRATE INFORMATION

	CEREAL	WITH SKIM MILK
COMPLEX CARBOHYDRATES	20 g	20 g
MALTOSE & OTHER SUGARS†	2 g	8 g
DIETARY FIBER	2 g	2 g
TOTAL CARBO-HYDRATES	24 g	30 g

†NO SUGAR ADDED. ALL SUGARS IN NUTRI-GRAIN CEREAL OCCUR NATURALLY IN THE WHEAT AND MALT FLAVORING.

The government has been very closely involved in the monitoring and testing of foods, drugs, and cosmetics over time. There is some debate today whether the Food and Drug Administration is demanding *too much* testing of drugs. Critics argue that overtesting keeps lifesaving drugs off the market that are available in other countries. "Better safe than sorry" has been the rule, but too much restriction can also be detrimental. Because of such legislation, though, you can be assured of the quality and safety of the food and drugs you buy. You are also much better informed because of the new labeling requirements.

The Tort System

In Chapter 24, we talked about several cases where businesses were sued for actions that are not covered in the legislation just discussed. For example, we explored cases of people who were injured by products and sued and patients who sued doctors because of alleged negligent treatment. Many such cases could be cited that show where wrongful conduct by a businessperson resulted in injury to someone else. Wrongful conduct that causes injury to another person's body, property, or reputation is called a **tort.**

tort
Wrongful conduct that causes injury to another person's body, property, or reputation.

What constitutes wrongful conduct is not spelled out in laws. Rather, it has emerged from court decisions over time (common law). A major issue of the 1980s, as learned in discussing risk management, is that more and more people are suing businesses for wrongful conduct, and the rewards for such litigation are very high.

Because there is so much uncertainty regarding the nature of torts and the likely cost if injury is found, state and federal government agencies are beginning to pass new legislation that spells out more clearly the limits of such suits. The tort system is likely to go through a major revision in the late 1980s. You may be interested in following these changes as they occur, because they will have a significant impact on the cost of doing business.

PROGRESS CHECK

■ What are some of the specific practices prohibited by the Robinson-Patman Act?

■ What government agency regulates false and deceptive advertising?

Recent Legislation

Businesspeople have gotten the message that Congress is going to force them to be more socially responsive and responsible if businesses do not regulate themselves more closely. In 1966, for example, Congress passed the National Traffic and Safety Act to create compulsory safety standards for automobiles and tires, something the automobile industry could have done on its own. The Child Protection Act was also passed in 1966. It banned the sale of hazardous toys and articles, certainly something that industry should have been careful to do.

In 1967 the U.S. government required that cigarette packs have a label that said, "Warning: The Surgeon General Has Determined That Cigarette Smoking is Dangerous to Your Health." The Environmental Protection Agency was created in 1970. The Consumer Product Safety Commission was formed in 1972.

Warnings on cigarette packs.

SURGEON GENERAL'S WARNING: Smoking Causes Lung Cancer, Heart Disease, Emphysema, And May Complicate Pregnancy.

SURGEON GENERAL'S WARNING: Quitting Smoking Now Greatly Reduces Serious Risks to Your Health.

SURGEON GENERAL'S WARNING: Smoking By Pregnant Women May Result in Fetal Injury, Premature Birth, And Low Birth Weight.

SURGEON GENERAL'S WARNING: Cigarette Smoke Contains Carbon Monoxide.

By 1980, there were laws and regulations covering almost every aspect of business. There was concern that there were too many laws and regulations, and that these laws and regulations were costing the public money (see Figure 25-1). Thus began the movement toward deregulation. **Deregulation** means that the government is withdrawing certain laws and regulations that seem to hinder competition. Perhaps the most publicized example is the deregulation of the airlines. At one time, airlines were restricted by the government as to where they could land and fly. When such restrictions were lifted, the airlines began competing for different routes and charging lower prices. This was a clear benefit to consumers, but it put tremendous pressure on the airlines to be more competitive. New airlines were born to take advantage of the opportunities. Similar deregulation of the trucking industry has made it more competitive as well.

deregulation
Government withdrawal of certain laws and regulations that seem to hinder competition (for example, airline regulations).

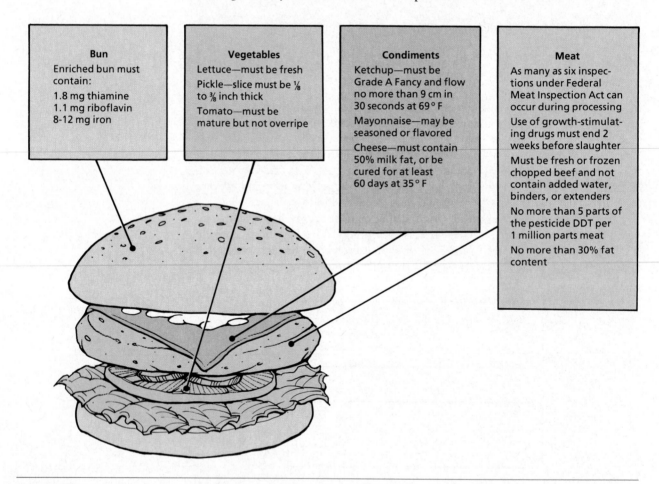

Bun
Enriched bun must contain:
1.8 mg thiamine
1.1 mg riboflavin
8-12 mg iron

Vegetables
Lettuce—must be fresh
Pickle—slice must be ⅛ to ⅜ inch thick
Tomato—must be mature but not overripe

Condiments
Ketchup—must be Grade A Fancy and flow no more than 9 cm in 30 seconds at 69° F
Mayonnaise—may be seasoned or flavored
Cheese—must contain 50% milk fat, or be cured for at least 60 days at 35° F

Meat
As many as six inspections under Federal Meat Inspection Act can occur during processing
Use of growth-stimulating drugs must end 2 weeks before slaughter
Must be fresh or frozen chopped beef and not contain added water, binders, or extenders
No more than 5 parts of the pesticide DDT per 1 million parts meat
No more than 30% fat content

FIGURE 25-1   Hamburger regulations. Does this amount of regulation seem just right, too little, or too much to you?

Today there appears to be more dialogue and more cooperation between business and government than in the past. Businesses have adapted to the laws and regulations, and have done much toward producing safer, more effective products (see Figure 25-2). Competition is getting fierce, as many small and innovative firms have been started to capture selected markets. Overseas competition is also increasing. In addition to this climate, there seems to be a growing awareness of environmental issues and other social concerns. We shall explore these issues next.

AGENCY	FUNCTION
Federal Trade Commission (FTC)	Enforces laws and guidelines regarding unfair business practices and acts to stop false and deceptive advertising and labeling
Food and Drug Administration (FDA)	Enforces laws and regulations to prevent distribution of adulterated or misbranded foods, drugs, medical devices, cosmetics, veterinary products, and hazardous consumer products
Consumer Products Safety Commission	Ensures compliance with the Consumer Product Safety Act and seeks to protect the public from unreasonable risk of injury from any consumer product not covered by other regulatory agencies
Interstate Commerce Commission (ICC)	Regulates rates, finances, and franchises of interstate rail, bus, truck, and water carriers
Federal Communications Commission (FCC)	Regulates wire, radio, and television communication in interstate and foreign commerce
Environmental Protection Agency (EPA)	Develops and enforces environmental protection standards and researches the effects of pollution
Federal Power Commission (FPC)	Regulates rates and sales of natural gas producers, wholesale rates for electricity and gas, pipeline construction, and imports and exports of natural gas and electricity to and from the United States

FIGURE 25-2

Federal regulatory agencies.

CONSUMERISM

Consumerism has been defined as a social movement that seeks to increase and strengthen the rights and powers of buyers in relation to sellers. President John F. Kennedy proposed four basic rights of consumers: (1) the right to safety, (2) the right to be informed, (3) the right to choose, and (4) the right to be heard. These rights will not be gained if consumers passively wait for organizations to recognize them; they will come partially from consumer action in the marketplace. Consumerism is the people's way of getting their fair share in marketing exchanges. Although consumerism is not a new movement, it has taken on new vigor and direction in the last decade or so. Figure 25-3 lists the major consumer protection laws.

consumerism
A social movement that tries to increase the rights and powers of buyers in relation to sellers.

FIGURE 25-3

Consumer protection laws.

LEGISLATION	PURPOSE
Pure Food and Drug Act (1906)	Protects against the adulteration and misbranding of foods and drugs sold in interstate commerce
Food, Drug, and Cosmetic Act (1938)	Protects against the adulteration and sale of foods, drugs, cosmetics, or therapeutic devices and allows the Food and Drug Administration to set minimum standards and guidelines for food products
Wool Products Labeling Act (1940)	Protects manufacturers, distributors, and consumers from undisclosed substitutes and mixtures in manufactured wool products
Fur Products Labeling Act (1951)	Protects consumers from misbranding, false advertising, and false invoicing of furs and fur products
Flammable Fabrics Act (1953)	Prohibits the interstate transportation of dangerously flammable wearing apparel and fabrics
Automobile Information Disclosure Act (1958)	Requires automobile manufacturers to put suggested retail prices on all new passenger vehicles
Textile Fiber Products Identification Act (1958)	Protects producers and consumers against misbranding and false advertising of fiber content of textile fiber products
Cigarette Labeling Act (1965)	Requires cigarette manufacturers to label cigarettes as potentially hazardous to health
Fair Packaging and Labeling Act (1966)	Makes unfair or deceptive packaging or labeling of certain consumer commodities illegal
Child Protection Act (1966)	Removes from sale potentially harmful toys and allows the FDA to pull dangerous products from the market
Truth-in-Lending Act (1968)	Requires full disclosure of all finance charges on consumer credit agreements and in advertisements of credit plans
Child Protection and Toy Safety Act (1969)	Protects children from toys and other products that contain thermal, electrical, or mechanical hazards
Fair Credit Reporting Act (1970)	Requires that consumer credit reports contain only accurate, relevant, and recent information and are confidential unless a proper party requests them for an appropriate reason
Consumer Product Safety Act (1972)	Created an independent agency to protect consumers from unreasonable risk of injury arising from consumer products and to set safety standards
Magnuson-Moss Warranty-Federal Trade Commission Improvement Act (1975)	Provides for minimum disclosure standards for written consumer product warranties and allows the FTC to prescribe interpretive rules and policy statements regarding unfair or deceptive practices

Environmental Issues

We have come a long way from the days when industrial plants were noisy, dirty, and dangerous. Most businesses have recognized their obligation to guard the health and safety of their workers and have spent millions of dollars on safety devices, exercise rooms, medical care, and the like. Nevertheless, the need for vigilance has not ended.

In the Silicon Valley of California, employees often work in "clean rooms" that are far more sterile than operating rooms in hospitals. Despite its clean, nonpolluting image, the semiconductor business "provides a complete spectrum of occupational hazards . . . including exposures to chemicals, gases [and] metals," according to Dr. Joseph LaDou of the University of California.[5]

Workers may be exposed to the sulfuric acid and nitric acid used to clean silicon wafers. They also handle solvents and may be exposed to deadly arsine and phosphine gases used in creating the circuits on computer chips. In short, workers today could be exposed to entirely new kinds of industrial hazards, and business has a moral and ethical obligation to protect workers from such hazards.

Environmental concerns will grow in the 1990s as people become more concerned about acid rain, nuclear waste storage, and other issues. In any pollution control effort there are trade-offs between costs and the environment. Those trade-offs must be made explicit and decisions made accordingly. Wise decisions demand cooperation between business and government.

Modern workers are still exposed to environmental hazards.

Environmental issues are just one of the many issues that will dominate corporate policymaking in the 1990s. The new corporate environment calls for active social performance by companies. We shall explore these issues next.

CORPORATE SOCIAL RESPONSIBILITY

John Filer, Chairman of Aetna Life & Casualty, says this about corporate social responsibility[6]:

> Justice, equality, recognition, freedom, mobility, and self-determination are unevenly distributed in the United States today, and corporate America can either do something about the inequities or be required to do something. . . . I suggest that each corporation give attention to the social consequences of each of its activities and, further, that each corporation examine its own special characteristics, strengths, and particular areas of interest and plan how it may best contribute to the fulfillment of one or more unmet public needs.

Harvey Kapnick, former chairman of Arthur Andersen & Company, says, "Part of the price we pay to maintain our free society is to accept voluntarily the necessity of self-regulation and self-discipline in the public interest in order to keep the role of government limited." He recommends a four-step social responsibility program[7]:

Corporate philanthropy supports the arts.

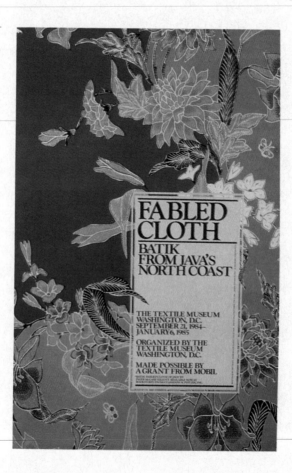

1 Specifically assign executive responsibility for the program.

2 Develop a plan that will ensure maximum benefits to society consistent with the company's particular goals, capabilities, earning capacity, and available resources.

3 Establish clear-cut priorities.

4 Communicate the results, including cost-benefit data, in a specific and meaningful way to those parts of the business which are actively engaged.

Dozens of other top executives who could be quoted agree that business has a social responsibility and needs to accept that responsibility in a structured way. The social performance of a company has several dimensions:

- **Corporate philanthropy** includes charitable donations to nonprofit groups of all kinds. Corporations gave approximately $3.5 billion to charity in 1984.[8]

- **Corporate responsibility** includes everything from minority hiring practices to the making of safe products, minimization of pollution, wise energy use, provision of a safe work environment, and more.

- **Corporate policy** refers to the position a firm takes on issues that affect the firm and society, including political issues.

Corporations are less likely to give to other organizations (charities) than they are to start their own programs of social responsibility. The Profile on William Norris discussed the many programs supported by Control Data and Commercial Credit Corporations. It would be instructive for you to read about the thousands of programs sponsored by leading U.S. firms. So much news coverage is devoted to the social *problems* caused by corporations that people tend to get a one-sided view of the social impact of companies. In fact, many corporations are publishing reports that document their net social contribution. To do that, a company must measure its social contributions and subtract its negative social impacts. We shall discuss that process next.

Social Auditing

It is nice to talk about having organizations become more socially responsible. It is also hopeful to see some efforts made toward creating safer products, more honest advertising, and so forth. But is there any indication that organizations are making social responsiveness an integral part of top management's decision making? The answer is yes, and the term that represents that effort is *social auditing*.

A **social audit** is a systematic evaluation of an organization's progress toward implementing programs that are socially responsible and responsive. One of the more difficult problems with social auditing is how to define what is meant exactly by "socially responsible and responsive." Is it being socially responsible to delay putting in the latest technology (for example, robots and computers) to save jobs, even if that makes the firm less competitive? There are literally hundreds of such questions that make the design of social audits difficult.

Another major problem is establishing procedures for measuring a firm's activities and their effects on society. What should be measured? Business activities that could be considered socially responsible include the following:

- Community-related activities such as participating in local fund-raising campaigns, donating executive time to various nonprofit organizations (including local government), and participating in urban planning and development.

- Employee-related activities such as equal opportunity programs, flextime, improved benefits, job enrichment, job safety, and employee development programs.

corporate philanthropy
Includes charitable donations made by the corporation to nonprofit groups of all kinds.

corporate responsibility
Encompasses various issues such as setting minority hiring practices, manufacturing safe products, and minimizing pollution.

corporate policy
The position a firm takes on issues that affect the corporation as well as society.

social audit
A systematic evaluation of an organization's progress toward implementing programs that are socially responsible and responsive.

- Political activities such as taking a position on issues such as nuclear safety, gun control, pollution control, and consumer protection; and working more closely with local, state, and federal government officials.
- Support for higher education, the arts, and other nonprofit social agencies.
- Consumer activities such as product safety, honest advertising, prompt complaint handling, honest pricing policies, and extensive consumer education programs.

There is some question whether positive actions such as these should be added up and then negative effects subtracted (for example, pollution, lay-offs) to get a *net social contribution*. Or should just positive actions be recorded?

The American Institute for Certified Public Accountants has created a Committee on Social Measurement to look into ways of measuring social responsiveness and responsibility. In general, therefore, social auditing has become a concern of business. It is becoming one of the aspects of corporate success that business evaluates, measures, and develops.

INFANT FORMULA: A LONG-TERM MORAL ISSUE

In 1986, Third World nations were still trying to enforce a 1981 decision by the World Health Organization to adopt a worldwide code to restrict the marketing of infant formula. This issue goes back to the 1950s, 1960s, and 1970s, when health authorities had identified bottle feeding as a source of infant diarrhea, malnutrition, and death. The cause of the sickness and death was traced to the fact that mothers in poor countries were mixing polluted water with the formula or using too much water to make it cheaper, and they were using nonsterile bottles.

The Nestlé company was targeted as the main culprit in the problem, because it was promoting the infant formula to illiterate and poverty-stricken mothers. "Mothercraft nurses," who distributed free infant formula samples in hospitals, were found not to be nurses, but saleswomen in costume. Pediatricians were given gifts, travel, and so forth to promote the formulas. Nestlé's advertisements said that formula was better than mother's milk. Efforts to end these practices failed until 1981 when the World Health Organization passed a code governing industry marketing practices that were "detrimental to breast feeding." Most companies complied, and Nestlé got a new leader who promised to comply with the new code. A boycott called against Nestlé products was then lifted.

Although promotional abuses have been largely stopped, the 1986 World Health Organization concluded that babies should be given infant formula as a first choice only during war, famine, or earthquake. If a mother is taking drugs or has died, the suggestion is to find a wet nurse or go to a breast milk bank. Both suggestions were considered "far-fetched" by a consultative group in Third World countries.

This problem has persisted and has received much media attention because the firms involved, especially Nestlé, did not react as soon as problems were discovered. Rather, the situation had to become a worldwide issue before action was taken.

People are now asking about U.S. firms that sell drugs that are banned in the United States in other countries. The same questions have been raised about sales of banned pesticides and other such products in less developed countries. Moral and ethical behavior must be followed by organizations engaged in international trade, or else organizations such as the World Health Organization will intervene. Boycotts, new laws, and sanctions will be used to force such behavior.

Most of the trade laws in the United States were passed because companies would not change their behavior without the force of the law. Now international laws may be needed for the same reason. An alternative, of course, would be for businesses to adopt codes of conduct that would preclude new legislation and show the world that American businesses are the technological *and* ethical leaders of the world.

Sources: Carol Adelman, "Closing the Book on Infant-Formula Fears," *The Wall Street Journal*, June 19, 1986, p. 30; and Richard K. Manoff, "Learning a Lesson From Nestle," *Advertising Age*, February 14, 1984, p. 16.

BUSINESS INTEGRITY BEGINS AT THE TOP

Integrity is caught more than it is taught. That is, people learn their standards and values from observing what others do, not what they say. This is as true in business as it is at home. Corporate values are instilled by the leadership and example of strong top managers. The result is what we have called *corporate culture*.

Companies such as IBM, Xerox, McDonald's, Disney, Marriott, and dozens of others have strong, effective, and ethical leadership. Within these firms, a high value system has become pervasive, and employees feel part of a corporate mission that is socially beneficial.

> Without the civilizing force of universal moral standards, particularly honesty, trust, self-respect, integrity, and loyalty, the marketplace quickly degenerates.
>
> Warren Brooks in
> *Goodness and the GNP*

INTERNATIONAL ETHICAL DECISIONS

The one situation in the 1980s that perhaps best illustrates ethical decision making on an international level is that of South Africa. The government of South Africa has long practiced apartheid, separation of the races. The blacks in South Africa protested apartheid throughout the 1980s, and hundreds of people were killed in clashes between blacks who had differences of opinion about the apartheid system and between blacks and the white ruling government.

Virtually all nations of the world, including the government of South Africa, felt that something had to be done about the system of apartheid. Some small steps were made to change some of the rules, but the changes were few and slow. Protestors in the United States demanded that American organizations, such as universities, stop investing in firms that did business in South Africa. The idea was to pressure the South African government to end apartheid more quickly. The protests grew more insistent when increased violence erupted in South Africa. Soon, protestors called for U.S. firms to pull out of South Africa entirely.

In 1986, an advertisement sponsored by 80 American companies operating in South Africa, including Citibank, IBM, Coca-Cola, and Union Carbide, called for a complete end of all forms of apartheid. One possibility is that all such U.S. firms would pull their subsidiaries out of South Africa. Many people proposed that very solution. The problem is that U.S. firms employ many black employees and are some of the fairest and most liberal employers in the country. If they were to pull out, it would hurt the economy of South Africa badly. That means both whites and blacks would suffer, and other nations would be less likely to lend money to businesses in the area. The government might fall, but what would remain would be a country with a weaker business base to build on. This would hurt blacks more than whites in the long run, because blacks are in the majority.

American businesses with subsidiaries in South Africa faced a serious ethical problem. Should they stay in South Africa and try to get the government to be more liberal with blacks? They do have a significant influence. Or should they pull out in protest and potentially hasten the end of apartheid, but increase black unemployment and remove a source of pressure on other businesses to be as fair as U.S. businesses are with blacks? American businesses have subsidiaries in many countries with poor race relations or suppressive governments. Should they pull out of all such countries or stay and try to promote change? What is the moral and ethical position for businesses to take relative to other governments? These are the kinds of international ethical questions that will have to be answered in the next decade.

Source: Steve Mufson, "South Africa Regime is Confident Sanctions Could Be Circumvented," *The Wall Street Journal*, June 20, 1986, p. 23. Reprinted by permission of *The Wall Street Journal*, © Dow Jones & Company, Inc., 1986. All rights reserved.

Ethics is the study of standards of conduct. *Integrity* refers to the honesty, sincerity, and morality of a person. *Morality* refers to ethical, virtuous, and upright behavior.

A rise in ethics and morality begins with each of us living lives of integrity. We teach others a higher level of ethics and morality through example. Strong ethical *leadership* from corporate executives may be the best source for maintaining America's "goodness."

THINKING IT THROUGH

What signs of moral progress, if any, do you see in society? What signs of moral and ethical decay, if any, do you see in society?

Ethical Standards

What should be the guiding philosophy for business in the twenty-first century? For most of the twentieth century, there has been uncertainty regarding the position top managers should take. Three different views of corporate responsibility have been presented[9]:

1 *The Invisible Hand.* Under this philosophy, "the true and only social responsibilities of business organizations are to make profits and obey the laws . . . the common good is best served when each of us and our economic institutions pursue not the

---

FIGURE 25-4

American Marketing Association Code of Ethics.

Source: Draft proposal (abbreviated) in *Marketing News,* May 9, 1986, pp. 1 & 11.

Honesty and fairness

Marketers shall uphold and advance the integrity, honor, and dignity of the marketing profession by:

1 Being honest and impartial in serving the public, employers, suppliers, and clients;
2 Communications that are truthful and avoid misleading omissions of pertinent details; and
3 Avoiding any conflict of interest and avoiding being a party to bribery.

Rights of the consumer

In March, 1962, President John F. Kennedy presented his now famous Consumer Bill of Rights: (1) the right to safety, (2) the right to be informed, (3) the right to choose, and (4) the right to be heard. To meet these objectives, the AMA encourages adherence to the following:

1 Communications should be clear so that the recipient can understand the message.
2 Risks connected with products and services should be fully disclosed.
3 No attempt should be made to disparage or maintain a limited stock or availability of an advertised product or service in an attempt to switch a customer to a more expensive one.
4 Those products or services which do not perform as advertised or represented should be subject to a refund or allowance.
5 Added features at extra cost must not be included without the customer's specific approval.
6 Attempts to sell or to raise funds must not be carried out under the guise of marketing research.
7 Customers have the right to have their names deleted from lists used or sold for further marketing efforts.
8 Names obtained during the course of marketing research studies must not be used for purposes other than research.

common good or moral purpose . . . but competitive advantage. Morality, responsibility, and conscience reside in the invisible hand of the free market system, not in the hands of the organizations within the system, much less the hands of managers within the system."

2 *The Hand of Government.* Under this philosophy, "the corporation would have no moral responsibility beyond political and legal obedience . . . corporations are to seek objectives that are rational and purely economic. The regulatory hands of the law and the political process rather than the invisible hand of the marketplace turn these objectives to the common good."

3 *The Hand of Management.* This philosophy "encourages corporations to exercise independent, noneconomic judgment over matters [of morals and ethics] that face them in their short- and long-term plans and operations." It [seeks] "moral reasoning and intent" from the corporation, and for managers to apply . . . individual morality to corporate decisions.

In corporations today, you can find examples of all three philosophies in action. Some organizations are totally profit oriented and leave social results to the marketplace. Others operate within the letter of the law, but provide no moral or ethical leadership. Managers such as William Norris (see the Profile), however, are going far beyond the narrow goals of profit to act as social citizens and ethical leaders.

The trend today is for society to demand moral and ethical leadership from business. Few business leaders are taking a public stand on such issues, but many are doing so in their own firms. The American Marketing Association published a Code of Ethics in 1986 (see Figure 25-4). It is just one example of many similar codes being proposed by business organizations. Notice that it goes beyond being honest and calls for active efforts to satisfy consumer rights to safety, to be informed, to choose among competing goods, and to be heard.

PROGRESS CHECK

■ Can you cite most of the 15 consumer protection laws discussed in this chapter?

■ What is a social audit? Which of the three philosophies of corporate responsibility does a social audit reflect?

SUMMARY

1 *Business law* refers to rules, statutes, codes, and regulations established to provide a legal framework within which business may be conducted that is enforceable by court action.

■ What makes a contract enforceable under the law?

It must meet six conditions: (1) an offer must be made, (2) the offer must be voluntarily accepted, (3) both parties must give consideration, (4) both parties must be competent, (5) the contract must be legal, and (6) the contract must be in proper form.

■ What is the Uniform Commercial Code?

It is the law that covers sales law and other commercial law in all states.

■ What are the bankruptcy laws?

The Bankruptcy Code was amended in 1984. *Chapter 7* of the code calls for straight bankruptcy, in which assets are divided among creditors after exemptions. *Chapter 11* is for companies; it allows a firm to reorganize and continue operation after paying only a limited portion of its debts. *Chapter 13* permits individuals to pay their creditors over a 3- to 5-year period.

2 Several terms are important to know when discussing business law.
- Which terms should I learn?

  Key terms are listed at the end of the chapter. Be sure to spend some time learning them.

3 Several laws were passed to promote fair and competitive practices.
- What does the Sherman Act cover?

  It forbids contracts, combinations, or conspiracies in restraint of trade and actual monopolies or attempts to monopolize any part of trade or commerce. Note that this language is indefinite.

- What does the Clayton Act add?

  It prohibits practices that will "substantially lessen competition," such as selling or leasing goods with the condition that the buyer will not deal in goods supplied by a competitor (exclusive dealing). It also prohibits *interlocking directorates*—serving on a competitor's board of directors.

- Which act regulates false and deceptive advertising?

  The Federal Trade Commission Act.

- Which act prohibits price discrimination and demands proportional promotional allowances?

  The Robinson-Patman Act.

- Which laws made producers put ingredients on labels?

  The Food, Drug, and Cosmetic Act and the Fair Packaging and Labeling Act (1966).

4 There are many government regulatory agencies.
- What are the major agencies?

  See Figure 25-2 (p. 679) for a brief description of each.

5 Organizations have social responsibilities beyond merely obeying laws and following regulations.
- How are such efforts measured?

  A *corporate social audit* measures the effects of positive social programs and subtracts the negative effects of business (for example, pollution) to get a net social benefit.

- Who is taking a leadership role in raising the moral and ethical standards of business and society?

  Individuals must begin the process. Business leaders can take a leadership role and many have done so within the firm. Few businesspeople speak out on such issues in the public, however. Is it time for such public commitment, or are ethics and morality not the concern of businesspeople? Case Two is designed to give you an opportunity to explore that issue.

KEY TERMS

bankruptcy p. 671	**consideration** p. 669
breach of contract p. 669	**consumerism** p. 679
business law p. 668	**contract** p. 669
Clayton Act p. 673	**contract law** p. 669
common law p. 671	**copyright** p. 671

corporate philanthropy p. 683
corporate policy p. 683
corporate responsibility p. 683
deregulation p. 678
express warranties p. 670
Fair Packaging and Labeling Act
  p. 675
Federal Trade Commission Act
  p. 674

implied warranties p. 670
negotiable instruments p. 670
patent p. 670
Robinson-Patman Act p. 674
Sherman Act p. 672
social audit p. 683
statutory law p. 671
tort p. 676
Uniform Commercial Code p. 670

GETTING INVOLVED

1 Go to the library and look up the Uniform Commercial Code. Take a few minutes to review what it covers, and report your findings back to class.

2 While at the library, check to see if they have any books on business law. Go through a business law book and read some of the cases cited. Get a feel for both statutory law and common law. Does the subject seem interesting enough to take a course in it? You should in any case, because the law is extremely important to business.

3 Discuss the merits of increased legislation versus self-regulation to prevent deceptive business practices. Which is better for society and business in the long run? Defend your answer.

4 Where do you see leadership emerging to improve the moral standards of the United States? What could you do to support such leadership?

PRACTICING MANAGEMENT DECISIONS

CASE ONE TYLENOL PULLS ITS CAPSULES OFF THE MARKET

One company that has demonstrated its social responsiveness and social responsibility is Johnson & Johnson. Its troubles began in 1982, when seven Chicagoans died after taking poisoned Tylenol capsules. It cost Johnson & Johnson and its McNeil Laboratories subsidiary $100 million to pull Tylenol capsules off the shelf and reintroduce a new package. The new package had three tamper-resistant features—a sealed carton, a shrink-wrapped seal over the bottle cap, and a foil seal under the cap. Johnson & Johnson received much favorable publicity for its quick action, and sales of Tylenol went back up.

In 1986, a 23-year-old woman died from another poisoned Tylenol capsule. A second tainted bottle was found in a store nearby. Johnson & Johnson again responded by pulling all the product off the shelves and replacing them with "caplets," or capsule-shaped tablets. The cost was estimated to be $150 million this time. Johnson & Johnson has said it will not return Tylenol capsules to the market. The Tylenol brand is a $525 million product for the company. It hopes consumers will adapt to the new "caplets" that are tamper resistant, but not tamper proof.

DECISION QUESTIONS

1 There is no way to make products on the shelves tamper proof. Was Tylenol wise to cease production of capsules while other companies continue selling them?

2 It is not against the law to sell over-the-counter drugs in capsules. Is it ethical? What obligation do producers of such capsules have to the public, if any?

3 Pieces of glass were allegedly found in baby food bottles. The manufacturer refused to pull the bottles off the shelf. A producer has an obligation to stockholders and employees as well as the public. Debate *both sides* of the issue of whether or not the producer should have pulled this product.

Source: "2-Time Loser," *Advertising Age,* February 17, 1986, pp. 1 ff; and Bill Powell and Marton Kasindorf, "The Tylenol Rescue," *Newsweek,* March 3, 1986, pp. 52-53.

PRACTICING MANAGEMENT DECISIONS

CASE TWO   THE PROFIT OBJECTIVE AND SOCIAL RESPONSIBILITY

Milton Friedman, an economist from the University of Chicago, has argued that "Few trends could thoroughly undermine the very foundation of our free society as the acceptance by corporate officials of a social responsibility other than to make as much money for stockholders as possible." Basically, Friedman's argument for this position goes like this:

a. Business exists to make a profit.
b. When a business makes a profit, it uses scarce resources efficiently, provides desired products and services, creates jobs, and serves society.
c. Business involvement in the social/political process will only increase the political influence of business. Because big business has more to spend, influence will be concentrated in big business.
d. The business of business is business.
e. Business profits belong to stockholders, not the public.

On the other hand, there is a sizeable body of literature which says that business has a social responsibility beyond profit. Some points of this argument include the following:

a. As part of society, business should be involved in solving society's problems.
b. It is in the self-interest of business to help solve society's problems.
c. Results have not come from leaving social problems to government.
d. Everyone has a responsibility to help his fellow citizen, including business-people.
e. Business has plenty of money to spend on social programs if it wanted.

DECISION QUESTIONS

1 Does the president of a firm have a right and obligation to use corporate profits for social programs? To whom do the profits belong?
2 Does a business executive have the same social responsibility as any other citizen, or is his or her responsibility greater? Why?
3 What socially responsible behavior could be profitable as well as socially beneficial?

Source: Milton Friedman, *Capitalism and Freedom* (The University of Chicago Press, 1963), p. 133.

LOOKING AHEAD

The business world extends beyond the borders of the United States. The future of American business is directly tied to the future of world business. Environmental issues such as acid rain are *world* problems. International trade directly affects the economies of individual nations. This book ends by looking at international business. People over much of the world go to bed hungry; poverty and disease still exist in the world (including the United States). One answer to such world problems is free world trade conducted by compassionate, honest, and committed businesspeople. We shall explore the fascinating subject of international business.

INTERNATIONAL BUSINESS

LEARNING GOALS

After you have read and studied this chapter, you should be able to:

▓ Discuss the increasing importance of the international market.

▓ Define the terminology used in international business.

▓ Explain the theory of comparative advantage.

▓ Distinguish between various types of restrictions on foreign trade.

▓ Describe several ways to participate in international business.

▓ Explain multinational and global corporations.

▓ Identify and describe several international trade organizations and trade agreements.

▓ Discuss the future of world trade.

PROFILE   RICHARD ARENDSEE, INTERNATIONAL MOVER

There has been much talk about the growth of the service sector in the United States. Much less is said about the fact that the selling of services overseas is one of the fastest-growing elements of international trade. One man who recognized the opportunity to sell services overseas is Richard Arendsee of Four Winds Enterprises (55 offices worldwide and 3,000 employees).

Four Winds is the world's largest international mover of household goods. In Saudi Arabia, for instance, Four Winds recently outbid three Saudi companies to handle all moving problems for the 20,000 or so employees of Arabian American Oil Company. It is believed to be the largest commercial moving contract ever ($60 million).

Four Winds was not always a big, international moving firm. In 1963, Arendsee bought his father-in-law's bankrupt moving and storage company for $17,000. He began bidding on military contracts to move military personnel in and out of Vietnam. Some 40% of his business is still in the form of government contracts.

When the United States pulled out of Vietnam, Arendsee had to look for new markets. The domestic market was tough in that six companies (North American, Allied, United, Mayflower, Bekins, and Atlas) had 85% of the market. On the other hand, competition in international markets was less stiff. By 1983, 85% of Four Winds' profits were coming from the international side of the business.

Richard Arendsee.

We have to accept the fact that we are going to be increasingly dependent on the international economy, while the international economy is likely to be less dependent on us. . . . Indeed, both economic growth and full employment will increasingly depend on success in competing in the international economy.

PETER F. DRUCKER

Arendsee owns 86% of the business. Employees own the rest. Profits are good, as are profit margins (2% vs. the U.S. average of 1.25%). The business must be doing rather well; recently, Richard Arendsee bought the presidential yacht *Sequoia* for $1.7 million.

Mr. Arendsee saw an opportunity for selling moving services overseas. Other entrepreneurs are selling services such as auto rentals, insurance, overnight delivery, consulting, telecommunications, and fast-food retailing. The market is huge and the opportunities many. ■

Source: "Moving Up," *Forbes,* March 12, 1984, pp. 194-196. Reprinted by permission of *Forbes* Magazine; © *Forbes* Inc., 1984.

THE INTERNATIONAL MARKET

Throughout this book we have been talking about opportunities in various careers. There is no question that there will be many challenging careers available in high-tech industries, in the service sector in general, and in small businesses. What doesn't show up as clearly in most projections of future careers is the potential for careers in international business, especially international marketing.

Have you stopped to think about the possibilities of a career in international business? Maybe a few statistics will awaken more interest:

- There are about 240 *million* people in the United States, but there are over 5 *billion* potential customers in the world market. That means that about 95% of the total market is outside the United States.
- Every year, the world's population increases by over 72 million people. That means as many people as live in all of England, Wales, Scotland, Ireland, Sweden, and Norway are added to world markets *every year*. Think of all those potential customers.

Schick display in Tokyo, Japan.

- Between 1977 and 1980, four of every five new manufacturing jobs were export related, and those trends continue today.[1]
- Combined world exports and imports exceed $4 *trillion* per year!
- The United States is now importing about 20% of its steel, 30% of its cars, 40% of its calculators, 50% of its computerized machine tools, and 60% of its TV sets, radios, tape recorders and phonographs—and over 95% of its motorcycles.[2]
- It is estimated that 30% of the world's gross national product (GNP) consists of world trade.[3]
- The United States is the largest importer and exporter in the world.

These figures show that international trade is big business today and will be even more important in the coming decades. Will you be ready? Are you studying a foreign language in school? Have you talked with anyone about the excitement and rewards of traveling to and trading with other countries?

The purpose of this chapter is to expose you to international business, including its potential and problems. Because most career advisors do not say much about international business, there are not many students preparing for such a career. That means that the demand for students with such training is likely to exceed the supply as international trade grows. Maybe you will be one of the lucky ones to find a challenging and rewarding career in international business.

TERMS OF INTERNATIONAL TRADE

When you read business periodicals or listen to news reports, you will see and hear terms relating to international business. Many of these terms may be familiar to you, but it will be helpful to review them before we discuss international business

PURCHASERS OF U.S. EXPORTS	SUPPLIERS OF U.S. IMPORTS
Canada	Japan
Japan	Canada
Mexico	West Germany
United Kingdom	Mexico
West Germany	Taiwan
Netherlands	United Kingdom
South Korea	South Korea
France	France
Australia	Italy
Italy	Hong Kong
Belgium/Luxembourg	Brazil
Taiwan	Venezuela
Saudi Arabia	Indonesia
Singapore	Sweden
U.S.S.R.	Singapore
China	Netherlands
Venezuela	China
Hong Kong	Belgium/Luxembourg
Israel	Switzerland
Brazil	Algeria

FIGURE 26-1

Top 20 purchasers of U.S. exports and suppliers of U.S. imports. Note that the U.S.S.R. buys many goods from the U.S. Also, note that China is one of America's biggest suppliers.

Source: *U.S. Foreign Trade Highlights,* U.S. Department of Commerce, 1985, p. 20.

in more detail. The first two terms refer to buying and selling goods and services with other countries:

exporting
Selling products to another country.

- **Exporting** is *selling* products to another country.
- **Importing** is *buying* products from another country.

Figure 26-1 shows the countries to which we *export* the most products, including Canada, Japan, Mexico and the United Kingdom. It also lists the countries from which we import the most products, including Japan, Canada, West Germany, and Mexico.

importing
Buying products from another country.

For many years, the United States exported more goods and services than it imported. Recently, however, it has begun buying more than it sells.

- *Balance of trade* is the relationship of exports to imports.
- A *favorable balance of trade* occurs when exports exceed imports.
- An *unfavorable balance of trade* occurs when imports exceed exports.

It is easy to understand why countries prefer to export more than they import. If I sell you $200 worth of goods and buy only $100 worth, I have an extra $100 available to buy other things. At least, that is how the thinking goes in international trade.

balance of payments
The difference between money coming into a country (from exports) and money leaving the country (for imports) *plus* money flows from other factors such as tourism, foreign aid, and military expenditures.

- **Balance of payments** is the difference between money coming into a country (from exports) and money leaving the country (for imports) *plus* money flows from other factors such as tourism, foreign aid, and military expenditures.

Other Terms Regarding World Trade

The amount of money flowing into or out of a country for tourism and other reasons may offset a trade imbalance. The goal is always to have a net inward flow of money. This is called a **favorable balance of payments.** In 1985, the United States had a trade deficit of $124 billion. Figure 26-2 shows where some of those deficits come from. Some U.S. firms are complaining that foreign firms sell products in the United States for less than they charge for the same products in their own country. The term used to describe such practices is **dumping.** The United States has laws against dumping, specifying that foreign firms must have 10% overhead costs plus 8% profit margin. Dumping is hard to prove, however. Charges of dumping have been made against manufacturers of several products, including steel, motorcycles, and microwave ovens.

favorable balance of payments
Occurs when the amount of money flowing into a country exceeds the flow out.

dumping
Selling products for less in a foreign country than is charged in the producing country.

Economic powers (markets) — UNITED ~~BOTH~~ EROPE IN 1992, UNITED GERMANY

Pacific (— Japan
Rim (— FOUR DRAGONS — TAIWAN, SOUTH KOREA, HONK KONG, SINGAPORE

FIGURE 26-2

Major U.S. trading partners, 1983.
Source: "U.S. Trade Outlook," *Business America*, February 20, 1984, pp. 2-6.

COUNTRY	U.S. IMPORTS ($ billions)	U.S. EXPORTS ($ billions)	TRADE DEFICIT ($ billions)
1 Canada	52.1	38.2	13.9
2 Japan	41.2	21.9	19.3
3 Mexico	16.8	9.1	7.7
4 West Germany	12.7	8.7	4.0
5 United Kingdom	12.5	10.6	1.9
6 Taiwan	11.2	4.7	6.5
7 South Korea	7.1	5.9	1.2
8 Hong Kong	6.4	2.6	3.8
9 France	6.0	6.0	0.0
10 Italy	5.5	3.9	1.6

+ trade deficit reasons
- fell behind in quality
- cheaper labor overseas.
- U.S. doesn't have export mentality
- early 80's high dollar

New Markets
Russia
Eastern Europe
China?

Solutions — raise import tariffs.
- lower value of the dollar.
- improve quality
- emphasize exports for U.S. companies

To protect themselves against dumping and foreign competition that hurts domestic industry, countries often use measures to protect their industries. **Trade protectionism** is the use of government regulations to limit the import of goods and services so that domestic producers can survive and grow, producing more jobs—in theory.

Much has been said in the business journals about the exchange rate of the dollar against foreign currencies all through the 1980s. The reason is that the value of the dollar was so high in the early 1980s that foreign goods were cheaper to buy. U.S. citizens began buying more overseas, which hurt the U.S. balance of trade. A "group of five" countries got together to lower the value of the dollar (successfully) and thus (1) increase the export market for U.S. goods and (2) decrease imports. Terms that are critical to understanding such matters are defined here.

- The *exchange rate* is the value of one currency relative to the currencies of other countries.
- *High value of the dollar* means that a dollar would buy more foreign goods (or would be traded for more foreign currency) than normal.
- The *group of five* are the top five industrial nations in the view of the World Bank: U.S., Britain, France, West Germany, and Japan.

Efforts by the group of five succeeded, and the value of the dollar fell. One more new term comes up in this discussion: the *World Bank*.

The formal title of the World Bank is *the International Bank for Reconstruction and Development,* a more descriptive term. The *World Bank* borrows from the more prosperous countries and lends at favorable rates to less developed countries.

The **International Monetary Fund** (IMF) is an international bank that makes short-term loans to countries experiencing problems with their balance of trade.

Now that you understand some terms, we can begin discussing international trade in more depth. The first question to answer is how the United States is doing in world trade.

THE TRADE DEFICIT

In 1985, the United States bought more goods from other nations than it sold to other nations. This is called a **merchandise trade deficit.** Figure 26-3 shows that the United States has had such deficits for the last several years. In 1985, the merchandise trade deficit reached over $124 billion. The United States has a surplus in the trading of services, however. In 1985, the U.S. sold over $35 billion more services than it purchased from other nations.

Figure 26-4 shows the nations with which the United States has a trade deficit. The highest trade deficit is with Japan. For that reason, the U.S. and the Japanese governments are trying to devise strategies to make the trade balance more even. To lessen the trade imbalance with Canada, the United States restricted the sale of some Canadian wood products in 1986. In general, the United States is trying to develop policies and strategies to restore a more favorable trade balance.

The broadest measure of foreign trade in goods, services, and investments is called the balance of payments. It measures the net flow of money between a country and other countries with which it trades. In 1985, the U.S. had a balance of payments deficit of over $117 billion. In fact, the United States has now become a **debtor nation.** That is, the U.S. owes other countries more money than they

trade protectionism
The use of government regulations to limit the import of goods and services so that domestic producers can survive and grow, producing more jobs–in theory.

International Monetary Fund
An international bank that makes short-term loans to countries experiencing problems with their balance of trade.

merchandise trade deficit
Buying more goods from other nations than are sold to them.

debtor nation
Country that owes more money to other nations than they owe it.

FIGURE 26-3

U.S. merchandise trade deficit.

Source: U.S. Department of Commerce, Bureau of Labor Statistics, 1986.

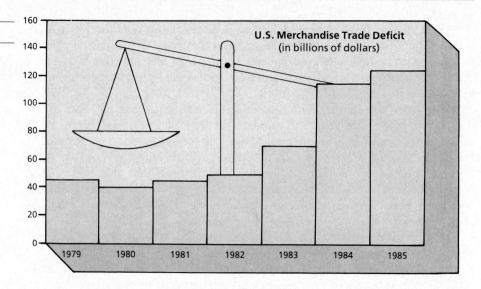

owe the U.S. Commerce Secretary Malcolm Baldridge noted that this is the first time since 1914 that the U.S. has been a debtor nation.[4]

In 1986 the U.S. Congress was planning to correct trade imbalances. The problem is that restricting trade from other nations may result in those nations cutting back on purchases from the United States. Such trade wars hurt the nations involved and the world economy in general. Later, we shall explore all the advantages and disadvantages of such policies. First, let's start at the beginning and discuss the reasons for international trade.

FIGURE 26-4

Nations with which the U.S. has a trade deficit.

Source: U.S. Department of Commerce, Bureau of Labor Statistics, 1985.

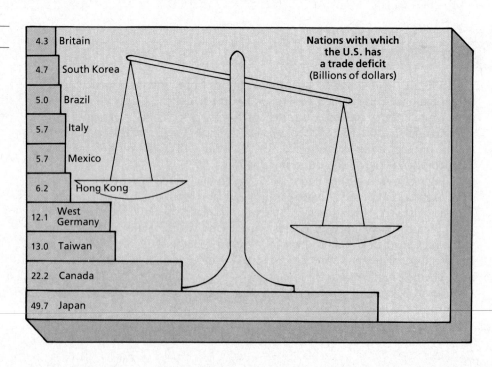

PROGRESS CHECK

■ What is the difference between balance of trade and balance of payments?

■ What is a favorable balance of trade?

■ What is the present status of the United States relative to trade in merchandise and services with other countries?

WHY TRADE WITH OTHER NATIONS?

There are several reasons why one country would trade with other countries. First, no country, even a technologically advanced one, can produce all the products that its people want and need. Second, even if a country became self-sufficient, other countries would demand trade with that country to meet the needs of their people. Third, some countries have an abundance of natural resources and a lack of technological know-how. Other countries (for example, Japan) have vast technological skills, but few natural resources. Trade relations enable each country to produce what it is most capable of producing and to buy what it needs in a mutually beneficial exchange relationship.

International trade is the exchange of goods and services across national borders. Exchanges between and among countries involve more than goods and services, however. Countries also exchange art, athletes (for international competition and friendly relations), cultural events (plays, dance performances, and so forth), medical advances, space exploration (for example the U.S.-Soviet space programs), and labor. The guiding principle behind international economic exchanges is the economic **comparative advantage theory.** This theory states that a country should produce and sell to other countries those products that it produces most effectively and efficiently and should buy from other countries those products it cannot produce as effectively or efficiently.

comparative advantage theory
Theory which asserts that a country should produce and sell to other countries those products that it produces most efficiently and effectively and should buy from other countries those products it cannot produce as effectively or efficiently.

An Otis Elevator repairman in Hong Kong.

Some of the major industries in the United States receive a significant percentage of their income from overseas. Of the 500 largest U.S. industrial firms, at least 40% make more than half of their profit from overseas operations. Examples are: 60% for Otis Elevator, 60% for Pfizer Pharmaceutical, 59% for Coca-Cola, 54% for IBM, and 72% for Citibank.[5] The United States has a comparative advantage in producing many goods and services. On the other hand, it does not have a comparative advantage in producing some shoes, clothes, videotape recorders, and other products that it imports. Figure 26-5 lists some of the leading import and export products for the United States.

FIGURE 26-5

Leading export and import goods, 1985. What comparative advantage enables other countries to sell shoes to the United States?

Source: *U.S. Foreign Trade Highlights*, U.S. Department of Commerce, 1985.

TEN LEADING U.S. EXPORT GOODS	TEN LEADING U.S. IMPORT GOODS
Aircraft, spacecraft, and associated goods	Automobiles
Parts for road vehicles and tractors	Crude petroleum
Parts for office machines and data processing machines	Petroleum products
Automatic data processing machines	Auto parts
Corn	Electronic components and parts
Automobiles	Special purpose motor vehicles
General merchandise	Telecommunications equipment
Electronic components and parts	Paper and paperboard
Measuring and checking instruments	Footwear, including military
Organic chemicals	Parts of office machines

absolute advantage
When a country has a monopoly on producing a product or is able to produce it at a cost below that of all other countries.

A country has an **absolute advantage** if it has a monopoly on the production of a specific product or is able to produce it more cheaply than all other countries. There are few examples of absolute advantage in today's competitive economy.

International trade is a challenging and interesting career because of the competitive situation today. Tomorrow's college graduates will find many opportunities to export and import more merchandise. We shall now explore how to get started.

THINKING IT THROUGH

Some 95% of the world's population lives outside the United States, but only a small percentage of U.S. companies engage in world trade. Why is that? What do such figures indicate about the future potential for increasing U.S. exports? What do they say about future careers in international business?

In which countries would you enjoy living other than the United States? What languages do they speak? What are the trade possibilities? Are you missing out on an opportunity by failing to take other languages in school and courses in international business?

Getting Involved

Students often wonder which U.S. firms are best for finding a job in international business. Naturally, the discussion focuses on *large* multinational firms (for example, GM, Ford, GE, IBM, du Pont, and Kodak) that have large overseas accounts (see Figure 26-6). But the real secret to success in overseas business may be with *small* businesses. Getting started is often a matter of observation, determination, and risk. What does that mean? First of all, it is important to travel overseas to get some feel for the culture and life-styles of various countries to see if you really want to work and trade overseas. When you are in foreign countries, notice that most have few of the material advantages (goods and services) that are widely available in the United States.

For example, a traveler in one part of Africa noticed that there was no ice available for drinks, for keeping foods fresh, and so on. Further research showed that, in fact, there was no ice factory for hundreds of miles, yet the market seemed huge. The man returned to the United States, found some venture capital, and returned to Africa to build an ice-making plant. Much negotiation was necessary with the authorities (negotiation best done by locals who know the system), and the plant was built. Now the man is indeed wealthy.

Lyle Fox was in Japan working as a journalist. He discovered that there were no bagels in the part of Japan in which he lived. Using an old family recipe, Mr. Fox and his Japanese wife began producing bagels and selling them in the local market.

Mike Solomko bought a franchise to sell West Bend Cookware in Japan. Today his company has 400 salespeople selling pots and pans door-to-door in Japan. Mike appears on Japanese TV as "Super Solomko."[6] You can see that international business is something like domestic business in that the goal is to "find a need and fill it." The difference is that one has to do much more preparation to buy and sell in foreign markets.

Importing

Students often find that *importing* goods into the United States can be quite profitable. Foreign students attending U.S. universities often notice that some products widely available in their countries are not available in the United States,

FIGURE 26-6

Top 20 U.S. exporters, 1984.

RANK	COMPANY
1	General Motors
2	Ford
3	GE
4	Boeing
5	IBM
6	Chrysler
7	du Pont
8	United Technologies
9	McDonnell-Douglas
10	Kodak
11	Caterpillar Tractor
12	Hewlett Packard
13	Digital Equipment
14	Westinghouse
15	Union Carbide
16	Motorola
17	Philip Morris
18	Exxon
19	Monsanto
20	Signal Companies

Source: *Fortune,* August 5, 1985.

Tullycross Fine Irish Imports store in Philadelphia.

or are more costly here. Such products include food (witness the growth of Vietnamese restaurants in large American cities), household goods (including furniture, art, rugs, lamps, tile, and pottery), and manufactured goods (motorcycles, watches, cameras, videotape recorders, autos, and TV sets). By working with foreign producers and finding some working capital, these students have become major importers.

Executives from Minnetonka, Inc. of Chaska, Minnesota were browsing in a West German supermarket when they noticed a fascinating new product—toothpaste in a pump dispenser. The company contacted Henkel, the German manufacturer, and together they introduced the product into the United States as Check-Up toothpaste. It was so popular that Colgate, Crest, and other brands soon followed with their own versions of the pump.

"We made grocery shopping a regular part of our business trips to Europe," says Grant Wood, V.P. of Marketing at Minnetonka. "In this case, it helped give us a jump on our bigger competitors."[7] Maybe you too could find such products to bring back to the United States (see the box below).

KEN HAKUTA'S WACKY WALLWALKER

One day in the fall of 1982, 3½-year-old Kenzo Hakuta received a present from his grandparents in Tokyo. It was a plastic toy that looked like a giant spider. You threw the toy against the wall. It stuck there briefly, and then began flipping over and creeping down the wall in a twitching motion. The toy was great fun to watch. It was called a WallWalker.

Kenzo's father, Ken, a Harvard graduate, thought the toy had great potential. He learned that nobody had bought the North American rights to the toy, and so he acquired them and began selling the toys himself. He began with an order of 300,000. Soon he had orders for 15 million WallWalkers from stores like Woolworth's, K-mart, and Revco.

Eventually, Mr. Hakuta built a WallWalker plant in Korea and began promoting the toy as a premium to be given away with other products. By the end of 1983, Ken had sold over 27 million WallWalkers and was going strong. Mr. Hakuta believes the potential for this toy is fantastic.

Mr. Hakuta kept his eyes open and found a product overseas that he felt could be popular in the U.S., and made a fortune. His story is just one of hundreds, or even thousands, that describe the success of importing foreign goods to the U.S. Why don't more people get involved? We'll explore that question next.

Source: Robert B. Harrow, Jr., "D.C. Entrepreneur Sticks With Wacky WallWalker Idea," *The Washington Post,* February 4, 1985, p. 7 of Washington Business. © *The Washington Post,* 1985.

RESTRICTIONS ON FOREIGN TRADE

People who have been successful in international trade have reported that one of the necessary ingredients for successful exchanges in many countries is knowing how to deal with foreign government bureaucracy. It is usually not enough to have a good product and ready markets, they say. Government administrators overseas will often insist on some under-the-table payment to get the necessary permits and the permission to begin trade.[8] That was the case when the man tried to build an ice manufacturing plant in Africa. Usually only natives to that country are suitably skilled to conduct such matters. Successful businesspeople in foreign countries are used to the procedures, know who to see and what to say, and can minimize the necessary fees. To be a successful trader in foreign countries, therefore, one might have to begin by contacting local businesspeople and gaining their cooperation and sponsorship. The problem is that foreign bureaucracies are often stumbling blocks to successful foreign trade; to penetrate those barriers, often one must find a local sponsor who can pay the necessary fees to gain government permission.

Trade Protectionism

In reality, it is relatively easy to manage the problem of foreign bureaucrats who demand payments for permits and the like. What is often a much greater barrier to international trade is the overall political atmosphere between nations. This barrier is best understood through a review of some economic history of world trade.

Business, economics, and politics have always been closely linked. In fact, economics was once referred to as "political economy," indicating the close ties between politics (government) and economics. For centuries, businesspeople have tried to influence economists and government officials. Back in the sixteenth, seventeenth, and eighteenth centuries, nations were trading goods (mostly farm products) with one another. Businesspeople at that time advocated an economic principle called **mercantilism.** Basically, the idea of mercantilism was to sell more goods to other nations than you bought from them; that is, to have a favorable balance of trade. This results in a flow of money to the country that sells the most. Governments assisted in this process by charging a tariff (basically a tax) on imports, making them more expensive.

There are two different kinds of tariffs: revenue and protective. **Protective tariffs** are designed to raise the retail price of imported products so that domestic products will be more competitive. These tariffs are meant to save jobs for domestic workers and to keep industries from closing down entirely because of foreign competition. The U.S. shoe industry, for example, has been almost totally taken over by imports. **Revenue tariffs,** on the other hand, are designed to raise money for the government.

Today, there is still much debate about the degree of protectionism a government should practice. For example, the U.S. government is concerned about protecting domestic auto producers and workers from Japanese producers. The government convinced Japanese producers to voluntarily limit the number of Japanese cars sold here.

The term that describes limiting the number of products in certain categories that can be imported is *import quota.* The U.S. has import quotas on a number of products such as beef and steel. Again, the goal is to protect industry to preserve jobs. An *embargo* is a complete ban on the import or export of certain products. The ban on the sale of Cuban cigars in the United States is one example. The U.S. also prohibits the export of some products. For example, the Trans-Alaskan Pipeline Authorization Act prohibits the export of oil from North Slope fields in Alaska. Another law bans the export of timber from federal lands. The Export Administration Act prohibits exporting goods that would endanger national security (for example, military hardware to the U.S.S.R.).[9]

Consequences of Protectionism

Today, nations throughout the world are debating how much protectionism they should use to keep foreign competition from driving their firms out of business.

mercantilism
The economic principle advocating the selling of more goods to other nations than a country buys.

protective tariff
Designed to raise the price of imported products so that domestic products are more competitive.

revenue tariff
Designed to raise money for the government.

Few measures that we could take would do more to promote the cause of freedom at home and abroad than complete free trade.

Milton Friedman

You can read about this trend in current business periodicals. As you do, keep in mind that the severity of the Great Depression of 1929 and the early 1930s was attributed by some people to the passage of the highly protectionist Smoot-Hawley Tariff Act of 1930. Economists were almost unanimous in opposition to the bill. Nonetheless, to protect American business, the government put tariffs on goods from England, France, and other foreign nations. The result was that other countries raised tariffs in return. This hurt U.S. businesses badly. By 1932, exports to England were at one third the 1929 level, exports to France were only one fourth of 1929, and exports to Australia were one fifth of 1929. Wheat exports fell from $200 million to $5 million, and auto exports fell from $541 million to $76 million.[9] In short, protectionist policies of the government (based on old mercantilist thinking) helped create the greatest depression in the history of the United States. Unemployment reached 24%. You can see the need for care when such policies are proposed. (See the box below for both sides of the tariff issue.)

TWO SIDES OF THE TARIFF ISSUE

Some people feel that tariffs are necessary to protect national markets from foreign competition. Some of the arguments they use include:

- *Tariffs save jobs.* Tariffs should be used to keep cheap foreign labor from taking over American jobs, thus increasing employment in the United States.
- *Tariffs are imposed on the United States by its competitors.* It is generally accepted that the United States has consistently followed a policy favoring open trade. Other countries, such as Japan, have nevertheless imposed severe tariffs on our products. To make competition fair we have to take reciprocal measures.
- *Tariffs protect industries vital to American security.* The U.S. government has been protecting certain industries that are sensitive for our defense, such as the automobile, aerospace, and shipbuilding industries.
- *Tariffs are needed to protect new domestic industries from established foreign competitors.* The so-called infant-industry argument supports tariffs for new industries until they can compete with foreign competitors.

The opponents of tariffs counterargue by presenting the following negative effects tariffs can have:

- *Tariffs reduce competition.* Any tool used to restrain international trade in effect reduces competition, with all the negative implications this has on the economy.
- *Tariffs tend to increase inflationary pressure.* Tariffs raise consumer prices and as such act as a stimulant for inflation.
- *Tariffs tend to support special interest groups.* Tariffs in general benefit special interest groups, such as local manufacturers, but overall hurt the public who are forced to pay higher prices for imported products.
- *Tariffs can lead to foreign retaliation and subsequently to trade wars.* If the United States imposes tariffs on products imported from certain countries, this might result in reciprocal tariffs on the part of the affected countries, which would escalate trade wars.

Debate over trade restrictions will be a major part of international politics for the next decade. You may want to stay current with such discussions, because the future of world growth depends on open trade.

Other Trade Constraints

Trade protectionism in the form of tariffs and quotas is just one of the barriers to open international trade. If you stop to think about it, it becomes obvious that different countries have different cultures, languages, money systems, and religions, all of which can cause potential problems for companies wishing to trade.

First, there is the real problem of different political beliefs. One country might be communist and another capitalist. To prove that its own system is "better," each country may try to keep its products from benefiting the other. In fact, political considerations have caused many countries to establish embargoes (legal constraints) that prevent their companies from trading with other countries. For example, the United States placed an embargo on grain sales to the U.S.S.R. for a while after it invaded Afghanistan.

Second, economic constraints often hinder international trade. For example, some nations are so poor that they have little or nothing with which to trade. Other countries have found that international trade drains money they cannot afford to lose from their economy.

Third, technological constraints may make it difficult or impossible to carry on effective trade. For example, some less developed countries have such primitive transportation and storage systems that international food exchanges are ineffective, because the food is spoiled by the time it reaches those in need. These constraints are further complicated by the tremendous geographic distances that separate some countries.

James Thwaits, president of international operations of the 3M Company, says that as much as *half* of all trade is limited by *nontariff* barriers. In other words, countries have established many strategies to prevent foreign competition that go beyond tariffs. For example, France tried to protect its videotape recorder industry by requiring that all imported recorders be sent through an undermanned customs post that was 100 miles from the nearest port. Denmark requires that beverages be sold in returnable bottles; this effectively cut off French mineral water producers who found the cost of returning bottles prohibitive. Margarine must be sold in cubes in Belgium, closing the market to countries that sell margarine in tubs.

Such constraints on world trade could be viewed as good reasons to *avoid* world trade. In fact, most companies in the United States do just that. But such constraints could also be viewed as a tremendous opportunity. Learn to hurdle such barriers, and you will have access to markets of billions of people! We shall now explore some ways of entering world markets.

PROGRESS CHECK

- What is the theory of comparative advantage?
- What is mercantilism and how do tariffs and embargos fit into the theory?

TRADING IN WORLD MARKETS

In spite of the tremendous potential of foreign markets, United States producers have lagged far behind most of the developed nations, as a percent of GNP, in tapping this resource. One reason has been the huge potential in domestic (U.S.) markets. Domestic firms were able to grow rapidly at home. Another reason, as we have noted, is the complexity of foreign markets; there are different political systems, legal systems, monetary systems, economic systems, communication systems, languages, values, standards of living, and more.

An organization may participate in international trade in many ways, including exporting and importing, joint venturing, licensing, creating subsidiaries, franchising, and forming a multinational organization.

Exporting

Firms just beginning to reach the international market are likely to use an independent export house (trading company) to handle all such sales. Eventually the function may be absorbed internally in the form of an export department or an export section in marketing.

Licensing

A firm may decide to service a growing overseas market by licensing the manufacture of its product by a foreign producer on a royalty basis. The company sends representatives to the foreign producer to help set up the production process and may provide a variety of services such as marketing advice. Coke and Pepsi often enter foreign markets in this way.

Creating Subsidiaries

As the size of a foreign market expands, a firm may want to establish a wholly owned foreign subsidiary. Such a subsidiary would operate much like a domestic branch.

A Dunkin' Donuts franchise in Indonesia.

Franchising

Franchising is popular both domestically and in international markets. Firms such as McDonald's, 7-Eleven, Kentucky Fried Chicken, Ramada Inn, Avis, Hertz, Travelodge, and Dunkin' Donuts have many overseas units operated by franchisees.

Franchisors have to be careful to adapt in the countries they serve. For example, Kentucky Fried Chicken's eleven Hong Kong outlets failed within 2 years. Apparently, the chicken was too greasy and messy to be eaten with fingers by the fastidious people of Hong Kong. McDonald's also made a mistake when entering the Amsterdam market. It originally set up operations in the suburbs, as it does in the United States, but soon learned that Europeans mostly live in the cities. Therefore McDonald's began to open outlets downtown. U.S. marketers learn fast, and there are now thousands of franchises operating internationally. McDonald's franchises now serve beer in Germany and wine in France. Other franchises are doing well also. In fact, automobile and truck rentals are first and food restaurants second in total international sales.

The mistakes franchisors have made bring up the subject of global marketing strategies. The debate concerns whether or not firms can develop a strategy that works everywhere. Let's review the debate.

GLOBAL MARKETING

Global marketing is the term used to describe selling the same product in essentially the same way everywhere in the world.[11] The growth of satellite systems will soon make it possible to have worldwide promotions. Rupert Murdoch, for example, has a satellite based in the United Kingdom that transmits to nearly 2.5 million homes in Norway, Finland, Switzerland, Austria, West Germany, and the United Kingdom itself. Many U.S. programs reach Canada, of course. The question is whether or not international promotions will be successful. Some companies *can* develop universal appeals. Sky Channel, Murdoch's European system, successfully promotes Coca-Cola, Wrigley, Ford, Polaroid, Kodak, and other companies whose products have wide appeal.

Some past experiences are revealing of the problems of global marketing, however. For example, translating a theme into a different language can be disastrous:

- "Body by Fisher" became "Corpse by Fisher."
- The Chevrolet Nova had little appeal in Spanish-speaking countries, because "no va" in Spanish means "it doesn't go."
- Campbell soup failed in Brazil because housewives felt they were not fulfilling their role by serving ready-made soup. They preferred dehydrated products that they could use as a soup starter, and then add their own creative touch.

Thousands of similar stories could be told. The truth is that most U.S. manufacturers simply do not *think* multinational yet. For example, they don't adapt automobiles to drive on the left side of the road as is done in many countries. They often print instructions only in English. Parts can be hard to get. Some electrical outlets can't handle American-style plugs. The problems go on and on. Only when U.S. producers begin to thoroughly research foreign markets before attempting sales will such problems be solved. Global marketing works only in limited cases. International marketing usually calls for careful marketing research (listening) and

global marketing
Term used to describe selling the same product in essentially the same way everywhere in the world.

adaptation to the specific wants and needs of various countries and to the differences between countries.

Export Trading Firms

export trading companies
Companies that attempt to match buyers and sellers from different countries.

Because so many U.S. firms are reluctant to go through the fuss and bother of establishing trading relationships overseas, it makes sense that some organization would step in to negotiate such exchanges for them. In fact, Congress authorized such organizations in 1982. They are called **export trading companies.** Their function is to match buyers and sellers from different countries. Although the idea sounds great, the implementation of such trades has been less than expected.

Sears World Trade Inc., for example, recently lost $16.3 million over a 15-month period on revenues of $120 million. Other companies that were slow getting started include Security Pacific Corporation, First Chicago Corporation, and Union Bancorp. *The Wall Street Journal* reported that, "A principal problem of the U.S. export trading companies is that they tend to lack experience and expertise."[12] International trade is so new to most U.S. firms that hardly anyone knows how to do it well.

G.E. has 60 bilingual workers with MBAs (Masters of Business Administration) in its trading department, and 70% of them are foreign born. Students *who learn foreign languages in school* and enter international trade have an opportunity to improve the status of export trading firms and make good money besides.

By the time you graduate from college, firms such as G.E. Trading will be doing billions of dollars worth of foreign trade. The opportunities are there for those who prepare. Opportunities also exist for smaller entrepreneurs who are internationally oriented.

One such entrepreneur is A.H. Farouki, a Jordanian who received a master's degree in engineering management at The George Washington University in Washington, D.C. Mr. Farouki's American Export Groups International Services, Inc. (Aegis) did more than $100 million in business in 1 year recently, and has become one of the largest independently owned trading corporations in the United States.[13] The company does not work as an agent for individual U.S. manufacturers; rather, it shops for the best equipment for specific jobs and handles the order all the way from the manufacturing process to installation. For example, Aegis was responsible for designing, supplying, and installing Somalia's first color TV system. It also handled the complete furnishing of King Saud University in Saudi Arabia (75,000 pieces of furniture), a $30 million trade. Aegis operates worldwide to seek markets for U.S. merchandise. It supplied a workshop and spare parts to help Pakistan rebuild old agricultural machinery ($6 million), worked on a 50-bed hospital and a candy factory in Burma, and is installing telephone equipment in Bangladesh. The idea is that there are great opportunities in the United States for marketers to establish trading companies that can find markets for U.S. products overseas and manage the shipment and installation of those goods.

Joint Ventures

international joint venture
A partnership in which companies from two different countries join to undertake a major project.

An **international joint venture** is a partnership in which companies from two different countries join to undertake a major project. Two of the more heavily publicized international joint ventures in the 1980s were the GM-Toyota plant in California and the Ford-Toyo Kogyo (Mazda) plant in Mexico. Both GM and

Ford needed a small car to compete with the small Japanese cars. What better place to find the technology and experience than Japan? The GM-Toyota plant is equally owned by the two companies. Ford owns the assembly plant in Mexico, but the car is one designed by Japan's Toyo Kogyo to replace the GLC model that was being sold in the U.S.

These auto company ventures are merely the most *publicized* cooperative efforts. Joint ventures are nothing new in international trade. Perhaps the most visible example is the cooperation between major department stores and foreign producers of TV sets, videotape recorders, and other such goods (especially Japan). The foreign company produces the goods, and U.S. corporations provide the distribution and promotion expertise. In the U.S., names such as Panasonic and Sony are as familiar as GE and Westinghouse because of joint ventures.

Nova automobiles are a joint venture of U.S. and Japanese firms.

The benefits of international joint ventures are rather clear—shared technology, shared marketing expertise, entry into markets where foreign goods are not allowed unless produced locally, and shared risk. The drawbacks are not so obvious. One important one is that the partner can learn your technology and practices and go off on its own as a competitor—a rather common practice. Over time, the technology may become obsolete or the partnership may be too large to be as flexible as needed. Because of these drawbacks, such agreements need to include some provision for shared information, shared management, and procedures for evaluating the agreement and potential separation. Given such arrangements, cooperative ventures promise to be a growing phenomenon as business firms seek to expand markets overseas.

JAPANESE ROBOTS BUILD AMERICAN CARS

The dominant robotics company in the United States is GMF Robotics, a 50-50 joint venture between General Motors Corporation and Fanic, Ltd., a Japanese robotics company. What makes the company so big is the number of robots it sells to General Motors for its auto manufacturing plants. The company sold just 332 robots in 1983, but increased sales to 1,208 in 1984.

Almost all of GMF's robots are built by Fanic in Japan, and are then integrated into custom-built robotics systems by GMF engineers. The only line of robots made in the United States are expensive, computer paint systems for automobile plants.

Other robot makers complain that GMF has an unfair advantage selling to GM. Some have even turned in lower bids, they say, but an old-boy network has been established that gives GMF preference.

GM denies giving any special advantage to GMF. Would it be in GM's best interest to open the bidding for robots to all firms, or should they buy from their own joint-venture firm? How could a U.S. robotics firm such as Cincinnati Milacron win business from GMF?

Countertrading

bartering
The exchange of merchandise for merchandise.

countertrading
Bartering among several countries.

One of the oldest forms of trade is called **bartering,** the exchange of merchandise for merchandise with no money involved. **Countertrading** is more complex than bartering in that several countries may be involved, each trading goods for goods. It has been estimated that countertrading accounts for 25% to 30% of all international exchanges.[14]

Examples of countertrade and bartering agreements are many. Chrysler traded its vehicles in Jamaica for bauxite. McDonnell-Douglas traded jets in Yugoslavia for canned hams. General Motors has traded vehicles with China for industrial gloves and cutting tools. Telelex Media has traded television shows for advertising time in several foreign countries.

Barter is especially important to poor countries that have little cash available for trade. Such countries may barter with all kinds of raw materials, food, or whatever resources they have. Colombia has traded coffee for buses. Romania traded cement for steam engines.

With the world currency markets fluctuating so widely in the 1980s, there is no question that countertrading will grow in importance. Trading products for products often solves problems of monetary differences.

MULTINATIONAL CORPORATIONS

There has been much discussion recently about the power of multinational corporations. It is helpful to first understand what they are and what they mean for international business. A **multinational corporation (MNC)** is an organization that does manufacturing and marketing in many different countries; it has multinational stock ownership and multinational management. The more multinational a company is, the more it attempts to operate without being influenced by restrictions from various governments.

multinational corporation
An organization that does manufacturing and marketing in many different countries; it has multinational stock ownership and multinational management.

The multinational corporation is constantly checking opportunities for expansion all over the globe. It aggressively markets its products, capitalizing on its technological and managerial expertise. Companies such as IBM, Procter and Gamble, du Pont, Shell, Exxon, Mobil, Toyota, Coca-Cola and Nestlé are examples of multinational corporations (see Figure 26-7). Caution should be exercised, however, before calling a company "multinational." Not all firms involved in international business are multinationals. A company may be exporting its entire product, thus deriving 100% of its sales and profits overseas, but that alone would not make it a multinational. Only firms that have manufacturing capacity or other physical presence in various nations can be called multinational.

Global Corporations

The global corporation is a step beyond the multinational corporation. The **global corporation** is a supranational entity that bears no national allegiance to any single country. The modern global corporation strives against any government's jurisdiction over its operations. In essence, it attempts to establish its own sovereignty in world markets. Barnett and Muller in their best-selling book *Global Reach* argued that:

global corporation
A supernational entity that bears no national allegiance to any country.

> The rise of the planetary enterprise is producing an organizational revolution as profound in its implications for modern man as the industrial revolution and the rise of the nation-state itself. The growth rate of global corporations in recent years is so spectacular that it is now easy to assemble an array of dazzling statistics. If we compare the annual sales of corporations with the gross national product of countries . . . we discover that GM is bigger than Switzerland, Pakistan and South Africa, that Royal Dutch Shell is bigger than Iran, Venezuela and Turkey and that Goodyear Tire is bigger than Saudi Arabia.

These global corporations are a major source of social and economic change, especially in the lesser developed countries (LDCs). By promoting the same products in many different countries, global corporations are homogenizing the world's needs. It has been the traditional view of international marketing that companies should adapt their products and promotions to each country individually. Recently, this view has been changing. Theodore Levitt, an international business consultant, argues that global corporations such as Coca-Cola, McDonald's, Toyota, and Nissan-Datsun are globalizing the world market. Levitt believes that because of the emergence of global markets for standardized consumer products on a previously unimagined scale of magnitude, corporations must learn to operate as if the world were one large market—ignoring superficial regional and national differences. This era has not yet arrived, but the globalization of business is definitely a trend.

FIGURE 26-7

The 50 top U.S. multinational corporations.

Source: "The 100 Largest U.S. Multinationals," *Forbes,* July 29, 1985, pp. 186-187.

RANK	COMPANY	FOREIGN REVENUE AS PERCENT OF TOTAL
1	Exxon	69.4%
2	Mobil	55.9
3	Texaco	50.1
4	Chevron	38.9
5	IBM	40.4
6	Phibro-Salomon	59.8
7	Ford Motor	29.7
8	General Motors	17.3
9	E.I. du Pont de Nemours	32.0
10	Citicorp	49.8
11	ITT	37.4
12	Dow Chemical	53.6
13	BankAmerica	41.3
14	Chase Manhattan	55.4
15	Amoco	19.3
16	Safeway Stores	23.4
17	Occidental Petroleum	25.1
18	J.P. Morgan	58.0
19	Procter & Gamble	28.9
20	General Electric	12.6
21	United Technologies	21.0
22	Sun Company	22.5
23	Xerox	27.6
24	Eastman Kodak	30.1
25	Goodyear	30.7
26	Manufacturers Hanover	37.5
27	Phillips Petroleum	19.8
28	Sears, Roebuck	7.6
29	Coca-Cola	38.0
30	Beatrice	21.9
31	American Express	21.4
32	Union Carbide	28.8
33	Bankers Trust New York	55.4
34	Pan Am Corporation	71.8
35	Dart & Kraft	26.9
36	Colgate-Palmolive	52.3
37	CPC International	58.5
38	Allied Corporation	23.7
39	Hewlett-Packard	41.6
40	Minnesota Mining & Manufacturing	32.6
41	Johnson & Johnson	39.0
42	Chrysler	11.9
43	Nabisco Brands	36.8
44	F.W. Woolworth	39.6
45	Chemical New York	37.1
46	Tenneco	14.6
47	InterNorth	28.1
48	GTE	14.2
49	Burroughs	40.4
50	American International Group	45.9

THE GLOBALIZATION OF K-MART

Recently, K-mart imported $2 billion worth of goods for its 2,100 stores; that's 12% of its inventory. A walk through the store will reveal the impact of importing on U.S. retailing. At K-mart you will see:

- Men's corduroy slacks and button-down shirts from China
- Lambskin rugs from Argentina
- Plush dolls from Korea
- Barbie dolls made in Taiwan
- Fiberfill jackets from China
- Wool rugs from Israel
- Fishing rods from Korea, and lures from Taiwan and Japan

- Woolen sweaters from Korea
- Tape-cassette holders from Taiwan
- Work gloves sewn in Mexico
- Flannel pajamas manufactured in the Dominican Republic
- Cabbage Patch doll earmuffs brought in from Taiwan

U.S. retailers get 46% of their shoes and 22% of their men's and boys' clothes overseas. These products come from all over the world, as you can see from the K-mart example.

Source: "Made Abroad—A Label You Can't Escape," *U.S. News and World Report,* November 19, 1984, p. 83.

International Trade Organizations

Most nations recognize the need to expand world trade. Consequently, some nations have joined together to form trading partnerships and to write up trade agreements that facilitate open trade. For example, after World War II, a spirit of intergovernmental cooperation emerged to encourage international trade. The International Monetary Fund was signed into existence by 44 nations at Bretton Woods, New Hampshire in 1944. The basic objectives were to promote exchange stability, maintain orderly exchange arrangements, avoid competitive currency depreciation, establish a multilateral system of payments, eliminate exchange restrictions, and create standby reserves.

The **World Bank,** an autonomous United Nations agency, is concerned with the development of the infrastructure (roads, schools, hospitals, power plants) in less-developed countries. In 1948 the General Agreement on Tariffs and Trade (GATT) was established. This agreement among 23 countries provided a forum for negotiating mutual reductions in trade restrictions. In short, government leaders from nations throughout the world have cooperated to create monetary and trade agreements that facilitate the exchange of goods, services, ideas, and cultural programs. (See Figure 26-8 for other examples.)

World Bank
Borrows money from the more prosperous countries and lends it at favorable rates to less-developed countries.

Some countries felt that their economies would be strengthened if they were to establish more detailed trade agreements with other countries in the same region. Some of these agreements are described here:

Producers' Cartels

Producers' cartels are organizations of commodity-producing countries. They are formed to stabilize or increase prices, optimizing overall profits in the long run. The most obvious example, and potentially the most dominant economically today, is OPEC (the Organization of Petroleum Exporting Countries). No doubt you have experienced the disruptions caused by the price changes instituted by OPEC. Similar arrangements have been made to manage prices for copper (the Council of Copper Exporting Countries), iron ore, bauxite, bananas, tungsten, and rubber.

producers' cartels
Organizations of commodity-producing countries that are formed to stabilize or increase prices to optimize overall profits in the long run. (An example is OPEC, the Organization of Petroleum-Exporting Countries.)

FIGURE 26-8

Other organizations that assist in foreign trade.

ORGANIZATION	OBJECTIVE
The Export-Import Bank	Government bank designed to reduce domestic unemployment. It makes loans to exporters who cannot secure financing through private sources and to foreign countries who use the funds to buy American goods.
Foreign Trade Zones	Places where goods can be imported without being subject to customs duties or quotas. The imported materials are then manufactured into finished products. If re-exported, they are not subject to any tariffs, but if they enter into domestic commerce, they are subject to regular tariffs.
The International Finance Corporation (IFC)	This organization makes loans to private businesses when they cannot obtain loans from more conventional sources (affiliated with the World Bank).
The International Development Association (IDA)	This organization makes loans to private businesses and to member countries of the World Bank.
Domestic International Sales Corporation (DISC)	U.S. firms can form tax-sheltered subsidiaries (DISCs) to handle their export sales. The purpose is to encourage exports and get American firms to enter the export market.
Overseas Private Investment Corporation (OPIC)	Sells insurance to U.S. firms that operate overseas. Covers damages caused by war, revolution, or insurrection, inability to convert local currencies into U.S. dollars, and expropriation (take-over by foreign governments).
The Foreign Credit Insurance Association (FCIA)	Sells insurance to cover political risk (e.g., expropriation). Comprehensive coverage can cover business risks (e.g., credit default). The company also sells insurance coverage on credit sales to foreign customers.

common market
A regional group of countries that have no internal tariffs, a common external tariff, and a coordination of laws to facilitate exchange. (An example is the European Economic Community.)

Common Markets

A **common market** is a regional group of countries that have no internal tariffs. Common markets have a common external tariff and a coordination of laws to facilitate exchange. Notable are the European Economic Community (EEC), the Central American Common Market (CACM), and the Caribbean Common Market (CCM).

There are many more such arrangements including *negotiating groups* (such as the Special Coordinating Committee for Latin America) that join together to negotiate trade agreements; *commodity associations* that bring together countries who are concerned with specific commodities (the group gathers statistics, does research, provides forums for buyers and sellers of products such as cotton and wool); *commodity agreements*, which are multilateral agreements among buyers and sellers to stabilize prices and earnings (such as for cocoa, sugar, tea, and coffee); and more.

You are likely to see more such agreements in the future. For example, the United States is negotiating better trade relations with China; the less-developed countries of the world are starting to join together to become more powerful traders; and the world community in general is becoming more aware of the need for further agreements covering fishing rights, the mining of ore from the ocean bottom, international pollution control, and more open trade agreements to minimize international tensions.

EEC MEMBER NATIONS

Belgium/Luxembourg
Denmark
France
Greece
Ireland
Italy
Netherlands
United Kingdom
West Germany

THINKING IT THROUGH

Many countries in the world are called less-developed countries. Why are they less developed? Is it the lack of natural resources? Then how do you explain the success of Japan, which has few natural resources? Does lack of free markets keep countries from developing? Why would a government restrict free trade? What could happen to the world's standard of living and quality of life if all countries engaged in free trade? What is keeping that from happening?

THE FUTURE OF WORLD TRADE

World trade now is a tiny percentage of what it could be. Where do you suppose is the biggest market for U.S. goods? Some would guess Canada ($52.1 billion), others Japan ($41.2 billion), and others the United Kingdom ($12.5 billion). But the true answer is the less-developed nations of the world. Together, 99 nations buy $59 billion worth of manufactured goods from the United States. The LDCs (less-developed countries) are the same areas that we read are suffering from drought, famine, war, and hunger. They are the nations that are worst off, and thus have the most potential for growth through trade.

Maxwell House coffee being unloaded in Singapore.

In India, there are 500,000 villages that don't have electric power and cannot afford to tie into some central power source, as towns do in most developed nations. One answer to this problem is solar power. The potential of this market is about $20 billion per year.[15]

You may think that the less-developed countries have nothing to export but food, natural resources, and labor. The truth is that the 39 nations that the World Bank classifies as lower-middle income (for example, Kenya, Senegal, Bolivia, Honduras) now derive an average of 35% of their gross domestic product (GDP)* from industry and 43% from services, while agriculture's share of production has fallen to an average 22%.[16] In short, the less-developed nations of the world have a GDP equal to that of the United States and are growing more rapidly. The Third World is where the future of world trade lies, along with the trade relations already established among the developed countries. The Third World nations include less developed countries such as Zimbabwe and newly industrialized countries such as Mexico and Taiwan. See Figure 26-9 for a list of developing nations and what they trade.

FIGURE 26-9

Ten best developing nations for world trade.

Source: "Making It in the Third World," *Grey Matter*, 1981.

COUNTRY	POPULATION (IN $MILLIONS)	PER CAPITA GNP (IN DOLLARS)	TRADE RESOURCES
Mexico	65.4	1,290	Oil, silver, copper, gold, lead, zinc, gas, timber
Singapore	2.3	3,290	Labor
Taiwan	17.1	1,400	Timber, camphor
Venezuela	14	2,910	Oil, gas, iron ore, gold, hydroelectric power
Yugoslavia	22	2,380	Coal, copper, iron ore, lead, zinc, oil, bauxite, gas
Argentina	26.4	1,910	Oil, gas, copper, iron ore, coal, lead, zinc, silver
Indonesia	13.6	360	Oil, tin, rubber, bauxite, nickel, copper, gas, coal
Malaysia	13.3	1,090	Tin, oil, copper, iron, timber
Zimbabwe	6.9	490	Gold, copper, chrome, asbestos, manganese, coal
Nigeria	80.6	560	Tin, oil, columbite, iron ore, coal, limestone, lead, zinc, timber

Here are some figures (1982) regarding the sum of import and export trade with some Pacific Basin nations:

- Taiwan, $13.3 billion

---

*GDP is income produced in a country; that is, it excludes overseas income.

- South Korea, $11 billion
- Hong Kong, $8 billion
- Indonesia, $6.2 billion
- Singapore, $5.4 billion
- The Philippines, $3.7 billion
- Malaysia, $3.6 billion

Clearly, the Third World nations are emerging as the international traders of the future. In fact, the fastest-growing group of multinational firms are located in newly industrialized countries (NICs). The Biria Group of India, United Laboratories of the Philippines, and Rutlan of Mexico are representative of the several hundred multinationals from NICs whose overseas subsidiaries grew from a few dozen in 1960 to a few thousand today.[17]

The United States has taken a leadership role in establishing mutually beneficial trade relations with Third World countries. Clearly there is much more to be done. Much of the world still goes to bed hungry. Much of the world is miserably poor. Disease kills millions everyday. There are world problems that can only be solved by worldwide efforts. Enough food exists to feed the world. We have all the medicine we need to conquer much of the illness that is decimating the populations of less-developed countries. What is missing? The political, social, and spiritual will and desire to end such problems through open world trade. The leadership for the needed political and social change will come from today's students, you included. The possibilities are great. Are you ready to accept the challenge?

PROGRESS CHECK

- Can you name three ways for a U.S. firm to enter world markets?

- Can you define the terms *multinational corporation* and *joint venture?*

- Can you name five organizations that assist in international trade?

SUMMARY

1 The world market for trade is huge. Some 95% of the people in the world live outside the United States, world population grows by 72 million per year, and 30% of the world's GNP consists of world trade.

- What terms should I know to read about world trade?

  Exporting is selling products to other countries.

  Importing is buying products from other countries.

  Balance of trade is the relationship of exports to imports.

  A *favorable balance of trade* is when exports exceed imports.

  Balance of payments is balance of trade *plus* other money flows such as tourism and foreign aid.

  Dumping is selling products for less in a foreign country.

  Trade protectionism is the use of government regulations to limit the importation of products. See other terms in the Key Terms section to be sure you know the important ones.

- Why should nations trade with other nations?

  (1) No country is self-sufficient, (2) other countries need products that prosperous countries produce, (3) there is a world imbalance of natural resources and technological skills.

- Is there a theory behind world trade?

  Yes, the *theory of comparative advantage* says that a country should produce and sell those products it produces most efficiently and buy those it cannot produce as efficiently.

2 Students can get involved in world trade through importing and exporting; they do not have to work for big multinational corporations.

- Who are the large exporters in the U.S.?

  They include the auto companies, G.E, Boeing, IBM, du Pont, United Technologies, McDonnell Douglas, Kodak, and more (See Figure 26-6).

3 There are many restrictions on our foreign trade, including foreign government bureaucracy, trade protectionism, different political beliefs, cultural values, and more.

- Is trade protectionism good for domestic producers?

  That is debatable. Trade protectionism hurt the United States badly during the Great Depression.

- Why do governments continue such practices?

  The theory of mercantilism started the practice of trade protectionism and it has persisted, in a lesser form, ever since.

- What are tariffs?

  There are two kinds of tariffs: *protective tariffs* raise the price of foreign products and *revenue tariffs* raise money for the government.

- How does a tariff differ from an embargo?

  An embargo *prohibits* the importing or exporting of products.

4 A company can enter world markets through exporting, licensing, creating subsidiaries, or franchising.

- Can the same marketing strategies be used worldwide as used in the United States?

  The use of the same marketing strategy as at home is called *global marketing*.

  It works for a few products, but generally it is better to adapt to the country and its people.

- Are there firms to assist companies in world trade?

  Yes, there are export trading firms that match buyers and sellers.

- What is an *international joint venture*?

  It is a partnership of companies from different countries.

- Is countertrading an important practice?

  Yes, some 25% to 30% of all trades involve the trading of goods for goods among countries.

5 Multinational corporations have a huge impact on world trade. The GNP of General Motors is bigger than that of Switzerland, Pakistan, or South Africa.

- What is the difference between a multinational corporation and a global corporation?

  A *global corporation* has no national allegiance. It goes where the action is and produces where labor is cheapest.

6 There are many organizations that facilitate world trade such as the World Bank, the International Monetary Fund, Common markets and the Export-Import Bank.

- Is the future of world trade with large, developed nations?

  No, more growth will be in less-developed countries such as China, India, Mexico, South Korea, Taiwan, Hong Kong, and Singapore.

7 Can you believe this is the end of the text material?
- No, it is not the end. This book is meant to be a resource for your life and career. I hope you read and reread it many times until you truly *understand* business.

KEY TERMS

absolute advantage p. 700
balance of payments p. 696
bartering p. 710
common market p. 714
comparative advantage theory p. 699
countertrading p. 710
debtor nation p. 697
dumping p. 696
exporting p. 696
export trading companies p. 708
favorable balance of payments p. 696
global corporation p. 711
global marketing p. 707
importing p. 696
International Monetary Fund p. 697
international joint venture p. 708
mercantilism p. 703
merchandise trade deficit p. 697
multinational corporation p. 711
producers' cartels p. 713
protective tariff p. 703
revenue tariff p. 703
trade protectionism p. 697
World Bank p. 713

GETTING INVOLVED

1 Visit an Oriental rug dealer or some other importer of foreign goods. Talk with the owner/manager about the problems and joys of being involved in international trade. Visit several such organizations and compile a list of advantages and disadvantages. Then get together with others in the class and compare notes.

2 Let's dream for a minute. Imagine yourself living in an exotic country where the weather is great, the living easy, and the people friendly. Have you ever visited such a place? Well, picture yourself living there. What language would you have to learn, if any? What could you import there that would be fun to sell? Share your vision with others. What's keeping you from having that dream come true?

3 Presently, we have a world where some countries are rich and have an overabundance of food. Some countries are poor and people are starving. Some countries have few natural resources, but are prosperous (for example, Japan, Singapore). Others are relatively rich in natural resources, but are poor (for example, Ghana). What trade barriers cause such disparities to continue? Is the problem economic, social, political, or some combination? Discuss.

4 Write a short essay describing the benefits and disadvantages of trade protectionism. Have your class divide into two sides and debate this issue: "Resolved that the United States should increase trade protection to save American jobs and American companies."

5 Many U.S. firms have made embarrassing mistakes selling overseas. Sometimes the product is not adapted to the needs of the country, sometimes the advertising makes no sense, sometimes the color is wrong, and so forth. Discuss the steps U.S. businesses should follow to be more responsive to the needs of foreign markets. Discuss your list with others, and together form a plan for improving U.S. trade overseas.

PRACTICING MANAGEMENT DECISIONS

CASE ONE   THE GHOSTS OF SMOOT-HAWLEY

No subject of this chapter has received more interest in the 1980s than that of trade protectionism. In 1985, there were 400 bills before Congress calling for some form or other of trade protection. Everywhere headlines referred to "Smoot-Hawley." Some history may help clarify the issue.

The date: June 13, 1930 (Friday the 13th). The time: 2:13 PM. The place: the U.S. Senate. The Great Depression had started and the air was full of talk about trade protection. Over 1,000 economists warned the government that protectionism was dangerous and petitioned it not to pass the Smoot-Hawley Act. But, by a vote of 44 to 42, the bill passed. It was an act conceived by Republican congressmen, passed by a Republican Congress, and signed into law by conservative President Herbert Hoover.

The bill imposed duties of up to 60% on almost everything imported into the United States. World trade fell by one third, and a global trade war started. The concept was to protect the Western beet sugar farmer by raising the duty for sugar; protect the Northwestern wheat farmer by raising the duty on wheat; and protect the Imperial Valley cotton farmer by raising the duty on cotton from Egypt. The list went on: cattle and dairy products, hides, shoes, velvet, silk, china, pocket knives, watch parts, and so on.

Hawley was a professor of economics at Willamette University. Smoot was a banker and wool manufacturer. Both men lost in the 1932 election (after a combined 56 years in Congress) when Franklin Roosevelt was elected President. That was the end of Republican dominance in the Senate for a long time to come. In 1934, Congress passed the Reciprocal Trade Agreement Act to reduce tariffs, but it was too little too late.

Exports dropped from $4.8 billion to $1.7 billion from 1929 to 1932. Imports chopped from $5.4 billion to $2.4 billion. Other countries were plunged into depression also as world trade fell.

In 1985, the 400 bills before Congress covered many of the same products covered by Smoot-Hawley: shoes, textiles, beef, and so on. This time, though, it was the Democrats who were pushing trade protection and the Republicans resisting. In 1985, Republicans had a slight edge in numbers of senators. Trade protection could make or break that slight margin in the next election.

DECISION QUESTIONS

1   Why do you suppose some Democrats were pushing for trade protection in 1985 and 1986? What were the economic conditions?
2   Has Congress learned the lessons of the early 1930s such that we will never again make the mistake of passing overly restrictive legislation on world trade? What is happening now in Congress on this issue?
3   What should the role of the U.S. government be in regard to world trade? How much effort should be made to protect American workers from foreign competition?

CASE TWO ENTERING THE IMPORT/EXPORT BUSINESS

Gordon and Carole Segal went to the Caribbean on their honeymoon. While there, they were fascinated by the variety of elegant, functional housewares they saw: French copper, German cutlery, and so on. A few months later, Gordon was doing the dishes (Arzberg dinnerware) when he got the inspiration to start an importing firm. He had experience in restaurants and real estate. Carole was a teacher. Neither had any experience in retailing.

With $17,000 in capital and one employee, the couple opened the first Crate & Barrel store in an old elevator factory in Chicago's Old Town district. It took a while to learn the business. In fact, the couple forgot to buy a cash register, and went several days without one. This was in 1962.

At first, the Segals and their company, Euromarket Designs, Inc., imported only quality items they had seen and used themselves. Eventually, they toured the continent searching for more items. They learned that European tradespeople were often reluctant to sell to Americans because of past bad experiences with department store buyers. These buyers would do things like place large orders; the manufacturers would expand to fill the orders; and then no reorders, and the manufacturers were stuck. Often the Segals had to spend days negotiating to buy goods.

When the store opened, sales were $8,000 the first month. The second month they fell to $4,000, the third month $2,000. About half the initial inventory was sold at cost due to ignorance, not charity. Eventually things got straightened out, and the Segals opened a second store in 1968 in suburban Wilmette, Illinois (outside Chicago). A third store opened in 1971.

The Segals now have 17 stores. They were the ones who set the image for all the new houseware stores. Glassware, dinnerware, flatware, and cookware are piled floor to ceiling on open shelves. Emphasis is on the product, not the display case.

The honeymoon shopping trip in the Caribbean led to a major retail chain in the United States. Total revenue in 1984: $46 million.

DECISION QUESTIONS

1   How much thought have you given to the import/export business as a career? The Segals imported European goods to America. Would you enjoy selling American goods in Europe?

2   What are some of the successful stores you have seen that sell imported goods? Have you ever talked to the owners about their experiences? Do so and report back to the class.

3   Why is the world market an attractive career possibility for tomorrow's college graduates relative to the U.S. market?

Source: Joseph P. Kahn, "On Display," *Inc.*, Nov., 1985, pp. 110-122.

GLOSSARY

absolute advantage When a country has a monopoly on producing a product or is able to produce it at a cost below that of all other countries.

absolute liability Means a manufacturer can be held liable for failure to warn of a hazard, even if the hazard was scientifically unknowable at the time of sale.

accounting The recording, classifying, summarizing, and interpreting of financial events and transactions that affect the organization. It may also be viewed as the measurement and reporting (inside and outside the organization) of financial information about the economic activities of the firm to various users.

active listening The asking of questions and feeding back what you have heard to let others know you are truly interested in what they say.

actuaries People who predict future losses based on the analysis of historical data.

adjustable life insurance Gives the policyholder the freedom to switch from whole life to term and back as life's circumstances change.

administered system The management by producers of all the marketing functions at the retail level.

advertising Paid, nonpersonal communication through various media by organizations and individuals who are in some way identified in the advertising message.

agency shop One where employers may hire anyone and employees do not have to join the union but must pay union fees.

American Federation of Labor (AFL) A craft union formed in 1886.

analytic systems Break down raw materials into components to extract other products.

apprenticeship A time when a new worker works alongside a master technician to learn the skills and procedures.

artificial intelligence The ability of computers to mimic human thought processes.

assembly process Puts together components.

assets Economic resources owned by a firm, such as land, buildings, and machinery.

authority The right to make decisions and take actions.

automated teller machines (ATMs) Machines that allow bank customers to use access cards to make deposits and withdrawals at a variety of outlets, including supermarkets and department stores as well as outside the bank.

aviation insurance Covers aircraft and damage and liability from the use of aircraft.

balance of merchandise trade The difference between the sales of merchandise to foreign countries and the purchase of merchandise from other countries.

balance of payments The difference between money coming into a country (from exports) and money leaving the country (for imports) plus money flows from other factors such as tourism, foreign aid, and military expenditures.

balance sheet Reports the financial position of a firm at a specific date. Balance sheets are composed of assets, liabilities, and owners' equity.

bankruptcy The legal process by which a person or business, unable to meet financial obligations, is relieved of those debts by having the court divide any assets among creditors, freeing the debtor to begin anew.

bartering The exchange of merchandise for merchandise.

bears Investors who expect stock prices to decline.

benefit segmentation Divides the market by benefits desired.

beta Measures the riskiness of a stock relative to the stock market as a whole.

bodily injury insurance Covers bodily injury to others resulting from the ownership, maintenance, or use of a car.

bond A contract of indebtedness issued by a corporation or governmental unit that promises payment of a principal amount at a specified future time plus interest.

brand A name, symbol, or design (or combination of these) that identifies the goods or services of one seller or group of sellers and distinguishes them from those of competitors.

brand name That part of the brand consisting of a word, letter, or group of words or letters comprising a name that differentiates the goods or services of a seller from those of competitors.

breach of contract Means that one party fails to follow the terms of a contract.

break-even analysis Tells managers whether the firm will make money (or break even) at a particular price, given a certain sales volume.

brokerage firms Organizations that buy and sell securities for their customers and provide other financial services.

bulls Investors who believe that stock prices are going to rise.

bureaucrat A middle manager whose function is to implement top management's orders.

business Any organization that seeks profit by providing needed goods and services.

business interruption insurance Provides protection for a business that shuts down because of fire, storm, or other insured causes; it covers lost income, continuing expenses, and utility expenses.

business law Rules, statutes, codes, and regulations established to provide a legal framework within which business may be conducted and that is enforceable in court.

business plan A detailed written statement that describes the nature of the business, the target market, the advantages the business will have over competitors, and the resources and qualifications of the owners.

buying on margin The purchase of stocks by borrowing some of the purchase cost from the broker.

CAD/CAM (computer aided design/computer aided manufacturing) The integration of computers into the design and manufacturing of products.

CAE (computer aided engineering) The computer-generated design and analysis of products, programming of robots and machine tools, designing of molds and tools, and planning of the production process and quality control.

call provision Gives the issuer of a bond the right to retire a bond before its maturity.

capital goods Products that cost a lot of money and last a long time, such as factories and machinery.

capitalism An economic system in which all or most of the means of production and distribution are privately owned and operated for profit.

capitalist systems Systems in which resources are allocated by consumers bargaining in the marketplace and trading goods and services.

CAPP (computer aided process planning) A system of converting engineering designs into manufacturing instructions.

cash flow The difference between cash receipts and cash disbursements.

cash-and-carry wholesalers Serve mostly smaller retailers with a limited assortment of products they sell for cash.

cellular phone systems The latest mobile phone technology that transfers calls between "cells" as the user moves from one geographical area to another.

centralized authority Maintaining decision making authority with the top level of management at its headquarters.

certificate of deposit (CD) A savings account that earns a high rate of interest to be delivered at the end of the CD's period.

certified public accountant (CPA) An individual who is certified by one of the states after passing a rigorous examination and meeting certain educational, moral, and job experience requirements.

channel captain One organization in the channel that gets the other members to work together in a cooperative effort.

channel of distribution All the firms involved in moving goods from producer to consumer.

CIM (computer-integrated manufacturing) Computer aided design (CAD) combined with computer aided manufacturing (CAM). It then further integrates CAD/CAM with other corporate functions such as purchasing, inventory control, cost accounting, materials handling, and shipping.

Clayton Act Prohibits practices whose effect will be to substantially lessen competition or to create a monopoly.

closed-shop agreement Specified that workers had to be members of a union before being hired (outlawed by the Taft-Hartley Act).

coinsurance clause Requires businesses to carry insurance equal to a certain percentage of a building's actual value, usually 80%.

commercial bank A profit-making organization that receives deposits from individuals and corporations in the form of checking and saving accounts and uses some of these funds to make loans.

commercial credit insurance Protects manufacturers and wholesalers from credit losses due to insolvency or default.

commercial paper A short-term corporate equivalent of an IOU that is sold in the marketplace by a firm. They mature in 270 days or less.

commodity exchange Specializes in the buying and selling of goods such as wheat, cattle, silver, sugar, gasoline, and foreign currencies.

common law The body of law that comes from judges' decisions; also known as "unwritten law."

common market A regional group of countries that have no internal tariffs, a common external tariff, and a coordination of laws to facilitate exchange. (An example is the European Economic Community.)

common stock The most basic form of ownership of firms; it includes voting rights and dividends, if dividends are offered by the firm.

communist systems Systems in which resource allocation is largely government controlled.

comparable worth The demand for equal pay for jobs requiring similar levels of education, training, and skills.

comparative advantage theory Theory which asserts that a country should produce and sell to other countries those products that it produces most efficiently and effectively and should buy from other countries those products it cannot produce as effectively or efficiently.

compressed work week Four 10-hour days.

computer hardware Includes all the tangible machines that process and store data.

computer operators Responsible for monitoring the overall computer operation for a system and troubleshooting problems that occur.

computer software The instructions for telling the computer what to do.

consideration Something of value; it is one of the requirements of a legal contract.

consumer advisory boards Panels of consumers who meet on a regular basis over time to advise managerial decision makers on ideas and products.

consumer finance companies Offer short-term loans to individuals at rates higher than those of commercial banks.

consumer orientation Means finding out and giving consumers what they want.

consumer price index (CPI) Measures changes in the prices of about 400 goods and services that consumers buy.

consumer services Products such as rental housing and medical care that service organizations provide consumers.

consumerism A social movement that tries to increase the rights and powers of buyers in relation to sellers.

contingency planning The preparation of alternative courses of action that may be used if the primary plans are not achieving the objectives.

continuous process One in which long production runs turn out finished goods over time.

contract A legally enforceable agreement between two or more parties.

contract law Specifies what constitutes a legally enforceable agreement between two or more parties.

contractual system One whose members are bound to cooperate through contractual agreements.

control Checking to determine whether or not an organization is progressing toward its objectives and taking corrective action if it is not.

control function Measuring performance relative to objectives and standards and taking corrective action when necessary.

convenience goods and services Products that the consumer wants to purchase frequently and with a minimum of effort.

convenience services Consumer services that the public purchases rather frequently and with a minimum of effort.

cooperative An organization owned by members/customers who pay an annual membership fee and share in any profits, if it is a profit-making organization.

copyright Protects an individual's rights to materials such as books, articles, photos, and cartoons.

core time The time when all employees are present in a flextime system.

corporate culture The use of stories, slogans, and legends to convey clearly felt values so that those values become part of what the corporation is.

corporate philanthropy Includes charitable donations made by the corporation to nonprofit groups of all kinds.

corporate policy The position a firm takes on issues that affect the corporation as well as society.

corporate responsibility Encompasses various issues such as setting minority hiring practices, manufacturing safe products, and minimizing pollution.

corporate system One in which all the organizations in this channel are owned by one firm.

corporation A state-chartered legal entity with authority to act and have liability separate from its owners.

cost of goods sold A particular type of expense measured by the total cost of merchandise sold (including costs associated with the acquisition, storage, transportation in, and packaging of goods).

cost-push inflation Refers to inflation caused by rising business costs.

countertrading Bartering among several countries.

CPM (critical path method) A production scheduling method through which a manager follows the path a product takes from the beginning of the production process until the end and assigns specific times for each step.

credit life insurance Guarantees the payment of the amount due on a loan if the debtor dies.

credit unions Nonprofit, member-owned financial cooperatives that offer basic banking services such as accepting deposits and making loans; they may also sell life insurance.

criminal loss protection Insurance against theft, burglary, or robbery.

culture The set of values, attitudes, and ways of doing things that are transmitted from one generation to another in a given society.

currency All coin and paper money issued by the Federal Reserve Banks and all gold coins.

current assets Include cash or noncash items that can be converted to cash within 1 year.

cyclical unemployment Occurs because of a recession or a similar downturn in the business cycle.

debenture A bond that is unsecured; i.e., not backed with any collateral such as equipment.

debt capital Funds from borrowing money through the sale of bonds or from banks and other lending institutions.

debtor nation Country that owes more money to other nations than other nations owe it.

decentralized authority Delegating decision-making authority to lower-level managers who are more familiar with local conditions.

deductible clause States that the insurance company will pay only that part of a loss that exceeds some figure (the deductible amount) stated in the policy.

delegating Assigning authority and accountability to others while keeping responsibility for results.

delegation of authority Assigning part of a manager's duties to subordinates.

demand The quantity of products that people are willing to buy at different prices at a specific time.

demand curve Shows the relationship between quantity demanded and price.

demand deposit The technical name for a checking account because the money is available on demand from the depositor.

demand-pull inflation Refers to inflation caused by excessive demand for goods and services.

demographic segmentation Divides the market into groups by age, sex, income, and similar categories.

departmentalization Dividing tasks into homogeneous departments such as manufacturing and marketing.

depression A severe form of recession (see *recession*).

deregulation Government withdrawal of certain laws and regulations that seem to hinder competition (for example, airline regulations).

discount bonds Bonds that sell below face value.

discount rate The interest rate that the Federal Reserve Bank charges other banks for loans.

distribution mix All those functions marketers perform to move goods from producers to consumers.

diversification Buying several different general investment vehicles to spread the risk.

dividend Part of the firm's profits that goes to stockholders.

door-to-door sales Selling to consumers in their homes.

Dow Jones Industrial Averages The average cost of 30 industrial stocks.

drop shippers Solicit orders from retailers and other wholesalers and have the merchandise shipped directly from a producer to a buyer.

dumping Selling products for less in a foreign country than is charged in the producing country.

duration The length of time assets are committed.

economics The study of the allocation of scarce resources among competing individuals.

electronic funds transfer system (EFTS) A system that allows for the payment of bills electronically; your paycheck may also be deposited electronically.

employee orientation The activity that introduces new employees to the organization, to fellow employees, to their immediate supervisors, and to the policies, practices, and objectives of the firm.

employee stock ownership plan (ESOP) A plan whereby employees can buy part or total ownership of the firm where they work.

entrepreneur An innovator who organizes, manages, and assumes the risks of starting a business.

entrepreneurial team A group of experienced people from different areas of business who join together to form a managerial team with the skills needed to develop, make, and market new products.

entrepreneurial venture A business enterprise founded by an entrepreneur or entrepreneurial team that provides not only employment for the founders, but also for a significant group of other people.

equilibrium point Point at which supply and demand are equal.

equity financing A means a company uses to obtain capital that involves the public sale of stock shares.

exchange An organization whose members can buy and sell securities to the public.

exclusive distribution The use of only one retail outlet in a given geographic area.

expense items Less costly goods that are used up relatively quickly, such as cleaning fluids and light bulbs.

expenses Costs incurred in operating the business, such as rent, utilities, and salaries.

expert systems Store and manipulate knowledge and rules of thumb as well as data.

export trading companies Companies that attempt to match buyers and sellers from different countries.

exporting Selling products to another country.

exports Goods and services sold to other countries.

express warranties Specific representations by the seller regarding the goods.

external information sources Include discussions with competitors, suppliers, dealers, customers, consultants, trade associations, previous customers, potential customers, and others who have some interests in the firm.

factoring Selling accounts receivable for cash.

factors of production Land, materials, human labor, and capital.

Fair Packaging and Labeling Act Gave the Food and Drug Administration authority to require information on labels.

favorable balance of payments Occurs when the amount of money flowing into a country exceeds the flow out.

federal deficit The difference between government revenue from taxes and government spending.

Federal Deposit Insurance Corporation (FDIC) Insures accounts in some banks against bank failures (up to a limit of $100,000 per account).

Federal Reserve System Consists of 12 Federal Reserve District banks that serve as a deposit for excess bank funds (for members) and loan member banks money.

Federal Savings and Loan Insurance Corporation (FSLIC) Insures accounts in some savings and loan associations against failures (up to a limit of $100,000 per account).

Federal Trade Commission Act Prohibits unfair methods of competition in commerce.

fidelity bond Protects an employer from financial loss resulting from employee dishonesty such as theft or forgery.

finance The function in a business responsible for acquiring funds for the firm, managing funds within the firm, and planning for the expenditure of funds on various assets.

financial accounting The preparation of financial statements for people outside of the firm (for example, investors).

financial control A process that periodically compares the actual revenue, costs, and expenses with projections.

financial plan Specifies the amount of money needed for various time periods and the most appropriate sources and uses of funds.

financial planners People who assist families in developing a comprehensive program that covers investments, taxes, insurance, and other financial matters.

financial planning Designed to provide a short-run and long-run picture of money flows to and from the firm with the objective of optimizing profits and making the best use of money.

financial statements Report the success and position (condition) of a firm; they include the income statement and balance sheet.

fire insurance Covers losses to buildings and their contents from fire.

fiscal policy Government efforts to keep the economy stable by increasing or decreasing taxes or government spending.

fixed assets Items of a permanent nature, such as land, buildings, furniture, and fixtures.

flat organization structure One with relatively few layers of management.

flextime plans Give employees some freedom to adjust when they work as long as they work the required number of hours.

float The delay between the time a check is given to a seller and the time it is cashed at the bank.

FMS (flexible manufacturing systems) Totally automated production centers that include robots, automatic materials-handling equipment, and computer-controlled machine tools.

focus group studies Unstructured interviews with 6 to 15 people who represent a target market to obtain their beliefs and feelings about a company and its products and other, similar subjects.

form utility The value added by the creation of finished goods and services using raw materials, components, and other inputs.

formal organization The structure that details lines of responsibility, authority, and position. It is the structure that is shown on organizational charts.

four *P*'s of marketing Product, place, promotion, and price.

franchise An arrangement whereby someone with a good idea for a business sells the rights to use the business name and sell its products or services in a given territory.

franchisee A person who buys a franchise (see franchise).

franchisor A company that develops a product concept and sells others the rights to make and sell the products.

free market system System in which decisions about what to produce and in what quantities are decided by the market; that is, by buyers and sellers negotiating prices for goods and services.

frictional unemployment Occurs because of people who have quit work and have not yet found a new job and also because of new entrants in the labor force.

fringe benefits Benefits such as sick-leave pay, vacation pay, pension plans, and health plans that represent additional compensation to employees.

full-service wholesalers Perform all eight distribution functions.

functional discount One given to wholesalers and retailers for the functions they perform.

fundamental accounting equation Assets = liability + owners' equity; it is the basis for the balance sheet.

futures trading The purchase and sale of goods for delivery some time in the future.

general partner An owner (partner) who has unlimited liability and is active in managing the firm.

generic name The name of a product category.

geographic segmentation Divides the market into separate geographic areas.

global corporation A supernational entity that bears no national allegiance to any country.

global marketing Term used to describe selling the same product in essentially the same way everywhere in the world.

globalization Involves searching the world for the plant site that offers the best financial breaks, building or using production facilities there, and shipping products back in finished form.

goods Tangible products that can be examined, purchased, stored, resold, and transported—for example, TV sets and furniture.

gross margin Net sales minus cost of goods sold.

gross national product (GNP) The total value of a country's output of goods and services.

group cohesiveness A feeling of group loyalty.

group life policy Covers all employees of a firm or members of a group.

group norms The informal rules and procedures that guide the behavior of group members.

group technology (GT) The process of grouping or assembling parts based on the similarity of their geometry, size, and manufacturing processes with the objective of designing a parts supply system so that robots can select and assemble the parts.

growth stocks Stock of corporations whose earnings have grown rapidly in the past in comparison with the economy and are expected to continue above-average growth in the future.

Hay Guide Chart Profile Method A technique for measuring pay equity based on an employee's knowledge, problem-solving ability, accountability, and working conditions.

hedging In its pure form, buying or selling commodities in the futures market equal and opposite to what you now have.

high-tech industries Industries that make and use the most advanced equipment in industries such as computers, robotics, computer chips, solar panels, and electronics.

homeowner's insurance Protects farmers and other individuals from losses associated with residential living.

human orientation The broadening of the profit orientation to include other corporate objectives, especially the satisfaction of the wants and needs of managers and employees.

human resource management The process of evaluating human resource needs and finding people to fill those needs (hiring); optimizing this important resource by providing the right compensation and fringe benefits (motivating); and providing job enrichment (training and education); all with the goal of meeting the organization's objectives.

implied warranties Legally imposed on the seller and assume products are safe; if not, legal remedies may be enforced.

importing Buying products from another country.

imports Goods and services bought from other countries.

income statement Reports revenues and expenses for a specific period of time, showing the results of operations during that period. It summarizes all the resources that came into the firm (revenues), and all the resources that left the firm and the resulting net income.

individual retirement account (IRA) A tax-deferred investment plan that enables one's self and one's spouse to save part of their income for retirement.

industrial advertising Advertising from manufacturers to other manufacturers.

industrial goods Products used in factories, utilities, mines, institutions, government agencies, and wholesale and retail outlets.

industrial marketing The marketing of goods and services to manufacturers, institutions, commercial operations, and the government.

industrial sector Industries such as mining, manufacturing, and construction.

industrial services Services that are provided to organizations engaged in such fields as mining, agriculture, and government.

inflation A general rise in the prices of goods and services over time.

informal organization The system of relationships and lines of authority that develops spontaneously as employees meet and form power centers. It is the human side of the organization and does not show on any formal charts.

infrastructure A country's network of facilities and plants, such as bridges, roads, dams, water systems, and utilities that are essential for the operation of the economy. (A country's infrastructure can also be visualized as the skeleton on which the economy is built.)

injunction A court order directing someone to do something or refrain from doing something.

inland marine insurance Covers transportation-related or transportable property while goods are being transported by ship, rail, truck, or plane.

institutional advertising Designed to create an attractive image for an organization.

insurance adjuster Person who calculates the extent of a loss.

insurance policy A written contract between the insured and an insurance company that promises to pay for all or part of a loss.

intensive distribution Puts products into as many retail outlets as possible.

interest The payment the issuer of a bond makes to bondholders for the use of borrowed money.

intermittent process An operation where the production run is short and the machines are shut down frequently or changed to produce different products.

internal auditor Accountant who makes sure that all transactions have been treated in accordance with established accounting rules and procedures.

internal information sources Include employee discussions, accounting records, and other internal reports and data.

internal marketing program One designed to commit employees to the objectives of the firm.

international joint venture A partnership in which companies from two different countries join to undertake a major project.

international monetary fund An international bank that makes short-term loans to countries experiencing problems with their balance of trade.

intrapreneur A person with entrepreneurial skills who is employed in a corporation to launch new products; such people take hands-on responsibility for creating innovation of any kind in an organization.

inventory financing Financing that uses inventory such as raw materials as collateral for a loan.

investing Committing capital with the expectation of making a profit.

investment risk The chance that an investment and all its accumulated yields will be worth less at some future time than when it is made.

invisible hand The idea that countries prosper when individuals within the country prosper because the way to make money is to provide needed goods and services to others through trade; the invisible hand turns self-directed gain into social benefit.

job analysis A study of what is done by employees who fill various job titles.

job descriptions Specify the objectives of a job, the type of work, the responsibilities of the job, the necessary skills, the working conditions, and the relationship of the job to other functions.

job enrichment Describes efforts to make jobs more interesting, challenging, and rewarding.

job sharing An arrangement whereby two part-time employees share one full-time job.

job simulation The use of equipment that duplicates job conditions and tasks so that trainees can learn skills before attempting them on the job.

job specifications Written descriptions of the qualifications required of workers.

joint venture An agreement whereby two or more corporations join together to accomplish some objective.

journals   Recording devices used for the first recording of all transactions.

just-in-time (JIT) inventory control   Delivery of the smallest possible quantities at the latest possible time to keep inventory as low as possible.

Knights of Labor   The first national labor union (1869).

Labor Management Reporting and Disclosure Act (Landrum-Griffin Act)   1959 law that gave individual rights to union members to nominate candidates, vote in union elections, attend union meetings, examine union records, and required annual financial reports from unions to be filed with the Department of Labor.

Labor-Management Relations Act (Taft-Hartley Act)   1974 law that permitted states to pass right-to-work laws; prohibited secondary boycotts, closed-shop agreements, and featherbedding; and set up methods to deal with strikes.

LAN (local area networks)   Unified systems that integrate the appropriate software and hardware and the computers, robots, and machines to use programs, as well as provide communication lines with the various functions of the organization.

law of large numbers   States that if a large number of people or organizations are exposed to the same risk, a predictable number of losses will occur.

leadership   Getting others to work willingly and enthusiastically to achieve the objectives of the organization.

learning   Involves changes in an individual's behavior resulting from previous experiences and information.

ledgers   Recording devices in which information from accounting journals is categorized into homogeneous groups and posted so that managers can find all the information about one account in the same place.

liabilities   Amounts owned by the organization to others. Current liabilities are due in 1 year or less.

limit order   Tells the broker to purchase stock at a specific price.

limited liability   Means that the owners of a business are responsible for losses only up to the amount they invest.

limited partner   Invests money in the business, but does not have any management responsibility or liability for losses (see limited liability).

limited-function wholesalers   Perform only selected distribution functions, such as transportation.

line of credit   The amount of unsecured short-term credit a bank will lend a borrower that is agreed to ahead of time.

line organization structure   One in which there are direct two-way lines of responsibility, authority, and communication running from the top to the bottom of the organization, with all employees reporting to only one supervisor.

line personnel   Perform functions that contribute directly to the primary goals of the organization.

liquidity   How quickly one can get back invested funds when they are desired.

lockouts   A tool for putting pressure on unions by closing the business.

long-term financing   Money obtained from the owners of the firm and lenders who do not expect repayment within 2 or more years.

long-term forecast   A prediction of revenues, costs, and expenses for a period longer than 1 year, sometimes extending 5 or 10 years into the future.

long-term loans   Loans that are payable in a period that exceeds 1 year.

macroeconomics   The study of the nation's economy as a whole.

mail order retailer   Sends catalogs to consumers who then order goods by mail (or phone).

maintenance-of-membership shop   One in which members of the union must remain in good standing.

manageability   Organization such that everyone knows who is responsible for what, who reports to whom, what to do when problems arise, and so forth.

management   The art of getting things done through people and other sources.

management by objectives (MBO)   A system of goal setting and implementation that involves a cycle of discussion, review, and evaluation of objectives among top level managers, middle level managers, supervisors, and employees.

management by walking around   Getting out of the office to personally interact with employees and customers.

management development   The process of training and educating employees to become good managers and then developing managerial skills over time.

manager   Person who is able to get things done through others.

managerial accounting   Provides information and analyses to managers within the organization to assist them in decision making.

manufacturing   Making goods by hand or with machinery as opposed to extracting things from the earth (mining or fishing) or producing services.

market economy   Economy in which free trade is encouraged and people have the freedom and incentives to profit from that free trade.

market order   Tells the broker to buy stock at the best price obtainable in the market now.

market price   Price determined by supply and demand.

market segmentation   Process of dividing the total market into several submarkets (segments) that have similar characteristics.

marketing   The process of studying wants and needs and then planning and executing the conception, pricing, promotion, and distribution of ideas, goods, or services to meet those needs, thus creating exchanges that satisfy individual and organizational objectives and also creating profits for sellers.

marketing communication   A two-way exchange of information between buyers and sellers; the process of talking with target markets to verify that the product, price, and all other aspects of the exchange situation are what is needed.

marketing communication system Listening to various publics, responding to that information, and promoting the organization and its product.

marketing concept Refers to a three-part business philosophy: (1) a consumer orientation, (2) the coordination and integration of the firm, and (3) a profit orientation.

marketing intelligence A constant stream of data from many sources, many of them unplanned.

marketing manager Plans and executes the conception, pricing, promotion, and distribution of ideas, goods, and services to create exchanges that satisfy individual and organizational goals.

marketing mix The strategic combination of product decisions with decisions regarding packaging, pricing, distribution, credit, branding, service, complaint handling, and other marketing activities.

marketing research The periodic, structured gathering of data; a major function in finding needs and determining the most effective and efficient ways to satisfy those needs.

market targeting The process by which an organization decides which markets to serve.

markup Selling price minus cost.

markup percentage Markup in dollars over selling price.

materials handling The movement of goods within a warehouse, factory, or store.

materials requirement planning A computer-based operations management system that uses sales forecasts to make sure that needed parts and materials are available at the right place and time.

matrix organization One where specialists from different parts of the organization are brought together to work on specific projects, but still remain part of a traditional line and staff structure.

mentors Corporate managers who supervise, coach, and guide lower level people by introducing them to the right people and groups and generally being their organizational sponsors.

mercantilism The economic principle advocating the selling of more goods to other nations than a country buys.

merchandise trade deficit Buying more goods from other nations than are sold to them.

merchant wholesalers Independently owned firms that take title to goods that they handle.

metaneeds Needs that go beyond self, such as the needs for justice, truth, and honesty.

microeconomics The study of the behavior of people and organizations in particular markets.

Minority Business Development Agency Awards grants to other organizations to assist minority enterprises, maintains an information clearing house for minority business development, conducts research, and otherwise helps minority enterprises.

MIPS Million instructions per second.

mixed economy An economy that combines free markets with some government allocation of resources.

modem Converts data into a form that can be sent over phone lines so that one computer can "talk" to another.

monetary policy The management of the amount of money placed into the economy by the government and the management of interest rates.

money supply The sum of all the funds that the public has immediately available for buying goods and services.

MRP (materials requirement planning) A computer-based operations management system that uses sales forecasts to make sure that needed parts and materials are available at the right place and time.

multiline policies Insurance "packages" that include both property and liability coverage.

multinational corporation An organization that does manufacturing and marketing in many different countries; it has multinational stock ownership and multinational management.

mutual fund An organization that buys stocks and bonds and then sells shares in those securities to the public.

mutual insurance company Firm owned by its policyholders.

mutual savings bank Similar to an S & L, but owned by its depositors.

NASDAQ National Association of Securities Dealers Automated Quotation system.

national brand The brand name of a national manufacturer (for example, Xerox).

national debt The sum of money the government has borrowed and not paid back.

national exchanges Exchanges that handle stocks of companies all over the United States (the New York Stock Exchange and the American Stock Exchange).

National Labor Relations Act (Wagner Act) 1935 law that gave employees the right to join a union, to collectively bargain, and to engage in union activities such as strikes, picketing, and boycotts.

negotiable instruments Forms of commercial paper that are transferrable among businesses and individuals, such as checks.

negotiated labor-management agreement Sets the tone and clarifies the terms under which management and labor agree to function over a period of time.

net income Revenue minus expenses.

net national product (NNP) The output of goods and services beyond that which is needed to replace worn-out machinery, equipment, and capital goods.

net sales Sales revenue minus discounts, returns, and other adjustments made for customers.

networking (1) The process of establishing and maintaining contacts with key managers in one's own organization and in other organizations and using those contacts to weave strong relationships that serve as informal development systems. (2) A business relationship where a small central organization relies on other companies and suppliers to perform manufacturing, marketing, or other crucial business functions on a contractual basis.

nonbanks   Financial organizations that accept no deposits, but offer many of the services provided by regular banks.

nonperformance loss protection   Insurance against failure of a contractor, supplier, or other person to fulfill an obligation.

nonprofit marketing   The use of marketing concepts and tools to establish exchange relationships among individuals or groups and organizations, other than businesses, that can partially satisfy their wants and needs.

nonprofit organization   Provides goods and services to the economic system, but does not have profit as an objective.

nonprofit sector   All organizations whose goals do not include making a profit.

Norris-La Guardia Act   1932 law that prohibited courts from using injunctions against nonviolent union activities and outlawed the use of yellow-dog contracts.

ocean marine insurance   Protects shippers from losses of property from damage to a ship or its cargo while at sea or in port.

odd lots   A purchase of less than 100 shares of stock.

odd pricing   Pricing items a few cents under a round price ($9.98 instead of $10) to make the product appear less expensive.

off-the-job training   Internal and external programs to develop a variety of skills and faster personal development away from the workplace.

on-the-job training   The employee immediately begins his or her tasks and learns by doing or watches others for a while and then imitates them, all right at the workplace.

open-market operations   Involve the buying and selling of U.S. government securities by the Federal Reserve to control the money supply.

operating expenses   The various costs incurred in running a business, including rent, salaries, and utilities.

organization   (1) A group of people working together to accomplish a goal. (2) The process of creating an organization; includes designing the structure, attracting staff, and creating conditions and systems that ensure that everyone and everything works together to achieve organizational objectives.

organizational culture   Widely shared values within an organization that provide coherence and cooperation to achieve common goals.

organizational design   The establishment of manageable groups of people who have clear responsibilities and who know how to accomplish the objectives of the organization and the group.

other (intangible) assets   Items that are not included in the current and fixed assets categories. This catch-all category includes items such as patents and copyrights.

over-the-counter market   Exchange that provides a means to trade stocks not listed on the national exchanges.

owners' equity   Assets minus liabilities.

Pacific Rim countries   Countries on the edge of the Pacific furthest from California: North Korea, South Korea, Japan, China, Taiwan, Hong Kong, and Singapore.

par value   An arbitrary dollar amount printed on the front of a stock certificate.

parallel processes   Links hundreds or thousands of processors to build faster computers.

Pareto analysis   A strategy that originated in Japan and ranks the problems of the production process in the order of frequency or importance.

partnership (general)   A legal form of business with two or more owners.

patent   Exclusive rights for inventors to their inventions for 17 years.

penetration strategy   One in which a product is priced low to attract more customers and discourage competitors.

penny stock   A stock that sells for less than $1.00.

pension funds   Amounts of money designated by corporations, nonprofit organizations, or unions to cover part of the financial needs of members when they retire.

performance appraisal   An evaluation of the performance level of employees against standards to make decisions about promotions, compensation, additional training, or firing.

peripheral equipment operators   Run the equipment (such as printers and disk drives) that is part of the computer system.

personal selling   The face-to-face presentation and promotion of products and services plus the searching out of prospects and follow-up service.

PERT (program evaluation and review technique)   A method for analyzing the activities involved in performing a given task, evaluating alternative means of meeting the goal, choosing the best method, and setting up controls that ensure the completion of the task on time.

physical distribution   The movement of goods from producer to consumer.

physical distribution manager   Responsible for coordinating and integrating all movement of materials, including transportation, internal movement, and warehousing.

physiological needs   The needs for basic life-giving elements such as food, water, and shelter.

planning   Anticipating future trends and determining the best strategies and tactics to achieve organizational objectives.

political marketing   The application of marketing strategies in the political arena.

preferred stock   Stock that gives owners preference in the payment of dividends and an earlier claim on assets if the business is sold but does not include voting rights.

premium   The fee charged by an insurance company.

premium bonds   Bonds that sell above face value.

price lining   Pricing products at a certain set price rather than having separate prices for individual items.

primary boycott   Union encouragement of members not to buy products of a firm involved in a labor dispute.

primary data   Refers to results of one's own research.

prime rate   The most favorable interest rate that businesses can get from banks.

principal   The face amount of a bond.

private brand   The name given products by distributors or retailers (also known as "house" or "distributor" brands).

process manufacturing   Physically or chemically changing materials.

producer price index   Measures changes in the prices businesses pay for goods and services over time.

producers' cartels   Organizations of commodity-producing countries that are formed to stabilize or increase prices to optimize overall profits in the long run. (An example is OPEC, the Organization of Petroleum-Exporting Countries.)

product   Consists of all the tangibles and intangibles that consumers evaluate when deciding whether or not to buy something.

product differentiation   The creation of benefits and an image for a product that captures the imagination of the public and sets it apart from other, similar products.

product life cycle   The five-stage theoretical depiction of the process from birth to death of a product class: introduction, rapid growth, maturity, saturation, and decline.

product line   A group of products that are physically similar or are intended for a similar market.

product manager   Coordinates all the marketing efforts for a particular product (or product line) or brand.

product mix   The combination of products offered by a manufacturer.

production process   Uses basic inputs (land, labor, capital) to produce outputs (products, services, ideas).

production orientation   Means businesses focused on producing goods rather than marketing them.

productivity   The total output of goods and services in a given period of time divided by work hours (output per work hour).

professional services   Services provided by experts to other businesses, the government, and consumers.

profit orientation   Marketing those goods and services which will earn the firm a profit.

programmers   People who write the instructions for the computer.

promotion   A one-way attempt by marketers to persuade others to participate in an exchange relationship with them.

promotion mix   Some combination of promotional tools (for example, advertising, personal selling, public relations, publicity, sales promotions, and word-of-mouth) that can be used to communicate to various publics.

prospectus   A condensed, printed version of material submitted to the Securities and Exchange Commission that is sent to prospective purchasers to enable them to evaluate a stock offering.

protective tariff   Designed to raise the price of imported products so that domestic products are more competitive.

proxy   A temporary transfer of voting rights from stockholders to managers.

psychographic segmentation   Divides the market by values, attitudes, and interests.

public   Any group that has a potential or actual relationship with an organization.

public liability insurance   Protects against losses resulting from personal injuries or damage to the property of others for which the insured is responsible.

public relations   The management function that evaluates public attitudes, identifies the policies and procedures of an individual or an organization with the public interest, and executes a program of action to earn public understanding and acceptance.

publicity   Any information about an individual, a product, or an organization that is distributed to the public through the media and that is not paid for or controlled by the sponsor.

pull strategy   One in which heavy advertising and sales promotion is directed toward consumers.

pure risk   The threat of loss with no chance for profit.

push strategy   Means that the producer uses advertising, personal selling, sales promotion, and all other promotional tools to convince wholesalers and retailers to stock and sell merchandise.

quality circles   Groups of employees that are formed to develop ideas for solving quality problems and other problems in the work place.

quality control   The measurement of products and services against set standards.

rack jobber   Furnishes racks or shelves to retailers, displays products, and sells on consignment.

rational decision making   Consists of five steps: (1) define the problem, (2) develop alternatives, (3) decide which alternative is best, (4) do what is indicated, and (5) determine whether the decision was a good one and follow up.

real wages   Money wages divided by the price level.

real yield   The yield after taxes and inflation are subtracted.

reasonable prudence   States that a product is unreasonably dangerous if the manufacturer knew, or through the exercise of reasonable prudence should have known, about the danger that allegedly caused the claimant's harm and if a reasonably prudent person in the same or similar circumstances would not have manufactured the product.

recession   Two consecutive quarters of negative growth in real GNP (GNP adjusted for inflation).

recruitment   The set of activities used to legally obtain a sufficient number of the right people at the right time to select those who best meet the needs of the organization.

reference group The group that an individual uses as a reference point in the formation of his or her beliefs, attitudes, values or behavior.

reindustrialization The rebuilding of factories to make them more competitive in world markets.

reserve requirement A percentage of member-bank funds that must be deposited in the Federal Reserve Bank.

responsibility Means that when a person is given a task to do, he or she has an obligation to do it.

retailer A marketing middleman that sells to consumers.

retained earnings The amount left after a company distributes some of its net income (profit) to stockholders in the form of dividends.

retained earnings Earnings that are retained rather than paid out in dividends.

revenue The value of what is received for goods sold, services rendered, and other sources.

revenue tariff Designed to raise money for the government.

revolving credit agreement A line of credit that is guaranteed by the bank.

rider Addition to a fire insurance policy that covers losses from wind, hail, explosion, riot, smoke, and falling aircraft.

right-to-work laws Give workers the right, under an open shop, to join a union—if it is present—or not.

risk The chance of loss, the degree of probability of loss, and the amount of possible loss.

risk managers People who do sophisticated analyses of corporate risks and design elaborate solutions to those problems.

Robinson-Patman Act Makes it unlawful to discriminate in price, to grant false brokerage fees, or to make disproportional payments to buyers; protects merchants, the public, and manufacturers from unfair competition.

robot A computer-controlled machine capable of performing many tasks that require the use of materials and tools.

robotics The use of computer-driven machines to do work formerly done by humans.

round lots 100 shares of stock

rule of indemnity States that an insured person or organization cannot collect more than the actual loss from an insurable risk.

safety needs Include the needs for peace and security.

sales branch A manufacturer-owned wholesale facility that stocks the goods it sells and processes orders from its own inventory.

sales office A manufacturer-owned wholesale facility in which sales are made, but no inventory is carried.

sales orientation Means a firm focuses all of its attention on the salesperson, teaching him or her techniques for winning customers.

sales promotion Consists of those marketing activities that stimulate consumer purchasing and dealer interest by means of such things as displays, shows, exhibitions, and contests.

savings and loan associations Financial institutions that accept both savings and checking deposits and provide home mortgage loans.

Scanlon plan Uses committees to set performance standards, and if the employees exceed the standards, a bonus is created, with 75% going to the employee.

scientific management The process of studying workers to find the most efficient way of doing things and then teaching people those techniques.

scrambled merchandising The adding of product lines that are not normally carried to a retail store.

seasonal unemployment Occurs where the demand for labor varies over the year.

secondary boycott An attempt by labor to force an employer to stop doing business with a firm that is the subject of a primary boycott.

secondary data Already published research results from journals, trade associations, the government, information services, libraries, and other sources.

secured bonds Bonds backed by some tangible asset that is pledged to the investor if the principal is not paid back.

secured loan Loan backed by something valuable, such as property.

Securities Act of 1933 Protects investors by requiring full disclosure of financial information by firms selling new stocks and bonds.

Securities and Exchange Commission (SEC) Has responsibility at the federal level for regulating the various exchanges.

securities markets Organizations that enable businesses and investors to buy and sell stocks, bonds, and mutual funds.

selection The process of gathering information to decide who should be hired, under legal guidelines, for the best interests of the individual and the organization.

selective distribution The use of only a preferred group of the available retailers in an area.

self-actualization needs The needs for achievement and to be all you can be.

self-esteem needs Include the needs for self confidence and status.

selling short Borrowing stock from a broker and selling it, hoping to buy the stock later at a lower price and return it to the broker.

Service Corps of Retired Executives (SCORE) Provides consulting services to small businesses for free (except expenses).

service sector Industries such as transportation and utilities, wholesale trade, retail trade, real estate, consumer services, health and education, and the government.

services Intangible products that often cannot be examined before purchase and cannot be stored, resold, or transported.

Sherman Act Forbids contracts, combinations, or conspiracies in restraint of trade and actual monopolies or attempts to monopolize any part of trade or commerce.

shopping goods and services Products or services that the consumer buys only after comparing quality and price from a variety of sellers.

short-term forecast A prediction of revenues, costs, and expenses for a period of 1 year or less.

short-term loans Loans that have to be paid in 1 year.

simple recognition shop One where the employer recognizes the union as the sole bargaining agent for all employees.

sinking fund Fund that requires the issuer to retire, on a periodic basis, some part of the bond issue prior to maturity.

situation segmentation Separates out those situations in which the product may be used.

skimming price strategy One in which the product is priced high to make optimum profit while there is little competition.

skunkworks A highly innovative, fast-moving entrepreneurial unit operating at the fringes of a corporation.

small business Business that is independently owned and operated, is not dominant in its field of operation, and meets certain standards of size in terms of employees (less than 100) or annual receipts.

Small Business Institute Sponsors college students who consult with small businesses, write a report, and are paid a fee by the Small Business Administration.

Small Business Investment Company (SBIC) Provides seed money for new ventures.

Small Marketers' Aids (SMAs) Booklets published by the Small Business Administration that cover topics such as keeping records, cash management, public relations, and advertising.

social audit A systematic evaluation of an organization's progress toward implementing programs that are socially responsible and responsive.

social catalyst A person or organization that recognizes a social need and mobilizes others to support the cause.

social marketing The marketing of programs that seek to foster the acceptance of a social idea, cause, or practice.

social needs The need to feel loved, accepted, and part of the group.

socialist systems Systems in which allocation of resources is done partially by the market (the free trade of goods and services), and partially by the government.

societal orientation Includes a consumer orientation, but adds programs designed to improve the community, reduce pollution, and satisfy other social goals.

sole proprietorship The ownership of an organization by one person.

span of control The optimum number of subordinates a manager should supervise.

specialty goods and services Products that have a special attraction to consumers, who are willing to go out of their way to obtain them.

specialty services Consumer services for which buyers are willing to make a special purchasing effort by traveling out of their way or paying a premium.

speculative risk A type of risk that involves a chance of either profit or loss.

spot trading The purchase and sale of commodities for immediate delivery.

spreadsheet analysis A technique for determining the effect on one account of changes in other accounts.

staff personnel Perform functions that assist line personnel in performing their goals.

stagflation Stagnant economic conditions (no growth) combined with inflation.

statutory law State and federal constitutions, legislative enactments, treaties, and ordinances (written laws).

stock Shares of ownership in a company.

stock certificate Evidence of stock ownership.

stock exchange An organization whose members can buy and sell securities to the public.

stock insurance company Owned by stockholders, just like any other investor-owned company.

stock splits Giving stockholders two or more shares of stock for each one they own.

stockbroker A middleman who buys and sells securities for clients.

strategic (long-range) planning Determines major objectives of the organization and the policies and strategies for obtaining and using resources to achieve those objectives.

strict liability States that there is no legal defense for placing a product on the market that is dangerous to the consumer because of a known or knowable defect.

strikebreakers Workers hired to do the jobs of striking workers until the labor dispute is resolved.

structural unemployment That unemployment caused by people losing jobs because their occupation is no longer part of the main structure of the economy.

Subchapter S corporation A hybrid, half-corporate, half-partnership entity that looks like a corporation, but is taxed like a partnership.

subculture The set of values, attitudes, and ways of doing things that result from belonging to a certain nationality group, religious group, racial group, or other group to which one closely identifies.

supply The quantity of products that manufacturers or owners are willing to sell at different prices at a specific time.

supply curve Shows the relationship between price and the quantity supplied.

supply-side economics The policy of lowering taxes so that more money is invested in production, leading to an increase in production activity, causing a drop in unemployment.

surety bond Protects against the failure of a second party to fulfill an obligation.

survey research Includes a variety of techniques designed to get the personal views of some sample of the target market.

synthetic systems Either change raw materials into other products or combine raw materials or parts into a finished product.

systems analysts Study the many functions of the firm and design a computer system to perform those functions more efficiently.

tactical planning The process of developing detailed short-term decisions about what is to be done, who is to do it, and how it is to be done.

tall organization structure One with many levels of management.

tax management The analysis of the tax implications of various managerial decisions and minimization of the taxes paid by the firm.

teleconference Conducting business meetings over phone lines and TV screens so that executives located in different geographic areas can see and talk to each other.

telemarketing Uses the telephone to allow consumers to order merchandise, ask questions, and keep in contact with businesses.

term insurance Pure insurance protection for a given number of years that must be renewed periodically.

term loan agreement A promissory note that requires the borrower to repay the loan in installments that are specified.

term to maturity The period from the purchase date of a bond to the final principal-payment date.

thrift institutions Savings and loan associations.

time deposit The technical name for a savings account, because the bank can require prior notice before withdrawal.

time-motion studies Studying the most efficient way of doing a job using a stopwatch.

tort Wrongful conduct that causes injury to another person's body, property, or reputation.

total quality control Includes planning for quality, preventing quality defects, correcting any defects that occur, and a philosophy of continuous effort to build quality into products.

total yield The increase in the value of an investment over time, usually a year.

trade credit The practice of buying goods now and paying for them early and getting a discount.

trade deficit The situation where imports (purchases from abroad) exceed exports (sales abroad).

trade protectionism The use of government regulations to limit the import of goods and services so that domestic producers can survive and grow, producing more jobs—in theory.

trademark A brand that has been given legal protection.

training and development All attempts to improve employee performance by increasing an employee's ability to perform through learning.

transcendence needs See metaneeds.

treasurer The chief financial officer of a company.

trickle-down theory Assumes that when wealthy people get wealthier, they will buy goods and services that will boost the economy so that their wealth will trickle down to less wealthy people.

truck jobber Delivers goods by truck to retailers.

Uniform Commercial Code Covers sales laws and other commercial law.

union shop agreement One where workers do not have to be members of a union to be hired, but must agree to join the union within a prescribed period.

universal life insurance A combination of term insurance and an accumulation fund usually based mostly on short-term debt instruments (bonds).

unlimited liability Means that the owner's personal assets (for example, home and car) are vulnerable to claims against the business; sole proprietors and general partners have unlimited liability.

unsecured loan A loan not backed by any collateral.

utility Value added to raw materials.

variable life insurance A whole life policy whose benefits vary based on the success of the insurance company in investing those funds.

vending machine Dispenses convenience goods when consumers deposit sufficient money in the machine.

venture capital Money that is invested in new companies with great profit potential.

vestibule training Done in schools where employees are given instructions on equipment similar to that used on the job.

videotex A system that allows the general public to access a central computer that provides various services such as news, games, banking, and electronic mail.

volume segmentation Divides the market into user categories: heavy, medium, light, and nonusers.

whole life insurance A combination insurance plan and savings plan that was popular in the past, but has declined in popularity in recent years.

wholesaler A marketing middleman who sells to organizations and individuals, but not final consumers.

Wilshire Index A stock average based on all domestic common stock on the New York and American stock exchanges plus 2,500 OTC stocks.

word-of-mouth promotion Encourages people to tell other people about products they have enjoyed.

workers' compensation insurance Provides compensation for workers injured on the job.

World Bank Borrows money from the more prosperous countries and lends it at favorable rates to less-developed countries.

yellow-dog contract A contract agreement whereby employees agreed not to join a union as a condition of employment.

Chapter Notes

CHAPTER ONE

1 Ronald K. Shelp, "Bum Rap on the Service Economy," *The Wall Street Journal* (April 13, 1984), p. 32.
2 "Giving Is Growing," *Forbes* (February 27, 1984), p. 10.
3 John Naisbitt, *Megatrends* (New York: Warner Books, Inc., 1984).
4 Naisbitt, p. 16.
5 If you are interested in reading about the exciting new high-tech careers, see S. Norman Feingold and Norma Reno Miller, *Emerging Careers: New Occupations for the Year 2000 and Beyond* (Garrett Park, Maryland: Garrett Park Press, 1985).
6 These data are from Jane Seaberry, "Unprecedented Changes Forecast for Population," *The Washington Post* (January 22, 1984), p. G7.
7 Peter Francese, "Baby Boom's Echo Keeps Economy Moving," *Advertising Age* (July 19, 1984), p. 12.
8 Francese.
9 Nancy Josephson, "Interesting Lives Are in Their Cards," *Advertising Age* (April 2, 1984), p. M-10.
10 Statistics are from "Women Managers Rise in High-Tech Firms, But They're Still a Rare Breed," *The Wall Street Journal* (August 28, 1984), p. 1.
11 Sarah Ban Breathnach, "Trends: Women Entrepreneurs," *The Washington Post* (May 3, 1984), p. D5.
12 Breathnach.
13 David Astor, "Black Spending Power: $140 Billion and Growing," *Marketing Communications* (July, 1982), p. 13.
14 Astor, p. 14.
15 Charles Murray, "Those the Great Society Left Behind," *The Wall Street Journal* (July 30, 1984).
16 Anne Mackay Smith, "Large Shortage of Black Professors in Higher Education Grows Worse," *The Wall Street Journal* (June 12, 1984), p. 37.
17 Figures are from Ronald Alsop, "Firms Translate Sales Pitches to Appeal to Asian-Americans," *The Wall Street Journal* (April 10, 1986), p. 35.
18 Johnnie L. Roberts, "After Rough Start, Venture-Capital Firm Finds Success Backing Minority Business," *The Wall Street Journal* (February 10, 1984), p. 29.
19 Bengt Anderson, "Developing New Markets with Global Strategies," *Marketing Communications* (February, 1984), p. 16.
20 Peter Behr, "Foreign Rivals Gain Ground on U.S. Firms," *The Washington Post* (April 22, 1984), p. G2.
21 Stephen Kindel and Robert Tietelman, "If Only . . . ," *Forbes* (August 29, 1983), pp. 126-130.
22 "No Yen to Bail Out," *Forbes* (September 10, 1984).

CHAPTER TWO

1 Lowdon Wingo and Alan Evans, eds., *Public Economics and the Quality of Life* (Washington, D.C.: Resources for the Future, Inc., 1977).
2 Donella H. Meadows, Dennis L. Meadows, Jorgen Randers, and William W. Behrens III, *The Limits to Growth* (New York: Potomac Association, 1972).
3 Julian L. Simon, *The Ultimate Resource* (New Jersey: Princeton University Press, 1986).
4 Karl Marx, *The Communist Manifesto* (Chicago: Henry Regnery Company, 1954), p. 41.
5 Marx, p. 55.
6 Michael Novak, *The Spirit of Democratic Capitalism* (New York: Simon & Schuster, 1982), pp. 16-17.
7 See P.T. Bauer, *Equality, the Third World, and Economic Delusion* (Cambridge: Harvard University Press, 1981), Chapter 4.
8 Ove Guldberg, "What's Rotten in Denmark?" *The Wall Street Journal* (April 23, 1986), p. 31.
9 Remy Dessarts, *L'Expansion,* February 3-16, 1984, condensed in *Reader's Digest* (August, 1984), pp. 49-50.
10 Richard F. Janssen, "Trouble on the Road to Utopia," *The Wall Street Journal* (November 10, 1977).
11 Quoted in Stephen D. Moore, "Swedish Taxman Goes After Executives Who Use Dodges to Avoid 85% Tax Rate," *The Wall Street Journal* (September 9, 1983), p. 36.
12 Marcia Berss, "A Mouse That's Roaring," *Forbes* (October 21, 1985), pp. 112-116.
13 "Promises, Dreams—4 Voices from Moscow's Streets," *U.S. News and World Report* (July 29, 1985), pp. 40-42.
14 "A System That Doesn't Work," *Newsweek* (April 12, 1982), pp. 36-44.
15 "Russia's Nuclear Nightmare," *Business Week* (May 12, 1986), pp. 24-26.

CHAPTER THREE

1 Paul McCracken, "Gobbling Up the Economic Pie," *The Wall Street Journal* (February 28, 1984), p. 32.
2 Allison T. French, "Poverty Rates and the Incentive to Be Unemployed," *The Wall Street Journal* (August 23, 1983), p. 32.

CHAPTER FOUR

1 Berkeley, California: Ten Speed Press, 1981.
2 Robert A. Esperti and Renno L. Peterson, *Incorporating Your Talents* (New York: McGraw-Hill Book Company, 1984).
3 Esperti and Peterson (reference cited).

1 Peter F. Drucker, "Why America's Got So Many Jobs," *The Wall Street Journal* (January 24, 1984).

2 Drucker (reference cited).

3 The story of Parsley Patch, Inc. is based on an article by Sanford L. Jacobs, "A Dash of Cost-Control Savvy Helps Turn Spice Firm Around," *The Wall Street Journal* (March 26, 1984), p. 31.

4 Figures are from Seymour Jones and M. Bruce Cohen, *The Emerging Business: Managing for Growth* (New York: John Wiley & Sons, 1983).

5 Sanford L. Jacobs, "Update on How Some Firms' Programs Progressed in 1983," *The Wall Street Journal* (January 16, 1984), p. 25.

6 "What Makes an Up and Comer?" *Forbes* (December 19, 1983), p. 103.

7 "How to Start a Successful Small Business," *Family Circle* (April 24, 1979), p. 50.

8 Barry R. Bronfin, "Who's Running America's Fastest Growing Companies," *Inc.* (August, 1983), p. 45.

9 Joel Kotkin, "A Call to Action," *Inc.* (November, 1983), pp. 85-96.

10 Joan G. Ford, "Overseas Customers Prefer Small Companies," *Inc.* (September, 1981), pp. 83-86.

11 Ford (reference cited).

CHAPTER SIX

1 Joseph R. Mancuso, *Have You Got What It Takes?* (Englewood Cliffs, N.J.: Prentice-Hall, Inc., 1982), pp. 44-45.

2 Robert Bond, *The Source Book of Franchise Opportunities* (Homewood, Ill.: Dow Jones-Irwin, 1985), p. 3.

3 This section is based on John Naisbitt and Patricia Aburdene, *Re-Inventing the Corporation* (New York: Warner Books, Inc., 1985).

4 Naisbitt and Aburdene (reference cited), pp. 110-111.

5 Naisbitt and Aburdene (reference cited), p. 111.

6 This section is based on Joel Kotkin, "The Smart Team at Compaq Computer," *Inc.* (February, 1986), pp. 48-56.

7 *The State of Small Business* (Washington, D.C.: The United States Small Business Administration, 1985), p. xv.

8 *The State of Small Business* (reference cited), p. 339.

9 These stories are from Carol Hymowitz, "Many Blacks Jump Off the Corporate Ladder to Be Entrepreneurs," *The Wall Street Journal* (August 2, 1982), pp. 1, 16.

10 *The State of Small Business* (reference cited).

11 This and other interesting stories about skunkworkers can be found in Tom Peters and Nancy Austin, *A Passion for Excellence* (New York: Random House, 1985).

12 Gifford Pinchot III, *Intrapreneuring* (New York: Harper & Row, Publishers, 1985), pp. xxi-xxiii.

13 Steven P. Galante, "Small Franchisers Put Accent on Growth in Markets Abroad," *The Wall Street Journal* (April 14, 1986), p. 31.

CHAPTER SEVEN

1 Thomas J. Peters and Robert H. Waterman, Jr., *In Search of Excellence* (New York: Harper & Row, Publishers, 1982).

2 Tom Peters and Nancy Austin, *A Passion for Excellence* (New York: Random House, 1985).

3 Peters and Waterman (reference cited), pp. 156, 193.

4 Peters and Austin (reference cited), p. 7.

5 See Robert Bartels, *The History of Marketing Thought,* 2nd ed. (Columbus, Ohio: Grid, Inc., 1976).

6 From a speech by John G. Marder, executive vice-president of Grey Advertising, published in *Grey Matter,* a publication of Grey Advertising, Inc. (January-February, 1975).

7 Philip Kotler, *Marketing Management: Analysis, Planning, and Control,* 4th ed. (Englewood Cliffs, N.J.: Prentice-Hall, Inc., 1980), pp. 206, 209-210.

8 Milton Friedman, *Capitalism and Freedom* (Chicago: The University of Chicago Press, 1963), p. 133.

9 "Iacocca's Marketing Fundamentals," *Advertising Age* (January 9, 1984), p. 12.

10 Gay Jervey, "Polaroid Develops Marketing Orientation," *Advertising Age* (January 30, 1984), p. 4.

11 "Doing Well By Doing Good," *Newsweek* (June 11, 1984), p. 62.

12 "Doing Well By Doing Good," (reference cited), p. 65.

13 Philip Kotler, *Marketing for Nonprofit Organizations* (Englewood Cliffs, N.J.: Prentice-Hall, Inc., 1982).

CHAPTER EIGHT

1 John Prestbo, "At Procter & Gamble, Success Is Largely Due to Heeding Customer," *The Wall Street Journal* (April 29, 1980), p. 1.

2 This is the basic message in Tom Peters and Nancy Austin, *A Passion for Excellence* (New York: Random House, 1985).

3 See William G. Nickels, "Word-of-Mouth Communication," *Marketing Communication and Production,* 3rd ed. (New York: John Wiley & Sons, Inc., 1984), pp. 265-280.

CHAPTER NINE

1 John Koten, "Fast-Food Firms' New Items Undergo Exhaustive Testing," *The Wall Street Journal* (January 5, 1984), p. 25.

2 Koten (reference cited).

3 John J. Ryan, "With a Little Luck, You May Even Find Books in the Library," *The Wall Street Journal* (May 7, 1975), p. 1.

4 "Survey Finds 67% of New Products Succeed," *Marketing News* (February 8, 1980), p. 1.

CHAPTER TEN

1 "Direct Marketing Sales Far Outpace Estimates," *Marketing News (Collegiate Edition)* (January 1, 1985), p. 1.

2 "Telemarketing and Technology," *Forbes* (October 7, 1985), p. 50.

3 "Telemarketing and Technology" (reference cited), p. 61.

4 Eric N. Berkowitz, Roger A. Kerin, and William Rudelius, *Marketing* (St. Louis: Times Mirror/Mosby College Publishing, 1986), p. 358.

CHAPTER ELEVEN

1 If you're interested in more details about this topic, see Philip Kotler, *Marketing for Nonprofit Organizations,* 2nd ed. (Englewood Cliffs, N.J.: Prentice-Hall, Inc., 1982).

CHAPTER TWELVE

1 Tom Peters and Nancy Austin, *A Passion for Excellence* (New York: Random House, 1985), pp. 8-33.

2 Don Hellriegel and John W. Slocum, Jr. *Management,* 4th ed. (Reading, Mass.: Addison-Wesley Publishing Company, 1986), pp. 12-14.

3 Edgar Huse, *Management,* 2nd ed. (St. Paul, Minn.: West Publishing Company, 1982), pp. 8-9.

4 This example is from "Presidential Forum," *Small Business Report* (August, 1984), pp. 44-45.

5 See Thomas J. Peters and Robert H. Waterman, Jr., *In Search of Excellence* (New York: Harper & Row, Publishers, 1982), pp. 319-320.

6 Peters and Austin (reference cited), pp. 324-377.

7 See, for example, B. Bass, *Stogdill's Handbook of Leadership* (New York: Free Press, 1981).

CHAPTER THIRTEEN

1 Thomas J. Peters and Robert H. Waterman, Jr., *In Search of Excellence* (New York: Harper & Row, Publishers, 1982) pp. 271-272.

2 "Small Is Beautiful Now in Manufacturing," *Business Week* (October 22, 1984), p. 152.

3 Peters and Waterman (reference cited), p. 353.

4 See Peters and Waterman (reference cited), Chapter 11, "Simple Form, Lean Staff."

5 Joe Kelly, *How Managers Manage* (Englewood Cliffs, N.J.: Prentice-Hall, 1980).

6 Martin J. Gannon, *Management* (Boston: Little, Brown & Company, 1982), p. 219.

7 Andrew S. Grove, *High Output Management* (New York: Random House, 1983), p. 66.

8 This example comes from Aimée Stern, "The New . . . Souped Up Campbell," *Marketing Communications* (February, 1984), pp. 29-54.

CHAPTER FOURTEEN

1 "Revitalizing the U.S. Economy," *Business Week* (June 30, 1980), p. 56.

2 A *Business Week* special report called "The Hollow Corporation" (March 3, 1986), pp. 57-80.

3 John W. Wilson and Judith H. Dobrzynski, "And Now the Post-Industrial Corporation," *Business Week* (March 3, 1986), pp. 64-71.

4 Wilson and Dobrzynski (reference cited).

5 If you are as fascinated as I was by this interesting writing style, you'll want to read Andrew S. Grove, *High Output Management* (New York: Random House, 1983).

6 W.P. Patterson, "The Software Solution: Forging Manufacturing's Missing Link," *Industry Week* (September 17, 1984), pp. 92ff.

7 James Cook, "Kanban, American-Style," *Forbes* (October 8, 1984), p. 66.

8 D. Whiteside and J. Arbose, "Unsnarling Industrial Production: Why Top Management Is Starting to Care," *International Management* (March, 1984), pp. 20-26.

9 B.S. Moskal, "Just In Time: Putting the Squeeze on Suppliers," *Industry Week* (July 9, 1984), pp. 59ff.

10 Dexter Hutchins, "Having a Hard Time with Just-In-Time," *Fortune* (June 9, 1986), pp. 64-66.

11 See Amal Nag, "To Build a Small Car, GM Tries to Redesign Its Production System," *The Wall Street Journal* (May 14, 1984), pp. 1, 16.

12 See Stephen Kindel, "The Workshop Economy," *Forbes* (April 30, 1984), p. 62.

13 See Thomas M. Hout and George Stalk, Jr., "The Big Revolution on the Factory Floor," *The Wall Street Journal* (July 12, 1982), p. 32.

14 James A. Baker, "The Automation Evolution," *Digital Design* (March, 1983), p. 42.

15 Baker (reference cited), p. 43.

16 "Computer Integrated Manufacturing: The Focus of Manufacturing Control," *Assembly Engineering* (May, 1983), p. 14.

17 Robert E. Harvey, "Factory 2000," *Iron Age* (June 4, 1984), p. 36.

18 John Teresko, "CAD/CAM Goes to Work," *Industry Week* (February 7, 1983), p. 43.

19 Based largely on Richard C. Winfrey, "Implications of Distributed Processing in Computer Integrated Manufacturing," Society of Manufacturing Engineers Technical Paper #MS82-417, 1982.

20 C.C. Harwood, "The View From the Top," *Quality Progress* (October, 1984), pp. 26-30.

21 See Don Hellreigel and John W. Slocum, Jr., *Management,* 4th ed. (Reading, Mass.: Addison-Wesley Publishing Company, 1986), pp. 690-691.

22 Robert C. Wood, "Squaring Off on Quality Circles," *Inc.* (August, 1982), p. 98.

23 Theodore Levitt, "Production-Line Approach to Service," *Harvard Business Review* (September-October, 1972), pp. 41-52.

24 Levitt (reference cited).

25 Levitt (reference cited).

CHAPTER FIFTEEN

1 William M. Bulkeley, "Computers Take on New Role as Experts in Financial Affairs," *The Wall Street Journal* (February 7, 1986), p. 23.

2 Bulkeley (reference cited).

3 Bob Davis, "Superfast Computers Mimic the Structure of the Human Brain," *The Wall Street Journal* (February 19, 1986), p. 1ff.

4 Figures are from Ellen Benoit, "Filling the Gap," *Forbes* (March 11, 1985), pp. 166-170.

5 William M. Bulkeley, "Who Built the First PC? Hint: His Name Isn't Wozniak or Jobs," *The Wall Street Journal* (May 14, 1986), p. 33.

6 John W. Wilson and Jonathan B. Levine, "Superchips: The New Frontier," *Business Week* (June 10, 1985), pp. 82-89.

7 Robert B. Forest and F. Douglas DeCarlo, "Computer Information Strategies for Smaller Corporations," *Inc.* (November, 1984), p. 132.

8 Forest and DeCarlo (reference cited), p. 140.

9 "Office Automation," *Business Week* (October 8, 1984), p. 59.

10 "Office Automation" (reference cited).

11 Figures are from Peter Behr, "Alterations Ahead in Apparel," *The Washington Post* (May 13, 1984), p. G1.

12 Behr (reference cited).

13 See Judith Rosenfeld, "Making the Most Out of Meetings," *Marketing Communications* (November, 1984), pp. 20-33.

14 Steven B. Weissman, "Videotex: A Technology in Search of a Market," *Marketing Communications* (September, 1983), pp. 30-34.

CHAPTER SIXTEEN

1 Abraham H. Maslow, *Motivation and Personality* (New York: Harper & Brothers, 1954).

2 See Abraham Maslow, *The Further Reaches of Human Nature* (New York: The Viking Press, 1971).

3 Andrew Grove, *High Output Management* (New York: Random House, 1983), pp. 157-180.

4 For more on Theory Y, see Douglas McGregor, *The Human Side of Enterprise* (New York: McGraw-Hill Publishing Co., 1970).

5 William G. Ouchi, *Theory Z: How American Business Can Meet the Japanese Challenge* (Menlo Park, Calif.: Addison-Wesley, 1981).

6 Harold Geneen, *Managing* (New York: Avon Books, 1984), p. 20.

7 Frederick Herzberg, *Work and the Nature of Man* (World Publishers, 1966).

8 See Henry L. Tose and Stephen J. Carroll, *Management,* 2nd ed. (New York: John Wiley & Sons, 1982), pp. 420-421.

9 See J. Richard Hackman and Greg Oldhorm, *Work Redesign* (Reading, Mass.: Addison-Wesley, 1980), pp. 78-80.

10 A. Poza and M. Markus, "Success Story: The Team Approach to Work Restructuring," *Organizational Dynamics* (Winter, 1980), pp. 3-25.

11 For more details, see "Letting Labor Share the Driver's Seat," *Business Week* (February 13, 1984), p. 110.

12 Thomas J. Peters and Robert H. Waterman, Jr., *In Search of Excellence* (New York: Harper & Row, Publishers, 1982), p. 262.

CHAPTER SEVENTEEN

1 These illustrations come from "Obsolete Workers Are More Often Retrained than Replaced by Their Firms," *The Wall Street Journal* (May 9, 1984), p. 1.

2 Julian L. Simon, *The Ultimate Resource* (Princeton, N.J.: Princeton University Press, 1981).

3 Arthur R. Bechan and William F. Glueck, *Management,* 3rd ed. (Chicago: The Dryden Press, 1983), pp. 440-441.

4 Amanda Bennett, "Bu Xinsheng: China's Model Manager," *The Wall Street Journal* (May 30, 1984), p. 36.

5 A. Gary Shilling, "We're Out of Choppy Waters, But Keep Cost Hatches Battened," *The Wall Street Journal* (April 25, 1984), p. 31.

CHAPTER EIGHTEEN

1 Report from June O'Neill of the Urban Institute in "It's Not Worth It," *The Wall Street Journal* (February 7, 1984).

2 "Boola Moola," *The Wall Street Journal* (November 17, 1984), p. A22.

3 Cathy Trost, "In Minnesota, 'Pay Equity' Passes Test, But Foes See Trouble Ahead," *The Wall Street Journal* (May 10, 1985), p. 27.

4 Figures are from Nelson W. Aldrich, Jr., "ESOP's Rising Stock," *Inc.* (April, 1985), p. 59.

5 Bruce G. Posner, "In Search of Equity," *Inc.* (April, 1985), pp. 51-60.

6 Posner (reference cited), p. 53.

7 John Hoerr, Gelvin Stevenson, and James R. Norman, "ESOPs: Revolution or Ripoff?" *Business Week* (April 15, 1985), pp. 94-108.

8 Hoerr, Stevenson, and Norman (reference cited), pp. 94-95.

CHAPTER NINETEEN

1 Definitions in this section are from Jack E. Kiger, Stephen E. Loeb, and Goron May, *Accounting Principles* (New York: Random House, 1984), pp. 1-2.

2 Personal interview.

CHAPTER TWENTY

1 Karen Pennar, "The '20s and '80s: Can Deflation Turn Into Depression?," *Business Week* (June 9, 1986), pp. 62-63.

2 Pennar (reference cited).

3 For a review of the troubled state of the economy, see the cover story in *Business Week* (June 9, 1986), pp. 52-63. It is titled, "America's Deflation Belt." The 1980s and 1920s are directly compared on pp. 62-63.

CHAPTER TWENTY-ONE

1 Roger Lopata, "Capital Formation for Smaller Corporations," *Inc.* (December, 1984), pp. 189-207.

2 Lopata (reference cited), p. 192.

3 Susan Benner, "Dear Jon," *Inc.* (February, 1985), pp. 79-86.

4 The examples cited are from Richard Taggs, "If the Grid Fits," a special *Newsweek Access* publication, 1984.

CHAPTER TWENTY-TWO

1 See John Case "Money Traps," *Forbes* (February 1985), pp. 132-140.

CHAPTER TWENTY-THREE

1 Johnnie L. Roberts, "Generation Gap Seems to Disappear If Investing Is Issue," *The Wall Street Journal* (January 16, 1985), p. 58.

CHAPTER TWENTY-FOUR

1 Jill Andresky, Mary Kuntz, and Barbara Kallen, "A World Without Insurance?" *Forbes* (July 15, 1985), p. 40.

2 Andresky, Kuntz, and Kallen (reference cited).

3 "Do-It-Yourself Coverage Wins Converts in a Tight Insurance Market," *The Wall Street Journal* (August 22, 1985), p. 1.

4 "Businesses Struggling to Adapt as Insurance Crisis Spreads," *The Wall Street Journal* (January 21, 1986), p. 31.

5 Robert J. Samuelson, "The Business of Conflict," *The Washington Post* (March 5, 1986), p. C1.

6 Examples are from "Businesses Struggling to Adapt as Insurance Crisis Spreads" (reference cited).

7 T.R. Reid, "Insurance Famine Plagues Nation," *The Washington Post* (February 23, 1986), pp. 1, 6.

8 Samuelson (reference cited), pp. C1-C2.

9 *Business Week* (May 21, 1979), p. 68.

10 These examples are from Roger Lekoy Miller, "Drawing Limits on Liability," *The Wall Street Journal* (April 7, 1984), p. 21.

CHAPTER TWENTY-FIVE

1 Ferdinand F. Mauser and David J. Schwartz, *American Business,* 6th ed. (Orlando, Fla.: Harcourt, Brace, Jovanovich, Inc., 1986), p. 597.

2 Mauser and Schwartz (reference cited), p. 594.

3 Paul Hoffman, *Lions of the Eighties* (New York: Doubleday, 1982).

4 *Statistical Abstract of the United States* (Washington, D.C.: United States Government, 1985), p. 520.

5 Reported in "Toxic Trouble in Silicon Valley," *Newsweek* (May 7, 1984), p. 85.

6 John H. Filer, "The Social Goals of a Corporation," in Thomas Bradshaw and David Vogel, eds., *Corporations and Their Critics* (New York: McGraw-Hill Book Company, 1981), p. 271.

7 Filer (reference cited), pp. 245-247.

8 *American Association of Fund-Raising Council Annual Report,* Washington, D.C., 1985.

9 Kenneth E. Goodpaster and John B. Matthews, Jr., "Can a Corporation Have a Conscience?," *Harvard Business Review* (January-February, 1982), pp. 132-141.

CHAPTER TWENTY-SIX

1 Alfred L. Malabre, Jr., "Tracking a Trend," *The Wall Street Journal* (August 9, 1983), p. 60.

2 Bengt Anderson, "Developing New Markets with Global Strategies," *Marketing Communications* (February, 1984), pp. 15-17.

3 Bureau of Economic Analysis, U.S. Department of Commerce, Survey of Current Business, *Business America* (February 20, 1984), p. 5.

4 Stuart Auerbach, "U.S. Now Debtor Nation as Trade Deficit Rises," *The Washington Post* (September 17, 1985), p. D17.

5 C. William Voris, "Tomorrow's International Managers," *The Collegiate Forum* (Spring, 1982), p. 10.

6 Reported in Urban C. Lehner, "Some Americans Find Success Running Own Firms in Japan," *The Wall Street Journal* (May 2, 1983), p. 33.

7 Ronald Alsop, "U.S. Concerns Seek Inspiration for Products from Overseas," *The Wall Street Journal* (January 3, 1985), p. 13.

8 See Brad Reid and Ed Timmerman, "Marketing, Morality and Multinational Firms," *The Collegiate Forum* (Spring, 1982), p. 5.

9 See Murray L. Weidenbaum, "U.S. Export Curbs Contribute to the Trade Deficit," *The Wall Street Journal* (April 2, 1985), p. 28.

10 Leonard Silk, *Economics in Plain English* (New York: Simon & Schuster, 1978), p. 120.

11 Wally O'Brien, "Realities of Global Marketing," *Advertising Age* (December 10, 1984), pp. 18-20.

12 Steve Weiner and Robert Johnson, "Export-Trading Firms in U.S. Are Failing to Fulfill Promise," *The Wall Street Journal* (May 24, 1984), pp. 1, 29.

13 Stuart Auerbach, "Low-Profile Firm Blooms Under Aegis of World Trade," Washington Business Section of *The Washington Post* (November 28, 1983), pp. 1, 15.

14 "New Restrictions on World Trade," *Business Week* (July 19, 1982), pp. 118-122.

15 Stephen Kindel and Robert Teitelman, "If Only . . .," *Forbes* (August 19, 1983), pp. 126-130.

16 Kindel and Teitelman (reference cited).

17 Louis T. Wells, Jr., "Guess Who's Creating the World's Newest Multinationals?" *The Wall Street Journal* (December 12, 1983), p. 26.

AUTHOR INDEX

A

Aburdene, Patricia, 443
Adelman, Carol, 684
Aguilar, Luis Jr., 166
Andersen, Kurt, 328
Andresky, Jill, 450
Apear, Leonard M., 310

B

Barnett, Richard J., 711
Beach, Dale S., 493
Bean, Ed, 142
Bennett, Amanda, 66
Berkowitz, Eric N., 475
Beynon, Roger, 409
Blood, Katherine, 377
Blumenthal, Karen, 148
Bond, Robert, 156
Breathnach, Sarah Ban, 34
Britt, Stewart H., 194
Brooks, Warren, 685
Browning, E.S., 643
Bruno, R. Richard, 130
Buchanan, James, 422
Buzzotta, V.R., 210

C

Celello, Michael, 131
Coen, Robert J., 203
Crosby, Philip, 386

D

Daft, R., 337
Drucker, Peter F., 48, 121, 166, 694
Dubin, Reggi Ann, 488
Dudek, Virginia, 415

E

Ellis, James E., 488
Emerson, Ralph Waldo, 222
Estren, Mark, 97

F

Fayol, 337, 338, 350
Ferrigno, Robert, 190
Flexman, Nancy, 148
Frank, John N., 601
Franklin, Benjamin, 548, 576
Freedman, Alix M., 576
Friedman, Milton, 690, 703

Frost, Robert, 488
Fulvio, Joseph, 409

G

Garcia, Beatrice E., 613
Geneen, Harold, 338, 429
Gray, Harry J., 140
Gray, Ralph, 223
Green, Cynthia, 354
Grierre, Richard, 121
Grove, Andrew S., 426, 427

H

Hall, Trish, 43
Harrow, Robert B. Jr., 702
Hartman, Curtis, 280
Hartrich, Edwin, 62
Havner, Judith A., 124
Hefner, Christie, 302
Heizer, Ned, 131
Heller, Haren, 302
Herzberg, Frederick, 431, 432, 437, 441, 442, 444
Heuer, Mark, 668
Hilden, David B., 642

J

Jacobs, Sanford L., 37, 146, 644, 664
Jaffe, Henry, 422
Johnson, Robert, 142

K

Kahn, Joseph P., 721
Kasindorf, Martin, 209, 690
Katz, Michael, 506
Kerin, Roger A., 475
Keynes, John Maynard, 48, 69
King, Resa W., 657
Kingstone, Brett, 98
Kinnear, Thomas C., 262
Kippen, Alexander, 166
Krishman, Harikar, 472

L

Lanson, Gerald, 188
Lee, Carmen J., 464
Levering, Robert, 506
Levitt, Theodore, 223
Lewyn, Mark, 564
Lowry, Albert, 116, 117

M

Mancuso, Joseph R., 146
Manoff, Richard K., 684
Marx, Karl, 53, 64
Maslow, Abraham, 424, 425, 426, 432, 437, 440, 441, 444, 448
Maxwell, John C. Jr., 190
Mayo, Elton, 424, 437, 441
McCoy, Charles F., 363
McGregor, Douglas, 427, 432, 441, 444
McInnes, William, 264
McNatt, Robert, 624
McVey, Philip, 250
Meisler, Laurie, 330
Mintz, David, 308
Moscowitz, Milt, 506
Mufson, Steve, 685
Muller, Peter, 536
Muller, Ronald E., 711
Murphy, Fred, 98

N

Naisbitt, John, 20, 24, 25, 40, 443
Nicholas, Ted S., 109
Norman, James R., 488
Novak, Michael, 57

O

Oates, Sarah, 31
O'Boyle, Thomas F., 592
Ouchi, William, 429, 430

P

Perrin, Noel, 407
Peters, Thomas J., 324, 354, 436
Pinchot, Gifford, 152
Powell, Bill, 209, 690
Powell, Michael A., 185

R

Raspberry, William, 8
Reiling, Lynn G., 206
Richman, Tom, 443
Roberts, Johnnie L., 119
Rosenthal, David W., 185
Rowan, Roy, 303
Rudelius, Wit, 475

S

Sanoff, Alvin P., 354
Scanlan, Thomas, 148

Schumpeter, Joseph A., 47
Schwartz, Bob, 147, 150
Sease, Douglas A., 250
Silver, David, 160
Simon, Ruth, 603
Smith, Adam, 52, 53
Smith, Timothy K., 194
Stamos, Theo, 645
Stratford, S., 346

T

Taylor, Frederick, 422, 423, 437, 440, 441
Thoreau, Henry David, 70
Tracy, Eleanor Johnson, 500
Trask, Reed, 409
Twain, Mark, 551

V

Vise, David A., 581

W

Waterman, Robert H. Jr., 324, 436
Waters, Craig R., 358, 386
Weber, Max, 336, 337, 338, 350
Weigner, Kathleen K., 155
Weisskopf, Michael, 66
Wessel, David, 511
Whalen, Bernie, 222
Williams, Mary, 390
Wojahn, Ellen, 142
Wynter, Leon, 554

Company and Product Index

A

AAMCO, 153, 161, 270
Acme-Cleveland Corporation, 70, 339
Adam Smith's Money World, 6
Adidas, 169
Administration Industrielle et Générale, 335
Advertising Age, 181, 223
Aetna Life & Casualty, 104, 647, 650, 682
Air Atlanta, 37
Aircraft Engine Group, 332
Ajax Manufacturing Company, 353
Albertson's, 257
Alcoa, 237
Allen-Edmonds Shoe Corporation, 64
Allied Corporation, 693, 712
All-Star Sports Edition of Trivial Pursuit, 188
Allstate, 650
Alpha Graphics, 162
Altair, 398
American Airlines, 511
American Can Co., 358
American Enterprise Institute, 84
American Export Groups International Services, Inc. (Aegis), 708
American Express, 34, 628, 712
American Federation of Labor, 490
American Financial, 650
American Home Products, 195
American International Group, 650, 712
American Library Association, 224
American Management Association, 320
American Medical International, 218
American Motors, 113, 120
American Orthodontics, 306
American Stock Exchange, 580, 603, 612, 613, 618
American Stores, 257
American Telephone & Telegraph, 195
American West Airlines, 506
AMEX; *see* American Stock Exchange
Amigo Sales, 447
Amoco, 104, 712
Mark Andy, Incorporated, 310
Anheuser-Busch Cos., 195
A&P, 257, 276, 277
Apple I, 398
Apple Computer, 7, 113, 147, 149, 159, 359, 414, 415, 507
Apple Jacks, 189

Arabian American Oil Company, 693
Army, 297
The Art of Getting Your Own Sweet Way, 386
Arthur Andersen & Company, 682
Arthur J. Gallagher & Company, 643
The Artists Foundation, Inc., 42
Asia Cola, 66
Ask Computers, 34
Aspen Music Festival, 42
Aspirin, 230
Asset Management International, 151
Association for Systems Management, 394
Atari, 159
Atlanta Exchange, 464
Atlantic Richfield, 104
Atlas, 693
AT&T, 104, 332, 333, 353, 504, 613, 668
AT&T Technologies, Inc., 333
Automatic Data Processing (ADP), 402
Avis, 139, 707
Avon, 146, 258

B

Baby Boomer Edition of Trivial Pursuit, 188
The Baltimore Aquarium, 289
BankAmerica, 712
Bankers Trust New York, 712
Baranco Pontiac, Inc., 151
Barron's, 583, 611
Barucci's Restaurant, 196, 217
Baskin-Robbins, 154, 270
Batten, Barton, Durstine, and Osborne, 151
Bausch & Lomb, 345, 346
Bayer, 230
Beatrice Company, 195, 311, 500, 712
Beijing Television Factory, 66
Bekins Moving & Storage, 279, 693
Bell Labs, 507
Bendix, 500
Beneficial Corporation, 613
Best Products, 257
Best Western, 286
Bethlehem Steel Corporation, 591, 592
Beverly Enterprises, 501
Big Daddy's Lounge and Package Liquor Stores, 162
Big Mac, 141, 222
Bing Steel, 151
BL, 113
Black & Decker, 303

Black Enterprise, 151
Blackwelder Furniture Company, 249
Blue Cross/Blue Shield, 631, 632
BMW, 516
Boeing, 345, 701, 718
Borden, 229
Boston Visual Artists Union, Inc., 42
Boy Scouts, 208
Bran Products, 189
Brim, 219
Britannica, 258
British American Arts Assn., 42
British Motors, Ltd., 104
Broderund Software, 613
Burger King, 153, 154, 158, 222
Burlington Northern Railroad, 613
Burroughs, 712
Business and Management Jobs, 15
Business Week, 10, 11, 12, 322, 357, 359, 360, 383, 470, 482, 487
Byte, 393

C

Cadillac, 225
Caminos, 35
Campbell Soup Company, 146, 178, 228, 229, 246, 331, 341, 342, 707
Capitalism, Socialism, and Democracy, 47
Cap'n Crunch, 189
Career Lab, 3, 4
Careers in Marketing, 15
Carte Blanche, 628
Catalyst, 473
Caterpillar Tractor, 701
C.B. Sports, 225
Celanese, 501
Celestial Seasonings, 507
The Center for Entrepreneurial Management, 147
Center for Entrepreneurship, 148
Cessna Aircraft Company, 644
Cetus, 7
Champion International, 613
Chase Manhattan Bank, 547, 712
Check-Up, 702
Cheerios, 189
Chemical New York, 712
The Cheney Florist, 128
Chevrolet, 229, 245
Chevron, 104, 598, 712

Chex, 189
Chicago Board of Trade, 601, 610
Chicago Mercantile Exchange, 610-611
Chicken McNuggets, 222
Chiquita, 169
Chrysler, 104, 120, 181, 195, 223, 317, 328, 367, 377, 488, 500, 501, 701, 710, 712
Chubb, 650
Cigna, 104, 650
Citadel Holding, 501
Citibank, 685, 700
Citicorp, 104, 317, 404, 712
City Arts Workshop, Inc., 42
Liz Claiborne, 360
Claire's Stores, 623
Clarkin, 296
CNA, 650
Coca-Cola, 66, 195, 685, 700, 707, 711, 712
Coke, 141, 218, 219, 228, 229, 235, 246, 252
Coke Classic, 245, 246
Coldwell Banker & Co., 116
Colgate, 229, 702, 712
College Store Journal, 119
Commander, 352
Commercial Credit Corporation, 667, 668, 683
Commonwealth Edison, 613
Commonwealth Savings Company of Lincoln, Nebraska, 572
The Communist Manifesto, 53
Compaq Computer, 150, 415, 543
Comprehensive Accounting Corporation, 526
Compuserve, 402
Compute!, 393
ComputerLand, 155
Computers & Electronics, 393
Congress of Industrial Organization, 490
Connecticut General, 647
Conoco, 598
Consumer Reports, 176
Continental Illinois Bank, 404
Continental Insurance, 650
Control Data Corporation, 373, 404, 667, 668, 683
Cookie Crisp, 189
Corcoran Gallery of Art, 42
Corn Flakes, 189
Corning Glass, 310
The Corporate Job Hunting Guide for the College Student, 14
CPC International, 712
Cracklin' Oat Bran, 189
Creative Computing, 393
Crest, 702
Crown Zellerbach, 448
Crum & Forster, 650

Crystal Brands, Incorporated, 303
C.W. Post Hearty Granola, 189

D

Dallas Museum of Fine Arts, 42
Dan River, Incorporated, 506
Dana Corporation, 339, 436
Danny Noble, Ltd., 575, 590, 591
Dart & Kraft, 712
Datapoint, 150
Data Processing Management Association, 394
David's Cookies, 442
Day's Ease, Inc., 156
Dayton Hudson, 613
Dean Witter Reynolds, 116
DeArmos Hispanic Magazine Network, 35
John Deere, 377, 495
Del Monte, 229
Delco Products, 510
Delta, 507
Denver Art Museum, 42
Designing Creative Resumes, 15
Deskpro, 150, 286
Detroit Free Press, 328
El Diario, 35
Dick Griffey Productions, 151
Diehard, 230
Digital Equipment Corporation, 396, 701
Diners Club, 628
Dinky Donuts, 189
Dip'N' Strip, 159
Diphtheria-tetanus-pertussis vaccine, 653
DISCOVER, 4
Walt Disney, 113, 114, 308, 348, 581, 685
Disneyland, 347
Disneyworld, 347
Domino's Pizza, Inc., 221
Donald Duck, 66
Donkey Kong, 189
Donnelley, 416
Donutz, 189
Dow Chemical, 712
Dow Jones Industrials, 613
Dr. Pepper, 207
du Pont, 104, 146, 237, 598, 613, 701, 711, 712, 718
Dunkin' Donuts, 707
DWG, 501

E

Eastern Air Lines, 613
Eastern Canvas Products, Inc., 119
Eastman Kodak Co., 195, 613, 712
East-Pak, 119
Edison, 113
Egg McMuffin, 222
Eggers Industries, 310
E.I. du Pont de Nemours, 712
Electrolux, 258

Electronic Data Systems, 385
Electronistore, 415, 416
Endata, Incorporated, 402
Energy Conversion Devices, 7
Entrepreneurial Megabucks, 160
Equitable, 647
Esprit, 360
Euromarket Designs, Inc., 721
Every Woman's Place, Incorporated, 124
Excedrin, 229
The Experienced Hand: A Student Manual for Making the Most of an Internship, 14
Exxon, 104, 125, 229, 501, 668, 701, 711, 712

F

Fanic, Ltd., 710
FAR-MAR-CO, 111, 114
Farmers Insurance, 650
Farmland Industries, Inc., 111
Fast Breaks, 141
The Fast Track to the Top Jobs in Accounting Career, 536
Federal Deposit Insurance Corporation (FDIC), 555
Federal Express, 268, 269, 275, 337, 613
Federal Reserve Bank, 81, 82, 547, 559
Federal Savings and Loan Insurance Corporation, 555
Federated Department Stores, 257
Filet-O-Fish, 222
Financial World, 10
Fireman's Fund, 650
First Boston, 501
First Chicago Corporation, 708
Florida Power & Light Company, 310
Florsheim Shoes, 258
Folger's Coffee, 218, 219
Forbes, 10, 11, 12, 48, 84, 127, 155, 322, 327, 482, 544, 545, 602
Ford Aerospace, 363
Ford Motor Company, 104, 113, 120, 146, 151, 327, 328, 339, 352, 353, 374, 377, 433, 510, 668, 701, 707, 709, 712
Ford Mustang, 152, 160, 327
Ford of Europe Inc., 358
Ford-Toyo Kogyo, 708
Foresight Group, 152
Fortune, 11, 12, 121, 303, 354, 367, 482
Foster Grant, 169
Foundation for the Community of Artists, 42
Four Winds Enterprises, 693
Franchise Opportunities Handbook, 160
The Fred Meyer Store, 257
Frito-Lay, 301
Froot Loops, 189
Funk & Company, 601
F.W. Woolworth, 712

G

Arthur J. Gallagher & Company, 643
GE Space Division, 395
Gemco, 257
Genentech, 7
General and Industrial Management, 335
General Dynamics, 501
General Electric, 104, 229, 237, 332, 358, 373, 398, 406, 449, 500, 507, 598, 613, 668, 701, 708, 709, 712, 718
General Foods Corp., 189, 195, 414, 415
General Mills, 189, 301
General Motors Corporation, 104, 113, 120, 179, 195, 237, 332, 338, 363, 367, 368, 373, 377, 385, 439, 449, 510, 511, 701, 710, 712, 718
General Theory of Employment, Interest and Money, 69
Genus Edition of Trivial Pursuit, 188
G.I. Joe Dolls of Trivial Pursuit, 182
Giant Stores, 257
Dick Giffey Productions, 151
Girl Scouts, 208
Global Reach, 711
GMF Robotics, 7, 710
G&M Oil Co., Inc., 151
GM-Toyota, 708, 709
Golden Girls action figures, 360
Golden Grahams, 189
Goldman Sacks, 507
Goodman Equipment, 269
Goodness and the GNP, 685
Goodwill, 625
Goodyear Tire and Rubber, 238, 510, 712
Gore, 507
Gracie's Corner, 43
Grand Union, 257
Grape-Nuts, 189
Grey Advertising, 171
Greyhound, 510
Gromer's, 276, 277
GTE, 104, 712
Gulf, 598
Gymboree, 159

H

Halfsies, 189
Robert Hall, 259
Hallmark, 507
John Hancock, 608, 647
Harley-Davidson, 368
Hartford, 650
HCA, 217
Healthdyne, 7
Heidrick & Struggles, 317
Helmerick & Payne, 613
Henkel, 702
Hercules Corporation, 404
Heritage Communications, 7
Hertz, 139, 140, 158, 707

Hewlett-Packard Company, 152, 244, 333, 346, 359, 386, 430, 448, 449, 507, 701, 712
Hickory Farms, 257
High's, 275
Hillenbrand Industries, 623
Hispanic Employment: A Recruitment Source Booklet, 15
H.J. Russell Construction, Inc., 151
Holiday, 501
Holiday Inn, 286
Home Emergency Kits, 141
Home Insurance, 650
Honda, 66, 113, 363
Honey Nut Cheerios, 189
Honey-Nut Crunch Raisin Bran, 189
Honey Smacks, 189
Honeywell, 363
Hormel, 497
Horn Abbot Ltd., 188
Household International, 257
How to Be a Franchisor, 162
How to Become Financially Successful by Owning Your Own Business, 116
How to Form Your Own Corporation Without a Lawyer for Under $500, 109
Howard Johnson's, 286
HP-150, 244
H&R Block, 153
Hughes Aircraft, 511
Humana, 218
Hyatt-Clark Industries, 506

I

Iacocca, 327
IBM, 34, 104, 143, 150, 195, 199, 210, 213, 317, 332, 346, 373, 386, 398, 415, 449, 501, 507, 509, 613, 685, 701, 711, 712, 718
IBM Sierra, 396
IGA food stores, 270
In Search of Excellence, 162, 166, 309, 323, 354, 443
Inc., 10, 11, 12, 43, 141, 160, 279, 322
InfoWorld, 393
Ingersoll Milling Machine Company, 373
An Inquiry into the Nature and Causes of the Wealth of Nations, 52
Institute for Movement Exploration, Inc., 42
Intel Corporation, 339, 365, 426, 436
Intelledex, 7
Intel's Bubble Memory, 152
Internal Revenue Service, 106, 541
International Business Machines; *see* IBM
International Harvester Company, 358, 544, 653
International Sculpture Center, 42
International Telephone and Telegraph, 430, 712
InterNorth, 712

Interstate Landscaping Co., 151
Intrapreneuring, 152
Introduction to Economics, 64
IRS, 289
Is Franchising for You?, 162
ITT, 430, 712
ITT Financial Corporation, 585

J

Jacklyn Inc., 623
J.C. Penney Co., 113, 195, 257
Jialing Machinery, 66
Jobs! What They Are . . . Where They Are . . . What They Pay, 15
John F. Kennedy Center for the Performing Arts Education Program, 42
John Hancock, 608, 647
John Hancock Funds, 608
John Michael Kohler Arts Center, 42
Johnson & Johnson, 195, 209, 339, 689, 712
Johnson Publishing Co., Inc., 151
Jordache, 229
J.P. Morgan, 712
Judson's Zippers, 233
Junior Achievement, 208, 292

K

K-mart, 104, 195, 257, 702, 713
Kaman Corporation, 7
Kellogg, 189
Kemper, 650
Kenbak I, 398
Kenmore, 230
John F. Kennedy Center for the Performing Arts Education Program, 42
Kentucky Fried Chicken, 139, 153, 158, 270, 707
Kodak, 146, 229, 670, 671, 701, 707, 718
John Michael Kohler Arts Center, 42
Kollmorgen Corporation, 333
Korvette's, 259
Kraft, 270
Kroger, 104, 257, 276, 509, 510

L

L'Opinion, 36
Lay's Potato Chips, 189
Levi Strauss, 113, 245
Levitz Furniture, 250
Lewis Galoob Toys Inc., 360
Liberty Mutual, 650
Life Cereal, 189
Lincoln Electric Company of Cleveland, 93
Liz Claiborne, 360
L.L. Bean, 258
Lockheed, 345, 501
Lockheed California Company, 152

Los Angeles Contemporary Exhibitions, Inc., 42
Los Angeles Dodgers, 507
Los Angeles Institute of Contemporary Art, 42
Lucky Charms, 189
Lucky Stores, 257
Lum's, 153

M

Macintosh, 245
MADD, 293
Madonna calendar, 148
Malcolm Forbes, 113
El Manana, 36
Manor Care, 31
Manufacturers Hanover, 712
Manville Corporation, 652, 657
Marathon Oil, 598
Mark Andy, Incorporated, 310
Marlboro, 228
Marriott, 308, 685
Mary Kay Cosmetics, 410
Massey-Ferguson, 544
MasterCard, 628
Master Charge, 152
Master Game Edition, 188
Max Ule & Company, 603
Maxwell House, 219
Mayflower, 693
Mazda, 708
MCA, 501
McCormick Company, 421
McCormick Spices, 440
McDonald Steel Company, 358
McDonald's, 19, 113, 139, 140, 141, 146, 153, 154, 156, 158, 159, 161, 195, 222, 229, 270, 340, 341, 348, 379, 380, 613, 685, 707, 711
McDonnell Douglas, 345, 579, 613, 701, 710, 718
MCI, 332
McNeil Laboratories, 689
Medicare, 29, 67
Megatrends, 24, 443
Mercedes, 516
Merchandising Your Job Talents, 15
Mesa Petroleum, 487, 488, 501
Mesbics, 37
Metroplex, 280
Metroplex Maintenance Services, Inc., 279
Metropolitan, 647
Miami Mensual, 35
Michelob, 229
Micro Peripheral, Inc., 37
Ming-Jones Advertising, Incorporated, 151
Minneapolis Institute of Arts, 42
Minnesota Mining & Manufacturing, 712
Minnetonka, Inc., 702
Minority Business Development Agency, 151

Minority Enterprise Small Business Investment Companies, 37
M&M Products Co., Inc., 151
Mobil, 104, 711, 712
Monet, 303
Money, 10
Monsanto, 701
Montgomery Ward, 296, 340, 341
Moody's Manuals, 482
J.P. Morgan, 712
Morton Salt Company, 227
Mothers Against Drunk Driving, 293
Motorola, 701
Motorola Radar Operations Service, 395
Motown Industries, 151
Moving Comfort, Inc., 389, 390
Mr. T's Cereal, 189
Mrs. Fields Chocolate Chippery, 442, 443
Murata Erie North American, Incorporated, 386
Museum of Northern Arizona, 42

N

Nabisco, 189
Nabisco Brands, 195, 712
NASA, 395
National Association of Business Economists, 89
National Association of Securities Dealers, 616
National Association of Women Business Owners, 34
National Center for Employee Ownership, 506
The National Center for Voluntary Action, 292
National Dance Assn., 42
National Education Association, 499
National Institute on Drug Abuse, 289
National Management Association, 320
National Opera Institute, 42
National Steel, 238
Nationwide, 650
Navistar, 358; *see also* International Harvester Company
NCR, 363, 510
Neighborhood Landscaping Service, 539
Neighborhood Watch, 293
Neiman-Marcus, 275
Nestlé, 684, 711
New Coke, 235, 245
Newsweek, 61, 327
New York Life, 647
New York Stock Exchange, 116, 580, 603, 612, 613, 618
New York Times, 442
New York Twist Drill, 200
Nightly Business Report, 7
Nike, 169, 360
1986 Internships, 14

1986 Madonna calendar, 148
Nissan, 363
Nissan-Datsun, 711
Nisshin Steel Co., 113
Noble Order of the Knights of Labor, 490
North American Van Lines, 693
Northeastern Pharmaceutical Chemical Company, 658
Northwest Instrument Systems, 580
Northwest Mutual Life, 507
Northwestern Mutual, 647
Nutri-Grain, 189
NYSE, 603

O

Occidental Petroleum, 712
Occupational Outlook Handbook, 89
Ocean Pacific (OP) Company, 360
Office of Education, 289
Ohio Foundation on the Arts, Inc/Statewide Arts Services Program, 42
101 Challenging Government Jobs for College Graduates, 14
Onion McNuggets, 222
Open Pantry, 257
Opportunities in Accounting, 15
Opportunities Resources for the Arts, 289
Oriental Land, 113
Osborne Computer, 149
Otis Elevator, 700

P

Pacific Gas and Electric, 613
Pacific Telephone & Telegraph, 279
Pan Am Corporation, 712
Pan American World Airways, 487, 506
Panasonic, 709
Pantry Pride, 500
Paragon Steel, 377
Parsley Patch, Inc., 125
A Passion for Excellence, 162, 166, 309
PC, 414
P.C. Magazine, 393
PC World, 393
Pedus, 280
Pedus International, 279
Pedus Security Services, Inc., 279
People Express, 507
People's Commercial Bank, 131
Pepperidge Farm, 342
Pepsi, 218, 245, 302
Pepsico, Incorporated, 195, 301, 500
Pepsico Foods/Japan, 301
Pepsi-Cola USA, 301, 303
Personal Computing, 393
Peterson's Business and Management Jobs, 1985, 14
Pettibone, 544
Pfizer Pharmaceutical, 700
Phibro-Salomon, 104, 501, 712

Philadelphia Coca-Cola Bottling Company, 151
Philip Morris Inc., 195, 701
Phillips Petroleum, 104, 712
Pillsbury Company, 195, 369
PIP, 162
Pitney Bowes, 507
Pizza Hut, 153, 158
Polaroid, 181, 229, 670, 671, 707
Pontiac Fiero, 152
Popular Computing, 393
Porterfield Wilson Pontiac-GMC Truck-Mazda, Inc., 151
Post Grape Nuts, 189
Post Raisin Bran, 189
Postal Instant Press, 162
Postal Service, 289
Post-It Note Pads, 152, 161
Prab Robots, 7
Preston Trucking Company, 437, 438, 439, 442
Prevention, 410
The Principles of Scientific Management, 422
Procter & Gamble Co., 146, 194, 195, 199, 212, 218, 230, 507, 509, 711, 712
PromoView Inc., 206
Prudential, 647
Purolator, 337

Q

Quaker Oats, 189
Quality Is Free, 386
Quality Without Tears, 386

R

Radio Shack, 257, 415
Radio Shack Computer, 414
Raisin Bran, 189
Ralston Purina Co., 189, 195
Ramada Inn, 707
RCA, 500, 598
Reader's Digest, 507
Reader's Guide to Business Literature, 482
Red Cross, 293
Redd Pest Control Company, Inc., 156
Reebok, 169
Re-entering: Successful Back-to-Work Strategies for Women Seeking a Fresh Start, 15
Re-Inventing the Corporation, 443
Renault, 113
Resources for Affirmative Action, 15
Revco, 702
Revising Your Resume, 15
Revlon, 204, 500
Rice Krispies, 189, 276
Dan River Incorporated, 506
R.J. Reynolds Industries, 195
Roadhandler mini-van, 352
Robert Hall, 259
Rock and Roll Replay, 188

Rockefeller Foundation, 142
Rockwell International, 303, 501
Rollins Environmental Service, 616
Running Your Own Business, 148
H.J. Russell Construction, Inc., 151

S

Safeway, 104, 257, 276, 488, 712
Saks Fifth Avenue, 575
Santa Fe Railroads, 598
Santic Corporation, 37
Saturday Evening Post, 178
Saturn, 363, 385
S.C. Johnson & Son, Inc., 310, 333
Schlumberger, 373
Schwinn Bicycle Company, 360
SCORE, 137, 140
Scotchgard, 161
Sears Roebuck and Co., 104, 113, 115, 116, 188, 195, 230, 257, 258, 271, 275, 296, 488, 599, 613, 625, 712
Sears World Trade Inc., 708
Securities and Exchange Commission, 619
Securities Industry Association, 617
Securities Industry Foundation for Economic Education, 616
Security Pacific Corporation, 708
Seiyu's, 253
Sell Overseas America, 139
Service Corps of Retired Executives, 137, 140
Service Merchandise, 257
7-Eleven, 158, 257, 275, 707
Sharper Image, 258
Shearson Lehman Brothers, 501
Shell, 711
Sherwin Williams, 432
Shopping Center Age, 275
Shredded Wheat, 189
SIGI, 4
Signal Companies, 701
Signetics, 378
Singer, 501
Sky Channel, 707
Small Business Administration, 34, 120, 129, 137, 138, 140
Small Business Institute, 137
Smithsonian Institution, Academic Internship Program, 42
Smurf-Berry Crunch, 189
Soft Sheen Products, Inc., 151
Sony, 229, 709
The Source, 402
South Street Dance Co., 42
Southern California Edison, 613
Southern California Rapid Transit District, 646
Southern Pacific, 598
Southland, 257
Spectrum Control, Incorporated, 386

Special K, 189
Sperry Univac, 297, 373
Sports Illustrated, 410
Squibb, 501
Standard & Poors, 482, 598
Stanford University Center for Integrated Systems, 398
State Farm, 650
The Statistical Abstract of the United States, 176
The Stock Market Game, 616
Stop & Shop, 257
Strong-Campbell Interest Inventory, 4
Studebaker's, 159
The Student Entrepreneur Guide, 98
Styrofoam, 230
Sugar Golden Crisp, 189
Sugar Pops, 189
Sugar Smacks, 189
Summer Jobs, 14
Sun Company, 712
Sunkist, 169
Super Sugar Crisp, 189
Supermarkets General, 257
System for Interactive Guidance and Information, 4
Systems and Applied Sciences Corp., 151

T

Taco Bell, 141
Tandon Corporation, 149
Target, 257
Taster's Choice, 219
The Tax State, 47
Teachers Insurance & Annuity, 647
Teledyne Semiconductor Plant, 378
Telelex Media, 710
Texaco, 104, 712
Texas Instruments, 150, 363
T.G.& Y., 257
Theodore Barry & Associates, Inc., 504
The Theory of Economic Development, 47
The Theory of Social and Economic Organizations, 336
Theory Z: How American Business Can Meet The Japanese Challenge, 429
Thinking Machines Corporation, 395
Thompson Financial Partners I, 601
3M Company, 152, 161, 436, 705
Thrift Guaranty Corporation, 572
Tide, 228
Tiffany Restaurant, 43
Time, 327
TLC Group, Inc., 151
To Work: A Guide for Women College Graduates, 15
Toffuti, 97, 308
TOFU, 97
Tofu Time, Inc., 97
Tokyo Disneyland, 113

Tommy's Charboiled Hamburger, 37
Toy Go Round, 182
Toyota, 113, 193, 339, 378, 711
Toys R' Us, 257
Trammell Crow, 507
Trans World Airlines, 497, 510, 613
Travelers Insurance, 647, 650
Travelodge, 707
The Triad Development Process, 152
Trivial Pursuit, 188
Trivial Pursuit T-shirts, 188
Trix, 189
TRW, 363
Tupperware, 258
Tylenol, 209, 210, 675, 689

U

Max Ule & Company, 603
Uniforce Temporary Personnel, 162
Unilever U.S., 195
Union Bancorp, 708
Union Carbide, 613, 658, 685, 701, 712
United Airlines, 487, 693
United Appeal, 292
United Mine Workers, 490
United Parcel Service, 269, 337
United Technologies Corporation, 353, 363, 701, 712, 718
United Way, 488
UPS, 269, 337
Urban National Corporation, 37
U.S. Defense Department, 433
U.S. News and World Report, 61
U.S. Postal Service, 337

U.S. Steel, 104, 332, 357, 358, 510, 598, 613
U.S. Travel Service, 289
U.S. Treasury Bonds, 610
USF&G, 650
USX; *see* U.S. Steel

V

Value Line, 598
Vector Graphic, Incorporated, 149
Venture, 148, 160, 598
Video Update, Inc., 158
V.I.P., 206
Visa, 628
VisiCalc, 594
VisiCorp, 594
Visual Information Package, 206
Vornado, 257

W

Waffelos, 189
Wall Drug, 253
The Wall Street Journal, 10, 11, 12, 43, 76, 131, 470, 580, 583, 599, 602, 603, 611, 612, 614, 615, 619, 620, 621, 708
Wall Street Week, 6, 611
WallWalker, 702
Wal-mart, 257
Walt Disney, 113, 114, 308, 347, 348, 581, 685
Wang Laboratories, 415, 488
Wardoco, Inc., 151
Warehouse Appliance, 516
Warner Amex, 501
Warner Communications, 501
Warner-Lambert Co., 195

Washington Post, 8, 646
Washington Project for the Arts, 42
WATS Lines, 177
Wealth of Nations, 53
Wendy's International Inc., 158, 193, 222
West Bend Cookware, 701
Western Auto, 258
Western Community Money Center, 572
Western Electric Company, 333, 423
Westinghouse, 104, 332, 358, 701, 709
Wetterau Inc., 510
What Color Is Your Parachute?, 15, 474
Wheeling-Pittsburgh Steel Corp., 113
White Hen, 257
Wilshire Index, 613
Winn-Dixie, 257, 276
Winston, 229
Wisconsin Conservatory of Music, 42
Women's InterArt Center, Inc., 42
Woolworth, 613, 702
World Bank, 697
World Health Organization, 684
Wrigley, 707
Wurlitzer jukebox, 159

X

Xerox, 104, 143, 152, 229, 230, 260, 368, 373, 685, 712

Y

Yellow Pages, 412
Youngstown Sheet & Tube, 357

Z

Zales, 257

GENERAL INDEX

A

Abilities assessment, 5
Absolute liability, 652
Accessory equipment, 227
Account; *see also* Accounting
  individual retirement, 633-634
  personal capital, 624-626
  types of, 522-525
Accounting, 515-545
  balance sheet and, 528
  bookkeeping versus, 519-522
  careers in, 520, 535-537
  cash flow problems and, 532-534
  computers in, 529
  creativity in, 531-533
  definitions of, 517-519, 538
  documents in, 521
  equation for, 530-531
  financial statements and, 525-528
  importance of, 516-517
  journals and, 525
  ledgers and, 525
  managerial, 518
  poor practices of, 540-541
  small business and, 132
  terms in, 529
Active investing, 606, 618
Active listening, 319
Actuary, 659-660, 661
Adaptive pricing, 241
Adjustable life insurance, 631
Adjuster, insurance, 659, 661
Administered system, 270-271
Advertising, 202
  careers in, 185
  classes of, 205
  deceptive, 674
  nonprofit, 290
  statistics in, 203
  television, 204, 205
AFL; *see* American Federation of
    Labor
Age of population, 29, 31
Agency, federal regulatory, 679
Agency shop, 494
Agent, insurance, 137
Agreement
  closed-shop, 493
  commodity, 715
  negotiated, labor-management, 493

Agreement—cont'd
  revolving credit, 590, 597
  term loan, 586
Airline, 268
Alien corporation, 109
Alternate compensation techniques, 460
American Federation of Labor, 490
American Stock Exchange, 603
AMEX; *see* American Stock Exchange
Analysis
  break-even, 239, 243
  job, 451
  location, 130
  Pareto, 378
  product, 233
  spreadsheet, 594-595, 597
Analyst, systems, 393, 394
Analytic production system, 365, 366
Apartment insurance, 656-657
Apprentice, 128, 456
Arendsee, Richard, 693-694
Army, marketing for, 297
Articles of incorporation, 108-109
Artificial intelligence, 395, 412
Asians
  marketing to, 36
  in small business, 37
Assembly process, 365
Assessment of skills, 4-5
Assets, 522-523
Assistant manager, 129
Association
  of College Entrepreneurs, 148
  commodity, 714
Auditing, social, 683-684, 688
Auditor, 537
Authority
  centralization versus decentralization of,
    340-341
  definition of, 350
  organization and, 331
Autocratic leadership
  fading of, 311
  managers and, 310
Automated teller machines, 550
Automation
  General Motors and, 385
  salesperson and, 380
Automobile Information Disclosure Act,
    680

Automobile insurance, 650-651
Aviation insurance, 651

B

Baby boom children, 29-31
Backpacks, 119
Balance
  of merchandise trade, 39
  of payments, 696, 697, 717
  of trade, 717
Balance sheet, 528, 538
Banking, 547-573
  accounting documents from, 521
  career information about, 568
  cash flow and, 534
  commercial, 549, 569
  failure of, 570
  history of, 565-568
  mutual savings, 569
  new developments in, 557
  small business and, 131
  world, 713
Bankruptcy, 106-107, 671, 687-688
Bartering, 710
Bear investor, 605, 618
Behavior, consumer, 175-176
Benefits
  fringe, 101
  segmentation variables and, 174
  unemployment, 76-77
Beta, 607
Blackwelder, John, 249-250
Blacks
  as entrepreneurs, 19-20, 151
  marketing to, 36
  networking and, 464
Blanket farm insurance, 656
Blue-sky laws, 615
Bodily injury insurance, 650
Bond, 590, 597
  definition of, 584, 596
  discount, 585
  fidelity, 662
  investment in, 620
  market for, 609-610
  premium, 585
  quotations of, 615
  secured, 586
  surety, 654, 662
Bonus plan, 461

Bookkeeping, 519-522
Boycott, 495
Branch, sales, 264
Branding, 229-230, 243
    new, 232
Breach of contract, 669-670
Break-even analysis, 239, 243
Brochures as management aid, 138
Budgeting, 593-594, 597
    personal, 628
Bull investor, 605, 618
Bureaucracy, 336, 337
Bureaucratic leadership, 310
Business; see also Business law
    capitalism and, 47-67
    careers in, 4-7
    definition of, 98
    insurance for
        interruption, 654, 662
        life, 655
        risk, 649
    nonprofit organizations as, 294
    organization of, 327-355; see also Orga-
        nization
    plan outline for, 130-131
    productivity and, 73
    small; see Small business
Business law, 667-690
    bankruptcy laws and, 671
    common, 671
    consumerism and, 679-682
    contract law and, 669-670
    definition of, 687
    fair practice, 672-679
    patent law and, 670-671
    statutory, 671
    uniform commercial code, 670
Buying
    career information, 263
    franchise and, 157
    on margin, 605, 618
    marketing and, 172
    of own business, 116-117

C

CACM; see Central American Common
    Market
CAD/CAM, 369-371
Caffeine, 219
Call provision, 585
Capital
    business plan and, 130
    debt, 579
    equity, 596
    personal, 624-626
    venture, 578, 579-580, 596
Capital goods, 227
Capitalism, 47-67
    in China, 65-66

Capitalism—cont'd
    communism and, 61-62
    definition of, 48, 53
    economics and, 48-54
    free market system and, 54-57
    mixed economy and, 62
    productivity and, 72
    socialism and, 60
    third world, 62
Captain, channel, 271
Car(s)
    Automobile Information Disclosure Act
        and, 680
    insurance and, 650-651
    Japanese robots in manufacture of, 710
Career
    in accounting, 534-536
    in banking, 568
    in computer operations, 391-394, 411
    as economist, 89
    in financial services sales, 617
    as manager, 320
    as manufacturer's representative, 214
    in marketing, 185
    as peripheral equipment operator, 411
    as production supervisor, 382
    in retail and wholesale buying, 263
    resources for, 3-8
    in risk management, 658-661
    as stockbroker, 617
    in traffic and shipping, 272
Caribbean Common Market, 714
Cartel, producers', 713
Cash budget, 597
Cash flow, 533-534, 538-539
Cash-and-carry wholesaler, 262
Catalog store, 257
Catalyst, social, 292
CCM; see Caribbean Common Market
CD; see Certificate of deposit
Celler-Kefauver Act, 674
Cellular telephones, 407-409
Center for Entrepreneurship, 148
Central American Common Market, 714
Centralization of authority, 336
    decentralization versus, 25, 340-341
Certificate
    of deposit, 550
    stock, 581
Certified Management Accountant, 535-536
Certified Public Accountant, 136, 535-536
Chain
    hospital and, 218
    store and, 258
Channel systems, 269-272, 274
Chapter 7, 671
Chapter 11, 106-107, 114, 671
Chapter 13, 671
Charities, 23-24; see also Nonprofit organi-
    zation

Charities—cont'd
    marketing for, 292
Child Protection Act, 680
Child Protection and Toy Safety Act, 680
China, capitalism in, 65-66
Chip, computer, 398
Cigarette Labeling Act, 680
CIM; see Computer-integrated manufac-
    turing
Classmates as career resource, 9, 12-13
Clause, insurance, 648, 649
Clayton Act, 673-674, 688
Clerk, accounting, 520
Closed corporation, 109
Closed-shop agreement, 493
Closing of union stores and factories, 509-
    510
CMA; see Certified Management Accountant
Coaching, 435
Coffee
    case report and, 218-219
    product life cycle and, 235-236
Coinsurance clause, 648
Collection period, 542
Collective bargaining, 492-497
College major, importance of, 8
Collegiate entrepreneurs, 148
Collision insurance, 650
Commercial, television, 193-194
Commercial bank, 549, 569
Commercial credit insurance, 654, 662
Commercial loan officer, 137
Commercial multiline insurance policies,
    654
Commercial paper, 591
Commission plan, 461
Commodity agreement, 715
Commodity associations, 714
Commodity exchange, 610-611, 618
Commodity fund manager, 601
Common law, 671
Common Market, 714-715
Common stock, 582, 596
Communication, 193-219
    computers and, 404
    importance of, 194-196
    marketing and, 171, 196-201
    motivation through, 435-436
    promotion and, 201-213
        advertising and, 202-205
        personal selling and, 210-213
        public relations and, 209-210
        sales and, 205-207
        word-of-mouth, 207-208
Communism, 61-62
    capitalism versus, 53-54
    definition of, 48
    economic consequences of, 64-65
Community
    liability and, 657

Community—cont'd
  organization and, 295
  social responsibility to, 683
Community service, 292-294
Comparable worth, 502-504
Comparative advantage theory, 699
Compensation
  comparable worth and, 502-504
  consideration and, 669
  differences in, 5
  fair, 508
  real wages and, 54
  types of, 460-461, 471
  unemployment, 76-77
Competition
  as basic right, 53
  foreign, 705
  franchise and, 158
  laws and, 672-679
  nonprice, 242
  pricing and, 241
  supermarket, 276-277
  tariffs and, 704
  unfair, 674
Complexity, functional, 339
Component parts, 227
Comprehensive automobile insurance, 651
Compressed work week, 466
Computer-aided design, 369-371
Computer-aided manufacturing, 369-371
Computer-integrated manufacturing, 373-374, 383
ComputerLand franchises, 155
Computers, 389-419
  accounting and, 529
  add-ons for, 244-245
  CAD/CAM and, 369-377
  careers in, 391-395, 411
  case report and, 414-415
  electronic shopping and, 415-416
  factory and, 371-373
  generations of, 395
  hardware for, 394, 396-399, 413
  languages for, 393, 411
  managers and, 319-320
  manufacturing and, 373-374, 383
  revolution, 27-29
  securities trading and, 603
  selection of, 140
  small business and, 135-136
  software for, 399-404, 413
  terminology and, 417-418
Concentrated marketing, 172
Conceptual skills, 316
Conflict, labor-management, 495-497
Consideration, 669; see also Compensation
Constraints, trade, 704-705
Construction firms, 122
Consultant
  computer, 393

Consultant—cont'd
  small business and, 136, 137
Consumer
  behavior of, 175-176
  choice and, 222
  marketing and, 179-180
  protection laws and, 680
  services and, 283-284, 285
Consumer finance companies, 556
Consumer goods, 226
  classes of, 242-243
Consumer price index, 77
Consumer Product Safety Act, 680
Consumer Products Safety Commission, 679
Consumerism, 679
Contacts as resource, 9, 13-14
Contingency planning, 306
Continuous process, 365, 366
  planning and, 306
Contracts, 669-670
  distribution and, 270
  yellow-dog, 496
Control, 321-322
  financial, 594
  manager and, 304, 313-315
  procedures for, 374-377
  quality, 378-379
  span of, 351
Convenience goods and services, 226, 228, 257, 285
Cooperative, 110-111, 114
Cooperative channel system, 270
Coordination
  control span and, 339
  marketing and, 180-181
Copyright, 671
Core time, 465
Corporate system, 270
Corporation, 98, 104-110
  culture of, 308
  global, 711, 718
  hospitals as, 217-218
  nonprofit, 106
  re-invention of, 443-444
  skunkworks and, 152
  social responsibility and, 682-684
Cost
  corporation and, 106
  cutting of, 383
  of goods sold, 526
  pricing, 238-239, 241
  site selection and, 362-363
Cost-push inflation, 77, 90
Countertrading, 710
Cover letter, 476, 480-483
CPA; see Certified Public Accountant
CPI; see Consumer price index, 77
Creativity, accounting, 531-533
Credit
  controls and, 562-563

Credit—cont'd
  line of, 590
  revolving, 597
  terms of, 543
  trade, 587
Credit cards, 628-629
  commercial bank service and, 551
Credit history, 551
Credit insurance, 653, 662
Credit union, 554, 569
Criminal loss protection, 654, 662
Crisis
  farm, 59
  insurance, 646
Critical path method, 375
Crop-failure insurance, 656
Culture
  corporate, 308
  marketing and, 176
  organizational, 347, 351
Currency, 563-564
Current assets, 523
Curve, supply or demand, 56
Customary pricing, 241
Cycle, product life, 243
Cyclical unemployment, 75, 90

D

Damages, 669
Data
  primary, 177
  secondary, 176
Data processing department, 401-402
  manager of, 393
Dealing, exclusive, 673
Death indemnity, 651
Debenture, 586
Debt
  financing of, 583-584
  national, 84, 85-88
Debt capital, 579
Debtor nation, United States as, 697-698
Debt-to-equity ratio, 544-545
Decaffeinated coffee, 219
Decentralization, 25, 340-341, 351
Deceptive advertising, 674
Decision making, 318
Deductible clause, 649
  automobile insurance and, 651
Deduction, tax, 627
Deep pocket rules, 645
Deficit, 88-89
  federal, 82
  trade, 91, 697-699
Delegation of authority, 317, 341
Demand
  definition of, 56
  planning and, 339
  pricing and, 241
  world markets and, 57
Demand deposit, 550

Demand-pull inflation, 77, 90
Democracy, 25
    management and, 310
Demographic segmentation, 173
Department store, 257
Departmentalization, 333-335
Deposit, 550
Depression, 80, 90
    tariffs and, 704
Deregulation, 678
Design
    computer-aided, 369-371
    organizational, 338-342, 351
        importance of, 332-335
Development
    employee, 471
    of labor unions, 489-492
    management, 462-464, 471
    product, 221-247; see also Product, de-
        velopment of
Differentiation, product, 168, 169
Diphtheria-tetanus-pertussis vaccine, 653
Diplomatic leadership, 310
Direct mail advertising, 204
Directorate, interlocking, 673
Directors liability insurance, 651
Disabled persons, protection laws and, 468
Disability income insurance, 651
Discharge of obligation, 670
Discount, 261
Discount bond, 585
Discount rate, 561
Discount store, 257
Distribution, 249-277
    channel systems and, 269-272, 274
    complexity of, 265
    definitions of, 260, 264, 273
    marketing and, 168
    middlemen and
        need for, 251-255
        retail, 255-260
        wholesale, 260-264
    physical, 264-269, 274
    place and, 250
    retail furniture, 249-250
    selection criteria for, 268-269
Distribution mix, 250
Diversification, 607
Dividend, 581
Documents, accounting, 521
Dollar
    exchange rate for, 697
    inflation and, 85
Domestic corporation, 109
Door-to-door sales, 258
Dott, Dick, 279
Double taxation, 107
Dow Jones Average, 613, 619
Drop shippers, 264
Drug Listing Act, 675
Drug testing, 676

Dual career planning, 473
Dumping, 696-697, 717
Duration, 607

E

Earnings
    economists and, 89
    manufacturers' sales workers, 214
    retained, 528, 578, 596
Economics, 48-67; see also Economy
    early theories of, 50-51
    Keynes's theory of, 69-70
    macro-, 49-50
    micro-, 50
    supply-side, 80-81
Economy, 69-94; see also Economics
    capitalist, 52-54
        Third World and, 62
    communist, 61-62
    constraints and, 705
    fiscal policy and, 83-84
    free-market system of, 54-57
        limitations of, 58-59
    gross national product and, 71-73
    high-tech production and, 363-364
    inflation and, 77-80
    interest rates and, 70-71
    market, 53
    mixed, 62
    monetary policy and, 82
    national, 25
    national debt and, 85-88
    recession versus inflation and, 80-81
    socialist, 60
    trade deficits and, 88
    unemployment and, 74-77
Education as investment, 632
EEC; see European Economic Community
EFTS; see Electronic funds transfer system,
    557
Electrical equipment case, 672
Electronic funds transfer system, 556-557
Electronic shopping, 415-416
Embargo, 703
Employee; see also Employee-management
    issues
    community programs and, 683
    orientation for, 470-471
        planning and, 454-456
    small business and, 134
    training and development and, 456-462,
        471
Employee-controlled leadership, 310
Employee-management issues, 487-515
    comparable worth and, 502-504
    employee ownership and, 504-506, 508
    employee satisfaction and, 506-507
    executive compensation and, 500-501
    labor and
        labor-management relations and, 497-
            500

Employee-management issues—cont'd
    labor and—cont'd
        legislation and collective bargaining,
            492-497
        unions and, 489-491
Employee stock ownership plan, 504-506
Engineer, computer, 393
Enrico, Roger, 301-302
Entertainment records, 521
Enthusiasm, 294
Entrepreneur, 16, 145-162
    blacks as, 19-20
    definition of, 159
    spirit of, 127-128, 146-152
    team and, 149-150
    woman as, 34
Environment
    assessment of, 5
    damage insurance and, 657-658
    laws affecting, 681-682
    liability insurance and, 651
Environmental Protection Agency, 679
Equation, accounting, 530-531
Equilibrium price, 56-57
Equipment
    peripheral, 411
    production goals and, 366
Equity
    organization theory, 336
    owners', 524, 538
Equity capital, 596
Equity financing, 580
ESOP; see Employee stock ownership plan,
    504
Esprit de corps, 336
Ethics, 685-686, 688
European Economic Community, 714-715
Exchange
    commodity, 610-611, 618
    dollar, 697
    middlemen and, 254
    stock, 602-603
Exclusive dealing, 673
Exclusive distribution, 260
Executive
    compensation to, 500-502
    insurance for, 655-656
Expense accounts, 524
Expense items, 227
Expenses, 538
    definition of, 522
    operating, 528
Experience as resource, 9, 12-13
Experimental research, 178
Expert systems, 395
    artificial intelligence and, 413
Export-Import Bank, 714
Exporting, 696, 700
    definition of, 717
    trading companies and, 708
    by United States, 695

Exporting—cont'd
world markets and, 706
Express warranties, 670
Extended product liability insurance, 651
External sources of information, 197

F

Factoring, 590
Factors of production, 48
Factory; *see also* Manufacturing
closing of, 509-510
computerized, 371-373
Failure
financial, 578
matrix-style, 346
small business and, 138
Fair Credit Reporting Act, 680
Fair Packaging and Labeling Act, 230, 675-676, 680
Fair practice laws, 672-679
Family structures, change in, 44
Farm
cooperatives and, 111
crisis and, 59
insurance and, 656, 662
profit and, 142
Fast-food organizations, 333
Favorable balance of payments, 696
Favorable balance of trade, 717
Fayo, Henri, 335-336
FCC; *see* Federal Communications Commission
FDA; *see* Food and Drug Administration
FDIC; *see* Federal Deposit Insurance Corporation
Federal Communications Commission, 679
Federal deficit, 82
Federal Deposit Insurance Corporation, 555
Federal funds, 561
Federal Power Commission, 679
Federal regulatory agencies, 679
securities and, 616
Federal Reserve System, 81-83, 559-565, 570
Paul Volcker and, 547-548
Federal Savings and Loan Insurance Corporation, 555
Federal Trade Commission, 679
Federal Trade Commission Act, 674
Ferris, Richard, 487-488
Fidelity bond, 662
FIFO; *see* First-in, First-out accounting system
Fifth generation computer, 412
File, resource, 5-7
Finance
control and, 594
definition of, 576, 596
franchise and, 154
media coverage and, 611-615
partnership and, 102-103

Finance—cont'd
role of, 576-578
romance of, 591
small business and, 132-133
Finance company, 556
Financial accounting, 519
Financial institutions, 547-573
banks as, 548-555
computerization and, 564-565
failures and, 567-568
history of, 565-566
electronic funds transfer systems, 556-558
Federal Reserve system and, 559-564
financial supermarkets and, 558-559
money supply regulation and, 560-562
nonbanks, 555-556
savings and loan associations and, 553-555
Financial management, 575-599
accounting and, 519; *see also* Accounting
budgeting and, 593-594
career information for, 617
financial controls, 594-595
long-term financing, 578-587
personal, 623-639
capital account and, 624-626
education and, 632
insurance coverage and, 630-632
management and, 624
money management and, 628-629
real estate and, 626-627
retirement planning and, 632-636
planning and, 130, 578, 592-593
role of finance in, 576-578
romance of finance and, 591-592
short-term financing, 587-591
tax preparation and, 595
Financial planner, 635-636
Financial statements, 525-528
Financial supermarkets, 558-559, 635-636
case report and, 599
Financing
inventory, 590
minority, 133
Finland, 60
Fire insurance, 650
Firing employees
case report and, 472
difficulty of, 450-451
First-in, first-out accounting system, 532-533, 538
Fiscal policy, 83-84, 91
Fixed assets, 523
Flammable Fabrics Act, 680
Flat organization, 338-339
Flexible Manufacturing Systems, 373
Flextime plan, 465
Float, 557
FMS; *see* Flexible Manufacturing Systems
Focus Group Studies, 177
Follow-up, 211

Food and Drug Administration, 679
Food, Drug, and Cosmetic Act, 680
Forecast
long-term, 592-593
production goals and, 366
short-term, 592
Foreign corporation, 109
Foreign Credit Insurance Association, 714
Foreign trade, 693-721
future of, 715-717
global marketing and, 707-710
international market and, 694-695, 705-707
multinational corporations and, 711-715
purpose of, 699-702
restrictions on, 702-705
terminology of, 695-696
trade deficit and, 697-699
Foreign Trade Zones, 714
Form utility, 364
Formal organization, 331-332, 350
For-profit corporations, hospitals as, 217-218
Four Ps of marketing, 168, 186
FPC; *see* Federal Power Commission
Franchise, 153-159
case report and, 161-162
world markets and, 707
Free market system, 54-57
limitations of, 58-59
Freedom, 53
entrepreneurial spirit and, 127-128
Frictional unemployment, 74, 90
Fringe benefits, 461
sole proprietorship and, 101
FSLIC; *see* Federal Savings and Loan Insurance Corporation
FTC; *see* Federal Trade Commission
Full-service wholesaler, 262
Functional complexity, 339
Functional discounts, 261
Fund; *see also* Funds
commodity, manager of, 601
international monetary, 697
mutual, 607-609, 618
pension, 556
sinking, 585
Fundamental accounting equation, 530-531
Funds; *see also* Financial management; Fund
electronic transfer of, 556-557
federal, 561
source of, for small business, 133
Funk, Christopher, 601
Fur Products Labeling Act, 680
Future
number of jobs in, 6
of computers, 404-405
of labor-management relations, 497-500
Future channel system, 271-272
Futures trading, 611

G

Games, investment, 613
Gantt Chart, 376
General Foods, 414-415
General Motors, 385
General partner, 103
General store, 257
Generation of new product ideas, 231-232
Generic name, 230
Geographic considerations
    control span and, 339
    segmentation and, 173
Global corporation, 711, 718
Global marketing, 707-710, 718
Globalization, 359-360, 383
GNP; *see* Gross National Product
Golden parachutes, 500
Goldman, Mark, 119
Gonzalez, Gilberto, 165-166
Goods
    convenience, 226
    cost of, 526
    definition of, 281
    import and export of, 700
    types of, 226-227
    and services, 281-283
Government
    economist for, 89
    ethical standards and, 687
    free market system and, 58-59
    mixed economy and, 62
Great Depression, 704
Greenmail, 581
Gross margin, 528
Gross National Product, 71-73
Gross sales, 527-528
Group cohesiveness, 349
Group life insurance, 655
Groups, negotiating, 714-715
Growth, 6
Growth stock, 582
Guaranteed loan, 590, 597

H

Hand of government philosophy, 687
Hand of management philosophy, 687
Handling of materals, 269
Hardware, computer, 394, 413
Hawthorne studies, 423-424
Hay Guide Chart Profile Method, 503
Health care
    marketing and, 217-218
    preventive, 632
Health insurance, 631, 662
    business, 655
Health maintenance organization, 655
Hedging, 611, 619
Help, managerial, 339
Hierarchies, 25

High technology
    economic growth and, 363-364
        computers and, 405-411
    industries in, 27
    supermarkets and, 253
High-tech/high-touch, 25
Hispanic market, 35-36
Home ownership
    insurance and, 656-657
    tax deductions and, 627
Hospitals, 217-218
Houck, David, 357-358
Hourly wage, 460
Human relations skills, 316, 320
Human resource management, 447-485
    career information and, 469-470
    comparable worth and, 502-504
    definition of, 470
    employee ownership and, 504-506
    employee satisfaction and, 506-507
    executive compensation, 500-501
    labor and
        legislation and collective bargaining,
        492-497
        unions and, 489-491
    laws affecting, 467-470
    management development and, 462-464
    management-employee issues and, 488-
        489
    personnel function in, 448-451
    planning in, 451-456
    problem of, 450
    small business and, 134
    training and development and, 456
    worker needs and, 464-466
Hypermarket, 257

I

Iacocca, Lee, 327
ICC; *see* Interstate Commerce Commission
Image, brand, 230
Implied warranties, 670
Import quota, 703
Importing, 38, 696, 700, 701-702
    definition of, 717
    United States and, 695
In Search of Excellence, 323-324
Incentive
    entrepreneurial spirit and, 127-128
    free market and, 54
    freedom and, 53
Income
    division of, 92-93
    net, 528
Income statement, 526, 538
    case report and, 539-540
    definition of, 524
Incorporation, 108-109
Indemnity
    auto death, 651

Indemnity—cont'd
    rule of, 648
Independence of entrepreneur, 147
Index
    consumer price, 77
    producer price, 79
    Wilshire, 613
Individual retirement account, 633-634
Industry
    advertising and, 205
    economist and, 89
    goods and, 227
    high-tech, 27
    marketing and, 183-184, 187, 277
    products and, 243
    service, 21
Industrial average, Dow Jones, 613
Industrial sector, 20
Industrial services, 285
    marketing of, 288
Industrial society, 25
Infant formula, 684
Inflation, 77-80
    dollar and, 85
    major causes of, 90
    recession versus, 80-81
    tariffs and, 704
Informal organization, 349-350
    formal versus, 331-332
Information
    distribution of, 24-29
    external sources of, 197
    internal sources of, 197
    system of, 5-7
    as utility, 253
Information age, 390-391
Information society, 25
Infrastructure, 359
Inheritance, investment of, 620-621
Injunction, 496
Injury
    bodily, insurance against, 650
    personal, 645, 651
    tort system and, 676-677
Inland marine insurance, 651
Installations, 227
Instant coffee, 235-236
Institutional advertising, 205
Instructor as resource, 9, 10
Instruments, negotiable, 670
Insurance, 641-664
    business interruption, 654
    business risk, 649
    careers in, 658-661
    credit, 654
    criminal loss and nonperformance, 654
    crisis in, 646
    environmental damage, 657-658
    farm, 656
    health, 655

Insurance—cont'd
  homeowner's, 656-657
  law of large numbers and, 648-649
  liability, 651-654
  life, 630, 636
    business, 655, 662
    credit, 654, 662
    group, 655
  personal, 630-632
  property, 650-651
  risk avoidance and, 644
  risk identification and, 642-643
  risk management and, 642
  self-, 643-644
  small business and, 137, 641
  types of companies, 647
Integration, marketing and, 180-181
Integrity, 685
Intelligence
  artificial, 395, 412
  marketing, 215
Intelligent robots, 406-407
Intensive distribution, 260
Interest
  definition of, 585
  small business and, 70-71
Interlocking directorates, 673
Intermittent process, 365, 366
Internal auditor, 578
Internal marketing program, 196
Internal sales promotion, 207
Internal sources of information, 197
International Bank for Reconstruction and
  Development, 697
International business, 693-721
  ethical issues and, 685-686
  future of, 715-717
  global marketing and, 707-708, 709-710
  market and, 38-40, 694-695
    franchising in, 158-159
  multinational corporations and, 711-715
  purpose of, 699-702
  restrictions on, 702-705
  small business and, 138-139
  trade deficit and, 697-699
  trade terminology and, 695-696
  world markets and, 705-707
International Finance Corporation, 714
International Franchise Association, 162
International monetary fund, 697
Interruption insurance, business, 654
Interstate Commerce Commission, 679
Interviews
  rating sheet and, 477
  skills development and, 474
  unstructured, 177
Intrapreneur, 152, 160
  case report and, 161
Inventory
  control of, 366-368

Inventory—cont'd
  financing and, 590
  raw material, 366
  self-analysis, 474
  turnover of, 544
Investment
  bonds and, 620
  choosing of, 606
  corporation and, 104
  definition of, 606, 618
  education as, 632
  games of, 613
  inheritance and, 620-621
  real estate as, 626-627
  return on, 543-544
  risk and, 607
Investment company, 133
Investment Company Act, 616
Investors
  bulls or bears, 605
  student, 616
Invisible hand philosophy, 868-867
IRA; see Individual retirement account

J
Japan, 40
Job
  characteristics of, 5
  description of, 451; see also Career
  enrichment and, 432-433, 441
  interview preparation and, 482-483
  planning and, 451
  rotation of, 463
  sharing and, 465
  simulation of, 457
  tariffs and, 704
Job Search Strategy, 474-476
Jobber, truck, 264
Joint venture, 111-113, 114
  international, 708-710, 718
Journal, 521, 538
  accounting, 525
Just-in-time inventory control, 366-368

K
Kellogg Breakfast Cereal, 189
Keough plans, 635
Key executive insurance, 655-656
Keynes, John Maynard, 69-70
Knights of Labor, 490, 508
Korea, 62
Kutz, Alan, 3

L
Labeling legislation, 230
  Fair Packaging and Labeling Act and, 675,
    676
Labor unions, 489-492
Labor-management relations
  conflict and, 495-497

Labor-management relations—cont'd
  future of, 497-500
  legislation and
    collective bargaining and, 492-497
    Labor-Management Reporting and
      Disclosure Act, 491
    Landrum-Griffin Act, 491
    major, 491
    Taft-Hartley Act and, 491
  negotiated agreement and, 508
Laissez-faire leadership, 310
LAN; see Local area networks
Landrum-Griffin Act, 491
Last-in, first-out accounting system, 532-
  533, 538
Law
  business, 667-690
    bankruptcy and, 671
    blue sky, 615
    common, 671
    consumerism and, 679-682
    contract and, 669-670
    fair practice, 672-679
    patent, 670-671
    statutory, 671
    uniform commercial code and, 670
  human resource management and, 467-
    469
    planning and, 471
  of large numbers, 648-649, 661
  protection for handicapped and, 468
  right-to-work, 493
Lawyers
  number of, 647
  small business and, 136-137
Leadership, 321, 422
  definition of, 321
  manager and, 304, 308-310
  pricing terms and, 241
  traits of, 309
  twelve rules for, 312
  types of, 310
Learning
  marketing and, 176
  of managerial skills, 318-321
Ledger, 525, 538
Legislation, 677-679; see also Law
  labeling, 230
Less-developed nations, 715-717
Letter, cover, 476, 480-483
Liability, 538
  accounts and, 524
  community, 657
  definition of, 114, 524
  insurance and, 651-654, 662
    cost of, 664
    farm and, 656
  limited
    corporation and, 104-105
    definition of, 104, 114
    legislation and, 645

Liability—cont'd
  unlimited, 114
    partnership and, 103
    sole proprietorship and, 101
Librarian, computer, 393
Library
  product of, 223-224
  as resource, 14-15
Licensing, 706; *see also* Franchise
Life cycle, product, 243
Life insurance, 630, 636
  business, 655, 662
  credit, 654, 662
  group, 655
LIFO; *see* Last-in, first-out accounting system
Limit order, 604
Limited-function wholesaler, 262
Limited liability
  corporation and, 104-105
  definition of, 104, 114
  legislation and, 645
Limited partner, 102
Line of credit, 597
  definition of, 590
Line organization, 343, 351
Line personnel, 343
Liquidity, 607
Listening, 198-200
Loan, 551-552
  guaranteed, 590, 597
  long-term, 552
  secured, 590
  short-term, 551
  term, 586
  unsecured, 589, 597
Loan officer, 137
Local area networks, 374, 383
Location
  analysis of, 130
  economic growth and, 364
Lockout, 496
Long-range planning, 306
Long-term financing, 578-587, 596
Long-term forecast, 592-593
Long-term loans, 552
Loss, risk of, in sole proprietorship, 100; *see also* Insurance; Risk; Risk management

M

Machines versus people, 377
Macroeconomics, 49-50
Magazines
  advertising and, 204
  for computer users, 393
Magnuson-Moss Warranty-Federal Trade Commission Improvement Act, 680
Mail order retailer, 258-259
Mail promotions, 206-207
Mainframe computers, 396

Maintenance-of-membership shop, 494
Major, college, 8
Malaysia, 62
Malthus, Thomas R., 50
Management, 487-515
  career information on, 320
  changing role of, 302-303
  control and, 313-315
  definition of, 302, 321
  development and, 462-464, 471
  employee-management issues and, 487-515
    comparable worth and, 502-504
    employee ownership and, 504-507
    executive compensation and, 500-501
    labor legislation and collective bargaining and, 492-497
    labor-management relations, future of, 497-500
    labor unions and, 489-491
  ethical standards and, 687
  financial, 575-599
  franchise and, 153-154, 155
  human resource, 447-485
    employee training and development, 456-462
    laws affecting, 467-470
    management development in, 462-464
    personnel function in, 448-451
    planning and, 451-456
    worker needs and, 464-466
  job of, 304
  labor and; *see* Labor-management relations
  leadership and, 301-325; *see also* Leadership
  learning skills of, 318-321
  levels of, 315-318
  middle, 316
  money, 628-629
  nonprofit organization, 288-294
  by objectives, 433-435, 441
  organization and, 307, 333
  participative, 310
  partnership and, 103
  personal financial, 624
  planning and, 305-306
  product, 230-234
    careers in, 185
  production; *see* Production management
  risk, 642
  scientific, 423
  small business, 119-143
    banking and, 131
    business plan and, 130-131
    international, 138-139
    large business versus, 120-124
    starting of, 125-129
    success and, 132
  sole proprietorship and, 101
  supervisory, 316

Management—cont'd
  tax, 576
  team of, 130
  top, 316
  by walking around, 302, 439-440
Management Aids brochures, 138
Manager
  accounting and, 518
  assistant, 129
  career information and, 320-321
  commodity fund, 601
  definition of, 313
  marketing, 167
  physical distribution, 266-269
  product, 230-231, 243
  responsibilities of, 304-310
  span of control of, 339
  styles of, 311
Managerial accounting, 518
Manpower, 366
Manufacturer-owned wholesale outlet, 264
Manufacturer's sales representative, 214
Manufacturing
  base of, 358-360
  definition of, 365
  growth in, 121-122
  plan and, 130
  small business and, 123
Margin, buying on, 605, 618
Marginal rates, 60
Marine insurance, 651
Market
  bond, 609-610
  common, 714-715
  franchise and, 157
  free, 54-57
  Hispanic, 35-36
  international, 38-40, 694-695
    franchising in, 158-159
  over-the-counter, 603
  securities, 602, 618
  segmentation of, 172
  world, 705-707
Market economy, 53
Market order, 604, 618
Market price
  definition of, 56-57
  pricing terms and, 241
Market research, 176, 215
  careers in, 185
  study, 137
Marketing, 165-190
  Army and, 294
  to Asians, 36
  to blacks, 36
  careers in, 185
  communication and, 193-219
    importance of, 194-196
  promotion and, 201-213; *see also* Promotion
  systems of, 199-201

Marketing—cont'd
concept of, 179-183
consumer goods versus industrial goods, 243
convenience service strategies and, 285-286
definition of, 166-167
different classes of goods and, 226
global, 707-710
importance of, 166
industrial, 183-184, 227, 288
intelligence and, 215
managers and, 167
new brands and, 232
nonprofit organizations, 288-294
plan for, 130
professional services and, 288
promotion and, 201-213
advertising and, 202-205
personal selling and, 210-213
public relations and, 208-210
sales promotion and, 205-207
word of mouth and, 207-208
service, 279-288, 295
services and, strategies for, 285-288
tasks of, 169-179
Marketing mix, 167, 186, 250
Marketing publics, 196
Markup, 241
Maslow, Abraham, 424-426, 440
Materials
handling of, 269
requirement planning and, 366, 373, 383
Matrix organization, 344-346, 351
Maturity, term to, 585
Mayo, Elton, 423-424, 441
MBDA; *see* Minority Business Development Agency
MBO; *see* Management by objectives
MBWA; *see* Management by walking around
McCormick, Charles P., 421-422
McCormick, Willouby, 440
McDonald's Corporation, 156
McGregor, Douglas, 427-429, 441
MCS; *see* Marketing communication system
Media, financial data in, 611-615
Medical payments insurance, 651
Megatrends, 24-29
Mentor, 464, 471
Mercantilism, 703
Merchandise
deficit and, 697
trade balance of, 39
Merchandising, scrambled, 259, 273
Merchant wholesaler, 262
Mergers and takeovers, 330-332
case report and, 598
Metaneeds, 425
Microcomputers, 396
Microeconomics, 50
Middle management, 316

Middlemen, 273
necessity of, 251-253
retail, 255-260
value of, 252-253
wholesale, 260-264
Minimum wage legislation, 468
Minisupercomputers, 396
Minorities
as entrepreneurs, 19-20, 151, 159
case report and, 43-44
financing and, 133
opportunities for, 37-38
Minority Business Development Agency, 151
Mix, product, 225
Mixed economy, 62
Modem, 405
Monaghan, Thomas S., 221-222
Monetary fund, international, 697
Money
lost value of, 571
management of, 628-629; *see also* Financial management
plastic, 628-629
policy concerning, 82, 91
supply of, 564, 570
regulation of, 560-562
Monopoly
international trade and, 700
Sherman Act and, 672
Moral issues, 684, 685, 688
Motivation, 421-445
concept implementation, 437-439
early management studies and, 422-424
Herzberg study and, 430-432
job enrichment and, 432
leadership and, 422
management by objectives and, 433-437
management by walking around and, 439-440
Maslow's need hierarchy and, 424-427
McGregor's Theory X and Theory Y and, 427-429
small business and, 134-135
source of, 426
Motor vehicles, 267
Moving company, international, 693-694
MRP; *see* Materials requirement planning
Multiline insurance policies, commercial, 654
Multinational corporation, 711-715, 718
Mutual fund, 607-609
definition of, 618
quotations of, 614
Mutual insurance company, 647, 661
Mutual savings bank, 554, 569

N

Name
brand, 229
generic, 230
recognition and, 154

NASD; *see* National Association of Securities Dealers
NASDAQ; *see* National Association of Securities Dealers
National Association of Securities Dealers, 603, 616
National brand, 229
National Center for Voluntary Action, 292
National debt, 84, 85-88
National economy, 25
National Labor Relations Act, 491
Negotiable instruments, 670
Negotiated labor-management agreement, 493, 508
Negotiating groups, 714-715
Net income, 528
Net national product, 72
Net sales, 527
Networking
definition of, 464
globalization and, 383
from hierarchies to, 25
importance of, 463-464
job search strategy and, 474
production management and, 360
New products, 231-233
New York Stock Exchange, 603, 618
Newspapers, 204
No load mutual fund, 614
Nobel, Danny, 575-576
Nobel, Annette, 575-576
Nonbanks, 555-556
Nonperformance loss protection, 654
Nonprice competition, 242
Nonprofit organization, 23-24, 98, 294-295
advertising and, 290
career in, 185, 295
as corporation, 106
marketing and, 289-294
types of, 290-292
Norms, group, 349
Norris, William C., 667-668
Norris-LaGuardia Act, 491
North Korea, 62
Nursing home, 31
NYSE; *see* New York Stock Exchange

O

Objective(s)
management by, 433-435, 441
pricing, 243
profit, 690
Obligation, discharge of, 670
Observation techniques, 178
Occupational disease insurance, 651
Ocean marine insurance, 651
Odd lot trading, 605
Odd pricing, 240
Office, sales, 264
Officer liability insurance, 651

Off-the-job training, 457, 463
Old Age, Survivors, and Diability Insurance Program, 633
One Minute Manager, 324-325
On-line remote processing, 402
On-the-job training, 456, 463
Open communication application, 436-437
Open corporation, 109
Open-market operations, 561
Operating budget, 597
Operating expenses, 528
Operations management, 357-387
  automation and
    problems with, 374-377
    of service sector, 379-381
  computerized factory and, 371-374
  future in, 381
  manufacturing base and, 358-360
  open-market, 561
  people versus machines and, 377
  production and
    fundamentals of, 360-364
    process and, 365-371
    as utility, 364-365
Operator
  computer, 392, 411
  peripheral equipment, 411
Opportunity
  career, 7
  entrepreneur and, 148
  repair worker, 27
Options, multiple, 25
Order
  limit, 604
  market, 604, 618
  organization theory, 336
Organization, 321, 327-355, 331
  community, 295
  cooperatives, 110-111
  corporation and, 104-110
  culture of, 347-349
  definition of, 321, 350
  design and
    importance of, 332-335
    types of, 338-342
  flat, 339
  formal, 331-332
  forms of, 97-118
  health maintenance, 655
  human resource management, 307
  informal, 331
  international trade, 713
  joint ventures and, 111, 113
  lines of authority and, 350
  management and, 322
  manager and, 304
  matrix, 344-346
  ownership and, 98
  partnership and, 98, 102-103
  restructure of, 350
  sole proprietorship and, 99-101

Organization—cont'd
  structure of, 293
    definition of, 330-332
    tall versus flat, 338-339
  theory of, 335-337, 350
  trends in, 328-330
  types of, 343-347
Organized labor, 490-491
Orientation
  consumer, 179-180
  employee, 470-471
  planning and, 454-456
Outdoor advertising, 204
Out-of-store shopping, 258-259
Outside readings as resource, 9, 10, 11
Overseas Private Investment Corporation, 714
Over-the-counter market, 603, 618
Owner insurance, 655-656
Ownership; *see also* Entrepreneur
  corporation and, 105
  employee, 508
    stock and, 504-506
  forms of, 98
  franchise and, 154
  home, 627
Owners' equity, 524, 538

P

Pacific Rim countries, 38
Packaging
  changes in, 227-229, 243
  Fair Packaging and Labeling Act, 675-676
  functions of, different, 228-229
  growing importance of, 228
  tamper-proof, 689
Paper, commercial, 591
Paperwork, 107
Par value, 581
Parallel processing, 395, 413
Pareto analysis, 378
Parkinson, Dave, 623-624
Parkinson, Jan, 623-624
Participating insurance, 647
Participative management, 310
Participatory democracy, 25
Partnership, 98, 102-103
  international, 708-710
Passive investing, 606, 618
Patent, 670-671
Payment
  balance of, 696
  breach of contract and, 669
  to executives, 500-501
  systems of, 460-461
Payroll records, 521
Pedus International, 279-280
Penetration strategy, 240
Penny stock, 582
Pension funds, 556
People versus machines, 377

Percentage of markup, 241
Peripheral equipment operator, 392, 411
Personal assessment scale, 475
Personal computers, 244-245; *see also* Computers
Personal financial planning, 623-639
  capital account and, 624-626
  education as investment and, 632
  insurance coverage and, 630-632
  management and, 624
  money management and, 628-629
  real estate and, 626-627
  retirement planning and, 632-636
Personal injury, 645
  insurance and, 651
Personal selling, 210-214
Personality assessment, 4-5
Personnel, 448; *see also* Human resource management
  career information and, 469-470
  importance of, 448-449
  line or staff, 343
PERT; *see* Program evaluation and review technique
Philanthropy, 683
Philosophy, ethical, 686-687
Phone system, 407-408
Physical distribution, 264-265, 274
  management and, 266-269
Physiological needs, 425
Piecework
  case report and, 93
  pay system and, 460
Pipeline, 267
Place, marketing and, 168, 250
  middlemen and, 253
Plan, Keough, 635
Planner, financial, 635-636
Planning
  contingency, 306
  financial, 130, 492-493, 578
    personal, 623-639; *see also* Financial planning, personal
  human resource, 451-456
  manager and, 304
  manufacturing, 130
  marketing, 130
  outline of, 130-131
  procedures for, 305
  retirement, 632-634
  span of control and, 339
  strategic, 306, 321
  tactical, 306
Plastic money, 628-629
Pledging, 590, 597
Policy
  commercial multiline, 654
  corporate, 683
  fiscal, 83-84, 91
  insurance, 648, 661; *see also* Insurance
  monetary, 82, 91

Political issues, economics and, 70
Political marketing, 291
Popp, Heinz, 641
Population
  age of, 29
  economic progress and, 51
  shifts in, 29-33
Possession utility, 253
Preapproach, 211
Preferred stock, 596
  definition of, 583
Premium, insurance, 648
Premium bond, 585
Preparation
  automation and, 381-382
  career, 7-8
  of resume and cover letter, 476-482
Presentation, sales, 211
Preston Trucking Company, 437-438, 442
Preventive health care, 632
Price; *see also* Pricing
  determination of, 55-57, 238-239
  free market and, 54
  market, 56-57
Price index
  consumer, 77
  producer, 79
Price lining, 240
Pricing, 236-242; *see also* Price
  cost-based, 238-239
  importance of, 236-237
  marketing and, 168
  objectives, 237-241, 243
  Robinson-Patman Act and, 674-675
  strategies in, 239-241
  terminology and, 241
  uniform, 241
Primary boycott, 495
Primary data, 177
Prime rate, 590
Principal, 585
Private brand, 230
Private property, 53
Process
  manufacturing, 365
  parallel, 395
  production, 364-365
Producer price index, 79
Producers' cartels, 713
Product
  add-ons and, 244-245
  analysis of, 233
  classes of, 242-243
  definition of, 223, 242
  development, 221-236
    branding and, 229-230
    chart of, 233
    example of, 221-222
    history of, 233
    packaging and, 227-229
    product life cycle, 234-236

Product—cont'd
  development—cont'd
    product management and, 230-233
  differentiation and, 168, 169
  importance of, 222-227
  liability insurance and, 652-653
  life cycle of, 234-236, 243
  line of, 226
  management of, 230-234, 243
    careers in, 185
  mix of, 225
  safety of, 679
  screening and, 233
  strategy and, 234-236
  success of, 231
  testing and, 233
Production management, 357-387
  automation and
    problems with, 374-377
    service sector and, 379-381
  computerized factory and, 371-377
  factors of, 48
  fundamentals of, 360-364
  future in, 381
  manufacturing base and, 358-360
  marketing and, 178-179
  orientation and, 179
  people versus machines in, 377
  process of, 365-371
    changes in, 368-371
    definition of, 383
    indicators of, 383
    manufacturing and, 364-365
  quality control and, 378-379
  supervisor of, 382
  utility and, 364-365
Productivity, 72, 362
Product-line pricing, 241
Professional services, 288
Professor as resource, 9, 10
Profit
  as basic right, 53
  entrepreneur and, 147
  farm, 142
  franchise and, 155
  orientation and, 181
  partnership and, 103,
  social responsibility and, 690
  sole proprietorship and, 100
Profit-sharing plan, 461
Program evaluation and review technique, 374
Programmers, 392
Promotion, 201-213
  advertising and, 202-205
  communication and, 195, 215
  mail, 206-207
  marketing and, 168
  personal selling and, 210-213
  public relations and, 208-210
  sales, 205-207

Promotion—cont'd
  video, 206-207
  word-of-mouth, 207-208, 216
Promotion mix, 202
Property
  insurance and, 650-651
  private, 53
  tort system and, 676-677
Proprietorship, sole, 98, 99-101
Prospect, sales, 211
Prospectus, 616
  definition of, 581
Protection, consumer, 680
Protectionism, trade, 697, 704-705, 717, 718
Protective tariff, 703
Provision, call, 585
Proxy, 582
Prudence, reasonable, 653
Psychographic segmentation variables, 174
Public
  definition of, 194
  responding to, 200-201
Public relations, 208-209
Publicity
  negative versus positive, 209-210
  problems with, 216
Pull strategies, 207
Purchasing documents, 521
Pure Food and Drug Act, 675, 680
Pure risk, 643
Push strategies, 207

Q

Quality
  as goal, 366
  of life, 48-49
Quality circles, 378
Quality control, 378-379, 384
  case report and, 386-387
Quota, import, 703
Quotations
  bond, 615
  mutual fund, 614
  securities, 619
  stock, 612

R

Rack jobber, 262
Radio advertising, 204
Railroads, 266-267
Rate discount, 561
  dollar exchange, 697
  marginal, 60
Ratio, debt-to-equity, 544-545
Rational decision making, steps of, 318
Raw materials
  industrial products and, 227
  inventory and, 366
Readings, outside, as resource, 9, 10, 11
Real estate as investment, 626-627

Real wages, 54
Real yield, 607
Reasonable prudence, 653
Recession, 90
  inflation versus, 80-81
Recruitment, 470
  planning and, 452-453
Recycling center, toy, 182
Reference group, marketing, 176
Regulation
  federal, 679
  management, 155
  of money supply, 560-562
  securities, 615-616
Reindustrialization, 359
Re-invention of corporation, 443-444
Remote processing, 402
Repair job opportunities, 27
Representative, sales, 214
Representative democracy, 25
Reputation, damage to, 676-677
Research
  experimental, 178
  marketing, 176, 215
    small business and, 137
  survey, 177
Reserve requirement, 560
Resources
  career, 3-7
  course, 8-16
  financial, 102-103
Responsibility
  corporate social, 682-684, 690
  organization and, 331
Restrictions, foreign trade, 702-705, 718
Restructuring, organizational, 350
  case report and, 353-354
Resumé, 476-480
  examples of, 478, 479
  job search strategy and, 474
Retailer, 273
  definition of, 256
Retailing
  advertising and, 205
  buying and, 263
  careers in, 185
  distribution strategy in, 259-260
  middlemen and, 255-260
  packaging and, 228
  pricing markups and, 241
  sales and, 256
  shopping mall and, 275
  small business and, 122
  store categories and, 257-258
  wheel of, 273
Retained earnings, 528, 578, 596
Retirement
  individual retirement account and, 633-
    634
  planning of, 623, 632-634, 636
    business and, 656

Return on investment, 543-544
Returning student, 12
Revenue, 526
  accounts and, 524
  tariff and, 703
Revolution
  computer, 27-29
  service, 20-24
  social, 29, 41
Revolving credit agreement, 590, 597
Rider, insurance, 650
Rights, capitalism versus communism and,
    53-54
Right-to-work laws, 493
Risk; see also Risk management
  definition of, 642
  investment, 607
  reduction of, 643
  sharing of, 663-664
  sole proprietorship and, 100
Risk management, 641-664
  careers in, 658-661
  identification of risk, 642-643
  insurance and, 646-661
    business interruption, 654
    business risk and, 649
    careers in, 658-661
    company types, 647-648
    criminal loss and nonperformance pro-
      tection, 654
    environmental damage and, 657-658
    farms and, 656-657
    health insurance and, 655
    law of large numbers and, 648-649
    liability insurance and, 651-654
    life insurance for business, 655-656
    property and, 650-651
  risk avoidance, 644
  self-insurance and, 643-644
  small business and, 641
Robinson-Patman Act, 674-675
Robot, 368, 405, 413
  automobile industry and, 710
  capabilities of, 407
  intelligent, 406-407
Role, management, 302
Rotation, job, 463
Rule
  of 72, 79
  of indemnity, 648
  of leadership, 312

S

Safety
  of money, 572
  as need, 425
Salary; see also Compensation
  comparable worth and, 502-504
  differences and, 5
  pay system and, 460

Sales
  accounting documents and, 521
  automation and, 380-381
  careers in, 185
  financial services, 617
  manufacturer's representative and, 214
  marketing and, 172
  net, 527
  office and, 264
  orientation and, 179
  personal, 210-214
  product life cycle and, 234
  production goals and, 366
  promotion and, 205-207
  retail, 256
Saving, 624
Savings bank, mutual, 569
Savings and loan association, 553
SBI; see Small Business Institute
SBIC; see Small Business Investment Com-
    pany
Scabs, 497
Scanlon plan, 461
Scheduled farm personal property insurance,
    656
School
  activities in, 476
  small business at, 141-142
Schuman, Douglas, 145
Schumpeter, Joseph A., 47-48
Scientific management, 423
SCORE; see Service Corps of Retired Ex-
    ecutives
Scrambled merchandising, 259, 273
Screening, product, 233
Sears, Roebuck and Company, 115-116
Seasonal unemployment, 75, 90
SEC; see Securities and Exchange Commis-
    sion
Secondary boycott, 495
Secondary data, 176
Sector
  industrial, 20
  nonprofit, 23-24
  service, 21, 280-283, 294-295; see also
    Services
    automation of, 379-381
    future of, 295
    international, 693
    productivity in, 73
Secured bond, 586
Secured loan, 590
Securities
  markets in, 602
  quotations of, 619
  regulation of, 615-616
Securities and Exchange Commission, 616
Securities Industry Association, 617, 618
Security specialist, computer, 393
Segmentation, 172, 186

Selective distribution, 260
Self-actualization, 425
Self-analysis inventory, 474
Self-assessment programs, 4-5
Self-esteem as need, 425
Self-insurance, 643-644
Selling; see Sales
Service Corps of Retired Executives, 137
Services, 279-288
  automation and, 379-381
  commercial banks and, 550-552
  convenience, 226
  definition of, 21, 281, 282
  financial, 617
  franchise and, 153
  future of, 295
  industrial products and, 227
  international, 693
  involvement with, 283-284
  marketing of, 280-283, 295
    strategies for, 285-288
  opportunities and, 27
  productivity in, 73
  revolution in, 20-24
  shopping malls and, 296
  small business and, 122
  types of, 281
Sherman Act, 672, 688
Shipper, drop, 264
Shipping
  accounting documents and, 521
  transportation mode and, 267
Shop
  types of, 494
  union, 493, 508
Shopping
  electronic, 415-416
  mall and, 296
  out-of-store, 258-259
  as service, 286
Shopping goods, 226
Short-term financing, 587-591, 597
Short-term forecast, 592
Short-term loans, 551
Simple recognition shop, 494
Sinking fund, 585
Site selection, 362-363
Situation segmentation, 174
Skills
  assessment of, 4-5
  computer, 319-320
  conceptual, 316
  human relations, 316, 320
  management, 322
  technical, 316
  verbal, 319
  writing, 319
Skimming price strategy, 239
Skunkworks, 151-152
Small business
  Asian, 37

Small business—cont'd
  categories of, 122-123, 139-140
  big versus, 120
  consultant and, 137
  failure of, 125-126
  importance of, 120-122
  insurance and, 641
  interest rates and, 70-71
  international, 138-139
  life insurance for, 656
  management of, 129-138
  market research and, 200
  minority-owned, 43-44
  at school, 141-142
  starting of, 125, 128-129
  success of, 125-126
  taking over of, 128
  trend toward, 24, 26
  women in, 34, 124
Small Business Administration, 137-138
Small Business Institute, 137
Small Business Investment Company, 133
Small Marketers' Aids, 138
SMAs; see Small Marketers' Aids
Smith, Adam, 52-54
Smoot-Hawley Tariff Act, 704
Social audit, corporate, 688
Social auditing, 683-684
Social catalyst, 292
Social issues
  corporation and, 682-684, 688, 690
  economic issues and, 70
  marketing of, 291
Social needs, 425
Social revolution, 29, 41
Social Security, 633
  case report and, 638
  corporation and, 107
  national debt and, 85
Socialism, 48, 60
Societal marketing, 182
Societal orientation, 180
Software, 399-404, 413
Sole proprietorship, 98-101
South Korea, 62
Soviet Union, 61-62
Span of control, 339, 351
Specialty goods, 226
Specialty service, 287
Specialty store, 257
Specific performance, breach of contract and, 669
Specifications, job, 451
Speculative risk, 642, 661
Spending, 83-84
Split, stock, 605
Spot trading, 611
Spreadsheet analysis, 594-595, 597
Staff organization, 351
Staff personnel, 343
Stagflation, 80-81

Standard
  ethics and, 685-686, 688
  of living, 48-49
  setting of, 314
Statement
  financial, 525-528
  income, 524, 526, 538
Statistics, advertising, 203
Statutory law, 671
Stephens, Charlotte, 19-20
Stock(s), 580, 601-621
  buying of, 604-605
  choosing investment in, 606-610
  commodity fund manager and, 601
  common, 582, 596
  financial data in media and, 611-615
  growth, 582
  how to buy, 604-605
  insurance company and, 647
  ownership by employees and, 504-506
  penny, 582
  preferred, 583, 596
  quotations of, 612
  regulation and, 615-616
  securities markets and, 602
  split of, 605
  stock exchange and, 602-603
  terminology of, 581-587
Stock certificate, 581
Stock exchange, 602-603
Stock insurance company, 647
Stockbroker, 604, 617, 618
Stockholders, 104
Strategy
  long-range, 306
  planning of, 321
  product, 234-236
  promotion and, 207
Strict liability, 652
Strike breakers, 497
Strikes, 495
Structural unemployment, 75, 90
Structure, organizational, 293, 338-339
Student
  as investor, 616
  returning, 12
Study
  focus group, 177
  marketing research, 137
Stutt, Brian, 515-516
Subchapter S corporation, 110, 114
Subculture, 176
Subordination, 336
Subsidiaries, 706
Success, 34
  new product, 231
  profile for, 132
  small business, 128
  visible, 293
Super Bowl marketing, 205
Supercomputers, 396

Supermarket
    category and, 257
    competition and, 276-277
    financial, 558-559, 635-636
        Sears as, 599
    high technology, 253
Supermicrocomputers, 396
Supervisory management, 316
Supply
    industrial products and, 227
    money, 564
    price and, 55-56
    world markets and, 57
Supply curve, 56
Supply-side economics, 80-81
Surety bond, 654, 662
Survey research, 177
Sweden, 60
Synthetic systems, 365
System
    computer, 393, 394
    information, 5-7
    pay, 460-461
    phone, 408
    synthetic, 365
Systems analyst, 393, 394

T

Tactical planning, 306
Taft-Hartley Act, 491
Takeover
    mergers and, 598
    of successful small business, 129
Tall organization, 338-339
Tamper-proof packaging, 689
Targeting
    market, 172
    pricing and, 241
Targeting volunteers, 292-293
Tariff, 703, 704, 718
Taxes
    corporation and, 105, 107
    home ownership and, 627
    management of, 576
    preparation of, 595
    rich and, 84
    sole proprietorship and, 100
    spending and, 83-84
Team
    entrepreneurial, 149-150
    management, 130
Technical skills, 316
Technical writers, 393
Technology
    computers and, 398
    high; see High technology
    telephone, 407-409
Teleconference, 409
Telemarketing, 258, 410
Telephone, 407-409

Television advertising, 204, 205
Teller, automated, 550
Term insurance, 630
Term loan agreement, 586
Term to maturity, 585
Terminology
    accounting, 529
    international trade, 695-696
    pricing, 241
Testing
    drug, 676
    product, 233
Textile Fiber Products Identification Act, 680
Theory
    comparative advantage, 699
    management, 427-432
    organizational, 350
    X, 441
        explanation of, 428, 429
        case report and, 442-443
    Y, 428-429, 441
    Z, 430
Thieme, Allan R., 447
Third World Countries, 716-717
    capitalism and, 62
Thrift organization, 553, 569
Time deposit, 550
Time utility, 252
Time-motion studies, 422
Time-sharing, 402
Top management, 316, 317
Tort, 645, 676-677
Total quality control, 378
Total yield, 607
Toy recycling center, 182
Trade, international
    deficit and, 88-89, 91, 697-699
    future of, 715-717
    global marketing and, 707-710
    multinational corporations and, 711-715
    protectionism and, 697, 704-705, 717
    purpose of, 699-702
    restrictions on, 702-705
    terminology and, 695-696
    world markets and, 705-707
Trade advertising, 205
Trade credit, 587
Trade organizations, 697
Trade wars, 704
Trademark, 229
Trading
    computer, of securities, 603
    futures, 611
    marketing and, 172
    odd lot, 605
    spot, 611
Trading company, export, 708
Training
    computer usage and, 403
        career information and, 393

Training—cont'd
    definition of, 456
    employee, 471
Traits chart, 484
Transcendence needs, 425
Transportation mode, 266-268
Travel records, 521
Treasurer, 576
Trends, 19-45
    international markets and, 38-40
    megatrends, 24-29
    organizational, 328-330
    service revolution and, 20-24
    social revolution and, 29-38
Trickle-down theory, 65
Trivial Pursuit, 188
Trucks, 264, 267
Truth-in-Lending Act, 680
Turnover, inventory, 544
Twelve rules for leadership, 312
Two-income families, 34
Two-tier wage contracts, 510-511
Tylenol, 689

U

Umbrella liability insurance, 651, 662
Underinsured motorist insurance, 651
Understudy positions, 463
Undifferentiated marketing, 172
Unemployment, 74-77
    types of, 90
Unfair competition, 674
Uniform Commercial Code, 670, 687
Uniform pricing, 241
Uninsured motorist insurance, 650-651
Union
    credit, 554, 569
    employee-management issues, 489-491;
        see also Labor-management relations
    membership of, 499
Union shop, 493, 508
Union store, 509-510
Universal life insurance, 630
Unlimited liability, 114
    definition of, 114
    partnership and, 103
    sole proprietorship and, 101
Unsecured loan, 589, 597
Unstructured interviews, 177
Utility
    definition of, 252
    form, 364
Utility average, 613

V

Vaccine, diphtheria-tetanus-pertussis, 653
Variable life insurance, 630
Varney, Jim, 193
Vending machine, 258
Venture

Venture—cont'd
  entrepreneurial, 146
  joint, 708-710, 718
Venture capital, 578, 579-580, 596
Verbal skills, 319
Vestibule training, 457
Video promotions, 206-207
Videotex, 412
Visibility, packaging, 228
Visual Information Package, 206
Volcker, Paul, 547-548
Volume segmentation, 174
Volunteers, 295
  targeting of, 292-293

W

Wages
  fair, 508
  real, 54
Wagner Act, 491
Warranties, 670
Wars, trade, 704
Weber, Max, 336-337
Wessel, Ellen, 389
Wheel of retailing, 259, 273

Wheeler-Lea Act, 674
Whole life insurance, 630
Wholesale outlet, 264
Wholesaling, 260, 273-274
  buying and, 263
  distribution, 249-277
  middlemen and, 260-264
  small business and, 122-123
Wilshire Index, 613
Women
  as entrepreneurs, 150, 159
  fair wages for, 508
  in small business, 124
  in work force, 33-34
Wool Products Labeling Act, 680
Word-of-mouth promotion, 207-208, 216
Work rule changes, 498
Work week, compressed, 466
Workers
  motivation of, 421-445
    concept implementation, 437-439
    early management studies and, 422-424
    Herzberg study and, 430-432
    job enrichment and, 432-433
    leadership and, 422

Workers—cont'd
  motivation of—cont'd
    management by objectives and, 433-437
    management by walking around, 439-440
    Maslow's needs hierarchy and, 424-427
    McGregor's Theory X and Theory Y, 427-429
    Theory Z, 430
  needs of, 464-466
  women as, 33-34
Workers compensation, 662
Workers compensation insurance, 651-652
World Bank, 697, 713
World economy, 25
World markets, 57, 705-707
Writer, technical, 393
Writing skills, 319

Y

Yellow-dog contract, 496
Yield, 607

CREDITS

p. 280, Photo compliments of Safety-Kleen Corporation. p. 280, Courtesy Sears, Roebuck, and Company. p. 286, Bob Barrie, art director; Mike Lescarbeau, copywriter. p. 287, Courtesy of Humana Inc. p. 288, Courtesy of Hyatt Legal Services. p. 289, © 1986 United States Government as represented by the Secretary of the Army. All rights reserved. Permission to use does not constitute an endorsement. p. 290, Reprinted by permission from Livingston and Company Advertising. p. 293, Courtesy of VOLUNTEER—The National Center.

CHAPTER 12

p. 300, Courtesy of Pepsi-Cola USA.
p. 301, Courtesy of Pepsi-Cola USA.
p. 305, © Susan McElhinney Archive.
p. 308, © The Walt Disney Company.
p. 314, © John Coletti, Stock Boston.
p. 315, Photo courtesy of Cincinnati Reds.
p. 319, Photo courtesy of Hewlett-Packard Company.

CHAPTER 13

p. 326, Photograph by A. Sacks. p. 329, Courtesy of *Anchora* of Delta Gamma. p. 332, Photo courtesy of Hewlett-Packard Company. p. 336, The Granger Collection. p. 337, Photo by Dana Duke. p. 341, Courtesy of Campbell Soup Company. p. 348, Photography by Voyles.

CHAPTER 14

p. 356, Photo courtesy Bethlehem Steel Company. p. 357, Photo courtesy Roman Sapecki Photography. p. 363, Courtesy of South Carolina State Development Board. p. 364, The Stock Shop. p. 367, Photo courtesy Leaseway Inc. p. 370, Courtesy of Converse, Inc. p. 372, Photograph reprinted with the permission of General Motors Corporation. p. 375, Reprinted by permission of Apollo Computer Inc. p. 379, Photography by Voyles. p. 380, Fingertip Banking ®, Mercantile Bancorporation Inc., St. Louis, Mo. p. 381, Photo courtesy of Hewlett-Packard Company.

CHAPTER 15

p. 388, © Kachaturian. p. 389, Courtesy of Moving Comfort. p. 391, Photo courtesy of Hewlett-Packard Company. p. 397, Courtesy of International Business Machines Corporation. p. 397, Photo courtesy of Digital Equipment Corporation. p. 397, Graphics courtesy of Convex Computer Corporation. p. 397, Courtesy of Cray Research, Inc. p. 399, Courtesy of ComputerLand Corporation. p. 401,

Photo courtesy of Hewlett-Packard Company. p. 403, Courtesy of Airborne Express. p. 406, Photograph reprinted with the permission of General Motors Corporation. p. 408, Courtesy of Cybertel Cellular Telephone Co. p. 410, Photo courtesy of Southwestern Bell Telephone.

CHAPTER 16

p. 420, Courtesy of McCormick & Co., Inc. p. 421, Courtesy of McCormick & Co., Inc. p. 423, Reproduced with the permission of AT&T Corporate Archive. p. 429, Courtesy of Apple Computer, Inc. p. 433, Courtesy of The Sherwin-Williams Company. p. 436, 3M Company photo by Mark Joseph. p. 437, Photo courtesy Southwestern Bell Telephone. p. 438, Courtesy of Preston Trucking Company, Inc.

CHAPTER 17

p. 446, Tom Ebenhoh/Photographic Resources. p. 447, Courtesy of Amigo Sales, Inc. p. 449, Courtesy of General Electric Transportation Systems. p. 455, Photo courtesy of General Dynamics. p. 457, Courtesy of American Airlines, photo by Bob Takis. p. 459, Courtesy of Nationwide Insurance, photograph by Tom Brunk. p. 461, © Harold Stucker. p. 462, Dick Luria/The Stock Shop. p. 463, © Friend & Denny. All rights reserved.

CHAPTER 18

p. 486, © Joan Liftin, Archive Pictures, Inc. p. 487, Courtesy United Airlines Inc. p. 488, Reprinted by permission from TIME. p. 489, © Martin Rogers 1985; all rights reserved; Stock Boston. p. 496, © James R. Holland, Stock Boston. p. 502, Studio 7L Ltd. Dick Luria, Medichrome, Div./The Stock Shop, Inc. p. 507, Courtesy of The Procter & Gamble Company. p. 514, Photography by Voyles.

CHAPTER 19

p. 514, Photography by Voyles. p. 515, John Grossman/ Black Star. p. 518, Courtesy of The Coca-Cola Company. p. 521, Photography by Voyles. p. 523, Courtesy NWA, Inc. p. 532, Courtesy of Converse, Inc.

CHAPTER 20

p. 546, Courtesy of the Federal Reserve Bank, Chicago, Ill. p. 547, Courtesy of Paul Volcker. p. 549, © American Bankers Association. Reprinted with permission. All rights reserved. p. 552, Courtesy of The Boeing Company. p. 553, The Stock Shop. p. 558, Courtesy of Discover Card

Services, Inc. p. 564, Courtesy of U.S. Department of the Treasury.

CHAPTER 21

p. 574, Courtesy of Danny Noble, Ltd.
p. 575, Courtesy of Danny Noble, Ltd.
p. 582, Courtesy of Apple Computer, Inc.
p. 584, Courtesy of International Business Machines Corporation. p. 589, Photo courtesy of the Hewlett-Packard Company.
p. 594, Courtesy of Lotus, Inc.

CHAPTER 22

p. 600, The Gladstone Studio, Ltd. p. 601, Photo courtesy of Christopher Funk. p. 602, Ethan Hoffman/Archive Pictures. p. 604, Jon Riley/The Stock Shop. p. 608, Courtesy of Twentieth Century Investors, Inc. p. 609, Courtesy of The Department of the Treasury Fiscal Service. p. 610, Courtesy of the Chicago Board of Trade.

CHAPTER 23

p. 622, Courtesy of BMW of North America, Inc. p. 623, Bill Ballenberg Photography. p. 625, Richard Pasley/Stock Boston. p. 627, Courtesy of American Express Travel Related Services Company, Inc.; Copyright 1986. p. 629, Courtesy of American Express Travel Related Services Company, Inc.; Copyright 1986. p. 631, Tom Morton/ Barnes Hospital. p. 633, Four by Five, Inc.

CHAPTER 24

p. 640, Permission granted by CIGNA Corporation. p. 641, Courtesy of Heinz Popp. p. 647, © *The New Yorker*, 1986. p. 652, Photography by Voyles. p. 653, Jeffrey Reed/Medichrome Div./The Stock Shop, Inc. p. 658, St. Louis *Globe-Democrat.* p. 659, Courtesy of Nationwide Insurance Companies.

CHAPTER 25

p. 666, Everett C. Johnson/Folio, Inc. p. 667, Courtesy of Control Data Corporation. p. 673, Courtesy of AT&T. p. 676, Photography by Voyles. p. 681, Courtesy of TRW Inc. p. 682, Design Kiyoshi Karai. Reprinted with permission from Mobil Corporation.

CHAPTER 26

p. 692, Courtesy of The Southland Corporation. p. 693, Courtesy of Four Winds Enterprises, Inc. p. 694, Copyrighted 1986, Caroline Parsons. p. 699, Courtesy of Otis Elevator Company. p. 706, Courtesy of Dunkin' Donuts. p. 715, Four by Five, Inc.